ALL·IN·ONE

CompTIA A+® Certification

EXAM GUIDE

Sixth Edition

ABOUT THE AUTHOR

Mike Meyers, lovingly called the "AlphaGeek" by those who know him, is the industry's leading authority on CompTIA A+ Certification. He is the president and co-founder of Total Seminars, LLC, a provider of PC and network repair seminars, books, videos, and courseware for thousands of organizations throughout the world. Mike has been involved in the computer and network repair industry since 1977 as a technician, instructor, author, consultant, and speaker. Author of numerous popular PC books and videos, Mike is also the series editor for the highly successful Mike Meyers' Certification Passport series, the Mike Meyers' Computer Skills series, and the Mike Meyers' Guide to series, all published by McGraw-Hill/Osborne.

ALL ·IN· ONE

CompTIA A+® Certification
Exam Guide
Sixth Edition

Mike Meyers

New York • Chicago • San Francisco • Lisbon
London • Madrid • Mexico City • Milan • New Delhi
San Juan • Seoul • Singapore • Sydney • Toronto

McGraw-Hill books are available at special quantity discounts to use as premiums and sales promotions, or for use in corporate training programs. For more information, please write to the Director of Special Sales, Professional Publishing, McGraw-Hill, Two Penn Plaza, New York, NY 10121-2298. Or contact your local bookstore.

CompTIA A+® Certification All-in-One Exam Guide, Sixth Edition

567890 DOC DOC 0198

ISBN-13: Book P/N 978-0-07-226312-1 and CD P/N 978-0-07-226313-8
of set 978-0-07-226311-4

ISBN-10: Book P/N 0-07-226312-1 and CD P/N 0-07-226313-X
of set 0-07-226311-3

Sponsoring Editor
Timothy Green

Editorial Supervisor
Patty Mon

Developmental Editor
Laura Stone

Acquisitions Coordinator
Jennifer Housh

Technical Editor
Ed Jennings

Copy Editors
Laura Stone, Lisa Theobald,
LeeAnn Pickrell, Andy Carroll

Proofreaders
Susie Elkind, Paul Tyler

Indexer
Jack Lewis

Production Supervisor
James Kussow

Composition
Apollo Publishing Services

Illustration
Apollo Publishing Services

Art Director, Cover
Jeff Weeks

Cover Designer
Pattie Lee

CompTIA Authorized Quality Curriculum

The logo of the CompTIA Authorized Quality Curriculum (CAQC) program and the status of this or other training material as "Authorized" under the CompTIA Authorized Quality Curriculum program signifies that, in CompTIA's opinion, such training material covers the content of CompTIA's related certification exam.

The contents of this training material were created for the CompTIA A+ exams covering CompTIA certification objectives that were current as of November 2006.

CompTIA has not reviewed or approved the accuracy of the contents of this training material and specifically disclaims any warranties of merchantability or fitness for a particular purpose. CompTIA makes no guarantee concerning the success of persons using any such "Authorized" or other training material in order to prepare for any CompTIA certification exam.

How to Become CompTIA Certified:

This training material can help you prepare for and pass a related CompTIA certification exam or exams. In order to achieve CompTIA certification, you must register for and pass a CompTIA certification exam or exams.

In order to become CompTIA certified, you must:

1. Select a certification exam provider. For more information please visit http://www.comptia.org/certification/general_information/exam_locations.aspx

2. Register for and schedule a time to take the CompTIA certification exam(s) at a convenient location.

3. Read and sign the Candidate Agreement, which will be presented at the time of the exam(s). The text of the Candidate Agreement can be found at http://www.comptia.org/certification/general_information/candidate_agreement.aspx

4. Take and pass the CompTIA certification exam(s).

For more information about CompTIA's certifications, such as its industry acceptance, benefits or program news, please visit www.comptia.org/certification.

CompTIA is a not-for-profit information technology (IT) trade association. CompTIA's certifications are designed by subject matter experts from across the IT industry. Each CompTIA certification is vendor-neutral, covers multiple technologies, and requires demonstration of skills and knowledge widely sought after by the IT industry.

To contact CompTIA with any questions or comments, please call (1) (630) 678 8300 or email questions@comptia.org

I dedicate this book to Tiffany JaAda Roosa,
the quiet eye of serenity around which the Mike vortex whirls.

—Mike Meyers

CONTENTS AT A GLANCE

CONTENTS

ACKNOWLEDGMENTS

Scott Jernigan, my Editor-in-Chief, Counter Strike Foe, Master Bard, and Bon Vivant, was the glue that made this product happen. There's not a word or picture I put into this book that he hasn't molded and polished into perfection.

My acquisitions editor, Tim Green, did a fabulous job keeping me motivated and excited about this project. Tim, you're the poster child for "Californians who can actually get along with loud, obnoxious Texans." Let's do another one!

My in-house Graphics Guru and Brother Tech, Michael Smyer, took every bizarre graphics idea I could toss at him and came back with exactly what I needed.

Cindy Clayton's title might be "Editor" but it should be "Go to Gal," as she was always there for any job we needed to get done.

Cary Dier and Brian Schwarz came in at the 11th hour to save our bacon with technical editing and copy edits. Thanks, guys!

On the McGraw-Hill side, their crew worked with the diligence of worker bees and the patience of saints to put this book together.

Laura Stone did it all this time, a true pleasure to work with as developmental editor, copy editor, and frequent long-distance companion during many late nights. I could not have asked for a better editor, Laura. Thanks!

Jenni Housh offered a quiet voice and helpful spirit as acquisitions coordinator. I enjoyed our Monday meetings and am looking forward to the next project.

My technical editor, Ed Jennings, kept a close eye on me throughout the book and made great suggestions and corrections. Thanks for the excellent work!

To the copy editors, page proofers, and layout folks—Lisa Theobald, LeeAnn Pickrell, Andy Carroll, Susie Elkind, Paul Tyler, and the folks at Apollo Publishing—thank you! You did a marvelous job.

The Path of the PC Tech

In this chapter, you will learn how to
- Explain the importance of gaining skill in managing and troubleshooting PCs
- Explain the importance of CompTIA A+ certification
- Describe how to become a CompTIA A+ certified technician

Computers have taken over the world, or at least many professions. Everywhere you turn, a quick dig beneath the surface sawdust of construction, the grease of auto mechanics, and the hum of medical technology reveals one or more personal computers (PCs) working away, doing essential jobs. Because the PC evolved from novelty item to essential science tool to everyday object in a short period of time, there's a huge demand for a workforce that can build, maintain, troubleshoot, and repair PCs.

The Importance of Skill in Managing and Troubleshooting PCs

The people who work with computers—the *Information Technology (IT)* workforce—do such varied jobs as design hardware, write computer programs that enable you to do specific jobs on the PC, and create small and large groupings of computers—*networks*—that enable people to share computer resources. IT people built the Internet, one of the most phenomenal inventions of the 20th century. IT people maintain the millions of computers that make up the Internet. Computer technicians, or *PC techs* as those of us in the field call each other, make up the core of the IT workforce. Without the techs, none of the other stuff works. Getting workers with skill in building, maintaining, troubleshooting, and fixing PCs is essential for success for every modern business.

In the early days of the personal computer, anyone who used a PC had to have skills as a PC tech. The PC was new, buggy, and prone to problems. You didn't want to rely on others to fix your PC when the inevitable problems arose. Today's PCs are much more robust and have fewer problems, but they're also much more complex machines. Today's IT industry, therefore, needs specialized workers who know how to make the machines run well.

The Concept of Certifications

Every profession requires specialized skills. For the most part, if you want to *get* or *keep* a job that requires those specialized skills, you need some type of *certification* or license. If you want a job fixing automobiles, for example, you get the *Automotive Service Excellence (ASE)* certification. If you want to perform companies' financial audits, you get your *Certified Public Accountant (CPA)* certification.

Nearly every profession has some criteria that you must meet to show your competence and ability to perform at a certain level. While the way this works varies widely from one profession to another, all of them will at some point make you take an exam or series of exams. Passing these exams proves that you have the necessary skills to work at a certain level in your profession, whether you're an aspiring plumber, teacher, barber, or lawyer.

If you successfully pass these exams, the organization that administers those exams grants you certification. You receive some piece of paper or pin or membership card that you can show to potential clients or employers. This certification gives those clients or employers a level of confidence that you can do what you say you can do. Without this certification, either you will not find suitable work in that profession or no one will trust you to do the work. Until relatively recently, PC technicians have been the exception to this rule.

The Importance of CompTIA A+ Certification

Although microcomputers were introduced in the late 1970s, for many years PC technicians did not have a universally recognized way to show clients or employers that they know what to do under the hood of a personal computer. Sure, there were vendor-specific certifications, but the only way to get them was to get a job at an authorized warranty or repair facility first, and then get the certification. Not that there's anything wrong with vendor-specific training; it's just that no one manufacturer has taken enough market share to make IBM training, for example, something that works for any job. (Then there is always that little detail of getting the job first before you can get certified!)

The software/networking side of our business has not suffered from the same lack of certifications. Due to the dominance of certain companies at one time or another (for example, Microsoft and Novell), the vendor-specific certifications have provided a great way to get and keep a job. For example, Microsoft's *Microsoft Certified Systems Engineer (MCSE)*, Novell's *Certified Novell Engineer (CNE)*, and Cisco's *Cisco Certified Internetwork Expert (CCIE)* have opened the doors for many.

But what about the person who runs around all day repairing printers, installing hard drives, upgrading device drivers, and building systems? What about the PC hobbyists who want to get paid for their skills? What about the folks who, because they had the audacity to show that they knew the difference between CMOS and a command prompt, find themselves with a new title like "PC Support Technician" or "Electronic Services Specialist?" On the other hand, how about the worst title of them all:

"The Person Who Doesn't Get a Nickel Extra but Who Fixes the Computers?" CompTIA A+ certification fills that need.

What Is CompTIA A+ Certification?

CompTIA A+ certification is an industry-wide, vendor-neutral certification program developed and sponsored by the *Computing Technology Industry Association (CompTIA)*. The CompTIA A+ certification shows that you have a basic competence in supporting microcomputers. You achieve this certification by taking two computer-based, multiple-choice examinations. The tests cover what technicians should know after nine months of full-time PC support experience. CompTIA A+ certification enjoys wide recognition throughout the computer industry. To date, more than 600,000 technicians have become CompTIA A+ certified, making it the most popular of all IT certifications.

Who Is CompTIA?

CompTIA is a nonprofit, industry trade association based in Oakbrook Terrace, Illinois. It consists of over 20,000 members in 102 countries. You'll find CompTIA offices in such diverse locales as Amsterdam, Dubai, Johannesburg, Tokyo, and São Paulo.

CompTIA provides a forum for people in these industries to network (as in meeting people), represents the interests of its members to the government, and provides certifications for many different aspects of the computer industry. CompTIA sponsors A+, Network+, i-Net+, Security+, and other certifications. CompTIA works hard to watch the IT industry and constantly looks to provide new certifications to meet the ongoing demand from its membership. Check out the CompTIA Web site at www.comptia.org for details on the other certifications that you can obtain from CompTIA.

Virtually every company of consequence in the IT industry is a member of CompTIA. Here are a few of the biggies:

Adobe Systems	AMD	Best Buy	Brother International
Canon	Cisco Systems	CompUSA	Fujitsu
Gateway	Hewlett-Packard	IBM	Intel
Kyocera	McAfee	Microsoft	NCR
Novell	Panasonic	Sharp Electronics	Siemens
Symantec	Toshiba	Total Seminars, LLC (that's my company)	Plus many thousands more!

CompTIA began offering CompTIA A+ certification back in 1993. When it debuted, the IT industry largely ignored CompTIA A+ certification. Since that initial stutter, however, the CompTIA A+ certification has grown to become the *de facto* requirement for entrance into the PC industry. Many companies require CompTIA A+ certification for all of their PC support technicians, and the CompTIA A+ certification is widely recognized both in the United States and internationally. Additionally, many other certifications recognize CompTIA A+ certification and use it as credit toward their certifications.

The Path to Other Certifications

Most IT companies—big and small—see CompTIA A+ certification as the entry point to IT. From CompTIA A+, you have a number of certification options, depending on whether you want to focus more on hardware and operating systems, or move into network administration (although these aren't mutually exclusive goals). The following three certifications are worth serious consideration:

- CompTIA Network+ certification
- Microsoft Certified Professional certifications
- Cisco certifications

CompTIA Network+ Certification

If you haven't already taken the CompTIA Network+ certification exam, make it your next certification. Just as CompTIA A+ certification shows that you have solid competency as a PC technician, *CompTIA Network+* demonstrates your skills as a network technician, including understanding of network hardware, installation, and troubleshooting. CompTIA's Network+ certification is a natural step for continuing toward your Microsoft, Novell, or Cisco certifications. Take the CompTIA Network+—it's your obvious next certification!

Microsoft Certified Professional Certifications

Microsoft operating systems control a huge portion of all installed networks, and those networks need qualified support people to make them run. Microsoft's series of certifications for networking professionals are a natural next step after the CompTIA certifications. They offer a whole slew of tracks and exams, but you should first pursue the *Microsoft Certified Professional (MCP)*. The MCP is the easiest Microsoft certification to get, as it only requires you to pass one of many different exams—and all of these exams count toward more advanced Microsoft certifications.

When it comes to advanced certifications, Microsoft's ever-popular Microsoft Certified Systems Engineer (MCSE) certification holds a lot of clout in the job market. The MCSE consists of seven exams: six core exams covering three study areas—client operating system, networking system, and design—and one elective. You can find more details on Microsoft's training Web site at www.microsoft.com/learning/mcp/default.asp.

Cisco Certification

Cisco routers pretty much run the Internet and most intranets in the world. A *router* is a networking device that controls and directs the flow of information over networks, such as e-mail messages, Web browsing, and so on. Cisco provides three levels of certification for folks who want to show their skills at handling Cisco products. Nearly everyone interested in Cisco certification starts with the *Cisco Certified Network Associate (CCNA)*. The CCNA can be yours for the price of only one completed exam, after which you can happily slap the word Cisco on your resume! After your CCNA, you should consider the *Cisco Certified Network Professional (CCNP)* certification. See the Cisco certification Web site here for more details: www.cisco.com/web/learning/le3/learning_career_certifications_and_learning_paths_home.html.

How Do I Become CompTIA A+ Certified?

You become CompTIA A+ certified, in the simplest sense, by taking and passing two computer-based, multiple-choice exams. No prerequisites are required for taking the CompTIA A+ certification exams. There is no required training course, and there are no training materials to buy. You *do* have to pay a testing fee for each of the two exams. You pay your testing fees, go to a local testing center, and take the tests. You immediately know whether you have passed or failed. By passing both exams, you become a *Comp-TIA A+ Certified Service Technician*. There are no requirements for professional experience. You do not have to go through an authorized training center. There are no annual dues. There are no continuing education requirements. You pass; you're in. That's it. Now for the details.

 NOTE In June of 2006, CompTIA announced comprehensive changes to the CompTIA A+ certification exams. Up to this point, the CompTIA A+ certification consisted of two exams very different from what we now use. CompTIA gave these two exams a number of different official names over the years, but regardless of the name they boiled down to what we called the "hardware" exam and the "operating system" exam. That split always seemed forced because you can't have a functional computer without both hardware and operating systems working together to get things done.

In keeping with the idea of a PC as a single system instead of the PC as two separate entities—a pile of hardware and a pile of software—CompTIA reshaped the exams into a basic, conceptual exam followed by a more in-depth configuration/maintenance/repair exam, for which you have three choices. This book will get you through all of the current exam paths.

The Basic Exam Structure

CompTIA offers three tracks to CompTIA A+ certification: a primary (referred to as the IT Technician track) and two secondary (Help Desk and Depot Technician tracks). All three tracks require you to take two exams, the first of which is called the *CompTIA A+ Essentials.*

The Essentials exam concentrates on understanding terminology and technology, how to do fundamental tasks such as upgrading RAM, and basic Windows operating system support.

To follow the primary track, you would also take the *CompTIA A+ 220-602* exam, called the "602" or "IT Technician exam." The IT Technician exam builds on the Essentials exam, concentrating on advanced configuration and troubleshooting, including using the command line to accomplish tech tasks. This exam also includes network and Internet configuration questions.

To attain CompTIA A+ Certification on one of the two secondary tracks, you would take Essentials and follow with either the *CompTIA A+ 220-603* exam (Help Desk Technician) or the *CompTIA A+ 220-604* exam (Depot Technician). Both exams test on a subset of the information covered in the IT Technician exam, but go more in-depth on some subjects and have less coverage on other subjects. Nearly a third of all questions on the Help Desk Technician exam ask about managing, configuring, and troubleshooting operating systems, for example, whereas only one in five questions on the IT Technician exam hits that subject.

All of the exams are extremely practical, with little or no interest in theory. All questions are multiple-choice or "click on the right part of the picture" questions. The following is an example of the type of question you will see on the exams:

A dot-matrix printer is printing blank pages. Which item should you check first?

A. Printer drivers
B. Platen
C. Print head
D. Ribbon

The correct answer is D, the ribbon. You can make an argument for any of the others, but common sense (and skill as a PC technician) tells you to check the simplest possibility first.

The 2006 tests use a regular test format, in which you answer a set number of questions and are scored based on how many correct answers you get, rather than the adaptive format used in recent years. These exams will have no more than 100 questions each.

Be aware that CompTIA may add new questions to the exams at any time to keep the content fresh. The subject matter covered by the exams won't change, but new questions may be added periodically at random intervals. This policy puts stronger emphasis on understanding concepts and having solid PC-tech knowledge rather than trying to memorize specific questions and answers that may have been on the tests in the past. Going forward, no book or Web resource will have all the "right answers" because those answers will constantly change. Luckily for you, however, this book does not just teach you what steps to follow in a particular case, but how to be a knowledgeable tech who understands *why* you're doing those steps, so that when you encounter a new problem (or test question), you can work out the answer. Not only will this help you pass the exams, you'll be a better PC tech!

To keep up to date, my staff and I monitor the CompTIA A+ exams for new content and update the special Tech Files section of the Total Seminars Web site (www.totalsem. com) with new articles covering subjects we believe may appear on future versions of the exams.

A Note on Adaptive Exams

Even though the current CompTIA A+ certification exams use a regular, multiple-choice exam format, CompTIA has in the past used an adaptive exam format. It's worth your time to make sure you know the difference between the two types of exams. The main difference between a regular exam and an adaptive exam is that on an adaptive exam, each question is assigned a difficulty level (for example, easy, medium, or difficult). When you answer a medium question correctly, the exam adapts and asks you a harder question. If you miss one, the exam adapts and asks an easier question.

There is a maximum number of questions the test will offer you, but not a set number of questions against which you are scored, like you'd find on a regular exam. To get a passing score on an adaptive exam, you need to answer enough difficult-level questions to prove your mastery of the material. Adaptive exams need far fewer questions than regular exams before the test ends, usually less than half the number of questions. Another big difference is that you cannot go back and check previous questions within adaptive exams, so make sure you have the answer you want before you move on to the next question!

Essentials

The questions on the CompTIA A+ Essentials exam fit into one of eight categories or *domains*. The number of questions for each domain is based on the following percentages shown in Table 1-1.

The Essentials exam tests your knowledge of computer components, expecting you to be able to identify just about every common device on PCs, including variations within device types. Here's a list:

- Floppy drives
- Hard drives
- CD- and DVD-media drives
- Solid state drives
- Motherboards
- Power supplies
- CPUs
- RAM
- Monitors
- Input devices, such as keyboards, mice, and touchscreens
- Video and multimedia cards
- Network and modem cards
- Cables and connectors
- Heat sinks, fans, and liquid cooling systems
- Laptops and portable devices
- Printers
- Scanners
- Network switches, cabling, and wireless adapters
- Biometric devices

The Essentials exam tests your ability to install, configure, and maintain all the standard technology involved in a personal computer. You need to be able to install and set up a hard drive, for example, and configure devices in Windows 2000 or Windows XP. You have to understand drivers. You have to know your way around Windows and understand the tasks involved in updating, upgrading, and installing the operating

Domain	Percentage
1.0 Personal Computer Components	21%
2.0 Laptop and Portable Devices	11%
3.0 Operating Systems	21%
4.0 Printers and Scanners	9%
5.0 Networks	12%
6.0 Security	11%
7.0 Safety and Environmental Issues	10%
8.0 Communication and Professionalism	5%

Table 1-1 Essentials exam domains and percentages

systems. You need to know the standard diagnostic tools available in Windows—not so you can fix everything, but so that you can work with higher-level techs to fix things.

You're tested on your knowledge of computer security, including identifying, installing, and configuring security hardware and software. You need to know security tools and diagnostic techniques for troubleshooting. Again, you're not expected to know everything, just enough to be competent.

Finally, the Essentials exam puts a lot of emphasis on safety and environmental issues, and on communication and professionalism. You need to know how to recycle and dispose of computer gear properly. You have to understand and avoid hazardous situations. The exams test your ability to communicate effectively with customers and coworkers. You need to understand professional behavior and demonstrate that you have tact, discretion, and respect for others and their property.

IT Technician (Exam 220-602)

The CompTIA A+ 220-602 exam covers the same eight domains, although they're weighted differently and emphasize different aspects of the tasks involved. Table 1-2 lists the domains and percentages.

The IT Technician exam covers the same hardware and software as Essentials, but with much more focus on determining the appropriate technology for a situation—running diagnostics, troubleshooting—rather than identification of hardware or operating system utilities. The exam tests your knowledge of computer components and programs so you can make informed recommendations to customers. You need to understand how all the technology should work, know the proper steps to figure out why something doesn't work, and then fix it.

The first domain, "Personal Computer Components," provides a stark example of the difference in focus between the exams. Essentials talks about identifying names, purposes, and characteristics of various devices. The IT Technician exam, in contrast, goes into more depth: "Add, remove, and configure personal computer components, *including selection and installation of appropriate components.*" [Emphasis mine.]

"Laptops and Portable Devices" gives another great example. Domain 2.1 is the same for both exams, "Identify fundamental principles of using laptops and portable devices." Digging a little deeper into the domains shows the differences. Essentials: "Identify

Domain	Percentage
1.0 Personal Computer Components	18%
2.0 Laptop and Portable Devices	9%
3.0 Operating Systems	20%
4.0 Printers and Scanners	14%
5.0 Networks	11%
6.0 Security	8%
7.0 Safety and Environmental Issues	5%
8.0 Communication and Professionalism	15%

Table 1-2   Exam 220-602 domains and percentages

names, purposes, and characteristics of laptop-specific [devices such as] peripherals, expansion slots, [and] communication devices." IT Technician: "Identify appropriate applications for laptop-specific communication connections such as Bluetooth, infra-red, cellular WAN, and Ethernet." The former has you identify the technology; the latter requires you to understand it in detail.

The two exams differ greatly in the "Operating Systems" domain. Essentials tests you on standard installation, configuration, and diagnostic tools, for example, but the IT Technician exam goes much deeper. You need to understand intimately how to use the command line to manage the operating systems. You're expected to know all sorts of disk structures and run all the major disk management tools. Finally, the IT Technician exam grills you on operating system recovery tools and techniques, so you can help customers get back up and running quickly.

 EXAM TIP   The IT Technician exam puts a lot of emphasis on the last domain, "Communication and Professionalism." As this domain makes up 15 percent of the exam, expect many questions about ethics, proper behavior in the work place, ways to communicate with customers to get the most information in troubleshooting situations, and more.

Help Desk Technician (Exam 220-603)

The CompTIA A+ 220-603 exam emphasizes skills you need to succeed as a help desk technician, remotely helping people who run into problems on their PCs. As such, you'll be tested a lot more intensely on operating system questions than on the IT Technician exam. In fact, almost a third of the questions cover OS diagnostic and trouble-shooting problems. Perhaps even more interesting is the coverage of "Communication and Professionalism." *One out of every five questions* is about the proper way to talk with people, working to get the most information and being polite and kind when speaking to angry and upset people. Table 1-3 lists the domains and percentages.

Although the Help Desk exam removes mention of portable computers, the percentages on the "Security" and "Safety and Environmental Issues" domains go up a lot (from 8 percent and 5 percent to 15 percent for both). You've got to know these topics very well to succeed on this exam.

A fundamental difference between the IT Technician and Help Desk Technician exams is that the former covers installing devices in detail, whereas the latter emphasizes troubleshooting even more. Of the two, the Help Desk Technician exam is clearly the more difficult. You should go that route only if your employer insists upon it!

Table 1-3 Exam 220-603 domains and percentages	Domain	Percentage
	1.0 Personal Computer Components	15%
	2.0 Operating Systems	29%
	3.0 Printers and Scanners	10%
	4.0 Networks	11%
	5.0 Security	15%
	6.0 Communication and Professionalism	20%

Depot Technician (Exam 220-604)

The CompTIA A+ 220-604 exam is targeted at folks who work behind the scenes fixing computers. These are the techs who don't interact with customers much, so the emphasis on this exam is hardware, hardware, and even more hardware. If you can't build, maintain, troubleshoot, and repair any personal computer—desktop and portable—on the planet, this path is not for you! Table 1-4 lists the domains and percentages.

A quick glance at the domain percentages tells the tale. Almost half of all questions are on installing, configuring, optimizing, and upgrading PCs. Although operating systems as a domain has been removed, you definitely need to know a lot about them to install, configure, and troubleshoot devices. "Laptop and Portable Devices" and "Printers and Scanners" domains leap up to 40 percent of the exam questions. You'll be grilled on fixing portables and printers! Because the exam assumes you'll be in a lab environment rather than in an office space, security is de-emphasized. The presumed lack of communication between tech and customer caused the "Communication and Professionalism" objective to go completely away.

Help! Which Exam Should I Take?

With three different tracks to becoming a CompTIA A+ Certified Technician, the inevitable question revolves around choosing the proper track. *The bottom line is that unless you have an employer specifically telling you otherwise, do the primary track.* Take Essentials and follow that with the 220-602 IT Technician exam. This is by far the more common track and the one the vast majority of employers will want to see on your résumé! When you complete a track, your test results will show which track you chose.

If you choose the primary IT Technician track, potential employers will know they're getting a properly well-rounded tech who can be thrown into pretty much any IT situation and handle it well. The Help Desk and Depot Technician tracks target very specific jobs, so unless that job is yours, completing one of these tracks—and not doing the IT Technician track—limits your employment opportunities.

A glance at the competencies for the three Technician exams (602, 603, and 604) might suggest that it would be easier to take 603 or 604 because they have fewer domains than 602, but that assumption could prove very painful indeed. The Help Desk and Depot Technician exams test you on the same material as the IT Technician exam, but emphasize different aspects or different ways to tackle personal computer issues.

Table 1-4 Exam 220-604 domains and percentages	Domain	Percentage
	1.0 Personal Computer Components	45%
	2.0 Laptop and Portable Devices	20%
	3.0 Printers and Scanners	20%
	4.0 Security	5%
	5.0 Safety and Environmental Issues	10%

Help! What Chapters Cover the Help Desk and Depot Technician Exams?

The *All-in-One A+ Certification Exam Guide* teaches you what you need to know to become a great tech, first and foremost. It just so happens that by learning how to become a great tech, you learn enough to pass the CompTIA A+ certification exams. Because the book focuses on tech and not exclusively on certification, the sections covered under the IT Tech banner in each chapter pertain to all three advanced exams, 220-602, 220-603, and 220-604.

To pass the 603 or 604 exams, focus more time on chapters weighted more heavily in the CompTIA domains for those exams. Table 1-5 shows the full eight domains for Essentials and IT Technician exams, with a series of check marks that tell you where to focus for which exam. The key is pretty straightforward. One check means around 10 percent on the domains. Two checks means approximately 20 percent, three checks approximately 30 percent, and so on. For a complete breakdown by sub-domain, see the "Mapping to the CompTIA A+ Objectives," Appendix A in this book.

How Do I Take the Exams?

Two companies, Prometric and Pearson/VUE, administer the actual CompTIA A+ testing. There are thousands of Prometric and Pearson/VUE testing centers across the United States and Canada, and the rest of the world. You may take the exams at any testing center. Both Prometric and Pearson/VUE offer complete listings online of all available testing centers. You can select the closest training center and schedule your exams right from the comfort of your favorite Web browser:

www.prometric.com
www.vue.com

Alternatively, in the United States and Canada, call Prometric at 800-776-4276 or Pearson/VUE at 877-551-PLUS (7587) to schedule the exams and to locate the nearest testing center. International customers can find a list of Prometric and Pearson/VUE international contact numbers for various regions of the world on CompTIA's Web site at www.comptia.org by selecting the Find Your Test Center link on the CompTIA A+ certification page.

Domain	Essentials	220-602	220-603	220-604
Personal Computer Components	✓✓	✓✓	✓✓	✓✓✓✓
Laptop and Portable Devices	✓	✓	✓✓✓	✓✓
Operating Systems	✓✓	✓✓	✓	
Printers and Scanners	✓	✓	✓	✓✓
Networks	✓	✓	✓	
Security	✓	✓	✓✓	✓
Safety and Environmental Issues	✓	✓		✓
Communication and Professionalism	✓	✓✓	✓✓	

Table 1-5   Where to focus your study time

You must pay for the exam when you call to schedule. Be prepared to sit on hold for a while. Have your Social Security number (or international equivalent) and a credit card ready when you call. Both Prometric and Pearson/VUE will be glad to invoice you, but you won't be able to take the exam until they receive full payment.

If you have special needs, both Prometric and Pearson/VUE will accommodate you, although this may limit your selection of testing locations.

How Much Does the Exam Cost?

The cost of the exam depends on whether you work for a CompTIA member or not. At this writing, the cost for non-CompTIA members is $158 (U.S.) for each exam. International prices vary, but you can check the CompTIA Web site for international pricing. Of course, the prices are subject to change without notice, so always check the CompTIA Web site for current pricing!

Very few people pay full price for the exam. Virtually every organization that provides CompTIA A+ training and testing also offers discount vouchers. You buy a discount voucher and then use the voucher number instead of a credit card when you schedule the exam. Vouchers are sold per exam, so you'll need two vouchers for the two CompTIA A+ exams. Total Seminars is one place to get discount vouchers. You can call Total Seminars at 800-446-6004 or 281-922-4166, or get vouchers via the Web site: www.totalsem.com. No one should ever pay full price for CompTIA A+ exams!

How to Pass the CompTIA A+ Exams

The single most important thing to remember about the CompTIA A+ certification exams is that CompTIA designed the exams to test the knowledge of a technician with only nine months' experience—so keep it simple! The exams aren't interested in your ability to overclock CAS timings in CMOS or whether you can explain the exact difference between the Intel 975X Express and the NVIDIA nForce590 SLI chipsets. Don't bother with a lot of theory—think in terms of practical knowledge. Read the book, do whatever works for you to memorize the key concepts and procedures, take the practice exams on the CD in the back of the book, review any topics you miss, and you should pass with no problem.

 NOTE Those of you who just want more knowledge in managing and troubleshooting PCs can follow the same strategy as certification-seekers. Think in practical terms and work with the PC as you go through each chapter.

Some of you may be in or just out of school, so studying for exams is nothing novel. But if it's been a while since you've had to study for and take an exam, or if you think maybe you could use some tips, you may find the next section valuable. It lays out a proven strategy for preparing to take and pass the CompTIA A+ exams. Try it. It works.

Obligate Yourself

The very first step you should take is to schedule yourself for the exams. Have you ever heard the old adage, "heat and pressure make diamonds?" Well, if you don't give yourself a little "heat," you'll end up procrastinating and delay taking the exams, possibly forever! Do yourself a favor. Using the information below, determine how much time you'll need to study for the exams, and then call Prometric or VUE and schedule them accordingly. Knowing the exams are coming up makes it much easier to turn off the television and crack open the book! You can schedule an exam as little as a few weeks in advance, but if you schedule an exam and can't take it at the scheduled time, you must reschedule at least a day in advance or you'll lose your money.

Set Aside the Right Amount of Study Time

After helping thousands of techs get their CompTIA A+ certification, we at Total Seminars have developed a pretty good feel for the amount of study time needed to pass the CompTIA A+ certification exams. Table 1-6 provides an estimate to help you plan how much study time you must commit to the CompTIA A+ certification exams. Keep in mind that these are averages. If you are not a great student or are a little on the nervous side, add 10 percent; if you're a fast learner or have a good bit of computer experience, you may want to reduce the figures.

Tech Task	Amount of Experience			
	None	Once or Twice	Every Now and Then	Quite a Bit
Installing an adapter card	12	10	8	4
Installing hard drives	12	10	8	2
Installing modems and NICs	8	6	6	3
Connecting a computer to the Internet	8	6	4	2
Installing printers and scanners	4	3	2	1
Installing RAM	8	6	4	2
Installing CPUs	8	7	5	3
Fixing printers	6	5	4	3
Fixing boot problems	8	7	7	5
Fixing portable computers	8	6	4	2
Building complete systems	12	10	8	6
Using the command line	8	8	6	4
Installing/optimizing Windows	10	8	6	4
Using Windows 2000	6	6	4	2
Using Windows XP	6	6	4	2
Configuring NTFS permissions	6	4	3	2
Configuring a wireless network	6	5	3	2
Configuring a software firewall	6	4	2	1
Installing a sound card	2	2	1	0
Using OS diagnostic tools	8	8	6	4
Using a Volt-Ohm Meter	4	3	2	1

Table 1-6 Analyzing skill levels

To use the table, just circle the values that are most accurate for you and add them up to get your estimated total hours of study time.

To that value, add hours based on the number of months of direct, professional experience you have had supporting PCs, as shown in Table 1-7.

A total neophyte usually needs around 200 hours of study time. An experienced tech shouldn't need more than 40 hours.

Total hours for you to study: _____.

A Strategy for Study

Now that you have a feel for how long it's going to take, it's time to develop a study strategy. I'd like to suggest a strategy that has worked for others who've come before you, whether they were experienced techs or total newbies. This book is designed to accommodate the different study agendas of these two different groups of students. The first group is experienced techs who already have strong PC experience, but need to be sure they're ready to be tested on the specific subjects covered by the CompTIA A+ exams. The second group is those with little or no background in the computer field. These techs can benefit from a more detailed understanding of the history and concepts that underlie modern PC technology, to help them remember the specific subject matter information they must know for the exams. I'll use the shorthand terms Old Techs and New Techs for these two groups. If you're not sure which group you fall into, pick a few chapters and go through some end-of-chapter questions. If you score less than 70 percent, go the New Tech route.

I have broken most of the chapters into four distinct parts:

- **Historical/Conceptual**   Topics that are not on the CompTIA A+ exams, but will help you understand what is on the CompTIA A+ exams more clearly.

- **Essentials**   Topics that clearly fit under the CompTIA A+ Essentials exam domains.

- **IT Tech**   Topics that clearly fit under the CompTIA A+ IT Technician exam domains.

- **Beyond A+**   More advanced issues that probably will not be on the CompTIA A+ exams—yet.

 NOTE   Not all chapters will have all four sections!

Months of Direct, Professional Experience...	To Your Study Time...
0	Add 50
Up to 6	Add 30
6 to 12	Add 10
Over 12	Add 0

Table 1-7   Adding up your study time

The beginning of each of these areas is clearly marked with a large banner that looks like this:

Historical/Conceptual

Those of you who fall into the Old Tech group may want to skip everything but the Essentials and IT Tech areas in each chapter. After reading those sections, jump immediately to the questions at the end of the chapter. The end-of-chapter questions concentrate on information in the Essentials and IT Tech sections. If you run into problems, review the Historical/Conceptual sections in that chapter. Note that you may need to skip back to previous chapters to get the Historical/Conceptual information you need for later chapters.

After going through every chapter as described, Old Techs can move directly to testing their knowledge using the free practice exams on the CD-ROM that accompanies the book. Once you start scoring in the 85 to 95 percent range, you're ready to take the exams!

If you're a New Tech or if you're an Old Tech who wants the full learning experience this book can offer, start by reading the book, *the whole book*, as though you were reading a novel, from page one to the end without skipping around. Because so many computer terms and concepts build on each other, skipping around greatly increases the odds you will become confused and end up closing the book and firing up your favorite PC game. Not that I have anything against PC games, but unfortunately that skill is *not* useful for the CompTIA A+ exams!

Your goal on this first read is to understand concepts, the *whys* behind the *hows*. It is very helpful to have a PC nearby as you read so you can stop and inspect the PC to see a piece of hardware or how a particular concept manifests in the real world. As you read about floppy drives, for example, inspect the cables. Do they look like the ones in the book? Is there a variation? Why? It is imperative that you understand why you are doing something, not just how to do it on one particular system under one specific set of conditions. The exams don't work that way, and neither does life as a PC tech!

If you're reading this book as part of a managing and troubleshooting PCs class, rather than a certification-prep course, then I highly recommend going the New Tech route, even if you have a decent amount of experience. The book contains a lot of details that can trip you up if you focus only on the test-specific sections of the chapters. Plus, your program might stress historical and conceptual knowledge as well as practical, hands-on skills.

The CompTIA A+ certification exams assume that you have basic user skills. The exams really try to trick you with questions on processes that you may do every day and not really think about. Here's a classic: "In order to move a file from the C:\WINDOWS folder to the A:\ drive using Windows Explorer, what key must you hold down while dragging the file?" If you can answer that without going to your keyboard and trying a few likely keys, you're better than most techs! In the real world, you can try a few wrong answers before you hit on the right one, but for the exams, you have to *know* it! Whether Old Tech or New Tech, make sure you are proficient at user-level Windows skills, including the following:

- Recognizing all the components of the standard Windows Desktop (Start Menu, System Tray, etc.)
- Manipulating windows—resizing, moving, and so on
- Creating, deleting, renaming, moving, and copying files and folders within Windows
- Understanding file extensions and their relationship with program associations
- Using common keyboard shortcuts/hotkeys

Any PC technician who has been around a while will tell you that one of the great secrets in the computer business is that there's almost never anything completely new in the world of computer technology. Faster, cleverer, smaller, wider—absolutely—but the underlying technology, the core of what makes your PC and its various peripheral devices operate, has changed remarkably little since PCs came into widespread use a few decades ago. When you do your initial read-through, you may be tempted to skip the Historical/Conceptual sections—don't! Understanding the history and technological developments behind today's PCs really helps you understand why they work—or don't work—the way they do. Basically, I'm passing on to you the kind of knowledge you might get by apprenticing yourself to an older, more experienced PC tech.

After you've completed the first read-through, go through the book again, this time in textbook mode. If you're an Old Tech, this is where you start your studying. Try to cover one chapter at a sitting. Concentrate on the Essentials and IT Tech sections. Get a highlighter and mark the phrases and sentences that bring out major points. Be sure you understand how the pictures and illustrations relate to the concepts being discussed.

Once you feel you have a good grasp of the material in the book, you can check your knowledge using the practice exams included on the CD-ROM in the back of the book. These can be taken in Practice mode or Final mode. In Practice mode, you can use the Assistance window to get a helpful hint for the current questions, find the chapter that covers the question using the Reference feature, check your answer for the question, and see an explanation of the correct answer. In Final mode, you answer all the questions and are given an exam score at the end, just like the real thing.

Both modes show you an overall grade, expressed as a percentage, as well as a breakdown of how well you did on each exam domain. The Review Questions feature lets you see what questions you missed and what the correct answers are. Use these results to guide further studying. Continue reviewing the topics you miss and taking additional exams until you are consistently scoring in the 85 percent to 95 percent range. When you get there, you are ready to pass the CompTIA A+ certification exams!

Study Strategies   Perhaps it's been a while since you had to study for a test. Or perhaps it hasn't, but you've done your best since then to block the whole experience from your mind! Either way, savvy test-takers know there are certain techniques that make studying for tests more efficient and effective.

Here's a trick used by students in law and medical schools who have to memorize reams of information: write it down. The act of writing something down (not typing, writing) in and of itself helps you to remember it, even if you never look at what you wrote again. Try taking separate notes on the material and re-creating diagrams by hand to help solidify the information in your mind.

Another oldie but goodie: make yourself flash cards with questions and answers on topics you find difficult. A third trick: take your notes to bed and read them just before you go to sleep. Many people find they really do learn while they sleep!

A Side Note on Windows Vista   Microsoft's Windows Vista operating system debuts in late 2006/early 2007, and although CompTIA won't immediately put it on the CompTIA A+ certification exams, every tech will need to know it. Do yourself and your customers a favor and work with Windows Vista as soon as you can *after* you finish getting CompTIA A+ certified, even if it's using a school computer or making a lot of trips to computer stores.

I suggest waiting only because you'll want to keep the details of how to do things in Windows 2000 and Windows XP as fresh as possible before you take the exams. If you're studying simply to gain knowledge and are not worried about getting certified, then jump right in!

Once you have access to a Windows Vista computer, skim through this book and ask yourself these questions. What's different about setting up drives? What about installation? What diagnostic and troubleshooting tools does Vista offer that you can't find or that differ significantly from tools in Windows 2000 or Windows XP?

Contact

If you have any problems, any questions, or if you just want to argue about something, feel free to send an e-mail to the author—michaelm@totalsem.com, or to the editor—scottj@totalsem.com.

For any other information you might need, contact CompTIA directly at their Web site: www.comptia.org.

Chapter Review Questions

1. Which certification is considered required for entrance into the PC industry?

   A. Certified Cisco Network Associate

   B. CompTIA A+ certification

   C. CompTIA Network+ certification

   D. Microsoft Certified Professional

2. How many exams do you need to pass to become CompTIA A+ certified?

   A. One

   B. Two

   C. Three

   D. Four

3. Which of the following exams, combined with CompTIA A+ Essentials, gets you CompTIA A+ certified? (Select all that apply.)

   A. CompTIA A+ 220-602

   B. CompTIA A+ 220-604

     C. CompTIA A+ Advanced

     D. None of the above—passing the CompTIA A+ Essentials exam is all you need to get certified.

4. What is the primary CompTIA Web site?

     A. www.comptia.com

     B. www.comptia.edu

     C. www.comptia.net

     D. www.comptia.org

5. Which of the following best describes an adaptive exam format?

     A. An adaptive exam enables you to adapt to the exam format by giving you several free questions at the beginning before the real questions start.

     B. An adaptive exam offers weighted questions and adapts to your testing style by lowering the difficulty of questions when you get one right. Once you answer enough easy questions, you get a passing score.

     C. An adaptive exam offers weighted questions and adapts to your testing style by raising the difficulty of questions when you get one right. Once you answer enough difficult questions, you get a passing score.

     D. An adaptive exam offers questions in many formats, such as multiple choice, fill in the blank, and true/false, so that it can adapt to many testing styles. This enables adaptive exams to be more inclusive.

6. Of the eight domains listed for the CompTIA A+ Essentials exam and the IT Technician exam, which do you need to study for each exam?

     A. Domains 1–4 for Essentials; 5–8 for IT Technician

     B. Domains 1–3 for Essentials; 4–8 for IT Technician

     C. Domains 1–3 for Essentials; 4–7 for IT Technician; 8 ("Communication and Professionalism") is optional

     D. Domains 1–8 for Essentials; 1–8 for IT Technician

7. What companies administer the CompTIA A+ certification exams? (Select all that apply.)

     A. CompTIA

     B. Microsoft

     C. Pearson/VUE

     D. Prometric

8. Of the four possible exams, which requires the most in-depth understanding of the domain "Personal Computer Components"?

     A. Essentials

     B. 220-602 (IT Technician)

    C. 220-603 (Help Desk Technician)

    D. 220-604 (Depot Technician)

9. Of the four possible exams, which requires the most in-depth understanding of the domain "Security"?

    A. Essentials

    B. 220-602 (IT Technician)

    C. 220-603 (Help Desk Technician)

    D. 220-604 (Depot Technician)

10. Of the four possible exams, which requires the most in-depth understanding of the domain "Communication and Professionalism"?

    A. Essentials

    B. 220-602 (IT Technician)

    C. 220-603 (Help Desk Technician)

    D. 220-604 (Depot Technician)

Answers

1. **B.** The CompTIA A+ certification is considered required for entrance into the PC industry.

2. **B.** You need to pass two exams to become CompTIA A+ certified.

3. **A, B.** You can combine any of the three numbered exams (220-602, 220-603, and 220-604) with CompTIA A+ Essentials to become a CompTIA A+ Certified Technician.

4. **D.** The primary CompTIA Web site is www.comptia.org (although the .com and .net addresses will redirect you to the main site).

5. **C.** An adaptive exam offers weighted questions and adapts to your testing style by raising the difficulty of questions when you get one right. Once you answer enough difficult questions, you get a passing score.

6. **D.** All eight domains apply to both exams.

7. **C, D.** Pearson/VUE and Prometric administer the CompTIA A+ certification exams.

8. **D.** At 45 percent, the Depot Technician exam requires the most in-depth understanding of the domain "Personal Computer Components."

9. **C.** At 15 percent, the Help Desk Technician exam requires the most in-depth understanding of the domain "Security."

10. **C.** At 20 percent, the Help Desk Technician exam requires the most in-depth understanding of the domain "Communication and Professionalism."

The Visible PC

In this chapter, you will learn how to
- Describe how the PC works
- Identify the essential tools of the trade and avoid electrostatic discharge
- Identify the different connectors on a typical PC system unit
- Identify the major internal and external components of a PC

Mastering the craft of a PC technician requires you to learn a lot of details about the many pieces of hardware in the typical PC. Even the most basic PC contains hundreds of discrete hardware components, each with its own set of characteristics, shapes, sizes, colors, connections, and so on. By the end of this book, you will be able to discuss all of these components in detail.

This chapter takes you inside a typical PC, starting with an overview of how computers work. Because it's always good to follow the physician's rule, "First, do no harm," the second section of the chapter gives you the scoop on how to avoid damaging anything when you open up the computer.

Remember the children's song that goes, "Oh, the leg bone connects to the thigh bone...."? Well, think of the rest of the chapter in that manner, showing you what the parts look like and giving you a rough idea as to how they work and connect. In later chapters, you'll dissect all these PC "leg bones" and "thigh bones" and get to the level of detail you need to install, configure, maintain, and fix computers. Even if you are an expert, do not skip this chapter! It introduces a large number of terms that will be used throughout the rest of the book. Many of these terms you will know, but some you will not, so take some time and read it.

It is handy, although certainly not required, to have a PC that you can take the lid off of and inspect as you progress. Almost any old PC will help—it doesn't even need to work. So get thee a screwdriver, grab your PC, and see if you can recognize the various components as you read about them.

Historical/Conceptual

How the PC Works

You've undoubtedly seen a PC in action—a nice, glossy monitor displaying a picture that changes according to the actions of the person sitting in front of it, typing away on a keyboard, clicking a mouse, or twisting a joystick. Sound pours out of tiny speakers that flank the screen, and a box whirs happily beneath the table. The PC is a computer: a machine that enables you to do work, produce documents, play games, balance your checkbook, and check up on the latest sports scores on the Internet.

Although the computer is certainly a machine, it's also *programming:* the commands that tell the computer what to do to get work done. These commands are just ones and zeroes that the computer's hardware understands, enabling it to do amazing actions, such as perform powerful mathematic functions, move data (also ones and zeroes), realize the mouse has moved, and put pretty icons on the screen. So a computer is a complex inter-action between hardware and computer programming, created by your fellow humans.

Ever heard of Morse code? Morse code is nothing more than dots and dashes to those who do not understand it, but if you send dots and dashes (in the right order) to a guy who understands Morse code, you can tell him a joke. Think of programming as Morse code for the computer. You may not understand those ones and zeroes, but your computer certainly does! (See Figure 2-1.)

Figure 2-1   Computer musing that a string of ones and zeroes makes perfect sense to him

There's more to the ones and zeroes than just programming. All of the data on the computer—the Web pages, your documents, your e-mail—is also stored as ones and zeroes. Programs know how to translate these ones and zeroes into a form humans understand.

Programming comes in two forms. First are the applications—the programs that get work done. Word processing programs, Web browsers, and e-mail programs are all considered applications. But applications need a main program to support them. They need a program that enables you to start and stop applications, copy/move/delete data, talk to the hardware, and perform lots of other jobs. This program is called the *operating system (OS)*. Microsoft Windows is the most popular OS today, but there are other computer operating systems, such as Apple Macintosh OS X (Figure 2-2) and the popular (and free) Linux. Computer people lump operating systems and applications into the term *software* to differentiate them from the hardware of the computer.

Understanding the computer at this broad conceptual level—in terms of hardware, OS, and programs—can help you explain things to customers, but good techs have a much more fundamental appreciation and understanding of the complex interplay of all the software and the individual pieces of hardware. In short, techs need to know the processes going on behind the scenes.

NOTE The CompTIA A+ certification exams focus on hardware and operating systems; other certifications cover many of the programs in common use today. Two examples are the Microsoft Office Specialist (MOS) and Macromedia Certified Professional certifications.

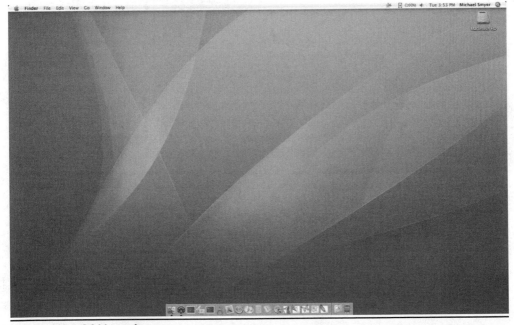

Figure 2-2 OS X interface

From the CompTIA A+ tech's perspective, the computer functions through four stages: input, processing, output, and storage. Knowing which parts participate in a particular stage of the computing process enables you to troubleshoot on a fundamental and decisive level.

Input

To illustrate this four-step process, let's walk through the steps involved in a fairly common computer task: preparing your taxes. [Insert collective groan here.] February has rolled around and, at least in the United States, millions of people install their favorite tax software, TurboTax from Intuit, onto their computers to help them prepare their taxes (Figure 2-3). After starting TurboTax, your first job is to provide the computer with data—essential information, such as your name, where you live, how much you earned, and how many dollars you gave to federal and state governments.

Figure 2-3   Turbo
Tax glamour shot

Various pieces of hardware enable you to input data, the most common of which are the keyboard and mouse. Most computers won't react when you say, "Hey you!"—at least anywhere outside of a Star Trek set. Although that day will come, for now you must use something decidedly more mechanical: a keyboard to type in your data. The OS provides a fundamental service in this process as well. You can bang on a keyboard all day and accomplish nothing without the OS translating your keystrokes into code that the hardware can understand.

Processing

Next, the computer processes your data. It places information in various appropriate "boxes" in TurboTax, and then it does the math for you. Processing takes place inside the computer case and happens almost completely at a hardware level, although that hardware functions according to rules laid out in the OS. Thus, again you have a complex interaction between hardware and software.

The processing portion is the magical part—you can't see it happen. The first half of this book demystifies this stage because good techs understand all the pieces of the process. I won't go through the specific hardware involved in the processing stage here because the pieces change according to the type of process.

Output

Simply adding up your total tax for the year is useless unless the computer shows you the result. That's where the third step—output—comes into play. Once the computer finishes processing data, it must put the information somewhere for you to inspect it. Often it places data on the monitor so you can see what you've just typed. It might send the data over to the printer if you tell it so you can print out copies of your tax return to mail to the Internal Revenue Service (or whatever the Tax Man is called where you live). A hardware device does the actual printing, but the OS controls the printing process. Again, it's a fundamental interaction of hardware and software.

Storage

Once you've sent in your tax return, you most likely do not want all that work simply to disappear. What happens if the IRS comes back a couple of months later with a question about your return? Yikes! You need to keep permanent records; plus, you need to keep a copy of the tax program. The fourth stage in the computing process is storage. A lot of devices are used in the storage process, the most visible of which are the external storage parts, such as floppy diskettes and CD-R discs (Figure 2-4).

Figure 2-4 Typical storage (CD-R discs)

The Art of the PC Technician

Using the four stages of the computing process—input, processing, output, and storage—to master how the PC works and, in turn, become a great technician, requires that you understand all the pieces of hardware and software involved **and** the interactions between them that make up the various stages. You have to know what the parts do, in other words, and how they work together. The best place to start is with a real computer. Let's go through the process of inspecting a typical, complete PC, including opening up a few important pieces to see the components inside. Hopefully, you've got a real computer in front of you right now that you may dismantle a bit. No two computers are exactly the same, so you'll see differences between your PC and the one in this chapter—and that's okay. You'll gain an appreciation of the fact that all computers have the same main parts that do the same jobs even though they differ in size, shape, and color.

By the time you reach the end of this book, you'll have a deeper, more nuanced understanding of the interaction of hardware and software in the four-stage computing process. Just as great artists have mastered fundamental skills of their trade before creating a masterpiece, you'll have the fundamentals of the art of the computer technician and be on your road to mastery.

Tools of the Trade and ESD Avoidance

Before we dive into the PC, you need two pieces of information: an overview of the most common tools you'll find in a tech's toolkit and how *not* to destroy hardware inadvertently through electrostatic discharge.

Tools of the Trade

The basic technician toolkit consists of a Phillips-head screwdriver and not much else—seriously—but a half dozen tools round out a fully-functional toolkit. Most kits have a star-headed Torx wrench, a nut driver or two, a pair of tweezers, a little grabber tool, and a hemostat to go along with Phillips-head and flat-head screwdrivers (Figure 2-5).

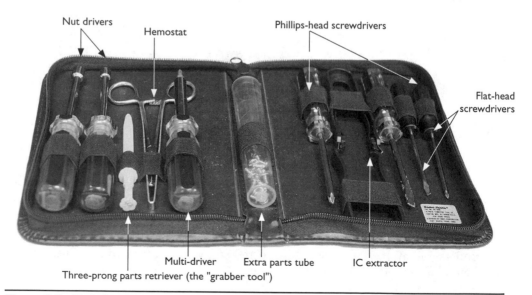

Figure 2-5 Typical technician toolkit

A lot of techs will throw in a magnifying glass and a flashlight for those hard-to-read numbers and text on the printed circuit boards (PCBs) that make up a large percentage of devices inside the system unit (Figure 2-6). Contrary to what you might think, techs rarely need a hammer.

Figure 2-6   Close-up of a printed circuit board (PCB)

Essentials

Avoiding Electrostatic Discharge

If you decide to open a PC while reading this chapter, as I encourage you to do, you must take proper steps to avoid the greatest killer of PCs—*electrostatic discharge (ESD)*. ESD simply means the passage of a static electrical charge. Have you ever rubbed a balloon against your shirt, making the balloon stick to you? That's a classic example of static electricity. When that static charge discharges, you may not notice it happening—although on a cool, dry day, I've been shocked so hard by touching a doorknob that I could see a big, blue spark! I've never heard of a human being getting anything worse than a rather nasty shock from ESD, but I can't say the same thing about computers. ESD will destroy the sensitive parts of your PC, so it is essential that you take steps to avoid ESD when working on your PC.

 NOTE   All PCs are well protected against ESD on the outside—unless you take a screwdriver and actually open up your PC, you really don't need to concern yourself with ESD.

Anti-static Tools

ESD only takes place when two objects that store different amounts (the hip electrical term to use is *potential*) of static electricity come in contact. The secret to avoiding ESD is to keep you and the parts of the PC you touch at the same electrical potential. You can accomplish this by connecting yourself to the PC via a handy little device called an *anti-static wrist strap*. This simple device consists of a wire that connects on one end to an alligator clip and on the other end to a small metal plate that secures to your wrist with an elastic strap. You snap the alligator clip onto any handy metal part of the PC and place the wrist strap on either wrist. Figure 2-7 shows a typical anti-static wrist strap in use.

Figure 2-7
Anti-static wrist
strap in use

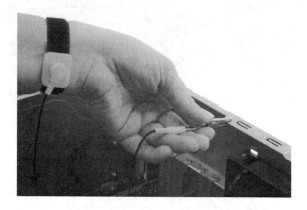

 EXAM TIP   Static electricity, and therefore the risk of ESD, is much more prevalent in dry, cool environments.

Anti-static wrist straps are standard equipment for anyone working on a PC, but other tools might come in handy. One of the big issues when working with a PC stems from the fact that in many situations you find yourself pulling out parts from the PC and setting them aside. The moment you take a piece out of the PC, it no longer has contact with the systems and may pick up static from other sources. Techs use *anti-static mats* to eliminate this risk. An anti-static mat acts as a point of common potential—it's very common to purchase a combination anti-static wrist strap and mat that all connect together to keep you, the PC, and any loose components at the same electrical potential (Figure 2-8).

Figure 2-8 Anti-
static wrist strap and
mat combination

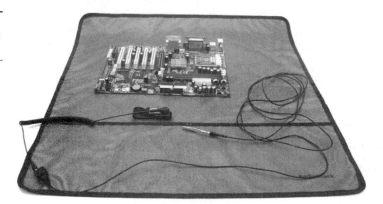

Anti-static wrist straps and mats use tiny *resistors*—devices that stop or *resist* the flow of electricity—to prevent anti-static charge from racing through the device. These resistors can fail over time, so it's always a good idea to read the documentation that comes with your anti-static tools to see how to test those small resistors properly.

Any electrical component not in a PC needs to be stored in an *anti-static bag*, a specially designed bag that sheds whatever static electricity you have when you touch it, thus preventing any damage to components stored within (Figure 2-9). Almost all PC components come in an anti-static bag when purchased. Experienced techs never throw these bags away, as you never know when you'll want to pull a part out and place it on a shelf for a while!

Figure 2-9
Anti-static bag

Although it would be ideal to have an anti-static wrist strap with you at all times, the reality is that from time to time you'll find yourself in situations where you lack the proper anti-static tools. This shouldn't keep you from working on the PC—if you're careful! Before working on a PC in such a situation, take a moment to touch the power supply—I'll show you where it is in this chapter—every once in a while as you work to keep yourself at the same electrical potential as the PC. Although this isn't as good as a wrist strap, it's better than nothing at all!

The last issue when it comes to preventing ESD is that never-ending question—should you work with the PC plugged in or unplugged? The answer is simple—do you really want to be physically connected to a PC that is plugged into an electrical outlet? Granted, the chances of electrocution are slim, but why take the risk?

 EXAM TIP Always unplug a PC when working inside it.

Have I convinced you that ESD is a problem? Good! So now it's safe to start looking at the components of the PC.

The Complete PC

Sometimes I hate the term "personal computer." That term implies a single device, like a toaster. A typical PC is more than one device, and you need all the parts (or at least most) to make the PC work. The most important part of the PC is the box that usually sits underneath your desk—the one that all the other parts connect to, called the *system unit*. All of the processing and storage takes place in the system unit. All of the other parts of the PC—the printer, the keyboard, the monitor—connect to the system unit and are known collectively as *peripherals*. Figure 2-10 shows a typical desktop PC, with the system unit and peripherals as separate pieces.

Figure 2-10   Typical desktop computer with peripherals

Most computers have a standard set of peripherals to provide input and output. You'll see some variation in color, bells, and whistles, but here's the standard set:

- **Monitor**   The big television thing that provides a visual output for the computer.
- **Keyboard**   Keypad for providing keyed input. Based on a typewriter.
- **Mouse**   Pointing device used to control a graphical pointer on the monitor for input.
- **Speakers/headphone**   Speakers provide sound output.
- **Printer**   Provides printed paper output.

A typical PC has all of these peripherals, but there's no law that requires a PC to have them. Plenty of PCs may not have a printer. Some PCs won't have speakers. Some computers don't even have a keyboard, mouse, or monitor—but they tend to hide in unlikely places, such as the inside of a jet fighter or next to the engine in an automobile. Other PCs may have many more peripherals. It's easy to install four or five printers on a single PC if you so desire. There are also hundreds of other types of peripherals, such as Web cameras and microphones, that you'll find on many PCs. You add or remove peripherals depending on what you need from the system. The only limit is the number of connections for peripherals available on the system unit.

External Connections

Every peripheral connects to the system unit through one of the many types of ports. The back of a typical system unit (Figure 2-11) has lots of cables running from the system unit to the different peripherals. You may even have a few connectors in the front. All these connectors and ports have their own naming conventions, and a good tech knows all of them. It's not acceptable to go around saying things like "that's a printer port" or "that's a *little-type* keyboard connector." You need to be comfortable with the more commonly used naming conventions so you can say "that's a female DB-25" or "that's a USB connector."

Figure 2-11
Connections on the back of a PC

Plugs, Ports, Jacks, and Connectors

Although PCs use close to 50 different types of connections, almost all fit into one of six major types: DIN, USB, FireWire, DB, RJ, and audio. Read the next paragraph to get your terminology straight, and then you can jump into the various connectors with gusto.

No one seems to use the terms *plug, port, jack,* or *connector* correctly, so let's get this right from the start. To connect one device to another, you need a cable containing the wires that make the connection. On each device, as well as on each end of the connecting cable, you need standardized parts to make that connection. Because these are usually electrical connections, you need one part to fit inside another to make a snug, safe connection.

A *plug* is a part with some type of projection that goes into a *port*. A port is a part that has some type of matching hole or slot that accepts the plug. You never put a port into a plug; it's always the other way around. The term *jack* is used as an alternative to port, so you may also put a plug into a jack. The term *connector* describes either a port or a plug. (See Figure 2-12.) As you progress through this chapter and see the different plugs and ports, this will become clearer.

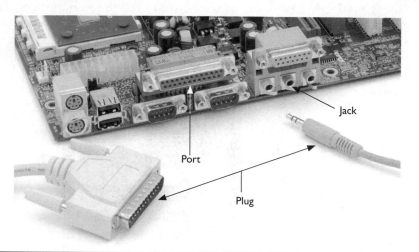

Figure 2-12   Plug, port, and jack

Mini-DIN Connectors

Most PCs sport the European-designed *mini-DIN* connectors. The original DIN connector was replaced by mini-DIN a long time ago, so you'll only see mini-DIN connectors on your PC (see Figure 2-13). Older-style keyboards and mice plug into mini-DIN ports.

Figure 2-13
DIN (top) and mini-
DIN connectors

USB Connectors

Universal serial bus (USB) provides the most common general-purpose connection for PCs. You'll find USB versions of many different devices, such as mice, keyboards, scanners, cameras, and printers. USB connections come in three different sizes: *A* (very common), *B*, and *mini-B* (less common). The USB A connector's distinctive rectangular shape makes it easily recognizable (Figure 2-14).

Figure 2-14
USB A connector
and port

You never see a USB B connector on your computer. USB B connectors are for the other end of the USB cable where it attaches to the USB device (Figure 2-15).

Figure 2-15
USB B connector

NOTE You'll sometimes hear USB ports and plugs described as *upstream* or *downstream*, terms that create rather amusing conversation and confusion. It's all about whether you refer to the plug or the port, so here's the scoop. The USB A plugs go upstream to USB A ports on the host or hub. USB A ports provide downstream output from the host or hub. So, the plug is upstream and the port is downstream. Just to add more fun to the mix, USB B plugs go downstream to devices. USB B ports provide upstream output from the device to the host or hub. My advice? Stick with A or B and nobody will get confused.

The USB B connector's relatively large size makes it less than optimal for small devices such as cameras, so the USB folks also make the smaller mini-B–style connector, as shown in Figure 2-16.

Figure 2-16
USB mini-B
connector

USB has a number of features that make it particularly popular on PCs. First, USB devices are *hot-swappable,* which means you can insert or remove them without restarting your PC. Almost every other type of connector requires you to turn the system off, insert or remove the connector, and then turn the system back on. Hot-swapping completely eliminates this process.

Second, many USB devices get their electrical power through the USB connection, so they don't need batteries or a plug for an electrical outlet. You can even recharge some devices, such as cellular telephones, by plugging them into a USB port (Figure 2-17).

Figure 2-17 Cell phone charging via a USB connection

FireWire Connectors

FireWire, also known as *IEEE 1394,* moves data at incredibly high speeds, making it the perfect connection for highly specialized applications, such as streaming video from a digital video camera onto a hard drive. FireWire consists of a special 6-wire connector, as shown in Figure 2-18. There's also a smaller, 4-pin version, usually seen on peripherals. Like USB, FireWire devices are hot-swappable.

Figure 2-18 FireWire connector and port

DB Connectors

Over the years, *DB connectors* have been used for almost any type of peripheral you can think of, with the exception of keyboards. They have a slight *D* shape, which allows only one proper way to insert a plug into the socket and makes it easier to remember what they're called. Technically, they're known as *D-sub* or *D-subminiature* connectors, but most techs call them DB.

Each male DB plug has a group of small pins that connect to DB ports. Female DB plugs connect to male DB ports on the system unit. DB connectors in the PC world can have from 9 to 37 pins or sockets, although you rarely see a DB connector with more than 25 pins or sockets. Figure 2-19 shows an example. DB-type connectors are some of the oldest and most common connectors used in the back of PCs.

Figure 2-19
DB-25 connector
and port

NOTE   Each size D-sub connector—called the *shell size*—has a specific name in the D-sub manufacturing world. A two-row, nine-pin connector, for example, is officially a DE-9 connector, rather than a DB-9. The E refers to the 9-pin shell size. Why all the DA, DB, DC, DD, and DE connectors became DB-*x* in the world of personal computers is a mystery, but most techs simply call them DB connectors.

It wasn't that long ago that a typical PC used at least three or more different DB connectors. Over the past few years, the PC world has moved away from DB connectors. A typical modern system might only have one or two, usually for a printer or video.

RJ Connectors

You have more than likely seen an *RJ connector,* whether or not you knew it by that name. The little plastic plug used to connect your telephone cord to the jack (techs don't use the word "port" to describe RJ connectors) is a classic example of an RJ plug. Modern PCs use only two types of RJ jacks: the RJ-11 and the RJ-45. The phone jack is an RJ-11. It is used

Figure 2-20
RJ-11 (top) and
RJ-45 (bottom)

almost exclusively for modems. The slightly wider RJ-45 jack is used for your network connection. Figure 2-20 shows an RJ-11 jack (top) and an RJ-45 jack (bottom).

Audio Connectors

Speakers and microphones connect to audio jacks on the system unit. The most common type of sound connector in popular use is the *mini-audio connector*. These small connectors have been around for years; they're just like the plug you use to insert headphones into an iPod or similar device (Figure 2-21). Traditionally, you'd find the audio jacks on the back of the PC, but many newer models sport front audio connections as well.

Figure 2-21
Mini-audio jacks
and plug

NOTE Keep in mind that the variety of connectors is virtually endless. The preceding types of connectors cover the vast majority, but many others exist in the PC world. No law or standard requires device makers to use a particular connector, especially if they have no interest in making that device interchangeable with similar devices from other manufacturers.

Devices and Their Connectors

Now that you have a sense of the connectors, let's turn to the devices common to almost every PC to learn which connectors go with which device.

NOTE Almost all connectors are now color coordinated to help users plug the right device into the right port. These color codes are not required, and not all PCs and devices use them.

Cards Versus Onboard

All of the connectors on the back of the PC are just that—connectors. Behind those connectors are the actual devices that support whatever peripherals plug into those connectors. These devices might be built into the computer, such as a keyboard port. Others might be add-on expansion cards that a tech installed into the PC.

Most PCs have special expansion slots inside the system unit that enable you to add more devices on expansion cards. Figure 2-22 shows a typical card. If you want some new device and your system unit doesn't have that device built into the PC, you just go to the store, buy a card version of that device, and snap it in! Later chapters of the book go into great detail on how to do this, but for now just appreciate that a device might be built in or it might come on a card.

Figure 2-22
Typical expansion card

Figure 2-23
Keyboard plug
and port

Keyboard

Today's keyboards come in many shapes and sizes, but connect into either a dedicated mini-DIN keyboard port or a USB port. Many keyboards ship with an adapter so you can use either port. Most keyboard plugs and mini-DIN ports are colored purple (see Figure 2-23).

Monitor

A monitor connects to the video connector on the system unit. You'll usually see one of two types of video connectors: the older 15-pin female DB *video graphics array (VGA)* connector or the unique *digital video interface* (DVI) connector. VGA connectors are colored blue, whereas DVI connectors are white. Many video cards have both types of connectors (Figure 2-24), or two VGA or two DVI connectors. Video cards with two connectors support two monitors, a very cool thing to do!

Occasionally you'll run into a video card with a mini-DIN connector, such as the S-Video connector you can see at the left in Figure 2-24. These mini-DIN connectors support all sorts of interesting video jobs, such as connecting to output to a television or input from a video camera.

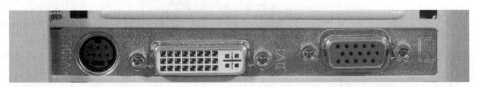

Figure 2-24   Video card with three ports. From left to right, S-Video, DVI, and VGA.

The newest video connector is called *High-Definition Multimedia Interface (HDMI)*, shown in Figure 2-25. HDMI is still very new to the video scene, but brings a number of enhancements, such as the ability to carry both video and sound on the same cable. Primarily designed for home theater, you'll see video cards with HDMI connectors growing more common over the next few years.

Figure 2-25
HDMI connector

Sound

The sound device on your card performs two functions. First, it takes digital information and turns it into sound, outputting the sound through speakers. Second, it takes sound that is input through a microphone and turns it into digital data.

To play and record sounds, your sound device needs to connect to at least a set of speakers and a microphone. All PCs have at least two miniature audio jacks: one for a microphone and another for stereo speakers. Better cards provide extra miniature audio jacks for surround sound. A few sound cards provide a female 15-pin DB port that enables you to attach an electronic musical instrument interface or add a joystick to your PC (see Figure 2-26).

Figure 2-26
Legacy joystick/MIDI
port

Adding more and more audio jacks to sound cards made the back of a typical sound card a busy place. In an effort to consolidate all of the different sound signals, the industry invented the *Sony/Philips Digital Interface Format (S/PDIF)* connection (Figure 2-27). One S/PDIF connection replaces all of the mini-audio connections, assuming your surround speaker system also comes with an S/PDIF connection.

Figure 2-27 S/PDIF connection

The color scheme for sound connections is complex, but for now remember one color—green. That's the one you need to connect a standard pair of stereo speakers.

Network

Networks are groups of connected PCs that share information. The PCs most commonly connect via some type of cabling that usually looks like an extra-thick phone cable. A modern PC uses an RJ-45 connection to connect to the network. Figure 2-28 shows a typical RJ-45 network connector. Network connectors do not have a standard color.

Figure 2-28
Typical network
connection

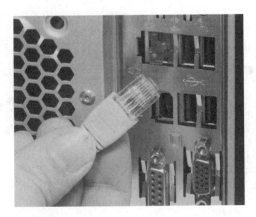

NOTE Modern PCs have built-in network connections, but this is a fairly recent development. For many years, network devices only came on an expansion card, called a *network interface card (NIC)*. The term is so common that even built-in network connections—which most certainly are not cards—are still called NICs.

Mouse

Most folks are pretty comfortable with the function of a mouse (Figure 2-29)—it enables you to select graphical items on a graphical screen. A PC mouse has at least two buttons (as opposed to the famous one-button mouse that came with Apple Macintosh computers until recently), while a better mouse provides a scroll wheel and extra buttons. A mouse uses either a USB port or a dedicated, light-green mini-DIN connector (see Figure 2-30).

Figure 2-29
Mouse

Figure 2-30
Typical mouse
mini-DIN connection

A variation of the mouse is a *trackball* (Figure 2-31). A trackball does the same job as a mouse, but instead of being pushed around like a mouse, the trackball stays in one place as you roll a ball with your fingers or thumb.

Figure 2-31
Trackball

Modem

A *modem* enables you to connect your PC to a telephone. A modem is another easily identifiable device in PCs. Most modems have two RJ-11 sockets. One connects the modem to the telephone jack on the wall, and the other is for an optional telephone so that you can use the phone line when the modem is not in use (see Figure 2-32).

Figure 2-32 Internal modem

External modems traditionally connected to a male 9-pin or 25-pin D-subminiature port on the system unit called a *serial port* (Figure 2-33). Although just about every external modem today connects to USB, most computers come with a serial port for legacy devices. Serial ports are one of the few connectors on modern systems that were also used in the first PCs more than 20 years ago!

Figure 2-33
Serial port

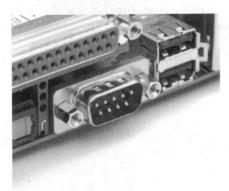

Printer

For many years, printers only used a special connector called a *parallel port*. Parallel ports use a 25-pin female DB connector that's usually colored fuchsia (see Figure 2-34).

Figure 2-34
Parallel port

After almost 20 years of domination by parallel ports, almost all printers now come with USB ports. Some better models even offer FireWire connections.

Figure 2-35
Joystick

Joystick

Joysticks (Figure 2-35) weren't supposed to be used just for games. When the folks at IBM added the 15-pin female DB joystick connector to PCs, they envisioned joysticks as hard-working input devices, just as the mouse is today. Except in the most rare circumstances, however, the only thing a joystick does today is enable you to turn your PC into a rather expensive game machine! But is there a more gratifying feeling than easing that joystick over, pressing the Fire button, and watching an enemy fighter jet get blasted by a well-placed Sidewinder missile? I think not. Traditional joystick connectors are colored orange, but most joysticks today connect to USB ports.

Plenty More!

Keep in mind that there are lots more devices and connectors out there! These are only the most common and the ones you're most likely to see. As we progress through this book, you'll see these less common connectors and where they are used.

Inside the System Unit

Now that you've seen the devices that connect to the PC, let's open up the system unit to inspect the major internal components of a typical PC. A single PC is composed of thousands of discrete components. Although no one can name every tiny bit of electronics in a PC, a good technician should be able to name the major internal components that make up the typical PC. Let's open and inspect a system unit to see these components and gain at least a concept of what they do. In later chapters, you'll see all of these components in much more detail.

Case

The system unit's case is both the internal framework of the PC and the external skin that protects the internal components from the environment. Cases come in an amazing variety of styles, sizes, and colors. Figure 2-36 shows the front and back of a typical PC case. The front of the case holds the buttons used to turn the system on and off, lights to tell you the status of the system, and access doors to removable media drives such as floppy, CD-ROM, and DVD drives. This system also provides USB, FireWire, and audio connections in the front for easy access if you want to use a device that needs these connections.

Figure 2-36
Front and back of
a typical PC case
showing various
buttons and ports

 NOTE Front connections are most commonly used for temporary devices, such as headphones. If you have a device you don't intend to remove very often, you should install it in one of the back connections.

The back of the case holds the vast majority of the system unit connections. You will also notice the power supply—almost always at the top of the case—distinguished by its cooling fan and power plug. Note that one area of the back of the case holds all the onboard connections, while another area contains slots for cards. The onboard ports need holes so you can plug devices into them (see Figure 2-37). Similarly, the case uses slots to enable access to the external connectors on cards installed in the system unit.

Figure 2-37 Onboard devices

NOTE You'll hear the PC case called the *enclosure*, especially at the more expensive end of the spectrum. Case, enclosure, and system unit are interchangeable terms.

Opening a case is always … interesting. There's no standard way to open a case, and I'm convinced that the folks making system units enjoy some sick humor inventing new and complex ways to open them. In general, you detach the sides of a case by removing a few screws in the back of the system unit, as shown in Figure 2-38. Use common sense and you won't have too many problems. Just don't lose track of your screws or where each one was inserted!

Figure 2-38
Opening a
system unit

Once you've opened the case, take a look inside. You see metal framework, all kinds of cables, and a number of devices. As you inspect the devices, you may gently push cables to the side to get a better view. Don't forget to wear an anti-static wrist strap or touch the metal case occasionally to prevent ESD.

CPU

The *central processing unit (CPU)*, also called the *microprocessor,* performs all the calculations that take place inside a PC. CPUs come in a variety of shapes and sizes, as shown in Figure 2-39.

Figure 2-39
Typical CPUs

Modern CPUs generate a lot of heat and thus require a cooling fan and heat sink assembly to avoid overheating (see Figure 2-40). A heat sink is a big slab of copper or aluminum that helps draw heat away from the processor. The fan then blows the heat out into the case. You can usually remove this cooling device if you need to replace it, although some CPU manufacturers have sold CPUs with a fan permanently attached.

Figure 2-40
CPU with fan in PC

CPUs have a make and model, just like automobiles do. When talking about a particular car, for example, most people speak in terms of a Ford Taurus or a Toyota Camry. When they talk about CPUs, people say Intel Pentium 4 or AMD Athlon. Over the years, there have been only a few major CPU manufacturers, just as there are only a few major auto manufacturers. The two most common makes of CPUs used in PCs are AMD and Intel.

Although only a few manufacturers of CPUs have existed, those manufacturers have made hundreds of models of CPUs. Some of the more common models made over the last few years have names such as Celeron, Athlon, Sempron, Pentium III, and Pentium 4.

Finally, CPUs come in different packages. The package defines how the CPU looks physically and how it connects to the computer. The predominant package type is called *pin grid array (PGA)*. Every package type has lots of variations.

Chapter 3, "Microprocessors," goes into great detail on CPUs, but for now remember that every CPU has a make, a model, and a package type.

RAM

Random access memory (RAM) stores programs and data currently being used by the CPU. The maximum amount of programs and data that a piece of RAM can store is measured in units called *bytes*. Modern PCs have many millions, even billions, of bytes of RAM, so RAM is measured in units called *megabytes (MB)* or *gigabytes (GB)*. An average PC will have from 256 MB to 2 GB of RAM, although you may see PCs with far more or far less RAM. Each piece of RAM is called a *stick*. One common type of stick found in today's PC is called a *dual inline memory module (DIMM)*. Figure 2-41 shows two examples of DIMMs used in PCs.

Figure 2-41
Two DIMMs

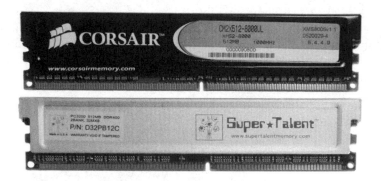

Your PC takes only one type of DIMM, and you must know the type so you can add or replace RAM when needed. Chapter 4, "RAM," covers everything you need to know to work comfortably with RAM.

 CAUTION Some parts of your PC are much more sensitive to ESD than others. Your CPU and RAM are very sensitive to ESD. If you touch the metal parts of your CPU or RAM and you have even the tiniest amount of charge, it can destroy them.

Motherboard

You can compare a motherboard to the chassis of an automobile. In a car, everything connects to the chassis either directly or indirectly. In a PC, everything connects to the motherboard either directly or indirectly. A motherboard is a thin, flat piece of circuit board, usually green or gold, and often slightly larger than a typical piece of notebook paper (see Figure 2-42).

Figure 2-42
Typical
motherboard

A motherboard contains a number of special sockets that accept various PC components. The CPU and RAM, for example, plug directly into the motherboard. Other devices, such as floppy drives, hard drives, CD and DVD drives, connect to the motherboard sockets through short cables. Motherboards also provide onboard connectors for external devices such as mice, printers, joysticks, and keyboards.

All motherboards use multipurpose expansion slots that enable you to add adapter cards. Different types of expansion slots exist for different types of cards (see Figure 2-43).

Figure 2-43 Expansion slots

Power Supply

The *power supply,* as its name implies, provides the necessary electrical power to make the PC operate. The power supply takes standard (in the United States) 110-volt AC power and converts it into 12-volt, 5-volt, and 3.3-volt DC power. Most power supplies are about the size of a shoebox cut in half and are usually a gray or metallic color (see Figure 2-44).

Figure 2-44
Power supply

A number of connectors lead out of the power supply. Every power supply provides special connectors to power the motherboard and a number of other general-use connectors that provide power to any device that needs electricity. Figure 2-45 shows both the motherboard power and typical general-use connectors. Check out Chapter 8, "Power Supplies," for more information.

Figure 2-45
Power connectors

Floppy Drive

The *floppy drive* enables you to access removable floppy disks (diskettes). The floppy drive used in PCs today is called a 3.5" floppy drive (Figure 2-46). Floppy drives only store a tiny amount of data and are disappearing from many PCs.

The floppy drive connects to the computer via a *ribbon cable,* which in turn connects to the motherboard. The connection to the motherboard is known as the *floppy drive controller* (Figure 2-47).

Figure 2-46
Floppy drive

Figure 2-47
Floppy drive
connected to
motherboard

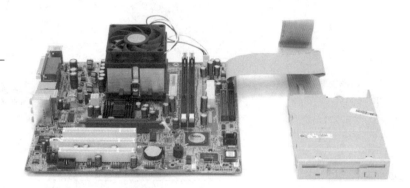

Hard Drive

Hard drives store programs and data that are not currently being used by the CPU (Figure 2-48). Even though both hard drives and RAM use the same storage units (megabytes and gigabytes), a PC's hard drive stores much more data than a typical PC's RAM—up to hundreds of gigabytes.

Figure 2-48
Typical hard drive

An average PC has one hard drive, although most PCs accept more. Special PCs that need to store large amounts of data, such as a large corporation's main file storage computer, can contain many hard drives—8 to 16 drives in some cases.

By far the most common type of hard drive seen in today's PC fall under the *AT Attachment (ATA)* standard. These drives come in two types: the older *parallel ATA (PATA)* or the more modern *serial ATA (SATA)*. PATA drives use a ribbon cable very similar to the one used by floppy drives, whereas SATA drives use a very narrow cable. Figure 2-49 shows a SATA drive (left) next to a PATA drive (right). Most motherboards come with connections for both types of drives.

Figure 2-49
SATA and
PATA drives

 NOTE A very few PCs use *small computer system interface (SCSI)* drives. SCSI drives are generally faster and more expensive, so they usually show up only in high-end PCs such as network servers or graphics workstations.

Almost all CD-ROM and DVD drives are actually PATA drives and connect via a ribbon cable just like a PATA hard drive. Figure 2-50 shows a DVD drive connected to a ribbon cable with a PATA hard drive—a very common sight inside a PC.

Figure 2-50
Hard drive and
DVD drive

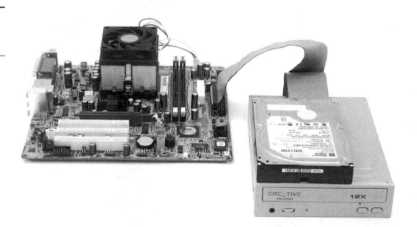

Optical Media

CDs, DVDs—there are so many types of those shiny discs to put in computers (Figure 2-51)! The term *optical media* describes all of them. Generally, you may break optical media into two groups: CDs and DVDs. CDs store around 700 MB and come in three varieties: CD-ROM (*read only memory:* you can't change the data on them), CD-R (*recordable:* you can change the data once), and CD-RW (*rewritable:* you can change the data on them over and over). DVDs store much more data—around 4 GB, enough for a Hollywood movie—and come in even more varieties: DVD-ROM, DVD+R, DVD-R, DVD+RW, and DVD-RW, just to name the more famous ones.

Figure 2-51
Assorted optical
media discs

All of these different optical-media discs require an optical drive that knows how to read them. If you want to do anything with a CD-RW disc, for example, you need a CD-RW drive. If you want to use a DVD+R disc, you need a DVD+R drive. Luckily, most optical drives support many different types of discs, and some support every common type of optical media available! Figure 2-52 shows typical optical drives. Note that some of them advertise the types of media they use. Others give no clue whatsoever.

 NOTE Chapter 11, "Removable Media," goes into great detail on the assorted disc and drive types.

Figure 2-52
Optical drives

Know Your Parts

The entire goal of this chapter was to get you to appreciate the names and functions of the different parts of the PC: peripherals, connectors, and components. You also learned about ESD and other issues that come into play when working with a PC. By starting with the Big Picture view, you may now begin breaking down the individual components on a chapter-by-chapter basis and truly understand at great depth how each component works and how they interconnect with the PC system as a whole.

Chapter Review Questions

1. What do you call the commands that tell the computer what to do?

    A. Data

    B. Morse code

    C. Programming

    D. Output

2. What is the essential tool for computer techs?

    A. File

    B. Phillips-head screwdriver

    C. Pliers

    D. Flat-head screwdriver

3. Where do you connect an anti-static wrist strap? (Select the best answer.)

    A. To an anti-static plate on the computer

    B. To an electrical outlet

    C. To a handy metal part of the case

    D. Non-static wrist strap

4. What sort of connector does a typical network card have?

    A. DB-9

    B. Mini-DIN

    C. RJ-11

    D. RJ-45

5. Modern keyboards connect to which of the following ports? (Select all that apply.)

    A. DIN

    B. FireWire

    C. Mini-DIN

    D. USB

6. Which end of the USB cable plugs into the PC?

   A. A

   B. B

   C. Mini-A

   D. Mini-B

7. A printer usually plugs into which of the following ports? (Select two.)

   A. DB-9

   B. DB-25

   C. Mini-DIN

   D. USB

8. What do you plug into a three-row, 15-pin port?

   A. Joystick

   B. Keyboard

   C. Monitor

   D. Mouse

9. What connector was designed to connect your PC to a high-end television set?

   A. DB-HD

   B. DVI

   C. HDMI

   D. VGA

10. What connector was designed to connect your PC to a high-end audio system?

    A. DB-HA

    B. DVI

    C. Mini-audio

    D. S/PDIF

Answers

1. **C.** Programming is the general term for commands that tell the computer what to do.

2. **B.** A Phillips-head screwdriver is the essential tool for computer techs.

3. **C.** Connect an anti-static wrist strap to any handy metal part of the computer. The metal plate, by the way, is the section on the strap where you connect the cable from the PC.

4. **D.** A typical network card sports an RJ-45 port.

5. **C, D.** Modern keyboards connect to either mini-DIN or USB ports.

6. **A.** Plug the USB A connector into the PC.

7. **B, D.** A printer usually plugs into either DB-25 or USB (although some can use FireWire, it's not as common).

8. **C.** You plug a monitor into a three-row, 15-pin port.

9. **C.** HDMI was designed to connect your PC to a high-end television set.

10. **D.** S/PDIF was designed to connect your PC to a high-end audio system.

Microprocessors

In this chapter, you will learn how to
- Identify the core components of a CPU
- Describe the relationship of CPUs and RAM
- Explain the varieties of modern CPUs
- Identify specialty CPUs
- Install and upgrade CPUs

For all practical purposes, the terms *microprocessor* and *central processing unit (CPU)* mean the same thing: it's that big chip inside your computer that many people often describe as the brain of the system. From the previous chapter, you know that CPU makers name their microprocessors in a fashion similar to the automobile industry: CPU names get a make and a model, such as Intel Core 2 Duo or AMD Athlon 64. But what's happening inside the CPU to make it able to do the amazing things asked of it every time you step up to the keyboard?

Historical/Conceptual

CPU Core Components

Although the computer might seem to act quite intelligently, comparing the CPU to a human brain hugely overstates its capabilities. A CPU functions more like a very powerful calculator than a brain—but, oh, what a calculator! Today's CPUs add, subtract, multiply, divide, and move billions of numbers per second. Processing that much information so quickly makes any CPU look quite intelligent. It's simply the speed of the CPU, rather than actual intelligence, that enables computers to perform feats such as accessing the Internet, playing visually stunning games, or creating graphics.

A good PC technician needs to understand some basic CPU functions in order to support PCs, so let's start with an analysis of how the CPU works. If you wanted to teach someone how an automobile engine works, you would use a relatively simple example engine, right? The same principle applies here. Let's begin our study of the CPU using the granddaddy of all CPUs: the famous Intel 8088, invented in the late 1970s. Although this CPU first appeared over 25 years ago, it defined the idea of the modern microprocessor and contains the same basic parts used in even the most advanced CPUs today. Stick with me, my friend. Prepare to enter that little bit of magic called the CPU.

The Man in the Box

Let's begin by visualizing the CPU as a man in a box (Figure 3-1). This is one clever guy in the box. He can perform virtually any mathematical function, manipulate data, and give answers *very quickly.*

Figure 3-1
Imagine the CPU as a man in a box.

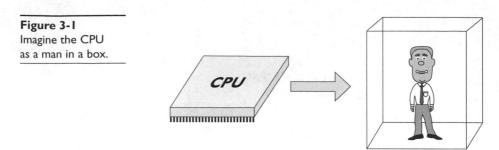

This guy is potentially very useful to us, but there's a catch—he lives closed up in a tiny black box. Before he can work with us, we must come up with a way to exchange information with him (Figure 3-2).

Figure 3-2
How do we talk to the Man in the Box?

Imagine that we install a set of 16 light bulbs, 8 inside his box and 8 outside his box. Each of the 8 light bulbs inside the box connects to one of the 8 bulbs outside the box to form a pair. Each pair of light bulbs is always either on or off. You can control the 8 pairs of bulbs using a set of 8 switches outside the box, and the Man in the Box can also control them using an identical set of 8 switches inside the box. This light bulb communication device is called the *external data bus* (*EDB*).

Figure 3-3 shows a cutaway view of the external data bus. When either you or the Man in the Box flip a switch on, *both* light bulbs go on, and the switch on the other side is also flipped to the on position. If you or the Man in the Box turn a switch off, the light bulbs on both sides are turned off, along with the other switch for that pair.

Figure 3-3
Cutaway of the external data bus—note that one light bulb is on

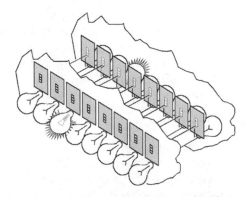

Can you see how this will work? By creating on/off patterns with the light bulbs that represent different pieces of data or commands, you can send that information to the Man in the Box, and he can send information back in the same way—*assuming that you agree ahead of time on what the different patterns of lights mean.* To accomplish this, you need some sort of codebook that assigns meanings to the many different patterns of lights that the external data bus might display. Keep this thought in mind while we push the analogy a bit more.

Before going any further, make sure you're clear on the fact that this is an analogy, not reality. There really is an external data bus, but you won't see any light bulbs or switches

Figure 3-4
Close-up of the underside of a CPU

on the CPU. You can, however, see little wires sticking out of the CPU (Figure 3-4). If you apply voltage to one of these wires, you in essence flip the switch. Get the idea? So if that wire had voltage, and if a tiny light bulb were attached to the wire, that light bulb would glow, would it not? By the same token, if the wire had no power, then the light bulb would not glow. That is why the switch-and-light bulb analogy may help you picture these little wires constantly flashing on and off.

Now that the external data bus enables you to communicate with the Man in the Box, you need to see how it works by placing voltages on the wires. This brings up a naming problem. It's a hassle to say terms such as "on-off-off-off-on-on-off-off" when talking about which wires have voltage. Rather than saying that one of the external data bus wires is on or off, use the number 1 to represent on and the number 0 to represent off (Figure 3-5). That way, instead of describing the state of the lights as "on-off-off-off-on-on-off-off," I can instead describe them by writing "10001100."

Figure 3-5
Here "1" means on; "0" means off.

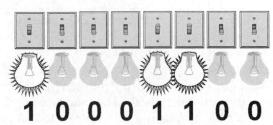

1 0 0 0 1 1 0 0

In the world of computers, we constantly turn wires on and off. As a result, this "1 and 0" or *binary* system is used to describe the state of these wires at any given moment. (See, and you just thought computer geeks spoke in binary to confuse normal people! Ha!) There's much more to binary numbering in the world of computing, but this is a great place to start. This binary numbering system will be revisited in greater detail in Chapter 6, "Expansion Bus."

Registers

The Man in the Box provides good insight into the workspace inside a CPU. The EDB gives you a way to communicate with the Man in the Box so you can give him work to do. But to do this work, he needs a worktable; in fact, he needs at least four worktables. Each of these four worktables has 16 light bulbs. These light bulbs are not in pairs; they're just 16 light bulbs lined up straight across the table. Each light bulb is controlled by a single switch, operated only by the Man in the Box. By creating On/Off patterns like the ones on the EDB, the Man in the Box can work math problems using these four sets of light bulbs. In a real computer, these worktables are called *registers* (Figure 3-6).

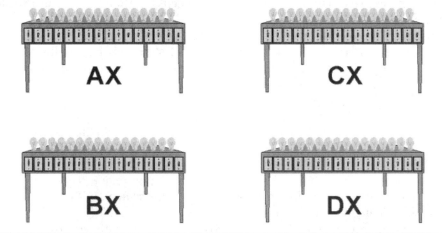

Figure 3-6   The four general-purpose registers

Registers provide the Man in the Box with a workplace for the problems you give him. All CPUs contain a large number of registers, but for the moment let's concentrate on the four most commonly used ones: the *general-purpose registers.* Intel gave them the names AX, BX, CX, and DX.

NOTE   The 8088 was the first CPU to use the four now famous AX–DX general-purpose registers, but they still exist in even the latest CPUs. (But they've got a lot more light bulbs!)

Great! We're just about ready to put the Man in the Box to work, but before you close the lid on the box, you must give the Man one more tool. Remember the codebook we mentioned earlier? Let's make one to enable us to communicate with him. Figure 3-7 shows the codebook we'll use. We'll give one copy to him and make a second for us.

In this codebook, for example, 10000111 means *Move the number 7 into the AX register.* These commands are called the microprocessor's *machine language.* The commands

Figure 3-7
CPU codebook

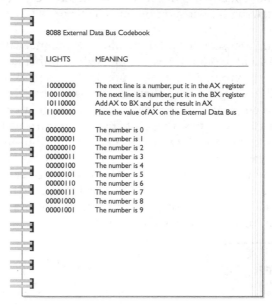

8088 External Data Bus Codebook

LIGHTS	MEANING
10000000	The next line is a number, put it in the AX register
10010000	The next line is a number, put it in the BX register
10110000	Add AX to BX and put the result in AX
11000000	Place the value of AX on the External Data Bus
00000000	The number is 0
00000001	The number is 1
00000010	The number is 2
00000011	The number is 3
00000100	The number is 4
00000101	The number is 5
00000110	The number is 6
00000111	The number is 7
00001000	The number is 8
00001001	The number is 9

listed in the figure are not actual commands—as you've probably guessed, I've simplified dramatically. The Intel 8088 CPU, invented in the late 1970s, actually used commands very similar to these, plus a few hundred others.

Here are some examples of real machine language for the Intel 8088:

10111010	The next line of code is a number. Put that number into the DX register.
01000001	Add 1 to the number already in the CX register.
00111100	Compare the value in the AX register with the next line of code.

By placing machine language commands—called *lines of code*—onto the external data bus one at a time, you can instruct the Man in the Box to do specific tasks. All of the machine language commands that the CPU understands make up the CPU's *instruction set.*

So here is the CPU so far: the Man in the Box can communicate with the outside world via the external data bus; he has four registers he can use to work on the problems you give him; and he has a codebook—the instruction set—so he can understand the different patterns (machine language commands) on the external data bus (Figure 3-8).

Figure 3-8
The CPU so far

Clock

Okay, so you're ready to put the Man in the Box to work. You can send the first command by lighting up wires on the EDB. How does he know when you're done setting up the wires and it's time to act?

Have you ever seen one of those old-time manual calculators with the big crank on one side? To add two numbers, you pressed a number key, the + key, and another number key, but then to make the calculator do the calculation and give you the answer, you had to pull down the crank. That was the signal that you were done entering data and instructions and ready for the calculator to give you an answer.

Well, a CPU also has a type of crank. To return to the Man in the Box, imagine there's a buzzer inside the box activated by a button on the outside of the box. Each time you press the button to sound the buzzer, the Man in the Box reads the next set of lights on the external data bus. Of course, a real computer doesn't use a buzzer. The buzzer on a real CPU is a special wire called the CLOCK wire (most diagrams label the clock wire CLK). A charge on the CLK wire tells the CPU there's another piece of information waiting to be processed (Figure 3-9).

Figure 3-9
The CPU does
nothing until
activated by
the clock!

For the CPU to process a command placed on the external data bus, a certain minimum voltage must be applied to the CLK wire. A single charge to the CLK wire is called a *clock cycle*. Actually, the CPU requires at least two clock cycles to act on a command, and usually more. Using the manual calculator analogy, you need to pull the crank at least twice before anything happens. In fact, a CPU may require hundreds of clock cycles to process some commands (Figure 3-10).

Figure 3-10
The CPU often
needs more than
one clock cycle
to get a result.

The maximum number of clock cycles that a CPU can handle in a given period of time is referred to as its *clock speed*. The clock speed is the fastest speed at which a CPU can operate, determined by the CPU manufacturer. The Intel 8088 processor had a clock speed of 4.77 MHz (4.77 million of cycles per second), extremely slow by modern standards, but still a pretty big number compared to using a pencil and paper! CPUs today run at speeds in excess of 3 GHz (3 billion cycles per second).

1 hertz (1 Hz) = 1 cycle per second
1 megahertz (1 MHz) = 1 million cycles per second
1 gigahertz (1 GHz) = 1 billion cycles per second

NOTE CPU makers sell the exact make and model of CPU at a number of different speeds. All of these CPUs come off of the same assembly lines, so why different speeds? Every CPU comes with subtle differences—flaws, really—in the silicon that makes one CPU run faster than another. The speed difference comes from testing each CPU to see what speed it can handle.

Understand that a CPU's clock speed is its *maximum* speed, not the speed at which it *must* run. A CPU can run at any speed, as long as that speed does not exceed its clock speed. Manufacturers used to print the CPU's clock speed directly onto the CPU, but for the last few years they've used cryptic codes (Figure 3-11). As the chapter progresses, you'll see why they do this.

Figure 3-11
Where is the
clock speed?

> **AMD Athlon™64**
> ADA3200AEP5AP
> CAAKC 0334TPMW
> 9441535240617

The *system crystal* determines the speed at which a CPU and the rest of the PC operate. This is called the *system bus speed*. The system crystal is usually a quartz oscillator, very similar to the one in a wristwatch, soldered to the motherboard (Figure 3-12). The quartz oscillator sends out an electric pulse at a certain speed, many millions of times per second. This signal goes first to a clock chip that adjusts the pulse, usually increasing the pulse sent by the crystal by some large multiple. (The folks who make motherboards could directly connect the crystal to the CPU's clock wire, but then if you wanted to replace your CPU with a CPU with a different clock speed, you'd need to replace the crystal too!) As long as the PC is turned on, the quartz oscillator, through the clock chip, fires a charge on the CLK wire, in essence pushing the system along.

Figure 3-12
One of many types
of system crystals

Visualize the system crystal as a metronome for the CPU. The quartz oscillator repeatedly fires a charge on the CLK wire, setting the beat, if you will, for the CPU's activities. If the system crystal sets a beat slower than the CPU's clock speed, the CPU will work just fine, but it will operate at the slower speed of the system crystal. If the system crystal forces the CPU to run faster than its clock speed, it can overheat and stop working.

NOTE Aggressive users sometimes intentionally overclock CPUs by telling the clock chip to multiply the pulse faster than the CPU's designed speed. They do this to make slower (cheaper) CPUs run faster. This is a risky business that can destroy your CPU, but those willing to take that risk often do it. See the "Overclocking" section later in this chapter.

Before you install a CPU into a system, you must make sure that the crystal and clock chip send out the correct clock pulse for that particular CPU. In the not so old days, this required very careful adjustments. With today's systems, the motherboard talks to the CPU (at a very slow speed), the CPU tells the motherboard the clock speed it needs, and the clock chip automatically adjusts for the CPU, making this process invisible.

NOTE Some motherboards enable you to override the default or automatic settings by changing a jumper or making a change in CMOS. A few enthusiasts' motherboards even enable you to make software changes to alter the speed of your CPU.

Back to the External Data Bus

One more reality check. We've been talking about tables with racks of light bulbs, but of course real CPU registers don't use light bulbs to represent on/1 and off/0. Registers are tiny storage areas on the CPU, microscopic semiconductor circuits. When one of these circuits holds a charge, you can think of the light bulb as on; no charge, the light bulb is off.

Figure 3-13 is a diagram of a real 8088 CPU, showing the wires that comprise the external data bus and the single clock wire. Because the registers are inside the CPU, they can't be shown in this figure.

Figure 3-13
Diagram of an Intel 8088 showing the external data bus and clock wires

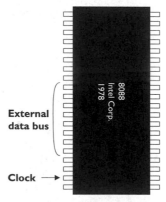

External data bus

Clock →

Now that you have learned what components are involved in the process, try the following simple exercise to see how the process works. In this example, you tell the CPU to add 2 + 3. To do this, you must send a series of commands to the CPU—the CPU will act on each command, eventually giving you an answer. Refer to the codebook in Figure 3-7 to translate the instructions you're giving the Man in the Box into binary commands.

Did you try it? Here's how it works:

1. Place 10000000 on the external data bus (EDB).

2. Place 00000010 on the EDB.

3. Place 10010000 on the EDB.

4. Place 00000011 on the EDB.

5. Place 10110000 on the EDB.

6. Place 11000000 on the EDB.

When you finish Step 6, the value on the EDB will be 00000101, the decimal number 5 written in binary.

Congrats! You just added 2 + 3 using individual commands from the codebook. This set of commands is known as a *program*, which is a series of commands sent to a CPU in a specific order for the CPU to perform work. Each discrete setting of the external data bus is a line of code. This program, therefore, has six lines of code.

Memory

Now that you've seen how the CPU executes program code, let's work backward in the process for a moment and think about how the program code gets to the external data bus. The program itself is stored on the hard drive. In theory, you could build a computer that sends data from the hard drive directly to the CPU, but there's a problem—the hard drive is too slow. Even the ancient 8088, with its clock speed of 4.77 MHz, could conceivably process several million lines of code every second. Modern CPUs crank out billions of lines every second. Hard drives simply can't give the data to the CPU at a fast enough speed.

Computers need some other device that takes copies of programs from the hard drive and then sends them, one line at a time, to the CPU quickly enough to keep up with its demands. Because each line of code is nothing more than a pattern of eight ones and zeroes, any device that can store ones and zeroes eight across will do. Devices that in any way hold ones and zeroes that the CPU accesses are known generically as *memory*.

Many types of device store ones and zeroes perfectly well—technically even a piece of paper counts as memory—but computers need memory that does more than just store groups of eight ones and zeroes. Consider this pretend program:

1. Put 2 in the AX register.

2. Put 5 in the BX register.

3. If AX is greater than BX, run line 4; otherwise, go to line 6.

4. Add 1 to the value in AX.

5. Go back to line 1.

6. Put the value of AX on the EDB.

This program has an IF statement, also called a *branch* by CPU makers. The CPU needs a way to address each line of this memory—a way for the CPU to say, "Give me the next line of code" or "Give me line 6" to the memory. Addressing memory takes care of another problem: the memory must store not only programs, but also the result of the programs. If the CPU adds 2 + 3 and gets 5, the memory needs to store that 5 in such a way that other programs may later read that 5, or possibly even store that 5 on a hard drive. By addressing each line of memory, other programs will know where to find the data.

Memory and RAM

Memory must store not only programs, but also data. The CPU needs to be able to read and write to this storage medium. Additionally, this system must enable the CPU to jump to *any* line of code as easily as to any other line of code that it stores. All of this must be done at or at least near the clock speed of the CPU. Fortunately, this magical device has existed for many years: *random access memory (RAM)*.

In Chapter 4 the concept of RAM is developed in detail, so for now let's look at RAM as an electronic spreadsheet, like one you can generate in Microsoft Excel (Figure 3-14). Each cell in this spreadsheet can store only a one or a zero. Each cell is called a *bit*. Each row in the spreadsheet is eight bits across to match the external data bus of the 8088. Each row of eight bits is called a *byte*. In the PC world, RAM transfers and stores data to and from the CPU in byte-sized chunks. RAM is therefore arranged in byte-sized rows. Here are the terms used when talking about quantities of bits:

- Any individual 1 or 0 = a *bit*
- 4 bits = a *nibble*
- 8 bits = a *byte*
- 16 bits = a *word*
- 32 bits = a *double word*
- 64 bits = a *paragraph* or *quad word*

Figure 3-14
RAM as a spreadsheet

I	0	0	0	0	0	I	I	I
0	I	0	0	0	0	0	0	0
0	0	0	0	I	I	0	I	I
0	I	0	I	0	0	0	0	I
0	0	0	0	0	0	0	I	0
0	I	0	I	I	0	I	0	I
0	0	I	I	I	I	0	0	0
0	0	0	0	I	0	0	I	I
I	I	I	0	0	0	0	0	0
0	0	I	0	I	I	I	0	I
I	0	0	0	0	0	0	0	0
I	0	I	0	I	0	I	0	I

The number of bytes of RAM varies from PC to PC. In the earlier PCs, from around 1980 to 1990, the typical system would have only a few hundred thousand bytes of RAM. Today's systems often have billions of bytes of RAM.

Let's stop here for a quick reality check. Electronically, RAM looks like a spreadsheet, but real RAM is made of groups of semiconductor chips soldered onto small cards that snap into your computer (Figure 3-15). In the next chapter, you'll see how these groups of chips actually make themselves look like a spreadsheet. For now, don't worry about real RAM and just stick with the spreadsheet idea.

Figure 3-15
Typical RAM

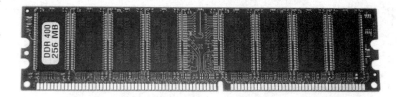

The CPU accesses any one row of RAM as easily and as fast as any other row, which explains the "random access" part of RAM. Not only is RAM randomly accessible, it's also fast. By storing programs on RAM, the CPU can access and run programs very quickly. RAM also stores any data that the CPU actively uses.

Computers use *dynamic RAM* (*DRAM*) for the main system memory. DRAM needs both a constant electrical charge and a periodic refresh of the circuits, otherwise it loses data—that's what makes it dynamic, rather than static in content. The refresh can cause some delays, as the CPU has to wait for the refresh to happen, but modern CPU manufacturers have clever ways to get by this issue, as you'll see when you read about the generations of processors later in this chapter.

Don't confuse RAM with mass storage devices like hard drives and floppy drives. You use hard drives and floppy drives to store programs and data permanently. Chapters 9 through 11 discuss permanent storage in intimate detail.

Address Bus

So far, the entire PC consists of only a CPU and RAM. But there needs to be some connection between the CPU and the RAM so they can talk to each other. To do so, extend the external data bus from the CPU so that it can talk to the RAM (Figure 3-16).

Figure 3-16
Extending the EDB

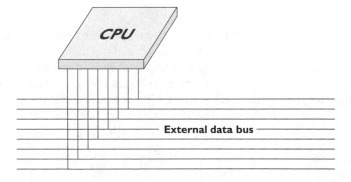

Wait a minute. How can you connect the RAM to the external data bus? This is not a matter of just plugging it into the external data bus wires! RAM is a spreadsheet with thousands and thousands of discrete rows, and you only need to look at the contents of one row of the spreadsheet at a time, right? So how do you connect RAM to the external data bus in such a way that the CPU can see any one given row, but still give the CPU the capability to look at *any* row in RAM? We need some type of chip between RAM and the CPU to make the connection. The CPU needs the ability to say which row of RAM it wants, and the chip should handle the mechanics of retrieving that row of data from RAM and putting it on the external data bus. Wouldn't you know I just happen to have such a chip? This chip comes with many names, but for right now just call it the *memory controller chip* (MCC).

The MCC contains special circuitry that enables it to grab the contents of any single line of RAM and place that data or command on the external data bus. This in turn enables the CPU to act on that code (Figure 3-17).

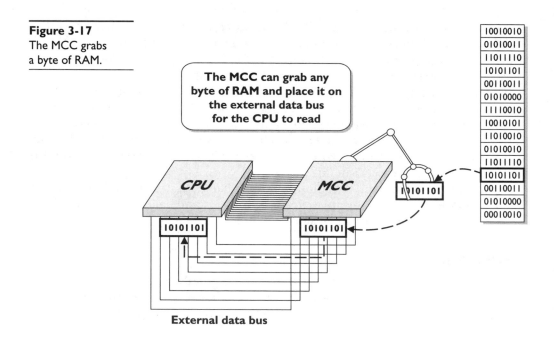

Figure 3-17
The MCC grabs a byte of RAM.

The MCC can grab any byte of RAM and place it on the external data bus for the CPU to read

CPU

MCC

External data bus

Once the MCC is in place to grab any discrete byte of RAM, the CPU needs the capability to tell the MCC which line of code it needs. The CPU, therefore, gains a second set of wires, called the *address bus,* that enables it to communicate with the MCC. Different CPUs have different numbers of wires (which, you will soon see, is very significant). The 8088 had 20 wires in its address bus (Figure 3-18).

Figure 3-18
Address bus

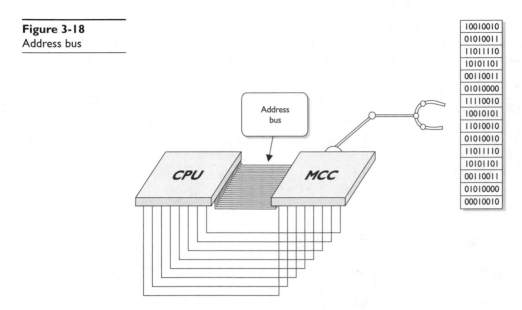

By turning the address bus wires on and off in different patterns, the CPU tells the MCC which line of RAM it wants at any given moment. Every different pattern of ones and zeroes on these 20 wires points to one byte of RAM. There are two big questions here. First, how many different patterns of "on" and "off" wires can exist with 20 wires? And second, which pattern goes to which row of RAM?

How many patterns?

Mathematics can answer the first question. Each wire in the address bus exists in only one of two different states: on or off. If the address bus consisted of only one wire, that wire would be at any given moment either on or off. Mathematically, that gives you (pull out your old pre-algebra books) $2^1 = 2$ different combinations. If you have two address bus wires, the address bus wires create $2^2 = 4$ different combinations. If you have 20 wires, you would have 2^{20} (or 1,048,576) combinations. Because each pattern points to one line of code and each line of RAM is one byte, *if you know the number of wires in the CPU's address bus, you know the maximum amount of RAM that a particular CPU can handle.* Because the 8088 had a 20-wire address bus, the most RAM it could handle was 2^{20} or 1,048,576 bytes. The 8088, therefore, had an *address space* of 1,048,576 bytes. This is not to say that every computer with an 8088 CPU had 1,048,576 bytes of RAM. Far from it! The original IBM PC only had a measly 64 kilobytes—but that was considered plenty back in the Dark Ages of Computing in the early 1980s.

Okay, so you know that the 8088 had 20 address wires and a total address space of 1,048,576 bytes. Although this is accurate, no one uses such an exact term to discuss the address space of the 8088. Instead, you say that the 8088 had one *megabyte* (1 MB) of address space.

What's a "mega"? Well, let's get some terminology down. Dealing with computers means constantly dealing with the number of patterns a set of wires can handle. Certain powers of 2 have names used a lot in the computing world. The following list explains:

1 kilo = 2^{10} = 1,024 (abbreviated as "K")

1 kilobyte = 1,024 bytes (abbreviated as "KB")

1 mega = 2^{20} = 1,048,576 (abbreviated as "M")

1 megabyte = 1,048,576 bytes (abbreviated as "MB")

1 giga = 2^{30} = 1,073,741,824 (abbreviated as "G")

1 gigabyte = 1,073,741,824 bytes (abbreviated as "GB")

1 tera = 2^{40} = 1,099,511,627,776 (abbreviated as "T")

1 terabyte = 1,099,511,627,776 bytes (abbreviated as "TB")

1 kilo is *not* equal to 1,000 (one thousand)

1 mega is *not* equal to 1,000,000 (one million)

1 giga is *not* equal to 1,000,000,000 (one billion)

1 tera is *not* equal to 1,000,000,000,000 (one trillion)

(But they are pretty close!)

NOTE Of course 1 kilo is equal to 1,000 when you talk in terms of the metric system. It also means 1,000 when you talk about the clock speed of a chip, so 1 KHz is equal to 1,000 Hz. When you talk storage capacity, though, the binary numbers kick in, making 1 KB = 1,024 bytes. Got it? This same bizarre, dual meaning applies all the way up the food chain, so 1 MHz is 1,000,000 Hz, but 1 MB is 1,048,576 bytes; 1 GHz is 1 billion Hz, but 1 GB is 1,073,741,824 bytes; and so on.

NOTE Bits and bytes are abbreviated differently. Bytes get a capital B whereas bits get a lowercase b. So, for example, 4 KB is four kilobytes, but 4 Kb is four kilobits!

Which Pattern Goes to Which Row?

The second question is a little harder: "Which pattern goes to which row of RAM?" To understand this, let's take a moment to discuss binary counting. In binary, only two numbers exist, 0 and 1, which makes binary a handy way to work with wires that turn on and off. Let's try to count in binary: 0, 1...what's next? It's not 2—you can only use 0s and 1s.

The next number after 1 is 10! Now let's count in binary to 1000: 0, 1, 10, 11, 100, 101, 110, 111, 1000. Try counting to 10000. Don't worry; it hardly takes any time at all.

Super, you now count in binary as well as any math professor. Let's add to the concept. Stop thinking about binary for just a moment and think about good old base 10 (regular numbers). If you have the number 365, can you put zeroes in front of the 365, like this: 000365? Sure you can—it doesn't change the value at all. The same thing is true in binary. Putting zeroes in front of a value doesn't change a thing! Let's count again to 1000 in binary. In this case, add enough zeroes to make 20 places:

00000000000000000000

00000000000000000001

00000000000000000010

00000000000000000011

00000000000000000100

00000000000000000101

00000000000000000110

00000000000000000111

00000000000000001000

Hey! This would be a great way to represent each line of RAM on the address bus, wouldn't it? The CPU identifies the first byte of RAM on the address bus as 00000000000000000000. The CPU identifies the last RAM row with 11111111111111111111. When the CPU turns off all the address bus wires, it wants the first line of RAM; when it turns on all the wires, it wants the 1,048,576th line of RAM. Obviously, the address bus also addresses all the other rows of RAM in between. So, by lighting up different patterns of 1s and 0s on the address bus, the CPU can access any row of RAM it needs.

Essentials

Modern CPUs

Modern CPUs retain the core structures of the Intel 8088, such as registers, instruction sets, and, of course, the *arithmetic logic unit (ALU)*—our friend, the Man in the Box. But in the decades of the personal computer, many manufacturers have risen to challenge Intel's dominance—some have even survived—and all processor makers have experimented with different processor shapes, connectors, and more. The amazing variety of modern CPUs presents unique challenges to a new tech. Which processors go on which motherboards? Can a motherboard use processors from two or more manufacturers? Aren't processors all designed for PCs and thus interchangeable?

This section maps out the modern processor scene. I'll start with a brief look at the manufacturers, so you know who the players are. Once you know who's making the CPUs, we'll go through the generations of CPUs in wide use today, starting with the Intel Pentium. All modern processors share fundamental technology first introduced by Intel in the Pentium CPU. I use the Pentium, therefore, to discuss the details of the shared technology, and then add specific bonus features when discussing subsequent processors.

Manufacturers

When IBM awarded Intel the contract to provide the CPUs for its new IBM PC back in 1980, it established for Intel a virtual monopoly on all PC CPUs. The other CPU makers of the time faded away: Tandy, Commodore, Texas Instruments—no one could compete directly with Intel. Over time, other competitors have risen to challenge Intel's market segment share dominance. In particular, a company called Advanced Micro Devices (AMD) began to make clones of Intel CPUs, creating an interesting and rather cutthroat competition with Intel that lasts to this day.

Intel

Intel Corporation thoroughly dominated the personal computer market with its CPUs and motherboard support chips. At nearly every step in the evolution of the PC, Intel has led the way with technological advances and surprising flexibility for such a huge corporation. Intel CPUs—and more specifically, their instruction sets—define the personal computer. Intel currently produces a dozen or so models of CPU for both desktop and portable computers, most of which use the name Pentium, such as the Pentium 4 and the Pentium M. Their lower-end CPUs use the Celeron branding; their highest-end ones are called Xeon.

AMD

You can't really talk about CPUs without mentioning Advanced Micro Devices—the Cogswell Cogs to Intel's Spacely Sprockets. AMD makes superb CPUs for the PC market and has grabbed roughly half of the CPU market. Like Intel, AMD doesn't just make CPUs, but their CPU business is certainly the part that the public notices. AMD has made CPUs that "clone" the function of Intel CPUs. If Intel invented the CPU used in the original IBM PC, how could AMD make clone CPUs without getting sued? Well, chipmakers have a habit of exchanging technologies through cross-license agreements. Way back in 1976, AMD and Intel signed just such an agreement, giving AMD the right to copy certain types of CPUs.

The trouble started with the Intel 8088. Intel needed AMD to produce CPUs. The PC business was young back then, and providing multiple suppliers gave IBM confidence in their choice of CPUs. Life was good. But after a few years, Intel had grown tremendously and no longer wanted AMD to make CPUs. AMD said, "Too bad. See this agreement you signed?" Throughout the 1980s and into the 1990s, AMD made pin-for-pin identical CPUs that matched the Intel lines of CPUs (Figure 3-19). You could yank an Intel CPU out of a system and snap in an AMD CPU—no problem!

Figure 3-19
Identical Intel and
AMD 486 CPUs
from the early 1990s

   In January 1995, after many years of legal wrangling, Intel and AMD settled and decided to end the licensing agreements. As a result of this settlement, AMD chips are no longer compatible—even though in some cases the chips look similar. Today, if you want to use an AMD CPU, you must purchase a motherboard designed for AMD CPUs. If you want to use an Intel CPU, you must purchase a motherboard designed for Intel CPUs. So you now have a choice: Intel or AMD. You'll look at both brands as you learn more about modern processors in this chapter.

CPU Packages

One of the many features that make PCs attractive is the ability for users (okay, maybe advanced users) to replace one CPU with another. If you want a removable CPU, you need your CPUs to use a standardized package with matching standardized socket on the motherboard. CPUs have gone through many packages, with manufacturers changing designs like snakes shedding skins. The fragile little DIP package of the 8088 (Figure 3-20) gave way to rugged slotted processors in the late 1990s (Figure 3-21), which have in turn given way to CPUs using the now prevalent grid array packaging.

Figure 3-20
The dual inline
pin package of
the Intel 8088

Figure 3-21
An AMD Athlon
Slot A processor

The grid array package has been popular since the mid-1980s. The most common form of grid array is the pin grid array (PGA). PGA CPUs are distinguished by their square shape with many—usually hundreds—of tiny pins (Figure 3-22).

Collectively, Intel and AMD have used close to 100 variations of the PGA package over the years for hundreds of different CPU models with names like staggered-PGA, micro-PGA, ball grid array (which uses tiny balls instead of pins) and land grid array (which uses flat pads instead of pins). There are also many different varieties of PGA CPUs based on the number of pins sticking out of the CPU. These CPUs snap into special sockets on the motherboard, with each socket designed to match the pins (or balls or pads) on the CPU. To make CPU insertion and removal easier, these sockets—officially called *zero insertion force (ZIF) sockets*—use a small arm on the side of the socket (Figure 3-23) or a cage that fits over the socket (Figure 3-24) to hold the CPU in place. ZIF sockets are universal and easily identified by their squarish shape.

NOTE Although there are many types of PGA packages, most techs just call them all "PGA."

Figure 3-23
ZIF socket with
arm on side

Figure 3-24
ZIF socket with cage
over the top

The first generations of sockets used a numbering system that started with Socket 1 and went through Socket 8. The hassle of trying to remember how many pins went with each type of socket made it clear after a while that the CPU makers might as well give all sockets a name based on the number of pins. Most sockets today have names like Socket 940 and Socket 775 to reflect the number of pins.

NOTE AMD CPUs and sockets have totally different numbering systems than Intel CPUs and sockets, so techs often use the name of the socket instead of AMD or Intel. For example: "Hey, did you see that Socket 775 motherboard?"

It's very important to know the more common CPU/socket types. As you go through each type of CPU in this chapter, pay attention to the socket types used by those particular CPUs.

The Pentium CPU: The Early Years

Since the advent of the 8088 way back in the late 1970s, CPU makers have added a large number of improvements. As technology has progressed from the 8088 to the most current CPUs, the sizes of the external data bus, address bus, and registers have grown dramatically. In addition, the clock speeds at which CPUs run have kept pace, getting faster and faster with each successive generation of processor. The 1980s were an exciting time for CPU technology. The 8088 CPU was supplanted by a series of improved processors with names such as 80286, 80386, and 80486 (Figure 3-25). Each of these CPU families incorporated wider buses, increasingly higher clock speeds, and other improvements.

Figure 3-25
Old CPUs

In the early 1990s, Intel unveiled the Pentium CPU. Although no longer manufactured, the Pentium CPU was the first Intel CPU to contain all of the core functions that define today's modern CPUs.

NOTE Many of the CPU features attributed here to the Pentium actually appeared earlier, but the Pentium was the first CPU to have *all* of these features!

Man in Box Redux

Let's take a look at these improvements by evolving the friendly Man in the Box to the standards of an Intel Pentium processor. The Pentium retained the core features of the 8088 and subsequent processors, although the clock was much faster, the address bus and external data bus were wider, and the registers had more bits. You'll also see a number of other improvements that simply didn't exist on the original 8088.

The Rise of 32-bit Processing

The old 8088 had 16-bit registers, an 8-bit EDB, and a 20-bit address bus. Old operating systems (like DOS and early versions of Windows) were written to work on the 8088. Over the years, later CPUs gradually increased their address bus and general-purpose register sizes to 32-bits, allowing much more powerful operating systems (such as Linux, Windows XP, and Windows Vista) to work with the Pentium to process larger numbers at a single time and to address up to $2^{32} = 4,294,967,296 =$ four gigabytes of RAM. (See Figure 3-26.) Running 32-bit operating systems on 32-bit hardware is called *32-bit processing*.

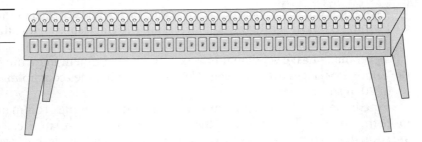

Figure 3-26
A 32-bit register

For the most part, modern PCs run 32-bit operating systems, like Windows, but that's about to change. Both AMD and Intel now make 64-bit processors that address up to 2^{64} = 18,446,744,073,709,551,616 bytes of RAM. You'll learn more about 64-bit processors later in this chapter.

Pipelining

Remember earlier when we talked about the idea that you needed to pull the crank multiple times to get an answer out of the CPU? The main reason for this stems from the fact that the CPU's process of getting a command from the EDB, doing the calculation, and then getting the answer back out on the EDB requires at least four steps (each of these steps is called a *stage*):

1. **Fetch**   Get the data from the EDB
2. **Decode**   Figure out what type of command needs to be done
3. **Execute**   Perform the calculation
4. **Write**   Send the data back onto the EDB

Smart, discrete circuits inside your CPU handle each of these stages. In early CPUs, when a command was placed on the EDB, each stage did its job and the CPU handed back the answer before starting the next command, requiring at least four clock cycles to process a command. In every clock cycle, three of the four circuits sat idle. Today, the circuits are organized in a conveyer belt fashion called a *pipeline*. With pipelining, each stage does its job with each clock cycle pulse, creating a much more efficient process. The CPU has multiple circuits doing multiple jobs, so let's add pipelining to the Man in Box analogy. Now, it's *Men* in Box (Figure 3-27)!

Figure 3-27
Simple pipeline

Fetch   Decode   Execute   Write

Pipelines keep every stage of the processor busy on every click of the clock, making a CPU run more efficiently without increasing the clock speed. Note that at this point, the CPU has four stages—fetch, decode, execute, and write—a four-stage pipeline. No CPU ever made has fewer than four stages, but advancement in caching have increased the number of stages over the years. Current CPU pipelines contain many more stages, up to 20 in some cases.

Pipelining isn't perfect. Sometimes a stage hits a complex command that requires more than one clock cycle, forcing the pipeline to stop. These stops, called *pipeline stalls*, are something your CPU tries to avoid. The decode stage tends to cause the most pipeline stalls—certain commands are complex and therefore harder to decode than other commands. The Pentium used two decode stages to reduce the chance of pipeline stalls due to complex decoding (Figure 3-28).

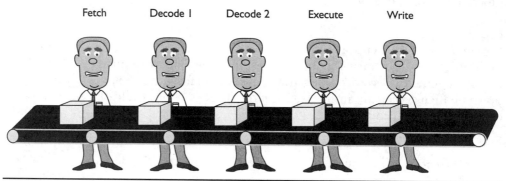

| Fetch | Decode 1 | Decode 2 | Execute | Write |

Figure 3-28 Pentium pipeline

After the Pentium, pipelines kept getting longer, reaching up to 20 stages in the Pentium 4. Since then, Intel and AMD have kept their pipeline around 12 stages (although this could change again).

Pipelining certainly helped the Pentium run more efficiently, but there's another issue—the execute stage. The inside of the CPU is composed of multiple chunks of circuitry to handle the different types of calculations your PC needs to do. For example, one part, the *integer unit*, handles integer math—basic math for numbers with no decimal point. 2 + 3 = 5 is a perfect example of integer math. The typical CPU spends more than 90 percent of its work doing integer math. But the Pentium also had special circuitry to handle complex numbers, called the *floating point unit* (FPU). With a single pipeline, only the integer unit or the floating point unit worked at any execution stage. Worse yet, floating point calculation often took many, many clock cycles to execute, forcing the CPU to stall the pipeline until the floating point finished executing the complex command (Figure 3-29).

NOTE You'll see the integer unit referred to as the arithmetic logic unit (ALU) in many sources. Either term works.

Figure 3-29
Bored ALU

Execute

To keep things moving, the folks at Intel gave the Pentium two pipelines—one main, "do everything" pipeline and one that only handled integer math. Although this didn't *stop* pipeline stalls, it at least had a second pipeline that kept running when the main one stalled! (See Figure 3-30.)

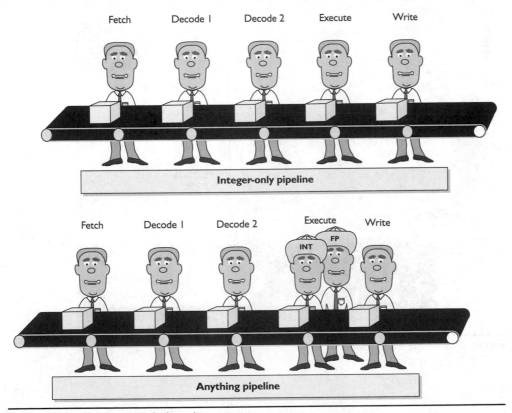

Figure 3-30 The Pentium dual pipeline

The two pipelines on the old Pentium were so successful that Intel and AMD added more and more pipelines to subsequent CPUs, to the point that most CPUs today have around eight pipelines, although there's tremendous variance from CPU to CPU.

 NOTE One of the biggest differences between equivalent AMD and Intel processors is the pipelines. AMD tends to go for lots of short pipelines whereas Intel tends to go with just a few long pipelines.

CPU Cache

When you send a program to the CPU, you actually run lots of little programs all at the same time. Okay, let's be fair here—*you* didn't send all these little programs—you just started your Web browser or some other program. The moment you double-clicked on that icon, Windows started sending lots of different programs to the CPU. Each of these programs breaks down into some number of little pieces called *threads*. Each thread is a tiny part of the whole program, designed to do a particular job. Take a look at Figure 3-31. It shows four programs in RAM, numbered 1, 2, 3, and 4. Note they are not the same size. Some programs need more RAM than others.

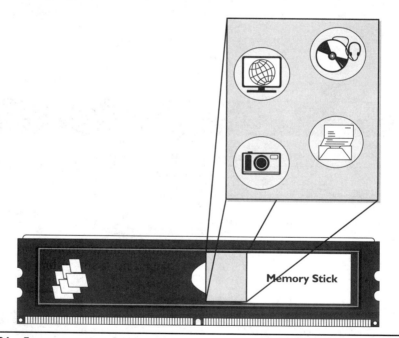

Figure 3-31 Four programs in RAM

Each of these programs is broken down into threads. If you zoom in on a small portion of Program 2, it would look like Figure 3-32.

Figure 3-32
Lots of threads!

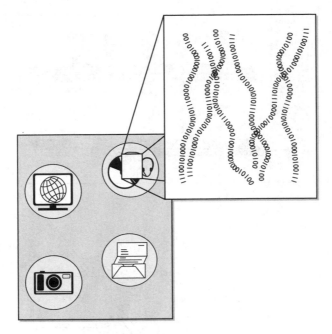

Pipelining CPUs work fantastically well as long as the pipelines stay filled with threads. Because the CPU runs faster than the RAM can supply it with code, however, you'll always get pipeline stalls—called *wait states*—due to the RAM not keeping up with the CPU. To reduce wait states, the Pentium came with built-in, very high speed RAM called *static RAM* (SRAM). This SRAM would preload as many threads as possible and would also keep copies of already run threads in the hope that the CPU would need to run it again (it's very common to run a thread over and over). See Figure 3-33. SRAM used in this fashion is called a *cache*.

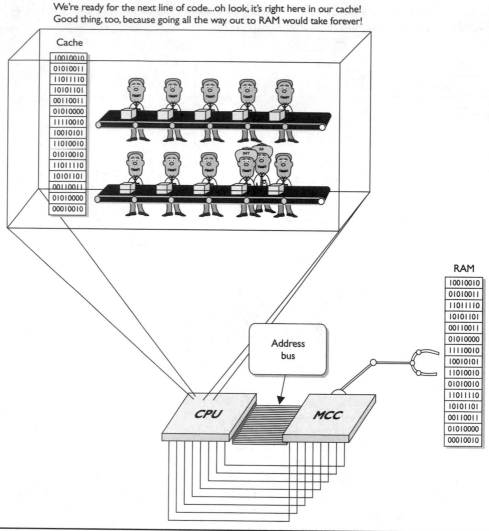

Figure 3-33 RAM cache

The SRAM cache inside the CPU was tiny, only about 16 KB, but it helped tremendously with performance. In fact, it helped so much that many motherboard makers began adding cache directly to the Pentium motherboards. These caches were much larger, usually around 128 to 512 KB. When the CPU looked for a line of code, it first went to the built-in cache, but if the code wasn't there, the CPU would go to the cache on the motherboard. The cache on the CPU was called the *L1 cache* because it was the one the CPU first tried to use. The cache on the motherboard was called the *L2 cache*; not because it was on the motherboard, but because it was the second cache the CPU checked. Later engineers took this cache concept even further and added the L2 cache onboard the CPU. A few CPU makers even went so far as to include three caches: an L1, an L2, and an L3 cache on the CPU. L3 caches are only seen on very powerful and specialized CPUs—never on more common CPUs.

NOTE You'll hear cache referred to as Level 1, Level 2, and Level 3 for L1, L2, and L3 cache, respectively. Any of the terms are acceptable.

 NOTE It's tempting to ask why processor manufacturers didn't just include bigger L1 caches instead of making onboard L1 and L2 caches. The answer is that a very small L1 and a larger L2 are much more efficient than a single fast L1!

The Pentium cache was capable of *branch prediction*, a process whereby the cache attempted to anticipate program branches before they got to the CPU itself. An IF statement provides a nice example of this: "If the value in the AX register = 5, stop running this code and jump to another memory location." Such a jump would make all of the data in the cache useless. The L1 cache in the Pentium could recognize a branch statement. Using a counter that kept a record about the direction of the previous branch, the L1 would guess which way the branch was going to go and make sure that side of the branch was in cache. The counter wasn't perfect, but it was right more often than it was wrong.

Clock Speed and Multipliers

In the earliest motherboards, the clock chip pushed every chip on the motherboard, not just the CPU. This setup worked great for a while until it became obvious that CPU makers (really Intel) could make CPUs with a much higher clock speed than the rest of the chips on the motherboard. So Intel had a choice: either stop making faster CPUs or come up with some way to make CPUs run faster than the rest of the computer (Figure 3-34).

Figure 3-34
Motherboards can't
run as fast as CPUs!

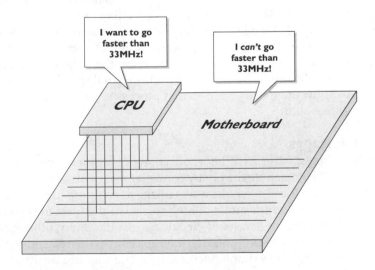

To overcome this problem, Intel developed clock-multiplying CPUs. A *clock-multiplying CPU* takes the incoming clock signal and multiplies it inside the CPU to let the internal circuitry of the CPU run faster. The secret to making clock multiplying work is caching. CPUs with caches spend the majority of their clock cycles performing calculations and moving data back and forth within the caches, not sending any data on the external buses.

NOTE Clock multiplying first surfaced during the reign of the Intel 80486 CPUs. All the first clock multipliers exactly doubled the clock speed, resulting in the term *clock doubling*. This term is used interchangeably with *clock multiplying*, even though modern CPUs multiply far more than just times two!

All modern CPUs are clock multipliers. So in reality, every CPU now has two clock speeds: the speed that it runs internally and the speed that it runs when talking on the address bus and the external data bus. Multipliers run from 2× up to almost 30×! Multipliers do not have to be whole numbers. You can find a CPU with a multiplier of 6.5× just as easily as you would find one with a multiplier of 7×. A late-generation Pentium would have an external speed of 66 MHz multiplied by 4.5× for an internal speed of 300 MHz. The Intel Pentium 4 3.06-GHz CPU runs at an external speed of 133 MHz with a 23× multiplier to make—yes, you've got it—3.06 GHz. Without the invention of multiplying, modern CPUs would be nowhere near their current blazing speeds.

The system bus speed and the multiplier on Pentium CPU systems had to be manually configured via jumpers on the motherboard (Figure 3-35). Today's CPUs actually report to the motherboard through a function called *CPUID* (CPU Identifier), and the system bus speed and multiplier are set automatically.

Figure 3-35
Jumper settings on an old motherboard

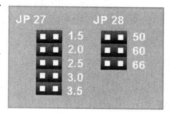

For years, users pushed for faster and faster CPU clock speeds, as clock speed was considered the most important way to differentiate one CPU from another. By 2003, advancements in caching, pipelining, and many other internal aspects of the CPU made using clock speed an inaccurate way to compare one CPU to another. CPU makers give their processors model numbers—nothing more than marketing names—to tell one processor from another. The Intel Core Duo T2300, for example, actually runs 1.66 GHz (166 MHz external speed with a 10× multiplier). If you want to know the speed of a particular processor, you must go to the CPU maker's Web site or other source.

CPU Voltages

In the simplest sense, a CPU is a collection of *transistors*, tiny electrical switches that enable the CPU to handle the binary code that makes up programs. Transistors, like every other electrical device, require a set voltage to run properly. Give a transistor too much and you fry it; too little and it doesn't work. For the first ten years of the personal computer, CPUs ran on 5 volts of electricity, just like every other circuit on the motherboard. To increase the complexity and capability with new generations of CPUs, microprocessor developers simply increased the number of transistors. But eventually they altered this strategy to increase the efficiency of the CPUs and keep the size down to something reasonable.

Intel and AMD discovered that by reducing the amount of voltage used, you could reduce the size of the transistors and cram more of them into the same space. Intel released the Pentium, for example, that required only 3.3 volts. AMD responded with its versions of the Pentium-class CPUs with even lower voltages.

Intel Pentium Pro

- External speed range: 60–66 MHz
- Internal speed range: 166–200 MHz
- Multiplier range: 2.5×–3×
- L1 cache: 16 KB
- L2 cache: 256 KB, 512 KB, 1 MB
- Package: PGA
- Socket(s) used: Socket 8

Superscalar Execution

The P6 had four pipelines, twice as many as the Pentium. These pipelines were deeper and faster. With this many pipelines, the P6 was guaranteed to always, no matter what, run at least two processes at the same time. The ability to run more than one process in any one clock cycle is called *superscalar execution*.

Out-of-Order Processing/Speculative Execution

From time to time, a CPU must go to system memory to access code, no matter how good its cache. When a RAM access takes place, the CPU must wait a few clock cycles before processing. Sometimes the wait can be 10 or 20 clock cycles. Plus, because system memory is dynamic RAM and needs to be refreshed (charged up) periodically, this can cause further delays. When the P6 was forced into wait states, it took advantage of the wait to look at the code in the pipeline to see if any commands could be run while the wait states were active. If it found commands it could process that were not dependent on the data being fetched from DRAM, it would run these commands out of order, a feature called *out-of-order processing*. After the DRAM returned with the code, it rearranged the commands and continued processing.

The P6 improved on the Pentium's branch prediction by adding a far more complex counter that would predict branches with a better than 90 percent success rate. With the combination of out-of-order processing and the chance of a branch prediction so high, the CPU could grab the predicted side of the branch out of the cache and run it out of order in one pipeline, even before the branch itself was run! This was called *speculative execution*.

On-Chip L2 Cache

The P6 had both an L1 and an L2 cache on the CPU. Because the L2 cache was on the chip, it ran almost as fast as the L1 cache (Figure 3-41). Be careful with the term "on-chip." Just because it was on the chip, that doesn't mean that the L2 cache was built into the CPU. The CPU and the L2 cache shared the same package, but physically they were separate.

The inclusion of the L2 cache on the chip gave rise to some new

Figure 3-41
A P6 opened to show separate CPU and L2 cache
(Photo courtesy Intel Corp)

terms to describe the connections between the CPU, MCC, RAM, and L2 cache. The address bus and external data bus (connecting the CPU, MCC, and RAM) were lumped into a single term called the *frontside bus*, and the connection between the CPU and the L2 cache became known as the *backside bus*.

Figure 3-42 shows a more modern configuration, labeling the important buses. Note that the external data bus and address bus are there, but the chipset provides separate address buses and external data buses—one set just for the CPU and another set for the rest of the devices in the PC. No official name has been given to the interface between the RAM and the chipset. On the rare occasions when it is discussed, most techs simply call it the *RAM interface*.

Figure 3-42
Frontside and backside buses

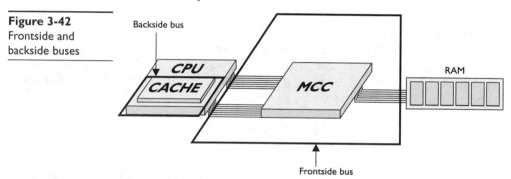

The Pentium Pro had a unique PGA case that fit into a special socket, called Socket 8. No other CPU used this type of socket. The Pentium Pro made strong inroads in the high-end server market, but its high cost made it unacceptable for most people's desktop computer.

Although the Pentium Pro never saw a large volume of sales compared with the Pentium, many people in the industry consider it to be the most important chip ever created by Intel. Its feature set was the prototype for all CPUs designed ever since.

Later Pentium-Class CPUs

Intel's usual game plan in the rough-and-tumble business of chip making is to introduce a new CPU and simultaneously declare all previous CPUs obsolete. That did not happen with the Pentium Pro, however, because Intel never really developed the P6 for most users. It was to be the CPU for powerful, higher-end systems. This kept the Pentium as the CPU of choice for all but the most power-hungry systems.

While the Pentium Pro languished on the high end for several years, Intel and AMD developed new Pentium-class CPUs that incorporated a series of powerful improve-

Figure 3-43
Later-generation Pentium

ments, some of which were taken from the Pentium Pro. These improvements required that they be regarded as a new family of CPUs, which I call the "later Pentium-class CPUs" (Figure 3-43). Although certainly some profound differences exist between these CPUs, they all have three groups of similar improvements: multimedia extensions (MMX), increased multipliers/clocks, and improved processing.

Later Pentium CPUs

- External speed range: 66–75 MHz
- Internal speed range: 166–200 MHz
- Multiplier range: 2.5×–4.5×
- L1 cache: 32 KB
- Package: PGA
- Socket(s) used: Socket 7

Later-generation Pentiums were pin-compatible with earlier Pentiums, but included a large number of improvements. The most important improvement was increases in multipliers, and therefore clock speeds, but other improvements took place—some borrowed from the P6 and some developed just for this new breed of Pentium.

MMX

In 1996, Intel added a new enhancement to its Pentium CPU, called *multimedia extensions* (MMX), in response to the large number of programs with heavy graphic needs coming out at this time. MMX was designed to work with large graphics by calculating on large chunks of data and performing vector math (vector math is needed to handle graphical issues such as spinning a 3D object). MMX was not heavily supported by the folks who wrote graphics programs, but MMX did start the idea that CPUs should have special circuitry just for such programs. Over time, the graphics community began to work with Intel to improve MMX, eventually replacing it with better solutions.

Increased Clocks and Multipliers

Later Pentiums all have vastly increased multipliers, resulting in higher speeds. Most early Pentiums used 2.5× multipliers at best, but later Pentium-class processors had up to 4.5× multipliers.

Pentium II

Intel's next major CPU was the Pentium II. Although highly touted as the next generation of CPU, the Pentium II was little more than a faster Pentium Pro with MMX and a refined

Figure 3-44
Pentium II
(Photo courtesy of
Intel Corp)

instruction set. The Pentium II came in a distinctive single edge cartridge (SEC) that gave more space for the L2 cache and made CPU cooling easier while freeing up more room on the mother-board (Figure 3-44). Aggressive advertising and pricing made the Pentium II extremely popular.

Intel Pentium II CPUs

- External speed range: 66–100 MHz
- Internal speed range: 233–450 MHz
- Multiplier range: 3.5×–4.5×
- L1 cache: 32 KB
- L2 cache: 512 KB
- Package: SEC
- Socket(s) used: Slot 1

The Pentium II initially achieved the higher clock speeds by using high multiples of a 66-MHz external speed. During this time, however, AMD began to sell CPUs designed to run on 100-MHz motherboards. Although the final Pentium II models also ran on 100-MHz motherboards, Intel's slow adoption of 100-MHz external speed CPUs lost market share for Intel.

The SEC cartridge also created another problem: it was not free to copy. This prevented other CPU manufacturers from making CPUs that fit in the SEC's special Slot 1 connection. This move forced AMD to create its own SEC packages that were incompatible with Intel's. From the Pentium II to today, AMD and Intel CPUs are no longer interchangeable. We live in a world where AMD CPUs have motherboards designed for AMD, while Intel CPUs must have motherboards designed for Intel.

AMD K6 Series

From 1997 to 2000, AMD produced a series of processors called the K6 that matched—and in many people's view, surpassed—the Pentium II, propelling AMD into serious competition with Intel (Figure 3-45). Four models were included in the K6 series: the K6, K6-2, K6-2+, and K6-III, each incorporating more advanced features than the previous model. The K6 processors incorporated a number of improvements, including 64-KB L1 cache, extremely advanced pipelining, and support for motherboard speeds of up to 100 MHz (on later models). The K6-2 added AMD's proprietary 3DNow! instruction set—a direct competitor to Intel's MMX and a significant advancement in graphics-handling capabilities—and increased clock speeds. The K6-III included even more advancements in pipelining and added a 256-KB L2 cache, all on a standard Socket 7 PGA package.

Figure 3-45
AMD K6 (Courtesy of AMD)

AMD K6-Family CPUs

- External speed range: 66–100 MHz
- Internal speed range: 200–550 MHz
- Multiplier range: 3×–5.5×
- L1 cache: 32 KB or 64 KB
- L2 cache: 256 KB (some had none)
- Package: PGA
- Socket(s) used: Socket 7

Intel Celeron (Pentium II)

In an attempt to capture more market share of low-end PCs, Intel developed an off-shoot of the Pentium II called the Celeron (Figure 3-46). The first Celerons were SEC, but lacked the protective covering of the Pentium II. Intel calls this the *single edge processor* (SEP) package.

 CAUTION Intel uses the name Celeron for its entire family of lower-end CPUs. There's a Celeron based on the Pentium II, a Celeron based on the Pentium III, and a Celeron based on the Pentium 4; and they are all called Celeron. When in doubt, ask.

Although touted by Intel as a low-end solution and limited to only a 66-MHz bus speed, the Celeron CPU's cheap price made it a huge success in the marketplace.

Figure 3-46
Pentium II Celeron

Intel Pentium II–Based Celeron CPUs

- External speed range: 66 MHz
- Internal speed range: 266–700 MHz
- Multiplier range: 4×–10.5×
- L1 cache: 32 KB
- L2 cache: None in the first versions. Later versions had 128 KB
- Package: SEP, PGA
- Socket(s) used: Slot 1, Socket 370

Pentium III

The Pentium III improved on the Pentium II by incorporating *Streaming SIMD Extensions* (*SSE*), Intel's direct competitor to AMD's 3DNow!; a number of internal processing/pipelining improvements; full support for 100-MHz and 133-MHz motherboard speeds; and high-speed L2 cache. The Pentium III was first produced using an SEC package, but improvements in die technology enabled Intel to produce PGA versions later (Figure 3-47), ending the short reign of the SEC-package CPUs.

Figure 3-47
Intel Pentium III

Intel Pentium III CPUs

- External speed range: 100–133 MHz
- Internal speed range: 450 MHz–1.26 GHz
- Multiplier range: 4×–10×
- L1 cache: 32 KB
- L2 cache: 256 KB or 512 KB
- Package: SEC-2, PGA
- Socket(s) used: Slot 1, Socket 370

Just as the Pentium II had a Celeron, so did the Pentium III. Unfortunately, Intel makes no differentiation between classes of Celerons, making buying a challenge unless you ask. The Pentium III–based Celerons were PGA and used Socket 370 (Figure 3-48).

Figure 3-48
Intel Celeron

Intel Pentium III–Based Celeron CPUs

- External speed range: 66–100 MHz
- Internal speed range: 533–700 MHz
- Multiplier range: 8×–11.5×
- L1 cache: 32 KB
- L2 cache: 128 KB
- Package: PGA
- Socket(s) used: Socket 370

Early AMD Athlon CPUs

The Athlon CPU has evolved from the name of a single class of CPUs into a term covering a number of very different CPUs that compete head to head against the latest Intel chips. The Athlon was AMD's first product to drop any attempt at pin compatibility with Intel chips. Instead, AMD decided to make its own AMD-only slots and sockets. The first Athlon CPUs, often referred to now as "classic Athlon" CPUs, used an SEC package called *Slot A* (Figure 3-49).

Figure 3-49
Early Athlon CPU

Classic AMD Athlon CPUs

- External speed range: 100 MHz
- Internal speed range: 500 MHz–1 GHz
- Multiplier range: 5×–10×
- L1 cache: 128 KB
- L2 cache: 512 KB
- Package: SEC
- Socket(s) used: Slot A

IT Technician

EXAM TIP If you're studying for the CompTIA A+ 220-604 (Depot Technician) exam, pay extra attention to the CPU variations covered in this chapter. Selecting and installing the appropriate CPU is your bread and butter!

Processing and Wattage

To make smarter CPUs, Intel and AMD need to increase the number of microscopic transistor circuits in the CPU. The more circuits you add, the more power they need. CPUs measure their power use in units called watts, just like a common light bulb. Higher wattage also means higher heat, forcing modern CPUs to use very powerful cooling methods. Good techs know how many watts are needed by a CPU, as this tells them how hot the CPU will get inside a PC. Known hot CPUs are often avoided for general-purpose PCs, as these CPUs require more aggressive cooling.

 NOTE As you read the wattages for the various CPUs, imagine a light bulb with that wattage inside your system unit!

CPU makers really hate heat, but they still want to add more circuits—so they constantly try to reduce the size of the circuits because smaller circuits use less power. CPUs are made from silicon wafers. The electrical circuitry is etched onto the wafers using a process called photo lithography. Photo lithography is an amazingly complex process, but basically requires placing a thin layer of chemicals on the wafer. These chemicals are sensitive to ultraviolet light—if a part of this mask gets exposed to UV light, it gets hard and resistant. If it doesn't get exposed, it's easy to remove. To make the circuitry, a mask of the circuits is placed over the wafer, and then the mask and wafer are exposed to UV light. The mask is removed and the wafer is washed in chemicals, leaving the circuits. If you want microscopic circuits, you need a mask with the pattern of the microscopic circuits. This is done through a photographic process. The old 8088 used a 3-micrometer (one millionth of a meter) process to make the mask. Some of today's CPUs were created with a 65-nanometer process, and 45-nanometer is just around the corner. The same CPU created with a smaller process is usually cooler.

 NOTE A nanometer is one billionth of a meter.

CPU Codenames

The Pentium 4 and the Athlon started the most aggressive phase of the Intel/AMD CPU wars. From the year 2000 and continuing to today, Intel and AMD fight to bring out new CPUs with an almost alarming frequency, making the job of documenting all these CPUs challenging. Luckily for us, the CPU makers use special CPU codenames for new CPUs, such as "Willamette" and "Barton" to describe the first version of the Pentium 4 and the last version of the 32-bit Athlon, respectively. These codenames are in common use, and a good tech should recognize these names—plus, they make a dandy way to learn about what's taking place in the CPU business!

 NOTE CPU codenames predate the Pentium 4 and Athlon, but the slower pace of new CPU models made them less important.

You've already seen up to this point how Intel and AMD were trying to one-up each other with earlier processors. Now you'll see how the Intel/AMD wars really got going!

AMD Athlon Thunderbird

AMD's first major improvement to the Athlon CPU was codenamed Thunderbird (Figure 3-50). The Thunderbird Athlon marked AMD's return to a PGA package with the adoption of the proprietary 462-pin socket called *Socket A*.

Figure 3-50
Athlon Thunderbird
(Photo courtesy of
AMD)

The change between the Classic and the Thunderbird wasn't just cosmetic. Thunderbird had an interesting *double-pumped frontside bus* that doubled the data rate without increasing the clock speed. Athlon Thunderbird CPUs have a smaller but far more powerful L2 cache, as well as a number of other minor improvements.

AMD Thunderbird Athlon CPUs

- Process: 180 nm
- Watts: 38–75
- External speed range: 100–133 MHz (Double-pumped)
- Internal speed range: 650 MHz–1.4 GHz
- Multiplier range: 6.5×–14×
- L1 cache: 128 KB
- L2 cache: 256 KB
- Package: PGA
- Socket(s) used: Socket A

AMD Duron

Duron is the generic name given to all lower-end CPUs based on the Athlon processor. Basically an Athlon with a smaller cache, the Duron supported the same 200-MHz frontside bus as the Athlon, giving it a slight edge over the Celeron. The Duron connected to the same 462-pin Socket A as the later Athlon CPUs (Figure 3-51).

Figure 3-51
AMD Duron
(Photo courtesy of
AMD)

AMD Duron CPUs

- Process: 180 nm
- Watts: 21–57
- External speed range: 100 MHz (Double-pumped)
- Internal speed range: 600 MHz–1.8 GHz
- Multiplier range: 6×–13.5×
- L1 cache: 128 KB
- L2 cache: 64 KB
- L3 cache: No
- Package: PGA
- Socket(s) used: Socket A

Intel Pentium 4 Willamette

While the Pentium II and III were little more than improvements on the Intel Pentium Pro, the Pentium 4 introduced a completely redesigned core, called *NetBurst*. NetBurst centered around a totally new 20-stage pipeline combined with other features to support this huge pipeline. Each stage of the pipeline performed fewer operations than typical pipeline stages in earlier processors, which enabled Intel to crank up the clock speed for the Pentium 4 CPUs. The first Pentium 4s included a new version of SSE called SSE2, and later versions introduced SSE3.

The Pentium 4 achieved a 400-MHz frontside bus speed—twice the Athlon's 200 MHz—by using four data transfers per clock cycle on a 100-MHz bus. Intel used this same *quad-pumped frontside bus* technology on a 133-MHz bus to achieve a 533-MHz frontside bus.

There were two packages of early Pentium 4 CPUs. The first Pentium 4 CPUs came in a 423-pin PGA package and had a 256-KB L2 cache. These were replaced by the 512-KB L2 cache Pentium 4 with a 478-pin PGA package (Figure 3-52). Even though the new package has more pins, it is considerably smaller than the earlier package.

Figure 3-52
Pentium 4 (423-
and 478-pin)

Intel Pentium 4 Willamette CPUs

- Process: 180 nm

- Watts: 49–100

- External speed range: 100 MHz, 133 MHz (Quad-pumped)

- Internal speed range: 1.3–2.0 GHz

- Multiplier range: 13×–20×

- L1 cache: 128 KB

- L2 cache: 256 KB

- Package: 423-pin PGA, 478-pin PGA

- Socket(s) used: Socket 423, Socket 478

AMD Athlon XP (Palomino and Thoroughbred)

Not to be left in the dust by Intel's Pentium 4, AMD released an upgraded version of the Athlon Thunderbird called the Athlon XP, codenamed Palomino, quickly followed by the Thoroughbred. Both processors used the 462-pin PGA package, but AMD incorporated a number of performance enhancements to the Athlon core, including support for Intel's SSE instructions. The Thoroughbred increased the external speed to a double-pumped 166 MHz and increased the clock speeds, while its 150-nm process reduced wattage.

One interesting aspect of the Athlon XP was AMD's attempt to ignore clock speeds and instead market the CPUs using a *performance rating* (PR) number that matched the equivalent power of an Intel Pentium 4 processor. For example, the Athlon XP 1800+ actually ran at 1.6 GHz, but AMD claimed it processed as fast or better than a Pentium 4 1.8 GHz—*ergo* "1800+."

AMD Athlon XP CPUs

- Process: 180 nm (Palomino), 150 nm (Thoroughbred)

- Watts: 60–72 (Palomino), 49–70 (Thoroughbred)

- External speed range: 133 MHz, 166 MHz (Double-pumped)

- Internal speed range: 1.3 GHz (1500+)–2.2 GHz (2800+)
- Multiplier range: 13×–16.5×
- L1 cache: 128 KB
- L2 cache: 256 KB, 512 KB
- Package: 462-pin PGA
- Socket(s) used: Socket A.

Intel Pentium 4 (Northwood and Prescott)

The Pentium 4 versus Athlon XP war really started to heat up with the next generation of Pentium 4 processors. These P4s increased the frontside bus speed to 800 MHz (200 MHz quad-pumped) and introduced hyperthreading.

NOTE P4 Prescotts and Northwoods came in hyperthreaded and non-hyperthreaded versions.

With *hyperthreading,* each individual pipeline can run more than one thread at a time—a very tricky act to achieve. A single Intel P4 with hyperthreading looks like two CPUs to the operating system. Figure 3-53 shows the Task Manager in Windows XP on a system running a hyperthreaded Pentium 4. Note how the CPU box is broken into two groups—Windows thinks this one CPU is two CPUs.

Figure 3-53
Windows Task Manager with the Performance Tab displayed for a system running a hyperthreaded Pentium 4

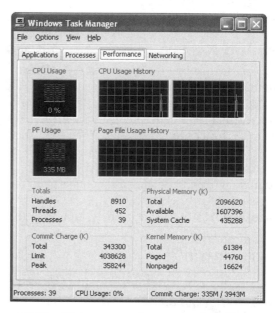

Hyperthreading enhances a CPU's efficiency, but has a couple of limitations. First, the operating system and the application have to be hyperthreading-aware to take advantage of the feature. Second, although the CPU uses idle processing power to simulate the actions of a second processor, it doesn't double the processing power because the main execution resources are not duplicated. Even with the limitations, hyperthreading is an interesting advancement in superscalar architecture.

Figure 3-54
Pentium 4 LGA 775

The Northwood used a 130-nm process, and the Prescott used a 90-nm process. The Northwood had the same 478-pin PGA package (as did the very first Prescotts), but Intel switched to the *Land Grid Array* (LGA) 775 package with the Prescott CPUs (Figure 3-54). Even though the LGA 775 package has more pins than a Socket 478 package, it is considerably smaller.

Starting with the LGA 775 Prescotts, Intel dumped the convention of naming CPUs by their clock speed and adopted a very cryptic three-digit model-numbering system. All Prescott Pentium 4s received a three-digit number starting with a 5 or a 6. One of the 2.8-GHz Pentium 4 CPUs is a 521, for example, and one of the 3-GHz processors is called the 630.

These Pentiums reached the apex of clock speeds, approaching 4 GHz. After this, Intel (and AMD) stopped the CPU clock speed race and instead began to concentrate on parallel and 64-bit processing (both to be discussed later in this chapter).

Intel Pentium 4 CPUs

- Process: 130 nm (Northwood), 90 nm (Prescott), 65 nm (Cedar Mill)
- Watts: 45–68 (Northwood), ~84 (Prescott), 86 (Cedar Mill)
- External speed range: 100 MHz (Quad-pumped); 133 MHz (Quad-pumped); 200 MHz (Quad-pumped)
- Internal speed range: 1.3–3.80 GHz
- Multiplier range: 13×–23×
- L1 cache: 128 KB
- L2 cache: 256 KB, 512 KB
- Package: 478-pin PGA, 775-pin LGA
- Socket(s) used: Socket 478, Socket LGA 775

AMD Athlon XP (Thorton and Barton)

The Athlon XP Thorton and Barton CPUs were the last generation of 32-bit Athlon XPs and the last to use the 462-pin PGA package. The only major difference between the two was the L2 cache. The Thorton had a 256-KB cache whereas the Barton had a 512-KB cache. Using a 130-nm process, AMD could produce faster CPUs without any real increase in wattage. Later versions of each processor increased the frontside bus to 200 MHz (double-pumped).

AMD Athlon XP CPUs

- Process: 130 nm
- Watts: 60–70

- External speed range: 133 MHz, 166 MHz, 200MHz (Double-pumped)
- Internal speed range: 1.6 GHz (2000+)–2.2 GHz (3100+)
- Multiplier range: 10×–16×
- L1 cache: 128 KB
- L2 cache: 256 KB (Thorton), 512 KB (Barton)
- Package: 462-pin PGA
- Socket(s) used: Socket A

After the Barton Athlon XPs, AMD stopped making 32-bit processors, concentrating exclusively on 64-bit. Intel, on the other hand, continued to make 32-bit processors.

Pentium 4 Extreme Edition

The Pentium 4 Extreme Edition was designed to place Intel at the top of the CPU performance curve. The Extreme Edition CPUs used a Socket 478 or LGA 775 package, making them identical to other Pentium 4s, but packed some powerful features. Most interesting was the 2-MB L3 cache—the only non-server CPU to carry an L3 cache. The Pentium 4 Extreme Edition also had some of the highest wattages ever recorded on any Intel desktop CPU—over 110 watts! Extreme Edition CPUs ran incredibly fast, but their high price kept them from making any significant impact on the market.

- Process: 130 and 90 nm
- Watts: 85–115
- External speed range: 200 MHz (Quad-pumped), 266 MHz (Quad-pumped)
- Internal speed range: 3.2 GHz–3.7 GHz
- Multiplier range: 14×–17×
- L1 cache: 128 KB
- L2 cache: 512 KB
- L3 cache 2 MB
- Package: 478-pin PGA, 775-pin LGA
- Socket(s) used: Socket 478, Socket LGA-775

Mobile Processors

The inside of a laptop PC is a cramped, hot environment, where no self-respecting CPU should ever need to operate. Since the mid-1980s, CPU manufacturers have endeavored to make specialized versions of their processors to function in the rugged world of laptops. Over the years, a number of CPU laptop solutions have appeared. Virtually every CPU made by Intel or AMD has come in a mobile version. You can usually tell a mobile version by the word "mobile" or the letter "M" in its name. Here are a few examples:

- Mobile Intel Pentium III
- Intel Pentium M

- Mobile AMD Athlon 64
- AMD Turion 64 (All Turions are mobile processors, but don't say "mobile" or "M" in their name. AMD usually adds "mobile technology" as part of the Turion description.)
- Intel Core Duo (See the "Intel Core" section later in the chapter.)

A mobile processor uses less power than an equivalent desktop model. This provides two advantages. First, it enables the battery in the laptop to last longer. Second, it makes the CPU run cooler, and the cooler the CPU, the fewer cooling devices you need.

Almost every mobile processor today runs at a lower voltage than the desktop version of the same CPU. As a result, most mobile CPUs also run at lower speeds—it takes juice if you want the speed! Mobile CPUs usually top out at about 75 percent of the speed of the same CPU's desktop version.

 NOTE Intel uses the marketing term *Centrino* to define complete mobile solutions including a mobile processor, support chips, and wireless networking. There is no Centrino CPU, only Centrino solutions that include some type of Intel mobile CPU.

Reducing voltage is a good first step, but making a smart CPU that can use less power in low-demand situations will reduce power usage even more. The first manifestation of this was the classic *System Management Mode* (*SMM*). Introduced back in the times of the Intel 80386 processor, SMM provided the CPU with the capability to turn off devices that use a lot of power, such as the monitor or the hard drives. Although originally designed just for laptops, SMM has been replaced with more advanced power management functions that are now built into all AMD and Intel CPUs.

CPU makers have taken power reduction one step further with *throttling*—the capability of modern CPUs to slow themselves down during low demand times or if the CPU detects that it is getting too hot. Intel's version of throttling is called *SpeedStep*, while AMD's version is known as *PowerNow!*

Intel Xeon Processors

Just as the term *Celeron* describes a series of lower-end processors built around the Pentium II, Pentium III, and Pentium 4, the term *Xeon* (pronounced "Zee-on") defines a series of high-end processors built around the Pentium II, Pentium III, and Pentium 4. Xeon CPUs built on the Pentium II and III core processors via the addition of massive L2 caches, but their strength comes from strong multiprocessor support. Both the Pentium II Xeon and the Pentium III Xeon used a unique SEC package that snapped into a Xeon-only slot called *Slot 2* (Figure 3-55). In general, people buy Xeons because they want to run a system with more than one processor. Most modern CPUs can run with one other identical CPU, but putting together two CPUs that were never designed to work together requires an incredibly complex MCC. Xeon processors, on the other hand, are carefully designed to work together in sets of two, four, or even eight CPUs. Although very expensive, their immense power lets them enjoy broad popularity in the high-horsepower world of server systems.

Figure 3-55
Intel Pentium
III Xeon (Photo
courtesy of
Intel Corp)

The Pentium 4 Xeon is quite a different beast from the previous Xeon types. First, the Pentium 4 Xeon's caches are smaller than other Xeons; advancements in pipelining make anything larger less valuable. Second, Intel sells two lines of Pentium 4 Xeons. One line, simply called the *Pentium 4 Xeon*, is for single or dual processor systems; and the second line, called the *Pentium 4 Xeon MP*, is for four or eight multiprocessor systems. Last, Intel went back to the PGA package with the Pentium 4 Xeons, a Xeon-only 603-pin package (Figure 3-56).

Figure 3-56
Intel Pentium 4 Xeon
(Photo courtesy of
Intel Corp)

Early 64-Bit CPUs

Both AMD and Intel currently produce the newest thing in microprocessing: 64-bit CPUs. A 64-bit CPU has general-purpose, floating point, and address registers that are 64 bits wide, meaning they can handle 64-bit-wide code in one pass—twice as wide as a 32-bit processor. And, they can address much, much more memory.

With the 32-bit address bus of the Pentium and later CPUs, the maximum amount of memory the CPU can address is 2^{32}, or 4,294,967,296 bytes. With a 64-bit address bus, CPUs can address 2^{64} bytes of memory, or more precisely, 18,446,744,073,709,551,616 bytes of memory—that's a lot of RAM! This number is so big that gigabytes and terabytes are no longer convenient, so we now go to an exabyte (2^{60}). A 64-bit address bus can address 16 exabytes of RAM.

No 64-bit CPU uses an actual 64-bit address bus. Right now, the most RAM anybody uses is 4 GB, so there's not much motivation for creating a CPU or a motherboard that can handle and hold 16 EB. Every 64-bit processor gets its address bus "clipped" down to something reasonable. The Intel Itanium, for example, only has a 44-bit address bus for a maximum address space of 2^{44}, or 17,592,186,044,416 bytes.

Initially, both AMD and Intel raced ahead with competing 64-bit processors. Interestingly, they took very different paths. Let's look at the two CPUs that made the first wave of 64-bit processing: the Intel Itanium and the AMD Opteron.

Intel Itanium (Original and Itanium 2)

Intel made the first strike into the 64-bit world for PCs with the Itanium CPU. The Itanium was more of a proof of concept product than one that was going to make Intel any money, but it paved the way for subsequent 64-bit processors. The Itanium had a unique 418-pin *pin array cartridge* (PAC) to help house its 2- or 4-MB Level 3 cache (Figure 3-57).

Figure 3-57
Intel Itanium
(Photo courtesy
of Intel Corp)

The Intel Itanium 2 was Intel's first serious foray into the 64-bit world. To describe the Itanium 2 simply in terms of bus sizes and clock speeds is simply unfair. The power of this processor goes far deeper. Massive pipelines, high speed caching, and literally hundreds of other improvements make the Itanium 2 a powerful CPU for high-end PCs. The Itanium 2 uses a unique form of PGA that Intel calls *organic land grid array* (OLGA). See Figure 3-58.

Figure 3-58
Intel Itanium 2
(Photo courtesy
of Intel Corp)

Intel Itanium 2

- Physical address: 50 bits
- Frontside bus width: 128 bit
- External speed range: 100 MHz (Quad-pumped)
- Internal speed range: 900 MHz, 1 GHz
- Watts: 90–100
- Multiplier range: 9×–10×
- L1 cache: 32 KB
- L2 cache: 256 KB
- L3 cache: 1.5 MB, 3 MB
- Package: OLGA
- Socket(s) used: Socket 611

Intel made a bold move with the Itanium and the Itanium 2 by not making them backward compatible to 32-bit programming. In other words, every OS, every application, and every driver of every device has to be rewritten to work on the Itanium and Itanium 2. In theory, developers would create excellent new applications and devices that dump all the old stuff (and problems) and thus would be more efficient and streamlined. If a company has a lot invested in 32-bit applications and can't make the jump to 64-bit, Intel continues to offer the Pentium 4 or Pentium Xeon. If you need 64-bit, get an Itanium 2. AMD didn't agree with Intel and made 64-bit processors that also ran 32-bit when needed. Intel would eventually follow AMD in this decision.

AMD Opteron

Coming in after the Itanium, AMD's Opteron doesn't try to take on the Itanium head to head. Instead, AMD presents the Opteron as the lower-end 64-bit CPU. But don't let the moniker "lower-end" fool you. Although the Opteron borrowed heavily from the Athlon, it included an I/O data path known as HyperTransport. Think of HyperTransport as a built-in memory controller chip, providing direct connection to other parts of the PC—and to other CPUs for multiprocessing—at a blistering speed of over 6 GB per second! The Opteron comes in a micro-PGA package, looking remarkably like a Pentium 4 (Figure 3-59).

Figure 3-59
AMD Opteron
(Image courtesy
of AMD)

AMD Opteron CPUs

- Physical address: 40 bits
- Frontside bus width: 128 bit
- External speed range: 6.4 GHz (HyperTransport)
- Internal speed range: 1.4–1.8 GHz
- Watts: 82–103
- Multiplier range: 14×–20×
- L1 cache: 128 KB
- L2 cache: 1 MB
- Package: micro-PGA
- Socket(s) used: Socket 940

Unlike the Itanium, the Opteron runs both 32-bit and 64-bit code. AMD gives customers the choice to move slowly into 64-bit without purchasing new equipment. This was the crucial difference between AMD and Intel in the early days of 64-bit processing.

Intel and AMD pitch the Itanium 2 and Opteron CPUs at the server market. This means that as a CompTIA A+ tech, you won't see them unless you go to work for a company that has massive computer needs. Newer CPUs from both companies fight for the desktop dollar.

Athlon 64

It's hardly fair to place the Athlon 64 with the early generation CPUs. The Athlon 64 was the first for-the-desktop 64-bit processor, so in that aspect it is an early 64-bit CPU.

Through careful evolution it continues on as AMD's top-of-the-line desktop CPU offering (Figure 3-60). AMD makes two lines of Athlon CPUs: the "regular" Athlon 64 and the Athlon 64 FX series. The FX series runs faster than the regular Athlon 64 CPUs, uses more wattage, and is marketed to the power users who are willing to pay a premium. Underneath those two lines, AMD has almost 20 sublines of Athlon 64 CPUs in different codenames, making the act of listing all of them here unwieldy. To simplify, let's just break down all Athlon 64 CPUs into two groups based on the processes used in all Athlon 64 CPUs to date: 130 nm and 90 nm.

NOTE Although the Athlon 64 may not have a true frontside bus, it does have a system clock that runs at 200 MHz to talk to RAM. This is still multiplied to get the internal speed of the CPU.

The Athlon 64 CPUs have a number of enhancements beyond simply moving into the 64-bit world. The most fascinating is the inclusion of a memory controller into the CPU, eliminating the need for an external MCC and for all intents also eliminating the idea of the frontside bus! The RAM directly connects to the Athlon 64. The Socket 754 and 939 Athlon 64 CPUs support DDR RAM; the Socket AM2 CPUs support DDR2. All Athlon 64 CPUs support Intel's SSE and SSE2 graphics extensions (later versions support SSE3).

The various mobile Athlon 64 processors offer AMD PowerNow! technology to reduce the wattage used and to extend the battery life in portable PCs. The two models to date are the Mobile AMD Athlon 64 processor and the AMD Athlon 64 for DTR. DTR stands for *desktop replacement,* the highest of the high end in portable PCs.

While regular Athlon 64 processors use the AMD PR numbers to describe CPUs, Athlon 64 FX processors uses a two-digit model number that's just as cryptic as Intel's current three-digit numbers.

Figure 3-60
Athlon 64

AMD Athlon 64 130nm CPUs

- Watts: 89
- Physical address: 40 bits
- External speed range: 200 MHz (System clock)
- Internal speed range (Regular): 1.8 (2800+)–2.4 (4000+) GHz

- Internal speed range (FX): 2.2 (FX-51)–2.6 (FX-55) GHz
- Multiplier range: 14×–20×
- L1 cache: 128 KB
- L2 cache: 512 KB, 1 MB
- Package: micro-PGA
- Socket(s) used (Regular): Socket 754, 939
- Socket(s) used (FX): Socket 940, 939

AMD Athlon 64 90nm CPUs

- Watts: 67
- Physical address: 40 bits
- External speed range: 200 MHz (System clock)
- Internal speed range (Regular): 1.8 (3000+)–2.4 (4000+) GHz
- Internal speed range (FX): 2.6 (FX-51)–2.8 (FX-57) GHz
- Multiplier range: 9×–12×
- L1 cache: 128 KB
- L2 cache: 512 KB, 1 MB
- Package: micro-PGA
- Socket(s) used (Regular and FX): Socket 754, 939, AM2

AMD Sempron CPUs

AMD produces various Sempron CPUs for the low end of the market. Semprons come in two socket sizes and have less cache than the Athlon 64, but offer a reasonable trade-off between price and performance.

AMD Sempron CPUs

- Watts: 35–62
- Physical address: 40 bits
- External speed range: 200 MHz (Double-pumped)
- Internal speed range: 1600–2000 MHz
- Multiplier range: 8×–10×
- L1 cache: 128 KB
- L2 cache: 128 KB, 256 KB
- Package: micro-PGA
- Socket(s) used: 754, AM2

Dual-Core CPUs

CPU clock speeds hit a practical limit of roughly 4 GHz around 2002–2003, motivating the CPU makers to find new ways to get more processing power for CPUs. Although

Intel and AMD had different opinions about 64-bit CPUs, both decided at virtually the same time to combine two CPUs into a single chip, creating a *dual-core architecture*. Dual-core isn't just two CPUs on the same chip. A dual-core CPU has two execution units—two sets of pipelines—but the two sets of pipelines share caches (how they share caches differs between Intel and AMD) and RAM.

 NOTE Putting more than two execution cores onto a single chip is called *multicore*.

Pentium D

Intel won the race for first dual-core processor with the Pentium D line of processors (Figure 3-61). The Pentium D is simply two late-generation Pentium 4s molded onto the same chip with each CPU using its own cache—although they do share the same frontside bus. One very interesting aspect to the Pentium D is the licensing of AMD's *AMD64* extensions—the "smarts" inside AMD CPUs that enables AMD CPUs to run either 64- or 32-bit code. Intel named their version *EM64T*. Even though the Pentium D is technically a 32-bit processor, it has extra address wires and 64-bit registers to

Figure 3-61
Pentium D
(Photo courtesy
of Intel Corp)

accommodate 64-bit code. There are two codenames for Pentium D processors: the "Smithfield" (model numbers 8*xx*), using a 90-nm process, and the "Presler" (model numbers 9*xx*), using a 65-nm process. Pentium Ds use the same LGA 775 package as seen on the later Pentium 4s.

Intel Pentium D

- Process: 90 nm and 65nm
- Watts: 95–130
- External speed range: 166 MHz, 200 MHz (Quad-pumped)
- Internal speed range: 2.6 GHz–3.6 GHz
- Multiplier range: 14×–20×
- L1 cache: Two 128-KB caches
- L2 cache: Two 1-MB caches or two 2-MB caches
- Package: 775-pin LGA
- Socket(s) used: Socket LGA-775

Athlon Dual Cores

AMD's introduction to dual-core came with the Athlon 64 X2 CPUs. The X2s are truly two separate cores that share L1 caches, unlike the Intel Pentium D. Athlon 64 X2s initially came in both "regular" and FX versions packaged in the well-known AMD Socket 939. To upgrade from a regular Athlon 64 to an Athlon 64 X2, assuming you have a Socket 939 motherboard, is often as easy as simply doing a minor motherboard update, called *flashing the BIOS*. Chapter 5, "BIOS and CMOS," goes through this process in detail, or you can simply check your motherboard manufacturer's Web site for the information on the process. In 2006, AMD announced the *Socket AM2*, designed to replace the Socket 939 across the Athlon line (Figure 3-62).

Figure 3-62
Socket AM2
(Photo courtesy
of Nvidia)

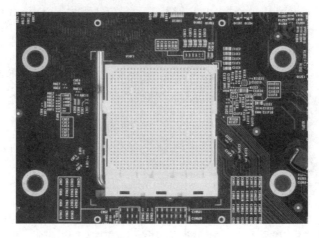

AMD Athlon 64 X2

- Watts: 89–110
- Physical address: 40 bits
- External speed range: 200 MHz (System clock)
- Internal speed range: 2.0 (3800+)–2.4 (4000+) GHz
- Multiplier range: 10×–12×
- L1 cache: 128 KB
- L2 cache: Two 512-KB caches or two 1-MB caches
- Package: micro-PGA
- Socket(s) used: Socket 939, Socket AM2

Intel Core—Goodbye, Pentium

Intel signaled the end of the Pentium name in 2006 with the introduction of the *Intel Core* CPUs. They followed up with the Core 2 processors, the first generation of CPUs to use the Intel Core architecture. Are you confused yet? Let's look a little closer at the Core and Core 2 CPUs.

Intel Core

Intel based the first generation of core processors, simply called "Core," on the Pentium M platform. Like the Pentium M, Core processors don't use the NetBurst architecture, instead falling back to a more Pentium Pro–style architecture (codenamed "Yonah") with a 12-stage pipeline. Core CPUs come in single- (Solo) and dual-core (Duo) versions, but they all use the same 478-pin FCPGA package. Core also dispenses with the three-digit Pentium numbering system, using instead a letter followed by four numbers, such as T2300.

Intel Core

- Process: 65 nm
- Watts: 5.5–31
- External speed range: 133 MHz, 166 MHz (Quad-pumped)
- Internal speed range: 1.06 GHz–2.33 GHz
- Multiplier range: 8×–14×
- L1 cache: One (Core Solo) or two (Core Duo) 32-KB caches
- L2 cache: One 2048-KB cache
- Package: 478-pin microFCPGA
- Socket(s) used: Socket microFCPGA

Intel Core 2

With the Core 2 line of processors, Intel released a radically revised processor architecture, called Core. Redesigned to maximize efficiency, the Core 2 processors spank their Pentium D predecessors by up to 40 percent in energy savings at the same performance level. To achieve the efficiency, Intel cranked up the cache size (to 2 or 4 MB) and went with a wide, short pipeline. The CPU can perform multiple actions in a single clock cycle and, in the process, run circles around the competition.

NOTE Intel's naming conventions can leave a lot to be desired. Note that the Core Solo and Core Duo processors were based on the Pentium M architecture. The Core 2 processors are based on the Core architecture.

Figure 3-63
Intel Core 2 CPU
(Photo courtesy
of Intel Corp)

Intel has released two Core 2 versions for the desktop, the Core 2 Duo and Core 2 Extreme, as well as a mobile version (Figure 3-63). At the end of 2006, Intel released a quad-core version of the Core 2 Extreme. All versions incorporate AMD's 64-bit technology, rebranding it as EM64T, so they can run Windows Vista in 64-bit mode natively.

Core 2

- Process: 65 nm
- Watts: 45–95
- External speed range: 266 MHz (Quad-pumped)
- Internal speed range: 1.8 GHz–3.2 GHz
- Multiplier range: 7×–12×
- L1 cache: Two 64-KB caches

- L2 cache: One 2048-KB or 4096-KB cache
- Package: 775-pin LGA
- Socket(s) used: Socket LGA-775

Installing CPUs

Installing or replacing a CPU is a remarkably straightforward process. You take off the fan and heat sink assembly, remove the CPU, put a new CPU in, and snap the fan and heat sink assembly back on. The trick to installing or replacing a CPU begins with two important questions. Do you need to replace your CPU? What CPU can you put in the computer?

Why Replace a CPU?

The CPU is the brain of your system, so it seems a natural assumption that taking out an old, slow CPU and replacing it with some new, fast CPU would make your computer run faster. No doubt it will, but before you do you need to consider a few issues, such as cost, cooling, and performance.

Cost

If you have an older CPU, there's a better than average chance that a faster version of your CPU is no longer available for retail purchase. In that case, replacing your CPU with a new one would require you to replace the motherboard and probably the RAM too. This is doable, but does it make sense cost-wise? How much would this upgrade compare to a whole new system?

Cooling

Faster CPUs run hotter than slower ones. If you get a new CPU, you will almost certainly need a new fan to dissipate the heat generated by the more powerful processor. In addition, you may discover your case fans are not sufficient, causing the CPU to overheat and making the system lock up. Adding improved cooling can be done, but it might require a new case.

Performance

A faster CPU will make your computer run faster, but by how much? The results are often disappointing. As you go through this book, you will discover many other areas where upgrading might make a much stronger impact on your system's performance.

Determining the Right CPU

So you go through all the decision-making and decide to go for a new CPU. Perhaps you're building a brand-new system or maybe you're ready to go for that CPU upgrade. The single most import bit of documentation is called the motherboard book (Figure 3-64). Every computer should come with this important booklet. This book contains all the details about what CPUs you can use as well as any special considerations for installing a CPU. Usually in the first few pages, the motherboard book will tell you exactly which CPUs your system can handle (as shown in Figure 3-65).

Figure 3-64
Sample motherboard
books

Figure 3-65
Allowed CPUs

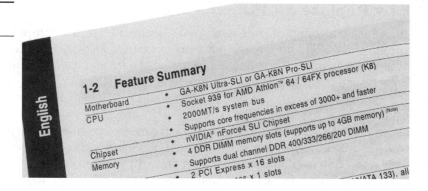

If you don't have a motherboard book, call the place where you got the PC and ask for it. If they don't have it, get online and find it—I'll show you where to look in later chapters.

Your first concern is the socket. You can't install an Athlon 64 X2 into a Pentium D's Socket 775—it won't fit! If your motherboard book lists the CPU you want to install, you're ready to start shopping.

Buying a CPU

Buying a CPU is a tricky game because most stores will not accept returns unless the CPU is bad. If you're not careful, you could get stuck with a useless CPU. Here are a few tricks.

CPUs come packaged two ways, as retail-boxed CPUs or OEM CPUs. Retail-boxed CPUs have two advantages. First, they are the genuine article. There are a surprising number of illegal CPUs on the market. Second, they come with a fan that is rated to work with that CPU.

Most stores have an installation deal and will install a new CPU for very cheap. I will take advantage of this sometimes, even though it may mean I don't have my PC for a few days. Why does your humble author, the Alpha Geek, have others do work he can do himself? Well, that way I'm not out of luck if there is a problem! Heck, I can change my own oil in my car, but I let others do that, too!

If you buy an OEM CPU, you will need the right fan. See "The Art of Cooling" section later in this chapter.

Preparing to Install

Once you're comfortable that your new CPU will work with your motherboard, get back to that motherboard book and see if there are any tiny jumpers or switches that you must adjust for your CPU. These jumpers might adjust the motherboard speed, the multiplier, or the voltage. Take your time, read the motherboard book, and set those jumpers or switches properly. Locate the fan power connector, usually called the CPU fan, as shown in Figure 3-66.

Figure 3-66
Fan connection

NOTE Many motherboards have no jumpers or switches.

CAUTION Before attempting to do anything inside the system unit, make sure you have adequate ESD protection. Make sure the power is off and the system is unplugged.

Most CPUs use some form of mounting bracket for the CPU fan. Some of these brackets require mounting underneath the motherboard, which means removing the motherboard from the system case.

If you're removing an old CPU, you'll need to take off the old fan. Removing CPU fans scares me more than any other physical act I do on a PC. Many (not all) CPU fans use a metal clamp on both sides of the socket. These clamps usually require you to pry them off to remove them using a flat-head screwdriver (Figure 3-67). You need a lot of force—usually far more than you think you should use, so take your time and pry that old fan off!

CAUTION It's a good idea to use a new fan when you replace a CPU—even if the old fan works with your new CPU. Fans get old and die, too!

Figure 3-67
Removing an old fan

Inserting a PGA-Type CPU

Inserting and removing PGA CPUs is a relatively simple process; just *don't touch the pins* or you might destroy the CPU. Figure 3-68 shows a technician installing a Sempron into a Socket 754. Note the pins on the CPU only fit in one orientation. These *orientation markers* are designed to help you align the CPU correctly. Although the orientation marks make it very difficult to install a CPU improperly, incorrectly installing your CPU will almost certainly destroy the CPU or the motherboard, or both!

Figure 3-68
Orienting the CPU

To install, lift the arm or open the metal cover, align the CPU, and it should drop right in (Figure 3-69). If it doesn't, verify your alignment and check for bent pins on the CPU. If you encounter a slightly bent pin, try a mechanical pencil that takes thick (0.9mm) lead. Take the lead out of the mechanical pencil, slide the pencil tip over the bent pin, and straighten it out. Be careful! A broken CPU pin ruins the CPU. Make sure the CPU is all the way in (no visible pins) and then snap down the arm or drop over the metal cover.

Figure 3-69
CPU inserted

Now it's time for the fan! Before inserting the fan, you need to add a small amount of thermal compound (also called *heat dope*). Many fans come with thermal compound already on them; the thermal compound on these pre-doped fans is covered by a small square of tape—take it off before you snap down the fan. If you need to put thermal compound on from a tube (see Figure 3-70), know that it only takes a tiny amount of this compound! Spread it on as thinly, completely, and evenly as you can. Unlike so many other things in life, you *can* have too much thermal compound!

Figure 3-70
Applying thermal
compound

Securing fans makes even the most jaded PC technician a little nervous (Figure 3-71). In most cases, you must apply a fairly strong amount of force to snap the fan into place—far more than you might think. Also, make certain that the fan you install works with your CPU package.

Figure 3-71
Installing the fan

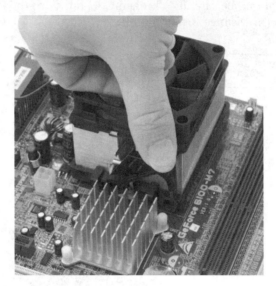

Testing Your New CPU

The next step is to turn on the PC and see if the system boots up. If life were perfect, every CPU installation would end right here as you watch the system happily boot up. Unfortunately, the reality is that sometimes nothing happens when you press the On button. Here's what to do if this happens.

First, make sure the system has power—we'll be going through lots of power issues throughout the book. Second, make sure the CPU is firmly pressed down into the socket. Get your head down and look at the mounted CPU from the side—do you see any of the CPU's wires showing? Does the CPU look level in its mount? If not, reinstall the CPU. If the system still does not boot, double-check any jumper settings—it's very easy to mess them up.

As the computer starts, make sure the CPU fan is spinning within a few seconds. If it doesn't spin up instantly, that's okay, but it must start within about 30 seconds at the least.

The Art of Cooling

There once was a time long ago when CPUs didn't need any type of cooling device. You just snapped in the CPU and it worked. Well, those days are gone. Long gone. If you're installing a modern CPU, you will have to cool it. Fortunately, you have choices.

- **OEM Fans**   OEM fans are included with a retail-boxed CPU. OEM CPUs, on the other hand, don't normally come bundled with fans. Crazy, isn't it? OEM fans have one big advantage: you know absolutely that they will work with your CPU.

- **Specialized Fans** Lots of companies sell third-party fans for different CPUs. These usually exceed the OEM fans in the amount of heat they dissipate. These fans invariably come with eye-catching designs to look really cool inside your system—some are even lighted! (See Figure 3-72.)

Figure 3-72
Cool retail fan

The last choice is the most impressive of all—liquid cooling! That's right, you can put a little liquid cooling system right inside your PC case! Liquid cooling works by running some liquid—usually water—through a metal block that sits on top of your CPU, absorbing heat. The liquid gets heated by the block, runs out of the block and into something that cools the liquid, and the liquid is then pumped through the block again. Any liquid cooling system consists of three main parts:

- A hollow metal block that sits on the CPU
- A pump to move the liquid around
- Some device to cool the liquid

And, of course, you need plenty of hosing to hook them all together! Figure 3-73 shows a typical liquid-cooled CPU.

Figure 3-73
Liquid-cooled CPU

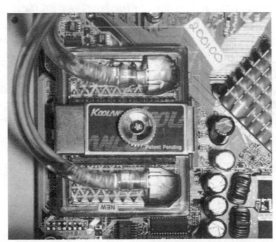

A number of companies sell these liquid-cooling systems. Although they look really impressive and certainly cool your CPU, the reality is that unless you're overclocking or want a quiet system, a good fan will more than suffice.

Whether you have a silent or noisy cooling system for your CPU, always remember to keep everything clean. Once a month or so, take a can of compressed air and clean dust off the fan or radiator. CPUs are very susceptible to heat; a poorly working fan can create all sorts of problems, such as system lockups, spontaneous reboots, and more.

 EXAM TIP CPUs are *thermally sensitive devices*—keep those fans clean!

Know Your CPUs

In this chapter, you have seen the basic components and functions of a PC's CPU. A historical view has been provided to help you better understand the amazing evolution of CPUs in the more than 20-year life span of the personal computer.

The information in this chapter will be referred to again and again throughout the book. Take the time to memorize certain facts, such as the size of the L1 and L2 caches, CPU speeds, and clock-doubling features. These are facts that good technicians can spout off without having to refer to a book.

Beyond A+

Overclocking

For the CPU to work, it must have the motherboard speed, multiplier, and voltage set properly. In most modern systems, the motherboard uses the CPUID functions to set these options automatically. Some motherboards enable you adjust these settings manually by moving a jumper, changing a CMOS setting, or with software, however, so many enthusiasts deliberately change these settings to enhance performance.

Starting way back in the days of the Intel 80486 CPU, people intentionally ran their systems at clock speeds higher than the CPU was rated, a process called *overclocking*, and they worked. Well, *sometimes* the systems worked, and sometimes they didn't. Intel and AMD have a reason for marking a CPU at a particular clock speed—that's the highest speed they guarantee will work.

Before I say anything else, I must warn you that intentional overclocking of a CPU immediately voids any warranty. Overclocking has been known to destroy CPUs. Overclocking might make your system unstable and prone to lockups and reboots. I neither applaud nor decry the practice of overclocking. My goal here is simply to inform you of the practice. You make your own decisions.

CPU makers dislike overclocking. Why would you pay more for a faster processor when you can take a cheaper, slower CPU and just make it run faster? To that end, CPU makers, especially Intel, have gone to great lengths to discourage the practice. For example, both AMD and Intel now make all their CPUs with locked multipliers and special overspeed electronics to deter the practice.

I don't think Intel or AMD really care too much what *end users* do with their CPUs. You own it; you take the risks. A number of criminals, however, learned to make a good business of remarking CPUs with higher than rated speeds and selling them as legitimate CPUs. These counterfeit CPUs have created a nightmare where unsuspecting retailers and end users have been given overclocked CPUs. When they run into trouble, they innocently ask for warranty support, only to discover that their CPU is counterfeit and the warranty is void.

If you want to know exactly what type of CPU you're running, download a copy of the very popular and free CPU-Z utility from www.cpuid.com. CPU-Z gives you every piece of information you'll ever want to know about your CPU (Figure 3-74).

Figure 3-74
CPU-Z in action

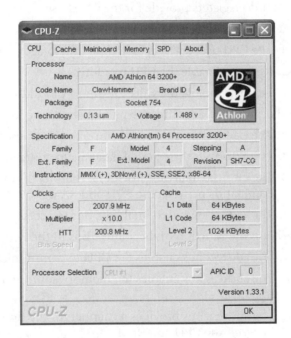

Most people make a couple of adjustments to overclock successfully. First, through jumpers, CMOS settings, or software configuration, increase the bus speed for the system. Second, you often have to increase the voltage going into the CPU by just a little to provide stability. You do that by changing a jumper or CMOS setting.

Overriding the defaults can completely lock up your system, to the point where even removing and reinstalling the CPU doesn't bring the motherboard back to life. (There's also a slight risk of toasting the processor, although all modern processors have circuitry that shuts them down quickly before they overheat.) Most motherboards have a jumper setting called *CMOS clear* (Figure 3-75) that makes the CMOS go back to default settings. Before you try overclocking on a modern system, find the CMOS clear jumper and make sure you know how to use it! Hint: Look in the motherboard manual.

Figure 3-75
CMOS clear jumper

Chapter Review Questions

1. What do registers provide for the CPU?

    A. Registers determine the clock speed.

    B. The CPU uses registers for temporary storage of internal commands and data.

    C. Registers enable the CPU to address RAM.

    D. Registers enable the CPU to control the address bus.

2. What function does the external data bus have in the PC?

    A. The external data bus determines the clock speed for the CPU.

    B. The CPU uses the external data bus to address RAM.

    C. The external data bus provides a channel for the flow of data and commands between the CPU and RAM.

    D. The CPU uses the external data bus to access registers.

3. What is the function of the address bus in the PC?

    A. The address bus enables the CPU to communicate with the chipset.

    B. The address bus enables the memory controller chip to communicate with the RAM.

    C. The address bus provides a channel for the flow of data and commands between the CPU and RAM.

    D. The address bus enables the CPU to access registers.

4. What is the size of the data bus and L1 cache on a Core 2 Duo CPU?

    A. 32-bit data bus, 32-KB L1 cache

    B. 64-bit data bus, two 32-KB L1 caches

    C. 64-bit data bus, two 64-KB L1 caches

    D. 128-bit data bus, two 128-KB L1 caches

5. When a tech adds a new Athlon 64 X2 processor to a motherboard, which of the following should he or she check? (Choose the *best* answer.)

    A. Clock speed of the CPU, clock multiplier for the CPU

    B. Clock speed of the CPU, clock multiplier for the CPU, voltage settings on the motherboard

    C. Clock speed of the CPU, clock multiplier for the CPU, voltage settings on the motherboard, system clock speed

    D. Voltage settings on the motherboard, system clock speed

6. The Intel Core Duo has which of the following advantages over the Pentium M?

    A. Level 1 cache

    B. 64-bit data bus

    C. Quad pipelining

    D. Dual processors

7. The Intel Core Duo processor has two 32-KB Level 1 caches, whereas the Athlon 64 X2 has one 128-KB Level 1 cache. What does the cache provide for the processor(s)?

    A. It enables the CPU to continue working during pipeline stalls.

    B. It enables the CPU to continue working during hard drive refreshes.

    C. It enables the CPU to access RAM.

    D. It enables the CPU to access the chipset memory controller.

8. What distinguishes the Athlon Thunderbird from the original Athlon? (Select all that apply.)

    A. Athlon Thunderbird used an SEC cartridge

    B. Athlon Thunderbird used a PGA package

    C. Athlon Thunderbird ran on a double-pumped frontside bus

    D. Athlon Thunderbird ran on a quad-pumped frontside bus

9. Jane, the hardware technician for a nonprofit corporation, has ten systems that she needs to upgrade with new microprocessors. Each system currently has a Socket 939 motherboard with an Athlon 64 3200+ CPU installed. To keep the upgrade costs low, her boss has told her to use the existing motherboards if possible.

    Primary objective   Upgrade the systems with faster CPUs.

    Optional objectives   Use existing motherboards and avoid adding any hardware aside from the CPU, fan, and heat sink assembly.

    Proposed solution   Jane places an order for ten PPGA Core 2 Duo processors and ten PPGA to Socket 939 converters.

    The proposed solution:

    A. Meets only the primary objective

    B. Meets the primary objective and one of the optional objectives

    C. Meets the primary objective and both of the optional objectives

    D. Meets none of the objectives

10. A donor gives five Socket 939 Athlon X2 processors to the nonprofit corporation for which Jane works as a technician. She has several systems with Socket 939 motherboards and Athlon 64 CPUs installed. Her boss wants her to upgrade five systems with the new processors but to keep the upgrade costs low if possible by using the existing motherboards.

Primary objective   Upgrade the systems with faster CPUs.

Optional objective   Use existing motherboards.

Proposed solution   Remove the Athlon 64 CPUs on five systems and replace them with the new Athlon 64 X2 CPUs. Update the motherboards following the motherboard manufacturer's guidelines.

The proposed solution:

A. Meets only the primary objective

B. Meets only the optional objective

C. Meets the primary and optional objectives

D. Meets neither objective

Answers

1. **B.** The CPU uses registers for temporary storage of internal commands and data.

2. **C.** The external data bus provides a channel for the flow of data and commands between the CPU and RAM.

3. **A.** The address bus enables the CPU to communicate with the chipset.

4. **C.** The Core 2 Duo CPU has a 64-bit data bus and two 64-KB L1 caches.

5. **C.** Even with the CPUID built into modern processors, a good tech should check the motherboard settings for speed, clock multiplier, and voltage. He or she should also know the speed of the CPU.

6. **D.** The Intel Core Duo has dual processors, a definite advantage over the Pentium M.

7. **A.** Cache enables the CPU to continue working during pipeline stalls.

8. **B, C.** The Athlon Thunderbird used a PGA package and ran on a double-pumped frontside bus.

9. **D.** What was Jane thinking? You can't install Intel processors on AMD-based motherboards! Her proposed solution accomplishes none of the objectives.

10. **C.** That's a little more like it. With a minor motherboard update, Jane can put those Athlon 64 X2 processors to work!

RAM

In this chapter, you will learn how to
- Identify the different types of RAM packaging
- Explain the varieties of DRAM
- Install RAM properly
- Perform basic RAM troubleshooting

Anytime someone comes up to me and starts professing their computer savvy, I ask them a few questions to see how much they really know. Just in case you and I ever meet and you decide you want to "talk tech" with me, I'll tell you my first two questions just so you'll be ready. Both involve *random access memory (RAM)*, the working memory for the CPU.

1. "How much RAM is in your computer?"

2. "What is RAM and why is it so important that every PC have some?"

Can you answer either of these questions? Don't fret if you can't—you'll know how to answer both of them before you finish this chapter. Let's start by reviewing what you know about RAM thus far.

 EXAM TIP The CompTIA A+ certification domains use the term *memory* to describe the short-term storage used by the PC to load the operating system and running applications. The more common term in the industry is *RAM*, for random access memory, the kind of short-term memory you'll find in every computer. More specifically, the primary system RAM is *dynamic random access memory (DRAM)*. For the most part, this book uses the terms RAM and DRAM.

When not in use, programs and data are held in mass storage, which usually means a hard drive, but could also mean a USB thumb drive, a CD-ROM, or some other device that can hold data when the computer is turned off (Figure 4-1). When you load a program by clicking an icon in Windows, the program is copied from the mass storage device to RAM and then run (Figure 4-2).

Figure 4-1
Mass storage holds
unused programs.

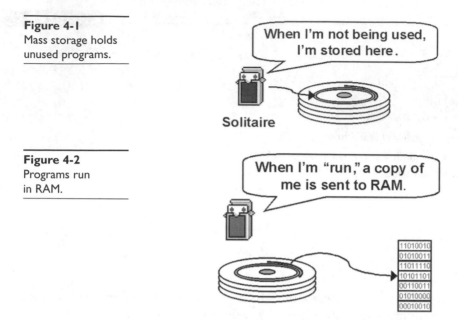

Figure 4-2
Programs run
in RAM.

You saw in the previous chapter that the CPU uses dynamic random access memory (DRAM) as RAM for all PCs. Just like CPUs, DRAM has gone through a number of evolutionary changes over the years, resulting in improved DRAM technologies with names such as SDRAM, RDRAM, and DDR RAM. This chapter starts by explaining how DRAM works, and then moves into the types of DRAM used over the last few years to see how they improve on the original DRAM. The third section, "Working with RAM," goes into the details of finding and installing RAM. The chapter finishes with troubleshooting RAM problems.

Historical/Conceptual

Understanding DRAM

As discussed in Chapter 3, DRAM functions like an electronic spreadsheet, with numbered rows containing cells and each cell holding a one or zero. Now let's look at what's physically happening. Each spreadsheet cell is a special type of semiconductor that can hold a single bit—one or zero—using microscopic capacitors and transistors. DRAM makers put these semiconductors into chips that can hold a certain number of bits. The bits inside the chips are organized in a rectangular fashion using rows and columns.

Each chip has a limit on the number of lines of code it can contain. Think of each line of code as one of the rows on the electronic spreadsheet; one chip might be able to store a million rows of code while another chip can store over a billion lines. Each chip also has a limit on the width of the lines of code it can handle, so one chip might handle 8-bit-wide data while another might handle 16-bit-wide data. Techs describe chips by bits rather than bytes, so ×8 and ×16, respectively. Just as you could describe a spreadsheet by the number of rows and columns—John's accounting spreadsheet is huge, 48 rows × 12 columns—memory makers describe RAM chips the same way. An individual DRAM chip that holds 1,048,576 rows and 8 columns, for example, would be a 1 M × 8 chip, with "M" as shorthand for "mega," just like in megabytes (2^{20} bytes). It is difficult if not impossible to tell the size of a DRAM chip just by looking at it—only the DRAM makers know the meaning of the tiny number on the chips (although sometimes you can make a good guess). See Figure 4-3.

Figure 4-3
What do these
numbers mean?

Organizing DRAM

Due to its low cost, high speed, and capability to contain a lot of data in a relatively small package, DRAM has been the standard RAM used in all computers—not just PCs—since the mid-1970s. DRAM can be found in just about everything, from automobiles to automatic bread makers.

The PC has very specific requirements for DRAM. The original 8088 processor had an 8-bit frontside bus. All the commands given to an 8088 processor were in discrete, 8-bit chunks. Therefore, you needed RAM that could store data in 8-bit (1-byte) chunks, so that each time the CPU asked for a line of code, the memory controller could put an 8-bit chunk on the data bus. This optimized the flow of data into (and out from) the CPU.

Although today's DRAM chips may have widths greater than 1 bit, back in the old days all DRAM chips were 1 bit wide. That means you only had sizes like 64 K × 1 or 256 K × 1—always 1 bit wide. So how was 1-bit-wide DRAM turned into 8-bit-wide memory? The answer was quite simple: just take eight 1-bit-wide chips and electronically organize them with the memory controller chip to be eight wide. First, put eight 1-bit-wide chips in a row on the motherboard (Figure 4-4), and then wire up this row

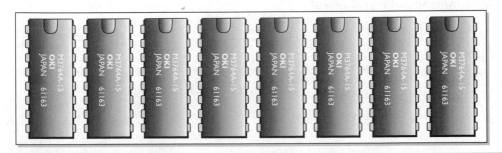

Figure 4-4   One row of DRAM

of DRAM chips to the memory controller chip (which has to be designed to handle this) to make byte-wide memory (Figure 4-5). You just made eight 1-bit-wide DRAM chips look like a single 8-bit-wide DRAM chip to the CPU.

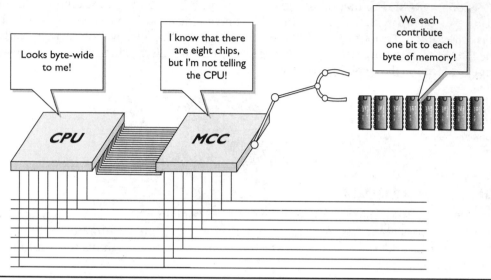

Figure 4-5 The MCC in action

Practical DRAM

Okay, before you learn more about DRAM, I need to make a critical point extremely clear. When you first saw the 8088's machine language in the previous chapter, all the examples in the "codebook" were exactly 1-byte commands. Figure 4-6 shows the code-book again—see how all the commands are 1 byte?

Well, the reality is slightly different. Most of the 8088 machine language commands are 1 byte, but a few more complex commands need 2 bytes. For example, the command below tells the CPU to move 163 bytes "up the RAM spreadsheet" and run whatever command is there. Cool, eh?

```
1110100110100011
```

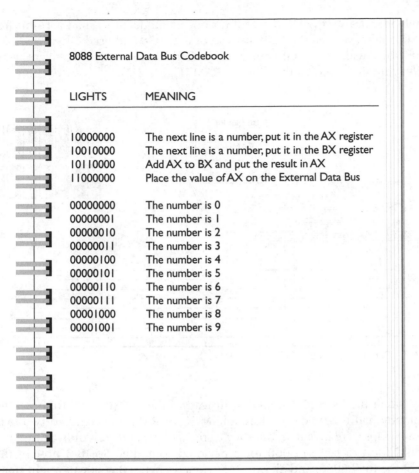

8088 External Data Bus Codebook

LIGHTS	MEANING
10000000	The next line is a number, put it in the AX register
10010000	The next line is a number, put it in the BX register
10110000	Add AX to BX and put the result in AX
11000000	Place the value of AX on the External Data Bus
00000000	The number is 0
00000001	The number is 1
00000010	The number is 2
00000011	The number is 3
00000100	The number is 4
00000101	The number is 5
00000110	The number is 6
00000111	The number is 7
00001000	The number is 8
00001001	The number is 9

Figure 4-6 Codebook again

The problem here is that the command is 2 bytes wide, not 1 byte wide! So how did the 8088 handle this? Simple—it just took the command 1 byte at a time. It took twice as long to handle the command because the MCC had to go to RAM twice, but it worked.

Okay, so if some of the commands are more than 1 byte wide, why didn't Intel make the 8088 with a 16-bit frontside bus? Wouldn't that have been better? Well, Intel did! Intel invented a CPU called the 8086. The 8086 actually predates the 8088 and was absolutely identical to the 8088 except for one small detail—it had a 16-bit frontside bus. IBM could have used the 8086 instead of the 8088 and used 2-byte-wide RAM instead of 1-byte-wide RAM. Of course, they would have needed to invent a memory controller chip that handled that kind of RAM (Figure 4-7).

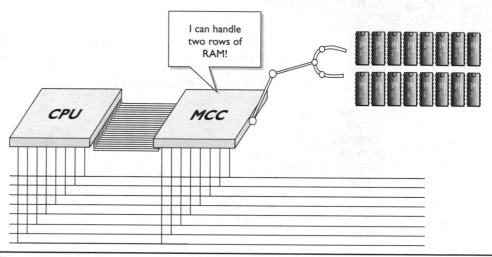

Figure 4-7 Pumped up 8086 MCC at work

Why didn't Intel sell IBM the 8086 instead of the 8088? There were two reasons. First, nobody had invented an affordable MCC or RAM that handled two bytes at a time. Sure, chips were invented, but they were *expensive* and IBM didn't think that anyone would want to pay $12,000 for a personal computer. So IBM bought the Intel 8088, not the Intel 8086, and all our RAM came in bytes. But as you might imagine, it didn't stay that way too long.

DRAM Sticks

As CPU data bus sizes increased, so too did the need for RAM wide enough to fill the bus. The Intel 80386 CPU, for example, had a 32-bit data bus and thus the need for 32-bit-wide DRAM. Imagine having to line up 32 1-bit-wide DRAM chips on a motherboard. Talk about a waste of space! Figure 4-8 shows an example of motherboard RAM run amuck.

Figure 4-8   That's a lot of real estate used by RAM chips!

DRAM manufacturers responded by creating wider DRAM chips, such as ×4, ×8, and ×16, and putting multiples of them on a small circuit board called a *stick* or *module*. Figure 4-9 shows an early stick, called a *single inline memory module (SIMM)*, with eight DRAM chips. To add RAM to a modern machine means you need to get the right stick or sticks for the particular motherboard. Your motherboard manual tells you precisely what sort of module you need and how much RAM you can install.

Figure 4-9
A 72-pin SIMM

Modern CPUs are a lot smarter than the old Intel 8088. Their machine languages have some commands that are up to 64 bits (8 bytes) wide. They also have at least a 64-bit front-side bus that can handle more than just 8 bits. They don't want RAM to give them a puny 8 bits at a time! To optimize the flow of data into and out of the CPU, the modern MCC provides at least 64 bits of data every time the CPU requests information from RAM.

NOTE   Some MCCs are 128 bits wide.

Dealing with Old RAM

Often in the PC world, old technology and ways of doing things get re-implemented with some newer technology. Learning how things worked back in the ancient days can stand a tech in good stead. Perhaps more importantly, many thousands of companies—including hospitals, auto repair places, and more—use very old, proprietary applications that keep track of medical records, inventory, and so on. If you're called to work on one of these ancient systems, you need to know how to work with old parts, so here's a suggestion.

Obtain an old computer, such as an 80386 or 80486. Ask your uncle or cousin or Great Aunt Edna if they have a PC collecting dust in a closet that you can use. Failing that, go to a secondhand store or market and buy one for a few dollars.

Open up the system and check out the RAM. Remove the RAM from the motherboard and then replace it to familiarize yourself with the internals. You never know when some critical system will go down and need repair immediately—and you're the one to do it!

Current RAM

Modern DRAM sticks come in 32-bit- and 64-bit-wide form factors with a varying number of chips. Many techs describe these memory modules by their width, so × 32 and × 64. Note that this number does *not* describe the width of the individual DRAM chips on the module! When you read or hear about *by whatever* memory, simply note that you need to know whether that person is talking about the DRAM width or the module width.

When the CPU needs certain bytes of data, it requests those bytes via the address bus. The CPU does not know the physical location of the RAM that stores that data, nor the physical makeup of the RAM—such as how many DRAM chips work together to provide the 64-bit-wide memory rows. The MCC keeps track of this and just gives the CPU whichever bytes it requests (Figure 4-10).

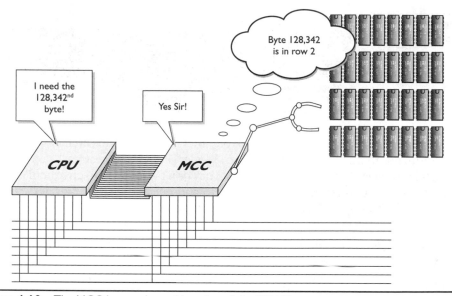

Figure 4-10 The MCC knows the real location of the DRAM.

Consumer RAM

So if modern DRAM modules come in sizes much wider than a byte, why do people still use the word "byte" to describe how much DRAM they have? Convention. Habit. Rather than using a label that describes the electronic structure of RAM, common usage describes the *total capacity of RAM on a stick in bytes.* John has a single 512-MB stick of RAM on his motherboard, for example, while Sally has two 256-MB sticks. Both systems have a total of 512 MB of system RAM. That's what your clients care about, after all, because having enough RAM makes their systems snappy and stable; not enough and the systems run poorly. As a tech, you need to know more, of course, to pick the right RAM for many different types of computers.

Essentials

Types of RAM

Development of newer, wider, and faster CPUs and MCCs motivate DRAM manufacturers to invent new DRAM technologies that deliver enough data at a single pop to optimize the flow of data into and out of the CPU.

EXAM TIP Old RAM—really old RAM—was called *fast page mode (FPM)* RAM. This ancient RAM used a totally different technology that was not tied to the system clock. If you ever hear of FPM RAM, it's going to be in a system that's over a decade old. Be careful! CompTIA likes to use older terms like this to throw you off!

SDRAM

Most modern systems use some form of *synchronous DRAM (SDRAM)*. SDRAM is still DRAM, but it is *synchronous*—tied to the system clock, just like the CPU and MCC, so the MCC knows when data is ready to be grabbed from SDRAM. This results in little wasted time.

SDRAM made its debut in 1996 on a stick called a *dual inline memory module (DIMM).* The early SDRAM DIMMs came in a wide variety of pin sizes. The most common pin sizes found on desktops were the 168-pin variety. Laptop DIMMs came in 68-pin, 144-pin (Figure 4-11), or 172-pin *micro-DIMM* packages; and the 72-pin, 144-pin, or 200-pin *small outline DIMM (SO DIMM)* form factors (Figure 4-12). With the exception of the 32-bit 72-pin SO DIMM, all these DIMM varieties delivered 64-bit-wide data to match the 64-bit data bus of every CPU since the Pentium.

Figure 4-11
144-pin micro-DIMM (photo courtesy of Micron Technology, Inc.)

Figure 4-12
A 168-pin DIMM
above a 144-pin
SO-DIMM

To take advantage of SDRAM, you needed a PC designed to use SDRAM. If you had a system with slots for 168-pin DIMMs, for example, your system used SDRAM. A DIMM in any one of the DIMM slots could fill the 64-bit bus, so each slot was called a *bank*. You could install one, two, or more sticks and the system would work. Note that on laptops that used the 72-pin SO DIMM, you needed to install two sticks of RAM to make a full bank because each stick only provided half the bus width.

SDRAM tied to the system clock, so it had a clock speed that matched the frontside bus. Five clock speeds were commonly used on the early SDRAM systems: 66, 75, 83, 100, and 133 MHz. The RAM speed had to match or exceed the system speed or the computer would be unstable or wouldn't work at all. These speeds were prefixed with a "PC" in the front based on a standard forwarded by Intel, so SDRAM speeds were PC66 through PC133. For a Pentium III computer with a 100-MHz frontside bus, you needed to buy SDRAM DIMMs rated to handle it, such as PC100 or PC133.

RDRAM

When Intel was developing the Pentium 4, they knew that regular SDRAM just wasn't going to be fast enough to handle the quad-pumped 400-MHz frontside bus. Intel announced plans to replace SDRAM with a very fast, new type of RAM developed by Rambus, Inc. called Rambus DRAM, or simply *RDRAM* (Figure 4-13). Hailed by Intel as the next great leap in DRAM technology, RDRAM could handle speeds up to 800 MHz, which gave Intel plenty of room to improve the Pentium 4.

Figure 4-13
RDRAM

NOTE The 400-MHz frontside bus speed wasn't achieved by making the system clock faster—it was done by making CPUs and MCCs capable of sending 64 bits of data two or four times for every clock cycle, effectively doubling or quadrupling the system bus speed.

RDRAM was greatly anticipated by the industry for years, but industry support for RDRAM proved less than enthusiastic due to significant delays in development, plus a price many times that of SDRAM. Despite this grudging support, almost all major PC makers sold systems that used RDRAM—for a while. From a tech's standpoint, RDRAM shares almost all of the characteristics of SDRAM. A stick of RDRAM is called a *RIMM*. In this case, however, the letters don't actually stand for anything; they just rhyme: SIMMs, DIMMs, and now RIMMs, get it?

RDRAM RIMMs came in two sizes: a 184-pin for desktops and a 160-pin SO-RIMM for laptops. RIMMs were keyed differently from DIMMs to ensure that even though they are the same basic size, you couldn't accidentally install a RIMM in a DIMM slot or vice versa. RDRAM also had a speed rating: 600 MHz, 700 MHz, 800 MHz, or 1066 MHz. RDRAM employed an interesting dual-channel architecture. Each RIMM was 64 bits wide, but the Rambus MCC alternated between two sticks to increase the speed of data retrieval. You were required to install RIMMs in pairs to use this dual-channel architecture.

RDRAM motherboards also required that all RIMM slots be populated. Unused pairs of slots needed a passive device called a *continuity RIMM* (CRIMM) installed in each slot to enable the RDRAM system to terminate properly. Figure 4-14 shows a CRIMM.

Figure 4-14
CRIMM

RDRAM offered dramatic possibilities for high-speed PCs, but ran into three roadblocks that betamaxed it. First, the technology was owned wholly by Rambus—if you wanted to make it, you had to pay the licensing fees they charged. That led directly to the second problem, expense. RDRAM cost substantially more than SDRAM. Third, Rambus and Intel made a completely closed deal for the technology. RDRAM worked only on Pentium 4 systems using Intel-made MCCs. AMD was out of luck. Clearly, the rest of the industry had to look for another high-speed RAM solution.

 NOTE *Betamaxed* is slang for "made it obsolete because no one bought it, even though it was a superior technology to the winner in the marketplace." Refers to the VHS versus Betamax wars in the old days of video cassette recorders.

DDR SDRAM

AMD and many major system and memory makers threw their support behind *double data rate SDRAM (DDR SDRAM)*. DDR SDRAM basically copied Rambus, doubling the throughput of SDRAM by making two processes for every clock cycle. This synchronized (pardon the pun) nicely with the Athlon and later AMD processors' double-pumped frontside bus. DDR SDRAM could not run as fast as RDRAM—although relatively low frontside bus speeds made that a moot point—but cost only slightly more than regular SDRAM.

 NOTE Most techs drop some or all of the SDRAM part of DDR SDRAM when engaged in normal geekspeak. You'll hear the memory referred to as DDR, DDR RAM, and the weird hybrid, DDRAM.

DDR SDRAM for desktops comes in 184-pin DIMMs. These DIMMs match 168-pin DIMMs in physical size, but not in pin compatibility (Figure 4-15). The slots for the two types of RAM appear similar as well, but have different guide notches, making it impossible to insert either type of RAM into the other's slot. DDR SDRAM for laptops comes in either 200-pin SO-DIMMs or 172-pin micro-DIMMs (Figure 4-16).

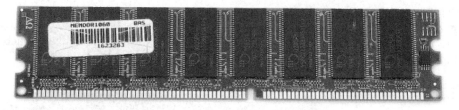

Figure 4-15   DDR SDRAM

Figure 4-16
172-pin DDR
SDRAM micro-
DIMM (photo
courtesy of
Kingston/Joint
Harvest)

 NOTE RAM makers use the term *single data rate SDRAM (SDR SDRAM)* for the original SDRAM to differentiate it from DDR SDRAM.

DDR sticks use a rather interesting naming convention—actually started by the Rambus folks—based on the number of bytes per second of data throughput the RAM can handle. To determine the bytes per second, take the MHz speed and multiply by 8 bytes (the width of all DDR SDRAM sticks). So 400 MHz multiplied by 8 is 3200 bytes per second. Put the abbreviation "PC" in the front to make the new term: PC3200. Many techs also use the naming convention used for the individual DDR chips; for example, *DDR400* refers to a 400-MHz DDR SDRAM chip running on a 200-MHz clock. Even though the term DDR*xxx* is really just for individual DDR chips and the term PC*xxxx* is for DDR sticks, this tradition of two names for every speed of RAM is a bit of a challenge as both terms are commonly used interchangeably. Table 4-1 shows all the speeds for DDR—not all of these are commonly used.

Clock Speed	DDR Speed Rating	PC Speed Rating
100 MHz	DDR200	PC1600
133 MHz	DDR266	PC2100
166 MHz	DDR333	PC2700
200 MHz	DDR400	PC3200
217 MHz	DDR433	PC3500
233 MHz	DDR466	PC3700
250 MHz	DDR500	PC4000
275 MHz	DDR550	PC4400
300 MHz	DDR600	PC4800

Table 4-1 DDR Speeds

Following the lead of AMD, VIA, and other manufacturers, the PC industry adopted DDR SDRAM as the standard system RAM. Intel relented and stopped producing motherboards and memory controllers that required RDRAM in the summer of 2003.

There's one sure thing about PC technologies—any good idea that can be copied will be copied. One of Rambus' best concepts was the dual-channel architecture—using two sticks of RDRAM together to increase throughput. Manufacturers have released motherboards with MCCs that support dual-channel architecture using DDR SDRAM. Dual-channel DDR motherboards use regular DDR sticks, although manufacturers often sell RAM in matched pairs, branding them as dual-channel RAM.

Dual-channel DDR works like RDRAM in that you must have two identical sticks of DDR and they must snap into two paired slots. Unlike RDRAM, dual-channel DDR doesn't have anything like CRIMMS—you don't need to put anything into unused slot pairs. Dual-channel DDR technology is very flexible, but also has a few quirks that vary with each system. Some motherboards have three DDR SDRAM slots, but the dual-channel DDR works only if you install DDR SDRAM in two of the slots (Figure 4-17). If you populate the third slot, the system will use the full capacity of RAM installed, but turns off the dual-channel feature—and no, it doesn't tell you! The dual slots are blue; the third slot is black, which you could clearly see if this weren't a black-and-white photo.

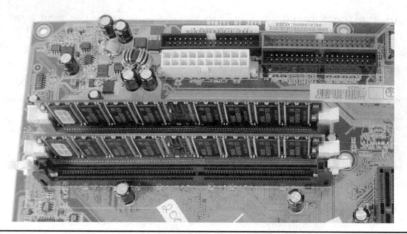

Figure 4-17   An nForce motherboard showing the three RAM slots. The two slots bracketing the slim space can run as dual channel as long as you don't populate the third slot.

DDR2

The fastest versions of DDR RAM run at a blistering PC4800. That's 4.8 gigabytes per second (GBps) of data throughput! You'd think that kind of speed would satisfy most users, and to be honest, DRAM running at approximately 5 GBps really is plenty fast—for now. However, the ongoing speed increases ensure that even these speeds won't be good enough in the future. Knowing this, the RAM industry came out with DDR2, the successor to DDR. *DDR2* is DDR RAM with some improvements in its electrical characteristics, enabling it to run even faster than DDR while using less power. The big speed increase from DDR2 comes by clock doubling the input/output circuits on the chips. This does not speed up the core RAM—the part that holds the data—but speeding up the input/output and adding special buffers (sort of like a cache) makes DDR2 runs much faster than regular DDR. DDR2 uses a 240-pin DIMM that's not compatible with DDR. You'll find motherboards running both single-channel and dual-channel DDR2 (Figure 4-18).

Figure 4-18
240-pin DDR2
DIMM

The following table shows some of the common DDR2 speeds.

Core RAM Clock Speed	DDR I/O Speed	DDR2 Speed Rating	PC Speed Rating
100 MHz	200 MHz	DDR2-400	PC2-3200
133 MHz	266 MHz	DDR2-533	PC2-4200
166 MHz	333 MHz	DDR2-667	PC2-5300
200 MHz	400 MHz	DDR2-800	PC2-6400
250 MHz	500 MHz	DDR2-1000	PC2-8000

RAM Variations

Within each class of RAM, you'll find variations in packaging, speed, quality, and the capability to handle data with more or fewer errors. Higher-end systems often need higher-end RAM, so knowing these variations is of crucial importance to techs.

Double-Sided DIMMs

Every type of RAM stick, starting with the old FPM SIMMs and continuing through to 240-pin DDR2 SDRAM, comes in one of two types: single-sided and double-sided. As their name implies, single-sided sticks only have chips on one side of the stick. Double-sided sticks have chips on both sides (Figure 4-19). The vast majority of RAM sticks are single-sided, but there are plenty of double-sided sticks out there. Double-sided sticks are basically two sticks of RAM soldered onto one board. There's nothing wrong with double-sided RAM other than the fact that some motherboards either can't use them or can only use them in certain ways—for example, only if you use a single stick and it goes into a certain slot.

Figure 4-19
Double-sided DDR SDRAM

Latency

If you've shopped for RAM lately, you may have noticed terms such as "CL2" or "low-latency" as you tried to determine which RAM to purchase. You might find two otherwise identical RAM sticks with a 20 percent price difference and a salesperson pressuring you to buy the more expensive one because it's "faster" even though both sticks say DDR400 (Figure 4-20).

Figure 4-20
Why is one more
expensive than
the other?

RAM responds to electrical signals at varying rates. When the memory controller starts to grab a line of memory, for example, there's a slight delay; think of it as the RAM getting off the couch. After the RAM sends out the requested line of memory, there's another slight delay before the memory controller can ask for another line—the RAM sat back down. The delay in RAM's response time is called its *latency*. RAM with a lower latency—such as CL2—is faster than RAM with a higher latency—such as CL3—because it responds more quickly.

Latency numbers reflect how many clicks of the system clock it takes before the RAM responds. If you speed up the system clock, say from 166 MHz to 200 MHz, the same stick of RAM might take an extra click before it can respond. When you take RAM out of an older system and put it into a newer one, you might get a seemingly dead PC, even though the RAM fits in the DIMM slot. Many motherboards enable you to adjust the RAM timings manually. If so, try raising the latency to give the slower RAM time to respond. See Chapter 5, "BIOS and CMOS," to learn how to make these adjustments (and how to recover if you make a mistake!).

From a tech's standpoint, you need to get the proper RAM for the system on which you're working. If you put a high latency stick in a motherboard set up for a low latency stick, you'll get an unstable or completely dead PC. Check the motherboard manual and get the quickest RAM the motherboard can handle and you should be fine.

NOTE CAS stands for *column array strobe*, one of the wires (along with the *row array strobe*) in the RAM that helps the memory controller find a particular bit of memory. Each of these wires require electricity to charge up before they can do their job. This is one of the aspects of latency.

Parity and ECC

Given the high speeds and phenomenal amount of data moved by the typical DRAM chip, it's possible that a RAM chip might occasionally give bad data to the memory controller. This doesn't necessarily mean that the RAM has gone bad. This could be an occasional hiccup caused by some unknown event that makes a good DRAM chip say a bit is a zero when it's really a one. In most cases, you won't even notice when such a rare event happens. In some environments, however, even these rare events are intolerable. A bank server handling thousands of online transactions per second, for example, can't risk even the smallest error. These important computers need a more robust, fault-resistant RAM.

The first type of error-detecting RAM was known as parity RAM (Figure 4-21). *Parity* RAM stored an extra bit of data (called the parity bit) that the MCC used to verify if the data was correct. Parity wasn't perfect—it wouldn't always detect an error, and if the MCC did find an error, it couldn't correct the error. For years, parity was the only available way to tell if the RAM made a mistake.

Figure 4-21
Ancient parity
RAM stick

Today's PCs that need to watch for RAM errors use a special type of RAM called *error correction code (ECC)* RAM. ECC is a major advance in error checking on DRAM. First, ECC detects any time a single bit is incorrect. Second, ECC fixes these errors on the fly. The checking and fixing come at a price, as ECC RAM is always slower than non-ECC RAM.

 NOTE Some memory manufacturers call the technology *Error Checking and Correction (ECC)*. Don't be thrown off if you see the phrase—it's the same thing, just a different marketing slant for error correction code.

ECC DRAM comes in every DIMM package type. You might be tempted to say "Gee, maybe I want to try this ECC RAM!" Well, don't! To take advantage of ECC RAM, you need a motherboard with an MCC designed to use ECC. Only expensive motherboards for high-end systems use ECC. The special-use-only nature of ECC makes it fairly rare. There are plenty of techs out there with years of experience who've never even seen ECC RAM.

Buffered/Registered DRAM

Your average PC motherboard accepts no more than four sticks of DRAM because more than four physical slots for sticks gives motherboard designers some serious electrical headaches. Yet some systems that use a lot of RAM need the capability to use more DRAM sticks on the motherboard, often six or eight. To get around the electrical hassles, special DRAM sticks add a buffering chip to the stick that acts as an intermediary between the DRAM and the MCC. These special DRAMs are called *buffered* or *registered* DRAM (Figure 4-22). The DDR2 version is called *fully buffered*. (See the "Beyond A+" section for more details.)

Figure 4-22
Buffered RAM

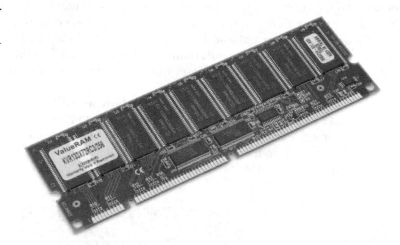

Like ECC, you must have a motherboard with an MCC designed to use this type of DRAM. Rest assured that such a motherboard will have a large number of RAM slots. Buffered/registered RAM is rare (maybe not quite as rare as ECC RAM), and you'll never see it in the typical desktop system.

Working with RAM

Whenever someone comes up to me and asks what single hardware upgrade they can do to improve their system performance, I always tell them the same thing—add more RAM. Adding more RAM can improve overall system performance, processing speed, and stability—if you get it right. Botching the job can cause dramatic system instability, such as frequent, random crashes and reboots. Every tech needs to know how to install and upgrade system RAM of all types.

To get the desired results from a RAM upgrade, you must first determine if insufficient RAM is the cause of system problems. Second, you need to pick the proper RAM for the system. Finally, you must use good installation practices. Always store RAM sticks in anti-static packaging whenever they're not in use, and use strict ESD handling procedures. Like many other pieces of the PC, RAM is *very* sensitive to ESD and other technician abuse (Figure 4-23)!

Figure 4-23
Don't do this!
Grabbing the
contacts is a
bad thing.

Do You Need RAM?

Two symptoms point to the need for more RAM in a PC: general system sluggishness and excessive hard drive accessing. If programs take forever to load and running programs seem to stall and move more slowly than you would like, the problem could stem from insufficient RAM. A friend with a new Windows XP Professional system complained that her PC seemed snappy when she first got it, but takes a long time to do the things she wants to do with it, such as photograph retouching in Adobe Photoshop and document layout for a print zine she produces. Her system had only 256 MB of RAM, sufficient to run Windows XP Professional, but woefully insufficient for her tasks—she kept maxing out the RAM and thus the system slowed to a crawl. I replaced her stick with a pair of 1-GB sticks and suddenly she had the powerhouse workstation she desired.

Excessive hard drive activity when you move between programs points to a need for more RAM. Every Windows PC has the capability to make a portion of your hard drive look like RAM in case you run out of real RAM. This is called the *page file* or *swap file.* This book discusses page files in Chapter 15, but for now appreciate the fact that if you fill your RAM up with programs, your PC will automatically start loading some programs into the page file. You can't see this process taking place just by looking at the screen—these swaps are done in the background. But you will notice the hard drive access LED going crazy as Windows rushes to move programs between RAM and the page file in a process called *disk thrashing.* Windows uses the page file all the time, but excessive disk thrashing suggests that you need more RAM.

You can diagnose excessive disk thrashing through simply observing the hard drive access LED flashing, or through various third-party tools. I like FreeMeter (www.tiler.com/freemeter/). It's been around for quite a while, runs on all versions of Windows, and is easy to use (Figure 4-24). Notice on the FreeMeter screenshot that some amount of the page file is being used. That's perfectly normal.

Figure 4-24
FreeMeter

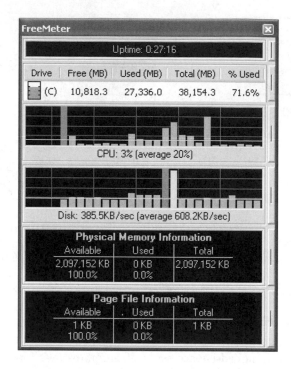

System RAM Recommendations

Microsoft sets the minimum RAM requirements listed for the various Windows operating systems very low to get the maximum number of users to upgrade or convert, and that's fine. A Windows XP Professional machine will run well enough on 128 MB of RAM. Just don't ask it to do any serious computing, like run Doom III! Here are my recommendations for system RAM.

Operating System	Reasonable Minimum	Solid Performance	Power User
Windows 2000	128 MB	256 MB	512 MB
Windows XP	256 MB	512 MB	1 GB
Windows Vista	512 MB	1 GB	2 GB

Determining Current RAM Capacity

Before you go get RAM, you obviously need to know how much RAM you currently have in your PC. Every version of Windows works the same way. Just select the Properties for My Computer to see how much RAM is in your system (Figure 4-25). If you have a newer keyboard, you can access the screen with the WINDOWS-PAUSE/BREAK keystroke combination. Windows 2000 and XP come with the handy Performance tab under the Task Manager (as shown in Figure 4-26).

Figure 4-25
Mike has a lot
of RAM!

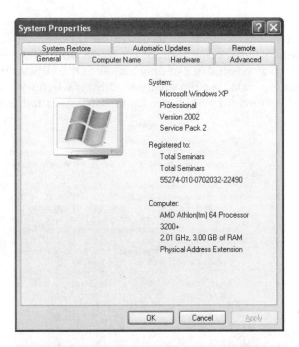

Figure 4-26
Performance tab on
the Windows XP
Task Manager

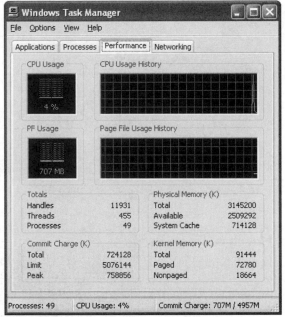

Getting the Right RAM

To do the perfect RAM upgrade, determine the optimum capacity of RAM to install and
then get the right RAM for the motherboard. Your first two stops toward these goals are
the inside of the case and your motherboard manual. Open the case to see how many

sticks of RAM you have installed currently and how many free slots you have open. Check the motherboard book to determine the total capacity of RAM the system can handle and what specific technology works with your system. You can't put DDR SDRAM into a system that can only handle SDR SDRAM, after all, and it won't do you much good to install a pair of 512-MB DIMMs when your system tops out at 784 MB! Figure 4-27 shows the RAM limits for my Gigabyte motherboard.

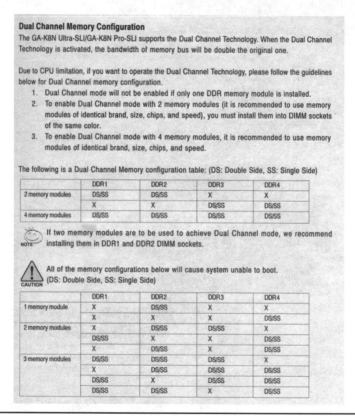

Dual Channel Memory Configuration

The GA-K8N Ultra-SLI/GA-K8N Pro-SLI supports the Dual Channel Technology. When the Dual Channel Technology is activated, the bandwidth of memory bus will be double the original one.

Due to CPU limitation, if you want to operate the Dual Channel Technology, please follow the guidelines below for Dual Channel memory configuration.

1. Dual Channel mode will not be enabled if only one DDR memory module is installed.
2. To enable Dual Channel mode with 2 memory modules (it is recommended to use memory modules of identical brand, size, chips, and speed), you must install them into DIMM sockets of the same color.
3. To enable Dual Channel mode with 4 memory modules, it is recommended to use memory modules of identical brand, size, chips, and speed.

The following is a Dual Channel Memory configuration table: (DS: Double Side, SS: Single Side)

	DDR1	DDR2	DDR3	DDR4
2 memory modules	DS/SS	DS/SS	X	X
	X	X	DS/SS	DS/SS
4 memory modules	DS/SS	DS/SS	DS/SS	DS/SS

NOTE: If two memory modules are to be used to achieve Dual Channel mode, we recommend installing them in DDR1 and DDR2 DIMM sockets.

CAUTION: All of the memory configurations below will cause system unable to boot. (DS: Double Side, SS: Single Side)

	DDR1	DDR2	DDR3	DDR4
1 memory module	X	DS/SS	X	X
	X	X	X	DS/SS
2 memory modules	X	DS/SS	DS/SS	X
	DS/SS	X	X	DS/SS
	X	DS/SS	X	DS/SS
3 memory modules	DS/SS	DS/SS	DS/SS	X
	X	DS/SS	DS/SS	DS/SS
	DS/SS	X	DS/SS	DS/SS
	DS/SS	DS/SS	X	DS/SS

Figure 4-27 The motherboard book shows how much RAM that Athlon 64 can handle.

Mix and Match at Your Peril

All motherboards can handle different capacities of RAM. If you have three slots, you may put a 512-MB stick in one and a 1-GB stick in the other with a high chance of success. To ensure maximum stability in a system, however, shoot for as close as you can get to uniformity of RAM. Choose RAM sticks that match in technology, capacity, and speed. Even on motherboards that offer slots for radically different RAM types, I recommend uniformity.

Mixing Speeds

With so many different DRAM speeds available, you may often find yourself tempted to mix speeds of DRAM in the same system. Although in many situations you can get away with mixing speeds on a system, the safest, easiest rule to follow is to use the speed of

DRAM specified in the motherboard book, and make sure that every piece of DRAM runs at that speed. In a worst-case scenario, mixing DRAM speeds can cause the system to lock up every few seconds or every few minutes. You might also get some data corruption. Mixing speeds sometimes works fine, but don't do your income tax on a machine with mixed DRAM speeds until the system has proven to be stable for a few days. The important thing to note here is that you won't break anything, other than possibly data, by experimenting.

Okay, I have mentioned enough disclaimers. Modern motherboards provide some flexibility regarding RAM speeds and mixing. First, you can use RAM that is faster than what the motherboard specifies. For example, if the system needs PC3200 DDR2 SDRAM, you may put in PC4200 DDR2 SDRAM and it should work fine. Faster DRAM is not going to make the system run any faster, however, so don't look for any system improvement.

Second, you can sometimes get away with putting one speed of DRAM in one bank and another speed in another bank, as long as all the speeds are as fast or faster than the speed specified by the motherboard. Don't bother trying to put different-speed DRAMs in the same bank with a motherboard that uses dual-channel DDR. Yes, it works once in a while, but it's too chancy. I avoid it.

Installing DIMMs and RIMMs

Installing DRAM is so easy that it's one of the very few jobs I recommend to non-techie folks. First, attach an anti-static wrist strap or touch some bare metal on the power supply to ground yourself and avoid ESD. Then swing the side tabs on the RAM slots down from the upright position. Pick up a stick of RAM—don't touch those contacts! A good hard push down is usually all you need to ensure a solid connection. Make sure that the DIMM snaps into position to show it is completely seated. You will also notice that the two side tabs will move in to reflect a tight connection (Figure 4-28).

Figure 4-28   Inserting a DIMM

SPD

Your motherboard should detect and automatically set up any DIMM or RIMM you install, assuming you have the right RAM for the system. RAM makers add a handy chip to modern sticks called the *serial presence detect (SPD)* chip (Figure 4-29). The SPD stores all the information about your DRAM, including size, speed, ECC or non-ECC, registered or unregistered, and a number of other more technical bits of information.

When a PC boots, it queries the SPD so that the MCC knows how much RAM is on the stick, how fast it runs, and other information. Any program can query the SPD. Take a look at Figure 4-30 with the results of the popular CPU-Z program showing RAM information from the SPD.

Figure 4-29
SPD chip on stick

Figure 4-30
CPU-Z showing
RAM information

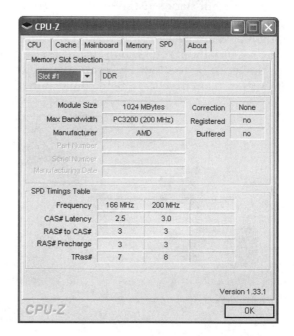

All new systems count on the SPD to set the RAM timings properly for your system when it boots. If you add a RAM stick with a bad SPD, you'll get a POST error message and the system will not boot. You can't fix a broken SPD; you just buy a new stick of RAM.

The RAM Count

After installing the new RAM, turn on the PC and watch the boot process closely. If you installed the RAM correctly, the RAM count on the PC will reflect the new value. If the RAM value stays the same, you probably have installed the RAM in a slot the motherboard doesn't want you to use (for example, if you need to use a particular slot first) or the RAM is not properly installed. If the computer does not boot and you've got a blank screen, you probably have not installed all the RAM sticks correctly. Usually, a good second look is all you need to determine the problem (Figures 4-31 and 4-32). Reseat or reinstall the RAM stick and try again.

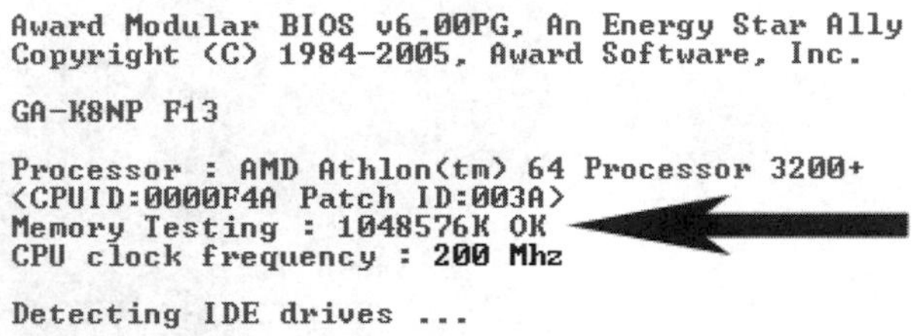

Figure 4-31
Hey, where's the rest of my RAM?!

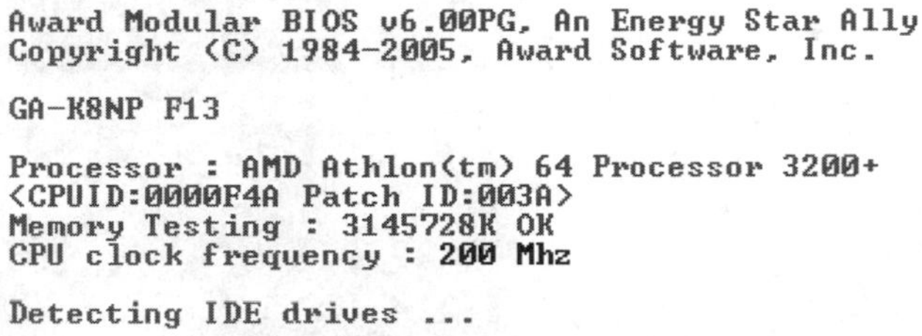

```
Award Modular BIOS v6.00PG, An Energy Star Ally
Copyright (C) 1984-2005, Award Software, Inc.

GA-K8NP F13

Processor : AMD Athlon(tm) 64 Processor 3200+
<CPUID:0000F4A Patch ID:003A>
Memory Testing : 1048576K OK  ◄─────────
CPU clock frequency : 200 Mhz

Detecting IDE drives ...
```

Figure 4-32
RAM count after proper insertion of DIMMs

```
Award Modular BIOS v6.00PG, An Energy Star Ally
Copyright (C) 1984-2005, Award Software, Inc.

GA-K8NP F13

Processor : AMD Athlon(tm) 64 Processor 3200+
<CPUID:0000F4A Patch ID:003A>
Memory Testing : 3145728K OK
CPU clock frequency : 200 Mhz

Detecting IDE drives ...
```

RAM counts are confusing because RAM uses megabytes and gigabytes as opposed to millions and billions. Here are some examples of how different systems would show 256 MB of RAM:

268435456 (exactly 256 x 1 MB)

256M (some PCs try to make it easy for you)

262,144 (number of KB)

You should know how much RAM you're trying to install and use some common sense. If you've got 512 MB and you add another 512-MB stick, you need a number that looks like one gigabyte. If after you add the second stick, you see a RAM count of 524582912—that sure looks like 512 MB, not the one gigabyte!

Installing SO-DIMMs in Laptops

It wasn't that long ago that adding RAM to a laptop was either impossible or required you to send the system back to the manufacturer. For years, every laptop maker had custom-made, proprietary RAM packages that were difficult to handle and staggeringly expensive. The wide acceptance of SO-DIMMs over the last few years has virtually erased these problems. All laptops now provide relatively convenient access to their SO-DIMMs, enabling easy replacement or addition of RAM.

Access to RAM usually requires removing a panel or lifting up the keyboard—the procedure varies among laptop manufacturers. Figure 4-33 shows a typical laptop RAM access panel. You can slide the panel off to reveal the SO-DIMMs. SO-DIMMs usually insert exactly like the old SIMMs—slide the pins into position and snap the SO-DIMM down into the retaining clips (Figure 4-34).

Figure 4-33
A RAM access panel on a laptop

Figure 4-34
Snapping in an SO-DIMM

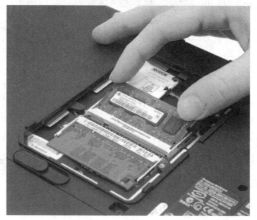

Before doing any work on a laptop, turn the system off, disconnect it from the AC wall socket, and remove all batteries. Use an anti-static wrist strap because laptops are far more susceptible to ESD than desktop PCs.

IT Technician

Troubleshooting RAM

"Memory" errors show up in a variety of ways on modern systems, including parity errors, ECC error messages, system lockups, page faults, and other error screens in Windows. These errors can indicate bad RAM, but often point to something completely unrelated to RAM.

This is especially true with intermittent problems. The challenge for techs is to recognize these errors and then determine which part of the system caused the memory error.

You can get two radically different types of parity errors: real and phantom. Real parity errors are simply errors that the MCC detects from the parity or ECC chips (if you have them). The operating system then reports the problem in an error message, such as "Parity error at *xxxx:xxxxxxxx*," where *xxxx:xxxxxxxx* is a hexadecimal value (a string of numbers and letters, like A5F2:004EEAB9). If you get an error like this, write down the value. A real parity/ECC error will show up at the same place in memory each time, and almost always indicates that you have a bad RAM stick.

Phantom parity errors show up on systems that don't have parity or ECC memory. If Windows generates parity errors with different addresses, you most likely do *not* have a problem with RAM. These phantom errors can occur for a variety of reasons, including software problems, heat or dust, solar flares, fluctuations in the Force … you get the idea.

System lockups and page faults (they often go hand in hand) in Windows can indicate a problem with RAM. A system lockup is when the computer stops functioning. A *page fault* is a milder error that can be caused by memory issues, but not necessarily system RAM problems. Certainly page faults *look* like RAM issues because Windows generates frightening error messages filled with long strings of hexadecimal digits, such as "KRNL386 caused a page fault at 03F2:25A003BC." (See Figure 4-35.) Just because the error message contains a memory address, however, does not mean that you have a problem with your RAM. Write down the address. If it repeats in later error messages, you probably have a bad RAM stick. If Windows displays different memory locations, you need to look elsewhere for the culprit.

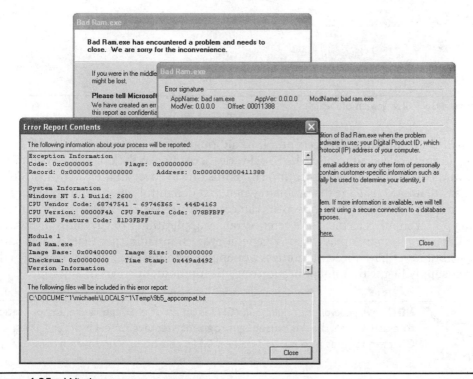

Figure 4-35   Windows error message

Every once in a while, something potentially catastrophic happens within the PC, some little electron hits the big red panic button, and the operating system has to shut down certain functions running in order to save data. This panic button inside the PC is called a *non-maskable interrupt (NMI)*, more simply defined as an interruption the CPU cannot ignore. An NMI manifests to the user as what techs lovingly call the *Blue Screen of Death (BSoD)*—a bright blue screen with a scary-sounding error message on it (Figure 4-36).

```
A problem has been detected and windows has been shut down to prevent damage
to your computer.

The problem seems to be caused by the following file: SPCMDCON.SYS

PAGE_FAULT_IN_NONPAGED_AREA

If this is the first time you've seen this stop error screen,
restart your computer. If this screen appears again, follow
these steps:

Check to make sure any new hardware or software is properly installed.
If this is a new installation, ask your hardware or software manufacturer
for any windows updates you might need.

If problems continue, disable or remove any newly installed hardware
or software. Disable BIOS memory options such as caching or shadowing.
If you need to use Safe Mode to remove or disable components, restart
your computer, press F8 to select Advanced Startup Options, and then
select Safe Mode.

Technical information:

*** STOP: 0x00000050 (0xFD3094C2,0x00000001,0xFBFE7617,0x00000000)


*** SPCMDCON.SYS - Address FBFE7617 base at FBFE5000, DateStamp 3d6dd67c
```

Figure 4-36   Blue Screen of Death

Bad RAM sometimes triggers an NMI, although often the culprit lies with buggy programming or clashing code. The BSoD varies according to the operating system, and it would require a much lengthier tome than this one to cover all the variations. Suffice it to say that RAM *could* be the problem when that delightful blue screen appears.

Finally, intermittent memory errors can come from a variety of sources, including a dying power supply, electrical interference, buggy applications, buggy hardware, and so on. These errors show up as lockups, general protection faults, page faults, and parity errors, but never have the same address or happen with the same applications. Try the power supply first with non-application-specific intermittent errors of any sort.

 NOTE   A *general protection fault (GPF)* is an error that can cause an application to crash. Often, they're caused by programs stepping on each others' toes. Chapter 15 goes into more detail on GPFs and other Windows errors.

Testing RAM

Once you discover that you may have a RAM problem, you have a couple of options. First, several companies manufacture hardware RAM testing devices, but unless you have a lot of disposable income, they're probably priced way too high for the average tech (US$1,500 and higher). Second, you can use the method I use—*replace and pray.* Open the system case and replace each stick, one at a time, with a known good replacement stick. (You have one of those lying around, don't you?) This method, although potentially time-consuming, certainly works. With PC prices as low as they are now, you could simply replace the whole system for less than the price of a dedicated RAM tester.

Third, you could run a software-based tester on the RAM. Because you have to load a software tester into the memory it's about to scan, there's always a small chance that simply starting the software RAM tester might cause an error. Still, you can find some pretty good free ones out there. My favorite is the venerable Memtest86 written by Mr. Chris Brady (www.memtest86.com). Memtest86 will exhaustively check your RAM and report bad RAM when it finds it (Figure 4-37).

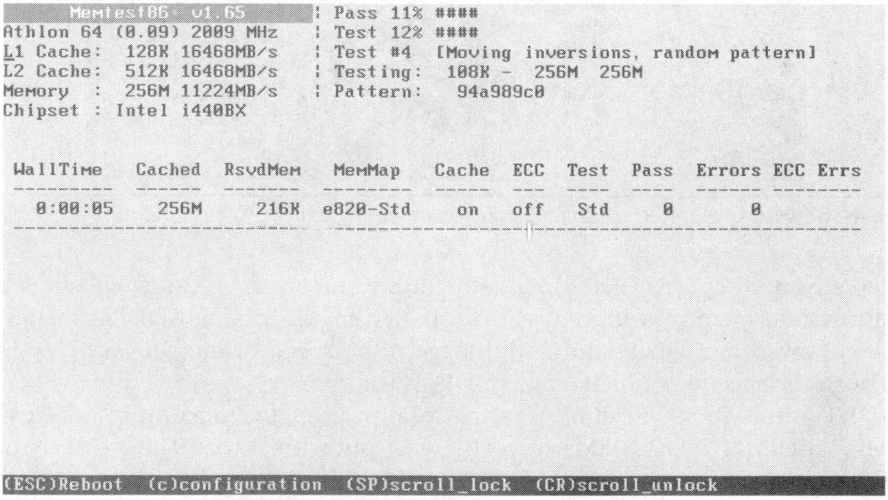

```
   Memtest86  v1.65        | Pass  11% ####
Athlon 64 (0.09) 2009 MHz  | Test  12% ####
L1 Cache:  128K 16468MB/s  | Test #4  [Moving inversions, random pattern]
L2 Cache:  512K 16468MB/s  | Testing:  108K -  256M 256M
Memory  :  256M 11224MB/s  | Pattern:   94a989c0
Chipset : Intel i440BX


  WallTime   Cached  RsvdMem   MemMap   Cache  ECC  Test  Pass  Errors ECC Errs
  --------   ------  -------   ------   -----  ---  ----  ----  ------ --------
   0:00:05    256M    216K   e820-Std   on   off   Std    0      0
  -----------------------------------------------------------------------------




(ESC)Reboot   (c)configuration   (SP)scroll_lock   (CR)scroll_unlock
```

Figure 4-37   Memtest86 in action

Beyond A+

The Next Generations

Computer games have done more for advances in PC hardware than anything else. Have you ever seen a late-generation game such as Half-Life 2 or Far Cry? These games require powerful video cards, and every video card comes with DRAM. To make these beautiful games, the video card's DRAM needs to be incredibly fast. Video card makers adopted many DRAM technologies such as DDR even before they were popular as system RAM on PCs. If you want to see where DRAM is going, check out video cards (Figure 4-38).

NOTE Go to Chapter 17 for a more detailed description of video memory.

Figure 4-38   Half-Life 2—these beautiful graphics are possible (in part) because of fast DRAM.

Two advancements to DDR2 originally found only in video cards will show up as primary system memory within a year of this writing: DDR3 and DDR4. DDR3 uses even less power than DDR2 and doubles again the speed of the DRAM's I/O. DDR4 chips push the speed even higher than DDR3!

DDR3 and DDR4 will almost certainly appear in the upcoming *fully buffered DIMMs (FB-DIMMs)*. FB-DIMMs are registered—but with a twist. They replace the 64-bit-wide DIMM data connection with a staggeringly fast serial connection, expected to reach as much as 4.8 GBps! That should be fast enough to keep our PCs happy for the next few years!

Chapter Review Questions

1. Steve adds a second 512-MB 240-pin DIMM to his PC, which should bring the total RAM in the system up to 1 GB. The PC has a Pentium 4 3.2-GHz processor and three 240-pin DIMM slots on the motherboard. When he turns on the PC, however, the RAM count only shows 512 MB of RAM. Which of the following is most likely to be the problem?

   A. Steve failed to seat the RAM properly.

   B. Steve put DDR SDRAM in a DDR 2 slot.

    C. The CPU cannot handle 1 GB of RAM.

    D. The motherboard can use only one RAM slot at a time.

2. Scott wants to add 512 MB of PC100 SDRAM to an aging but still useful desktop system. The system has a 100-MHz motherboard and currently has 256 MB of non-ECC SDRAM in the system. What else does he need to know before installing?

    A. What speed of RAM does he need?

    B. What type of RAM does he need?

    C. How many pins does the RAM have?

    D. Can the system handle that much RAM?

3. What is the primary reason that DDR2 RAM is potentially faster than DDR RAM?

    A. The core speed of the RAM chips is faster.

    B. The input/output speed of the RAM is faster.

    C. DDR RAM is single-channel and DDR2 RAM is dual-channel.

    D. DDR RAM uses 184-pin DIMMs and DDR2 uses 240-pin DIMMs.

4. What is the term for the delay in the RAM's response to a request from the MCC?

    A. Variance

    B. MCC gap

    C. Latency

    D. Fetch interval

5. Rico has a motherboard with four RAM slots that doesn't seem to work. He has two RDRAM RIMMs installed, for a total of 1 GB of memory, but the system won't boot. What is likely to be the problem?

    A. The motherboard requires SDRAM, not RDRAM.

    B. The motherboard requires DDR SDRAM, not RDRAM.

    C. The motherboard requires all four slots filled with RDRAM.

    D. The motherboard requires that the two empty slots be filled with CRIMMs for termination.

6. Silas has a new Athlon 64 motherboard with two sticks of DDR2 RAM installed in two of the three RAM slots, for a total of 2 GB of system memory. When he runs CPU-Z to test the system, he notices that the software claims he's running single-channel memory. What could be the problem? (Select the best answer.)

    A. His motherboard only supports single-channel memory.

    B. His motherboard only supports dual-channel memory with DDR RAM, not DDR2.

C. He needs to install a third RAM stick to enable dual-channel memory.

D. He needs to move one of the installed sticks to a different slot to activate dual-channel memory.

7. Motherboards that support more than four sticks of RAM may require what to function properly?

A. Buffered RAM

B. ECC RAM

C. Dual-channel RAM

D. DDR2 RAM

8. What is the best way to determine the total capacity and specific type of RAM your system can handle?

A. Check the motherboard book.

B. Open the case and inspect the RAM.

C. Check the Device Manager.

D. Check the System utility in the Control Panel.

9. Gregor installed a third stick of known-good RAM into his Athlon 64 system, bringing the total amount of RAM up to 768 MB. Within a few days, though, he started having random lockups and reboots, especially when doing memory intensive tasks like gaming. What is most likely the problem?

A. Gregor installed DDR RAM into a DDR2 system.

B. Gregor installed DDR2 RAM into a DDR system.

C. Gregor installed RAM that didn't match the speed or quality of the RAM in the system.

D. Gregor installed RAM that exceeded the speed of the RAM in the system.

10. Cindy installs a second stick of DDR2 RAM into her Core 2 Duo system, bringing the total system memory up to 2 GB. Within a short period of time, though, she begins experiencing Blue Screens of Death. What could the problem be?

A. She installed faulty RAM.

B. The motherboard could only handle 1 GB of RAM.

C. The motherboard needed dual-channel RAM.

D. There is no problem. Windows always does this initially, but gets better after crashing a few times.

Answers

1. **A.** Steve failed to seat the RAM properly.

2. **D.** Scott needs to know if the system can handle that much RAM.

3. **B.** The input/output speed of DDR2 RAM is faster than DDR RAM (although the latency is higher).

4. **C.** Latency is the term for the delay in the RAM's response to a request from the MCC.

5. **D.** RDRAM-based motherboards require empty slots to be filled with CRIMMs for termination.

6. **D.** Motherboards can be tricky and require you to install RAM in the proper slots to enable dual-channel memory access. In this case, Silas should move one of the installed sticks to a different slot to activate dual-channel memory. (And he should check the motherboard manual for the proper slots.)

7. **A.** Motherboards that support more than four sticks of RAM may require buffered RAM to function properly.

8. **A.** The best way to determine the total capacity and specific type of RAM your system can handle is to check the motherboard book.

9. **C.** Most likely, Gregor installed RAM that didn't match the speed or quality of the RAM in the system.

10. **A.** If you have no problems with a system and then experience problems after installing something new, then chances are the something new is at fault!

BIOS and CMOS

5

In this chapter, you will learn how to
- Explain the function of BIOS
- Distinguish among various CMOS setup utility options
- Describe BIOS and device drivers
- Troubleshoot the power-on self test (POST)

In Chapter 3, you saw how the address bus and external data bus connect RAM to the CPU via the memory controller chip (MCC) in order to run programs and transfer data. Assuming you apply power in the right places, you don't need anything else to make a simple computer. The only problem with such a simple computer is that it would bore you to death—there's no way to do anything with it! A PC needs devices such as keyboards and mice to provide input, and output devices such as monitors and sound cards to communicate the current state of the running programs to you. A computer also needs permanent storage devices, such as hard drives and optical drives, to store programs and data when you turn off the computer.

Historical/Conceptual

We Need to Talk

Simply placing a number of components into a computer is useless if the CPU can't communicate with them. Getting the CPU to communicate with a device starts with some kind of interconnection—a communication bus that enables the CPU to send commands to and from devices. To make this connection, let's promote the MCC, giving it extra firepower to act as not only the interconnection between the CPU and RAM, but also the interconnection between the CPU and the other devices on the PC. The MCC isn't just the memory controller anymore, so let's now call it the *Northbridge* because it acts as the primary bridge between the CPU and the rest of the computer (Figure 5-1).

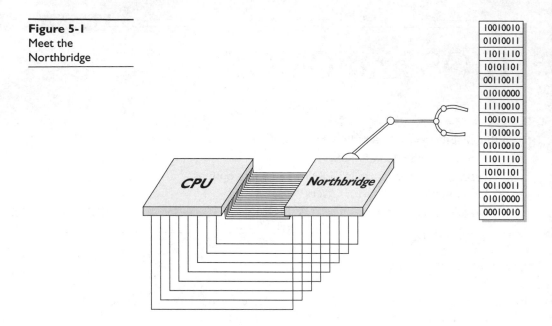

Figure 5-1
Meet the
Northbridge

Your PC is full of devices, so the PC industry decided to delegate some of the inter-connectivity work to a second chip called the *Southbridge.* The Northbridge only deals with high-speed interfaces such as the connection to your video card and RAM. The Southbridge works mainly with lower-speed devices such as the USB controller and hard drive controllers. Chip makers design matched sets of particular models of North-bridge and Southbridge to work together. You don't buy a Northbridge from one com-pany and a Southbridge from another—they're sold as a set. We call this set of Northbridge and Southbridge the *chipset.*

NOTE Chipset makers rarely use the terms "Northbridge" and "Southbridge" anymore, but because most modern chipsets consist of only two or three chips with basically the same functions, techs continue to use the terms.

The chipset extends the data bus to every device on the PC. The CPU uses the data bus to move data to and from all the devices of the PC. Data constantly flows on the external data bus among the CPU, chipset, RAM, and other devices on the PC (Figure 5-2).

The first use for the address bus, as you know, is for the CPU to tell the chipset to send or store data in memory and to tell the chipset which section of memory to access

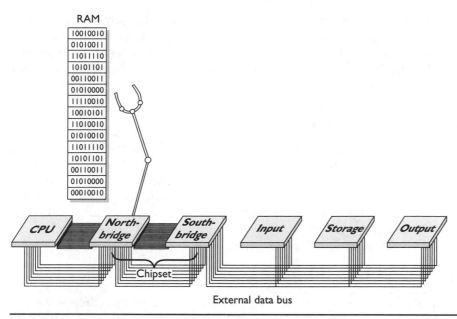

Figure 5-2 The chipset extending the data bus

or use. Just like with the external data bus, the chipset extends the address bus to all the devices, too (Figure 5-3). That way, the CPU can use the address bus to send commands to devices, just like it sends commands to the chipset. You'll see this in action a lot more in Chapter 6, "Expansion Bus," but for now just go with the concept.

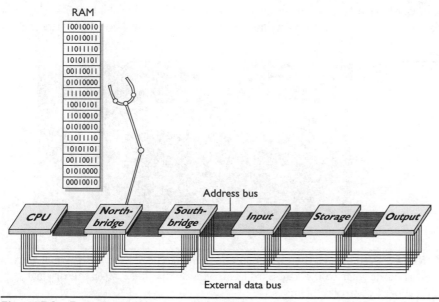

Figure 5-3 Every device in your computer connects to the address bus.

It's not too hard to swallow the concept that the CPU uses the address bus to talk to the devices, but how does it know what to *say* to them? How does it know all of the different patterns of ones and zeros to place on the address bus to tell the hard drive it needs to send a file? Let's look at the interaction between the keyboard and CPU for insight into this process.

Talking to the Keyboard

The keyboard provides a great example of how the buses and support programming help the CPU get the job done. In early computers, the keyboard connected to the external data bus via a special chip known as the *keyboard controller.* Don't bother looking for this chip on your motherboard—the keyboard controller functions are now handled by the Southbridge. The way the keyboard controller—or technically, the keyboard controller *circuitry*—works with the CPU, however, has changed only a small amount in the last 20 years, making it a perfect tool to see how the CPU talks to a device.

 NOTE It is very common for techs to talk about various functions of the chipset as if those functions were still handled by discrete chips. So you'll hear about memory controllers, keyboard controllers, mouse controllers, USB controllers, and so on, even though they're all just circuits on the Northbridge or Southbridge chips.

The keyboard controller was one of the last single-function chips to be absorbed into the chipset. For many years—in fact, well into the Pentium III/Early Athlon era—most motherboards still had separate keyboard controller chips. Figure 5-4 shows a typical keyboard controller from those days. Electronically, it looked like Figure 5-5.

Figure 5-4
A keyboard chip
on a Pentium
motherboard

 NOTE Even though the model numbers changed over the years, you'll still hear techs refer to the keyboard controller as the *8042,* after the original keyboard controller chip.

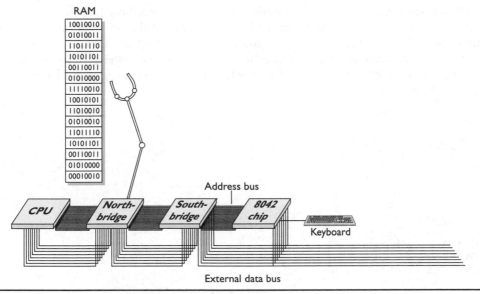

Figure 5-5   Electronic view of the keyboard controller

Every time you press a key on your keyboard, a scanning chip in the keyboard notices which key has been pressed. Then the scanner sends a coded pattern of ones and zeros—called the *scan code*—to the keyboard controller. Every key on your keyboard has a unique scan code. The keyboard controller stores the scan code in its own register. Does it surprise you that the lowly keyboard controller has a register similar to a CPU? Lots of chips have registers—not just CPUs! (See Figure 5-6.)

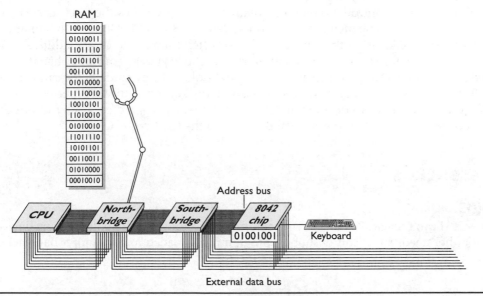

Figure 5-6   Scan code stored in keyboard controller's register

How does the CPU get the scan code out of the keyboard controller? (See Figure 5-7.) While we're at it, how does the CPU tell the keyboard to change the typematic buffer rate (when you hold down a key and the letter repeats) or turn the number lock LED on and off, to mention just a few other jobs the keyboard needs to do for the system? The point is that the keyboard controller must be able to respond to multiple commands, not just one.

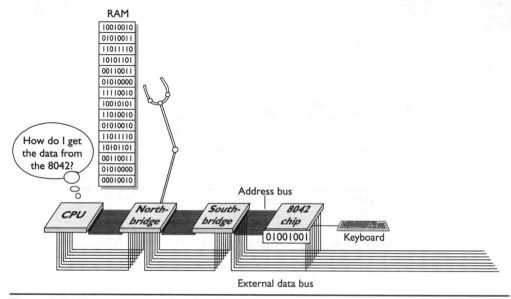

Figure 5-7 The CPU ponders its dilemma....

The keyboard controller accepts commands exactly as you saw the CPU accept commands in Chapter 3. Remember when you added 2 to 3 with the 8088? You had to use specific commands from the 8088's codebook to tell the CPU to do the addition and then place the answer on the external data bus. The keyboard controller has its own codebook—much simpler than any CPU's codebook, but conceptually the same. If the CPU wants to know what key was last pressed on the keyboard, the CPU needs to know the command (or series of commands) that orders the keyboard controller to put the scan code of the letter on the external data bus so the CPU can read it.

Essentials

BIOS

The CPU can't magically or otherwise automatically know how to talk with any device, but rather needs some sort of support programming loaded into memory that teaches it about a particular device. This programming is called *basic input/output services (BIOS)*. The programs dedicated to enabling the CPU to communicate with devices are called *services* (or *device drivers,* as you'll see later in the chapter). This goes well beyond the keyboard, by the way. In fact, *every* device on the computer needs BIOS! But let's continue with the keyboard for now.

Bringing BIOS to the PC   A talented programmer could write BIOS for a keyboard if he or she knew the keyboard's code book—keyboards are pretty simple devices. This begs the question: where would this support programming be stored? Well, programming could be incorporated into the operating system. Storing programming to talk to the hardware of your PC in the operating system is great—all operating systems have built-in code that knows how to talk to your keyboard, your mouse, and just about every piece of hardware you may put into your PC.

That's fine once the operating system's up and running, but what about a brand-new stack of parts you're about to assemble into a new PC? When a new system's being built, there is no operating system! The CPU must have access to BIOS for the most important hardware on your PC: not only the keyboard, but also the monitor, the hard drives, optical drives, USB ports, and RAM. So this code can't be stored on a hard drive or CD-ROM disc—these important devices need to be ready at any time the CPU calls them, even before installing a mass storage device or an operating system.

The perfect place to store the support programming is on the motherboard. That settles one issue, but another looms: What storage medium should the motherboard use? DRAM won't work because all the data would be erased every time the computer was turned off. You need some type of permanent program storage device that does not depend on other peripherals in order to work. And you need that storage device to sit on the motherboard.

ROM   Motherboards store the keyboard controller support programming, among other programs, on a special type of device called a *read-only memory (ROM)* chip. A ROM chip stores programs exactly like RAM: that is, like an 8-bit-wide spreadsheet. But ROM differs from RAM in two important ways. First, ROM chips are non-volatile, meaning that the information stored on ROM isn't erased when the computer is turned off. Second, traditional ROM chips are read-only, meaning that once a program is stored on one, it can't be changed. Modern motherboards use a type of ROM called *Flash ROM* that differs from traditional ROM in that you can update and change the contents through a very specific process called "flashing the ROM," covered later in this chapter. Figure 5-8 shows a typical Flash ROM chip on a motherboard. When the CPU wants to talk to the keyboard controller, it goes to the Flash ROM chip to access the proper programming (Figure 5-9).

Figure 5-8
Typical Flash ROM

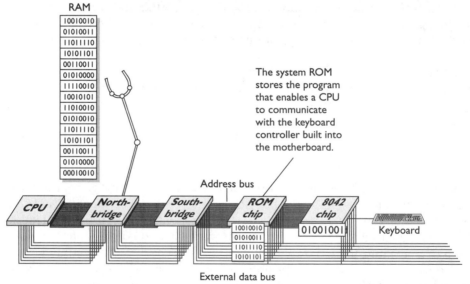

Figure 5-9   Function of the Flash ROM chip

Every motherboard has a Flash ROM, called the *system ROM* chip because it contains code that enables your CPU to talk to the basic hardware of your PC. As alluded to earlier, the system ROM holds BIOS for more than just the keyboard controller. It also stores programs for communicating with the floppy drives, hard drives, optical drives, video, USB ports, and other basic devices on your motherboard.

To talk to all of that hardware requires hundreds of little services (2 to 30 lines of code each). These hundreds of little programs stored on the system ROM chip on the motherboard are called, collectively, the *system BIOS*. (See Figure 5-10.)

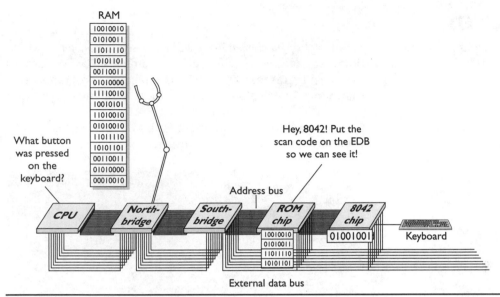

Figure 5-10   CPU running BIOS service

 EXAM TIP   Programs stored on ROM chips—Flash or any other kind of
ROM chip—are known collectively as *firmware*, as opposed to programs
stored on erasable media that are collectively called *software*.

The system ROM chips used on modern PCs store as much as 2 MB of programs,
although only 65,536 bytes are used to store the system BIOS. This allows for backward
compatibility with earlier systems. The rest of the ROM space is put to good use doing
other jobs.

System BIOS Support

Every system BIOS has two types of hardware to support. First, the system BIOS supports all the hardware that never changes, such as the keyboard. (You can change your
keyboard, but you can't change the keyboard controller built into the Southbridge.)
Another example of hardware that never changes is the PC speaker (the tiny one that
beeps at you, not the ones that play music). The system ROM chip stores the BIOS for
these and other devices that never change.

Second, the system BIOS supports all the hardware that might change from time to
time. This includes RAM (you can add RAM), hard drives (you can replace your hard
drive with a larger drive or add a second hard drive), and floppy drives (you can add
another floppy drive). The system ROM chip stores the *BIOS* for these devices, but the
system needs another place to store information about the specific *details* of a piece of
hardware. This enables the system to differentiate between a Western Digital Caviar
500-GB hard drive and a Seagate Barracuda 60-GB drive, and yet still support both
drives right out of the box.

CMOS

A separate memory chip, called the *complementary metal-oxide semiconductor (CMOS)* chip, stores the information that describes specific device parameters. CMOS does *not* store programs; it only stores data that is read by BIOS to complete the programs needed to talk to changeable hardware. CMOS also acts as a clock to keep the current date and time.

Years ago, CMOS was a separate chip on the motherboard, as shown in Figure 5-11. Today, the CMOS is almost always built into the Southbridge.

Figure 5-11
Old-style CMOS

Most CMOS chips store around 64 KB of data, but the PC usually needs only a very small amount—about 128 bytes—to store all the necessary information on the changeable hardware. Don't let the tiny size fool you. The information stored in CMOS is absolutely necessary for the PC to function!

If the data stored on CMOS about a particular piece of hardware (or about its fancier features) is different from the specs of the actual hardware, the computer will not be able to access that piece of hardware (or use its fancier features). It is crucial that this information be correct. If you change any of the previously mentioned hardware, you must update CMOS to reflect those changes. You need to know, therefore, how to change the data on CMOS.

Updating CMOS: The Setup Program

Every PC ships with a program built into the system ROM, called the *CMOS setup program* or the *system setup utility*, which enables you to access and update CMOS data. When you fire up your computer in the morning, the first thing you will likely see is the BIOS information. It might look like the example in Figure 5-12 or perhaps something like Figure 5-13.

NOTE The terms *CMOS setup program*, CMOS, and *system setup utility* are functionally interchangeable today. You'll even hear the program referred to as the *BIOS setup utility*. Most techs just call it the CMOS.

Figure 5-12
AMIBIOS
information

```
        American      Released: 07/12/2000
        Megatrends    AMIBIOS (C)1999 American Megatrends Inc.,
6VX7-4X F15

Check System Health OK.
CPU ID:0683 Patch ID:0010
Pentium III - 667 MHz
Checking NVRAM..
393216KB OK

WAIT...
Auto-Detecting Pri Master..IDE Hard Disk
Auto-Detecting Pri Slave...IDE Hard Disk
Auto-Detecting Sec Master..ATAPI CDROM
Auto-Detecting Sec Slave...Not Detected
Pri Master: 3.02     ST310212A
                     Ultra DMA Mode-4, S.M.A.R.T. Capable and Status OK
Pri Slave : 3.39     ST310211A
                     Ultra DMA Mode-4, S.M.A.R.T. Capable and Status OK
Sec Master: YYS7     CDU5211
```

Figure 5-13
Award/Phoenix BIOS
information

```
  Award Modular BIOS v6.00PG, An Energy Star Ally
  Copyright (C) 1984-2003 Phoenix Technologies, LTD

Main Processor : AMD Athlon(tm) 64 Processor 3200+
Memory Testing : 1048576K OK
CPU0 Memory Information: DDR 400 CL:3 ,1T Dual Channel, 128-bit

IDE Channel 1 Master : WDC WD1200JB-75CRA0 16.06V16
IDE Channel 1 Slave  : None
IDE Channel 2 Master : SONY     CD-RW  CRX175E2 S002
IDE Channel 2 Slave  : TOSHIBA CD=DVDW SDR5372V TV11

IDE Channel 3 Master : None
IDE Channel 4 Master : None

Detecting IDE drives ...




Press DEL to enter SETUP, ESC to Enter Boot Menu
07/01/2005-MF-CK804-6A61FA1DC-10
```

Who or what is AMIBIOS, and who or what is Phoenix Technologies? These are brand names of BIOS companies. They write BIOS programs and sell them to computer manufacturers. In today's world, motherboard makers rarely write their own BIOS. Instead, they buy their BIOS from specialized third-party BIOS makers like Award Software and Phoenix Technologies. Although several companies write BIOS, two big companies control 99 percent of the BIOS business: American Megatrends (AMI) and Phoenix Technologies. Phoenix bought Award Software a few years ago and still sells the Award brand name as a separate product line. These are the most common brand names in the field.

You always access a system's CMOS setup program at boot. The real question is, how do you access the CMOS setup at boot for your particular PC? AMI, Award, and Phoenix use different keys to access the CMOS setup program. Usually, BIOS manufacturers will tell you how to access the CMOS setup right on the screen as your computer boots up. For example, at the bottom of the screen in Figure 5-13, you are instructed to "Press DEL to enter SETUP." Keep in mind that this is only one possible example. Motherboard manufacturers can change the key combinations for entering CMOS setup. You can even set up the computer so the message does not show—a smart idea if you need to keep nosy people out of your CMOS setup! If you don't see an "enter setup" message, wait until the RAM count starts and then try one of the following keys or key combinations: DEL, ESC, F1, F2, CTRL-ALT-ESC, CTRL-ALT-INS, CTRL-ALT-ENTER, or CTRL-S. It may take a few tries, but you will eventually find the right key or key combination! If not, check the motherboard book or the manufacturer's Web site for the information.

A Quick Tour Through a Typical CMOS Setup Program

Every BIOS maker's CMOS setup program looks a little different, but don't let that confuse you. They all contain basically the same settings; you just have to be comfortable poking around. To avoid doing something foolish, *do not save anything* unless you are sure you have it set correctly.

 CAUTION It's perfectly fine to access the CMOS setup utility for a system, but do not make changes unless you fully understand that system!

As an example, let's say your machine has Award BIOS. You boot the system and press DEL to enter CMOS setup. The screen in Figure 5-14 appears. You are now in the Main menu of the Award CMOS setup program. The setup program itself is stored on the ROM chip, but it edits only the data on the CMOS chip.

Figure 5-14
Typical CMOS Main screen by Award

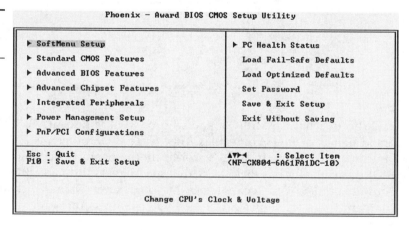

If you select the Standard CMOS Features option, the Standard CMOS Features screen appears (Figure 5-15). On this screen, you can change floppy drive and hard drive settings, as well as the system's date and time. You will learn how to set up the CMOS for these devices in later chapters. At this point, your only goal is to understand CMOS and know how to access the CMOS setup on your PC, so don't try to change anything yet. If you have a system that you are allowed to reboot, try accessing the CMOS setup now. Does it look anything like these examples? If not, can you find the screen that enables you to change the floppy and hard drives? Trust me, every CMOS setup has that screen somewhere! Figure 5-16 shows the same standard CMOS setup screen on a system with Phoenix BIOS. Note that this CMOS setup utility calls this screen "Main."

Figure 5-15
Standard CMOS
Features screen

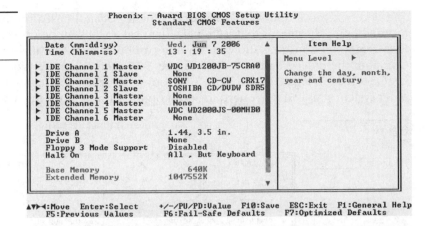

Figure 5-16
Phoenix BIOS
CMOS setup
utility Main screen

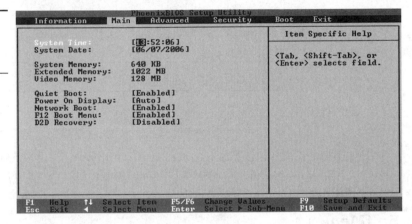

The first BIOS was nothing more than this standard CMOS setup. Today, all computers have many extra CMOS settings. They control items such as memory management, password and booting options, diagnostic and error handling, and power management. The following section takes a quick tour of an Award CMOS setup program. Remember that your CMOS setup will almost certainly look at least a little different from mine, unless you happen to have the *same* BIOS. The chances of that happening are quite slim!

NOTE All these screens tend to overwhelm new techs. When they first encounter the many options, some techs feel they need to understand every option on every screen in order to configure CMOS properly. Relax—every new motherboard comes with settings that befuddle even the most experienced techs! If I don't talk about a particular CMOS setting somewhere in this book, it's probably not important, either to the CompTIA A+ certification exams or to a real tech.

Phoenix has virtually cornered the desktop PC BIOS market with its Award Modular BIOS. Motherboard makers buy a "boilerplate" BIOS, designed for a particular chipset, and add or remove options (Phoenix calls them *modules*) based on the needs of each motherboard. This means that seemingly identical CMOS setup utilities can be extremely different. Options that show up on one computer might be missing from another. Compare the older Award screen in Figure 5-17 with the more modern main Award CMOS screen in Figure 5-14. Figure 5-17 looks different—and it should—as this much older system simply doesn't need the extra options available on the newer system!

Figure 5-17
Older Award
setup screen

```
                    ROM PCI/ISA BIOS (2A69HQ1A)
                         CMOS SETUP UTILITY
                       AWARD SOFTWARE, INC.

  ┌─────────────────────────────┬─────────────────────────────┐
  │ STANDARD CMOS SETUP         │ INTEGRATED PERIPHERALS       │
  │                             │                              │
  │ BIOS FEATURES SETUP         │ SUPERVISOR PASSWORD          │
  │                             │                              │
  │ CHIPSET FEATURES SETUP      │ USER PASSWORD                │
  │                             │                              │
  │ POWER MANAGEMENT SETUP      │ IDE HDD AUTO DETECTION       │
  │                             │                              │
  │ PNP/PCI CONFIGURATION       │ HDD LOW LEVEL FORMAT         │
  │                             │                              │
  │ LOAD BIOS DEFAULTS          │ SAVE & EXIT SETUP            │
  │                             │                              │
  │ LOAD SETUP DEFAULTS         │ EXIT WITHOUT SAVING          │
  ├─────────────────────────────┴─────────────────────────────┤
  │ Esc : Quit                   ↑ ↓ → ←  : Select Item         │
  │ F10 : Save & Exit Setup     (Shift)F2 : Change Color        │
  └────────────────────────────────────────────────────────────┘
```

I'll start the walkthrough of a CMOS setup utility with the SoftMenu, followed by some of the Advanced screens. Then I'll go through other common screens, such as Integrated Peripherals, Power, and more.

SoftMenu

The SoftMenu enables you to change the voltage and multiplier settings on the motherboard for the CPU from the defaults. Motherboards that cater to overclockers tend to have this option. Usually, you just set this to AUTO and stay away from this screen (Figure 5-18).

Figure 5-18
SoftMenu

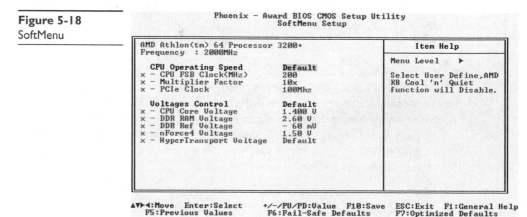

Advanced BIOS Features

Advanced BIOS Features is the dumping ground for all the settings that aren't covered in the Standard menu, but don't fit nicely under any other screen. This screen varies wildly from one system to the next. You most often use this screen to select the boot options (Figure 5-19).

Figure 5-19
Advanced BIOS Features

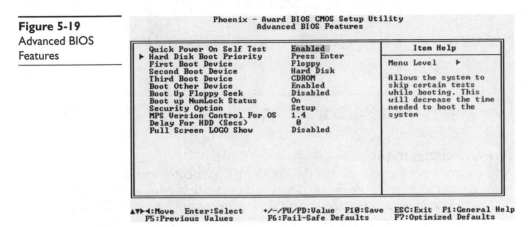

Advanced Chipset Features

The Advanced Chipset Features screen strikes fear into most everyone because it deals with extremely low-level chipset functions. Avoid this screen unless a high-level tech (like a motherboard maker's support tech) explicitly tells you to do something in here (Figure 5-20).

Figure 5-20
Advanced Chipset Features

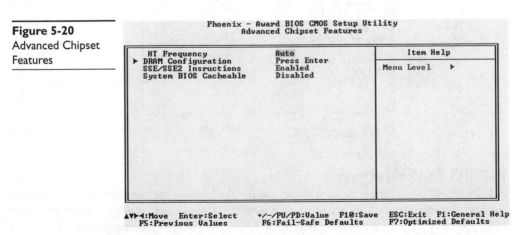

Integrated Peripherals

You will use the Integrated Peripherals screen quite often. It's here where you configure, enable, or disable the onboard ports, such as the serial and parallel ports. As you'll see when I discuss these ports in more detail in later chapters, you can use this screen to get important work done (Figure 5-21).

Figure 5-21
Integrated
Peripherals

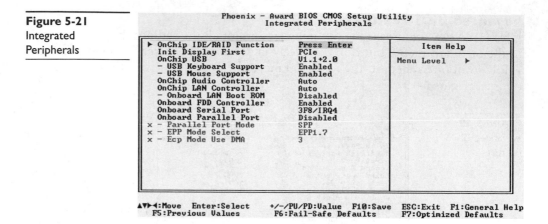

Power Management

As the name implies, you can use the Power Management screen to set up the power management settings for the system. These settings work in concert (sometimes in conflict) with Windows' power management settings to control how and when devices turn off and back on to conserve power (Figure 5-22).

Figure 5-22
Power Management

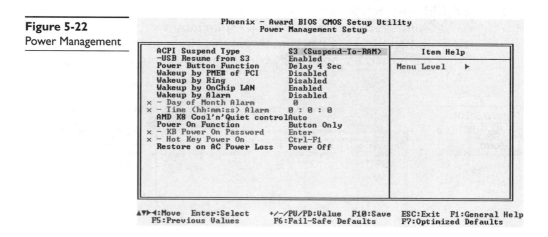

PnP/PCI Configurations

All CMOS setup utilities come with menu items that are for the most part no longer needed, but no one wants to remove. PnP/PCI is a perfect example. Plug and play (PnP) is how devices automatically work when you snap them into your PC. PCI is a type of slot used for cards. Odds are very good you'll never deal with this screen (Figure 5-23).

Figure 5-23
PnP/PCI

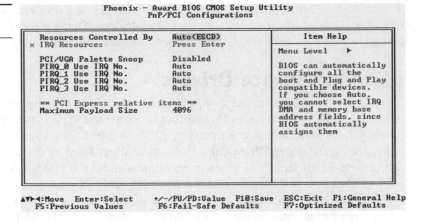

And the Rest of the CMOS Settings...

The other options on the main menu of an Award CMOS do not have their own screens. Rather, these simply have small dialog boxes that pop up, usually with, "Are you sure?" messages. The Load Fail-Safe/Optimized defaults options keep you from having to memorize all of those weird settings you'll never touch. Fail-Safe sets everything to very simple settings—you might occasionally use this setting when very low-level problems like freeze-ups occur, and you've checked more obvious areas first. Optimized sets the CMOS to the best possible speed/stability for the system. You would use this option after tampering with the CMOS too much when you need to put it back like it was!

Many CMOS setup programs enable you to set a password in CMOS to force the user to enter a password every time the system boots. Don't confuse this with the Windows logon password. This CMOS password shows up at boot, long before Windows even starts to load. Figure 5-24 shows a typical CMOS password prompt.

Figure 5-24
CMOS password
prompt

Some CMOS setup utilities enable you to create two passwords: one for boot and another for accessing the CMOS setup program. This extra password just for entering CMOS setup is a godsend for places such as schools where non-techs tend to wreak havoc in areas (like CMOS) that they should not access!

Of course, all CMOS setups provide some method to Save and Exit or to Exit *Without* Saving. Use these as needed for your situation. Exit Without Saving is particularly nice for those folks who want to poke around the CMOS setup utility but don't want to mess anything up. Use it!

The CMOS setup utility would meet all the needs of a modern system for BIOS if manufacturers would just stop creating new devices. That's not going to happen, of course, so let's turn now to devices that need to have BIOS loaded from elsewhere.

BIOS and Device Drivers

Every piece of hardware in your computer needs some kind of programming that tells the CPU how to talk to that device. When IBM invented the PC 25 years ago, they couldn't possibly have included all the necessary BIOS routines for every conceivable piece of hardware on the system ROM chip. How could they? Most of the devices in use today didn't exist on the first PCs! When programmers wrote the first BIOS, for example, network cards, mice, and sound cards did not exist. Early PC designers at IBM understood that they could not anticipate every new type of hardware, so they gave us a few ways to add programming other than on the BIOS. I call this *BYOB*—Bring Your Own BIOS. There are two ways you can BYOB: option ROM and device drivers. Let's look at both.

Option ROM

The first way to BYOB is to put the BIOS on the hardware device itself. Look at the card displayed in Figure 5-25. This is a serial ATA RAID hard drive controller—basically just a card that lets you add more hard drives to a PC. The chip in the center with the wires coming out the sides is a Flash ROM storing BIOS for the card. The system BIOS does not have a clue about how to talk to this card, but that's okay because this card brings its own BIOS on what's called an *option ROM* chip.

  NOTE Not all option ROMs say "flash"!

Figure 5-25
Option ROM on
expansion card

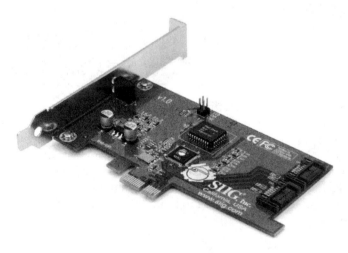

Most BIOS that come on option ROMs tell you that they exist by displaying information when you boot the system. Figure 5-26 shows a typical example of an option ROM advertising itself.

Figure 5-26
Option ROM at boot

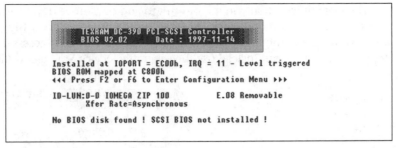

```
      TEXRAM DC-390 PCI-SCSI Controller
      BIOS V2.02       Date : 1997-11-14

Installed at IOPORT = EC00h, IRQ = 11 - Level triggered
BIOS ROM mapped at C800h
◄◄◄ Press F2 or F6 to Enter Configuration Menu ►►►

ID-LUN:0-0 IOMEGA ZIP 100            E.08 Removable
         Xfer Rate=Asynchronous

No BIOS disk found ! SCSI BIOS not installed !
```

In the early days of the PC, you could find all sorts of devices with BIOS on option ROMs. Today, option ROMs have mostly been replaced by more flexible software methods (more on that in the next section), with one major exception: video cards. Every video card made today contains its own BIOS. Option ROMs work well, but are hard to upgrade. For this reason, most hardware in PCs relies on software for BYOB.

Device Drivers

A *device driver* is a file stored on the PC's hard drive that contains all the commands necessary to talk to whatever device it was written to support. All operating systems employ a method of loading these device drivers into RAM every time the system boots. They know which device drivers to install by reading a file (or files) that lists which device drivers the system needs to load at boot time. All operating systems are designed to look at this list early on in the boot process and copy the listed files into RAM, thereby giving the CPU the capability to communicate with the hardware supported by the device drivers.

Device drivers come with the device when you buy it. When you buy a sound card, for example, it comes with a CD-ROM that holds all the necessary device drivers (and usually a bunch of extra goodies). The generic name for this type of CD-ROM is *installation disc*. In most cases, you install a new device, start the computer and wait for Windows to prompt you for the installation disc (Figure 5-27).

Figure 5-27
Windows asking for
the installation disc

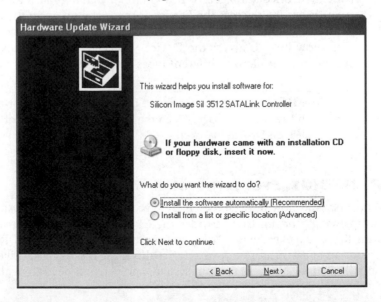

There are times when you might want to add or remove device drivers manually. Windows uses a special database called the *registry* that stores everything you want to know about your system, including the device drivers. You shouldn't access the registry directly to access these drivers, but instead use the venerable Device Manager utility (Figure 5-28).

Figure 5-28
Typical Device
Manager

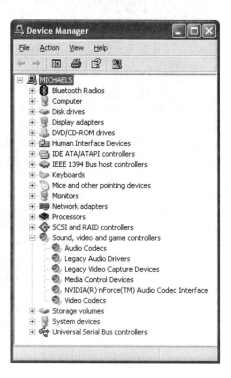

Using the Device Manager, you can manually change or remove the drivers for any particular device. You access the Device Manager by opening the System applet in the Control Panel; then select the Hardware tab and click the Device Manager button. Make sure you know how to access the Device Manager. You'll see lots more of the Device Manager as you learn about different types of devices in the rest of the book.

NOTE You can also access the Device Manager by right-clicking My Computer and selecting Manage. When the Computer Management dialog box comes up, click on Device Manager.

BIOS, BIOS, Everywhere!

As you should now understand, every piece of hardware on a system must have an accompanying program that provides the CPU with the code necessary to communicate with that particular device. This code may reside on the system ROM on the motherboard, on ROM on a card, or in a device driver file on the hard drive loaded into RAM at boot. BIOS is everywhere on your system, and you will need to deal with it occasionally.

IT Technician

Power-On Self Test (POST)

BIOS isn't the only program on your system ROM. When the computer is turned on or reset, it initiates a special program, also stored on the system ROM chip, called the *power-on self test (POST)*. The POST program checks out the system every time the computer boots. To perform this check, the POST sends out a standard command that says to all the devices, "Check yourselves out!" All the standard devices in the computer then run their own internal diagnostic—the POST doesn't specify what they must check. The quality of the diagnostic is up to the people who made that particular device.

Let's consider the POST for a moment. Suppose some device—let's say it's the keyboard controller chip—runs its diagnostic and determines that it is not working properly. What can the POST do about it? Only one thing really: Tell the human in front of the PC! So how does the computer tell the human? PCs convey POST information to you in two ways: beep codes and text messages.

Before and During the Video Test: The Beep Codes

The computer tests the most basic parts of the computer first, up to and including the video card. In early PCs, you'd hear a series of beeps—called *beep codes*—if anything went wrong. By using beep codes before and during the video test, the computer could communicate with you. The meaning of the beep code you'd hear varied among different BIOS manufacturers. You could find the beep codes for a specific motherboard in its motherboard manual.

Most modern PCs have only a single beep code, which is for bad or missing video—one long beep followed by three short beeps. Check the \SHAREWARE\SOUNDS folder on the CD-ROM that accompanies this book for a recording of an Award BIOS reporting a failed video test.

 CAUTION   You'll find lots of online documentation about beep codes, but it's usually badly outdated!

You'll hear three other beep sequences on most PCs (although they're not officially beep codes). At the end of a successful POST, the PC will produce one or two short beeps, simply to inform you that all is well. Most systems make a rather strange noise when the RAM is missing or very seriously damaged. Unlike traditional beep codes, this code repeats until you shut off the system. I've included a recording of one of the more common variations on the CD-ROM in the \SHAREWARE\SOUNDS folder. Finally, your speaker might make beeps for reasons that aren't POST or boot related. One of the more common is a series of short beeps after the system's been running for a while. That's a CPU alarm telling you the CPU is approaching its high heat limit.

 NOTE   Some newer motherboards can also talk to you if there is a problem during POST. To use this feature, all that is normally required is to plug a pair of speakers or headphones into the onboard sound card.

Text Errors

After the video has tested okay, any POST errors will display on the screen as a text error. If you get a text error, the problem is usually, but not always, self-explanatory (Figure 5-29). Text errors are far more useful than beep errors because you can simply read the screen to determine the bad device.

Figure 5-29
Text error messages

```
PhoenixBIOS 4.0 release 6.0
Copyright 1985-2000 Phoenixies Ltd.  ies Ltd.
All Rights Reserved


CPU = Pentium III  500MHz
640K System RAM Passed
47M Extended RAM Passed
USB upper limit segment address:  EEFE
Mouse initialized

HDD Controller Failure
Press <F1> to resume
```

POST Cards

Beep codes, numeric codes, and text error codes, although helpful, can sometimes be misleading. Worse than that, an inoperative device can sometimes disrupt the POST, forcing the machine into an endless loop. This causes the PC to act dead—no beeps and nothing on the screen. In this case, you need a device, called a *POST card*, to monitor the POST and identify which piece of hardware is causing the trouble.

POST cards are simple cards that snap into an expansion slot on your system. A small, two-character light-emitting diode (LED) readout on the card indicates what device the POST is currently testing (Figure 5-30). The documentation that comes with the POST card tells you what the codes mean. BIOS makers also provide this information on their Web sites. Manufacturers make POST cards for all types of desktop PCs. They will work with any BIOS, but you need to know the type of BIOS you have in order to interpret the readout properly.

Figure 5-30
POST card in action

I usually only pull out a POST card when the usual POST errors fail to appear. When a computer provides a beep or text error code that doesn't make sense, or if your machine keeps locking up, some device has stalled the POST. Because the POST card will tell you which device is being tested, the frozen system will stay at that point in the POST, and the error will stay on the POST card's readout.

Many companies sell POST cards today, with prices ranging from the affordable to the outrageous. Spend the absolute least amount of money you can. The more expensive cards add bells and whistles that you do not need, such as diagnostic software and voltmeters.

Using a POST card is straightforward. Simply power down the PC, install the POST card in any unused slot, and turn the PC back on. As you watch the POST display, notice the different hexadecimal readouts and refer to them as the POST progresses. Notice how quickly they change. If you get an "FF" or "00," that means the POST is over and everything passed—time to check the operating system. If a device stalls the POST, however, the POST card will display an error code. That's the problem device! Good technicians often memorize a dozen or more different POST codes because it's much faster than looking them up in a book.

So you got a beep code, a text error code, or a POST error. Now what do you do with that knowledge? Remember that a POST error does not fix the computer; it only tells you where to look. You then have to know how to deal with that bad or improperly configured component. If you use a POST card, for example, and it hangs at the "Initializing Floppy Drive" test, you'd better know how to work on a floppy drive!

Sometimes the POST card returns a bizarre or confusing error code. What device do you point at when you get a "CMOS shutdown register read/write error" beep code from an older system? First of all, read the error carefully. Let's say on that same system you got an "8042—gate A20 failure" beep code. What will you do? Assuming you know (and you should!) that the "8042" refers to the keyboard, a quick peek at the keyboard and its connection would be a good first step. Beyond that specific example, here is a good general rule: If you don't know what the error means or the bad part isn't replaceable, replace the motherboard. Clearly, you will stumble across exceptions to this rule, but more often than not, the rule stands.

The Boot Process

All PCs need a process to begin their operations. Once you feed power to the PC, the tight interrelation of hardware, firmware, and software enables the PC to start itself, to "pull itself up by the bootstraps" or boot itself.

When you first power on the PC, the power supply circuitry tests for proper voltage and then sends a signal down a special wire called the *power good* wire to awaken the CPU. The moment the power good wire wakes it up, every Intel and clone CPU immediately sends a built-in memory address via its address bus. This special address is the same on every Intel and clone CPU, from the oldest 8086 to the most recent microprocessor. This address is the first line of the POST program on the system ROM! That's how the system starts the POST.

After the POST has finished, there must be a way for the computer to find the programs on the hard drive to start the operating system. The POST passes control to the last BIOS function: the bootstrap loader. The *bootstrap loader* is little more than a few dozen lines of BIOS code tacked to the end of the POST program. Its job is to find the operating system. The bootstrap loader reads CMOS information to tell it where to look first for an operating system. Your PC's CMOS setup utility has an option that you configure to tell the bootstrap loader which devices to check for an operating system and in which order (Figure 5-31).

Figure 5-31
CMOS boot order

```
▶ Hard Disk Boot Priority    Press Enter
  First Boot Device          Floppy
  Second Boot Device         Hard Disk
  Third Boot Device          CDROM
  Boot Other Device          Enabled
```

Almost all storage devices—floppy disks, hard disks, CDs, DVDs, and even USB thumb drives—can be configured to boot an operating system by setting aside a specific location called the *boot sector*. (Later chapters show you how to do this.) If the device is bootable, its boot sector will contain special programming designed to tell the system where to locate the operating system. Any device with a functional operating system is called a bootable disk or a *system disk*. If the bootstrap loader locates a good boot sector, it passes control to the operating system and removes itself from memory. If it doesn't, it will go to the next device in the boot order you set in CMOS setup utility. Boot order is an important tool for techs because it enables you to load in special bootable devices so you can run utilities to maintain PCs without using the primary operating system.

Care and Feeding of BIOS and CMOS

BIOS and CMOS are areas in your PC that you don't go to very often. BIOS itself is invisible. The only real clue you have that it even exists is the POST. The CMOS setup utility, on the other hand, is very visible if you start it. Most CMOS setup utilities today work acceptably well without ever being touched. You're an aspiring tech, however, and all self-respecting techs start up the CMOS setup utility and make changes. That's when most CMOS setup utility problems take place.

If you mess with the CMOS setup utility, remember to make only as many changes at one time as you can remember. Document the original settings and the changes on a piece of paper. That way, you can put things back if necessary. Don't make changes unless you know what they mean! It's easy to screw up a computer fairly seriously by playing with CMOS settings you don't understand.

Losing CMOS Settings

Your CMOS needs a continuous trickle charge to retain its data. Motherboards use some type of battery, usually a coin battery like those used in wrist watches, to give the CMOS the charge it needs when the computer is turned off (Figure 5-32). This battery also keeps track of the date and time when the PC is turned off.

Figure 5-32
A CMOS battery

If the battery runs out of charge, you lose all of your CMOS information. If some mishap suddenly erases the information on the CMOS chip, the computer might not boot up or you'll get nasty-looking errors at boot. Any PC made after 2002 will boot to factory defaults if the CMOS clears, so the chances of not booting are slim—but you'll still get errors at boot. Here are a few examples of errors that point to lost CMOS information:

- CMOS configuration mismatch
- CMOS date/time not set
- No boot device available
- CMOS battery state low

Here are some of the more common reasons for losing CMOS data:

- Pulling and inserting cards
- Touching the motherboard
- Dropping something on the motherboard
- Dirt on the motherboard
- Faulty power supplies
- Electrical surges
- Chip creep

Most of these items should be fairly self-explanatory, but chip creep might be a new term for some of you. As PCs run, the components inside get warm. When a PC is turned off, the components cool off. This cycling of hot and cold causes the chips to expand and contract in their mounts. While the chip designers account for this, in some extreme cases this thermal expansion and contraction will cause a chip to work out of its mount and cause a failure called *chip creep*. Chip creep was a common problem in the earlier days of PCs, but after 20 years of experience, the PC industry has done a pretty good job of designing mounts that will hold all your chips in place dependably.

If you encounter any of these errors, or if the clock in Windows resets itself to January 1st every time you reboot the system, the battery on the motherboard is losing its charge and needs to be replaced. To replace it, use a screwdriver to pry the battery's catch gently back. The battery should pop up for easy removal. Before you install the new battery, double-check that it has the same voltage and amperage as the old battery. To retain your CMOS settings while replacing the battery, simply leave your PC plugged into an AC outlet. The 5-volt soft power on all modern motherboards will provide enough electricity to keep the CMOS charged and the data secure. Of course, I know you're going to be *extremely* careful about ESD while prying up the battery from a live system!

Clearing CMOS

All techs invariably do things in CMOS they want to undo, but sometimes simply making a change in CMOS prevents you from getting back to the CMOS setup utility to make the change back. A great example is when someone sets a CMOS password and then forgets the password. If you ever run into a system with an unknown CMOS password, you'll need to erase the CMOS and then reset everything. All motherboards have a clear CMOS jumper somewhere on the motherboard (Figure 5-33). Check your motherboard book for the correct location.

Figure 5-33
Clear CMOS
jumpers

To clear the CMOS, turn off the PC. Then locate one of those tiny little plastic pieces (officially called a *shunt*) and place it over the two jumper wires for a moment. Next, restart the PC and immediately go into CMOS and restore the settings you need.

Flashing ROM

Flash ROM chips can be reprogrammed to update their contents. With Flash ROM, when you need to update your system BIOS to add support for a new technology, you can simply run a small command-line program, combined with an update file, and voilà, you've got a new, updated BIOS! Different BIOS makers use slightly different processes for *flashing the BIOS*, but in general, you must boot from a floppy diskette and then run the relevant updating command from the A:\> prompt. This example shows how simple it can be:

```
A:\> aw athxpt2.bin
```

Some motherboard makers even provide Windows-based Flash ROM update utilities that will check the Internet for updates and download them for you to install (Figure 5-34). Most of these utilities will also enable you to back up your current BIOS so you can return to it if the updated version causes trouble. Without a good backup, you could end up throwing away your motherboard if a Flash BIOS update goes wrong, so you should always make one! Finally, don't update your BIOS unless you have some compelling reason to do so. As the old saying goes, "If it ain't broke, don't fix it!"

Figure 5-34
ROM updating
program for an
ASUS motherboard

Chapter Review Questions

1. What does BIOS provide for the computer? (Choose the best answer.)

   A. BIOS provides the physical interface for various devices such as USB and FireWire ports.

   B. BIOS provides the programming that enables the CPU to communicate with other hardware.

   C. BIOS provides memory space for applications to load into from the hard drive.

   D. BIOS provides memory space for applications to load into from the main system RAM.

2. What is the correct boot sequence for a PC?

   A. CPU, POST, power good, boot loader, operating system

   B. POST, power good, CPU, boot loader, operating system

   C. Power good, boot loader, CPU, POST, operating system

   D. Power good, CPU, POST, boot loader, operating system

3. Jill decided to go retro and added a second floppy disk drive to her computer. She thinks she got it physically installed correctly, but it doesn't show up in Windows. Which of the following options will most likely lead Jill where she needs to go to resolve the issue?

A. Reboot the computer and press the F key on the keyboard twice. This signals that the computer has two floppy disk drives.

B. Reboot the computer and watch for instructions to enter the CMOS setup utility (for example, a message may say to press the DELETE key). Do what it says to go into CMOS setup.

C. In Windows, press the DELETE key twice to enter the CMOS setup utility.

D. In Windows, go to Start | Run and type "floppy." Click OK to open the Floppy Disk Drive Setup Wizard.

4. Henry bought a new card for capturing television on his computer. When he finished going through the packaging, however, he found no driver disc, only an application disc for setting up the TV capture software. After installing the card and software, it all works flawlessly. What's the most likely explanation?

A. The device doesn't need BIOS, so there's no need for a driver disc.

B. The device has an option ROM that loads BIOS, so there's no need for a driver disc.

C. Windows supports TV capture cards out of the box, so there's no need for a driver disc.

D. The manufacturer made a mistake and didn't include everything needed to set up the device.

5. Which of the following most accurately describes the relationship between BIOS and hardware?

A. All hardware needs BIOS.

B. All hardware that attaches to the motherboard via ribbon cables needs BIOS.

C. All hardware built into the motherboard needs BIOS.

D. Some hardware devices need BIOS.

6. After a sudden power outage, Samson's PC rebooted, but nothing appeared on the screen. The PC just beeped at him, over and over and over. What's most likely the problem?

A. The power outage toasted his RAM.

B. The power outage toasted his video card.

C. The power outage toasted his hard drive.

D. The power outage toasted his CPU.

7. Davos finds that a disgruntled former employee decided to sabotage her computer when she left by putting a password in CMOS that stops the computer from booting. What can Davos do to solve this problem?

   A. Davos should boot the computer holding the left SHIFT key. This will clear the CMOS information.

   B. Davos should try various combinations of the former employee's name. The vast majority of people use their name or initials for CMOS passwords.

   C. Davos should find the CMOS clear jumper on the motherboard. Then he can boot the computer with a shunt on the jumper to clear the CMOS information.

   D. Davos should find a replacement motherboard. Unless he knows the CMOS password, there's nothing he can do.

8. Richard over in the sales department went wild in CMOS and made a bunch of changes that he thought would optimize his PC. Now most of his PC doesn't work. He can boot, but only to CMOS, not into Windows. Which of the following tech call answers would most likely get him up and running again?

   A. Reboot the computer about three times. That'll clear the CMOS and get you up and running.

   B. Open up the computer and find the CMOS clear jumper. Remove a shunt from somewhere on the motherboard and put it on the CMOS clear jumper. Reboot and then put the shunt back where you got it. Reboot, and you should be up and running in no time.

   C. Boot into the CMOS setup program and then find the option to load a plug-and-play operating system. Make sure it's set to On. Save and exit CMOS; boot normally into Windows. You should be up and running in no time.

   D. Boot into the CMOS setup program and then find the option to load Optimized Default settings. Save and exit CMOS; boot normally into Windows. You should be up and running in no time.

9. Jill boots up an older Pentium III system that has been the cause of several user complaints at the office. The system powers up and starts to run through POST, but then stops. The screen displays a "CMOS configuration mismatch" error. Of the following list, what is the most likely cause of this error?

   A. Dying CMOS battery

   B. Bad CPU

   C. Bad RAM

   D. Corrupt system BIOS

10. Where does Windows store device drivers?

   A. My Computer

   B. My Hardware

   C. Registry

   D. Drivers and Settings

Answers

1. **B.** BIOS provides the programming that enables the CPU to communicate with other hardware.

2. **D.** Here's the correct boot sequence: power good, CPU, POST, boot loader, operating system.

3. **B.** Jill should reboot the computer and watch for instructions to enter the CMOS setup utility (for example, a message may say to press the DELETE key). She should do what it says to go into CMOS setup.

4. **B.** Most likely the device has an option ROM because it works.

5. **A.** All hardware needs BIOS!

6. **A.** The long repeating beep and a dead PC most likely indicates a problem with RAM.

7. **C.** Davos should find the CMOS clear jumper on the motherboard. Boot the computer with a shunt on the jumper to clear the CMOS information.

8. **D.** Please don't hand Richard a screwdriver! Having him load Optimized Default settings will most likely do the trick.

9. **A.** The CMOS battery is likely dying.

10. **C.** Windows stores device drivers in the Registry.

Expansion Bus

6

In this chapter, you will learn how to
- Identify the structure and function of the expansion bus
- Explain classic system resources
- Identify the modern expansion bus slots
- Install expansion cards properly
- Troubleshoot expansion card problems

Expansion slots have been part of the PC from the very beginning. Way back then, IBM created the PC with an eye to the future; the original IBM PC had slots built into the motherboard for adding expansion cards and thus new functions to the PC. This expandability might seem obvious today, but think about the three big hurdles a would-be expansion card developer needed to cross to make a card that would work successfully in an expansion slot. First, any expansion card needed to be built specifically for the expansion slots—that would require the creation of industry standards. Second, the card needed some way to communicate with the CPU, both to receive instructions and to relay information. And third, the operating system would need some means of enabling the user to control the new device and thus take advantage of its functions. Here's the short form of those three hurdles:

- Physical connection
- Communication
- Drivers

This chapter covers the expansion bus in detail, starting almost at the very beginning of the PC—not because the history of the PC is inherently thrilling, but rather because the way the old PCs worked still affects the latest systems. Installation today remains very similar to installation in 1987 in that you must have physical connection, communication, and drivers for the operating system. Taking the time to learn the old ways first most definitely helps make current technology, terminology, and practices easier to understand and implement.

Historical/Conceptual

Structure and Function of the Expansion Bus

As you've learned, every device in the computer—whether soldered to the motherboard or snapped into a socket—connects to the external data bus and the address bus. The expansion slots are no exception. They connect to the rest of the PC through the chipset. Exactly *where* on the chipset varies depending on the system. On some systems, the expansion slots connect to the Southbridge (Figure 6-1). On other systems, the expansion slots connect to the Northbridge (Figure 6-2). Finally, many systems have more than one type of expansion bus, with slots of one type connecting to the Northbridge and slots of another type connecting to the Southbridge (Figure 6-3).

Figure 6-1
Expansion slots connecting to Southbridge

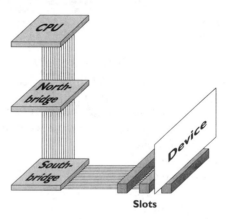

Figure 6-2
Expansion slots connecting to Northbridge

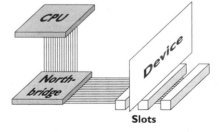

Figure 6-3
Expansion slots
connecting to both
Northbridge and
Southbridge

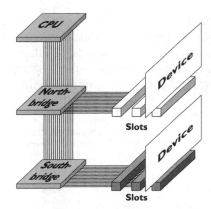

The chipset provides an extension of the address bus and data bus to the expansion slots, and thus to any expansion cards in those slots. If you plug a hard drive controller card into an expansion slot, it will function just as if it were built into the motherboard, albeit with one big difference: speed. As you'll recall from Chapter 3, the system crystal—the clock—pushes the CPU. The system crystal provides a critical function for the entire PC, acting like a drill sergeant calling a cadence, setting the pace of activity in the computer. Every device soldered to the motherboard is designed to run at the speed of the system crystal. A 133-MHz motherboard, for example, has at least a 133-MHz Northbridge chip and a 133-MHz Southbridge, all timed by a 133-MHz crystal (Figure 6-4).

Figure 6-4
The system crystal
sets the speed.

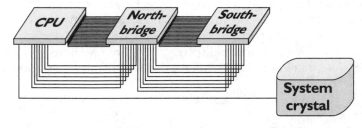

The system crystal
sits on its own bus.

Clock crystals aren't just for CPUs and chipsets. Pretty much every chip in your computer has a CLK wire and needs to be pushed by a clock chip, including the chips on your expansion cards. Suppose you buy a device that did not come with your computer—say, a sound card. The chips on the sound card need to be pushed by a CLK signal from a crystal. If PCs were designed to use the system crystal to push that sound card, sound card manufacturers would need to make sound cards for every possible motherboard speed. You would have to buy a 100-MHz sound card for a 100-MHz system or a 133-MHz sound card for a 133-MHz system.

This would be ridiculous, and IBM knew it when they designed the PC. They had to make an extension to the external data bus that *ran at its own standardized speed*. You would use this part of the external data bus to snap new devices into the PC. IBM achieved this goal by adding a different crystal, called the expansion bus crystal, which controlled the part of the external data bus connected to the expansion slots (Figure 6-5).

Figure 6-5
Function of system and expansion bus crystals

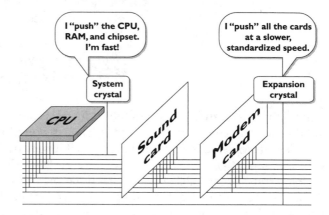

The expansion slots run at a much slower speed than the frontside bus. The chipset acts as the divider between the two buses, compensating for the speed difference with wait states and special buffering (storage) areas. No matter how fast the motherboard runs, the expansion slots run at a standard speed. In the original IBM PC, that speed was about 14.318 MHz ÷ 2, or about 7.16 MHz. The latest expansion buses run much faster, but remember that old speed of roughly 7 MHz; as you learn more about expansion slots, you'll see that it's still needed on even the most modern systems.

PC Bus

On first-generation IBM PCs, the 8088 CPU had an 8-bit external data bus and ran at a top speed of 4.77 MHz. IBM made the expansion slots on the first PCs with an 8-bit external bus connection. IBM wanted the bus to run as fast as the CPU, and even way back then 4.77 MHz was an easy speed to achieve. IBM settled on a standard expansion bus speed of about 7 MHz—faster than the CPU! (This was the only occurrence in the history of PCs that the expansion bus was faster than the CPU.) This expansion bus was called the *PC bus* or *XT bus*. Figure 6-6 shows these ancient, 8-bit expansion slots.

Figure 6-6
Eight-bit PC/XT slots

IBM certainly didn't invent the idea of the expansion bus—plenty of earlier computers, including many mainframes, had expansion slots—but IBM did something no one had ever done. They allowed competitors to copy the PC bus and make their own PCs without having to pay a licensing or royalty fee. They also allowed third parties to make cards that would snap into their PC bus. Remember that IBM invented the PC bus—it was (and still is) a patented product of IBM Corporation. By allowing everyone to copy the PC expansion bus technology, however, IBM established the industry standard and fostered the emergence of the clone market. If IBM had not allowed others to copy their patented technologies for free, companies such as Compaq, Dell, and Gateway never would have existed. Equally, component makers like Logitech, Creative, and 3Com would never be the companies they are today without the help of IBM. Who knows? If IBM had not opened the PC bus to the world, this book and the A+ Certification exams might have been based on Apple computers!

PC Bus

- 8 bits wide
- 7-MHz speed
- Manual configuration

ISA

When Intel invented the 286 processor, IBM wanted to create a new expansion bus that took advantage of the 286's 16-bit external data bus, yet also supported 8-bit cards. IBM achieved this by simply adding a set of connections to the end of the PC bus, creating a new 16-bit bus (Figure 6-7). Many techs called this bus the *AT bus* after the first system to use these slots, the 286-based IBM Advanced Technology (AT) computer. The AT bus ran at the same speed (approximately 7 MHz) as the earlier PC bus.

Figure 6-7
Sixteen-bit ISA or AT slots

Even though IBM allowed third parties to copy the PC and AT expansion bus architecture, they never released the complete specifications for these two types of expansion buses. A number of clone makers got together in the early 1980s and pooled their combined knowledge of the PC/XT and AT buses to create a book of standards called the Industry Standard Architecture (ISA) Bus Standards, coining the term *ISA* to describe these first-generation expansion slots.

The ISA bus enabled manufacturers to jump the first of the three hurdles for successful expansion cards, namely connectivity. If a company wanted to build a new kind of adapter card for the PC, they simply followed the specifications in the ISA standard.

ISA Bus

- 16 bits wide
- 7-MIIz speed
- Manual configuration

Essentials

Modern Expansion Buses

The ISA expansion bus was both excellent and cutting edge for its time, and was *the* expansion bus in every PC for the first ten years of the PC's existence. Yet ISA suffered from three tremendous limitations that began to cause serious bottlenecks by the late 1980s. First, ISA was slow, running at only about 7 MHz. Second, ISA was narrow—only 16 bits wide—and therefore unable to handle the 32-bit and 64-bit external data buses of more modern processors. Finally, techs had to configure ISA cards manually, making installation a time-consuming nightmare of running proprietary configuration programs and moving tiny jumpers just to get a single card to work.

Manufacturers clearly needed to come up with a better bus that addressed the many problems associated with ISA. They needed a bus that could take advantage of the 33-MHz motherboard speed and 32-bit-wide data bus found in 386 and 486 systems. They also wanted a bus that was self-configuring, freeing techs from the drudgery of manual configuration. Finally, they had to make the new bus backward-compatible, so end users wouldn't have to throw out their oftentimes substantial investment in ISA expansion cards.

False Starts

In the late 1980s, several new expansion buses designed to address these shortcomings appeared on the market. Three in particular—IBM's Micro Channel Architecture (MCA), the open standard Extended ISA (EISA), and the Video Electronics Standards Association's VESA Local Bus (VL-Bus)—all had a few years of modest popularity from the late 1980s to the mid 1990s. Although all of these alternative buses worked well, they each had shortcomings that made them less than optimal replacements for ISA. IBM charged a heavy licensing fee for MCA, EISA was expensive to make, and VL-Bus only worked in tandem with the ISA bus. By 1993, the PC world was eager for a big name to come forward with a fast, wide, easy-to-configure, and cheap new expansion bus. Intel saw the need and stepped up to the plate with the now famous PCI bus.

PCI

Intel introduced the *peripheral component interconnect (PCI)* bus architecture (Figure 6-8) in the early 1990s, and the PC expansion bus was never again the same. Intel made many smart moves with PCI, not the least of which was releasing PCI to the public domain to make PCI very attractive to manufacturers. PCI provided a wider, faster, more flexible alternative than any previous expansion bus. The exceptional technology of the new bus, combined with the lack of a price tag, made manufacturers quickly drop ISA and the other alternatives and adopt PCI.

Figure 6-8
PCI expansion
bus slots

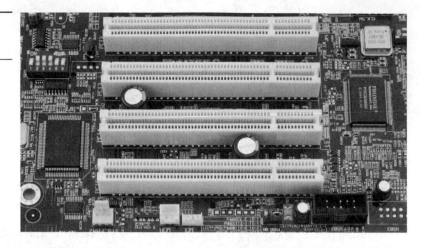

PCI really shook up the PC world with its capabilities. The original PCI bus was 32 bits wide and ran at 33 MHz, which was superb, but these features were expected and not earth-shattering. The coolness of PCI came from its capability to coexist with other expansion buses. When PCI first came out, you could buy a motherboard with both PCI and ISA slots. This was important because it enabled users to keep their old ISA cards and slowly migrate to PCI. Equally impressive was that PCI devices were (and still are) self-configuring, a feature that led to the industry standard that became known as plug and play. Finally, PCI had a powerful burst mode feature that enabled very efficient data transfers.

Before PCI, it was rare to see more than one type of expansion slot on a motherboard. Today, this is not only common—it's expected!

PCI Bus

- 32 bits wide
- 33-MHz speed
- Self-configuring

TIP   There was a 64-bit version of the original PCI standard, but it was quite rare.

The original PCI expansion bus has soldiered on in PCs for over ten years. Recently, PCI has begun to be replaced by more advanced forms of PCI. Although these new PCI expansion buses are faster than the original PCI, they're only improvements to PCI, not entirely new expansion buses. The original PCI might be fading away, but PCI in its many new forms is still "King of the Motherboard."

AGP

One of the big reasons for ISA's demise was video cards. When video started going graphical with the introduction of Windows, ISA buses were too slow and graphics looked terrible. PCI certainly improved graphics at the time it came out, but Intel was thinking ahead. Shortly after Intel invented PCI, they presented a specialized, video-only version of PCI called the *accelerated graphics port (AGP)*. An AGP slot is a PCI slot, but one with a direct connection to the Northbridge. AGP slots are only for video cards—don't try to snap a sound card or modem into one. You'll learn much more about this fascinating technology in Chapter 17, "Video." Figure 6-9 shows a typical AGP slot.

Figure 6-9
AGP slot

 NOTE The AGP slot is almost universally brown in color, making it easy to spot.

PCI-X

PCI-X, already available in systems such as the Macintosh G5, is a huge enhancement to current PCI that is also fully backward-compatible, in terms of both hardware and software. PCI-X is a 64-bit-wide bus (see Figure 6-10). Its slots will accept regular PCI cards. The real bonus of PCI-X is its much enhanced speed. The PCI-X 2.0 standard features four speed grades (measured in MHz): PCI-X 66, PCI-X 133, PCI-X 266, and PCI-X 533.

Figure 6-10
PCI-X slot

The obvious candidates for PCI-X are businesses using workstations and servers, because they have the "need for speed" and also the need for backward compatibility. Large vendors, especially in the high-end market, are already on board. HP, Dell, and Intel server products, for example, support PCI-X. A quick online shopping trip reveals tons of PCI-X stuff for sale: gigabit NICs, Fibre Channel cards, video adapters, and more.

Mini-PCI

PCI has even made it into laptops in the specialty Mini-PCI format (Figure 6-11). You'll find Mini-PCI in just about every laptop these days. Mini-PCI is designed to use low power and to lie flat—both good features for a laptop expansion slot! Mini-PCI returns in Chapter 19, "Portable Computing."

Figure 6-11
Tiny card in a Mini-PCI slot. See the contacts at the bottom of the picture?

PCI Express

PCI Express (PCIe) is the latest, fastest, and most popular expansion bus in use today. As its name implies, PCI Express is still PCI, but it uses a point-to-point serial connection instead of PCI's shared parallel communication. Consider a single 32-bit chunk of data moving from a device to the CPU. In PCI parallel communication, 32 wires each carry one bit of that chunk of data. In serial communication, only one wire carries those 32 bits. You'd think that 32 are better than one, correct? Well, first of all, PCIe doesn't share the bus. A PCIe device has its own direct connection (a point-to-point connection) to the Northbridge, so it does not wait for other devices. Plus, when you start going really fast (think gigabits per second), it's difficult to get all 32 bits of data to go from one device to another at the same time because some bits get there slightly faster than others. That means you need some serious, high-speed checking of the data when it arrives to verify that it's all there and in good shape. Serial data doesn't have this problem, as all the bits arrive one after the other in a single stream. When data is really going fast, a single point-to-point serial connection is faster than a shared, 32-wire parallel connection.

And boy howdy, is PCIe ever fast! A PCIe connection uses one wire for sending and one for receiving. Each of these pairs of wires between a PCIe controller and a device is called a *lane*. Each lane runs at 2.5 Gbps. Better yet, each point-to-point connection can use 1, 2, 4, 8, 12, 16, or 32 lanes to achieve a maximum bandwidth of 160 Gbps. The effective data rate drops a little bit because of the *encoding scheme*—the way the data is broken down and reassembled—but full duplex data throughput can go up to a whopping 12.8 GBps on a ×32 connection.

The most common PCIe slot is the 16-lane (×16) version most commonly used for video cards, as shown in Figure 6-12. The first versions of PCIe motherboards used a combination of a single PCIe ×16 slot and a number of standard PCI slots. (Remember, PCI is designed to work with other expansion slots, even other types of PCI.)

Figure 6-12
PCIe ×16 slot (black) with PCI slots (white)

NOTE When you talk about the lanes, such as ×1 or ×8, use "by" rather than "ex" for the multiplication mark. So "by 1" and "by 8" is the correct pronunciation. You'll of course hear it spoken as "by 8" and "8 ex" for the next few years until the technology has become a household term.

The bandwidth generated by a ×16 slot is far more than anything other than a video card would need, so most PCIe motherboards also contain slots with fewer lanes. Currently, ×1 (Figure 6-13) and ×4 are the most common general-purpose PCIe slots, but PCIe is still pretty new—so expect things to change as PCIe matures.

Figure 6-13
PCIe ×1 slots

System Resources

All devices on your computer, including your expansion cards, need to communicate with the CPU. Unfortunately, just using the word *communication* is too simplistic, because communication between the CPU and devices isn't like a human conversation. In the PC, only the CPU "talks" in the form of BIOS or driver commands—devices only react to the CPU's commands. You can divide communication into four aspects called *system resources*. The system resources are

- **I/O address** How the CPU sends commands to devices
- **IRQ** How devices tell the CPU they need communication
- **DMA** How the CPU enables devices to talk directly to RAM
- **Memory** How the CPU talks to RAM on devices

Not all devices use all four system resources. All devices use I/O addressing and most use IRQs, but very few use DMA or memory. System resources are not new—they've been with PCs since the first IBM PC over 25 years ago.

New devices must have their system resources configured. Configuration happens more or less automatically now through the plug and play process, but in the old days configuration was handled through a painstaking manual process. (You kids don't know how good you got it! Oops! Sorry—Old Man Voice.) Even though system resources are now automated, there are a few places on a modern PC where you still might run into them. On those rare occasions, you'll need to understand I/O addresses,

IRQs, DMAs, and memory to make changes as needed. Let's look at each system re-source in detail to understand what they are and how they work.

I/O Addresses

The chipset extends the address bus to the expansion slots, which makes two interesting things happen. First, you can place RAM on a card, and the CPU can address it just like it can your regular RAM. Devices like video cards come with their own RAM. The CPU draws the screen by writing directly to the RAM on the video card. Second, the CPU can use the address bus to talk to all the devices on your computer through I/O addressing.

Normally, the address bus on an expansion bus works exactly like the address bus on a frontside bus—different patterns of ones and zeroes point to different memory locations. If the CPU wants to send an I/O address, however, it puts the expansion bus into what can be called I/O mode. When the bus goes into I/O mode, all devices on the bus look for patterns of ones and zeroes to appear on the address bus.

Back in the old Intel 8088 days, the CPU used an extra wire, called the *input/output or memory (IO/MEM) wire,* to notify devices that it was using the address bus either to specify an address in memory or to communicate with a particular device (Figure 6-14). You won't find an IO/MEM wire on a modern CPU, as the process has changed and become more complex—but the concept hasn't changed one bit! The CPU sends com-mands to devices by placing patterns of ones and zeroes on the address bus. Every device in your computer has at least four discrete patterns of ones and zeroes; each pattern is a different command called an *I/O address.*

Figure 6-14
Sending out an I/O address on an old-fashioned IO/MEM wire

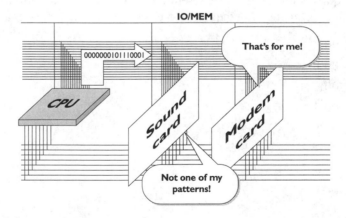

No two devices share the same I/O address because that would defeat the entire concept. To make sure no two devices share I/O addresses, all I/O addresses are either preset by standard (e.g., all hard drive controllers use the same I/O addresses on every PC) or are set at boot by the operating system. You can see the I/O addresses for all the devices on your computer by going into Device Manager. Go to the View menu option and select *Resources by type*. Click on the plus sign directly to the left of the Input/output (IO) option to see a listing of I/O addresses, as shown in Figure 6-15.

Figure 6-15
Viewing resources
by type, with I/O
addresses expanded

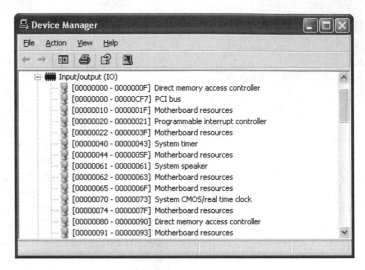

Whoa! What's with all the letters and numbers? The address bus is always 32 bits (even if you have a 64-bit processor, the Northbridge only allows the first 32 bits to pass to the expansion slots), so instead of showing you the raw ones and zeroes, Device Manager shows you the I/O address ranges in hexadecimal. Don't know hex? No worries—it's just quick shorthand for representing the strings of ones and zeroes—*binary*—that you *do* know. One hex character is used to represent four binary characters. Here's the key:

0000	=	0
0001	=	1
0010	=	2
0011	=	3
0100	=	4
0101	=	5
0110	=	6
0111	=	7
1000	=	8
1001	=	9
1010	=	A
1011	=	B
1100	=	C
1101	=	D
1110	=	E
1111	=	F

Let's pick an arbitrary string of ones and zeroes:

00000000000000000000000111110000

To convert to hex, just chop them into chunks of four:

0000 0000 0000 0000 0000 0001 1111 0000

Then use the key above to convert:

0 0 0 0 0 1 F 0

Then push the hex values together:

000001F0

You now understand what those values mean in Device Manager. Scroll down until you find the "[000001F0 - 000001F7] Primary IDE Channel" setting. Notice that there are two I/O addresses listed. These show the entire range of I/O addresses for this device; the more complex the device, the more I/O addresses it uses. Address ranges are generally referred to by the first value in the range, commonly known as the *I/O base address.*

NOTE All I/O addresses only use the last 16 bits (they all start with 0000). Sixteen bits makes 2^{16} = 65,536 I/O address ranges—plenty for even the most modern PCs. Should PCs begin to need more I/O addresses in the future, the current I/O addressing system is ready!

Here are the most important items to remember about I/O addresses. First, every device on your PC has an I/O address. Without it, the CPU wouldn't have a way to send a device commands! Second, I/O addresses are configured automatically—you just plug in a device and it works. Third, no two devices should share I/O addresses. The system handles configuration, so this is done automatically.

Interrupt Requests

Between the standardized expansion bus connections and BIOS using I/O addressing, the CPU can now communicate with all of the devices inside the computer, but a third and final hurdle remains. I/O addressing enables the CPU to talk to devices, but how does a device tell the CPU it needs attention? How does the mouse tell the CPU that it has moved, for example, or how does the keyboard tell the CPU that somebody just pressed the J key? The PC needs some kind of mechanism to tell the CPU to stop doing whatever it is doing and talk to a particular device (Figure 6-16). This mechanism is called *interruption.*

Figure 6-16
How do devices tell the CPU they need attention?

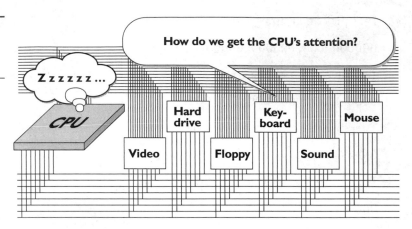

Every CPU in the PC world has an INT (interrupt) wire, shown in Figure 6-17. If a device puts voltage on this wire, the CPU will stop what it is doing and deal with the interrupting device. Suppose you have a PC with only one peripheral, a keyboard that directly connects to the INT wire. If the user presses the J key, the keyboard charges the INT wire. The CPU temporarily stops running the browser (or whatever program is active) and runs the necessary BIOS routine to query the keyboard.

Figure 6-17
The INT wire

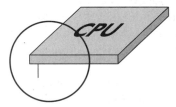

This would be fine if the computer had only one device. As you know, however, PCs have many devices, and almost all of them need to interrupt the CPU at some point. So the PC needs some kind of "traffic cop" to act as an intermediary between all the devices and the CPU's INT wire. This traffic cop chip, called the *I/O Advanced Programmable Interrupt Controller (IOAPIC)*, uses special interrupt wires that run to all devices on the expansion bus (Figure 6-18).

Figure 6-18
Eight interrupt wires (IRQs) run from the expansion bus to the IOAPIC.

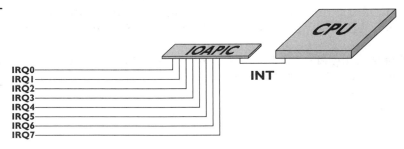

NOTE IOAPIC functions are usually built into the Southbridge.

If a device wants to get the CPU's attention, it lights the interrupt wires with a special pattern of ones and zeroes just for that device. The IOAPIC then interrupts the CPU. The CPU queries the IOAPIC to see which device interrupted, and then it begins to communicate with the device over the address bus (Figure 6-19).

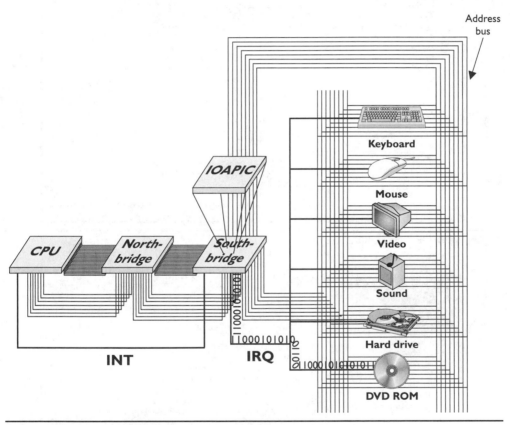

Figure 6-19 IOAPIC at work

These unique patterns of ones and zeroes manifest themselves as something called *interrupt requests (IRQs)*. Before IOAPICs, IRQs were actual wires leading to the previous generation of traffic cops, called PICs. It's easy to see if your system has a PIC or an IOAPIC. Go into the Device Manager and select Interrupt Request (IRQ).

Figure 6-20 shows 24 IRQs, numbered 0 through 23, making this an IOAPIC system. IRQ 9 is special—this IRQ is assigned to the controller itself and is the IOAPIC's connection to the CPU. If you look closely, you'll also notice that some IRQs aren't listed. These are unused or "open" IRQs. If you add another device to the system, the new device will take up one of these unused IRQs. Now look at the older PIC system in Figure 6-21—note that it only shows 16 IRQs.

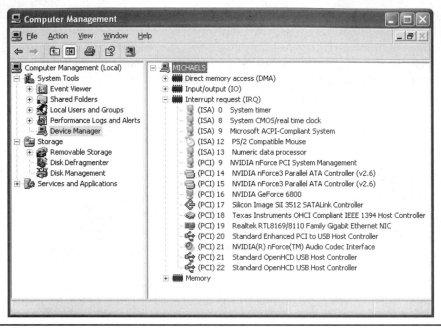

Figure 6-20   IRQs in an IOAPIC system

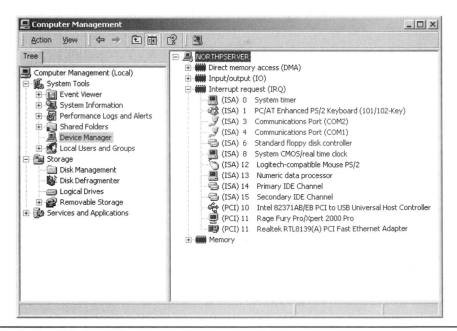

Figure 6-21   IRQs in a PIC system

Don't freak out if you have a PIC system—they work just fine, but with fewer IRQs. As of now, very few systems take advantage of the extra IRQs provided by IOAPIC systems. But like the extra I/O addresses, they are there should we need them in the future.

Look again at Figures 6-20 and 6-21. Do you see the little (PCI) and (ISA) text to the left of each IRQ number? Neither of these systems has ISA slots, so why does it say ISA? These ISA IRQ settings are the original IRQ numbers defined for these devices a long time ago. For backward compatibility with older equipment and older programs, your system makes these classically ISA devices look as though they use the old-style IRQs. As soon as the last few old devices go away, Microsoft will most likely remove these ISA values. What's interesting here is that you can still manually adjust the resources for a few of the old ISA devices, in particular the serial ports and the parallel ports. Let's look at the last serious vestige of the "bad old days" on your PC: COM and LPT ports.

COM and LPT Ports

When the PC first came out, every device had to have its I/O addresses and IRQ manually configured. How you did this varied from device to device: you moved jumpers, turned dials, or ran weird configuration programs. It was never easy. IBM tried to make configuration easier by creating preset I/O address and IRQ combinations for the serial and parallel ports, because they were the most commonly used ports on the original PC. These preset combinations were called "COM" ports for serial connections and "LPT" ports for parallel ports. Table 6-1 lists the early preset combinations of I/O addresses and IRQs.

 NOTE   The term "COM" for serial ports came from "communication," and the term LPT for parallel ports came from "line printer."

Table 6-1	Port	I/O Base Address	IRQ
COM and LPT assignments	COM1	03F8	4
	COM2	02F8	3
	COM3	03E8	4
	COM4	02E8	3
	LPT1	0378	7
	LPT2	0278	5

Notice that the four COM ports share two IRQs. In the old days, if two devices shared an IRQ, the system instantly locked up. The lack of available IRQs in early systems led IBM to double up the IRQs for the serial devices, creating one of the few exceptions to the rule that no two devices could share IRQs. You could share an IRQ between two devices, but only if one of the devices would never actually access the IRQ. You'd see this with a dedicated fax/modem card, for example, which has a single phone line connected to a single card that has two different functions. The CPU needed distinct sets of I/O addresses for fax commands and modem commands, but as there was only the one modem doing both jobs, it needed only a single IRQ.

Direct Memory Access

CPUs do a lot of work. They run the BIOS, operating system, and applications. CPUs handle interrupts and I/O addresses. CPUs also deal with one other item: data. CPUs constantly move data between devices and RAM. CPUs move files from the hard drive to RAM. They move print jobs from RAM to laser printers, and they move images from scanners to RAM, just to name a very few examples of this RAM-to-device-and-back process.

Moving all this data is obviously necessary, but it is a simple task—the CPU has better things to do with its power and time. Moreover, with all of the caches and such on today's CPUs, the system spends most of its time waiting around doing nothing while the CPU handles some internal calculation. Add these facts together and the question arises: Why not make devices that access memory directly, without involving the CPU (Figure 6-22)? The process of accessing memory without using the CPU is called *direct memory access (DMA)*.

Figure 6-22
Why not talk to the chipset directly?

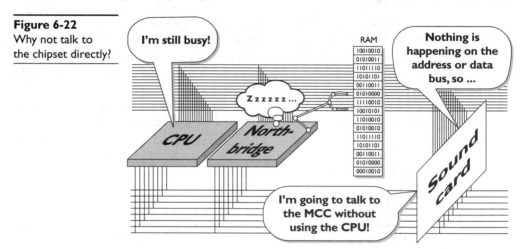

DMA is very common, and is excellent for creating background sounds in games and for moving data from floppy and hard drives into RAM (Figure 6-23).

Figure 6-23
DMA in action

Nice as it may sound, the concept of DMA as described above has a problem—there's only one expansion bus. What if more than one device wants to use DMA? What keeps these devices from stomping on the external data bus all at the same time? Plus, what if the CPU suddenly needs the data bus? How can you stop the device using DMA so the CPU, which should have priority, can access the bus? To deal with this, IBM added another traffic cop.

The *DMA controller,* which seasoned techs often call the *8237* after its old chip name, controls all DMA functions (Figure 6-24). DMA is similar to IRQ handling in that the DMA controller assigns numbers, called DMA channels, to enable devices to request use of the DMA. The DMA also handles the data passing from peripherals to RAM and vice versa. This takes necessary but simple work away from the CPU, so the CPU can spend time doing more productive work.

Figure 6-24
The DMA contoller handles all DMA transfers.

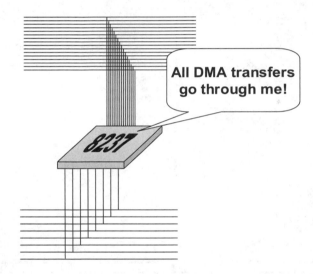

All DMA transfers go through me!

The DMA chip sends data along the external data bus when the CPU is busy with internal calculations and not using the external data bus. This is perfectly acceptable because the CPU accesses the external data bus only about five percent of the time on a modern CPU.

The DMA just described is called "classic DMA"; it was the first and for a long time the only way to do DMA. Classic DMA is dying out because it's very slow and only supports 16-bit data transfers, a silly waste in a world of much wider buses. On most systems, only floppy drives still use classic DMA.

All systems still support classic DMA, but most devices today that use DMA do so without going through the DMA controller. These devices are known as bus masters. *Bus mastering* devices have circuitry that enables them to watch for other devices accessing the external data bus; they can detect a potential conflict and get out of the way on their own. Bus mastering has become extremely popular in hard drives. All modern hard drives take advantage of bus mastering. Hard drive bus mastering is hidden under terms such as *Ultra DMA,* and for the most part is totally automatic and invisible. See Chapter 10, "Implementing Hard Drives," for more details on bus mastering hard drives.

NOTE Bus mastering devices ignore the DMA controller; they don't have DMA channels.

If you want to see your DMA usage, head back to Device Manager and change the view to *Resources by type.* Click on Direct Memory Access (DMA) and you'll see something like Figure 6-25. This system has only two DMA channels: one for the floppy drive and one for the connection to the CPU.

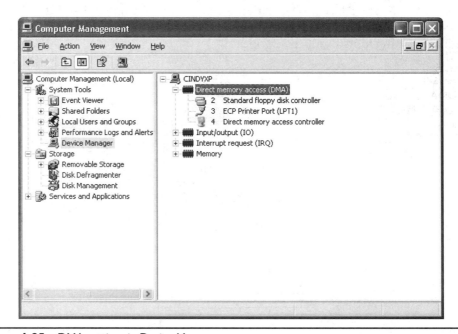

Figure 6-25   DMA settings in Device Manager

One interesting note to DMA is that neither PCI nor PCIe supports DMA, so you'll never find a DMA device that snaps into these expansion buses. A hard drive, floppy drive, or any other device that still wants to use DMA must do so through onboard connections. Sure, you can find hard drive and floppy drive cards, but they're not using DMA.

Memory Addresses

Some expansion cards need memory addresses. There are two reasons a card may need memory addresses. First, a card may have onboard RAM that the CPU needs to address. Second, a few cards come with an onboard ROM, the so-called adapter or option ROM you read about in Chapter 5. In either of these situations, the RAM or ROM must steal memory addresses away from the main system RAM to enable the CPU to access the RAM or ROM.

The key fact for techs is that, just like I/O addresses, IRQs, and DMA channels, memory addressing is fully automatic and no longer an issue.

Installing Expansion Cards

Installing an expansion card successfully—another one of those bread-and-butter tasks for the PC tech—requires at least four steps. First, you need to know that the card works with your system and your operating system. Second, you have to insert the card in an expansion slot properly and without damaging that card or the motherboard. Third, you need to provide drivers for the operating system—that's *proper* drivers for the *specific* OS. Fourth, you should always verify that the card functions properly before you walk away from the PC.

 NOTE   Some manufacturers insist on a different order for device installation than the traditional one described here. The most common variation requires you to install the drivers and support software for an expansion card *before* you insert the card. Failure to follow the manufacturer's directions with such a card can lead to hours of frustration while you uninstall the card and reinstall the drivers, sometimes manually removing some drivers and software from the system. The bottom line? Read the instructions that come with a particular card! I'll provide more specific examples of problem devices in later chapters.

Step 1: Knowledge

Learn about the device you plan to install—preferably before you purchase it! Does the device work with your system and operating system? Does it have drivers for your operating system? If you use Windows, the answer to these questions is almost always "yes." If you use an old operating system like Windows 98 or a less common operating system such as Linux, these questions become critical. A lot of older, pre-XP hardware simply won't work with Windows XP at all. Check the device's documentation and check the device manufacturer's Web site to verify that you have the correct drivers. While you're checking, make sure that you have the latest version of the driver; most devices get driver updates more often than the weather changes in Texas.

For Windows systems, your best resource for this knowledge is the Windows Marketplace. This used to be called the Hardware Compatibility List (HCL), and you'll still hear lots of people refer to it as such. You can check out the Web site (http://testedproducts.windowsmarketplace.com) to see if your product is listed, but most people just look on the box of the device in question (Figure 6-26)—all Windows certified devices will proudly display that they work with Windows.

Figure 6-26
Works with
Windows!

NOTE   Windows Marketplace is also a great resource to check if a particular software program works with your version of Windows.

Step 2: Physical Installation

To install an expansion card successfully, you need to take steps to avoid damaging the card, the motherboard, or both. This means knowing how to handle a card and avoiding electrostatic discharge (ESD) or any other electrical issue. You also need to place the card firmly and completely into an available expansion slot.

Optimally, a card should always be in one of two places: in a computer or in an anti-static bag. When inserting or removing a card, be careful to hold the card only by its edges. Do not hold the card by the slot connectors or touch any components on the board (Figure 6-27).

Figure 6-27
Where to handle
a card

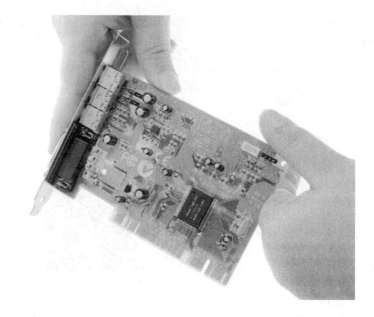

Use an anti-static wrist strap if possible, properly attached to the PC, as noted in Chapter 2. If you don't have a wrist strap, you can use the tech way of avoiding ESD by touching the power supply after you remove the expansion card from its anti-static bag. This puts you, the card, and the PC at the same electrical potential and thus minimizes the risk of ESD.

Modern systems have a trickle of voltage on the motherboard at all times when the computer is plugged into a power outlet. Chapter 8, "Power Supplies," covers power for the PC and how to deal with it in detail, but here's the short version: *Always unplug the PC before inserting an expansion card!* Failure to do so can destroy the card, the motherboard, or both. It's not worth the risk!

Never insert or remove a card at an extreme angle. This may damage the card. A slight angle is acceptable and even necessary when removing a card. Always screw the card to the case with a connection screw. This keeps the card from slipping out and potentially shorting against other cards. Also, many cards use the screw connection to ground the card to the case (Figure 6-28).

Figure 6-28
Always screw
down all cards.

Many technicians have been told to clean the slot connectors if a particular card is not working. This is almost never necessary after a card is installed, and if done improperly, can cause damage. You should clean slot connectors only if you have a card that's been on the shelf for a while and the contacts are obviously dull. *Never use a pencil eraser for this purpose.* Pencil erasers can leave behind bits of residue that wedge between the card and slot, preventing contact and causing the card to fail. Grab a can of contact cleaning solution and use it instead. Contact cleaning solution is designed exactly for this purpose, will clean the contact nicely, and won't leave any residue. You can find contact cleaning solution at any electronics store.

A fully inserted expansion card will sit flush against the back of the PC case—assuming the motherboard is mounted properly, of course—with no gap between the mounting bracket on the card and the screw hole on the case. If the card is properly seated, no contacts will be exposed above the slot. Figure 6-29 shows a properly seated (meaning fitted snugly in the slot) expansion card.

Figure 6-29
Properly seated
expansion card; note
the tight fit between
case and mounting
bracket and the
evenness of the
card in the slot

Step 3: Device Drivers

You know from Chapter 5 that all devices, whether built into the motherboard or added along the way, require BIOS. For almost all expansion cards, that BIOS comes in the form of device drivers loaded from a CD-ROM disc provided by the card manufacturer.

Installing device drivers is fairly straightforward. You should use the correct drivers—kind of obvious, but you'd be surprised by how many techs mess this up—and, if you're upgrading, you might have to unload current drivers before loading new drivers. Finally, if you have a problem, you may need to uninstall the drivers you just loaded or, with Windows XP, roll back to earlier, more stable drivers.

Getting the Correct Drivers

To be sure you have the best possible driver you can get for your device, you should always check the manufacturer's Web site. The drivers that come with a device may work well, but odds are good that you'll find a newer and better driver on the Web site. How do you know that the drivers on the Web site are newer? First, take the easy route: look on the CD. Often the version is printed right on the CD itself. If it's not printed there, you're going to have to load the CD in your CD-ROM drive and poke around. Many driver discs have an AutoRun screen that advertises the version. If there's nothing on the pop-up screen, look for a Readme file (Figure 6-30).

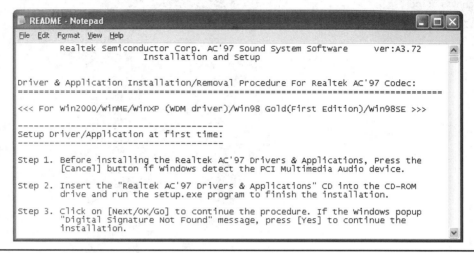

Figure 6-30 Part of a Readme file showing the driver version

Driver or Device?

In almost all cases, you should install the device driver after you install the device. Without the device installed, the driver installation will not see the device and will give an error screen. The only exceptions to this rule are USB and FireWire devices—with these you should always install the driver first!

Removing the Old Drivers

Some cards—and this is especially true with video cards—require you to remove old drivers of the same type before you install the new device. To do this, you must first locate the driver in Device Manager. Right-click the device driver you want to uninstall and select Uninstall (Figure 6-31). Many devices, especially ones that come with a lot of applications, will have an uninstall option in the Add/Remove Programs (Windows 2000) or Add or Remove Programs (Windows XP) applet in the Control Panel (Figure 6-32).

Figure 6-31
Uninstalling a device

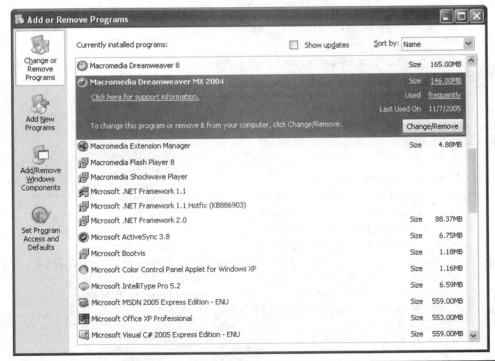

Figure 6-32   The Uninstall option in Add or Remove Programs

Unsigned Drivers

Not all driver makers use the Windows Certification program. When Windows runs into such a driver, it brings up a scary-looking screen (Figure 6-33) that says you're about to install an unsigned driver.

Figure 6-33
Unsigned driver
warning

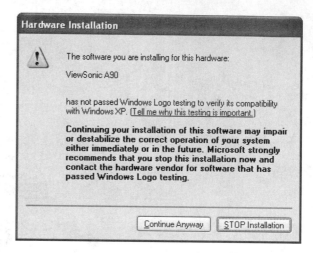

The fact that a company refuses to use the Windows Certification doesn't mean that its drivers are bad—it simply means that they haven't gone through Microsoft's exhaustive quality-assurance certification procedure. If I run into this, I usually check the driver's version to make sure I'm not installing something outdated, and then I just take my chances and install it. (I've yet to encounter a problem with an unsigned driver that I haven't also seen with Windows Certified drivers.)

Installing the New Driver

You've got two ways to install a new driver: using the installation CD directly or using the Add Hardware Wizard in the Control Panel. Most experienced techs prefer to run from the installation CD. Most devices come with extra programs. My motherboard comes with a number of handy applications for monitoring temperature and overclocking. The Add Hardware Wizard does not install anything but the drivers. Granted, some techs find this a blessing because they don't want all the extra junk that sometimes comes with a device, but most install discs give clear options to enable you to pick and choose what you want to install (Figure 6-34).

Figure 6-34
Installation menu

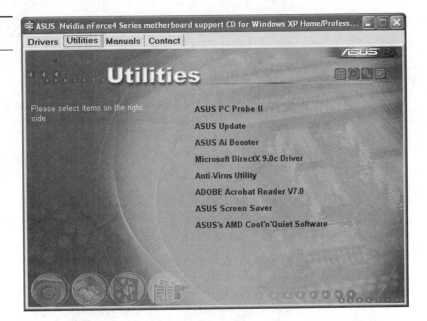

The other reason to use installation CDs instead of the Add Hardware Wizard stems from the fact that many expansion cards are actually many devices in one, and each device needs its own drivers. Sound cards often come with joystick ports, for example, and video cards often have built-in TV tuners. The Add Hardware Wizard will install all the devices, but the installation CD brings them to your attention. Go for the CD program first and save the Add Hardware Wizard for problems, as you'll see in the next section.

Driver Rollback

Windows XP offers the nifty feature of rolling back to previous drivers after an installation or driver upgrade. If you decide to live on the edge and install beta drivers for your video card, for example, and your system becomes frightfully unstable, you can back up to the drivers that worked before. (Not that I've ever had to use that feature, of course!) To access the rollback feature, simply open the Device Manager and access the properties for the device you want to adjust. On the Drivers tab (Figure 6-35), you'll find the Rollback Driver button.

Figure 6-35
Driver rollback
feature

NVIDIA GeForce 6800 Properties

General | Driver | Details | Resources

NVIDIA GeForce 6800

Driver Provider: NVIDIA
Driver Date: 3/9/2006
Driver Version: 8.4.2.1
Digital Signer: Microsoft Windows Hardware Compatibility Publ

Driver Details...   To view details about the driver files.

Update Driver...   To update the driver for this device.

Roll Back Driver   If the device fails after updating the driver, roll
                      back to the previously installed driver.

Uninstall   To uninstall the driver (Advanced).

OK   Cancel

NOTE Many PC enthusiasts try to squeeze every bit of performance out
of their PC components, much like auto enthusiasts tinker with engine
tunings to get a little extra horsepower out of their engines. Expansion
card manufacturers love enthusiasts, who often act as free testers for their
unpolished drivers, known as *beta drivers*. Beta drivers are fine for the most
part, but they can sometimes cause amazing system instability—never a good
thing! If you use beta drivers, make sure you know how to uninstall or roll
back to previous drivers.

Step 4: Verify

As a last step in the installation process, inspect the results of the installation and verify
that the device works properly. Immediately after installing, you should open the Device Manager and verify that Windows sees the device (Figure 6-36). Assuming that
Device Manager shows the device working properly, your next check is to put the device
to work by making it do whatever it is supposed to do. If you installed a printer, print
something; if you installed a scanner, scan something. If it works, you're done!

Figure 6-36
Device Manager
shows the device
working properly.

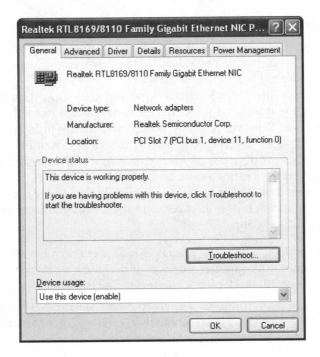

IT Technician

Troubleshooting Expansion Cards

A properly installed expansion card rarely makes trouble—it's the botched installations that produce headaches. Chances are high that you'll have to troubleshoot an expansion card installation at some point, usually from an installation that you botched personally.

The first sign of an improperly installed card usually shows up the moment you first try to get that card to do whatever it's supposed to do and it doesn't do it. When this happens, your primary troubleshooting process is a reinstallation—after checking in with Device Manager.

Other chapters in this book cover specific hardware troubleshooting—sound cards in Chapter 18, for example, and video cards in Chapter 17. Use this section as your general methodology to decide what to look for and how to deal with the problem.

Device Manager

The Device Manager provides the first diagnostic and troubleshooting tool in Windows. After you install a new device, Device Manager gives you many clues if something has gone wrong.

Occasionally, Device Manager may not even show the new device. If that happens, verify that you inserted the device properly and, if needed, that the device has power. Run the Add/Remove Hardware Wizard and see if Windows recognizes the device. If the Device Manager doesn't recognize the device at this point, you have one of two problems: either the device is physically damaged and you must replace it, or the device is an onboard device, not a card, and is turned off in CMOS.

It's rare that Device Manager completely fails to see a device. More commonly, device problems manifest themselves in the Device Manager via error icons—a black "!" or a red "X" or a blue "i."

- A black "!" on a yellow circle indicates that a device is missing, that Windows does not recognize a device, or that there's a device driver problem. A device may still work even while producing this error.

- A red "X" indicates a disabled device (Figure 6-37). This usually points to a device that's been manually turned off, or a damaged device. A device producing this error will not work.

Figure 6-37
An "X" in Device Manager, indicating a problem with the selected device

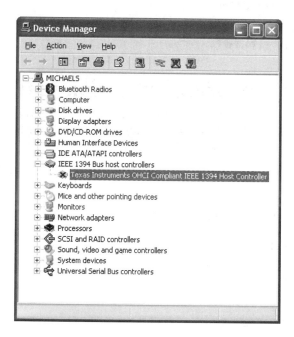

- A blue "i" on a white field indicates a device on which someone has configured the system resources manually. This only occurs on non-ACPI systems. This symbol merely provides information and does not indicate an error with the device.

The "!" symbol is the most common error symbol and usually the easiest to fix. First, double-check the device's connections. Second, try reinstalling the driver with the Update Driver button. To get to the Update Driver button, right-click the desired device in the Device Manager and select Properties. In the Properties dialog box, select the Driver tab. On the Driver tab, click the Update Driver button (Figure 6-38).

Figure 6-38
Updating the driver

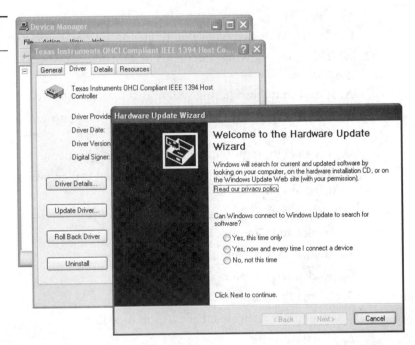

A red "X" error strikes fear into most technicians. If you get one, first check that the device isn't disabled. Right-click on the device and select Enable. If that doesn't work (it often will not), try rolling back the driver (if you updated the driver) or uninstalling (if it's a new install). Shut the system down and make triple-sure you have the card physically installed. Then redo the entire driver installation procedure, making sure you have the most current driver for that device. If none of these procedures works, return the card—it's almost certainly bad.

As you look at the errors in Device Manager, you'll notice error codes for the device that does not work properly. Windows has about 20 error codes, but the fixes still boil down to the same methods just shown. If you really want to frustrate yourself, try the Troubleshooter. It starts most fixes the same way—by reinstalling the device driver.

Chapter Review Questions

1. Which of the following statements about the expansion bus is true?

   A. The expansion bus runs at the speed of the system clock.

   B. The expansion bus crystal sets the speed for the expansion bus.

   C. The CPU communicates with RAM via the expansion bus.

   D. The frontside bus is another name for the expansion bus.

2. Which of the following statements best describes the hexadecimal numbering system?

   A. It is a binary numbering system that uses only two digits, a 0 and a 1.

   B. It is another name for the decimal numbering system with ten digits, 0 through 9.

   C. It is an eight-digit numbering system, using letters A through H.

   D. It is a sixteen-digit numbering system that can express all its values by using four wires.

3. AGP stands for _____ and is an expansion of the _____ bus.

   A. Accelerated Graphics Port, PCI

   B. Alternative Graphics Port, PCI

   C. Accelerated Graphics Port, ISA

   D. Alternative Graphics Port, ISA

4. Which of these devices is likely to still use DMA?

   A. USB flash drive

   B. Floppy drive

   C. Hard drive

   D. CD-ROM drive

5. What does a red "X" next to a device in Device Manager indicate?

   A. A compatible driver has been installed that may not provide all the functions for the device.

   B. The device is missing or Windows cannot recognize it.

   C. The system resources have been assigned manually.

   D. The device has been disabled because it is damaged or has a system resource conflict.

6. What are the standard system resource assignments for LPT2?

   A. I/O address 378 and IRQ7

   B. I/O address 3F8 and IRQ4

C. I/O address 278 and IRQ5

D. I/O address 2F8 and IRQ5

7. When installing an expansion card, which of these should you do?

A. Make sure the computer is plugged into the AC wall outlet.

B. Hold the card only by its slot connectors.

C. Use firm but not excessive force to snap the card into the slot.

D. Avoid letting the metal flange touch the PC case.

8. How does the CPU communicate with a device?

A. It uses the device's I/O addresses over the address bus.

B. It uses the device's IRQ addresses over the data bus.

C. It uses the device's COM port over the address bus.

D. It uses the device's DMA over the data bus.

9. Which of the following does a device use to initiate communication with the CPU?

A. IO/MEM wire

B. Bus mastering

C. DMA

D. IRQ

10. Which variation of the PCI bus was specifically designed for laptops?

A. PCI-X

B. PCIe

C. Mini-PCI

D. AGP

Answers

1. **B.** A separate expansion bus crystal enables the expansion bus to run at a different speed than the frontside bus.

2. **D.** The hexadecimal numbering system represents binary values using the characters 0–9 and A–F.

3. **A.** The Accelerated Graphics Port is a specialized PCI slot used for video cards.

4. **B.** On most modern PCs, only the floppy drive (if one is installed!) still uses classic DMA.

5. **D.** The dreaded red "X" can mean a bad connection, a bad driver, or even a bad card.

6. **C.** The LPT2 port is by default assigned I/O base address 278 and IRQ5.

7. **C.** After handling the card only by the edges and avoiding the slot connectors, you should snap it into an open slot on an unplugged system, pushing firmly and evenly until the metal flange is in contact with the slot on the case.

8. **A.** The CPU uses the device's I/O addresses over the address bus to communicate with that device.

9. **D.** A device uses its IRQ to get the CPU's attention and begin communication.

10. **C.** The Mini-PCI format conserves space and power, making it an ideal card type for use in laptops.

Motherboards

In this chapter, you will learn how to
- Explain how motherboards work
- Identify the types of motherboards
- Explain chipset varieties
- Upgrade and install motherboards
- Troubleshoot motherboard problems

The *motherboard* provides the foundation for the personal computer. Every piece of hardware, from the CPU to the lowliest expansion card, directly or indirectly plugs into the motherboard. The motherboard contains the wires—called *traces*—that make up the different buses of the system. It holds the vast majority of the ports used by the peripherals and it distributes the power from the power supply (Figure 7-1). Without the motherboard, you literally have no PC.

Figure 7-1
Traces visible beneath the CPU socket on a motherboard

How Motherboards Work

Three variable and interrelated characteristics define modern motherboards: form factor, chipset, and components. The *form factor* determines the physical size of the motherboard as well as the general location of components and ports. The *chipset* defines the type of processor and RAM required for the motherboard, and determines to a degree the built-in devices supported by a motherboard, including the expansion slots. Finally, the built-in components determine the core functionality of the system.

Any good tech should be able to make a recommendation to a client about a particular motherboard simply by perusing the specs. Because the motherboard determines function, expansion, and stability for the whole PC, it's essential that you know your motherboards!

Form Factors

Form factors are industry standardized shapes and layouts that enable motherboards to work with cases and power supplies. A single form factor applies to all three components. All motherboards come in a basic rectangular or square shape, for example, but vary in overall size and the layout of built-in components (Figure 7-2). You need to install a motherboard in a case designed to fit it, so the ports and slot openings on the back fit correctly.

The power supply and the motherboard need matching connectors, and different form factors define different connections. Given that the form factor includes the case, motherboard, and power supply—the three parts of the PC most responsible for moving air around inside the PC—the form factor also defines how the air moves around in the case.

Figure 7-2
Typical motherboard

To perform motherboard upgrades and provide knowledgeable recommendations to clients, techs need to know their form factors. The PC industry has adopted—and dropped—a number of form factors over the years with names such as AT, ATX, BTX, and others. Let's start with the granddaddy of all PC form factors, AT.

AT Form Factor

The AT form factor (Figure 7-3), invented by IBM in the early 1980s, was the predominant form factor for motherboards through the mid-1990s. AT is now obsolete. The AT type of motherboard had a large keyboard plug in the same relative spot on the motherboard, and it had a unique, split power socket called *P8/P9*.

Figure 7-3
AT-style
motherboard

The AT motherboard had a few size variations, ranging from large to very large (Figure 7-4). The original AT motherboard was huge, around 12 inches wide by 13 inches deep. PC technology was new and needed lot of space for the various chips needed to run the components of the PC, such as the keyboard.

Figure 7-4
AT motherboard
(bottom) and Baby
AT motherboard
(top)

The single greatest problem with AT motherboards was the lack of external ports. When PCs were first invented, the only devices plugged into the average PC were a monitor and a keyboard. That's what the AT was designed to handle—the only dedicated connector on an AT motherboard was the keyboard plug (Figure 7-5).

Figure 7-5
Keyboard connector on the back of an AT motherboard

Over the years, the number of devices plugged into the back of the PC has grown tremendously. Your average PC today has a keyboard, a mouse, a printer, some speakers, a monitor, and if your system's like mine, four to six USB devices connected to it at any given time. These added components created a demand for a new type of form factor, one with more dedicated connectors for more devices. Many attempts were made to create a new standard form factor. Invariably, these new form factors integrated dedicated connectors for at least the mouse and printer, and many even added connectors for video, sound, and phone lines.

One variation from the AT form factor that enjoyed a degree of success was the slimline form factor. The first slimline form factor was known as LPX (defined in some sources as *low profile extended,* although there's some disagreement). It was replaced by the NLX form factor. (NLX apparently stands for nothing, by the way. It's just a cool grouping of letters.) The LPX and NLX form factors met the demands of the slimline market by providing a central riser slot to enable the insertion of a special riser card (Figure 7-6). Expansion cards then fit into the riser card horizontally. Combining built-in connections with a riser card enabled manufacturers to produce PCs shorter than 4 inches.

Figure 7-6
Riser card on an older motherboard

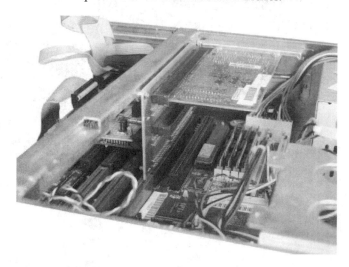

   The main problem with form factors like LPX and NLX was their inflexibility. Certainly, no problem occurred with dedicated connections for devices such as mice or printers, but the new form factors also added connectors for devices like video and sound—devices that were prone to obsolescence, making the motherboard useless the moment a new type of video or sound card came into popularity.

Essentials

ATX Form Factor

There continued to be a tremendous demand for a new form factor—a form factor that had more standard connectors, but at the same time was flexible enough for possible changes in technology. This demand led to the creation of the ATX form factor in 1995 (Figure 7-7). ATX got off to a slow start, but by around 1998 ATX overtook AT to become the most common form factor used today.

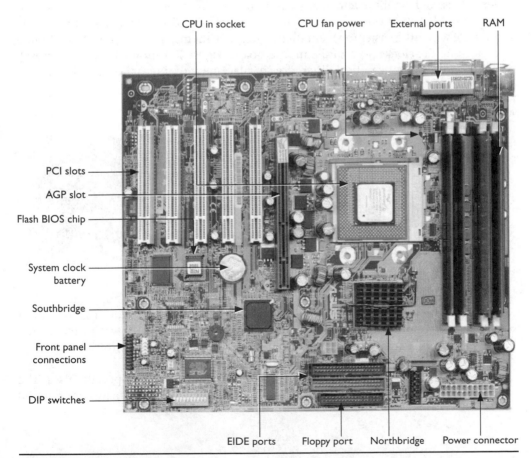

Figure 7-7 Early ATX motherboard

ATX is distinct from AT in the lack of an AT keyboard port, replaced with a rear panel that has all necessary ports built in. Note the mini-DIN (PS/2) keyboard and mouse ports in Figure 7-8, standard features on almost all ATX boards.

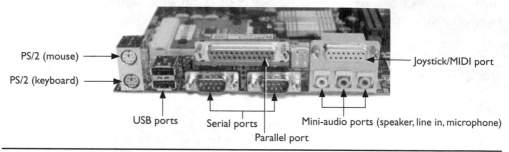

PS/2 (mouse)
PS/2 (keyboard)
Joystick/MIDI port
USB ports
Serial ports
Parallel port
Mini-audio ports (speaker, line in, microphone)

Figure 7-8 ATX ports

The ATX form factor includes many improvements over AT. The position of the power supply enables better air movement. The CPU and RAM are placed to enable easier access. Other improvements, such as placement of RAM closer to the North-bridge and CPU than on AT boards, offer users enhanced performance as well. The shorter the wires, the easier to shield them and make them capable of handling double or quadruple the clock speed of the motherboard. Figure 7-9 shows an AT and an ATX motherboard—note the radical differences in placement of internal connections.

Figure 7-9
AT (left) and ATX (right) motherboards for quick visual comparison

ATX motherboards use a feature called *soft power*. This means that they can use soft-ware to turn the PC on and off. The physical manifestation of soft power is the power switch. Instead of the thick power cord used in AT systems, an ATX power switch is little more than a pair of small wires leading to the motherboard. We delve into this in more detail in Chapter 8, "Power Supplies."

The success of ATX has spawned two form factor subtypes for specialty uses. The microATX motherboard (Figure 7-10) floats in at a svelte 9.6 by 9.6 inches or about 30

Figure 7-10
Micro-ATX

percent smaller than standard ATX, yet still uses the standard ATX connections. A micro-ATX motherboard fits into a standard ATX case or in the much smaller microATX cases. Note that not all microATX motherboards have the same physical size. You'll sometimes see microATX motherboards referred to with the Greek symbol for micro, as in μATX.

In 1999, Intel created a variant of the microATX called the FlexATX. FlexATX motherboards have maximum dimensions of just 9 by 7.5 inches, which makes them the smallest motherboards in the ATX standard. Although FlexATX motherboards can use a standard ATX power supply, most FlexATX systems use a special FlexATX-only power supply. This diminutive power supply fits into tight FlexATX cases.

NOTE   You'll find many techs and Web sites use the term *mini-ATX* to refer to motherboards smaller than a full ATX board. This is technically incorrect. The specifications for these small boards use only the terms *microATX* and *FlexATX*.

Keep in mind that each main type of form factor requires its own case. AT motherboards go into AT cases, NLX motherboards go into NLX cases, and ATX motherboards go into ATX cases. You cannot replace one form factor with another without purchasing a new case (Figure 7-11). The exception to this rule is that larger form factor ATX cases can handle any smaller-sized form factor motherboards.

Figure 7-11
That's not going
to fit!

BTX Form Factor

Even though ATX addressed ventilation, faster CPUs and powerful graphics cards create phenomenal amounts of heat, motivating the PC industry to create the "coolest" new form factor used today—the Balanced Technology eXtended (BTX) form factor (Figure 7-12). BTX defines three subtypes: standard BTX, microBTX, and picoBTX, designed to replace ATX, microATX, and FlexATX, respectively.

Figure 7-12
microBTX
motherboard

At first glance, BTX looks like ATX, but notice that the I/O ports and the expansion slots have switched sides. You can't put a BTX motherboard in an ATX case! BTX does not change the power connection, so there's no such thing as a BTX power supply.

> **NOTE** Many manufacturers sell what they call "BTX power supplies." These are actually marketing gimmicks. See Chapter 8, "Power Supplies," for details.

Everything in the BTX standard is designed to improve cooling. BTX cases vent in cool air from the front and warm air out the back. CPUs are moved to the front of the motherboard so they get cool air coming in from the front of the case. BTX defines a special heat sink and fan assembly called the *thermal unit*. The thermal unit's fan blows the hot CPU air directly out the back of the case, as opposed to the ATX method of just blowing the air into the case.

The BTX standard is clearly a much cooler option than ATX, but the PC industry tends to take its time when making big changes like moving to a new form factor. As a result, BTX has not yet made much of an impact in the industry, and BTX motherboards, cases, and thermal units are still fairly rare. BTX will take off to become the next big thing or disappear in a cloud of disinterest—only time will tell.

Proprietary Form Factors

Several major PC makers, including Dell and Sony, make motherboards that work only with their cases. These *proprietary* motherboards enable these companies to create systems that stand out from the generic ones and, not coincidently, push you to get service and upgrades from their authorized dealers. Some of the features you'll see in proprietary systems are riser boards like you see with the NLX form factor—part of a motherboard separate from the main one, but connected by a cable of some sort—and unique power connections. Proprietary motherboards drive techs crazy as replacement parts tend to cost more and are not readily available.

Chipset

Every motherboard has a chipset. The chipset determines the type of processor the motherboard accepts, the type and capacity of RAM, and what sort of internal and external devices the motherboard supports. As you learned in earlier chapters, the chips in a PC's chipset serve as electronic interfaces through which the CPU, RAM, and input/output devices interact. Chipsets vary in feature, performance, and stability, so they factor hugely in the purchase or recommendation of a particular motherboard. Good techs know their chipsets!

Because the chipset facilitates communication between the CPU and other devices in the system, its component chips are relatively centrally located on the motherboard (Figure 7-13). Most modern chipsets are composed of two primary chips—the Northbridge and the Southbridge.

Figure 7-13
Northbridge
(under the fan) and
Southbridge (lower
right, labeled VIA)

The Northbridge chip on Intel-based motherboards helps the CPU work with RAM, as mentioned in earlier chapters. On AMD-based motherboards, the Northbridge provides the communication with the video card, rather than memory, because the memory controller is built into the CPU. Current Northbridge chips do a lot and thus get pretty hot, so they get their own heat sink and fan assembly (Figure 7-14).

Figure 7-14
Heat sink and fan
on a Northbridge

The Southbridge handles some expansion devices and mass storage drives, such as hard drives. Most Southbridge chips don't need extra cooling, leaving the chip exposed or passively cooled with only a heat sink. This makes the Southbridge a great place to see the manufacturer of the chipset, such as Intel (Figure 7-15).

Figure 7-15
An Intel NH82801 Southbridge chip on a motherboard

Most motherboards support very old technologies such as floppy drives, infrared connections, parallel ports, and modems. Although supporting these old devices was once part of the Southbridge's job, hardly any modern chipsets still support these devices. Motherboard manufacturers add a third chip called the *Super I/O chip* to handle these chores. Figure 7-16 shows a typical Super I/O chip.

Figure 7-16
Super I/O chip on ASUS motherboard

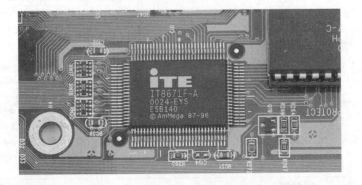

 NOTE Super I/O chips work with chipsets but are not part of the chipset. Motherboard makers purchase them separately from chipsets.

The system ROM chip provides part of the BIOS for the chipset, but only a bare-bones, generic level of support. The chipset still needs support for the rest of the things it can do. So, how do expansion devices get BIOS? Software drivers, of course, and the same holds true for modern chipsets. You have to load the proper drivers for the specific OS to support all the features of today's chipsets. Without software drivers, you'll never create a stable, fully functional PC. All motherboards ship with a CD-ROM disc with drivers, support programs, and extra special goodies such as anti-virus software (Figure 7-17).

Figure 7-17
Driver disc for ASUS
motherboard

There are a limited number of chipset makers. Both AMD and Intel make chipsets, but although they may control the CPU market, they have some serious competition in the chipset market. Two third-party chipset makers, VIA Technologies and NVIDIA Corporation, make some very popular chipsets. Motherboard manufacturers incorporate the chipsets into motherboards that match the feature set of the chipset. Some of the companies produce chipsets designed for both Intel and AMD CPUs, whereas others choose one or the other company to support. Chipset companies rise and fall every few years, with one company seeming to hold the hot position for a while until another company comes along to unseat them.

NOTE Due to the purchase by AMD of chipset (and video card) maker ATI in 2006, the chipset field has the potential to change again. ATI makes a nice line of mobile and desktop chipsets. Backed by AMD's muscle, the combined companies might give VIA and NVIDIA a run for their money. Only time will tell, but it's something for informed CompTIA A+ certified techs to watch.

NOTE In an average year, chipset makers collectively produce around one hundred new chipset models for the PC market.

Chipset makers don't always use the terms Northbridge and Southbridge. Chipsets for AMD-based motherboards tend to use the terms, but Intel-based motherboards prefer to use the terms Memory Controller Hub (MCH) for the Northbridge and I/O Controller Hub (ICH) for the Southbridge. Regardless of the official name, Northbridge and Southbridge are the commonly used terms. Figure 7-18 shows a schematic with typical chipset chores for a VIA K8T900 chipset.

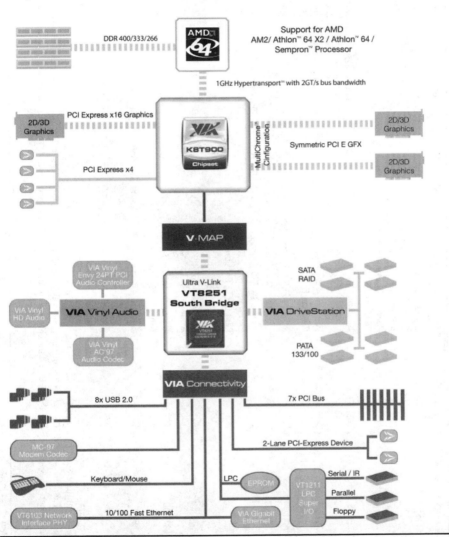

Figure 7-18 Schematic of a modern chipset (courtesy of VIA Technologies)

It would be impossible to provide an inclusive chipset chart here that wouldn't be obsolete by the time you pick this book up off the shelf at your local tech pub (doesn't everybody have one of those?), but Table 7-1 gives you an idea of what to look for as you research motherboards for recommendations and purchases.

Chipset	Northbridge	Southbridge	CPU	FSB (MHz)	RAM	HDD
Intel 975X Express	82955X MCH	82801GB ICH, 82801GR ICH, or 82801GDH ICH	LGA775 Core 2 Extreme, Core 2 Duo, Pentium 4, Pentium 4 with HT, Pentium Extreme Edition, Pentium D	1066, 800	Dual-channel DDR2 up to 8 GB	4× SATA 3 Gbps
Intel P965 Express	82P965 GMCH	P965 ICH8	All LGA775	533, 800, 1066	Dual-channel DDR2 up to 8 GB	6× SATA 3 Gbps
Intel 910GL Express	82910G GMCH	ICH6 or ICH6R	Pentium 4 with HT, Celeron D	533	DDR up to 2 GB	4× SATA 1.5 Gbps
NVIDIA nForce4	nForce4[1]	n/a[1]	Athlon 64, Athlon 64 FX, Sempron	n/a[2]	n/a[2]	4× SATA 1.5 Gbps
NVIDIA nForce 570 SLI Intel	nForce 570 SLI[1]	n/a[1]	Intel LGA 775: Core 2 Extreme, Core 2 Duo, Pentium D, Pentium 4, Celeron D	533, 800, 1066	Dual-channel DDR2	4× SATA 3 Gbps, 4× PATA
NVIDIA nForce 590 SLI AMD	nForce 590 SLI[1]	n/a[1]	Athlon 64, Athlon 64 FX, Athlon 64 X2	n/a[2]	n/a[2]	6× SATA 3 Gbps, 2× PATA
VIA K8 Series	K8T900	VT8251	Opteron, Athlon 64, Athlon FX, Sempron	n/a[2]	n/a[2]	4× SATA 3 Gbps, 4× PATA 133 MBps
VIA P4 Series	PT890	VT8237A	Pentium 4, Celeron	400, 533, 800, 1066	SDRAM with ECC, DDR, DDR2 up to 4 GB	2×/4× SATA 1.5 Mbps, 4× PATA 133 MBps

1. NVIDIA does not make a Northbridge/Southbridge distinction with the nForce chipset.
2. Because the Athlon 64 varieties and the Sempron CPUs have the memory controller built into the CPU, the Frontside bus and memory clock speeds depend on the motherboard speed rather than the chipset. The speed between the CPU and the chipset runs up to 1066 MHz, hyperthreaded. The amount of RAM supported likewise depends on the CPU rather than the chipset.

Table 7-1 PCI Express Chipset Comparison Chart

So why do good techs need to know the hot chipsets in detail? The chipset defines almost every motherboard feature short of the CPU itself. Techs love to discuss chipsets and expect a fellow tech to know the differences between one chipset and another. You also need to be able to recommend a motherboard that suits a client's needs.

Motherboard Components

The connections and capabilities of a motherboard sometimes differ from that of the chipset the motherboard uses. This disparity happens for a couple of reasons. First, a particular chipset may support eight USB ports, but to keep costs down the manufacturer might include only four ports. Second, a motherboard maker may choose to install extra features—ones not supported by the chipset—by adding additional chips. A common example is a motherboard that supports FireWire. Other technologies you might find are built-in sound, hard drive RAID controllers, and AMR or CNR slots for modems, network cards, and more.

USB/FireWire

Most chipsets support USB and most motherboards come with FireWire as well, but it seems no two motherboards offer the same port arrangement. My motherboard supports eight USB ports and two FireWire ports, for example, but if you look on the back of the motherboard, you'll only see four USB ports and one FireWire port. So, where are the other ports? Well, this motherboard has special connectors for the other four USB and one FireWire port, and the motherboard comes with the dongles you need to connect them (Figure 7-19). These dongles typically use an extra slot on the back of the case.

Figure 7-19
USB/FireWire
dongles

These dongle connectors are standardized, so many cases have built-in front USB/FireWire ports that have dongles attached. This is very handy for USB or FireWire devices you might want to plug and unplug frequently, such as a thumb drive or digital camera. You can also buy add-on front USB and FireWire devices that go into a 3.5-inch drive bay, like a floppy drive (Figure 7-20).

Figure 7-20
Front USB and
FireWire drive
bay device

Sound

Quite a few motherboards come with onboard sound chips. These sound chips are usually pretty low quality compared to even a lower-end sound card, but onboard sound is cheap and doesn't take up a slot. These connectors are identical to the ones used on sound cards, so we'll save more discussion for Chapter 18, "Sound."

RAID

RAID stands for *redundant array of independent devices* and is very common on motherboards. There are many types of RAID, but the RAID on motherboards usually only supports *mirroring* (the process of using two drives to hold the same data, which is good for safety because if one drive dies, the other still has all the data) or *striping* (making two drives act as one drive by spreading data across them, which is good for speed). RAID is a very cool but complex topic that's discussed in detail in Chapter 9, "Hard Drive Technologies."

AMR/CNR

The U.S. Federal Communications Commission (FCC) must certify any electronic device to ensure that it does not transmit unwanted electronic signals. This process is a bit expensive, so in the very late 1990s Intel came up with a special slot called the *audio modem riser (AMR)*. See Figure 7-21. An AMR slot was designed to take specialized AMR devices (modems, sound cards, and network cards). An AMR device would get one FCC certification and then be used on as many motherboards as the manufacturer wanted without going through the FCC certification process again. AMR was quickly replaced with the more advanced *communications and networking riser (CNR)*. Many motherboard manufacturers used these slots in the early 2000s, but they've lost popularity because most motherboard makers simply use onboard networking and sound.

Figure 7-21
AMR slot

Figure 7-21
AMR slot

Upgrading and Installing Motherboards

To most techs, the concept of adding or replacing a motherboard can be extremely intimidating. It really shouldn't be; motherboard installation is a common and necessary part of PC repair. It is inexpensive and easy, although it can sometimes be a little tedious and messy due to the large number of parts involved. This section covers the process of installation and replacement and will show you some of the tricks that make this necessary process easy to handle.

IT Technician

Choosing the Motherboard and Case

Choosing a motherboard and case, whether new or old, can prove quite a challenge for a tech. You first have to figure out the type of motherboard you want, such as AMD- or Intel-based. Then you need to think about the form factor, which of course influences the type of case you'll need. Third, how rich in features is the motherboard and how tough is it to configure? You've got to read the motherboard manual to find out! Finally, you need to select the case that matches your space needs, budget, and form factor. Let's look at each step in a little more detail.

EXAM TIP Every CompTIA A+ technician should know how to select and install a motherboard appropriate for a client or customer. This is particularly important if you're studying for the CompTIA A+ 220-604 Depot Technician exam, but less so for those working toward the CompTIA A+ 220-603 Help Desk Technician exam.

First, determine what motherboard you need. What CPU are you using? Will the motherboard work with that CPU? Because most of us buy the CPU and the motherboard at the same time, make the seller guarantee that the CPU will work with the motherboard. If you can, choose a motherboard that works with much higher speeds than the CPU you can afford; that way you can upgrade later. How much RAM do you intend to install? Are extra RAM sockets available for future upgrades?

A number of excellent motherboard manufacturers are available today. Some of the more popular brands are Abit, Asus, Biostar, DFI, Gigabyte, Intel, MSI, and Shuttle. Your supplier may also have some lesser-known but perfectly acceptable brands of motherboards. As long as the supplier has an easy return policy, it's perfectly fine to try one of these.

Second, make sure you're getting a form factor that works with your case. Don't try to put a regular ATX motherboard into a microATX case!

Third, all motherboards come with a technical manual, better known as the motherboard book (Figure 7-22). You must have this book! This book is your only source for all of the critical information about the motherboard. If you set up CPU or RAM timings incorrectly in CMOS, for example, and you have a dead PC, where would you find the CMOS clear jumper? Where do you plug in the speaker? Even if you let someone else install the motherboard, insist on the motherboard book; you will need it.

Figure 7-22
Motherboard
box and book

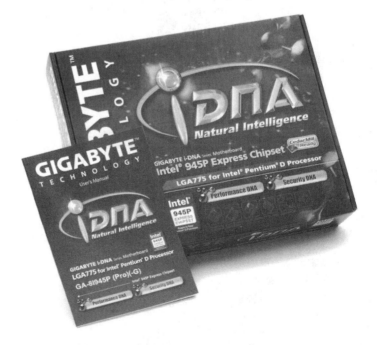

Fourth, pick your case carefully. Cases come in six basic sizes: slimline, desktop, mini-tower, mid-tower, tower, and cube. Slimline and desktop models generally sit on the desk, beneath the monitor. The various tower cases usually occupy a bit of floor space next to the desk. The mini-tower and mid-tower cases are the most popular choices. Make sure you get a case that will fit your motherboard—many microATX and all FlexATX cases are too small for a regular ATX motherboard. Cube cases generally require a specific motherboard, so be prepared to buy both pieces at once. A quick test fit before you buy saves a lot of return trips to the supplier.

Cases come with many different options, but three more common options point to a better case. One option is a removable face (Figure 7-23)—many cheaper cases will screw the face into the metal frame using wood screws. A removable face makes disassembly much easier.

Figure 7-23
Removable face

Another option is a detachable motherboard mount. Clearly, the motherboard will have to be attached to the case in some fashion. In better cases, this is handled by a removable tray or plate (Figure 7-24). This enables you to attach the motherboard to the case separately, saving you from the chore of sticking your arms into the case to turn screws.

Figure 7-24
Motherboard tray

The third option, front-mounted ports for USB, FireWire, and headphones, can make using a PC much easier. Better cases offer these ports, although you can also get add-on components that fit into the increasingly useless floppy drive bay to bring added front connectivity to the PC. Figure 7-25 shows a case with both types of front connectors.

Figure 7-25
Case with both front-mounted ports and an add-on flash memory card reader

Power supplies often come with the case. Watch out for "really good deal" cases, because that invariably points to a cheap or missing power supply. You also need to verify that the power supply has sufficient wattage. This issue is handled in Chapter 8, "Power Supplies."

Building a Recommendation

Family, friends, and potential clients often solicit the advice of a tech when they're thinking about upgrading their PC. This solicitation puts you on the spot to make not just any old recommendation, but one that works with the needs and budget of the potential upgrader. To do this successfully, you need to manage expectations and ask the right questions. Let's take a quick look at how you might do this.

Start by finding out what the upgrader wants to do that compels him or her to upgrade. Write it down! Some of the common motivations for upgrading are to play that hot new game or to take advantage of new technology. What's the minimum system needed to run tomorrow's action games? What do you need to make multimedia sing?

Does the motherboard need to have FireWire and Hi-Speed USB built in to accommodate digital video and better printers?

Your next line of inquiry should be to find out how much of the current system the upgrader wants to save. Upgrading a motherboard can very quickly turn into a complete system rebuild. How old is the case? If it's an AT case, you pretty much need to look at a full computer replacement, but if it's a generic ATX case, you can usually save that much. On the other hand, if you want to use front-mounted USB and FireWire ports, then you'll want a new case as well. You'll most likely want to replace the CPU, so your first decision is AMD vs. Intel. The former gives you more bang for the buck, but the latter offers peace of mind for non-techs. What about RAM? Do you stick with the SDRAM or DDR SDRAM currently in the PC and go for a lower-end board that supports the older technology, or buy a board that uses DDR2? Do you go for a motherboard that supports AGP—and thus keep the current video card—or go for a PCI Express board that will require a new video card as well?

Once you've gathered information on motivation and assessed the current PC of the upgrader, it's time to get down to business: field trip time! This is a great excuse to get to the computer store and check out the latest motherboards and gadgets. Don't forget to jot down notes and prices while you're there! By the end of the field trip, you should have the information to give the upgrader an honest assessment of what an upgrade will entail, at least in monetary terms. Be honest—in other words, don't just tell the upgrader what you think he or she wants to hear—and you won't get in trouble!

Installing the Motherboard

If you're replacing a motherboard, first remove the old motherboard. Begin by removing all the cards. Also remove anything else that might impede removal or installation of the motherboard, such as hard or floppy drives. Keep track of your screws—the best idea is to return the screws to their mounting holes temporarily, at least until you can reinstall the parts. Sometimes even the power supply has to be removed temporarily to enable access to the motherboard. Document the position of the little wires for the speaker, power switch, and reset button in case you need to reinstall them.

 EXAM TIP The CompTIA A+ Essentials exam will test you on the basics of installing a motherboard, so you need to know this section!

Unscrew the motherboard. *It will not simply lift out.* The motherboard mounts to the case via small connectors called *standouts* that slide into keyed slots or screw into the bottom of the case (Figure 7-26). Screws then go into the standouts to hold the motherboard in place. Be sure to place the standouts properly before installing the new motherboard.

 CAUTION Watch out for ESD here! Remember that it's very easy to damage or destroy a CPU and RAM with a little electrostatic discharge. It's also fairly easy to damage the motherboard with ESD. Wear your anti-static wrist strap!

Figure 7-26
Standout on a
case, ready for
the motherboard

A lot of techs install the CPU, CPU fan, and RAM into the motherboard before installing the motherboard into the case. This helps in several ways, especially with a new system. First, you want to make certain that the CPU and RAM work well with the motherboard and with each other—without that, you have no hope of setting up a stable system. Second, installing these components first prevents the phenomenon of *flexing* the motherboard. Some cases don't provide quite enough support for the motherboard, and pushing in RAM can make the board bend. Third, attaching a CPU fan can be a bear of a task, one that's considerably easier to do on a table top than within the confines of a case. Finally, on motherboards that require you to set jumpers or switches, it's much easier to read the tiny information stenciled on the PCB before you add the shadows from the case! If necessary, set any jumpers and switches for the specific CPU according to information from the motherboard manual.

When you insert the new motherboard, do not assume that you will put the screws and standouts in the same place as they were in your old motherboard. When it comes to the placement of screws and standouts, only one rule applies: anywhere it fits. Do not be afraid to be a little tough here! Installing motherboards can be a wiggling, twisting, knuckle-scraping process.

CAUTION Pay attention to the location of the standouts if you're swapping a motherboard. If you leave a screw-type standout beneath a spot on the motherboard where you can't add a screw and then apply power to the motherboard, you run the risk of shorting the motherboard.

Once you get the motherboard mounted in the case with the CPU and RAM properly installed, it's time to insert the power connections and test it. A POST card can be helpful with the system test because you won't have to add the speaker, a video card, monitor, and keyboard to verify that the system is booting. If you have a POST card, start the system and watch to see if the POST takes place—you should see a number of POST codes before the POST stops. If you don't have a POST card, install a keyboard, speaker, video card, and monitor. Boot the system and see if the BIOS information shows up on the screen. If it does, you're probably okay. If it doesn't, it's time to refer to the motherboard book to see where a mistake was made.

Wires, Wires, Wires

The last, and often the most frustrating, part of motherboard installation is connecting the LEDs, buttons, and front-mounted ports on the front of the box. These usually include the following:

- Soft power
- Reset button
- Speaker
- Hard drive activity LED
- Power LED
- USB
- FireWire
- Sound

These wires have specific pin connections to the motherboard. Although you can refer to the motherboard book for their location, usually a quick inspection of the motherboard will suffice for an experienced tech (Figure 7-27).

Figure 7-27
Motherboard wire connections labeled on the motherboard

A few rules need to be followed when installing these wires. First, the lights are LEDs, not light bulbs—they have a positive and negative side. If they don't work one way, turn the connector around and try the other. Second, when in doubt, guess. Incorrect installation only results in the device not working; it won't damage the computer. Refer to the motherboard book for the correct installation. The third and last rule is that with the exception of the soft power switch on an ATX system, you do not need any of these wires for the computer to run! Many techs often simply ignore these wires, although this would not be something I'd do to any system but my own!

No hard-and-fast rule exists for determining the function of each wire. Often, the function of each wire is printed on the connector (Figure 7-28). If not, track each wire to the LED or switch to determine its function.

Figure 7-28
Sample of case wires

Troubleshooting Motherboards

Motherboards fail. Not often, but motherboards and motherboard components can die from many causes: time, dust, cat hair, or simply slight manufacturing defects made worse by the millions of amps of current sluicing through the motherboard traces. Installing cards, electrostatic discharge, flexing the motherboard one time too many when swapping out RAM or drives—any of these factors can cause a motherboard to fail. The motherboard is a hard-working, often abused component of the PC! Unfortunately for the common tech, troubleshooting a motherboard problem can be very difficult and time-consuming. Let's wrap this chapter with a look at symptoms of a failing motherboard, techniques for troubleshooting, and the options you have when you discover a motherboard problem.

 EXAM TIP If you're studying for the CompTIA A+ 220-604 Depot Technician exam, pay particular attention to the techniques for troubleshooting motherboards.

Symptoms

Motherboard failures commonly fall into three types: catastrophic, component, and ethereal. With a catastrophic failure, the PC just won't boot. This sort of problem happens with brand-new systems due to manufacturing defects—often called a *burn-in fail-*

ure—and to any system that gets a shock of electrostatic discharge. Burn-in failure is uncommon, but usually happens in the first 30 days of use. Swap out the motherboard for a replacement and you should be fine. If you accidentally zap your motherboard when inserting a card or moving wires around, be chagrined. Change your daring ways and wear an anti-static wrist strap!

Component failure happens rarely, but appears as flaky connections between a device and motherboard, or as intermittent problems. A hard drive plugged into a faulty controller on the motherboard, for example, might show up in CMOS autodetect, but be inaccessible in Windows. A serial controller that worked fine for months until a big storm took out the external modem hooked to it, but doesn't work anymore, even with a replacement modem, is another example.

The most difficult of the three types of symptoms to diagnose are those I call *ethereal* symptoms. Stuff just doesn't work all the time. The PC reboots itself. You get blue screens of death in the midst of heavy computing, like right before you smack the villain and rescue the damsel. What can cause such symptoms? If you answered any of the following, you win the prize:

- Faulty component
- Buggy device driver
- Buggy application software
- Slight corruption of the operating system
- Power supply problems

Err…you get the picture.

What a nightmare scenario to troubleshoot! The Way of the Tech knows paths through such perils, though, so let's turn to troubleshooting techniques now.

Techniques

To troubleshoot a potential motherboard failure requires time, patience, and organization. Some problems will certainly be quicker to solve than others. If the hard drive doesn't work as expected, as in the example above, check the settings on the drive. Try a different drive. Try the same drive with a different motherboard to verify that it's a good drive. Like every other troubleshooting technique, all you try to do with motherboard testing is to isolate the problem by eliminating potential factors.

This three-part system—check, replace, verify good component—works for the simpler and the more complicated motherboard problems. You can even apply the same technique to ethereal-type problems that might be anything, but you should add one more verb: *document*. Take notes on the individual components tested so you don't repeat efforts or waste time. Plus, this can lead to the establishment of patterns. Being able to re-create a system crash by performing certain actions in a specific order can often lead you to the root of the problem. Document your actions. Motherboard testing is time-consuming enough without adding inefficiency!

Options

Once you determine that the motherboard has problems, you have several options for fixing the three types of failures. If you have a catastrophic failure, you must replace the motherboard. Even if it works somewhat, don't mess around. The motherboard should provide bedrock stability for the system. If it's even remotely buggy or problematic, get rid of it!

If you have a component failure, you can often replace the component with an add-on card that will be as good as or better than the failed device. Promise Technologies, for example, makes fine hard drive controller cards that can replace one or both hard drive controllers on the motherboard (Figure 7-29).

Figure 7-29
Promise Technology
PCI hard drive
controller card

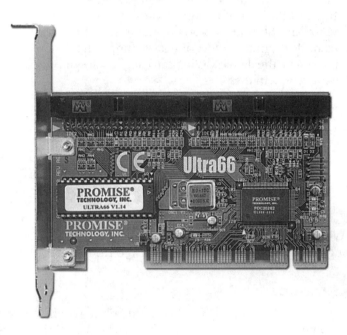

 CAUTION If you've lost components due to ESD or a power surge, then you would most likely be better off replacing the motherboard. The damage you *can't* see can definitely sneak up to bite you and create system instability.

If your component failure is more a technology issue rather than physical damage, then you can try upgrading the BIOS on the motherboard. As you'll recall from Chapter 5 on BIOS, every motherboard comes with a small set of code that enables the CPU to communicate properly with the devices built into the motherboard. You can quite readily upgrade this programming by *flashing the BIOS:* running a small command-line program to write new BIOS in the Flash ROM chip. Figure 7-30 shows a couple of typical Flash ROMs. Refer back to Chapter 5 for the details on flashing.

Figure 7-30
AMI and Award
Flash ROM chips

Flashing the BIOS for a motherboard can fix a lot of system stability problems and provide better implementation of built-in technology. What it cannot do for your system is improve the hardware. If AMD comes out with a new, improved, lower-voltage Athlon 64, for example, and your motherboard cannot scale down the voltage properly, then you cannot use that CPU—even if it fits in your motherboard's Socket AM2. No amount of BIOS flashing can change the hardware built into your motherboard.

Finally, if you have an ethereal, ghost-in-the-machine type of problem that you have finally determined to be motherboard related, you have only a couple of options for fixing the problem. You can flash the BIOS in a desperate attempt to correct whatever it is, which sometimes does work and is less expensive than the other option. Or, you can replace the motherboard.

Beyond A+

Shuttle Form Factor

In the early 2000s, Shuttle started making a very interesting line of tiny cube-shaped PCs called XPCs that became an overnight sensation and continue to be popular today (Figure 7-31). These boxes use a tiny, proprietary form factor motherboard, called *Shuttle Form Factor*, installed in a proprietary case with a proprietary power supply. Originally, these systems were sold *barebones*, meaning they came with only a motherboard, case and power supply. You had to supply a CPU, RAM, video card, keyboard, mouse, and monitor. Shuttle now produces a full line of computers.

Figure 7-31
Shuttle XPC (photo courtesy of Shuttle Computer Group, Inc.)

Many companies followed Shuttle's lead and started making cube or cube-like small cases. You'll hear these cases commonly referred to as *small form factor (SFF)*, but there's no industry-wide standard. Most SFF cases accommodate microATX and Flex-ATX motherboards.

Mini-ITX

If you really want to get small, check out Mini-ITX (Figure 7-32). Developed by VIA Technologies in 2001, mini-ITX has a maximum size of only 17 centimeters by 17 centimeters! These tiny systems only use the VIA C3 family of CPUs, so if you want to get really picky, mini-ITX is a proprietary computer system, not really a form factor. Mini-ITX also has its own tiny power supply standard. The low power requirements don't require a fan on some systems. The VIA C3 CPUS aren't as powerful as the latest offerings from Intel and AMD, but they're great for specialized jobs such as home theater systems or manufacturing.

Figure 7-32
Mini-ITX
motherboard

NOTE   Watch out for all the pretty colors on today's motherboards! To catch the consumer's eye, a lot of motherboard manufacturers have started making wildly colorful motherboard components. There is no universally accepted standard for connection colors on the inside of a motherboard.

Chapter Review Questions

1. Which of the following form factors dominates the PC industry?

   A. AT

   B. ATX

   C. BTX

   D. CTX

2. Which of the following form factors offers the best cooling?

   A. AT

   B. ATX

   C. BTX

   D. CTX

3. On Intel-based motherboards, which chip enables the CPU to interact with RAM?

   A. Memorybridge

   B. Northbridge

   C. Southbridge

   D. Super I/O

4. On modern motherboards, which chip most commonly supports floppy drives and infrared ports?

   A. Memorybridge

   B. Northbridge

   C. Southbridge

   D. Super I/O

5. Brian bought a new motherboard that advertised support for eight USB ports. When he pulled the motherboard out of the box, however, he found that it only had four USB ports! What's likely the issue here?

   A. The extra four USB ports will connect to the front of the case or via a dongle to an expansion slot.

   B. The extra four USB ports require an add-on expansion card.

   C. The FireWire port will have a splitter that makes it four USB ports.

   D. The motherboard chipset might support eight USB ports, but the manufacturer only included four ports.

6. Which of the following chips enables an Athlon 64 to use dual-channel DDR RAM?

   A. ATI 200 Express

   B. NVIDIA nForce 570 SLI Intel

   C. NVIDIA nForce 590 SLI AMD

   D. None of the above

7. Martin bought a new motherboard to replace his older ATX motherboard. As he left the shop, the tech on duty called after him, "Check your standouts!" What could the tech have meant?

   A. Standouts are the connectors on the motherboard for the front panel buttons, like the on/off switch and reset button.

   B. Standouts are the metal edges on some cases that aren't rolled.

   C. Standouts are the metal connectors that attach the motherboard to the case.

   D. Standouts are the dongles that enable a motherboard to support more than four USB ports.

8. Amanda bought a new system that, right in the middle of an important presentation, gave her a blue screen of death. Now her system won't boot at all, not even to CMOS. After extensive troubleshooting, she determined that the motherboard was at fault and replaced it. Now the system runs fine. What was the most likely cause of the problem?

   A. Burn-in failure

   B. Electro-static discharge

   C. Component failure

   D. Power supply failure

9. Solon has a very buggy computer that keeps locking up at odd moments and rebooting spontaneously. He suspects the motherboard. How should he test it?

   A. Check settings and verify good components.

   B. Verify good components and document all testing.

   C. Replace the motherboard first to see if the problems disappear.

   D. Check settings, verify good components, replace components, and document all testing.

10. Steve has been tasked to upgrade ten systems at his office. The systems currently have microATX motherboards with 512 MB of DDR RAM and Athlon XP CPUs.
    Primary objective: Upgrade ten systems.
    Optional objectives: Use the current cases and use the current RAM.
    Proposed solution: Purchase ten microATX motherboards with NVIDIA nForce 570 SLI Intel chipsets and ten Pentium D CPUs.
    The proposed solution:

    A. Accomplishes only the primary objective.

    B. Accomplishes the primary objective and one of the optional objectives.

    C. Accomplishes the primary objective and both of the optional objectives.

    D. Accomplishes neither the primary nor the optional objectives.

Answers

1. **B.** Almost all modern motherboards follow the ATX form factor.

2. **C.** Although not widely adopted by the industry, BTX motherboards offer superior cooling to AT or ATX systems.

3. **B.** The Northbridge enables the communication between the CPU and RAM.

4. **D.** The Super I/O chip handles older technologies such as floppy drives and infrared ports.

5. **A.** The extra four USB ports most likely connect to the front of the case or via a dongle to an expansion slot.

6. **D.** Athlon 64 CPUs have a memory controller built in; thus, none of the chips listed handles memory access for the CPU.

7. **C.** Standouts are the metal connectors that attach the motherboard to the case.

8. **A.** Although all the answers are plausible, the best answer here is that her system suffered burn-in failure.

9. **D.** Solon needs to check settings, verify good components, replace components, and document all testing.

10. **B.** The motherboards would fit just fine in the cases because the switch from AMD to Intel CPUs has nothing to do with the form factor of the motherboards. Steve slipped up, however, because the chipset on the new motherboards requires DDR2 rather than DDR RAM.

Power Supplies

In this chapter, you will learn how to
- Explain the basics of electricity
- Describe the details about powering the PC
- Install, maintain, and troubleshoot power supplies

Powering the PC requires a single box—the power supply—that takes electricity from the wall socket and transforms it into electricity to run the motherboard and other internal components. Figure 8-1 shows a typical power supply inside a case. All the wires dangling out of it connect to the motherboard and peripherals.

Figure 8-1
Typical power supply mounted inside the PC system unit

As simple as this appears on the surface, power supply issues are of critical importance for techs. Problems with power can create system instability, crashes, and data loss—all things most computer users would rather avoid! Good techs, therefore, know an awful lot about powering the PC, from understanding the basic principles of electricity to knowing the many variations of PC power supplies. Plus, you need to know how to recognize power problems and implement the proper solutions. Too many techs fall into the "just plug it in" camp and never learn how to deal with power, much to their clients' unhappiness.

EXAM TIP Some questions on the CompTIA A+ certification exams could refer to a power supply as a *PSU*, for power supply unit. A power supply also falls into the category of *field replaceable unit (FRU)*, which refers to the typical parts a tech should carry, such as RAM and a floppy disk drive.

Historical/Conceptual

Understanding Electricity

Electricity is simply a flow of negatively charged particles, called electrons, through matter. All matter enables the flow of electrons to some extent. This flow of electrons is very similar to the flow of water through pipes; so similar that the best way to learn about electricity is by comparing it to how water flows through pipes! So let's talk about water for a moment.

Water comes from the ground, through wells, aquifers, rivers, and so forth. In a typical city, water comes to you through pipes from the water supply company that took it from the ground. What do you pay for when you pay your water bill each month? You pay for the water you use, certainly, but built into the price of the water you use is the surety that when you turn the spigot, water will flow at a more or less constant rate. The water sits in the pipes under pressure from the water company, waiting for you to turn on the spigot.

Electricity works essentially the same way as water. Electric companies gather or generate electricity and then push it to your house under pressure through wires. Just like water, the electricity sits in the wires, waiting for you to plug something into the wall socket, at which time it'll flow at a more or less constant rate. You plug a lamp into an electrical outlet and flip the switch, electricity flows, and you have light. You pay for reliability, electrical pressure, and electricity used.

The pressure of the electrons in the wire is called *voltage* and is measured in units called *volts (V)*. The amount of electrons moving past a certain point on a wire is called the *current* or *amperage*, which is measured in units called *amperes (amps or A)*. The amount of amps and volts needed by a particular device to function is expressed as how much wattage (watts or W) that device needs. The correlation between the three is very simple math: $V \times A = W$. You'll learn more about wattage a little later in this chapter.

Wires of all sorts—whether copper, tin, gold, or platinum—have a slight resistance to the flow of electrons, just like water pipes have a slight amount of friction that resists the flow of water. Resistance to the flow of electrons is measured in ohms (Ω).

- Pressure = Voltage (V)
- Volume flowing = Amperes (A)
- Work = Wattage (W)
- Resistance = Ohms (Ω)

A particular thickness of wire only handles so much electricity at a time. If you push too much through, the wire will overheat and break, much like an overloaded water pipe will burst. To make sure you use the right wire for the right job, all electrical wires have an amperage rating, such as 20 amps. If you try to push 30 amps through a 20-amp wire, the wire will break and electrons will seek a way to return into the ground. Not a good thing, especially if the path back to ground is through you!

Circuit breakers and ground wires provide the basic protection from accidental over-flow. A circuit breaker is a heat-sensitive electrical switch rated at a certain amperage. If you push too much amperage through the circuit breaker, the wiring inside will detect the increase in heat and automatically open, stopping the flow of electricity before the wiring overheats and breaks. You reset the circuit breaker to reestablish the circuit and electricity will flow once more through the wires. A ground wire provides a path of least resistance for electrons to flow back to ground in case of an accidental overflow.

Many years ago, your electrical supply used fuses instead of circuit breakers. Fuses are small devices with a tiny filament designed to break if subjected to too much current. Unfortunately, that breaking meant fuses had to be replaced every time they blew, making circuit breakers much more preferable. Even though you no longer see fuses in a building's electrical circuits, many electrical devices—such as a PC's power supply—often still use fuses for their own internal protection.

EXAM TIP An electrical outlet must have a ground wire to be suitable for PC use!

Electricity comes in two flavors: *direct current (DC)*, in which the electrons flow in one direction around a continuous circuit, and *alternating current (AC)*, in which the flow of electrons alternates direction back and forth in a circuit (see Figure 8-2). Most electronic devices use DC power, but all power companies supply AC power because AC travels long distances much more efficiently than DC.

Figure 8-2
Diagrams showing
DC and AC flow
of electrons

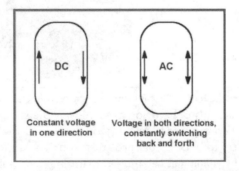

Essentials

Powering the PC

Your PC uses DC voltage, so some conversion process must take place so that the PC can use AC power from the power company. The power supply in a computer converts high-voltage AC power from the wall socket to low-voltage DC. The first step in powering the PC, therefore, is to get and maintain a good supply of AC power. Second, you need a power supply to convert AC to the proper voltage and amperage of DC power for the motherboard and peripherals. Finally, you need to control the byproduct of electricity use, namely heat. Let's look at the specifics of powering the PC.

Supplying AC

Every PC power supply must have standard AC power from the power company, supplied steadily rather than in fits and spurts, and protection against accidental blurps in the supply. The power supply connects to the power cord (and thus to an electrical outlet) via a standard *IEC-320* connector. In the United States, standard AC comes in somewhere between 110 and 120 volts, often written as ~115 VAC (volts of alternating current). The rest of the world uses 220–240 VAC, so most power supplies have a little switch in the back so you can use them anywhere. Figure 8-3 shows the back of a power supply. Note the three switches, from top to bottom: the hard on/off switch, the 115/230 switch, and IEC 320 connector.

Figure 8-3
Back of power supply showing typical switches and power connection.

 CAUTION Flipping the AC switch on the back of a power supply can wreak all kinds of havoc on a PC. Moving the switch to ~230 V in the U.S. makes for a great practical joke (as long as the PC is off when you do it)—the PC might try to boot up, but probably won't get far. You don't risk damaging anything by running at half the AC that the power supply is expecting. In countries that run ~230 standard, on the other hand, firing up the PC with the AC switch set to ~115 can cause the power supply to die a horrid, smoking death. Watch that switch!

Before plugging anything into an AC outlet, take a moment to test the outlet first using a multimeter or a device designed exclusively to test outlets. Failure to test AC outlets properly can result in inoperable or destroyed equipment, as well as possible electrocution. The IEC-320 plug has three holes, called hot, neutral, and ground. These names describe the function of the wires that connect to them behind the wall plate. The hot wire carries electrical voltage, much like a pipe that delivers water. The neutral wire carries no voltage, but instead acts like a water drain, completing the circuit by returning electricity to the local source, normally a breaker panel. The ground wire makes it possible for excess electricity to return safely to the ground. When testing AC power, you want to check for three things: that the hot outputs approximately 115 V (or whatever the proper voltage is for your part of the world), that the neutral connects to ground (0 V output), and that the ground connects to ground (again, 0 V). Figure 8-4 shows the voltages at an outlet.

Figure 8-4
Outlet voltages

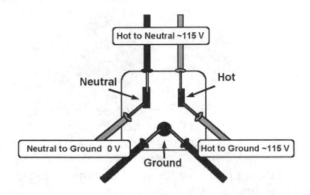

A *multimeter*—often also referred to as a *volt-ohm meter (VOM)* or *digital multimeter (DMM)*—enables you to measure a number of different aspects of electrical current. Most multimeters provide at least four major measurements: AC voltage, DC voltage, continuity, and resistance. A multimeter consists of two probes: an analog or digital meter, and a dial to set the type of test you want to perform. Refer to Figure 8-5 to become familiar with the different components of the multimeter.

Figure 8-5
Digital multimeter

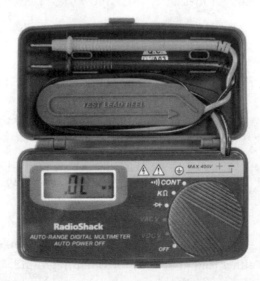

Note that some multimeters use symbols rather than letters to describe AC and DC settings. The *V* with the solid line above a dashed line, for example, in Figure 8-6, refers to direct current. The *V~* stands for alternating current.

Figure 8-6
Multimeter featuring DC and AC symbols

Most multimeters offer four types of electrical tests: continuity, resistance, AC voltage (VAC), and DC voltage (VDC). Continuity tests whether electrons can flow from one end of a wire to the other end. If so, you have continuity; if not, you don't. You can use this setting to determine if a fuse is good or to check for breaks in wires. If your multimeter doesn't have a continuity tester (many cheaper multimeters do not), you may use the resistance tester. A broken wire or fuse will show infinite resistance, while a good wire or fuse will show no resistance. Testing AC and DC voltages is a matter of making sure the measured voltage is what it should be.

Testing AC

Every competent technician knows how to use a multimeter to test an AC outlet, so if you haven't used one in the past, get hold of one and give it a whirl! First, you need to set up the meter for measuring AC. Follow these steps:

1. Move the selector switch to the AC V (usually red). If multiple settings are available, put it into the first scale higher than 120 V (usually 200 V). *Auto-range* meters set their own range; they don't need any selection except AC V.

2. Place the black lead in the common (–) hole. If the black lead is permanently attached, ignore this step.

3. Place the red lead in the V-Ohm-A (+) hole. If the red lead is permanently attached, ignore this step.

Once you have the meter set up for AC, go through the process of testing the various wires on an AC socket. Just don't put your fingers on the metal parts of the leads when you stick them into the socket! Follow these steps:

1. Put either lead in hot, the other in neutral. You should read 110 to 120 V AC.

2. Put either lead in hot, the other in ground. You should read 110 to 120 V AC.

3. Put either lead in neutral, the other in ground. You should read 0 V AC.

If any of these readings is different from what is described here, it's time to call an electrician.

Using Special Equipment to Test AC Voltage

A number of good AC-only testing devices are available. With these devices, you can test all voltages for an AC outlet by simply inserting them into the outlet. Be sure to test all the outlets the computer system uses: power supply, external devices, and monitor. Although convenient, these devices aren't as accurate as a multimeter. My favorite tester is made by Radio Shack, catalog number 22-141 (see Figure 8-7). This handy device provides three light-emitting diodes (LEDs) that describe everything that can go wrong with a plug.

Figure 8-7
Circuit tester

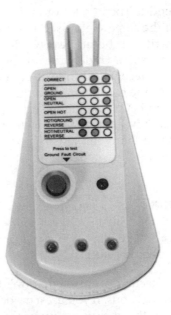

If all power companies could supply electricity in smooth, continuous flows with no dips or spikes in pressure, the next two sections of this chapter would be irrelevant. Unfortunately, no matter how clean the AC supply appears to be to a multimeter, the truth is that voltage from the power company tends to drop well below (sag) and shoot far above (surge or spike) the standard 115 Volts (in the U.S.). These sags and spikes usually don't affect lamps and refrigerators, but they can keep your PC from running or can even destroy a PC or peripheral device. Two essential devices handle spikes and sags in the supply of AC: surge suppressors and uninterruptible power supplies.

Surge Suppressors

Surges or spikes are far more dangerous than sags. Even a strong sag only shuts off or reboots your PC—any surge can harm your computer, and a strong surge destroys components. Given the seriousness of surges, every PC should use a *surge suppressor* device that absorbs the extra voltage from a surge to protect the PC. The power supply does a good job of surge suppression and can handle many of the smaller surges that take place fairly often. But the power supply takes a lot of damage from this and will eventually fail. To protect your power supply, a dedicated surge suppressor works between the power supply and the outlet to protect the system from power surges (see Figure 8-8).

Figure 8-8
Surge suppressor

Most people tend to spend a lot of money on their PC and for some reason suddenly get cheap on the surge suppressor. Don't do that! Make sure your surge suppressor has the Underwriters Laboratories UL 1449 for 330 V rating to ensure substantial protection for your system. Underwriters Laboratories (www.ul.com) is a U.S.-based, not-for-profit, widely recognized industry testing laboratory whose testing standards are very important to the consumer electronics industry. Additionally, check the joules rating before buying a new surge suppressor. A joule is a unit of electrical energy. Joules are used to describe how much energy a surge suppressor can handle before it fails. Most authorities agree that your surge suppressor should rate at a minimum of 800 joules—the more joules, the better the protection! My surge suppressor rates out at 1,750 joules.

 CAUTION   No surge suppressor in the world can handle the ultimate surge, the ESD of a lightning strike. If your electrical system takes such a hit, you can kiss your PC goodbye if it was plugged in at the time. *Always* unplug electronics during electrical storms!

While you're protecting your system, don't forget that surges also come from telephone and cable connections. If you use a modem, DSL, or cable modem, make sure to get a surge suppressor that includes support for these types of connections. Many manufacturers make surge suppressors with telephone line protection (see Figure 8-9).

Figure 8-9
Good surge
suppressor

No surge suppressor works forever. Make sure your surge suppressor has a test/reset button so you'll know when the device has—as we say in the business—turned into an extension cord. If your system takes a hit and you have a surge suppressor, call the company! Many companies provide cash guarantees against system failure due to surges, but only if you follow their guidelines.

If you want really great surge suppression, you need to move up to *power conditioning*. Your power lines take in all kinds of strange signals that have no business being in there, such as electromagnetic interference (EMI) and radio frequency interference (RFI). Most of the time, this line noise is so minimal that it's not worth addressing, but occasionally events (such as lightning) generate enough line noise to cause weird things to happen to your PC (keyboard lockups, messed up data). All better surge suppressors add power conditioning to filter out EMI and RFI.

UPS

An uninterruptible power supply (UPS) protects your computer (and, more importantly, your data) in the event of a power sag or power outage. Figure 8-10 shows a typical UPS. A UPS essentially contains a big battery that will provide AC power to your computer, regardless of the power coming from the AC outlet.

Figure 8-10
Uninterruptible
power supply

All uninterruptible power supplies are measured in both watts (the true amount of power they supply in the event of a power outage) and in *volt-amps (VA)*. Volt-amps is the amount of power the UPS could supply if the devices took power from the UPS in a perfect way. Your UPS provides perfect AC power, moving current smoothly back and forth 60 times a second. However, power supplies, monitors, and other devices may not take all the power the UPS has to offer at every point as the AC power moves back and forth, resulting in inefficiencies. If your devices took all the power the UPS offered at every point as the power moved back and forth, then VA would equal watts. If the UPS makers knew ahead of time exactly what devices you planned to plug into their UPSs, they could tell you the exact watts, but different devices have different efficiencies, forcing the UPS makers to go by what they can offer (VAs), not what your devices will take (watts). The watts value they give is a guess, and it's never as high as the VAs. The VA ratings is always higher than the watt rating. Since you have no way to calculate the exact efficiency of every device you'll plug into the UPS, go with the wattage rating. You add up the total wattage of every component in your PC and buy a UPS with a higher wattage. You'll spend a lot of time and mental energy figuring precisely how much wattage your computer, monitor, drives, and so on require to get the proper UPS for your system. But you're still not done! Remember, the UPS is a battery with a limited amount of power, so you then need to figure out how long you want the UPS to run when you lose power.

The quicker and far better method to use for determining the UPS you need is to go to any of the major surge suppressor/UPS makers' Web sites and use their handy power calculators. My personal favorite is on the American Power Conversion Web site: www. apc.com. APC makes great surge suppressors and UPSs, and the company's online calculator will show you the true wattage you need—and teach you about whatever new thing is happening in power at the same time.

Every UPS also has surge suppression and power conditioning, so look for the joule and UL 1449 ratings. Also look for replacement battery costs—some UPS replacement batteries are very expensive. Finally, look for a smart UPS with a USB or serial port connection. These handy UPSs come with monitoring and maintenance software (Figure 8-11) that tells you the status of your system and the amount of battery power available, logs power events, and provides other handy options.

Figure 8-11
APC PowerChute software

Table 8-1 gives you a quick look at the low end and the very high end of UPS products (as of November 2006).

Brand	Model	Outlets Protected	Backup Time	Price	Type
APC	BE350U	3 @ 120 V	2 min @ 200 W, 21 min @ 50W	$39.99	Standby
APC	BE725BB	4 @ 120 V	4 min @ 400 W, <1 hour @ 50W	$99.99	Standby
CyberPower	CPS825AVR	3 @ 120 V	25 to 60 minutes	$136.12	Line interactive
APC	SYH2K6RMT-P1	12 @ 120 V 2 @ 240 V	11.9 min @ 1400 W	$2,835.00	Online

Table 8-1   Typical UPS devices

Supplying DC

After you've assured the supply of good AC electricity for the PC, the power supply unit (PSU) takes over, converting high-voltage AC into several DC voltages (notably, 5.0, 12.0, and 3.3 volts) usable by the delicate interior components. Power supplies come in a large number of shapes and sizes, but the most common size by far is the standard 150 mm × 140 mm × 86 mm desktop PSU, shown in Figure 8-12.

Figure 8-12
Desktop PSU

The PC uses the 12.0-volt current to power motors on devices such as hard drives and CD-ROM drives, and it uses the 5.0-volt and 3.3-volt current for support of on-board electronics. Manufacturers may use these voltages any way they wish, however, and may deviate from these assumptions. Power supplies also come with standard connectors for the motherboard and interior devices.

Power to the Motherboard

Modern motherboards use a 20- or 24-pin P1 power connector. Some motherboards may require special 4-, 6-, or 8-pin connectors to supply extra power (Figure 8-13). We'll talk about each of these connectors in the form factor standards discussion later in this chapter.

Figure 8-13
Motherboard
power connectors

Power to Peripherals: Molex, Mini, and SATA

Many different devices inside the PC require power. These include hard drives, floppy drives, CD- and DVD-media drives, Zip drives, and fans. The typical PC power supply has up to three different types of connectors that plug into peripherals: Molex, mini, and SATA.

Molex Connectors   The most common type of power connection for devices that need 5- or 12-volts of power is the *Molex* connector (Figure 8-14). The Molex connector has notches, called *chamfers*, that guide its installation. The tricky part is that Molex connectors require a firm push to plug in properly, and a strong person can defeat the chamfers, plugging a Molex in upside down. Not a good thing. *Always* check for proper orientation before you push it in!

Figure 8-14
Molex connector

Testing DC

It is common practice for techs troubleshooting a system to test the DC voltages coming out of the power supply. Even with good AC, a bad power supply can fail to transform AC to DC at voltages needed by the motherboard and peripherals. So grab your trusty multimeter and try this on a powered up PC with the side cover removed. Note that you must have P1 connected to the motherboard and the system must be running (you don't have to be in Windows, of course).

1. Switch your multimeter to DC, somewhere around 20 V DC, if you need to make that choice. Make sure your leads are plugged into the multimeter properly, red to hot, black to ground. The key to testing DC is that it matters which lead you touch to which wire. Red goes to hot wires of all colors; black *always* goes to ground.

2. Plug the red lead into the red wire socket of a free Molex connector and plug the black lead into one of the two black wire sockets. You should get a reading of ~5 V. What do you have?

3. Now move the red lead to the yellow socket. What voltage do you get?

4. Testing the P1 connector is a little more complicated. You push the red and black leads into the top of P1, sliding in along side the wires until you bottom out. Leave the black lead in one of the black wire ground sockets. Move the red lead through all the colored wire sockets. What voltages do you find?

Mini Connectors   All power supplies have a second type of connector, called a *mini connector* (Figure 8-15), that supplies 5 and 12 volts to peripherals, although only floppy disk drives in modern systems use this connector. Drive manufacturers adopted the mini as the standard connector on 3.5-inch floppy disk drives. Often, these mini connectors are referred to as floppy power connectors.

Figure 8-15
Mini connector

Be extra careful when plugging in a mini connector! Whereas Molex connectors are difficult to plug in backward, you can insert a mini connector incorrectly with very little effort. As with a Molex connector, doing so will almost certainly destroy the floppy drive. Figure 8-16 depicts a correctly oriented mini connection.

Figure 8-16
Correct orientation
of a mini connector

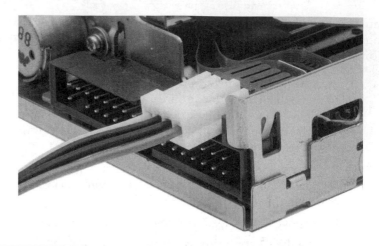

 CAUTION As with any power connector, plugging a mini connector into a device the wrong way will almost certainly destroy the device. Check twice before you plug one in!

SATA Power Connectors Serial ATA (SATA) hard drives need a special 15-pin *SATA* power connector (Figure 8-17). The larger pin count supports the SATA hot-swappable feature, and 3.3 V, 5.0 V, and 12.0 V devices. SATA power connectors are *L* shaped, making it almost impossible to insert one incorrectly into a SATA drive. No other device on your computer uses the SATA power connector. For more information about SATA drives, see Chapter 9, "Hard Drive Technologies."

Figure 8-17
SATA power
connector

 NOTE It's normal and common to have unused power connectors inside your PC case.

Splitters and Adapters You may occasionally find yourself without enough connectors to power all of the devices inside your PC. In this case, you can purchase splitters to create more connections (see Figure 8-18). You might also run into the phenomenon of needing a SATA connector but having only a spare Molex. Because the voltages on the wires are the same, a simple adapter will take care of the problem nicely.

Figure 8-18
Molex splitter

ATX

The original ATX power supplies had two distinguishing physical features: the motherboard power connector and soft power. Motherboard power came from a single cable with a 20-pin P1 motherboard power connector. ATX power supplies also had at least two other cables, each populated with two or more Molex or mini connectors for peripheral power.

When plugged in, ATX systems have 5 volts running to the motherboard. They're always "on" even when powered down. The power switch you press to power up the PC isn't a true power switch like the light switch on the wall in your bedroom. The power switch on an ATX system simply tells the computer whether it has been pressed. The BIOS or operating system takes over from there and handles the chore of turning the PC on or off. This is called *soft power*.

Using soft power instead of a physical switch has a number of important benefits. Soft power prevents a user from turning off a system before the operating system's been shut down. It enables the PC to use power saving modes that put the system to sleep and then wake it up when you press a key, move a mouse, or receive an e-mail. (See Chapter 19, "Portable Computing," for more details on sleep mode.)

All of the most important settings for ATX soft power reside in CMOS setup. Boot into CMOS and look for a Power Management section. Take a look at the Power On Function option in Figure 8-19. This determines the function of the on/off switch. You may set this switch to turn off the computer, or you may set it to the more common *4-second delay*.

Figure 8-19
Soft Power setting
in CMOS

```
              Phoenix - Award BIOS CMOS Setup Utility
                        Power Management Setup

    ACPI Suspend Typr          S3 <Suspend-To-RAM>         Item Help
    - USB Resume from S3       Enabled
    Power Button Function      Delay 4 Sec          Menu Level    ▶
    Wake by PME# of PCI        Disabled
    Wakeup by Ring             Disabled
    Wakeup by OnChip LAN       Enabled
    Wakeup by Alarm            Disabled
  x - Day of Month Alarm         0
  x - Time (hh:mm:ss) Alarm     0 : 0 : 0
    AMD K8 Cool'n'Quite controlAuto
    Power On Function          Button Only
  x - KB Power On Password     Enter
  x - Hot Key Power On         Ctrl-F1
    Restore on AC Power Loss   Power Off




▲▼►◄:Move  Enter:Select     +/-/PU/PD:Value  F10:Save   ESC:Exit  F1:General Help
       F5:Previous Values         F6:Fail-Safe Defaults      F7:Optimized Defaults
```

ATX did a great job supplying power for more than a decade, but over time more powerful CPUs, multiple CPUs, video cards, and other components began to need more current than the original ATX provided. This motivated the industry to introduce a number of updates to the ATX power standards: ATX12V 1.3, EPS12V, multiple rails, ATX12V 2.0, other form factors, and active PFC.

ATX12V 1.3 The first widespread update to the ATX standard, ATX12V 1.3, came out in 2003. This introduced a 4-pin motherboard power connector, unofficially but commonly called the P4, that provided more 12-volt power to assist the 20-pin P1 motherboard power connector. Any power supply that provides a P4 connector is called an ATX12V power supply. The term "ATX" was dropped from the ATX power standard, so if you want to get really nerdy you can say—accurately—that there's no such thing as an ATX power supply. All power supplies—assuming they have a P4 connector—are ATX12V or one of the later standards.

The ATX12V 1.3 standard also introduced a 6-pin auxiliary connector—commonly called an *AUX* connector—to supply increased 3.3- and 5.0-volt current to the motherboard (see Figure 8-20). This connector was based on the motherboard power connector from the precursor of ATX, called *AT*.

Figure 8-20
Auxiliary power
connector

The introduction of these two extra power connectors caused the industry some teething problems. In particular, motherboards using AMD CPUs tended to need the AUX connector, while motherboards using Intel CPUs needed only the P4. As a result, many power supplies came with only a P4 or only an AUX connector to save money. A few motherboard makers skipped adding either connector and used a standard Molex so people with older power supplies wouldn't have to upgrade just because they bought a new motherboard (Figure 8-21).

Figure 8-21
Molex power on
motherboard

The biggest problem with ATX12V was its lack of teeth—it made a lot of recommendations but few requirements, giving PSU makers too much choice (such as choosing or not choosing to add AUX and P4 connectors) that weren't fixed until later versions.

EPS12V   Server motherboards are thirsty for power and sometimes ATX12V 1.3 just didn't cut it. An industry group called the Server System Infrastructure (SSI) developed a non-ATX standard motherboard and power supply called EPS12V. An EPS12V power supply came with a 24-pin main motherboard power connector that resembled a 20-pin ATX connector, but it offered more current and thus more stability for motherboards. It also came with an AUX connector, an ATX12V P4 connector and a unique 8-pin connector. That's a lot of connectors! EPS12V power supplies were not interchangeable with ATX12V power supplies.

EPS12V may not have seen much life beyond servers, but it introduced a number of power features, some of which eventually became part of the ATX12V standard. The most important issue being something called *rails*.

Rails   Generally, all of the PC's power comes from a single transformer that takes the AC current from a wall socket and converts it into DC current that is split into three primary DC voltage rails: 12.0 volts, 5.0 volts, and 3.3 volts. Individual lines run from each of these voltage rails to the various connectors. That means the 12-volt connector on a P4 draws from the same rail as the main 12-volt connector feeding power to the motherboard. This works fine as long as the collective needs of the connectors sharing a rail don't exceed its capacity to feed them power. To avoid this, EPS12V divided the 12-volt supply into two or three separate 12-volt rails, each one providing a separate source of power.

ATX12V 2.0   The ATX12V 2.0 standard incorporated many of the good ideas of EPS12V into the ATX world, starting with the 24-pin connector. This 24-pin motherboard power connector is backward compatible with the older 20-pin connector so users don't have to buy a new motherboard if they use an ATX12V 2.0 power supply. ATX12V 2.0 requires two, 12-volt rails for any power supply rated higher than 230 watts. ATX12V 2.0 dropped the AUX connector and required SATA hard drive connectors.

NOTE   A few updates have been made to the ATX12V 2.0 standard, but these are trivial from a PC tech's standpoint.

In theory, a 20-pin motherboard power supply connector will work on a motherboard with a 24-pin socket, but doing this is risky in that the 20-pin connector may not provide enough power to your system. Try to use the right power supply for your motherboard to avoid problems. Many ATX12V 2.0 power supplies have a convertible 24- to 20-pin converter. These are handy if you want to make a nice "clean" connection as many 20-pin connectors have capacitors that prevent plugging in a 24-pin connector. You'll also see the occasional 24-pin connector constructed in such a way that you can slide off the extra four pins. Figure 8-22 shows 20-pin and 24-pin connectors; Figure 8-23 shows a convertible connector. Although they look similar, those extra four pins won't replace the P4 connector. They are incompatible!

Figure 8-22
20- and 24-pin connectors

Figure 8-23
Convertible
motherboard
power connector

The other notable additional connector is a 6-pin PCI Express (PCIe) connector (Figure 8-24). Some motherboards add a Molex socket for PCIe, and some cards come with a Molex socket as well. Higher end cards have a dedicated 6-pin connector.

Figure 8-24
PCI Express 6-pin
power connector

IT Technician

Niche Market Power Supply Form Factors The demand for smaller and quieter PCs and, to a lesser extent, the emergence of the BTX form factor has led to the development of a number of niche market power supply form factors. All use standard ATX connectors, but differ in size and shape from standard ATX power supplies.

NOTE You'll commonly find niche market power supplies bundled with computer cases (and often motherboards as well). These form factors are rarely sold alone.

- **TFX12V** A small power form factor optimized for low-profile ATX systems
- **SFX12V** A small power form factor optimized for systems using FlexATX motherboards (Figure 8-25)
- **CFX12V** An L-shaped power supply optimized for Micro BTX systems
- **LFX12V** A small power form factor optimized for low-profile BTX systems

Figure 8-25
SFX power supply

EXAM TIP The CompTIA A+ 220-602 and 220-604 exams test you pretty heavily on power supplies. You need to know what power supply will work with a particular system or with a particular computing goal in mind.

Active PFC Visualize the AC current coming from the power company as water in a pipe, smoothly moving back and forth, 60 times a second. A PC's power supply, simply due to the process of changing this AC current into DC current, is like a person sucking on a straw on the end of this pipe, taking gulps only when the current is fully pushing or pulling at the top and bottom of each cycle, creating an electrical phenomena—sort of a back pressure—that's called *harmonics* in the power industry. These harmonics create the humming sound that you hear from electrical components. Over time, harmonics damage electrical equipment, causing serious problems with the power supply and other electrical devices on the circuit. Once you put a few thousand PCs with power supplies in the same local area, harmonics can even damage the electrical power supplier's equipment!

Good PC power supplies come with *active power factor correction (active PFC)*, extra circuitry that smoothes out the way the power supply takes power from the power company and eliminates harmonics (Figure 8-26). Never buy a power supply that does not have active PFC—all power supplies with active PFC will proudly show you on the box.

Figure 8-26
Power supply
showing active PFC

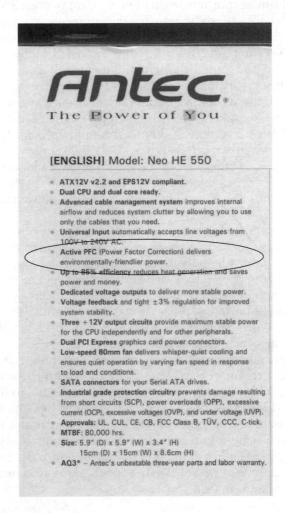

Wattage Requirements

Every device in a PC requires a certain amount of wattage in order to function. A typical hard drive draws 15 watts of power when accessed, for example, whereas some Athlon 64 X2 CPUs draw a whopping 110 watts at peak usage—with average usage around 70 watts. The total wattage of all devices combined is the minimum you need the power supply to provide.

EXAM TIP The CompTIA A+ Certification exams do not require you to figure precise wattage needs for a particular system. When building a PC for a client, however, you do need to know this stuff!

If the power supply cannot produce the wattage needed by a system, that PC won't work properly. Because most devices in the PC require maximum wattage when first starting, the most common result of insufficient wattage is a paper weight that looks like a PC. This can lead to some embarrassing moments. You might plug in a new hard drive for a client, for example, push the power button on the case, and nothing happens—a dead PC! Eek! You can quickly determine if insufficient wattage is the problem. Unplug the drive and power up the system. If the system boots up, the power supply is a likely suspect. The only fix for this problem is to replace the power supply with one that provides more wattage (or leave the new drive out—a less-than-ideal solution).

No power supply can turn 100 percent of the AC power coming from the power company into DC current. So all power supplies provide less power to the system than the wattage advertised on the box. ATX12V 2.0 standards require a power supply to be at least 70 percent efficient, but you can find power supplies with better than 80 percent efficiency. More efficiency can tell you how many watts the system puts out to the PC in actual use. Plus, the added efficiency means the power supply uses less power, saving you money.

One common argument these days is that people buy power supplies that provide far more wattage than a system needs and therefore waste power. This is untrue. A power supply provides only the amount of power your system needs. If you put a 1000-watt power supply (yes, they really exist) into a system that needs only 250 watts, that big power supply will put out only 250 watts to the system. So buying an efficient, higher wattage power supply gives you two benefits: First, running a power supply at less than 100 percent load lets it live longer. Second, you'll have plenty of extra power when adding new components.

As a general recommendation for a new system, use at least a 400-watt power supply. This is a common wattage and will give you plenty of extra power for booting as well as for whatever other components you might add to the system in the future.

Don't cut the specifications too tightly for power supplies. All power supplies produce less wattage over time, simply because of wear and tear on the internal components. If you build a system that runs with only a few watts of extra power available from the power supply initially, that system will most likely start causing problems within a year or less! Do yourself or your clients a favor and get a power supply that has a little more wattage than you need.

Installing, Maintaining, and Troubleshooting Power Supplies

Installing, maintaining, and troubleshooting power supplies take a little less math than selecting the proper power supply for a system but remain essential skills for any tech. Installing takes but a moment, and maintaining is almost as simple, but troubleshooting can cause headaches. Let's take a look.

Installing

The typical power supply connects to the PC with four standard computer screws, mounted in the back of the case (Figure 8-27). Unscrew the four screws and the power supply lifts out easily (Figure 8-28). Insert a new power supply that fits the case and attach it using the same four screws.

Figure 8-27
Mounting screws
for power supply

Figure 8-28
Removing power
supply from
system unit

Handling ATX power supplies requires special consideration. Understand that an ATX power supply *never turns off*. As long as that power supply stays connected to a power outlet, the power supply will continue to supply 5 volts to the motherboard. Always unplug an ATX system before you do any work! For years, techs bickered about the merits of leaving a PC plugged in or unplugged while you serviced it. ATX settled this issue forever. Many ATX power supplies provide a real on/off switch on the back of the PSU (see Figure 8-29). If you really need the system to shut down with no power to the motherboard, use this switch.

Figure 8-29
On/off switch for
an ATX system

When working on an ATX system, you may find using the power button inconvenient because you're not using a case or you haven't bothered to plug the power button's leads into the motherboard. That means there is no power button! One trick you can use when in that situation is to use a set of car keys or a screwdriver to contact the two wires to start and stop the system (see Figure 8-30).

Figure 8-30
Shorting the soft
on/off jumpers

Your first task after acquiring a new power supply is simply making sure it works. Insert the motherboard power connectors before starting the system. If you have video cards with power connectors, plug them in, too. Other connectors such as hard drives can wait until you've got one successful boot—or if you're cocky, just plug everything in!

Cooling

Heat and computers are not the best of friends. Cooling is, therefore, a vital consideration when building a computer. Electricity equals heat. Computers, being electrical devices, generate heat as they operate, and too much can seriously damage a computer's internal components.

The power supply fan (Figure 8-31) provides the basic cooling for the PC. It not only cools the voltage regulator circuits *within* the power supply, but it also provides a constant flow of outside air throughout the interior of the computer case. A dead power supply fan can rapidly cause tremendous problems, even equipment failure. If you ever turn on a computer and it boots just fine, but you notice that it seems unusually quiet, check to see if the power supply fan has died. If it has, quickly turn off the PC and replace the power supply.

Figure 8-31
Power supply fan

Some power supplies come with a built-in sensor to help regulate the airflow. If the system gets too hot, the power supply fan spins faster. The three-pin, three-wire fan sensor connector plugs into the motherboard directly (Figure 8-32).

Figure 8-32
Three-wire fan
sensor connector

Case fans (Figure 8-33) are large, square fans that snap into special brackets on the case or screw directly to the case, providing extra cooling for key components. Most cases come with a case fan, and no modern computer should really be without one or two.

Figure 8-33
Case fan

The single biggest issue related to case fans is where to plug them in. Most case fans come with standard Molex connectors, which are easy to plug in, but other case fans come with special three-pronged power connectors that need to connect to the motherboard. You can get adapters to plug three-pronged connectors into Molex connectors or Molex connectors into three-pronged connectors.

Maintaining Airflow

A computer is a closed system and computer cases help the fans keep things cool: everything is inside a box. Although many tech types like to run their systems with the side panel of the case open for easy access to the components, in the end they are cheating themselves. Why? A closed case enables the fans to create airflow. This airflow substantially cools off interior components. When the side of the case is open, you ruin the airflow of the system, and you lose a lot of cooling efficiency.

An important point to remember when implementing good airflow inside your computer case is that hot air rises. Warm air always rises above cold air, and you can use this principle to your advantage in keeping your computer cool.

In the typical layout of case fans for a computer case, an intake fan is located near the bottom of the front bezel of the case. This fan draws cool air in from outside the case and blows it over the components inside the case. Near the top and rear of the case (usually near the power supply), you'll usually find an exhaust fan. This fan works the opposite of the intake fan: it takes the warm air from inside the case and sends it to the outside.

Another important part of maintaining proper airflow inside the case is ensuring that all empty expansion bays are covered by slot covers (Figure 8-34). To maintain good airflow inside your case, you shouldn't provide too many opportunities for air to escape. Slot covers not only assist in maintaining a steady airflow; they help keep dust and smoke out of your case.

Figure 8-34
Slot covers

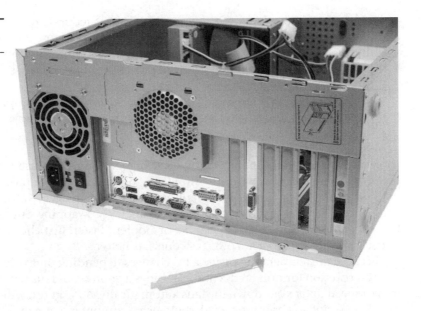

 EXAM TIP   Missing slot covers can cause the PC to overheat!

Reducing Fan Noise

Fans generate noise. In an effort to ensure proper cooling, many techs put several high-speed fans into a case, making the PC sound like a jet engine. You can reduce fan noise by getting manually adjustable-speed fans, larger fans, or specialty "quiet" fans. Many motherboards enable you to control fans through software.

Manually adjustable fans have a little knob you can turn to speed up or slow down the fan (Figure 8-35). This kind of fan can reduce some of the noise, but you run the risk of slowing down the fan too much and thus letting the interior of the case heat up. A better solution is to get quieter fans.

Figure 8-35
Manual fan
adjustment device

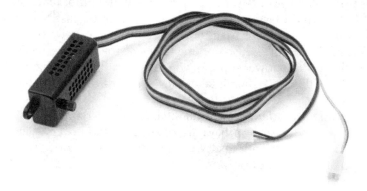

Larger fans that spin slower are another way to reduce noise while maintaining good airflow. Fans sizes are measured in millimeters (mm) or centimeters (cm). Traditionally, the industry used 80-mm power supply and cooling fans, but today you'll find 100 mm, 120 mm, and even larger fans in power supplies and cases.

NOTE When shopping for fans, remember your metric system. 80 mm = 8 cm; 120 mm = 12 cm. You'll find fans marketed both ways.

Many companies manufacture and sell higher-end, low-noise fans. The fans have better bearings than the run-of-the-mill fans, so they cost a little more, but they're definitely worth it. They market these fans as "quiet" or "silencer," or other similar adjectives. If you run into a PC that sounds like a jet, try swapping out the case fans for a low-decibel fan from Papst, Panasonic, or Cooler Master. Just check the decibel rating to decide which one to get. Lower, of course, is better.

Because the temperature inside a PC changes depending on the load put on the PC, the best solution for noise reduction combines a good set of fans with temperature sensors to speed up or slow down the fans automatically. A PC at rest will use less than half of the power of a PC running a video-intensive computer game and therefore makes a lot less heat. Virtually all modern systems support three fans through three, 3-pin fan connectors on the motherboard. The CPU fan uses one of these connectors, but the other two are for system fans or the power supply fan.

Most CMOS setup utilities provide a little control over fans plugged into the motherboard. Figure 8-36 shows a typical CMOS setting for the fans. Note that there's no way to tell the fans when to come on or off—only when to set off an alarm when they reach a certain temperature.

Figure 8-36
CMOS fan options

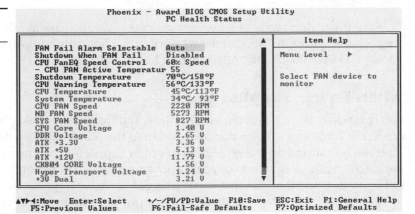

Software is the best way to control your fans. Some motherboards come with system monitoring software that enables you to set the temperature at which you want the fans to come on and off. If no program came with your motherboard and the manufacturer's Web site doesn't offer one for download, try the popular freeware SpeedFan utility (Figure 8-37), written by Alfredo Milani Comparetti, that monitors voltages, fan speeds, and temperatures in computers with hardware monitor chips. SpeedFan can even access S.M.A.R.T. information (see Chapter 9, "Hard Drive Technologies") for hard disks that support this feature and shows hard disk temperatures too, if supported. You can find SpeedFan at www.almico.com/speedfan.php.

Figure 8-37
SpeedFan

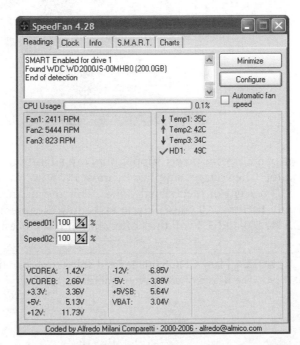

CAUTION SpeedFan is a powerful tool that does far more than work with fans. Don't tweak any settings that you don't understand!

Even if you don't want to mess with your fans, always make a point to turn on your temperature alarms in CMOS. If the system gets too hot, an alarm will warn you. There's no way to know if a fan dies other than to have an alarm.

When Power Supplies Die

Power supplies fail in two ways: sudden death and slowly over time. When they die suddenly, the computer will not start and the fan in the power supply will not turn. In this case, verify that electricity is getting to the power supply before you do anything! Avoid the embarrassment of trying to repair a power supply when the only problem is a bad outlet or an extension cord that is not plugged in. Assuming that the system has electricity, the best way to verify that a power supply is working or not working is to check the voltages coming out of the power supply with a multimeter (see Figure 8-38).

Figure 8-38
Testing one of the 5-volt DC connections

Do not panic if your power supply puts out slightly more or less voltage than its nominal value. The voltages supplied by most PC power supplies can safely vary by as much as ±10 percent of their stated values. This means that the 12-volt line can vary from roughly 10.5 to 12.9 volts without exceeding the tolerance of the various systems in the PC. The 5.0 and 3.3 volt lines offer similar tolerances.

 NOTE Many CMOS utilities and software programs monitor voltage, saving you the hassle of using a multimeter.

Be sure to test every connection on the power supply—that means every connection on your main power as well as every Molex and mini. Because all voltages are between –20 and +20 VDC, simply set the voltmeter to the 20-V DC setting for everything. If the power supply fails to provide power, throw it into the recycling bin and get a new one—even if you're a component expert and a whiz with a soldering iron. Don't waste your or your company's time; the price of new power supplies makes replacement the obvious way to go.

No Motherboard

Power supplies will not start unless they're connected to a motherboard, so what do you do if you don't have a motherboard you trust to test? First, try an ATX tester. Many companies make these devices. Look for one that supports both 20- and 24-pin motherboard connectors as well as all of the other connectors on your motherboard. Figure 8-39 shows a power supply tester.

Figure 8-39
ATX power
supply tester

Switches

Broken power switches form an occasional source of problems for power supplies that fail to start. The power switch is behind the on/off button on every PC. It is usually secured to the front cover or inside front frame on your PC, making it a rather challenging part to access. To test, try shorting the soft power jumpers as described earlier. A key or screwdriver will do the trick.

When Power Supplies Die Slowly

If all power supplies died suddenly, this would be a much shorter chapter. Unfortunately, the majority of PC problems occur when power supplies die slowly over time. This means that one of the internal electronics of the power supply has begun to fail.

The failures are *always* intermittent and tend to cause some of the most difficult to diagnose problems in PC repair. The secret to discovering that a power supply is dying lies in one word: intermittent. Whenever you experience intermittent problems, your first guess should be that the power supply is bad. Here are some other clues you may hear from users:

- "Whenever I start my computer in the morning, it starts to boot, and then locks up. If I press CTRL-ALT-DEL two or three times, then it will boot up fine."
- "Sometimes when I start my PC, I get an error code. If I reboot it goes away. Sometimes I get different errors."
- "My computer will run fine for an hour or so. Then it locks up, sometimes once or twice an hour."

Sometimes something bad happens and sometimes it does not. That's the clue for replacing the power supply. And don't bother with the voltmeter; the voltages will show up within tolerances, but only *once in a while* they will spike and sag (far more quickly than your voltmeter can measure) and cause these intermittent errors. When in doubt, change the power supply. Power supplies break in computers more often than any other part of the PC except the floppy disk drives. You might choose to keep power supplies on hand for swapping and testing.

Fuses and Fire

Inside every power supply resides a simple fuse. If your power supply simply pops and stops working, you might be tempted to go inside the power supply and check the fuse. This is not a good idea. First off, the capacitors in most power supplies carry high voltage charges that can hurt a lot if you touch them. Second, fuses blow for a reason. If a power supply is malfunctioning inside, you want that fuse to blow, because the alternative is much less desirable.

Failure to respect the power of electricity will eventually result in the most catastrophic of all situations: a fire. Don't think it won't happen to you! Keep a fire extinguisher handy. Every PC workbench needs a fire extinguisher, but you need to make sure you have the right one. The fire prevention industry has divided fire extinguishers into three fire classes:

- **Class A** Ordinary free-burning combustible, such as wood or paper
- **Class B** Flammable liquids, such as gasoline, solvents, or paint
- **Class C** Live electrical equipment

As you might expect, you should only use a Class C fire extinguisher on your PC if it should catch fire. All fire extinguishers are required to have their type labeled prominently on them. Many fire extinguishers are multi-class in that they can handle more than one type of fire. The most common fire extinguisher is type ABC—it works on all common types of fires.

Beyond A+

Power supplies provide essential services for the PC, creating DC out of AC and cooling the system, but that utilitarian role does not stop the power supply from being an enthusiast's plaything. Plus, server and high-end workstations have somewhat different needs than more typical systems, so naturally they need a boost in power. Let's take a look Beyond A+ at these issues.

It Glows!

The enthusiast community has been modifying, or *modding,* their PCs for years, cutting holes in the cases, adding fans to make overclocking feasible, and slapping in glowing strips of neon and cold cathode tubes. The power supply escaped the scene for a while, but it's back. A quick visit to a good computer store off or online, such as Directron. com, reveals a line of power supplies that light up, sport a fancy color, or have more fans than some rock stars. Figure 8-40 shows a quartet of four-fan PSUs.

Figure 8-40
Colorful, four-fan power supplies (photo courtesy of Directron)

On the other hand, you also find super-quiet stealth power supplies (Figure 8-41), with single or double high-end fans that react to the temperature inside your PC—speeding up when necessary but running slowly and silently when not. One of these would make a perfect power supply for a home entertainment PC, because it would provide function without adding excessive decibels of noise.

Figure 8-41
High-end power supply

Modular Power Supplies

It's getting more and more popular to make PCs that look good on both the inside and the outside. Unused power cables dangling around inside PCs creates a not-so-pretty picture. To help out stylish people, manufacturers created power supplies with modular cables (Figure 8-42).

Figure 8-42
Modular cable
power supply

Modular cables are pretty cool, because you add only the lines you need for your system. On the other hand, some techs claim that modular cables hurt efficiency because the modular connectors add resistance to the lines. You make the choice: is a slight reduction in efficiency worth a pretty look?

Rail Power

When you start using more powerful CPUs and video cards, you can run into a problem I call "rail power." Every ATX12V power supply using multiple rails supplies only a certain amount of power, measured in amps (A), on each rail. The problem is with the 12-V rails. The ATX12V standard requires up to 18 A for each 12-V rail—more than enough for the majority of users, but not enough when you're using a powerful CPU and one or more PCIe video cards. If you've got a powerful system, get online and read the detailed specs for your power supply. Figure 8-43 shows sample power supply specs. Many power supply makers do not release detailed specs—avoid them!

Figure 8-43
Sample specs

NeoHE 550

FEATURES	
Switches	ATX Logic on-off Additional power rocker switch
Maximum Power	550W
Transient Response	+12V, +5Vand +3.3V independent output circuitry provides stable power and tighter cross regulation (+/- 3%)
P. G. Signal	100-500ms
Over Voltage Protection recycle AC to reset	+5V trip point < +6.5V +3.3V trip point < +4.1V +12V trip point < +14.3V
Special Connectors	ATX12V/EPS12V Compatible 4 + 4 pin +12V Molex Peripheral Floppy SATA PCI Express
Leakage Current	<3.5mA @ 115VAC

OUTPUT							
Output Voltage	+3.3V	+5V	+12V1	+12V2	+12V3	-12V	+5Vsb
Max. Load	24A	20A	18A	18A	18A	0.8A	2.5A
Min. Load	0.5A	0.3A	1A	1A	1A	0A	0A
Regulation	3%	3%	3%	3%	3%	6%	3%
Ripple & Noise(mV)	50	50	120	120	120	120	50
Available Power	79.2W	100W	504W			9.6W	12.5W
Total Power	550W continuous output @ 50C ambient temperature						

Look for power supplies that offer about 16 to 18 A per rail. These will be big power supplies—400 W and up. Nothing less will support a big CPU and one or two PCIe video cards.

Watch out for power supplies that list their operating temperature at 25° C—about room temperature. A power supply that provides 500 W at 25° C will supply substantially less in warmer temperatures, and the inside of your PC is usually 15° C warmer than the outside air. Sadly, many power supply makers—even those who make good power supplies—fudge this fact.

Chapter Review Questions

1. When testing an AC outlet in the U.S., what voltage should the multimeter show between the hot and ground wires?

    A. 120 V

    B. 60 V

    C. 0 V

    D. –120 V

2. What voltages does an ATX12V P1 connector provide for the motherboard?

   A. 3.3 V, 5 V

   B. 3.3 V, 12 V

   C. 5 V, 12 V

   D. 3.3 V, 5 V, 12 V

3. What sort of power connector does a floppy disk drive typically use?

   A. Molex

   B. Mini

   C. Sub-mini

   D. Micro

4. Joachim ordered a new power supply but was surprised when it arrived because it had an extra, 4-wire connector. What is that connector?

   A. P2 connector for plugging in auxiliary components

   B. P3 connector for plugging in case fans

   C. P4 connector for plugging into Pentium 4 and later motherboards

   D. Aux connector for plugging into a secondary power supply

5. What should you keep in mind when testing DC connectors?

   A. DC has polarity. The red lead should always touch the hot wire; the black lead should touch a ground wire.

   B. DC has polarity. The red lead should always touch the ground wire; the black lead should always touch the hot wire.

   C. DC has no polarity, so you can touch the red lead to either hot or ground.

   D. DC has no polarity, so you can touch the black lead to either hot or neutral, but not ground.

6. What voltages should the two hot wires on a Molex connector read?

   A. Red = 3.3 V; Yellow = 5 V

   B. Red = 5 V; Yellow = 12 V

   C. Red = 12 V; Yellow = 5 V

   D. Red = 5 V; Yellow = 3.3 V

7. Why is it a good idea to ensure that the slot covers on your computer case are all covered?

   A. To maintain good airflow inside your case.

   B. It helps keep dust and smoke out of your case.

   C. Both A and B are correct reasons.

   D. Trick question! Leaving a slot uncovered doesn't hurt anything.

8. A PC's power supply provides DC power in what standard configuration?

   A. Two primary voltage rails, 12 volts and 5 volts, and an auxiliary 3.3 volt connector.

   B. Three primary voltage rails, one each for 12-volt, 5-volt, and 3.3-volt connectors.

   C. One primary DC voltage rail for 12-volt, 5-volt, and 3.3-volt connectors.

   D. One voltage rail with a 12-volt connector for the motherboard, a second voltage rail with a 12-volt connector for the CPU, and a third voltage rail for the 5-volt and 3.3-volt connectors.

9. What feature of ATX systems prevents a user from turning off a system before the operating system's been shut down?

   A. Motherboard power connector

   B. CMOS setup

   C. Sleep mode

   D. Soft power

10. How many pins does a SATA power connector have?

   A. 6

   B. 9

   C. 12

   D. 15

Answers

1. **A.** The multimeter should show 120 V (or thereabouts) between the hot and ground of a properly wired outlet.

2. **D.** An ATX12V power supply P1 connector provides 3.3, 5, and 12 volts to the motherboard.

3. **B.** Floppy drives commonly use a mini connector.

4. **C.** The P4 connector goes into the motherboard to support faster processors.

5. **A.** DC has polarity. The red lead should always touch the hot wire; the black lead should touch a ground wire.

6. **B.** A Molex connector's red wires should be at 5 volts; the yellow wire should be at 12 volts.

7. **C.** Both A and B are correct reasons—keeping the slots covered helps keep a good airflow in your case, and it keeps dust and smoke away from all those sensitive internal components.

8. **B.** The standard PC power supply configuration has three primary voltage rails, one each for 12-volt, 5-volt, and 3.3-volt connectors.

9. **D.** The soft power feature of ATX systems prevents a user from turning off a system before the operating system's been shut down.

10. **D.** SATA power connectors have 15 pins.

Hard Drive Technologies

In this chapter, you will learn how to
- Explain how hard drives work
- Identify and explain the ATA hard drive interfaces
- Identify and explain the SCSI hard drive interfaces
- Describe how to protect data with RAID
- Explain how to install drives
- Configure CMOS and install drivers
- Troubleshoot hard drive installation

Of all the hardware on a PC, none gets more attention—or gives more anguish—than the hard drive. There's a good reason for this: if the hard drive breaks, you lose data. As you probably know, when the data goes, you have to redo work or restore from backup—or worse. It's good to worry about the data, because the data runs the office, maintains the payrolls, and stores the e-mail. This level of concern is so strong that even the most neophyte PC users are exposed to terms such as *IDE, ATA,* and *controller*—even if they don't put the terms into practice!

This chapter focuses on how hard drives work, beginning with the internal layout and organization of the hard drive. You'll look at the different types of hard drives used today (PATA, SATA, and SCSI), how they interface with the PC, and how to install them properly into a system. The chapter covers how more than one drive may work with other drives to provide data safety and improve speed through a feature called RAID. Let's get started.

 NOTE Chapter 10, "Implementing Hard Drives," continues the hard drive discussion by adding in the operating systems, showing you how to prepare drives to receive data, and teaching you how to maintain and upgrade drives in all versions of Windows.

How Hard Drives Work

All hard drives are composed of individual disks, or *platters*, with read/write heads on actuator arms controlled by a servo motor—all contained in a sealed case that prevents contamination by outside air (see Figure 9-1).

Figure 9-1   Inside the hard drive

The aluminum platters are coated with a magnetic medium. Two tiny read/write heads service each platter, one to read the top and the other to read the bottom of the platter (see Figure 9-2).

Figure 9-2 Top and bottom read/write heads and armatures

The coating on the platters is phenomenally smooth! It has to be, as the read/write heads actually float on a cushion of air above the platters, which spin at speeds between 3,500 and 10,000 rpm. The distance (flying height) between the heads and the disk surface is less than the thickness of a fingerprint. The closer the read/write heads are to the platter, the more densely the data packs onto the drive. These infinitesimal tolerances demand that the platters never be exposed to outside air. Even a tiny dust particle on a platter would act like a mountain in the way of the read/write heads and would cause catastrophic damage to the drive. To keep the air clean inside the drive, all hard drives use a tiny, heavily filtered aperture to keep the air pressure equalized between the interior and the exterior of the drive.

Data Encoding

Although the hard drive stores data in binary form, visualizing a magnetized spot representing a one and a non-magnetized spot representing a zero grossly oversimplifies the process. Hard drives store data in tiny magnetic fields—think of them as tiny magnets that can be placed in either direction on the platter, as shown in Figure 9-3. Each tiny magnetic field, called a *flux*, can switch back and forth through a process called a *flux reversal* (see Figure 9-4). Electronic equipment can read and write flux reversals much faster and easier than it can magnetize or not magnetize a spot to store a one or a zero.

Figure 9-3
Data is stored in
tiny magnetic fields.

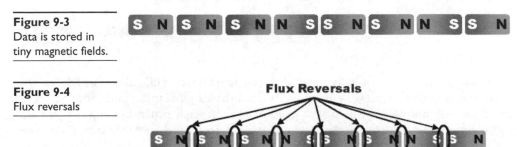

Figure 9-4
Flux reversals

In early hard drives, as the read/write head moved over a spot, the direction of the flux reversal defined a one or a zero. As the read/write head passed from the left to the right, it recognized fluxes in one direction as a zero and the other direction as a one (Figure 9-5). Hard drives read these flux reversals at a very high speed when accessing or writing data.

Figure 9-5
Fluxes are read in one direction as 0 and the other direction as 1.

Today's hard drives use a more complex and efficient method to interpret flux reversals using special data encoding systems. Instead of reading individual fluxes, a modern hard drive reads groups of fluxes called *runs*. Starting around 1991, hard drives began using a data encoding system known as *run length limited (RLL)*. With RLL, any combination of ones and zeroes can be stored in a preset combination of about 15 different runs. The hard drive looks for these runs and reads them as a group, resulting in much faster and much more dense data. Whenever you see RLL, you also see two numbers: the minimum and the maximum run length, such as RLL 1,7 or RLL 2,7. Figure 9-6 shows two sequential RLL runs.

Figure 9-6
Sequential RLL runs

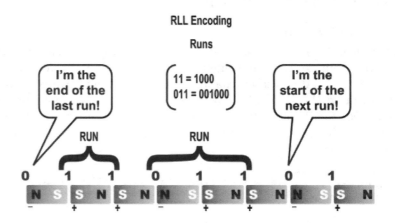

Current drives use an extremely advanced method of RLL called *Partial Response Maximum Likelihood (PRML)* encoding. As hard drives pack more and more fluxes on the drive, the individual fluxes start to interact with each other, making it more and more difficult for the drive to verify where one flux stops and another starts. PRML uses powerful, intelligent circuitry to analyze each flux reversal and to make a "best guess" as to what type of flux reversal it just read. As a result, the maximum run length for PRML drives reaches up to around 16 to 20 fluxes, far more than the 7 or so on RLL drives. Longer run lengths enable the hard drive to use more complicated run combinations so that the hard drive can store a phenomenal amount of data. For example, a run of only 12 fluxes on a hard drive might equal a string of 30 or 40 ones and zeroes when handed to the system from the hard drive.

The size required by each magnetic flux on a hard drive has reduced considerably over the years, resulting in higher capacities. As fluxes become smaller, they begin to interfere with each other in weird ways. I have to say *weird* since to make sense of what's going on at this subatomic level (I told you these fluxes were small!) would require that you take a semester of quantum mechanics! Let's just say that laying fluxes flat against the platter has reached its limit. To get around this problem, hard drive makers recently began to make hard drives that store their flux reversals vertically (up and down) rather than longitudinally (forward and backward), enabling them to make hard drives in the 1 terabyte (1,024 gigabyte) range. Manufacturers call this vertical storage method *perpendicular recording* (Figure 9-7).

Figure 9-7 Perpendicular versus traditional longitudinal recording

For all this discussion and detail on data encoding, the day-to-day PC technician never deals with encoding. Sometimes, however, knowing what you don't need to know helps as much as knowing what you do need to know. Fortunately, data encoding is inherent to the hard drive and completely invisible to the system. You're never going to have to deal with data encoding, but you'll sure sound smart when talking to other PC techs if you know your RLL from your PRML!

Moving the Arms

The read/write heads move across the platter on the ends of *actuator arms*. In the entire history of hard drives, manufacturers have used only two technologies to move the arms: *stepper motor* and *voice coil*. Hard drives first used stepper motor technology, but today they've all moved to voice coil.

Stepper motor technology moved the arm in fixed increments or steps, but the technology had several limitations that doomed it. Because the interface between motor and actuator arm required minimal slippage to ensure precise and reproducible movements, the positioning of the arms became less precise over time. This physical deterioration caused data transfer errors. Additionally, heat deformation wreaked havoc with stepper motor drives. Just as valve clearances in automobile engines change with operating temperature, the positioning accuracy changed as the PC operated and various hard drive components got warmer. Although very small, these changes caused problems. Accessing the data written on a cold hard drive, for example, became difficult after the disk warmed. In addition, the read/write heads could damage the disk surface if not "parked" (set in a non-data area) when not in use, requiring techs to use special parking programs before transporting a stepper motor drive.

 NOTE Floppy disk drives still use stepper motors.

All hard drives made today employ a linear motor to move the actuator arms. The linear motor, more popularly called a voice coil motor, uses a permanent magnet surrounding a coil on the actuator arm. When an electrical current passes, the coil generates a magnetic field that moves the actuator arm. The direction of the actuator arm's movement depends on the polarity of the electrical current through the coil. Because the voice coil and the actuator arm never touch, no degradation in positional accuracy takes place over time. Voice coil drives automatically park the heads when the drive loses power, making the old stepper motor park programs obsolete.

Lacking the discrete "steps" of the stepper motor drive, a voice coil drive cannot accurately predict the movement of the heads across the disk. To make sure voice coil drives land exactly in the correct area, the drive reserves one side of one platter for navigational purposes. This area essentially "maps" the exact location of the data on the drive. The voice coil moves the read/write head to its best guess about the correct position on the hard drive. The read/write head then uses this map to fine-tune its true position and make any necessary adjustments.

Now that you have a basic understanding of how a drive physically stores data, let's turn to how the hard drive organizes that data so we can use that drive.

Geometry

Have you ever seen a cassette tape? If you look at the actual brown Mylar (a type of plastic) tape, nothing will tell you whether sound is recorded on that tape. Assuming the tape is not blank, however, you know *something* is on the tape. Cassettes store music in distinct magnetized lines. You could say that the physical placement of those lines of magnetism is the tape's "geometry."

Geometry also determines where a hard drive stores data. As with a cassette tape, if you opened up a hard drive, you would not see the geometry. But rest assured that the drive has geometry; in fact, every model of hard drive uses a different geometry. We describe the geometry for a particular hard drive with a set of numbers representing three values: heads, cylinders, and sectors per track.

Heads

The number of *heads* for a specific hard drive describes, rather logically, the number of read/write heads used by the drive to store data. Every platter requires two heads. If a hard drive has four platters, for example, it would need eight heads (see Figure 9-8).

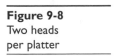

Figure 9-8
Two heads
per platter

Four platters = eight heads

Based on this description of heads, you would think that hard drives would always have an even number of heads, right? Wrong! Most hard drives reserve a head or two for their own use. Therefore, a hard drive can have either an even or an odd number of heads.

Cylinders

To visualize cylinders, imagine taking a soup can and opening both ends of the can. Wash off the label and clean out the inside. Now look at the shape of the can; it is a geometric shape called a cylinder. Now imagine taking that cylinder and sharpening one end so that it easily cuts through the hardest metal. Visualize placing the ex-soup can over the hard drive and pushing it down through the drive. The can cuts into one side and out the other of each platter. Each circle transcribed by the can is where you store data on the drive, and is called a *track* (Figure 9-9).

Figure 9-9
Tracks

**Two tracks - one on top and
another underneath**

**Every head has many hundreds
of tracks on each side**

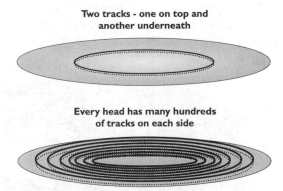

Each side of each platter contains tens of thousands of tracks. Interestingly enough, the individual tracks themselves are not directly part of the drive geometry. Our interest lies only in the groups of tracks of the same diameter, going all of the way through the drive. Each group of tracks of the same diameter is called a *cylinder* (see Figure 9-10).

Figure 9-10
Cylinder

**All tracks of the same diameter
are called a cylinder**

There's more than one cylinder! Go get yourself about a thousand more cans, each one a different diameter, and push them through the hard drive. A typical hard drive contains thousands of cylinders.

Sectors per Track

Now imagine cutting the hard drive like a birthday cake, slicing all the tracks into tens of thousands of small slivers. Each sliver is called a *sector,* and each sector stores 512 bytes of data (see Figure 9-11). Note that *sector* refers to the sliver when discussing geometry, but it refers to the specific spot on a single track within that sliver when discussing data capacity.

Figure 9-11
Sectors

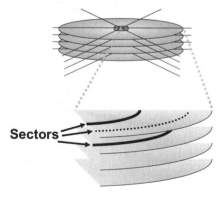

Sectors

The sector is the universal "atom" of all hard drives. You can't divide data into anything smaller than a sector. Although sectors are important, the number of sectors is not a geometry. The geometry value is called *sectors per track* (sectors/track). The sectors/track value describes the number of sectors in each track (see Figure 9-12).

Figure 9-12
Sectors per track

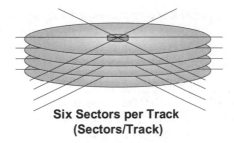

Six Sectors per Track
(Sectors/Track)

The Big Three

Cylinders, heads, and sectors/track combine to define the hard drive's geometry. In most cases, these three critical values are referred to as *CHS*. The importance of these three values lies in the fact that the PC's BIOS needs to know the drive's geometry to know how to talk to the drive. Back in the old days, a technician needed to enter these values into the CMOS setup program manually. Today, every hard drive stores the CHS information in the drive itself, in an electronic format that enables the BIOS to query the drive automatically to determine these values. You'll see more on this later in the chapter in the section called "Autodetection."

Two other values—write precompensation cylinder and landing zone—no longer have relevance in today's PCs; however, these terms still are tossed around and a few CMOS setup utilities still support them—another classic example of a technology appendix! Let's look at these two holdouts from another era so when you access CMOS, you won't say, "What the heck are these?"

Write Precompensation Cylinder

Older hard drives had a real problem with the fact that sectors toward the inside of the drives were much smaller than sectors toward the outside. To handle this, an older drive would spread data a little farther apart once it got to a particular cylinder. This cylinder was called the write precompensation (write precomp) cylinder, and the PC had to know which cylinder began this wider data spacing. Hard drives no longer have this problem, making the write precomp setting obsolete.

Landing Zone

On older hard drives with stepper motors, the landing zone value designated an unused cylinder as a "parking place" for the read/write heads. As mentioned earlier, old stepper motor hard drives needed to have their read/write heads parked before being moved in order to avoid accidental damage. Today's voice coil drives park themselves whenever they're not accessing data, automatically placing the read/write heads on the landing zone. As a result, the BIOS no longer needs the landing zone geometry.

Essentials

ATA—The King

Over the years, many interfaces existed for hard drives, with such names as ST-506 and ESDI. Don't worry about what these abbreviations stood for; neither the CompTIA A+

certification exams nor the computer world at large has an interest in these prehistoric interfaces. Starting around 1990, an interface called ATA appeared that now virtually monopolizes the hard drive market. Only one other type of interface, the moderately popular small computer system interface (SCSI), has any relevance for hard drives.

 NOTE The term *IDE* (integrated drive electronics) refers to any hard drive with a built-in controller. All hard drives are technically IDE drives, although we only use the term IDE when discussing ATA drives.

ATA drives come in two basic flavors: parallel ATA (PATA) and serial ATA (SATA). PATA drives dominated the industry for more than a decade but are being replaced by SATA drives. The leap from PATA to SATA is only one of a large number of changes that have taken place over the years with ATA. To appreciate these changes, we'll run through the many ATA standards forwarded over the years.

 NOTE Modern external drives connect to a FireWire, Hi-Speed USB 2.0, or eSATA port. All three interfaces offer high data transfer rates and hot-swap capability, making them ideal for transporting huge files such as digital video clips. Regardless of the external interface, however, inside the casing you'll find an ordinary PATA or SATA drive, just like those described in this chapter.

ATA-1

When IBM unveiled the 80286-powered IBM PC AT in the early 1980s, it introduced the first PC to include BIOS support for hard drives. This BIOS supported up to two physical drives, and each drive could be up to 504 MB—far larger than the 5-MB and 10-MB drives of the time. Although having built-in support for hard drives certainly improved the power of the PC, at that time, installing, configuring, and troubleshooting hard drives could at best be called difficult.

To address these problems, Western Digital and Compaq developed a new hard drive interface and placed this specification before the *American National Standards Institute (ANSI)* committees, which in turn put out the *AT Attachment (ATA)* interface in March of 1989. The ATA interface specified a cable and a built-in controller on the drive itself. Most importantly, the ATA standard used the existing AT BIOS on a PC, which meant that you didn't have to replace the old system BIOS to make the drive work—a very important consideration for compatibility but one that would later haunt ATA drives. The official name for the standard, ATA, never made it into the common vernacular until recently, and then only as PATA to distinguish it from SATA drives.

 NOTE The ANSI subcommittee directly responsible for the ATA standard is called Technical Committee T13. If you want to know what's happening with ATA, check out the T13 Web site: www.t13.org.

Early ATA Physical Connections

The first ATA drives connected to the computer via a 40-pin plug and a controller. Figure 9-13 shows the "business end" of an early ATA drive, with the connectors for the controller and the power cable.

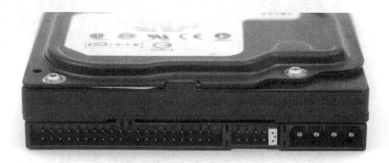

Figure 9-13 Back of IDE drive showing 40-pin connector (left), jumpers (center), and power connector (right)

The controller is the support circuitry that acts as the intermediary between the hard drive and the external data bus. Electronically, the setup looks like Figure 9-14.

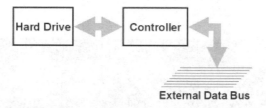

Figure 9-14 Relation of drive, controller, and bus

Wait a minute! If ATA drives are IDE, they already have a built-in controller. Why do they then have to plug into a *controller* on the motherboard? Well, this is a great example of a term that's not used properly, but everyone (including the motherboard and hard drive makers) uses it this way. What we call the ATA controller is really no more than an interface providing a connection to the rest of the PC system. When your BIOS talks to the hard drive, it actually talks to the onboard circuitry on the drive, not the connection on the motherboard. But, even though the *real* controller resides on the hard drive, the 40-pin connection on the motherboard is called the controller. We have a lot of misnomers to live with in the ATA world!

The ATA-1 standard defined that no more than two drives attach to a single IDE connector on a single ribbon cable. Because up to two drives can attach to one connector via a single cable, you need to be able to identify each drive on the cable. The ATA standard identifies the two different drives as "master" and "slave." You set one drive as master and one as slave using tiny jumpers on the drives (Figure 9-15).

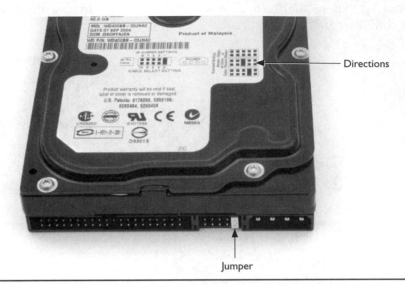

Figure 9-15 A typical hard drive with directions (top) for setting a jumper (bottom)

The controllers are on the motherboard and manifest themselves as two 40-pin male ports, as shown in Figure 9-16.

Figure 9-16
IDE interfaces on
a motherboard

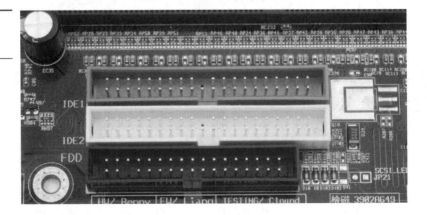

PIO and DMA Modes

If you're making a hard drive standard, you must define both the method and the speed at which the data's going to move. ATA-1 defined two different methods, the first using programmed I/O (PIO) addressing and the second using direct memory access (DMA) mode.

PIO is nothing more than the traditional I/O addressing scheme, where the CPU talks directly to the hard drive via the BIOS to send and receive data. Three different PIO speeds called *PIO modes* were initially adopted:

- PIO mode 0: 3.3 MBps (megabytes per second)
- PIO mode 1: 5.2 MBps
- PIO mode 2: 8.3 MBps

DMA modes defined a method to enable the hard drives to talk to RAM directly using old-style DMA commands. (The ATA folks called this *single word DMA*.) This old-style DMA was slow, and the resulting three ATA single word DMA modes were also slow:

- Single word DMA mode 0: 2.1 MBps
- Single word DMA mode 1: 4.2 MBps
- Single word DMA mode 2: 8.3 MBps

When a computer booted up, the BIOS queried the hard drive to see what modes it could use and would then automatically adjust to the fastest mode.

ATA-2

In 1990, the industry adopted a series of improvements to the ATA standard called ATA-2. Many people called these new features *Enhanced IDE (EIDE)*. EIDE was really no more than a marketing term invented by Western Digital, but it caught on in common vernacular and is still used today, although its use is fading. Regular IDE drives quickly disappeared, and by 1995, EIDE drives dominated the PC world. Figure 9-17 shows a typical EIDE drive.

Figure 9-17   EIDE drive

NOTE The terms *ATA, IDE,* and *EIDE* are used interchangeably.

ATA-2 was the most important ATA standard, as it included powerful new features such as higher capacities; support for non-hard drive storage devices; support for two more ATA devices, for a maximum of four; and substantially improved throughput.

Higher Capacity with LBA

IBM created the AT BIOS to support hard drives many years before IDE drives were invented, and every system had that BIOS. The developers of IDE made certain that the new drives would run from the same AT BIOS command set. With this capability, you could use the same CMOS and BIOS routines to talk to a much more advanced drive. Your motherboard or hard drive controller wouldn't become instantly obsolete when you installed a new hard drive.

NOTE Hard drive makers talk about hard drive capacities in millions and billions of bytes, not megabytes and gigabytes!

Unfortunately, the BIOS routines for the original AT command set allowed a hard drive size of only up to 528 million bytes (or 504 MB—remember that a mega = 1,048,576, not 1,000,000). A drive could have no more than 1,024 cylinders, 16 heads, and 63 sectors/track:

1,024 cylinders × 16 heads × 63 sectors/track × 512 bytes/sector = 504 MB

For years, this was not a problem. But when hard drives began to approach the 504 MB barrier, it became clear that there needed to be a way of getting past 504 MB. The ATA-2 standard defined a way to get past this limit with *logical block addressing (LBA)*. With LBA, the hard drive lies to the computer about its geometry through an advanced type of sector translation. Let's take a moment to understand sector translation, and then come back to LBA.

Sector Translation Long before hard drives approached the 504 MB limit, the limits of 1,024 cylinders, 16 heads, and 63 sectors/track gave hard drive makers fits. The big problem was the heads. Remember that every two heads means another platter, another physical disk that you have to squeeze into a hard drive. If you wanted a hard drive with the maximum number of 16 heads, you would need a hard drive with eight physical platters inside the drive! Nobody wanted that many platters: it made the drives too tall, it took more power to spin up the drive, and that many parts cost too much money (see Figure 9-18).

Figure 9-18
Too many heads

Looks a little high!

Manufacturers could readily produce a hard drive that had fewer heads and more cylinders, but the stupid 1,024/16/63 limit got in the way. Plus, the traditional sector arrangement wasted a lot of useful space. Sectors toward the inside of the drive, for example, are much shorter than the sectors on the outside. The sectors on the outside don't need to be that long, but with the traditional geometry setup, hard drive makers had no choice. They could make a hard drive store a lot more information, however, if hard drives could be made with more sectors/track on the outside tracks (see Figure 9-19).

Figure 9-19
Multiple sectors/
track

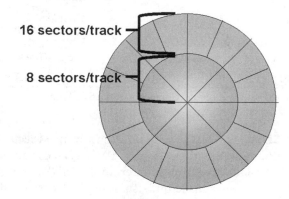

16 sectors/track

8 sectors/track

The ATA specification was designed to have two geometries. The *physical geometry* defined the real layout of the CHS inside the drive. The *logical geometry* described what the drive told the CMOS. In other words, the IDE drive "lied" to the CMOS, thus side-stepping the artificial limits of the BIOS. When data was being transferred to and from the drive, the onboard circuitry of the drive translated the logical geometry into the physical geometry. This function was, and still is, called *sector translation*.

Let's look at a couple of hypothetical examples in action. First, pretend that Seagate came out with a new, cheap, fast hard drive called the ST108. To get the ST108 drive fast and cheap, however, Seagate had to use a rather strange geometry, shown in Table 9-1.

ST108 Physical			BIOS Limits
Cylinders	2,048	Cylinders	1,024
Heads	2	Heads	16
Sectors/Track	52	Sectors/Track	63
Total Capacity	108 MB		

Table 9-1 Seagate's ST108 Drive Geometry

Notice that the cylinder number is greater than 1,024. To overcome this problem, the IDE drive performs a sector translation that reports a geometry to the BIOS that is totally different from the true geometry of the drive. Table 9-2 shows the actual geometry and the "logical" geometry of our mythical ST108 drive. Notice that the logical geometry is now within the acceptable parameters of the BIOS limitations. Sector translation never changes the capacity of the drive; it changes only the geometry to stay within the BIOS limits.

Physical		Logical	
Cylinders	2,048	Cylinders	512
Heads	2	Heads	8
Sectors/Track	52	Sectors/Track	52
Total Capacity	108 MB	Total Capacity	108 MB

Table 9-2 Physical and Logical Geometry of the ST108 Drive

Back to LBA Now let's watch how the advanced sector translation of LBA provides support for hard drives greater than 504 MB. Let's use an old drive, the Western Digital WD2160, a 2.1-GB hard drive, as an example. This drive is no longer in production but its smaller CHS values make understanding LBA easier. Table 9-3 lists its physical and logical geometries.

Physical		Logical	
Cylinders	16,384	Cylinders	1,024
Heads	4	Heads	64
Sectors/Track	63	Sectors/Track	63
Total Capacity	2.1 GB	Total Capacity	2.1 GB

Table 9-3 Western Digital WD2160's Physical and Logical Geometries

Note that, even with sector translation, the number of heads is greater than the allowed 16! So here's where the magic of LBA comes in. The WD2160 is capable of LBA. Now assuming that the BIOS is also capable of LBA, here's what happens. When the computer boots up, the BIOS asks the drives if they can perform LBA. If they say yes, the BIOS and the drive work together to change the way they talk to each other. They can do this without conflicting with the original AT BIOS commands by taking advantage of unused commands to use up to 256 heads. LBA enables support for a maximum of $1,024 \times 256 \times 63 \times 512$ bytes = 8.4-GB hard drives. Back in 1990, 8.4 GB was hundreds of time larger than the drives used at the time. Don't worry, later ATA standards will get the BIOS up to today's huge drives!

Not Just Hard Drives Anymore: ATAPI

ATA-2 added an extension to the ATA specification, called Advanced Technology Attachment Packet Interface (ATAPI), that enabled non-hard drive devices such as CD-ROM drives and tape backups to connect to the PC via the ATA controllers. ATAPI drives have the same 40-pin interface and master/slave jumpers as ATA hard drives. Figure 9-20 shows an ATAPI CD-RW drive attached to a motherboard. The key difference between hard drives and every other type of drive that attaches to the ATA controller is in how the drives get BIOS support. Hard drives get it through the system BIOS, whereas non-hard drives require the operating system to load a software driver.

Figure 9-20 ATAPI CD-RW drive attached to a motherboard via a standard, 40-pin ribbon cable

NOTE With the introduction of ATAPI, the ATA standards are often referred to as ATA/ATAPI instead of just ATA.

More Drives with ATA-2

ATA-2 added support for a second controller, raising the total number of supported drives from two to four. Each of the two controllers is equal in power and capability. Figure 9-21 is a close-up of a typical motherboard, showing the primary controller marked as *IDE1* and the secondary marked as *IDE2*.

Figure 9-21 Primary and secondary controllers labeled on a motherboard

Increased Speed

ATA-2 defined two new PIO modes and a new type of DMA called *multi-word DMA* that was a substantial improvement over the old DMA. Technically, multi-word DMA was still the old-style DMA, but it worked in a much more efficient manner so it was much faster.

- PIO mode 3: 11.1 MBps
- PIO mode 4: 16.6 MBps
- Multi-word DMA mode 0: 4.2 MBps

- Multi-word DMA mode 1: 13.3 MBps
- Multi-word DMA mode 2: 16.6 MBps

ATA-3

ATA-3 came on quickly after ATA-2 and added one new feature called *Self-Monitoring, Analysis, and Reporting Technology* (*S.M.A.R.T.*, one of the few PC acronyms that requires the use of periods after each letter). S.M.A.R.T. helps predict when a hard drive is going to fail by monitoring the hard drive's mechanical components.

S.M.A.R.T. is a great idea and is popular in specialized server systems, but it's complex, imperfect, and hard to understand. As a result, only a few utilities can read the S.M.A.R.T. data on your hard drive. Your best sources are the hard drive manufacturers. Every hard drive maker has a free diagnostic tool (that usually works only for their drives) that will do a S.M.A.R.T. check along with other tests. Figure 9-22 shows Western Digital's Data Lifeguard Tool in action. Note that it says only whether the drive has passed or not. Figure 9-23 shows some S.M.A.R.T. information.

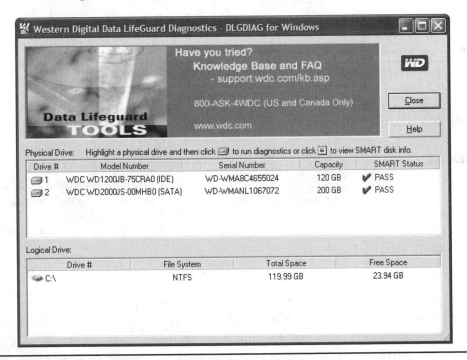

Figure 9-22   Data Lifeguard

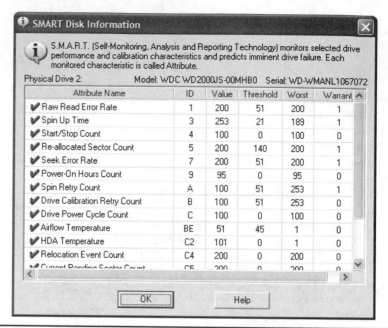

Figure 9-23 S.M.A.R.T. information

Although you can see the actual S.M.A.R.T. data, it's generally useless or indecipherable. It's best to trust the manufacturer's opinion and run the software provided.

ATA-4

Anyone who has opened a big database file on a hard drive appreciates that a faster hard drive is better. ATA-4 introduced a new DMA mode called Ultra-DMA that is now the primary way a hard drive communicates with a PC. Ultra DMA uses DMA bus mastering to achieve far faster speeds than was possible with PIO or old-style DMA. ATA-4 defined three Ultra DMA modes:

- Ultra DMA mode 0: 16.7 MBps
- Ultra DMA mode 1: 25.0 MBps
- Ultra DMA mode 2: 33.3 MBps

 NOTE Ultra DMA mode 2, the most popular of the ATA-4 DMA modes, is also called ATA/33.

INT13 Extensions

Here's an interesting factoid for you: The original ATA-1 standard allowed for hard drives up to 137 GB! It wasn't the ATA standard that caused the 504-MB size limit, it was the fact that the standard used the old AT BIOS and the BIOS, not the ATA standard, could support only 504 MB. LBA was a work-around that told the hard drive to lie to the BIOS to get it up to 8.4 GB. But eventually hard drives started edging close to the LBA limit and something had to be done. The T13 folks said, "This isn't *our* problem! It's the ancient BIOS problem. You BIOS makers need to fix the BIOS!" And they did.

In 1994, Phoenix Technologies (the BIOS manufacturer) came up with a new set of BIOS commands called *Interrupt 13 (INT13) extensions*. INT13 extensions broke the 8.4-GB barrier by completely ignoring the CHS values and instead feeding the LBA a stream of addressable sectors. A system with INT13 extensions can handle drives up to 137 GB. The entire PC industry quickly adopted INT13 extensions and every system made since 2000–2001 supports INT13 extensions.

ATA-5

Ultra DMA was such a huge hit that the ATA folks adopted two faster Ultra DMA modes with ATA-5:

- Ultra DMA mode 3: 44.4 MBps
- Ultra DMA mode 4: 66.6 MBps

NOTE Ultra DMA mode 4, the most popular of the ATA-5 DMA modes, is also called ATA/66.

Ultra DMA modes 4 and 5 ran so quickly that the ATA-5 standard defined a new type of ribbon cable of handling the higher speeds. This cable still has 40 pins on the connectors, but it includes another 40 wires in the cable that act as grounds to improve the cable's ability to handle high-speed signals. Previous versions of ATA didn't define where the different drives were plugged into the ribbon cable, but ATA-5 defined exactly where the controller, master, and slave drives connected, even defining colors to identify them. Take a look at the ATA/66 cable in Figure 9-24. The connector on the left is colored blue (which you could see if the photo was in color!)—that connector must be the one used to plug into the controller. The connector in the middle is grey—that's for the slave drive. The connector on the right is black—that's for the master drive. Any ATA/66 controller connections are colored blue to let you know it is an ATA/66 controller.

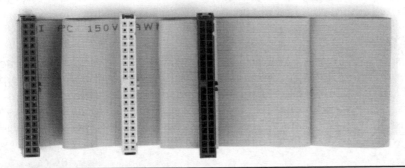

Figure 9-24   ATA/66 cable

ATA/66 is backward compatible, so you may safely plug an earlier drive into an ATA/66 cable and controller. If you plug an ATA/66 drive into an older controller it will work—just not in ATA/66 mode. The only risky action is to use an ATA/66 controller and hard drive with a non-ATA/66 cable. Doing so will almost certainly cause nasty data losses!

ATA-6

Hard drive size exploded in the early 21st century and the seemingly impossible-to-fill 137-GB limit created by INT13 extensions became a barrier to fine computing more quickly than most people had anticipated. When drives started hitting the 120-GB mark, the T13 committee adopted an industry proposal pushed by Maxtor (a major hard drive maker) called *Big Drive* that increased the limit to more than 144 petabytes (approximately 144,000,000 GB). T13 also thankfully gave the new standard a less-silly name, calling it ATA-6. Big Drive was basically just a 48-bit LBA, supplanting the older 24-bit addressing of LBA and INT13 extensions. Plus, the standard defined an enhanced block mode, enabling drives to transfer up to 65,536 sectors in one chunk, up from the measly 256 sectors of lesser drive technologies.

ATA-6 also introduced Ultra DMA mode 5, kicking the data transfer rate up to 100 MBps. Ultra DMA mode 5 is more commonly referred to as ATA/100, which requires the same 80-wire connectors as ATA/66.

ATA-7

ATA-7 brought two new innovations to the ATA world—one evolutionary and the other revolutionary. The evolutionary innovation came with the last of the parallel ATA Ultra DMA modes; the revolutionary was a new form of ATA called *serial ATA (SATA)*.

ATA/133

ATA-7 introduced the fastest and probably least adopted of all the ATA speeds, Ultra DMA mode 6 (ATA/133). Even though it runs at a speed of 133 MBps, the fact that it came out with SATA kept many hard drive manufacturers away. ATA/133 uses the same cables as Ultra DMA 66 and 100.

While you won't find many ATA/133 hard drives, you will find plenty of ATA/133 controllers. There's a trend in the industry to color the controller connections on the hard drive red, although this is not part of the ATA-7 standard.

Serial ATA

The real story of ATA-7 is SATA. For all its longevity as the mass storage interface of choice for the PC, parallel ATA has problems. First, the flat ribbon cables impede air-flow and can be a pain to insert properly. Second, the cables have a limited length, only 18 inches. Third, you can't hot-swap PATA drives. You have to shut down completely before installing or replacing a drive. Finally, the technology has simply reached the limits of what it can do in terms of throughput.

Serial ATA addresses these issues. SATA creates a point-to-point connection between the SATA device—hard disk, CD-ROM, CD-RW, DVD-ROM, DVD-RW, and so on—and the SATA controller. At a glance, SATA devices look identical to standard PATA devices. Take a closer look at the cable and power connectors, however, and you'll see significant differences (Figure 9-25).

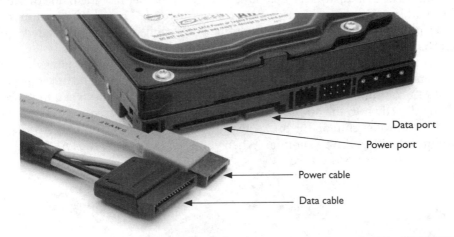

Data port
Power port
Power cable
Data cable

Figure 9-25   SATA hard drive cables and connectors

Because SATA devices send data serially instead of in parallel, the SATA interface needs far fewer physical wires—seven instead of the eighty wires that is typical of PATA—resulting in much thinner cabling. This might not seem significant, but the benefit is that thinner cabling means better cable control and better airflow through the PC case, resulting in better cooling.

Further, the maximum SATA device cable length is more than twice that of an IDE cable—about 40 inches (1 meter) instead of 18 inches. Again, this might not seem like a big deal, unless you've struggled to connect a PATA hard disk installed into the top bay of a full-tower case to an IDE connector located all the way at the bottom of the motherboard!

SATA does away with the entire master/slave concept. Each drive connects to one port, so no more daisy-chaining drives. Further, there's no maximum number of drives—many motherboards are now available that support up to eight SATA drives. Want more? Snap in a SATA host card and load 'em up!

The big news, however, is in data throughput. As the name implies, SATA devices transfer data in serial bursts instead of parallel, as PATA devices do. Typically, you might not think of serial devices as being faster than parallel, but in this case, that's exactly the case. A SATA device's single stream of data moves much faster than the multiple streams of data coming from a parallel IDE device—theoretically up to 30 times faster! SATA drives come in two common varieties, the 1.5Gb and the 3Gb, that have a maximum throughput of 150 MBps and 300 MBps, respectively.

Number-savvy readers might have noticed a discrepancy between the names and throughput of the two SATA drives. After all, 1.5 Gb per second throughput translates to 192 MB per second, a lot higher than the advertised speed of a "mere" 150 MBps. The same is true of the 3Gb/300 MBps drives. The encoding scheme used on SATA drives takes about 20 percent of the overhead for the drive, leaving 80 percent for pure bandwidth. The 3Gb drive created all kinds of problems, because the name of the committee working on the specifications was called the SATA II committee, and marketers picked up on the SATA II name. As a result, you'll find many brands called SATA II rather than 3Gb. The SATA committee now goes by the name SATA-IO.

SATA is backward-compatible with current PATA standards and enables you to install a parallel ATA device, including a hard drive, CD-media drive, and other devices, to a serial ATA controller by using a SATA *bridge*. A SATA bridge manifests as a tiny card that you plug directly into the 40-pin connector on a PATA drive. As you can see in Figure 9-26, the controller chip on the bridge requires separate power; you plug a Molex connector into the PATA drive as normal. When you boot the system, the PATA drive shows up to the system as a SATA drive.

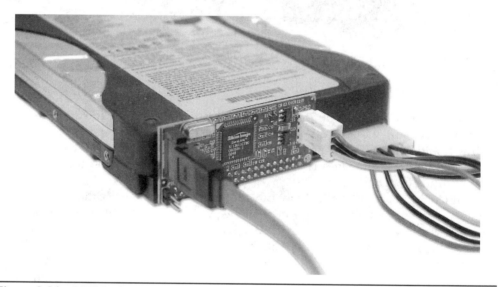

Figure 9-26   SATA bridge

SATA's ease of use has made it the choice for desktop system storage, and its success is already showing in the fact that more than 90 percent of all hard drives sold today are SATA drives.

eSATA

External SATA (eSATA) extends the SATA bus to external devices, as the name would imply. The eSATA drives use similar connectors to internal SATA, but they're keyed differently so you can't mistake one for the other. Figure 9-27 shows eSATA connectors on the back of a motherboard. eSATA uses shielded cable lengths up to 2 meters outside the PC and is hot pluggable. The beauty of eSATA is that it extends the SATA bus at full speed, so you're not limited to the meager 50 or 60 MBps of FireWire or USB.

Figure 9-27
eSATA connectors
(center; that's a
FireWire port
on the left)

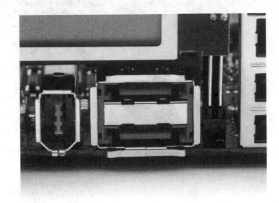

SCSI: Still Around

Many specialized server machines and enthusiasts' systems use the SCSI technologies for various pieces of core hardware and peripherals, from hard drives to printers to high-end tape backup machines. SCSI is different from ATA in that SCSI devices connect together in a string of devices called a *chain*. Each device in the chain gets a SCSI ID to distinguish it from other devices on the chain. Last, the ends of a SCSI chain must be terminated. Let's dive into SCSI now, and see how SCSI chains, SCSI IDs, and termination all work.

SCSI is an old technology dating from the late 1970s, but it has been continually updated. SCSI is faster than ATA (though the gap is closing fast), and until SATA arrived SCSI was the only choice for anyone using RAID (see the "RAID" section a little later). SCSI is arguably fading away, but it still deserves some mention.

SCSI Chains

SCSI manifests itself through a SCSI chain, a series of SCSI devices working together through a host adapter. The host adapter provides the interface between the SCSI chain and the PC. Figure 9-28 shows a typical PCI host adapter. Many techs refer to the host adapter as the *SCSI controller*, so you should be comfortable with both terms.

Figure 9-28   SCSI host adapter

All SCSI devices can be divided into two groups: internal and external. Internal SCSI devices are attached inside the PC and connect to the host adapter through the latter's internal connector. Figure 9-29 shows an internal SCSI device, in this case a CD-ROM drive. External devices hook to the external connector of the host adapter. Figure 9-30 is an example of an external SCSI device.

Figure 9-29   Internal SCSI CD-ROM

Figure 9-30   Back of external SCSI device

Internal SCSI devices connect to the host adapter with a 68-pin ribbon cable (Figure 9-31). This flat, flexible cable functions precisely like a PATA cable. Many external devices connect to the host adapter with a 50-pin high density (HD) connector. Figure 9-32 shows a host adapter external port. Higher end SCSI devices use a 68-pin high density (HD) connector.

Figure 9-31   Typical 68-pin ribbon cable

Figure 9-32   50-pin HD port on SCSI host adapter

Multiple internal devices can be connected together simply by using a cable with enough connectors. Figure 9-33, for example, shows a cable that can take up to four SCSI devices, including the host adapter.

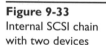

Figure 9-33
Internal SCSI chain
with two devices

Assuming the SCSI host adapter has a standard external port (some controllers don't have external connections at all), plugging in an external SCSI device is as simple as running a cable from device to controller. The external SCSI connectors are D-shaped, so you can't plug them in backward. As an added bonus, some external SCSI devices have two ports, one to connect to the host adapter and a second to connect to another SCSI device. The process of connecting a device directly to another device is called *daisy-chaining*. You can daisy-chain up to 15 devices to one host adapter. SCSI chains can be internal, external, or both (see Figure 9-34).

Figure 9-34
Internal and external
devices on one SCSI
chain

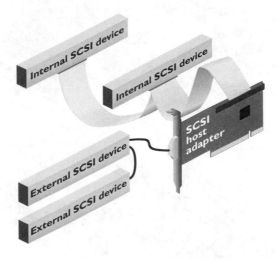

SCSI IDs

If you're going to connect a number of devices on the same SCSI chain, you must provide some way for the host adapter to tell one device from another. To differentiate devices, SCSI uses a unique identifier called the *SCSI ID*. The SCSI ID number can range from 0 to 15. SCSI IDs are similar to many other PC hardware settings in that a SCSI device can theoretically have any SCSI ID, as long as that ID is not already taken by another device connected to the same host adapter.

NOTE Old SCSI equipment allowed SCSI IDs from 0 to 7 only.

Some conventions should be followed when setting SCSI IDs. Typically, most people set the host adapter to 7 or 15, but you can change this setting. Note that there is no order for the use of SCSI IDs. It does not matter which device gets which number, and you can skip numbers. Restrictions on IDs apply only within a single chain. Two devices can have the same ID, in other words, as long as they are on different chains (Figure 9-35).

Figure 9-35
IDs don't conflict
between separate
SCSI chains.

Every SCSI device has some method of setting its SCSI ID. The trick is to figure out how as you're holding the device in your hand. A SCSI device may use jumpers, dip switches, or even tiny dials; every new SCSI device is a new adventure as you try to determine how to set its SCSI ID.

Termination

Whenever you send a signal down a wire, some of that signal reflects back up the wire, creating an echo and causing electronic chaos. SCSI chains use *termination* to prevent this problem. Termination simply means putting something on the ends of the wire to prevent this echo. Terminators are usually pull-down resistors and can manifest themselves in many different ways. Most of the devices within a PC have the appropriate termination built in. On other devices, including SCSI chains and some network cables, you have to set termination during installation.

The rule with SCSI is that you *must* terminate *only* the ends of the SCSI chain. You have to terminate the ends of the cable, which usually means that you need to terminate the two devices at the ends of the cable. Do *not* terminate devices that are not on the ends of the cable. Figure 9-36 shows some examples of where to terminate SCSI devices.

Figure 9-36
Location of the
terminated devices

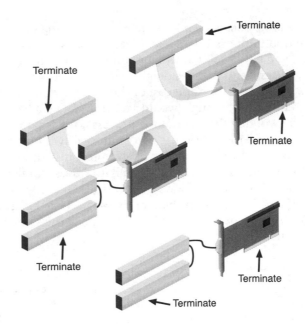

Because any SCSI device might be on the end of a chain, most manufacturers build SCSI devices that can self-terminate. Some devices will detect that they are on the end of the SCSI chain and will automatically terminate themselves. Most devices, however, require that you set a jumper or switch to enable termination (Figure 9-37).

Figure 9-37
Setting termination

Protecting Data with RAID

Ask experienced techs, "What is the most expensive part of a PC?" and they'll all answer in the same way: "It's the data." You can replace any single part of your PC for a few hundred dollars at most, but if you lose critical data—well, let's just say I know of two small companies that went out of business just because they lost a hard drive full of data.

Data is king; data is your PC's *raison d'être*. Losing data is a bad thing, so you need some method to prevent data loss. Now, of course, you can do backups, but if a hard drive dies, you have to shut down the computer, reinstall a new hard drive, reinstall the operating system, and then restore the backup. There's nothing wrong with this as long as you can afford the time and cost of shutting down the system.

A better solution, though, would save your data if a hard drive died and enable you to continue working throughout the process. This is possible if you stop relying on a single hard drive and instead use two or more drives to store your data. Sounds good, but how do you do this? Well, first of all, you could install some fancy hard drive controller that reads and writes data to two hard drives simultaneously (Figure 9-38). The data on each drive would always be identical. One drive would be the primary drive and the other drive, called the *mirror* drive, would not be used unless the primary drive failed. This process of reading and writing data at the same time to two drives is called *disk mirroring*.

Figure 9-38
Mirrored drives

RAID 1 (Mirroring)
- **Exactly two (redundant) drives**
- **Safe but Slow**
- **Both drives are assigned the same drive letter**

If you really want to make data safe, you can use two separate controllers for each drive. With two drives, each on a separate controller, the system will continue to operate, even if the primary drive's controller stops working. This super-drive mirroring technique is called *disk duplexing* (Figure 9-39). Disk duplexing is also much faster than disk mirroring because one controller does not write each piece of data twice.

Figure 9-39
Duplexing drives

RAID 1 (Duplexing)
- **Exactly two (redundant) drives**
- **Faster and safer!**
- **Both drives are assigned the same drive letter**

Even though duplexing is faster than mirroring, they both are slower than the classic one drive, one controller setup. You can use multiple drives to increase your hard drive access speed. *Disk striping* (without parity) means spreading the data among multiple (at least two) drives. Disk striping by itself provides no redundancy. If you save a small Microsoft Word file, for example, the file is split into multiple pieces; half of the pieces go on one drive and half on the other (Figure 9-40).

Figure 9-40
Disk striping

RAID 0 (Striping)
- **Two or more (non-redundant) drives**
- **Fast, but not really safe**
- **Both drives are assigned the same drive letter**

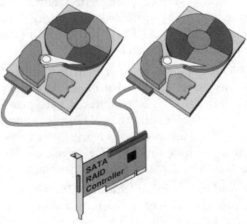

The one and only advantage of disk striping is speed—it is a fast way to read and write to hard drives. But if either drive fails, *all* data is lost. Disk striping is not something you should do—unless you're willing to increase the risk of losing data to increase the speed at which your hard drives save and restore data.

Disk striping with parity, in contrast, protects data by adding extra information, called *parity data,* that can be used to rebuild data should one of the drives fail. Disk striping with parity requires at least three drives, but it is common to use more than three. Disk striping with parity combines the best of disk mirroring and plain disk striping. It protects data and is quite fast. The majority of network servers use a type of disk striping with parity.

RAID

A couple of sharp guys in Berkeley back in the 1980s organized the many techniques for using multiple drives for data protection and increasing speeds as the *random array of inexpensive disks* or *redundant array of independent disks (RAID)*. They outlined seven levels of RAID, numbered 0 through 6.

 NOTE An *array* in the context of RAID refers to a collection of two or more hard drives.

- **RAID 0—Disk Striping**   Disk striping requires at least two drives. It does not provide redundancy to data. If any one drive fails, all data is lost.

- **RAID 1—Disk Mirroring/Duplexing**   RAID 1 arrays require at least two hard drives, although they also work with any even number of drives. RAID 1 is the ultimate in safety, but you lose storage space since the data is duplicated—you need two 100-GB drives to store 100 GB of data.

- **RAID 2—Disk Striping with Multiple Parity Drives**   RAID 2 was a weird RAID idea that never saw practical use. Unused, ignore it.

- **RAID 3 and 4—Disk Striping with Dedicated Parity**   RAID 3 and 4 combined dedicated data drives with dedicated parity drives. The differences between the two are trivial. Unlike RAID 2, these versions did see some use in the real world but were quickly replaced by RAID 5.

- **RAID 5—Disk Striping with Distributed Parity**   Instead of dedicated data and parity drives, RAID 5 distributes data and parity information evenly across all drives. This is the fastest way to provide data redundancy. RAID 5 is by far the most common RAID implementation and requires at least three drives. RAID 5 arrays effectively use one drive's worth of space for parity. If, for example, you have three 200-GB drives, your total storage capacity is 400 GB. If you have four 200-GB drives, your total capacity is 600 GB.

- **RAID 6—Disk Striping with Extra Parity**   If you lose a hard drive in a RAID 5 array, your data is at great risk until you replace the bad hard drive and rebuild the array. RAID 6 is RAID 5 with extra parity information. RAID 6 needs at least five drives, but in exchange you can lose up to two drives at the same time. RAID 6 is gaining in popularity for those willing to use larger arrays.

After these first RAID levels were defined, some manufacturers came up with ways to combine different RAIDs. For example, what if you took two pairs of striped drives and mirrored the pairs? You would get what is called RAID 0+1. Or what (read this carefully now) if you took two pairs of mirrored drives and striped the pairs? You then get what we call RAID 1+0 or what is often called RAID 10. Combinations of different types of single RAID are called Multiple RAID solutions. Multiple RAID solutions, while enjoying some support in the real world, are quite rare when compared to single RAID solutions RAID 0, 1, and 5.

NOTE There is actually a term for a storage system composed of multiple independent disks, rather than disks organized using RAID: *JBOD*, which stands for Just a Bunch of Disks (or Drives).

Implementing RAID

RAID levels describe different methods of providing data redundancy or enhancing the speed of data throughput to and from groups of hard drives. They do not say *how* to implement these methods. Literally thousands of different methods can be used to set up RAID. The method used depends largely on the desired level of RAID, the operating system used, and the thickness of your wallet.

The obvious starting place for RAID is to connect at least two hard drives in some fashion to create a RAID array. For many years, if you wanted to do RAID beyond RAID 0 and RAID 1, the only technology you could use was good-old SCSI. SCSI's chaining of multiple devices to a single controller made it a natural for RAID. SCSI drives make superb RAID arrays, but the high cost of SCSI drives and RAID-capable host adapters kept RAID away from all but the most critical systems—usually big file servers.

In the last few years, substantial leaps in ATA technology have made ATA a viable alternative to SCSI drive technology for RAID arrays. Specialized ATA RAID controller cards support ATA RAID arrays of up to 15 drives—plenty to support even the most complex RAID needs. In addition, the inherent hot-swap capabilities of serial ATA have virtually guaranteed that serial ATA will quickly take over the lower end of the RAID business. Personally, I think the price and performance of serial ATA mean SCSI's days are numbered.

Once you have a number of hard drives, the next question is whether to use hardware or software to control the array. Let's look at both options.

Hardware versus Software

All RAID implementations break down into either hardware or software methods. Software is often used when price takes priority over performance. Hardware is used when you need speed along with data redundancy. Software RAID does not require special controllers—you can use the regular ATA controllers or SCSI host adapters to make a software RAID array. But you do need "smart" software. The most common software implementation of RAID is the built-in RAID software that comes with Windows 2000 Server and Windows Server 2003. The Disk Management program in these Windows Server versions can configure drives for RAID 0, 1, or 5, and it works with ATA or SCSI

(Figure 9-41). Disk Management in Windows 2000 Professional and Windows XP Professional, in contrast, can only do RAID 0.

Figure 9-41
Disk Management
in Windows
Server 2003

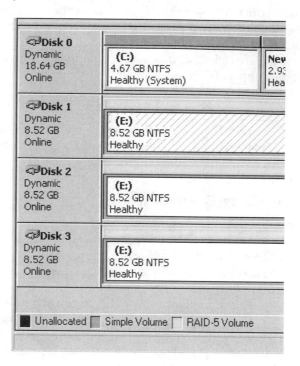

NOTE You can use Disk Management in Windows 2000 and Windows XP Professional to create RAID 1 and RAID 5 arrays, but you can use Disk Management only remotely on a server version of Windows (2000 Server or Server 2003). In other words, the capability is there, but Microsoft has limited the OS. If you want to use software RAID in Windows 2000 or XP (Home or Professional), you need to use a third-party tool to set it up.

Windows Disk Management is not the only software RAID game in town. A number of third-party software programs can be used with Windows or other operating systems.

Software RAID means the operating system is in charge of all RAID functions. It works for small RAID solutions but tends to overwork your operating system easily, creating slowdowns. When you *really* need to keep going, when you need RAID that doesn't even let the users know a problem has occurred, hardware RAID is the answer.

Hardware RAID centers around an *intelligent* controller—either a SCSI host adapter or an ATA controller that handles all of the RAID functions (Figure 9-42). Unlike a regular ATA controller or SCSI host adapter, these controllers have chips that know how to "talk RAID."

Most RAID setups in the real world are hardware-based. Almost all of the many hardware RAID solutions provide *hot-swapping*—the ability to replace a bad drive without disturbing the operating system. Hot swapping is common in hardware RAID.

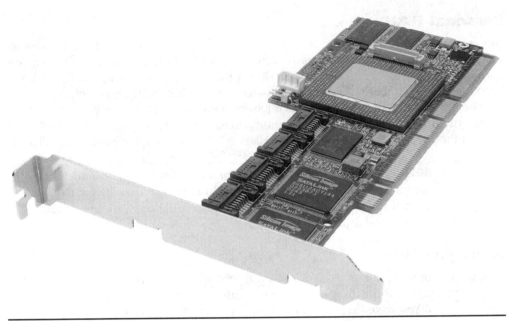

Figure 9-42   Serial ATA RAID controller

Hardware-based RAID is invisible to the operating system and is configured in several ways, depending on the specific chips involved. Most RAID systems have a special configuration utility in Flash ROM that you access after CMOS but before the OS loads. Figure 9-43 shows a typical firmware program used to configure a hardware RAID solution.

```
FastBuild (tm) Utility (c) 2004-2005 Promise Technology, Inc.
========================[ View Drives Assignments ]========================

      Channel:ID      Drive Model           Capacity (MB)  Assignment
         1:Mas  HDT722525DLA380               250059
                Extent 1                      249992        LD   1-1
         2:Mas  HDT722525DLA380               250059
                Extent 2                      249992        LD   1-2
         3:Mas  HDT722525DLA380               250059
                Extent 3                      249992        LD   1-3
         4:Mas  HDT722525DLA380               250059
                Extent 4                      249992        LD   1-4




                        ===========[ Keys Available ]===========

   [↑] Up    [↓] Down    [ESC] Exit
```

Figure 9-43   RAID configuration utility

Personal RAID

Due to drastic reductions in the cost of ATA RAID controller chips, in the last few years we've seen an explosion of ATA-based hardware RAID solutions built into mainstream motherboards. While this "ATA RAID on the motherboard" began with parallel ATA, the introduction of serial ATA made motherboards with built-in RAID extremely common.

These personal RAID motherboards might be quite common, but they're not used too terribly often given that these RAID solutions usually provide only RAID 0 or RAID 1. If you want to use RAID, spend a few extra dollars and buy a RAID 5–capable controller.

 NOTE RAID controllers aren't just for internal drives; some models can handle multiple eSATA drives configured using any of the different RAID levels. If you're feeling lucky, you can create a RAID array using both internal and external SATA drives.

Managing Heat

Adding three or more fast hard drives into a cramped PC case can be a recipe for disaster to the unwary tech. All those disks spinning constantly create a phenomenal amount of heat. Heat kills PCs! You've got to manage the heat inside a RAID-enabled system or risk losing your data, drives, and basic system stability. The easiest way to do this is to add fans.

Open up your PC case and look for built-in places to mount fans. Note how many case fans you currently have installed and the sizes you can use. (Most cases use 80 mm fans, but 60 and 120 mm fans are common as well.) Jot down the particulars of your system and take a trip to the local PC store to check out the fans.

Before you get all fan-happy and grab the biggest and baddest fans to throw in your case, don't forget to think about the added noise level. Try to get a compromise between keeping your case cool enough and not causing early deafness!

The Future Is RAID

RAID has been with us for about 20 years, but until only recently it was the domain of big systems and deep pockets. During those 20 years, however, a number of factors have come together to make RAID a reality for both big servers and common desktop systems. Imagine a world where dirt-cheap RAID on every computer means no one ever again losing critical data. I get goose bumps just thinking about it!

Connecting Drives

Installing a drive is a fairly simple process if you take the time to make sure you've got the right drive for your system, configured the drive properly, and made a few quick tests to see if it's running properly. Since PATA, SATA, and SCSI have different cabling requirements, we'll look at each of these separately.

Choosing Your Drive

First, decide where you're going to put the drive. Look for an open ATA connection. Is it PATA or SATA? Is it a dedicated RAID controller? Many motherboards with built-in RAID controllers have a CMOS setting that enables you to turn the RAID on or off (Figure 9-44). Do you have the right controller for a SCSI drive?

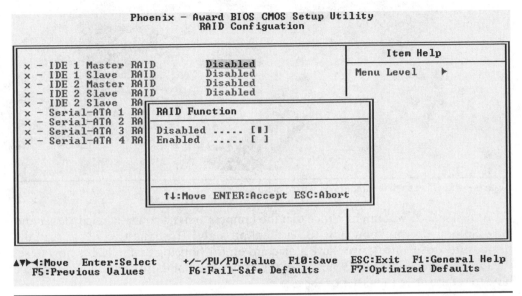

Figure 9-44 Settings for RAID in CMOS

Second, make sure you have room for the drive in the case. Where will you place it? Do you have a spare power connector? Will the data and power cables reach the drive? A quick test fit is always a good idea.

Don't worry about PIO Modes and DMA—a new drive will support anything your controller wants to do.

Jumpers and Cabling on PATA Drives

If you have only one hard drive, set the drive's jumpers to master or standalone. If you have two drives, set one to master and the other to slave. Figure 9-45 shows a close-up of a PATA hard drive showing the jumpers.

Figure 9-45   Master/slave jumpers on a hard drive

At first glance, you might notice that the jumpers aren't actually labeled *master* and *slave*. So how do you know how to set them properly? The easiest way is to read the front of the drive; most drives have a diagram on the housing that explains how to set the jumpers properly. Figure 9-46 shows the front of one of these drives, so you can see how to set the drive to master or slave.

Figure 9-46
Drive label showing master/slave settings

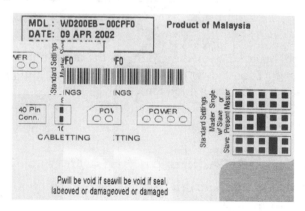

Hard drives may have other jumpers that may or may not concern you during installation. One common set of jumpers is used for diagnostics at the manufacturing plant or for special settings in other kinds of devices that use hard drives. Ignore them. They have no bearing in the PC world. Second, many drives provide a third setting, which is used if only one drive connects to a controller. Often, master and single drive are the same setting on the hard drive, although some hard drives require separate settings. Note that the name for the single drive setting varies among manufacturers. Some use Single; others use 1 Drive or Standalone.

Many current PATA hard drives use a jumper setting called *cable select,* rather than master or slave. As the name implies, the position on the cable determines which drive will be master or slave: master on the end, slave in the middle. For cable select to work properly with two drives, both drives must be set as cable select and the cable itself must be a special cable-select cable. If you see a ribbon cable with a pinhole through one wire, watch out! That's a cable-select cable.

NOTE   Most of the high speed ATA/66/100/133 cables support cable select—try one and see!

If you don't see a label on the drive that tells you how to set the jumpers, you have several options. First, look for the drive maker's Web site. Every drive manufacturer lists its drive jumper settings on the Web, although it can take a while to find the information you want. Second, try phoning the hard drive maker directly. Unlike many other PC parts manufacturers, hard drive producers tend to stay in business for a long period of time and offer great technical support.

Hard drive cables have a colored stripe that corresponds to the number-one pin—called *Pin 1*—on the connector. You need to make certain that Pin 1 on the controller is on the same wire as Pin 1 on the hard drive. Failing to plug in the drive properly will also prevent the PC from recognizing the drive. If you incorrectly set the master/slave jumpers or cable to the hard drives, you won't break anything; it just won't work.

Finally, you need to plug a Molex connector from the power supply into the drive. All modern PATA drives use a Molex connector.

Cabling SATA Drives

Installing SATA hard drives is even easier than installing IDE devices due to the fact that there's no master, slave, or cable select configuration to mess with. In fact, there are no jumper settings to worry about at all, as SATA supports only a single device per controller channel. Simply connect the power and plug in the controller cable as shown in Figure 9-47—the OS automatically detects the drive and it's ready to go! The keying on SATA controller and power cables makes it impossible to install either incorrectly.

Figure 9-47
Properly connected
SATA cable

The biggest problem with SATA drives is that many motherboards come with four or more. Sure, the cabling is easy enough, but what do you do when it comes time to start the computer and the system is trying to find the right hard drive to boot up! That's where CMOS comes into play.

Connecting SCSI Drives

Connecting SCSI drives requires three things. You must use a controller that works with your drive. You need to set unique SCSI IDs on the controller and the drive. Finally, you need to connect the ribbon cable and power connections properly. With SCSI, you need to attach the data cable correctly. You can reverse a PATA cable, for example, and nothing happens except the drive doesn't work. If you reverse a SCSI cable, however, you can seriously damage the drive. Just as with PATA cables, Pin 1 on the SCSI data cable must go to Pin 1 on both the drive and the host adapter.

BIOS Support: Configuring CMOS and Installing Drivers

Every device in your PC needs BIOS support, and the hard drive controllers are no exception. Motherboards provide support for the ATA hard drive controllers via the system BIOS, but they require configuration in CMOS for the specific hard drives attached. SCSI drives require software drivers or firmware on the host adapter.

In the old days, you had to fire up CMOS and manually enter CHS information whenever you installed a new ATA drive to ensure the system saw the drive. Today, this process still takes place, but it's much more automated. Still, there's plenty to do in CMOS when you install a new hard drive.

CMOS settings for hard drives vary a lot among motherboards. The following information provides a generic look at the most common settings, but you'll need to look at your specific motherboard manual to understand all the options available.

Configuring Controllers

As a first step in configuring controllers, make certain they're enabled. It's easy to turn off controllers in CMOS, and many motherboards turn off secondary ATA controllers by default. Scan through your CMOS settings to locate the controller on/off options (see Figure 9-48 for typical settings). This is also the time to check whether your on-board RAID controllers work in both RAID and non-RAID settings.

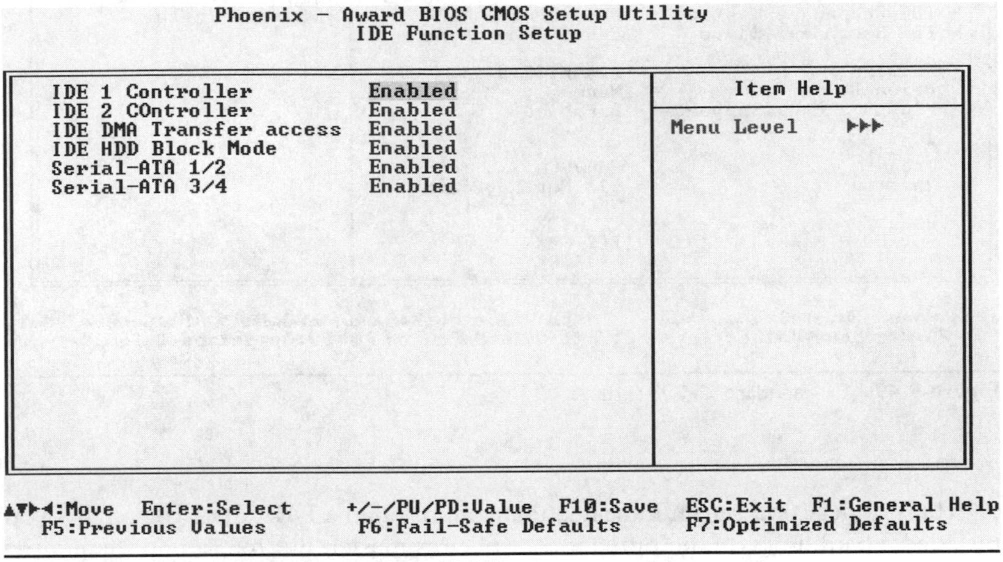

```
            Phoenix - Award BIOS CMOS Setup Utility
                    IDE Function Setup
 ┌─────────────────────────────────────────────┬──────────────────────┐
 │ IDE 1 Controller          Enabled            │     Item Help        │
 │ IDE 2 COntroller          Enabled            │                      │
 │ IDE DMA Transfer access   Enabled            │  Menu Level    ▶▶▶   │
 │ IDE HDD Block Mode        Enabled            │                      │
 │ Serial-ATA 1/2            Enabled            │                      │
 │ Serial-ATA 3/4            Enabled            │                      │
 │                                              │                      │
 │                                              │                      │
 │                                              │                      │
 │                                              │                      │
 │                                              │                      │
 │                                              │                      │
 │                                              │                      │
 │                                              │                      │
 │                                              │                      │
 └─────────────────────────────────────────────┴──────────────────────┘
 ▲▼►◄:Move   Enter:Select    +/-/PU/PD:Value  F10:Save   ESC:Exit  F1:General Help
    F5:Previous Values       F6:Fail-Safe Defaults       F7:Optimized Defaults
```

Figure 9-48 Typical controller settings in CMOS

Autodetection

If the controllers are enabled and the drive is properly connected, the drive should appear in CMOS through a process called *autodetection*. Autodetection is a powerful and handy feature, but it seems every CMOS has a different way to manifest it, and how it is manifested may affect how your computer decides which hard drive to try to boot when you start your PC.

One of your hard drives stores the operating system needed when you boot your computer, and your system needs a way to know where to look for this operating system. The traditional BIOS supported a maximum of only four ATA drives on two controllers, called the *primary controller* and the *secondary controller*. The BIOS looked for the master drive on the primary controller when the system booted up. If you used only one controller, you used the primary controller. The secondary controller was used for CD-ROMs, DVDs, or other non-bootable drives.

Older CMOS made this clear and easy, as shown in Figure 9-49. When you booted up, the CMOS would query the drives—a process called *autodetection*—and whatever drives the CMOS saw would show up here. Some even older CMOS had a special menu option called Autodetect that you had to run to see the drives in this screen. There are places for up to four devices—notice not all of them actually have a device.

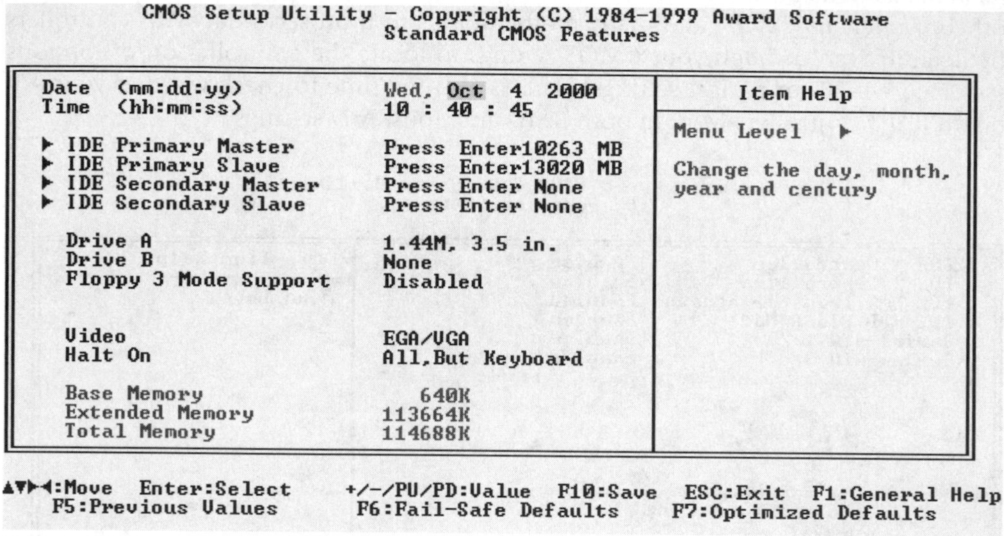

```
        CMOS Setup Utility - Copyright (C) 1984-1999 Award Software
                        Standard CMOS Features

   Date  (mm:dd:yy)           Wed, Oct  4  2000          Item Help
   Time  (hh:mm:ss)           10 : 40 : 45
                                                    Menu Level   ▶
   ▶ IDE Primary Master       Press Enter10263 MB
   ▶ IDE Primary Slave        Press Enter13020 MB    Change the day, month,
   ▶ IDE Secondary Master     Press Enter None       year and century
   ▶ IDE Secondary Slave      Press Enter None

     Drive A                  1.44M, 3.5 in.
     Drive B                  None
     Floppy 3 Mode Support    Disabled


     Video                    EGA/VGA
     Halt On                  All,But Keyboard

     Base Memory                 640K
     Extended Memory          113664K
     Total Memory             114688K


▲▼▶◀:Move   Enter:Select    +/-/PU/PD:Value   F10:Save    ESC:Exit  F1:General Help
   F5:Previous Values        F6:Fail-Safe Defaults       F7:Optimized Defaults
```

Figure 9-49 Old standard CMOS settings

The autodetection screen indicated that you installed a PATA drive correctly. If you installed a hard drive on the primary controller as master, but messed up the jumper and set it to slave, it would show up in the autodetection screen as the slave. If you had two drives and set them both to master, one drive or the other (or sometimes both) didn't appear, telling you that something was messed up in the physical installation. If you forgot to plug in the ribbon cable or the power, the drives wouldn't autodetect.

SATA messed up the autodetection happiness. There's no such thing as master, slave, or even primary and secondary controller in the SATA world. To get around this, motherboards with PATA and SATA today use a numbering system—and every motherboard uses its own numbering system! One common numbering method uses the term *channels* for each controller. The first boot device is channel 1, the second is channel 2, and so on. PATA channels may have a master and a slave, but a SATA channel has only a master, as SATA controllers support only one drive. So instead of names of drives, you see numbers. Take a look at Figure 9-50.

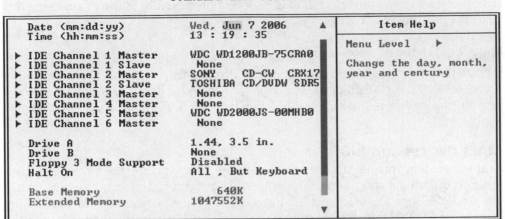

Figure 9-50 New standard CMOS features

Whew! Lots of hard drives! This motherboard supports the traditional four PATA drives, but it also supports four SATA drives. Each controller is assigned a number—note that channel 1 and channel 2 have master/slave settings, and that's how you know channel 1 and 2 are the PATA drives. Channels 3 through 6 are SATA, even though the listing says *master*. (SATA's still somewhat new, and a CMOS using incorrect terms like *master* is common.)

Boot Order

If you want your computer to run, it's going to need an operating system to boot. While the PCs of our forefathers (those of the 1980s and early 1990s) absolutely required you to put the operating system on the primary master, most BIOS makers by 1995 enabled you to put the OS on any of the four drives and then tell the system through CMOS which hard drive to boot. Additionally, you may need to boot from a floppy, CD-ROM, or even a thumb drive at times. CMOS takes care of this by enabling you to set a *boot order*.

Figure 9-51 shows a typical boot order screen. It has a first, second, and third boot option. Many users like to boot first from floppy or CD-ROM, and then from a hard drive. This enables them to put in a bootable floppy or CD-ROM if they're having problems with the system. Of course, you can set it to boot first from your hard drive and then go into CMOS and change it when you need to—it's your choice.

Figure 9-51
Boot order

```
▶ Hard Disk Boot Priority     Press Enter
  First Boot Device           Floppy
  Second Boot Device          Hard Disk
  Third Boot Device           CDROM
  Boot Other Device           Enabled
```

Most modern CMOS lump the hard drive boot order onto a second screen. This screen works like an autodetect in that it shows only actual hard drives attached. This beats the heck out of guessing!

Device Drivers

Devices that do not get BIOS via the system BIOS routines naturally require some other source for BIOS. For ATAPI devices and many SATA controllers, the source of choice is software device drivers, but both technologies have a couple of quirks you should know about.

ATAPI Devices and BIOS

ATAPI drives plug into an ATA controller on the motherboard and follow the same conventions on cabling and jumpers used by PATA hard drives. In fact, all current CMOS setup utilities *seem* to autodetect CD-media ATAPI drives. If you go into CMOS after installing a CD-ROM drive as master on the secondary IDE controller, for example, the drive will show up just fine, as in Figure 9-52.

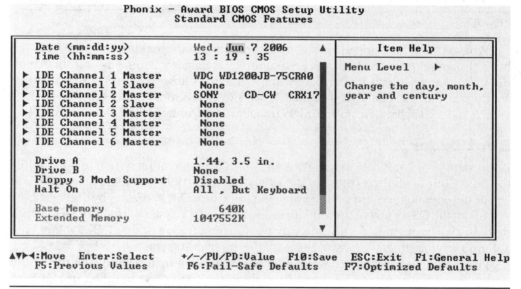

Figure 9-52 CMOS screen showing a CD-ROM drive detected

The reporting of installed CD-media drives in CMOS serves two purposes. First, it tells the technician that he or she has good connectivity on the ATAPI drive. Second, it shows that you have the option to boot to CD media, such as a Windows XP disc. What it doesn't do, however, is provide true BIOS support for that drive! That has to come with a driver loaded at boot-up.

Troubleshooting Hard Drive Installation

The best friend a tech has when it comes to troubleshooting hard drive installation is the autodetection feature of the CMOS setup utility. When a drive doesn't work, the biggest question, especially during installation, is, "Did I plug it in correctly?" With autodetection, the answer is simple; if it doesn't see the drives, something is wrong with the hardware configuration. Either a device has physically failed or, more likely, you didn't give the hard drive power, plugged a cable in backwards, or messed up some other connectivity issue.

It takes three things to get a drive installed and recognized by the system: jumpers (PATA only), data cable, power, and CMOS setup recognizing the drive. If any of these steps are missed or messed up, you have a drive that simply doesn't exist according to the PC! To troubleshoot hard drives, simply work your way through each step to figure out what went wrong.

First, set the drive to master, slave, standalone, or cable select, depending on where you decide to install the drive. If a drive is alone on the cable, set it to master or standalone. With two drives, one must be master and the other slave. Alternatively, you can set both drives to cable select and use a cable-select cable.

Second, the data cable must be connected to both the drive and controller, pin 1 to pin 1. Reversing the data cable at one end is remarkably easy to do, especially with the rounded cables. They obviously don't have a big red stripe down the side to indicate the location of pin 1! If you can't autodetect the drive, check the cabling.

Third, be sure to give the hard drive power. Most hard drives use a standard Molex connector. If you don't hear the whirring of the drive, make certain you plugged in a Molex from the power supply, rather than from another source such as an otherwise disconnected fan. You'd be surprised how often I've seen that!

Fourth, you need to provide BIOS for the controller and the drive. This can get tricky as the typical CMOS setup program has a lot of hard drive options. Plus, you have an added level of confusion with RAID settings and non-integrated controllers that require software drivers.

Once you've checked the physical connections, run through these issues in CMOS. Is the controller enabled? Is the storage technology—LBA, INT13, ATA/ATAPI- 6—properly set up? Similarly, can the motherboard support the type of drive you're installing? If not, you have a couple of options. You can flash the BIOS with an upgraded BIOS from the manufacturer or you can get a hard drive controller that goes into an expansion slot.

Finally, make certain with non-integrated hard drive controllers, such as those that come with many SATA drives, that you've installed the proper drivers for the controller. Driver issues can crop up with new, very large drives, and with changes in technology. Always check the manufacturer's Web site for new drivers.

Beyond A+

Spindle (or Rotational) Speed

Hard drives run at a set spindle speed, measured in *revolutions per minute (RPM)*. Older drives run at the long-standard speed of 3,600 RPM, but new drives are hitting 15,000 RPM! The faster the spindle speed, the faster the controller can store and retrieve data. Here are the common speeds: 4,500, 5,400, 7,200, and 10,000 RPM.

Faster drives mean better system performance, but they can also cause the computer to overheat. This is especially true in tight cases, such as minitowers, and in cases containing many drives. Two 4,500 RPM drives might run forever, snugly tucked together in your old case. But slap a hot new 10,000 RPM drive in that same case and watch your system start crashing right and left!

You can deal with these hotrod drives by adding drive bay fans between the drives or migrating to a more spacious case. Most enthusiasts end up doing both. Drive bay fans sit at the front of a bay and blow air across the drive. They range in price from $10 to $100 (U.S.) and can lower the temperature of your drives dramatically. Figure 9-53 shows a picture of a double-fan drive bay cooler.

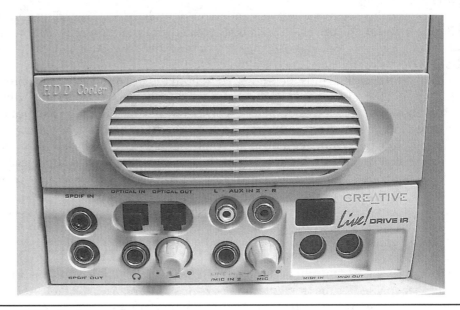

Figure 9-53   Bay fans

Airflow in a case can make or break your system stability, especially when you add new drives that increase the ambient temperature. Hot systems get flaky and lock up at odd moments. Many things can impede the airflow—jumbled-up ribbon cables, drives squished together in a tiny case, fans clogged by dust or animal hair, and so on.

Technicians need to be aware of the dangers when adding a new hard drive to an older system. Get into the habit of tying off ribbon cables, adding front fans to cases when systems lock up intermittently, and making sure the fan(s) run well. Finally, if a client wants a new drive and his system is a tiny minitower with only the power supply fan to cool it off, be gentle, but definitely steer him to one of the slower drives!

Chapter Review Questions

1. John's system is running INT13 extensions. What is the maximum size hard drive it can support?

   A. 504 GB

   B. 137 GB

    C. 10 GB

    D. 8.4 GB

2. How many IDE hard drives can you have on a system with two hard drive controllers?

    A. 1

    B. 2

    C. 3

    D. 4

3. How do you differentiate two IDE drives on the same cable?

    A. The flat ribbon cable has a seven-wire twist that determines which is which.

    B. Set jumpers on the individual drives to determine which is master and which is slave.

    C. The IDE controller determines the hierarchy.

    D. Both drives are considered equal.

4. What happens if you cable an IDE hard drive incorrectly?

    A. You can destroy that hard drive.

    B. The data will be erased, but the hard drive will be okay.

    C. The system will not be able to communicate with that hard drive.

    D. Nothing. It doesn't matter how the cable is set up; it doesn't have the seven-wire twist.

5. John has just purchased an ATA/66-capable hard drive for his ATA/66-capable system. However, he notices that he forgot to get the special 80-wire cable. If he installs the ATA/66 drive with a 40-pin EIDE cable, what will happen?

    A. The drive will work, but will not run at the ATA/66 speed.

    B. He might damage the motherboard.

    C. He won't be able to install the drive, because the cables are incompatible.

    D. He will not be able to run in ATA mode.

6. What is the maximum cable length of an internal serial ATA device ?

    A. 2 meters

    B. 12 inches

    C. 18 inches

    D. 1 meter

7. Which of the following is part of the ATA-7 standard?

    A. Red controller connections on the motherboard

    B. SATA

    C. ATA/100

    D. 1 meter maximum cable length

8. What is the maximum number of SATA drives you can have on a system?

   A. One master, one slave

   B. Two, with no master/slave distinction

   C. Eight

   D. There is no maximum other than the limitations of your motherboard.

9. Simon wants to connect his old PATA hard drive to the SATA controller in his new computer. What does he need to do this?

   A. A SATA bridge to plug into the connector on the PATA drive

   B. A PATA converter to plug into the SATA bridge on the controller

   C. Nothing at all; he can just connect the PATA drive directly to the SATA controller

   D. He can't do it; the SATA controller is not backward compatible with PATA drives

10. What do you call a series of SCSI devices working together through a host adapter?

    A. A SCSI controller

    B. A SCSI chain

    C. RAID

    D. Cabled SCSI

Answers

1. **B.** A system running INT13 extensions can support up to a 137-GB hard drive.

2. **D.** Each controller supports two drives.

3. **B.** Drives use master/slave jumpers to differentiate between the two drives.

4. **C.** Nothing will be damaged or lost—there just won't be any communication.

5. **A.** ATA/66 drives work fine with a 40-pin cable—they just won't run at ATA/66 speed.

6. **D.** The maximum cable length for an internal SATA device is 1 meter.

7. **B.** Serial ATA is part of the ATA-7 standard.

8. **D.** There is no maximum number of SATA drives you can have on a system, beyond the limits imposed by the number of ports on your motherboard/host card.

9. **A.** Simon needs a SATA bridge to plug into the connector on the PATA drive in order to connect his old PATA hard drive to the SATA controller.

10. **B.** A series of SCSI devices working together through a host adapter is a SCSI chain.

Implementing Hard Drives

In this chapter, you will learn how to
- Explain the partitions available in Windows
- Discuss the formatting options
- Partition and format hard drives
- Maintain and troubleshoot a hard drive

From the standpoint of your PC, a new hard drive successfully installed is nothing more than a huge pile of sectors. CMOS sees the drive; it shows up in your autodetect screen and BIOS knows how to talk to the drive; but as far as an operating system is concerned, that drive is unreadable. Your operating system must organize that big pile of sectors so you can create two things: folders and files. This chapter covers that process.

Historical/Conceptual

After you've successfully installed a hard drive, you must perform two more steps to translate a drive's geometry and circuits into something usable to the system: partitioning and formatting. *Partitioning* is the process of electronically subdividing the physical hard drive into groups of cylinders called *partitions* (or *volumes*). A hard drive must have at least one partition, and you can create multiple partitions on a single hard drive if you wish. In Windows, each of these partitions typically is assigned a drive letter such as C: or D:. After partitioning, you must *format* the drive. This step installs a *file system* onto the drive that organizes each partition in such a way that the operating system can store files and folders on the drive. Several different types of file systems are used in the Windows world. This chapter will go through them after covering partitioning.

The process of partitioning and formatting a drive is one of the few areas remaining on the software side of PC assembly that requires you to perform a series of fairly complex manual steps. The CompTIA A+ certification exams test your knowledge of *what* these processes do to make the drive work, as well as the steps needed to partition and format hard drives in Windows 2000/XP.

This chapter continues the exploration of hard drive installation by explaining partitioning and formatting and then going through the process of partitioning and formatting hard drives. The chapter wraps with a discussion on hard drive maintenance and troubleshooting issues.

Hard Drive Partitions

Partitions provide tremendous flexibility in hard drive organization. Partitions enable you to organize a drive in a way that suits your personal taste. For example, I partitioned my 500-GB hard drive into a 150-GB partition, where I store Windows XP and all my programs, and a 350-GB partition, where I store all my personal data. This is a matter of personal choice—in my case, it makes backups simpler because the data is stored in one partition, and that partition alone can be backed up without including the applications.

Partitioning enables a single hard drive to store more than one operating system (OS). One OS could be stored in one partition and another OS stored in a second, for example. Granted, most people use only one OS, but if you want to choose to boot Windows or Linux, partitions are the key to enabling you to do so.

Windows 2000 and XP support two different partitioning methods: the older but more universal master boot record (MBR) partitioning scheme and the newer (but proprietary to Microsoft) dynamic storage partitioning scheme. Microsoft calls a hard drive that uses the MBR partitioning scheme a *basic disk* and a drive using the dynamic storage partitioning scheme a *dynamic disk*. A single Windows system with two hard drives may have one of the drives partitioned as a basic disk and the other as a dynamic disk, and the system will run perfectly well. The bottom line? You get to learn about two totally different types of partitioning! Yay! Given that basic disks are much older, we'll start there.

Basic Disks

Basic disk partitioning creates two very small data structures on a drive, the *master boot record (MBR)* and a partition table, and stores them on the first sector of the hard drive—called the *boot sector*. The MBR is nothing more than a tiny bit of code that takes control of the boot process from the system BIOS. When the computer boots to a hard drive, BIOS automatically looks for MBR code on the boot sector. The MBR has only one job: to look in the partition table for a partition with a valid operating system (Figure 10-1).

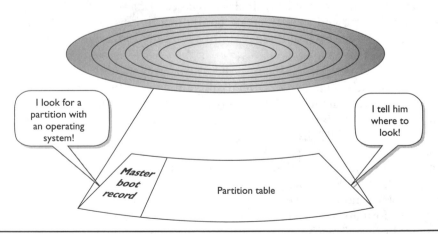

Figure 10-1 Functions of the MBR and partition table

> **NOTE** Only one MBR and one partition table exist per basic disk.

All basic disk partition tables support up to four partitions. The partition table supports two types of partitions: primary partitions and extended partitions. *Primary partitions* are designed to support bootable operating systems. *Extended partitions* are not bootable. A single basic disk may have up to three primary partitions and one extended partition. If you do not have an extended partition, you may have up to four primary partitions.

Each partition must have some unique identifier to enable users to recognize it as an individual partition. Microsoft operating systems (DOS and Windows) traditionally assign primary partitions a drive letter from C: to Z:. Extended partitions do not get drive letters.

After you create an extended partition, you must create logical drives within that extended partition. A logical drive traditionally gets a drive letter from D: to Z:. (The drive letter C: is always reserved for the first primary partition in a Windows PC.)

Windows 2000 and Windows XP partitions are not limited to drive letters. With the exception of the partition that stores the boot files for Windows (which will always be C:), any other primary partitions or logical drives may get either a drive letter or a folder on a primary partition. You'll see how all of this works later in this chapter.

If a primary partition is a bootable partition, then why does a basic drive's partition table support up to four primary partitions? Remember when I said that partitioning allows multiple operating systems? This is how it works! You can install up to four different operating systems, each OS installed on its own primary partition, and boot to your choice each time you fire up the computer.

Every primary partition on a single drive has a special setting called *active* stored in the partition table. This setting is either on or off on each primary partition. At boot, the MBR uses the active setting in the partition table to determine which primary partition to choose to try to load an OS. Only one partition at a time can be the active partition, because you can run only one OS at a time (see Figure 10-2).

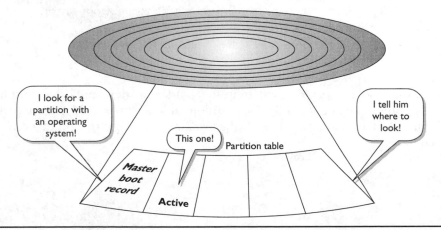

Figure 10-2 The MBR checks the partition table to find the active partition.

The boot sector at the beginning of the hard drive isn't the only special sector on a hard drive. The first sector of the first cylinder of each partition also has a special sector called the *volume boot sector*. While the "main" boot sector defines the partitions, the volume boot sector stores information important to its partition, such as the location of the OS boot files. Figure 10-3 shows a hard drive with two partitions. The first partition's volume boot sector contains information about the size of the partition and the code pointing to the boot files on this partition. The second volume boot sector contains information about the size of the partition.

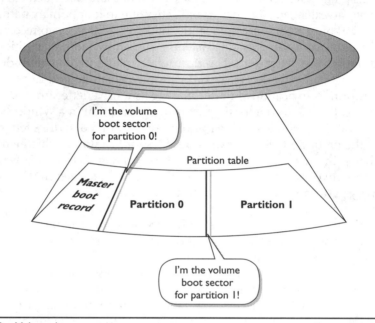

Figure 10-3   Volume boot sector

   NOTE   Every partition on a hard drive has a volume boot sector.

Primary Partitions

If you want to boot an operating system from a hard drive, that hard drive must have a primary partition. The MBR checks the partition table for the active primary partition (see Figure 10-4). In Windows 2000/XP, the primary partition is C:, and that cannot be changed.

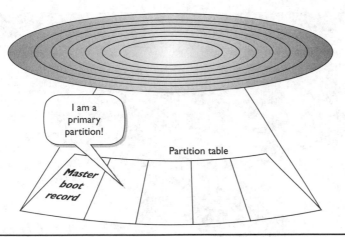

Figure 10-4 The MBR checks the partition table to find a primary partition.

NOTE Don't confuse primary partition with primary controller. The latter, as you'll recall from Chapter 9, refers to the first PATA drive controller on a motherboard.

Even though hard drives support up to four primary partitions, you almost never see four partitions used in the Windows world. Both Windows 2000 and Windows XP support up to four primary partitions on one drive, but how many people (other than nerdy CompTIA A+ people like you and me) really want to boot up more than one OS? We use a number of terms for this function, but *dual-boot* and *multiboot* are the most common. The system in my house, for example, uses four primary partitions, each holding one OS: Ubuntu Linux, Windows 2000, Windows XP, and Windows Vista. In other words, I chopped my drive up into four chunks and installed a different OS in each. To do multiboot, I used a third-party tool—System Commander 8 by VCOM—to set up the partitions. Windows 2000/XP and Linux come with similar tools that can do this, but I find them messy to use and prefer System Commander. When my computer boots, System Commander yanks control from the MBR and asks me which OS I wish to boot (see Figure 10-5). I select my OS and it appears. As you look at this figure, you'll notice more than four operating systems. This particular system gets around the four primary partitions/disk limitation by using two hard drives.

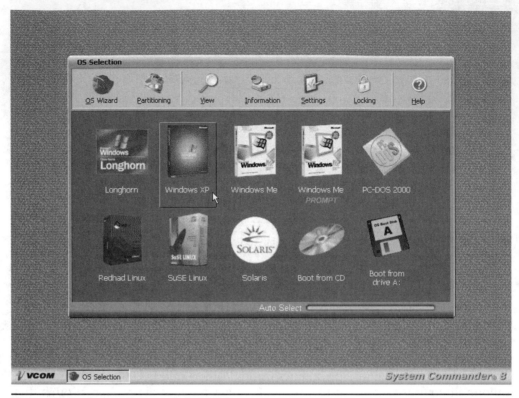

Figure 10-5 System Commander's OS Selection menu

Again, few systems use more than one primary partition. You may work on PCs for years and never see a system with more than one primary partition. The CompTIA A+ certification exams certainly don't expect you to demonstrate how to create a system with multiple primary partitions, but they assume that you know you *can* add more than one primary partition to a hard drive if you so desire. The rest of this book assumes that you want only one primary partition.

 EXAM TIP If you get the error "No Fixed Disks Present," you can bet you forgot to tell the CMOS to look for the drive. Reboot, access CMOS, and try setting up the drive again.

Active Partition

When you create a primary partition and decide to place an OS on that partition, you must set that partition as active. This must take place even if you use only a single primary partition. Luckily, this step is automated in the Windows installation process. Consider this: When would you want to go through the steps to define a partition as active? That would be when you install an OS on that partition! So when you install Windows on a new system, the install program automatically sets up your first primary partition as the active partition. It never actually says this in the install, it just does it for you.

So if you raise your right hand and promise to use only Microsoft Windows and make only single primary partitions on your hard drives, odds are good you'll never have to mess with manually adjusting your active partitions. Of course, since you're crazy enough to want to get into PCs, that means within a year of reading this text you're going to want to install other operating systems like Linux on your PC (and that's OK—all techs want to try this at some point). The moment you do, you'll enter the world of boot manager programs of which the just-described System Commander is only one of many, many choices. You also might use tools that enable you to change the active partition manually—exactly when and how this is done varies tremendously for each situation and is way outside the scope of the CompTIA A+ exams, but make sure you know why you might need to set a partition as active.

When my System Commander boot screen comes up, it essentially asks me, "What primary partition do you want me to make active?"

Extended Partition

Understanding the purpose of extended partitions requires a brief look at the historical PC. The first versions of the old DOS operating system to support hard drives only supported primary partitions up to 32 MB. As hard drives went past 32 MB, Microsoft needed a way to support them. Instead of rewriting DOS to handle larger drives, Microsoft developers created the idea of the extended partition. That way, if you had a hard drive larger than 32 MB, you could make a 32-MB primary partition and the rest of the drive an extended partition. Over the years, DOS and then Windows were rewritten to support large hard drives, but the extended partition is still fully supported.

The beauty of an extended partition is in the way it handles drive letters. When you create a primary partition, it gets a drive letter and that's it. But when you create an extended partition, it does not automatically get a drive letter. Instead, you then go through a second step, where you divide the extended partition into one or more logical drives. An extended partition may have as many logical drives as you wish. By default, Windows gives each logical drive in an extended partition a drive letter and most Windows users use drive letters. However, if you'd like, you may even "mount" the drive letter as a folder on any lettered drive. You can set the size of each logical drive to any size you want. You'll learn how to mount drives later in this chapter—for now, just get the idea that a partition may be mounted with a drive letter or as a folder.

 EXAM TIP Primary partitions and logical drives on basic disks are also called *basic volumes*.

Extended partitions are completely optional; you do not have to create an extended partition on a hard drive. So, if you can't boot to an extended partition and your hard drive doesn't need an extended partition, why would you want to create one? First of all, the majority of systems do not use extended partitions. Most systems use only one hard drive and that single drive is partitioned as one big primary partition—nothing wrong with that! Some users like having an extended partition with one or more logical drives, and they use the extended partitions as a way to separate data. For example, I might store all my movie files on my G: logical drive.

Instead of assigning drive letters, you can mount logical drives as folders on an existing drive. It's easy to make a logical drive and call it C:\STORAGE. If the C:\STORAGE folder fills up, you could add an extra hard drive, make the entire extra drive an extended partition with one logical drive, unmount the old C:\STORAGE drive, and then mount the new huge logical drive as C:\STORAGE! It's as though you made your C: drive bigger without replacing it.

Dynamic Disks

With the introduction of Windows 2000, Microsoft defined an entirely new type of partitioning called *dynamic storage partitioning,* better known as *dynamic disks.* Dynamic disks drop the word *partition* and instead use the term *volume.* There is no dynamic disk equivalent to primary vs. extended partitions. A volume is still technically a partition, but it can do things a regular partition cannot do, such as spanning. A *spanned volume* goes across more than one drive. Windows allows you to span up to 32 drives under a single volume. Dynamic disks also support RAID 0 in Windows 2000 Professional and Windows XP Professional. Windows 2000 Server and Windows Server/2003 support RAID 0, 1, and 5.

 NOTE Windows XP Home and Windows Media Center do not support dynamic disks.

Dynamic disks use an MBR and a partition table, but these older structures are there only for backward compatibility. All of the information about a dynamic disk is stored in a hidden partition that takes up the last 1 MB of the hard drive. Every partition in a partition table holds a 2-byte value that describes the partition. For example, an extended partition gets the number 05. Windows adds a new number, 42, to the first partition on a dynamic disk. When Windows 2000 or XP reads the partition table for a dynamic disk, it sees the number 42 and immediately jumps to the 1-MB hidden partition, ignoring the old style partition table. By supporting an MBR and partition table, Windows also prevents other disk partitioning programs from messing with a dynamic disk. If a third-party partitioning program is used, it simply sees the entire hard drive as either an unformatted primary partition or a non-readable partition.

 NOTE A key thing to understand about dynamic drives is that the technology is *proprietary.* Microsoft has no intention of telling anyone exactly how dynamic disks work. Only fairly recent Microsoft operating systems (Windows 2000, XP, 2003, and Vista) can read a drive configured as a dynamic disk.

You can use five volume types with dynamic disks: simple, spanned, striped, mirrored, and RAID 5. Most folks stick with simple volumes.

Simple volumes work much like primary partitions. If you have a hard drive and you want to make half of it C: and the other half D:, you create two volumes on a dynamic disk. That's it—no choosing between primary and extended partitions. Remember that you were limited to four primary partitions when using basic disks. To make more than four volumes with a basic disk, you first had to create an extended partition and then make logical drives within the extended partition. Dynamic disks simplify the process by treating all partitions as volumes, so you can make as many as you need.

Spanned volumes use unallocated space on multiple drives to create a single volume. Spanned volumes are a bit risky—if any of the spanned drives fail, the entire volume is permanently lost.

Striped volumes are RAID 0 volumes. You may take any two unallocated spaces on two separate hard drives and stripe them. But again, if either drive fails, you lose all your data.

Mirrored volumes are RAID 1 volumes. You may take any two unallocated spaces on two separate hard drives and mirror them. If one of the two mirrored drives fails, the other will keep running.

RAID 5 volumes, as the name implies, are for RAID 5 arrays. A RAID 5 volume requires three or more dynamic disks with equal-sized unallocated spaces.

Other Partitions

The partition types supported by Windows are not the only partition types you may encounter—other types exist. One of the most common is called the *hidden partition*. A hidden partition is really just a primary partition that is hidden from your operating system. Only special BIOS tools may access a hidden partition. Hidden partitions are used by some PC makers to hide a backup copy of an installed OS that you can use to restore your system if you accidentally trash it—by, for example, learning about partitions and using a partitioning program incorrectly.

A *swap partition* is another special type of partition, but they're only found on Linux and BSD systems. A swap partition is an entire partition whose only job is to act like RAM when your system needs more RAM than you have installed. Windows has a similar function called a *page file* that uses a special file instead of a partition. Most OS experts believe a swap partition is a little bit faster than a page file. You'll learn all about page files and swap partitions in Chapter 13.

NOTE   Early versions of Windows (3.x and 9x/Me) called the page file a *swap file*. Most techs use the terms interchangeably today.

When to Partition

Partitioning is not a common task. The two most common situations likely to require partitioning are when you're installing an OS on a new system, and when you are adding a second drive to an existing system. When you install a new OS, the installation CD will at some point ask you how you would like to partition the drive. When you're adding a new hard drive to an existing system, every OS has a built-in tool to help you partition it.

Each version of Windows offers a different tool for partitioning hard drives. For more than 20 years, through the days of DOS and early Windows (up to Windows Me), you used a command line program called FDISK to partition drives. Figure 10-6 shows the FDISK program. Windows 2000 and Windows XP use a graphical partitioning program called Disk Management (Figure 10-7).

```
                    Microsoft Windows 98
                   Fixed Disk Setup Program
             (C)Copyright Microsoft Corp.  1983 - 1998

                       FDISK Options

  Current fixed disk drive: 1

  Choose one of the following:

  1. Create DOS partition or Logical DOS Drive
  2. Set active partition
  3. Delete partition or Logical DOS Drive
  4. Display partition information


  Enter choice: [1]



  Press Esc to exit FDISK
```

Figure 10-6   FDISK

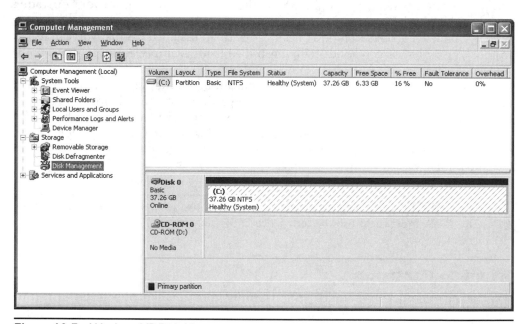

Figure 10-7   Windows XP Disk Management

Linux uses a number of different tools for partitioning. The oldest is called FDISK—yup, the exact same name as the DOS/Windows version. However, that's where the similarities end, as Linux FDISK has a totally different command set. Even though every copy of Linux comes with the Linux FDISK, it's rarely used because so many better partitioning tools are available. One of the newer Linux partitioning tools is called GParted.

GParted is graphical like Disk Management and is fairly easy to use (Figure 10-8). GParted is also a powerful partition management tool—so powerful that it also works with Windows partitions.

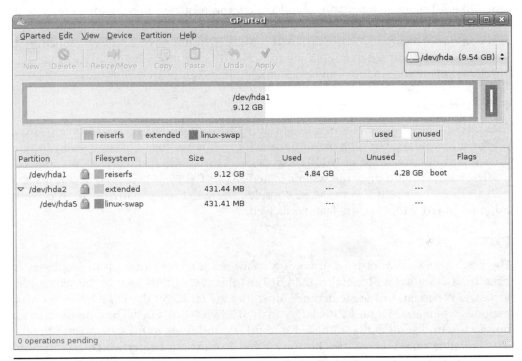

Figure 10-8   GParted in action

Traditionally, once a partition is made, you cannot change its size or type other than by erasing it. You might, however, want to take a hard drive partitioned as a single primary partition and change it to half primary and half extended. Before Windows 2000, there was no way to do this non-destructively. As a result, a few third-party tools, led by Symantec's now famous Partition Magic, gave techs the tools to resize partitions without losing the data they held. Windows 2000 and XP can non-destructively resize a partition to be larger but not smaller. Vista lets users non-destructively resize partitions any way they wish!

NOTE   This chapter explains how to partition a hard drive *before* it explains formatting, because that is the order in which you as a PC tech will actually perform those tasks. You'll learn all the specifics of the various file systems—such as FAT32 and NTFS—when I explain formatting in the next section, but until then, just accept that there are several different systems for organizing the files on a hard drive, and that part of setting up a hard drive involves choosing among them.

Hard Drive Formatting

Once a hard drive has been partitioned, there's one more step you must perform before your OS can use that drive: formatting. *Formatting* does two things: it creates a file system—like a library's card catalog—and makes the root directory in that file system. Every partition and volume you create needs to be formatted to enable it to hold data that you can easily retrieve. The various versions of Windows you're likely to encounter today can use several different file systems, so we'll look at those in detail next. The *root directory* provides the foundation upon which the OS builds files and folders.

File Systems in Windows

Every version of Windows comes with a built-in formatting utility that enables it to create one or more file systems on a partition or volume. The versions of Windows in current use support three separate Microsoft file systems: FAT16, FAT32, and NTFS.

The simplest hard drive file system, called FAT or FAT16, provides a good introduction to how file systems work. More complex file systems fix many of the problems inherent in FAT and add extra features as well.

FAT

The base storage area for hard drives is a sector; each sector stores up to 512 bytes of data. If an OS stores a file smaller than 512 bytes in a sector, the rest of the sector goes to waste. We accept this waste because most files are far larger than 512 bytes. So what happens when an OS stores a file larger than 512 bytes? The OS needs a method to fill one sector, find another that's unused, and fill it, continuing to fill sectors until the file is completely stored. Once the OS stores a file, it must remember which sectors hold that file so that file can be retrieved later.

MS-DOS version 2.1 first supported hard drives using a special data structure to keep track of stored data on the hard drive, and Microsoft called this structure the *file allocation table (FAT)*. Think of the FAT as nothing more than a card catalog that keeps track of which sectors store the various parts of a file. The official jargon term for a FAT is *data structure,* but it is more like a two-column spreadsheet.

The left column (see Figure 10-9) gives each sector a number, from 0000 to FFFF (in hex, of course). This means there are 65,536 (64 K) sectors.

Notice that each value in the left column contains 16 bits. (Four hex characters make 16 bits, remember?) We call this type of FAT a *16-bit FAT* or *FAT16*. Not just hard drives have FATs. Some USB thumb drives also use FAT16. Floppy disks use FATs, but their FATs are only 12 bits since they store much less data.

Figure 10-9
16-bit FAT

0000	
0001	
0002	
0003	
0004	
0005	
0006	

FFF9	
FFFA	
FFFB	
FFFC	
FFFD	
FFFE	
FFFF	

The right column of the FAT contains information on the status of sectors. All hard drives, even brand-new drives fresh from the factory, contain faulty sectors that cannot store data because of imperfections in the construction of the drives. The OS must locate these bad sectors, mark them as unusable, and then prevent any files from being written to them. This mapping of bad sectors is one of the functions of high-level formatting (we'll talk about low-level formatting later in this chapter). After the format program creates the FAT, it proceeds through the entire partition, writing and attempting to read from each sector sequentially. If it finds a bad sector, it places a special status code (FFF7) in the sector's FAT location, indicating that sector is unavailable for use. Formatting also marks the good sectors as 0000.

Using the FAT to track sectors, however, creates a problem. The 16-bit FAT addresses a maximum of 64 K (2^{16}) locations. Therefore, the size of a hard-drive partition should be limited to 64 K × 512 bytes per sector, or 32 MB. When Microsoft first unveiled FAT16, this 32-MB limit presented no problem because most hard drives were only 5 MB to 10 MB. As hard drives grew in size, you could use FDISK to break them up into multiple partitions. You could divide a 40-MB hard drive into two partitions, for example, making each partition smaller than 32 MB. But as hard drives started to become much larger, Microsoft realized that the 32-MB limit for drives was unacceptable. We needed an improvement to the 16-bit FAT, a new and improved FAT16 that would support larger drives while still maintaining backward compatibility with the old style 16-bit FAT. This need led to the development of a dramatic improvement in FAT16, called *clustering*, that enabled you to format partitions larger than 32 MB (see Figure 10-10). This new FAT16 appeared way back in the DOS 4 days.

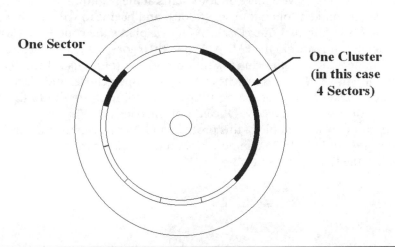

Figure 10-10   Cluster versus sector

Clustering simply refers to combining a set of contiguous sectors and treating them as a single unit in the FAT. These units are called *file allocation units* or *clusters*. Each row of the FAT addressed a cluster instead of a sector. Unlike sectors, the size of a cluster is not fixed. Clusters improved FAT16, but it still only supported a maximum of 64 K storage units, so the formatting program set the number of sectors in each cluster according to the size of the partition. The larger the partition, the more sectors per cluster. This method kept clustering completely compatible with the 64-K locations in the old 16-bit FAT. The new FAT16 could support partitions up to 2 GB. (The old 16-bit FAT is so old it doesn't really even have a name—if someone says "FAT16," they mean the newer FAT16 that supports clustering.) Table 10-1 shows the number of sectors per cluster for FAT16.

If FDISK makes a partition this big:	You'll get this many sectors/clusters:
16 to 127.9 MB	4
128 to 255.9 MB	8
256 to 511.9 MB	16
512 to 1023.9 MB	32
1024 to 2048 MB	64

Table 10-1 FAT16 Cluster Sizes

FAT16 in Action

Assume you have a copy of Windows using FAT16. When an application such as Microsoft Word tells the OS to save a file, Windows starts at the beginning of the FAT, looking for the first space marked "open for use" (0000), and begins to write to that cluster. If the entire file fits within that one cluster, Windows places the code *FFFF* (last cluster) into the cluster's status area in the FAT. Windows then goes to the folder storing the file and adds the filename and the cluster's number to the folder list. If the file requires more than one cluster, Windows searches for the next open cluster and places the number of the next cluster in the status area, filling and adding clusters until the entire file is saved. The last cluster then receives the end-of-file code (FFFF).

Let's run through an example of this process, and start by selecting an arbitrary part of the FAT: from 3ABB to 3AC7. Assume you want to save a file called MOM.TXT. Before saving the file, the FAT looks like Figure 10-11.

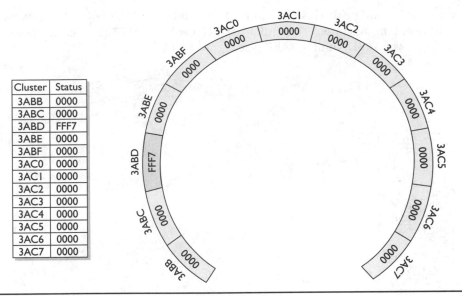

Cluster	Status
3ABB	0000
3ABC	0000
3ABD	FFF7
3ABE	0000
3ABF	0000
3AC0	0000
3AC1	0000
3AC2	0000
3AC3	0000
3AC4	0000
3AC5	0000
3AC6	0000
3AC7	0000

Figure 10-11   The initial FAT

Windows finds the first open cluster, 3ABB, and fills it. But not all of the MOM.TXT file fits into that cluster. Needing more space, the OS goes through the FAT to find the next open cluster. It finds cluster 3ABC. Before filling 3ABC, the value *3ABC* is placed in 3ABB's status (see Figure 10-12).

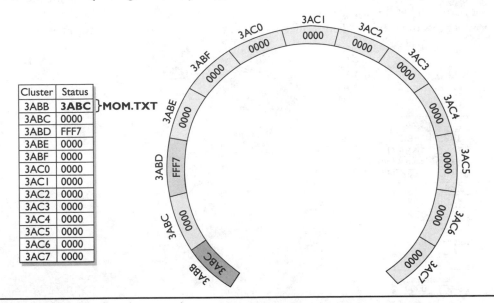

Cluster	Status
3ABB	**3ABC** }MOM.TXT
3ABC	0000
3ABD	FFF7
3ABE	0000
3ABF	0000
3AC0	0000
3AC1	0000
3AC2	0000
3AC3	0000
3AC4	0000
3AC5	0000
3AC6	0000
3AC7	0000

Figure 10-12   The first cluster used

Even after filling two clusters, more of the MOM.TXT file remains, so Windows must find one more cluster. The 3ABD has been marked FFF7 (bad cluster), so Windows skips over 3ABD, finding 3ABE (see Figure 10-13).

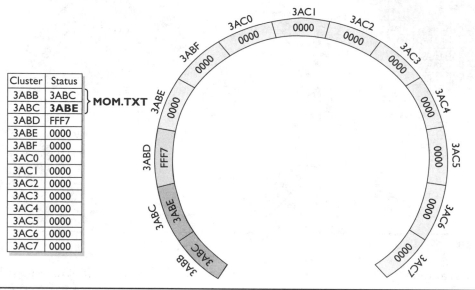

Figure 10-13 The second cluster used

Before filling 3ABE, Windows enters the value *3ABE* in 3ABC's status. Windows does not completely fill 3ABE, signifying that the entire MOM.TXT file has been stored. Windows enters the value *FFFF* in 3ABE's status, indicating the end of file (see Figure 10-14).

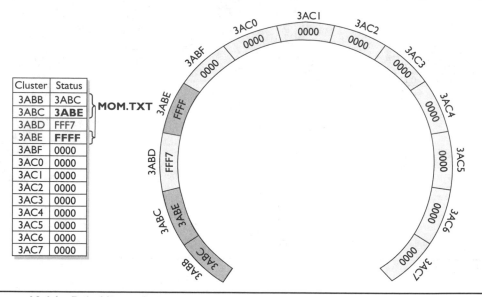

Figure 10-14 End of file reached

After saving all the clusters, Windows now locates the file's folder (yes, folders also get stored on clusters, but they get a different set of clusters, somewhere else on the disk) and records the filename, size, date/time, and starting cluster, like this:

MOM.TXT 19234 05-19-07 2:04p 3ABB

If a program requests that file, the process is reversed. Windows locates the folder containing the file to determine the starting cluster and then pulls a piece of the file from each cluster until it sees the end-of-file cluster. Windows then hands the reassembled file to the requesting application.

Clearly, without the FAT, Windows cannot locate files. FAT16 automatically makes two copies of the FAT. One FAT backs up the other to provide special utilities a way to recover a FAT that gets corrupted—a painfully common occurrence.

Even when FAT works perfectly, over time the files begin to separate in a process called *fragmentation*.

Fragmentation

Continuing with the example, let's use Microsoft Word to save two more files: a letter to the IRS (IRSROB.DOC) and a letter to IBM (IBMHELP.DOC). IRSROB.DOC takes the next three clusters—3ABF, 3AC0, and 3AC1—and IBMHELP.DOC takes two clusters—3AC2 and 3AC3 (see Figure 10-15).

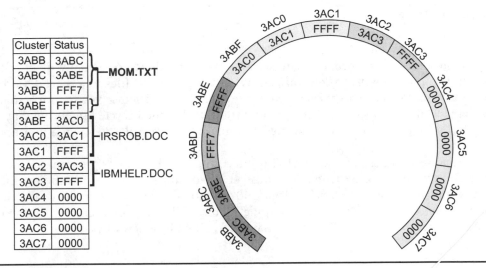

Figure 10-15 Three files saved

Now suppose you erase MOM.TXT. Windows does not delete the cluster entries for MOM.TXT when it erases a file. Windows only alters the information in the folder, simply changing the first letter of MOM.TXT to a hex code that can be translated as the Greek letter Σ (sigma). This causes the file to "disappear" as far as the OS knows. It won't show up, for example, in Windows Explorer, even though the data still resides on the hard drive for the moment (see Figure 10-16).

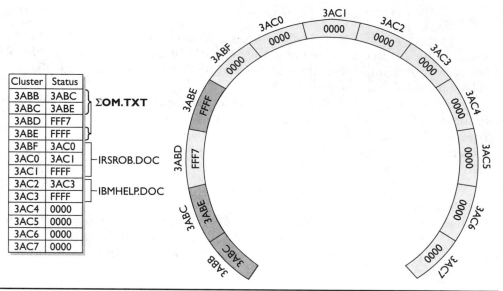

Cluster	Status
3ABB	3ABC
3ABC	3ABE
3ABD	FFF7
3ABE	FFFF
3ABF	3AC0
3AC0	3AC1
3AC1	FFFF
3AC2	3AC3
3AC3	FFFF
3AC4	0000
3AC5	0000
3AC6	0000
3AC7	0000

ΣOM.TXT

IRSROB.DOC

IBMHELP.DOC

Figure 10-16   MOM.TXT erased

Note that under normal circumstances, Windows does not actually delete files when you press the DELETE key. Instead, Windows moves the files to a special hidden directory that you can access via the Recycle Bin. The files themselves are not actually deleted until you empty the Recycle Bin. (You can skip the Recycle Bin entirely if you wish, by highlighting a file, and then holding down the SHIFT key when you press DELETE.)

Because all the data for MOM.TXT is intact, you could use some program to change the Σ back into another letter, and thus get the document back. A number of third party undelete tools are available. Figure 10-17 shows one such program at work. Just remember that if you want to use an undelete tool, you must use it quickly. The space allocated to your deleted file may soon be overwritten by a new file.

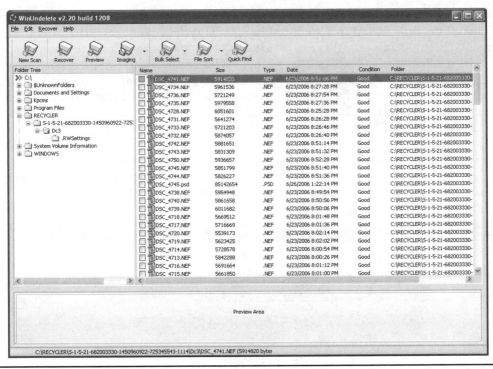

Figure 10-17   WinUndelete in action

Let's say you just emptied your Recycle Bin. You now save one more file, TAXREC. XLS, a big spreadsheet that will take six clusters, into the same folder that once held MOM.TXT. As Windows writes the file to the drive, it overwrites the space that MOM. TXT used, but it needs three more clusters. The next three available clusters are 3AC4, 3AC5, and 3AC6 (see Figure 10-18).

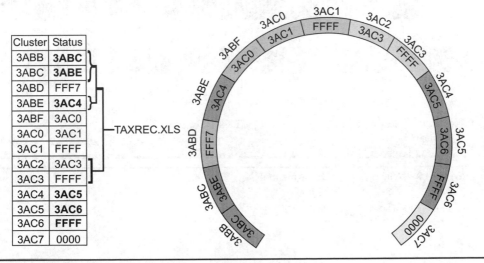

Figure 10-18   TAXREC.XLS fragmented

Notice that TAXREC.XLS is in two pieces, thus *fragmented*. Fragmentation takes place all the time on FAT16 systems. Although the system easily negotiates a tiny fragmented file split into only two parts, excess fragmentation slows down the system during hard drive reads and writes. This example is fragmented into two pieces; in the real world, a file might fragment into hundreds of pieces, forcing the read/write heads to travel all over the hard drive to retrieve a single file. The speed at which the hard drive reads and writes files can be improved dramatically by eliminating this fragmentation.

Every version of Windows (with the exception of NT) comes with a program called Disk Defragmenter, which can rearrange the files back into neat contiguous chunks (see Figure 10-19). Defragmentation is crucial for ensuring the top performance of a hard drive. The "Maintaining and Troubleshooting Hard Drives" section of this chapter gives the details on working with the various Disk Defragmenters in Windows.

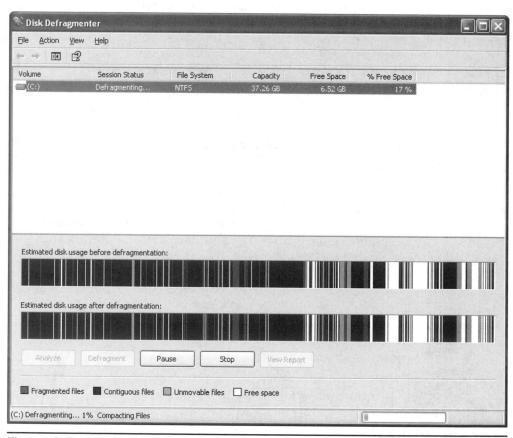

Figure 10-19   Windows Disk Defragmenter

FAT32

When Microsoft introduced Windows 95 OSR2 (OEM Service Release 2), it also unveiled a totally new file format called FAT32 that brought a couple of dramatic improvements. First, FAT32 supports partitions up to 2 terabytes (more than 2 trillion bytes). Second, as its name implies, FAT32 uses 32 bits to describe each cluster, which means clusters can drop to more reasonable sizes. FAT32's use of so many FAT entries gives it the power to use small clusters, making the old "keep your partitions small" rule obsolete. A 2-GB volume using FAT16 would use 32-KB clusters, while the same 2-GB volume using FAT32 would use 4-KB clusters. You get far more efficient use of disk space with FAT32 without the need to make multiple small partitions. FAT32 partitions still need defragmentation, however, just as often as FAT16 partitions.

Table 10-2 shows cluster sizes for FAT32 partitions.

Table 10-2 FAT32 Cluster Sizes	Drive Size	Cluster Size
	512 MB or 1023 MB	4 KB
	1024 MB to 2 GB	4 KB
	2 GB to 8 GB	4 KB
	8 GB to 16 GB	8 KB
	16 GB to 32 GB	16 KB
	>32 GB	32 KB

NTFS

The Windows format of choice these days is the *NT File System (NTFS)*. NTFS came out a long time ago with the first version of Windows NT, thus the name. Over the years, NTFS has undergone a number of improvements. The version used in Windows 2000 is NTFS 3.0; the version used in Windows XP and Vista is called NTFS 3.1, although you'll see it referred to as NTFS 5.0/5.1 (Windows 2000 was unofficially Windows NT version 5). NTFS uses clusters and file allocation tables but in a much more complex and powerful way compared to FAT or FAT32. NTFS offers six major improvements and refinements: redundancy, security, compression, encryption, disk quotas, and cluster sizing.

NTFS Structure

NTFS utilizes an enhanced file allocation table called the *Master File Table (MFT)*. An NTFS partition keeps a backup copy of the most critical parts of the MFT in the middle of the disk, reducing the chance that a serious drive error can wipe out both the MFT and the MFT copy. Whenever you defragment an NTFS partition, you'll see a small, immovable chunk in the middle of the drive; that's the backup MFT (Figure 10-20).

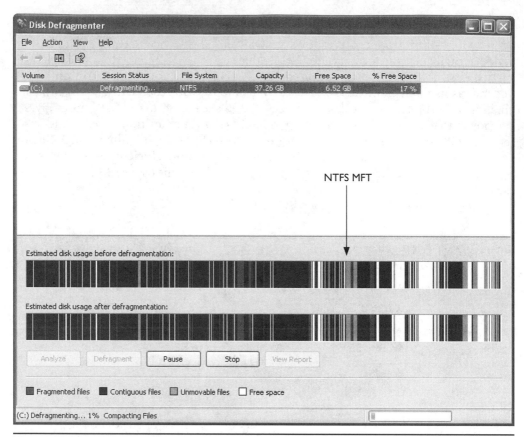

Figure 10-20 An NTFS MFT appearing in a defragmenter program

 NOTE Microsoft has never released the exact workings of NTFS to the public.

Security

NTFS views individual files and folders as objects and provides security for those objects through a feature called the *access control list (ACL)*. Future chapters go into this in much more detail, but a quick example here should make the basic concept clear.

Suppose Bill the IT Guy sets up a Windows XP PC as a workstation for three users: John, Wilma, and Felipe. John logs into the PC with his username and password (johns and f3f2f1f0, respectively, in case you're curious) and begins to work on his project. The project folder is stored on the C: drive as C:\Projects\JohnSuperSecret. When John saves his work and gets ready to leave, he alters the permissions on his folder to deny access to anyone but him. When curious Wilma logs into the PC after John leaves, she cannot access the C:\Programs\JohnSuperSecret folder contents at all, although she can see the entry in Explorer. Without the ACL provided by NTFS, John would have no security over his files or folders at all.

Compression

NTFS enables you to compress individual files and folders to save space on a hard drive. Compression makes access time to the data slower, because the OS has to uncompress files every time you use them, but in a space-limited environment, sometimes that's what you have to do.

Encrypting File System

One of the big draws with NTFS is file encryption, the black art of making files unreadable to anybody who doesn't have the right key. You can encrypt a single file, a folder, and a folder full of files. Microsoft calls the encryption utility in NTFS the *encrypting file system (EFS)*, but it's simply an aspect of NTFS, not a standalone file system. To encrypt a file or folder, right-click it in My Computer and select Properties to open the Properties dialog box (Figure 10-21). Click the Advanced button to open the Advanced Properties dialog box. As you can see in Figure 10-22, encryption (and compression) is simply a selectable check box. Click the box next to *Encrypt contents to secure data*, and then click the OK button—instantly your file is safe from prying eyes!

Figure 10-21
Folder Properties

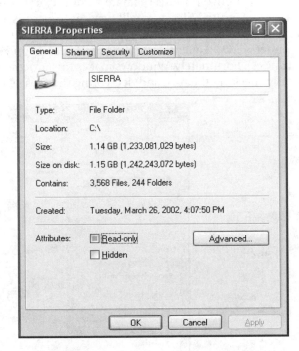

Figure 10-22
Options for
compression
and encryption

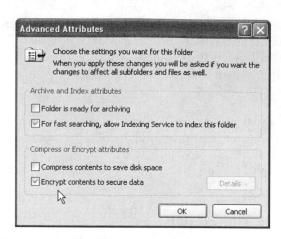

Encryption does not hide files; it simply makes them unreadable to other users. Figure 10-23 shows a couple of encrypted image files. Note that in addition to the pale green color of the filenames (that you can't tell are pale green in this black-and-white image), the files seem readily accessible. Windows XP can't provide a thumbnail, however, even though it can read the type of image file (JPEG) easily. Further, double-clicking the files opens the Windows Picture and Fax Viewer, but you still can't see the image (Figure 10-24). Better still, you can try to access the files across your network and the encryption does precisely what it's supposed to do—blocks unwanted access to sensitive data.

Remember that encryption is separate from the NTFS file security provided by the ACL—to access encrypted files, you will need both permission to access the files based on the ACL and the keys used to encrypt the files (which are stored in your user profile, typically under C:\Documents and Settings\%username%\Application Data\Microsoft\Crypto\RSA). Fortunately, Windows makes this process transparent to the end user, automatically checking the ACL and decrypting the files as needed.

Figure 10-23
Encrypted files

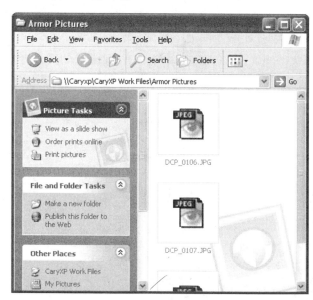

Figure 10-24
Windows Picture
and Fax Viewer
blocked by file
encryption

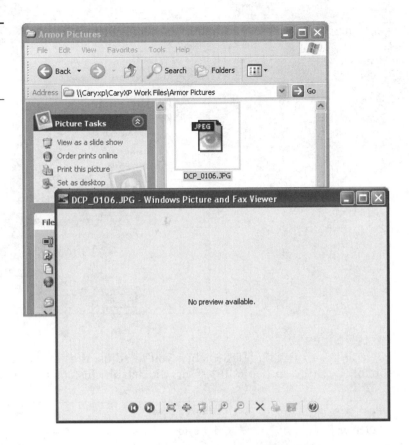

EXAM TIP Windows XP Home and Media Center editions do not support EFS.

NOTE Encryption protects against other users, but only if you log out. It might seem obvious, but I've had lots of users get confused by encryption, thinking that the PC *knows* who's clicking the keyboard! All protections and security are based on user accounts. If someone logs into your computer with a different account, the encrypted files will be unreadable. We'll get to user accounts, permissions, and such in later chapters in detail.

Disk Quotas

NTFS supports *disk quotas,* enabling administrators to set limits on drive space usage for users. To set quotas, you must log in as an Administrator, right-click the hard drive name, and select Properties. In the Drive Properties dialog box, select the Quota tab and make changes. Figure 10-25 shows configured quotas for a hard drive. While rarely used on single-user systems, setting disk quotas on multi-user systems prevents any individual user from monopolizing your hard disk space.

Figure 10-25
Hard drive quotas
in Windows XP

Cluster Sizes

Unlike FAT16 or FAT32, NTFS enables you to adjust the cluster sizes, although you'll probably rarely do so. Table 10-3 shows the default cluster sizes for NTFS.

Drive Size	Cluster Size	Number of Sectors
512 MB or less	512 bytes	1
513 MB to 1024 MB (1 GB)	1,024 bytes (1 KB)	2
1,025 MB to 2048 MB (2 GB)	2,048 bytes (2 KB)	4
2,049 MB and larger	4,096 bytes (4 KB)	8

Table 10-3 NTFS Cluster Sizes

By default, NTFS supports partitions up to 2 terabytes (2,199,023,255,552 bytes). By tweaking the cluster sizes, you can get NTFS to support partitions up to 16 exabytes, or 18,446,744,073,709,551,616 bytes! That might support any and all upcoming hard drive capacities for the next 100 years or so.

NTFS Naming

Most computer writers, including those at Microsoft (until recently), label the version of NTFS that shipped with a particular version of Windows by the version number of Windows. So, the NTFS that shipped with Windows NT 4.0 is frequently called NTFS 4, although that's not technically correct. Similarly, since the NTFS that shipped with Windows 2000 offered great improvements over the earlier versions, it became NTFS 5 in the minds of most techs.

Current Microsoft Knowledge Base articles refer to the NTFS that ships with Windows XP specifically as NTFS 3.1. Windows Vista is still in beta at the time of this writing, so whether Microsoft will update NTFS in the final version shipped is unknown. Table 10-4 summarizes the names used to refer to each version of NTFS.

Official Microsoft Name	Also Known as	Shipped With
NTFS 1.x	n/a	Windows NT 3.51 and Windows NT 4
NTFS 3.0	NTFS 4	Windows 2000
NTFS 3.1	NTFS 5	Windows XP, Windows Server 2003

Table 10-4 NTFS Version Names

With so many file systems, how do you know which one to use? In the case of internal hard drives, you should use the most feature-rich system your OS supports. If you have Windows 2000/XP/2003/Vista, use NTFS. FAT32 is still often used on external hard drives because NTFS features such as the ACL and encryption can make access difficult when moving the drive between systems, but with that exception the benefits of NTFS make it your best choice on a Windows-based system.

The Partitioning and Formatting Process

Now that you understand the concepts of formatting and partitioning, let's go through the process of setting up an installed hard drive using different partitioning and formatting tools. If you have access to a system, try following along with these descriptions. Remember, don't make any changes to a drive you want to keep, because both partitioning and formatting are destructive processes!

Bootable Disks

Imagine you've built a brand-new PC. The hard drive has no OS so you need to boot up something to set up that hard drive. Any software that can boot up a system is by definition an operating system. You need a floppy disk, CD-ROM, or USB thumb drive with a bootable OS installed. Any removable media that has a bootable OS is generically called a *boot device* or *boot disk*. Your system boots off the boot device, which then loads some kind of OS that enables you to partition, format, and install an OS on your new hard drive. Boot devices come from many sources. All Windows OS installation CDs are boot devices, as are Linux installation CDs. You can make your own bootable devices, and most techs do, because a boot device often has a number of handy tools included to do certain jobs.

In the next chapter, "Removable Media," I go through the steps to make a number of different types of boot devices for different jobs. If you want to follow along with some of the steps in this chapter, you may want to jump ahead to the next chapter to make a boot device or two and then return here.

Partitioning and Formatting with the Windows Installation CD

When you boot up a Windows installation CD and the installation program detects a hard drive that is not yet partitioned, it prompts you through a sequence of steps to partition (and format) the hard drive. Chapter 12, "Installing and Upgrading Windows," covers the entire installation process, but we'll jump ahead and dive into the partitioning part of the installation here to see how this is done, working through two examples using one, then two partitions. This example uses the Windows XP Installation CD—but don't worry, this part of the Windows 2000 installation is almost identical.

Single Partition

The most common partitioning scenario involves turning a new, blank drive into a single, bootable C: drive. To accomplish this goal, you need to make the entire drive a primary partition and then make it active. Let's go through the process of partitioning and formatting a single, brand-new, 200-GB hard drive.

The Windows installation begins by booting from a Windows installation CD-ROM like the one shown in Figure 10-26. The installation program starts automatically from the CD. The installation first loads some needed files but will eventually prompt you with the screen shown in Figure 10-27. This is your clue that partitioning is about to start!

Figure 10-26
Windows
installation CD

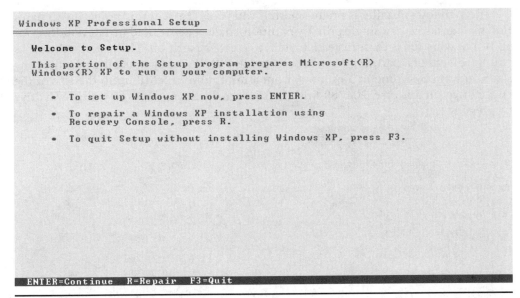

```
Windows XP Professional Setup

Welcome to Setup.

This portion of the Setup program prepares Microsoft(R)
Windows(R) XP to run on your computer.

    • To set up Windows XP now, press ENTER.

    • To repair a Windows XP installation using
      Recovery Console, press R.

    • To quit Setup without installing Windows XP, press F3.

ENTER=Continue   R=Repair   F3=Quit
```

Figure 10-27   Welcome to Setup

Press the ENTER key to start a new Windows installation and accept the license agreement to see the main partitioning screen (Figure 10-28). The bar that says Unpartitioned Space is the drive.

```
Windows XP Professional Setup

The following list shows the existing partitions and
unpartitioned space on this computer.

Use the UP and DOWN ARROW keys to select an item in the list.

    • To set up Windows XP on the selected item, press ENTER.

    • To create a partition in the unpartitioned space, press C.

    • To delete the selected partition, press D.

204798 MB Disk 0 at Id 0 on bus 0 on atapi [MBR]
        Unpartitioned space                 204797 MB

ENTER=Install   C=Create Partition   F3=Quit
```

Figure 10-28   Partitioning screen

The Windows installer is pretty smart. If you press ENTER at this point, it will partition the hard drive as a single primary partition, make it active, and install Windows for you—but what fun is that? Instead, press C to create a partition. The installer then asks you how large of a partition to make (Figure 10-29). You may make the partition any size you want by typing in a number, from a minimum of 8 MB up to the size of the entire drive (in this case, 204789 MB). Let's just make the entire drive a single C: drive by pressing ENTER.

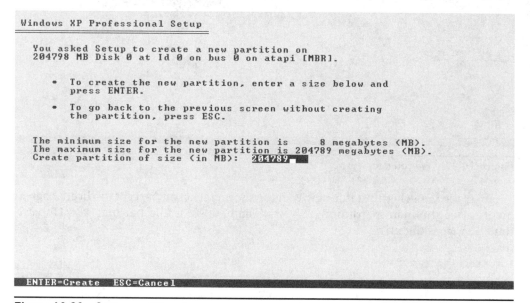

Figure 10-29 Setting partition size

Ta-da! You just partitioned the drive! Now Windows asks you how you want to format that drive (Figure 10-30). So you might be asking—where's the basic vs. dynamic? Where do you tell Windows to make the partition primary instead of extended? Where do you set it as active?

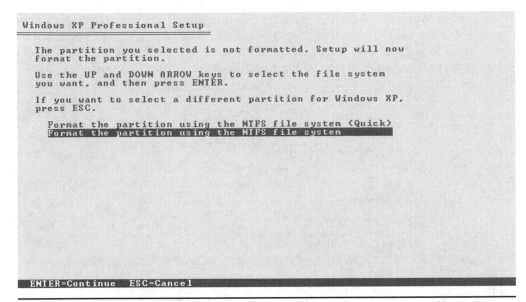

Figure 10-30 Format screen

The Windows installer makes a number of assumptions for you, such as always making the first partition primary and setting it active. The installer also makes all hard drives basic disks. You'll have to convert it to dynamic later (if you even want to convert it at all).

Select NTFS for the format. Either option—quick or full—will do the job here. (Quick format is quicker, as the name would suggest, but the full option is more thorough and thus safer.) After Windows formats the drive, the installation continues, copying the new Windows installation to the C: drive.

Two Partitions Well, that was fun! So much fun that I'd like to do another new Windows install, with a bit more complex partitioning. This time, you still have the 200-GB hard drive, but you want to split the drive into three drive letters of roughly 66 GB each. That means you'll need to make a single 66-GB primary partition, then a 133-GB extended partition, and then split that extended partition into two logical drives of 66 GB each.

Back at the Windows installation main partitioning screen, first press C to make a new partition, but this time change the 204789 to 66666, which will give you a partition of about 66 GB. When you press ENTER, the partitioning screen should look like Figure 10-31. Even though the installation program doesn't tell you, the partition is primary.

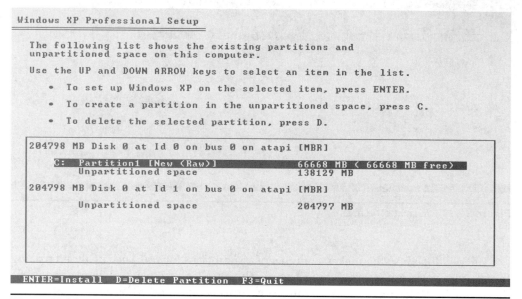

```
Windows XP Professional Setup

    The following list shows the existing partitions and
    unpartitioned space on this computer.

    Use the UP and DOWN ARROW keys to select an item in the list.

    •  To set up Windows XP on the selected item, press ENTER.

    •  To create a partition in the unpartitioned space, press C.

    •  To delete the selected partition, press D.

  204798 MB Disk 0 at Id 0 on bus 0 on atapi [MBR]
    C:   Partition1 [New (Raw)]              66668 MB ( 66668 MB free)
         Unpartitioned space                138129 MB
  204798 MB Disk 0 at Id 1 on bus 0 on atapi [MBR]

         Unpartitioned space                204797 MB




  ENTER=Install   D=Delete Partition   F3=Quit
```

Figure 10-31   66-GB partition created

 NOTE   Windows will almost always adjust the number you type in for a partition size. In this case, it changed **66666** to **66668**, a number that makes more sense when translated to binary. Don't worry about it!

Notice that two-thirds of the drive is still unpartitioned space. Move the selection down to this option and press C to create the next partition. Once again, enter **66666** in the partition size screen and press ENTER, and you'll see something similar to Figure 10-32.

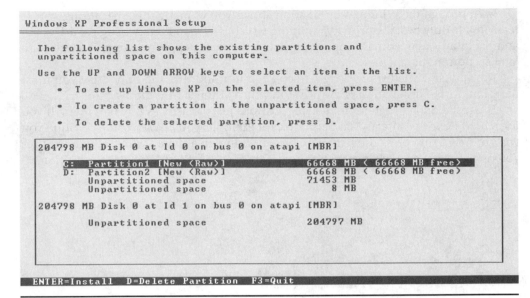

Figure 10-32 Second partition created

Create your last partition exactly as you made the other two to see your almost-completely partitioned drive (Figure 10-33). (Note that the example is not realistic in one respect: you would never leave any unpartitioned space on a drive in a typical PC.)

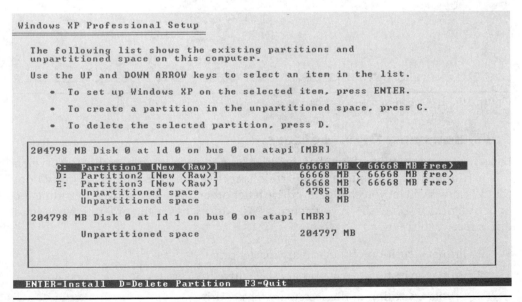

Figure 10-33 Fully partitioned drive

Even though the Windows installation shows you've made three partitions, you've really made only two: the primary partition, which is C:, and then two logical drives (D: and E:) in an extended partition. Once again, the next step, formatting, is saved for a later section in this chapter.

You've just created three drive letters. Keep in mind that the only drive you must partition during installation is the drive on which you install Windows.

The installation program can delete partitions just as easily as it makes them. If you use a hard drive that already has partitions, for example, you just select the partition you wish to delete and press the letter D. This will bring up a dialog where Windows gives you one last change to change your mind (Figure 10-34). Press L to kill the partition.

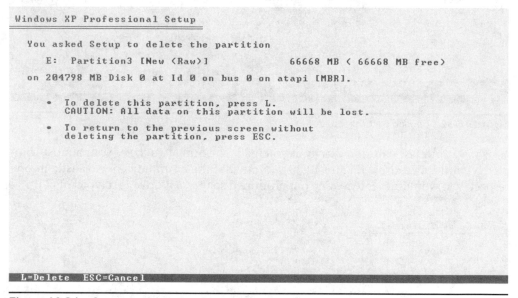

Figure 10-34 Option to delete partition

Partitions and Drive Letters

Folks new to partitioning think that the drive letter gets "burned into the drive" when it is partitioned. This is untrue. The partitions receive their drive letters at every boot (but Windows will let you change any drive letter other than the C: drive, overriding the boot ordering, if you wish). If you're using PATA drives, here's the order in which hard drives receive their letters:

1. Primary partition of the primary master drive
2. Primary partition of the primary slave drive
3. Primary partition of the secondary master drive
4. Primary partition of the secondary slave drive
5. All logical drives in the extended partition of the primary master drive

6. All logical drives in the extended partition of the primary slave drive

7. All logical drives in the extended partition of the secondary master drive

8. All logical drives in the extended partition of the secondary slave drive

If you're using SATA drives, this order still exists, but given that SATA no longer uses the concept of master or slave, the drive letter is based on the order you set in CMOS:

1. Primary partition of the first drive in the boot order

2. Primary partition of the second drive in the boot order

3. Primary partition of the third drive in the boot order

Keep going through the boot order for all the Primary partitions of the rest of the SATA drives!

4. All logical drives in the extended partition of the first drive in the boot order

5. All logical drives in the extended partition of the second drive in the boot order

6. All logical drives in the extended partition of the third drive in the boot order

Keep going through the boot order for all the Logical partitions of the rest of the SATA drives!

If you've got both PATA and SATA drives, things get a bit complicated and boot order depends on your motherboard. The first generations of motherboard with both PATA and SATA always had you first boot to the PATA drives and then the SATA drives. Later, motherboards with both PATA and SATA will have a special setting in CMOS that shows all of the drives currently seen by the system, including hard drives, CD media, floppy drives, and even USB drives. Figure 10-35 shows a sample of this more modern CMOS.

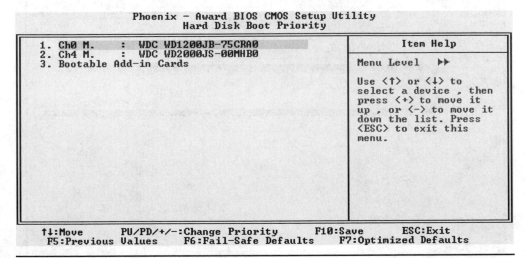

Figure 10-35 Modern boot order

In these systems, the boot order is determined not by whether the drives are PATA or SATA, but simply by the order of the hard drives in this list (other devices get their drive letters after the hard drives). If you have a particular drive you want to be the C: drive, just move it to the top of the list.

At boot, the system uses this order to assign drive letters. If you install a single drive with one primary partition and one extended partition with one logical drive, for example, at boot the primary partition would become C: and the logical drive would become D:.

If you install a second drive, say one with a single primary partition, this changes. The system first finds the primary partition on the primary master and assigns it the letter C:, just as before. It then continues to look for any other primary partitions, finding the primary partition on the primary slave and assigning that primary partition the letter D:. Not seeing any more primary partitions, it then goes back up to the primary master drive, now looking for logical drives in extended partitions. It finds one logical drive and assigns it the letter E:. If the system had found two logical drives on the primary master, they would receive the letters E: and F:. After giving the drive letter E: to the one logical drive in the extended partition, the system continues down the list, looking for more logical drives in more extended partitions.

Disk Management

The real tool for partitioning and formatting is the Disk Management utility. Disk Management enables you to do everything you want to do to a hard drive in one handy tool. You can access Disk Management by going to the Control Panel and opening the Computer Management applet. If you're cool, you can click Start | Run, type in **diskmgmt.msc**, and press ENTER. Windows 2000, XP, and Vista come with Disk Management (Figure 10-36).

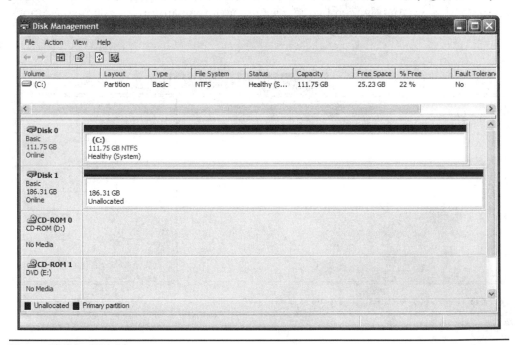

Figure 10-36   Disk Management

Disk Management works only within Windows, so you can't use Disk Management from a boot device. If you install Windows from an installation CD, in other words, you must use the special partitioning/formatting software built into the installation program you just saw in action.

One of the most interesting parts of Disk Management is disk initialization. Every hard drive in a Windows system has special information placed onto the drive. This initialization information includes identifiers that say "this drive belongs in this system" and other information that defines what this hard drive does in the system. If the hard drive is part of a RAID array, its RAID information is stored in the initialization. If it's part of a spanned volume, this is also stored there. All new drives must be initialized before you can use them. When you install an extra hard drive into a Windows system and start Disk Management, it notices the new drive and starts the Hard Drive Initialization Wizard. If you don't let the wizard run, the drive will be listed as unknown (Figure 10-37).

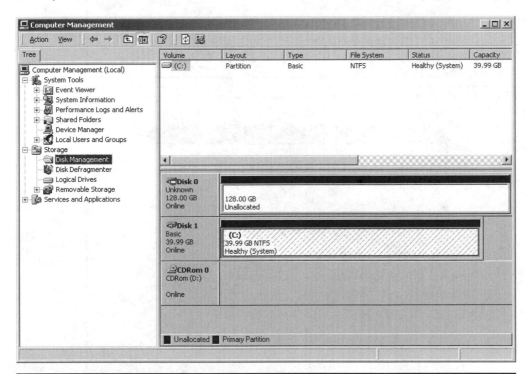

Figure 10-37   Unknown drive in Disk Management

To initialize a disk, right-click the disk icon and select Initialize. Once a disk is initialized, you can see the status of the drive—a handy tool for troubleshooting.

A newly-installed drive is always set as a basic disk. There's nothing wrong with using basic disks, other than that you miss out on some handy features. To create partitions, right-click the unallocated part of the drive and select New Partition. Disk Management will run the New Partition Wizard, enabling you to select a primary or extended partition (Figure 10-38). Afterward, you'll see a screen where you specify the size partition you prefer (Figure 10-39).

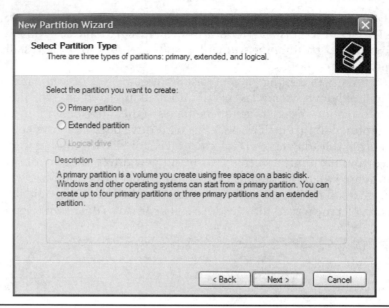

Figure 10-38   The New Partition Wizard

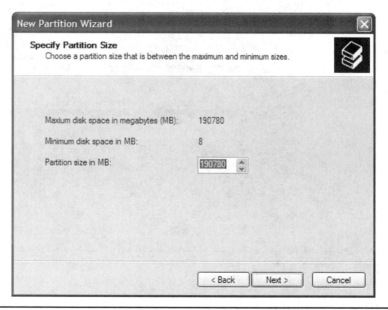

Figure 10-39   Specifying the partition size

If you choose to make a primary partition, the wizard asks if you want to assign a drive letter to the partition, mount it as a folder to an existing partition, or do neither (Figure 10-40). (If you choose to make an extended partition, you just get a confirmation screen and you are returned to Disk Management.) In almost all cases, we give primary partitions a drive letter.

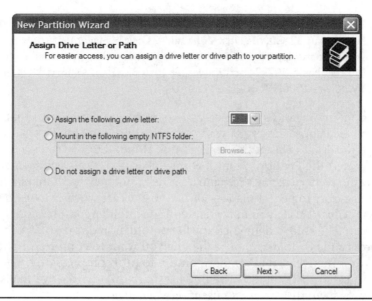

Figure 10-40   Assigning a drive letter to a primary partition

The last screen of the New Partition Wizard asks for the type of format you want to use for this partition (Figure 10-41). If your partition is 4 GB or less, you may format it as FAT, FAT32, or NTFS. If your partition is greater than 4 GB but less than 32 GB, you can make the drive FAT32 or NTFS. Windows requires NTFS on any partition greater than 32 GB. Although FAT32 supports partitions up to 2 TB, Microsoft wants you to use NTFS on larger partitions and creates this limit. In today's world of big hard drives, there's no good reason to use anything other than NTFS.

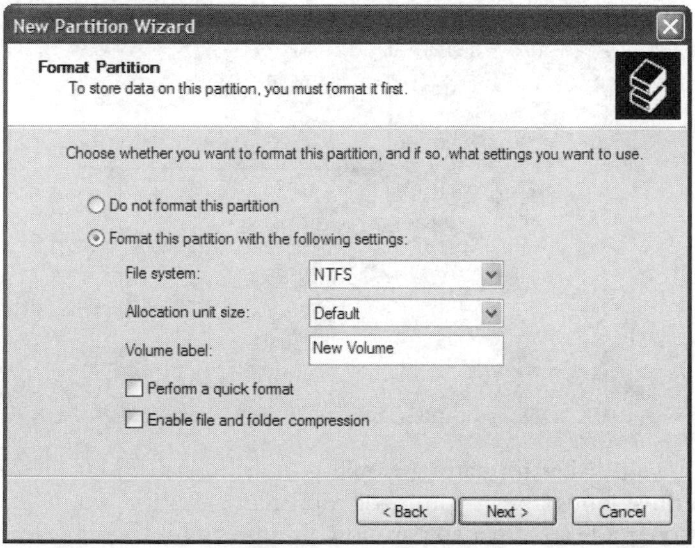

Figure 10-41   Choosing a file system type

NOTE Windows 2000, XP, and Vista read and write to FAT32 partitions larger than 32 GB; they just don't allow Disk Management to make them! If you ever stumble across a drive from a system that ran the old Windows 9x/ Me that has a FAT32 partition larger than 32 GB, it will work just fine in your Windows 2000, XP, or Vista system.

You have a few more tasks to complete at this screen. You can add a volume label if you want. You can also choose the size of your clusters (Allocation Unit Size). There's no reason to change the default cluster size, so leave that alone—but you can sure speed up the format if you select the Perform A Quick Format check box. This will format your drive without checking every cluster. It's fast and a bit risky, but new hard drives almost always come from the factory in perfect shape—so you must decide whether to use it or not.

Last, if you chose NTFS, you may enable file and folder compression. If you select this option, you'll be able to right-click any file or folder on this partition and compress it. To compress a file or folder, choose the one you want to compress, right-click, and select Properties. Then click the Advanced button to turn compression on or off (Figure 10-42). Compression is handy for opening up space on a hard drive that's filling up, but it also slows down disk access, so use it only when you need it.

Figure 10-42
Turning on
compression

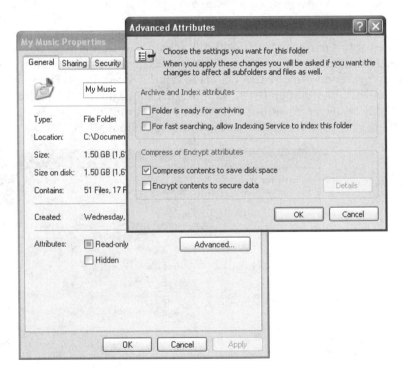

After the drive finishes formatting, you'll go back to Disk Management and see a changed hard drive landscape. If you made a primary partition, you will see your new drive letter. If you made an extended partition, things will look a bit different. Figure 10-43 shows the extended partition as free space because it has no logical drive yet. As you can easily guess from Figure 10-44, to create a logical drive, simply right-click in that extended partition and choose New Logical Drive. Disk Management will fire up the New Partition Wizard again, this time with the option to create a logical drive (Figure 10-45).

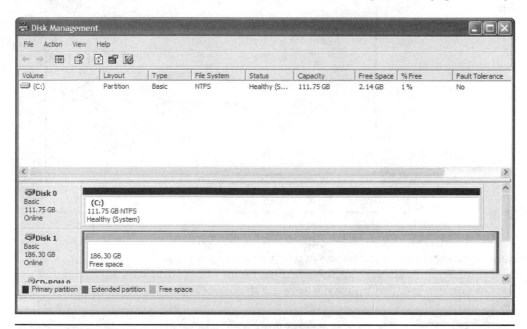

Figure 10-43 Extended partition with no logical drives

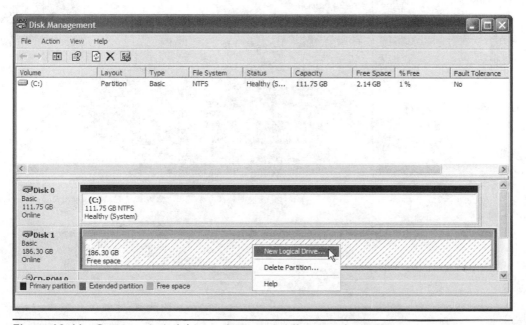

Figure 10-44 Creating a logical drive in the extended (free space) partition

Figure 10-45
New Partition
Wizard for logical
drive

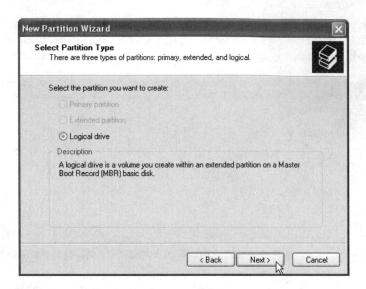

When you create a logical drive, the New Partition Wizard automatically gives you the same options to format the partition using one of the three file systems you saw earlier with primary partitions (Figure 10-46). You'll get another confirmation screen, and then the Disk Management console will show you the newly created drive (see Figure 10-47).

Figure 10-46
The New Partition
Wizard offering
formatting options

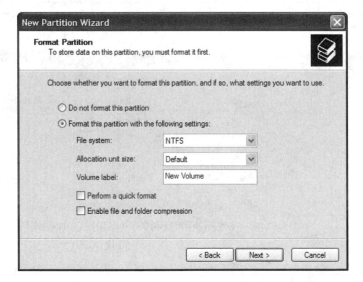

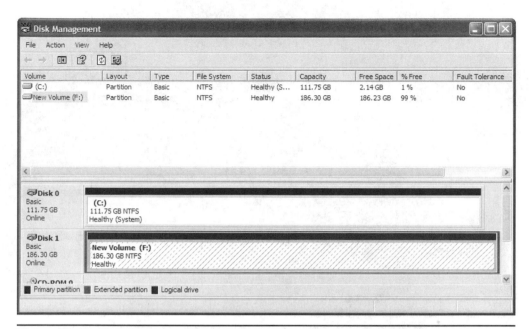

Figure 10-47   The Disk Management console showing newly created logical drive

One interesting aspect of Windows is the tiny (approximately 8 MB) mysterious unallocated partition that shows up on the C: drive. This is done by the Windows installation program when you first install Windows on a new system, to reserve a space Windows needs to convert the C: drive to a dynamic disk. It doesn't hurt anything and it's tiny, so just leave it alone. If you want to make a volume and format it, feel free to do so.

Dynamic Disks

You create dynamic disk from basic disks in Disk Management. Once you convert a drive from a basic to a dynamic disk, primary and extended partitions no longer exist; dynamic disks are divided into volumes instead of partitions.

To convert a basic disk to dynamic, just right-click the drive icon and select Convert to Dynamic Disk (Figure 10-48). The process is very quick and safe, although the reverse is not true. The conversion from dynamic disk to basic disk first requires you to delete all partitions off the hard drive.

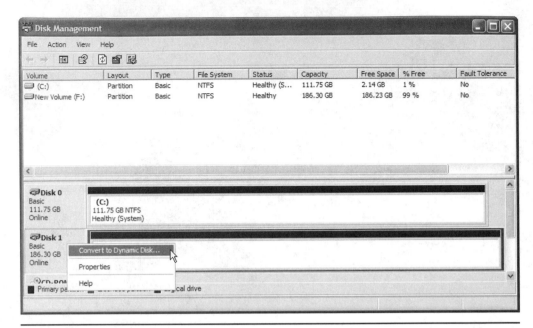

Figure 10-48 Converting to a dynamic disk

Once you've converted, no partitions exist, only volumes. You can make five types of volumes on a dynamic disk: simple, spanned, striped, mirrored, and RAID 5, although you'll commonly see only the first three in a Windows 2000 Professional or Windows XP Professional environment. You'll next learn how to implement the three most common volume types. The final step involves assigning a drive letter or mounting the volume as a folder.

EXAM TIP Windows XP Home does not support dynamic disks.

NOTE Disk Management enables you to create mirrored and striped with parity volumes, but only on Windows 2000 or 2003 Server machines. The cool thing is that you can do this remotely across a network. You can sit at your Windows XP Professional workstation, in other words, and open Disk Management. Surf to a Windows 2000/2003 Server that you want to work with and poof! You have two new options for configuring volumes. By limiting the implementation of mirroring and RAID 5 to server machines, Microsoft clearly meant to encourage small businesses to pony up for a copy of Server rather than using the less-expensive Professional OS for the company server! Both mirrored and striped with parity volumes are included here for completeness and because they show up in the Windows Help Files when you search for dynamic disks. Both are cool, but definitely way beyond CompTIA A+!

Simple Volumes

A simple volume acts just like a primary partition. If you have only one dynamic disk in a system, it can have only a simple volume. It's important to note here that a simple volume may act like a traditional primary partition, but it is very different. If you install a hard drive partitioned as a simple volume dynamic disk into any version of Windows prior to Windows 2000, you would see no usable partition.

In Disk Management, right-click any unallocated space on the dynamic disk and choose New Volume (Figure 10-49) to run the New Volume Wizard. You'll see a series of screens that prompt you on size and file system, and then you're done. Figure 10-50 shows Disk Management with three simple volumes.

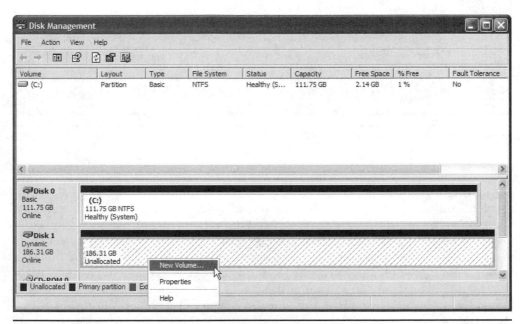

Figure 10-49 Opening the New Volume Wizard

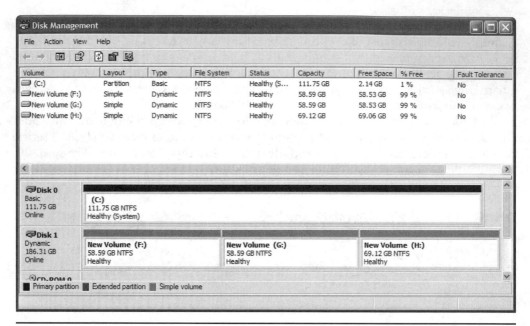

Figure 10-50 Simple volumes

Spanning Volumes

Dynamic disks enable you to extend the size of a simple volume to any unallocated space on a dynamic disk. You can also extend the volume to grab extra space on completely different dynamic disks, creating a *spanned* volume. To extend or span, simply right-click the volume you want to make bigger, and choose Extend Volume from the options (Figure 10-51). This opens the Extend Volume Wizard that will prompt you for the location of free space on a dynamic disk and the increased volume size you want to assign (Figure 10-52). If you have multiple drives, you can span the volume just as easily to one of those drives.

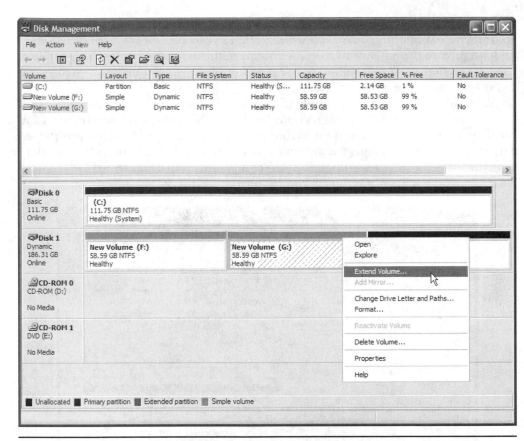

Figure 10-51   Selecting the Extend Volume option

Figure 10-52
The Extend Volume
Wizard

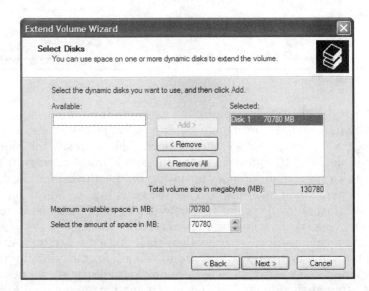

The ability to extend and span volumes makes dynamic disks worth their weight in gold! If you start running out of space on a volume, you can simply add another physical hard drive to the system and span the volume to the new drive. This keeps your drive letters consistent and unchanging so your programs don't get confused, yet enables you to expand drive space when needed.

You can extend or span any simple volume on a dynamic disk, not just the "one on the end" in the Disk Management console. You simply select the volume to expand and the total volume increase you want. Figure 10-53 shows a simple 4-GB volume named Extended that has been enlarged an extra 7.91 GB in a portion of the hard drive, skipping the 2-GB section of unallocated space contiguous to it. This created an 11.91-GB volume. Windows has no problem skipping areas on a drive.

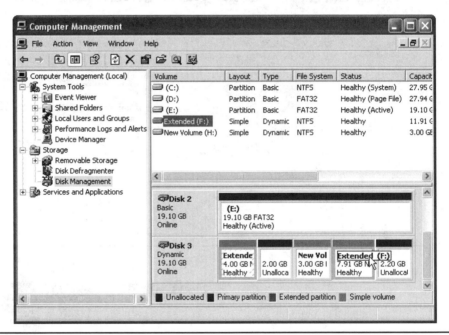

Figure 10-53   Extended volume

Striped Volumes

If you have two or more dynamic disks in a PC, Disk Management enables you to combine them into a *striped* volume. A striped volume spreads out blocks of each file across multiple disks. Using two or more drives in a group called a *stripe set*, striping writes data first to a certain number of clusters on one drive, then on the next, and so on. It speeds up data throughput because the system has to wait a much shorter time for a drive to read or write data. The drawback of striping is that if any single drive in the stripe set fails, all data in the stripe set is lost.

To create a striped volume, right-click unused space on a drive and choose New Volume, and then Striped. The wizard will ask for the other drives you want to add to the stripe, and you need to select two unallocated spaces on other dynamic disks. Select the other unallocated spaces and go through the remaining screens on sizing and formatting until you've created a new striped volume (Figure 10-54). The two stripes in the figure may seem as though they have different sizes, but if you look closely you'll see they are both 4 GB. All stripes must be the same size on each drive.

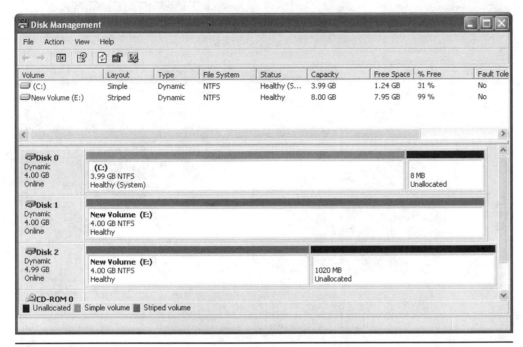

Figure 10-54   Two striped drives

Mount Points

The one drive that can't take full advantage of being dynamic is the drive containing the operating system, your primary master C: drive. You can make it dynamic, but that still won't let you do all the cool dynamic things, like extending and spanning. So what good is the ability to allocate more space to a volume if you can't use it when you start to fill up your C: drive? If you can't add to that drive, your only option is to replace it with a new, bigger drive, right?

Not at all! Earlier we discussed the idea of mounting a drive as a folder instead of a drive letter, and here's where you get to do it. A *volume mount point* (or simply *mount point*) is a place in the directory structure of an existing volume that you can point to a volume or partition. The mounted volume will then function just like a folder, but all files stored in that segment of the directory structure will go to the mounted volume. After partitioning and formatting the drive, you don't give it a drive letter; instead, you *mount* the volume to a folder on the C: drive and make it nothing more than just another folder (Figure 10-55). You can load programs to that folder, just as you would to your Program Files folder. You can use it to store data files or backed-up system files. In *function*, therefore, the new hard drive simply extends the capacity of the C: drive, so neither you nor your client need ever trouble yourselves with dealing with multiple drive letters.

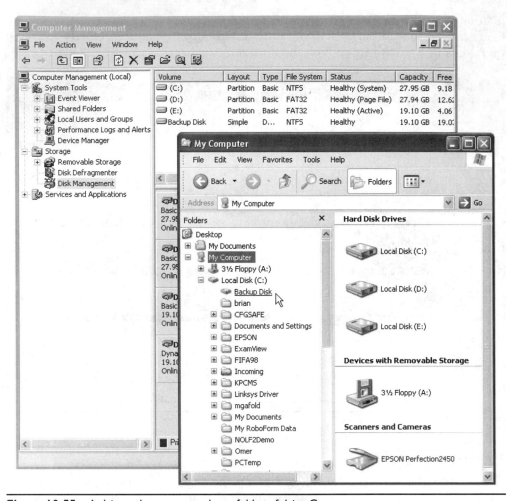

Figure 10-55 A drive volume mounted as a folder of drive C:

To create a mount point, right-click an unallocated section of a dynamic disk and choose New Volume. This opens the New Volume Wizard. In the second screen, you can select a mount point rather than a drive letter (Figure 10-56). Browse to a blank folder on an NTFS-formatted drive or create a new folder and you're in business.

Figure 10-56
Choosing to create
a mounted volume

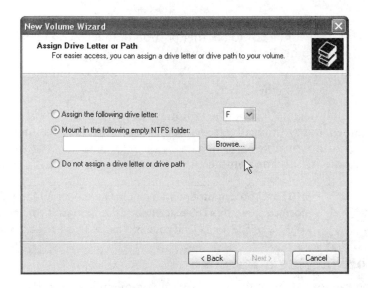

With mount points, Microsoft dramatically changed the way you can work with hard drives. You're no longer stuck in the rut of adding drive letters that mess up Windows' mapping of the CD-ROM drive. You don't have to confuse clients with multiple drive letters when they just want a little more space. You can resurrect smaller hard drives, making them a functional part of today's computer. With the Disk Management console in Windows 2000 and XP, Microsoft got it right.

Working with Dynamic Drives and Mount Points

You can't begin to appreciate the ease and elegant simplicity of dynamic drives until you play with them. Get a couple of spare drives and install them into a PC running Windows 2000 or Windows XP. Fire up the Disk Management console and try the following setups. Convert both spare drives to dynamic drives.

CAUTION Once you convert a drive to dynamic, you cannot revert it to a basic disk without losing all the data on that drive. Be prepared to back up all data before you revert.

1. Make a mirror set.

2. Make a stripe set.

3. Make them into a single volume, spanned between both drives.

4. Make a single volume that takes up a portion of one drive, and then extend that volume onto another portion of that drive. Finally, span that volume to the other hard drive as well.

5. Create a volume of some sort—you decide—and then mount that volume to a folder on the C: drive.

You'll need to format the volumes after you create them so you can see how they manifest in My Computer. (See the next section of this chapter for details on formatting.) Also, you'll need to delete volumes to create a new setup. To delete volumes, simply right-click the volume and choose Delete Volume. It's almost too easy.

 NOTE You can mount a volume to an empty folder only on a drive formatted with NTFS 5. In theory, the mounted volume can be formatted as FAT16, FAT32, or NTFS5, but you almost never see anything but NTFS5.

Formatting a Partition

You can format any Windows partition/volume in My Computer. Just right-click the drive name and choose Format (Figure 10-57). You'll see a dialog box that asks for the type of file system you want to use, the cluster size, a place to put a volume label, and two other options. The Quick Format option tells Windows not to test the clusters and is a handy option when you're in a hurry—and feeling lucky. The Enable Compression option tells Windows to give users the ability to compress folders or files. It works well but slows down your hard drive.

Figure 10-57
Choosing Format
in My Computer

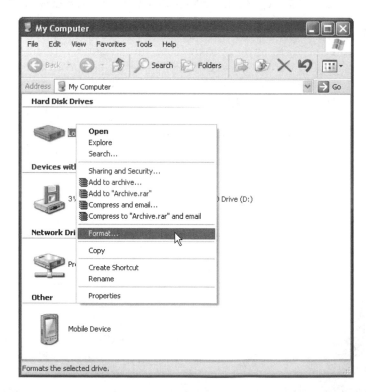

Disk Management is today's preferred formatting tool for Windows 2000, XP, and Vista. When you create a new volume on a dynamic disk or a new partition on a basic disk, the New Volume Wizard will also ask you what type of format you want to use. Always use NTFS unless you're that rare and strange person that wants to dual-boot Windows XP or Windows Vista with some ancient version of Windows.

All OS installation CD-ROMs will partition and format as part of the OS installation. Windows simply prompts you to partition and then format the drive. Read the screens and you'll do great.

Maintaining and Troubleshooting Hard Drives

Hard drives are complex mechanical and electrical devices. With platters spinning at thousands of rotations per minute, they also generate heat and vibration. All of these factors make hard drives susceptible to failure. In this section, you will learn some basic maintenance tasks that will keep your hard drives healthy, and for those inevitable instances when a hard drive fails, you will also learn what you can do to repair them.

Maintenance

Hard drive maintenance can be broken down into two distinct functions: checking the disk occasionally for failed clusters and keeping data organized on the drive so that it can be accessed quickly.

Error-Checking

Individual clusters on hard drives sometimes go bad. There's nothing you can do to prevent this from happening, so it's important that you check occasionally for bad clusters on drives. The tools used to perform this checking are generically called error-checking utilities, although the terms for two older Microsoft tools—ScanDisk and CHKDSK (pronounced "Checkdisk")—are often used. Microsoft calls the tool Error-checking in Windows XP. Whatever the name of the utility, each does the same job: when the tool finds bad clusters, it puts the electronic equivalent of orange cones around them so that the system won't try to place data in those bad clusters.

Most error-checking tools do far more than just check for bad clusters. They go through all of the drive's filenames, looking for invalid names and attempting to fix them. They look for clusters that have no filenames associated with them (we call these *lost chains*) and erase them. From time to time, the underlying links between parent and child folders are lost, so a good error-checking tool checks every parent and child folder. With a folder such as C:\TEST\DATA, for example, they make sure that the folder DATA is properly associated with its parent folder, C:\TEST, and that C:\TEST is properly associated with its child folder, C:\TEST\DATA.

To access Error-Checking on a Windows 2000 or Windows XP system, open My Computer, right-click the drive you want to check, and choose Properties to open the drive's Properties dialog box. Select the Tools tab and click the Check Now button (Figure 10-58) to display the Check Disk dialog box, which has two options (Figure 10-59). Check the box next to Automatically Fix File System Errors, but save the option to Scan For and Attempt Recovery of Bad Sectors for times when you actually suspect a problem, because it takes a while on bigger hard drives.

Figure 10-58
The Tools tab in the Properties dialog box in Windows XP

Figure 10-59
The Check Disk dialog box

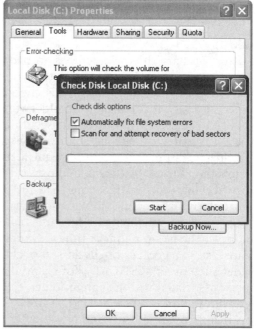

Now that you know how to run Error-checking, your next question should be, "How often do I run it?" A reasonable maintenance plan would include running it about once a week. Error-checking is fast (unless you use the Scan For and Attempt Recovery option), and it's a great tool for keeping your system in top shape.

Defragmentation

Fragmentation of clusters can make your drive access times increase dramatically. It's a good idea to defragment—or *defrag*—your drives as part of monthly maintenance. You access the defrag tool that runs with Windows 2000, XP, and Vista, called Disk Defragmenter, the same way you access Error-checking—right-click a drive in My Computer and choose Properties—except you click the Defragment Now button on the Tools tab to open the Defragmenter (Figure 10-60).

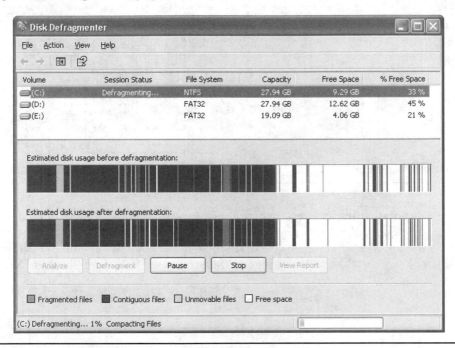

Figure 10-60 Disk Defragmenter in Windows XP

Defragmentation is interesting to watch—once. From then on, schedule it to run late at night. You should defragment your drives about once a month, although you could run it every week, and if you run it every night it takes only a few minutes. The longer you go between defrags, the longer it takes. If you don't run Disk Defragmenter, your system will run slower. If you don't run Error-checking, you may lose data.

Disk Cleanup

Did you know that the average hard drive is full of trash? Not the junk you intentionally put in your hard drive like the 23,000 e-mail messages that you refuse to delete from your e-mail program. This kind of trash is all the files that you never see that Windows keeps for you. Here are a few examples:

- **Files in the Recycle Bin** When you delete a file, it isn't really deleted. It's placed in the Recycle Bin in case you decide you need the file later. I just checked my Recycle Bin and found 3 GB worth of files (Figure 10-61). That's a lot of trash!

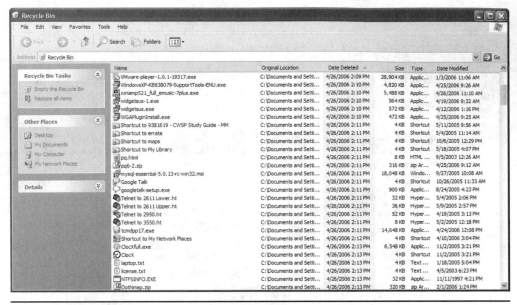

Figure 10-61   Mike's Recycle Bin

- **Temporary Internet Files**   When you go to a Web site, Windows keeps copies of the graphics and other items so that the page will load more quickly the next time you access the page. You can see these files by opening the Internet Options applet on the Control Panel. Figure 10-62 shows my temporary Internet files.

Figure 10-62
Lots of temporary
Internet files

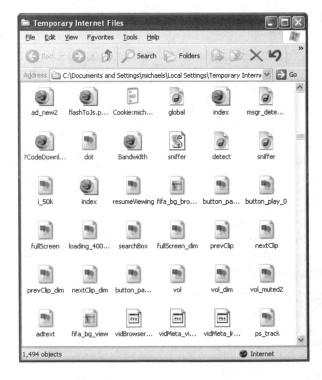

- **Downloaded Program Files** Your system always keeps a copy of any Java or ActiveX applets that it downloads. You can see these in the Internet Options applet. You'll generally find only a few tiny files here.

- **Temporary Files** Many applications create temporary files that are supposed to be deleted when the application is closed. For one reason or another, these temporary files sometimes aren't deleted. The location of these files varies with the version of Windows, but they always reside in a folder called TEMP.

Every hard drive will eventually become filled with lots of unnecessary trash. All versions of Windows tend to act erratically when the drives run out of unused space. Fortunately, all versions of Windows have a powerful tool called Disk Cleanup (Figure 10-63). You can access Disk Cleanup in all versions of Windows by choosing Start | Program | Accessories | System Tools | Disk Cleanup.

Figure 10-63
Disk Cleanup

Disk Cleanup gets rid of the four types of files just described (and a few others). Run Disk Cleanup once a month or so to keep plenty of space available on your hard drive.

Troubleshooting

There's no scarier computer problem than an error that points to trouble with a hard drive. This section looks at some of the more common problems that occur with hard drives and how to fix them. These issues fall into three broad categories: installation, data corruption, and dying hard drives.

Installation Errors

Installing a drive and getting to the point where it can hold data requires four distinct steps: connectivity, CMOS, partitioning, and formatting. If you make a mistake at any point on any of these steps, the drive won't work. The beauty of this is that if you make an error, you can walk back through each step and check for problems.

Connectivity   A connectivity error means something isn't plugged in correctly or something has managed to unplug itself. These problems virtually always show themselves at boot time. Here are some classics:

- Hard drive error
- No fixed disks present
- HDD controller failure
- No boot device available
- Drive not found

If you plug the data cable in backward for an IDE drive, for example, the computer simply won't see the drive—it's a famous error and everyone who has ever installed a hard drive has done it. Just reinsert the cable properly and turn the machine back on. The power connectors aren't nearly as forgiving. If you install the power cable backward, you will destroy the drive in a dazzling display of sparks and smoke. Fortunately, the chamfers on Molex connectors make this mistake difficult to do.

You can usually conquer connectivity errors by carefully inspecting the entire connection system (including electricity) and finding the silly mistake (welcome to the club). Always remove and reseat the controller (if it's on an expansion card) if you get an HDD controller failure, as they are prone to static build-up. It is also a good idea to keep an extra controller around to verify whether the controller is bad or good. Cables can go bad, but it is rare unless the cable is obviously ripped or pinched. If your BIOS has an autodetection function, use it. It will not detect a drive unless everything is installed correctly. It's a great, quick connectivity verifier.

If you've just installed the drive, check the jumper settings. You can't have two masters or two slaves on a single controller. And don't forget the 1 Drive or Standalone setting on some drives!

Installing two drives on the same controller increases the chances of errors dramatically. For example, adding a slave drive to an existing single drive requires you to check the first drive to see if its jumper needs to change from single to master. You need to make sure to install the slave drive properly or neither drive will work, causing the system to fail on boot. Additionally, some ATA drives are simply incompatible and will not work on the same controller. I've worked on many systems where I had to add a second drive to the secondary controller since it would not work with the existing drive.

CMOS   Modern systems rarely get CMOS errors, because the autodetection feature handles most drives. The errors that do occur generally fall into two groups: forgetting to run Autodetect and selecting the wrong sector translation in Autodetect. Two rules apply here: Always run Autodetect and *always* select LBA.

Older systems could lose CMOS data for a variety of reasons, including static electricity, inserting an expansion card, and blinking with too much force. It takes nothing to do a quick CMOS check to verify that the drive's geometry is correct using autodetection. Here are some of the more common errors that might point to CMOS problems:

- CMOS configuration mismatch
- No boot device available
- Drive not found
- Missing OS

If Autodetect fails to see the drive in question, it's probably a connectivity problem. Grab a screwdriver and look inside the system. This is also the one time where your hard drive's S.M.A.R.T. functions may help. Unplug the drive and make it an extra drive on a working system. Go to the hard drive manufacturer's Web site and download its diagnostic tool and run it. If you get a failure, the drive is dead and there's nothing you can do except be really happy that you back up your data all the time.

Uh, you do back up your system, right? Backing up a system is an incredibly important job, so important that we'll give it substantial discussion in Chapters 15 and 23.

Partitioning   Partitioning errors generally fall into two groups: failing to partition at all and making the wrong size or type of partition. You'll recognize the former type of error the first time you open My Computer after installing a drive. If you forgot to partition it, the drive won't even show up in My Computer, only Disk Management! If you made the partition too small, that'll become painfully obvious when you start filling it up with files.

The fix for partitioning errors is simply to open Disk Management and do the partitioning correctly. If you've added files to the wrongly sized drive, don't forget to back them up before you repartition!

Formatting   Failing to format a drive makes the drive unable to hold data. Accessing the drive in Windows will result in a drive "is not accessible" error, and from a C:\ prompt, you'll get the famous "Invalid media" type error. Format the drive unless you're certain that the drive has a format already. Corrupted files can create the Invalid media type error. Check one of the sections on corrupted data later in this chapter for the fix.

Most of the time, formatting is a slow, boring process. But sometimes the drive makes "bad sounds" and you start seeing errors like the one shown in Figure 10-64 at the bottom of the screen.

```
A:\>format C:/s

WARNING:   ALL DATA ON NON-REMOVABLE DISK
DRIVE C:   WILL BE LOST!
Proceed with Format   (Y/N)?y


Formatting  30709.65M

Trying to recover lost allocation unit 37,925
```

Figure 10-64   The "Trying to recover lost allocation unit" error

An *allocation unit* is FORMAT's term for a cluster. The drive has run across a bad cluster and is trying to fix it. For years, I've told techs that seeing this error a few (610) times doesn't mean anything; every drive comes with a few bad spots. This is no longer true. Modern ATA drives actually hide a significant number of extra sectors that they use to replace bad sectors automatically. If a new drive gets a lot of "Trying to recover lost allocation unit" errors, you can bet that the drive is dying and needs to be replaced. Get the hard drive maker's diagnostic to be sure. Bad clusters are reported by S.M.A.R.T.

Mental Reinstall   Focus on the fact that all of these errors share a common thread—you just installed a drive! Installation errors don't show up on a system that has been running correctly for three weeks; they show up the moment you try to do something with the drive you just installed. If a newly installed drive fails to work, do a "mental reinstall." Does the drive show up in the CMOS Autodetect? No? Then recheck the cables, master/slave settings, and power. If it does show up, did you remember to partition and format the drive? Did it need to be set to active? These are common-sense questions that come to mind as you march through your mental reinstall. Even if you've installed thousands of drives over the years, you'll be amazed at how often you do things such as forget to plug in power to a drive, forget CMOS, or install a cable backward. Do the mental reinstall—it really works!

Data Corruption
All hard drives occasionally get corrupted data in individual sectors. Power surges, accidental shutdowns, corrupted installation media, and viruses, along with hundreds of

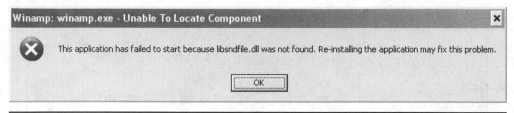

Figure 10-65   A corrupted data error

other problems, can cause this corruption. In most cases, this type of error shows up while Windows is running. Figure 10-65 shows a classic example.

You may also see Windows error messages saying one of the following:

- "The following file is missing or corrupt"
- "The download location information is damaged"
- "Unable to load file"

If core boot files become corrupted, you may see text errors at boot, such as the following:

- "Cannot find COMMAND.COM"
- "Error loading operating system"
- "Invalid BOOT.INI"

On older programs, you may see a command prompt open with errors such as this one:

```
Sector not found reading drive C: Abort, Retry, Fail?
```

The first fix for any of these problems is to run the Error-Checking utility. Error-Checking will go through and mark bad clusters and hopefully move your data to a good cluster.

Extract/Expand   If Error-Checking fails to move a critically important file, such as a file Windows needs in order to load, you can always resort to the command line and try to extract the file from the Windows cabinet files. Most Windows programs store all files in a compressed format called CAB (which is short for cabinet file). One CAB file contains many files, and most installation disks have lots of CAB files (see Figure 10-66).

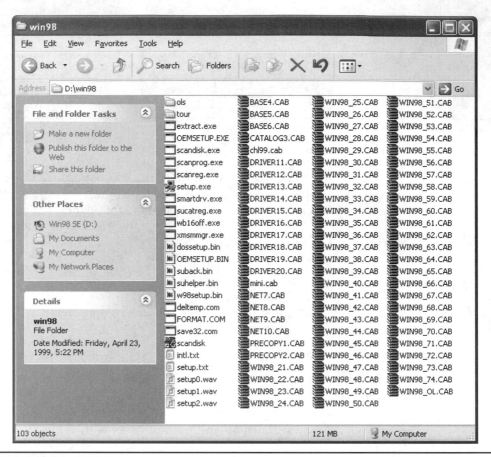

Figure 10-66 CAB files

To replace a single corrupt file this way, you need to know two things: the location of the CAB file that contains the file you need, and how to get the file out so you can copy it back to its original spot. Microsoft supplies the EXPAND program to enable you to get a new copy of the missing file from the CAB files on the installation CD-ROM. Also notice how they are numbered—that's the secret to understanding these programs.

In most cases, all the CAB files for a program are piled into some folder, as shown in Figure 10-66. Let's say you need a file called OLEPRO32.DLL. (I have no idea what this file does. I only know that Windows can't find it, and you need to put it back!) Get to a command prompt within Windows and tell EXPAND to check *all* the CAB files on your installation CD (drive E: in this example) with this command:

```
EXPAND e:\I386\*.CAB -F:OLEPRO32.DLL
```

EXPAND goes through all the CAB files and finds the file. If you want to see details on the EXPAND command, use Windows Help or type **EXPAND /?** at a command prompt.

NOTE Chapter 14 goes into a lot of detail on using the command line.

Corrupted Data on Bad Sectors If the same errors continue to appear after running the disk-checking utility, there's a chance that the drive has bad sectors.

Almost all drives today take advantage of built-in error correction code (ECC) that constantly checks the drive for bad sectors. If the ECC detects a bad sector, it marks the sector as bad in the drive's internal error map. Don't confuse this error map with a FAT. The partitioning program creates the FAT. The drive's internal error map was created at the factory on reserved drive heads and is invisible to the system. If the ECC finds a bad sector, you will get a corrupted data error as the computer attempts to read the bad sector. Disk-checking utilities fix this problem most of the time.

Many times, the ECC thinks a bad sector is good, however, and fails to update the internal error map. In this case, you need a program that goes back into the drive and marks the sectors as bad. That's where the powerful SpinRite utility from Gibson Research comes into play. SpinRite marks sectors as bad or good more accurately than ECC and does not disturb the data, enabling you to run SpinRite without fear of losing anything. And if it finds a bad sector with data in it, SpinRite has powerful algorithms that usually recover the data on all but the most badly damaged sectors (see Figure 10-67).

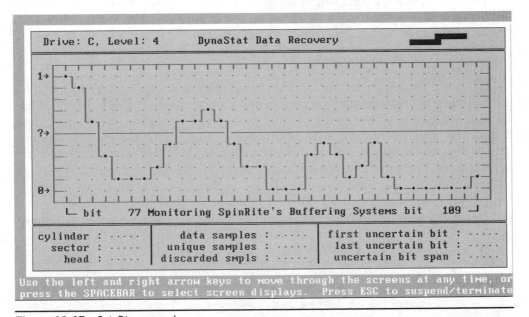

Figure 10-67 SpinRite at work

Without SpinRite, you must use a low-level format program supplied by the hard-drive maker, assuming you can get one (not all are willing to distribute these). These programs work like SpinRite in that they aggressively check the hard drive's sectors and update the internal error map. Unfortunately, all of them wipe out all data on the drive. At least the drive can be used, even if it means repartitioning, formatting, and reinstalling everything.

Dying Hard Drive

Physical problems are rare but devastating when they happen. If a hard drive is truly damaged physically, there is nothing that you or any service technician can do to fix it. Fortunately, hard drives are designed to take a phenomenal amount of punishment without failing. Physical problems manifest themselves in two ways: either the drive works properly but makes a lot of noise, or the drive seems to disappear.

All hard drives make noise—the hum as the platters spin and the occasional slight scratching noise as the read/write heads access sectors are normal. However, if your drive begins to make any of the following sounds, it is about to die:

- Continuous high-pitched squeal
- Series of clacks, a short pause, and then another series of clacks
- Continuous grinding or rumbling

Back up your critical data and replace the drive. Windows comes with great tools for backing up data.

You'll know when a drive simply disappears. If it's the drive that contains your operating system, the system will lock up. When you try to restart the computer, you'll see this error message:

```
No Boot Device Present
```

If it's a second drive, it will simply stop showing up in My Computer. The first thing to do in this case is to fire up the System Setup program and see if Autodetect sees the drive. If it does, you do not have a physical problem with the drive. If Autodetect fails, shut off the system and remove the ribbon cable, but leave the power cable attached. Restart the system and listen to the drive. If the drive spins up, you know that the drive is getting good power. In most cases, this is a clue that the drive is probably good. In that case, you need to look for more mundane problems such as an unplugged power cord or jumpers incorrectly set. If the drive doesn't spin up, try another power connector. If it still doesn't spin up and you've triple-checked the jumpers and ribbon cable, you have a problem with the onboard electronics, and the drive is dead.

 NOTE If you ever lose a hard drive that contains absolutely critical information, you can turn to a company that specializes in hard drive data recovery. The job will be expensive—prices usually start around US$1,000— but when you have to have the data, such companies are your only hope. Do a Web search for "data recovery" or check the Yellow Pages for companies in this line of business.

Beyond A+

Modern hard drives have many other features that are worth knowing about, but that rarely impact beginning techs. A couple of the more interesting ones are spindle speed and third-party hard drive tools. If you have a burning desire to dive into hard drives in all their glory, you need not go any farther than the Storage Review, an excellent site dedicated solely to hard drives. Here's the link: www.storagereview.com.

Third-Party Partition Tools

Disk Management is a good tool, but is limited for some situations. Some really great third-party tools on the market can give you incredible flexibility and power to structure and restructure your hard drive storage to meet your changing needs. They each have interesting unique features, but in general they enable you to create, change, and delete partitions on a hard drive *without* destroying any of the programs or data stored there. Slick! These programs aren't on the CompTIA A+ exams, but all PC techs use at least one of them, so let's explore three of the most well-known examples: Symantec's PartitionMagic, VCOM's Partition Commander Professional, and the open source Linux tool, GParted.

Probably the most well-known third-party partition tool is PartitionMagic, up to version 8 as of this writing (Figure 10-68). It supports every version of Windows and just about every other operating system, too. It enables you to create, resize, split, merge, delete, undelete, and convert partitions without destroying your data. Among the additional features it advertises are: the ability to browse, copy, or move files and folders between supported partitions; expand an NTFS partition—even if it's a system partition—without rebooting; change NTFS cluster sizes; and add new partitions for multiple OSs using a simple wizard.

Figure 10-68
PartitionMagic

VCOM offers a variety of related products, one of which is the very useful Partition Commander Professional 10. Like PartitionMagic, it supports all versions of Windows and enables you to play with your partitions without destroying your data. Among its niftier features are the ability to convert a Windows 2000/XP/2003 dynamic disk to a basic disk nondestructively (which Windows 2000/XP/2003 can't do); defrag the Master File Table on an NTFS partition; and move unused space from one partition to another on the same physical drive, automatically resizing the partitions based on the amount of space you tell it to move. Figure 10-69 shows the Partition Commander dialog box for moving unused space between partitions.

Figure 10-69
Partition
Commander

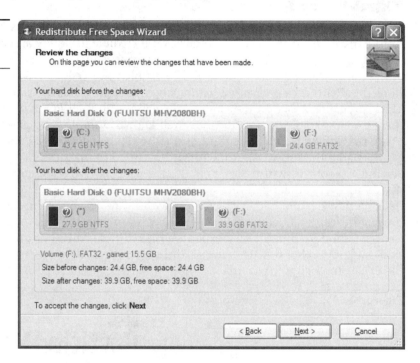

The only problem with PartitionMagic and Partition Commander is that they cost money. There's nothing wrong with spending money on a good product, but if you can find something that does the job for free, why not try it? If you think like I do, check out the Gnome Partition Editor, better known as GParted. You can find it at http://sourceforge.net/.

GParted is an incredibly powerful partition editor and does almost everything the for-pay partition editors do, but it's free. It's still in beta—which means it's constantly changing and it's got a few bugs (that are constantly being fixed)—but I use it all the time and love it. If you look closely at Figure 10-70, you'll notice that it uses strange names for the partitions such as HDA1 or HDB3. These are Linux conventions and are well documented in GParted's help screens. Take a little time and you'll love GParted, too.

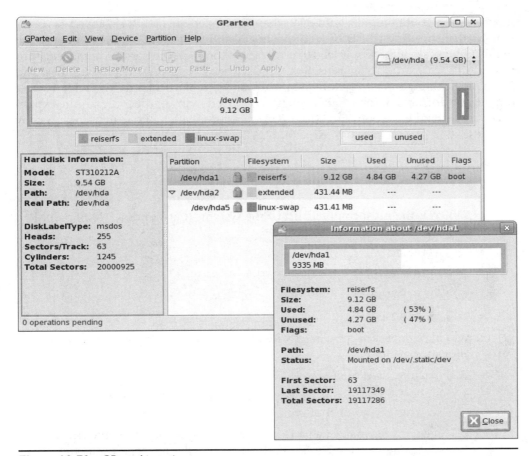

Figure 10-70   GParted in action

The one downside to GParted is that it is a Linux program—because no Windows version exists, you need Linux to run it. So how do you run Linux on a Windows system without actually installing Linux on your hard drive? The answer is easy—the folks at GParted will give you the tools to burn a live CD that boots Linux so you can run GParted!

A live CD is a complete OS on a CD. Understand this is not an installation CD like your Windows installation disk. The OS is already installed on the CD. You boot from the live CD and the OS loads into RAM, just like the OS on your hard drive loads into RAM at boot. As the live CD boots, it recognizes your hardware and loads the proper drivers into RAM so everything works. You get everything you'd expect from an OS with one big exception: a live CD does not touch your hard drive. Of course you may run programs (like GParted) that work on your hard drive, which makes live CDs popular with PC techs, because you can toss them into a cranky system and run utilities.

The truly intrepid might want to consider using The Ultimate Boot CD (UBCD), basically a huge pile of useful freeware utilities compiled by frustrated technician Ben

Burrows, who couldn't find a boot disk when he needed one. His Web site is www.ulti-matebootcd.com. The UBCD has more than 100 different tools, all placed on a single live CD. It has all of the low-level diagnostic tools for all of the hard drive makers, four or five different partitioning tools, S.M.A.R.T. viewers, hard drive wiping utilities, and hard drive cloning tools (nice for when you want to replace a hard drive with a larger one). Little documentation is provided, however, and many of the tools require experience way beyond the scope of the CompTIA A+ exams. I will tell you that I have a copy and I use it.

Chapter Review Questions

1. Which is the most complete list of file systems that Windows 2000 and XP can use?

    A. FAT16, FAT32, NTFS

    B. FAT16, FAT32, FAT64, NTFS

    C. FAT16, FAT32

    D. FAT16, NTFS

2. Which of the following correctly identifies the four possible entries in a file allocation table?

    A. Filename, date, time, size

    B. Number of the starting cluster, number of the ending cluster, number of used clusters, number of available clusters

    C. An end of file marker, a bad sector marker, code indicating the cluster is available, the number of the cluster where the next part of the file is stored

    D. Filename, folder location, starting cluster number, ending cluster number

3. What program does Microsoft include with Windows 2000 and Windows XP to partition and format a drive?

    A. Format

    B. Disk Management console

    C. Disk Administrator console

    D. System Commander

4. What does NTFS use to provide security for individual files and folders?

    A. Dynamic disks

    B. ECC

    C. Access Control List

    D. MFT

Chapter 10: Implementing Hard Drives

411

5. Adam wants to create a new simple volume in some unallocated space on his hard drive, but when he right-clicks the space in Disk Management he sees only an option to create a new partition. What is the problem?

    A. The drive has developed bad sectors.

    B. The drive is a basic disk and not a dynamic disk.

    C. The drive has less than 32 GB of unallocated space.

    D. The drive is jumpered as a slave.

6. Jaime wants to check her hard drive for errors. What tool should she use?

    A. FDISK

    B. Format

    C. Disk Management

    D. Error-Checking

7. To make your files unreadable by others, what should you use?

    A. Clustering

    B. Compression

    C. Disk quotas

    D. Encryption

8. How can you effectively expand the capacity of an NTFS drive?

    A. Create an extended partition to extend the capacity.

    B. Install a second drive and mount it to a folder on the original smaller NTFS drive.

    C. Convert the drive to a dynamic disk and create a mirrored set.

    D. Format the drive with the Quick Format option.

9. Which volume configuration uses parity for fault tolerance?

    A. RAID 5

    B. Mirrored set

    C. Spanned volume

    D. Striped volume

10. You will almost certainly destroy your hard drive if you reverse which of the following?

    A. Power cable

    B. Data cable

    C. Jumpers

    D. Pins

Answers

1. **A.** Windows 2000 and XP can use FAT16, FAT32, and NTFS.

2. **C.** The four possible entries in a file allocation table are an end of file marker, a bad sector marker, code indicating the cluster is available, and the number of the cluster where the next part of the file is stored.

3. **B.** Windows 2000 and XP use the Disk Management console to partition and format a drive.

4. **C.** Because NTFS views individual files and folders as objects, it can provide security for those objects through an Access Control List.

5. **B.** The drive is a basic disk and not a dynamic disk. Partitions are created on basic disks, while volumes are created on dynamic disks.

6. **D.** Error-Checking is used to check a drive for errors.

7. **D.** To make your files unreadable by others, use encryption.

8. **B.** You can effectively expand the capacity of an NTFS drive by installing a second drive and mounting it to a folder on the original smaller NTFS drive.

9. **A.** RAID 5 uses parity for fault tolerance.

10. **A.** You will almost certainly destroy your hard drive if you reverse the power cable.

Removable Media

In this chapter, you will learn how to
- Explain and install floppy disk drives
- Demonstrate the variations among flash drives and other tiny drives
- Identify and install optical media technology
- Troubleshoot removable-media drives

Removable media is any type of mass storage device that you may use in one system and then physically remove from that system and use in another. Removable media has been a part of the personal PC from its first introduction back in 1980. Granted, back then the only removable media available were floppy disks, but the ability to easily move programs and data from one machine to another was quickly established as one of the strongest points of the personal computer. Over time, higher capacity removable media technologies were introduced. Some technologies—CDs, DVDs, and thumb drives, for example—have become very common. Other technologies (that you may or may not have heard of) like the Iomega Zip drives were extremely popular for a time but faded away. The history of PCs has also left a trash heap of removable media technologies that were trumpeted in with fanfare and a lot of money but never really saw any adoption.

Today's highly internetworked computers have reduced the need for removable media as a method of sharing programs and data, but removable media has so many other uses that this hasn't slowed things down a bit. Removable media is the perfect tool for software distribution, data archiving, and system backup. Figure 11-1 shows my software toolbox. As a PC technician, you'll not only need to install, maintain, and troubleshoot removable media on a system working for users, but you'll also find yourself turning to removable media (remember the live CDs in the previous chapter?) as a way to store and run software tools to perform all types of PC support!

Figure 11-1
Author's toolbox

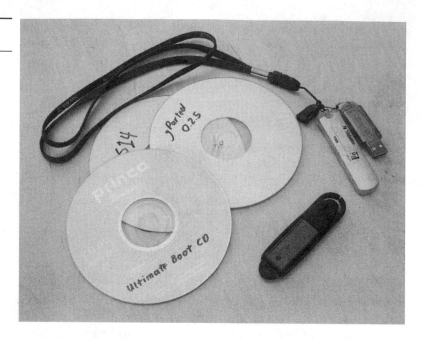

This chapter covers the most common types of removable media used today. For the sake of organization, all removable media are broken down into these groups:

- **Floppy drives** The traditional floppy drive
- **Flash memory** From flash memory cards to USB thumb drives
- **Optical media** Any shiny disc technology from CD-ROMs to DVDs
- **External drives** Any hard drive or optical drive that connects to a PC via an external cable

If you go by the earlier description of removable memory, then two other technologies, PC Cards and tape backups, also fit as removable media. PC Cards are a laptop-centric technology and are covered in Chapter 19, "Portable Computing," whereas tape backups are part of the big world of backups and are covered in Chapter 15, "Maintaining and Troubleshooting Windows."

Historical/Conceptual

Floppy Drives

Good old floppies! These little disks, storing a whopping 1.44 MB of data per disk, have been part of PCs from the beginning. For decades, the PC industry has made one attempt after another to replace the floppy with some higher capacity removable media, only to keep falling back to the floppy disk. Floppy drive technology was well entrenched: motherboard makers found it easy to add, all BIOS supported them, and they were almost always the first boot device, so techs loved floppies when they helped boot a system.

Only in the last few years have we finally seen systems without floppy drives due to an industry push called *legacy-free computing:* an initiative forwarded by Microsoft and Intel back in 2001 to rid computers of old technologies such as PS/2 ports, serial ports, parallel ports—and floppy drives (interesting how long it took to start getting adopted by PC makers). Thus, the venerable floppy drive will probably soon disappear from PCs. Until then, the floppy drive, that artifact from the Dark Ages of the PC world, will continue to be a viable technology you must know.

Floppy Drive Basics

If you've used computers at all, you've probably used a floppy drive. When you insert a floppy disk into a floppy drive, the protective slide on the disk opens, revealing the magnetic media inside the plastic casing. A motor-driven spindle snaps into the center of the drive to make it spin. A set of read/write heads then moves back and forth across the disk, reading or writing tracks on the disk as needed. The current floppy disks are 3½ inches wide and store 1.44 MB (Figure 11-2).

Figure 11-2
Floppy drive and
floppy disk

Whenever your system accesses a floppy disk in its floppy drive, a read/write LED on the outside front of the drive will flash on. You should not try to remove the floppy disk from the drive when this light is lit! That light means that the read/writes heads are accessing the floppy drive, and pulling the disk out while the light is on can damage the floppy disk. When the light is off, you can push in the small release button on the front of the drive to eject the floppy disk.

NOTE The term "floppy" comes from the fact that early floppy disks were actually floppy. You could easily bend one. Modern floppy disks come in much more robust rigid plastic casings, but the term has stuck—we still call them floppies!

The first PC floppy drives used a 5¼-inch floppy drive format (Figure 11-3). The 5¼-inch measurement actually described the drive, but most users also called the disks for those drives 5¼-inch disks. In the 1970s and early 1980s, before PCs became predominant, you would occasionally see an 8-inch format floppy drive in computers. Fortunately, these never saw any noticeable use in PCs. If you happen to run into an 8-inch drive or disk, keep it! Collectors of old computers pay big money for these old drives!

Figure 11-3
A 5¼-inch floppy
drive and disk

Around 1986, the 3½-inch drives appeared, and within a few years came to dominate the floppy world completely. If you are really interested, however, you can still purchase 5¼-inch floppy drives on the Internet!

Essentials

Installing Floppy Drives

All Windows systems reserve the drive letters A: and B: for floppy drives. You cannot name them anything other than A: or B:, but you can configure a floppy to get either drive letter. However, convention dictates that if you have only one floppy drive, you should call it A:. The second floppy drive will then be called B:.

Floppy drives connect to the computer via a *34-pin ribbon cable*. If the cable supports two floppy drives, it will have a seven-wire twist in the middle, used to differentiate electronically between the A: and B: drives (Figure 11-4). Given that the majority of users do not want two floppy drives, many system makers have dropped the twist and saved a couple of pennies on a simpler cable (Figure 11-5).

Figure 11-4
Floppy cable that
supports two drives

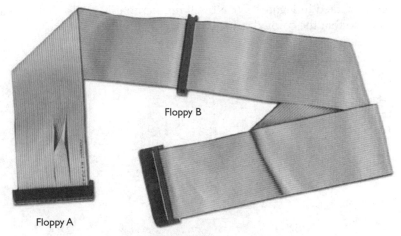

Floppy B

Floppy A

Floppy controller plug

Figure 11-5
Floppy cable for
only one drive

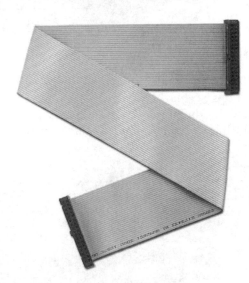

By default, almost all PCs (well, the ones that still support floppy drives) first try to boot to a floppy before any other boot device, looking for an operating system. This process enables technicians to insert a floppy disk into a sick computer to run programs when the hard drives fail. It can also enable hackers to insert bootable floppy disks into servers and do bad things. You do have a choice, however, as most systems have special CMOS settings that enable you to change this default boot order to something other than the default drive A: and then C:; I'll show you how in a minute.

Inserting Ribbon Cables

Look at the floppy cable in Figure 11-5. Notice the connector on the left side. This connector, identical to the other connectors on the same cable, plugs into the floppy controller on the motherboard, as shown in Figure 11-6. Notice how clearly the motherboard has *pin 1* marked in Figure 11-6. Not all motherboards are so clear. Make sure to orient the cable so that the colored stripe is aligned with pin 1.

Figure 11-6
Plugging a floppy
cable into a
controller, pin
1 labeled at left

Here are a few tips on cable orientation. By the way, these rules work for all ribbon cables, not just floppy cables! Ribbon cable connectors usually have a distinct orientation notch in the middle. If they have an orientation notch and the controller socket has a slot in which the orientation notch will fit, your job is easy (Figure 11-7).

Figure 11-7
Floppy controller
with notch

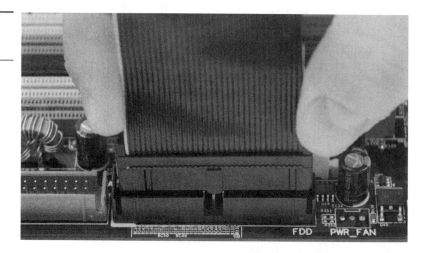

Unfortunately, not all connectors use the orientation notch. Try looking in the motherboard book. All motherboard books provide a graphic of the motherboard showing the proper orientation position. Look at other ribbon cables on the motherboard. In almost all motherboards, all plugs orient the same way. Last of all, just guess! You will not destroy anything by inserting the cable backwards. When you boot up, the floppy drive will not work. This is not a big deal; turn off the system and try again!

After you insert the floppy ribbon cable into the floppy controller, you need to insert the ribbon cable into the floppy drive. Watch out here! You still need to orient the cable by pin 1—all the rules of ribbon cable insertion apply here, too. Before you plug in the floppy ribbon cable to the floppy drive, you need to know which connector on the cable to use; it makes a big difference. The specific connector that you insert into the floppy drive determines its drive letter!

 EXAM TIP In the past, the CompTIA A+ certification exams have been very focused on the pins on cables! Know the number (34) and orientation (pin 1 to pin 1) for the pins on the floppy drive ribbon cable.

If the floppy drive is installed on the end connector, it becomes the A: drive; if the drive is installed on the middle connector, it is the B: drive (Figure 11-8). If you're installing only one floppy, make sure you install it in the A: drive position!

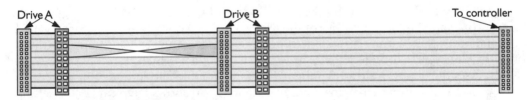

Figure 11-8   Cable placement determines the drive letter.

Power

Floppy drives need electricity in order to work, just like every other device in the PC. Modern 3½-inch floppy drives use the small *mini power connector*. Be careful! It is easy to insert a mini connector incorrectly, and if you install it incorrectly, you'll destroy the floppy drive and make what we call "The Nasty Smell." Look at Figure 11-9, a bottom view of a properly installed mini connector—note the chamfers (beveled edges) that show correct orientation. The problem lies in the plastic used to make the connector. The plastic connector bends easily, giving even the least brawny techs the ability to put the plug in a mini backward or to hit only three of the four pins.

Figure 11-9
Properly installed
mini connector

Great! You have installed a floppy drive! Once you have physically installed the floppy drive, it's time to go into CMOS.

CAUTION Installing *any* power connector incorrectly will destroy whatever device is unfortunate enough to be so abused. However, with the exception of minis, most power connectors are constructed so that it's almost impossible to do so unintentionally.

CMOS

After the floppy drive is installed, the next step is configuring the CMOS settings, which must correspond to the capacities of the drives. Look in your CMOS for a menu called "Standard CMOS Features" (or something similar to that) to see your floppy settings. Most CMOS setups configure the A: drive by default as a 3½-inch, 1.44 MB drive, so in most cases the floppy is already configured. Simply double-check the setting in CMOS; if it's okay, exit without changing anything. Figure 11-10 shows a typical CMOS setting for a single floppy drive.

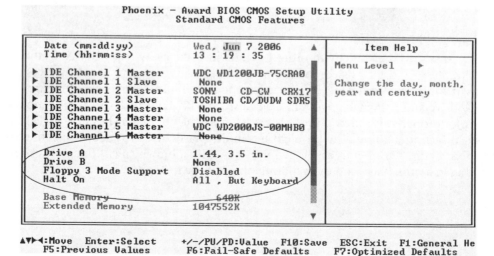

Figure 11-10   CMOS setting for one standard floppy drive

On the rare occasion that you require a different setting from the typical 3½-inch, 1.44-MB A: drive, simply select the drive (A: or B:) and enter the correct capacity. Figure 11-11 shows a CMOS with another 3½-inch floppy drive on B:.

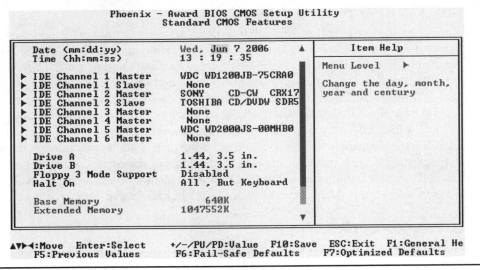

Figure 11-11 CMOS setting for two floppy drives

Disabling the Boot Up Floppy Seek option tells the PC not to check the floppy disk during the POST, which isn't very handy except for slightly speeding up the boot process (Figure 11-12).

```
        Phoenix - Award BIOS CMOS Setup Utility
                 Advanced BIOS Features

   Quick Power On Self Test      Enabled          Item Help
 ▶ Hard Disk Boot Priority       Press Enter
   First Boot Device             Floppy        Menu Level    ▶
   Second Boot Device            Hard Disk
   Third Boot Device             CDROM         Select User Define,AMD
   Boot Other Device             Enabled       K8 Cool 'n' Quite
   Boot Up Floppy Seek           Disabled      Function will Disable
   Boot up NumLock Status        On
   Security Option               Setup
   MPS Version Control For OS    1.4
   Delay For HDD (Secs)          0
   Full Screen LOGO Show         Disabled



▲▼▶◄:Move  Enter:Select   +/-/PU/PD:Value  F10:Save  ESC:Exit  F1:General Help
   F5:Previous Values      F6:Fail-Safe Defaults   F7:Optimized Defaults
```

Figure 11-12 CMOS Boot Up Floppy Seek option

Many CMOS setup utilities have an option called Floppy 3 Mode Support. Refer to Figure 11-11 to see an example of a CMOS with this option. A Mode 3 floppy is a special

1.2-MB format used outside the United States, primarily in Japan. Unless you live in Japan and use Mode 3 floppy disks, ignore this option.

Flash Memory

Flash memory, the same flash memory that replaced CMOS technology for your system BIOS, found another home in PCs in the form of removable mass storage devices. Flash memory comes in two different families: USB thumb drives and memory cards. *USB thumb drives* are flash devices that contain a standard USB connection. *Memory cards* is a generic term for a number of different tiny cards that are used in cameras, PDAs, and other devices. Both of these families can manifest themselves as drives in Windows, but they usually perform different jobs. USB thumb drives have replaced virtually all other rewritable removable media as the way people transfer files or keep copies of important programs. My thumb drives (yes, I have two on me at all times) keep backups of my current work, important photos, and a stack of utilities I need to fix computers. Memory cards are very small and make a great way to store data on small devices and then transfer that data to your PC.

USB Thumb Drives

Moving data between computers is always a pain, and even more so since digital photography and multimedia storage has littered hard drives with huge files that won't fit on a single floppy disk. The latest entry into the floppy disk replacement sweepstakes is a winner: the USB Flash memory drive, also known as the thumb drive, jump drive, or flash drive. These tiny new drives (Figure 11-13) are incredibly popular. For a low price in US$, you can get a 2-GB thumb drive that holds as much data as 1400 standard 3½-inch floppy disks.

Figure 11-13
USB thumb drives

The smallest thumb drives are slightly larger than an adult thumbnail, whereas others are larger and more rounded. The drives are hot-swappable in Windows 2000/XP/ Vista. You simply plug one into any USB port and it will appear as a removable storage device in My Computer. After you plug the drive into a USB port, you can copy or move data to or from your hard disk and then unplug the unit and take it with you. You can read, write, and delete files directly from the drive. Because these are USB devices, they don't need an external power source. The non-volatile flash memory is solid-state, so it's shock resistant and is supposed to retain data safely for a decade. One big improvement over floppies is cross-platform compatibility—you can transfer files among Macintosh, Windows, and Linux operating systems.

The latest systems enable you to boot to a thumb drive. With a bootable thumb drive, you can replace both bootable floppies and bootable CDs with fast flash drives. Making a thumb drive bootable is a bit of a challenge, so most of the classic bootable utility CD makers have created USB versions that seek out your thumb drive and add an operating system with the utilities you wish to use. Most of these are simply versions of Linux-based live CDs. At this point, there's no single magic USB thumb drive to recommend, as bootable USB drives are still quite new and updated versions come out almost daily. If you just have to try this new technology now, check out the GParted LiveUSB at http://gparted.sourceforge.net and click on the LiveUSB link.

Flash Cards

Flash cards are the way people store data on small appliances. Every digital camera, virtually every PDA, and many cell phones come with slots for some type of memory card. Memory cards come in a number of different incompatible formats, so let's start by making sure you know the more common ones.

CompactFlash

CompactFlash (CF) is the oldest, most complex, and physically largest of all removable flash media cards (Figure 11-14). Roughly one inch wide, CF cards use a simplified PCMCIA bus (see Chapter 19, "Portable Computing," for details) for interconnection. CF cards come in two sizes: CF I (3.3 mm thick) and CF II (5 mm thick). CF II cards are too thick to fit into CF I slots.

Figure 11-14
CF Card

Clever manufacturers have repurposed the CF form factor to create the microdrive (Figure 11-15). *Microdrives* are true hard drives, using platters and read/write heads that fit into the tiny CF form factor. Microdrives are slower and use more power than flash drives but cost much less than an equivalent CF flash card. From the user's standpoint, CF flash cards and microdrives look and act exactly the same way, although the greater power consumption of microdrives makes them incompatible with some devices.

Figure 11-15
Microdrive

SmartMedia

SmartMedia came out as a competitor to CF cards and for a few years was quite popular in digital cameras (Figure 11-16). The introduction of SD media reduced SmartMedia's popularity, and no new devices use this media.

Figure 11-16
SmartMedia

Secure Digital

Secure Digital (SD) cards are arguably the most common flash media format today. About the size of a small postage stamp, you'll see SD cards in just about any type of device that uses flash media. SD comes in two types: the original SD and SDIO. SD cards store only data. The more advanced SDIO (the "IO" denoting input/output rather than storage) cards also support devices such as GPS and cameras. If you want to use an SDIO device, you must have an SDIO slot. There is no way to tell an SD slot from an SDIO slot, so read the technical specs for your device!

SD cards also come in two tiny forms called *Mini Secure Digital (MiniSD)* and *Micro Secure Digital (MicroSD)* cards. They're extremely popular in cellular phones that use flash memory, but see little use in other devices. Figure 11-17 shows all three types of SD cards.

Figure 11-17
SD, MiniSD, and
MicroSD cards

 NOTE SD cards developed out of an older, slower flash memory technology called *MultiMediaCard (MMC)*. If you happen to have an MMC card laying around, you can use it in almost any SD card slot. SD cards are a little thicker than MMC cards, though, so the reverse is not true.

Memory Stick

Sony always likes to use proprietary formats, and their *Memory Stick* flash memory is no exception. If you own something from Sony and it uses flash memory, you'll need a Memory Stick (Figure 11-18). There are several Memory Stick formats, including Standard, Pro, Duo, Pro Duo, and Micro.

Figure 11-18
Memory Stick

xD Picture Card

Extreme Digital (xD) Picture Cards (Figure 11-19) are about half the size of an SD card. They're almost exclusively used in digital cameras, although Olympus (the developer of the xD technology) produces a USB housing so you can use an xD Picture Card like any other USB flash memory drive. xD Picture Cards come in three flavors: original, Standard (Type M), and Hi-Speed (Type H). The Standard cards are faster than the original cards, which were only available for a short time; the Hi-Speed cards are two to three times faster than the others and enable you to capture full-motion video (assuming the camera has that capability, naturally!).

Figure 11-19
xD card

Card Readers

Whatever type of flash memory you use, your PC must have a card reader in order to access the data on the card directly. There are a number of inexpensive USB card readers available today (Figure 11-20), and some PCs, especially those tuned to home theater use, often come with built-in readers—handy to have when someone pulls out an SD card and says, "Let's look at the pictures I just took!"

NOTE Of course, if the person just happened to bring his or her camera and the usually-proprietary USB cable along, you could connect the camera to the PC and pull pictures in that way. Just make sure you have spare batteries, too! Wouldn't a card reader be a more elegant solution?

Figure 11-20
USB card reader

Whichever type of flash memory you have, understand that it acts exactly like a hard drive. If you wish, you can format a memory card as well as copy, paste, and rename files.

Optical Drives

CD- and DVD-media discs and drives come in a variety of flavors and formats, enabling you to back up data, record music, master a home video, and much, much more. Generically, we call them *optical-media discs* and the drives that support them *optical drives.* This section examines CD-media and DVD-media, finishing with the details about installing both types of drives.

The phrase *optical media* is an umbrella phrase for all those shiny, 12-cm-wide discs that, if you're a slob like me, collect around your PC like pizza boxes in a fraternity house. *CD* stands for *compact disc,* a medium that was originally designed more than 20 years ago as a replacement for vinyl records. The CD now reigns as the primary method of long-term storage for sound and data. The *DVD (digital versatile disc)* first eliminated VHS cassette tapes from the home movie market, but has also grown into a contender for backups and high-capacity storage. Optical media include a number of technologies with names such as CD-ROM, CD-R, CD-RW, DVD, DVD+RW, HD-DVD, and so on. Each of these technologies will be discussed in detail in this chapter—for now, understand that although *optical media* describes a number of different, exciting formats, they all basically boil down to the same physical object: that little shiny disc.

CD-Media

The best way to understand the world of optical discs is to sort out the many types of technologies available, starting with the first, the compact disc. All you're about to read is relevant and fair game for the CompTIA A+ certification exams. Let's begin by looking at how CDs work.

How CDs Work

CDs—the discs that you buy in music stores or may find in software boxes—store data via microscopic pits. CD producers use a power laser to burn these pits into a glass master CD. Once the CD producer creates a master, expensive machines create plastic copies using a very high-tolerance injection molding process. The copies are coated with a reflective metallic covering and then finished with lacquer for protection. CDs only store data on one side of the disc—we don't flip a CD as we used to flip vinyl records (did I just sound really old?). The data on a CD is near the top of the CD, where the label is located (see Figure 11-21).

Figure 11-21
Location of the data

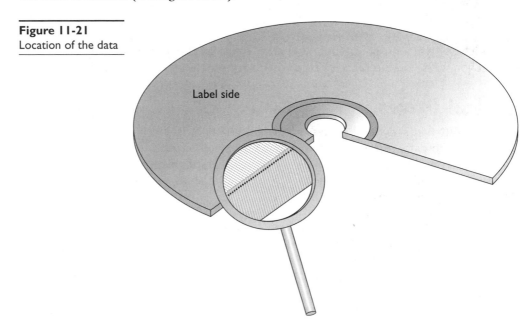

Many people believe that scratching a CD on the bottom makes it unreadable. This is untrue. If you scratch a CD on the bottom (the shiny side), just polish out the scratches—assuming that they aren't too deep—and reread the CD. A number of companies sell inexpensive CD polishing kits. It's the scratches on the *top* of the disc that wreak havoc on CDs. Avoid writing on the top with anything other than a soft-tipped pen, and certainly don't scratch the top!

CD readers (like the one in your car or the one in your PC) use a laser and mirrors to read the data from the CD. The metallic covering of the CD makes a highly reflective surface—the pits create interruptions in that surface, while the non-pitted spots, called *lands,* leave it intact. The laser picks up on the reflected pattern that the pits and lands create, and the CD drive converts this pattern into binary ones and zeroes. Because the pits are so densely packed on the CD, a vast amount of data can be stored: A standard CD holds up to 5.2 billion bits, or 650 million bytes, of data.

CD Formats

The first CDs were designed for playing music and organized the music in a special format called CD-Digital Audio (CDDA), which we usually just call CD-audio. CD-audio divides the CD's data into variable-length tracks; on music CDs, each song gets one track. CD-audio is an excellent way to store music, but it lacks any error checking, file support, or directory structure, making it a terrible way to store data! For this reason, The Powers That Be created a special method for storing data on a CD, called—are you ready—CD-ROM. The CD-ROM format divides the CD into fixed sectors, each holding 2353 bytes.

Most CD-ROM drives also support a number of older, less known formats. You may never come across these formats—CD-I, CD-ROM/XA, and so forth—although you may see them listed among compatible formats on the packaging for a new drive (Figure 11-22). Don't let these oddball formats throw you—with few exceptions, they've pretty much fallen by the wayside. All CD-ROM drives read all of these formats, assuming that the system is loaded with the proper software.

Figure 11-22
Crazy CD formats

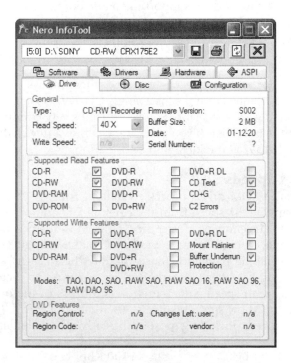

There are two other formats called CD-R and CD-RW—perhaps you've heard of them? Well, I cover these in detail in a moment, but first I need to explain a bit more about CD-ROM. The CD-ROM format is something like a partition in the hard drive world.

CD-ROM may define the sectors (and some other information), but it doesn't enable a CD-ROM disc to act like a hard drive with a file structure, directories, and such. To make CD-ROMs act like a hard drive, there's another layer of formatting that defines the file system used on the drive.

At first glance, you might think, "Why don't CD-ROMs just use a FAT or an NTFS format like hard drives?" Well, first of all, they could! There's no law of physics that prevented the CD-ROM world from adopting any file system. The problem is that the CD makers did not want CD-ROM to be tied to Microsoft's or Apple's or anyone else's file format. In addition, they wanted non-PC devices to read CDs, so they invented their own file system just for CD-ROMs, called *ISO-9660*. This format is sometimes referred by the more generic term, CD File System (CDFS). The vast majority of data CD-ROMs today use this format.

Over the years, extensions of the ISO-9660 have addressed certain limitations such as the characters used in file and directory names, filename length, and directory depth. It's important to know these IUSO-9660 extensions:

- **Joliet** Microsoft's extension of the ISO-9660. Macintosh and Linux also support Joliet formatted discs.
- **Rock Ridge** An open standard to provide UNIX file system support for discs; rarely used outside of UNIX systems.
- **El Torito** Added support to enable bootable CD-media. All bootable CDs use the El Torito standard, which is supported by the BIOS on all modern PCs.
- **Apple Extensions** Apple's added support for their HFS file system. Windows systems cannot read these CDs without third-party tools.

It is important to appreciate that all of these file systems are extensions, not replacements to ISO-9660. That means a single CD/DVD can have both regular ISO-9660 information and the extension. For example, it's very common to have a CD-media that is ISO-9660 and Joliet. If you place the CD into a device that cannot read Joliet, it will still be able to read the ISO-9660 information.

CD-ROM Speeds

The first CD-ROM drives processed data at roughly 150,000 bytes per second (150 KBps), copying the speed from the original CD-audio format. Although this speed is excellent for listening to music, the CD-ROM industry quickly recognized that installing programs or transferring files from a CD-ROM at 150 KBps was the electronic equivalent of watching paint dry. Since the day the first CD-ROM drives for PCs hit the market, there has been a desire to speed them up to increase their data throughput. Each increase in speed is measured in multiples of the original 150 KBps drives and given an × to show speed relative to the first (1×) drives. Here's a list of the common CD-ROM speeds, including most of the early speeds that are no longer produced:

1×	150 KBps	10×	1500 KBps	40×	6000 KBps
2×	300 KBps	12×	1800 KBps	48×	7200 KBps
3×	450 KBps	16×	2400 KBps	52×	7800 KBps

4×	600 KBps	24×	3600 KBps	60×	9000 KBps
6×	900 KBps	32×	4800 KBps	72×	10800 KBps
8×	1200 KBps	36×	5400 KBps		

Keep in mind that these are maximum speeds that are rarely met in real-life operation. You can, however, count on a 32× drive reading data faster than an 8× drive. As multipliers continue to increase, so many other factors come into play that telling the difference between a 48× and a 52× drive, for example, becomes difficult. High-speed CD-ROM drives are so inexpensive, however, that most folks buy the fastest drive possible—at least installations go faster!

CD-R

Making CD-ROMs requires specialized, expensive equipment and substantial expertise, and it's done by a relatively small number of CD-ROM production companies. Yet, since the day the first CD-ROMs came to market, demand has been terrific for a way that normal PC users could make their own CDs. The CD industry made a number of attempts to create a technology that would let users record, or *burn,* their own CDs.

In the mid-1990s, the CD industry introduced the CD-recordable (CD-R) standard, which enables affordable CD-R drives, often referred to as *CD burners,* to add data to special CD-R discs. Any CD-ROM drive can then read the data stored on the CD-R, and all CD-R drives can read regular CD-ROMs. CD-R discs come in two varieties: a 74-minute disc that holds approximately 650 MB, and an 80-minute variety that holds approximately 700 MB (see Figure 11-23). A CD-R burner must be specifically designed to support the longer 80-minute CD-R format, but most drives you'll encounter can do this.

Figure 11-23
A CD-R disc, with its capacity clearly labeled

 NOTE Some music CD players can't handle CD-R discs.

CD-R discs function similarly to regular CD-ROMs, although the chemicals used to make them produce a brightly colored recording side on almost all CD-R discs. CD-ROM discs, in contrast, have a silver recording side. CD-R technology records data using special organic dyes embedded into the disc. This dye is what gives the CD-R its distinctive bottom color. CD-R burners have a second burn laser, roughly ten times as powerful as the read laser, which heats the organic dye. This causes a change in the reflectivity of the surface, creating the functional equivalent of a CD-ROM's pits.

Once the CD-R drive burns data onto a CD-R, the data cannot be erased or changed short of destroying the disc itself. Early CD-R drives required that the entire disc be burned in one burn session, wasting any unused part of the CD-R disc. These were called single-session drives. All modern CD-R drives are multisession drives that enable you to go back and burn additional data onto the CD-R disc until the disc is full. Multisession drives also have the capability to "close" a partially filled CD-R so that no more data may be burned onto that disc.

CD-R drives have two speeds that matter: the record speed and the read speed, both expressed as multiples of the 150-KBps speed of the original CD-ROM drives. The record speed, which is listed first, is always equal to or slower than the read speed. For example, a CD-R drive with a specification of 8×24× would burn at 8× and read at 24×.

CD-RW

For all their usefulness, CD-R drives have disappeared from the market. Notice that I didn't say CD-R *discs* have disappeared; more CD-R discs get burned now than ever before. Just as CD-R drives could both burn CD-R discs and read CD-ROMs, a newer type of drive called CD-rewritable (CD-RW) has taken over the burning market from CD-R drives. Although this drive has its own type of CD-RW discs, it also can burn to CD-R discs, which are much cheaper.

CD-RW technology enables you not only to burn a disc, but to *burn over* existing data on a CD-RW disc. This is not something you need for every disc—for example, I create CD-R archives of my completed books to store the text and graphics for posterity—this is data I want to access later, but do not need to modify. While I'm working on content for the CD that accompanies this book, however, I may decide to delete an item—I couldn't do that with a CD-R. The CD-RW format, on the other hand, essentially takes CD-media to the functional equivalent of a 650-MB floppy disk. Once again, CD-RW discs look exactly like CD-ROM discs, with the exception of a colored bottom side. Figure 11-24 shows all three formats.

Figure 11-24
CD-ROM, CD-R,
and CD-RW discs

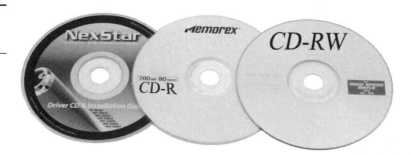

CAUTION You can rewrite CD-RW discs a limited number of times. The number varies according to the source, but expect a maximum life of about 1000 rewrites, although in real life you'll get considerably fewer.

A CD-RW drive works by using a laser to heat an amorphous (noncrystalline) substance that, when cooled, slowly becomes crystalline. The crystalline areas are reflective, whereas the amorphous areas are not. Because both CD-R and CD-RW drives require a powerful laser, it was a simple process to make a drive that could burn CD-Rs and CD-RWs, making plain CD-R drives disappear almost overnight. Why buy a CD-R drive when a comparably priced CD-RW drive could burn both CD-R and CD-RW discs?

CD-RW drive specs have three multiplier values. The first shows the CD-R write speed, the second shows the CD-RW rewrite speed, and the third shows the read speed. Write, rewrite, and read speeds vary tremendously among the various brands of CD-RW drives; here are just a few representative samples: 8×4×32×, 12×10×32×, and 48×24×48×.

One of the goals of introducing CD-RWs was to make a CD-RW act like a hard drive so that you could simply drag a file onto the CD-RW (or CD-R) and just as easily drag it off again. This goal was difficult for two reasons: first, the different file formats made on-the-fly conversion risky. Second, CD-RWs don't store data exactly the same way as hard drives and would quickly wear out if data was copied in the same manner.

Two developments, UDF and packet writing, now allow us to treat a CD-RW just like a hard drive—with a few gotchas. The not-so-new kid in town with CD-media file formats is the Universal Data Format (UDF). UDF is a replacement for ISO-9660 and all of its various extensions, resulting in a single file format that any drive and operating system can read. UDF has already taken over the DVD world (all movie DVDs use this format) and is poised to also become the CD-media file format in the near future. UDF handles very large files and is excellent for all rewritable CD-media.

UDF has been available for quite a while, but until Windows Vista came out, no version of Windows could write to UDF formatted discs. They could *read* the discs, but if you wanted to *write* to them in Windows you had to use one of a number of third-party UDF tools like Roxio's DirectCD and Nero's InCD. UDF also supports a feature called Mount Rainier, better known as packet writing, that works with UDF to enable you to copy individual files back and forth like a hard drive. With UDF and packet writing, rewritable CD-media is as easy to use as a hard drive.

Windows and CD-Media

Virtually all CD-media drives are ATAPI compliant, so there's no need to install drivers. You just plug in the drive and assuming you didn't make any physical installation mistakes, the drive will appear in Windows (Figure 11-25).

Figure 11-25
CD-media drive
in Windows

Windows XP displays a CD-media drive in My Computer with the typical CD-media icon and assigns it a drive letter. If you want to put data onto a CD-R disc, however, you need special *burner software* to get that data onto the disc. Windows XP comes with burning support—you just drop a CD-R disc into your CD-R drive, open the drive in My Computer, drag the files you wish to copy, and click Write to Disc. However this support doesn't enable you to make bootable CDs, music CDs, or other specialties. No worries, almost every new CD-R drive comes with some type of burner software, so you rarely need to go out and buy your own unless you have a preference for a particular brand. Figure 11-26 shows the opening menu of one that I like, the popular Nero Express CD-burning program.

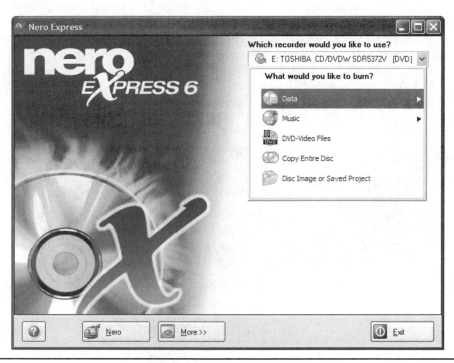

Figure 11-26 Nero Express CD-burning program

When I buy a new program on CD, the first thing I do is make a backup copy; then I stash the original under lock and key. If I break, melt, or otherwise destroy the backup, I quickly create a new one from the original. I can easily copy the disc because my system, like many, has both a regular CD-ROM and a CD-RW drive (even though CD-RW drives read CD-ROM discs). I can place a CD in the CD-ROM drive and a CD-R or CD-RW disc in the CD-RW drive. Then I run special software such as Adaptec's DiskCopy to quickly create an exact replica of the CD. CD-RW drives work great for another, bigger type of backup—not the archival "put it on the disc and stash it in the closet" type of backup, but rather the daily/weekly backups that most of us do (or should do!) on our systems. Using CD-R discs for these backups is wasteful; once a disc fills up, you throw it away at the next backup. But with CD-RW, you can use the same set of CD-RW discs time and again to perform backups.

Music CDs

Computers do not hold a monopoly on CD burning. Many companies offer consumer CD burners that work with your stereo system. These come in a wide variety of formats, but they're usually dual-deck player/recorder combinations (see Figure 11-27). These recorders do not use regular CD-R or CD-RW discs. Instead, under U.S. law, these home recorders must use a slightly different disc called a *Music CD-R*. Makers of Music CDs pay a small royalty for each CD (and add it to your price).

Figure 11-27   CD recorder

You can record *to* a Music CD-R or CD-RW, but you cannot record *from* one—the idea being to restrict duplication. If you decide to buy one of these burners, make sure to buy the special Music CD-Rs. Music CD-Rs are designed specifically for these types of devices and may not work well in a PC.

DVD-Media

For years, the video industry tried to create a optical-media replacement for videotape. The 12-inch diameter *laserdisc* format originally introduced by Philips gained some ground in the 1980s and 1990s. But the high cost of both the discs and the players, plus various marketing factors, meant there was never a very large laserdisc market. You may still find one of them sitting around, however, or you may know someone who invested in a small collection during the laserdisc's heyday (see Figure 11-28).

Figure 11-28
Sample laserdisc with a CD-ROM disc for size comparison

The DVD was developed by a large consortium of electronics and entertainment firms during the early 1990s and released as digital *video* discs in 1995. The transformation of DVD to a data storage medium quickly required a name change, to digital *versatile* discs. You'll still hear both terms used. The industry also uses the term *DVD-video* to distinguish the movie format from the data formats.

With the exception of the DVD logo stamped on all commercial DVDs (see Figure 11-29), DVDs look exactly like CD-media discs; but that's pretty much where the similarities end. DVD has become the fastest growing media format in history and has completely overtaken VHS as the preferred media for video. Additionally, one variant of DVD called DVD-RAM has enjoyed some success as a mass storage medium.

Figure 11-29
Typical DVD-video

The single best word to describe DVD is *capacity.* All previous optical media stored a maximum of 700 MB of data or 80 minutes of video. The lowest capacity DVD holds 4.37 GB of data, or two hours of standard definition video. The highest capacity version DVDs store roughly 16 GB of data, or more than eight hours of video! DVD achieves these amazing capacities using a number of technologies, but three are most important. First, DVD uses smaller pits than CD-media, and packs them much more densely. Second, DVD comes in both *single-sided (SS)* and *dual-sided (DS)* formats. As the name implies, a DS disc holds twice the data of an SS disc, but it also requires you to flip the disc to read the other side. Third, DVDs come in *single-layer (SL)* and *dual-layer (DL)* formats. DL formats use two pitted layers on each side, each with a slightly different reflectivity index. Table 11-1 shows the common DVD capacities.

DVD Version	Capacity
DVD-5 (12 cm, SS/SL)	4.37 GB, more than two hours of video
DVD-9 (12 cm, SS/DL)	7.95 GB, about four hours of video
DVD-10 (12 cm, DS/SL)	8.74 GB, about four and a half hours of video
DVD-18 (12 cm, DS/DL)	15.90 GB, more than eight hours of video

Table 11-1   DVD Versions/Capacities

DVD-Video

The most beautiful trait of DVD-video lies in its capability to store two hours of video on one side. You drop in a DVD-video and get to watch an entire movie without flipping it over. DVD-video supports TV-style 4:3 aspect ratio screens as well as 16:9 theater screens, but it is up to the producer to decide which to use. Many DVD-video producers distribute DVD movies on DS media with a 4:3 ratio on one side and 16:9 ratio on the other. DVD-video relies on the MPEG-2 standard of video and audio compression to reach the magic of two hours of video per side. *Moving Picture Experts Group (MPEG)* is a group of compression standards for both audio and video. The MPEG-2 standard offers resolutions of up to 1280 × 720 at 60 frames per second (fps), with full CD-quality audio (standard DVDs only offer 480 vertical resolution, the same as regular television).

MPEG Standards   Reproducing video and sound on the PC provides interesting challenges for developers. How do you take a motion picture from film, translate it into ones and zeroes that the CPU understands, process those bits, and then send high-quality video and sound to the monitor and speakers for the pleasure of the computer user? How much data do you think is required to display even a two-minute clip of a car racing through a city street, in all the minute detail of the shops, people, screeching tires, road debris, and so on? For that matter, how do you *store* the obviously huge amount of data required to do this?

To handle these chores, the Moving Pictures Experts Group (MPEG) has released various coding standards such as MPEG-1, MPEG-2, and MPEG-4. Each standard provides a different *compression algorithm*, which makes the files manageable. The standards also implement various technologies to handle movement, called *motion compensation*. The details of the standards matter a lot to the folks producing the movies and other video and audio content, but here's the short answer that should suffice for the purposes of a PC tech.

MPEG-1 is the standard upon which video and MP3, among other technologies, are based. The most common implementations of this standard provide a resolution of 352 × 240 at 30 fps. This video quality falls just below that of a conventional VHS video.

One very well-known subset of MPEG-1 is better known for audio than video. MPEG-1 Layer 3, better known as MP3 format, dominates the world of audio. MP3 takes an uncompressed audio file and compresses it dramatically, but the algorithm is so tight that the music that comes out of the speakers remains almost completely faithful to the original audio file. To paraphrase a catch phrase from the '80s—*I want my MP3s!*

MPEG-2 provides resolutions of 720 × 480 and 1280 × 720 at 60 fps (as well as others), plus CD-quality audio, making it adequate for all major TV standards, even HDTV. MPEG-2 is the standard that covers DVD-ROM technology—it can compress two hours of video into a file no larger than a few gigabytes. Although encoding video into MPEG-2 format requires a computer with some serious firepower, even a modest PC can decompress and play such a video.

The MPEG-4 standard is based on MPEG-1, MPEG-2, and Apple's QuickTime technology. MPEG-4 graphics and video files use what's known as *wavelet* compression to create files that are more compact than either JPEG or QuickTime files. This superior compression makes MPEG-4 popular for delivering video and images over the Web.

DVD-ROM

DVD-ROM is the DVD equivalent of the standard CD-ROM data format except that it's capable of storing up to almost 16 GB of data. Almost all DVD-ROM drives also fully support DVD-video, as well as most CD-ROM formats. Most DVD drives sold with PCs are DVD-ROM drives.

Recordable DVD

The IT industry has no fewer than *six* distinct standards of recordable DVD-media: DVD-R for general use, DVD-R for authoring, DVD-RW, DVD+R, DVD+RW, and DVD-RAM. Both DVD-R standard discs and DVD+R discs work like CD-Rs. You can write to them but not erase or alter what's written. DVD-RW, DVD+RW, and DVD-RAM discs can be written and rewritten, just like CD-RW discs. Most DVD drives can read all formats with the exception of DVD-RAM. DVD-RAM is the only DVD format that uses a cartridge, so it requires a special drive (Figure 11-30). DVD-RAM is still around but fading away.

Figure 11-30
DVD-RAM disc

Although there is little if any difference in quality among the standards, the competition between corporations pushing their preferred standards has raged for years. Sony and Phillips, for example, pushed the + series, whereas other manufacturers pushed the – series. Worse, no recordable DVD drive manufactured before 2003 could write any format except its own. You could plop down US$250 on a brand-new DVD+RW drive and still find yourself unable to edit a disc from your friend who used the DVD-RW format! Half of the time, the drive couldn't even *read* the competing format disc.

The situation is much better today, as DVD±RW combo drives in PCs will play just about anyone else's DVDs. The challenge is DVD players. If you want to make a DVD of your family picnic and then play it on the DVD player hooked to your television, take the time to read the documentation for your player to make sure it reads that particular DVD format—not all players read all formats.

Installing Optical Drives

From ten feet away, CD-ROM, CD-R, CD-RW, DVD-RW, and DVD+RW drives look absolutely identical. Figure 11-31 shows a CD-ROM, CD-RW, and a DVD drive. Can you tell them apart just by a glance? In case you were wondering, the CD-RW is on the top, the CD-ROM is in the center, and the DVD is on the bottom. If you look closely at an optical drive, its function is normally either stamped on the front of the case or printed on a label somewhere less obvious (see Figure 11-32).

Figure 11-31
CD-ROM, CD-RW, and DVD

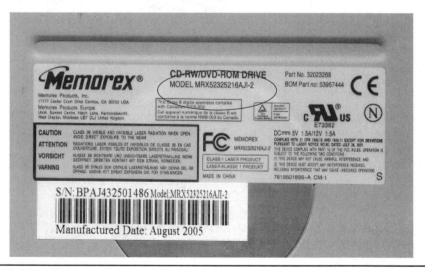

Figure 11-32 Label on optical drive indicating its type and speeds

Connections

Most CD drives use PATA or SATA connections and support the ATAPI standard. (Other connections, such as SCSI and USB, are possible but less common.) ATAPI treats a CD-media drive exactly as though it were an ATA drive. PATA CD drives have regular 40-pin IDE connectors and master/slave jumpers. SATA CD drives use standard SATA cables.

You install them the same way you would install any ATA hard drive. Figure 11-33 shows a typical DVD installation using PATA. The DVD is configured as slave with a master hard drive on a system's primary IDE controller.

Figure 11-33 Typical DVD installation

ATAPI drives require no CMOS changes as part of the install process. When the industry first introduced ATAPI drives, techs familiar with hard-drive installations swamped the CD-ROM makers' service departments asking how to set up the drives in CMOS. To reduce these calls, BIOS makers added a CD-ROM option in many CMOS setup utilities, just to give the techs something to do! You can find this option in many older CMOS setup utilities. This setting actually didn't do anything at all; it just kept users from bothering the CD-ROM makers with silly support calls. Modern motherboards report the actual model numbers of optical drives, giving a tech a degree of assurance that he or she configured and installed the drive correctly (Figure 11-34).

Figure 11-34
Autodetect settings
for two optical
drives

```
           Phoenix - Award BIOS CMOS Setup Ut
                 Standard CMOS Features

    Date (mm:dd:yy)           Wed, Jun 7 2006       ▲
    Time (hh:mm:ss)           13 : 19 : 35

  ▶ IDE Channel 1 Master      WDC WD1200JB-75CRA0
  ▶ IDE Channel 1 Slave       None
  ▶ IDE Channel 2 Master      SONY      CD-CW   CRX17
  ▶ IDE Channel 2 Slave       TOSHIBA CD/DVDW SDR5
  ▶ IDE Channel 3 Master      None
```

External Optical Drives   Almost all new PCs have one or both external expansion buses, USB and FireWire, and the makers of optical drives have quickly taken this fact to heart. Many manufacturers have released external versions of CD and DVD drives, both readers and burners. Of the two expansion options, I prefer FireWire simply because it's the standard for most digital video cameras and the 400 Mbps *sustained* data transfer rate easily trumps the Hi-Speed USB 480 Mbps burst rate for transferring huge files.

The only benefit to the USB versions is that USB is still more common than FireWire, particularly on portable computers. In fact, quite a few super-light laptops don't have an optical drive built in; the only way to load an OS on them is through an external drive! (Note that some external drives for laptops connect via the IEEE1284 DB 25 parallel port.) If you can't decide which expansion type to use, several manufacturers have taken pity on you.

Device Manager

When you install a new CD-ROM into an existing system, the first question to ask is, "Does Windows recognize my CD-ROM?" You can determine this by opening the My Computer icon and verifying that a CD-ROM is present (see Figure 11-35). When you want to know more, go to Device Manager.

Figure 11-35   CD-ROM drive letter in My Computer

The Device Manager contains most of the information about the CD-ROM. The General tab tells you about the current status of the CD-ROM, basically saying whether the device is working properly or not—rather less useful than actually trying the device. Other tabs, such as the Driver tab shown in Figure 11-36, provide other pertinent information about the drive.

Figure 11-36
Driver tab in the
Device Manager

Auto Insert Notification

Another setting of note is the Auto Insert Notification option, often referred to as *Auto-Play* in Windows 2000/XP. This setting enables Windows to detect automatically the presence of audio or data CD-ROMs when they are placed in the drive.

Windows 2000 and Windows XP have very different ways of dealing with AutoPlay. In Windows 2000, if the CD is an audio disc, track 1 plays automatically. If the CD-ROM is a data disc, Windows searches the disc's root directory for a special text file called AUTORUN.INF.

Although handy, this option can sometimes be annoying and unproductive. Windows 2000 does not provide a simple method to turn off AutoPlay. The only way to turn it off is to edit the registry. You can use the REGEDT32 version of the Registry Editor and do it directly. In REGEDT32, access this subkey:

HKEY_LOCAL_MACHINE\SYSTEM\CurrentControlSet\Services\Cdrom

Change Autorun 0 x 1 to 0 x 0.

Most techs will use Group Policy to make the change because it gives you much more control in multiple CD and DVD drive situations. With Group Policy, you can turn off AutoPlay on your CD-RW drive, for example, but leave it enabled for your DVD drive. Group Policy is a very powerful tool that goes well beyond CompTIA A+, so be careful with what you're about to do. To run Group Policy, go to Start | Run and type **gpedit.msc** in the Run dialog box. Click OK to open the MMC. To turn off AutoPlay, navigate down in the menu to the left as follows: Local Computer Policy | Computer Configuration |

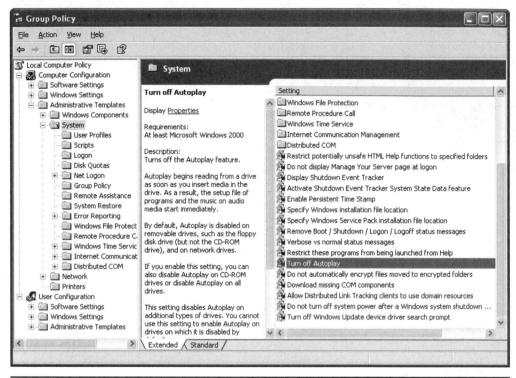

Figure 11-37 Group Policy MMC with Turn off Autoplay selected

Administrative Templates. Select the System option and you'll see the *Turn off Autoplay* option in the Setting section on the right pane of the MMC (Figure 11-37).

Double-click or right-click Turn off Autoplay to open the Properties. Note in Figure 11-38 that the default option is Not Configured, but you can enable or disable it here. The words are messy here, so make sure you know what you're doing. Enabling Turn off Autoplay gives you the option to stop an optical drive from automatically playing a disc. *Disabling* Turn off Autoplay prevents you or any other user from stopping any optical drive from automatically playing a disc. Got the distinction?

Figure 11-38
Turn off Autoplay
Properties dialog box

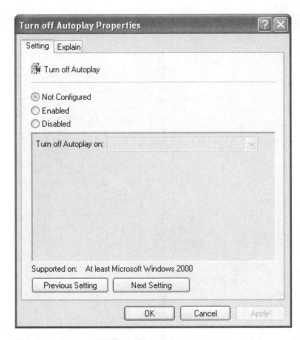

Windows XP provides a much more sophisticated and simpler approach to Auto-Play. By default, when you insert a CD- or DVD-media disc that doesn't have an AUTO-RUN.INF file, XP asks you what you want to do (Figure 11-39). You can change the default behavior simply by accessing the properties for a particular drive in My Computer and making your selection on the AutoPlay tab. Figure 11-40 shows some of the options for a typical Windows XP machine.

Figure 11-39
XP prompting user
for action

Figure 11-40
AutoPlay tab for
a DVD-RW drive

As a final note, Windows 2000 and XP enable you to change the drive letter for a CD- or DVD-media drive, just like you can change the letter of a hard drive. You'll find that option in Disk Management (Figure 11-41).

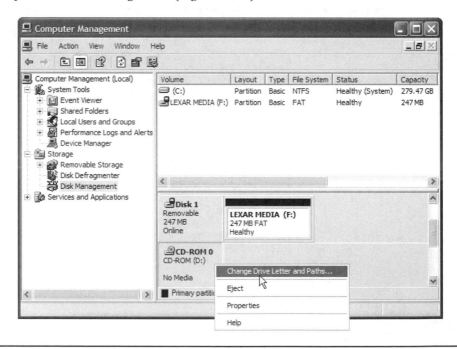

Figure 11-41   Change CD drive letter option in Disk Management.

Applications

A regular CD-ROM drive installation involves no applications. You install it, Windows sees it, and you're done. CD-R and CD-RW drives, in contrast, require applications to enable their burning features. DVD-media drives need software to enable you to watch movies, burn DVDs, and so on. As of this writing, Nero Burning ROM (www.nero.com) and Roxio's Easy Media Creator (www.roxio.com) suites of programs share the reigns as the most popular CD-burning software programs. If you're looking for a free burner, try CDBurnerXP Pro, pictured in Figure 11-42 (www.cdburnerxp.se). Windows XP contains basic CD-burning capabilities built into the operating system. With XP, you can readily drag and drop files to your CD-R or CD-RW drive and move those files from PC to PC. Almost all CD- and DVD-media drives will read the discs burned in an XP system.

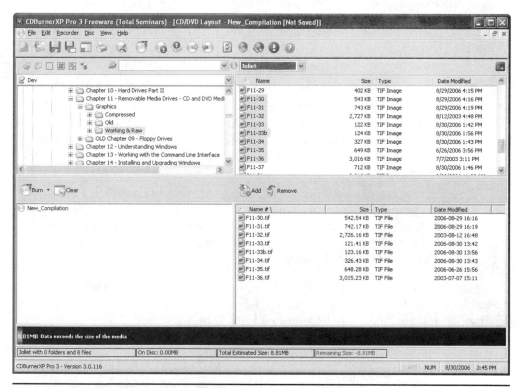

Figure 11-42 Typical third-party CD-burning program

Windows Media Player that comes free with Windows makes an excellent DVD-watching application, but for DVD burning you need to turn to a third-party tool. Nero and Roxio make excellent software that handles every DVD recordable standard (as well as CD-R and CD-RW) that your drive can use.

Burning Digital Music Files to a CD   Almost all computers and many portable CD players now have the ability to play recordable CDs loaded with MP3 files. This enables you to mix songs from your music collection and fit a lot of songs on a disc (MP3s are smaller than CD-audio files). That's a great feature—but where do digital audio files come from and how do you put them on a CD?

You can create MP3s from your favorite CDs by using a *ripper*. A ripper is a piece of software that takes standard CD-audio files and compresses them, using specialized algorithms, into much smaller files while maintaining most of the audio qualities of the original file. One legal note, however—you should only make MP3s from CDs that you have purchased. Borrowing a CD from a friend and ripping MP3s from it is illegal! Likewise, downloading MP3s from unauthorized sources on the Internet is also illegal. You don't want to go to jail because you just had to listen to the latest, greatest single from your favorite artist, right?

Now that I've taken care of the legal disclaimer, get ready to rip your MP3s. You need three things—a recordable/rewritable optical drive, some CD authoring software, and of course, a blank disc. I recommend a CD-R. (Audio-only devices stand a much better chance of playing a CD-R successfully rather than a CD-RW.)

1. Confirm that you have a CD-R/RW drive installed in your computer. You don't have to have a drive like this in order to rip audio files *from* a CD, but you must have one in order to burn digital audio to a CD-R.

2. Launch your favorite CD authoring software. Popular titles in this category include Nero Burning ROM and Easy CD Creator.

3. Most CD authoring programs use a simple drag-and-drop interface, similar to the Windows Explorer interface. Browse to the location of the audio files and select them. Then drag them into the appropriate area—this is often called the *queue*.

4. After you've selected all the files you want to have on your CD, it's time to burn! The procedure for initiating the CD-burning sequence is different for each program. You should always make sure to *close* the CD after you've burned it. Most standalone CD players (even ones that play MP3s) won't play CD-Rs that haven't been closed.

Once you get all the configuration information keyed in, just sit back and watch the fireworks. Always be sure to use CD-media that is rated appropriately for your drive, for both speed and media type. In no time at all, you'll be listening to MP3s while jogging around the park!

Burning ISO Images Ever wanted to make a perfect copy of a CD so that you can keep your original in a safe place? You can do so using a special file type called an ISO file. An ISO file is a complete copy—an ISO image as we say—of a CD. As you might imagine, they are huge files, but they are also very important to techs. Techs use ISO images to send each other copies of bootable utility CDs. For example, if you want a copy of the Ultimate Boot CD, you go to their Web site and download an ISO image. You then take your third-party burning program (Windows XP built-in burning software can't do this) and go through a special process called burning an ISO image. Learn how to burn ISO images with your burning program, you'll use it all the time!

IT Technician

Troubleshooting Removable Media

Floppy disk drives, flash memory, and optical drives are fairly robust devices that rarely require troubleshooting due to an actual hardware failure. Most problems with removable media stem from lack of knowledge, improper installation, abuse, and incorrect use of associated applications. There's no way to repair a truly broken flash memory—once a flash card dies, you replace it—so let's concentrate on troubleshooting floppy drives and optical drives.

Floppy Drive Maintenance and Troubleshooting

No single component fails more often than the floppy drive. This is not really that surprising because floppy drives have more exposure to the outside environment than anything but the keyboard. Only a small door (or in the case of 5¼-inch drives, not even a door) divides the read/write heads from dust and grime. Floppy drives are also exposed to the threat of mechanical damage. Many folks destroy floppy drives by accidentally inserting inverted disks, paper clips, and other foreign objects. Life is tough for floppy drives!

In the face of this abuse, the key preventative maintenance performed on floppy drives is cleaning. You can find floppy drive *cleaning kits* at some electronics stores, or you can use a cotton swab and some denatured alcohol to scour gently inside the drive for dust and other particles.

Repairing Floppy Drives

When a floppy drive stops working, follow these steps to resolve the problem:

1. Check for a bad floppy disk.
2. Check for data errors on the disk.
3. Check the CMOS settings.
4. Blame the floppy controller.
5. Check the cable.
6. Replace the floppy drive.

First, Check the Floppy Disk

The vast majority of the time, when the floppy drive decides it won't read a floppy disk, the bad guy is the floppy disk, not the floppy drive. When the floppy drive refuses to read a floppy disk, you usually get an error like the one shown in Figure 11-43.

Figure 11-43 Floppy disk read error

If you get this error, first try inserting another floppy disk. If a new disk from a fresh box won't work, don't insert another one from the same box. Find another disk, preferably from another box or one just lying around, to retest. If the floppy drive refuses to read two floppy disks, then suspect the floppy drive is the problem. Otherwise, blame the disk!

Sometimes pieces of a floppy disk—the metal shutter, for example, or the spring—can get jammed into the drive by users who keep trying to shove a disk into the drive. The user won't notice anything different except that the disk doesn't work and sometimes sticks in the drive. If you have any trouble inserting the floppy disk, take a flashlight and peer inside the drive to check for stray bits that don't belong!

Second, Check for Data Errors on the Disk

If other floppy disks work in the drive, then you know the floppy disk has a problem. If a floppy disk fails, you have three options. First, just throw it away. Second, reformat the floppy disk. The only downside to these two options is that you lose the data on the floppy disk, and sometimes that is not an acceptable option. Your third option is to run some sort of recovery/fixing software on the disk.

Figure 11-44
Formatting a floppy disk

Floppy disks come preformatted from the manufacturer. We reformat floppies for one of two reasons: either as a handy way to completely erase a floppy disk or as a last-ditch effort to try to fix a bad floppy. To reformat a floppy disk in any version of Windows, go to My Computer and right-click the floppy icon. Select Format to see the dialog box shown in Figure 11-44.

Note that in Windows XP, although the first three settings appear to be pull-down menus, you don't actually get any format options besides the ones showing. In Windows 2000, the Capacity pull-down menu does let you format the floppy as an ancient 720 KB as well as a modern 1.44 MB type. The Format Type radio button group enables you to choose between Quick Format (just erases data), or Create an MS-DOS Startup Disk (don't format the floppy—save the data, just make it bootable). You can add a Volume Label, which simply enables you to place a small amount of text on the floppy to help describe the contents. Volume labels were quite popular in the DOS days but are almost never used today.

The third option (recovery software) may save the data—and possibly the disk! A bad floppy disk often holds data that you need. Don't panic! Unless the floppy disk has substantial physical damage—for example, your dog chewed on it for 20 minutes—certain utility programs can retrieve the data. The process for repairing floppy disks is identical to the process for repairing hard drives. Refer to Chapter 10 to review the process of running the Error-Checking/SpinRite combination for data repair.

Third, Check the CMOS Settings

CMOS settings for floppy drives rarely cause problems. All BIOS makers default the CMOS settings for the A: drive to 3½-inch high density if the CMOS is accidentally erased. So although an erased CMOS might keep everything else on your computer from running, at least the floppy will still work (assuming you have a 3½-inch A: drive). The rare instances of a problem with CMOS can be dangerous because technicians rarely look there. Double-check the CMOS: A quick peek can save a lot of time!

Next, Blame the Floppy Controller

If the data cable or power plug is loose, the POST will flag with either "FDD Controller Failure" or "Drive Not Ready" errors. At this point, open the machine and verify the connections. If the connections are good, it's possible that your motherboard has a bad floppy drive controller. Checking the floppy drive controller requires two basic steps. First, turn off the onboard controller. To turn off the controller, go into CMOS and find the Onboard FDD Controller option (or something like that), shown in Figure 11-45, and disable it. Some motherboards don't give you the option to do this, in which case you need to disable the controller in Device Manager.

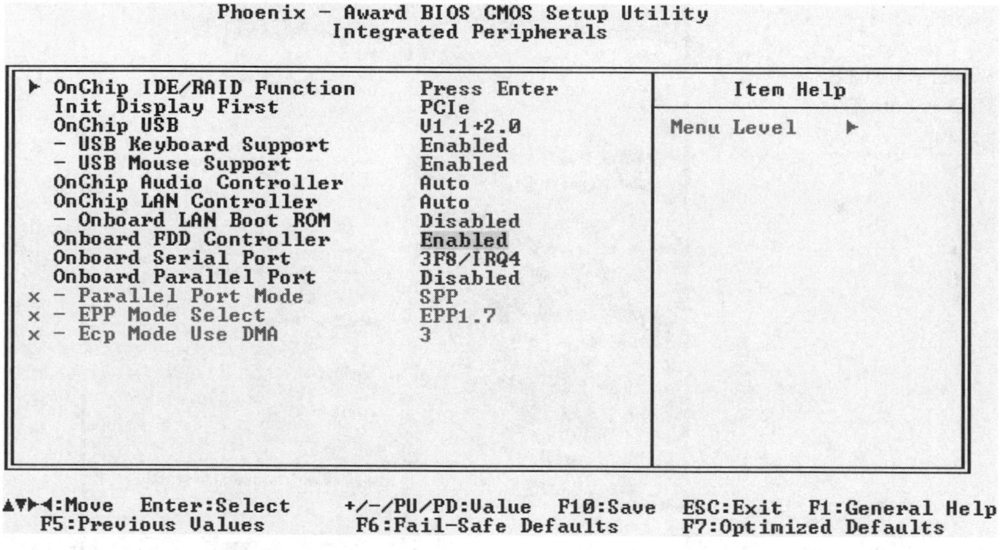

```
             Phoenix - Award BIOS CMOS Setup Utility
                      Integrated Peripherals

 ► OnChip IDE/RAID Function    Press Enter          Item Help
   Init Display First          PCIe
   OnChip USB                  V1.1+2.0       Menu Level    ►
   - USB Keyboard Support      Enabled
   - USB Mouse Support         Enabled
   OnChip Audio Controller     Auto
   OnChip LAN Controller       Auto
   - Onboard LAN Boot ROM      Disabled
   Onboard FDD Controller      Enabled
   Onboard Serial Port         3F8/IRQ4
   Onboard Parallel Port       Disabled
 x - Parallel Port Mode        SPP
 x - EPP Mode Select           EPP1.7
 x - Ecp Mode Use DMA          3




▲▼►◄:Move   Enter:Select    +/-/PU/PD:Value  F10:Save   ESC:Exit  F1:General Help
   F5:Previous Values       F6:Fail-Safe Defaults     F7:Optimized Defaults
```

Figure 11-45 Onboard FDD Controller option

Second, go to the computer store (hooray!) and buy one of two items. On the off chance that the store has a PCI FDD controller card, pick it up. You can install it and plug in the floppy drive. If the drive works then, suspect the onboard controller. If the floppy drive still doesn't work, remove the card and reenable the CMOS setting for the onboard controller.

Alternatively, you can get an external USB floppy drive (Figure 11-46). This won't give you a bootable floppy drive, but you can bypass the internal components altogether and access it in Windows. Figure 11-47 shows My Computer in a system with only a USB FDD installed. Note that the USB device shows up as D:, but that you have the option of clicking on the A: drive as well. Clicking on either drive icon will access the same floppy disk.

Figure 11-46
USB floppy disk drive

Figure 11-47
My Computer
showing the USB
FDD as both D:
and A:

Maybe It's the Cable ...

Your next investigation should focus on whether the cable is the culprit. The 34th wire on the floppy-drive cable is called the *drive change signal* (or disk change signal). When a floppy disk is inserted or removed, this wire is active. When Windows first reads a floppy disk, it keeps a copy of the directory in RAM and will not update that information unless the floppy drive detects a disk removal and activates the drive change signal. This keeps the system from constantly accessing the very slow floppy drive. Windows waits until it knows it needs to reread the disk. However, if the drive change signal disconnects because of a bent pin or bad cable, you will keep seeing the same directory, even if you change the disk! This problem almost always traces back to a bad floppy cable, so replace it and retry.

Connectivity plays a big (and sometimes embarrassing) role in floppy drive failure. One of the most common errors techs make installing floppy drives is reversing the ribbon cable on one or both ends. If you reverse it on *one end*, invariably the LED on the drive (the light) comes on the moment you turn on the system and *stays on*. Always check the light on the floppy drive when installing a new floppy! If you reverse the cable on *both ends*, the LED *will not come on at all*—most of the time. Usually, you will get an FDD error at POST, and the drive simply will not work. As mentioned earlier, newer systems key the floppy drive connector and ribbon cable to minimize this issue, but no rule requires the floppy drive manufacturers to abide by this standard! Always check the cable!

Last, Replace the Floppy Drive

At this point, if the floppy drive isn't working, the only recourse is to replace the drive. When you replace a bad drive, throw it away. Keeping a bad floppy drive is a study in frustration because almost all bad floppy drives aren't consistently bad—just sometimes bad. Technicians are often tempted to give a bad floppy drive one more chance. They install the drive, and it works! They're convinced they made a mistake and declare the drive good. If the drive is reinstalled somewhere else, however, it will soon die again. Throw it away.

Troubleshooting Optical Drives and Discs

Optical drives are extremely reliable and durable PC components. However, there are times when that reliable and durable device decides to turn into an unreliable, nondurable pile of plastic and metal frustration. This section covers a few of the more common problems with optical drives and discs—installation issues, burning issues, and firmware updates—and how to fix them.

Installation Issues

The single biggest problem with optical drives, especially in a new installation, is the connection. Your first guess should be that the drive has not been properly installed in some way. A few of the common culprits are forgetting to plug in a power connector, inserting a cable backward, and misconfiguring jumpers/switches. Although you need to know the type of drive, the test for an improper physical connection is always the same: using BIOS to see whether the system can see the optical drive.

The way in which a BIOS detects an optical drive really depends on the system. Most BIOS makers have created intelligent BIOS software that can see an installed optical drive. Figure 11-48 shows a modern Award Software, Inc., BIOS recognizing a CD-RW during startup.

```
 Award Modular BIOS v6.00PG, An Energy Star Ally
 Copyright (C) 1984-2003 Phonix Technologies, LTD


Main Processor : AMD Athlon(tm) 64 Processor 3200+
Memory Testing : 1048576K OK
CPU0 Memory Information: DDR 400 CL:3 ,1T Dual Channel, 128-bit

IDE Channel 1 Master : WDC WD1200JB-75CRA0 16.06V16
IDE Channel 1 Slave  : None
IDE Channel 2 Master : TOSHIBA CD=DVDW SDR5372V TV11
IDE Channel 2 Slave  : None
```

Figure 11-48   BIOS recognizing an optical drive at boot

If the device is detected in BIOS, Windows will recognize the drive and you'll see it in My Computer and Device Manager.

If the drive won't read a CD-R or CD-RW disc, first try a commercial CD-ROM disc that is in good condition. CD-R and CD-RW discs sometimes have compatibility issues with CD-ROM drives. The same goes for a DVD-RW or any other writable DVD disc in your DVD drive. As noted earlier, DVD drives have issues with media incompatibility. Also, no CD- or DVD-media drive will read badly scratched discs.

If the drive still does not see a disc, try cleaning the drive. Most modern optical drives have built-in cleaning mechanisms, but from time to time, you need to use a commercial optical-drive cleaning kit (see Figure 11-49).

Figure 11-49
Optical drive
cleaning kit

Optical drives are not cleaned too often, but the discs are. Although a number of fine optical disc cleaning kits are available, most discs can be cleaned quite well with nothing more than a damp soft cloth. Occasionally, a mild detergent can be added. Always wipe from the center of the optical disc to the edge—never clean a CD or DVD using a circular motion! A common old tech's tale about cleaning optical discs is that they can be washed in a dishwasher! Although this may seem laughable, the tale has become so common that it requires a serious response. This is *not true* for two reasons:

First, the water in most dishwashers is too hot and can cause the discs to warp. Second, the water pushes the discs around, causing them to hit other objects and get scratched. Don't do it!

The final problem with optical drives—stuck discs—comes from *technician* error and is not actually the fault of the drives. I can't tell you the number of times I've pulled an optical drive out of a system to replace it, only to discover that I or my customer left an essential disc inside the now-powerless drive. Luckily, most optical drives have a small hole in the front, usually just below the drive opening, into which you can insert a wire—an unbent paper clip is the standard tool for this purpose—and push on an internal release lever that will eject the disc. Try it!

Burning Issues

The tremendous growth of the CD-R and CD-RW industry—and to a lesser extent, the recordable DVD industry—has led to a substantial number of incompatibility issues between discs and drives. Some of these incompatibilities trace back to serious *IO* (Ignorant Operator) problems; people try to make these discs do jobs they aren't designed to do. Even when people read the manuals and jump through the proper hoops, real problems do arise, many of which you can easily solve with a few checks.

Know What It Can Do   Most mistakes take place at the point of purchase, when someone buys a drive without completely understanding its capabilities. Don't just assume that the device will do everything! Before I purchase a CD-RW drive, for example, I make it a point to get my hands on every technical document provided by the maker to verify exactly what capabilities the drive possesses. I make sure that the drive has a good reputation—just use any search engine and type in **review** and the model number of the drive to get several people's opinions.

Media Issues   The CD-R and CD-RW standards committees refused to mandate the types of materials used in the construction of discs. As a result, you see substantial quality differences among CD-R and CD-RW discs of different brands and sources (they are made in several different countries). As mentioned earlier, CD-R discs use organic inks as part of the burning process. Fellow techs love to talk about which color to use or which color gives the best results. Ignore them—the color itself means nothing. Instead, try a few different brands of CD-R discs when you first get your drive to determine what works best for you. If you have a particular reason for burning CDs, such as music recording, you may want to ask for opinions and recommendations among folks in online communities with the same focus. They're usually happy to share their hard-won knowledge about what's good.

In general, two items can affect media quality: speed and inks. Most CD-R and CD-RW media makers certify their CDs to work up to a certain speed multiplier. A media maker often has two product lines: a quality line guaranteed to work at a certain speed, and a generic line where you take your chances. As a rule, I buy both. I primarily use cheap discs, but I always stash five to ten good quality discs in case I run into a problem. Again, this will in large part depend on what you want them for—you may want to pull out the cheapies for temporary backups, but stick with the high-end discs for archiving musical performances.

All of the discussion above about CD-Rs and CD-RWs definitely holds true for recordable DVD discs and drives as well. Factor in the incompatibility of standards and you're looking at a fine mess. Do your homework before you buy or advise a client to buy a DVD-writable or -rewritable drive.

Buffer Underrun   Every CD and DVD burner comes with onboard RAM, called *buffer RAM*—usually just called the buffer—that stores the incoming data from the recording source. Buffer underrun, the inability of the source device to keep the burner loaded with data, creates more *coasters*—that is, improperly burned and therefore useless CDs and DVDs—than any other single problem. Buffer underrun most often occurs when copying from CD-ROM to CD-R/RW or from DVD-ROM to DVD-writable of all stripes. Many factors contribute to buffer underrun, but two stand out as the most important. The first factor is buffer size. Make sure you purchase drives with large buffers, a minimum of 2 MB. Unlike with system RAM, you can't get a buffer upgrade. Second is multitasking. Most systems won't enable you to run any other programs while the burner is running.

One trick to reduce underrun is using an ISO. Unlike some CD and DVD media drives, *any* hard drive can keep up with a CD or DVD burner. Doing a bit-by-bit copy from disc to disc dramatically reduces the chance of a buffer underrun adding to your coaster collection.

All current CD-RW and DVD burners include the BURN-Proof technology developed by Sanyo, which has eliminated the underrun issue. These drives can literally turn off the burning process if the buffer runs out of information and automatically restart as soon as the buffer refills. I love this feature, as I can now burn CDs in the background and run other programs without fear of underrun. If you're buying a new CD-RW drive, make sure you get one that uses the BURN-Proof technology.

Firmware Updates
Almost all optical drives come with an upgradeable flash ROM chip. If your drive doesn't read a particular type of media, or if any other non-intermittent reading/writing problems develop, check the manufacturer's Web site to see if it offers a firmware upgrade. Almost every optical drive seems to get one or two firmware updates during its production cycle.

Conclusion
The world of removable media continues to change at a pretty hectic pace. Within the last couple of years, floppy drives have just about died out; thumb drives have become the rewritable media of choice for most users; high-definition optical drives and discs (HD-DVD and Blu-ray, see the "Beyond A+" section) have hit the store shelves, although they're both outrageously expensive as of this writing. Manufacturers keep inventing new and exciting technologies that seem to appear out of nowhere. A CompTIA A+ certified technician would be wise to keep removable media on his or her radar, well after taking and passing the CompTIA A+ exams!

Beyond A+

Color Books

The term *color books* is often used in the world of CD-media. Books are—well, books! In this case, they're the standards developed in the industry to describe various media. For example, the Red book describes the original audio CD format. If you have a lot of money—say, US$3000—you may purchase copies of these books, and yes, their covers really match the colors of the standards. You might hear a fellow computer support person using these terms. Instead of saying, "Does your CD-ROM read CD-RWs?" they will say, "Is that CD-ROM of yours Orange book?" Technical specifications also use these terms. I personally don't like the way many people refer to these book colors, but the terms are used enough that you should memorize the meanings of at least three book colors: Red, Yellow, and Orange. Table 11-2 shows a complete list of CD-media book colors.

Application	Book	Subtypes	
Audio CDs	Red book	N/A	
Data CDs	Yellow book	Mode 1	Original Format
		Mode 2	Form 1 and Form 2
CD-I	Green book	N/A	
Recordable CDs	Orange book	Part I	CD-MO (Magneto-Optical)
		Part II	CD-R, includes Photo-CD
		Part III	CD-RW
Video CD	White book	N/A	
CD Extra	Blue Book	N/A	

Table 11-2   CD-media Book Colors

High-Definition Optical Drives

At the time of this writing, two optical standards are duking it out to see which will become the Next Great Thing™ in optical media: HD DVD and Blu-ray. HD DVD (High-Density DVD) offered the initial salvo, coming out with 30-GB optical discs that could contain 8 hours of High-Definition video. Sweet! Blu-ray (no special meaning aside from using blue lasers rather than red lasers) responded with 50-GB discs, and the gloves were off. Right now it appears that HD DVD will be the eventual winner on the video front, but Blu-ray might win on the data-storage front. Time will tell. For more information, check out the respective camps' Web sites:

www.thelookandsoundofperfect.com (I am not making this up!)

www.blu-raydisc.com

Chapter Review Questions

1. To install a floppy drive as the A: drive, what must you do?

   A. Attach the mini connector

   B. Plug it into the end connector of the ribbon cable

   C. Plug it into the middle connector on the ribbon cable

   D. Attach the Molex connector

2. If the floppy disk you used last week will not work today in your floppy drive, what should you do first to determine if the problem is the drive or the disk?

   A. Try another disk in the drive or try the disk in another drive.

   B. Open the computer and check the ribbon cable.

   C. Replace the floppy drive.

   D. Check the CMOS settings.

3. Which term describes the capability to burn files to a CD-R and then come back later and burn additional files?

   A. MultiBurn

   B. Multisession

   C. MultiDrive

   D. Multibuffer

4. Which type of flash memory card is currently the most popular?

   A. CompactFlash

   B. Memory Stick

   C. Secure Digital

   D. SmartMedia

5. What type of device must be installed on your system in order to access data on a flash memory card?

   A. Scanner

   B. Card reader

   C. Floppy drive

   D. Zip drive

6. Which of the following can be bootable media? (Select the best answer.)

   A. CD-R disc

   B. Floppy disc

C. USB thumb drive

D. All of the above

7. When a CD is inserted, the AutoPlay feature of Windows looks for what file?

A. AUTOPLAY.INF

B. AUTORUN.INF

C. AUTORUN.INI

D. AUTORUN.EXE

8. A copy of a CD or DVD can be saved as what type of file?

A. ISO

B. ISO-9660

C. INF

D. CDDA

9. A CD-RW has a speed rating of 12×10×32×. What do the three numbers refer to, in order?

A. Write, rewrite, read

B. Read, write, rewrite

C. Rewrite, read, write

D. Write, read, rewrite

10. Which standard covers DVD-ROM technology?

A. MPEG-1

B. MPEG-2

C. MPEG-3

D. MPEG-4

Answers

1. **B.** Plug the floppy drive into the end of the ribbon cable to make it the A: drive.

2. **A.** If the floppy disk won't read in the drive, try another disk first.

3. **B.** The term *multisession* describes the capability to burn files to a CD-R and then come back later and burn additional files.

4. **C.** Secure Digital cards are the current kings of the marketplace.

5. **B.** You need some sort of card reader to read a flash memory card.

6. **D.** You can make a boot disk out of optical media, floppy disks, or flash memory drives.

7. **B.** By default, Windows looks for AUTORUN.INF when you insert a CD.

8. **A.** You can save a complete CD or DVD as an ISO image.

9. **A.** The three speeds listed for CD-RW drives stand for write, rewrite, and read.

10. **B.** The MPEG-2 standard covers DVD-ROM technology (among other things).

Installing and Upgrading Windows

In this chapter, you will learn how to
- Identify and explain the basic functions of an operating system
- Describe the features and characteristics of Windows 2000 and Windows XP
- Upgrade to or install the Windows 2000 and Windows XP operating systems

An operating system provides the fundamental link between the hardware that makes up the PC and the user. Without an operating system, all the greatest, slickest PC hardware in the world is but so much copper, silicon, and gold wrapped up as a big, beige paperweight. The operating system creates the interface between human and machine, enabling you to unleash the astonishing power locked up in the sophisticated electronics of the PC to create amazing pictures, games, documents, business tools, medical miracles, and much more.

All operating systems are not created equal. They don't look the same or, on the surface, act the same. But every OS shares essential characteristics that, once you have the concepts, help lead you to answers when troubleshooting: "I know that the OS formerly known as Y must enable me to access programs; therefore, no matter how odd the interface, the option must be here!"

This chapter starts with an analysis of all operating systems, examining the functions and traits they all share. After that, we'll delve into the features common to every version of Microsoft Windows (or at least those covered on the CompTIA A+ certification exams). We'll then go through the process of installing Windows on a new system, as well as upgrading earlier versions of Windows. The chapter finishes with an in-depth examination of the core structures of Windows 2000 and XP systems. Let's get started.

Historical/Conceptual

Functions of the Operating System

An operating system (OS) is a program that performs four basic functions. First, it must communicate, or at least provide a method for other programs to communicate, with the hardware of the PC. It's up to the OS to access the hard drives, respond to the keyboard, and output data to the monitor. Second, the OS must create a user interface—a visual representation of the computer on the monitor that makes sense to the people using the computer. The OS must also take advantage of standard input devices, such as mice and keyboards, to enable users to manipulate the user interface and thereby make changes on the computer. Third, the OS, via the user interface, must enable users to determine the available installed programs and run, use, and shut down the program(s) of their choice. Fourth, the OS should enable users to add, move, and delete the installed programs and data.

In a nutshell, the OS should be able to do four things:

- Communicate with hardware
- Provide a user interface
- Provide a structure for accessing applications
- Enable users to manipulate programs and data

Operating System Traits

To achieve these four functions, all operating systems share certain common traits.

First, an OS works only with a particular type of processor. For example, Microsoft Windows XP Professional 64-bit Edition only runs on systems using Intel or AMD CPUs with 64-bit support, like the AMD Athlon 64. For many years, other platforms used different CPUs that were completely incompatible with the Intel and AMD lines, such as the IBM/Motorola PowerPC CPU used inside Macintosh computers until 2005. The Macintosh OS used on those systems would not run on an Intel/AMD based system. (This changed in 2005 when Apple switched to the Intel/AMD platform—you can now run Windows on a newer Mac with a few tweaks.) The OS must understand important aspects of the CPU, such as the amount of memory the CPU can handle, what modes of operation it is capable of performing, and the CPU commands (the codebook) needed to perform the operations. Certain OSs, such as Linux, can run on more than one type of processor, but they achieve this by having versions for each type of processor they support.

Second, an OS always starts running immediately after the PC has finished its POST, taking control of the PC. The OS continues running until the PC is rebooted or turned off. The OS cannot be turned off unless the PC is also turned off.

Third, *application programs,* such as word processors, spreadsheets, and Web browsers, cannot run on a PC without an OS. Therefore, programmers write application programs to function under the control of a certain OS. You cannot write one version of an application that works under different OSs. Table 12-1 shows a selection of OSs and applications written specifically for them. The creators of an OS always provide a "rule book" that tells programmers how to write programs for a particular OS. These rule books are known as *application programming interfaces (APIs).*

 NOTE The popularity of programming paradigms such as Java might make some folks want to challenge the idea that every application must come in different versions for different operating systems. Although a piece of Java code may run on any computer, each computer must have some programming installed that can interpret that Java code. That programming is OS-specific.

Table 12-1	Operating System	Application
Operating Systems and Applications	Mac OS X	Microsoft Office 2004
	Windows XP	Microsoft Office 2006
	Linux	OpenOffice

Last, an OS must have flexibility and provide some facility for using new software or hardware that might be installed. It just wouldn't do, for example, to be stuck with the same game year after year! (See Figure 12-1.)

Figure 12-1   Progress is good: Half-Life 2 above Wolfenstein 3-D.

Communicating with Hardware

In earlier chapters you learned that the system BIOS, stored on some type of non-volatile memory (ROM or Flash ROM) on the motherboard, stores programs that know how to talk to the most basic and important parts of the computer. These include the hard drives, floppy drives, keyboard, and basic video. The OS must work with the system BIOS to deal with these devices. If users want to access the hard drive to retrieve a program, the OS must take the request and pass it to the appropriate hard drive BIOS instruction that tells the drive to send the program to RAM. Plus, if for some reason the BIOS lacks the ability to perform its function, the OS should bypass the system BIOS and talk to the piece of hardware directly. Most recent OSs, including Windows, skip the system BIOS and talk directly to almost every piece of hardware, reducing your system BIOS to little more than a relic of the past.

For the OS to take control of a new piece of hardware, it needs to communicate with that hardware. Therefore, the OS needs a method to add the programming necessary to talk to that device, preferably in some simple and flexible way. Most OSs use *device drivers* to add this necessary code. An OS maker (such as Microsoft) tells hardware makers how to create these programs (and makes money selling the development tools) and also creates a method of adding the device driver to the OS code. Because makers of a particular piece of hardware usually supply the device drivers with the hardware, and because drivers act something like BIOS, this solution can be jokingly, although accurately, thought of as BYOB (Bring Your Own BIOS).

Because the OS handles communicating with hardware, it should provide some type of error handling, or at least error notification. If someone attempts to use a piece of hardware that isn't working properly, the OS should either try to fix the problem or at least attempt to communicate with the device a few more times. If the device continues to fail, the OS should provide an error message to notify the user of the problem.

Creating a User Interface

Most users have fairly straightforward needs. First, they want to know which applications are available; second, they want easy access to those programs; and third, they want to be able to save the data they generate with some easy-to-use label by which they can retrieve it later.

A shoe store makes a good analogy for a user interface. The front of the shoe store is filled with attractive displays of shoes, organized and grouped by gender (men and women), age (adults and children), function (dress or sports), and style. Shoe sellers do this so consumers can see everything that's available and to make it much easier to select the shoes they want to purchase. If a customer wants to buy a pair of shoes, what happens? The customer points out the shoes he or she wants to try on. The salesperson looks at the inside of the shoe and disappears through a small door. Wonder why the salesperson looked in the shoe? To read an inventory code that shoe manufacturers print inside every shoe.

Have you ever seen the back of a shoe store? It's scary. All the shoes are organized, not by gender, age, function, or style, but by inventory code, and the salesperson reads the inventory code to know where to look for that particular shoe. Without understanding the code, no one would know where to search for a pair of shoes, but it's the best way to organize an inventory of 25,000 pairs of shoes. What a customer sees in the store is not all the shoes as they really are in the back, but a "user interface" of what's available. The front display in the store—the user interface—is a pretty, easy to use, but entirely unrealistic display of the shoes in stock (Figure 12-2).

Figure 12-2
Shoe display

A computer's user interface performs the same function by offering the user a display of the programs and data on the PC. The customers (users) look at the display (the user interface) and tell the salesperson (the OS) what they want, without ever really knowing how all the shoes (programs and data) are really organized.

Finishing the analogy, the shoe store's displays are not permanent. Salespeople can easily add shoes and replace old displays. They can change a rack of men's shoes into a rack of women's shoes, for example, relatively easily. Like the shoe store, a user interface should also be flexible and scalable, depending on the system in which it is installed.

Accessing and Supporting Programs

An OS must enable users to start a program. This is a simple but important concept. When a program starts, the user interface must move away from the main part of the screen and set itself to the top, bottom, or side. While the application runs, the OS must still provide whatever access to hardware the application needs, such as updating the screen, saving data, or printing. If a program loses control, the OS should have some way to stop it or at least to recognize what's happening and generate an error message. Finally, the OS should instantly return to the user interface when the application shuts down, so that the user can choose another application.

Organizing and Manipulating Programs and Data

A single PC might store hundreds of programs and thousands of separate pieces of data. Simply making all the programs and data visible would be like taking all the shoes in the back of the shoe store and setting them neatly on the display room floor. Yes, you could locate shoes in this fashion, but it would be an overly complicated mess. Much better to have some method of organizing the programs and data.

Okay, I hear you saying, I'll buy into that, but how? Let's break it down. First question: [holds up chunk of binary code] Is this a program or a piece of data used by a program? Read the label! The OS must provide a label or name for each program and each individual piece of data that identifies it as either a program or a piece of data. If it's data, there must also be some method by which the OS can identify what type of program uses it.

Next question: How can I distinguish between the various places I might store this chunk of data or program? Each floppy disk, hard drive, and optical drive needs some sort of identifier, again provided by the OS. It can be as simple as a letter of the alphabet or as complex as a fully descriptive phrase.

Third question: [picks up several more chunks of data] How can I make sure that related chunks of data or programs are stored in a way that permits efficient retrieval and alteration? Data and programs must be stored in distinct groups on each drive, and the OS user interface must enable users to interact with each of these groups individually. Users must be able to open and close these groups, and copy, move, or delete both programs and data. Finally, a good OS will have a user interface that enables users to perform these functions easily and accurately, especially in the case of deletions. Clearly, a good OS has a lot of work to do!

Essentials

Today's Operating Systems

The CompTIA A+ certification concentrates almost exclusively on one operating system: Microsoft Windows. To be even more specific, CompTIA A+ certification only concentrates on two versions of Microsoft Windows: Microsoft Windows 2000 Professional and Microsoft Windows XP. That's not a bad idea on CompTIA's part, given that these two versions of Windows are easily the most common operating systems used today! Still, it's important that you understand there are a lot of operating systems available today beyond just these two, including a large number of Windows versions. You may only need to know Windows 2000 and XP in detail for the exams, but life as a tech will test you on the capabilities of others.

Microsoft Windows

Windows is the trade name for a very large family of Microsoft operating systems created over the last 20 years. The earliest versions of Windows were little more than pretty graphical front ends for the ancient DOS operating system. Windows as a full-blown

OS really got its start with Windows NT 3.1 way back in 1993. Windows NT was the first Microsoft product designed from the ground up to take advantage of 32-bit processing, and it included a number of important new features such as the now common NTFS file system, enhanced security, and robust network support.

NOTE The first version of Windows NT was numbered 3.1 to match up with the then-popular version of old-style Windows called 3.1.

Windows NT 3.1 came out in two versions: Workstation and Advanced Server. The Workstation version was for—duh—workstations. The Advanced Server version was basically just the Workstation version with lots of extra built-in software to support servers.

Windows NT went through a number of upgrades, with each version adding improvements, such as better network support, and enhancements in NTFS. Figure 12-3 shows Windows NT version 4.0.

Figure 12-3 Windows NT version 4.0

The only problem with NT was that it had high hardware requirements and didn't play well with older programs written for earlier versions of Windows. To keep lower-end users happy, Microsoft upgraded the old Windows into a patched-together operating system called Windows 95. Windows 95, along with its successors, Windows 98 (Figure 12-4) and the infamous Windows Me, were tasked with the difficult job of trying to be 32-bit operating systems that had virtually complete backward compatibility with every program ever written for Windows 3.*x* or even the old DOS. As a result, these versions of Windows (we call the entire family Windows 9*x*) only used FAT or FAT32, had a zillion little configurations files, and were prone to many problems.

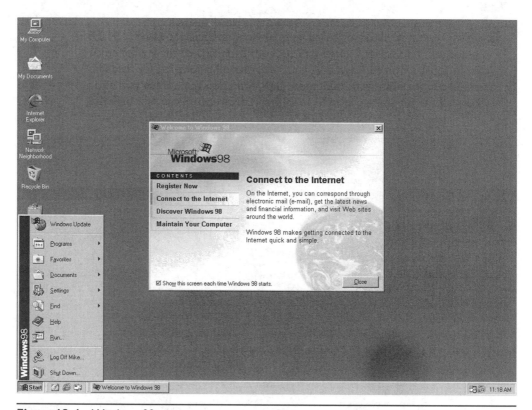

Figure 12-4   Windows 98

Windows 2000 (Figure 12-5) was really just Windows NT with a number of very nice improvements, such as plug and play—the ability to just insert a device and have it work—and a greatly improved interface. Like NT, Windows 2000 came out in a workstation version (called Windows 2000 Professional) and a server version (called Windows 2000 Server). Microsoft kept selling Windows 9x versions, but a large number of users liked Windows 2000 so much that even more casual users (like home users) went to Windows 2000 Professional.

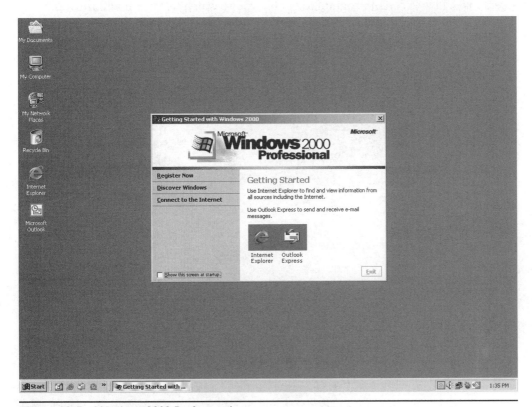

Figure 12-5 Windows 2000 Professional

Microsoft officially ended the Windows 9*x* product line with the introduction of Windows XP in 2001. Windows XP was designed for everyone from casual home users to the heaviest workstation users. XP is based on the NT/2000 operating systems and uses NTFS. There is no server version of Windows XP, but there are five user versions. Windows XP Professional (Figure 12-6) is designed to work in Windows networks that use Active Directory (I discuss Active Directory in Chapter 23). Windows XP Home Edition is designed for single users or small networks that do not use Active Directory. Windows XP Media Center is a version of Windows XP Home Edition that comes with a Personal Video Recorder program to enable you to watch television and movies. Windows XP Tablet PC Edition is a version of Windows XP Professional with additional support for tablet PCs. Finally Windows XP Professional x64 is for 64-bit CPUs.

Figure 12-6 Windows XP Professional

The current server version is called Windows Server 2003 (Figure 12-7). It's very similar to Windows 2000 Server but adds a few handy extras that people who run large networks really like. Windows 2003 comes in 32-bit and 64-bit versions.

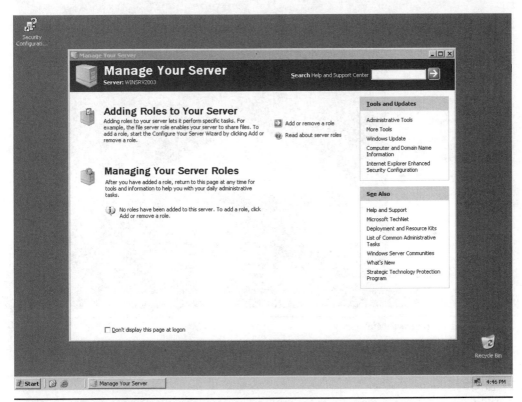

Figure 12-7 Windows Server 2003

The latest version of Windows is called Windows Vista (Figure 12-8). Vista, which comes in multiple versions, is basically a rewritten Windows XP in terms of its structure and function, but it comes with a broad array of new desktop enhancements that improve usability.

Figure 12-8   Windows Vista

Mac OS

Apple Computer has a reputation for making great operating systems to run on their computers. Macintosh computers were running graphical user interfaces (GUIs) back in the days when PCs were still using DOS, and Microsoft has (arguably) been playing catch up with Apple ever since. It's a bit easier for Apple to add features to their computers, since all Apple computers are proprietary.

There is no one cover name for Macintosh operating systems like "Windows"—Apple just calls their operating systems Mac OS. Figure 12-9 shows the latest version: OS X (pronounced "ten," not "ex"). Originally, Macs ran on non-Intel CPUs, but starting in 2006, Macs run on Intel CPUs, just like PCs that run Windows.

Figure 12-9 Apple's Mac OS X

Apple always made their own operating systems with names such as System 7, Mac OS 8, and Mac OS 9. However, in 2001 Apple switched to Mac OS X, an OS based on the BSD variant of UNIX. Mac OS is now a flavor of UNIX—although heavily customized by Apple.

UNIX

UNIX is the oldest, most powerful, and most influential operating system ever invented. Though old, UNIX has gone through generation after generation of updates and is the operating system chosen by those geeky folks who need detailed control and raw power out of their operating system. UNIX was first developed by Bell Labs in the early 1970s and has spawned not only new versions but also entire subclasses of UNIX. It's hard to say how many variations of UNIX exist, as sometimes the variations are subtle. A good but unscientific guess would be in the area of 500 clearly defined versions!

Every popular operating system—Windows, Mac OS, even the ancient DOS—used concepts from UNIX as a starting point. Mac OS may be the leader in cool ways to make an OS user interface, but UNIX has always defined how your OS worked behind the scenes. So many things we never think about came from UNIX: hard drive volumes and tree-structured directories are just two of thousands of innovations that come from UNIX. So even if you don't use UNIX, many of the aspects of the OS you do use came from UNIX.

Linux

Linux is a UNIX clone written by a fellow named Linus Torvalds in 1991, and it has been updated constantly—almost daily—since then (Figure 12-10). Linux was designed from the beginning to run on Intel/AMD processors and has one aspect that makes it unique among popular operating systems—it's totally free. Not only is it totally free, all of the source code (the actual code the programmers wrote to make Linux) is also freely available to be used and changed. To do this, Linux uses the GNU public license, which is managed by the Free Software Foundation, a nonprofit organization that promotes open source software.

Figure 12-10   Linux operating system

Technically, Linux is only the core operating system part of the big GNU picture. Other parts of GNU include the interface, device drivers, and lots of other parts that Linux doesn't have any part of developing. The GNU license covers literally tens of thousands of different programs, from games to fonts to word processing programs, so no one would ever download everything. Instead, companies (and sometimes just groups of people) take the Linux core and add different bits and pieces of GNU (or other) software to make what are called *Linux distributions (distros)*. There are quite a few Linux distributions available, but here are a few of the more famous ones:

- **Fedora Core**   A popular general-purpose Linux, derived from Red Hat Linux.
- **Debian**   Used for everything from individual systems to powerful servers.
- **Slackware**   A favorite distro for folks who are good at Linux—flexible but not as user friendly.
- **Ubuntu**   Based on Debian but designed for easy use by individual users.
- **SuSE**   Another popular general-purpose distro.

Installing/Upgrading Windows

Installing or upgrading an OS is like any good story: it has a beginning, a middle, and an end. In this case, the beginning is the several tasks you need to do before you actually do the installation or upgrade. If you do your homework here, the installation process is a breeze, and the post-installation tasks are minimal. In the next section, I'll give you my short list of preparation tasks, the generic procedure for installing Windows, and the tasks you need to do after the installation.

Preparing for Installation or Upgrade

Working with PCs gives us many exciting opportunities for frustrating delays and unproductive side trips! Because installing an OS can be a time-consuming task, even when everything goes right, the Windows installation process holds great potential for lost time. Nothing sets the teeth to grinding as much as encountering an indecipherable or ambiguous error message or the infamous Blue Screen of Death 55 minutes into an hour-long system installation.

NOTE   Never heard of the Blue Screen of Death? Stay tuned—you will!

Don't get discouraged at all the preparation tasks. They usually go pretty fast, and skipping them can cause you gobs of grief later when you're in the middle of installing and things blow up. Well, maybe there isn't a real explosion, but the computer might lock up and refuse to boot into anything usable. With that in mind, let's look at the nine tasks you need to complete *before* you insert that CD or DVD. Here's the list; discussion follows:

1. Identify hardware requirements.
2. Verify hardware and software compatibility.
3. Decide whether to perform a clean installation or an upgrade.
4. Determine how to back up and restore existing data, if necessary.
5. Select an installation method.
6. Determine how to partition the hard drive and what file system to use.
7. Determine your computer's network role.
8. Decide on your computer's language and locale settings.
9. Plan for post-installation tasks.

Identify Hardware Requirements

Hardware requirements help you decide whether a computer system is a reasonable host for a particular operating system. Requirements include the CPU model, the amount of RAM, the amount of free hard disk space, and the video adapter, display, and storage devices that may be required to install and run the operating system. They are stated as minimums or, more recently, as recommended minimums. Although you could install an operating system on a computer with the old minimums that Microsoft published, they were not realistic if you wanted to actually accomplish work. With the last few versions of Windows, Microsoft has published recommended minimums that are much more realistic. You will find the published minimums on the packaging and at Microsoft's Web site (www.microsoft.com). Later in this chapter, I'll also tell you what I recommend as minimums for Windows 2000 and Windows XP.

Verify Hardware and Software Compatibility

Assuming your system meets the requirements, you next need to find out how well Windows supports the brand and model of hardware and the application software you intend to use under Windows. You have two basic sources for this information: Microsoft and the manufacturer of the device or software. How do you actually access this information? Use the Web!

If you're installing Windows XP, the Setup Wizard automatically checks your hardware and software and reports any potential conflicts. But please don't wait until you are all ready to install to check this out. With any flavor of Windows, *first do your homework!*

Microsoft goes to great lengths to test any piece of hardware that might be used in a system running Windows through their *Windows Marketplace* (Figure 12-11). Windows Marketplace, formerly known as the *Hardware Compatibility List (HCL)*, is the definitive authority as to whether your component is compatible with the OS. Every component listed on the Windows Marketplace Web site has been extensively tested to verify it works with Windows 2000 and XP and is guaranteed by Microsoft to work with your installation. The URL for Windows Marketplace is www.windowsmarketplace.com.

Figure 12-11 Windows Marketplace

 NOTE The Windows Catalog also lists compatible software.

When you install a device that's not tested by Microsoft, a rather scary screen appears (Figure 12-12). This doesn't mean the component won't work, only that it's not been tested. Not all component makers go through the rather painful process of getting the Microsoft approval so they can list their component in the Windows Marketplace. As a rule of thumb, unless the device is more than five years old, go ahead and install it. If it still doesn't work, you can simply uninstall it later.

Figure 12-12
Untested device!

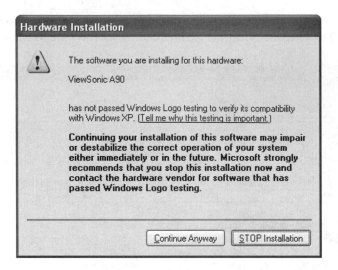

Hardware Installation

⚠ The software you are installing for this hardware:

ViewSonic A90

has not passed Windows Logo testing to verify its compatibility with Windows XP. (Tell me why this testing is important.)

Continuing your installation of this software may impair or destabilize the correct operation of your system either immediately or in the future. Microsoft strongly recommends that you stop this installation now and contact the hardware vendor for software that has passed Windows Logo testing.

[Continue Anyway]   [STOP Installation]

Don't panic if you don't see your device on the list; many supported devices aren't on it. Check the floppies or CD-ROMs that came with your hardware for proper drivers. Better yet, check the manufacturer's Web site for compatible drivers. Even when the Windows Marketplace lists a piece of hardware, I still make a point of checking the manufacturer's Web site for newer drivers.

When preparing to upgrade, check with the manufacturers of the applications already installed in the previous OS. If there are software compatibility problems with the versions you have, the manufacturer should provide upgrade packs that can be installed during the Windows setup process.

Decide Whether to Perform a Clean Installation or an Upgrade

A clean installation of an OS involves installing it onto an empty hard drive with no previous OS installed. An upgrade installation is an installation of an OS on top of an earlier installed version, thus inheriting all previous hardware and software settings.

You may think the choice between doing a clean installation and an upgrade installation is simple: you do a clean installation on a brand new computer with an empty hard drive, and you do an upgrade of a preexisting installation. It isn't necessarily so! I'll tell you why as we look at this issue more closely.

EXAM TIP CompTIA tests you on your ability to upgrade a Windows 9x or Windows NT system to Windows 2000 or Windows XP. You do not need to know about Windows 9x or NT for the tests, but you do need to know how to upgrade them!

Clean Installation   A clean installation usually begins with a completely empty hard disk. The advantage to doing a clean installation is that you don't carry problems from the old OS over to the new one, but the disadvantage is that all applications have to be reinstalled and the desktop and each application reconfigured to the user's preferences. You perform a clean install by resetting your CMOS to tell the system to boot from the CD-media drive before your hard drive. You then boot off a Windows 2000 or XP Installation CD-ROM, and Windows will give you the opportunity to partition and format the hard drive and then install Windows.

Upgrade Installation   In an upgrade installation, the new OS installs into the same folders as the old OS, or in tech speak, the new installs *on top of* the old. The new OS replaces the old OS but retains all saved data and inherits all the previous settings (such as font styles, desktop colors and background, and so on), hardware, and applications. You don't have to reinstall your favorite programs!

TIP   Before starting an OS upgrade, make sure you have shut down all other open applications!

To begin the upgrade of Windows, you must run the appropriate program from the CD-ROM. This usually means inserting a Windows 2000 or Windows XP installation CD-ROM into your system while your old OS is running, which will start the install program. Then, to do an upgrade, you indicate that Windows 2000 or XP should install into a directory that already contains an installation of Windows (it will do this by default). You will be asked whether it is an upgrade or a new installation; if you select new installation, it will remove the existing OS before installing.

If for some reason the install program doesn't start automatically, go to My Computer, open the CD-ROM, and locate WINNT32.EXE. This program starts an upgrade to Windows 2000 or XP.

Multiboot   A third option that you need to be aware of is dual boot. Both Windows 2000 and Windows XP can install in a separate folder from your existing copy of Windows. Then every time your computer boots, you'll get a menu asking you which version of Windows you wish to boot. Multiboot sounds great, but it has lots of nasty little problems. For example, let's say you've got a system running Windows Me that you would like to upgrade to Windows XP. Windows Me must use either a FAT or a FAT32 file system; Windows XP can use these old file systems, but you'll miss out on the benefits of using NTFS.

When configuring a computer for multibooting, there are two basic rules: first, the system partition must be formatted in a file system that is common to all installed OSs, and second, if you're including Windows 98, you must install it first, and then install the other operating systems in order from oldest to newest.

Other Installation Methods   In medium to large organizations, more advanced installation methods are often employed, especially when many computers need to be identically configured. A common method is to place the source files in a shared directory on a network server. Then, whenever a tech needs to install a new OS, it is a simple task of booting up the computer, connecting to the source location on the network, and starting the installation from there. This method alone has many variations, and it can be automated with special scripts that automatically select the options and components needed. The scripts can even install the necessary applications at the end of the OS installation—all without user intervention once the installation has been started.

TIP Scripting OS and application installations is a full-time job in many organizations. There are many scripting tools and methods available from both Microsoft and third-party sources.

Another type of installation that is very popular for re-creating standard configurations is an *image installation*. An image is a complete copy of a hard disk volume on which an operating system and, usually, all required application software has been preinstalled. Images can be on CD-media, in which case the tech runs special software on the computer that copies the image onto the local hard drive. Images can also be stored on special network servers, in which case the tech connects to the image server using special software and copies the image from the server to the local hard drive. A leader in this technology has been Norton Ghost, which is available from Symantec. Other similar programs are PowerQuest's Drive Image and Acronis's True Image.

Beginning with Windows 2000 Server, Microsoft added *Remote Installation Services (RIS)*, which can be used to initiate either a scripted installation or an installation of an image.

Determine How to Back Up and Restore Existing Data, if Necessary

Whether you are installing or upgrading, you may need to back up existing user data before installing or upgrading because things can go very wrong either way, and the data on the hard drive might be damaged. You'll need to find out where the user is currently saving data files. If they are being saved onto the local hard drive, it must be backed up before the installation or replacement takes place, in order to preserve the data. However, if all data has been saved to a network location, you are in luck because the data is safe from damage during installation.

If the user saves data locally, and the computer is connected to a network, save the data, at least temporarily, to a network location until after the upgrade or installation has taken place. If the computer is not connected to a network, but the computer has a burnable CD-media or DVD drive, copy the data to CDs or DVDs. Wherever you save the data, you will need to copy or restore any lost or damaged data back to the local hard disk after the installation.

Select an Installation Method

Once you've backed up everything important, you need to select an installation method. You have two basic choices: insert the CD-ROM disc into the drive and go, or install over a network. The latter method falls into the realm of CompTIA Network+ technicians or even network administrators, so this book assumes you'll install from disc.

Determine How to Partition the Hard Drive and What File System to Use

If you are performing a clean installation, you need to decide ahead of time how to partition the disk space on your hard disk drive, including the number and size of partitions and the file system you will use. Actually, in the decision process, the file system comes first, and then the space issue follows, as you will see.

If you are not planning a multiboot installation, use NTFS. If you are planning a multiboot configuration, the highest common denominator rule applies, at least for the system volume, and for any volumes you want usable by the oldest OS. Once you know which file system you are using, deciding the size and number of partitions will follow, because if you decide to use FAT16, you will have the size limitations of FAT16 to deal with.

Determine Your Computer's Network Role

The question of your computer's network role comes up in one form or another during a Windows installation. A Windows computer can have one of several roles relative to a network (in Microsoft terms). One role, called *standalone*, is actually a non-network role, and it simply means that the computer does not participate on a network. Any version of Windows can be installed on a standalone computer, and this is the only role that a Windows XP Home computer can play on a network. Every other modern version of Windows can be a member of either a workgroup or domain. You will learn more about the workgroup and domain member roles in Chapter 21.

Decide on Your Computer's Language and Locale Settings

These settings are especially important for Windows 2000 and Windows XP, because these versions have greatly increased support for various spoken languages and locale conventions. The locale settings determine how date and time information is displayed, and which math separators and currency symbols are used for various locations.

Plan for Post-Installation Tasks

After installing Windows, you will need to install the latest service pack or update. You may also need to install updated drivers and reconfigure any settings, such as network settings, that were found not to work. You will also need to install any applications (word processor, spreadsheet, database, etc.) required by the user of the computer. Finally, don't forget to restore any data backed up before the installation or upgrade.

Performing the Installation or Upgrade

When doing a Windows installation (also called setup) you'll notice that the screen progresses from simple textual information on a plain background to a full graphical interface. During text mode, the computer is inspecting the hardware, and it will then display the *End User License Agreement (EULA)*, which must be accepted for setup to continue. It is during the text display portion of an installation that you can partition your hard disk. Also during this time, the computer copies files to the local hard disk, including a base set of files for running the graphical portion of the setup.

When finished with the text part of the setup, the computer reboots, which starts the graphical portion of the installation. You are prompted to enter the product key, which is invariably located on the CD/DVD case. Most techs learn the hard way that these covers tend to disappear when you need them most, and they write the product code directly on the CD or DVD itself. (Just don't use a ballpoint pen; it'll scratch the surface of the disc.) See Figure 12-13.

Figure 12-13
Product key written
on the installation
CD-ROM

Most of the installation process takes place in the graphical portion. This is where you select configuration options and choose optional Windows components.

No matter your version of Windows, the installation process always gets to the point where Windows begins to install itself on the system. I call this "The Big Copy" and use this time to catch up on my reading, eat a sandwich, or count ceiling tiles.

 TIP Windows comes in both upgrade and full versions. Make sure you use the correct CD-ROM! Some systems, particularly laptops, require a special OEM version made just for that system. Don't bother trying to use an upgrade version to install on a blank drive unless you also possess a CD-ROM with a full earlier version of Windows.

Post-Installation Tasks

You might think that's enough work for one day, but there are a few more things on your task list. They include updating the OS with patches and service packs, upgrading drivers, restoring user data files, and identifying installation problems (if they occur).

Identifying Installation Problems

After you install or upgrade Windows, you only need to use your powers of observation to check whether you had a serious installation problem. The worst problems show up early in the installation process, but others may show up later as you work in Windows. If your installation wasn't successful, check out the last major section of this chapter ("Troubleshooting Installation Problems"), where I will tell you about common installation problems.

Patches, Service Packs, and Updates

Someone once described an airliner as consisting of millions of parts flying in close formation. I think that's also a good description for an operating system. And we can even carry that analogy further by thinking about all the maintenance required to keep an airliner safely flying. Like an airliner, the parts (programming code) of your OS were created by different people, and some parts may even have been contracted out. Although each component is tested as much as possible, and the assembled OS is also tested, it's not possible to test for every possible combination of events. Sometimes a piece is simply found to be defective. The fix for such a problem is a corrective program called a *patch*.

In the past, Microsoft would provide patches for individual problems. They would also accumulate patches until they reached some sort of "critical mass" and then bundle them together as a *service pack*. They still do this. But they also make it easier for you to find and install the appropriate patches and service packs, which, when combined together, are called *updates*. They make these updates available at their Web site or on CD-ROM. Many organizations make the updates available for distribution from network servers. Immediately after installing Windows, install the latest updates on the computer. Chapter 15 covers this process more fully.

Upgrading Drivers

Even if you did all your pre-installation tasks, you may decide to go with the default drivers that come with Windows, and then upgrade them to the latest drivers after the fact. In fact, this is a good strategy, because installation is a complicated task, and you can simplify it by installing old but adequate drivers. Maybe those newest drivers are just a week old—waiting until after the Windows install to install new drivers will give you a usable driver to go back to if the new driver turns out to be a lemon. In Chapters 15 and 16 you'll learn more about working with drivers, including a little driver magic called driver rollback.

Restoring User Data Files (if Applicable)

Remember when you backed up the user data files before installation? You don't? Well, check again, because now is the time to restore that data. Your method of restoring will depend on how you backed up the files in the first place. If you used a third-party backup program, you will need to install it before you can restore those files, but if you used Windows Backup, you are in luck, because it is installed by default. If you did something simpler, like copying to CD-media or a network location, all you have to do is copy the files back to the local hard disk. Good luck!

Installing or Upgrading to Windows 2000 Professional

On the face of it, installing Windows 2000 Professional seems fairly simple. You insert the CD-ROM, access the setup routine, and go! But that conceptualization does not hold up in practice.

Hardware Requirements

The minimum specs represent what Microsoft says you need in order to install the Windows 2000 Professional OS. However, you need to take these specifications and at least double them if you want to be happy with your system's performance!

Here is a more realistic recommendation for a useful Windows 2000 Professional computer system:

Component	Minimum for a Windows 2000 Professional Computer	Recommended for a Windows 2000 Professional Computer
CPU	Intel Pentium 133 MHz	Intel Pentium II 350 MHz
Memory	64 MB	128 MB
Hard disk	2 GB with 650 MB of free space	6.4 GB with 2 GB of free space
Network	None	Modern network card
Display	Video adapter and monitor with VGA resolution	Video adapter and monitor with SVGA resolution, capable of high-color (16-bit) display
Optical drive	If you don't have an optical drive, you must use a floppy disk drive or install over a network	If you don't have an optical drive, you must use a floppy disk drive or install over a network

If your test system(s) exceeds the recommended configuration, all the better! You can never have too fast a processor or too much hard disk space.

Installing or Upgrading to Windows XP Professional

You prepare for a Windows XP installation just as you do for installing Windows 2000. Windows XP has a few different aspects to it that are worth considering as a separate issue.

Upgrade Paths

You can upgrade to Windows XP Professional from all the following versions of Windows:

- Windows 98 (all versions)
- Windows Me
- Windows NT 4.0 Workstation (Service Pack 5 and later)
- Windows 2000 Professional (including service packs)
- Windows XP Home Edition

XP Hardware Requirements

Hardware requirements for Windows XP Professional are higher than for previous versions of Windows but quite in line with even a modestly priced computer today.

Microsoft XP runs on a wide range of computers, but you need to be sure that your computer meets the minimum hardware requirements as shown here. Also shown is my recommended minimum for a system running a typical selection of business productivity software.

Component	Minimum for a Windows XP Computer	Recommended for a Windows XP Computer
CPU	Any Intel or AMD 233 MHz or higher processor	Any Intel or AMD 300 MHz or higher processor
Memory	64 MB of RAM (though Microsoft admits XP will be somewhat crippled with only this amount)	256 MB of RAM or higher
Hard disk	1.5 GB of available hard drive space	4 GB of available hard drive space
Network	None	Modern network card
Display	Video card that supports DirectX 8 with at least 800×600 resolution	Video card that supports DirectX 8 with at least 800×600 resolution
Optical drive	Any CD- or DVD-media drive	Any CD- or DVD-media drive

Hardware and Software Compatibility

You'll need to check hardware and software compatibility before installing Windows XP Professional—either as an upgrade or a new installation. Of course, if you purchase a computer with Windows XP preinstalled, you're spared this task, but you'll still need to verify that the application software you plan to add to the computer will be compatible.

Luckily, you have two tools for determining whether your hardware is compatible: the Windows Catalog and the Upgrade Advisor on the Windows XP CD-ROM.

Upgrade Advisor In my experience, Windows XP has supported a wide range of hardware and software, including some rather old "no name" computers, but I like to be proactive when planning an installation, especially an upgrade. You may not have the luxury of time in upgrading a computer, however. You may be asked by your boss or client to perform an upgrade *now*. Fortunately, the Upgrade Advisor is the first process that runs on the XP installation CD-ROM. It examines your hardware and installed software (in the case of an upgrade) and provides a list of devices and software that are known to have issues with XP. Be sure to follow the suggestions on this list!

The Upgrade Advisor can also be run separately from the Windows XP installation. You can run it from the Windows XP CD-ROM, or, if you want to find out about compatibility for an upgrade before purchasing Windows XP, you can download the Upgrade Advisor from Microsoft's Web site (www.microsoft.com—search for "Upgrade Advisor"). Follow the instructions in the sidebar to use the online Upgrade Advisor.

I ran the advisor on a test computer at the office that was running Windows 98. It produced a report that found only one incompatibility—an antivirus program. The details stated that the program was compatible only if installed after Windows XP was installed. Therefore, it suggested removing the program before installing the OS, and then reinstalling it after the OS was installed. Don't ignore the instructions provided by the Upgrade Advisor!

Booting into Windows XP Setup

The Windows XP CD-ROMs are bootable, and Microsoft no longer includes a program to create a set of setup boot disks. This should not be an issue, because PCs manufactured in the last several years have the ability to boot from the optical drive. This system BIOS setting, usually described as "boot order," is controlled through a PC's BIOS-based setup program.

In the unlikely event that your lab computer can't be made to boot from CD-media, you can create a set of six (yes!) Windows XP setup boot floppy disks using a special program you can download from Microsoft's Web site. Note that Microsoft provides separate boot disk programs for XP Home and XP Pro.

Registration Versus Activation

During setup, you will be prompted to register your product and activate it. Many people confuse activation with registration, but these are two separate operations. Registration is informing Microsoft who the official owner or user of the product is, providing contact information such as name, address, company, phone number, e-mail address, and so on. Registration is still entirely optional. Activation is a way to combat software piracy, meaning that Microsoft wishes to ensure that each license for Windows XP is used solely on a single computer. It's more formally called *Microsoft Product Activation (MPA)*.

Mandatory Activation Within 30 Days of Installation   Activation is mandatory, but you can skip this step during installation. You will have 30 days in which to activate the product, during which time it will work normally. If you don't activate it within that time frame, it will be disabled. Don't worry about forgetting, though, because once it's installed, Windows XP frequently reminds you to activate it with a balloon message over the tray area of the taskbar. The messages even tell you how many days you have left.

Activation Mechanics   Here is how product activation works. When you choose to activate, either during setup or later when XP reminds you to do it, the product ID code that you entered during installation is combined with a 50-digit value that identifies your key hardware components to create an installation ID code. You must send this code to Microsoft, either automatically if you have an Internet connection, or verbally via a phone call to Microsoft. Microsoft then returns a 42-digit product activation code. If you are activating online, you don't have to enter the activation code; it will happen automatically. If you are activating over the phone, you must read the installation ID to a representative and enter the resulting 42-digit activation code into the Activate Windows by Phone dialog box.

No personal information about you is sent as part of the activation process. Figure 12-14 shows the dialog box that will open when you start activation by clicking on the reminder message balloon.

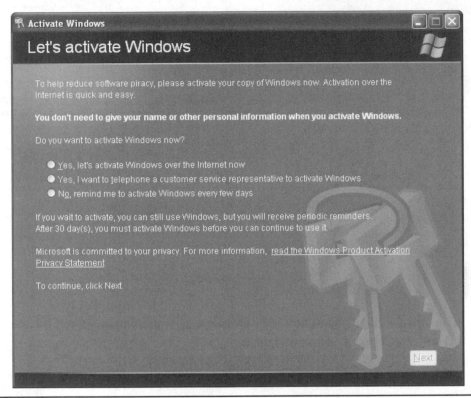

Figure 12-14   Activation will take just seconds with an Internet connection.

Upgrading Issues for Windows 2000 and Windows XP

Upgrading your computer system from an earlier version of Windows can be a tricky affair, with its own set of pitfalls. It is important to note that you have a somewhat higher risk of running into errors during an upgrade than you do when performing a "clean" installation.

Here are some of the issues that you should be aware of before performing an upgrade:

- You can upgrade directly to Windows 2000 Professional from Windows 95/98 (but not Windows Me) and Windows NT Workstation.

- Because of differences between Windows 9*x* and Windows 2000/XP, you might find that some programs that ran well under Windows 9*x* will not run under Windows 2000/XP. Not only does Windows 2000/XP have new hardware requirements, it also does not like a lot of Windows 9*x* software!

- Third-party disk compression applications are not supported by Windows 2000/XP.

- Third-party power management applications are also likely to cause problems with a Windows 2000/XP installation.

Obviously, it's worth your time to take a few extra steps before you pop in that installation CD-ROM! If you plan to upgrade rather than perform a clean installation, follow these steps first:

1. Check out the Windows Marketplace Web site or run a compatibility report using the Check Upgrade utility provided with Windows 2000 Professional or the Upgrade Advisor for Windows XP. These utilities generate a detailed list of potentially problematic devices and applications. You can run the utility in both 2000 and XP as follows: Insert the Windows Installation CD-ROM and, from your current OS, open a command prompt or use the Start Run dialog box to run the WINNT32.EXE program with the CHECKUPGRADEONLY switch turned on. The command line will look like this: `d:\i386\winnt32 /checkupgradeonly` (where `d:` is the optical drive).

2. Have an up-to-date backup of your data and configuration files handy.

3. Perform a "spring cleaning" on your system by uninstalling unused or unnecessary applications and deleting old files.

4. Perform a disk scan and a disk defragmentation.

5. Uncompress all files, folders, and partitions.

6. Perform a virus scan, and then remove or disable all virus-checking software.

7. Disable virus checking in your system CMOS.

8. Keep in mind that if worse comes to worst, you may have to start over and do a clean installation anyway. This makes step 2 exceedingly important! Back up your data!

The Windows 2000/XP Clean Install Process

The steps involved in a clean installation of Windows 2000 Professional and Windows XP are virtually identical. The only differences are the order of two steps and some of the art on the screens that appear, so we can comfortably discuss both installations at the same time.

 NOTE Not all screens in the install process are shown!

A clean install begins with your system set to boot to your optical drive and the Windows Install CD-ROM in the drive. You start your PC, and assuming you've got the boot order right, the install program starts booting (Figure 12-15). Note at the bottom that it says to press F6 for a third-party SCSI or RAID driver. This is only done if you want to install Windows onto a strange drive and Windows does not already have the driver for that drive. Don't worry about this—Windows has a huge assortment of drivers for just about every hard drive ever made, and in the rare situation where you need a third-party driver, the folks who sell you the SCSI or RAID array will tell you ahead of time.

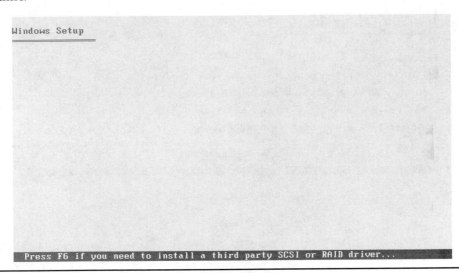

```
Windows Setup




















   Press F6 if you need to install a third party SCSI or RAID driver...
```

Figure 12-15   Windows Setup text screen

After the system copies a number of files, you'll see the Welcome screen (Figure 12-16). This is an important screen! As you'll see in later chapters, techs often use the Windows Install CD-ROM as a repair tool, and this is the screen that lets you choose between installing Windows or repairing an existing installation. Since you're making a new install, just press ENTER.

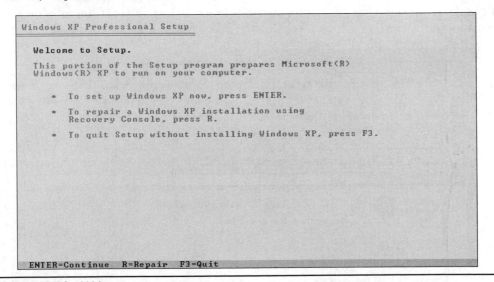

```
Windows XP Professional Setup

  Welcome to Setup.

  This portion of the Setup program prepares Microsoft(R)
  Windows(R) XP to run on your computer.

     •  To set up Windows XP now, press ENTER.

     •  To repair a Windows XP installation using
        Recovery Console, press R.

     •  To quit Setup without installing Windows XP, press F3.












  ENTER=Continue   R=Repair   F3=Quit
```

Figure 12-16   Welcome text screen

You're now prompted to read and accept the End User License Agreement (EULA). Nobody ever reads this—it just gives you a stomachache when you see what you're really agreeing to—so just press F8 and move to the next screen to start partitioning the drive (Figure 12-17).

```
Windows XP Professional Setup

   The following list shows the existing partitions and
   unpartitioned space on this computer.

   Use the UP and DOWN ARROW keys to select an item in the list.

     •  To set up Windows XP on the selected item, press ENTER.

     •  To create a partition in the unpartitioned space, press C.

     •  To delete the selected partition, press D.

   ┌──────────────────────────────────────────────────────────────┐
   │ 8190 MB Disk 0 at Id 0 on bus 0 on atapi [MBR]                 │
   │       Unpartitioned space                        8189 MB       │
   │                                                                │
   │                                                                │
   │                                                                │
   │                                                                │
   │                                                                │
   └──────────────────────────────────────────────────────────────┘

   ENTER=Install   C=Create Partition   F3=Quit
```

Figure 12-17   Partitioning text screen

If your hard disk is unpartitioned, you will need to create a new partition when prompted. Follow the instructions. In most cases, you can make a single partition, although you can easily make as many partitions as you wish. You can also delete partitions if you're using a hard drive that was partitioned in the past (or if you mess up your partitioning). Note that there is no option to make a primary or extended partition; this tool makes the first partition primary and the rest extended.

 NOTE   Many techie types, at least those with bigger (> 100 GB) hard drives, will only partition half of their hard drive for Windows. This makes it easy for them to install an alternative OS (usually Linux) at a later date!

After you've made the partition(s), you must select the partition on which to install XP (sort of trivial if you only have one partition), and then you need to decide which file system format to use for the new partition. Unless you have some weird need to support FAT or FAT32, format the partition using NTFS (Figure 12-18).

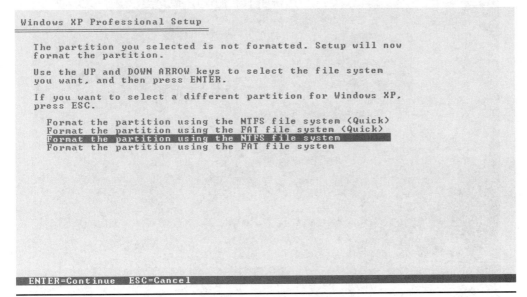

```
Windows XP Professional Setup

    The partition you selected is not formatted. Setup will now
    format the partition.

    Use the UP and DOWN ARROW keys to select the file system
    you want, and then press ENTER.

    If you want to select a different partition for Windows XP,
    press ESC.

        Format the partition using the NTFS file system (Quick)
        Format the partition using the FAT file system (Quick)
        Format the partition using the NTFS file system
        Format the partition using the FAT file system




    ENTER=Continue   ESC=Cancel
```

Figure 12-18   Choosing NTFS

Setup will now format the drive and copy some basic installation files to the newly formatted partition, displaying another progress bar. Go get a book to read while you wait.

After it completes copying the base set of files to the hard drive, your computer reboots, and the graphical mode of Windows setup begins. This is where 2000 and XP begin to vary in appearance, even though they are performing the same steps. The rest of this section shows Windows XP. If you're running a Windows 2000 install, compare it to the screens you see here—it's interesting to see the different presentation doing the same job.

You will see a generic screen during the install that looks like Figure 12-19. On the left of the screen, uncompleted tasks have a white button, completed tasks have a green button, and the current task has a red button. You'll get plenty of advertising to read as you install.

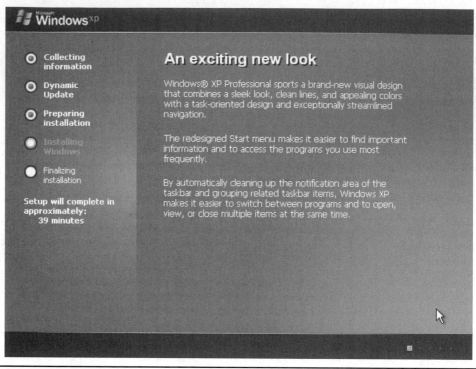

Figure 12-19   Beginning of graphical mode

The following screens ask questions about a number of things the computer needs to know. They include the desired region and language the computer will operate in, your name and organization for personalizing your computer, and a valid product key for Windows XP (Figure 12-20). Be sure to enter the product key exactly, or you will be unable to continue.

   NOTE   Losing your product key is a bad idea! Document it—at least write it on the install CD-ROM.

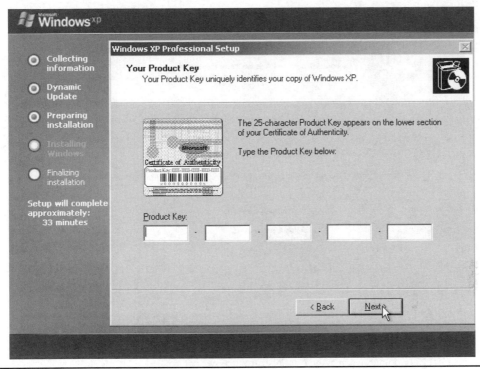

Figure 12-20   Product key

Next, you need to give your computer a name that will identify it on a network. Check with your system administrator for an appropriate name. If you don't have a system administrator, just enter a simple name like MYPC for now—you can change this at any time—and read up on networking later in this book. You also need to create a password for the Administrator user account (Figure 12-21). Every Windows system has an Administrator user account that can do anything on the computer. Techs will need this account to modify and fix the computer in the future.

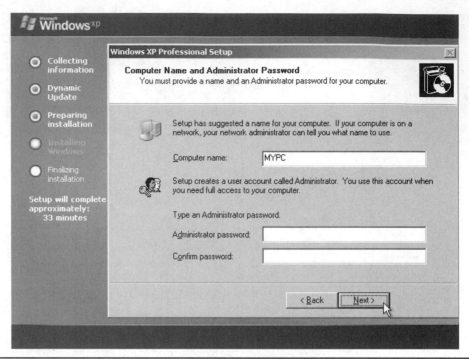

Figure 12-21   Computer name and Administrator password

Last, you're asked for the correct date, time, and time zone. Then Windows tries to detect a network card. If a network card is detected, the network components will be installed and you'll have an opportunity to configure the network settings. Unless you know you need special settings for your network, just select the Typical Settings option (Figure 12-22). Relax; XP will do most of the work for you. Plus it's easy to change network settings after the installation.

NOTE   Even experienced techs usually select the Typical Settings option! Installation is not the time to be messing with network details unless you need to!

Install now begins the big copy of files from the CD-ROM to your hard drive. This is a good time to pick your book back up, because watching the ads is boring (Figure 12-23).

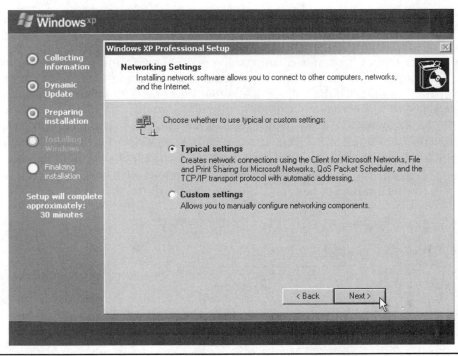

Figure 12-22 Selecting typical network settings

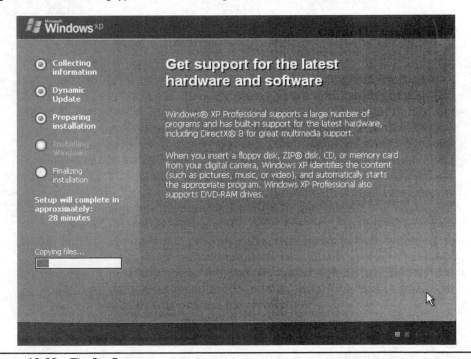

Figure 12-23 The Big Copy

After the files required for the final configuration are copied, XP will reboot again. During this reboot, XP determines your screen size and applies the appropriate resolution. This reboot can take several minutes to complete, so be patient.

Once the reboot is complete, you can log on as the Administrator. Balloon messages may appear over the tray area of the taskbar—a common message concerns the display resolution. Click the balloon and allow Windows XP to automatically adjust the display settings.

The final message in the installation process reminds you that you have 30 days left for activation. Go ahead and activate now over the Internet or by telephone. It's painless and quick. If you choose not to activate, simply click the Close button on the message balloon. That's it! You have successfully installed Windows XP and should have a desktop with the default Bliss background, as shown in Figure 12-24.

Figure 12-24   Windows XP desktop with Bliss background

Automating the Install

As you can see, you may have to sit around for quite a while. Instead of having to sit there answering questions and typing in CD keys, wouldn't it be nice just to boot up the machine and have the install process finish without any intervention on your part? Especially if you have 30 PCs that need to be ready to go tomorrow morning? Fortunately, Windows offers two good options for automating the install process: scripted installations and disk cloning.

Scripting Installations with Setup Manager

Microsoft provides *Setup Manager* to help you create a text file—called an *answer file*—containing all of your answers to the installation questions. Windows doesn't come with Setup Manager, but you can download it from the Microsoft Download Center (www .microsoft.com/downloads) as part of the Windows XP Service Pack 2 Deployment Tools. Setup Manager supports creating answer files for three different types of setups: unattended, sysprep, and Remote Installation Services (Figure 12-25). The current version of the tool can create answer files for Windows XP Home Edition, Windows XP Professional, and Windows Server 2003 (Standard, Enterprise, or Web Edition). See Figure 12-26.

Figure 12-25
Setup Manager can create three different types of answer files.

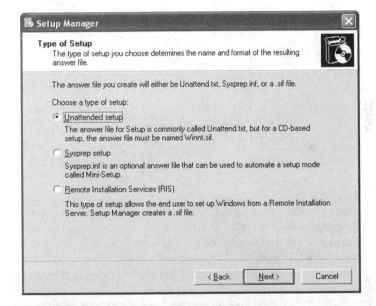

Figure 12-26
Setup Manager can create answer files for five different versions of Windows.

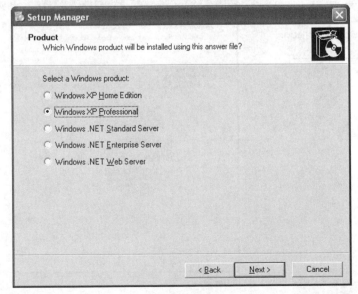

Setup Manager can create an answer file to completely automate the process, or it can be used to set default options. You'll almost always want to create an answer file that automates the entire process (Figure 12-27).

Figure 12-27
Setup Manager can create several kinds of answer files.

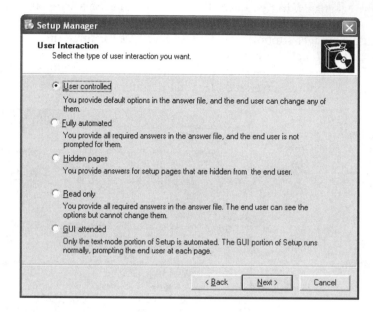

When running a scripted install, you have to decide how to make the installation files themselves available to the PC. While you can always boot your new machine from an installation CD, you can save yourself a lot of CD swapping if you just put the install files on a network share and install your OS over the network (Figure 12-28).

Figure 12-28
Choose where to store the installation files.

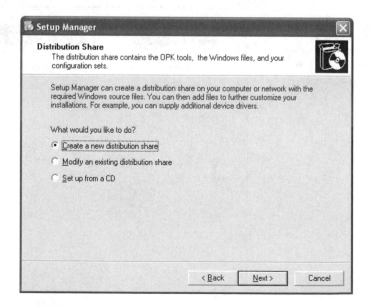

When you run Setup Manager, you get to answer all those pesky questions. As always, you will also have to "accept the terms of the License Agreement" (Figure 12-29) and specify the product key (Figure 12-30), but at least by scripting these steps you can do it once and get it over with.

Figure 12-29
Don't forget to accept the license agreement!

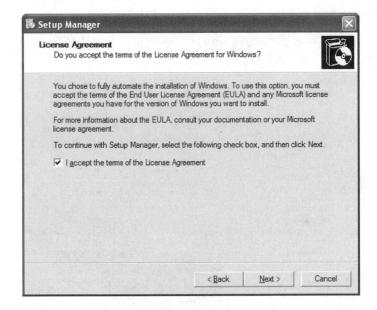

Figure 12-30   Enter the product key.

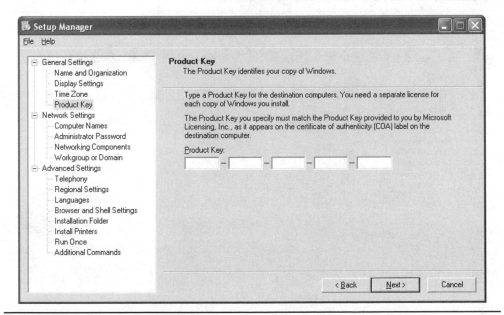

Now it's time to get to the good stuff—customizing your installation. Using the graphical interface, decide what configuration options you want to use—screen resolutions, network options, browser settings, regional settings, and so on. You can even add finishing touches to the installation, installing additional programs such as Microsoft Office and Adobe Reader, by automatically running additional commands after the Windows installation finishes (Figure 12-31). You can also set programs to run once (Figure 12-32).

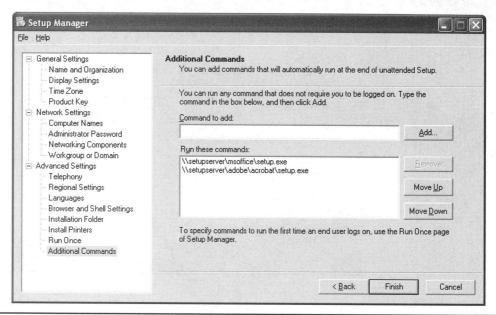

Figure 12-31   Run additional commands.

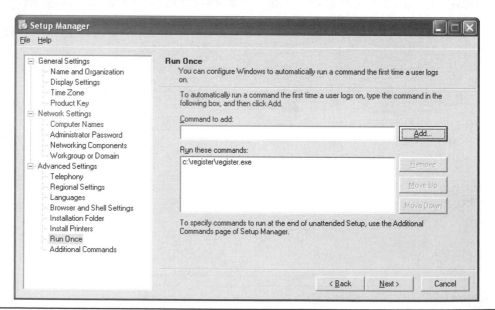

Figure 12-32   Running a program once

Remember that computer names have to be unique on the network. If you're going to use the same answer files for multiple machines on the same network, you need to make sure that each one gets its own unique name. You can either provide a list of names to use, or you can have the setup program randomly generate names (Figure 12-33).

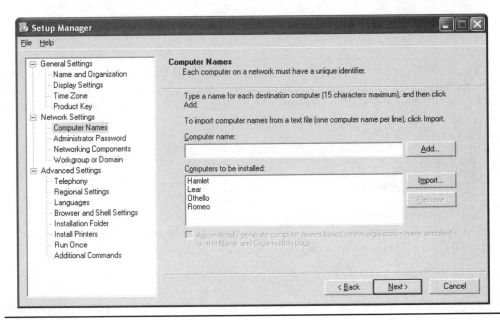

Figure 12-33 Pick your computer names.

When you're done, Setup Manager prompts you to save your answers as a text file. The contents of the file will look something like this:

```
;SetupMgrTag
[Data]
    AutoPartition=1
    MsDosInitiated="0"
    UnattendedInstall="Yes"

[Unattended]
    UnattendMode=FullUnattended
    OemSkipEula=Yes
    OemPreinstall=No
    TargetPath=\WINDOWS

[GuiUnattended]
    AdminPassword=414c11f760b0064 ... [out to 64 characters]
    EncryptedAdminPassword=Yes
    OEMSkipRegional=1
    TimeZone=85
    OemSkipWelcome=1
    AutoLogon=Yes
    AutoLogonCount=1

[UserData]
    ProductKey=FFFFF-FFFFF-FFFFF-FFFFF-FFFFF
```

```
        FullName="Scott"
        OrgName="Total Seminars"
        ComputerName=*

[Identification]
    JoinDomain=TOTAL
    DomainAdmin=admin09
    DomainAdminPassword=my-password


    [
```

The list goes on for another hundred lines or so, and this is a fairly simply answer file. One thing to note is that if you provide a domain administrator's user name and password for the purpose of automatically adding new PCs to your domain, that user name and password will be in the text file in clear text:

```
[Identification]
    JoinDomain=TOTAL
    DomainAdmin=admin09
    DomainAdminPassword=my-password
```

In that case, you will want to be very careful about protecting your setup files.

Once you have your answer file created, you can start your installation with this command, and go enjoy a nice cup of coffee while the installation runs:

```
D:\i386\winnt32 /s:%SetupFiles% /unattend:%AnswerFile%
```

For `%SetupFiles%`, substitute the location of your setup files—either a local path (`D:\i386` if you are installing from a CD) or a network path. If you use a network path, don't forget to create a network boot disk so that the install program can access the files. For `%AnswerFile%`, substitute the name of the text file that you created with Setup Manager (usually `unattend.txt`).

Of course, you don't have to use Setup Manager to create your answer file. Feel free to pull out your favorite text editor and write one from scratch. Most techs, however, will find it much easier to use the provided tool than to wrestle with the answer file's sometimes arcane syntax.

NOTE If you need help creating a network boot floppy or CD, check out www.netbootdisk.com/bootcd.htm.

Scripted installations are a fine option, but they don't necessarily work well in all scenarios. Creating a fully scripted install, including the installation of all additional drivers, software updates, and applications, can be a time-consuming process involving lots of trial-and-error adjustments. Wouldn't it be easier, at least some of the time, to go ahead and take one PC, manually set it up exactly the way you want it, and then automatically create exact copies of that installation on other machines? That's where disk cloning comes into play.

NOTE You can save time by modifying your installation files to include the latest patches by "slipstreaming" your installation files. See the following sites for instructions on how to merge (slipstream) Service Pack 2 into your Windows XP installation files:
www.helpwithwindows.com/WindowsXP/winxp-sp2-bootcd.html
www.winsupersite.com/showcase/windowsxp_sp2_slipstream.asp

Disk Cloning

Disk cloning simply takes an existing PC and makes a full copy of the drive, including all data, software, and configuration files. That copy can then be transferred to as many machines as you like, essentially creating "clones" of the original machine. In the old days, making a clone was pretty simple. You just hooked up two hard drives and copied the files from the original to the clone using something like the venerable XCOPY program (as long as the hard drive was formatted with FAT or FAT32). Today, you'll want to use a more sophisticated program, such as Norton Ghost, which enables you to make an image file that contains a copy of an entire hard drive, and then lets you copy that image either locally or over the network.

 NOTE Norton Ghost is not the only disk imaging software out there, but it is so widely used that techs often refer to disk cloning as "ghosting the drive."

Windows complicates the process of cloning machines because each PC generates a unique security identifier, called the *SID*. Each PC must have its own SID, but if you clone a system, each clone will have the same SID, causing a variety of problems whenever two such machines interact over the network. After cloning a PC, you must somehow change the SID of each clone. The easiest way to do this is to use a utility such as Ghostwalker (included with Norton Ghost) or NewSID (available for download at www.microsoft.com/technet/sysinternals/Security/NewSid.mspx).

Sysprep

Cloning a Windows PC and changing its SID works great for some situations, but what if you need to send the same image out to machines that have slightly different hardware? What if you need the customer to go through the final steps of the Windows installation (creating a user account, accepting the license agreement, etc.)? That's when you need to combine a scripted setup and cloning by using the System Preparation Tool, *sysprep*, which can undo portions of the Windows installation process.

After installing Windows and adding any additional software (Microsoft Office, Adobe Acrobat, Yahoo Instant Messenger, etc.), run sysprep (Figure 12-34) and then create your disk image using the cloning application of your choice. The first time a new system cloned from the image boots, an abbreviated version of setup, Mini-Setup, runs and completes the last few steps of the installation process: creating the new system's SID, installing drivers for hardware, prompting the user to accept the license agreement and create user accounts, and so on. Optionally, you can use Setup Manager to create an answer file to customize Mini-Setup, just as you would with a standard scripted install.

Figure 12-34 Sysprep, the System Preparation Tool

Troubleshooting Installation Problems

The term "installation problem" is rather deceptive. The installation process itself almost never fails. Usually, something else fails during the process that is generally interpreted as an "install failure." Let's look at some typical installation problems and how to correct them.

Text Mode Errors

If you're going to have an install problem, this is the place to get one. It's always better to have the error right off the bat, as opposed to when the installation is nearly complete. Text mode errors most often take place during clean installs and usually point to one of the following problems:

No Boot Device Present When Booting Off the Startup Disc
Either the startup disc is bad or the CMOS is not set to look at that disc drive first.

Windows Setup Requires XXXX Amount of Available Drive Space
You forgot to format the C: drive, or there's a bunch of stuff on the drive already.

Not Ready Error on Optical Drive
You probably just need to give the optical drive a moment to catch up. Press R for retry a few times. You may also have a damaged installation disc, or the optical drive may be too slow for the system.

A Stop Error (Blue Screen of Death) After the Reboot at the End of Text Mode
This is most common during a Windows 2000/XP installation and may mean that you didn't do your homework in checking hardware compatibility, especially the BIOS. I'll tell you more about stop errors in Chapter 15, but if you encounter one of these errors during installation, check out the Microsoft Knowledge Base, especially article 165863, "Troubleshooting 'Stop 0x0A' Messages in Windows 2000 and Windows NT."

Graphical Mode Errors

Once the install passes the text mode and moves into graphical mode, a whole new crop of problems may arise.

Hardware Detection Errors

Failure to properly detect hardware by any version of Setup can be avoided by simply researching compatibility beforehand. Or, if you decided to skip that step, you might be lucky and only have a hardware detection error involving a non-critical hardware device. You can troubleshoot this problem at your leisure. In a sense, you are handing in your homework late, checking out compatibility and finding a proper driver after Windows is installed. Windows 2000 and Windows XP inherited the underpinnings of Windows NT. They all depend on the Setup program properly detecting the computer type (motherboard and BIOS stuff, in particular) and installing the correct Hardware Abstraction Layer (HAL). (See Chapter 13 for discussion about the HAL.)

Can't Read CAB Files

This is probably the most common of all installation errors. CAB (as in cabinet) files are special compressed files, recognizable by their .cab file extension, that Microsoft uses to distribute copies of Windows. If your system can't read them, first check the CD-ROM for scratches. Then try copying all the files from the source directory on the CD (\i386) into a directory on your local hard drive. Then run Setup from there, remembering to use the correct program (WINNT32.EXE). If you can't read any of the files on the CD-ROM, you may have a defective drive.

Lockups During Install

Lockups are one of the most challenging problems that can take place during install, as they don't give you a clue as to what's causing the problem. Here are a few things to check if you get a lockup during install.

Smart Recovery, Repair Install

Most system lockups occur when Windows Setup queries the hardware. If a system locks up once during setup, turn off the computer—literally. Unplug the system! Do *not* press CTRL-ALT-DEL. Do *not* click Reset. Unplug it! Then turn the system back on, boot into Setup, and rerun the Setup program. Windows will see the partial installation and either restart the install process automatically (Smart Recovery) or prompt you for a "Repair Install." Both of these look at the installation progress and complete the installation.

Optical Drive, Hard Drive

Bad CD- or DVD-media discs, optical drives, or hard drives may cause lockups. Check the CD or DVD for scratches or dirt, and clean it up or replace it. Try a known good disc in the drive. If you get the same error, you may need to replace the drive.

Log Files

Windows generates a number of special text files called log files that track the progress of certain processes. While Windows creates a number of different log files for different purposes, two files most interest us:

- SETUPLOG.TXT tracks the complete installation process, logging the success or failure of file copying, Registry updates, reboots, and so on.

- SETUPAPI.LOG tracks each piece of hardware as it is installed. This is not an easy log file to read, as it uses Plug and Play code, but it will show you the last device installed before Windows locked up.

Windows 2000 and Windows XP store these log files in the WINNT or Windows directory (the location in which the OS is installed). These OSs have powerful recovery options, so, honestly, the chances of your ever actually having to read a log file, understand it, and then get something fixed as a result of that understanding are pretty small. What makes log files handy is when you call Microsoft or a hardware manufacturer. They *love* to read these files, and they actually have people who understand them. Don't worry about trying to understand log files for the CompTIA A+ exams; just make sure you know the names of the log files and their location. Leave the details to the über geeks.

No Installation Is Perfect

Even when the installation seems smooth, issues may slowly surface, especially in the case of upgrades. Be prepared to reinstall applications or deal with new functions that were absent in the previous OS. If things really fall apart, you can always go back to the previous OS.

The procedures I've laid out in this chapter may seem like a lot of work—how bad could it really be to simply grab an installation CD-ROM, fling a copy of Windows onto a system, and as the saying goes, let the chips fall where they may? Plenty bad, is how bad. Not only is it important that you understand these procedures for the CompTIA A+ Certification exams, they can save your, ah, hide, once you're a working PC tech and you're tasked to install the latest version of Windows on the boss's new computer!

Chapter Review Questions

1. Which of the following is an advantage of running Windows 2000 on NTFS as opposed to FAT32?

   A. Security

   B. Support for DOS applications

   C. Long filenames

   D. Network support

2. Ricardo's Windows XP installation has failed. What file should he check to see what files failed to copy?

   A. INSTALL.LOG

   B. SETUP.LOG

   C. SETUP.TXT

   D. SETUPLOG.TXT

3. Which of the following *best* describes the operating system's user interface?

   A. It enables the system to communicate with peripheral devices.

   B. It provides a display of the programs and data on a system to the user.

   C. It provides a display of the system hardware to the user.

   D. It provides error handling or notification displays when communicating with hardware.

4. If you do not complete the activation process for Windows XP, what will happen to your computer?

   A. Nothing. Activation is optional.

   B. The computer will work fine for 30 days and then Windows XP will be disabled.

   C. Microsoft will not know how to contact you to provide upgrade information.

   D. You will have to use a floppy disk set to boot to XP.

5. If Windows locks up during the installation, what should you do?

   A. Press CTRL-ALT-DEL to restart the installation process.

   B. Push the Reset button to restart the installation process.

   C. Press the ESC key to cancel the installation process.

   D. Unplug the computer and restart the installation process.

6. You can upgrade directly to Windows 2000 from which of these operating systems?

   A. Windows 3.11

   B. Windows 95

   C. Windows Me

   D. All of the above

7. The Windows XP CD-ROM contains which two tools for checking hardware and software compatibility?

   A. The HCL and the HAL

   B. The HCL and the Windows Catalog

   C. The Windows Catalog and the Upgrade Advisor

   D. The Upgrade Advisor and the HCL

8. Which term describes a combination of many updates and fixes?

   A. Hot fix

   B. Hot pack

   C. Service pack

   D. Service release

9. Which operating system is made freely available under the GNU public license?

   A. Linux

   B. Mac OS X

   C. UNIX

   D. Windows 3.1

10. If you are experiencing problems with Windows Me and wish to install Windows XP, what type of installation is preferred?

   A. Clean install

   B. Upgrade install

   C. Network install

   D. Image install

Answers

1. **A.** Security is an advantage of running Windows 2000 on NTFS as opposed to FAT32.

2. **D.** Ricardo should check SETUPLOG.TXT.

3. **B.** An operating system's user interface provides a display of the programs and data on a system to the user.

4. **B.** If you do not complete the activation process for Windows XP, the computer will work fine for 30 days and then Windows XP will be disabled.

5. **D.** If Windows locks up during the installation, you should unplug the computer and restart the installation process.

6. **B.** You can upgrade directly to Windows 2000 from Windows 95.

7. **C.** The Windows XP CD-ROM contains the Windows Catalog and the Upgrade Advisor for checking hardware and software compatibility.

8. **C.** A service pack is a combination of many updates and fixes.

9. **A.** Linux is freely available under the GNU public license.

10. **A.** If you are experiencing problems with any OS, a clean install is preferred so you don't migrate the trouble to the new OS.

Understanding Windows

In this chapter, you will learn how to
- Explain the Windows interface
- Identify the features and characteristics of Windows 2000 and Windows XP
- Describe the current versions of Windows

So, you've now got Windows installed and you're staring at the desktop. Pretty, eh? Well, as a tech, you need to understand Windows at a level that no regular user would dare. This chapter introduces you to and shows you the functions of some of the more powerful aspects of Windows, such as NTFS and the Registry. Not only must techs run through the standard Windows features that everyone uses every day (My Computer, Recycle Bin, and so on), they must also be comfortable drilling down underneath that user-friendly surface to get their hands a little dirty.

This chapter takes you through the Windows interface in detail, including the user interface, tech utilities, and folder structure. The second section looks in more detail at the techie aspects of Windows, including the structure of the OS, NTFS, and the boot process. The final short section runs through the many variations of Windows on the market today, going through the "Beyond A+" section to Windows Vista and non-desktop versions of Windows. Let's get started!

Windows Interface

All versions of Windows share certain characteristics, configuration files, and general look and feel. Here's some good news: you'll find the same, or nearly the same, utilities in almost all versions of Windows, and once you master one version—both GUI and command line interface—you've pretty much got them all covered. This section covers the essentials: where to find things, how to maneuver, and what common utilities are available. Where versions of Windows differ in concept or detail, I'll point that out along the way. We'll get to the underlying structure of Windows in the subsequent two sections of this chapter. For now, let's look at the common user interface, tech-oriented utilities, and typical OS folders.

User Interface

Windows offers a set of utilities, or *interfaces,* that every user should know about—both how and why to access them. And since every user should know about them, certainly every CompTIA A+ certified tech should as well! Let's take a quick tour of the typical Windows GUI.

Login

Every version of Windows supports multiple users on a single machine, so the starting point for any tour of the Windows user interface starts with the *login screen.* Figure 13-1 shows a Windows 2000 login screen; Figure 13-2 shows a Windows XP login screen.

The login screen for Windows 9*x*/Me offered no security for the system—you could simply press ESC to bypass the screen and access the OS. Bowing to the home user's

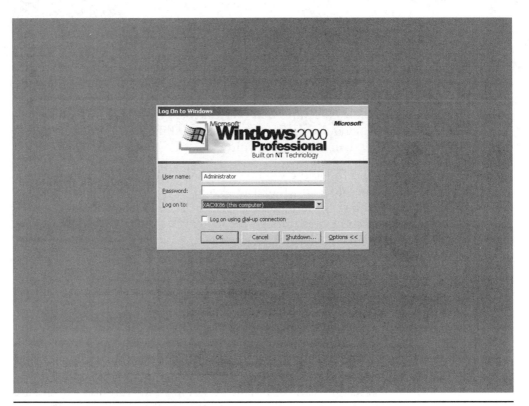

Figure 13-1   Windows 2000 login screen

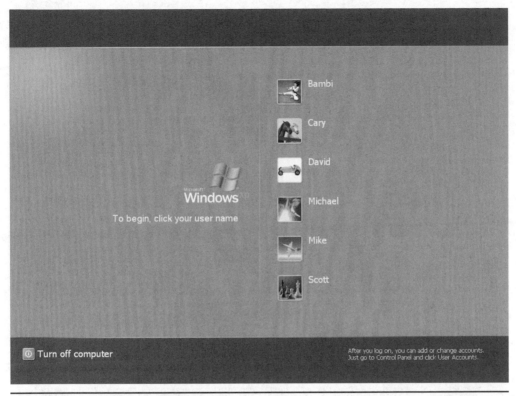

To begin, click your user name

Bambi

Cary

David

Michael

Mike

Scott

Turn off computer

After you log on, you can add or change accounts. Just go to Control Panel and click User Accounts.

Figure 13-2 Windows XP login screen

focus on convenience, Windows XP Home also allows users to access their accounts without requiring a login password, but by enabling password-protected individual user logins, the NT, 2000, and XP versions of Windows offer the security-conscious user a higher degree of security.

Desktop

The Windows desktop is your primary interface to the computer. It's always there, underneath whatever applications you have open. The desktop analogy appeals to most people—we're used to sitting down at a desk to get work done. Figure 13-3 shows a nice, clean Windows 2000 desktop; note the icons on the left and the various graphical elements across the bottom. You can add folders and files to the desktop, and customize the background to change its color or add a picture. Most people like to do so—certainly, I do! As an example, Figure 13-4 shows my desktop from my home system—a Windows XP PC.

Figure 13-3   Windows 2000 desktop

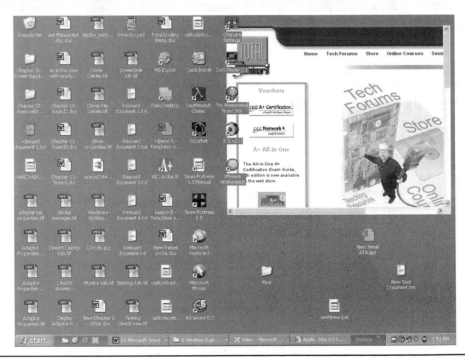

Figure 13-4   Mike's messy desktop

Taskbar and Start Menu

The *taskbar* runs along the bottom of all Windows desktops and includes up to four sections (depending on the version of Windows and your configuration). Starting at the left side, these are: the Start button, the Quick Launch toolbar, the running programs area, and the system tray. Although the taskbar by default sits at the bottom of the desktop, you can move it to either side or the top of the screen.

One of the main jobs of the taskbar is to show the Start button, probably the most clicked button on all Windows systems. You can find the Start button on the far left end of the taskbar (Figure 13-5). Click the Start button to bring up the Start menu, which enables you to see all programs loaded on the system and to start them. Now, move your mouse cursor onto All Programs. When the All Programs menu appears, move the cursor to the Accessories menu. Locate the Notepad program and click it, as shown in Figure 13-6. By default, Windows hides lesser-used menu options, so if you don't see Notepad, click the double down-arrows at the bottom of the Accessories menu. Notepad will then appear.

Figure 13-5
Start button

Figure 13-6
Opening Notepad
in Windows XP

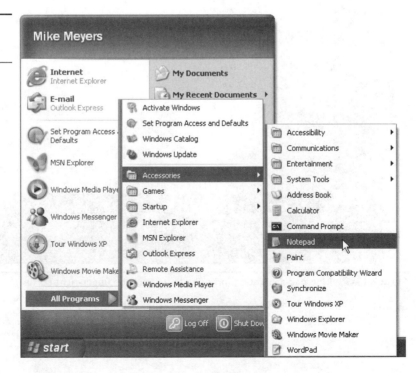

NOTE You have a lot of clicking to do in this chapter, so take a moment to reflect on what I lovingly call the "General Rules of Clicking." With a few exceptions, these rules always apply, and they really help in manipulating the Windows interface to do whatever you need done:

- Click menu items once to use them.
- Click icons once to select them.
- Click icons twice to use them.
- Right-click anything to see its properties.

Great! If you opened Notepad properly, you should see something like Figure 13-7, with Notepad displaying an untitled text page. Notice how Notepad shows up on the taskbar at the bottom of the screen. Most running programs will appear on the taskbar in this way. Close the Notepad program by clicking on the button with the "X" in the upper right corner of the Notepad window. Look again at the taskbar to see that Notepad no longer appears there.

Figure 13-7 Notepad application (note the buttons in the upper-right corner)

Now look all the way to the right end of the taskbar. This part of the taskbar is known as the *system tray*. You will at a minimum see the current time displayed in the system tray, and on most Windows systems you'll also see a number of small icons there. Figure 13-8 shows the system tray on my PC.

Figure 13-8
System tray showing seven icons and the time

These icons show programs running in the background. You'll often see icons for network status, volume controls, battery state (on laptops), and PC Card status (also usually on laptops). What shows up on yours depends on your version of Windows, what hardware you use, and what programs you have loaded. For example, the icon at the far left in Figure 13-8 is my McAfee Antivirus program, and the one at the far right is my UPS program, both humming away in the background protecting my precious data!

Near the left end of the taskbar, next to the Start button, you will find the Quick Launch toolbar (Figure 13-9). This handy extra enables you to select often-used programs with a single click. On Windows XP systems, the Quick Launch toolbar is not displayed on the taskbar by default, so before you can use this convenient feature, you must right-click the taskbar, select Properties, and check Show Quick Launch. To change the contents of the Quick Launch toolbar, simply drag icons onto or off of it.

Figure 13-9
Quick Launch toolbar

My Computer

My Computer provides access to all drives, folders, and files on the system. To open My Computer, simply double-click the My Computer icon on the desktop. When you first open My Computer in Windows 2000, it displays all the drives on the system (Figure 13-10). Windows XP offers a more sophisticated My Computer, with all details and common tasks displayed in the left pane (Figure 13-11). Windows XP does not include My Computer on the desktop by default, but you can readily access it through the Start menu.

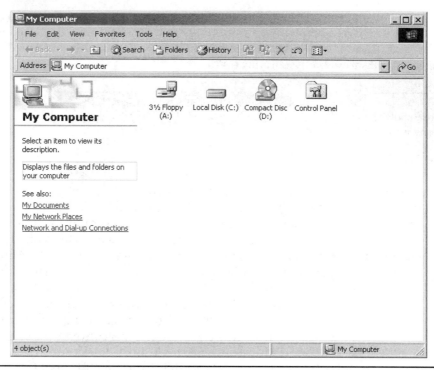

Figure 13-10 My Computer in Windows 2000

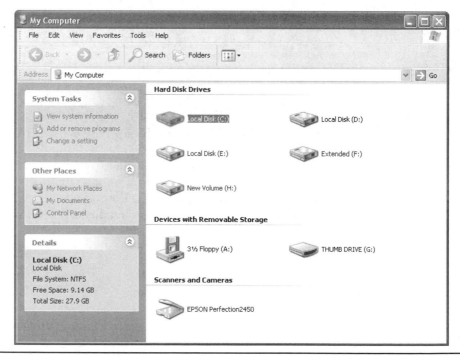

Figure 13-11 My Computer in Windows XP

Note the interesting icons Windows XP gives for all the different devices on your computer! Most of these are storage devices, like the hard drive and optical drives—but what the heck is a scanner doing in there? The answer is that any program can add to the My Computer screen, and the folks who wrote the drivers for the scanner thought that it should go into My Computer.

To view the contents of any device, double-click its icon in My Computer. For example, let's say you want to see the contents of a floppy diskette. Just insert the diskette into the floppy drive, then double-click the floppy drive icon to see what's inside. Figure 13-12 shows the contents of a USB thumb drive I had lying around.

Figure 13-12   Displaying the contents of a thumb drive using My Computer

Notice the different icons? Windows assigns different icons to different types of files based on their *extensions*, the set of characters at the end of a filename, such as .EXE, .TXT, or .JPG. The oldest extensions, starting from back in the DOS era, are usually three characters, but newer programs may use two-character extensions, like .JS (JavaScript) or .AU (audio), or even four-character extensions, like the ubiquitous .HTML for Web pages. In rare cases, such as the system file NTLDR, a filename might actually have no extension.

As you look at these icons on your own screen, some of you might say, "But I don't see any extensions!" That's because Windows hides them by default. To see the extensions, select Tools | Folder Options to open the Folder Options dialog box (Figure 13-13). Click the View tab and uncheck Hide Extensions for Known File Types.

Figure 13-13
Folder Options
dialog box

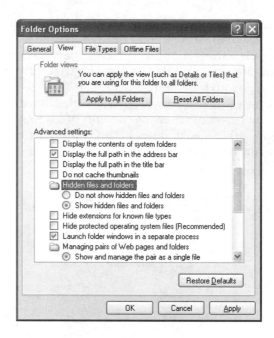

There are two other very handy settings under the View tab, but to best see the results, you need to be in the C: drive of My Computer, as shown in Figure 13-14.

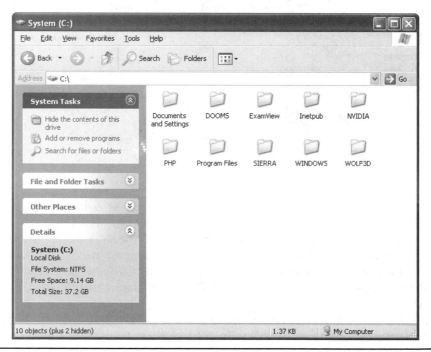

Figure 13-14   Default My Computer View

Go back into the View tab under Folder Options, click the Show Hidden Files and Folders radio button, and then uncheck Hide Protected Operating System Files. Click the Apply to All Folders button in Windows XP, or the Apply button (bottom right) in Windows 2000. Your C: drive should look like Figure 13-15 (it shows the Windows XP version) when you are done. As before, when you return to examining the folder contents, you will see the file extensions, and possibly some previously hidden files.

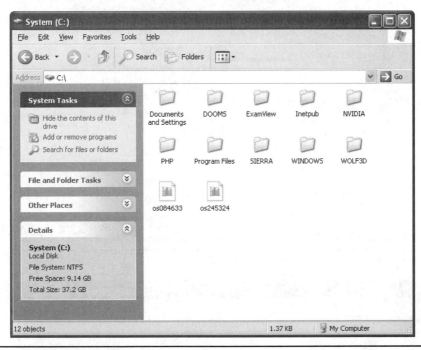

Figure 13-15   My Computer displaying hidden files and folders

Now that those files are visible, you have the awesome responsibility of keeping them safe! In general, the less you handle your vital system files, the better. You'll learn some ways to do useful things with files that were previously hidden, but unless you really know what you're doing, it's best to leave them alone. Before you turn a PC over to someone who isn't a trained PC tech, you'll probably want to hide those system files again.

Windows Explorer

In every version of Windows prior to XP, Windows Explorer acts like a separate and distinct tool from My Computer, showing file and folder information in a double-paned fashion rather than all in a single pane (Figure 13-16). Windows XP merged the two into a single tool, but you can still get the Explorer-like interface by right-clicking a folder and selecting Explore from the options, or by clicking on the Folder button on the toolbar. Figure 13-17 shows My Computer exploring an important folder on my hard drive.

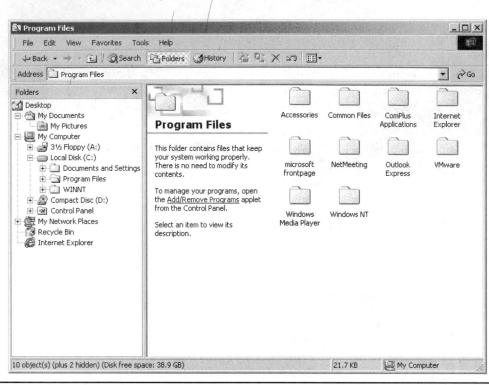

Figure 13-16 Windows Explorer in Windows 2000

Figure 13-17 My Computer in Windows XP masquerading as Windows Explorer

My Documents, My [Whatever]

Windows provides a special folder called My Documents. Early versions of Windows lacked a single location for users to place their files, and Microsoft discovered that users dumped their files all over the hard drive, and they often had trouble remembering where they'd put them! Microsoft recognized this issue and created My Documents as a central default storage area for all files created by applications. Many Windows programs, such as Office 2003, store their files in My Documents unless you explicitly tell them to use a different folder.

As with My Computer, most Windows XP installations do not show My Documents on the desktop. You can access it readily through the Start menu, or you can add it to your desktop. Right-click the desktop and select Properties to open the Display Properties dialog box. Select the Desktop tab, and then click on the Customize Desktop button to open the Desktop Items dialog box (Figure 13-18). On the General tab, select the check box next to My Documents, My Computer, or both, and then click OK to close the dialog box and make the icon(s) appear on the desktop.

Figure 13-18
Desktop Items
dialog box

NOTE As with most tools in Windows, Microsoft gives you more than one way to accomplish tasks. To make My Documents and other default folders appear on the desktop, you can right-click the icon in the Start menu and select Show on Desktop from the options. That's it!

Windows XP adds a number of subfolders to My Documents: My Pictures (which offers filmstrip and thumbnail views of pictures you store there), My Music (which will fire up Media Player to play any file), My Videos (which, again, starts Media Player), and more. Figure 13-19 shows My Pictures, using thumbnail view. Many applications have since jumped on the bandwagon and added their own My [Whatever] folders in My Documents. On my PC right now, I have My eBooks, My Webs, My Received Files, My Virtual Machines … My Goodness!

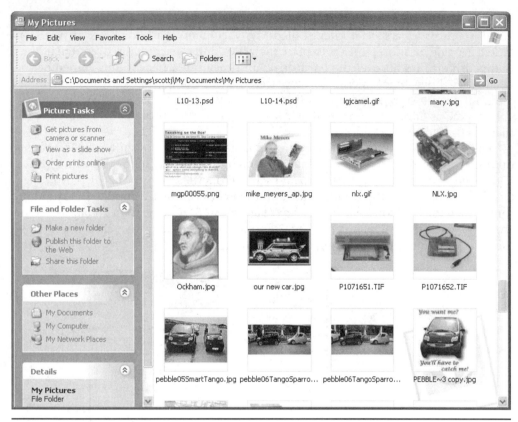

Figure 13-19   My Pictures subfolder in My Documents

Recycle Bin

In Windows, a file is not erased when you delete it. Windows adds a level of protection in the form of a special folder called the *Recycle Bin.* When you delete a file in Windows, it moves into the Recycle Bin. It stays there until you empty the Recycle Bin or restore the file, or until the Recycle Bin reaches a preset size and starts erasing its oldest contents.

To access its properties, right-click the Recycle Bin and select Properties. The Recycle Bin's properties look different in different versions of Windows, but they all work basically the same. Figure 13-20 shows the properties of a typical Windows XP Recycle Bin. Note that you set the amount of drive space to use for the Recycle Bin, 10 percent being the default amount. If a hard drive starts to run low on space, this is one of the first places to check!

Figure 13-20
Windows XP
Recycle Bin
Properties

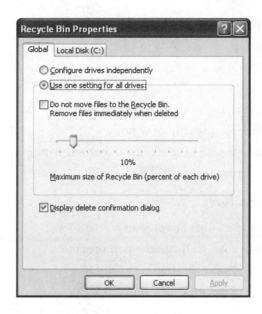

My Network Places

Systems tied to a network, either via a network cable or by a modem, have a folder called *My Network Places* (see Figure 13-21). This shows all the current network connections available to you. You'll learn about My Network Places in Chapter 21.

Figure 13-21
My Network Places
in Windows XP

 NOTE Microsoft called the Windows 9x/Me network space *Network Neighborhood*. You'll still hear many techs use that term instead of My Network Places, simply because it doesn't sound so awkward. "Simply open your My ..."

Hot Keys

Windows has a number of key combinations that enable you to go directly to different programs and places. Here's a fairly extensive list of general purpose commands for Windows. Be aware that some applications may change the use of these commands!

Function Keys

- F1   Help
- F2   Rename
- F3   Search menu
- F4   Open the Address Bar options
- F5   Refresh the current window
- F6   Move among selections in current windows
- F10   Activate menu bar options

Popular Hot Keys

- CTRL-ESC   Open Start menu
- ALT-TAB   Switch between open programs
- ALT-F4   Quit program
- CTRL-Z   Undo the last command
- CTRL-A   Select all the items in the current window
- SHIFT-DELETE   Delete item permanently
- SHIFT-F10   Open a shortcut menu for the selected item (this is the same as right-clicking an object)
- SHIFT   Bypass the automatic-run feature for optical media (by pressing and holding down the SHIFT key while you insert optical media)
- ALT-SPACE   Display the main window's System menu (from this menu you can restore, move, resize, minimize, maximize, or close the window)
- ALT-ENTER   Open the properties for the selected object

Working with Text

- CTRL-C   Copy
- CTRL-X   Cut
- CTRL-V   Paste
- CTRL-Z   Undo
- CTRL-B   Bold
- CTRL-U   Underline
- CTRL-I   Italic

Windows Key Shortcuts   These shortcuts use the special Windows key:

- Windows key   Start menu

- **Windows key-D**   Show desktop
- **Windows key-E**   Windows Explorer
- **Windows key-F**   Search menu
- **Windows key-L**   Log off Windows
- **Windows key-P**   Start Print Manager
- **Windows key-R**   Run dialog box
- **Windows key-S**   Toggle CAPS LOCK
- **Windows key-V**   Open the Clipboard
- **Windows key-CTRL-F**   Find computer
- **Windows key-TAB**   Cycle through taskbar buttons
- **Windows key-break**   Open the System Properties dialog box

 NOTE   I've covered only the most basic parts of the Windows desktop in this chapter. The typical Windows desktop will include many other parts, but for techs and for the CompTIA A+ certification exams, what you've learned here about the desktop is more than enough!

Tech Utilities

Windows offers a huge number of utilities that enable techs to configure the OS, optimize and tweak settings, install hardware, and more. The trick is to know where to go to find them. This section shows the seven most common locations in Windows where you can go to access utilities: right-click, Control Panel, Device Manager, System Tools, command line, Microsoft Management Console, and Administrative tools. Note that these are locations for tools, not tools themselves, and many tools may be accessed from more than one of these locations. However, you'll see some of the utilities in many of these locations. Stay sharp in this section, as you'll need to access utilities to understand the inner workings of Windows in the next section.

Right-Click

Windows, being a graphical user interface OS, covers your monitor with windows, menus, icons, file lists—all kinds of pretty things you click on to get work done. Any single thing you see on your desktop is called an *object*. If you want to open any object in Windows, you double-click on it. If you want to change something about an object, you right-click on it.

Right-clicking on an object brings up a small menu, and it works on everything in Windows. In fact, try to place your mouse somewhere in Windows where right-clicking does *not* bring up a menu (there are a few places, but they're not easy to find). What you see on the little menu when you right-click varies dramatically, depending on the item you decide to right-click. If you right-click a running program in the running program area on the taskbar, you'll see items that relate to a window, such as move, resize, and so on (Figure 13-22). If you right-click on your desktop, you get options for changing the appearance of the desktop (Figure 13-23). Even different types of files will show different results when you right-click on them!

Figure 13-22
Right-clicking
on a program

Restore	
Move	
Size	
Minimize	
Maximize	
X Close	Alt+F4

35513w (Read-Only) ...

Figure 13-23
Right-clicking on
the desktop

Arrange Icons By	▶
Refresh	
Paste	
Paste Shortcut	
Undo Move	Ctrl+Z
New	▶
Properties	

One menu item you'll see almost anywhere you right-click is Properties. Every object in Windows has properties. When you right-click on something and can't find what you're looking for, select Properties. Figure 13-24 shows the results of right-clicking on My Computer—not very exciting. But if you click Properties, you'll get a dialog box like the one shown in Figure 13-25.

Figure 13-24
Right-clicking on
My Computer

Open
Explore
Search...
Manage
Map Network Drive...
Disconnect Network Drive...
Create Shortcut
Delete
Rename
Properties

My Com...

Figure 13-25
My Computer
properties

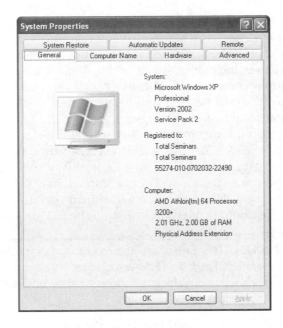

Control Panel

The Control Panel handles most of the maintenance, upgrade, and configuration aspects of Windows. As such, the Control Panel is the first set of tools for every tech to explore. Select Start | Settings | Control Panel to open the Control Panel in Windows 2000. In Windows XP, it's a Start menu item.

The Control Panel in Windows 2000 opens in the traditional icon-littered view. In Windows XP and Vista, the Control Panel opens into the Category view, in which all the icons are grouped into broad categories such as "Printers and Other Hardware." This view requires an additional click (and sometimes a guess about which category includes the icon you need), so most techs use the Switch to Classic View link to get back to the icons. Figure 13-26 shows the Windows XP Control Panel in both Category (left) and Classic (right) views.

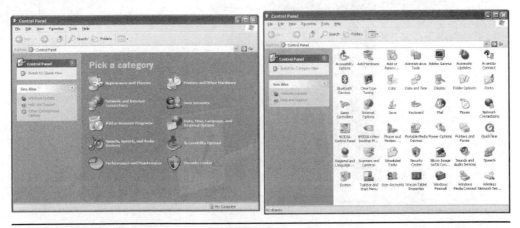

Figure 13-26   Windows XP Control Panel—two views

A large number of programs, called *applets*, populate the Control Panel. The names and selection of applets will vary depending on the version of Windows and whether any installed programs have added applets. But all versions of Windows share many of the same applets, including Display, Add or Remove Programs, and System—what I call the *Big Three* applets for techs. Display enables you to make changes to the look and feel of your Windows desktop, and to tweak your video settings. Add or Remove Programs enables you to add or remove programs. The System applet gives you access to essential system information and tools, such as the Device Manager.

Every icon you see in the Control Panel is actually a file with the extension .CPL, and any time you get an error opening the Control Panel, you can bet you have a corrupted CPL file. These are a pain to fix. You have to rename all of your CPL files with another extension (I use .CPB), and then rename them back to .CPL one at a time, each time reopening the Control Panel, until you find the CPL file that's causing the lockup.

 EXAM TIP Even these common applets vary slightly among Windows versions. The CompTIA A+ certification exams do not test you on every little variance among the same applets in different versions—just know what each applet does!

The Control Panel applets enable you to do an amazing array of things to a Windows system, and each applet displays text that helps explain its functions. The Add Hardware applet (Figure 13-27), for example, says quite clearly, "Installs and troubleshoots hardware." They are all like that. Figure 13-28 shows the User Accounts applet. Can you determine its use? (If not, don't sweat it. I'll cover users in Chapter 15, "Maintaining and Troubleshooting Windows.") Each Control Panel applet relevant to the CompTIA A+ exams is discussed in detail in the relevant chapter—for example, the Modems applet is discussed in Chapter 22, "The Internet."

Figure 13-27
Add Hardware Wizard of the Add Hardware applet

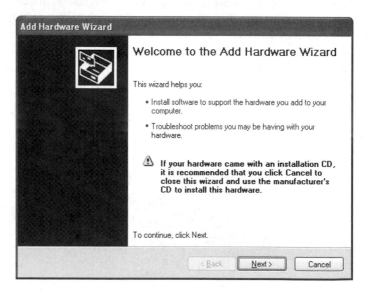

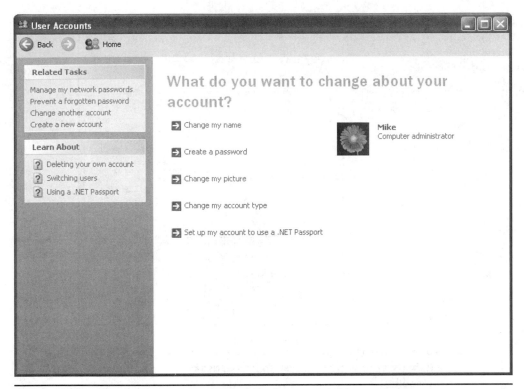

Figure 13-28   User Accounts window of the User Accounts applet

Device Manager

The *Device Manager* enables techs to examine and configure all the hardware and drivers in a Windows PC. As you might suspect from that description, every tech spends a lot of time with this tool! You've seen it at work in several earlier chapters, and you'll work with the Device Manager many more times during the course of this book and your career as a PC tech.

There are many ways to get to the Device Manager—make sure you know all of them! The first way is to open the Control Panel and double-click the System applet icon. This brings up the System Properties dialog box. From here, you access the Device Manager by selecting the Hardware tab and then clicking the Device Manager button. Figure 13-29 shows the Hardware tab of the System Properties dialog box in Windows XP.

You can also get to the System Properties dialog box by right-clicking My Computer and selecting Properties. From there, the path to Device Manager is the same as when you access this dialog box from the Control Panel.

Figure 13-29
Windows XP
System applet with
the Hardware tab
selected

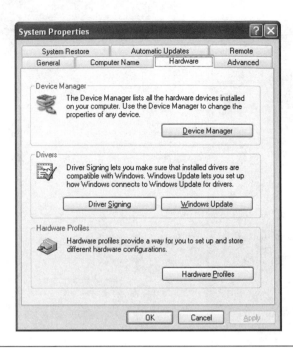

NOTE Holding down the Windows key and pressing the PAUSE key is yet another way to get to the System Properties dialog box. Keyboard shortcuts are cool!

The second (and more streamlined) method is to right-click My Computer and select Manage (Figure 13-30). This opens a window called Computer Management, where you'll see Device Manager listed on the left side of the screen, under System Tools (Figure 13-31). Just click on Device Manager and it will open. You can also access Computer Management by opening the Administrative Tools applet in the Control Panel and then selecting Computer Management.

Figure 13-30
Right-clicking on My
Computer to select
the Manage option

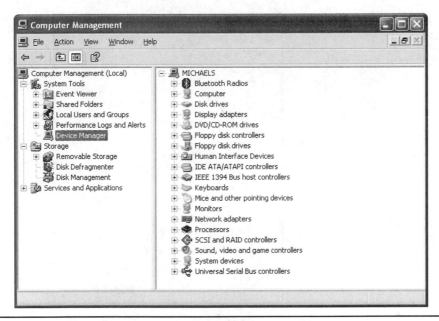

Figure 13-31 Device Manager in Computer Management

Why are there so many ways to open Device Manager? Well, remember that we're only looking at locations in Windows from which to open utilities, not at the actual utilities themselves. Windows wants you to get to the tools you need when you need them, and it's better to have multiple paths to a utility rather than just one.

The Device Manager displays every device that Windows recognizes, organized in special groups called *types*. All devices of the same type are grouped under the same type heading. To see the devices of a particular type, you must open that type's group. Figure 13-32 shows a typical Windows XP Device Manager screen with all installed devices in good order—which makes us techs happy. If Windows detects a problem, it shows the device with a red "X" or a yellow exclamation point, as in the case of the network adapter in Figure 13-33.

Figure 13-32
Happy Device
Manager

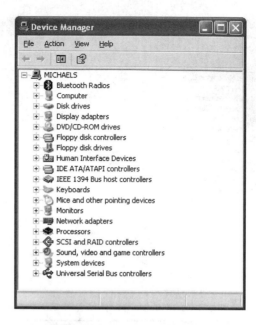

Figure 13-33
Sad Device Manager

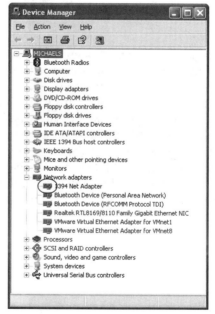

NOTE There is one other "problem" icon you might see on a device in Device Manager—a blue *i*. According to Microsoft, this means you turned off automatic configuration for a device. This is probably good to know for the exams, but you'll never see this error on a working machine unless you're intentionally messing with I/O address or IRQ settings for a device.

The red "X" means the device is disabled—right-click on the device to enable it. The tough one is the yellow exclamation point. If you see this, right-click on the device and select Properties; you'll see a dialog box like the one shown in Figure 13-34. Read the error code in the Device Status pane, and then look up Microsoft Knowledge Base article 310123 to see what to do. There are around 40 different errors—nobody bothers to memorize them!

Figure 13-34
Problem device

The Device Manager isn't just for dealing with problems! It also enables you to update drivers with a simple click of the mouse (assuming you have a driver downloaded or on disc). Right-click a device and select Update Driver from the menu to get the process started. Figure 13-35 shows the options in Windows XP.

Figure 13-35
Selecting Update Driver in the Windows XP Device Manager

By double-clicking a device (or by selecting the device and clicking the Properties button) and then clicking the Resources tab, you can see the resources used by that device. Figure 13-36 shows the resources for an NVIDIA GeForce 7900 GT video card.

Figure 13-36
Resources revealed in the Windows XP Device Manager

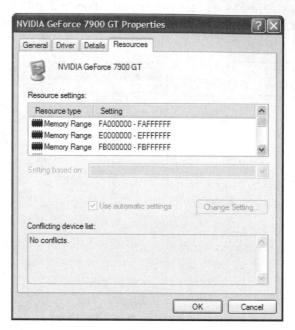

Make sure you can get to Device Manager! You will come back to it again and again in subsequent chapters, because it is the first tool you should access when you have a hardware problem.

System Tools

The Start menu offers a variety of tech utilities collected in one place: select Start | Programs | Accessories | System Tools. In the *System Tools* menu, you'll find commonly accessed tools, such as System Information and Disk Defragmenter (Figure 13-37).

Figure 13-37
System Tools menu options

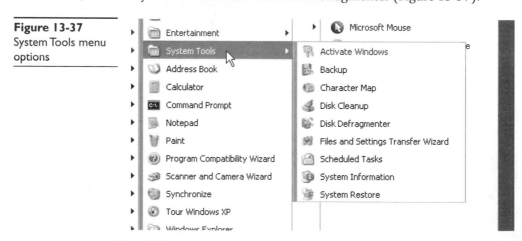

Many techs overlook memorizing how to find the appropriate Windows tool to diagnose problems, but nothing hurts your credibility with a client like fumbling around, clicking a variety of menus and applets, mumbling "I know it's around here somewhere." The CompTIA A+ certification exams therefore test you on a variety of paths to appropriate tools. One of those paths is Start | Programs | Accessories | System Tools! Windows XP has all the same tools as Windows 2000, plus a few more, so for each tool I discuss, I'll say whether the tool is in Windows 2000 or only in XP.

Activate Windows (XP only)   Windows XP unveiled a copy protection scheme called *activation*. Activation is a process where your computer sends Microsoft a unique code generated on your machine based on the installation CD's product key and a number of hardware features, such as the amount of RAM, the CPU processor model, and other ones and zeros in your PC. Normally activation is done at install time, but if you choose not to activate at install or if you make "substantial" changes to the hardware, you'll need to use the Activate Windows utility (Figure 13-38). The Activate Windows utility enables you to activate over the Internet or over the telephone.

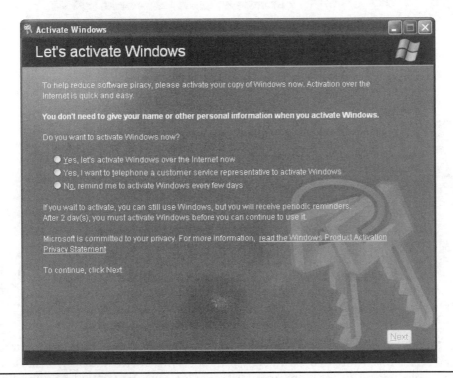

Figure 13-38   Activate Windows

 NOTE   Once you've activated Windows, this applet goes away.

Backup   The Backup utility enables you to back up selected files and folders to removable media like tape drives. Backing up is an important function that's covered in detail in Chapters 15 and 23.

> **NOTE**   Neither Windows XP Home nor Windows Media Center automatically include Backup! You must install the Backup program from the Windows installation CD by running the \Valueadd\MSFT\Ntbackup\NTbackup.msi program.

Character Map   Ever been using a program only to discover you need to enter a strange character such as the euro character € but your word processor doesn't support it? That's when you need the Character Map. It enables you to copy any Unicode character into the clipboard (Figure 13-39).

Figure 13-39
Character Map

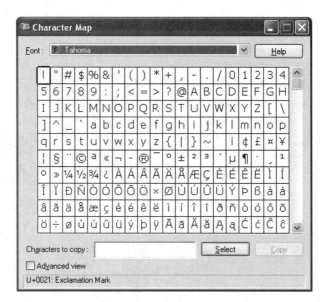

Disk Cleanup   Disk Cleanup looks for unneeded files on your computer, which is handy when your hard drive starts to get full and you need space! You must run Disk Cleanup manually in Windows 2000, but Windows XP starts this program whenever your hard drive gets below 200 MB of free disk space.

Disk Defragmenter   We first discussed Disk Defragmenter back in Chapter 10. You can access this utility in the same way you access the Device Manager; Disk Defragmenter is also found in the Computer Management console. A simpler method is to select Start | Programs | Accessories | System Tools—you'll find Disk Defragmenter listed there. You can also right-click on any drive in My Computer, select Properties, and click the Tools tab, where you'll find a convenient Defragment Now button.

Files and Settings Transfer Wizard (XP Only)   Suppose you have an old computer full of files and settings, and you just got yourself a brand-new computer. You want to copy everything from your old computer onto your new computer—what to do? Microsoft touts the Files and Settings Transfer Wizard (Figure 13-40) as just the tool you need. This utility copies your desktop files and folders, and most conveniently, your settings from Internet Explorer and Outlook Express; however, it won't copy over your programs, not even the Microsoft ones, and it won't copy settings for any programs other than IE and Outlook Express. If you need to copy everything from an old computer to a new one, you'll probably want to use a disk imaging tool like Norton Ghost.

Figure 13-40
Files and Settings
Transfer Wizard

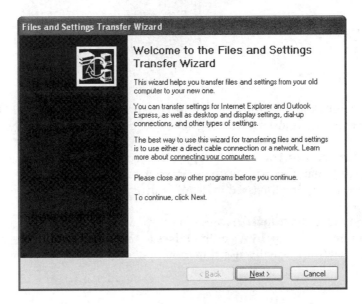

Scheduled Tasks   The Scheduled Tasks utility enables you to schedule any program to start and stop any time you wish. The only trick to this utility is that you must enter the program you want to run as a command on the command line, with all the proper switches. Figure 13-41 shows the configuration line for running the Disk Defragmenter program.

Figure 13-41
Task Scheduler

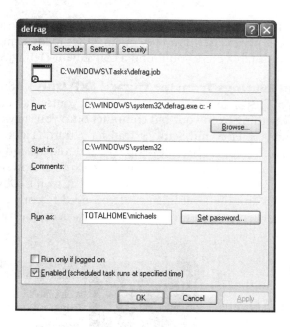

Don't know anything about the command line or switches? Don't worry, the entire next chapter is just for learning about the command line—and switches!

Security Center (XP Only)   The Security Center is a one-stop location for configuring many security features on your computer. All of these security features, and many more, are discussed in detail in their related chapters.

System Information   System Information is one of those tools that everyone (including the CompTIA A+ exams) likes to talk about, but it's uncommon to meet techs who say they actually use this tool. System Information shows tons of information about the hardware and software on your PC (Figure 13-42). You can also use it as a launch point for a number of programs by clicking on the Tools menu.

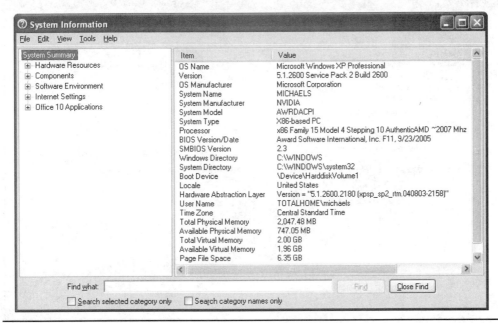

Figure 13-42 System Information

System Restore (XP Only)   System Restore is not only handy, it's also arguably the most important single utility you'll ever use in Windows when it comes to fixing a broken system. System Restore enables you to take a "snapshot"—a copy of a number of critical files and settings—and return to that state later (Figure 13-43). System Restore holds multiple snapshots, any of which you may restore to in the future.

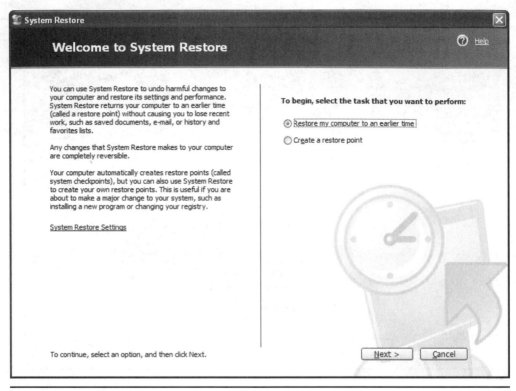

Figure 13-43   System Restore

Imagine you're installing some new device in your PC, or maybe a piece of software. Before you actually install, you take a snapshot and call it "Before Install." You install the device, and now something starts acting weird. You go back into System Restore and reload the previous snapshot, and the problem goes away.

System Restore isn't perfect. It only backs up a few critical items, and it's useless if the computer won't boot, but it's usually the first thing to try when something goes wrong—assuming, of course, you made a snapshot!

Command Line

The Windows command line is a throwback to how Microsoft operating systems worked a long, long time ago, when text commands were entered at a command prompt. Figure 13-44 shows the command prompt from DOS, the first operating system commonly used in PCs.

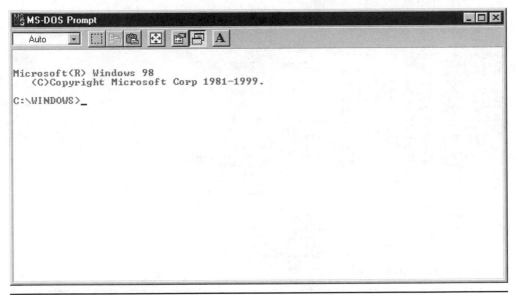

Figure 13-44 DOS command prompt

NOTE The command line goes back to the early days of computing, but it continues to be an essential tool in all modern operating systems, including Linux, Mac OS X, and all versions of Windows. Chapter 14 goes into the command line in detail.

DOS is dead, but the command prompt is alive and well in Windows—including Vista. Every good tech knows how to access and use the command prompt. It is a lifesaver when the GUI part of Windows doesn't work, and it is often faster than using a mouse, if you're skilled at using it. Since the entire next chapter is devoted to the command line, I'll mention only one thing here, and that's how to access a command prompt from within Windows. Select Start | Run, and type **cmd** in the dialog box. Click OK and you'll get to a command prompt (Figure 13-45).

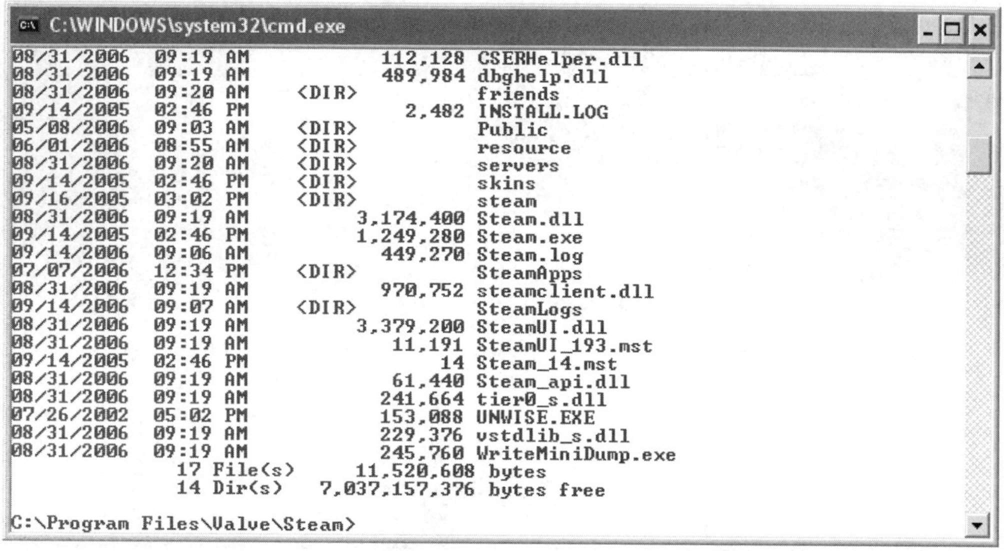

```
C:\WINDOWS\system32\cmd.exe                                    _ □ ×
08/31/2006    09:19 AM              112,128 CSERHelper.dll      ▲
08/31/2006    09:19 AM              489,984 dbghelp.dll
08/31/2006    09:20 AM      <DIR>           friends
09/14/2005    02:46 PM                2,482 INSTALL.LOG
05/08/2006    09:03 AM      <DIR>           Public
06/01/2006    08:55 AM      <DIR>           resource
08/31/2006    09:20 AM      <DIR>           servers
09/14/2005    02:46 PM      <DIR>           skins
09/16/2005    03:02 PM      <DIR>           steam
08/31/2006    09:19 AM            3,174,400 Steam.dll
09/14/2005    02:46 PM            1,249,280 Steam.exe
09/14/2006    09:06 AM              449,270 Steam.log
07/07/2006    12:34 PM      <DIR>           SteamApps
08/31/2006    09:19 AM              970,752 steamclient.dll
09/14/2006    09:07 AM      <DIR>           SteamLogs
08/31/2006    09:19 AM            3,379,200 SteamUI.dll
08/31/2006    09:19 AM               11,191 SteamUI_193.mst
09/14/2005    02:46 PM                   14 Steam_14.mst
08/31/2006    09:19 AM               61,440 Steam_api.dll
08/31/2006    09:19 AM              241,664 tier0_s.dll
07/26/2002    05:02 PM              153,088 UNWISE.EXE
08/31/2006    09:19 AM              229,376 vstdlib_s.dll
08/31/2006    09:19 AM              245,760 WriteMiniDump.exe
              17 File(s)        11,520,608 bytes
              14 Dir(s)      7,037,157,376 bytes free

C:\Program Files\Valve\Steam>                                  ▼
```

Figure 13-45   Command prompt in Windows XP

Microsoft Management Console

One of the biggest complaints about earlier versions of Windows was the wide dispersal of the many utilities needed for administration and troubleshooting. Despite years of research, Microsoft could never find a place for all the utilities that would please even a small minority of support people. In a moment of sheer genius, Microsoft determined that the ultimate utility was one that the support person made for him or herself! This brought on the creation of the amazing Microsoft Management Console.

The *Microsoft Management Console (MMC)* is simply a shell program in Windows 2000 and XP that holds individual utilities called *snap-ins*. You can start the MMC by selecting Start | Run and typing in **MMC** to get a blank MMC. Blank MMCs aren't much to look at (Figure 13-46).

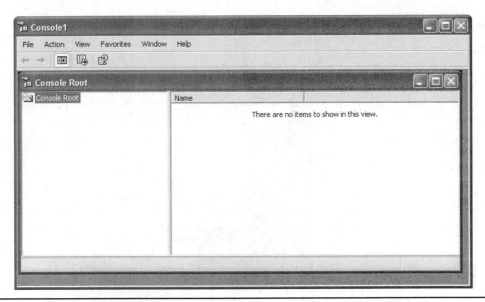

Figure 13-46   Blank MMC

You make a blank MMC console useful by adding snap-ins, and most of the utilities you use in Windows are really snap-ins. Even the good old Device Manager is a snap-in. You can add as many snap-ins as you like, and there are many to choose from. Many companies sell third-party utilities as MMC snap-ins.

For example, to add the Device Manager snap-in, open the blank MMC, select File (Console in Windows 2000) | Add/Remove Snap-in, and then click the Add button to open the Add Standalone Snap-in dialog box. Here you will see a list of available snap-ins (Figure 13-47). Select Device Manager, and click the Add button to open a dialog box that prompts you to choose the local or a remote PC for the snap-in to work with. Choose Local Computer for this exercise, and click the Finish button. Click the Close button to close the Add Standalone Snap-in dialog box, and then click OK to close the Add/Remove Snap-in dialog box.

Figure 13-47
Available snap-ins

You should see Device Manager listed in the console. Click it. Hey, that looks kind of familiar, doesn't it? (See Figure 13-48.)

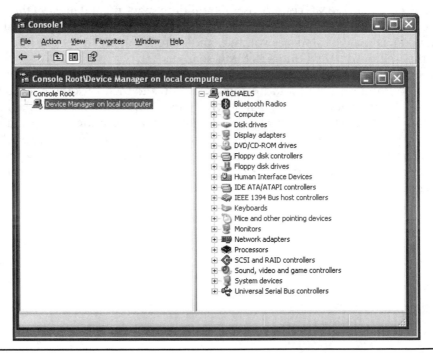

Figure 13-48   Device Manager as a snap-in

Once you've added the snap-ins you want, just save the console under any name, anywhere you want. I'll save this console as Device Manager, for example, and drop it on my desktop (see Figure 13-49). I'm now just a double-click away from the Device Manager!

Figure 13-49
The Device Manager shortcut on the desktop

Administrative Tools

Windows 2000 and XP have combined almost all of the snap-ins into an applet in the Control Panel called *Administrative Tools.* Open the Control Panel and open Administrative Tools (Figure 13-50).

Figure 13-50
Administrative Tools

Administrative Tools is really just a folder that stores a number of pre-made consoles. As you poke through these, you'll notice that many of the consoles share some of the same snap-ins—nothing wrong with that. Of the consoles in a standard Administrative Tools collection, the ones you'll spend the most time with are Computer Management, Event Viewer, Performance, and Services.

EXAM TIP The CompTIA A+ certification exams have little interest in some of these snap-ins, so I won't cover them all. If I don't mention it, it's almost certainly not on the test!

Computer Management The *Computer Management* applet is a tech's best buddy, or at least a place where you'll spend a lot of time when building or maintaining a system (Figure 13-51). You've already spent considerable time with two of its components, System Tools and Storage. System Tools offers System Information, Performance Logs and Alerts, Device Manager, and more. Storage is where you'll find Disk Management. Each of these tools is of particular interest to techs, as you've seen earlier and will see again in Chapters 15 and 23.

Figure 13-51
Computer
Management applet

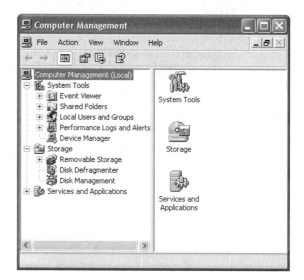

Event Viewer Event Viewer enables you to tell at a glance what has happened in the last day, week, or more, including when people logged in and when the PC had problems (Figure 13-52). You'll see more of Event Viewer in Chapter 23.

Figure 13-52
Event Viewer
reporting system
errors

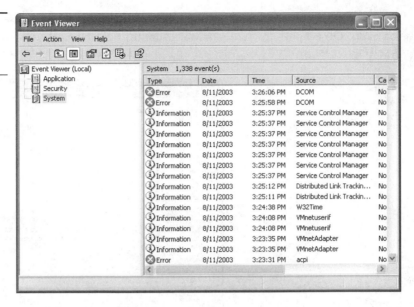

Performance   The Performance console consists of two snap-ins: System Monitor and
Performance Logs and Alerts. You can use these for reading *logs*—files that record information over time. The System Monitor can also monitor real-time data (Figure 13-53).

Figure 13-53
System Monitor
in action

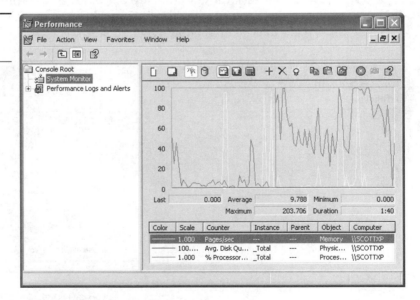

Suppose you just got a new cable modem and you want to know just how fast you can
download data. Click the plus sign (+) on the toolbar to add a counter. Click the Use Lo-

cal Computer Counters radio button, and then choose Network Interface from the Performance Object pull-down menu. Make sure the Select Counters from List radio button is selected. Last, select Bytes Received/Sec. The dialog box should look like Figure 13-54.

Figure 13-54
Setting up a throughput test

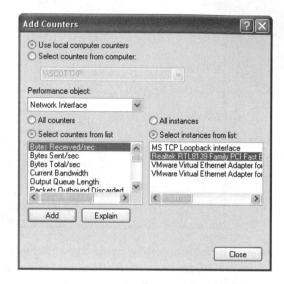

Click Add, and then click Close—probably not much is happening. Go to a Web site, preferably one where you can download a huge file. Start downloading and watch the chart jump; that's the real throughput (Figure 13-55).

Figure 13-55
Downloading with blazing speed

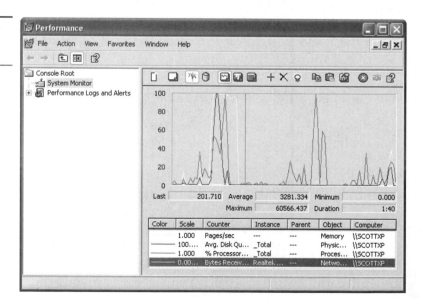

NOTE You'll learn more about the Performance console in Chapter 15.

Services Windows runs a large number of separate programs called *services*. The best way to visualize a service is to think of it as something that runs, yet is invisible. Windows comes with about 100 services by default, and they handle a huge number of tasks, from application support to network functions. The Services applet enables you to see the status of all services on the system, including services that are not running (Figure 13-56).

Figure 13-56
Services applet

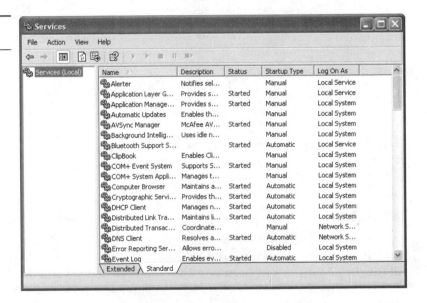

Right-click a service and select Properties to modify its settings. Figure 13-57 shows the properties for the Alerter service. See the Startup Type pull-down menu? It shows three options: Automatic, Manual, and Disabled. Automatic means it starts when the system starts, Manual means you have to come to this tab to start it, and Disabled prevents anything from starting it. Make sure you know these three settings, and also make sure you understand how to start, stop, pause, and resume services (note the four buttons underneath Startup Type).

Figure 13-57
Alerter service
properties

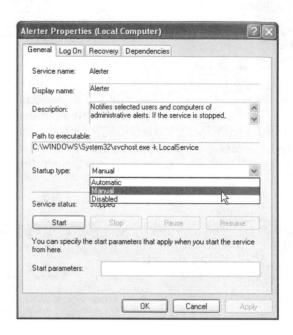

EXAM TIP   The CompTIA A+ certification exams are not interested in
having you memorize all of these services—just make sure you can manipulate
them!

OS Folders

Each modern version of Windows organizes essential files and folders in a similar fashion. All have a primary system folder for storing most Windows internal tools and files.
All use the Registry to keep track of all the hardware loaded and the drivers that enable
you to use that hardware. Finally, every version has a RAM cache file, enabling more
robust access to programs and utilities.

System Folder

SystemRoot is the tech name given to the folder in which Windows has been installed.
In most cases, as you might expect, Windows XP's SystemRoot is C:\WINDOWS, but
that's not always the case; during the installation process, you can change where Windows is installed, and for Windows 2000, SystemRoot by default is C:\WINNT.

It's handy to know about SystemRoot. You'll find it cropping up in many other tech
publications, and it can also be specified when adjusting certain Windows settings, to
make sure that they work under all circumstances. When used as part of a Windows
configuration setting, it's often written as %SystemRoot%.

If you don't know where Windows is installed on a particular system, here's a handy
trick. Go to a command prompt, type **cd %systemroot%**, and press ENTER. The prompt
will change to the directory in which the Windows OS files are stored. Slick!

Other Important Folders

Windows has a number of important folders other than the system folder. Here's a list of the ones you'll most likely encounter. For simplicity, let's assume the system root is C:\WINNT.

 NOTE Windows XP has more system folders than Windows 2000. This list only contains folders common to both Windows 2000 and XP.

- **C:\Program Files**   This is the default location for all of the installed programs.

- **C:\Documents and Settings**   This is where all of the personal settings for each user are stored. Every user has their own subfolder in Documents and Settings. In each user folder, you'll find another level of folders with familiar names such as Desktop, My Documents, and Start Menu. These folders hold the actual contents of these items.

- **C:\WINNT**   The SystemRoot has a number of critical subfolders, but surprisingly holds no critical files in the folder itself. About the most interesting file found here is good old notepad.exe. Remember that this is C:\WINDOWS on a Windows XP system!

- **C:\WINNT\FONTS**   All of the fonts installed in Windows live here.

- **C:\WINNT\SYSTEM32**   This is the *real* Windows! All of the most critical programs that make Windows run are stored here.

Registry

The *Registry* is a huge database that stores everything about your PC, including information on all the hardware in the PC, network information, user preferences, file types, and virtually anything else you might run into with Windows. Almost any form of configuration done to a Windows system involves editing the Registry. In Windows 2000/XP, the numerous Registry files (called *hives*) are in the \%SystemRoot%\System32\config folder. Fortunately, you rarely have to access these massive files directly. Instead, you can use a set of relatively user-friendly applications to edit the Registry.

The CompTIA A+ certification exams do not expect you to memorize every aspect of the Windows Registry. You should, however, understand the basic components of the Registry, know how to edit the Registry manually, and know the best way to locate a particular setting.

Accessing the Registry   Before we look in the Registry, let's look at how you access the Registry directly using a Registry editor. Once you know that, you can open the Registry on your machine and compare what you see to the examples in this chapter.

Windows 2000 comes with two Registry editors: REGEDT32.EXE, shown in Figure 13-58, and the much older REGEDIT.EXE (Figure 13-59). You start either of these programs by going to a command prompt and typing its name.

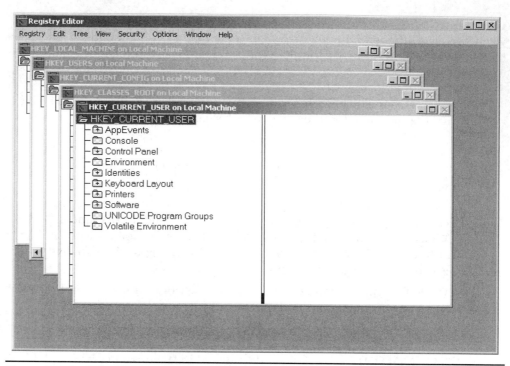

Figure 13-58 REGEDT32 in Windows 2000

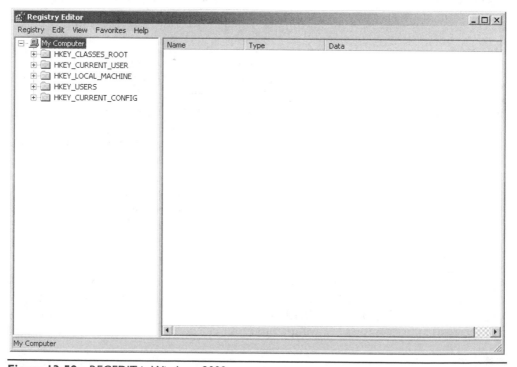

Figure 13-59 REGEDIT in Windows 2000

The reason for having two different Registry editors is long and boring, and explaining it would require a very dull 15-minute monologue (preferably with an angelic chorus singing in the background) about how the Registry worked in Windows 9x and Windows NT. Suffice it to say that in Windows 2000 only REGEDT32 is safe to use for actual editing, but you can use the older REGEDIT to perform searches, because REGEDT32's search capabilities are not very good.

Windows XP and Vista have eliminated the entire two-Registry-editor nonsense by creating a new REGEDT32 that includes strong search functions. No longer are there two separate programs, but interestingly, entering either REGEDIT or REGEDT32 at a command prompt will bring up the same program, so feel free to use either program name. Figure 13-60 shows REGEDIT on a typical Windows XP system.

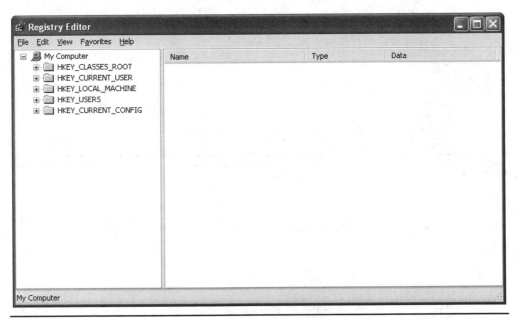

Figure 13-60   Registry Editor in Windows XP

Registry Components   The Registry is organized in a tree structure similar to the folders in the PC. Once you open the Registry Editor in Windows, you will see five main subgroups, or *root keys*:

- HKEY_CLASSES_ROOT
- HKEY_CURRENT_USER
- HKEY_USERS
- HKEY_LOCAL_MACHINE
- HKEY_CURRENT_CONFIG

Try opening one of these root keys by clicking on the plus sign to its left; note that more subkeys are listed underneath. A subkey also has other subkeys, or *values*. Figure 13-61 shows an example of a subkey with some values. Notice that REGEDIT shows keys on the left and values on the right, just as Windows Explorer shows directories on the left and files on the right.

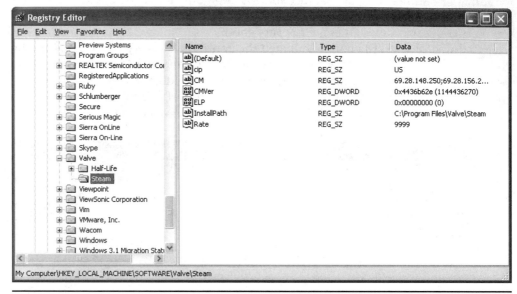

Figure 13-61   Typical Registry keys and values

NOTE   When writing about keys and values, I'll use the expression *key = value.*

The secret to understanding the Registry is to understand the function of the five root keys first. Each of these root keys has a specific function, so let's take a look at them individually.

HKEY_CLASSES_ROOT   This root key defines the standard *class objects* used by Windows. A class object is a named group of functions that define what you can do with the object it represents. Pretty much everything that has to do with files on the system is defined by a class object. For example, the Registry defines the popular MP3 sound file using two class objects. If you search the Registry for the .MP3 file extension, you will find the first class object, which associates the .MP3 file extension with the name "Winamp.File" on this computer (Figure 13-62).

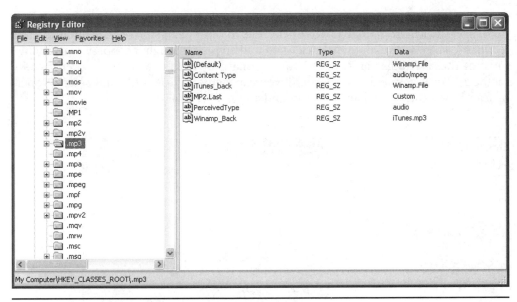

Figure 13-62   Association of .MP3 with Winamp

Ah, but what are the properties of Winamp.File? That's what the HKEY_CLASSES_ROOT root key is designed to handle. Search this section again for "Winamp.File" (or whatever it said in the value for your MP3 file) and look for a subkey called "open." This variable determines the *file association* (Figure 13-63), which is the Windows term for what program to use to open a particular type of file.

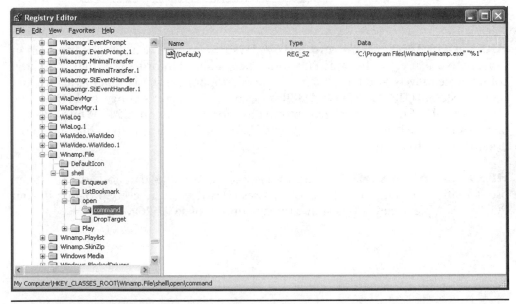

Figure 13-63   Winamp file settings

This subkey tells the system everything it needs to know about a particular software item, from which program to use to open a file, to the type of icon used to show the file, to what to show when you right-click on that file type. Although it is possible to change most of these settings via REGEDIT, the normal way is to choose more user-friendly methods. For example, in Windows XP you can right-click on a file and select Properties, and then click the Change button under Open With (Figure 13-64).

Figure 13-64
Changing the file
association the
easy way

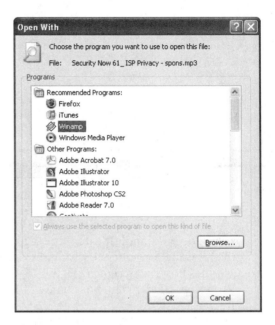

HKEY_CURRENT_USER and HKEY_USERS   Windows is designed to support more than one user on the same PC, storing personalized information such as desktop colors, screen savers, and the contents of the desktop for every user that has an account on the system. HKEY_CURRENT_USER stores the current user settings, and HKEY_US-ERS stores all of the personalized information for all users on a PC. While you certainly can change items like the screen saver here, the better way is to right-click on the desktop and select Properties!

HKEY_LOCAL_MACHINE   This root key contains all the data for a system's non-user-specific configurations. This encompasses every device and every program in your PC. For example, Figure 13-65 shows the description of a CD-ROM drive.

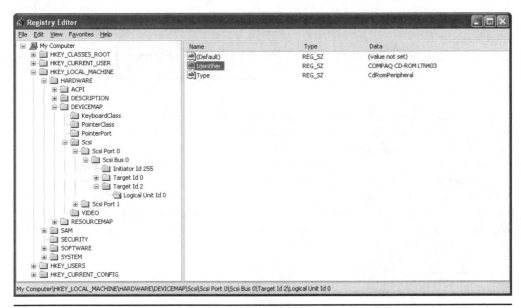

Figure 13-65   Registry information for a CD-ROM drive

HKEY_CURRENT_CONFIG   If the values in HKEY_LOCAL_MACHINE have more than one option, such as two different monitors, this root key defines which one is currently being used. Because most people have only one type of monitor and similar equipment, this area is almost never touched.

Swap File or Page File

Windows uses a portion of the hard drive as an extension of system RAM, through what's called a *RAM cache*. A RAM cache is a block of cylinders on a hard drive set aside as what's called a swap file, page file, or *virtual memory*. When the PC starts running out of real RAM because you've loaded too many programs, the system swaps programs from RAM to the swap file, opening more space for programs currently active. All versions of Windows use a swap file, so let's look at how one works.

Let's assume you have a PC with 256 MB of RAM. Figure 13-66 shows the system RAM as a thermometer with gradients from 0 to 256 MB. As programs load, they take up RAM, and as more and more programs are loaded (labeled A, B, and C in the figure), more RAM is used (Figure 13-67).

Figure 13-66
A RAM
thermometer

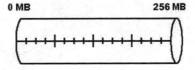

Figure 13-67
More programs
take more RAM

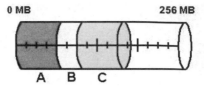

At a certain point, you won't have enough RAM to run any more programs (Figure 13-68). Sure, you could close one or more programs to make room for yet another program, but you can't keep all the programs running simultaneously. This is where virtual memory comes into play. Windows' virtual memory starts by creating a swap file that resides somewhere on your hard drive. The swap file works like a temporary storage box. Windows removes running programs temporarily from RAM into the swap file so other programs can load and run. If you have enough RAM to run all your programs, Windows does not need to use the swap file—Windows brings the swap file into play only when insufficient RAM is available to run all open programs.

Figure 13-68
Not enough RAM
to load program D

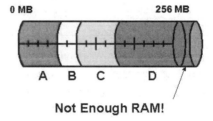

 NOTE Virtual memory is a fully automated process and does not require any user intervention. Tech intervention is another story!

To load, Program D needs a certain amount of free RAM. Clearly, this requires that some other program (or programs) be unloaded from RAM without actually closing the program(s). Windows looks at all running programs, in this case A, B, and C, and decides which program is the least used. That program is then cut out of or swapped from RAM and copied into the swap file. In this case, Windows has chosen Program B (Figure 13-69). Unloading Program B from RAM provides enough RAM to load Program D (Figure 13-70).

Figure 13-69
Program B being
unloaded from
memory

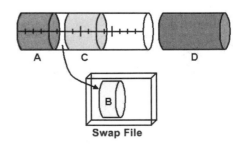

Figure 13-70
Program B stored in
the swap file—room
is made for
Program D

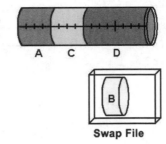

Swap File

It is important to understand that none of this activity is visible on the screen! Program B's window is still visible along with those of all the other running programs. Nothing tells the user that Program B is no longer in RAM (Figure 13-71).

Figure 13-71
You can't tell
whether a program
is swapped or not.

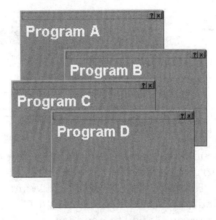

Program A

Program B

Program C

Program D

So what happens if you click on Program B's window to bring it to the front? The program can't actually run from the swap file; it must be reloaded back into RAM. First, Windows decides which program must be removed from RAM, and this time Windows chooses Program C (Figure 13-72). Then it loads Program B into RAM (Figure 13-73).

Figure 13-72
Program C is
swapped to the
swap file.

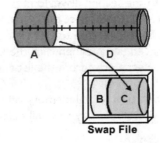

Swap File

Figure 13-73
Program B is
swapped back
into RAM.

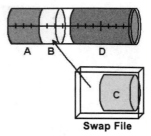

Swap File

Swapping programs to and from the swap file and RAM takes time. Although no visual clues suggest that a swap is taking place, the machine will slow down quite noticeably as Windows performs the swaps. However, the alternative (Figure 13-74) is far less acceptable. Swap files are a crucial aspect of Windows operation.

Figure 13-74
The alternative
to swap files

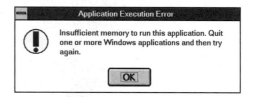

Windows handles swap files automatically, but occasionally you'll run into problems and need to change the size of the swap file or delete it and let Windows re-create it automatically. The swap file, or page file in Windows 2000 and XP, is PAGEFILE.SYS. You can often find it in the root directory of the C: drive, but again, that can be changed. Wherever it is, the swap file will be a hidden system file (see Chapter 14 for a discussion of file attributes), which means in practice that you'll have to play with your folder viewing options to see it.

NOTE If you have a second hard drive installed in your PC, you can often get a nice performance boost by moving your page file from the C: drive (the default) to the second drive. To move your page file, go to the Control Panel | System applet and select the Advanced tab. In the Performance section, click the Settings button to open the Performance Options dialog box. Select the Advanced tab, and then click the Change button in the Virtual Memory section. Select a drive from the list and give it a size or range, and you're ready to go!

Just don't turn virtual memory off completely. Although Windows can run without virtual memory, you will definitely take a performance hit.

Features and Characteristics of Windows 2000/XP

Microsoft Windows 2000 and XP are stable, high-performance operating systems that offer scalability and, above all else, security. Windows 2000 and Windows XP share the same core structure, files, and features, so the discussion that follows applies to both operating systems. Let's cover both in detail and then discuss the differences between the two OSs.

OS Organization

Three words best describe Windows 2000/XP organization: robust, scalable, and cross-platform. Microsoft takes an object-oriented approach to the OS, separating it into three distinct parts: the drivers, the NT Executive, and the subsystems (Figure 13-75).

Figure 13-75
Windows NT
organization

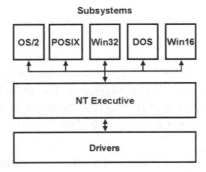

The NT Executive is the core power of the Windows 2000/XP OS, handling all of the memory management and multitasking. The NT Executive uses a Hardware Abstraction Layer (HAL) to separate the system-specific device drivers from the rest of the operating system (Figure 13-76).

Figure 13-76
NT Executive and
the HAL

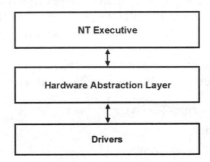

Windows 2000/XP's robustness comes from the separation of running processes into a myriad of subsystems. Each of these subsystems supports different types of applications in separate areas; that way, if one program locks up, it won't cause the entire system to lock up. Windows supports DOS and older programs designed for earlier versions of Windows, as well current Windows applications, via these numerous subsystems (Figure 13-77).

Figure 13-77
NT Executive can handle a lot of different OSs.

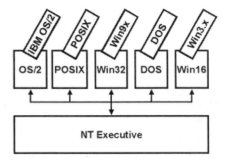

Windows 2000/XP's scalability makes them the only Microsoft OSs to support *symmetric multiprocessing (SMP)*, providing support for systems with up to 32 CPUs. Yee hah! The server versions of Windows go beyond SMP by adding the power of clustering, enabling multiple computers to share redundant data for ultimate protection. (Say that three times fast—I dare you!) If one system goes down, the other systems continue to run.

 TIP For those of you a little weak on networking, take a moment to read through Chapter 21. You need to understand basic networking to appreciate Windows 2000/XP.

NT File System (NTFS)

From the beginning, Microsoft designed and optimized every aspect of Windows 2000/XP for multi-user, networked environments. This is most evident in the NT file system. Whereas all previous Microsoft OSs used either FAT16 or FAT32, Windows 2000 and XP use a far more powerful and robust file system, appropriately called *NT File System (NTFS)*.

Chapter 10 contains a good basic description of NTFS, but let's go into a bit more detail. NTFS offers the following excellent features:

- Long filenames (LFNs)
- Redundancy
- Backward compatibility
- Recoverability
- Security

Long Filenames
NTFS supported LFNs long before FAT32 even existed. NTFS filenames can be up to 255 characters.

Redundancy
NTFS has an advanced FAT called the *Master File Table (MFT)*. An NTFS partition keeps a backup copy of the most critical parts of the MFT in the middle of the disk, reducing the chance that a serious drive error can wipe out both the MFT and the MFT copy. Whenever you defrag an NTFS partition, you'll see a small, immovable "chunk" in the middle of the drive; that's the backup MFT.

Backward Compatibility
For all its power, NTFS is amazingly backward compatible. You can copy DOS or Windows 9*x*/Me programs to an NTFS partition—Windows will even keep the LFNs.

Recoverability
Accidental system shutdowns, reboots, and lockups in the midst of a file save or retrieval wreak havoc on most systems. NTFS avoids this with *transaction logging*. Transaction logging identifies incomplete file transactions and restores the file to the original format automatically and invisibly.

Security
NTFS truly shines with its powerful security functions. When most people hear the term "security," they tend to think about networks, and NTFS security works perfectly in a networked environment, but it works equally well on single systems that support multiple users. Let's look at three major features of NTFS security: accounts, groups, and permissions.

Accounts   To use a Windows 2000/XP system, you must have a valid account (and, frequently, a password). Without an account, you cannot use the system (Figure 13-78).

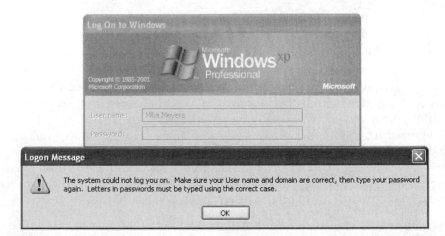

Figure 13-78   Login failure

Every Windows 2000/XP system has a "super" account called *administrator*. Remember when you saw the installation of Windows and it prompted you for a password for the administrator account? As you might imagine, this account has access to everything—a dangerous thing in the wrong hands!

Groups   The administrator creates user accounts with a special program called Users and Passwords in Windows 2000 (Figure 13-79) and User Accounts in Windows XP. Note that the account list has three columns: User Name, Domain, and Group. To understand domains requires an extensive networking discussion, so we'll leave that for Chapter 20. We'll instead focus here on user names and groups. A *user name* defines an account for a person who has access to the PC. A *group* is simply a collection of accounts that share the same access capabilities. A single account can be a member of multiple groups.

Figure 13-79
Users and Passwords
dialog box in
Windows 2000

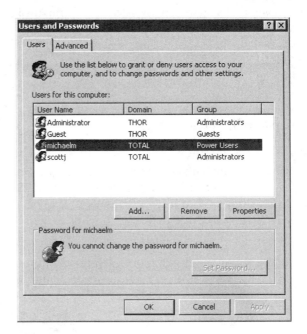

Groups make Windows administration much easier in two ways. First, you can assign a certain level of access for a file or folder to a group, instead of to just a single user account. For example, you can make a group called Accounting and put all the accounting user accounts in that group. If a person quits, you don't need to worry about assigning all the proper access levels when you create a new account for her replacement. After you make an account for the new person, you just add the new account to the appropriate access group!

Second, Windows provides seven built-in groups: Administrators, Power Users, Users, Backup Operators, Replicator, Everyone, and Guests. These built-in groups have a number of preset abilities. You cannot delete these groups.

- **Administrators**   Any account that is a member of this group has complete administrator privileges. It is common for the primary user of a Windows 2000/XP system to have his or her account in the Administrators group.

- **Power Users**   Power users are almost as powerful as administrators, but they cannot install new devices or access other users' files or folders unless the files or folders specifically provide them access.

- **Users**   Users cannot edit the Registry or access critical system files. They can create groups but can manage only those they create.

- **Backup Operators**   Backup operators have the same rights as users, except that they can run backup programs that access any file or folder—for backup purposes only.

- **Replicator**   Members of the Replicator group can replicate files and folders in a domain.

- **Everyone**   This group applies to any user who can log onto the system. You cannot edit this group.

- **Guests**   Someone who does not have an account on the system can log on using a Guest account if the system has been set up to enable that option. This group is useful in certain network situations.

Windows XP diverges a lot from Windows 2000 on user accounts. If you're running XP Professional and you are on a Windows domain, XP offers all the accounts listed above, but it adds four other specialized types, including Help Services Group and Remote Desktop Users. Windows XP Home and XP Professional, when it's installed as a standalone PC or connected to a workgroup but not a domain, run in a specialized networking mode called *simple file sharing*. A Windows XP system running simple file sharing has only three account types: Computer Administrator, Limited User, and Guest. Computer Administrators can do anything, as you might suspect. Limited Users can access only certain things and have limits on where they can save files on the PC.

NTFS Permissions   In the 2000/XP world, every folder and file on an NTFS partition has a list that contains two sets of data. First, the list details every user and group that has access to that file or folder. Second, the list specifies the level of access that each user or group has to that file or folder. The level of access is defined by a set of restrictions called NTFS permissions.

Permissions define exactly what a particular account can or cannot do to the file or folder and are thus quite detailed and powerful. You can make it possible, for example, for a person to edit a file but not delete it. You can let someone create a folder and not allow other people to make subfolders. NTFS file and folder permissions are so complicated that entire books have been written on them! Fortunately, the CompTIA A+ certification exams test your understanding of only a few basic concepts of NTFS permissions: Ownership, Take Ownership permission, Change permissions, Folder permissions, and File permissions.

- **Ownership**   When you create a new file or folder on an NTFS partition, you become the *owner* of that file or folder. A newly created file or folder by default gives everyone full permission to access, delete, and otherwise manipulate that file or folder. Owners can do anything they want to the files or folders they own, including changing the permissions to prevent anybody, even administrators, from accessing them.

- **Take Ownership permission** This special permission enables anyone with the permission to seize control of a file or folder. Administrator accounts have Take Ownership permission for everything. Note the difference here between owning a file and accessing a file. If you own a file, you can prevent anyone from accessing that file. An administrator who you have blocked, however, can take that ownership away from you and *then* access that file!

- **Change permissions** Another important permission for all NTFS files and folders is the Change permission. An account with this permission can give or take away permissions for other accounts.

- **Folder permissions** Let's look at a typical folder in my Windows XP system to see how this one works. My E: drive is formatted as NTFS, and on it I created a folder called E:\MIKE. In My Computer, it looks like Figure 13-80. I set the permissions for the E:\MIKE folder by accessing the folder's properties and clicking the Security tab (see Figure 13-81).

- **File permissions** File permissions are similar to Folder permissions. We'll talk about File permissions right after we cover Folder permissions.

Figure 13-80
My E:\MIKE folder—isn't it lovely?

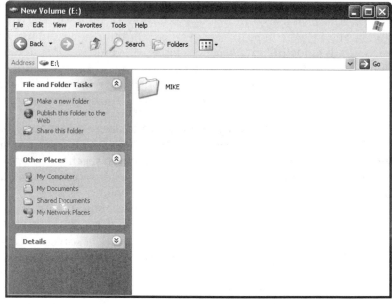

Figure 13-81
The Security tab lets
me set permissions.

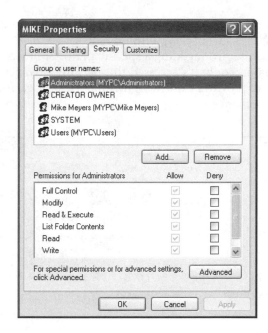

In Windows 2000/XP, just about everything in the computer has a Security tab in its properties, and every Security tab contains two main areas. The top area shows the list of accounts that have permissions for that resource. The lower area shows exactly what permissions have been assigned to the selected account.

Here are the standard permissions for a folder:

- **Full Control**   Enables you to do anything you want!
- **Modify**   Enables you to do anything except delete files or subfolders.
- **Read & Execute**   Enables you to see the contents of the folder and any subfolders.
- **List Folder Contents**   Enables you to see the contents of the folder and any subfolders. (This permission seems the same as the Read & Execute permission, but it is only inherited by folders.)
- **Read**   Enables you to read any file in the folder.
- **Write**   Enables you to write to files and create new files and folders.

If you look at the bottom of the Security tab in Windows 2000, you'll see a little check box that says Allow Inheritable Permissions from Parent to Propagate to This

Object. In other words, any files or subfolders created in this folder get the same permissions for the same users/groups that the folder has. Unchecking this option enables you to stop a user from getting a specific permission via inheritance. Windows XP has the same feature, only it's accessed through the Advanced button in the Security tab. Windows also provides explicit Deny functions for each option (Figure 13-82). Deny overrules inheritance.

Figure 13-82
Special permissions

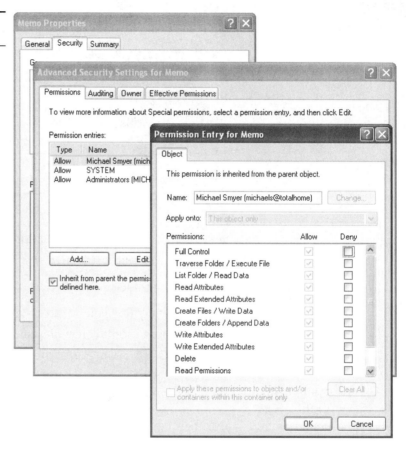

 EXAM TIP Don't panic about memorizing special permissions; just appreciate that they exist and that the permissions you see in the Security tab cover the vast majority of our needs.

File permissions are quite similar to folder permissions. Take a look at the Security tab on a typical file (Figure 13-83).

Figure 13-83
Security tab

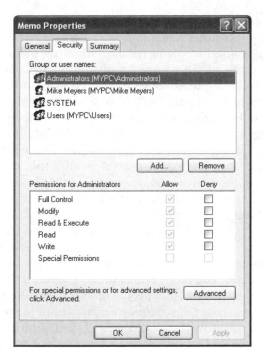

- **Full Control** Enables you to do anything you want!
- **Modify** Enables you to do anything except take ownership or change permissions on the file.
- **Read & Execute** If the file is a program, you can run it.
- **Read** If the file is data, you can read it.
- **Write** Enables you to write to the file.

Take some time to think about these permissions. Why would Microsoft create them? Think of situations where you might want to give a group Modify permission. Also, you can assign more than one permission. In many situations, we like to give users both the Read as well as the Write permission.

Permissions are cumulative. If you have Full Control on a folder and only Read permission on a file in the folder, you get Full Control permission on the file.

NOTE Windows XP Home has only a limited set of permissions you can assign. As far as folder permissions go, you can assign only one: Make This Folder Private. To see this in action, right-click a file or folder and select Sharing and Security from the options. Note that you can't just select the properties and see a Security tab as you can in Windows 2000 and XP Professional. Windows XP Home does not have file-level permissions.

Techs and Permissions   Techs, as a rule, hate NTFS permissions. You must have administrative privileges to do almost anything on a Windows 2000/XP machine, and most administrators hate giving out administrative permissions (for obvious reasons). If one does give you administrative permission for a PC, and something goes wrong with that system while you're working on it, you immediately become the primary suspect!

If you're working on an 2000/XP system administered by someone else, make sure he or she understands what you are doing and how long you think it will take. Have the administrator create a new account for you with administrator privileges. Never ask for the password for a permanent administrator account! That way, you won't be blamed if anything goes wrong on that system: "Well, I told Janet the password when she installed the new hard drive ... maybe she did it!" When you have fixed the system, make sure that the administrator deletes the account you used.

This "protect yourself from passwords" attitude transcends just Windows 2000/XP. PC support folks get lots of passwords, scan cards, keys, and ID tags. Most newer techs tend to get an "I can go anywhere and access anything" attitude, and this is dangerous. I've seen many jobs lost and friendships ruined when a tape backup suddenly disappears or a critical file gets erased. Everybody points to the support tech in these situations. In physical security situations, make other people unlock doors for you. In some cases, I've literally made the administrator or system owner sit behind me reading a magazine, jumping up and punching in passwords as needed. What you don't have access to can't hurt you.

The Boot Process

Windows 2000 and XP distinguish between the files that start the operating system (called the *system files*) and the rest of the operating system files (usually in the \WINDOWS or \ WINNT folders). The system files (memorize these!) consist of three required files: NTLDR, BOOT.INI, and NTDETECT.COM. If you're using a SCSI hard drive, there's a fourth file called NTBOOTDD.SYS. NTLDR (pronounced *NT loader*), begins the boot process.

You know from earlier chapters that to make a drive bootable requires an active, primary partition, right? Let's look at the process in a PC with a hard drive partitioned as C: and D:. Ready?

The CPU wakes up and runs the system BIOS, and then the BIOS sends out a routine looking for a valid operating system in the boot sector of the primary, master hard drive. The master file table (MFT) lives in the boot sector of the C: partition. It points to the location of the Windows 2000/XP system files, also on the C: drive, because that's the bootable drive. Windows calls the primary, active partition the *system partition* or the *system volume* (if it's a dynamic disk).

The Windows 2000/XP *boot files* consists of NTOSKRNL.EXE (the Windows kernel), the \WINNT\SYSTEM32\CONFIG\SYSTEM file (which controls the loading of device drivers), and the device drivers. Even though these files are the core of the Windows 2000/XP OS, they are not capable of booting, or starting, the system. For that feat, they require NTLDR, NTDETECT.COM, and BOOT.INI—the system files.

The system files start the PC and then, at the end of that process, point the CPU to the location of the boot files. The CPU goes over and chats with NTOSKRNL, and the GUI starts to load. The operating system is then up and running, and you're able to do work.

The odd part about all this is that Microsoft decided to make the OS files mobile. *The Windows operating system files can reside on any partition or volume in the PC.* The \

WINDOWS folder, for example, could very well be on drive D:, not drive C:. Whichever drive holds the core OS files is called the *boot partition*. This can lead to a little confusion when you say the system files are on my C: drive, but Windows is on my D: drive, but that's just the way it is. The vast majority of Windows 2000/XP systems have the system partition and the boot partition both on the same big C: partition.

You've got the process now in general, so let's look more specifically at the makeup and function of the individual files involved in the boot process.

System Partition Files

Windows 2000 and XP require the three system files in the root directory of the system partition:

- NTLDR
- BOOT.INI
- NTDETECT.COM

To see these files, go into My Computer and open the C: drive. Then open Folder Options, as shown in the "My Computer" section earlier in the chapter. Click on the Show Hidden Files and Folders radio button, uncheck the Hide Protected Operating System Files (Recommended) option, and click OK. Now when you return to viewing the folder in My Computer, you will see certain critical files that Windows otherwise hides from you, so you don't accidentally move, delete, or change them in some unintended way (Figure 13-84).

Figure 13-84 My Computer showing the system files

NTLDR

When the system boots up, the master boot record (MBR) or MFT on the hard drive starts the NTLDR program. The NTLDR program then launches Windows 2000/XP or another OS. To find the available OSs, the NTLDR program must read the BOOT.INI configuration file, and to do so it loads its own minimal file system, which enables it to read the BOOT.INI file off the system partition.

BOOT.INI File

The BOOT.INI file is a text file that lists the OSs available to NTLDR and tells NTLDR where to find the boot partition (where the OS is stored) for each of them. The BOOT. INI file has sections defined by headings enclosed in brackets. A basic BOOT.INI in Windows XP looks like this:

```
[boot loader]
timeout=30
default=multi(0)disk(0)rdisk(0)partition(1)\WINDOWS
[operating systems]
multi(0)disk(0)rdisk(0)partition(1)\WINDOWS="Microsoft Windows XP
Professional" /fastdetect
```

A more complex BOOT.INI may look like this:

```
[boot loader]
timeout=30
default=multi(0)disk(0)rdisk(0)partition(1)\WINDOWS
[operating systems]
multi(0)disk(0)rdisk(0)partition(1)\WINDOWS="Microsoft Windows XP
Professional" /fastdetect
multi(0)disk(0)rdisk(0)partition(1)\WINNT="Microsoft Windows 2000
Professional" /fastdetect
```

Such a BOOT.INI would result in the boot menu that appears in Figure 13-85.

Figure 13-85 Boot loader in Windows 2000 with System Recovery Console	Please select the operating system to start: Microsoft Windows 2000 Professional Microsoft Windows 2000 Recovery Console Previous Operating system on C: Use ↑ and ↓ to move the highlight to your choice. Press Enter to choose. Seconds until highlighted choice will be started automatically: 26 For troubleshooting and advanced startup options for Windows 2000, press F8.

This crazy `multi(0)disk(0)rdisk(0)partition(1)` is an example of the Advanced RISC Computing (ARC) naming system. It's a system that's designed to enable your PC to use any hard drive, including removable devices, to boot Windows. Let's take a quick peek at each ARC setting to see how it works.

`Multi(x)` is the number of the adapter and always starts with 0. The adapter is determined by how you set the boot order in your CMOS setting. For example, if you have a single PATA controller and a SATA controller, and you set the system to boot first from the PATA, any drive on that controller will get the value `multi(0)` placed in their ARC format. Any SATA drive will get `multi(1)`.

`Disk(x)` is only used for SCSI drives, but the value is required in the ARC format, so with ATA systems it's always set to `disk(0)`.

`Rdisk(x)` specifies the number of the disk on the adapter. On a PATA drive, the master is `rdisk(0)` and the slave is `rdisk(1)`. On SATA drives, the order is usually based on the number of the SATA connection printed on the motherboard, though some systems allow you to change this in CMOS.

`Partition(x)` is the number of the partition or logical drive in an extended partition. The numbering starts at 1, so the first partition is `partition(1)`, the second is `partition(2)`, and so on.

The `\WINDOWS` is the name of the folder that holds the boot files. This is important to appreciate! The ARC format looks at the folder, so there's no problem running different versions of Windows on a single partition. You can simply install them in different folders. Of course, you have other limitations, such as file system type, but in general, multibooting in Windows is pretty trivial. Better yet, this is all handled during the install process.

ARC format can get far more complicated. SCSI drives get a slightly different ARC format. For example, if you installed Windows on a SCSI drive, you might see this ARC setting in your BOOT.INI:

```
scsi(0)disk(1)rdisk(0)partition(1)
```

If you want to boot to a SCSI drive, Windows will add a fourth file to your system files called NTBOOTDD.SYS. This file will only exist if you want to boot to a SCSI drive. Most people don't boot to a SCSI, so don't worry if you don't see this file with the other three system files.

On rare occasions, you might find yourself needing to edit the BOOT.INI file. Any text editor handily edits this file, but most of us prefer to edit BOOT.INI via the System Setup dialog box. In Windows 2000/XP, open the System applet from the Control Panel. Click the Advanced tab and then click the Startup and Recovery button. The BOOT. INI options show up at the top (Figure 13-86).

Figure 13-86
BOOT.INI options

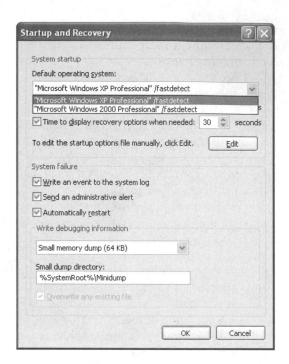

BOOT.INI has some interesting switches at the end of the ARC formats that give special instructions on how the operating system should boot. Sometimes Windows puts these in automatically, and sometimes you will add them manually for trouble-shooting. Here are a few of the more common ones:

- **/BOOTLOG**   Tells Windows to create a log of the boot process and write it to a file called Ntbtlog.txt.

- **/CMDCONS**   Tells Windows to start the Recovery Console (see Chapter 15).

- **/LASTKNOWNGOOD**   Tells Windows to boot the Last Known Good set of files (see Chapter 15).

- **/NOEXECUTE**   Newer CPUs come with Data Execute Protection (DEP) to prevent unruly programs from causing system lockups. The setting for this, /NOEXECUTE=OPTIN, is the default on Windows systems.

NTDETECT.COM

If the NTLDR determines that you have chosen to start Windows 2000/XP, it boots the system into protected mode and then calls on NTDETECT.COM to detect the installed hardware on the system. NTLDR then refers to the BOOT.INI file to locate the Windows boot files.

Critical Boot Files

Naming all of the critical boot files for Windows 2000/XP is akin to naming every mus-cle in the human body—completely possible, but time-consuming and without any real benefit. However, a few of the *most* important files certainly deserve a short mention.

Once NTLDR finishes detections, it loads NTOSKRNL.EXE, HAL.DLL, some of the Registry, and some basic device drivers; then it passes control to the NTOSKRNL.EXE file. NTOSKRNL.EXE completes the Registry loading, initializes all device drivers, and starts the WINLOGON.EXE program, which displays the Windows 2000/XP logon screen (Figure 13-87).

Figure 13-87
Where do you
want to go today?

Take the time to memorize the primary boot files and the boot process for Windows 2000/XP. Most boot errors are easily repaired if you know which files are used for booting and in which order they load.

Windows Versions

Up to this point we've been talking about two different versions of Windows: Windows 2000 Professional and Windows XP Professional. This is a great way to look at the big picture with Windows operating systems, but if you want to get detailed—and we need to get detailed—Windows 2000 and Windows XP are really families of Windows operating systems. In this section, we'll look at every version of Windows 2000 and XP, as well as a few other versions of Windows, and see the differences in detail.

Before Windows XP came along, Windows was in a bit of a mess. Microsoft had two totally different operating systems—each called Windows—that it sold for two different markets. Microsoft sold the old Windows 9x series (Windows 95, Windows 98, and Windows Me) for the home user and small office, and the much more powerful Windows NT was for corporate environments. The Windows 9x operating systems were little more than upgrades from the old DOS operating system, still tied to old 8088 programs (we call these 16-bit programs), unable to use the powerful NTFS file system and generally unstable for any serious work. Windows NT had all the power and security we love in Windows 2000 and XP, but it lacked a powerful interface and many other little niceties we expect in our Windows today.

Windows 2000 was the first step towards changing this mess. It was based on the old Windows NT, but for the first time it included a great interface, support for dang near any program, and was generally substantially easier to use than the old Windows NT. Microsoft originally presented Windows 2000 as a replacement for Windows NT, but its stability and ease of use motivated many knowledgeable Windows 9x users to upgrade. Windows 2000 is still very popular today, even with Windows XP and Windows Vista now available.

Windows 2000 comes in two versions: Professional and Server. Every description of Windows 2000 thus far has referred to the Professional version, so let's talk about Server. If you were to look at the Windows 2000 Server desktop, you'd be hard-pressed to see any obvious differences from Windows 2000. Windows 2000 Server (Figure 13-88) is the heavy-duty version, loaded with extra software and features that make it superb for running an office server. Windows 2000 Server is also extremely expensive, costing on average around $200 per computer that accesses the server.

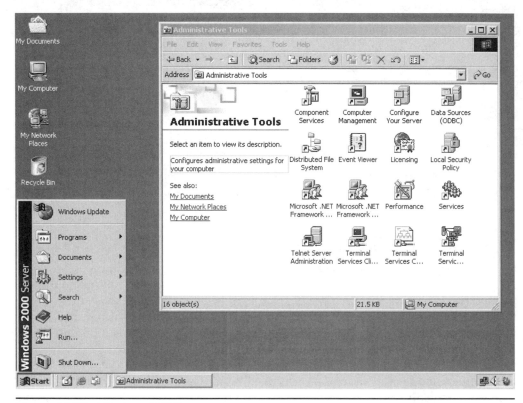

Figure 13-88 Windows 2000 Server

Windows XP was designed to be the one-stop OS for everyone. And because Microsoft sees three types of users—professionals, home users, and media junkies—Windows XP comes in three different versions: Windows XP Professional, Windows XP Home, and Windows XP Media Center. There is no official server version of Windows XP.

NOTE Windows Server 2003 is not an official XP version, but it is the server Microsoft likes folks to use with Windows XP.

Windows XP Professional

Microsoft Windows XP Professional offers a complete computing solution, tuned for office environments that support multiple users. It provides full-blown data security, and it is the only version of Windows with the capability of logging into a special Windows Server-controlled network called a *domain*. (Windows domains are discussed in detail in Chapter 21, "Local Area Networking.")

Windows XP Home

As its name implies, Windows XP Home is designed for the home and small office user. The best way to describe Windows XP Home is to list the Windows XP Professional features that Windows XP Home lacks. Windows XP Home does *not* have:

- **The ability to log on to a Windows domain** A Windows Home PC may log into any single Windows server, but you must have a username and password on every single server. With a domain, you can have one username and password that works on all computers that are members of the domain.

- **Encrypting File System** With Windows XP Professional you can encrypt a file so that only you can read it.

- **Support for multiple processors** Windows XP Home does not support more than one CPU. Surprisingly, it does support dual-core CPUs!

- **Support for Remote Desktop** A Windows XP Professional PC may be remotely accessed from another computer using the Remote Desktop (Figure 13-89). You cannot access a Windows XP Home system in this fashion.

Figure 13-89   Remote Desktop

- **Support for NTFS Access Control** Remember all those neato NTFS permissions like Full Control, Modify, and Read & Execute? Well, Windows XP Home doesn't give you the ability to control these NTFS permissions individually. When you look at the properties of a file or folder in Windows XP Home, you'll notice that there is no Security Tab. Instead, Windows XP Home's Sharing Tab (Figure 13-90) shows that only one folder, the Shared Documents folder, is open for sharing—very different from XP Professional!

Figure 13-90
Windows XP
Home Sharing tab

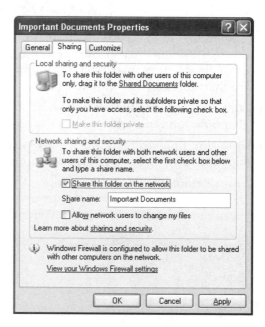

- **Support for group policies** Do you need to keep users from using a certain program? Do you want to prevent them from changing the screensaver? What do you want to do if they try to log in three times unsuccessfully? That's the job of group polices. Well, if you want this level of control on your system, get Windows XP Professional as XP Home doesn't support them. Group policies are discussed in detail in Chapter 23.

There are a few more differences between Windows XP Professional and XP Home, but these are the ones you're most likely to run into. Basically, if you want serious control of the folders, files, users, and network, you need XP Professional.

Windows XP Media Center

Microsoft Media Center is a specialized XP version that includes the very handy Windows Media Center program (Figure 13-91). Media Center is a powerful Personal Video

Recorder (PVR) program that enables you to watch and record television (you'll need a TV tuner card) and organize all of your media, from photos to music.

Figure 13-91
Microsoft Media
Center

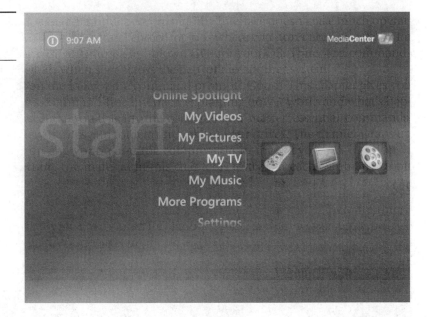

On the Microsoft Media Center Web site, Microsoft declares that the Windows XP Microsoft Media Center edition is based on Windows XP Professional; however, other than the Media Center program, Windows XP Media Center's capabilities are identical to those of Windows XP Home.

Windows 64-Bit Versions

Microsoft has multiple versions of Windows designed to support 64-bit CPUs. If you remember from the CPU chapter, there are two families of 64-bit CPUs: the ones that don't support 32-bit processors (like the Intel Itanium2) and ones that can run both 64-bit and 32-bit (like the Intel Core 2). The 64-bit-only version of Windows is called Windows XP 64-bit Edition (apparently Microsoft decided not to get cute when naming that one). Given that it only works on Intel Itanium processors, the chance of you seeing this operating system is pretty small unless you decide to work in a place with powerful server needs. The Windows XP Professional x64 Edition is much more common, as it runs on any AMD or Intel processor that supports both 32 and 64 bits (Figure 13-92).

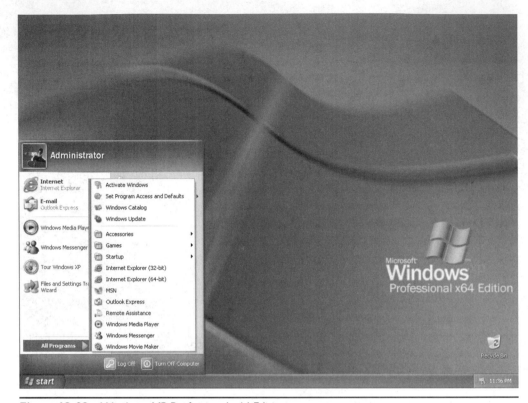

Figure 13-92 Windows XP Professional x64 Edition

 NOTE Windows Server 2003 also has a 64-bit version.

Windows XP 64-bit versions have had some impact, as they were the first stable Windows versions that truly supported 64-bit processing, but it was the introduction of Microsoft Vista that really started the move into the 64-bit world.

Beyond A+

There are a few more versions of Windows you should know about, starting with the newest version, Windows Vista. It's not on the CompTIA A+ exam (yet), but if you're working as a PC tech, you'll soon start encountering it. There are also several specialized versions that you won't find on regular PCs but that are very popular on PDAs, tablet PCs, and embedded systems.

Windows Vista

Even though Windows Vista is not a part of the current CompTIA A+ exams, it's important to at least recognize what Vista is, and know what choices you have when deciding which version of Vista you need for a particular PC. Windows has a number of different versions of Vista, each geared toward a particular market segment. Let's look at the different version of Vista.

Windows Vista Home Basic

Vista Home Basic is roughly equivalent to XP Home. Microsoft gears it to home users not needing more advanced multimedia support.

Windows Vista Home Premium

Vista Home Premium is the same as Vista Home Basic, but it adds PVR capabilities similar to those of Windows XP Media Center.

Windows Vista Business

Vista Business is the basic business version and has all the security, file sharing, and access controls seen in Windows XP Professional.

Windows Vista Enterprise

Windows Vista Enterprise adds a few features to Vista Business, including more advanced encryption and support for multiple languages from a single install location. This version is only available to enterprise (large corporate) buyers of Windows.

Windows Vista Ultimate

Vista Ultimate combines all of the features of every other Vista version and includes some other features, such as a game performance tweaker and DVD ripping capability.

Windows Mobile

Windows Mobile is a very small version of Windows designed for PDAs and phones. Windows Mobile is only available as an Original Equipment Manufacturer (OEM) product, which means you buy the device and it comes with Windows Mobile—you can't buy some PDA or phone and then buy Windows Mobile separately.

Windows XP Tablet PC

A tablet PC is a laptop with a built-in touch screen. The idea behind a tablet PC is to drastically reduce, if not totally eliminate, the use of a keyboard (Figure 13-93). In some situations tablet PCs have started to become quite popular. Windows XP Tablet PC edition is Microsoft's operating solution for tablet PCs. Tablet PC is still Windows XP, but it adds special drivers and applications to support the tablet.

Figure 13-93
Tablet PC

NOTE   You'll see more of Windows XP Tablet PC Edition in Chapter 19, "Portable Computing."

Windows Embedded

The world is filled with PCs in the most unlikely places. Everything from cash registers to the F-22 Raptor fighting plane contain some number of tiny PCs. These aren't the PCs you're used to seeing, though. They almost never have mice, monitors, keyboards, and the usual I/O you'd expect to see, but they are truly PCs, with a CPU, RAM, BIOS, and storage.

These tiny PCs need operating systems just like any other PC, and there are a number of different companies that make specialized OSs for embedded PCs. Microsoft makes Windows Embedded just for these specialized embedded PCs.

Chapter Review Questions

1. Which of the following is an advantage of running Windows 2000 on NTFS as opposed to FAT32? (Select two.)

   A. Security

   B. Encryption

   C. Long filenames

   D. FDISK

2. Which folder permission allows file creation and editing, but not deleting?

    A. Full Control

    B. Full Access

    C. Modify

    D. Read & Execute

3. What type of files are NTLDR, BOOT.INI, and NTDETECT.COM?

    A. Boot files

    B. System files

    C. Starter files

    D. NTFS files

4. What folder is a central storage location for user files?

    A. Program Files

    B. My Documents

    C. My Files

    D. My Network Places

5. Which utility is helpful in troubleshooting hardware?

    A. System Properties

    B. Device Manager

    C. Disk Management

    D. Security Center

6. Which Windows XP utility backs up critical files and settings and enables you to roll back to a previous state?

    A. Registry

    B. System Restore

    C. System Information

    D. Microsoft Management Console

7. Many tech tools are grouped together in which location?

    A. Start | All Programs | Tools

    B. Start | All Program | Tools | System Tools

    C. Start | All Programs | System Tools | Accessories

    D. Start | All Programs | Accessories | System Tools

8. Which utility is missing from the default Windows XP Home installation?

    A. Backup

    B. Character Map

    C. Computer Management

    D. User Accounts

9. What is displayed in the My Computer window?

    A. All the drives on your system

    B. All the Control Panel applets

    C. Installed programs

    D. Other computers on the network

10. Which Registry root key contains information about file types?

    A. HKEY_CLASSES_ROOT

    B. HKEY_LOCAL_MACHINE

    C. HKEY_CURRENT_CONFIG

    D. HKEY_USERS

Answers

1. **A, B.** NTFS offers security and encryption, two things you don't get with FAT32.

2. **C.** Modify permission enables you to create and edit files, but not delete them.

3. **B.** NTLDR, BOOT.INI, and NTDETECT.COM are the Windows 2000/XP system files.

4. **B.** Most users put files in My Documents.

5. **B.** For hardware in general, turn to the Device Manager.

6. **B.** System Restore does the trick here, enabling you to back up and restore your system.

7. **D.** You'll find many useful tools in Start | All Programs | Accessories | System Tools.

8. **A.** Backup is not installed by default in Windows XP Home.

9. **A.** My Computer shows your drives.

10. **A.** You'll find file information in HKEY_CLASSES_ROOT.

CHAPTER 14

Working with the Command-Line Interface

In this chapter, you will learn how to
- Explain the operation of the command-line interface
- Execute fundamental commands from the command line
- Manipulate files and folders from the command line

Whenever I teach a class of new techs and we get to the section on working with the command line, I'm invariably met with a chorus of moans and a barrage of questions and statements. "Why do we need to learn this old stuff?" "We're running Windows XP Professional, not Windows 3.1!" "Is this ritualistic hazing appropriate in an IT class?"

For techs who master the interface, the command line provides a powerful, quick, and elegant tool for working on a PC. Learning that interface and understanding how to make it work is not only useful, but necessary for all techs who want to go beyond baby-tech status. You simply cannot work on all PCs without knowing the command line! It's not just me who thinks this way. The CompTIA A+ certification exams test you on a variety of command-line commands for doing everything from renaming a file to rebuilding a system file.

If you're interested in moving beyond Windows and into other operating systems such as Linux, you'll find that pretty much all of the serious work is done at a command prompt. Even the Mac OS, for years a purely graphical operating system, now supports a command prompt. Why is the command prompt so popular? Well, for three reasons: First, if you know what you're doing, you can get most jobs done more quickly typing a text command than clicking through a GUI. Second, a command-line interface doesn't take much operating system firepower, so it's the natural choice for jobs where you don't need or don't want (or can't get to, in the case of Linux) a full-blown GUI for your OS. Third, text commands take very little bandwidth when sent across the network to another system.

So, are you sold on the idea of the command prompt? Good! This chapter gives you a tour of the Windows command-line interface, explaining how it works and what's happening behind the scenes. You'll learn the concepts and master essential commands, and then you'll work with files and folders throughout your drives. The chapter wraps up with a brief section on encryption and file compression in the "Beyond A+" section. A good tactic for absorbing the material in this chapter is to try out each command or bit of information as it is presented. If you have some experience working with a command prompt, many of these commands should be familiar to you. If the command line is completely new to you, please take the red pill and join me as we step into the Matrix.

Historical/Conceptual

Operating systems existed long before PCs were invented. Ancient, massive computers called *mainframes* and *minicomputers* employed sophisticated OSs. It wasn't until the late 1970s that IBM went looking for an OS for a new *microcomputer*—the official name for the PC—the company was developing, called the IBM Personal Computer, better known as the PC. After being rebuffed by a company called Digital Research, IBM went to a tiny company that had written a popular new version of the programming language called BASIC. They asked the president of his company if he could create an OS for the IBM PC. Although his company had never actually written an OS, he brazenly said, "Sure!" That man was Bill Gates, and the tiny company was Microsoft.

After shaking hands with IBM representatives, Bill Gates hurriedly began to search for an OS based on the Intel 8086 processor. He found a primitive OS called *Quick-and-Dirty Operating System (QDOS)*, which was written by a one-man shop, and he purchased it for a few thousand dollars. After several minor changes, Microsoft released it as MS-DOS (Microsoft Disk Operating System) version 1.1. Although primitive by today's standards, MS-DOS 1.1 could provide all the functions needed for an OS. Over the years, MS-DOS went through version after version until the last Microsoft version, MS-DOS 6.22, was released in 1994. Microsoft licensed MS-DOS to PC makers so they could add their own changes and then rename the program. IBM called its version PC-DOS.

DOS used a command-line interface, as you know from Chapter 12. You typed a command at a prompt, and DOS responded to that command. When Microsoft introduced Windows 95 and Windows NT, many computer users and techs thought that the DOS interface would go away, but it turned out that techs not only continued to use the command line, they *needed it* to troubleshoot and fix problems! With Windows 2000, it seemed once again that the command line would die, but again, that just didn't turn out to be the case.

Finally recognizing the importance of the command-line interface, Microsoft beefed it up in Windows XP. The command line in Windows XP offers commands and options for using various commands that go well beyond anything seen in previous Microsoft operating systems. This chapter starts with some essential concepts of the command line and then turns to more specific commands.

IT Technician

Deciphering the Command-Line Interface

So how does a command-line interface work? It's a little like having an Instant Message conversation with your computer. The computer tells you it's ready to receive commands by displaying a specific set of characters called a *prompt*.

```
Computer: Want to play a game?
Mike: _
```

You type a command and press ENTER to send it.

```
Mike: What kind of game?
Computer: _
```

The PC goes off and executes the command, and when it's done it displays a new prompt, often along with some information about what it did.

```
Computer: A very fun game...
Mike: _
```

Once you get a new prompt, it means the computer is ready for your next instruction. You give the computer commands in the graphical user interface (GUI) of Windows as well, just in a different way, by clicking buttons and menu options with your mouse instead of typing on the keyboard. The results are basically the same: you tell the computer to do something and it responds.

When you type in a command from the command line, you cause the computer to respond. As an example, suppose you want to find out the contents of a particular folder. From the command line, you'd type a command (in this case **DIR**, but more on that in a minute), and the computer would respond by displaying a screen like the one in Figure 14-1.

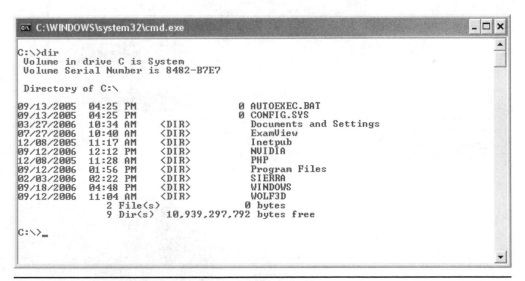

Figure 14-1 Contents of C: directory from the command line

In the GUI, you would open My Computer and click the C: drive icon to see the contents of that directory. The results might look like Figure 14-2, which at first glance isn't much like the command-line screen; however, simply by choosing a different view (Figure 14-3), you can make the results look quite a bit like the command-line version, albeit much prettier (Figure 14-4). The point here is that whichever interface you use, the information available to you is essentially the same.

Figure 14-2
Contents of C: in My Computer—Icon view

Figure 14-3
Selecting Details view in My Computer

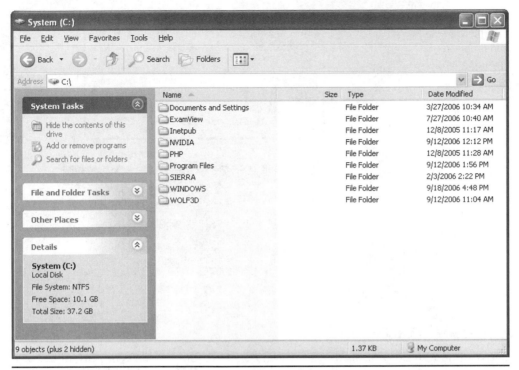

Figure 14-4 Contents of C: in My Computer—Details view

Accessing the Command Line

Before you can use the command-line interface, you've got to open it. You can use various methods to do this, depending on the flavor of Windows that you might be using. Some methods are simpler than others—just make sure that you know at least one, or you'll never get off the starting line!

One easy way to access the command-line interface is by using the Run dialog box. Click the Start button, and then select Run. If you're using Windows 2000 or Windows XP, type **CMD** and press the ENTER key (Figure 14-5). A window will pop up on your screen with a black background and white text—this is the command-line interface. Alternatively, buried in the Start menu of *most* computers, under Programs | Accessories, is a link to the command-line interface. In Windows 2000 and XP, it's called Command Prompt. These links, just like the Run dialog box, pull up a nice command line–interface window (Figure 14-6). To close the command line–interface window, you can either click the Close box, like on any other window, or simply type **EXIT** at any command prompt and press ENTER.

Figure 14-5
Type CMD in the
Run dialog box to
open a command-
line window.

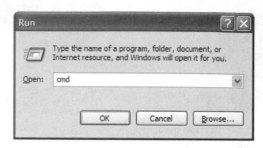

Figure 14-6
The command line-
interface window
with a C:\ prompt

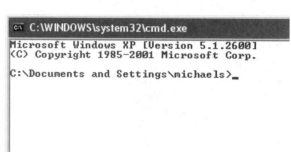

The Command Prompt

The command prompt is always *focused* on a specific folder. This is important because
any commands you issue are performed *on the files in the folder* on which the prompt is
focused. For example, if you see a prompt that looks like the line below you know that
the focus is on the root directory of the C: drive:

```
C:\>
```

If you see a prompt that looks like Figure 14-7, you know that the focus is on the
C:\Diploma\APLUS\ folder of the C: drive. The trick to using a command line is first to
focus the prompt on the drive and folder where you want to work.

Figure 14-7
Command prompt
indicating focus on
the C:\Diploma\
APLUS\ folder

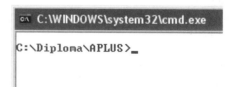

NOTE   You can hold down the F5 or F8 key during boot up to access the
Windows 2000 or Windows XP Advanced Options menu. This has an option
to boot to Safe Mode with Command Prompt. This loads the GUI into Safe
Mode and then overlays that with a command-line interface for rapid access
to a prompt. This saves you the step of going to Start | Run and typing CMD.
This is not the old-style command-prompt–only interface!

Filenames and File Formats

Windows manifests each program and piece of data as an individual file. Each file has a name, which is stored with the file on the drive. Windows inherits the idea of files from older operating systems—namely DOS—so a quick review of the old-style DOS filenames helps in understanding how Windows filenames work. Names are broken down into two parts: the filename and the extension. In true DOS, the filename could be no longer than eight characters, so you'll often see oddly named files on older systems. The extension, which is optional, could be up to three characters long in true DOS, and most computer programs and users continue to honor that old limit, even though it does not apply to modern PCs. No spaces or other illegal characters (/ \ [ ] | ÷ + = ; , * ?) could be used in the filename or extension. The filename and extension are separated by a period, or *dot*. This naming system was known as the 8.3 (eight-dot-three) naming system.

Here are some examples of acceptable true DOS filenames:

FRED.EXE   SYSTEM.INI   FILE1.DOC

DRIVER3.SYS   JANET   CODE33.H

Here are some unacceptable true DOS filenames:

4CHAREXT.EXEC   WAYTOOLONG.FIL   BAD÷CHAR.BAT   .NO

I mention the true DOS limitations for a simple reason: *backward compatibility.* All versions of Windows starting with 9*x* did not suffer from the 8.3 filename limitation, instead supporting filenames of up to 255 characters (but still using the three-character extension) using a trick called Long File Names (LFN). Windows systems using LFN retained complete backward compatibility by automatically creating two names for every file, an 8.3 filename and a long filename. Modern Windows using NTFS work almost exactly the same way as LFNs.

Whether you're running an ancient DOS system or the latest version of Windows Vista, the extension is very important, because the extension part of the filename tells the computer the type or function of the file. Program files use the extension .EXE (for executable) or .COM (for command). Anything that is not a program is some form of data to support a program. Different programs use different types of data files. The extension usually indicates which program uses that particular data file. For example, Microsoft Word uses the extension .DOC, while WordPerfect uses .WPD, and Power-Point uses .PPT. Graphics file extensions, in contrast, often reflect the graphics standard used to render the image, such as .GIF for CompuServe's Graphics Interchange Format or .JPG for the JPEG (Joint Photographic Experts Group) format.

Changing the extension of a data file does not affect its contents, but without the proper extension, Windows won't know which program uses it. You can see this clearly in My Computer. Figure 14-8 shows a folder with two identical image files. The one on top shows the Photoshop icon, which is the program that Windows will use to open that file; the one on the bottom shows a generic icon, because I deleted the extension.

Windows GUI doesn't show file extensions by default. Figure 14-9 shows the contents of that same folder from the command line.

Figure 14-8
What kind of file is the one on the lower right?

Figure 14-9
One file has no extension.

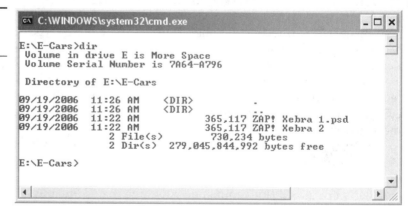

All files are stored on the hard drive in binary format, but every program has its own way of reading and writing this binary data. Each unique method of binary organization is called a file *format*. One program cannot read another program's files unless it has the ability to convert the other program's format into its format. In the early days of DOS, no programs were capable of performing this type of conversion, yet people wanted to exchange files. They wanted some type of common format that any program could read. The answer was a special format called *American Standard Code for Information Interchange (ASCII)*.

The ASCII standard defines 256, eight-bit characters. These characters include all the letters of the alphabet (uppercase and lowercase), numbers, punctuation, many foreign characters (such as accented letters for French and Spanish—é, ñ, ô—and other typical non-English characters), box-drawing characters, and a series of special characters for commands such as a carriage return, bell, and end of file (Figure 14-10). ASCII files, more commonly known as *text files*, store all data in ASCII format. The ASCII standard, however, is for more than just files. For example, the keyboard sends the letters of keys you press, in ASCII code, to the PC. Even the monitor outputs in ASCII when you are running DOS.

Figure 14-10
ASCII characters

000	(nul)	032	sp	064	@	096	`	128	Ç	160	á	192	└	224	α
001	☺ (soh)	033	!	065	A	097	a	129	ü	161	í	193	┴	225	ß
002	☻ (stx)	034	"	066	B	098	b	130	é	162	ó	194	┬	226	Γ
003	♥ (etx)	035	#	067	C	099	c	131	â	163	ú	195	├	227	π
004	♦ (eot)	036	$	068	D	100	d	132	ä	164	ñ	196	─	228	Σ
005	♣ (enq)	037	%	069	E	101	e	133	à	165	Ñ	197	┼	229	σ
006	♠ (ack)	038	&	070	F	102	f	134	å	166	ª	198	╞	230	µ
007	• (bel)	039	'	071	G	103	g	135	ç	167	º	199	╟	231	τ
008	◘ (bs)	040	(	072	H	104	h	136	ê	168	¿	200	╚	232	Φ
009	(tab)	041	)	073	I	105	i	137	ë	169	⌐	201	╔	233	Θ
010	(lf)	042	*	074	J	106	j	138	è	170	¬	202	╩	234	Ω
011	♂ (vt)	043	+	075	K	107	k	139	ï	171	½	203	╦	235	δ
012	♀ (np)	044	,	076	L	108	l	140	î	172	¼	204	╠	236	∞
013	(cr)	045	-	077	M	109	m	141	ì	173	¡	205	═	237	φ
014	♫ (so)	046	.	078	N	110	n	142	Ä	174	«	206	╬	238	∈
015	☼ (si)	047	/	079	O	111	o	143	Å	175	»	207	╧	239	∩
016	► (dle)	048	0	080	P	112	p	144	É	176	░	208	╨	240	≡
017	◄ (dc1)	049	1	081	Q	113	q	145	æ	177	▒	209	╤	241	±
018	↕ (dc2)	050	2	082	R	114	r	146	Æ	178	▓	210	╥	242	≥
019	‼ (dc3)	051	3	083	S	115	s	147	ô	179	│	211	╙	243	≤
020	¶ (dc4)	052	4	084	T	116	t	148	ö	180	┤	212	╘	244	⌠
021	§ (nak)	053	5	085	U	117	u	149	ò	181	╡	213	╒	245	⌡
022	▬ (syn)	054	6	086	V	118	v	150	û	182	╢	214	╓	246	÷
023	↨ (etb)	055	7	087	W	119	w	151	ù	183	╖	215	╫	247	≈
024	↑ (can)	056	8	088	X	120	x	152	ÿ	184	╕	216	╪	248	°
025	↓ (em)	057	9	089	Y	121	y	153	Ö	185	╣	217	┘	249	·
026	→ (eof)	058	:	090	Z	122	z	154	Ü	186	║	218	┌	250	·
027	← (esc)	059	;	091	[	123	{	155	¢	187	╗	219	█	251	√
028	∟ (fs)	060	<	092	\	124	|	156	£	188	╝	220	▄	252	ⁿ
029	↔ (gs)	061	=	093	]	125	}	157	¥	189	╜	221	▌	253	²
030	▲ (rs)	062	>	094	^	126	~	158	₧	190	╛	222	▐	254	■
031	▼ (us)	063	?	095	_	127	⌂	159	ƒ	191	┐	223	▀	255	

ASCII was the first universal file format. Virtually every type of program—word processors, spreadsheets, databases, presentation programs—can read and write text files. However, text files have severe limitations. A text file can't store important information such as shapes, colors, margins, or text attributes (bold, underline, font, and so on). Therefore, even though text files are fairly universal, they are also limited to the 256 ASCII characters.

Even in the most basic text, you need to perform a number of actions beyond just printing simple characters. For example, how does the program reading the text file know when to start a new line? This is where the first 32 ASCII characters come into play. These first 32 characters are special commands (actually, some of them are both commands and characters). For example, the ASCII value 7 can be either a large dot or a command to play a note (bell) on the PC speaker. ASCII value 9 is a Tab. ASCII value 27 is an Escape.

ASCII worked well for years, but as computers became used worldwide, the industry began to run into a problem—there's a lot more than 256 characters used all over the world! Nobody could use Arabic, Greek, Hebrew, or even Braille! In 1991, the Unicode Consortium, an international standards group, introduced *Unicode*. Basic Unicode is a 16-bit code that covers every character for the most common languages plus a few thousand symbols. With Unicode, you can make just about any character or symbol you might imagine—plus a few thousand more you'd never even think of. The first 256 Unicode characters are exactly the same as ASCII characters, making for easy backward compatibility.

A lot of e-mail programs can use Unicode characters, as can Internet message boards such as my Tech Forums. You can use Unicode characters to accent your writing or simply to spell a person's name correctly—Martin *Acuña*—when you address him. Working with Unicode is fun, so try it!

1. Open a text editing program, such as Notepad in the Windows GUI.

2. Hold down the ALT key on your keyboard, and, referring to Figure 14-10, press numbers on your keyboard's number pad to enter special characters. For example, pressing ALT-164 should display an ñ, whereas ALT-168 will show a ¿.

3. If you have access to the Internet, surf over to the Tech Forums (www. totalsem.com) and say howdy! Include some Unicode in your post, of course!

Drives and Folders

When working from the command line, you need to be able to focus the prompt at the specific drive and folder that contains the files or programs with which you want to work. This can be a little more complicated than it seems, especially in Windows 2000 and Windows XP.

At boot, Windows assigns a drive letter (or name) to each hard drive partition and to each floppy or other disk drive. The first floppy drive is called A:, and the second, if installed, is called B:. Hard drives usually start with the letter C: and can continue to Z: if necessary. CD-media drives by default get the next available drive letter after the last hard drive. Windows 2000 and XP enable you to change the default lettering for drives, so you're likely to see all sorts of lettering schemes. On top of that, Windows 2000 and XP let you mount a hard drive as a volume in another drive.

Whatever the names of the drives, Windows uses a hierarchical directory tree to organize the contents of these drives. All files are put into groups Windows calls *folders,* although you'll often hear techs use the term *directory* rather than *folder,* a holdover from the true DOS days. Any file not in a folder *within* the tree—that is, any file in the folder at the root of the directory tree—is said to be in the *root directory.* A folder inside another folder is called a *subfolder.* Any folder can have multiple subfolders. Two or more files with the same name can exist in different folders on a PC, but two files in the same folder cannot have the same name. In the same way, no two subfolders under the same folder can have the same name, but two subfolders under different folders can have the same name.

When describing a drive, you use its letter and a colon. For example, the hard drive would be represented by C:. To describe the root directory, put a backslash (\) after the C:, as in C:\. To describe a particular directory, add the name of the directory. For example, if a PC had a directory in the root directory called TEST, it would be C:\TEST. Subdirectories in a directory are displayed by adding backslashes and names. If the TEST directory had a subdirectory called SYSTEM, it would be shown like this: C:\TEST\SYSTEM. This naming convention provides for a complete description of the location and name of any file. If the C:\TEST\SYSTEM directory included a file called TEST2.TXT, it would be C:\TEST\SYSTEM\TEST2.TXT.

The exact location of a file is called its *path*. The path for the TEST2.TXT file is C:\ TEST\SYSTEM. Here are some examples of possible paths:

```
C:\PROGRAM FILES
C:\WINNT\system32\1025
F:\FRUSCH3\CLEAR
A:\REPORTS
D:\
```

Here are a few items to remember about folder names and file names.

- Folders and files may have spaces in their names.
- The only disallowed characters are the following eleven: * " / \ [ ] : ; | = ,
- Files aren't required to have extensions, but Windows won't know the file type without an extension.
- Folder names may have extensions—but they are not commonly used.

Mastering Fundamental Commands

It's time to try using the command line, but before you begin, a note of warning is in order: the command-line interface is picky and unforgiving. It will do what you *say*, not what you *mean*, so it always pays to double-check that those are one and the same before you press ENTER and commit the command. One careless keystroke can result in the loss of crucial data, with no warning and no going back. In this section, you'll explore the structure of commands and then play with four commands built into all versions of Microsoft's command-line interface: DIR, CD, MD, and RD.

Structure: Syntax and Switches

All commands in the Windows command-line interface use a similar structure and execute in the same way. You type the name of the command followed by the target of that command and any modifications of that command that you want to apply. The modifications are called up by using extra letters and numbers, called *switches* or *options*, which may follow either the command or the target, depending on the command. The proper way to write a command is called its *syntax*. The key with commands is that you can't spell anything incorrectly or use a \ when the syntax calls for a /. The command line is completely inflexible, so you have to learn the correct syntax for each command.

```
[command] [target (if any)] [switches]
```

or

```
[command] [switches] [target (if any)]
```

How do you know what switches are allowed? How do you know whether the switches come before or after the target? If you want to find out the syntax and switches used by a particular command, always type the command followed by a /? to get help.

DIR Command

The DIR command shows you the contents of the directory where the prompt is focused. DIR is used more often than any other command at the command prompt. When you open a command-line window in Windows XP, it opens focused on your user folder. You will know this because the prompt will look like this: `C:\Documents and Settings\username>`. By typing in **DIR** and then pressing the ENTER key (remember that you must always press ENTER to execute a command from the command line), you will see something like Figure 14-11.

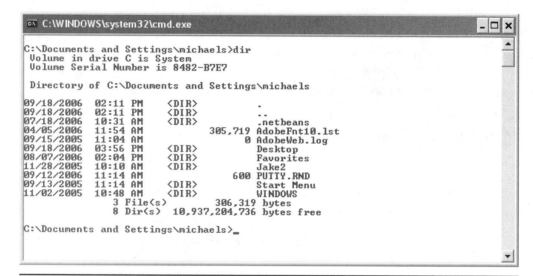

Figure 14-11 DIR in a user's folder

If you are following along on a PC, remember that different computers contain different files and programs, so you will absolutely see something different from what's shown in Figure 14-11! If a lot of text scrolls quickly down the screen, try typing **DIR /P** (pause). Don't forget to press ENTER. The DIR /P command is a lifesaver when you're looking for something in a large directory.

Some commands give you the same result, by the way, whether you include spaces or not. DIR/P and DIR /P, for example, provide the same output. Some commands, however, require spaces between the command and switches. In general, get into the habit of putting spaces between your command and switches and you won't run into problems.

 NOTE Extra text typed after a command to modify its operation, such as the /W or /P after DIR, is called a *switch*. Almost all switches can be used simultaneously to modify a command. For example, try typing **DIR /W /P**.

When you type a simple DIR command, you will see that some of the entries look like this:

```
09/04/2008    05:51 PM        63,664 bambi.jpg
```

All of these entries are files. The DIR command lists the creation date, creation time, file size in bytes, filename, and extension. Any entries that look like this are folders:

```
12/31/2004  10:18 AM    <DIR>         WINDOWS
```

The DIR command lists the creation date, creation time, *<DIR>* to tell you it is a folder, and the folder name. If you ever see a listing with *<JUNCTION>* instead of *<DIR>*, you're looking at a hard drive partition that's been mounted as a folder instead of a drive letter:

```
08/06/2006  02:28 PM    <JUNCTION>    Other Drive
```

Now type the **DIR /W** command. Note that the DIR /W command shows only the filenames, but they are arranged in five columns across your screen. Finally, type **DIR /?** to see the screen shown in Figure 14-12, which lists all possible switches for the command.

```
C:\Documents and Settings\michaels>dir /?
Displays a list of files and subdirectories in a directory.

DIR [drive:][path][filename] [/A[[:]attributes]] [/B] [/C] [/D] [/L] [/N]
  [/O[[:]sortorder]] [/P] [/Q] [/S] [/T[[:]timefield]] [/W] [/X] [/4]

  [drive:][path][filename]
              Specifies drive, directory, and/or files to list.

  /A          Displays files with specified attributes.
  attributes   D  Directories           R  Read-only files
               H  Hidden files          A  Files ready for archiving
               S  System files          -  Prefix meaning not
  /B          Uses bare format (no heading information or summary).
  /C          Display the thousand separator in file sizes.  This is the
              default.  Use /-C to disable display of separator.
  /D          Same as wide but files are list sorted by column.
  /L          Uses lowercase.
  /N          New long list format where filenames are on the far right.
  /O          List by files in sorted order.
  sortorder    N  By name (alphabetic)      S  By size (smallest first)
               E  By extension (alphabetic) D  By date/time (oldest first)
               G  Group directories first   -  Prefix to reverse order
  /P          Pauses after each screenful of information.
Press any key to continue . . .
```

Figure 14-12   Typing DIR /? lists all possible switches for DIR command.

Typing any command followed by a /? brings up a help screen for that particular command. Although these help screens can sometimes seem a little cryptic, they're useful when you're not too familiar with a command or you can't figure out how to get a command to do what you need. Even though I have almost every command memorized, I still refer to these help screens—you should use them as well. If you're really lost, type **HELP** at the command prompt for a list of commands you may type. Once you find one, type **HELP** and then the name of the command. For example, if you type **HELP DIR**, you'll see the information shown in Figure 14-12.

Directories: The CD Command

The CD (or CHDIR) command enables you to change the focus of the command prompt to a different directory. To use the CD command, type CD\ followed by the name of the directory on which you want the prompt to focus. For example, to go to the C:\OBIWAN directory, you would type CD\OBIWAN, and then press ENTER. If the system has an OBIWAN directory, the prompt will change focus to that directory, and appear as C:\OBIWAN>. If no OBIWAN directory exists or if you accidentally typed something like **OBIWAM**, you get the error "The system cannot find the path specified." If only I had a dollar for every time I've seen those errors! I usually get them due to typing too fast. If you get this error, check what you typed and try again.

To return to the root directory, type **CD** and press ENTER. You can use the CD command to point DOS to any directory. For example, you could type CD\FRED\BACKUP\TEST from a C:\ prompt, and the prompt would change to C:\FRED\BACKUP\TEST>— assuming, of course, that your system *has* a directory called C:\FRED\BACKUP\TEST.

Once the prompt has changed, type **DIR** again. You should see a different list of files and directories. Every directory holds different files and subdirectories, so when you point DOS to different directories, the DIR command will show you different contents.

The CD command allows you to use a space instead of a backslash, a convenient shortcut. For example, you could go to the C:\WINDOWS directory from the root directory simply by typing **CD WINDOWS** at the C:\ prompt. You can use the **CD [space]** command to move one level at a time, like this:

```
C:\>CD FRED
C:\FRED\>CD BACKUP
C:\FRED\BACKUP>CD TEST
```

Or, you can jump multiple directory levels in one step, like this:

```
C:\>CD FRED\BACKUP\TEST
C:\FRED\BACKUP\TEST>
```

A final trick: if you want to go *up* a single directory level, you can type **CD** followed immediately by two periods. So, for example, if you're in the C:\FRED\BACKUP directory and you want to move up to the C:\FRED directory, you can simply type **CD..** and you'll be there:

```
C:\FRED\BACKUP>CD..
C:\FRED>
```

Take some time to move the DOS focus around the directories of your PC using the CD and DIR commands. Use DIR to find a directory, and then use CD to move the focus to that directory. Remember, CD\ will always get you back to the root directory.

Moving Between Drives

The CD command is *not* used to move between drives. To get the prompt to point to another drive ("point" is command-line geek-speak for "switch its focus"), just type the drive letter and a colon. If the prompt points at the C:\Sierra directory and you want to see what is on the floppy (A:) drive, just type **A:** and DOS will point to the floppy drive. You'll see the following on the screen:

```
C:\Sierra>A:
A:\>
```

To return to the C: drive, just type **C:** and you'll see the following:

```
A:\>C:
C:\Sierra>
```

Note that you return to the same directory you left. Just for fun, try typing in a drive letter that you know doesn't exist. I know that my system does not have a W: drive. If I type in a nonexistent drive on a Windows system, I get the following error:

```
The system cannot find the drive specified.
```

Try inserting a floppy disk and using the CD command to point at its drive. Do the same with a CD-media disc. Type **DIR** to see the contents of the floppy or CD-media. Type **CD** to move the focus to any folders on the floppy or CD-media. Now return focus to the C: drive.

Using the DIR, CD, and drive letter commands, you can access any folder on any storage device on your system. Make sure you can use these commands comfortably to navigate inside your computer.

Making Directories

Now that you have learned how to navigate in a command-prompt world, it's time to start making stuff, beginning with a new directory.

To make a directory, use the MD (or MKDIR) command. To create a directory called STEAM under the root directory C:, for example, first ensure that you are in the root directory by typing **CD**. You should see the prompt

```
C:\>
```

Now that the prompt points to the root directory, type the following:

```
C:\>MD STEAM
```

Once you press ENTER, Windows will execute the command, but it won't volunteer any information about what it did. You must use the DIR command to see that you have, in fact, created a new directory. Note that the STEAM directory in this example is not listed last, as you might expect.

```
C:\>DIR
 Volume in Drive C is
 Volume Serial Number is 1734-3234
 Directory of C:\

07/12/2006  04:46 AM    <DIR>          Documents and Settings
06/04/2008  10:22 PM    <DIR>          STEAM
09/11/2006  11:32 AM    <DIR>          NVIDIA
08/06/2007  02:28 PM    <JUNCTION>     Other Drive
09/14/2006  11:11 AM    <DIR>          Program Files
09/12/2006  08:32 PM                21 statusclient.log
07/31/2005  10:40 PM               153 systemscandata.txt
03/13/2006  09:54 AM         1,111,040 t3h0
04/21/2006  04:19 PM    <DIR>          temp
07/12/2006  10:18 AM    <DIR>          WINDOWS
              3 file(s)      1,111,214 bytes
                        294,182,881,834   bytes free
```

What about uppercase and lowercase? Windows will support both but it always interprets all commands as uppercase. Use the MD command to make a folder called steam (note the lowercase) and see what happens. This also happens in the graphical Windows. Go to your Desktop and try to make two folders, one called STEAM and the other called steam, and see what Windows tells you.

To create a FILES subdirectory in the STEAM directory, first use the CD\ command to point the prompt at the STEAM directory:

```
CD\STEAM
```

Then run the MD command to make the FILES directory:

```
MD FILES
```

Make sure that the prompt points to the directory in which you want to make the new subdirectory before you execute the MD command. When you're done, type **DIR** to see the new FILES subdirectory. Just for fun, try the process again and add a GAMES directory under the STEAM directory. Type **DIR** to verify success.

Removing Directories

Removing subdirectories works exactly like making them. First, get to the directory that contains the subdirectory you want to delete, and then execute the RD (or RMDIR) command. In this example, let's delete the FILES subdirectory in the C:\STEAM directory. First, get to where the FILES directory is located—C:\STEAM—by typing **CD\STEAM**. Then type **RD FILES**. If no response was received from Windows, you probably did it right! Type **DIR** to check that the FILES subdirectory is gone.

The plain RD command will not delete a directory in Windows if the directory contains files or subdirectories. If you want to delete a directory that contains files or subdirectories, you must first empty that directory using the DEL (for files) or RD (for subdirectories) command. You can use the RD command followed by the /S switch to delete a directory as well as all files and subdirectories. RD followed by the /S switch is handy but dangerous, because it's easy to delete more than you want. When deleting, always follow the maxim "check twice and delete once."

Let's delete the STEAM and GAMES directories with RD followed by the /S switch. Because the STEAM directory is in the root directory, point to the root directory with CD\. Now execute the command **RD C:\STEAM /S**. In a rare display of mercy, Windows will respond with the following:

```
C:\>rd steam /s
steam, Are you sure (Y/N)?
```

Press the Y key and both C:\STEAM and C:\STEAM\GAMES will be eliminated.

Running a Program

To run a program from the command line, simply change the prompt focus to the folder where the program is located, type the name of the program, and then press the ENTER key on your keyboard. Try this safe example. Go to the C:\WINNT\System32 or C:\WINDOWS\System32—the exact name of this folder varies by system. Type **DIR/P** to see the files one page at a time. You should see a file called MEM.EXE (Figure 14-13).

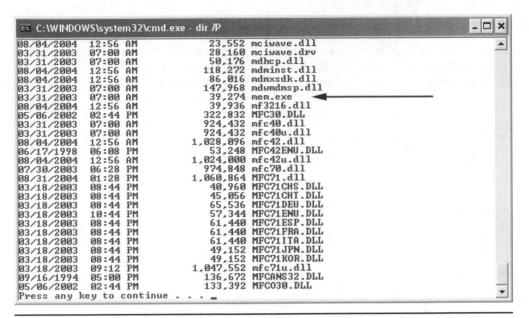

```
C:\WINDOWS\system32\cmd.exe - dir /P                                    _ □ ×
08/04/2004  12:56 AM            23,552 mciwave.dll
03/31/2003  07:00 AM            28,160 mciwave.drv
03/31/2003  07:00 AM            50,176 mdhcp.dll
08/04/2004  12:56 AM           118,272 mdminst.dll
08/04/2004  12:56 AM            86,016 mdmxsdk.dll
03/31/2003  07:00 AM           147,968 mdwmdmsp.dll
03/31/2003  07:00 AM            39,274 mem.exe        ◄─────────────────
08/04/2004  12:56 AM            39,936 mf3216.dll
05/06/2002  02:44 PM           322,832 MFC30.DLL
03/31/2003  07:00 AM           924,432 mfc40.dll
03/31/2003  07:00 AM           924,432 mfc40u.dll
08/04/2004  12:56 AM         1,028,096 mfc42.dll
06/17/1998  06:08 PM            53,248 MFC42ENU.DLL
08/04/2004  12:56 AM         1,024,000 mfc42u.dll
07/30/2004  06:28 PM           974,848 mfc70.dll
08/31/2004  01:28 PM         1,060,864 MFC71.dll
03/18/2003  08:44 PM            40,960 MFC71CHS.DLL
03/18/2003  08:44 PM            45,056 MFC71CHT.DLL
03/18/2003  08:44 PM            65,536 MFC71DEU.DLL
03/18/2003  10:44 PM            57,344 MFC71ENU.DLL
03/18/2003  08:44 PM            61,440 MFC71ESP.DLL
03/18/2003  08:44 PM            61,440 MFC71FRA.DLL
03/18/2003  08:44 PM            61,440 MFC71ITA.DLL
03/18/2003  08:44 PM            49,152 MFC71JPN.DLL
03/18/2003  08:44 PM            49,152 MFC71KOR.DLL
03/18/2003  09:12 PM         1,047,552 mfc71u.dll
09/16/1994  05:00 PM           136,672 MFCANS32.DLL
05/06/2002  02:44 PM           133,392 MFCO30.DLL
Press any key to continue . . . _
```

Figure 14-13   MEM.EXE displayed in the System32 folder

As mentioned earlier, all files with extensions .EXE and .COM are programs, so MEM.EXE is a program. To run the MEM.EXE program, just type the filename, in this case **MEM**, and press ENTER (Figure 14-14). Note that you do not have to type the .EXE extension, although you can. Congratulations! You have just run your first program from the command line!

Figure 14-14
Running MEM
in Windows XP

```
C:\WINDOWS\system32\cmd.exe

C:\WINDOWS\system32>mem

     655360 bytes total conventional memory
     655360 bytes available to MS-DOS
     598576 largest executable program size

   1048576 bytes total contiguous extended memory
         0 bytes available contiguous extended memory
    941056 bytes available XMS memory
           MS-DOS resident in High Memory Area

C:\WINDOWS\system32>
```

NOTE Windows includes a lot of command-line tools for specific jobs such as starting and stopping services, viewing computers on a network, converting hard drive file systems, and more. The book discusses these task-specific tools in the chapters that reflect their task. Chapter 21, "Local Area Networking," goes into detail on the versatile and powerful NET command, for example. You'll read about the CONVERT command in Chapter 23, "Computer Security." I couldn't resist throwing in two of the more interesting tools, COMPACT and CIPHER in the Beyond A+ section of this chapter.

Working with Files

This section deals with basic file manipulation. You will learn how to look at, copy, move, rename, and delete files. You'll look at the ins and outs of batch files. The examples in this section are based on a C: root directory with the following files and directories:

```
C:\>dir
 Volume in drive C has no label.
 Volume Serial Number is 4C62-1572

 Directory of C:\

05/26/2006  11:37 PM                    0 AILog.txt
05/29/2006  05:33 PM                5,776 aoedoppl.txt
05/29/2006  05:33 PM                2,238 aoeWVlog.txt
07/12/2006  10:38 AM    <DIR>          books
07/15/2005  02:45 PM                1,708 CtDrvStp.log
07/12/2006  04:46 AM    <DIR>          Documents and Settings
06/04/2006  10:22 PM    <DIR>          Impressions Games
09/11/2005  11:32 AM    <DIR>          NVIDIA
08/06/2006  02:28 PM    <JUNCTION>     Other Drive
01/03/2005  01:12 PM    <DIR>          pers-drv
09/14/2006  11:11 AM    <DIR>          Program Files
09/12/2006  08:32 PM                   21 statusclient.log
07/31/2005  10:40 PM                  153 systemscandata.txt
03/13/2006  09:54 AM            1,111,040 t3h0
04/21/2006  04:19 PM    <DIR>          temp
01/10/2006  07:07 PM    <DIR>          WebCam
12/31/2004  10:18 AM    <DIR>          WINDOWS
09/14/2006  12:48 PM    <DIR>          WINNT
01/03/2005  09:06 AM    <DIR>          WUTemp
               7 File(s)      1,120,936 bytes
              12 Dir(s)  94,630,002,688 bytes free
```

Because you probably don't have a PC with these files and directories, follow the examples but use what's on your drive. In other words, create your own folders and copy files to them from various folders currently on your system.

Once you get beyond navigation, command-line commands take on a bit more complexity. To alter a file or folder with a command, for example, you would follow this syntax:

Command | Source | Destination.

So, in a simple example using the rename command (REN), here is the command to change a file name from RICO.TXT to ARTURO.TXT.

```
REN RICO.TEX ARTURO.TXT
```

REN is the command; RICO.TXT is the source file; ARTURO.TXT is the intended destination or culmination of the command.

Now that you're armed with a basic grasp of the format for command-line commands, let's check out some of the common commands. You'll end up using most, if not all, of these commands as a PC tech.

Attributes

Remember back in the last chapter when you had to make changes to the folder options in My Computer to see NTLDR, NTDETECT.COM, and other files? You were actually seeing files with special attributes.

All files have four special values, or *attributes*, which determine how programs (like My Computer) treat the file in special situations. The first attribute is the hidden attribute. If a file is hidden, it will not be displayed when the DIR command is issued. Next is the read-only attribute. A read-only file cannot be modified or deleted. Third is the system attribute, which is used only for system files such as NTLDR and BOOT.INI. In reality, it does nothing more than provide an easy identifier for these files. Fourth is the archive attribute, which is used by backup software to identify files that have been changed since their last backup.

ATTRIB.EXE is an external command-line program that enables you to inspect and change file attributes. To inspect a file's attributes, type the **ATTRIB** command followed by the name of the file. To see the attributes of the file AILog.txt, type **ATTRIB AILOG.TXT**. The result is

```
A       AILog.txt
```

The letter *A* stands for archive, the only attribute of AILog.txt.

Go to the C:\ directory and type **ATTRIB** by itself. You'll see a result similar to the following:

```
C:\>attrib
A               C:\AILog.txt
A               C:\aoedoppl.txt
A               C:\aoeWVlog.txt
A   H           C:\AUTOEXEC.BAT
A   SH          C:\boot.ini
A   H           C:\CONFIG.SYS
A               C:\CtDrvStp.log
A   SH          C:\hiberfil.sys
A   SHR         C:\IO.SYS
A   SHR         C:\MSDOS.SYS
A   SHR         C:\NTDETECT.COM
A   SHR         C:\ntldr
A   SH          C:\pagefile.sys
A               C:\statusclient.log
A               C:\systemscandata.txt
A               C:\t3h0
```

The letter *R* means read-only, *H* is hidden, and *S* is system. Hey! There are some new files there! That's right, some were hidden. Don't panic if you see a number of files different from those just listed. No two C:\ directories are ever the same. In most cases, you'll see many more files than just these. Notice that important files, NTLDR and NT-DETECT.COM, have the system, hidden, and read-only attributes set. Microsoft does this to protect them from accidental deletion.

The ATTRIB command is also used to change a file's attributes. To add an attribute to a file, type the attribute letter preceded by a plus sign (+) as an option, and then type the filename. To delete an attribute, use a minus sign (–). For example, to add the read-only attribute to the file AILog.txt, type this:

```
ATTRIB +R AILOG.TXT
```

To remove the archive attribute, type this:

```
ATTRIB -A AILOG.TXT
```

Multiple attributes can be added or removed in one command. Here's an example of removing three attributes from the NTDETECT.COM file:

```
ATTRIB -R -S -H NTDETECT.COM
```

You can also automatically apply ATTRIB to matching files in subdirectories by using the /s switch at the end of the statement. For example, if you had lots of files in your My Music folder that you wanted to hide, but they were neatly organized in many subdirectories, you could readily use ATTRIB to change all of them with a simple command. Change directories from the prompt until you're at the My Music folder and then type the following:

```
ATTRIB +H *.MP3 /S
```

When you press the ENTER key, all your music files in My Music and any My Music subdirectories will become hidden files.

Wildcards

Visualize having 273 files in one directory. A few of these files have the extension .DOC, but most do not. You are looking only for files with the .DOC extension. Wouldn't it be nice to type the DIR command so that only the .DOC files come up? You can do this using wildcards.

A wildcard is one of two special characters, asterisk (*) and question mark (?), that can be used in place of all or part of a filename, often to enable a command-line command to act on more than one file at a time. Wildcards work with all command-line commands that take filenames. A great example is the DIR command. When you execute a plain DIR command, it finds and displays all the files and folders in the specified directory; however, you can also narrow its search by adding a filename. For example, if you type the command **DIR AILOG.TXT** while in your root (C:\) directory, you get the following result:

```
C:\>dir AILOG.TXT
 Volume in drive C has no label.
 Volume Serial Number is 4C62-1572
 Directory of C:\
05/26/2006  11:37 PM                    0 AILog.txt
               1 File(s)              0 bytes
               0 Dir(s)  94,630,195,200 bytes free
```

If you just want to confirm the presence of a particular file in a particular place, this is very convenient. But suppose you want to see all files with the extension .TXT. In that case, you use the * wildcard, like this: **DIR *.TXT**. A good way to think of the * wildcard is *"I don't care."* Replace the part of the filename that you don't care about with an asterisk (*). The result of DIR *.TXT would look like this:

```
Volume in drive C has no label.
 Volume Serial Number is 4C62-1572

 Directory of C:\

05/26/2006  11:37 PM                 0 AILog.txt
05/29/2006  05:33 PM             5,776 aoedoppl.txt
05/29/2006  05:33 PM             2,238 aoeWVlog.txt
07/31/2005  10:40 PM               153 systemscandata.txt
               4 File(s)          8,167 bytes
               0 Dir(s)  94,630,002,688 bytes free
```

Wildcards also substitute for parts of filenames. This DIR command will find every file that starts with the letter *a:*

```
C:\>dir a*.*
 Volume in drive C has no label.
 Volume Serial Number is 4C62-1572

 Directory of C:\

05/26/2006  11:37 PM                 0 AILog.txt
05/29/2006  05:33 PM             5,776 aoedoppl.txt
05/29/2006  05:33 PM             2,238 aoeWVlog.txt
               3 File(s)          8,014 bytes
               0 Dir(s)  94,629,675,008 bytes free
```

We've used wildcards only with the DIR command, but virtually every command that deals with files will take wildcards. Let's examine the REN and DEL commands and see how they use wildcards.

Renaming Files

To rename files, you use the REN or RENAME command, which seems pretty straightforward. To rename the file IMG033.jpg to park.jpg, type this and press the ENTER key:

```
ren img033.jpg park.jpg
```

"That's great," you might be thinking, "but what about using a more complex and descriptive filename, like Sunny day in the park.jpg?" Type what should work, like this:

```
ren img033.jpg Sunny day in the park.jpg
```

But you'll get an error message (Figure 14-15). Even the tried-and-true method of seeking help by typing the command followed by /? doesn't give you the answer.

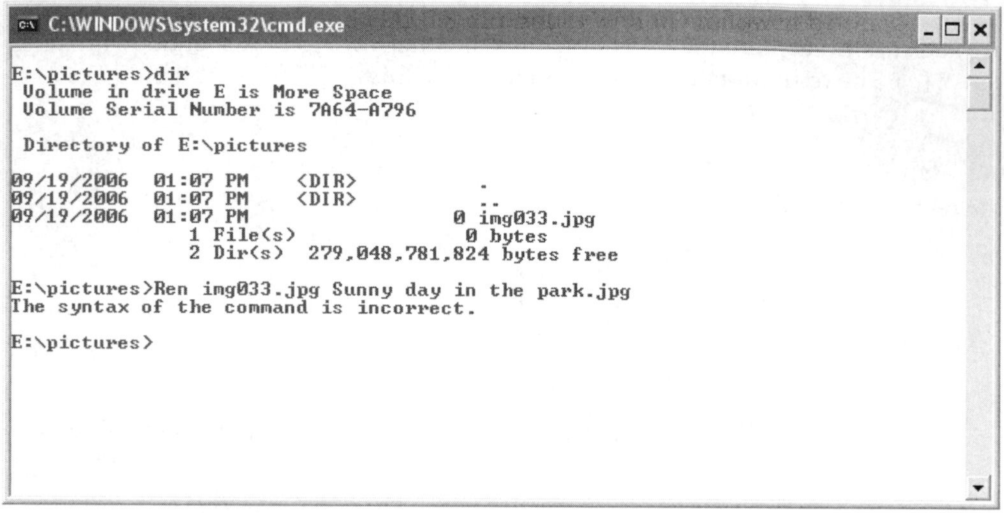

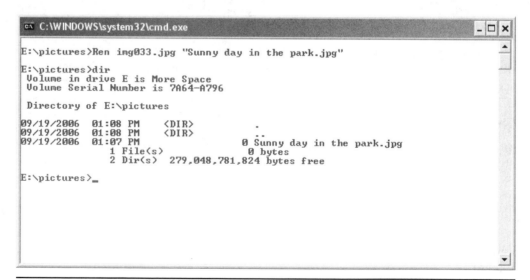

Figure 14-15   Rename failed me.

You can use more complicated names by putting them in quotation marks. Figure 14-16 shows the same command that failed but now succeeds because of the quotation marks.

Figure 14-16   Success at last!

Deleting Files

To delete files, you use the DEL or ERASE command. DEL and ERASE are identical commands and can be used interchangeably. Deleting files is simple—maybe too simple. Windows' users enjoy the luxury of retrieving deleted files from the Recycle Bin on those "Oops, I didn't mean to delete that" occasions everyone encounters at one time or another. The command line, however, shows no such mercy to the careless user. It has no function equivalent to the Windows Recycle Bin. Once a file has been erased, it can be recovered only by using a special recovery utility such as Norton's UNERASE. Again, the rule here is to *check twice and delete once.*

To delete a single file, type the **DEL** command followed by the name of the file to delete. To delete the file AILOG.TXT, for example, type this:

```
DEL AILOG.TXT
```

Although nothing will appear on the screen to confirm it, the file is now gone. To confirm that the AILOG.TXT file is no longer listed, use the DIR command.

As with the DIR command, you can use wildcards with the DEL and ERASE commands to delete multiple files. For example, to delete all files with the extension .TXT in a directory, you would type this:

```
DEL *.TXT
```

To delete all files with the filename CONFIG in a directory, type **DEL CONFIG.***. To delete all the files in a directory, you can use the popular *.* wildcard (often pronounced "star-dot-star"), like this:

```
DEL *.*
```

This is one of the few command-line commands that will elicit a response. Upon receiving the DEL *.* command, Windows will respond with "Are you sure? (Y/N)," to which you respond with a *Y* or *N*. Pressing Y will erase every file in the directory, so be careful when using *.*!

Don't confuse deleting *files* with deleting *directories.* DEL deletes files, but it will not remove directories. Use RD to delete directories.

Copying and Moving Files

The ability to copy and move files in a command line is crucial to all technicians. Due to its finicky nature and many options, the COPY command is also rather painful to learn, especially if you're used to dragging icons in Windows. The following tried-and-true, five-step process will make it easier, but the real secret is to get in front of a C:\ prompt and just copy and move files around until you're comfortable. Keep in mind that the only difference between copying and moving is whether the original is left behind (COPY) or not (MOVE). Once you've learned the COPY command, you've learned the MOVE command!

Mike's Five-Step COPY/MOVE Process

I've been teaching folks how to copy and move files for years using this handy process. Keep in mind that hundreds of variations on this process exist. As you become more confident with these commands, try doing a COPY /? or MOVE /? at any handy prompt to see the real power of these commands. But first, follow this process step-by-step:

1. Point the command prompt to the directory containing the files to be copied or moved.

2. Type **COPY** or **MOVE** and a space.

3. Type the *name(s)* of the file(s) to be copied/moved (with or without wildcards) and a space.

4. Type the *path* of the new location for the files.

5. Press ENTER.

Let's try an example. The directory C:\STEAM contains the file README.TXT. We'll copy this file to the floppy drive (A:).

1. Type **CD\STEAM** to point command prompt to the STEAM directory.

   ```
   C:\>CD\STEAM
   ```

2. Type **COPY** and a space.

   ```
   C:\STEAM>COPY _
   ```

3. Type **README.TXT** and a space.

   ```
   C:\STEAM>COPY README.TXT _
   ```

4. Type **A:**.

   ```
   C:\STEAM>COPY README.TXT A:\
   ```

5. Press ENTER.

   The entire command and response would look like this:

   ```
   C:\STEAM>COPY README.TXT A:\
   1 file(s) copied
   ```

If you point the command prompt to the A: drive and type **DIR**, the README.TXT file will be visible. Let's try another example. Suppose 100 files are in the C:\DOCS directory, 30 of which have the .DOC extension, and suppose you want to move those files to the C:\STEAM directory. Follow these steps:

1. Type **CD\DOCS** to point the command prompt to the DOCS directory.

   ```
   C:\>CD\DOCS
   ```

2. Type **MOVE** and a space.

   ```
   C:\DOCS>MOVE _
   ```

3. Type ***.DOC** and a space.

   ```
   C:\DOCS>MOVE *.DOC _
   ```

4. Type **C:\STEAM**.

   ```
   C:\DOCS>MOVE *.DOC C:\STEAM
   ```

5. Press ENTER.

   ```
   C:\DOCS>MOVE *.DOC C:\STEAM
   30 file(s) copied
   ```

The power of the COPY/MOVE command makes it rather dangerous. The COPY/ MOVE command not only lets you put a file in a new location, but it lets you change the name of the file at the same time. Suppose you want to copy a file called AUTO-EXEC.BAT from your C:\ folder to a floppy disk, for example, but you want the name of the copy on the floppy disk to be AUTO1.BAT. You can do both things with one COPY command, like this:

```
COPY C:\AUTOEXEC.BAT A:\AUTO1.BAT
```

Not only does the AUTOEXEC.BAT file get copied to the floppy disk, but the copy also gets the new name AUTO1.BAT.

As another example, move all of the files with the extension .DOC from the C:\ DOCS directory to the C:\BACK directory and simultaneously change the DOC extension to .SAV. Here is the command:

```
MOVE C:\DOCS\*.DOC C:\BACK\*.SAV
```

This says, "Move all files that have the extension .DOC from the directory C:\DOCS into the directory C:\BACK, and while you're at it, change their file extensions to .SAV." This is very handy, but very dangerous!

Let's say, for example, that I made one tiny typo. Here I typed a semicolon instead of a colon after the second *C:*

```
MOVE C:\DOCS\*.DOC C;\BACK\*.SAV
```

The command line understands the semicolon to mean "end of command" and therefore ignores both the semicolon and anything I type after it. As far as the command line is concerned, I typed this:

```
MOVE C:\DOCS\*.DOC C
```

This, unfortunately for me, means "take all the files with the extension .DOC in the directory C:\DOCS and copy them back into that same directory, but squish them all together into a single file called C." If I run this command, Windows gives me only one clue that something went wrong:

```
MOVE C:\DOCS\*.DOC C
1 file(s) copied
```

See "1 file(s) copied"? Feeling the chilly hand of fate slide my spine, I do a DIR of the directory, and I now see a single file called C, where there used to be 30 files with the extension .DOC. All of my DOC files are gone, completely unrecoverable.

XCOPY

The standard COPY and MOVE commands can work only in one directory at a time, making them a poor choice for copying or moving files in multiple directories. To help with these multi-directory jobs, Microsoft added the XCOPY command. (Note that there is no XMOVE, only XCOPY.)

XCOPY works similar to COPY, but XCOPY has extra switches that give it the power to work with multiple directories. Here's how it works. Let's say I have a directory on my C: drive called \DATA. The \DATA directory has three subdirectories: \JAN, \FEB, and \ MAR. All of these directories, including the \DATA directory, contain about 50 files. If I wanted to copy all of these files to my D: drive in one command, I would use XCOPY in the following manner:

```
XCOPY C:\DATA D:\DATA /S
```

Because XCOPY works on directories, you don't have to use filenames as you would in COPY, although XCOPY certainly accepts filenames and wildcards. The /S switch, the most commonly used of all the many switches that come with XCOPY, tells XCOPY to copy all subdirectories except for empty ones. The /E switch tells XCOPY to copy empty subdirectories. When you have a lot of copying to do over many directories, XCOPY is the tool to use.

The power of XCOPY varies depending on the version of Windows you use. The XCOPY that comes with true DOS is fairly weak. Windows 9x comes with a second type of XCOPY called XCOPY32 that enables you to copy hidden, read-only, and system files. Windows 2000 no longer has XCOPY32 but has instead incorporated all the power of XCOPY and XCOPY32 into its version of XCOPY.

Their power and utility make the DEL, COPY/MOVE, and XCOPY commands indispensable for a PC technician, but that same power and utility can cause disaster. Only a trained Jedi, with The Force as his ally … well, wrong book, but the principle remains: Beware of the quick and easy keystroke, for it may spell your doom. Think twice and execute the command once. The data you save may be yours!

Working with Batch Files

Batch files are nothing more than text files that store a series of commands, one command per line. The only thing that differentiates a batch file from any other text file is the .BAT extension. Take a look at Figure 14-17 and note the unique icon used for a batch file compared to the icon for a regular text file.

Figure 14-17
Text and batch
file icons

Readme

Batch

You can create and edit batch files using any text editor program—good old Notepad is often the tool of choice. This is the command-line chapter, though, so let's dust off the ancient but still important Edit program—it comes with every version of Windows—and use it to create and edit batch files.

Edit

Get to a command prompt on any Windows system and use the CD\ command to get to the root directory (use C: to get to the C: drive if you're not on the C: drive by default). From there, type **EDIT** at the command prompt to see the Edit program's interface (Figure 14-18).

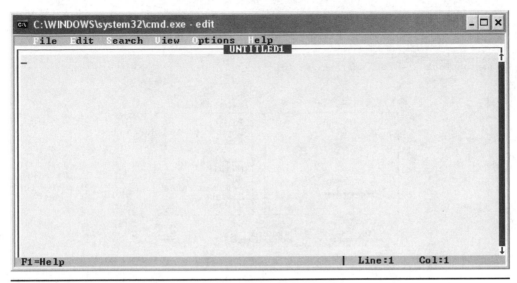

Figure 14-18   Edit interface

Now that you've started Edit, type in the two commands as shown in Figure 14-19. Make sure they look exactly the same as the lines shown in the figure.

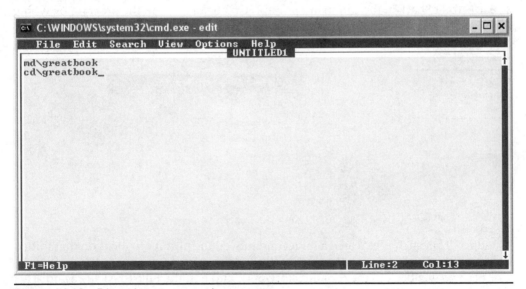

Figure 14-19   Edit with two commands

Great! You have just made your first batch file! All you need to do now is save it with some name—the name doesn't matter, but this example uses FIRST as the file-name. It is imperative, however, that you use the extension .BAT. Even though you could probably figure this out on your own later, do it now. Hold down the ALT key to activate the menu. Press the F (File) key. Then press S (Save). Type in the name **first.bat** as shown in Figure 14-20. Press ENTER and the file is now saved.

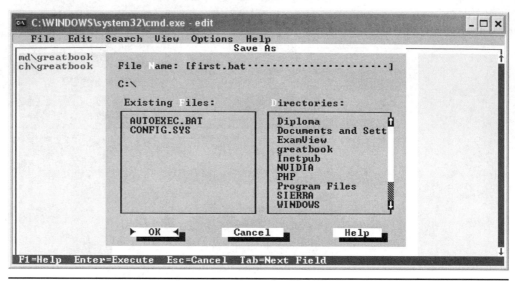

Figure 14-20   Saving the batch file

Now that you've saved the file, exit the Edit program by pressing ALT-F and then press X (Exit). You're back at the command prompt. Go ahead and run the program by typing **FIRST** and pressing ENTER. Your results should look something like Figure 14-21.

Figure 14-21
Running the
batch file

Super! The batch file created a folder and moved the prompt to focus on that folder. Don't run the first batch file again or you'll create another folder inside the first one!

Let's now get back to the root directory of C: and edit the FIRST.BAT file again. This time type **EDIT FIRST.BAT** and press ENTER. The batch file will come up, ready to edit. Now change the batch file to look like Figure 14-22. Use the arrow keys to move your cursor and the DELETE key to delete.

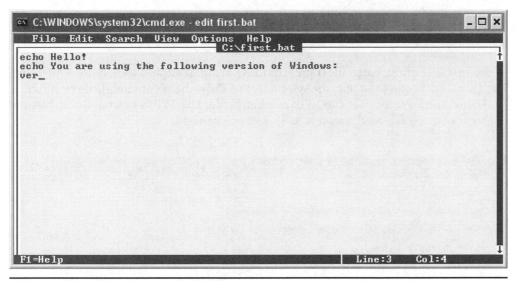

Figure 14-22   New version of FIRST.BAT

  NOTE   Most of the keyboard shortcuts used in WordPad, Word, and so on, were first used in the Edit program. If you know keyboard shortcuts for WordPad or Word, many will work in Edit.

The VER command shows the current version of Windows. The ECHO command tells the batch file to put text on the screen. Run the batch file, and it should look like Figure 14-23.

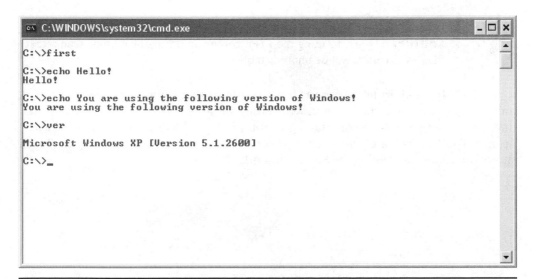

Figure 14-23   Running VER to show the current version of Windows

Gee, that's kind of ugly. Try editing the FIRST.BAT file one more time and add the line

```
@echo off
```

as the first line of the batch file. Run FIRST.BAT again. It should look quite a bit nicer! The @echo off command tells the system not to show the command, just the result.

Sometimes you just want to look at a batch file. The TYPE command displays the contents of a text file on the screen, as shown in Figure 14-24.

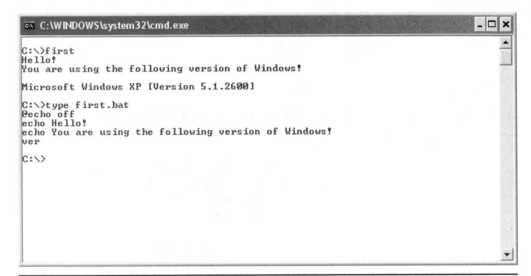

```
C:\>first
Hello!
You are using the following version of Windows!

Microsoft Windows XP [Version 5.1.2600]

C:\>type first.bat
@echo off
echo Hello!
echo You are using the following version of Windows!
ver

C:\>
```

Figure 14-24   Using the TYPE command to see file contents

CAUTION   Don't try using the TYPE command on anything other than a text files—the results will be unpredictable.

One of the more irritating aspects to batch files is that sometimes they don't work unless you run them in the folder in which they are stored. This is due to the path setting. Every time you open a command prompt, Windows loads a number of settings by default. You can see all of these settings by running the SET command. Figure 14-25 shows the results of running the SET command.

Figure 14-25   Using the SET command to see settings

Don't worry about understanding everything the SET command shows you, but do notice a line that starts with Path=. This line tells Windows where to look for a program (or batch file) if you run a program that's not in your current folder. For example, let's say I make a folder called C:\batch to store all my batch files. I can run the PATH command from the command prompt to see my current path (Figure 14-26).

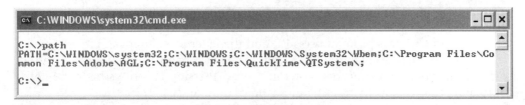

Figure 14-26   Using the PATH command to see the current path

I can then run the PATH command again, this time adding the C:\batch folder (Figure 14-27). I can now place all my batch files in this folder, and they will always work, no matter where I am in the system.

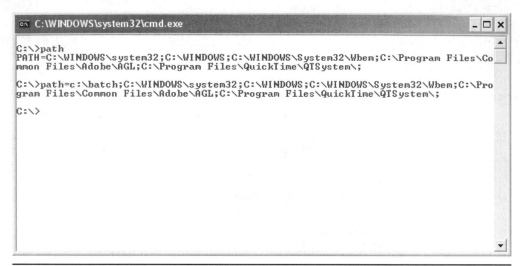

```
C:\>path
PATH=C:\WINDOWS\system32;C:\WINDOWS;C:\WINDOWS\System32\Wbem;C:\Program Files\Co
mmon Files\Adobe\AGL;C:\Program Files\QuickTime\QTSystem\;

C:\>path=c:\batch;C:\WINDOWS\system32;C:\WINDOWS;C:\WINDOWS\System32\Wbem;C:\Pro
gram Files\Common Files\Adobe\AGL;C:\Program Files\QuickTime\QTSystem\;

C:\>
```

Figure 14-27   Using PATH to add a folder

NOTE   You can edit the BOOT.INI file using the Edit program. Just make sure you turn off the System and Hidden attributes using ATTRIB first!

Beyond A+

Using Special Keys

You might find yourself repeatedly typing the same commands, or at least very similar commands, when working at a prompt. Microsoft has provided a number of ways to access previously typed commands. Type the **DIR** command at a command prompt. When you get back to a prompt, press F1, and the letter *D* will appear. Press F1 again. Now the letter *I* appears after the *D*. Do you see what is happening? The F1 key brings back the previous command one letter at a time. Pressing F3 brings back the entire command at once. Now try running these three commands:

DIR/W

ATTRIB

MD FRED

Now press the up arrow key. Keep pressing it till you see your original DIR command—it's a history of all your old commands. Now use the right arrow key to add /P to the end of you DIR command. Windows command history is very handy.

Compact and Cipher

Windows XP offers two cool commands at the command-line interface: COMPACT and CIPHER. COMPACT displays or alters the compression of files on NTFS partitions. CIPHER displays or alters the encryption of folders and files on NTFS partitions. If you type just the command with no added parameters, COMPACT and CIPHER display the compression state and the encryption state, respectively, of the current directory and any files it contains. You may specify multiple directory names, and you may use wildcards, as you learned earlier in the chapter. You must add parameters to make the commands change things. For example, you add /C to compress and /U to uncompress directories and/or files with the COMPACT command, and you add /E to encrypt and /D to decrypt directories and/or files with the CIPHER command. When you do these operations, you also mark the directories involved so that any files you add to them in the future will take on their encryption or compression characteristics. In other words, if you encrypt a directory and all its files, any files you add later will also be encrypted. The same thing applies if you compress a directory. I'll run through a quick example of each.

COMPACT

First, let's try the COMPACT command. Figure 14-28 shows the result of entering the COMPACT command with no switches. It displays the compression status of the contents of a directory called compact on a system's D: drive. Notice that after the file listing, COMPACT helpfully tells you that 0 files are compressed and 6 files (all of them) are not compressed, with a total compression ratio of 1.0 to 1.

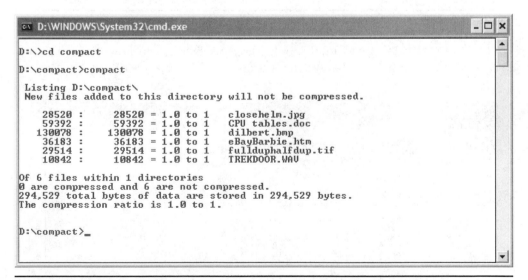

Figure 14-28   The COMPACT command with no switches

If you enter the COMPACT command with the /C switch, it will compress all the files in the directory, as shown in Figure 14-29. Look closely at the listing. Notice that it includes the original and compressed file sizes and calculates the compression ratio for you. Notice also that the JPG (a compressed graphics format) and WAV files didn't compress at all, while the Word file and the BMP file (an uncompressed graphics format) compressed down to less than a third of their original sizes. Also, can you spot what's different in the text at the bottom of the screen? COMPACT claims to have compressed *seven* files in *two* directories! How can this be? The secret is that when it compresses all the files in a directory, it must also compress the directory file itself, which is "in" the D: directory above it. Thus, it correctly reports that it compressed seven files: six in the compact directory and one in the D: directory.

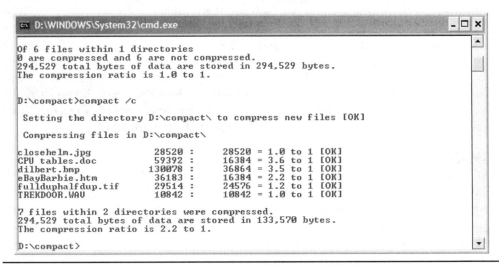

Figure 14-29 Typing COMPACT /C compresses the contents of the directory.

Typing **COMPACT** again shows you the directory listing, and now there's a C next to each filename, indicating that the file is compressed (Figure 14-30).

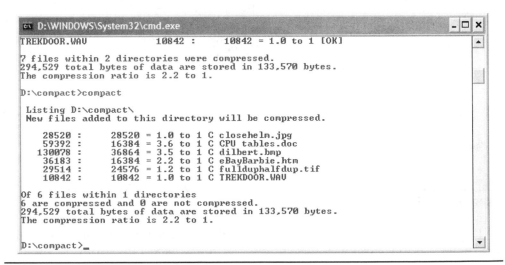

Figure 14-30 The contents of D:\COMPACT have been compressed.

Okay, now suppose you want to uncompress a file—the Dilbert image, dilbert.bmp. To do this, you must specify the decompression operation, using the /U switch and the name of the file you want decompressed, as shown in Figure 14-31. Note that COMPACT reports the successful decompression of one file only: dilbert.bmp. You could do the same thing in reverse, using the /C switch and a filename to compress an individual file.

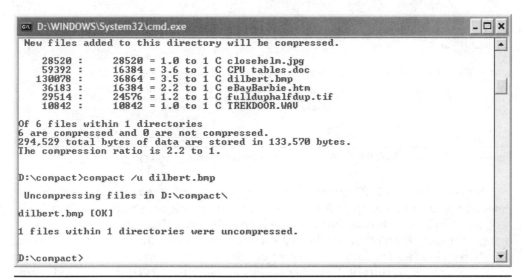

```
 D:\WINDOWS\System32\cmd.exe                                    _ □ ×
New files added to this directory will be compressed.

    28520 :     28520 = 1.0 to 1 C closehelm.jpg
    59392 :     16384 = 3.6 to 1 C CPU tables.doc
   130078 :     36864 = 3.5 to 1 C dilbert.bmp
    36183 :     16384 = 2.2 to 1 C eBayBarbie.htm
    29514 :     24576 = 1.2 to 1 C fullduphalfdup.tif
    10842 :     10842 = 1.0 to 1 C TREKDOOR.WAV

Of 6 files within 1 directories
6 are compressed and 0 are not compressed.
294,529 total bytes of data are stored in 133,570 bytes.
The compression ratio is 2.2 to 1.

D:\compact>compact /u dilbert.bmp

 Uncompressing files in D:\compact\

dilbert.bmp [OK]

1 files within 1 directories were uncompressed.

D:\compact>
```

Figure 14-31   Typing COMPACT /U DILBERT.BMP decompresses only that file.

CIPHER

The CIPHER command is a bit complex, but in its most basic implementation, it's pretty straightforward. Figure 14-32 shows two steps in the process. Like the COMPACT command, the CIPHER command simply displays the current state of affairs when entered with no switches. In this case, it displays the encryption state of the files in the D:\Work Files\Armor Pictures directory. Notice the letter *U* to the left of the filenames, which tells you they are unencrypted. The second command you can see on the screen in Figure 14-32 is this:

```
D:\Work Files\Armor Pictures>cipher /E /A
```

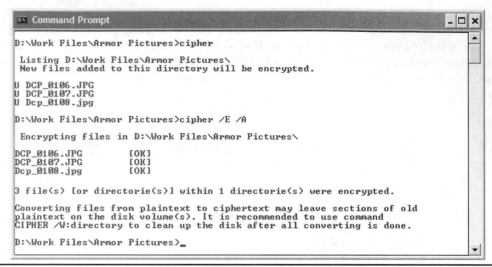

Figure 14-32 Typing CIPHER /E /A encrypts the contents of the directory.

This time the CIPHER command carries two switches: /E specifies the encryption operation, and /A says to apply it to the *files* in the directory, not just the directory itself. As you can see, the command-line interface is actually pretty chatty in this case. It reports that it's doing the encryption and then tells you what it's done, and it even warns you that you should clean up any stray unencrypted bits that may have been left in the directory.

To confirm the results of the cipher operation, enter the **CIPHER** command again, as shown in Figure 14-33. Note that the *U* to the left of each filename has been replaced with an *E*, indicating an encrypted file. The other indication that this directory has been encrypted is the statement above the file listing:

```
New files added to this directory will be encrypted.
```

Remember that the CIPHER command works on directories first and foremost, and it works on individual files only when you specifically tell it to do so.

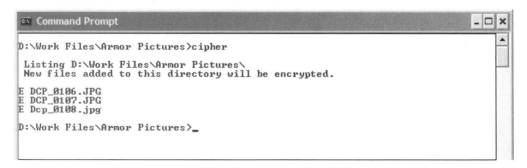

Figure 14-33 The CIPHER command confirms that the files were encrypted.

That's great, but suppose you want to decrypt just *one* of the files in the Armor Pictures directory. Can you guess how you need to alter the command? Simply add the filename of the file you want to decrypt after the command and the relevant switches. Figure 14-34 shows the CIPHER command being used to decipher DCP_0106.JPG, a single file.

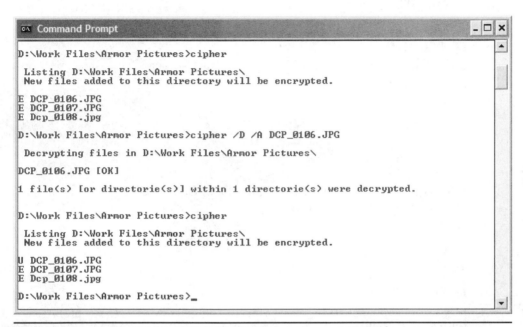

```
Command Prompt                                               _ □ ✕

D:\Work Files\Armor Pictures>cipher

 Listing D:\Work Files\Armor Pictures\
 New files added to this directory will be encrypted.

E DCP_0106.JPG
E DCP_0107.JPG
E Dcp_0108.jpg

D:\Work Files\Armor Pictures>cipher /D /A DCP_0106.JPG

 Decrypting files in D:\Work Files\Armor Pictures\

DCP_0106.JPG [OK]

1 file(s) [or directorie(s)] within 1 directorie(s) were decrypted.

D:\Work Files\Armor Pictures>cipher

 Listing D:\Work Files\Armor Pictures\
 New files added to this directory will be encrypted.

U DCP_0106.JPG
E DCP_0107.JPG
E Dcp_0108.jpg

D:\Work Files\Armor Pictures>_
```

Figure 14-34   Typing CIPHER /D /A DCP_0106.JPG decrypts only that file.

Chapter Review Questions

1. How many 8-bit characters does the ASCII standard define?

   A. 64

   B. 256

   C. 512

   D. 64,000

2. Which of the following is the correct path for a file named YODA.TXT on the C: drive in a directory called JEDI that's in a directory called REBELS that's in the root directory?

   A. C:\ROOT\JEDI\YODA.TXT

   B. C:\JEDI\REBELS\YODA.TXT

   C. C:\REBELS\JEDI\YODA.TXT

   D. C:\ROOT\REBELS\JEDI\YODA.TXT

3. Which of the following commands will delete all the files in a directory?

   A. DEL *.*

   B. DEL ALL

   C. DEL ?.?

   D. DEL *.?

4. What command enables you to make a new directory in a Windows XP Professional system?

   A. MF

   B. MKFOL

   C. MD

   D. MAKEDIR

5. What command do you type at the Run dialog box to access the command-line interface in Windows XP?

   A. CMD

   B. COMMAND

   C. MSDOS

   D. PROMPT

6. Joey wants to change the name of a file from START.BAT to HAMMER.BAT. Which of the following commands would accomplish this feat?

   A. REN HAMMER.BAT START.BAT

   B. REN START.BAT HAMMER.BAT

   C. RENAME /S START.BAT HAMMER.BAT

   D. RENAME /S HAMMER.BAT START.BAT

7. What types of characters are the asterisk (*) and the question mark (?)?

   A. Wildcards

   B. Optionals

   C. Designators

   D. Switches

8. What is the command to make MYFILE.TXT read-only?

   A. ATTRIB +R MYFILE.TXT

   B. ATTRIB –R MYFILE.TXT

   C. READONLY MYFILE.TXT

   D. MYFILE.TXT /READONLY

9. To learn the syntax of the DIR command, what can you type?

   A. HELP DIR

   B. DIR /?

   C. DIR /HELP

   D. Both A and B.

10. What is the command to quit the command-line interface?

   A. EXIT

   B. BYE

   C. QUIT

   D. STOP

Answers

1. **B.** The ASCII standard has 256 characters, because that's all 8 bits can handle!

2. **C.** You'll find the YODA.TXT file in the C:\REBELS\JEDI\ folder.

3. **A.** You can use the *.* wildcard combination to affect every file in a particular folder.

4. **C.** MD enables you to make a directory or folder. You can also use the older form of MKDIR.

5. **A.** Use the CMD command in the Run dialog box to access a command line in Windows 2000/WP.

6. **B.** The REN command with the proper syntax—REN START.BAT HAMMER. BAT—will rename the file.

7. **A.** The asterisk and question mark characters are wildcards when used with command-line commands.

8. **A.** The command ATTRIB +R MYFILE.TXT will make MYFILE.TXT read-only.

9. **D.** To learn the ins and outs of every command-line program, type either HELP followed by the command neme or the command followed by the /? switch.

10. **A.** Type EXIT and press the ENTER key to bail out of a command line–interface dialog box in Windows.

Maintaining and Troubleshooting Windows

In this chapter, you will learn how to
- Maintain Windows 2000/XP
- Optimize Windows 2000/XP
- Troubleshoot Windows 2000/XP

An installed Windows operating system needs occasional optimization, ongoing maintenance, and troubleshooting when it doesn't work correctly. Not that long ago, Windows had a bit of a bad rap as being difficult to maintain and challenging to troubleshoot problems. Microsoft used its 20-plus years of experience with operating systems searching for ways to make the tasks of maintaining and troubleshooting less onerous. They've done such a good job with the latest versions of Windows that, out of the box, they are easy to optimize and maintain, although troubleshooting—and all operating systems share this—is still a bit of a challenge.

The chapter starts with optimization and maintenance, so let's make sure we know what these two terms mean. CompTIA sees optimization as jobs you do to your Windows system to make it better—a good example is adding RAM. Maintenance means jobs you do from time to time to keep Windows running well, such as running hard drive utilities. This chapter covers the standard maintenance and optimization activities performed on Windows and the tools techs use to perform them.

The last part of this chapter dives into troubleshooting Windows 2000 and Windows XP, examining steps you can take to bring a system back from the brink of disaster. You'll learn techniques for recovering a PC that won't boot and a PC that almost boots into Windows but fails.

Maintaining Windows

Maintaining Windows can be compared to maintaining a new automobile. Of course, a new automobile comes with a warranty, so most of us just take it to the dealer to get work done. In this case, *you* are the mechanic, so you need to think as an auto mechanic would think. First, an auto mechanic needs to apply recalls when the automaker finds a serious problem. For a PC Tech, that means keeping the system patches announced by Microsoft up to date. You also need to check on the parts that wear down over time. On a car that might mean changing the oil or rotating the tires. In a Windows system that includes keeping the hard drive and Registry organized and uncluttered.

Patches, Updates, and Service Packs

Updating Windows has been an important, but often neglected, task for computer users. Typically, Microsoft finds and corrects problems with its software in a timely fashion. Because earlier versions of Windows let users decide when, if ever, to update their computers, the net result could be disastrous. The Blaster worm hammered computers all over the world in the summer of 2003, causing thousands of computers to start rebooting spontaneously—no small feat for a tiny piece of programming! Blaster exploited a flaw in Windows 2000/XP and spread like wildfire, but Microsoft had *already corrected* the flaw with a security update weeks earlier. If users had simply updated their computers, the virus would not have caused such widespread damage.

The Internet has enabled Microsoft to make updates available, and the *Windows Update* program can grab those updates and patch user systems easily and automatically. Even if you don't want to allow Windows Update to patch your computer automatically, it'll still nag you about updates until you patch your system. Microsoft provides the Windows Update utility in Windows 2000 and Windows XP.

Once Microsoft released Service Pack 2 for Windows XP, it began pushing for wholesale acceptance of automatic updates from Windows Update. You can also start Windows Update manually. When your computer is connected to the Internet, start the utility in Windows 2000 by selecting Start | Windows Update. In Windows XP you will find it at Start | All Programs | Windows Update. When you run Windows Update manually, the software connects to the Microsoft Web site and scans your computer to determine what updates may be needed. Within a few seconds or minutes, depending on your connection speed, you'll get a straightforward screen, like the one shown in Figure 15-1.

You have several choices here, although two are most obvious. If you click the Express button, Windows Update will grab any high-priority updates—these are security patches—and install them on your computer. If you click the Custom button, you can select from a list of optional updates.

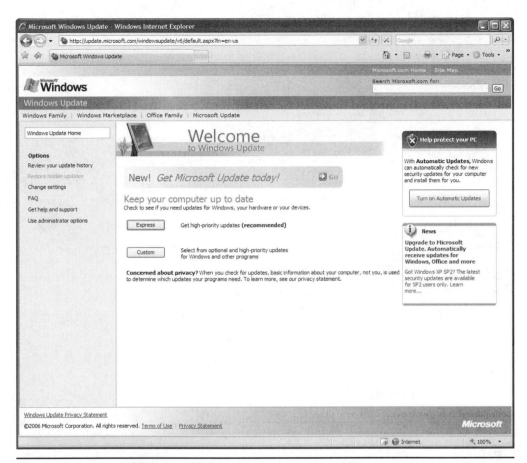

Figure 15-1 Microsoft Windows Update page

Figure 15-2 shows the updater with a list of patches and security updates. You can scroll through the list and review the description of each update. You can deselect the checkbox next to a patch or update, and Windows Update will not download or install it. If you click the Clear All button, as you might suspect, all the updates will be removed from the list. When you click Install Updates, all the updates remaining in the list will be installed. A dialog box like the one in Figure 15-3 appears during the copying and installing phases.

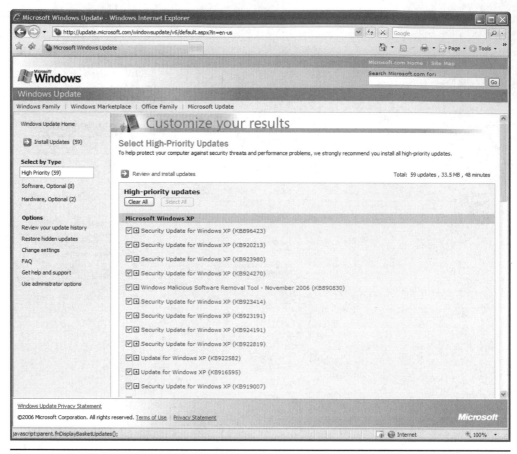

Figure 15-2 Choose updates to be installed

Figure 15-3
Windows Update
Installing Updates

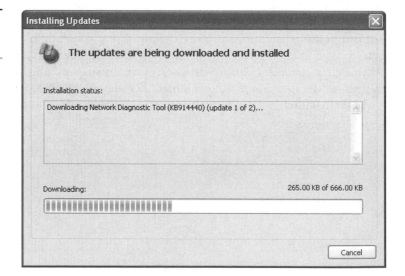

Automatic Update

Updates are so important that Microsoft gives you the option to update Windows automatically. Actually, it nags you about it! Soon after installing XP (a day or two, in my experience), a message balloon will pop up from the taskbar suggesting that you automate updates. If you click this balloon, the Automatic Updates Setup Wizard will run, enabling you to configure the update program. You say you've never seen this message balloon, but would like to automate the update process? No problem—simply right-click My Computer (on the Start menu), select Properties, click the Automatic Updates tab, and select Automatic Update options. Then, whenever your computer connects to the Web, it checks the Windows Update page. What happens next depends on the setting you choose. You have four choices:

- **Automatic (recommended)**   Windows Update will simply keep your computer patched up and ready to go. This is the best option for most users, although not necessarily good for users of portable computers. Nobody wants to log into a slow hotel dial-up connection and have most of your bandwidth sucked away by Automatic Update downloading hot fixes!

- **Download updates for me …**   Windows Update downloads all patches in the background and then, when complete, tells you about them. You have the option at that point to install or not install.

- **Notify me …**   Windows Update simply flashes you a dialog box that tells you updates are available, but does not download anything until you say go. This is the best option for users of portable computers. You can download files when it's convenient for you, such as when you're home rather than traveling on business.

- **Turn off Automatic Updates**   This does precisely what is advertised. You get neither automatic patches nor notification that patches are available. Only use this option on a system that does not or cannot connect to the Internet. If you're online, your computer needs to be patched!

When Windows Update works the way Microsoft wants it to work, it scans the Microsoft Web site periodically, downloads patches as they appear, and then installs them on your computer. If you opted for the download but don't install option, Windows Update simply notifies you when updates are downloaded and ready to install (Figure 15-4).

Figure 15-4
Windows Update
balloon message

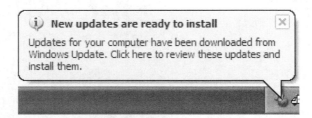

Managing User Accounts and Groups

The most basic element of Windows security is the user account. Each user must present a valid user name and the password of a user account in order to log on to a Windows computer. There are ways to make this logon highly simplified, even invisible in some cases, but there is no exception to this rule. Each user is also a member of one or more groups of users. Groups enable the system administrator to easily assign the same rights and permissions to all members of the group without the need to set those rights and permissions individually.

Windows 2000 and XP have several built-in groups and two user accounts created during installation—Administrator and Guest—with only the Administrator account enabled by default. When you install Windows, you supply the password for the Administrator account. This is the only usable account you have to log on to the computer, unless you joined the computer to a domain (a Chapter 21 topic) or until you create a new user account. I'll assume that your computer doesn't belong to a domain and show you how to create local accounts on your Windows 2000 or Windows XP computer.

You manage users and groups using the Local Users and Groups node in the Computer Management console, accessed by right-clicking on My Computer and selecting Manage. (I'll show you more in Chapter 21.) Local Users and Groups can also be used on standalone computers, but Microsoft includes simpler GUI tools for that purpose in Windows 2000 and Windows XP. In Windows XP, Microsoft made significant changes in the GUI tools for managing users and groups, so I'll break up this discussion between these two operating systems.

Using the Users and Passwords Applet in Windows 2000

When you install Windows 2000 Professional, assuming your computer is not made a member of a domain, you may choose to let the OS assume that you are the only user of the computer and do not want to see the logon dialog box. You can check this setting after installation by opening the Users and Passwords applet in Control Panel to see the setting for *Users must enter a user name and password to use this computer.* Figure 15-5 shows this choice selected, which means that you will see a logon box every time you restart your computer. Also notice that the only user is Administrator. That's the account you're using to log on!

Figure 15-5
Security begins with turning on *Users must enter a user name and password to use this computer*

Using the Administrator account is just fine when you're doing administrative tasks such as installing updates, adding printers, adding and removing programs and Windows components, and creating users and groups. Best practice for the workplace is to create one or more user accounts and only log in with the user accounts, not the Administrator account. This gives you a lot more control over who or what happens to the computer.

There's a second setting in Users and Passwords that's important to enable for the sake of security—the setting on the Advanced Tab under Secure Boot Settings. If checked, as shown in Figure 15-6, it requires users to press CTRL-ALT-DEL before logging on. This setting is a defense against certain viruses that try to capture your user name and password, sometimes by presenting a fake logon prompt. Pressing CTRL-ALT-DEL will remove a program like that from memory and allow the actual logon dialog box to appear.

Figure 15-6
Make your computer more secure by enabling Secure Boot Settings

 NOTE If the user name and password requirement is turned off or you have user accounts that aren't password protected in Windows 2000 (or XP, for that matter), anyone with physical access to your computer can turn it on and use it by pressing the power button. This is potentially a very bad thing!

Creating a New User in Windows 2000

Creating a new user account enables that user to log in with a user name and password. This enables an administrator to set the rights and permissions for the user as well as to audit access to certain network resources. For that reason, it is good practice to create users on a desktop computer. You are working with the same concepts on a small scale that an administrator must work with in a domain. Let's review the steps in this procedure for Windows 2000.

 NOTE To create and manage users, you must be logged on as the Administrator, be a member of the Administrators group, or have an Administrator account (in Windows XP). Assign a password to the Administrator account so that only authorized users can access this all-powerful account.

If you're logged on in Windows 2000 as the Administrator or a member of the local Administrators group, open the Users and Passwords applet from Control Panel and click the Add button. This opens the Add New User Wizard (Figure 15-7). Enter the user name that the user will use to log on. Enter the user's first and last names in the Full name field, and if you wish, enter some text that describes this person in the Description field. If this is at work, enter a job description in this field. The Full name and Description fields are optional.

Figure 15-7
Adding a new user

After entering the user information, click the Next button to continue. This opens a password dialog box (Figure 15-8) where you can enter and confirm the initial password for this new user. Click the Next button to continue.

Figure 15-8
Create user password

CAUTION Blank passwords or those that are easily visible on a sticky note provide *no security*. Always insist on non-blank passwords, and do not let anyone leave a password sitting out in the open. See the section on passwords later in the chapter.

Now you get to decide what groups the new user should belong to. Select one of the two suggested options—Standard User or Restricted User—or select the Other option button and choose a group from the drop-down list. Select Standard user, which on a Windows 2000 Professional desktop makes this person a member of the local Power Users Group as well as the local Users group. Click the Finish button to close the dialog box. You should see your new user listed in the Users and Passwords dialog box. While you're there, note how easy it is for an administrator to change a user's password. Simply select a user from the list and then click on the Set Password button. Enter and confirm the new password in the Set Password dialog box. Figure 15-9 shows the Set Password dialog box with the Users and Passwords dialog box in the background.

Figure 15-9
Set Password
dialog box

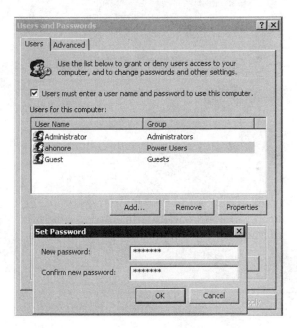

Now let's say you want to change a password. Select the new user in the *Users for this computer* list on the Users page. Then click the Set Password button on the Users page. Enter and confirm the new password and then click the OK button to apply the changes.

Managing Users in Windows XP

Although Windows XP has essentially the same type of accounts database as Windows 2000, the User Accounts Control Panel applet replaces the former Users and Passwords applet and further simplifies user management tasks.

Windows XP has two very different ways to deal with user accounts and how you log on to a system: the blank user name and password text boxes, reminiscent of Windows 2000 , and the Windows XP Welcome screen (Figure 15-10). If your Windows XP computer is a member of a Windows domain, your system automatically uses the Windows Classic style, including the requirement to press CTRL-ALT-DEL to get to the user name and password text boxes, just like in Windows 2000. If your Windows XP computer is not a member of a domain, you may use either method, although the Welcome screen is the default. Windows XP Home and Windows XP Media Center cannot join a domain, so these versions of Windows only use the Welcome screen. Windows Tablet PC Edition functions just like Windows XP Professional.

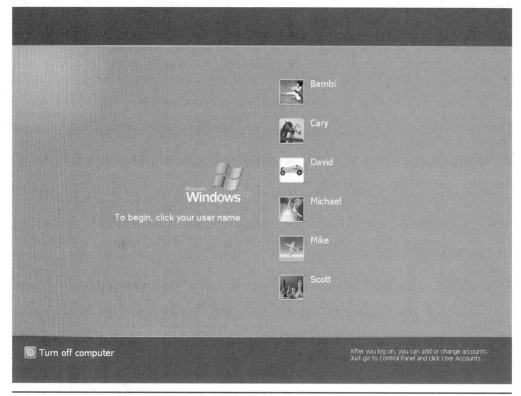

Figure 15-10 Windows XP Welcome screen

Assuming that your Windows XP system is *not* a member of a domain, I'll concentrate on the XP Welcome screen and some of the options you'll see in the User Accounts Control Panel applet.

The User Accounts applet is very different from the old Users and Passwords applet in Windows 2000. User Accounts hides the complete list of users, using a simplistic reference to account types that is actually a reference to its group membership. An account that is a member of the local Administrators group is said to be a Computer Administrator; an account that only belongs to the Local Users group is said to be a Limited account. Which users the applet displays depends on which type of user is currently logged on (see Figure 15-11). When an Administrator is logged on, she will see both types of accounts and the Guest account. A Limited user will only see his or her own account in User Accounts.

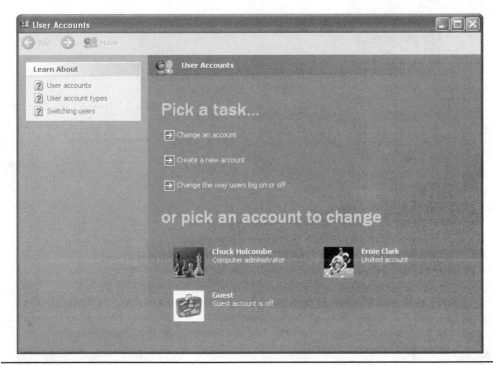

Figure 15-11 User Accounts dialog box showing a Computer Administrator, a Limited account, and the Guest account (disabled)

Windows requires you to create a second account that is a member of the Administrator's group during the initial Windows installation. This is for simple redundancy—if one administrator is not available or is not able to log on to the computer, another one can.

 NOTE If you upgrade from Windows NT, Windows 2000, or a Windows 9*x* installation in which user accounts were enabled, Setup will migrate the existing accounts to Windows XP.

Creating users is a straightforward process. You need to provide a user name (a password can be added later), and you need to know which type of account to create: Computer Administrator or Limited. To create a new user in Windows XP, open the User Accounts applet from the Control Panel and click *Create a new account*. On the *Pick an account type* page (Figure 15-12) you can create either type of account. Simply follow the prompts on the screen. After you have created your local accounts, you'll see them listed when you open the User Accounts applet. It will look something like Figure 15-13.

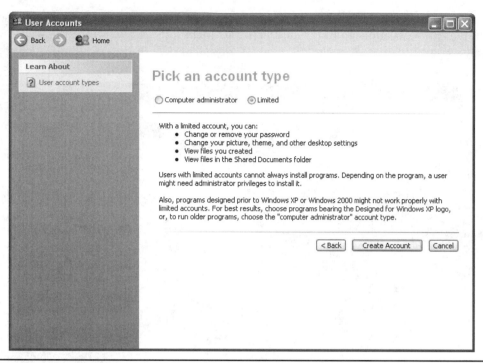

Figure 15-12 The *Pick an account type* page showing both options available

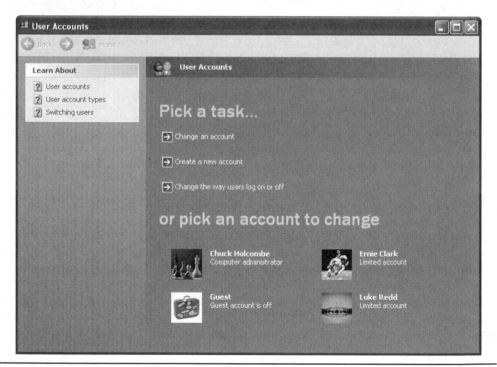

Figure 15-13 New Limited account listed in User Accounts

Head back to the User Accounts applet and look at the *Change the way users log on and off* option. Select it; you will see two checkboxes (Figure 15-14). If you select the Use the Welcome screen checkbox, Windows will bring up the friendly Welcome screen shown in Figure 15-15 each time users log in. If this box is unchecked, you'll have to enter a user name and password (Figure 15-16).

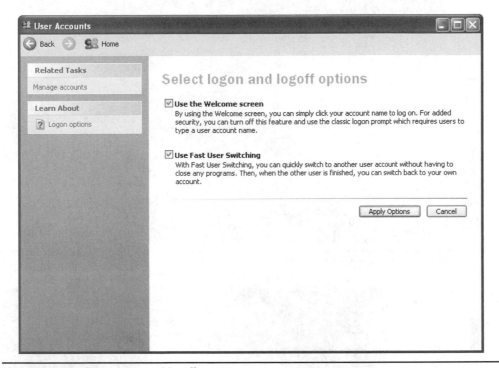

Figure 15-14 Select logon and logoff options

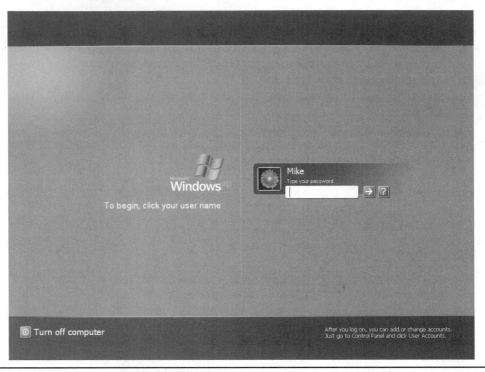

Figure 15-15 Single account logon screen

Figure 15-16
Classic Logon
screen, XP style

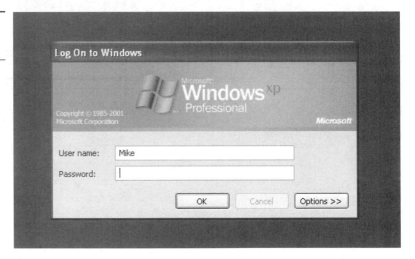

The second option, Use Fast User Switching, enables you to switch to another user without logging off the currently running user. This is a handy option when two people actively share a system, or when someone wants to borrow your system for a moment but you don't want to close all your programs. This option is only active if you have the Use the Welcome screen checkbox enabled. If Fast User Switching is enabled, when you click on the Log Off button on the Start menu, you get the option to switch users shown in Figure 15-17.

Figure 15-17
Switch Users option

Passwords

Passwords are the ultimate key to protecting your computers. A user account with a valid password will get you into any system. Even if the user account only has limited permissions, you still have a security breach. Remember: for a hacker, just getting into the network is half the battle.

Protect your passwords. Never give out passwords over the phone. If a user loses a password, an administrator should reset the password to a complex combination of letters and numbers, and then allow the user to change the password to something they want. All of the stronger operating systems have this capability.

Make your users choose good passwords. I once attended a security seminar, and the speaker had everyone stand up. She then began to ask questions about our passwords—if we responded yes to the question we were to sit down. She began to ask questions such as

"Do you use the name of your spouse as a password?" and

"Do you use your pet's name?"

By the time she was done asking about 15 questions, only 6 people out of some 300 were still standing! The reality is that most of us choose passwords that are amazingly easy to hack. Make sure you use strong passwords: at least six to eight characters in length, including letters, numbers, and punctuation symbols.

TIP Using non-alphanumeric characters makes any password much more difficult to crack for two reasons. First, adding non-alphanumeric characters forces the hacker to consider many more possible characters than just letters and numbers. Second, most password crackers use combinations of common words and numbers to try to hack a password.

Because non-alphanumeric characters don't fit into common words or numbers, including a character such as an exclamation point will defeat these common-word hacks. Not all serving systems allow you to use characters such as @, $, %, or \, however, so you need to experiment to see if a particular server will accept them.

Once you've forced your users to choose strong passwords, you should make them change passwords at regular intervals. While this concept sounds good on paper, in the real world it is a hard policy to maintain. For starters, users tend to forget passwords when they change a lot. This can lead to an even bigger security problem because users start writing passwords down!

If your organization forces you to change passwords often, one way to remember the password is to use a numbering system. I worked at a company that required me to change my password at the beginning of each month, so I did something very simple. I took a root password—let's say it was "m3y3rs5"—and simply added a number to the end representing the current month. So when June rolled around, for example, I would change my password to "m3y3rs56." It worked pretty well!

Resetting Forgotten Passwords in Windows XP Windows XP allows the currently logged-on user to create a password reset disk that can be used in case of a forgotten password. This is very important to have because if you forget your password, and an administrator resets the password using User Accounts or Local Users and Groups, then when you log on using the new password, you will discover that you cannot access some items, including files that you encrypted when logged on with the forgotten password. When you reset a password with a password reset disk, you can log on using the new password and still have access to previously encrypted files.

Best of all, with the password reset disk, users have the power to fix their own passwords. Encourage your users to create this disk; you only have this power if you remember to create a password reset disk *before* you forget the password! If you need to create a password reset disk for a computer on a network (domain), search the Help system for "password reset disk" and follow the instructions for password reset disks for a computer on a domain.

Error-Checking and Disk Defragmentation

Keeping drives healthy and happy is a key task for every tech. Error-checking and Disk Defragmenter, discussed way back in Chapter 10, "Implementing Hard Drives," are the key Windows maintenance tools you use to accomplish this task.

When you can't find a software reason (and there are many possible ones) for a problem like a system freezing on shutdown, the problem might be the actual physical hard drive. The tool to investigate that is Error-checking. Error-checking can be done from a command line using the chkdsk command, or you can access the tool through the GUI by opening My Computer, right-clicking on the drive you want to check, selecting Properties, and then clicking the Tools tab, where you can click Check Now to have Error-checking scan the drive for bad sectors, lost clusters, and similar problems, and repair them if possible.

Run the Disk Defragmenter (Figure 15-18) on a regular basis to keep your system from slowing down due to files being scattered in pieces on your hard drive. Before you click the Defragment button, click the Analyze button to have Windows analyze the disk and determine if defragmentation is actually necessary.

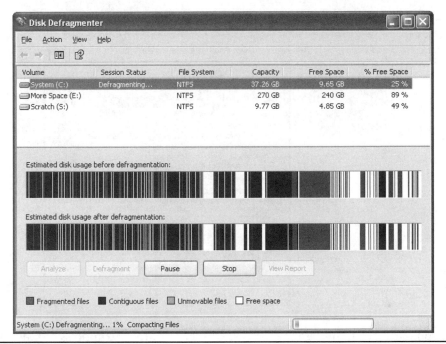

Figure 15-18 Disk Defragmenter

Temporary File Management with Disk Cleanup

Before you defrag a drive, you should run the Disk Cleanup utility to make sure you've cleared out the junk files that accumulate from daily use. All that late-night Web surfing doesn't just use up time, it uses up disk space, leaving behind hundreds of temporary Internet files. Those, and other bits and pieces such as those "deleted" files still hanging around in your Recycle Bin, can add up to a lot of wasted disk space if you don't periodically clean them out.

You can reach this tool through the Start menu (Start | All Programs | Accessories | System Tools), or you can open My Computer, right-click the drive you want to clean up, select Properties, and right there in the middle of the General tab you'll find the Disk Cleanup button. Disk Cleanup calculates the space you will be able to free up and then displays the Disk Cleanup dialog box (Figure 15-19), which tells you how much disk space it can free up—the total amount possible as well as the amount you'll get from each of the different categories of files it checks. In Figure 15-19, the list of Files to delete only has a few categories checked, and the actual amount of disk space to be gained by allowing Disk Cleanup to delete these files is much smaller than the estimate. As you select and deselect choices, watch the value for this total change.

Figure 15-19
Disk Cleanup
dialog box

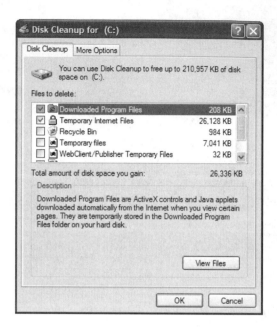

If you scroll down through the list, you will see a choice to compress old files. What do you know, Disk Cleanup does more than just delete files? In fact, this file compression trick is where Disk Cleanup really, uh, cleans up. This is one of the few choices where you will gain the most space. The other big heavyweight category is Temporary Internet Files, which it will delete. Try Disk Cleanup on a computer that gets hours of Internet use every day and you'll be pleased with the results.

Registry Maintenance

Your Registry is a huge database that Windows constantly updates. As a result, the Registry tends to get clogged with entries that are no longer valid. These usually don't cause any problems directly, but they can slow down your system. Interestingly, Microsoft does not provide a utility to clean up the Registry. (Back in the old Windows 9x days there was a Microsoft tool called REGCLEAN, but it was never updated for Windows 2000/XP). To clean your Registry, you need to turn to a third-party utility. There are quite a few Registry cleaner programs out there, but my favorite is the freeware EasyCleaner by ToniArts (Figure 15-20). You can download the latest copy at http://personal.inet.fi/business/toniarts/ecleane.htm.

 CAUTION The http://www.toniarts.com Web site is a scam—do not use anything from that Web site!

Figure 15-20 EasyCleaner

Before you start cleaning your Registry with wild abandon, keep in mind that all Registry cleaners are risky in that there is a chance that it may delete something you want in the Registry. I've used EasyCleaner for a while and it has worked well for me— your experience may differ! Always use EasyCleaner's handy undo feature so that you can restore what you deleted.

EasyCleaner is a powerful optimization tool that does far more than just clean your Registry. Check out the file duplicate finder, space usage, and other tools that come with this package. If you like this program, go to the Web site and donate some money to Toni.

Security: Spyware/Anti-Virus/Firewall

You simply cannot run a computer today without a large number of security programs to protect you from malicious attacks from spyware, malware, viruses, and hacking. In fact, the installation, monitoring, and updating of these programs (and possibly even hardware) is so important that they get their own chapter. Head to Chapter 23, "Computer Security" for a complete discussion of how to keep your computer safe!

Optimizing Windows

Maintenance is about keeping Windows' performance from degrading with time and use. Of course, we don't just want to keep trouble at bay—we want to make our systems better, stronger, faster! Anything you do that makes Windows better than it was before, such as adding a piece of software or hardware to make something run better, is an optimization.

Installing and Removing Software

The most common optimization performed on any PC is probably adding and removing applications. Installing and removing software is part of the normal life of any PC. Each time you add or remove software, you are making changes and decisions that can affect the system beyond whatever the program does, so it pays to know how to do it right.

Installing Software

Most application programs are distributed on CD-ROMs. Luckily, Windows supports Autorun, a feature that enables it to look for and read a special file called—wait for it—Autorun immediately after a CD-ROM is inserted, and then run whatever program is listed in Autorun.inf. Most application programs distributed on CD-ROM have an Autorun file that calls up the installation program.

 NOTE Programs keep getting bigger and bigger, and distributors have started using DVD discs for applications. Expect that trend to continue in a big way. Apple switched over to DVD for OS X some time ago, and Microsoft has followed suit with Windows Vista. Autorun works with DVDs just fine.

Sometimes, however, it is necessary to institute the installation sequence yourself. Perhaps the installation CD lacks an Autorun installation program, or perhaps Windows is configured so that programs on a CD-ROM must be started manually. In some cases, a CD-ROM may contain more than one program, and you must choose which of them to install. Regardless of the reason, beginning the installation manually is a simple and straightforward process using the Add or Remove Programs (Add/Remove Programs in Windows 2000) applet in the Control Panel. Click the Add New Programs button (Figure 15-21), follow the prompts, and provide the disk or location of the files.

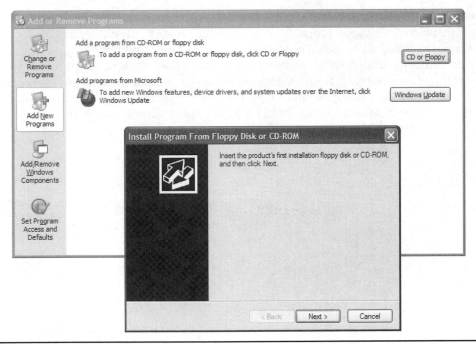

Figure 15-21   Add New Programs

As long as you have sufficient permissions to install an application—your account is a member of the Administrators group in Windows 2000, for example, or is an Administrator Account in Windows XP—the application will begin its install routine. If you don't have sufficient permissions to install an application, Windows will stop the installation.

Assuming all is well, you typically first must accept the terms of a software license before you are allowed to install an application. These steps are not optional—the installation simply won't proceed until you accept all terms the software manufacturer requires, and in many cases enter a correct code. You may also be asked to make several decisions during the installation process. For example, you may be asked where you would like to install the program and if you would like certain optional components installed. Generally speaking, it is best to accept the suggested settings unless you have a very specific reason for changing the defaults.

Removing Software

Each installed application program takes up space on your computer's hard drive, and programs that you no longer need simply waste space that could be used for other purposes. Removing unnecessary programs can be an important piece of optimization.

You remove a program from a Windows PC in much the same manner as you install it. That is, you use the application's own uninstall program, when possible. You normally find the uninstall program listed under the application's icon on the Start Menu, as shown in Figure 15-22.

Figure 15-22
Uninstall me!

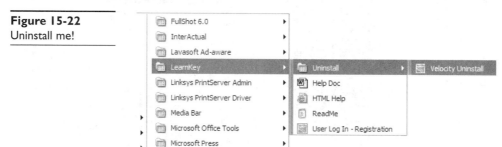

If an uninstall program is not available, then use Windows' Add or Remove Programs applet from Control Panel. Figure 15-23 shows this applet. You select the program you want to remove and click the Change/Remove button. You should not be surprised by now to hear that it does not disappear in a flash. First you'll see a message warning you that the program will be permanently removed from your PC. If you're certain you want to continue, click Yes.

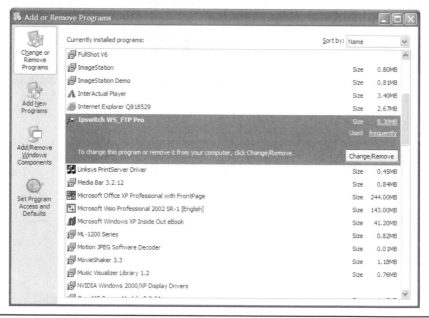

Figure 15-23   Add or Remove Programs applet

You may then see a message telling you that a shared file that appears to no longer be in use is about to be deleted, and asking your approval. Generally speaking, it's safe to delete such files. If you do not delete them, they will likely be orphaned and remain unused on your hard disk forever. In some cases, clicking the Change/Remove button will start the application's install program (the one you couldn't find before) so that you can modify the installed features. This is a function of the program you're attempting to remove. The end result should be the removal of the application and all of its pieces and parts, including files and Registry entries.

Adding or Removing Windows Components

When you installed Windows, it tried to guess which optional Windows components you would need. It installed Notepad, modem support, and games on your computer. These Windows components can be removed from your system if you like, and other components can be added as well. If you're adding components, you'll need a copy of your Windows CD, or another location where the Windows source files are stored. This task really hasn't changed from previous versions of Windows.

To add or remove a Windows component, open the Add or Remove Programs applet in the Control Panel (Add/Remove Programs in Windows 2000). From here select Add/Remove Windows Components, which opens the Windows Components Wizard (Figure 15-24). You can select an installed program; see how frequently it is used, how much disk space it uses, and (sometimes) the last time it was used.

Figure 15-24
Windows
Components Wizard

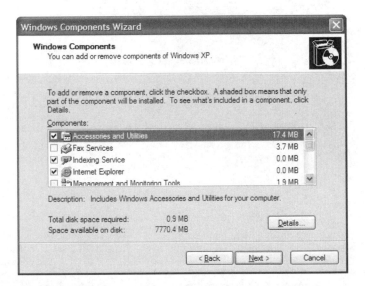

Installing/Optimizing a Device

The processes for optimizing hardware in Windows 2000 and Windows XP are absolutely identical, even down to the troubleshooting and backup utilities, and are very similar to the steps for installing a new device. The install process is covered in every chapter of this book that deals with one type of device or another, so this section concentrates on the issues that fit best under optimization.

Driver Updates

Device manufacturers occasionally update their drivers. Most of these updates take place to fix problems, but many updates incorporate new features. Whatever the case, when one of your devices gets an updated driver, it's your job to install it. Windows / Microsoft Update provides an easy method to update drivers from manufacturers that take advantage of the service. The only trick to this is that you usually need to select the Custom option to see these updates because Windows only installs high-priority updates using the Express option. When you click on the Custom option, look under Hardware, Optional (on the left) to see if Windows has any driver updates (Figure 15-25). Take some time and read what these updates do—sometimes you may choose not to install a driver update because it's not necessary or useful to your system.

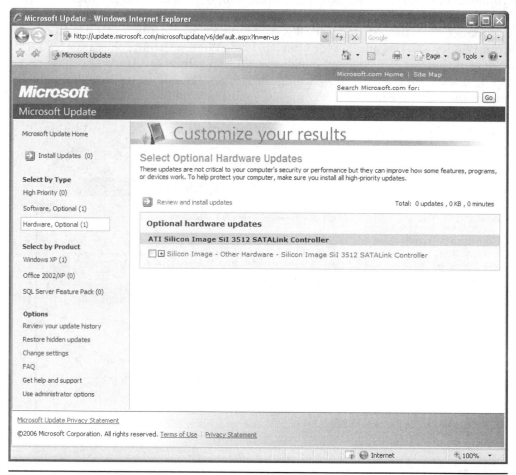

Figure 15-25 Hardware, Optional

If Windows does not put a driver update in the Windows Update tool, how do you know a device needs updating? The trick is to know your devices. Video card manufacturers update drivers quite often. Get in the habit of registering your video card with the manufacturer to stay up to date. Any very new device is also a good candidate for an update. When you buy that new cool toy for your system, make a point to head over to the manufacturer's Web site and see if any updates have come out since it was packaged for sale. That happens more often than you might think!

Driver Signing

Device drivers become part of the operating system and thus have the potential to cause lots of problems if they're written poorly. To protect Windows systems from bad device drivers, Microsoft introduced with Windows 2000 something called *driver signing*, which means that each driver has a digital signature. Digital signatures are issued by Microsoft to drivers that have been tested at the Windows Hardware Quality Lab (WHQL). Look on the packaging of a hardware device. If you see the Designed for Windows 2000 or Designed for Windows XP logo, the driver packaged with the device is digitally signed. Any drivers included on the Windows CD-ROM or at the Windows Update Web site are digitally signed.

Once you have installed a driver, you can look at its Properties to confirm that it was digitally signed. Figure 15-26 shows a digitally signed network card driver.

Figure 15-26
A digitally signed
driver

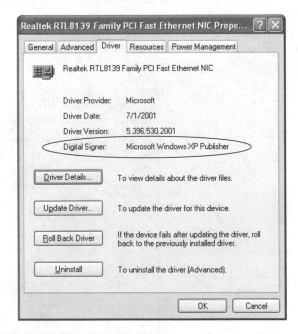

Many manufacturers issue drivers that are not digitally signed. I personally have installed many of them. When an unsigned driver is detected during hardware installation, you'll see the message in Figure 15-27 offering you the choice to stop or continue the installation. Signed drivers are more or less a sure thing, but that doesn't mean unsigned ones are a problem—just consider the source of the driver and ensure your device works properly after installation.

Figure 15-27
Stop or continue installation of an unsigned driver

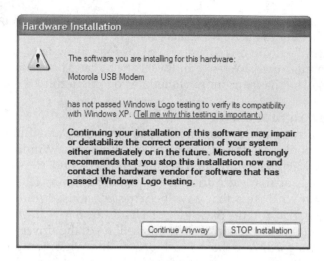

You can control how Windows behaves when drivers are being installed. Click the Driver Signing button on the Hardware tab of the System Properties dialog box to display the Driver Signing Options page shown in Figure 15-28. If you select Ignore, Windows will install an unsigned driver without warning you. If you select Warn, you will be prompted when Windows detects an unsigned driver during driver installation, and you will be given the opportunity to either stop or continue the installation. Choosing Block will prevent the installation of unsigned drivers.

Figure 15-28
Driver Signing Options

The default Driver Signing setting is Warn. This also is the default setting during installation, so you will always be warned when Windows detects an unsigned driver during Windows installation. This is no problem for an standard installation, when you are sitting at the computer, responding to all prompts—but it is a problem for automated, unattended installations. This is a good reason to check out all your device drivers before installing Windows.

Device Manager

You've worked with the Device Manager in other chapters when installing and trouble-shooting devices; it's also the tool to use when optimizing device drivers. Right-click on a device in Device Manager to display the context menu. From here you can update or uninstall the driver, disable the device, scan for hardware changes, or display the Properties dialog box. When you open the Properties dialog box, you'll see several tabs that vary according to the specific device. Most have General, Driver, Details, and Resources. The tab that matters most for optimization is the Driver tab.

The Driver tab has buttons labeled Driver Details, Update Driver, Roll Back Driver, and Uninstall. Driver Details lists the driver files and their locations on disk. Update Driver opens the Hardware Update Wizard—not very useful given that the install pro-grams for almost all drivers do this automatically. The Roll Back Driver option is a dif-ferent story. It enables you to remove an updated driver, thus rolling back to the previous driver version. Rollback (Figure 15-29) is a lifesaver when you install a new driver and suddenly discover it's worse than the driver it replaced! Uninstall removes the driver.

Figure 15-29
Rollback

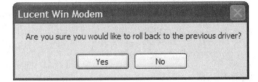

Adding a New Device

Windows should automatically detect any new device you install in your system. If Windows does not detect a newly connected device, use the Add Hardware Wizard (Figure 15-30) to get the device recognized and drivers installed. You'll find it on the Hardware tab of the System Properties dialog box.

Figure 15-30
Add Hardware
Wizard

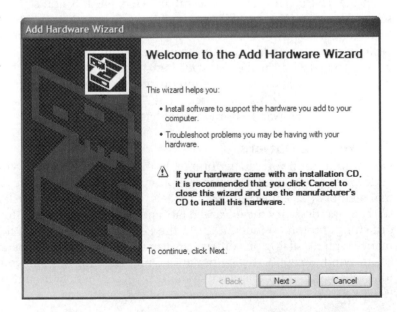

Click Next on the Welcome screen, and the wizard will search for hardware that has been connected but does not yet have a driver installed. If it detects the device, select the device, and the wizard will install the driver. You may have to point to the source location for the driver files. If it does not detect the device, which is very likely, it will ask you if the hardware is connected. When you answer yes and click Next, it will give you a list of installed hardware, similar to Figure 15-31.

Figure 15-31
List of installed
hardware

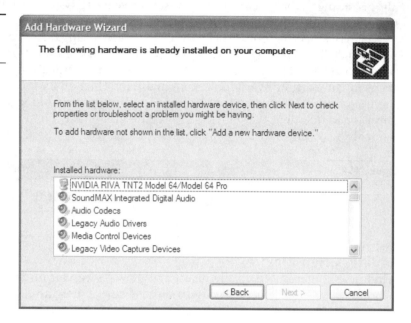

If the device is in the list, select it and click Next. If not, scroll to the bottom and select Add a New Hardware Device, and then click Next. If the device is a printer, network card, or modem, select *Search for and install the hardware automatically* and click Next. In that case, once it detects the device and installs the driver, you're done. If you do see your device on the list, your best hope is to select *Install the hardware that I manually select from a list.* In the subsequent screens, select the appropriate device category, select the device manufacturer and the correct model, and respond to the prompts from the Add Hardware Wizard to complete the installation.

Performance Options

One optimization you can perform on both Windows 2000 and Windows XP is setting Performance Options. Performance Options are used to configure CPU, RAM, and virtual memory (page file) settings. To access these options, right-click My Computer and select Properties, click the Advanced tab, and click the Options button (Windows 2000) or Settings button (Windows XP) in the Performance section of that tab. The Performance Options dialog box differs between the two families of operating systems.

In Windows 2000, the Performance Options dialog box shows a pair of radio buttons called Applications and Background Services. These radio buttons set how processor time is divided between the foreground application and all other background tasks. Set this to Applications if you run applications that need more processor time. Set it to Background Services to give all running programs the same processor usage. You can also adjust the size of the page file in this dialog box, but in most cases I don't mess with these settings and instead leave control of the page file to Windows.

The Windows XP Performance Options dialog box has three tabs: Visual Effects, Advanced, and Data Execution Prevention (Figure 15-32). The Visual Effects tab enables you to adjust visual effects that impact performance. Try clicking the top three choices in turn and watch the list of settings. Notice the tiny difference between the first two choices. The third choice, *Adjust for best performance*, turns off all visual effects, and the fourth option is an invitation to make your own adjustments. If you're on a computer that barely supports Windows XP, turning off visual effects can make a huge difference in the responsiveness of the computer. For the most part, though, just leave these settings alone.

Figure 15-32
Windows XP
Performance Settings
dialog box

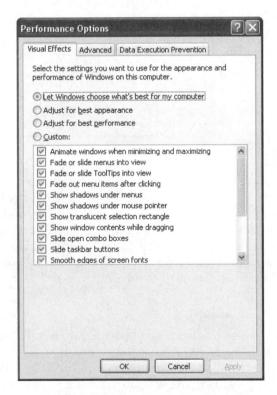

The Advanced tab, shown in Figure 15-33, has three sections: Processor scheduling, Memory usage, and Virtual memory. Under the Processor scheduling section, you can choose to adjust for best performance of either Programs or Background services. The Memory usage settings enable you to allocate a greater share of memory to programs or to the system cache. Finally, the Virtual memory section of this page enables you to modify the size and location of the page file.

Figure 15-33
Advanced tab of
Performance Settings

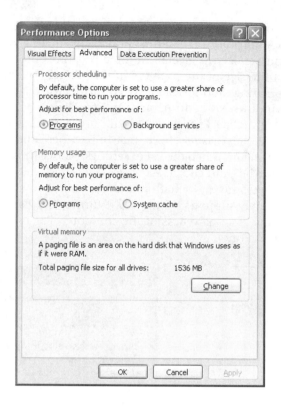

Microsoft introduced Data Execution Prevention (DEP) with Windows XP Service Pack 2. DEP works in the background to stop viruses and other malware from taking over programs loaded in system memory. It doesn't prevent viruses from being installed on your computer, but makes them less effective. By default, DEP monitors only critical operating system files in RAM, but the Data Execution Prevention tab enables you to have DEP monitor all running programs. It works, but you'll take a performance hit. Like other options in the Performance Options dialog box, leaving the DEP settings as default is the best option most of the time.

Resource Tracking

One big issue with optimization is knowing when something needs optimization. Let's say your Windows computer seems to be running more slowly. Resource tracking is very important for identifying the performance problem. Task Manager and the Performance Console are tools you can use to figure out what (if anything) has become a bottleneck.

Task Manager

The Task Manager has many uses. Most users are only aware of the Applications tab, used to shut down a troublesome program. For optimization purposes, Task Manager is a great tool for investigating how hard your RAM and CPU are working at any given moment and why. The quick way to open the Task Manager is to press CTRL-SHIFT-ESC. Click the Performance tab to reveal a handy screen with the most commonly used information: CPU usage, available physical memory, the size of the disk cache, commit charge (memory for programs), and kernel memory (memory used by Windows). Figure 15-34 shows a system with a dual-core processor, which is why you see two screens under CPU Usage History. A system with a single-core processor would have a single screen.

Figure 15-34
Task Manager

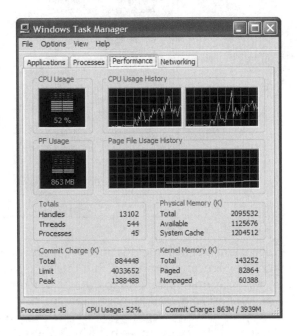

Not only does Task Manager tell you how much CPU and RAM usage is taking place, it also tells you what program is using those resources. Let's say your system is running slowly. You open up Task Manager and see that your CPU usage is at 100 percent. You then click on the Processes tab to see all the processes running on your system. Click on the CPU column to sort all processes by CPU usage to see who's hogging the CPU (Figure 15-35)! To shut off a process, just right-click on the process and select End Process. Many times a single process will open many other processes. If you want to be thorough, click on End Process Tree to turn off not only the one process, but also any other processes it started.

NOTE Every program that runs on your system is composed of one or more processes.

Figure 15-35
CPU Usage

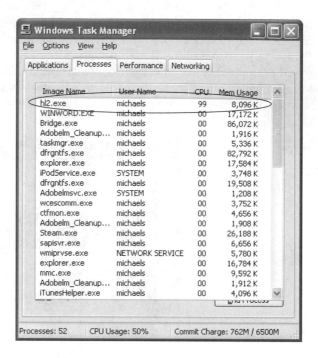

Task Manager is also a great tool for turning off processes that are hogging memory. Let's say you're experiencing a slowdown, but this time you also notice your hard drive light is flickering nonstop—a clear sign that you've run out of memory and the swapfile is now in use. You go into Task Manager and see that there is no available system memory—now you *know* the swapfile is in use! In order to make the PC run faster you have got to start unloading programs—but which ones? By going into the Processes tab in Task Manager, you can see exactly which processes are using the most memory. Just be careful not to shut down processes you don't recognize; they might be something the computer needs!

Performance Console

Task Manager is good for identifying current problems, but what about problems that happen when you're not around? What if your system is always running at a CPU utilization of 20 percent—is that good or bad? Windows provides a tool called Performance that is used to log resource usage so that you can track items such as CPU and RAM usage over time. Performance is an MMC console file, PERFMON.MSC, so you call it from Start | Run or through the Performance icon in Administrative Tools. Use either method to open the Performance Console (Figure 15-36). As you can see, there are two nodes, System Monitor and Performance Logs and Alerts.

Objects and Counters   To begin working with the Performance Console, you need to understand two terms: object and counter. An object is a system component that is given a set of characteristics and can be managed by the operating system as a

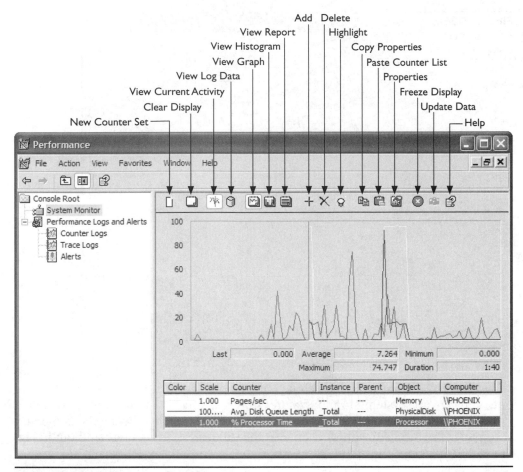

Figure 15-36 Performance Console

single entity. A counter tracks specific information about an object. For example, the Processor object has a counter, %Processor Time, which tracks the percentage of elapsed time the processor uses to execute a non-idle thread. There can be many counters associated with an object.

System Monitor   System Monitor gathers real-time data on objects such as memory, physical disk, processor, and network, and displays this data as a graph (line graph), histogram (bar graph), or a simple report. Think of System Monitor as a more detailed, customizable Task Manager. When you first open the Performance Console, the System Monitor shows data in graph form. The data displayed is from the set of three counters listed below the chart. If you want to add counters, click the Add button (the one that looks like a plus sign) or press CTRL-I to open the Add Counters dialog box. Click the Performance object drop-down list and select one of the many different objects you can monitor. The Add Counters dialog box includes a helpful feature; you can select a counter and click the Explain button to learn about the counter, just like Figure 15-37. Try that now.

Figure 15-37
Add Counters
dialog box

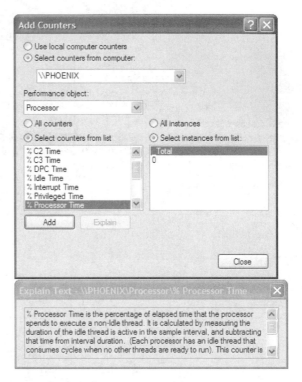

Even with just three counters selected, the graph can get a little busy. That's where one of my favorite System Monitor features shines. If you want the line of charted data from just one counter to stand out, select the counter in the list below the graph and then press CTRL-H. See how this trick makes the %Processor Time line stand out in Figure 15-38? Imagine how useful that is when you are monitoring a dozen counters.

Figure 15-38
CTRL-H makes one
set of data stand out

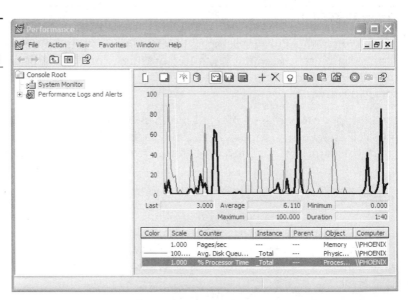

Performance Logs and Alerts   The Performance Logs and Alerts snap-in en-ables Windows 2000/XP to create a written record of just about anything that happens on your system. Do you want to know if someone is trying to log onto your system when you're not around? The following procedure is specific to Windows XP, but the steps are nearly identical in Windows 2000.

To create the new event log, right-click Counter Logs and select New Log Settings. Give the new log a name—in this example, "Unauthorized Accesses." Click OK, and a properties box for the new log will open, similar to that in Figure 15-39.

Figure 15-39
Creating a new
performance log

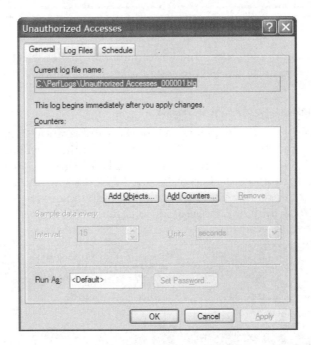

To select counters for the log, click Add Counters and then select the *Use local computer counters* radio button. Select Server from the Performance object pull-down menu, then select Errors Logon from the list of counters; click Add, and then Close.

Back in the properties box for your new log, click the Schedule tab and set up when you want this thing to start running—probably at the end of the workday today. Then select when it should stop logging—probably tomorrow morning when you start work. Click the Log Files tab to see where the log file will be saved—probably C:\PerfLogs—and make a note of the filename. The filename will consist of the name you gave the log and a number. In this example I named the new performance log "Unauthorized Accesses," so the file name is Unauthorized Accesses_000001.blg.

When you come back in the morning, open the Performance console, select Performance Logs and Alerts, and then select Counter Logs. Your log should be listed on the right. The icon by the log name will be green if the log is still running or red if it has stopped. If it has not stopped, select it and click the stop button (the one with the black square). See Figure 15-40.

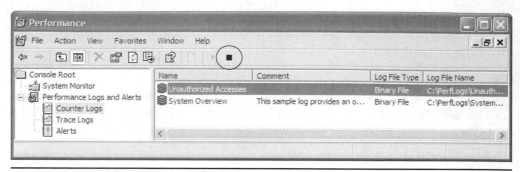

Figure 15-40 Stopping the performance log

To view the log, open the Performance Console, select System Monitor, change to Report view, and load the file as a new source using the Properties box.

Preparing for Problems

The secret to troubleshooting Windows is preparation. You must have critical system files and data backed up and tools in place for the inevitable glitches. The various versions of Windows offer five different tools for the job, although none offer them all: System Restore, the Backup or Restore Wizard (called NTBackup if you want to run it from the command prompt), Automated System Recovery (ASR), the Emergency Repair Disk (ERD), and the Recovery Console. Table 15-1 shows which OS gets which tool.

	System Restore	Backup or Restore Wizard	Automated System Recovery	Emergency Repair Disk	Recovery Console
Windows 2000 Professional	No	Yes, but called "Backup"	No	Yes	Yes
Windows XP Home[1]	Yes	No	No	No	No
Windows XP Professional[2]	Yes	Yes	Yes	No	Yes

1. Also applies to Windows XP Media Center Edition
2. Also applies to Windows XP Tablet PC Edition

Table 15-1 Backup and recovery tools in Windows

System Restore

Every technician has war stories about the user who likes to add the latest gadget and cool software to their computer. Then he's amazed when things go very, very wrong: the system locks up, refuses to boot, or simply acts "weird." This guy also can't remember what he added or when. All he knows is that you should be able to fix it—fast.

This is not news to the folks at Microsoft, and they have a solution to this problem. It's called System Restore, and they first introduced it in Windows Me, with further refinements in Windows XP. The System Restore tool enables you to create a restore point, a copy of your computer's configuration at a specific point in time. If you later crash or have a corrupted OS, you can restore the system to its previous state.

To create a restore point, go to Start | All Programs | Accessories | System Tools | System Restore. When the tool opens, select Create a Restore Point and then click Next (Figure 15-41). Type in a description on the next screen. There's no need to include the date and time because the System Restore adds them automatically. Click Create and you're done.

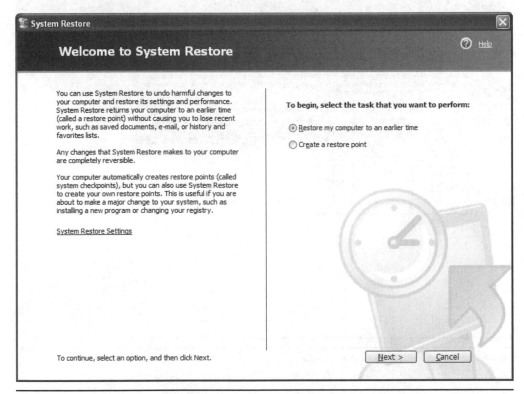

Figure 15-41   Create a restore point

The System Restore tool creates some of the restore points in time automatically. For instance, by default, every time you install new software, XP creates a restore point. Thus, if installation of a program causes your computer to malfunction, simply restore the system to a time point prior to that installation, and the computer should work again.

During the restore process, only settings and programs are changed. No data is lost. Your computer will include all programs and settings as of the restore date. This feature is absolutely invaluable for overworked techs. A simple restore will fix many user-generated problems.

To restore to a previous time point, start the System Restore Wizard by choosing Start | All Programs | Accessories | System Tools | System Restore. Then select the first radio button, Restore my computer to an earlier time, and then click Next. Figure 15-42 shows a calendar with restore points. Any day with a boldface date has at least one re-store point. These points are created after you add or remove software or install Windows updates and during the normal shutdown of your computer. Select a date on the calendar; then select a restore point from the list on the right and click Next.

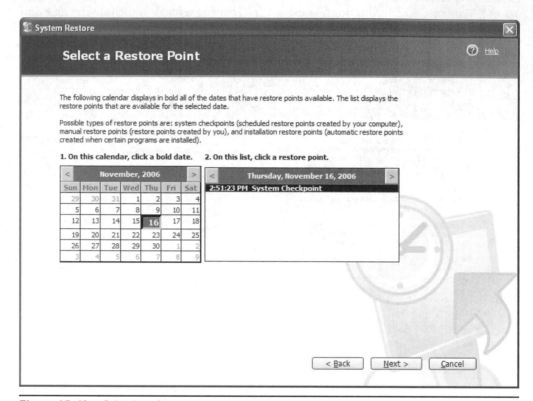

Figure 15-42   Calendar of restore points

The last screen before the system is restored shows a warning. It advises you to close all open programs and reminds you that Windows will shut down during the restore process. It also states that the restore operation is completely reversible. Thus, if you go too far back in time, you can restore to a more recent date.

You don't have to count on the automatic creation of restore points. You can open System Restore at any time and simply select Create a restore point. Consider doing this before making changes that might not trigger an automatic restore point, such as directly editing the Registry.

System Restore is turned on by default and uses some of your disk space to save information on restore points. To turn System Restore off or change the disk space usage, open the System Properties applet in Control Panel and select the System Restore tab (Figure 15-43).

Figure 15-43
System Restore tab
in System Properties
applet

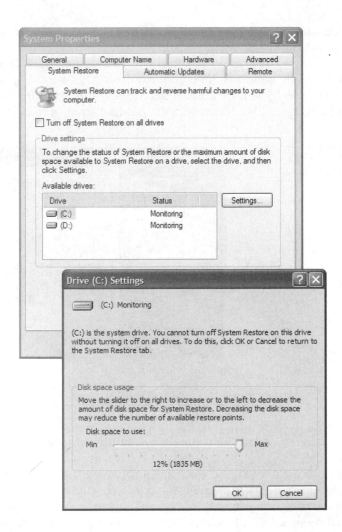

Backup or Restore Wizard (NTBackup)

Windows 2000/XP Backup provides almost all the tools you need. It has come a long way from its origins in Windows NT. It supports a greater variety of devices, enabling you to network drives, logical drives, tape, and removable disks (but not CD-R, CD-RW, or DVD-R). Most folks, however, still turn to third-party utilities to create system, e-mail, browser, and personal data backups.

NOTE The Backup utility is not included in the default installation of Windows XP Home. You must install it manually from the Windows CD-ROM.

You can start Backup by navigating the Start menu to Accessories | System Tools, or by clicking the Backup Now button on the Tools page of the local disk properties box. I prefer to start it from Start | Run with the command NTBACKUP. This technique works in both Windows 2000 and Windows XP. To use the XP version in Advanced Mode (Figure 15-44), click Advanced Mode on the opening screen. To have it always open in Advanced Mode, uncheck the *Always start in wizard mode* checkbox.

Figure 15-44
Advanced Mode

To create a backup, start the Backup utility, click Advanced Mode, and choose the Backup tab. Check the boxes next to the drives and files you want to include in the backup. To include your system state information, such as Registry and boot files (which you should do), click the System State checkbox. To specify where to put the backup file you're creating, either type the path and filename in the *Backup media or filename* box or click Browse, select a location, type the filename, and click Save. Click Start Backup. Choose whether you want to append this backup to a previous one or overwrite it. Click Advanced to open the Advanced Backup Options dialog box, select *Verify data after backup*, and click OK. Click Start Backup again. A dialog box will show you the utility's progress. When it's done, click Close and then close the Backup utility.

Both versions of Backup give you three choices after you click Advanced Mode: Backup Wizard (Advanced), Restore Wizard (Advanced), and a third choice that is very important. The third option in Windows 2000 is the Emergency Repair Disk. As you can see in Figure 15-45, the third option in Windows XP is the Automated System Recovery Wizard.

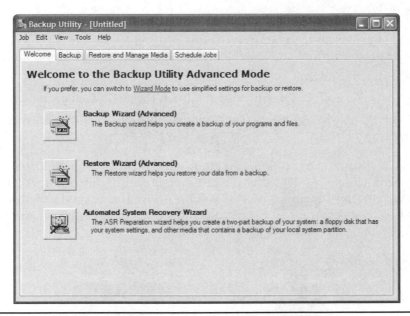

Figure 15-45   Windows XP Backup options

Windows 2000 Emergency Repair Disk (ERD)   Let's first consider the Windows 2000 Emergency Repair Disk (ERD). This disk saves critical boot files and partition information and is your main tool for fixing boot problems in Windows 2000. It is not a bootable disk, nor does it store very much information; the ERD does not replace a good system backup! It works with a special folder called \WINNT\REPAIR to store a copy of your Registry. It's not perfect, but it gets you out of most startup problems. It's good practice to make a new ERD before you install a new device or program. Then the ERD is ready if you need it.

So, we've got this great Emergency Repair Disk that'll take care of all of our system repair problems, we just pop it in the floppy drive and go, right?

Not just yet. As I mentioned, the ERD itself is not a bootable disk. To use the ERD, you must first boot the system using the Windows installation CD-ROM. Follow these steps to repair a system using the ERD:

1. Boot the system using either your set of boot diskettes or installation CD-ROM.

2. In the Welcome to Setup dialog box, press the R key to select the option to repair a Windows 2000 installation.

3. The Windows 2000 Repair Options menu appears. You have the option of either entering the Recovery Console or using the Emergency Repair Disk.

4. Press the R key to select the option to repair Windows 2000 using the emergency repair process.

5. The next screen offers the choice of Manual or Fast repair:

- Manual repair lets you select the following repair options: inspect the startup environment, verify the system files, and inspect the boot sector.

- Fast repair doesn't ask for any further input.

6. Follow the on-screen instructions and insert the ERD when prompted.

7. Your system will be inspected and, if possible, restored. When finished, the system will restart.

Windows XP Automated System Recovery (ASR)   The Windows XP Automated System Recovery (ASR) looks and acts very similar to the Windows 2000 ERD. The ASR Wizard lets you create a backup of your system. This backup includes a floppy disk and backup media (tape or CD-R) containing the system partition and disks containing operating system components (Figure 15-46).

Figure 15-46   Creating an ASR backup

The restore side of ASR involves a complete reinstall of the operating system, preferably on a new partition. This is something you do when all is lost. Run setup and press F2 when prompted during the text-mode portion of Setup. Follow the prompts on the screen, which will first ask for the floppy disk and then for the backup media.

Backup Wizard   Data files are not backed up by the ERD or by the ASR. Therefore, you have to back up data files. If you run the Backup utility and click Next rather than choosing Advanced Mode, you'll see the screen in Figure 15-47. You have three options here. The first two are fairly self-explanatory: You can back up everything or just selected drives and files.

Figure 15-47
Backup Wizard when not using Advanced Mode

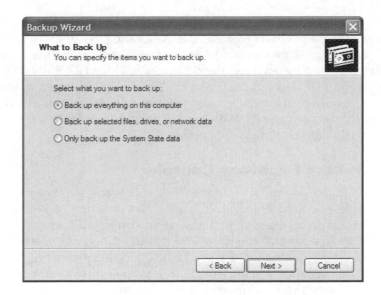

The third option needs some explanation. The *Only back up the System State data* radio button enables you to save "other" system-critical files, but with Windows 2000/XP, it's not much more than making an ERD with the Registry backup. This option really makes sense for Windows 2000 Server and Windows Server 2003 systems because it saves Active Directory information (which your Windows 2000/XP systems do not store) as well as other critical, server-specific functions. (More on these topics in Chapter 23.) But the CompTIA A+ certification exams may still expect you to know about it!

Tape Backup The odd fact that Microsoft has not updated the Backup or Restore Wizard to enable you to back up to optical media of any sort has kept alive the practice of tape backups. Tape drives connect to the ATA or SCSI bus, just like optical drives, but rather than using a shiny CD-R or DVD+R disc, you have to back up to magnetic tape (Figure 15-48).

Figure 15-48
Backup tapes

Tape drive manufacturers have done pretty much everything they can do to make tape backups as fast as possible, but the technology suffers from two huge drawbacks. First, it's tape, which means all data must be stored and restored in sequential access. The drive has to go through File 1 and 2 before reaching File 3, in other words. Second, tape is painfully slow in comparison to hard drives, optical drives, or Flash-media drives.

The only great benefit to tape is that it's relatively cheap to buy multiple tapes with a lot of storage capacity. With hard drive and recordable DVD prices at rock bottom today, though, tape's days are numbered.

Installing Recovery Console

When things get really bad on a Windows system, you need to turn to the Recovery Console. The Recovery Console is a text-based startup of Windows that gets you to a command prompt similar to the Windows command prompt.

If you have the Windows 2000/XP CD-ROM, you can start the Recovery Console by running Setup, selecting Repair, and then selecting Recovery Console. If you like to be proactive, however, you can install the Recovery Console on your hard drive so that it is one of your startup options and does not require the Windows 2000 or XP CD-ROM to run. The steps to do this in Windows 2000 and Windows XP are very nearly identical.

First, you need to log into the system with the Administrator account. Grab your Windows 2000 or XP installation CD-ROM and drop it in your system. If the Autorun function kicks in, just click the No button. To install the Recovery Console and make it a part of your startup options, click the Start button, select Run, and type the following:

```
d:\i386\winnt32 /cmdcons
```

If your CD-ROM drive uses a different drive letter, substitute it for the D: drive. Then just follow the instructions on the screen. If you are connected to the Internet, allow the Setup program to download updated files. From now on, every time the system boots, the OS selection menu will show your Windows OS (Windows 2000 Professional or Windows XP) and the Microsoft Windows Recovery Console. It may also show other choices if yours is a multi-boot computer.

Troubleshooting Windows

Chapters 10 and 12 through 14 introduced you to the essential tools for troubleshooting and repairing Windows. You know about Disk Management, Device Manager, Event Viewer, and more. You've spent countless hours preparing systems for disaster with NTBackup and System Restore. While learning about the tools, you also learned how to use them. This section puts it all together and shows you a plan to deal with potential disasters for a Windows computer.

This section looks at Windows problems from the ground up. It starts with catastrophic failure—a PC that won't boot—and then discusses ways to get past that problem. The next section covers the causes and workarounds when the Windows GUI fails to load. Once you can access the GUI, then the world of Windows diagnostic and troubleshooting tools that you've spent so much time learning about comes to your fingertips. First, though, you have to get there.

Failure to Boot

Windows boot errors take place in those short moments between the time the POST ends and the Loading Windows screen begins. For Windows to start loading the main operating system, the critical system files NTLDR, NTDETECT.COM, and BOOT.INI must reside in the root directory of the C: drive, and BOOT.INI must point to the Windows boot files. If any of these requirements aren't in place, the system won't get past this step. Here are some of the common errors you see at this point:

No Boot device Present
NTLDR Bad or Missing
Invalid BOOT.INI

Note that these text errors take place very early in the startup process. That's your big clue that you have a boot issue. If you get to the Windows splash screen and then lock up, that's a whole different game, so know the difference.

If you get one of the catastrophic error messages, you have a three-level process to get back up and running. You first should attempt to repair. If that fails, then attempt to restore from a backup copy of Windows. If restore is either not available or fails, then your only recourse is to rebuild. You will lose data at the restore and rebuild phases, so you definitely want to spend a lot of effort on the repair effort first!

Attempt to Repair Using Recovery Console

To begin troubleshooting one of these errors, boot from the installation CD-ROM and have Windows do a repair of an existing installation. Windows will prompt you if you want to use the Recovery Console or the emergency repair process (ASR/ERD). Start with the Recovery Console.

If you followed the instructions earlier in the lesson, then you've installed the Recovery Console onto your system and have it as an option when you boot the system. If not, start it as described earlier using the Windows 2000 or XP installation CD-ROM. When you select the Recovery Console, you will see a message about NTDETECT, another one that the Recovery Console is starting up, and then you will be greeted with the following message and command prompt:

```
Microsoft Windows XP<TM> Recovery Console.
The Recovery Console provides system repair and recovery functionality.
Type Exit to quit the Recovery Console and restart the computer.

1: C:\WINDOWS
Which Windows XP installation would you like to log onto
<To cancel, press ENTER>?
```

The cursor is a small, white rectangle sitting to the right of the question mark on the last line. If you are not accustomed to working at the command prompt, this may be disorienting. If there is only one installation of Windows XP on your computer, type the number 1 at the prompt and press the ENTER key. If you press ENTER before typing in a valid selection, the Recovery Console will cancel and the computer will reboot. The only choice you can make in this example is 1. Having made that choice, the only change to the screen above is a new line:

```
Type the Administrator password:
```

This is also followed by the cursor. Enter the Administrator password for that computer and press ENTER. The password will not display on the screen; you will see asterisks in place of the password. The screen still shows everything that has happened so far, unless something has happened to cause an error message. It now looks like this:

```
Microsoft Windows XP<TM> Recovery Console.
The Recovery Console provides system repair and recovery functionality.
Type Exit to quit the Recovery Console and restart the computer.

1: C:\WINDOWS
Which Windows XP installation would you like to log onto
<To cancel, press ENTER>? 1
Type the Administrator password: ********
C:\Windows>
```

By now, you've caught on and know that there is a rectangular prompt immediately after the last line. Now what do you do? Use the Recovery Console commands, of course. Recovery Console uses many of the commands that worked in the Windows command-line interface that you explored in Chapter 14, as well as some uniquely its own. Table 15-2 lists the common Recovery Console commands.

The Recovery Console shines in the business of manually restoring registries, stopping problem services, rebuilding partitions (other than the system partition), and using the EXPAND program to extract copies of corrupted files from a CD-ROM or floppy disk.

Using the Recovery Console, you can reconfigure a service so that it starts with different settings, format drives on the hard disk, read and write on local FAT or NTFS volumes, and copy replacement files from a floppy or CD-ROM. The Recovery Console enables you to access the file system, and is still constrained by the file and folder security of NTFS, which makes it a more secure tool to use than some third-party solutions.

The Recovery Console is best at fixing three items: repairing the MBR, reinstalling the boot files, and rebuilding BOOT.INI. Let's look at each of these.

A bad boot sector usually shows up as a No Boot Device error. If it turns out that this isn't the problem, the Recovery Console command to fix it won't hurt anything. At the Recovery Console prompt, just type:

```
fixmbr
```

This fixes the master boot record.

The second problem the Recovery Console is best at fixing is missing system files, usually indicated by the error NTLDR bad or missing. Odds are good that if NTDLR is missing, so are the rest of the system files. To fix this, get to the root directory (CD\—remember that from Chapter 14?) and type

```
copy d:\i386\ntldr
```

Then type

```
copy d:\i386\ntdetect.com
```

This takes care of two of the big three and leads us to the last issue, rebuilding BOOT.INI. If the BOOT.INI file is gone or corrupted, run this command from the recovery console:

```
bootcfg /rebuild
```

Command	Description
attrib	Changes attributes of selected file or folder
cd (or chdir)	Displays current directory or changes directories
chkdsk	Runs CheckDisk utility
cls	Clears screen
copy	Copies from removable media to system folders on hard disk. No wildcards
del (or delete)	Deletes service or folder
dir	Lists contents of selected directory on system partition only
disable	Disables service or driver
diskpart	Replaces FDISK—creates/deletes partitions
enable	Enables service or driver
extract	Extracts components from .CAB files
fixboot	Writes new partition boot sector on system partition
fixmbr	Writes new Master Boot Record for partition boot sector
format	Formats selected disk
listsvc	Lists all services on system
logon	Lets you choose which W2K installation to logon to if you have more than one
map	Displays current drive letter mappings
md (or mkdir)	Creates a directory
more (or type)	Displays contents of text file
rd (or rmdir)	Removes a directory
ren (or rename)	Renames a single file
systemroot	Makes current directory system root of drive you're logged into
type	Displays a text file

Table 15-2   Common Recovery Console Commands

The Recovery console will then try to locate all installed copies of Windows and ask you if you want to add them to the new BOOT.INI file it's about to create. Say yes to the ones you want.

If all goes well with the Recovery Console, then do a thorough backup as soon as possible (just in case something else goes wrong). If the Recovery Console does not do the trick, the next step is to restore Windows.

Attempt to Restore

If you've been diligent about backing up, you can attempt to restore to an earlier, working copy of Windows. You have two basic choices depending on your OS. In Windows 2000, you can try the Emergency Repair Disk (ERD). Windows XP limits you to the Automated System Recovery (ASR).

NOTE To use the Windows XP System Restore, you need to be able to get into Windows. "Restore" in the context used here means to give you an option to get into Windows.

If you elected to create an ERD in Windows 2000, you can attempt to restore your system with it. Boot your system to the Windows 2000 installation CD-ROM and select repair installation, but in this case opt for the ERD. Follow the steps outlined earlier in the chapter and you might have some success.

ASR can restore your system to a previously installed state, but you should use it as a last resort. You lose everything on the system that was installed or added after you created the ASR disk. If that's the best option, though, follow the steps outlined earlier in the chapter.

Rebuild

If faced with a full system rebuild, you have several options depending on the particular system. You could simply reboot to the Windows CD-ROM and install right on top of the existing system, but that's usually not the optimal solution. To avoid losing anything important, you'd be better off swapping the C: drive for a blank hard drive and installing a clean version of Windows.

Most OEM systems come with a misleadingly-named *Recover CD* or *recovery partition*. The Recover CD is a CD-ROM that you boot to and run. The recovery partition is a hidden partition on the hard drive that you activate at boot by holding down a key combination specific to the manufacturer of that system. (See the motherboard manual or users' guide for the key combination and other details.) Both "recover" options do the same thing—restore your computer to the factory-installed state. If you run one of these tools, you will wipe everything off your system—all personal files, folders, and programs will go away! Before running either tool, make sure all important files and folders are backed up on an optical disc or spare hard drive.

Failure to Load the GUI

Assuming that Windows gets past the boot part of the startup, it will then begin to load the real Windows OS. You will see the Windows startup image on the screen (Figure 15-49), hiding everything until Windows loads the Desktop.

Copyright © 1985-2001
Microsoft Corporation

Microsoft

Figure 15-49 GUI Time

Several issues can cause Windows to hang during the GUI-loading phase, such as buggy device drivers or Registry problems. Even autoloading programs can cause the GUI to hang on load. The first step in troubleshooting these issues is to use one of the Advanced Startup options (covered later in the chapter) to try to get past the hang spot and into Windows.

Device Drivers

Device driver problems that stop Windows GUI from loading look pretty scary. Figure 15-50 shows the infamous Windows *Stop error*, better known as the *Blue Screen of Death (BSoD)*. The BSoD only appears when something causes an error from which Windows cannot recover. The BSoD is not limited to device driver problems, but device drivers are one of the reasons you'll see the BSoD.

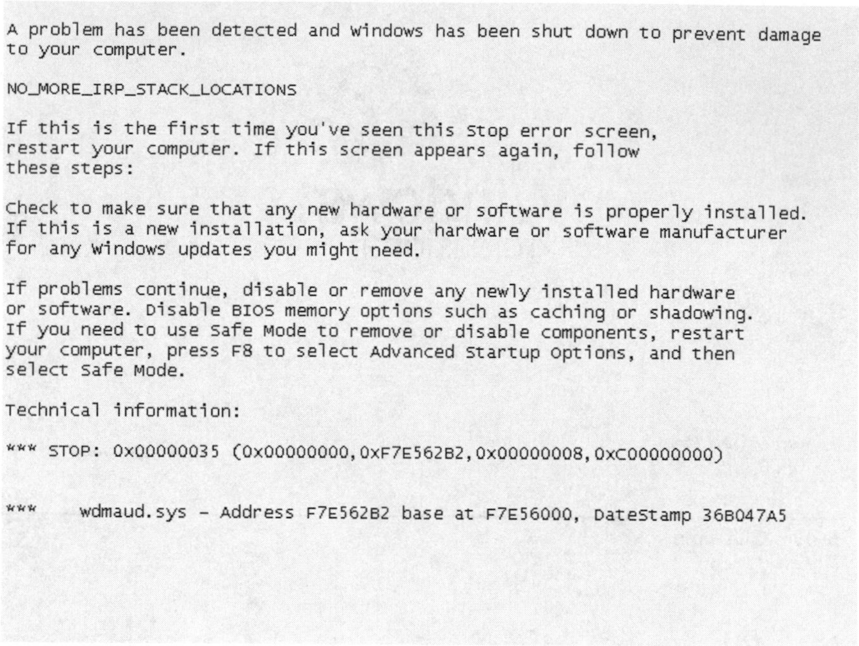

```
A problem has been detected and windows has been shut down to prevent damage
to your computer.

NO_MORE_IRP_STACK_LOCATIONS

If this is the first time you've seen this Stop error screen,
restart your computer. If this screen appears again, follow
these steps:

Check to make sure that any new hardware or software is properly installed.
If this is a new installation, ask your hardware or software manufacturer
for any windows updates you might need.

If problems continue, disable or remove any newly installed hardware
or software. Disable BIOS memory options such as caching or shadowing.
If you need to use Safe Mode to remove or disable components, restart
your computer, press F8 to select Advanced Startup Options, and then
select Safe Mode.

Technical information:

*** STOP: 0x00000035 (0x00000000,0xF7E562B2,0x00000008,0xC00000000)


***    wdmaud.sys - Address F7E562B2 base at F7E56000, DateStamp 36B047A5
```

Figure 15-50   BSoD

Whenever you get a BSoD, take a moment and read what it says. Windows BSoDs tell you the name of the file that caused the problem and usually suggest a recommended action. Once in a while these are helpful—but not often.

BSoD problems due to device drivers almost always take place immediately after you've installed a new device and rebooted. Take out the device and reboot. If Windows loads properly, head over to the manufacturer's Web site. A new device producing this type of problem is a serious issue that should have been caught before the device was released. In many cases the manufacturer will have updated drivers available for download or will recommend a replacement device.

The second indication of a device problem that shows up during the GUI part of startup is a freeze-up: the Windows startup screen just stays there and you never get a chance to log on. If this happens, try one of the Advanced Startup Options, covered below.

Registry

Your Registry files load every time the computer boots. Windows does a pretty good job of protecting your Registry files from corruption, but from time to time something may slip by Windows and it will attempt to load a bad Registry. These errors may show up as

BSoDs that say "Registry File Failure" or text errors that say "Windows could not start." Whatever the case, you need to restore a good Registry copy. The best way to do this is the Last Known Good Configuration boot option (see the upcoming section). If that fails, then you can restore an earlier version of the Registry through the Recovery Console.

Boot to the Windows installation CD-ROM, select the repair installation to get to the Recovery Console, and type these commands to restore a Registry. Notice I didn't say "your" Registry in the previous sentence. Your Registry is corrupted and gone, so you need to rebuild.

```
delete c:\windows\system32\config\system
delete c:\windows\system32\config\software
delete c:\windows\system32\config\sam
delete c:\windows\system32\config\security
delete c:\windows\system32\config\default

copy c:\windows\repair\system c:\windows\system32\config\system
copy c:\windows\repair\software c:\windows\system32\config\software
copy c:\windows\repair\sam c:\windows\system32\config\sam
copy c:\windows\repair\security c:\windows\system32\config\security
copy c:\windows\repair\default c:\windows\system32\config\default
```

Advanced Startup Options

If Windows fails to start up, use the Windows Advanced Startup Options menu to discover the cause. To get to this menu, restart the computer and press F8 after the POST messages, but before the Windows logo screen appears. Windows 2000 and Windows XP have similar menus. Central to these advanced options are Safe Mode and Last Known Good.

There are several differences between the two operating systems in this menu. First, the Windows 2000 option called Boot Normally is called Start Windows Normally in Windows XP. In addition, Windows XP has options not available in Windows 2000: *Disable automatic restart on system failure* and *Reboot*. A Windows system with multiple operating systems might also have the Return to OS Choices Menu. Here's a rundown of the menu options.

 NOTE Windows 9x had an option for Step-by-step confirmation, but that is not a choice in Windows 2000/XP. Look for it as a wrong answer on the exams!

Safe Mode

Safe Mode (Figure 15-51) starts up Windows but loads only very basic, non–vendor-specific drivers for mouse, VGA monitor, keyboard, mass storage, and system services. Some devices, such as your USB mouse, may not work!

Safe Mode   Microsoft (R) Windows XP (R) (Build 2600)   Safe Mode

Safe Mode   Safe Mode

Figure 15-51 Safe Mode

Once in Safe Mode, you can use tools like Device Manager to locate and correct the source of the problem. When you use Device Manager in Safe Mode, you can access the properties for all the devices, even those that are not working in Safe Mode. The status displayed for the device is the status for a normal startup. Even the network card will show as enabled. You can disable any suspect device or perform other tasks, such as removing or updating drivers. If a problem with a device driver is preventing the operating system from starting normally, check the Device Manager for yellow question mark warning icons that indicate an unknown device.

Safe Mode with Networking

This mode is identical to plain Safe Mode except that you get network support. I use this mode to test for a problem with network drivers. If Windows won't start up normally, but does start up in Safe Mode, I then reboot into Safe Mode with Networking. If it fails to start up with Networking, then the problem is a network driver. I reboot back to Safe Mode, open Device Manager, and start disabling network components, beginning with the network adapter.

Safe Mode with Command Prompt

When you start Windows in this mode, after you log on, rather than loading the GUI desktop, it loads the command prompt (CMD.EXE) as the shell to the operating system, as shown in Figure 15-52. This is a handy option to remember if the desktop does not display at all, which, after you have eliminated video drivers, can be caused by the corruption of the EXPLORER.EXE program. From the command prompt you can delete the corrupted version of EXPLORER.EXE and copy in an undamaged version. This requires knowing the command-line commands for navigating the directory structure, as well as knowing the location of the file that you are replacing. Although Explorer is not loaded, you can load other GUI tools that don't depend on Explorer. All you have to do is enter the correct command. For instance, to load Event Viewer, type **eventvwr.msc** at the command line and press ENTER.

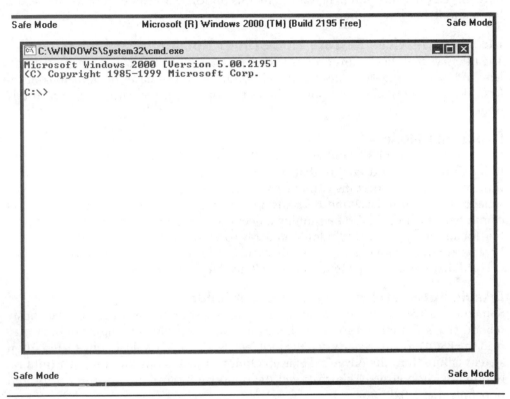

Figure 15-52   Safe Mode with Command Prompt

Enable Boot Logging

This option starts Windows normally and creates a log file of the drivers as they load into memory. The file is named Ntbtlog.txt and is saved in the %SystemRoot% folder. If the startup failed because of a bad driver, the last entry in this file may be the driver the OS was initializing when it failed.

Reboot and go into the Recovery Console. Use the Recovery Console tools to read the boot log (**type ntbtlog.txt**) and disable or enable problematic devices or services.

Enable VGA Mode

Enable VGA Mode starts Windows normally but only loads a default VGA driver. If this mode works, it may mean that you have a bad driver, or it may mean that you are using the correct video driver, but it is configured incorrectly (perhaps with the wrong refresh rate and/or resolution). Whereas Safe Mode loads a generic VGA driver, this mode loads the driver Windows is configured to use, but starts it up in standard VGA mode rather than using the settings for which it is configured. After successfully starting in this mode, open the Display Properties and change the settings.

Last Known Good Configuration
When Windows' startup fails immediately after installing a new driver, but before you have logged on again, you may want to try this option. This can be a rather fickle and limited tool, but it never hurts to try it.

Directory Services Restore Mode (Does Not Apply to Professional)
The title says it all here—this option only applies to Active Directory domain controllers, and Windows 2000 Professional and Windows XP can never be domain controllers. I have no idea why Microsoft includes this option. If you choose it, you simply boot into Safe Mode.

Debugging Mode
If you select this choice, Windows 2000/XP starts in kernel debug mode. It's a super-techie thing to do, and I doubt that even über techs do debug mode anymore. To do this, you have to connect the computer you are debugging to another computer via a serial connection, and as Windows starts up, a debug of the kernel is sent to the second computer, which must also be running a debugger program. I remember running debug for an early version of Windows 2000. My co-workers and I did it back then simply because we were studying for the MCSE exams and expected to be tested on it! We all decided that it was an experience that didn't need to be repeated.

Disable automatic restart on system failure
Sometimes a BSOD will appear at startup, causing your computer to spontaneously reboot. That's all well and good, but if it happens too quickly, you might not be able to read the BSOD to see what caused the problem. Selecting Disable automatic restart on system failure from the Advanced Startup Options menu stops the computer from rebooting on Stop errors. This gives you the opportunity to write down the error and hopefully find a fix.

Start Windows Normally
This choice will simply start Windows normally, without rebooting. You already rebooted to get to this menu. Select this if you changed your mind about using any of the other exotic choices.

Reboot
This choice will actually do a soft reboot of the computer.

Return to OS Choices Menu
On computers with multiple operating systems, you get an OS Choices Menu to select which OS to load. If you load Windows XP and press F8 to get the Advanced Startup Options menu, you'll see this option. This choice will return you to the OS Choices Menu, from which you can select the operating system to load.

Troubleshooting Tools in the GUI

Once you're able to load into Windows, whether through Safe Mode or one of the other options, the whole gamut of Windows tools are available for you. If a bad device driver caused the startup problems, for example, you can open Device Manager and begin troubleshooting just as you've learned in previous chapters. If you suspect some service or Registry issue caused the problem, head on over to Event Viewer and see what sort of logon events have happened recently.

NOTE Chapter 23, "Computer Security," goes into a lot more detail on using the Event Viewer, especially *auditing*, a way to troubleshoot a buggy system.

Event Viewer might reveal problems with applications failing to load, a big cause of Windows loading problems (Figure 15-53). It might also reveal problems with services failing to start. Finally, Windows might run into problems loading DLLs. You can troubleshoot these issues individually or you can use System Restore in Windows XP to load a restore point that predates the bugginess.

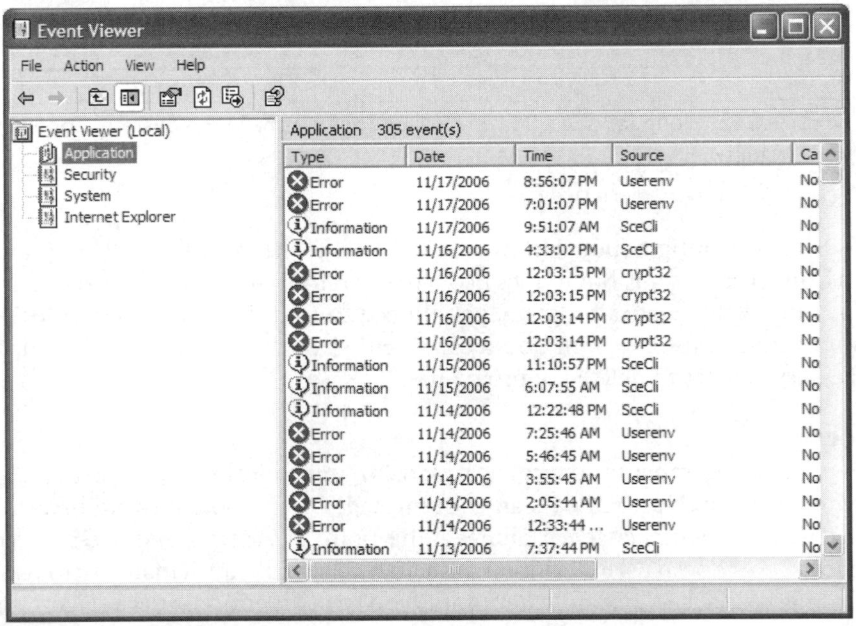

Figure 15-53 Event Viewer showing some serious application errors

Autoloading Programs

Windows loves to autoload programs so they start at boot. Most of the time this is an incredibly handy option, used by every Windows PC in existence. The problem with Autoloading programs is when one of them starts behaving badly—you need to shut off that program!

There are at least five different locations in folders, files, and the Registry that Windows accesses to autoload programs. To help you, Windows XP includes the handy System Configuration Utility (MSCONFIG.EXE), a one-stop spot to see and maintain every program (and service) that autoloads at startup (Figure 15-54).

Figure 15-54
MSCONFIG

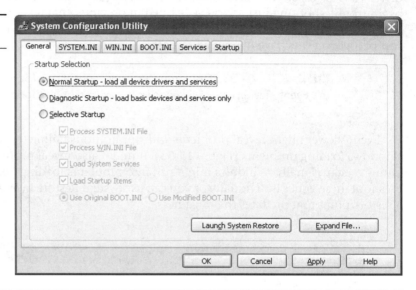

NOTE Windows 2000 Professional does not have the System Configuration Utility.

The System Configuration Utility enables you to keep individual programs and services from autoloading, but it does not actually remove the programs/services. If you want to completely delete a program, you'll need to find the uninstall or Add/Remove Program option. If the program doesn't have either of these, you'll need a third-party tool like EasyCleaner to delete the program.

Services

Windows loads a number of services as it starts. If any critical service fails to load, Windows will tell you at this point with an error message. The important word here is *critical*. Windows will not report *all* service failures at this point. If a service that is less than critical in Windows' eyes doesn't start, Windows usually waits until you actually try to use a program that needs that service before it prompts you with an error message (Figure 15-55).

Figure 15-55
Service error

To work with your system's services, go to the Control Panel | Administrative Tools | Services and verify that the Service you need is running. If not, turn it on. Also notice that each service has a Startup Type—Automatic, Manual, or Disabled—that defines when it starts. It's very common to find that a service has been set to Manual when it needs to be set to Automatic so that it starts when Windows boots (Figure 15-56).

Figure 15-56
Autostarting
a service

System Files

Windows lives on dynamic link library (DLL) files. Almost every program used by Windows—and certainly all of the important ones—call to DLL files to do most of the heavy lifting that makes Windows work. Windows protects all of the critical DLL files very carefully, but once in a while you may get an error saying Windows can't load a particular DLL. Although rare, the core system files that make up Windows itself may become corrupted, preventing Windows from starting properly. You usually see something like "Error loading XXXX.DLL," or sometimes a program you need simply won't start when you double-click on its icon. In these cases, the tool you need is the System File Checker. The System File Checker is a command prompt program (SFC.EXE) that is used to check a number of critical files, including the ever-important DLL cache. SFC takes a number of switches, but by far the most important is /scannow. Go to a command prompt and type the following to start the program:

```
SFC /scannow
```

SFC will automatically check all critical files and replace any it sees as corrupted. During this process, it may ask for the Windows installation CD-ROM, so keep it handy!

System Restore

Windows XP systems enable you to recover from a bad device or application installation by using System Restore to load a restore point. Follow the process explained earlier in the chapter. System Restore is the final step in recovering from a major Windows meltdown.

Chapter Review Questions

1. Your Windows XP Professional system fails to boot up. You suspect that the boot sector has become corrupted. You start the system using the set of boot disks and then launch the Recovery Console. Which command should you use to write a new boot sector into the system partition?

    A. chkdsk

    B. fdisk

    C. fixmbr

    D. fixboot

2. Which of the following commands would you use to install the Recovery Console?

    A. Start | Run; then type **d:\i386\winnt32 /cmdcons**

    B. Start | Run; then type **d:\i386\winnt32 /rc**

    C. Start | Run; then type **d:\i386\winnt32 /cmd:command_line**

    D. Start | Run; then type **d:\i386\winnt32 /copydir:recovery_console**

3. Which tool in Windows XP Home would you use to back up your essential system files?

    A. System Restore

    B. Backup and Recovery Wizard

    C. Emergency Repair Disk

    D. Recovery Console

4. Phil tried to install a printer on his Windows XP Professional machine, but found he didn't have permission. What could be the problem? (Select all that apply.)

    A. Phil is logged on with a Limited account.

    B. Phil is logged on as a Local User.

    C. Phil is logged on as a Local Administrator.

    D. Phil is logged on as Guest.

5. Mary wants to get a quick snapshot of her System Resources on a Windows XP Home machine. How does she get to the appropriate tool?

   A. Start | Run | Perfmon.

   B. Start | Control Panel | Administrative Tools | Performance.

   C. Start | All Programs | Accessories | System Resources.

   D. Press CTRL-ALT-DEL once and click the Performance tab.

6. What tool should Bill use to track who logs on and off of the busy library terminal for which he is responsible?

   A. Event Viewer

   B. Performance console

   C. System Resource Meter

   D. Task Manager

7. Sven loaded a new video card on his system, but now everything looks very bad. What should he do first?

   A. Go to Event Viewer and check the log

   B. Go to Device Manager

   C. Go to the printed manual

   D. Call tech support

8. Which of the following is a command-line utility?

   A. Event Viewer

   B. Microsoft Management Console

   C. Task Manager

   D. Recovery Console

9. Which of the following passwords will probably be the most secure one?

   A. MaryEllen

   B. MEO2144

   C. M-21e44

   D. MikeM

10. What's another name for a Windows Stop error?

   A. ASR

   B. BSOD

   C. ERD

   D. Virus

Answers

1. **D.** The Recovery Console command "fixboot" writes a new partition boot sector to the system partition. The Recovery Console command "chkdsk" runs the CheckDisk utility; "fixmbr" writes a new Master Boot Record for the partition boot sector; "fdisk" is not a valid command for the Recovery Console.

2. **A.** Start | Run; then type **d:\i386\winnt32 /cmdcons** is the correct command to install the Recovery Console.

3. **A.** System Restore is the only tool in Windows XP Home for backing up essential system files.

4. **A, D.** Phil needs to be logged on as an Administrator, not a Limited account or Guest.

5. **D.** Press CTRL-ALT-DEL once and click the Performance tab

6. **A.** Event Viewer is the tool he needs.

7. **B.** Always go to Device Manager first when hardware goes wrong.

8. **D.** The Recovery Console is a command-line utility.

9. **C.** The combination of letters, numbers, and non-alphanumeric characters makes M-21e44 the strongest password.

10. **B.** A Windows Stop error is better known as a Blue Screen of Death.

Input/Output

16

In this chapter, you will learn how to
- Explain how to support common input/output ports
- Identify certain common input/output devices on a PC
- Describe how certain specialty input/output devices work on a PC

In Chapter 2, you learned how to recognize and connect a number of common devices and the ports they use. Because these devices and their ports sometimes fail, it is important that you learn how they work and how to troubleshoot them when problems arise. This chapter reviews some of the major types of input ports, discusses a number of common and not-so-common input/output (I/O) devices, and deals with some of the troubleshooting issues you may encounter with I/O devices and their ports.

The CompTIA A+ certification exams split the domains of computer I/O devices into three groups: common, multimedia, and specialty. Common I/O devices, such as keyboards and mice, are found on virtually every PC. Multimedia I/O devices support video and sound functions. Specialty I/O devices run the gamut from common (touch screens) to rare (biometric devices). In fact, the exams deal with an entire set of I/O devices—networking devices—as completely distinct technologies. This book dedicates entire chapters to sound, printing, video, and networking, providing details about dealing with these types of devices and the ports they use. This chapter concentrates on two of the I/O device groups: the common devices and the specialty devices. You'll learn how to identify and support both the most common and some of the most unusual I/O devices used in today's PCs.

Supporting Common I/O Ports

Whenever you're dealing with an I/O device that isn't playing nice, you need to remember that you're never dealing with just a device—you're dealing with a device and the port to which it is connected. Before you start looking at I/O devices, you need to take a look into the issues and technologies of some of the more common I/O ports and see what needs to be done to keep them running well.

Serial Ports

It's difficult to find a new PC with a real serial port, because devices that traditionally used serial ports have for the most part moved on to better interfaces, in particular USB. Physical serial ports may be getting hard to find on new PC cases, but many devices, in particular the modems many people still use to access the Internet, continue to use built-in serial ports.

In Chapter 6, you learned that COM ports are nothing more than preset I/O addresses and interrupt request lines (IRQs) for serial ports. Want to see a built-in serial port? Open Device Manager on a system and see if you have an icon for Ports (COM and LPT). If you do, click the plus (+) sign to the left of the icon to open it and see the ports on your system—don't be surprised if you have COM ports on your PC. Even if you don't see any physical serial ports on your PC, the serial ports are really there; they're simply built into some other device, probably a modem.

 NOTE   Having trouble finding a PC with serial ports? Try a laptop—almost all laptops come with built-in modems.

Your PC's expansion bus uses parallel communication—multiple data wires, each one sending 1 bit of data at a time between your devices. Many I/O devices use serial communication—one wire to send data and another wire to receive data. The job of a serial port is to convert data moving between parallel and serial devices. A traditional serial port consists of two pieces: the physical, 9-pin DB connector (Figure 16-1), and a chip that actually does the conversion between the serial data and parallel data, called the *universal asynchronous receiver/transmitter (UART)* chip. If you want to be completely accurate, the UART *is* the serial port. The port on the back of your PC is nothing more than a standardized connector that enables different serial devices to use the serial port. The UART holds all the smarts that make the true serial port.

Figure 16-1
Serial port

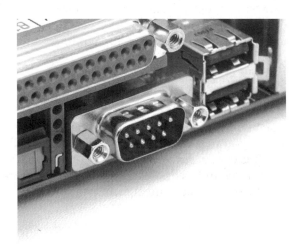

NOTE Serial ports might be dead on PCs, but they're still alive and cooking in other computer hardware. The standard way to make the initial configuration on most routers—the machines that form the backbone of many networks, including the Internet—is by connecting through a serial port. To get around the lack of traditional serial ports, networking people use a USB-to-serial dongle.

RS-232 is a very old standard that defines everything about serial ports: how fast they communicate, the "language" they use, even how the connectors should look. The RS-232 standard specifies that two serial devices must talk to each other in 8-bit chunks of data, but it also allows flexibility in other areas, such as speed and error checking. Serial came out back in the days when devices were configured manually, and the RS-232 standard has never been updated for automatic configuration. Serial ports are a throwback to the old days of computer maintenance and are the last manually configured port you'll find on a PC.

So what type of settings do you need to configure on a serial port? Find a PC with a real serial port (a real 9-pin connector on the back of the PC). Right-click the COM port and choose Properties to see the properties of that port in Device Manager. Open the Port Settings tab and click the Advanced button to see a dialog box that looks like Figure 16-2.

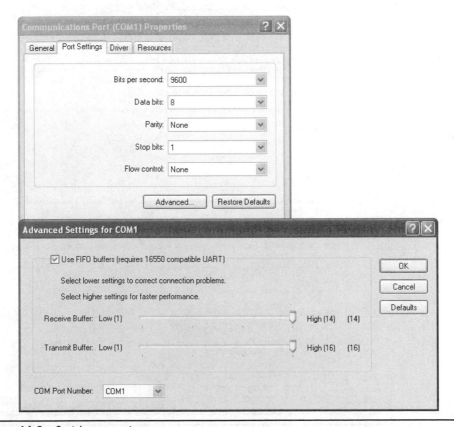

Figure 16-2 Serial port settings

Devices such as modems that have built-in serial ports don't have COM port icons in Device Manager, because there's nothing to change. Can you see why? Even though these devices are using a COM port, that port is never going to connect to anything other than the device it's soldered onto, so all the settings are fixed and unchangeable—thank goodness!

When you are configuring a serial port, the first thing you need to set is its speed in bits per second. A serial port may run as slowly as 75 bps up to a maximum speed of 128,000 bps. Next, you should set the parameters of the data "chunks": serial data moves up and down the cable connecting the serial device to your serial port in either 7- or 8-bit chunks, and it may or may not use a special "stop" bit to identify the end of each chunk. Serial ports use parity for error-checking and flow control to ensure that the sending device doesn't overload the receiving device with data. The convenient part about all this is that when you get a new serial device to plug into your serial port, the instructions will tell you what settings to use. Figure 16-3 shows an instruction sheet for a Cisco switch.

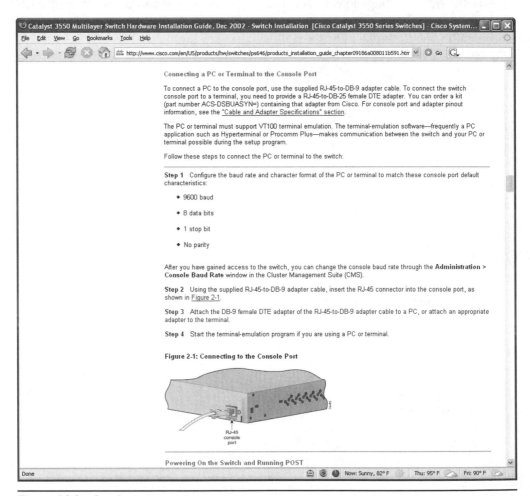

Figure 16-3 Serial port instructions

USB Ports

You should be familiar with the concept of USB, USB connectors, and USB hubs from the discussion of those concepts in Chapter 2. Here's a more in-depth look at USB and some of the issues involved with using USB devices.

Understanding USB

The cornerstone of a USB connection is the USB *host controller,* an integrated circuit that is usually built into the chipset, which controls every USB device that connects to it. Inside the host controller is a *root hub*—the part of the host controller that makes the physical connection to the USB ports. Every USB root hub is really just a bus—similar in many ways to an expansion bus. Figure 16-4 shows a diagram of the relationship between the host controller, root hub, and USB ports.

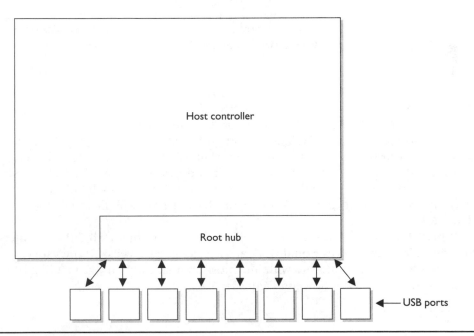

Figure 16-4   Host controller, root hub, and USB ports

No rule says how many USB ports a single host adapter may use. Early USB host adapters had two USB ports. The most recent ones support up to ten. Even if a host adapter supports a certain number of ports, there's no guarantee that the motherboard maker will supply that many ports. To give a common example, a host adapter might support eight ports while the motherboard maker only supplies four adapters.

The most important point to remember about this is that every USB device connected to a single host adapter/root hub *shares* that USB bus with every other device connected to it. The more devices you place on a single host adapter, the more the total USB bus slows down and the more power they use. These issues are two of the biggest headaches that take place with USB devices in the real world.

USB devices, like any electrical device, need power to run, but not all take care of their own power needs. A powered USB device comes with it own electrical cord that is usually connected in turn to an AC adapter. *Bus-powered* USB devices take power from the USB bus itself; they don't bring any AC or DC power with them. When too many bus-powered devices take too much power from the USB bus, bad things happen—devices that work only some of the time and devices that lock up. You'll also often get a simple message from Windows saying that the hub power has been exceeded and it just won't work.

Every USB device is designed to run at one of three different speeds. The first USB standard, version 1.1, defined two speeds: Low-Speed USB, running at a maximum of 1.5 Mbps (plenty for keyboards and mice), and Full-Speed USB, running up to 12 Mbps. Later, the USB 2.0 standard introduced Hi-Speed USB running at a whopping 480 Mbps. The industry sometimes refers to Low-Speed and Full-Speed USB as USB 1.1 and Hi-Speed as USB 2.0, respectively.

 NOTE USB 2.0 defined more than just a new speed. Many Low-Speed and Full-Speed USB devices are also under the USB 2.0 standard.

In addition to a much faster transfer rate, Hi-Speed USB is fully backward compatible with devices that operate under the slower USB standards. Those old devices won't run any faster than they used to, however. To take advantage of the fastest USB speed, you must connect Hi-Speed USB devices to Hi-Speed USB ports using Hi-Speed USB cables. Hi-Speed USB devices will function when plugged into Full-Speed USB ports, but they will run at only 12 Mbps. While backward compatibility at least allows you to use the newer USB device with an older port, a quick bit of math will tell you how much time you're sacrificing when you're transferring a 240 MB file at 12 Mbps instead of 480 Mbps!

When USB 2.0 came out in 2001, folks scrambled to buy USB 2.0 controllers so their new Hi-Speed devices would work at their designed speeds. Of the variety of different solutions people came up with, the most popular early on was to add a USB 2.0 adapter card like the one shown in Figure 16-5.

Figure 16-5
USB adapter card

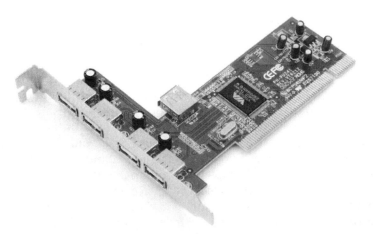

Motherboard makers quickly added a second USB 2.0 host controller—and they did it in a clever way. Instead of making the USB 2.0 host controller separate from the USB 1.1 host controller, they designed things so that both controllers share all of the connected USB ports (Figure 16-6). That way, no matter which USB port you choose, if you plug in a Low-Speed or Full-Speed device, the 1.1 host controller takes over, and if you plug in a Hi-Speed device, the USB 2.0 host controller takes over. Clever, and convenient!

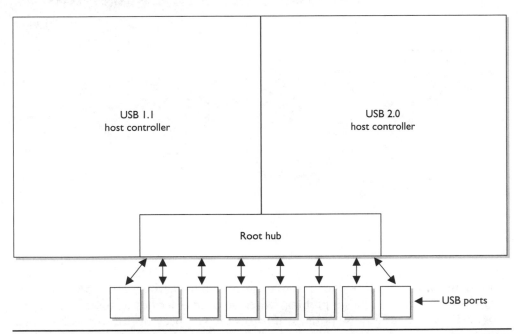

Figure 16-6 Shared USB ports

You can readily determine the speed of your USB ports and components. Using a PC running Windows 2000 or later, open the Device Manager and locate two controllers under the Universal Serial Bus icon. The one named Standard Enhanced Host Controller is the Hi-Speed controller. The Standard OpenHCD Host Controller is the Low- and Full-Speed controller.

USB Hubs and Cables

Each USB host controller supports up to 127 USB devices, but as mentioned earlier, most motherboard makers provide only six to eight real USB ports. So what do you do when you need to add more USB devices than the motherboard provides ports for? You can add more host controllers (in the form of internal cards), or you can use a USB hub. A USB hub is a device that extends a single USB connection to two or more USB ports, almost always directly from one of the USB ports connected to the root hub. Figure 16-7 shows a typical USB hub. USB hubs are sometime embedded into peripherals. The keyboard in Figure 16-8 comes with a built-in USB hub—very handy!

Figure 16-7
USB hub

Figure 16-8
USB keyboard
with built-in hub

USB hubs are one of those parts of a PC that tend not to work nearly as well in the real world as they do on paper. (Sorry, USB folks, but it's true!) USB hubs have a speed just like any other USB device; for example, the hub in the keyboard in Figure 16-8 runs at Full-Speed. This becomes a problem when someone decides to insert a Hi-Speed USB device into one of those ports, as it forces the Hi-Speed device to crawl along at only 12 Mbps. Windows XP is nice and will at least warn you of this problem with a bubble over the system tray like the one shown in Figure 16-9.

Figure 16-9
Windows XP speed
warning

Hubs also come in powered and bus-powered versions. If you choose to use a general purpose USB hub like the one shown in Figure 16-7, try to find a powered one, as too many devices on a single USB root hub will draw too much power and create problems.

Cable length is an important limitation to keep in mind with USB. USB specifications allow for a maximum cable length of 5 meters, although you may add a powered USB hub every 5 meters to extend this distance. Although most USB devices never get near this maximum, some devices, such as digital cameras, can come with cables at or near the maximum 5-meter cable length. Because USB is a two-way (bi-directional) connection, as the cable grows longer, even a standard, well-shielded, 20-gauge, twisted-pair USB cable begins to suffer from electrical interference. To avoid these problems, I stick to cables that are no more than about 2 meters long.

If you really want to play it safe, spend a few extra dollars and get a high-quality USB 2.0 cable like the one shown in Figure 16-10. These cables come with extra shielding and improved electrical performance to make sure your USB data gets from the device to your computer safely.

Figure 16-10
USB 2.0 cable

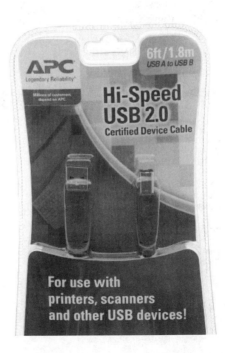

USB Configuration

The biggest troubleshooting challenge you encounter with USB is a direct result of its widespread adoption and ease of use. Pretty much every modern PC comes with multiple USB ports, and it's easy for anyone to pick up a cool new USB device at the local computer store. The problems arise when all this USB installation activity gets out of control, with too many devices using the wrong types of ports or pulling too much power. Happily, by following a few easy steps, you can avoid or eliminate these issues.

The first and often-ignored rule of USB installation is this: Always install the device driver for a new USB device *before* you plug it into the USB port. Once you've installed the device and you know the ports are active (running properly in Device Manager), feel free to plug in the new device and hot swap to your heart's content. USB device installation really is a breeze as long as you follow this rule!

Windows 2000 and XP have a large number of built-in drivers for USB devices. You can count on Windows 2000 and Windows XP to recognize keyboards, mice, and other basic devices with its built-in drivers. Just be aware that if your new mouse or keyboard has some extras, the default USB drivers will probably not support them. To be sure I'm not missing any added functionality, I always install the driver that comes with the device or an updated one downloaded from the manufacturer's Web site.

When looking to add a new USB device to a system, first make sure your machine has a USB port that supports the speed you need for the USB device. On more modern PCs, this is more likely to be a non-issue, but even then if you start adding hubs and such you can end up with devices that either won't run at all or, worse yet, exhibit strange behaviors. Your best tool for a quick check of your ports is the free Microsoft Utility UVCView. UVCView works on all versions of Windows. Do a Web search for "UVCView.exe" to locate a copy and download it; it's a single .EXE file that requires no installation. When you run UVCView, you see something like Figure 16-11, which shows an AMD64 system using only the onboard USB host controllers.

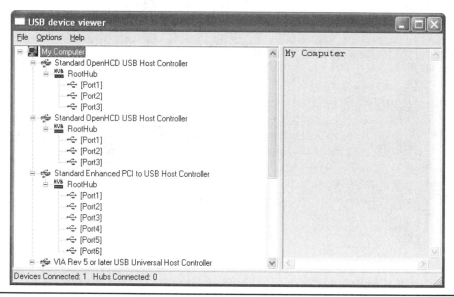

Figure 16-11 UVCView in action

 NOTE As of this printing, UVCView may be found at: www.microsoft.com/whdc/device/stream/vidcap/UVCView.mspx—but keep in mind Microsoft does change URLs rather frequently!

UVCView is a very powerful tool used by USB professionals to test USB devices; as such, it has a number of features that are not of interest to the typical PC tech. Nevertheless, two features make it worth the download. UVCView quickly answers the questions, "What and where are all the USB devices plugged into my system right now?" and "What speed is this USB device?" Figure 16-12 shows UVCView finding a number of installed USB devices, including a keyboard with a built-in hub. Look on the left side to see how easy it is to locate the USB hub and the thumb drive installed on that hub. Note that a USB thumb drive is selected. Look on the upper-right side of the program, where the details of the device are shown, to see that the thumb drive is a Hi-Speed USB device.

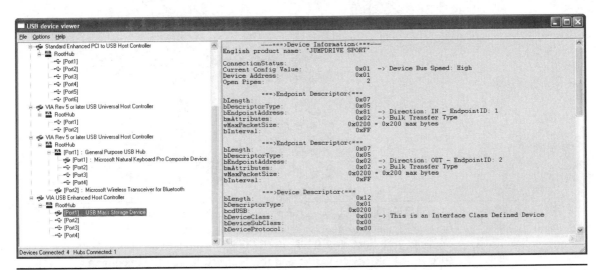

Figure 16-12 UVCView details

The last and toughest issue is power. A mismatch between available and required power for USB devices can result in non-functioning or malfunctioning USB devices. If you're pulling too much power, you must take devices off that root hub until the error goes away. Buy an add-in USB hub card if you need to use more devices than your current USB hub supports.

To check the USB power usage in Windows, open Device Manager and locate any USB hub under the Universal Serial Bus Controller icon. Right-click the hub and select Properties, and then select the Power tab. This will show you the current use for each of the devices connected to that root hub (Figure 16-13).

Figure 16-13
USB hub Power tab

USB Root Hub Properties

General | Power | Driver | Details | Power Management

Hub information

The hub is self-powered.

Total power available: 500 mA per port

Attached devices:

Description	Power Required
Microsoft Wireless Transceiver for Bluetooth	150 mA
2 port(s) available	0 mA

To update the list, click Refresh.   Refresh

                                           OK   Cancel

NOTE The USB Hub Power Properties tab shows you the power usage only for a given moment, so to ensure that you keep getting accurate readings, you must click the Refresh button to update its display. Make sure your USB device works, and then refresh to see the maximum power used.

Most root hubs provide 500 mA per port—more than enough for any USB device. Most power problems take place when you start adding hubs, especially bus-powered hubs, and then you add too many devices to them. Figure 16-14 shows the Power Tab for a bus-powered hub—note that it provides a maximum of 100 mA per port.

Figure 16-14
General purpose
bus-powered hub

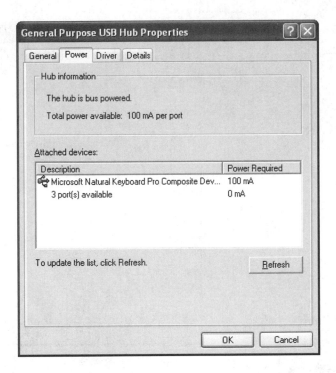

There's one more problem with USB power: sometimes USB devices go to sleep and don't wake up. Actually, the system is telling them to sleep, to save power. You can suspect this problem if you try to access a USB device that was working earlier, but that suddenly no longer appears in Device Manager. To fix this, head back in to Device Manager to inspect the hub's Properties, but this time open the Power Management tab and uncheck the *Allow the computer to turn off this device to save power* check box, as shown in Figure 16-15.

Figure 16-15
Power Management

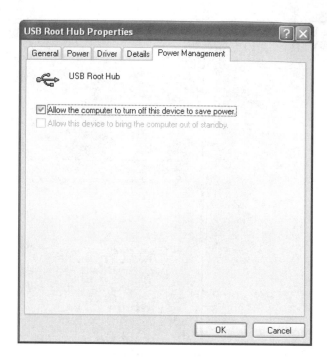

FireWire Ports

At first glance, FireWire, also known as IEEE 1394, looks and acts much like USB. FireWire has all the same features of USB, but it uses different connectors and is actually the older of the two technologies. For years, FireWire had the upper hand when it came to moving data quickly to and from external devices. The onset of Hi-Speed USB changed that, and FireWire has lost ground to USB in many areas. One area where FireWire still dominates is editing digital video. Most modern digital video cameras use the IEEE 1394 interface for transferring video from camera to PC for editing. The high transfer speed of FireWire makes transferring large video files quick and easy.

NOTE Even Apple, the inventors of FireWire, dropped FireWire for USB in its iPod.

Understanding FireWire

FireWire has two distinct types of connectors, both of which are commonly found on PCs. The first is a 6-pin *powered* connector, the type you see on many desktop PCs. Like USB, a FireWire port is capable of providing power to a device, and it carries the same cautions about powering high-power devices through the port. The other type of connector is a 4-pin *bus-powered* connector, which you see on portable computers and some FireWire devices such as cameras. This type of connector does not provide power to a device, so you will need to find another method of powering the external device.

FireWire comes in two speeds: 1394a, which runs at 400 Mbps, and 1394b, which runs at 800 Mbps. FireWire devices can also take advantage of bus mastering, enabling two FireWire devices—such as a digital video camera and an external FireWire hard drive—to communicate directly with each other. When it comes to raw speed, FireWire 800—that would be 1394b, naturally—is much faster than Hi-Speed USB.

FireWire does have differences from USB other than just speed and a different-looking connector. First, a USB device must connect directly to a hub, but a FireWire device may use either a hub or daisy chaining. Figure 16-16 show the difference between hubbed connections and daisy chaining. Second, FireWire supports a maximum of 63 devices, compared to USB's 127. Third, each cable in a FireWire daisy chain has a maximum length of 4.5 meters, as opposed to USB's 5 meters.

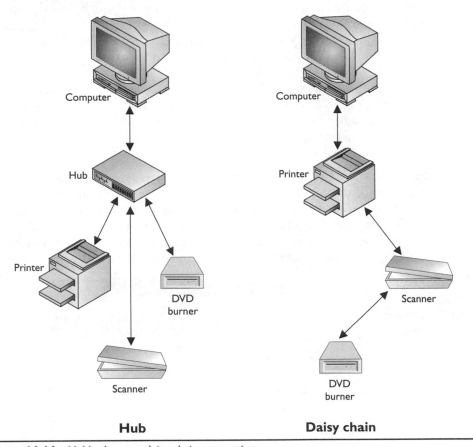

Hub | **Daisy chain**

Figure 16-16 Hubbed versus daisy chain connections

Configuring FireWire

FireWire was invented and is still controlled to a degree by Apple Computer. This single source of control makes FireWire more stable and more interchangeable than USB—in plain language, FireWire is ridiculously easy to use. In a Windows environment, FireWire is subject to many of the same issues as USB, such as the need to pre-install drivers, verify that onboard devices are active, and so on. But none of these issues is nearly as crucial with a FireWire connection. For example, as with USB, you really should install a FireWire device driver before attaching the device, but given that 95 percent of the FireWire devices used in PCs are either external hard drives or digital video connections, the pre-installed Windows drivers almost always work perfectly. FireWire devices do use much more power than USB devices, but the FireWire controllers are designed to handle higher voltages, and they'll warn you on the rare chance your FireWire devices pull too much power.

General Port Issues

No matter what type of port you use, if it's not working, you should always check out a few issues. First of all, make sure you can tell a port problem from a device problem. Your best bet here is to try a second "known good" device in the same port and see if that device works. If it does *not*, you can assume the port is the problem. It's not a bad idea to reverse this and plug the device into a known good port.

NOTE A "known good" device is simply a device that you know is in good working order. All techs count heavily on the use of known good devices to check other devices. For example, if you think a PC has a bad keyboard, borrow one from the PC next door and see if that keyboard works on the broken machine.

If you're pretty sure the port's not working, you can check three things: First, make sure the port is turned on. Almost any I/O port on a motherboard can be turned off in CMOS. Reboot the system and find the device and see if the port's been turned off. Windows Device Manager also enables you to disable most ports. Figure 16-17 shows a disabled parallel port in Device Manager—you'll see a red *X* over the device icon. To turn the port back on, right-click the device's icon and choose Enable.

Figure 16-17
An X marks a disabled parallel port in Device Manager.

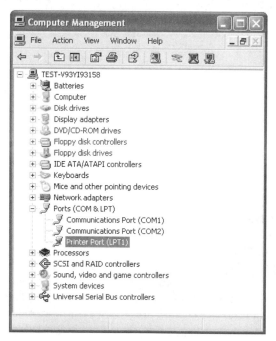

The fact that you can turn off a port in Device Manager points to another not-so-obvious fact: ports need drivers just as devices need drivers. Windows has excellent built-in drivers for all common ports, so if you fail to see a port in Device Manager (and you know the port is turned on in CMOS), you can bet there's a physical problem with the port itself.

Because ports have connectors inserted and removed from them repeatedly, eventually they can physically break. Figure 16-18 shows the back of a USB port that's been pushed on too hard for too long and has physically separated from the motherboard. Unless you're an expert solderer, you either must stop using those ports or replace the entire motherboard.

Figure 16-18
Broken USB port

Many ports (or the plugs that fit into those ports) use tiny pins or relatively delicate metal casings that are susceptible to damage. PS/2 plugs are some of the worst for bent pins or misshaped casings. Figure 16-19 shows what happened to a PS/2 plug when I was in a hurry and thought that force was an alternative to lining up the plug properly. Replacement plugs are available—but again, unless you're excellent at soldering, they're not a viable alternative. Still, if you're patient, you might be able to save the plug. Using needle-nose pliers and a pair of scissors, I was able to reshape the plug so that it once again fit in the PS/2 port.

Figure 16-19
Badly bent PS/2 plug

Common I/O Devices

So what is a "common" I/O device? I'm hoping you immediately thought of the mouse and the keyboard, two of the most basic, necessary, and abused I/O devices on a computer. Another fairly common input device that's been around a long time is the scanner. To these oldsters, you can add relative newcomers to the world of common devices: digital cameras and Web cameras.

NOTE If you want to get picky, these five common I/O devices enable a user only to *input* data; they don't provide any output at all.

Keyboards

Keyboards are both the oldest and still the primary way you input data into a PC. Windows comes with perfectly good drivers for any keyboard, although some fancier keyboards may come with specialized keys that require a special driver be installed to operate properly. About the only issue that might affect keyboard installation is if you're using a USB keyboard: make sure that the USB Keyboard Support option is enabled in your CMOS (Figure 16-20). Other than that, any keyboard installation issue you're likely to encounter is covered in the general port issues sections at the beginning of this chapter.

Figure 16-20
CMOS USB
Keyboard
Support option

```
OnChip USB                 U1.1+2.0
 - USB Keyboard Support     Enabled
 - USB Mouse Support        Enabled
```

There's not much to do to configure a standard keyboard. The only configuration tool you might need is the keyboard Control Panel applet. This tool enables you to change the repeat delay (the amount of time you must hold down a key before the keyboard starts repeating the character), the repeat rate (how quickly the character is repeated after the repeat delay), and the default cursor blink rate. Figure 16-21 shows the default Windows Keyboard Properties window—some keyboard makers provide drivers that add extra tabs.

Figure 16-21
Keyboard Control
Panel applet

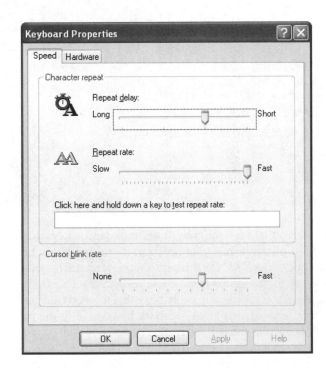

Keyboards might be easy to install, but they do fail occasionally. Given their location—right in front of you—the three issues that cause the most keyboard problems stem from spills, physical damage, and dirt.

Spilling a soda onto your keyboard can make for a really bad day. If you're quick and unplug the keyboard from the PC before the liquid hits the electrical components, you might be able to save the keyboard. It'll take some cleaning, though (keep reading for cleaning tips). More often than not, you'll get a sticky, ill-performing keyboard, which is not worth the hassle—just replace it!

Other common physical damage comes from dropping objects onto the keyboard, such as a heavy book (like the one in your hands). This can have bad results! Most keyboards are pretty resilient, though, and can bounce back from the hit.

Clean dirt and grime off the keys using a cloth dampened with a little water, or if the water alone doesn't do the job, use a bit of isopropyl alcohol on a cloth (Figure 16-22).

Figure 16-22
Cleaning keys

Dirty keys might be unsightly, but dirt under the keys might cause the keyboard to stop working completely. When your keys start to stick, grab a bottle of compressed air and shoot some air under the keys. Do this outside or over a trash can—you'll be amazed how much junk gets caught under the keys! If you really mess up a keyboard by dumping a chocolate milkshake on the keys, you're probably going to need to dismantle the keyboard to clean it. This is pretty easy as long as you keep track of where all the parts go. Keyboards are made of layers of plastic that create the electrical connections when you press a key. Unscrew the keyboard (keep track of the screws!) and gently peel away the plastic layers, using a damp cloth to clean each layer (Figure 16-23). Allow the sheets to dry and replace them.

Figure 16-23
Serious keyboard
surgery

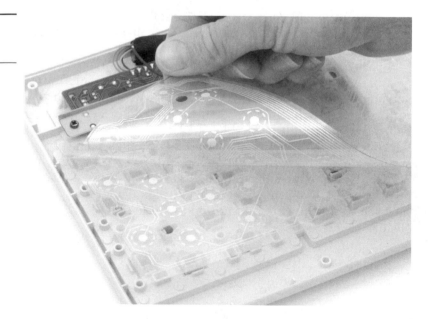

Sometimes dirt or foreign objects get under individual keys, requiring you to remove the key to get to the dirt or object. Removing individual keys from a keyboard is risky business, as keyboards are set up in many different ways. Most manufacturers use a process in which keys are placed on a single plastic post. In that case, you may use a screwdriver or other flat tool to safely pop off the key (Figure 16-24). Be careful! You'll need to use a good amount of force and the key will fly across the room. Other keyboard makers (mainly on laptops) use tiny plastic pins shaped like scissors. In that case, beware—if you try prying one of these off, you'll permanently break the key!

Figure 16-24
Prying off a key

The bottom line when it comes to stuck keys is that the keyboard's probably useless with the stuck key, so you might as well try to clean it. Worse comes to worst, you can always buy another keyboard.

Mice

Have you ever tried to use Windows without a mouse? It's not fun, but it can be done. All techs eventually learn the Windows navigation hotkeys for those times when mice fail, but all in all we do love our mice. Like keyboards, Windows comes with excellent drivers for all standard mice; the exception you're likely to encounter is the more advanced mice that come with extra buttons. Conveniently, the built-in Windows drivers consider a mouse's scroll wheel to be standard equipment and will support it.

 NOTE Everything in this section works equally well for trackballs.

You can adjust your mouse settings through the Mouse Control Panel applet. Figure 16-25 show the Windows 2000 version. Be aware that the Mouse Properties window in Windows 2000 uses a different layout than that of Windows XP (Figure 16-26).

All the settings you need for adjusting your mouse can be found in the Mouse Properties window. In particular, make sure to adjust the mouse speed, double-click speed, and

Figure 16-25
Windows 2000
Mouse Control
Panel applet

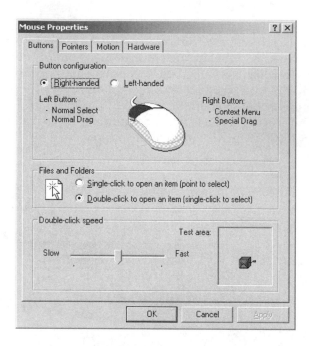

Figure 16-26
Windows XP Mouse
Control Panel applet

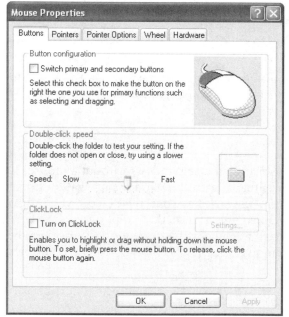

acceleration to fit your preferences. Mouse speed and double-click speed are obvious, but mouse acceleration needs a bit of explaining as it has changed from Windows 2000 to Windows XP. Originally, mouse *acceleration* referred to a feature that caused the mouse speed to increase when the mouse moved a relatively large distance across the screen. The Windows 2000 Mouse Properties window included a Motion tab where you could set the mouse speed and acceleration. Windows XP dropped the Motion tab in favor of an Enhanced pointer precision check box on the Pointer Options tab (Figure 16-27). Enhanced pointer precision is a much more advanced form of automatic acceleration. While it works well, it can cause erratic mouse movements in some applications.

Figure 16-27
Enhanced pointer
precision checkbox
on the Pointer
Options tab

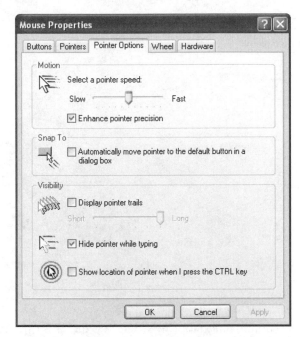

Currently, two types of mouse technologies dominate the market: ball mice and optical mice. Ball mice use a small round ball while optical mice use LED or lasers and a camera to track their movements. The problem with ball mice is that the ball inside the mouse picks up dirt over time and deposits the dirt on internal rollers that contact the ball. Dirt builds up to the point that the mouse stops responding smoothly. If you are struggling with your mouse to point at objects on your screen, you need to clean the mouse (Figure 16-28). Few mice manufacturers still make ball mice, as they tend to require far more maintenance than optical mice.

Figure 16-28
Dirty mouse
internals

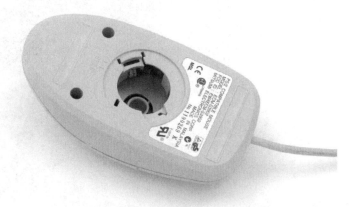

To access the internals of a ball mouse, turn it over and remove the protective cover over the mouse ball. The process of removing the cover varies, but it usually involves rotating the collar that surrounds the ball until the collar pops out (Figure 16-29). Be careful—without the collar, the mouse ball will drop out the instant you turn it upright.

Figure 16-29
Removing the collar

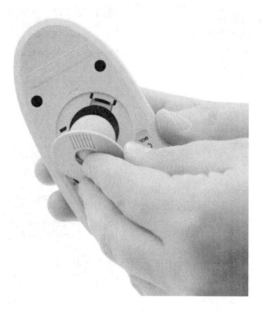

Use any non-metallic tool to scrape the dirt from the roller without scratching or gouging the device. Although you could use a commercial "Mouse cleaning kit," I find that a fingernail or a pencil eraser will clean the rollers quite nicely and at much less expense (Figure 16-30). Clean a ball mouse in this way at least every two or three months.

Figure 16-30
Cleaning the rollers

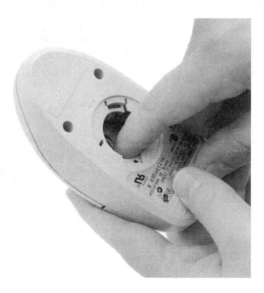

Optical mice require little maintenance and almost never need cleaning, as the optics that make them work are never in contact with the grimy outside world. On the rare occasion where an optical mouse begins to act erratically, try using a damp cotton swab to clean out any bits of dirt that may be blocking the optics (Figure 16-31).

Figure 16-31
Cleaning the optics

Scanners

A scanner enables you to make digital copies of existing paper photos, documents, drawings, and more. Better scanners give you the option of copying directly from a photographic negative or slide, providing images of stunning visual quality—assuming the original photo was halfway decent, of course! In this section, you'll look at how scanners work and then turn to what you need to know to select the correct scanner for you or your clients.

How Scanners Work

All consumer-level scanners—called *flatbed scanners*—work the same way. You place a photo or other object face down on the glass, close the lid, and then use software to initiate the scan. The scanner runs a bright light along the length of the glass tray once or more to capture the image. Figure 16-32 shows an open scanner.

Figure 16-32
Scanner open with
photograph face
down

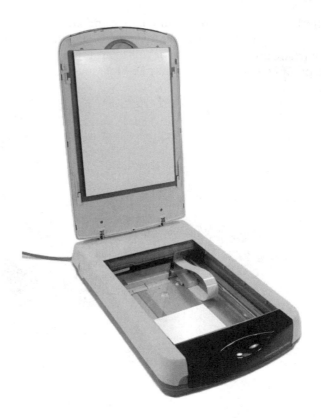

The scanning software that controls the hardware can be manifested in a variety of ways. Nearly every manufacturer will have some sort of drivers and other software to create an interface between your computer and the scanner. When you push the front button on the Epson Perfection scanner in Figure 16-33, for example, the Epson software opens the Photoshop program as well as its own interface.

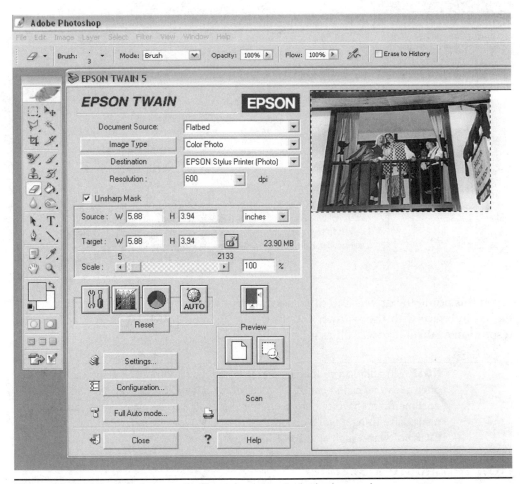

Figure 16-33   Epson software with Photoshop open in the background

You can also open your favorite image-editing software first, and then choose to acquire a file from a scanner. Figure 16-34 shows the process of acquiring an image from a scanner in the popular shareware image editing software, Paint Shop Pro. As in most such software, you choose File | Import and then select a source. In this case, the scanner uses the traditional TWAIN drivers. *TWAIN* stands for *Technology Without an Interesting Name*—I'm not making this up!—and has been the default driver type for scanners for a long time.

Figure 16-34
Acquiring an image
in Paint Shop Pro

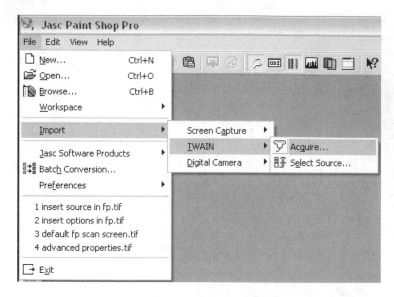

At this point, the drivers and other software controlling the scanner pop up, providing an interface with the scanner (as shown in Figure 16-33). Here, you can set the resolution of the image as well as many other options.

NOTE In addition to loading pictures into your computer, many scanners offer a feature called *optical character recognition (OCR)*, a way to scan a document and have the computer turn the picture into text that you can manipulate using a word processing program. Many scanners come with OCR software, such as ABBYY FineReader.

How to Choose a Scanner

You must consider five primary variables when choosing a scanner: resolution, color depth, grayscale depth, connection, and scan speed. You can and will adjust the first three during the scanning process, although probably only down from their maximum. You need to decide on the connection before you buy. The scan speed relates to all four of the other variables, and the maximum speed is hard-coded into the scanner.

Configurable Variables Scanners convert the scanned image into a grid of dots. The maximum number of dots determines how well you can capture an image and how the image will look when scaled up in size. Most folks use the term resolution to define the grid size. As you might imagine, the higher the resolution, the better the scanned image will look and scale.

Older scanners can create images of only 600 × 600 dots per inch (dpi), while newer models commonly achieve four times that density and high-end machines do much more. Manufacturers cite *two* sets of numbers for a scanner's resolution: the resolution it achieves mechanically—called the *optical resolution*—and the enhanced resolution it can achieve with assistance from some onboard software.

The enhanced resolution numbers are useless. I recommend at least 2400 × 2400 dpi optical resolution or better, although you can get by with a lower resolution for purely Web-destined images.

The *color depth* of a scan defines the number of bits of information the scanner can use to describe each individual dot. This number determines color, shade, hue, and so forth, so a higher number makes a dramatic difference in your picture quality. With binary numbers, each extra bit of information *doubles* the quality. An 8-bit scan, for example, can save up to 256 color variations per dot. A 16-bit scan, in contrast, can save up to 65,536 variations, not the 512 that you might expect!

Modern scanners come in 24-bit, 36-bit, and 48-bit variations. These days, 48-bit scanners are common enough that you shouldn't have to settle for less, even on a budget. Figures 16-35, 16-36, and 16-37 show pretty clearly the difference resolution makes when scanning.

Figure 16-35
Earring scanned
at 72 dpi and
24-bit color

Figure 16-36
Same earring,
scanned at 300 dpi
and 24-bit color

Figure 16-37
Same earring,
scanned at 1200 dpi
and 24-bit color

Scanners differ a lot in *grayscale depth,* a number that defines how many shades of gray the scanner can save per dot. This matters if you work with black-and-white images in any significant way, because grayscale depth is usually a much lower number than color depth. Current consumer-level scanners come in 8-bit, 12-bit, and 16-bit grayscale varieties. I recommend 16-bit or better.

Connection   Almost all modern scanners plug into the USB port on your PC, although some high-end models offer FireWire as well. Older scanners come in SCSI and parallel varieties.

Scanning Speed   Scanners have a maximum scanning speed defined by the manufacturer. The time required to complete a scan is also affected by the parameters you set—the time increases as you increase the amount of detail captured. A typical low-end scanner, for example, takes upwards of 30 seconds to scan a 4 × 6 photo at 300 dpi. A faster scanner, in contrast, can crank out the same scan in 10 seconds.

Raise the resolution of the scan to 600 dpi at 48-bit resolution, and that faster scanner can take a full minute to complete the scan. Adjust your scanning settings to optimize for your project. Don't always go for the highest possible scan if you don't need the resolution.

Connections matter as well. A good Hi-Speed USB scanner can scan an 8 × 10 image in about 12 seconds at 300 dpi. I made the mistake of taking the scanner to a friend's house to scan some of her jewelry, but she had only a Full-Speed USB port. I plugged the scanner into her PC and it took about 45 seconds to scan each 8 × 10 image. We were up all night finishing the project!

Installing and Scanning Tips

Most USB and FireWire devices require you to install the software drivers before you plug in the device for the first time. I have run into exceptions, though, so I strongly suggest you read the scanner's documentation before you install.

As a general rule, you should obtain the highest quality scan you can manage, and then play with the size and image quality when it's time to include it in a Web site or an e-mail. The amount of RAM in your system—and to a lesser extent, the processor speed—dictates how big a file you can handle.

For example, don't do 8 × 10 scans at 600 dpi if you have only 128 MB of RAM, because the image file alone weighs in at over 93 MB. Because your operating system, scanner software, image-editing program, and a lot of other things are taking up plenty of that RAM already, your system will likely crash.

If you travel a lot, you'll want to make sure to use the locking mechanism for the scanner light assembly. Just be sure to unlock before you try to use it or you'll get a light that's stuck in one position. That won't make for very good scans!

Digital Cameras

Another option available for those not-yet-taken pictures is to put away your point-and-shoot film camera and use a digital camera. Digital cameras are a wonderful tool for capturing a moment and then sending it to friends and relatives.

In a short period of time, digital camera prices have gone from levels that made them the province of a few wealthy technogeeks to being competitive with a wide range of electronic consumer goods. Because digital cameras interface with computers, Comp-TIA A+ certified techs need to know the basics.

Storage Media—Digital Film for Your Camera

Every consumer-grade camera saves the pictures it takes onto some type of *removable storage media*. Think of it as your digital film. Probably the most common removable storage media used in modern digital cameras (and probably your best choice) is the Secure Digital (SD) card (Figure 16-38). About the size of a Wheat Thin (roughly an inch square), you can find these tiny cards with capacities ranging from 64 MB to more than 1 GB. They are among the fastest of the various media types at transferring data to and from a PC, and they're quite sturdy.

Figure 16-38
Secure Digital card

Connection

These days, almost all digital cameras plug directly into a USB port (Figure 16-39). Another common option, though, is to connect only the camera's storage media to the computer, using one of the many digital media readers available.

Figure 16-39
Camera connecting
to USB port

You can find readers designed specifically for SD cards, as well as other types. Plenty of readers can handle multiple media formats. Many computers come with a decent built-in digital media reader (Figure 16-40).

Figure 16-40
Digital media reader
built into computer

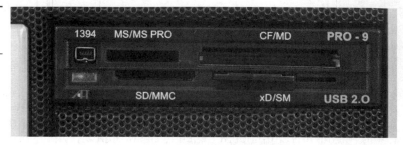

Quality

As with scanners, you should consider the amount of information a particular model of camera can capture, which in the digital camera world is expressed as some number of *megapixels*. Instead of light-sensitive film, digital cameras have one CCD (charged coupled device) or CMOS (complementary metal-oxide semiconductor) sensor covered with photosensitive pixels (called *photosites*) to capture the image; the more pixels on the sensor, the higher the resolution of the images it captures.

Not so long ago, a 1-megapixel digital camera was the bleeding edge of digital photographic technology, but now you can find cameras with ten times that resolution for a few hundred dollars. As a basis of reference, a 2-megapixel camera will produce snapshot-sized (4 × 6 inch) pictures with print photograph quality, whereas a 5-megapixel unit can produce a high-quality 8 × 10 inch print.

Another feature of most digital cameras is the ability to zoom in on your subject. The way you ideally want to do this is the way film cameras do it, using the camera's optics—that's the lens. Most cameras above the basic level have some optical zoom, but almost all models include multiple levels of digital zoom, accomplished by some very clever software in the camera. Choose your camera based on optical zoom—3× at a minimum, or better if you can afford it. Digital zoom is useless.

Form Factor

As was the case with film cameras, size matters on digital cameras. Digital cameras come in several form factors. They range from tiny, ultra compact models that readily fit in a shirt pocket to monster cameras with huge lenses. Although it's not universally true, the bigger the camera the more features and sensors it can have. Thus, bigger is usually better in terms of quality. In shape, they come in a rectangular package, in which the lens retracts into the body, or as an SLR-type, with a lens that sticks out of the body. Figure 16-41 shows both styles.

Figure 16-41
Typical digital
cameras

Web Cameras

PC cameras, often called *webcams* because their most common use is for Internet video communication, are fairly new to the world of common I/O devices. Too many people run out and buy the cheapest one, not appreciating the vast difference between a discount webcam and more expensive models; nor do they take the time to configure the webcam properly. Let's consider some of the features you should look for when buying webcams and some of the problems you can run into when using them.

The biggest issue with webcams is the image quality. Webcams measure their resolution in pixels. You can find webcams with resolutions of as few as 100,000 pixels, and webcams with millions of pixels. Most people who use webcams agree that 1.3 million pixels (megapixels) is pretty much the highest resolution quality you can use before your video becomes so large it will bog down even a broadband connection.

The next issue with webcams is the frame rate; that is, the number of times the camera "takes your picture" each second. Higher frame rates make for smoother video; 30 frames per second is considered the best. A good camera with a high megapixel resolution and fast frame rate will provide you with excellent video conferencing capabilities. Figure 16-42 shows the author using his headset to chat via webcam using Skype software.

NOTE   Read more about pixels and frame rates in Chapter 17, "Video."

Figure 16-42
Video chatting by
webcam with Skype

Most people who use online video will also want a microphone. Many cameras come with microphones, or you can use your own. Those who do a lot of video chatting may prefer to get a camera without a microphone, and then buy a good quality headset with which to speak and listen.

Many cameras now have the ability to track you when you move, to keep your face in the picture—a very handy feature for fidgety folks using video conferencing! This interesting technology recognizes a human face with little or no "training" and rotates its position to keep your face in the picture. Some companies even add funny extras which, while not very productive, are good for a laugh (Figure 16-43).

Figure 16-43
Funny pictures

Configuring Webcams

Almost all webcams use USB connections. Windows comes with a limited set of web-cam drivers, so always make sure to install the drivers supplied with the camera before you plug it in. Most webcams use Hi-Speed USB, so make sure you're plugging your webcam into a Hi-Speed USB port.

Once the camera's plugged in, you'll need to test it. All cameras come with some type of program, but finding the program can be a challenge. Some brands put the program in the system tray, some place it in My Computer, and others put it in the Control Panel—and some do all three! Figure 16-44 shows the Control Panel applet that appeared when I installed the webcam driver.

Figure 16-44
Camera Settings
applet

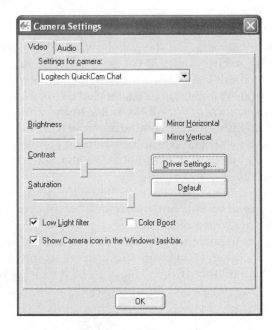

The biggest challenge to using webcams is getting your webcam applications to recognize that your webcam is available and configured for use. Every program does this differently, but conceptually the steps are basically the same (with plenty of exceptions):

1. Tell the program you want to use a camera.
2. Tell the program whether you want the camera to turn on automatically when you chat.
3. Configure the image quality.
4. Test the camera.

If you're having problems with a camera, always go through the general I/O problems first, as this will clear up most problems. If you're still having problems getting the camera to work in a program, be sure to turn off all other programs that may also be using the camera. Windows allows only one program at a time to use a webcam.

Specialty I/O Devices

The CompTIA A+ certification exams want to make sure you're aware of two other types of I/O devices: biometric scanners and touch screens. Let's look at these fairly specialized devices.

Biometric Devices

If you look up *biometrics* on the popular Wikipedia Web site, you'll get the following definition: "**Biometrics** (ancient Greek: *bios* ="life," *metron* ="measure") is the study of automated methods for uniquely recognizing humans based upon one or more intrinsic physical or behavioral traits." The field of biometrics also encompasses a number of security devices, such as door locks and security cameras, that don't really fit into the world of PCs. This section concentrates on the types of biometrics that you can actually buy and use on your PC. Within the realm of computers, biometrics includes a huge number of technologies, from thumb drives that read fingerprints, to software that does voice recognition.

PCs use biometrics for security. Biometric security devices scan and remember unique aspects of various body parts such as your retina, iris, head image, or fingerprint, using some form of sensing device such as a retinal scanner. This information is used as a key to prevent unauthorized people from accessing whatever the biometric device is securing. Most biometric devices currently used in PCs secure only themselves. The USB thumb drive in Figure 16-45 has a tiny fingerprint scanner. You slide your finger (any finger, you choose) over the drive to unlock the contents of the thumb drive.

Figure 16-45
USB thumb drive
with fingerprint
scanner (photo
courtesy of Lexar
Media, Inc.)

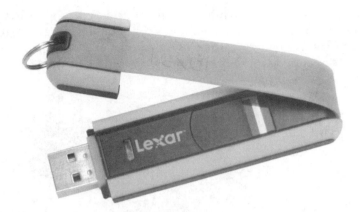

Less common are biometric security devices that secure entire computers. The Microsoft fingerprint scanner is a USB device that replaces standard user name and password security. Figure 16-46 shows the scanner built into a keyboard. When a program or Web site asks for a user name and password, you simply press your finger against the fingerprint scanner. It will confirm your identity (assuming your fingerprint matches), and then special software that comes with the scanner will supply the program or Web site with your stored user name and password.

Figure 16-46
Microsoft fingerprint
scanner on a
keyboard

Biometric devices are also used for recognition. Recognition is different from security in that the biometric device doesn't care who you are, it just wants to know what you're doing. The best example of this is voice recognition. Voice recognition programs convert human voice input into commands or text. Voice recognition for PCs has been around for some time. While it has never achieved enough accuracy to replace a keyboard completely, voice recognition is common in devices that have a limited number of commands to interpret, such as cell phones and PDAs. If you speak the words "Call Mike Meyers" into your PocketPC PDA/phone (Figure 16-47), your phone knows what to do—at least, *my* phone does!

Figure 16-47
Using voice
recognition to dial
a phone number

No matter what biometric device you use, you use the same steps to make it work:

1. Install the device.
2. Register your identity with the device by sticking your eye, finger, or other unique body part (why are you snickering?) into the device so it can scan you.
3. Configure its software to tell the device what to do when it recognizes your scanned identity.

Bar Code Readers

Bar code readers are designed to read standard Universal Product Code (UPC) bar codes (Figure 16-48). We read bar codes for only one reason—to track inventory. Bar code readers enable easy updating of inventory databases stored on PCs. Bar code readers are just about the oldest "specialty" I/O device used with PCs.

Figure 16-48
Typical UPC code

Two types of bar code readers are commonly found with PCs: pen scanners and hand scanners. Pen scanners (Figure 16-49) look like an ink pen and must be swiped across the barcode. Hand scanners are held in front of the UPC code while a button is pressed to scan. All barcode readers emit a tone to let you know the scan was successful.

Figure 16-49
Pen scanner
(photo courtesy of
Wasp® Barcode
Technologies)

Older barcode readers used serial ports, but all of the newer readers use either PS/2 or USB ports. No configuration is usually necessary, other than making sure that the particular bar code reader works with whatever database/point-of-sale software you use. When in doubt, most people find the PS/2 style bar code readers work best, as they simply act like a keyboard. You plug the reader into your keyboard port and then plug your keyboard into the reader. Then all you need is software that accepts keyboard input (and what one doesn't!), and it will work.

Touch Screens

A touch screen is a monitor with some type of sensing device across its face that detects the location and duration of contact, usually by a finger or stylus. All touch screens then supply this contact information to the PC as though it were a click event from a mouse. Touch screens are used in situations for which conventional mouse/keyboard input is either impossible or impractical. Here are a few places you'll see touch screens at work:

- Information kiosks
- PDAs
- Point of sale systems
- Tablet PCs

Touch screens can be separated into two groups: built-in screens like the ones in PDAs, and standalone touch screen monitors like those used in many point of sale systems. From a technician's standpoint, you can think of a standalone touch screen as a monitor with a built-in mouse. All touch screens will have a separate USB or PS/2 port for the "mouse" part of the device, along with drivers that you install just as you would for any USB mouse.

Chapter Review Questions

1. A serial port receives and sends serial data. What device translates that serial data into parallel data for the computer to use?

   A. Parallel translator chip

   B. Serial translator chip

   C. COM chip

   D. UART chip

2. What integrated circuit device controls USB devices connected to a USB port?

   A. Host controller

   B. IC-USB

   C. Serial port

   D. UART

3. What happens to bus speed and power usage when you plug multiple devices into a USB hub?

   A. The bus speed stays constant, but power usage increases.

   B. The bus speed increases because each device brings a little burst; power usage increases.

   C. The bus speed decreases because all devices share the same total bandwidth; power usage increases.

   D. The bus speed decreases because all devices share the same total bandwidth; power usage decreases.

4. Which port type offers the fastest transfer speed?

  A. IEEE 1394a

  B. IEEE 1394b

  C. Full-Speed USB

  D. Hi-Speed USB

5. You take a tech call from a user who complains that she gets an error message, "Hub power exceeded," when she plugs her new thumb drive into her USB keyboard's external USB port. Worse, the device won't work. What's most likely the problem?

  A. Her USB port is defective.

  B. She has a defective thumb drive.

  C. She plugged a Hi-Speed device into a Full-Speed port.

  D. She plugged one too many devices into the USB hub.

6. What is the fastest speed that Hi-Speed USB 2.0 can go?

  A. 12 Mbps

  B. 120 Mbps

  C. 400 Mbps

  D. 480 Mbps

7. USB 1.1 devices can run at two speeds. What are the speeds?

  A. 1 and 2 Mbps

  B. 1.5 and 12 Mbps

  C. 1.5 and 15 Mbps

  D. 12 and 48 Mbps

8. What's the maximum cable length for USB?

  A. 1.2 meters

  B. 1.2 yards

  C. 5 meters

  D. 5 feet

9. Which of the following mice technologies most needs to be cleaned?

  A. Ball

  B. Optical

  C. Parallel

  D. Serial

10. If you attempt to scan an item and the scanner light assembly does not move, what is most likely the problem?

   A. The scanner is frozen.

   B. The scanner is broken.

   C. The scanner light assembly is locked.

   D. The scanner light assembly is resetting.

Answers

1. **D.** The UART handles the serial to parallel and parallel to serial translation.

2. **A.** The host controller controls USB devices plugged into the USB bus via a USB port.

3. **C.** The bus speed decreases because all devices share the same total bandwidth; power usage increases.

4. **B.** FireWire 800 easily spanks the competition here.

5. **D.** Just like the error message said, the thumb drive drew too much power for the hub to handle.

6. **D.** Hi-Speed USB 2.0 has a theoretical maximum of 480 Mbps.

7. **B.** USB 1.1 devices can run at either 1.5 Mbps or 12 Mbps.

8. **C.** USB has a maximum cable length of 5 meters.

9. **A.** Ball mice get the dirtiest.

10. **C.** The scanner light assembly is most likely locked.

Video

In this chapter, you will learn how to
- Explain how video displays work
- Select the proper video card
- Install and configure video software
- Troubleshoot basic video problems

The term *video* encompasses a complex interaction among numerous parts of the PC, all designed to put a picture on the screen. The monitor shows you what's going on with your programs and operating system. It's the primary output device for the PC. The video card or *display adapter* handles all of the communication between the CPU and the monitor (see Figure 17-1). The operating system needs to know how to handle communication between the CPU and the display adapter, which requires drivers specific for each card and proper setup within Windows. Finally, each application needs to be able to interact with the rest of the video system.

Figure 17-1
Typical monitor
and video card

Let's look at monitors and video cards individually. I'll bring them back together as a team later in the chapter so that you can understand the many nuances that make video so challenging. Let's begin with the video display—a.k.a. the monitor—and then we'll move to the video card.

Video Displays

To understand displays, you need a good grasp of each component and how they work together to make a beautiful (or not so beautiful) picture on the screen. Different types of displays use different methods and technologies to accomplish this task. Video displays for PCs come in three varieties: CRT, LCD, and projectors. The first two you'll see on the desktop or laptop; the last you'll find in boardrooms and classrooms, splashing a picture onto a screen.

CRT Monitors

Cathode ray tube (CRT) monitors were the original computer monitors—those heavy, boxy monitors that take up half your desk. Although for the most part they've been replaced by LCD technology on new systems, there are plenty of CRT monitors still chugging away in the field. As the name implies, this type of display contains a large cathode ray tube, a type of airtight vacuum tube. One end of this tube is a slender cylinder that contains three electron guns. The other end of the tube, which is fatter and wider, is the display screen.

CAUTION Before we begin in earnest, a note of warning about the inside of a traditional monitor. I will discuss what can be repaired and what requires more specialized expertise. Make no mistake—the interior of a monitor might appear similar to the interior of a PC because of the printed circuit boards and related components, but that is where the similarity ends. No PC has voltages exceeding 15,000 to 30,000 V, but most monitors do. So let's get one thing perfectly clear: Opening up a monitor can kill you! Even when the power is disconnected, certain components retain a substantial voltage for an extended period of time. You can inadvertently short one of the components and fry yourself—to death. Given this risk, certain aspects of monitor repair lie outside the necessary skill set for a normal PC support person and definitely outside the CompTIA A+ certification exam domains! I will show you how to address the problems you can fix safely and make sure you understand the ones you need to hand over to a monitor shop.

The inside of the display screen has a phosphor coating. When power is applied to one or more of the electron guns, a stream of electrons shoots towards the display end of the CRT (see Figure 17-2). Along the way, this stream is subjected to magnetic fields generated by a ring of electromagnets called a *yoke* that controls the electron beam's point of impact. When the phosphor coating is struck by the electron beam, it releases its energy as visible light.

Figure 17-2
Electron stream
in the CRT

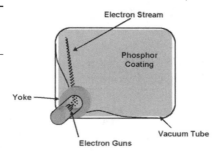

When struck by a stream of electrons, a phosphor quickly releases a burst of energy. This happens far too quickly for the human eye and brain connection to register. Fortunately, the phosphors on the display screen have a quality called *persistence,* which means the phosphors continue to glow after being struck by the electron beam. Too much persistence and the image is smeary; too little and the image appears to flicker. The perfect combination of beam and persistence creates the illusion of a solid picture.

NOTE   Several manufacturers still make CRT monitors, but only a couple of companies make the CRT—the tube inside the monitor—itself. All CRT tubes can be categorized into either of two types: traditional curved-screen CRTs and CRTs that are often referred to as *perfect flat*—using a kind of vacuum tube that has a completely flat screen and no bending around the edges. The perfect flat screens offer a wider viewing angle than standard CRT screens. About the only negative to the perfect flat screens is that they tend to lack true black, so pictures seem just shy of a natural richness of color and contrast.

Essentials

Refresh Rate

The monitor displays video data as the electron guns make a series of horizontal sweeps across the screen, energizing the appropriate areas of the phosphorous coating. The sweeps start at the upper-left corner of the monitor and move across and down to the lower-right corner. The screen is "painted" only in one direction; then the electron guns turn and retrace their path across the screen, to be ready for the next sweep. These sweeps are called *raster lines* (see Figure 17-3).

Figure 17-3
Electron guns sweep
from left to right.

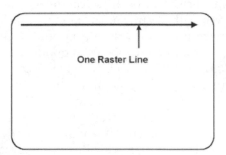

One Raster Line

The speed at which the electron beam moves across the screen is known as the *horizontal refresh rate (HRR),* as shown in Figure 17-4. The monitor draws a number of lines across the screen, eventually covering the screen with glowing phosphors. The number of lines is not fixed, unlike television screens, which have a set number of lines. After the guns reach the lower-right corner of the screen, they turn off and point back to the upper-left corner. The amount of time it takes to draw the entire screen and get the electron guns back to the upper-left corner is called the *vertical refresh rate (VRR),* shown in Figure 17-5.

Figure 17-4
Horizontal
refresh rate

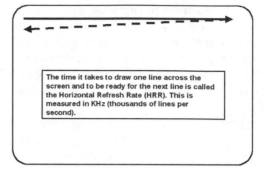

The time it takes to draw one line across the screen and to be ready for the next line is called the Horizontal Refresh Rate (HRR). This is measured in KHz (thousands of lines per second).

Figure 17-5
Vertical refresh rate

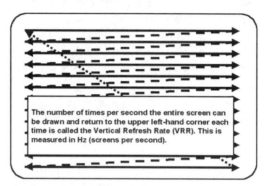

The number of times per second the entire screen can be drawn and return to the upper left-hand corner each time is called the Vertical Refresh Rate (VRR). This is measured in Hz (screens per second).

The monitor does not determine the HRR or VRR; the video card "pushes" the monitor at a certain VRR and then the monitor determines the HRR. If the video card is set to push at too low a VRR, the monitor produces a noticeable flicker, causing eyestrain and headaches for users. Pushing the monitor at too high of a VRR, however, causes a definite distortion of the screen image and will damage the circuitry of the monitor and eventually destroy it. The number one killer of monitors is improper VRR settings, and the number one reason your office is filled with crabby workers is due to the VRR being set too low. All good PC support techs understand this and take substantial time tweaking the VRR to ensure that the video card pushes the monitor at the highest VRR without damaging the monitor—this is the Holy Grail of monitor support!

You should know the refresh rate for all CRTs you service. Setting up monitors incorrectly can cause havoc in the work place. Most PCs have two places where you can discover the current refresh rate of the monitor. Many monitors offer a menu button for adjusting the display. Often it will show the refresh rate when pushed once. If that doesn't work, go to the Control Panel and open the Display applet. Select the Settings tab and then click the Advanced button. Select the Monitor tab in the Monitor Properties dialog box.

Phosphors and Shadow Mask

All CRT monitors contain dots of phosphorous or some other light-sensitive compound that glows *red, green,* or *blue* (RGB) when an electron gun sweeps over it. These phosphors are evenly distributed across the front of the monitor (see Figure 17-6).

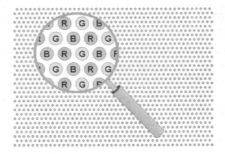

Figure 17-6
A monitor is a grid of red, green, and blue phosphors.

A normal CRT has three electron guns: one for the red phosphors, one for the blue phosphors, and one for the green phosphors. It is important to understand that the electron guns do not fire colored light; they simply fire electrons at different intensities, which then make the phosphors glow. The higher the intensity of the electron stream, the brighter the color produced by the glowing phosphor.

Directly behind the phosphors in a CRT is the *shadow mask*, a screen that allows only the proper electron gun to light the proper phosphors (see Figure 17-7). This prevents, for example, the red electron beam from "bleeding over" and lighting neighboring blue and green dots.

Figure 17-7
Shadow mask

The electron guns sweep across the phosphors as a group, turning rapidly on and off as they move across the screen. When the group reaches the end of the screen, it moves to the next line. It is crucial to understand that turning the guns on and off, combined with moving the guns to new lines, creates a "mosaic" that is the image you see on the screen. The number of times the guns turn on and off, combined with the number of lines drawn on the screen, determines the number of mosaic pieces used to create the image. These individual "pieces" are called *pixels*, from the term *picture elements*. You can't hold a pixel in your hand; it's just the area of phosphors lit at one instant when the group of guns is turned on. The size of pixels can change, depending on the number of times the group of guns is turned on and off and the number of lines drawn.

NOTE Not all CRT monitors use dots. The popular Sony Trinitron line of CRT monitors uses bars of red, green, and blue instead of dots. The holes in the shadow mask have a rectangular shape. Many people feel this makes the monitor's image much crisper and clearer. Somebody must agree with them since the Trinitron enjoys tremendous popularity. Even though the phosphors and shadow mask have a different shape, everything you learn here applies to Trinitrons also.

Resolution

Monitor *resolution* is always shown as the number of horizontal pixels times the number of vertical pixels. A resolution of 640 × 480, therefore, indicates a horizontal resolution of 640 pixels and a vertical resolution of 480 pixels. If you multiply the values together, you can see how many pixels are on each screen: 640 × 480 = 307,200 pixels per screen. An example of resolution affecting the pixel size is shown in Figure 17-8.

Figure 17-8
Resolution
versus pixel size

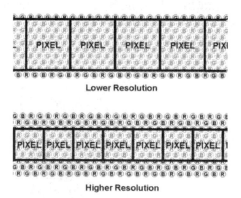

Some common resolutions are 640 × 480, 800 × 600, 1024 × 768, 1280 × 960, 1280 × 1024, and 1600 × 1200. Notice that most of these resolutions match a 4:3 ratio. This is called the *aspect ratio*. Many monitors are shaped like television screens, with a 4:3 aspect ratio, so most resolutions are designed to match—or at least be close to—that shape. Many monitors, generically called *wide-screen monitors*, have a 16:9 or 16:10 ratio. Two of the common resolutions you'll see with these monitors are 1366 × 768 and 1920 × 1200.

The last important issue is to determine the maximum possible resolution for a monitor. In other words, how small can one pixel be? Well, the answer lies in the phosphors. A pixel must be made up of at least one red, one green, and one blue phosphor to make any color, so the smallest theoretical pixel would consist of one group of red, green, and blue phosphors: a triad (see Figure 17-9). Various limitations in screens, controlling electronics, and electron gun technology make the maximum resolution much bigger than one triad.

Figure 17-9
One triad

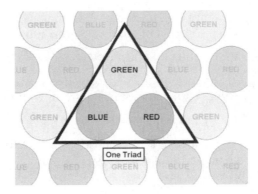

Dot Pitch

The resolution of a monitor is defined by the maximum amount of detail the monitor can render. The dot pitch of the monitor ultimately limits this resolution. The *dot pitch* defines the diagonal distance between phosphorous dots of the same color, and is measured in *millimeters (mm)*. Because a lower dot pitch means more dots on the screen, it usually produces a sharper, more defined image (see Figure 17-10). Dot pitch works in tandem with the maximum number of lines the monitor can support in order to determine the greatest working resolution of the monitor. It might be possible to place an image at 1600 × 1200 on a 15-inch monitor with a dot pitch of 0.31 mm, but it would not be very readable.

Figure 17-10
Measuring dot pitch

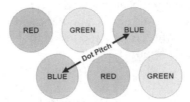

The dot pitch can range from as high as 0.39 mm to as low as 0.18 mm. For most Windows-based applications on a 17-inch monitor, many people find that 0.28 mm is the maximum usable dot pitch that still produces a clear picture.

Bandwidth

Bandwidth defines the maximum number of times the electron gun can be turned on and off per second. Bandwidth is measured in *megahertz (MHz)*. In essence, bandwidth tells us how fast the monitor can put an image on the screen. A typical value for a better-quality 17-inch color monitor would be around 150 MHz, which means that the electron beam can be turned on and off 150 million times per second. The value for a monitor's bandwidth determines the maximum VRR the video card should push the monitor for any given resolution. It reads as follows:

maximum VRR = bandwidth ÷ pixels per page

For example, what is the maximum VRR that a 17-inch monitor with a bandwidth of 100 MHz and a resolution of 1024 × 768 can support? The answer is

maximum VRR = 100,000,000 ÷ (1024 × 768) = 127 Hz

That's a pretty good monitor, as most video cards do not push beyond 120 Hz! At a resolution of 1200 × 1024, the vertical refresh would be

100,000,000 ÷ (1200 × 1024) = 81 Hz

So, we would make sure to set the video card's VRR to 80 Hz or less. If you had a monitor with a bandwidth of only 75 MHz, the maximum VRR at a 1200 × 1024 resolution would be only 61 Hz.

Most monitor makers know that people aren't going to take the time to do these calculations. Instead, they do the calculations for you and create tables of refresh rates at certain resolutions to show what a monitor can do.

Great! Now that you have the basics of CRT monitors, let's turn to LCD monitors. Although the technology differs dramatically between the monitor types, most of the terms used for CRTs also apply to LCD functions.

LCD Monitors

Liquid crystal displays (LCDs) are the most common type of display technology for PCs. LCD monitors have many advantages over CRTs. They are thinner and lighter, use much less power, are virtually flicker free, and don't emit potentially harmful radiation. LCDs still have resolution, refresh rates, and bandwidth, but LCDs also come with their own family of abbreviations, jargon, and terms that you need to understand in order to install, maintain, and support LCDs.

How LCDs Work

The secret to understanding LCD panels is to understand the concept of the polarity of light. Anyone who played with a prism in sixth grade or looked at a rainbow knows that light travels in waves (no quantum mechanics here, please!) and the wavelength of the light determines the color. What you might not appreciate is the fact that light waves emanate from a light source in three dimensions. It's impossible to draw a clear diagram of three-dimensional waves, so instead, let's use an analogy. To visualize this, think of light emanating from a flashlight. Now think of the light emanating from that flashlight as though someone was shaking a jump rope. This is not a rhythmic shaking, back and forth or up and down; it's more as if a person went crazy and was shaking the jump rope all over the place—up, down, left, right—constantly changing the speed.

That's how light really acts. Well, I guess we could take the analogy one step further by saying the person has an infinite number of arms, each holding a jump rope shooting out in every direction to show the three-dimensionality of light waves, but (a) I can't draw that and (b) one jump rope will suffice to explain LCD panels. The different speeds create wavelengths, from very short to very long. When light comes into your eyes at many different wavelengths, you see white light. If the light came in only one wavelength, you would see only that color. Light flowing through a polarized filter (like sunglasses) is like putting a picket fence between you and the people shaking the ropes. You see all of the wavelengths, but only the waves of similar orientation. You would still see all of the colors, just fewer of them because you only see the waves of the same orientation, making the image darker. That's why many sunglasses use polarizing filters.

Now, what would happen if we added another picket fence but put the slats in a horizontal direction? This would effectively cancel out all of the waves. This is what happens when two polarizing filters are combined at a 90-degree angle—no light passes through.

What would happen if a third fence was added between the two fences with the slats at a 45-degree angle? Well, it would sort of "twist" some of the shakes in the rope so that the waves could then get through. The same thing is true with the polarizing filters. The third filter twists some of the light so that it gets through. If you're really feeling scientific, go to any teacher's supply store and pick up three polarizing filters for about US$3 each and try it. It works.

Liquid crystals take advantage of the property of polarization. Liquid crystals are composed of a specially formulated liquid full of long, thin crystals that always want to orient themselves in the same direction, as shown in Figure 17-11. This substance acts exactly like a liquid polarized filter. If you poured a thin film of this stuff between two sheets of glass, you'd get a darn good pair of sunglasses.

Figure 17-11
Waves of similar
orientation

Imagine cutting extremely fine grooves on one side of one of those sheets of glass. When you place this liquid in contact with a finely grooved surface, the molecules naturally line up with the grooves in the surface (see Figure 17-12).

Figure 17-12
Liquid crystal
molecules tend to
line up together.

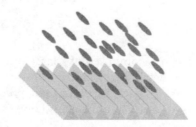

If you place another finely grooved surface, with the grooves at a 90-degree orientation to the other surface, opposite the first one, the molecules in contact with that side will attempt to line up with it. The molecules in between, in trying to line up with both sides, will immediately line up in a nice twist (see Figure 17-13). If two perpendicular polarizing filters are then placed on either side of the liquid crystal, the liquid crystal will twist the light and enable it to pass (see Figure 17-14).

Figure 17-13
Liquid crystal molecules twisting

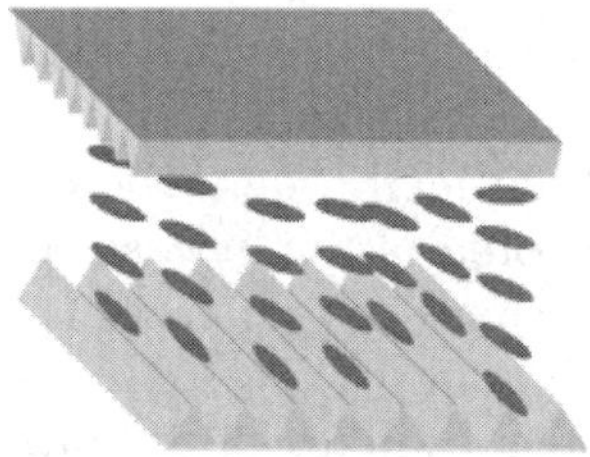

Figure 17-14
No charge, enabling light to pass

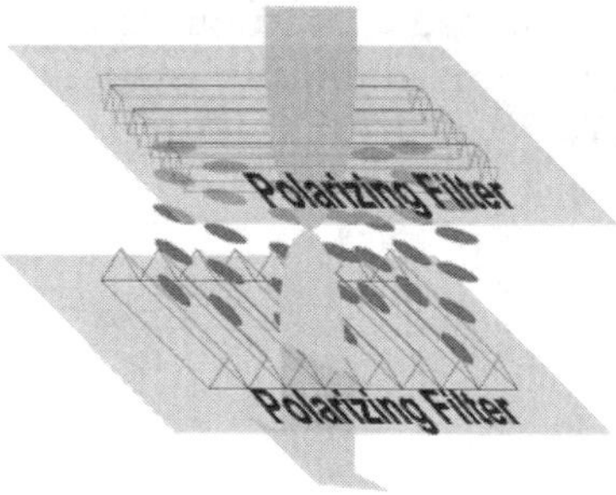

If you expose the liquid crystal to an electrical potential, however, the crystals will change their orientation to match the direction of the electrical field. The twist goes away and no light passes through (see Figure 17-15).

Figure 17-15
Electrical charge, enabling no light to pass

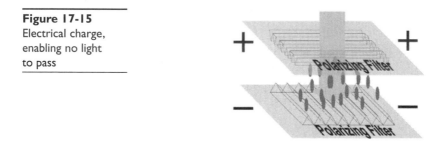

A color LCD screen is composed of a large number of tiny liquid crystal molecules (called *sub-pixels*) arranged in rows and columns between polarizing filters. A translucent sheet above the sub-pixels is colored red, green, or blue. Each tiny distinct group of three sub-pixels—one red, one green, and one blue—form a physical pixel, as shown in Figure 17-16.

Figure 17-16
LCD pixels

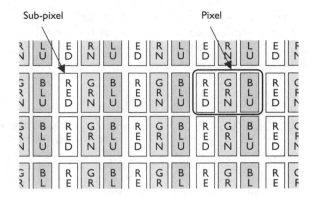

NOTE LCD pixels are very different from the pixels in a CRT. A CRT pixel's size will change depending on the resolution. The pixels in an LCD panel are fixed and cannot be changed. See the section on "LCD Resolution" below for the scoop.

Once all the pixels are laid out, how do you charge the right spots to make an image? Early LCDs didn't use rectangular pixels. Instead, images were composed of different-shaped elements, each electrically separate from the others. To create an image, each area was charged at the same time. Figure 17-17 shows the number zero, a display made possible by charging six areas to make an ellipse of sorts. This process, called *static charging,* is still quite popular in more basic numeric displays such as calculators.

Figure 17-17
Single character for
static LCD numeric
display

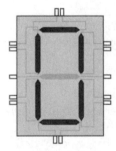

The static method would not work in PCs due to its inherent inflexibility. Instead, LCD screens use a matrix of wires (see Figure 17-18). The vertical wires, the Y wires, run to every sub-pixel in the column. The horizontal wires, the X wires, run along an entire row of sub-pixels. There must be a charge on both the X and Y wires to make enough voltage to light a single sub-pixel.

Figure 17-18
An LCD matrix
of wires

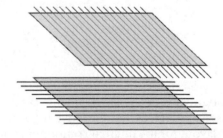

If you want color, you have three matrices. The three matrices intersect very close together. Above the intersections, the glass is covered with tiny red, green, and blue dots. Varying the amount of voltage on the wires makes different levels of red, green, and blue, creating colors (see Figure 17-19).

Figure 17-19
Passive matrix display

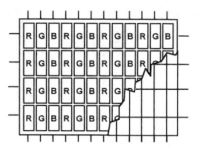

We call this usage of LCD technology *passive matrix*. All LCD displays on PCs used only passive matrix for many years. Unfortunately, passive matrix is slow and tends to create a little overlap between individual pixels. This gives a slightly blurred effect to the image displayed. Manufacturers eventually came up with a speedier method of display, called *dual-scan passive matrix*, in which the screen refreshed two lines at a time. Although other LCD technologies have since appeared, dual-scan continues to show up on some lower-end LCD panels.

NOTE You'll also find passive matrix displays in smaller, hand-held devices. See Chapter 19, "Portable Computing," for details about hand-held computing devices.

Thin Film Transistor

A vast improvement over dual scan is called active matrix or *thin film transistor (TFT)*. Instead of using X and Y wires, one or more tiny transistors control each color dot, providing faster picture display, crisp definition, and much tighter color control. TFT is the LCD of choice today, even though it is much more expensive than passive matrix (see Figure 17-20).

Figure 17-20
Active matrix display

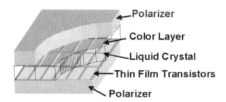

LCD Components

The typical LCD projector is composed of three main components: the LCD panel, the backlight(s), and the inverters. The LCD panel creates the image, the backlights illuminate the image so you can see it, and the inverters send power to backlights. Figure 17-21 shows a typical layout for the internal components of an LCD monitor.

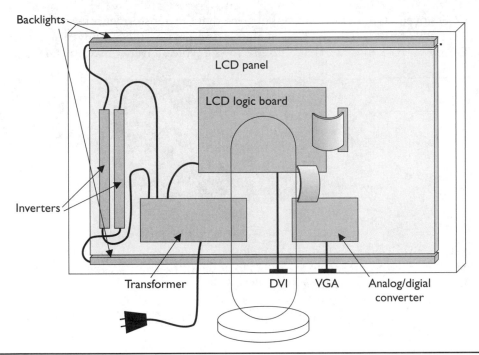

Figure 17-21 LCD internals

One of the great challenges to LCD power stems from the fact that the backlights need AC power while the electronics need DC power. The figure shows one of the many ways that LCD monitor makers handle this issue. The AC power from your wall socket goes into an AC/DC transformer that changes the power to DC. The LCD panel uses this DC power.

Note in Figure 17-21 that this monitor has two backlights: one at the top and one at the bottom. Most LCDs have two backlights, although many only have one. All LCD backlights use *cold cathode florescent lamp (CCFL)* technology, popular for its low power use, even brightness, and long life. Figure 17-22 shows a CCFL from an LCD panel.

Figure 17-22
CCFL backlight

CCFLs need AC power to operate, but given that the transformer converts the incoming AC power to DC, each CCFL backlight needs a device called an inverter to convert the DC power back into AC. Figure 17-23 shows a typical inverter used in an LCD.

Figure 17-23
Inverter

Back to the diagram in Figure 17-21, note the DVI and VGA inputs. DVI is a digital signal, so it connects directly to the LCD's logic circuitry. The VGA goes to an analog to digital converter before reaching the LCD logic board.

Keep in mind that Figure 17-21 is a generic illustration. The actual location and interconnections of the different components are as variable as the number of LCD panels available today!

LCD Resolution

All LCD monitors have a *native resolution*, such as 1680 × 1050, that enables them to display the sharpest picture possible. As mentioned earlier, the pixels are fixed. You simply cannot run an LCD monitor at a resolution higher than the native one. Worse, because LCDs have no equivalent to a shadow mask, they can't run at a *lower* than native resolution without severely degrading image quality. A CRT can simply use more dots and the filtering and smoothing of the shadow mask to make a picture at a lower resolution look as good and crisp as the same picture at a higher resolution, but an LCD cannot. The LCD has to use an edge-blurring technique called *anti-aliasing* to soften the jagged corners of the pixels when running at lower than native resolution, which simply does not look as good. The bottom line? Always set the LCD at native resolution!

NOTE Two LCD panels that have the same physical size may have different native resolutions.

The hard-wired nature of LCD resolution creates a problem for techs and consumers when dealing with bigger, better-quality monitors. A typical 15-inch LCD has a 1024 × 768 resolution, but a 17-inch usually has 1280 × 1024 or higher. These high resolutions make the menus and fonts on a monitor super tiny, a problem for people with less-than-stellar vision. Many folks throw in the towel and run these high-end LCDs at lower resolution and just live with the lower quality picture, but that's not the best way to resolve this problem.

With Windows XP (and to a lesser extent with the earlier versions of Windows), Microsoft allows incredible customizing of the interface. You can change the font size, shape, and color. You can resize the icons, toolbars, and more. You can even change the number of dots per inch (DPI) for the full screen, making everything bigger or smaller!

For basic customizing, start at the Control Panel | Display applet | Appearance tab. To change the DPI for the display, go to the Settings tab and click the Advanced button. Your clients will thank you!

Brightness

The strength of an LCD monitor's backlights determines the brightness of the monitor. The brightness is measured in *nits*. LCD panels vary from 100 nits on the low end to over 1,000 nits or more on the high end. Average LCD panels are around 300 nits, which most monitor authorities consider excellent brightness.

 NOTE One nit equals one candela/m^2. One candela is roughly equal to the amount of light created by a candle.

Response Rate

An LCD panel's *response rate* is the amount of time it takes for all of the sub-pixels on the panel to go from pure black to pure white and back again. This is roughly the same concept as the CRT refresh rate, but with one important difference. Once the electron gun on a CRT lights a phosphor, that phosphor begins to fade until it is lit again. Individual LCD sub-pixels hold their intensity until the LCD circuitry changes that sub-pixel, making the problem of flicker nonexistent on LCDs.

Manufacturers measure LCD response rates in milliseconds, with lower being better. A typical lower-end or older LCD will have a response rate of 20–25 ms. The screens look fine, but you'll get some ghosting if you try to watch a movie or play a fast-paced video game. In recent years, manufacturers have figured out how to overcome this issue, and you can find many LCD monitors with a response rate of 6–8 ms.

Contrast Ratio

A big drawback of LCD monitors is that they don't have nearly the color saturation or richness of contrast of a good CRT monitor—although LCD technology continues to improve every year. A good contrast ratio—the difference between the darkest and lightest spots that the monitor can display—is 450:1, although a quick trip to a computer store will reveal LCDs with lower levels (250:1) and higher levels (1000:1).

Projectors

Projectors are a third option for displaying your computer images and the best choice when displaying to an audience or in a classroom. There are two ways to project an image on a screen: rear-view and front-view. As the name would suggest, a *rear-view projector* (Figure 17-24) shoots an image onto a screen from the rear. Rear-view projectors are always self-enclosed and very popular for televisions, but are virtually unheard of in the PC world.

Figure 17-24
Rear-view projector
(photo courtesy of
Samsung)

A *front-view projector* shoots the image out the front and counts on you to put a screen in front at the proper distance. Front-view projectors connected to PCs running Microsoft PowerPoint have been the cornerstone of every meeting almost everywhere for at least the last ten years (Figure 17-25). This section deals exclusively with front-view projectors that connect to PCs.

Figure 17-25
Front-view projector
(photo courtesy of
Dell Inc.)

Projector Technologies

Projectors that connect to PCs have been in existence for almost as long as PCs themselves. Given all that time, there have been a number of technologies used in projectors. The first generation of projectors used CRTs. Each color used a separate CRT that projected the image onto a screen (Figure 17-26). CRT projectors create beautiful images but are expensive, large, and very heavy, and have for the most part been abandoned for more recent technologies.

Figure 17-26
CRT projector

Given that light shines through an LCD panel, LCD projectors are a natural fit for front projection. LCD projectors are light and very inexpensive compared to CRTs but lack the image quality. LCD projectors are so light that almost all portable projectors use LCD (Figure 17-27).

Figure 17-27
LCD projector
(photo courtesy
of ViewSonic)

 NOTE Another type of technology that's seen in projectors but is outside the scope of the CompTIA A+ exams is called digital light processing (DLP). Check out the "Beyond A+" section of this chapter for details.

All projectors share the same issues of their equivalent technology monitors. LCD projectors have a specific native resolution, for example. In addition, you need to understand three concepts specific to projectors: lumens, throw, and lamps.

Lumens

The brightness of a projector is measured in lumens. A *lumen* is the amount of light given off by a light source from a certain angle that is perceived by the human eye. The greater the lumen rating of a projector, the brighter the projector will be. The best lumen rating depends on the size of the room and the amount of light in the room.

There's no single answer for "the right lumen rating" for a projector, but use this as a rough guide. If you use a projector in a small, darkened room, 1,000 to 1,500 lumens will work well. If you use a projector in a mid-sized room with typical lighting, in contrast, you'll need at least 2,000 lumens. Projectors for large rooms have ratings over 10,000 lumens and are very expensive.

Throw

A projector's *throw* is the size of the image at a certain distance from the screen. All projectors have a recommended minimum and maximum throw distance that you need to take into consideration. A typical throw would be expressed as follows. A projector with a 16:9 image aspect ratio needs to be 11 to 12 feet away from the projection surface to create a 100-inch diagonal screen. A *long throw lens* has about a 1:2 ratio of screen size to distance, so to display a 4-foot screen, you'd have to put the projector 8 feet away. Some *short throw lenses* drop that ratio down as low as 1:1!

Lamps

The bane of every projector is the lamp. Lamps work hard in your projector, as they must generate a tremendous amount of light. As a result, they generate quite a bit of heat, and all projectors come with a fan to keep the lamp from overheating. When you turn off a projector, the fan will continue to run until the lamp is fully cooled. Lamps are also very expensive, usually in the range of a few hundred dollars (U.S.), which comes as a nasty shock to someone who's not prepared for that price when their lamp dies!

Common Features

CRT or LCD, all monitors share a number of characteristics that you need to know for purchase, installation, maintenance, and troubleshooting.

Size

You need to take care when buying CRT monitors. CRT monitors come in a large number of sizes, all measured in inches (although most metric countries provide the metric equivalent value). All monitors provide two numbers: the monitor size and the actual size of the screen. The monitor size measures from two opposite diagonal corners. The actual screen is measured from one edge of the screen to the opposite diagonal side. This latter measurement is often referred to as the *viewable image size (VIS)*; see Figure 17-28. You will commonly see a size difference of one to two inches between the two measurements. A 17-inch CRT monitor, for example, might have a 15.5-inch VIS.

Figure 17-28
Viewable image
size of a CRT

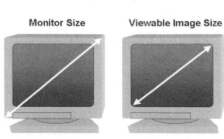

Monitor Size   Viewable Image Size

LCD monitors dispense with the two values and simply express the VIS value. You must consider this issue when comparing LCDs to CRTs. A 15-inch LCD monitor will have about the same viewing area as a 17-inch CRT.

Connections

CRT monitors for PCs all use the famous 15-pin, three-row, DB-type connector (see Figure 17-29) and a power plug. Larger or multipurpose monitors may have a few other connectors, but as far as the CRT is concerned, these are the only two you need for video.

Figure 17-29
A traditional CRT connection

 NOTE You'll often hear the terms *flat-panel display* or *LCD panels* to describe LCD monitors. I prefer the term LCD monitor, but be prepared to hear it a few different ways.

Unlike the analog CRTs, LCD monitors need a digital signal. This creates somewhat of an issue. The video information stored on a video card's RAM is clearly digital. All VGA and better video cards include a special chip (or function embedded into a chip that does several other jobs) called the *random access memory digital-to-analog converter (RAMDAC)*. As the name implies, RAMDAC takes the digital signal from the video card and turns it into an analog signal for the analog CRT (see Figure 17-30). The RAMDAC really defines the bandwidth that the video card outputs.

Figure 17-30
An analog signal sent to a CRT monitor

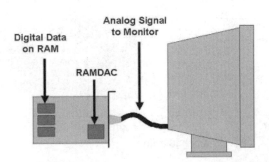

Digital Data on RAM

Analog Signal to Monitor

RAMDAC

Well, RAMDACs certainly make sense for analog CRT monitors. However, if you want to plug your LCD monitor into a regular video card, you need circuitry on the LCD monitor to convert the signal from analog to digital (see Figure 17-31).

Figure 17-31
Converting analog
back to digital on
the LCD

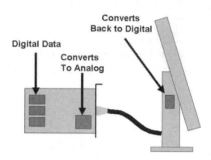

Many LCD monitors use exactly this process. These are called *analog LCD monitors.* The monitor really isn't analog; it's digital, but it takes a standard VGA input. These monitors have one advantage: You may use any standard VGA video card. But these monitors require adjustment of the analog timing signal to the digital clock inside the monitor. This used to be a fairly painful process, but most analog LCD monitors now include intelligent circuitry to make this process either automatic or very easy.

Why convert the signal from digital to analog and then back to digital? Well, many monitor and video card people agree. We now see quite a few digital LCD monitors and digital video cards. They use a completely different connector than the old 15-pin DB connector used on analog video cards and monitors. After a few false starts with connection standards, under names like P&D and DFP, the digital LCD world, with a few holdouts, moved to the *digital video interface (DVI)* standard. DVI is actually three different connectors that look very much alike: DVI-D is for digital, DVI-A is for analog (for backward compatibility if the monitor maker so desires), and the DVI-A/D or DVI-I (interchangeable) accepts either a DVI-D or DVI-A. DVI-D and DVI-A are keyed so that they will not connect.

DVI-D and DVI-I connectors come in two varieties, single link and dual link. *Single-link DVI* has a maximum bandwidth of 165 MHz which, translated into practical terms, limits the maximum resolution of a monitor to 1920 × 1080 at 60 Hz or 1280 × 1024 at 85 Hz. *Dual-link DVI* uses more pins to double throughput and thus grant higher resolutions (Figure 17-32). With dual link, you can have displays up to a whopping 2048 × 1536 at 60 Hz!

Figure 17-32
Dual-link DVI-I
connector

NOTE   You can plug a single-link DVI monitor into a dual-link DVI connector and it'll work just fine.

Digital connectors are quickly replacing analog in the monitor world. Digital makes both the monitor and the video card cheaper, provides a clearer signal because no conversion is necessary, and makes installation easy. The problem is that no video card or monitor maker wants to be the first to go all digital, so to hedge their bets, most continue to produce display products that offer both analog and digital support.

The video card people have it easy. They either include both a VGA and a DVI-D connector or they use a DVI-I connector. The advantage to DVI-I is that you can add a cheap DVI-I to VGA adapter (one usually comes with the video card) like the one shown in Figure 17-33 and connect an analog monitor just fine.

Figure 17-33
DVI to VGA adapter

 NOTE   Video cards with two video connectors support dual monitors, which I discuss later in the chapter.

Monitor makers have it tougher. Most LCD monitor makers have made the jump to DVI, but many include a VGA connector for those machines that still need it.

Unless you're buying a complete new system, you'll rarely buy a video card at the same time you buy a monitor. When you're buying a monitor or a video card, make sure that the new device will connect to the other!

Adjustments

Most adjustments to the monitor take place at installation, but for now, let's just make sure you know what they are and where they are located. Clearly, all monitors have an On/Off button or switch. Also, see if you can locate the Brightness and Contrast buttons. Beyond that, most monitors (at least the only ones you should buy) have an on-board menu system, enabling a number of adjustments. Every monitor maker provides a different way to access these menus, but they all provide two main functions: physical screen adjustment (bigger, smaller, move to the left, right, up, down, and others) and color adjustment. The color adjustment lets you adjust the red, green, and blue guns to give you the best color tones. All these settings are a matter of personal taste. Make sure the person who will use the computer understands how to adjust these settings (see Figure 17-34).

Figure 17-34
Typical menu controls

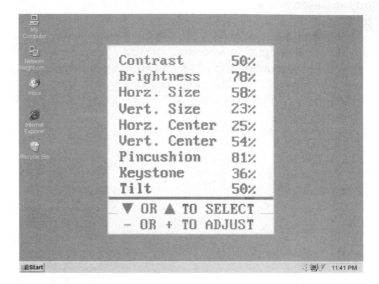

Power Conservation

CRT and LCD monitors differ greatly in the amount of electricity they require. The bottom line is that CRTs use a lot and LCDs use a lot less. Here's the scoop.

Approximately half the power required to run a desktop PC is consumed by the CRT monitor. Monitors that meet the *Video Electronics Standards Association (VESA)* specification for *display power-management signaling (DPMS)* can reduce monitor power consumption by roughly 75 percent. This is accomplished by reducing or eliminating the signals sent by the video card to the monitor during idle periods. By eliminating these pulses, the monitor essentially takes catnaps. The advantage over simply shutting the monitor off is in the time it takes to restore the display.

A typical CRT monitor consumes approximately 120 watts. During a catnap or power-down mode, the energy consumption is reduced to below 25 watts, while enabling the screen to return to use in less than ten seconds. Full shutoff is accomplished by eliminating all clocking pulses to the monitor. Although this reduces power consumption to below 15 watts, it also requires anywhere from 15 to 30 seconds to restore a usable display.

Turning off the monitor with the power switch is the most basic form of power management. The downside to this is the wear and tear on the CRT. The CRT is the most expensive component of a monitor, and turning it on and off frequently can damage the CRT. When using a non-DPMS monitor or video card, it is best to turn the monitor on once during the day and then turn it off only when you are finished for the day. This on-off cycle must be balanced against the life of the CRT display phosphors. The typical monitor will lose about half its original brightness after roughly 10,000 to 15,000 hours of display time. Leaving the monitor on all the time will bring a noticeable decrease in brightness in just over a year (8,766 hours). The only way around this is enabling the DPMS features of the monitor or taking care to turn the monitor off.

A typical LCD monitor uses less than half the electricity that a CRT uses. A 19-inch, 4:3 aspect-ratio flat panel, for example, uses around 33 watts at peak usage and less than 2 watts in DPMS mode. Larger LCDs use more power at peak usage than smaller ones. A 21-inch wide-screen model, for example, might draw ~75 watts at peak, but still drop down to less than 2 watts in DPMS mode. Swapping out CRTs with LCDs is a great way to save on your electric bill!

Video Cards

The video card, or display adapter, handles the video chores within the PC, processing information from the CPU and sending it out to the monitor. The video card is composed of two major pieces: the video RAM and the video processor circuitry. The video RAM stores the video image. On the first video cards, this RAM was good old dynamic RAM (DRAM), just like the RAM on the motherboard. Today's video cards often have better RAM than your system has! The video processing circuitry takes the information on the video RAM and shoots it out to the monitor. While early video processing circuitry was little more than an intermediary between the CPU and the video RAM, modern video processors are more powerful than all but the latest CPUs! It's not at all uncommon to see video cards that need fans to cool their onboard processors (see Figure 17-35).

Figure 17-35
Video card with
a cooling fan

The trick to understanding video cards is to appreciate the beginnings and evolution of video. Video output to computers was around long before PCs were created. At the time PCs became popular, video was almost exclusively text-based, meaning that the only image the video card could place on the monitor was one of the 256 ASCII characters. These characters were made up of patterns of pixels that were stored in the system BIOS. When a program wanted to make a character, it talked to DOS or to the BIOS, which stored the image of that character in the video memory. The character then appeared on the screen.

The beauty of text video cards was that they were simple to use and cheap to make. The simplicity was based on the fact that only 256 characters existed, and no color choices were available—just monochrome text (see Figure 17-36).

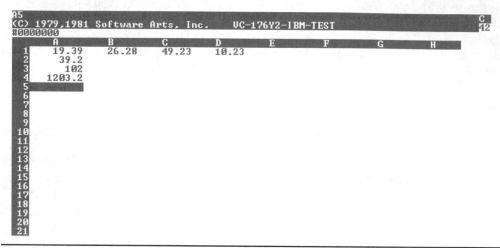

Figure 17-36 Text mode

You could, however, choose to make the character bright, dim, normal, underlined, or blinking. It was easy to position the characters, as space on the screen allowed for only 80 characters per row and 24 rows of characters.

Long ago, RAM was very expensive, so video-card makers were interested in using the absolute least amount of RAM possible. Making a monochrome text video card was a great way to keep down RAM costs. Let's consider this for a minute. First, the video RAM is where the contents of the screen are located. You need enough video RAM to hold all the necessary information for a completely full screen. Each ASCII character needs eight bits (by definition), so a monitor with 80 characters/row and 24 rows will need

80 characters × 24 rows = 1920 characters = 15,360 bits or 1920 bytes

The video card would need less than 2000 bytes of memory, which isn't much, not even in 1981 when the PC first came out. Now, be warned that I'm glossing over a few things—where you store the information about underlines, blinking, and so on. The bottom line is that the tiny amount of necessary RAM kept monochrome text video cards cheap.

Very early on in the life of PCs, a new type of video, called a *graphics video card*, was invented. It was quite similar to a text card. The text card, however, was limited to the 256 ASCII characters, whereas a graphics video card enabled programs to turn any pixel on the screen on or off. It was still monochrome, but programs could access any individual pixel, enabling much more creative control of the screen. Of course, it took more video RAM. The first graphics cards ran at 320 × 200 pixels. One bit was needed for each pixel (on or off), so

320 × 200 = 64,000 bits or 8000 bytes

That's a lot more RAM than what was needed for text, but it was still a pretty low amount of RAM—even in the old days. As resolutions increased, however, the amount of video RAM needed to store this information also increased.

Once monochrome video was invented, it was a relatively easy step to move into color for both text and graphics video cards. The only question was how to store color information for each character (text cards) or pixel (graphics cards). This was easy—just set aside a few more bits for each pixel or character. So now the question becomes, "How many bits do you set aside?" Well, that depends on how many colors you want. Basically, the number of colors determines the number of bits. For example, if you wanted four colors, you need two bits (two bits per pixel). Then, you could do something like this

00 = black	01 = cyan (blue)
10 = magenta (reddish pink)	11 = white

So if you set aside two bits, you could get four colors. If you want 16 colors, set aside four bits, which would make 16 different combinations. Nobody ever invented a text mode that used more than 16 colors, so let's start thinking in terms of only graphics mode and bits per pixels. To get 256 colors, each pixel would have to be represented with eight bits. In PCs, the number of colors is always a power of 2: 4, 16, 256, 64 K, and so on. Note that as more colors are added, more video RAM is needed to store the information. Here are the most common color depths and the number of bits necessary to store the color information per pixel:

2 colors = 1 bit (mono)

4 colors = 2 bits

16 colors = 4 bits

256 colors = 8 bits

64 K colors = 16 bits

16.7 million colors = 24 bits

Most technicians won't say, for example, "I set my video card to show over 16 million colors." Instead, they'll say, "I set my color depth to 24 bits." Talk in terms of bits, not colors. It is assumed that you know the number of colors for any color depth.

You can set the color depth for a Windows 2000 or Windows XP computer in the Display Properties applet on the Settings tab (Figure 17-37). If you set up a typical Windows XP computer, you'll notice that Windows offers you 32-bit color quality, which might make you assume you're about to crank out more than 4 billion colors, but that's simply not the case. The 32-bit color setting offers 24-bit color plus an 8-bit alpha channel. An alpha channel controls the opacity of a particular color. By using an alpha channel, Windows can more effectively blend colors to create the effect of semi-transparent images. In Windows XP, you see this in the drop shadow under a menu; in Windows Vista, almost every screen element can be semi-transparent (Figure 17-38).

Figure 17-37
Adjusting color
settings in
Windows XP

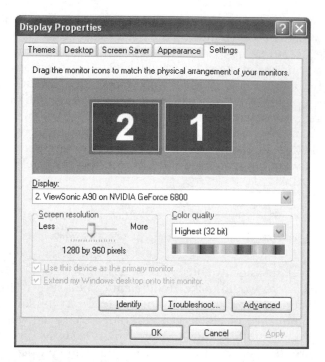

Figure 17-38   Semi-transparency in Windows Vista

Modes

Your video card and monitor are capable of showing Windows in a fixed number of different resolutions and color depths. The choices depend on the resolutions and color depths the video card can push to the monitor and the amount of bandwidth your monitor can support. Any single combination of resolution and color depth you set for you system is called a *mode*. For standardization, VESA defines a certain number of resolutions, all derived from the granddaddy of video modes: VGA.

VGA

With the introduction of the PS/2, IBM introduced the *video graphics array (VGA)* standard. This standard offered 16 colors at a resolution of 640 × 480 pixels. VGA supported such an amazing variety of colors by using an analog video signal instead of a digital one, as was the case prior to the VGA standard. A digital signal is either all on or all off. By using an analog signal, the VGA standard can provide 64 distinct levels for the three colors (RGB)—that is, 64^3 or 262,144 possible colors—although only 16 or 256 can be seen at a time. For most purposes, 640 × 480 and 16 colors defines VGA mode. This is typically the display resolution and color depth referred to on many software packages as a minimum display requirement. Every video card made in the last 15 years can output as VGA, but VGA-only cards are now obsolete.

Beyond VGA

The 1980s were a strange time for video. Until the very late 1980s, VGA was the highest mode defined by VESA, but demand grew for modes that went beyond VGA. This motivated VESA to introduce (over time) a number of new modes with names such as SVGA, XGA, and many others. Even today, new modes are being released! Table 17-1 shows the more common modes.

Video Mode	Resolution	Aspect Ratio	Typical Device
QVGA "Quarter" VGA	320 × 240	4:3	PDAs and small video players
WVGA	800 × 480	5:3	Car navigation systems and ultra mobile PCs
SVGA	800 × 600	4:3	Small monitors
XGA	1024 × 768	4:3	Monitors and portable projectors
WXGA	1280 × 800	16:10	Small widescreen laptops
HDTV 720p	1280 × 720	16:9	Lowest resolution that can be called HDTV
SXGA	1280 × 1024	5:4	Native resolution for many desktop LCD monitors
WSXGA	1440 × 900	16:10	Widescreen laptops

Table 17-1 Typical Display Modes

Video Mode	Resolution	Aspect Ratio	Typical Device
SXGA+	1400 × 1050	4:3	Laptop monitors and high-end projectors
WSXGA+	1680 × 1050	16:10	Large laptops and 20" widescreen monitors
UXGA	1600 × 1200	4:3	Larger CRT monitors
HDTV 1080p	1920 × 1080	16:9	Full HDTV resolution
WUXGA	1920 × 1200	16:10	Big 24" widescreen monitors
WQUXGA	2560 × 1600	16:10	Big 30" widescreen monitors; requires Dual-link DVI connector

Table 17-1 Typical Display Modes *(continued)*

Motherboard Connection

Using more color depth slows down video functions. Data moving from the video card to the display has to go through the video card's memory chips and the expansion bus, and this can happen only so quickly. The standard PCI slots used in almost all systems are limited to 32-bit transfers at roughly 33 MHz, yielding a maximum bandwidth of 132 MBps. This sounds like a lot until you start using higher resolutions, high color depths, and higher refresh rates.

For example, take a typical display at 800 × 600 with a fairly low refresh of 70 Hz. The 70 Hz means the display screen is being redrawn 70 times per second. If you use a low color depth of 256 colors, which is 8 bits ($2^8 = 256$), you can multiply all the values together to see how much data per second has to be sent to the display:

800 × 600 × 1 byte × 70 = 33.6 MBps

If you use the same example at 16 million (24-bit) colors, the figure jumps to 100.8 MBps. You might say, "Well, if PCI runs at 132 MBps, it can handle that!" That statement would be true if the PCI bus had nothing else to do but tend to the video card, but almost every system has more than one PCI device, each requiring part of that throughput. The PCI bus simply cannot handle the needs of many current systems.

AGP

Intel answered the desire for video bandwidth even higher than PCI with the *Accelerated Graphics Port (AGP)*. AGP is a single, special port, similar to a PCI slot, which is dedicated to video. You will never see a motherboard with two AGP slots. Figure 17-39 shows an early-generation AGP. AGP is derived from the 66-MHz, 32-bit PCI 2.1 specification. AGP uses a function called *strobing* that increases the signals two, four, and eight times for each clock cycle.

Figure 17-39
AGP

Simply describing AGP as a faster PCI would seriously misrepresent the power of AGP. AGP has several technological advantages over PCI, including the bus, internal operations, and the capability to handle 3-D texturing.

First, AGP currently resides alone on its own personal data bus, connected directly to the Northbridge (see Figure 17-40). This is very important because more advanced versions of AGP out perform every bus on the system except the frontside bus!

Figure 17-40
An AGP bus

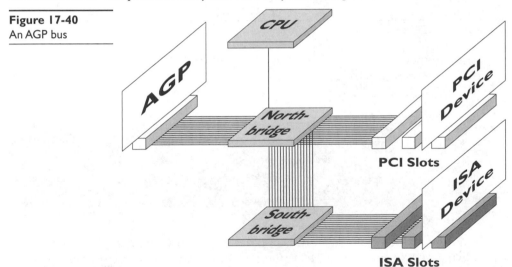

Second, AGP takes advantage of pipelining commands, similar to the way CPUs pipeline. Third, AGP has a feature called *sidebanding*—basically a second data bus that enables the video card to send more commands to the Northbridge while receiving other commands at the same time.

Video cards do all kinds of neat stuff with their RAM; for example, video cards store copies of individual windows so that they can display the windows at different points on the screen very quickly. Demanding applications can quickly max out the onboard

RAM on a video card, so AGP provides a pathway so that the AGP card may "steal" chunks of the regular system memory to store video information, especially textures. This is generically called a *system memory access* and is quite popular.

AGP has gone through three sets of specifications (AGP1.0, AGP2.0, and AGP3.0), but the official names tend to be ignored. Most techs and consumers refer to the various cards by their strobe multiplier, such as AGP 1×, 2×, 4×, and 8×. The only problem with blurring the distinctions between the specifications comes from the fact that many new motherboards simply don't support the older AGP cards because the older cards require a different physical connection than the new ones. Table 17-2 shows the AGP specifications.

	Bus Speed	Strobe	Width	Throughput	Side Band	Pipe	System Memory	Multiple Ports
AGP 1×	66 MHz	1×	32-bit	264 MBps	Yes	Yes	No	No
AGP 2×	66 MHz	2×	32-bit	528 MBps	Yes	Yes	Yes	No
AGP 4×	66 MHz	4×	32-bit*	1056 MBps	Yes	Yes	Yes	No
AGP 4×	66 MHz	4×	64-bit	2112 MBps	Yes	Yes	Yes	No
AGP 8×	66 MHz	8×	64-bit	4224 MBps	Yes	Yes	Yes	Yes

*AGP 4× can work at 64 bits, but many installations use only a 32-bit bus.

Table 17-2 AGP Types

Some motherboards support multiple types of AGP. Figure 17-41 shows an AGP slot that accommodates everything up to 8×, even the very rare AGP Pro cards. Note that the tab on the slot covers the extra pins required for AGP Pro.

Figure 17-41
AGP 8× slot

Because many AGP cards will run on older AGP motherboards, you can get away with mixing AGP specifications. To get the best, most stable performance possible, you should use an AGP card that's fully supported by the motherboard.

The only significant downside to AGP lies in the close connection tolerances required by the cards themselves. It's very common to snap in a new AGP card and power up just to get a no-video-card beep or a system that doesn't boot. Always take the time to ensure that an AGP card is snapped down securely and screwed in before starting the system.

PCIe

AGP is a great way to get video information to and from video cards very quickly, but it has the downside of being a unique connector in a world where saving money is important. AGP, being based on PCI, also uses a parallel interface. When the PCI Express (PCIe) interface was developed to replace PCI, the PCIe designers also worked hard to make sure it would replace AGP too. PCIe is a natural evolution for video as it is incredibly fast, using a serial communication method. Also, because PCIe is a true expansion bus designed to talk to the CPU and RAM, it also supports all the little extras found in AGP such as sidebanding and system memory access. All PCIe video cards use the PCIe ×16 connector (Figure 17-42).

Figure 17-42
PCIe video card connected in PCIe slot

Graphics Processor

The graphics processor handles the heavy lifting of taking commands from the CPU and translating them into coordinates and color information that the monitor understands and displays.

Video card discussion, at least among techs, almost always revolves around the graphics processor they use and the amount of RAM onboard. A typical video card might be called an ATI Radeon X1950 XTX 512 MB, so let's break that down. ATI is the manufacturer, Radeon X1950 XTX is the model of the card as well as the graphics processor, and 512 MB is the amount of video RAM.

Many companies make the hundreds of different video cards on the market, but only two companies produce the vast majority of graphics processors found on video cards: NVIDIA and ATI. NVIDIA and ATI make and sell graphics processors to third-party manufacturers who then design, build, and sell video cards under their own branding. ATI also makes and sells its own line of cards. Figure 17-43 shows an NVIDIA GeForce 7900 GT KO on a board made by EVGA.

Figure 17-43
NVIDIA GeForce
7900 GT KO

Your choice of graphics processor is your single most important decision in buying a video card. Low-end graphics processors will usually work fine for the run-of-the-mill user who wants to write letters or run a Web browser. High-end graphics processors are designed to support the beautiful 3-D games that are so popular today.

NVIDIA and ATI are extremely competitive, and both companies introduce multiple models of graphics processors (and therefore new models of cards) every year. However, unless you're using the Vista Aero glass desktop, all of these extra features you see in video cards are really only for the true driving force in video cards—3-D gaming. Your PC is capable of providing you with hours of incredible entertainment via a huge number of popular games that immerse you in 3-D environments full of light, shadows, explosions, and other amazing effects that create a fun and beautiful gaming experience.

These 3-D games have special needs to do all this amazing stuff. One need is textures. A *texture* is a small picture that is tiled over and over again on walls, floors, and other surfaces to create the 3-D world. Take a look at the wall in Figure 17-44. It's made up of only three textures that are repeated over and over again on the surface.

Figure 17-44
Wall of textures

Games also use hundreds of lighting effects such as transparency (water), shadows, reflection, and bump mapping—the process of laying multiple textures on the same spot to give a more textured (bumpy) look to the surface. These games are where the higher-quality graphics processors really shine. Learn more about 3-D issues in more depth in the "3-D Graphics" section later in the chapter.

Choosing a graphics processor is a challenge because the video industry is constantly coming out with new models. One of the best guides is price. The best (and newest) graphics cards usually cost around US$400–500. The cheapest cards cost around $50. I usually split the difference and go for a card priced around $180 to $200—such a card will have most of the features you want without breaking your bank account.

If you use your computer only for 2-D programs (most office applications such as word processors, e-mail, and Web browsers are 2-D), then almost all of the features of the more advanced graphics cards will do you little good. If you're not a gamer, cheap, low-end video cards will more than meet your needs.

Video Memory

Video memory is crucial to the operation of a PC. It is probably the hardest-working set of electronics on the PC. Video RAM constantly updates to reflect every change that takes place on the screen. Video memory can prove to be a serious bottleneck when working with heavy-duty applications (like games) in three ways: data throughput speed, access speed, and simple capacity.

Manufacturers have overcome these bottlenecks in three ways: upping the width of the bus between the video RAM and video processor; using specialized, super-fast RAM; and adding more and more total RAM.

First, manufacturers reorganized the video display memory on cards from the typical 32-bit-wide structure to 64, 128, or even 256 bits wide. This would not be of much benefit because the system bus is limited to 32 or 64 bits—if it weren't for the fact that video display cards are really coprocessor boards. Most of the graphics rendering and processing is handled on the card by the video processor chip rather than by the CPU. The main system simply provides the input data to the processor on the video card. By making the memory bus on the video card as much as eight times wider than the standard 32-bit pathway (256 bits), data can be manipulated and then sent to the monitor much more quickly (Figure 17-45).

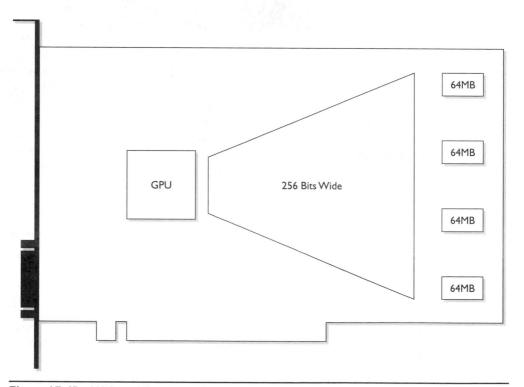

Figure 17-45   Wide path between video processor and video RAM

Specialized types of video RAM have been developed for graphics cards, and many offer substantial improvements in video speeds. The single most important feature that separates DRAM from video RAM is that video RAM can read and write data at the same time. Table 17-3 shows a list of common video memory technologies used yesterday and today—make sure you know these for the exams!

Acronym	Name	Purpose
VRAM	Video RAM	The original graphics RAM
WRAM	Window RAM	Designed to replace VRAM; never caught on
SGRAM	Synchronous Graphics RAM	A version of SDRAM with features to speed up access for graphics
DDR SDRAM	Double Data Rate Synchronous DRAM	Used on budget graphics cards and very common on laptop video cards
DDR2 SDRAM	Double Data Rate version 2, Synchronous DRAM	Popular on video cards until GDDR3; lower voltage than DDR memory
GDDR3 SDRAM	Graphics Double Data Rate, version 3	Similar to DDR2 but runs at faster speeds; different cooling requirements
GDDR4 SDRAM	Graphics Double Data Rate, version 4	Upgrade of GDDR3; faster clock

Table 17-3 Video RAM Technologies

Finally, many advanced 3-D video cards come with huge amounts of video RAM. It's very common to see cards with 64, 128, 256, or even 512 MB of RAM! Why so much? Even with PCI Express, accessing data in system RAM always takes a lot longer than accessing data stored in local RAM on the video card. The huge amount of video RAM enables game developers to optimize their games and store more essential data on the local video RAM.

Installing and Configuring Video

Once you've decided on the features and price for your new video card or monitor, you need to install them into your system. As long as you've got the right connection to your video card, installing a monitor is straightforward. The challenge comes when installing the video card.

During the physical installation of a video card, watch out for two possible issues: long cards and proximity of the nearest PCI card. Some high-end video cards simply won't fit in certain cases or block access to needed motherboard connectors such as the IDE sockets. There's no clean fix for such a problem—you simply have to change at least one of the components (video card, motherboard, or case). Because high-end video cards run very hot, you don't want them sitting right next to another card; make sure the fan on the video card has plenty of ventilation space. A good practice is to leave the slot next to the video card empty to allow better airflow (Figure 17-46).

Figure 17-46
Installing a
video card

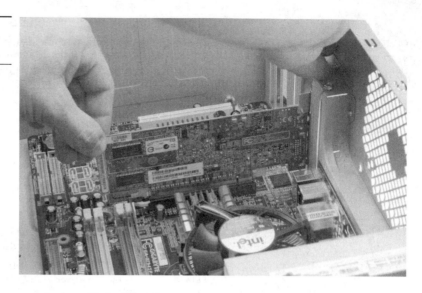

Once you've properly installed the video card and connected it to the monitor, you've conquered half the territory for making the video process work properly. You're ready to tackle the drivers and tweak the operating system, so let's go!

Software

Configuring your video software is usually a two-step process. First you need to load drivers for the video card. Then you need to open the Control Panel and go to the Display applet to make your adjustments. Let's explore how to make the video card and monitor work in Windows.

Drivers

Just like any other piece of hardware, your video card needs a driver to function. Video card drivers install pretty much the same way as all of the other drivers we've discussed thus far: either the driver is already built into Windows or you must use the installation CD that comes with the video card.

Video card makers are constantly updating their drivers. Odds are good that any video card more than a few months old will have at least one driver update. If possible, check the manufacturer's Web site and use the driver located there if there is one. If the Web site doesn't offer a driver, then it's usually best to use the installation CD. Always avoid using the built-in Windows driver as it tends to be the most dated.

We'll explore driver issues in more detail after we discuss the Display applet. Like so many things about video, you can't really fully understand one topic without understanding at least one other!

Using the Display Applet

With the driver installed, you're ready to configure your display settings. The Display applet on the Control Panel is your next stop. The Display applet provides a convenient, central location for all of your display settings, including resolution, refresh rate, driver information, and color depth.

The default Display applet window in Windows XP, called the Display Properties dialog box (Figure 17-47), has five tabs: Themes, Desktop, Screen Saver, Appearance, and Settings. Earlier versions of Windows have a subset of these tabs. The first four tabs have options that enable you to change the look and feel of Windows and set up a screen saver; the fifth tab is where you make adjustments that relate directly to your monitor and video card. Let's take a closer look at the tabs.

Figure 17-47
Display Properties
dialog box in
Windows XP

Making the Screen Pretty

Three tabs in the display applet have the job of adjusting the appearance of the screen: Themes, Desktop, and Appearance. Windows themes are preset configurations of the look and feel of the entire Windows environment. The Desktop Tab defines the background color or image. It also includes the handy Customize Desktop dialog box (Figure 17-48) that enables you to define the icons as well as any Web pages you want to appear on the Desktop.

Figure 17-48
Customize Desktop

The last of the tabs for the look and feel of the desktop is the Appearance Tab. Think of the Appearance tab as the way to fine-tune the theme to your liking. The main screen gives only a few options—the real power is when you click the Advanced button (Figure 17-49). Using this dialog box, you may adjust almost everything about the desktop including the types of fonts and colors of every part of a window.

Figure 17-49
Advanced
Appearance
dialog box

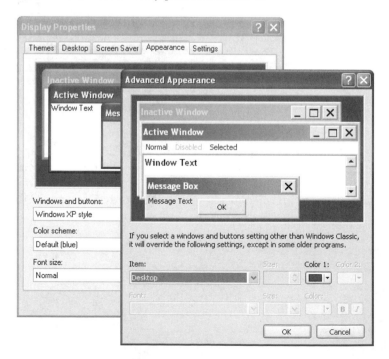

Screen Saver Tab

At first glance the Screen Saver tab seems to do nothing but set the Windows screen-saver—no big deal, just about everyone has set a screensaver. But there's another button on the screen saver tab that gets you to one of the most important settings of your system—power management. Click on the Power button to get to the Power Options Properties dialog box (Figure 17-50).

Figure 17-50
Power Options
Properties dialog box

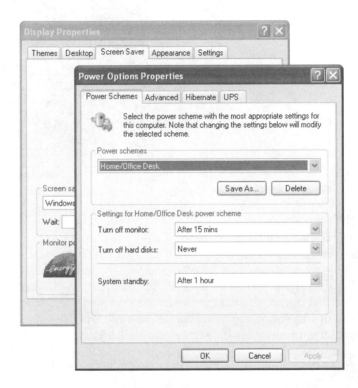

These tabs define all of the power management of the system. Power management is a fairly involved process, so we'll save the big discussion for where we need to save power the most—Chapter 19, "Portable Computing."

Settings Tab

The Settings Tab (Figure 17-51) is the centralized location for configuring all of your video settings. From the main screen, you can adjust both the resolution and the color depth. Windows will only display resolutions and color depths your video card/monitor combination can accept and that are suitable for most situations. Everyone has a favorite resolution, and higher isn't always better. Especially for those with trouble seeing small screen elements, higher resolutions can present a difficulty—already small icons are *much* smaller at 1,280 × 1024 than at 800 × 600. Try all of the resolutions to see which you like—just remember that LCD monitors look sharpest at their native resolution (usually the highest listed).

Figure 17-51
Settings tab

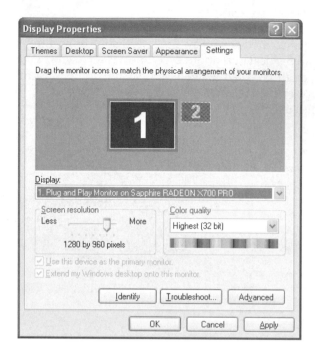

The color quality is the number of colors displayed on the screen. You can change the screen resolution with a simple slider, adjusting the color depth from 4-bit all the way up to 32-bit color. Unless you have an older video card or a significant video speed issue, you'll probably set your system for 32-bit color and never touch this setting again.

Another option you may see in the Settings tab is dual monitors. Windows supports the use of two (or more) monitors. These monitors may work together like two halves of one large monitor, or the second monitor might simply show a duplicate of what's happening on the first monitor. Dual monitors are very handy for those who need lots of screen space but don't want to buy a really large, expensive monitor (Figure 17-52).

Figure 17-52
My editor hard at work with dual monitors

There are two ways to set up dual monitors: plug in two video cards or use a single video card that supports two monitors (a "dual-head" video card). Both methods are quite common and work well. Dual monitors are easy to configure—just plug in the monitors and Windows should detect them. Windows will show both monitors in the Settings tab, as shown in Figure 17-53. By default, the second monitor is not enabled. To use the second monitor, just select the *Extend my Windows desktop onto this monitor* checkbox.

Figure 17-53
Enabling dual
monitors

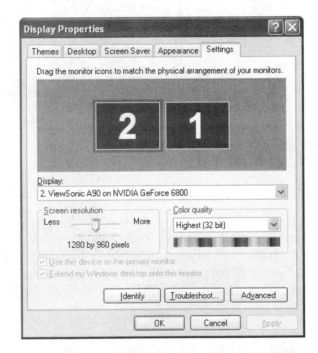

If you need to see more advanced settings, click on...that's right, the Advanced button (Figure 17-54). The title of this dialog box reflects the monitor and video card. As you can see in the screen shot, this particular monitor is a ViewSonic A90 running off an NVIDIA GeForce 6800 video card.

Figure 17-54
Advanced video
settings

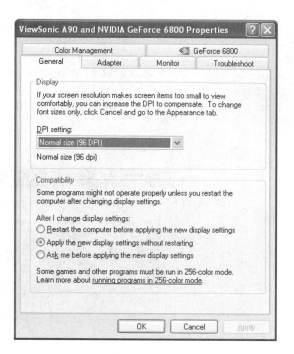

The two tabs you're most likely to use are the Adapter and Monitor tabs. The Adapter tab gives detailed information about the video card, including the amount of video memory, the graphics processor, and the BIOS information (yup, your video card has a BIOS, too!). You can also click on the *List all Modes* button to change the current mode of the video card, although there's no mode you may set here that you cannot set in the sliders on the main screen.

If you're still using a CRT, you'll find the Monitor tab a handy place. This is where you can set the refresh rate (Figure 17-55). Windows only shows refresh rates that the monitor says it can handle, but many monitors can take a faster—and therefore easier on the eyes—refresh rate. To see all the modes the video card can support, uncheck the *Hide modes that this monitor cannot display* option.

Figure 17-55
Monitor tab

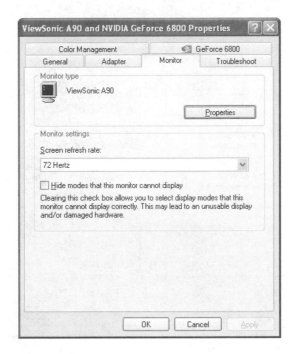

NOTE All LCD monitors have a fixed refresh rate.

If you try this, always increase the refresh rate in small increments. If the screen looks better, use it. If the screen seems distorted or disappears, wait a moment and Windows will reset back to the original refresh rate. Be careful when using modes that Windows says the monitor cannot display! Pushing a CRT past its fastest refresh rate for more than a minute or two can damage it!

Most video cards add their own tab to the Advanced dialog box like the one shown in Figure 17-56. This tab adjusts all of the specialized settings for that video card. What you see here varies by model of card and version of driver, but here's a list of some of the more interesting settings you might see.

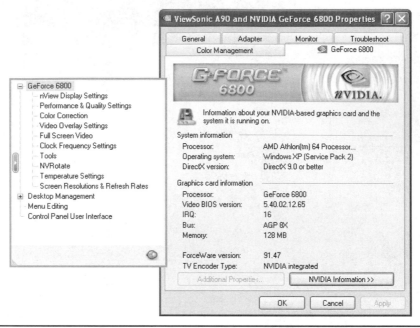

Figure 17-56 Third-party video tab

Color correction Sometimes the colors on your monitor are not close enough for your taste to the actual color you're trying to create. In this case, you can use color correction to fine-tune the colors on the screen to get the look you want.

Rotation All monitors are by default wider than they are tall. This is called landscape mode. Some LCD monitors can be physically rotated to facilitate users who like to see their desktops taller than they are wide (portrait mode). Figure 17-57 shows the author's LCDs rotated in portrait mode. If you wanted to rotate your screens, you must tell the system you're rotating them.

Figure 17-57
Portrait mode

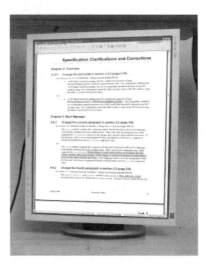

Modes   Most video cards add very advanced settings to enable you to finely tweak your monitor. These very dangerous settings have names such as "sync polarity" or "front porch" and are outside the scope of both CompTIA A+ and the needs of all but the most geeky techs. These settings are mostly used to display a non-standard resolution. Stay out of those settings!

Working with Drivers

Now that you know the locations of the primary video tools within the operating system, it's time to learn about fine-tuning your video. You need to know how to work with video drivers from within the Display applet, including how to update them, roll back updates, and uninstall them.

Windows is very persnickety when it comes to video card drivers. You can crash Windows and force a reinstall simply by installing a new video card and not uninstalling the old card's drivers. This doesn't happen every time, but certainly can happen. As a basic rule, always uninstall the old card's drivers before you install drivers for a new card.

When you update the drivers for a card, you have a choice of uninstalling the outdated drivers and then installing new drivers—which makes the process the same as for installing a new card—or if you're running Windows XP, you can let it flex some digital muscle and install the new ones right over the older drivers.

Updating

To update your drivers, go to the Control Panel and double-click the Display applet. In the Display Properties dialog box, select the Settings tab and click the Advanced button. In the Advanced button dialog box, click the Adapter tab and then click the Properties button. In the Properties dialog box for your adapter (Figure 17-58), select the Driver tab and then click the Update Driver button to run the Hardware Update wizard.

Figure 17-58
Adapter Properties
dialog box

IT Technician

3-D Graphics

No other area of the PC world reflects the amazing acceleration of technological improvements more than 3-D video—in particular, 3-D gaming. We are spectators to an amazing new world where software and hardware race to produce new levels of realism and complexity displayed on the computer screen. Powered by the wallets of tens of millions of PC gamers always demanding more and better, the video industry constantly introduces new video cards and new software titles that make today's games so incredibly realistic and fun. Although the gaming world certainly leads the PC industry in 3-D technologies, many other PC applications such as *Computer Aided Design (CAD)* programs quickly snatch up these technologies, making 3-D more useful in many ways other than just games. In this section, we'll add to the many bits and pieces of 3-D video encountered over previous chapters in the book and put together an understanding of the function and configuration of 3-D graphics.

Before the early 1990s, PCs did not mix well with 3-D graphics. Certainly, many 3-D applications existed, primarily 3-D design programs such as AutoCAD and Intergraph, but these applications used proprietary methods to generate 3-D graphics and often required the users to purchase complete systems as opposed to simply dropping an install disk into their desktop system. Even though these systems worked extremely well, their high cost and steep learning curves kept them hidden inside organizations such as design firms and government entities that needed them. UNIX systems enjoyed 3-D graphics very early on, but even the most powerful UNIX workstations of the early 1980s relegated almost all 3-D functions to CAD applications.

The big change took place in 1992 when a small company called id Software created a new game called Wolfenstein 3D that launched an entirely new genre of games, now called *first-person shooters (FPSs)* (see Figure 17-59). In these games, the player looks out into a 3-D world, interacting with walls, doors, and items, and shoots whatever bad guys the game provides.

Figure 17-59
Wolfenstein 3D

Wolfenstein 3D shook the PC gaming world to its foundations. An upstart little company suddenly appears with this new format, making Wolfenstein 3D and id Software overnight sensations. id Software knew that their 3-D game required substantial RAM and CPU strength for the time. They gambled that enough systems existed to handle the massive calculations required to keep track of the position of objects, keyboard inputs, and most importantly, the incredibly complex process of placing the 3-D world on the screen. The gamble paid off, making John Carmack and John Romero, the creators of id Software, the fathers of 3-D gaming.

Early 3-D games used fixed 3-D images called *sprites* to create the 3-D world. A sprite is nothing more than a bitmapped graphic like a BMP file. These early first-person shooters would calculate the position of an object from the player's perspective and place a sprite to represent the object. Any single object would only have a fixed number of sprites—if you walked around an object, you noticed an obvious jerk as the game replaced the current sprite with a new one to represent the new position. Figure 17-60 shows different sprites for the same bad guy in Wolfenstein 3D. Sprites weren't pretty, but they worked without seriously taxing the 486s and early Pentiums of the time.

Figure 17-60
Each figure has a limited number of sprites.

The second generation of 3-D began to replace sprites with true 3-D objects, which are drastically more complex than a sprite. A true 3-D object is composed of a group of points called *vertices*. Each vertex has a defined X, Y, and Z position in a 3-D world. Figure 17-61 shows the vertices for an airplane in a 3-D world.

Figure 17-61
Vertices for a 3-D airplane

The computer must track all the vertices of all the objects in the 3-D world, including the ones you cannot currently see. Keep in mind that objects may be motionless in the 3-D world (like a wall), may have animation (like a door opening and closing), or may be moving (like bad monsters trying to spray you with evil alien goo). This calculation process is called *transformation* and, as you might imagine, is extremely taxing to most CPUs. Intel's SIMD and AMD's 3DNow! processor extensions were expressly designed to perform transformations.

Once the CPU has determined the positions of all vertices, the system then begins to fill in the 3-D object. The process begins by drawing lines (the 3-D term is *edges*) between vertices to build the 3-D object into many triangles. Why triangles? Well, mainly by consensus of game developers. Any shape works, but triangles make the most sense from a mathematical standpoint. I could go into more depth here, but that would require talking about trigonometry, and I'm gambling you'd rather not read that detailed of a description! All 3-D games use triangles to connect vertices. The 3-D process then groups triangles together into various shapes called *polygons*. Figure 17-62 shows the same model from Figure 17-61, now displaying all the connected vertices to create a large number of polygons.

Figure 17-62
Connected vertices
forming polygons
on a 3-D airplane

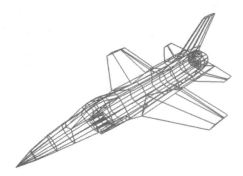

Originally, the CPU handled these calculations to create triangles, but now special 3-D video cards do the job, greatly speeding up the process.

The last step in second-generation games was texturing. Every 3-D game stores a number of bitmaps called *textures*. The program wraps textures around the object to give it a surface. Textures work well as they provide dramatic detail without the need to use a lot of triangles. A single object may take one texture or many textures applied to single triangles or groups of triangles (polygons). Figure 17-63 shows the finished airplane.

Figure 17-63
3-D airplane with
textures added

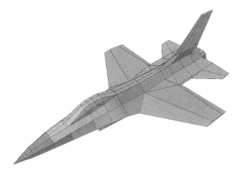

These second-generation games made a much more realistic environment, but the heavy demands of true 3-D often forced game designers to use both 3-D and sprites in the same game. Figure 17-64 shows the famous game Doom. Note that the walls, floors, doors, and such were 3-D images, whereas the bad guys continued to manifest as sprites. Notice how pixilated the bad guy looks compared to the rest of the scene.

Figure 17-64
A mix of 3-D objects
and sprites

Figure 17-64
A mix of 3-D objects
and sprites

True 3-D, more often referred to as *rendered* objects, immediately created the need for massively powerful video cards and much wider data buses. Intel's primary motivation for creating AGP was to provide a big enough pipe for massive data pumping between the video card and the CPU. Intel gave AGP the ability to read system RAM to support textures. If it weren't for 3-D games, AGP would almost certainly not exist.

3-D Video Cards

No CPU of the mid-1990s could ever hope to handle the massive processes required to render 3-D worlds. Keep in mind that in order to create realistic movement, the 3-D world must refresh at least 24 times per second. That means that this entire process, from transformation to texturing, must repeat once every 1/24th of a second! Furthermore, while the game re-creates each screen, it must also keep score, track the position of all the objects in the game, provide some type of intelligence to the bad guys, and so on. Something had to happen to take the workload off the CPU. The answer came from video cards.

Video cards were developed with smart onboard *graphical processing units (GPUs)*. The GPU helped the CPU by taking over some, and eventually all, the 3-D rendering duties. These video cards not only have GPUs but also have massive amounts of RAM to store textures.

But a problem exists with this setup: How do we talk to these cards? This is done by means of a device driver, of course, but wouldn't it be great if we could create standard commands to speed up the process? The best thing to do would be to create a standardized set of instructions that any 3-D program could send to a video card to do all the basic work, such as "make a cone" or "lay texture 237 on the cone you just made."

The video card instructions standards manifested themselves into a series of *application programming interfaces (APIs)*. In essence, an API is a library of commands that people who make 3-D games must use in their programs. The program currently using the video card sends API commands directly to the device driver. Device drivers must know how to understand the API commands. If you were to picture the graphics system of your computer as a layer cake, the top layer would be the program making a call to the video card driver that then directs the graphics hardware.

Several different APIs have been developed over the years with two clear winners among all of them: OpenGL and DirectX. The OpenGL standard was developed for UNIX systems, but has since been *ported*, or made compatible with, a wide variety of computer systems, including Windows and Apple computers. As the demand for 3-D video became increasingly strong, Microsoft decided to throw its hat into the 3-D graphics ring with its own API, called DirectX. We look at DirectX in-depth in the next section.

Although they might accomplish the same task (for instance, translating instructions and passing them on to the video driver), every API handles things just a little bit differently. In some 3-D games, the OpenGL standard might produce more precise images with less CPU overhead than the DirectX standard. In general, however, you won't notice a large difference between the images produced using OpenGL and DirectX.

DirectX and Video Cards

In the old days, many applications communicated directly with much of the PC hardware and, as a result, could crash your computer if not written well enough. Microsoft tried to fix this problem by placing all hardware under the control of Windows, but programmers balked because Windows added too much work for the video process and slowed down everything. For the most demanding programs, such as games, only direct access of hardware would work.

This need to "get around Windows" motivated Microsoft to unveil a new set of protocols called *DirectX*. Programmers use DirectX to take control of certain pieces of hardware and to talk directly to that hardware; it provides the speed necessary to play the advanced games so popular today. The primary impetus for DirectX was to build a series of products to enable Windows to run 3-D games. That's not to say that you couldn't run 3-D games in Windows *before* DirectX; rather, it's just that Microsoft wasn't involved in the API rat race at the time and wanted to be. Microsoft's goal in developing DirectX was to create a 100-percent stable environment, with direct hardware access, for running 3-D applications and games within Windows.

DirectX is not only for video; it also supports sound, network connections, input devices, and other parts of your PC. Each of these subsets of DirectX has a name like DirectDraw, Direct3D, or DirectSound.

- **DirectDraw** Supports direct access to the hardware for 2-D graphics.
- **Direct3D** Supports direct access to the hardware for 3-D graphics—the most important part of DirectX.
- **DirectInput** Supports direct access to the hardware for joysticks and other game controllers.
- **DirectSound** Supports direct access to the hardware for waveforms.

- **DirectMusic**   Supports direct access to the hardware for MIDI devices.
- **DirectPlay**   Supports direct access to network devices for multiplayer games.
- **DirectShow**   Supports direct access to video and presentation devices.

Microsoft constantly adds and tweaks this list. As almost all games need DirectX and all video cards have drivers to support DirectX, you need to verify that DirectX is installed and working properly on your system. To do this, use the DirectX diagnostic tool in the System Information program. After you open System Information (it usually lives in the Accessories | System Tools area of the Start menu), click the Tools menu and select DirectX Diagnostic Tool (see Figure 17-65).

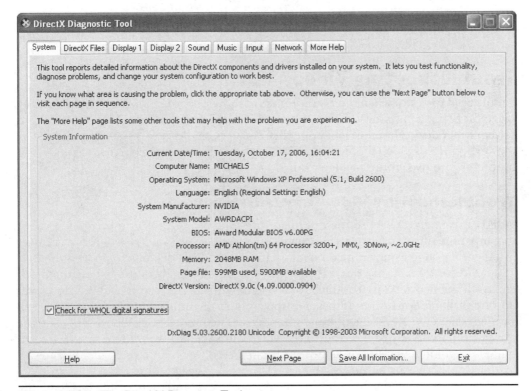

Figure 17-65   The DirectX Diagnostic Tool

The System tab gives the version of DirectX. The system pictured in Figure 17-65 runs DirectX 9.0c. You may then test the separate DirectX functions by running through the other tabs and running the tests.

So, what does DirectX do for video cards? Back in the bad old days before DirectX became popular with the game makers, many GPU makers created their own chip-specific APIs. 3dfx had Glide, for example, and S3 had ViRGE. This made buying 3-D games a mess. There would often be multiple versions of the same game for each card. Even worse, many games never used 3-D acceleration because it was just too much work to support all the different cards.

That all changed when Microsoft beefed up DirectX and got more GPU makers to support it. That in turn enabled the game companies to write games using DirectX and have it run on any card out there. The bottom line: When Microsoft comes out with a new version of DirectX, all the GPU companies hurry to support it or they will be left behind.

Trying to decide what video card to buy gives me the shakes—too many options! One good way to narrow down your buying decision is to see what GPU is hot at the moment. I make a point to check out these Web sites whenever I'm getting ready to buy in order to see what everyone says is the best.

- www.arstechnica.com
- www.hardocp.com
- www.tomshardware.com
- www.sharkyextreme.com

Troubleshooting Video

People tend to notice when their monitors stop showing the Windows desktop, making video problems a big issue for technicians. A user might temporarily ignore a bad sound card or other device, but they will holler like crazy when the screen doesn't look the way they expect. To fix video problems quickly, the best place to start is to divide your video problems into two groups—video cards/drivers and monitors.

Troubleshooting Video Cards/Drivers

Video cards rarely go bad, so the vast majority of video card/driver problems are bad or incompatible drivers or incorrect settings. Always make sure you have the correct driver installed. If you're using an incompatible driver, Windows defaults to good old 640 × 480, 16-color VGA. A driver that is suddenly corrupted usually doesn't show the problem until the next reboot. If you reboot a system with a corrupted driver, Windows will do one of the following: go into VGA mode, blank the monitor, lock up, or display a garbled screen. Whatever the output, reboot into Safe mode and roll back or delete the driver. Keep in mind that more advanced video cards tend to show their driver as an installed program under Add or Remove Programs, so always check there first before you try deleting a driver using Device Manager. Download the latest driver and reinstall.

Video cards are pretty durable but they do have two components that do go bad: the fan and the RAM. Lucky for you, if either of these go out, they tend to show the same error—bizarre screen outputs followed shortly by a screen lockup. Usually, Windows keeps running; you may see your mouse pointer moving around and windows refreshing, but the screen turns into a huge mess (Figure 17-66).

Figure 17-66 Serious video problem

Bad drivers sometimes also make this error, so always first try going into Safe mode to see if the problem suddenly clears up. If it does, you do not have a problem with the video card!

The last and probably the most common problem is nothing more than improperly configured video settings. Identifying the problem is just common sense—if your monitor is showing everything sideways, someone messed with your rotation settings; if your gorgeous wallpaper of a mountain pass looks like an ugly four-color cartoon, someone lowered the color depth. Go into your Display Properties and reset them to a setting that works! The one serious configuration issue is pushing the resolution too high. If you adjust your resolution and then your monitor displays an error message such as "sync out of range" (Figure 17-67), then you need to set your resolution back to something that works for your video card/monitor combination!

Figure 17-67
Pushing a monitor
too hard

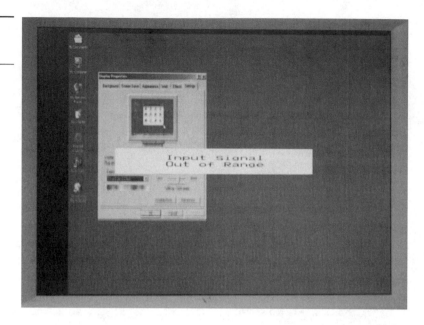

Troubleshooting Monitors

Because of the inherent dangers of the high-frequency and high-voltage power required by monitors, and because proper adjustment requires specialized training, this section concentrates on giving a support person the information necessary to decide whether a trouble call is warranted. Virtually no monitor manufacturers make schematics of their monitors available to the public because of liability issues regarding possible electrocution. To simplify troubleshooting, look at the process as three separate parts: common monitor problems, external adjustments, and internal adjustments.

Common Monitor Problems

Although I'm not super comfortable diving into the guts of a monitor, you can fix a substantial percentage of monitor problems yourself. The following list describes the most common monitor problems and tells you what to do—even when that means sending it to someone else.

- Almost all CRT and LCD monitors have replaceable controls. If the Brightness knob or Degauss button stops working or seems loose, check with the manufacturer for replacement controls. They usually come as a complete package.

- For problems with ghosting, streaking, and/or fuzzy vertical edges, check the cable connections and the cable itself. These problems rarely apply to monitors; more commonly, they point to the video card.

- If one color is missing, check cables for breaks or bent pins. Check the front controls for that color. If the color adjustment is already maxed out, the monitor will require internal service.

- As monitors age, they lose brightness. If the brightness control is turned all the way up and the picture seems dim, the monitor will require internal adjustment. This is a good argument for power-management functions. Use the power-management options in Windows to turn off the monitor after a certain amount of time or use the power switch.

Common Problems Specific to CRTs

The complexity of CRTs compared to LCDs requires us to look at a number of monitor problems unique to CRTs. Most of these problems require opening the monitor, so be careful! When in doubt, take it to a repair shop.

- Most out-of-focus monitors can be fixed. Focus adjustments are usually on the inside somewhere close to the flyback transformer. This is the transformer that provides power to the high-voltage anode.

- Hissing or sparking sounds are often indicative of an insulation rupture on the flyback transformer. This sound is usually accompanied by the smell of ozone. If your monitor has these symptoms, it definitely needs a qualified technician. Having replaced a flyback transformer once myself, I can say it is not worth the hassle and potential loss of life and limb.

- Big color blotches on the display are an easy and cheap repair. Find the Degauss button and use it. If your monitor doesn't have a Degauss button, you can purchase a special tool called a degaussing coil at any electronics store.

- Bird-like chirping sounds occurring at regular intervals usually indicate a problem with the monitor power supply.

- Suppose you got a good deal on a used 17-inch monitor, but the display is kind of dark, even though you have the brightness turned up all the way. This points to a dying CRT. So, how about replacing the CRT? Forget it. Even if the monitor was free, it just isn't worth it; a replacement tube runs into the hundreds of dollars. Nobody ever sold a monitor because it was too bright and too sharp. Save your money and buy a new monitor.

- The monitor displaying only a single horizontal or vertical line is probably a problem between the main circuit board and the yoke, or a blown yoke coil. This definitely requires a service call.

- A single white dot on an otherwise black screen means the high-voltage flyback transformer is most likely shot. Take it into the repair shop.

External Adjustments

Monitor adjustments range from the simplest—brightness and contrast—to the more sophisticated—pincushioning and trapezoidal adjustments. The external controls provide users with the opportunity to fine-tune the monitor's image. Many monitors have controls for changing the tint and saturation of color, although plenty of monitors put those controls inside the monitor. Better monitors enable you to square up the visible portion of the screen with the monitor housing.

Finally, most monitors have the ability to degauss themselves with the push of a button. Over time, the shadow mask picks up a weak magnetic charge that interferes with the focus of the electron beams. This magnetic field makes the image look slightly fuzzy and streaked. Most monitors have a special built-in circuit called a *degaussing coil* to eliminate this magnetic buildup. When the degaussing circuit is used, an alternating current is sent through a coil of wire surrounding the CRT, and this current generates an alternating magnetic field that demagnetizes the shadow mask. The degaussing coil is activated using the Degauss button or menu selection on the monitor. Degaussing usually makes a rather nasty thunk sound and the screen goes crazy for a moment—don't worry, that's normal. Whenever a user calls me with a fuzzy monitor problem, I always have them degauss first.

Troubleshooting CRTs

As shipped, most monitors do not produce an image out to the limits of the screen because of poor convergence at the outer display edges. Convergence defines how closely the three colors can meet at a single point on the display. At the point of convergence, the three colors will combine to form a single white dot. With misconvergence, a noticeable halo of one or more colors will appear around the outside of the white point. The farther away the colors are from the center of the screen, the more likely the chance for misconvergence. Low-end monitors are especially susceptible to this problem. Even though adjusting the convergence of a monitor is not difficult, it does require getting inside the monitor case and having a copy of the schematic, which shows the location of the variable resistors. For this reason, it is a good idea to leave this adjustment to a trained specialist.

I don't like opening a CRT monitor. I avoid doing this for two reasons: (1) I know very little about electronic circuits and (2) I once almost electrocuted myself. At any rate, the A+ exams expect you to have a passing understanding of adjustments you might need to perform inside a monitor. Before we go any further, let me remind you about a little issue with CRT monitors (see Figure 17-68).

Figure 17-68
Hey! That's 25,000 volts! Be careful!

This product includes critical mechanical and electrical parts which are essential for x-radiation safety. For continued safety replace critical components indicated in the service manual only with exact replacement parts given in the parts list. Operating high voltage for this product is 25kV at minimum brightness. Refer to service manual for measurement procedures and proper service adjustments.

265V ~

The CRT monitor contains a wire called a *high-voltage anode* covered with a suction cup. If you lift that suction cup, you will almost certainly get seriously electrocuted. The anode wire leads to the flyback transformer and produces up to 25,000 volts. Don't worry about what they do; just worry about what they can do to *you!* That charge is stored in a capacitor, which will hold that charge even if the monitor is turned off. It will hold the charge even if the monitor is unplugged. That capacitor (depending on the system) can hold a charge for days, weeks, months, or even years. Knowing this, you should learn how to discharge a CRT.

Discharging a CRT   There are 75,000 opinions on how to discharge a CRT properly. Although my procedure may not follow the steps outlined in someone's official handbook or electrical code, I know this works. Read the rules, and then look at Figure 17-69.

High-voltage anode

Figure 17-69   Discharging a CRT

1. Make sure everything is unplugged.

2. If possible, let the monitor sit for a couple of hours. Most good monitors will discharge themselves in two to three hours, and many new monitors discharge in just a few moments.

3. Get a heavy, well-insulated, flat-bladed screwdriver.

4. Get a heavy gauge wire with alligator clips on each end.

5. Do not let yourself be grounded in any way. Wear rubber-soled shoes, and no rings or watches.

6. Wear safety goggles to protect yourself in the very rare case that the CRT implodes.

7. Remove the monitor's case. Remember where the screw went in.

8. Attach one alligator clip to an unpainted part of the metal frame of the monitor.

9. Clip the other end to the metal shaft of the screwdriver.

10. Slide the screwdriver blade under the suction cup. Make triple-sure that neither you nor the screwdriver is in any incidental contact with anything metal.

11. Slide the blade under until you hear a loud pop—you'll also see a nice blue flash.

12. If anyone is in the building, they will hear the pop and come running. Tell them everything's okay.

13. Wait about 15 minutes and repeat.

The main controls that require you to remove the monitor case to make adjustments include those for convergence, gain for each of the color guns, and sometimes the focus control. A technician with either informal or formal training in component-level repair can usually figure out which controls do what. In some cases, you can also readily spot and repair bad solder connections inside the monitor case, and thus fix a dead or dying CRT. Still, balance the cost of repairing the monitor against the cost of death or serious injury— is it worth it? Finally, before making adjustments to the display image, especially with the internal controls, give the monitor at least 15 to 30 minutes of warm-up time. This is necessary for both the components on the printed circuit boards and for the CRT itself.

Troubleshooting LCDs

- If your LCD monitor cracks, it is not repairable and must be replaced.
- If the LCD goes dark but you can still barely see the image under bright lights, you lost either the lamp or the inverter.
- If your LCD makes a distinct hissing noise, an inverter is about to fail.
- You can find companies that sell replacement parts for LCDs, but repairing an LCD is difficult, and there are folks who will do it for you faster and cheaper than you can. Search for a specialty LCD repair company. Hundreds of these companies exist all over the world.
- An LCD monitor may have bad pixels. A bad pixel is any single pixel that does not react the way it should. A pixel that never lights up is a dead pixel. A pixel that is stuck on pure white is a lit pixel, and a pixel on a certain color is a stuck pixel. You cannot repair bad pixels; the panel must be replaced. All LCD panel makers allow a certain number of bad pixels, even on a brand-new LCD monitor! You need to check the warranty for your monitor and see how many they allow before you may return the monitor.

Cleaning Monitors

Cleaning monitors is easy. Always use antistatic monitor wipes or at least a general antistatic cloth. Some LCD monitors may require special cleaning equipment. Never use window cleaners or any liquid because the danger of liquid getting into the monitor may create a shocking experience! Many commercial cleaning solutions will also melt older LCD screens, which is never a good thing.

Beyond A+

Video and CMOS

I'm always impressed by the number of video options provided in CMOS, especially in some of the more advanced CMOS options. I'm equally impressed by the amount of disinformation provided on these settings. In this section, I'll touch on some of the most common CMOS settings that deal with video. You may notice that no power-management video options have been included.

Video

Every standard CMOS setup shows an option for video support. The default setting is invariably EGA/VGA. Many years ago, this setting told the BIOS what type of card was installed on the system, enabling it to know how to talk to that card. Today, this setting has no meaning. No matter what you put there, it will be ignored and the system will boot normally.

Init Display First

This CMOS setting usually resides in an advanced options or BIOS options screen. In multi-monitor systems, Init Display First enables you to decide between PCIe and PCI as to which monitor initializes at boot. This will also determine the initial primary monitor for Windows.

Assign IRQ for VGA

Many video cards do not need an *interrupt request (IRQ)*. This option gives you the ability to choose whether your video card gets an IRQ. In general, lower-end cards that do not provide input to the system do not need an IRQ. Most advanced cards will need one; try it both ways. If you need it, your system will freeze up without an IRQ assigned. If you don't need it, you get an extra IRQ.

VGA Palette Snoop

True-VGA devices only show 16 out of a possible 262,000 colors at a time. The 16 current colors are called the *palette*. VGA Palette Snoop opens a video card's palette to other devices that may need to read or temporarily change the palette. I am unaware of any device made today that still needs this option.

Video Shadowing Enabled

As mentioned in previous chapters, this setting enables you to shadow the Video ROM. In most cases, this option is ignored as today's video cards perform their own automatic shadowing. A few cards require this setting to be off, so I generally leave it off now after years of leaving it on.

TV and PCs

It wasn't that long ago that your television and your PC were two totally different devices, but those days are quickly changing. For years, all television signals (at least in the U.S.) used the NTSC standard of 480 interlaced lines and a refresh rate of 59.94 hertz. In the last few years, the high-definition television standards of 480 non-interlaced (480p), 720p, 1080i, and 1080p are bringing the technologies that made PC monitors so attractive into the realm of television sets. Let's talk about some of the new technologies and how you might see them on your PC ... err ... I mean television.

Tuner Cards

Okay, tuner cards aren't that new, but man are they now getting popular! A *tuner card* is simply a card that accepts television input signals from your cable television box or an antenna. Tuner cards come in regular TV versions (NTSC tuners) and now high-definition versions called ATSC tuners. All of these cards come with the necessary drivers and software so that you can watch television on your PC (Figure 17-70).

Figure 17-70
Tuner card

Have you ever used the popular TiVo brand *personal video recorder (PVR)*? TiVos are amazing! You plug them in between your cable box and your television and then connect the TiVo to a phone line or network connection (Figure 17-71). They enable you to pause live television and record television shows to a built-in hard drive. TiVo is proprietary and you have to pay the TiVo people an ongoing fee to use it.

Figure 17-71
TiVo (© TiVo Inc. All
Rights Reserved.)

TiVo is so popular that now others have copied the idea. You can turn your PC into a PVR using nothing but a tuner card, an Internet connection, and the right software. Companies such as SnapStream (www.snapstream.com) produce programs like Beyond TV that give you all the power of PVR for a very small, one-time price for the software. If you like free (and hard to configure), you might want to consider the Linux-based MythTV (www.mythtv.org). Even Microsoft has jumped into the PVR game with its Microsoft Windows XP Media Center edition.

Even if you don't want to turn your PC into a TV, you'll find a number of television technologies that have some overlap into the PC world. Let's look at those technologies and see how they fit into PCs.

HDMI

The newest video connector available today is the *High-Definition Multimedia Interface (HDMI)*. HDMI was developed to replace DVI for televisions by combining both video and sound connections in a single cable (Figure 17-72). HDMI also includes a feature called DDC. DDC is similar to your PC's plug-and-play feature. Imagine plugging a DVD player into your TV using an HDMI cable. When this happens, the two devices talk to each other and the TV tells the DVD player exactly what resolutions it will support, making a perfect setup with no user intervention.

Figure 17-72
HDMI

HDMI supports *High-Bandwidth Digital Content Protection (HDCP)*, an anti-copy feature (also called *digital rights management*) designed to prevent unauthorized use of copyrighted material (mainly High Definition DVDs). If you attempt to play an HD DVD without HDCP, you will only get to watch that content in 480p, much lower than the 1080p native resolution of HD DVD.

HDCP is controversial but it is here, even in PCs. You don't need an HDMI cable to support HDCP. Operating system programmers are working furiously to provide some way to support HDCP. If you decide you want to play an HD DVD movie on your Windows Vista systems, go right ahead, as HDCP support is built in!

Plasma

Plasma display panels (PDP) are a very popular technology for displaying movies. Unfortunately, plasma TVs have two issues that make them a bad choice for PC use. First, they have strange native resolutions (such as 1366 × 768) that are hard to get your video card to accept. Second is *burn-in*—the tendency for a screen to "ghost" an image even after the image is off the screen. Plasma TV makers have virtually eliminated burn-in, but even the latest plasma displays are subject to burn-in when used with PC displays.

DLP

The final projector technology to discuss is *Digital Light Processing (DLP)*. DLP is a relatively new technology that uses a chip covered in microscopically small mirrors (Figure 17-73).

Figure 17-73
DLP chip (photo courtesy of Texas Instruments)

These individual mirrors move thousands of times per second toward and away from a light source. The more times per second they move toward a light source, the whiter the image; the fewer times they move, the grayer the image. See Figure 17-74 for a diagram of how the mirrors would appear in a microscopic close-up of the chip.

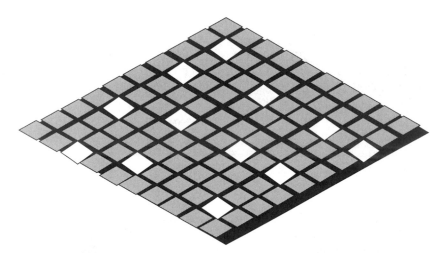

Figure 17-74   Microscopic close-up of DLP showing tiny mirrors—note some are tilted

Figure 17-75 shows a diagram of a typical DLP system. The lamp projects through a color wheel onto the DLP chip. The DLP chip creates the image by moving the tiny mirrors, which in turn reflect onto the screen.

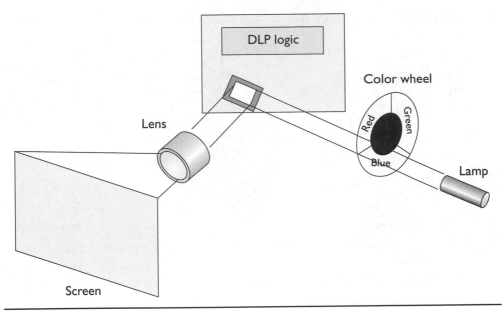

Figure 17-75   DLP in action

DLP is very popular in home theater systems, as it makes an amazingly rich image. DLP has had very little impact on PC monitors, but has had great success as projectors. DLP projectors are much more expensive than LCD projectors, but many customers feel the extra expense is worth the image quality.

Chapter Review Questions

1. What term refers to the amount of time it takes to draw an entire screen and get the electron guns back to the upper-left corner?

   A. Horizontal refresh rate

   B. Horizontal redraw rate

   C. Vertical refresh rate

   D. Vertical redraw rate

2. What does the dot pitch signify about a CRT monitor?

   A. The resolution, such as 1024 × 768

   B. The sharpness of the picture, such as 0.31 or 0.18

   C. The maximum refresh rate, such as 100 Hz

   D. The minimum refresh rate, such as 60 Hz

3. On an LCD monitor, what is the technology that uses a matrix of wires under colored glass?

   A. Active matrix

   B. Passive matrix

   C. Active TFT

   D. Passive TFT

4. What provides the illumination for LCD monitors?

   A. Backlights

   B. Inverter

   C. Lamp

   D. LCD panel

5. Which statement best describes the difference, if any, between CRT and LCD resolution?

   A. The CRT has a single native resolution; LCDs have no native resolution.

   B. The CRT has three native resolutions; LCDs have no native resolution.

   C. The CRT has no native resolution; LCDs have three native resolutions.

   D. The CRT has no native resolution; LCDs have a single native resolution.

6. Which typically uses more wattage?

   A. CRT

   B. DVI

   C. LCD

   D. VGA

7. What is WSXGA+ resolution?

   A. 1024 × 768

   B. 1280 × 1024

   C. 1680 × 1050

   D. 1920 × 1080

8. What is the processor on a video card called?

   A. CPU

   B. GPU

   C. GDDR

   D. MPU

9. What Microsoft API supports 3-D graphics?

   A. Active Desktop

   B. DirectX

   C. Glide

   D. OpenGL

10. How would you adjust your screen settings?

   A. Go to Start | Run and type DISPLAY to open the Display applet.

   B. Go to Start | Run and type MSCONFIG to open the Display applet.

   C. Go to Start | Control Panel and double-click the Display applet icon.

   D. Go to Start | All Programs and select the Display applet icon.

Answers

1. **C.** The vertical refresh rate is the amount of time it takes to draw the entire screen and get the electron guns back to the upper-left corner.

2. **B.** The dot pitch, measured in millimeters, tells you how fine the screen will be.

3. **B.** Passive matrix technology uses a matrix of wires under colored glass.

4. **A.** The backlights provide the illumination for the LCD panel.

5. **D.** The CRT has no native resolution; LCDs have a single native resolution.

6. **A.** CRTs use a lot more wattage than LCDs.

7. **C.** WSXGA+ resolution is 1680 × 1050.

8. **B.** You'll typically see video card processors referred to as GPUs.

9. **B.** Microsoft makes the DirectX API to support 3-D programs.

10. **C.** The Display applet is part of the Control Panel.

Sound

In this chapter, you will learn how to
- Describe how sound works in a PC
- Select the appropriate sound card for a given scenario
- Install a sound card in a Windows system
- Troubleshoot problems that might arise with sound cards and speakers

Racing down the virtual track, pixels flying across the screen, hearing the engine roar as you take another turn and press down the accelerator—or surfing the Web for lovely scenic nature photos with the sweet, mellifluous sounds of Mozart filling the room—sound has become an integral component of the computing experience. Setting up and optimizing sound for the PC has become an integral skill for all computer techs.

Correctly setting up sound for a PC requires that you know about quite a few things, because the sound process has many components. You need a properly installed sound card with the correct drivers loaded, reasonably high-quality speakers, support software such as the API for a particular game correctly configured in Windows, and a properly set up application that can use the features of the sound card. And every great tech needs to know troubleshooting to handle both routine and uncommon problems with sound.

Historical/Conceptual

How Sound Works in a PC

Like the ripples that roll across a pond when you drop a rock in the center, sound flows from a source in invisible but measurable waves that cause the membranes in your ears to vibrate and create sound. The sophistication of the human ear enables most people to differentiate the melodious from the raucous, the loud from the soft. Computers aren't nearly as sophisticated as the human ear and brain, so clear standards are a must for converting music into a format that a PC can use to record and play sound. Computer folks use the terms *capture* and *output* instead of record and play.

Sound-Capture Basics

Virtually every PC today comes with four critical components for capturing and output-ting sound: a sound card, speakers, microphone, and recording/playback software. Computers capture (record) sound waves in electronic format through a process called *sampling*. In its simplest sense, sampling means capturing the state or quality of a par-ticular sound wave a set number of times each second. The sampling rate is measured in units of thousands of cycles per second, or kilohertz (KHz). The more often a sound is sampled, the better the reproduction of that sound. Most sounds in the PC world are recorded with a sampling rate of from 11 KHz (very low quality, like a telephone) to 192 KHz (ultra-high quality, better than the human ear).

Sounds vary according to their loudness (*amplitude*), how high or low their tone (*frequency*), and the qualities that differentiate the same note played on different instru-ments (*timbre*). All the characteristics of a particular sound wave—amplitude, frequen-cy, timbre—need to be recorded and translated into ones and zeroes to reproduce that sound accurately within the computer and out to your speakers.

 NOTE The most famous of all sound cards is the Creative Labs SoundBlaster series.

The number of characteristics of a particular sound captured during sampling is measured by the *bit depth* of the sample, the number of bits used to describe the char-acteristics of a sound. The greater the bit depth used to capture a sample, the more characteristics of that sound can be stored and thus re-created. An 8-bit sample of a Jimi Hendrix guitar solo, for example, captures 2^8 (256) characteristics of that sound per sample. It would sound like a cheap recording of a recording, perhaps a little flat and thin. A 16-bit sample, in contrast, captures 2^{16} (65,536) different characteristics of his solo and reproduces all the fuzzy overtones and feedback that gave Hendrix his unique sound.

The last aspect of sound capture is the number of different tracks of sound you cap-ture. Most commonly, you can capture either a single track (*monaural*) or two tracks (*stereo*). More advanced captures record many more sound tracks, but that's a topic for a more advanced sound capture discussion.

The combination of sampling frequency and bit depth determines how faithfully a digital version of a sound captures what your ear would hear. A sound capture is con-sidered *CD quality* when recorded at 44.1 KHz, with 16-bit depth, and in stereo. Most recording programs let you set these values before you begin recording. Figure 18-1 shows the configuration settings for the Windows Sound Recorder.

Figure 18-1
Sound Recorder
settings

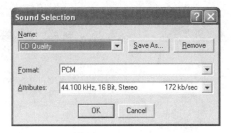

Hey, wait a minute! Did you notice the Format setting in Figure 18-1? What's that? You can save those sampled sounds in lots of different ways—and that's where the term *format* comes into play.

Recorded Sound Formats

The granddaddy of all sound formats is *pulse code modulation (PCM)*. PCM was developed in the 1960s to carry telephone calls over the first digital lines. With just a few minor changes to allow for use in PCs, the PCM format is still alive and well, although it's better known as the *WAV* format so common in the PC world. WAV files are great for storing faithfully recorded sounds and music, but they do so at a price. WAV files can be huge, especially when sampled at high frequency and depth. A 4-minute song at 44.1 KHz and 16-bit stereo, for example, weighs in at a whopping 40-plus MB!

What's interesting about sound quality is that the human ear cannot perceive anywhere near the subtle variations of sound recorded at 44.1 KHz and 16-bit stereo. Clever programmers have written algorithms to store full-quality WAV files as compressed files, discarding unnecessary audio qualities of that file. These algorithms—really nothing more than a series of instructions in code—are called compressor/decompressor programs, or, more simply, *codecs*. The most famous of the codecs is the Fraunhoffer MPEG-1 Layer 3 codec, more often called by its file extension, *MP3*.

NOTE WAV and MP3 are only two among a large number of file formats for sound. Not all sound players can play all of these formats; however, many sound formats are nothing more than some type of compressed WAV file, so with the right codec loaded, you can play most sound formats.

Playing Sounds

A large number of programs can play sounds on a typical Windows computer. First, virtually every Windows computer comes with Windows Media Player, possibly the most popular of all sound players. Figure 18-2 shows the default Media Player for Windows Vista. You can download many other players, of course, including iTunes, Apple's media program for Windows and OS X. This is good, because not all sound players can play all sounds.

Figure 18-2   Windows Media Player

NOTE   Using MP3 compression, it is possible to shrink a WAV file by a factor of 12 without losing much sound quality. When you compress a WAV file into an MP3 file, the key decision is the bit rate. The bit rate is the amount of information (number of bits) transferred from the compressed file to the MP3 decoder in one second. The higher the bit rate of an MP3 file, the higher the sound quality. The bit rate of MP3 audio files is commonly measured in thousands of bits per second, abbreviated *Kbps*. Most MP3 encoders support a range of bit rates from 24 Kbps up to 320 Kbps (or 320,000 bits per second). A CD-quality MP3 bit rate is 128 Kbps.

MIDI

Every sound card can produce sounds, in addition to playing prerecorded sound files. Every sound card comes with a second processor designed to interpret standardized *musical instrument digital interface (MIDI)* files. It's important to note that a MIDI file is not an independent music file, unlike a WAV file that will sound more or less the same on many different PCs. A MIDI file is a text file that takes advantage of the sound processing hardware to enable the PC to produce sound. Programmers use these small files to tell the sound card what notes to play, how long, how loud, on which instruments, and so forth. Think of a MIDI file as a piece of electronic sheet music, with the instruments built into your sound card.

NOTE MIDI files have the file extension .MID in the PC world.

The beauty of MIDI files is that they're tiny in comparison to equivalent WAV files. The first movement of Beethoven's 5th Symphony, for example, weighs in at a whopping 78 MB as a high-quality WAV file. The same 7-minute composition as a MIDI file, in contrast, slips in at a svelte 60 KB.

MIDI is hardware dependent, meaning the capabilities and quality of the individual sound card make all the difference in the world on the sound produced. Sound cards play MIDI files using one of two technologies: FM synthesis or wave table synthesis.

FM Synthesis

Early processors used electronic emulation of various instruments—a technique often called *FM synthesis*—to produce music and other sound effects. Software developers could tell the sound processor to reproduce a piano playing certain notes, for example, and a sound resembling a piano would pour forth from the speakers. The problem with FM synthesis is that although the modulation sounds okay for a single note, such as middle C, it sounds increasingly electronic the farther up or down the scale you go from that prime note.

Wave Table Synthesis

To address the odd techno-sound of early sound processors, manufacturers began embedding recordings of actual instruments or other sounds in the sound card. Modern sound cards use these recorded sounds to reproduce an instrument much more faithfully than with FM synthesis. When asked to play a C note on a piano or on a viola, for example, the sound processor grabs a prerecorded WAV file from its memory and adjusts it to match the specific sound and timing requested. This technique is called *wave table synthesis*. The number of instruments a sound card can play at once is called the polyphony of that card—typically 64 sounds on better cards. Most modern sound cards have samples of 128 instruments—a veritable symphony orchestra on a chip!

NOTE MIDI files are much less popular than other recorded formats on computers, but every Windows computer and every sound card still fully supports MIDI.

Other File Formats

The WAV, MP3, and MIDI formats may account for the majority of sound files, but plenty of other less common formats are out there. Here are the extensions of some other sound file formats you may run into in the PC world:

- **AAC**   Advanced Audio Coding is the native format for songs downloaded into the iTunes music library. This is Apple Computer's proprietary format, though, so it's not nearly as friendly as MP3, even though the compression algorithm is good.

- **AIFF**   Audio Interchange File Format files are a popular sound format used on Macintosh computers. These files are often seen at Web sites, and you can use the well-known QuickTime player to play them.

- **ASX**   Microsoft created the ASX format to facilitate streaming audio over the Internet through Windows Media Player. It's more than just a format, though; it acts like a super playlist and enables you to play other sound file types as well. The full name of the format is Microsoft Advanced Streaming Redirector.

- **AU**   This popular format is often seen in the Windows world. Many different players can play these files, including players on non-Windows systems, such as Sun, Next, UNIX, and Macintosh.

- **OGG**   The Vorbis format is an open-source compression codec that competes well with the proprietary AAC and WMA codecs, as well as MP3. Vorbis files are saved with the .OGG filename extension, so you'll hear them (incorrectly) referred to as "Ogg" files.

- **RM**   RealMedia files play either just audio or audio and video. They are proprietary to RealMedia, a popular player often used on the Internet. You must have RealMedia Player installed on your computer to play these files.

- **WMA**   Windows Media Audio is Microsoft's proprietary compression format.

This list scratches the surface of the 100-plus sound file formats available out there, but it represents those you're most likely to encounter.

Video

Recorded audio files and MIDI files aren't the only files that play sounds on your computer. Video files also have sound built into them. However, to play the sound that accompanies the video, the video player program must support the particular video file format. The most common video formats in the PC world are Audio Video Interleave (AVI), Moving Pictures Experts Group (MPEG), QuickTime (MOV), Advanced Streaming Format (ASF), Real Media (RM), Windows Media Video (WMV), DivX, and Flash. The popular video sharing site YouTube was made possible by the amazingly small size of Flash-based video.

Applications

Many applications, especially games, play sounds, too. In the not-too-distant past, a game or an application sometimes had its own sound format, but most applications and games today use standard WAV, MP3, or MIDI files.

Streaming Media

Streaming media is incredibly popular on the Internet. Streaming media is a broadcast of data that is played on your computer and immediately discarded. Streaming media has spawned an entire industry of Internet radio stations. The three most popular streaming media players are Windows Media Player, Winamp, and Apple's iTunes. ASF and RM are compressed audio/video file formats that were specially created to stream over the Internet. With the spread of broadband Internet, the quality of streaming radio has improved dramatically. In fact, it is common to see Internet stations streaming 128 Kbps and better MP3 files. Some sites even have surround-sound music for those who have the speakers to appreciate it.

Essentials

Getting the Right Sound Card

Sound cards come with many built-in features, including two separate sound processors (one for all of the recorded formats such as WAV and another for MIDI), support chips for joysticks and other pointing devices that plug into the game port, recording capabilities, support for MIDI instruments, and more. All sound cards, from the cheapest to the most expensive, can play music and drive a pair of speakers, so techs need to delve a little deeper to understand the crucial differences among low-, mid-, and high-end sound cards. Sound cards differ in five basic areas: processor capabilities, speaker support, recording quality, jacks, and extra features.

But the sound card itself is only one part of the equation. You also need good-quality speakers if you have any intention of listening to music or enjoying some of the more advanced features such as surround sound.

 NOTE The hardware portion of sound-processing equipment in the PC comes either as a chip built into the motherboard or on an expansion card. Techs call both forms *sound cards*, though technically the first type is not a card at all. Still, the generic term has stuck for the time being.

Processor Capabilities

Sound processor capabilities differ dramatically from the low end to the high end, even though the prices don't reflect the great divide. The sound processor handles the communication among the application, operating system, and CPU and translates commands into sounds coming out of the speakers. Low-end sound processors do little more than translate, which means that the CPU has to do the heavy lifting on the processing front.

Better sound processors, in contrast, shoulder much of the processing burden and bring a series of extra features to the table. By handling a lot of the processing on board, these better sound processors free up the CPU for other duties and, in effect and in name, *accelerate* the sound process. These decent sound processors also provide excellent sound reproduction, so your MP3s sound as awesome on your PC as they do on your stereo.

Most mid-range and all high-end sound processors offer support for various surround sound standards, enabling equally equipped games and other applications to provide positional audio effects and detailed sound modeling—features that make PC gaming take on a whole new dimension. You'll learn about the various standards in detail in the "Speakers" section of this chapter, but for now let an example suffice. With properly implemented positional audio, when you're sneaking down the hall, ready to steal the Pasha's treasure, you will hear behind you the sounds of the guards marching up to capture you. Such added realism has many potential benefits beyond games, but games are currently the primary beneficiary of this technology.

Speaker Support

Every sound card supports two speakers or a pair of headphones, but many better sound cards support five or more speakers in discrete channels. These multiple speakers provide surround sound—popular not only for games but also for those who enjoy playing DVDs on their PCs. The card shown in Figure 18-3, for example, supports up to eight speakers.

Figure 18-3
A sound card with multiple speaker connections

Another popular speaker addition is a subwoofer. Subwoofers provide the amazing low-frequency sounds that give all of your sounds, from the surround sound of a game to the music of a simple stereo MP3 file, an extra dimension. Almost all modern sound cards support both surround sound and a subwoofer and advertise this with a nomenclature such as Dolby Digital, DTS, or 5.1. The 5 denotes the number of speakers: two in front, two in back, and one in the center. The .1 denotes the subwoofer. Figure 18-4 shows one type of surround speaker system. (You'll learn more about surround sound in the upcoming "Speakers" section.)

Figure 18-4
Surround speakers (photo courtesy of Klipsch)

Recording Quality

Almost every sound card has an input for a powered microphone, but the high-end cards record with substantially lower amounts of noise or other audible artifacts. The measure that describes the relative quality of an input port is signal-to-noise ratio and is expressed in decibels. The smaller the number, the worse the card is for recording, because you'll more likely get noise. Most sound cards at the low end and in the mid range have a signal-to-noise ratio of 30 to 50 decibels, which makes them unacceptable for recording. High-end cards offer a 96 to 100+ signal-to-noise ratio, a level near what professional musicians use. Check the documentation (see Figure 18-5) before you buy or recommend a sound card for recording purposes.

Figure 18-5
The E-MU 1820 advertises its excellent 112-decibel signal-to-noise ratio for recording.

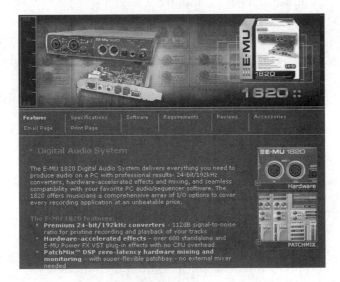

Jacks

Virtually every sound card comes with at least three connections: one for a stereo speaker system, one for a microphone, and one for a secondary output called line out. If you look at the back of a motherboard with a built-in sound card, you'll invariably see these three connections (Figure 18-6). On most systems, the main stereo speaker connector is green, the line-in connector is blue, and the microphone connector is pink. You'll often find plenty of other connectors as well (Figure 18-7).

Figure 18-6
Typical audio connections on a motherboard sound card

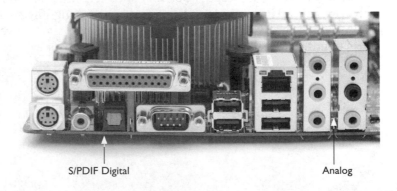

S/PDIF Digital   Analog

Figure 18-7
Lots of connections on a high-end sound card

Take a look at what these connectors do for your sound card:

- **Line out** The line out is a secondary connector that is often used to connect to an external device such as cassette or CD player to allow you to output sounds from your computer.

- **Line in** The line in port connects to an external device such as a cassette or CD player to allow you to import sounds into your computer.

- **Rear out** The rear out connector connects to the rear speakers for surround sound audio output.

- **Analog/digital out** The multifunction analog/digital out connection acts as a special digital connection to external digital devices or digital speaker systems, and it also acts as the analog connection to center and subwoofer channels. (See the "Speakers" section later in this chapter for a discussion of surround sound.)

- **Microphone** The microphone port connects to an external microphone for voice input.

- **Joystick** The joystick port connects a joystick or a MIDI device to the sound card. The joystick port is a two-row DB15 female connection, but as more and more peripherals go to USB, more motherboard and sound card makers are dropping this venerable port from their models.

Extra Features

With all motherboards including built-in sound these days, expansion sound card makers have responded by adding a host of extra goodies and abilities to their cards that, for some folks, prove irresistibly tempting. These include a digital output to integrate the PC with a home entertainment unit, DVD receiver, and surround sound speaker connection abilities; a breakout box that adds recording and output ports in a 5.25-inch bay; and a FireWire connection for direct gaming, file sharing, and immediate MP3 playing from a portable MP3 device. Figure 18-8 shows a version of the Creative Labs SoundBlaster breakout box. These features aren't for everyone, but they are compelling to many consumers.

Figure 18-8
Breakout box for a
SoundBlaster Live!
Platinum sound card

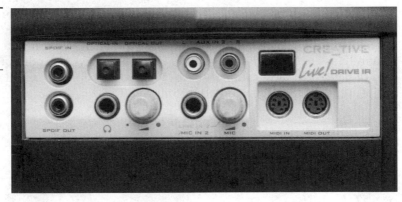

Audio Cables

In the days of yore, if you wanted to play audio CDs through your sound card, you needed a special cable that ran from your CD-ROM drive to the sound card. These cables have been around for a while, but the connectors were not standardized—for years, you had to use the cable that came with your sound card and hope that it would connect to your CD-ROM drive.

Today, a connector called *MPC2* is quite standard, and cables usually come with optical drives, not sound cards. To accommodate the many other types of connections that are still in use, a special cable called a *universal audio cable* is also available (Figure 18-9). Universal audio cables have a set of connectors to enable an optical drive to connect to any sort of audio card. Universal audio cables were important when CD-ROM audio connections were not standardized.

Figure 18-9
Universal audio cable

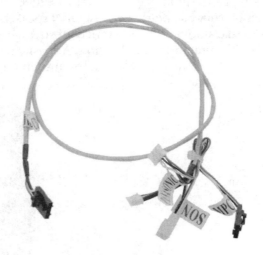

The early SoundBlaster line of audio cards came with a small, proprietary connection for CD-ROM drives. Because SoundBlaster dominated the field of sound cards for many years, you'll still run into audio cables with an MPC2 connector on one end and a SoundBlaster connector on the other end. These days, SoundBlaster cards use standard cables. You'll most commonly see MPC2 connections on sound cards, and MPC2/MPC2 audio cables (Figure 18-10) included with any new optical drive.

Figure 18-10
MPC2/MPC2
audio cable

Speakers

It always blows me away when I walk into someone's study and hear tinny music whining from a $10 pair of speakers connected to a $2000 computer. If you listen to music or play games on your computer, a decent set of speakers can significantly improve the experience. Speakers come in a wide variety of sizes, shapes, technologies, and quality and can stump the uninformed tech who can't easily tell that the $50 set on the right sounds 100 times better than the $25 pair on the left (Figure 18-11).

Figure 18-11
High-quality
speaker set (right)
versus another
manufacturer's low-
end speaker set (left)

Speaker Standards

The advent of surround sound in the computing world has created a number of speaker standards. You should know these standards so that you can choose the speakers that work best for you and your clients.

Stereo   Stereo is the oldest speaker technology that you'll see in the PC world. Stereo speakers are just what you might imagine: two speakers, a left and a right (Figure 18-12). The two speakers share a single jack that connects to the sound card. Most cheap speakers are stereo speakers.

Figure 18-12
Stereo speakers

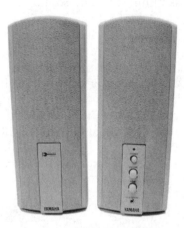

2.1 Systems   A 2.1 speaker system consists of a pair of standard stereo speakers—called *satellites*—combined with a subwoofer (Figure 18-13). The average 2.1 speaker system has a single jack that connects to the sound card and runs into the subwoofer. Another wire runs from the subwoofer to the two stereo speakers. If you want to enjoy great music and don't need surround sound, this is your speaker standard of choice.

Figure 18-13
Typical 2.1 speakers

Surround Speaker Standards   Going beyond standard two-channel (stereo) sound has been a goal in the sound world since the 1970s. However, it wasn't until the advent of Dolby Laboratory's *Dolby Digital* sound standard in the early 1990s that surround sound began to take off. The Dolby Digital sound standard is designed to support five channels of sound: front-left, front-right, front-center, rear-left, and rear-right. Dolby Digital also supports a subwoofer—thus, the term *5.1*. Another company, *Digital Theatre Systems (DTS)*, created a competing standard that also supported a 5.1 speaker system. When DVDs were introduced, they included both Dolby Digital and DTS 5.1 standards, making 5.1 speakers an overnight requirement for home theater. If you want to enjoy your DVDs in full surround sound on your PC, you must purchase a full 5.1 speaker system. A number of 5.1 speaker systems are available for PCs. The choice you make is usually determined by what sounds best to you.

Many sound cards also come with a special *Sony/Philips digital interface (S/PDIF)* connector that enables you to connect your sound card directly to a 5.1 speaker system or receiver (Figure 18-14). Using a single S/PDIF instead of a tangle of separate wires for each speaker greatly simplifies your sound setup. S/PDIF connections come in two types, optical and coaxial. The optical variety looks like a square with a small door (at right in Figure 18-14). The coaxial is a standard RCA connector (at left), the same type used to connect a CD player to your stereo. It doesn't matter which one you use; just make sure you have an open spot on your receiver or speakers.

Figure 18-14
S/PDIF connectors

 NOTE   Only a few 5.1 PC speaker sets come with S/PDIF. In most cases, you'll have to use the regular audio outputs on the sound card. You'll find the connector more common on 6.1 and 7.1 sets.

Games can also take advantage of 5.1, 6.1, and 7.1 speakers, but they use the DirectX standard. DirectX offers numerous commands, also known as APIs, that issue instructions such as "make a sound on the right speaker" or "play music in both the right and left channels." DirectX simplifies the programming needed to create sound and video: rather than having to program sounds in different ways for each sound card option, games can talk DirectX; the hardware manufacturers simply have to ensure that their sound cards are DirectX compatible.

DirectX version 3 introduced DirectSound3D (DS3D), which offered a range of commands to place a sound anywhere in 3-D space. Known as *positional audio*, it fundamentally changed the way most PC games were played. DS3D could not handle all sound information, but it supported extensions to its instructions for more advanced sound features. This challenged the sound card designers to develop more fully the concept of positional audio. Creative Labs responded by rolling out *environmental audio extensions (EAX)*, a set of audio presets that gave developers the capability to create a convincing sense of environment in entertainment titles and a realistic sense of distance between the player and audio events. Figure 18-15 shows an EAX setup screen.

Figure 18-15 EAX setup screen

In late 2000, a number of EAX effects were incorporated into the DirectX audio component of DirectX 8.0. This signaled the acceptance of EAX as the standard for audio effects in gaming. Shortly afterward, Creative Labs started releasing audio cards that were Dolby 5.1 compatible out of the box. This let you plug a 5.1 speaker system directly into your sound card. The sound card automatically decoded the Dolby/DTS sound track when you played a DVD and the EAX effects when you played a game that supports it. All current sound cards support DirectX and EAX.

NOTE Not all cards support Dolby Digital/DTS. Most software DVD players and some sound cards support Dolby Digital. DTS support is a little harder to come by. Check the manufacturer's Web site to determine whether your card will work with DTS.

Speaker Features

Speakers also come with a few other features that you should consider when choosing a set for yourself or your clients. Speakers offer a variety of power sources, controls accessibility, and headphone jacks.

Controls   All speakers have volume controls as well as an on/off switch. Get a system that provides easy access to those controls by placing them on an easy-to-reach speaker or on a special control box.

Headphone Jack   The problem with headphones is that you need to plug them into the back of the sound card and then tell Windows to output to them from the Sound applet on the Control Panel. Save yourself a lot of hassle and get a speaker system that has a handy microphone jack on one of the speakers or on a control box.

Installing Sound in a Windows System

You've got two choices for sound hardware on today's PCs: onboard sound built into the motherboard or a separate sound card. The installation process for a sound card is basically the same as the process for any other card. You snap the card into a slot, plug some speakers into the card, load a driver—and for the most part, you're done. With onboard sound, you need to make sure the sound is enabled in your CMOS and then load the driver. As with most of the devices discussed in this book, sound card installation consists of three major parts: physical installation, device driver installation, and configuration.

Physical Installation

Physical installation is easy. Onboard sound is already physically installed and most sound cards are run-of-the-mill PCI cards (Figure 18-16). The real trick to physical installation is deciding where to plug in the speakers, microphone, and so on. The surround sound devices so common today feature a variety of jacks, so you will probably want to refer to your sound card documentation for details, but here are a few guidelines:

- The typical stereo or 2.1 speaker system will use only a single jack. Look for the jack labeled Speaker or Speaker 1.
- Surround speakers either use a single digital (S/PDIF) connection, which in most cases runs from the sound card to the subwoofer, or they need three separate cables: one for the front two speakers that runs to the Speaker 1 connector, one for the back two speakers that runs to the Speaker 2 connector, and a third cable for the center channel and subwoofer that runs to the digital/ audio out or Speaker 3 connector.

Figure 18-16
Typical sound card

Here's a quick look at sound card installation. As with any PCI card, you'll need a Phillips-head screwdriver to install a sound card, as well as your electrostatic discharge (ESD) prevention equipment. Of course, you'll also need the sound card itself, a set of speakers, an audio cable, and a microphone if you want to be able to record sounds.

1. Shut down your computer, unplug it, and open the case.

2. Find an open PCI slot and snap in the sound card. Remember to handle the card with tender loving care—especially if you're installing an expensive, high-end card! Make sure that the card is securely seated, and secure it to the chassis with a hex screw.

3. Now connect the CD audio cable to the back of your optical drive, and plug the other end into the CD audio port on your sound card. Be sure to use the correct connector—many sound cards have multiple audio connectors. The one shown in Figure 18-17, for example, has separate connectors to use for an optical drive or modem.

Figure 18-17
Sound card with multiple audio connectors

Installing Drivers

Once the sound card is installed, start the system and let Windows install the card's drivers. This applies to expansion cards and onboard sound. As you might expect by now, you'll probably have a choice between the built-in Windows drivers and the driver that comes on a CD-ROM with your sound card. Just as with other cards, it's always best to install the driver that comes with the card. All sound devices have easy-to-use autoplay-enabled installation CD-ROMs that step you through the process (Figure 18-18).

Figure 18-18
Typical autoplay screen for a sound card

 NOTE Sound card drivers are updated occasionally. Take a moment to check the manufacturer's Web site to see whether your sound card has any driver updates.

You might run into one of the USB sound cards out on the market (Figure 18-19), in which case the installation process is reversed. The only secret to these devices is to follow the important rule of all USB devices: *install the drivers before you plug in the device.*

Windows, especially Windows XP and Vista, probably have basic drivers for these USB sound cards, but don't take a chance—always install the drivers first!

Figure 18-19 USB sound card (photo courtesy of Creative)

After your sound card and driver are installed, make a quick trip to the Device Manager to ensure that the driver was installed correctly, and you're two-thirds of the way there. Installing the driver is never the last step for a sound card. Your final step is to configure the sound card using configuration programs and test it using an application. Most sound cards come with both special configuration programs and a few sound applications on the same CD-ROM that supplies the drivers. Take a look at these extra bits of software that I call *sound programs*.

Installing Sound Programs

You've already seen that you need a program to play sounds on your PC: Windows Media Player, Winamp, or something similar. But two other classes of sound programs also reside on your computer: programs for the configuration of your sound card and special applications that may or may not come with your sound card.

Configuration Applications

Every Windows computer comes with at least one important sound configuration program built right into the operating system: the Control Panel applet called Sounds and Audio Devices in Windows XP or Sounds and Multimedia in Windows 2000. Whatever the name, this applet (or applets) performs the same job: it provides a location for performing most or all the configuration you need for your sound card. Consider the Sounds and Audio Devices applet in Windows XP, for example; the Sounds and Multimedia applet in Windows 2000 works roughly the same, although it may have one control or another in a different place.

The Sounds and Audio Devices applet has five tabs: Volume, Sounds, Audio, Voice, and Hardware. The Volume tab is the most interesting. This tab adjusts the volume for the speakers, and it allows you to set up the type of speaker system you have, as shown in Figure 18-20.

Figure 18-20
Advanced Audio
Properties dialog box

The Sounds tab allows you to add customized sounds to Windows events, such as the startup of a program or Windows shutdown. The Audio tab (Figure 18-21) and Voice tab do roughly the same thing: they allow you to specify the device used for input and output of general sounds (Audio tab) and voice (Voice tab). These settings are handy for folks like me who have a regular microphone and speakers but also use a headset with microphone for voice recognition or Internet telephone software. By telling Windows to use the microphone for normal sounds and to use the headset for voice recognition, I don't have to make any manual changes when I switch from listening to an MP3 to listening to my brother when he calls me over the Internet.

Figure 18-21
Audio tab (note the
MIDI Music Playback
options)

The Hardware tab isn't used very often, but it does have one interesting feature: it shows you all of the audio and video codecs installed in your system (Figure 18-22). Not long ago, you had to install codecs manually in your system to play certain compressed file formats. Today, most audio players automatically detect whether a file is using an unrecognized codec and will download the proper codec for you.

Figure 18-22
Audio codecs

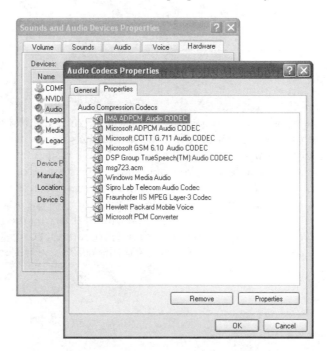

Proprietary Configuration Applications

Many sound cards install proprietary software to support configuration features not provided by Windows. Figure 18-23 shows one such application. This special configuration application comes with Creative Labs sound cards to add a few tweaks to the speaker setup that the Sounds and Audio Devices applet doesn't support.

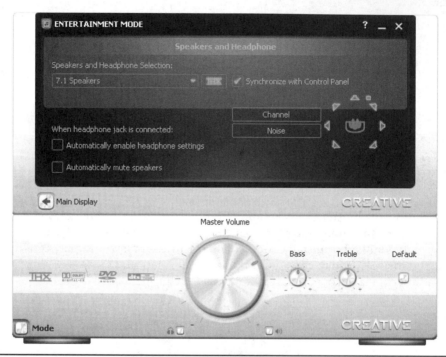

Figure 18-23   Creative Labs Speakers and Headphone panel

Most sound cards come with some form of configuration program that works with the Control Panel applet to tweak the sound the way you want it. Figure 18-24 shows the applet that came with my motherboard. One of its many interesting features is to detect what types of devices are installed into the sound ports and adjust the system to use them. In other words, I don't even have to look where I'm plugging in anything! If I plug a microphone into the front speakers port, the system just adjusts the outputs—very cool. Software and sound cards that can do this are called *autosensing*.

Take some time to experiment with the program that comes with your sound card—this is a great way to learn about some of the card's features that you might otherwise not even know are there!

Figure 18-24
Autosensing
software detecting
connected devices

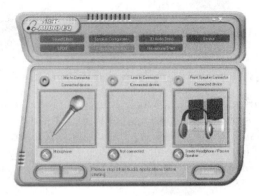

Installing Applications

Some sound cards—Creative Labs sound cards are by far the most infamous for this—
install one or more applications, ostensibly to improve your sound experience. These
are not the configuration programs just described. These programs do anything from
enabling you to compose music to organizing your sound files. Personally, I'm not a
big fan of, for example, an 3DMIDI Player program (Figure 18-25)—but you might be
just the type of person who loves it. Be sure at least to install the applications that come
with your card. If you don't like them, you can easily uninstall them.

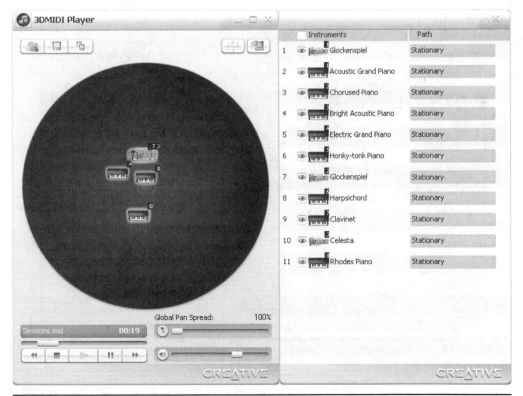

Figure 18-25   Creative Labs 3DMIDI Player program

IT Technician

Troubleshooting Sound

The problems you'll run into with sound seem to fall into one of two camps: those that are embarrassingly simple to repair and those that defy any possible logic and are seemingly impossible to fix. This section divides sound problems into three groups—hardware, configuration, and application problems—and gives you some ideas on how to fix these problems.

Hardware Problems

Hardware problems are by far the most common sound problems, especially if your sound card has worked for some amount of time already. Properly installed and configured sound cards almost never suddenly stop making sounds.

Volume

The absolute first item to check when a sound dies is the volume controls. Remember that you can set the volume in two places: in software and on the speakers. I can't tell you the number of times I've lost sound only to discover that my wife turned down the volume on the speakers. If the speaker volume is okay, open the volume controls in Windows (Figure 18-26) by clicking the little speaker icon on the System Tray, and make sure that both the master volume and the volume of the other controls are turned up.

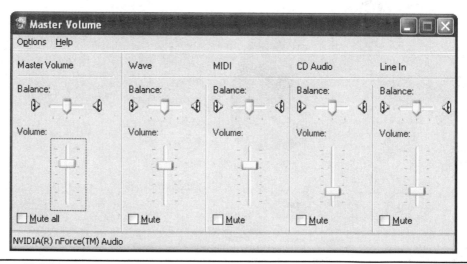

Figure 18-26   Volume controls in Windows

NOTE   If your System Tray is cluttered and the little speaker icon hard to find, you can access the Play Control dialog box by opening the Sounds and Audio Devices applet in the Control Panel. On the Volume tab—the one that's on top by default—click the Advanced button under Device Volume.

   If you don't have a little speaker in your System Tray at all, you can add it. Just check the checkbox next to the *Place volume icon in the taskbar* option on the Volume tab of the Sound and Audio Devices Properties dialog box. Presto!

Speakers

The second place to look for sound problems is the speakers. Make sure that the speakers are turned on and are getting good power. Then make sure the speakers are plugged into the proper connection on the back of the sound card. If this all checks out, try playing a sound using any sound program. If the sound program *looks* like it is playing—maybe the application has an equalizer that is moving or a status marker that shows that the application is playing the sound—you may have blown speakers. Try another pair and see if the sound returns.

Most of the time, speakers come in a matched set—whether it's a 2.1, 4.1, 5.1, or other system—and the manufacturer will include adequate connecting wires for the whole set. On occasion, you might run into a system in which the user has connected pairs of speakers from different sets or rigged a surround sound system by replacing the stock wires with much longer wires. Either option can create a perfectly functional surround sound system that works for a specific room, but you should make sure that all the speakers match in wattage required and that high-quality wire is used to connect them.

If you troubleshoot a system in which two of the speakers are very quiet and two very loud, the wattages are probably different between the two pairs. A simple check of the labels should suffice to troubleshoot, or you can swap out one pair for a different pair and see if that affects the volume issues. Cheap wire, on the other hand, simply degrades the sound quality. If the speakers sounded good before getting strung on long wires, but they now have a lot of low grade noise, blame the wires.

Configuration Problems

Configuration errors occur when the sound card is physically good but some setting hasn't been properly configured. I also include drive problems in this category. These errors happen almost exclusively at installation, but they can appear on a working system, too.

NOTE   Technically speaking, turning down the volume in the volume control program is not a configuration problem, but it's just something I always check at the same time I check the volume on the speakers.

The first place to check is the Device Manager. If the driver has a problem, you'll see it right there. Try reinstalling the driver. If the driver doesn't show any problems, again try playing a sound and see if the player acts as though the sound is playing. If that's the case, you need to start touring the Sounds and Audio Devices applet to see if you've made a configuration error—perhaps you have the system configured for 5.1 when you have a stereo setup, or maybe you set the default sound output device to some other device. Take your time and look—configuration errors always show themselves.

Application Problems

Application problems are always the hardest to fix and tend to occur on a system that was previously playing sounds without trouble.

First, look for an error message (Figure 18-27). If an error code appears, write it down *exactly* as you see it and head to the program's support site. Odds are very good that if you have the error text, you'll get the fix right away from the support site. Of course, you can always hope the built-in help has some support, but help systems tend to be a little light in providing real fixes.

Figure 18-27
Sample error
message

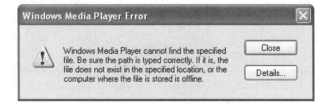

Don't always blame the sound application—remember that any sound file might be corrupted. Most sound players will display a clear error message, but not always. Try playing the sound file using another application.

Last, a good approach almost always is to reinstall the application.

Beyond A+

Sound Card Benchmarking

Sound cards can demand a huge share of system resources—particularly CPU time—during intense work (like gaming). Most techs who find an otherwise serviceable PC stuttering during games will immediately blame the video card or the video card drivers. What they don't realize is that sound cards can be the cause of the problem. A recent test of a client's built-in audio, for example, revealed that at peak usage the sound card took more than 30 percent of the CPU cycles. Thirty percent? Holy smokes! And he wondered why his Pentium III system bogged down on yesterday's games! He could just forget about playing Half-Life 2 or Doom 3.

The folks at iXBT.com/Digit-Life make an excellent suite of sound card benchmarking utilities that helps you analyze the particulars of any sound card: RightMark 3DSound (Figure 18-28). It will run a system through fairly serious tests, from regular sound to 3-D positional audio, and will reveal whether or not the sound processor—built-in or expansion card—is causing a problem with resource use. You can find the utility at http://audio.rightmark.org.

Figure 18-28
RightMark 3DSound

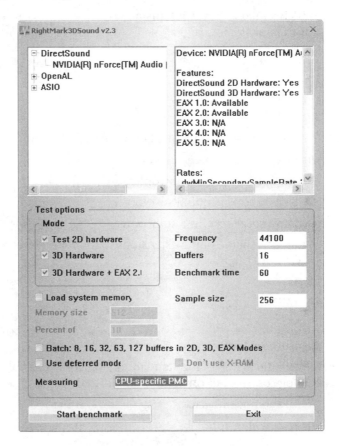

Chapter Review Questions

1. What refers to the number of characteristics of a particular sound captured when sampling?

    A. Sample rate

    B. Kilohertz

    C. Bit depth

    D. Quality rating

2. All recorded sound formats used in PCs today are derived from which format?

   A. WAV

   B. Fraunhoffer

   C. MP3

   D. PCM

3. Which sound format contains no actual sound recording, but only a series of commands stored in a text file for the sound card to interpret?

   A. WMA

   B. WAV

   C. MIDI

   D. MP3

4. How many speakers are in a Dolby Digital 5.1 setup?

   A. Five speakers plus a subwoofer

   B. Six speakers plus a subwoofer

   C. Seven speakers plus a subwoofer

   D. Eight speakers plus a subwoofer

5. What is the name of the extensions to the DirectSound3D standard developed by Creative Labs?

   A. EAX

   B. MP3

   C. Positional audio

   D. Reverberation

6. What is the name of the standard digital connection that replaces many analog connections on some sound cards?

   A. CD audio connector

   B. AUX connector

   C. TAD connector

   D. S/PDIF connector

7. Which sampling rate would produce the highest quality sound?

   A. 8 Hz

   B. 8 KHz

   C. 128 Hz

   D. 128 KHz

8. What must be installed on your system to decode a sound file?

  A. The proper codec

  B. Sound application software

  C. Speakers

  D. Universal audio cables

9. Which of the following are valid audio file formats?

  A. ASF, WMA, ASP

  B. PCI, MP3, ASX

  C. WAV, PCM, AU

  D. MID, MPEG, AVI

10. Which term describes the stereo speakers in a 2.1 sound system?

  A. Woofers

  B. Satellites

  C. Subwoofers

  D. Twins

Answers

1. C. The bit depth refers to the number of characteristics of a particular sound captured when sampling.

2. D. All recorded sound formats used in PCs today are derived from PCM format.

3. C. MIDI files contains no actual sound recording, but only a series of commands stored in a text file for the sound card to interpret.

4. A. A Dolby Digital 5.1 setup has five speakers and one subwoofer.

5. A. Creative Labs developed the EAX presets.

6. D. The S/PDIF connector can replace analog connections on some sound cards.

7. D. The bigger the number, the better the quality, so 128 KHz is the king here.

8. A. You need a proper codec installed to decode a sound file.

9. C. WAV, PCM, and AU are audio file formats.

10. B. Stereo speakers are called satellites.

CHAPTER 19

Portable Computing

In this chapter, you will learn how to
- Describe the many types of portable computing devices available
- Enhance and upgrade portable computers
- Manage and maintain portable computers
- Troubleshoot portable computers

There are times when the walls close in, when you need a change of scenery to get that elusive spark that inspires greatness … or sometimes you just need to get away from your co-workers for a few hours because they're driving you nuts! For many occupations, that's difficult to do. You've got to have access to your documents and spreadsheets; you can't function without e-mail or the Internet. In short, you need a computer to get your job done.

Portable computing devices combine mobility with accessibility to bring you the best of both worlds; put more simply, portables let you take some or even all of your computing abilities with you when you go. Some portable computers feature Windows XP systems with all the bells and whistles and all your Microsoft Office apps for a seamless transition from desk to café table. Even the smallest portable devices enable you to check your appointments and address book, or play Solitaire during the endless wait at the doctor's office. This chapter takes an in-depth look at portables, first going through the major variations you'll run into and then hitting the tech-specific topics of enhancing, upgrading, managing, and maintaining portable computers. Let's get started!

Essentials

Portable Computing Devices

All portable devices share certain features. For output, they have LCD screens, although these vary from 20-inch behemoths to microscopic 2-inch screens. Portable computing devices employ sound of varying quality, from simple beeps to fairly nice music reproductions. All of them run on DC electricity stored in batteries, although several different technologies offer a range of battery life, lifespan, and cost. Other than screen,

823

sound, and battery, portable computing devices come in an amazing variety of shapes, sizes, and intended uses.

 EXAM TIP   Note that this chapter does not have an Historical/Conceptual section. Everything in here is on the CompTIA A+ certification exams, so pay attention!

LCD Screens

Laptops come in a variety of sizes and at varying costs. One major contributor to the overall cost of a laptop is the size of the LCD screen. Most laptops offer a range between 12-inch to 17-inch screens (measured diagonally), while a few offer just over 20-inch screens. Not only are screens getting larger, but also wider screens are becoming the status quo. Many manufacturers are phasing out the standard 4:3 aspect ratio screen in favor of the widescreen format. *Aspect ratio* is the comparison of the screen width to the screen height. Depending on screen resolution, widescreens can have varying aspect ratios of 10:6, 16:9, 16:9.5, or 16:10. The 16:9 aspect ratio is the standard for widescreen movies while 16:10 is the standard for 17-inch LCD screens.

Laptop LCD screens come in a variety of supported resolutions, described with acronyms such as XGA, WXGA, WSXGA, and more. The *W* in front of the letters indicates widescreen. Table 19-1 lists commonly supported laptop display resolutions.

Acronym	Name	Native Resolution
XGA	eXtended Graphics Array	1024 × 768
SXGA	Super eXtended Graphics Array	1280 × 1024
SXGA+	Super eXtended Graphics Array Plus	1400 × 1050
WSXGA+	Widescreen SXGA	1680 × 1050
UXGA	Ultra eXtended Graphics Array	1600 × 1200
WUXGA	Widescreen UXGA	1920 × 1200

Table 19-1   Screen Resolutions

Laptop screens come with two types of finish: *matte* and *high gloss.* The matte finish was the industry standard for many years and offers a good trade-off between richness of colors and reflection or glare. The better screens have a wide viewing angle and decent response time. The major drawback for matte-finished laptop screens is that they wash out a lot in bright light. Using such a laptop at an outdoor café, for example, is almost hopeless during daylight.

Manufacturers released high-gloss laptop screens in 2006, and they've rapidly taken over many store shelves. The high-gloss finish offers sharper contrast, richer colors, and wider viewing angles when compared to the matte screens. Each manufacturer has a different name for high-gloss coatings. Dell calls theirs TrueLife; Acer calls theirs Crystal-Brite; and HP calls theirs BrightView. The drawback to the high-gloss screens is that, contrary to what the manufacturers' claim, they pick up lots of reflection from nearby objects, including the user! So while they're usable outside during the day, you'll need to contend with increased reflection as well.

Desktop Replacements

When asked about portable computing devices, most folks describe the traditional clamshell *laptop* computer, such as the one in Figure 19-1, with built-in LCD monitor, keyboard, and input device (a *touchpad*, in this case). A typical laptop computer functions as a fully standalone PC, potentially even replacing the desktop. The one in Figure 19-1, for example, has all of the features you expect the modern PC to have, such as a fast CPU, lots of RAM, a high-capacity hard drive, CD-RW and DVD drives, an excellent sound system, and a functioning copy of Windows XP. Attach it to a network and you can browse the Internet and send e-mail. Considering it weighs almost as much as a mini-tower PC (or at least it feels like it does when I'm lugging it through the airport!), such a portable can be considered a *desktop replacement*, because it does everything that most people want to do with a desktop PC and doesn't compromise performance just to make the laptop a few pounds lighter or the battery last an extra hour.

Figure 19-1
A notebook PC

NOTE There's no industry standard naming for the vast majority of styles of portable computing devices, and thus manufacturers let their marketing folks have fun with naming. What's the difference between a portable, a laptop, and a notebook? Nothing. One manufacturer might call its 12-inch LCD, four-pound portable a notebook, while another manufacturer might call its much larger desktop-replacement portable a notebook as well. A laptop refers in general to the clamshell, keyboard-on-the-bottom and LCD-screen-at-the-top design that is considered the shape of mobile PCs.

Laptop Input Devices

For input devices, desktop replacements (and other portables) used trackballs in the early days, often plugged in like a mouse and clipped to the side of the case. Other models with trackballs placed them in front of the keyboard at the edge of the case nearest the user, or behind the keyboard at the edge nearest the screen.

The next wave to hit the laptop market was IBM's *TrackPoint* device, a pencil eraser–sized joystick situated in the center of the keyboard. The TrackPoint enables you to move the pointer around without taking your fingers away from the "home" typing position. You use a forefinger to push the joystick around, and click or right-click using two buttons below the spacebar. This type of pointing device has since been licensed for use by other manufacturers, and it continues to appear on laptops today.

But by far the most common laptop pointing device found today is the *touchpad* (Figure 19-2)—a flat, touch-sensitive pad just in front of the keyboard. To operate a touchpad, you simply glide your finger across its surface to move the pointer, and tap the surface once or twice to single- or double-click. You can also click using buttons just below the pad. Most people get the hang of this technique after just a few minutes of practice. The main advantage of the touchpad over previous laptop pointing devices is that it uses no moving parts—a fact that can really extend the life of a hard-working laptop. Some modern laptops actually provide both a TrackPoint-type device and a touchpad, to give the user a choice.

Figure 19-2
Touchpad
on a laptop

Weighty Issues

Manufacturers advertise the weight of portable PCs, for the most part, without the weight of the battery or the removable drives. Although this deception is deplorable, it's pretty much universal in the industry because no manufacturer wants to be the first to say that their desktop-replacement portable, including battery and DVD-RW drive, weighs 15 pounds when their competitor advertises the same kind of machine at 7.5 pounds! They'd lose market share quickly.

So when you shop or recommend portable PCs, take the real weight into consideration. By the time you fill your laptop bag with power adapters, external mice, a spare battery, and all the extra accessories, you'll definitely be carrying more than the advertised 5–6 pounds.

Desktop Extenders

Manufacturers offer *desktop extender* portable devices that don't replace the desktop, but rather extend it by giving you a subset of features of the typical desktop that you can take away from the desk. Figure 19-3 shows a portable with a good but small 13.3-inch wide screen. The system has 512 MB of RAM, a 2-GHz processor, a 60-GB hard drive, and a battery that enables you to do work on it for more than five hours while disconnected from the wall socket. Even though it plays music and has a couple of decent, tiny speakers, you can't game on this computer (Solitaire, perhaps, but definitely not Half-Life 2!). But it weighs only five pounds, nearly half the weight of the typical desktop replacement portable.

Figure 19-3
Excellent mid-sized portable computer

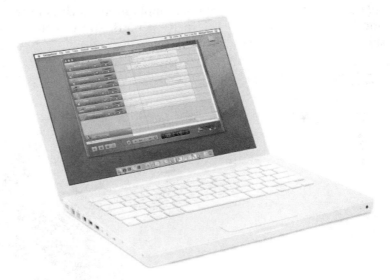

Desktop extenders enable you to go mobile. When I'm on a roll writing, for example, I don't want to stop. But sometimes I do want to take a break from the office and stroll over to my favorite café for a latté or a pint of fine ale. At moments like these, I don't need a fully featured laptop with a monster 15-inch or 17-inch screen, but just a good word processing system—and perhaps the ability to surf the Internet on the café's wireless network so I can research other important topics once I finish my project for the day. A lightweight laptop with a 12–13-inch screen, a reasonably fast processor, and gobs of RAM does nicely.

Ultralights

Ultralight portables are computers that normally weigh less than three pounds and are less than an inch in thickness. These machines usually have smaller displays, lower-capacity hard drives, and CPUs that operate at lower speeds than their more full-sized brethren. This class of portable computers is designed for the busy traveler who wants a nearly full-featured laptop in a small, easily transported package. Often, these laptops are much more expensive than larger, faster machines—think of it as paying more to get less! You'll hear the term *subnotebooks* used to describe ultralight portables; the terms aren't quite synonymous, but the marketing waters for all portable computing devices are pretty muddy.

PDAs

Having a few computing essentials on hand at all times eases the day and makes planning and scheduling much more likely to succeed. Several companies, such as Palm, Sony, Toshiba, Hewlett-Packard, Dell, and Microsoft, manufacture tiny handheld portable computing devices that hold data such as your address book, personal notes, appointment schedules, and more. Such machines are called *personal digital assistants (PDAs)*. All modern PDAs have many applications, such as word processors for jotting down notes or shopping lists, expense reports, and even image viewers. Figure 19-4 shows a Palm Zire 71 PDA.

Figure 19-4
Palm Zire 71
displaying a to-do list

PDAs don't run Windows XP or even 98, but rather require specialized OSs such as Windows CE, PocketPC, PalmOS, and Linux. All of these OSs provide a GUI that enables you to interact with the device by touching the screen directly. Many of today's

PDAs use handwriting recognition combined with modified mouse functions, usually in the form of a pen-like *stylus* to make a type of input called *pen-based computing*. To make an application load, for example, you would slide the stylus out of its holder in the PDA case and touch the appropriate icon with the stylus tip.

HotSync

PDAs make excellent pocket companions because you can quickly add a client's address or telephone number, check the day's schedule before going to your next meeting, and modify your calendar entries when something unexpected arises. Best of all, you can then update all the equivalent features on your desktop PC automatically! PDAs synchronize with your primary PC so you have the same essential data on both machines. Many PDAs come with a cradle, a place to rest your PDA and recharge its battery. The cradle connects to the PC most often through a USB port. You can run special software to synchronize the data between the PDA and the main PC. Setting up the Zire 71 featured previously, for example, requires you to install a portion of the Palm desktop for Windows. This software handles all the synchronization chores. You simply place the PDA in the properly connected cradle and click the button to synchronize. Figure 19-5 shows a PDA in the middle of a *HotSync* operation, PalmOS's term for the process of synchronizing.

Figure 19-5
HotSync in progress

Beaming

Just about every PDA comes with an infrared port that enables you to transfer data from one PDA to another, a process called *beaming*. For example, you can readily exchange business contact information at a conference or share pictures that you carry around in your PDA. The process is usually as simple as clicking a drop-down list and selecting Beam or Beaming from the menu. The PDA searches the nearby area—infrared has a very limited range—to discover any PDA close by. The receiving PDA flashes a message to its owner asking permission to receive. Once that's granted, you simply stand there and wait for a moment while the PDAs transfer data. Slick!

NOTE   Chapter 21 goes into more detail on infrared networking.

PDA Memory

Almost every PDA has both internal Flash ROM memory of 1 MB or more, and some sort of removable and upgradeable storage medium. Secure Digital (SD) technology has the strongest market share among the many competing standards, but you'll find a bunch of different memory card types out there. SD cards come in a variety of physical sizes (SD, Mini SD, and Micro SD) and fit in a special SD slot. Other popular media include CompactFlash (CF) cards and Sony's proprietary Memory Stick. You'll find capacities for all the standards ranging from 128 MB up to 8 GB—on a card the size of a postage stamp! Figure 19-6 shows some typical memory cards.

Figure 19-6
SD, Mini SD, and
Micro SD (photos
courtesy of SanDisk)

NOTE Memory cards of all stripes made the leap in 2003 from the exclusive realm of tiny devices such as PDAs and digital photographic cameras to fully featured portable PCs and even desktop models. Some Panasonic PCs sport SD card slots, for example, and you can expect nearly every Sony PC—portable or otherwise—made in 2003 and later to offer a Memory Stick port.

Tablet PCs

Tablet PCs combine the handwriting benefits of PDAs with the full-fledged power of a traditional portable PC to create a machine that perfectly meets the needs of many professions. Unlike PDAs, tablet PCs use a full-featured PC operating system such as Microsoft Windows XP Tablet PC Edition 2005. Instead of (or in addition to) a keyboard and mouse, tablet PCs provide a screen that doubles as an input device. With a special pen, called a *stylus,* you can actually write on the screen (Figure 19-7). Just make sure you don't grab your fancy Cross ball-point pen accidentally and start writing on the screen! Unlike many PDA screens, most tablet PC screens are not pressure sensitive—you have to use the stylus to write on the screen. Tablet PCs come in two main form factors: *convertibles,* which include a keyboard that can be folded out of the way, and *slates,* which do away with the keyboard entirely. The convertible tablet PC in Figure 19-7, for example, looks and functions just like the typical clamshell laptop shown back in Figure 19-1. But here it's shown with the screen rotated 180 degrees and snapped flat so it functions as a slate. Pretty slick!

Figure 19-7
A tablet PC

In applications that aren't "tablet-aware," the stylus acts just like a mouse, enabling you to select items, double-click, right-click, and so on. To input text with the stylus, you can either tap keys on a virtual keyboard (shown in Figure 19-8), write in the writing utility (shown in Figure 19-9), or use speech recognition software. With a little practice, most users will find the computer's accuracy in recognizing their handwriting to be sufficient for most text input, although speedy touch-typists will probably still want to use a keyboard when typing longer documents.

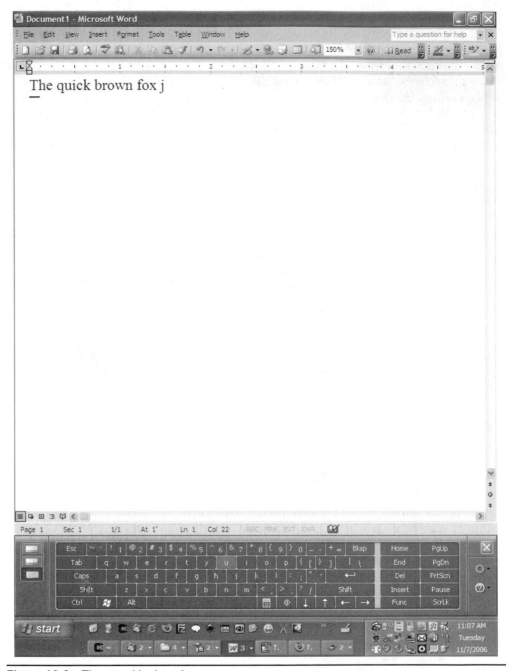

Figure 19-8   The virtual keyboard

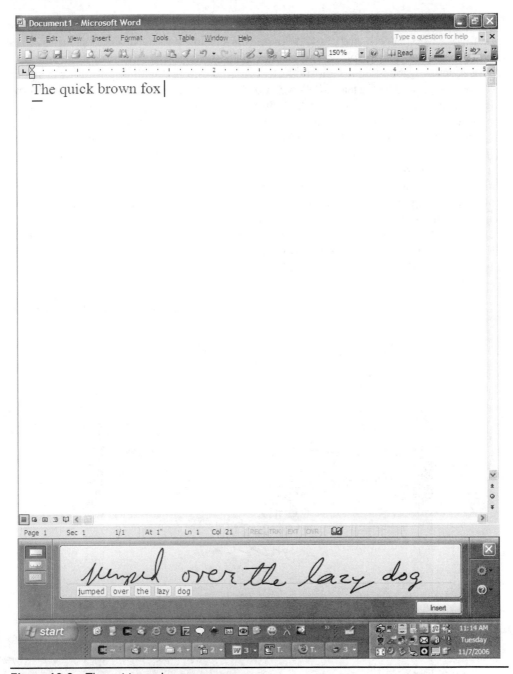

Figure 19-9 The writing pad

NOTE Handwriting recognition and speech recognition are two technologies that benefit greatly from increased CPU power. As multicore CPUs become more common, get ready to see more widespread adoption of these technologies!

Tablet PCs work well when you have limited space or have to walk around and use a laptop. Anyone who has ever tried to type with one hand, while walking around the factory floor holding the laptop with the other hand, will immediately appreciate the beauty of a tablet PC. In this scenario, tablet PCs are most effective when combined with applications designed to be used with a stylus instead of a keyboard. An inventory control program, for example, might present drop-down lists and radio buttons to the user, making a stylus the perfect input tool. With the right custom application, tablet PCs become an indispensable tool.

Microsoft encourages software developers to take advantage of a feature they call *digital ink*, which allows applications to accept pen strokes as input without first converting the pen strokes into text or mouse-clicks. Microsoft Journal (Figure 19-10), which comes with Windows-based tablet PCs, allows you to write on the screen just as though you were writing on a paper legal pad. Many other applications, including Microsoft Office, allow users to add ink annotations. Imagine sitting on an airplane reviewing a Microsoft Word document and simply scribbling your comments on the screen (Figure 19-11). No more printing out hard copy and breaking out the red pen for me! Imagine running a PowerPoint presentation and being able to annotate your presentation as you go. In the future, look for more applications to support Microsoft's digital ink.

Figure 19-10 Microsoft Journal preserves pen strokes as digital ink.

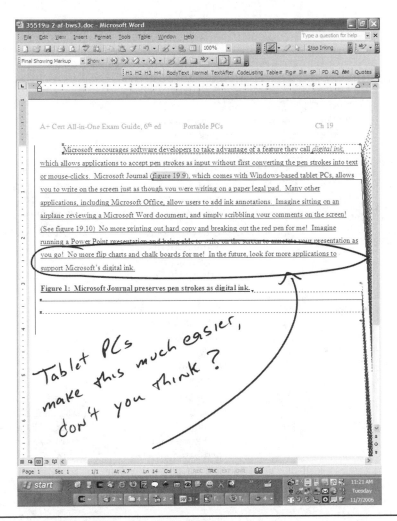

Figure 19-11   Microsoft Office supports digital ink.

There are many useful third-party applications designed specifically to take advantage of the tablet PC form factor. In fields such as law and medicine where tablet PCs have been especially popular, the choices are endless. One handy free utility that anyone who spends time in front of an audience (teachers, salespeople, cult leaders, and so on) will appreciate is InkyBoard (www.cfcassidy.com/Inkyboard/). Inkyboard provides a virtual dry-erase board, eliminating the need to find a flip chart or dry-erase board when holding meetings. Ever wished you could have a record of everything that was written on the chalkboard in a class (or at a business meeting)? If the professor had used Inkyboard, creating and distributing a copy would be a snap.

Portable Computer Device Types

Sorting out all the variations of portable computing devices out there would take entirely too much ink (and go well beyond CompTIA A+). Table 19-2 lists the seven most common styles of portable computing devices, some of their key features, and the intended use or audience for the product. This table is in no way conclusive, but lists the highlights.

	Screen Size	Weight	Features	Uses
Desktop replacements	14–20 inches+	8–12+ lbs	Everything on a desktop	Mobile multimedia editing, presentations, mobile gaming
Desktop extenders	10–14 inches	4–7 lbs	Almost everything you'll find on a desktop. Better battery life than desktop replacements	Presentations, note-taking in class or meetings, traveling companion for business folks
Ultralights	6–12 inches	2–3 lbs	Ultimate mobility without sacrificing full PC status. Excellent battery life. Few have internal optical drives	Long-term traveling companion, in the purse or pack for writing or doing e-mail on the road, coolness factor
Tablet PCs	10–12 inches	4 lbs	Pen-based interface enables you to use them like a paper notepad; no optical drives, but integrated wireless networking	Niche market for people who need handwritten notes that have to be transcribed to the PC
Ultra mobile PCs	4–7 inches	1–2 lbs	A variation of tablet PCs, UMPCs run Windows XP (Tablet or Home edition); pen-based interface and no optical drives	More of a niche market than tablet PCs, but similar audience; see the "Beyond A+" section for details
PDAs	3–4 inches	1 lb	Light, multifunction devices that carry address book, scheduler; many offer other features, such as MP3 and video playback	Helps busy people stay organized; helps get people organized; fun; can carry many electronic books (e-books) so you're never caught waiting in line and being bored
PDA phones	2 inches	< 1 lb	Tiny PDA built into a cell phone; some offer e-mail and other Internet connectivity	Reduces the number of gadgets some folks carry

Table 19-2 Portable Computing Devices

NOTE Portables come in such a dizzying variety of sizes, styles, features, and shapes that a simple table in a book cannot do justice to the ingenuity and engineering of the manufacturers of these devices. If you want to wander into the realm of extremes, check out www.dynamism.com. They specialize in bringing Japanese-only products to the English-speaking market. You'll find the hottest desktop replacement laptops and the sleekest subnotebooks at the site, with all the details beautifully converted from native Japanese to English.

IT Technician

Enhance and Upgrade the Portable PC

In the dark ages of mobile computing, you had to shell out top dollar for any device that would unplug, and what you purchased was what you got. Upgrade a laptop? Add functions to your desktop replacement? You had few if any options, so you simply paid for a device that would be way behind the technology curve within a year and functionally obsolete within two.

EXAM TIP If you're studying for the Help Desk Technician exam (Exam 220-603), you don't have to worry as much about portable PCs as you would studying for Depot Technician (Exam 220-604). The latter exam has fully one out of every five questions on laptops and portable devices. In other words, if you're studying for the Depot Tech exam, pay careful attention to this section! All of this material is relevant for the Essentials exam, so don't skip the rest of this chapter regardless of which exams you plan to take.

Portable PCs today offer many ways to enhance their capabilities. Internal and external expansion buses enable you to add completely new functions to portables, such as attaching a scanner or mobile printer or both! You can take advantage of the latest wireless technology breakthrough simply by slipping a card into the appropriate slot on the laptop. Further, modern portables offer a modular interior. You can add or change RAM, for example—the first upgrade that almost every laptop owner wants to make. You can increase the hard drive storage space and, at least with some models, swap out the CPU, video card, sound card, and more. Gone forever are the days of buying guaranteed obsolescence! Let's look at four specific areas of technology that laptops use to enhance functions and upgrade components: PC Cards, single- and multiple-function expansion ports, and modular components.

PC Cards

The *Personal Computer Memory Card International Association (PCMCIA)* establishes standards involving portable computers, especially when it comes to expansion cards, which are generically called PC Cards. *PC Cards* are roughly credit-card sized devices that enhance and extend the functions of a portable PC. PC Cards are as standard on today's mobile computers as the hard drive. PC Cards are easy to use, inexpensive, and convenient. Figure 19-12 shows a typical PC Card.

Figure 19-12
PC Card

 EXAM TIP CompTIA uses the older term *PCMCIA cards* to describe PC Cards. Don't be shocked if you get that as an option on your exams! You'll hear many techs use the phrase as well, though the PCMCIA trade group has not used it for many years.

Almost every portable PC has one or two PC Card slots, into which you insert a PC Card. Each card will have at least one function, but many have two, three, or more! You can buy a PC Card that offers connections for removable media, for example, such as combination SD and CF card readers. You can also find PC Cards that enable you to plug into multiple types of networks. All PC Cards are hot-swappable, meaning you can plug them in without powering down the PC.

 EXAM TIP Many manufacturers use the term *hot-pluggable* rather than hot-swappable to describe the ability to plug in and replace PC Cards on the fly. Look for either term on the exams.

The PCMCIA has established two versions of PC Cards, one using a parallel bus and the other using a serial bus. Each version, in turn, offers two technology variations as well as several physical varieties. This might sound complicated at first, but here's the map to sort it all out.

Parallel PC Cards

Parallel PC Cards come in two flavors, *16-bit* and *CardBus,* and each flavor comes in three different physical sizes, called Type I, Type II, and Type III. The 16-bit PC Cards, as the name suggests, are 16-bit, 5-V cards that can have up to two distinct functions or devices, such as a modem/network card combination. CardBus PC Cards are 32-bit,

3.3-V cards that can have up to eight (!) different functions on a single card. Regular PC Cards will fit into and work in CardBus slots, but the reverse is not true. CardBus totally dominates the current PC Card landscape, but you might still run into older 16-bit PC Cards.

Type I, II, and III cards differ only in the thickness of the card (Type I being the thinnest, and Type III the thickest). All PC Cards share the same 68-pin interface, so any PC Card will work in any slot that's high enough to accept that card type. Type II cards are by far the most common of PC Cards. Therefore, most laptops will have two Type II slots, one above the other, to enable the computer to accept two Type I or II cards or one Type III card (Figure 19-13).

Figure 19-13
PC Card slots

Although PCMCIA doesn't require that certain sizes perform certain functions, most PC Cards follow their recommendations. Table 19-3 lists the sizes and typical uses of each type of PC Card.

Type	Length	Width	Thickness	Typical Use
Type I	85.6 mm	54.0 mm	3.3 mm	Flash memory
Type II	85.6 mm	54.0 mm	5.0 mm	I/O (Modem, NIC, and so on)
Type III	85.6 mm	54.0 mm	10.5 mm	Hard drives

Table 19-3 PC Card Types and Their Typical Uses

NOTE Most PC Cards normally come with a hard plastic storage case. Always be sure to use this case to store the cards when you're not using them. If dust, dirt, or grime gets into the array of contacts at the end of the card, the card won't work when you try to use it next. Also, be careful when using PC Cards that extend out of the PC Card slot past the edge of your laptop. One dark night I set my laptop on the floor with a PC Card NIC sticking out of it while I went to get a drink of water. On my way back, I accidentally stepped on the card sticking out of my laptop and nearly snapped it in half. Luckily, my laptop wasn't damaged, but the card was toast!

ExpressCard

ExpressCard, the high-performance serial version of the PC Card, has begun to replace PC Card slots on newer laptop PCs. While ExpressCard offers significant performance benefits, keep in mind that ExpressCard and PC Cards are incompatible. You cannot use your PC Card in your new laptop's ExpressCard socket. The PC Card has had a remarkably long life in portable PCs, and you can still find it on some new laptops, but get ready to replace all your PC Card devices. ExpressCard comes in two widths: 54 mm and 34 mm. Figure 19-14 shows a 34-mm ExpressCard. Both cards are 75-mm long and 5-mm thick, which makes them shorter than all previous PC Cards and the same width as a Type II PC Card.

Figure 19-14
34-mm ExpressCard
(photo courtesy of
PCMCIA)

ExpressCards connect to either the Hi-Speed USB 2.0 bus or a PCI Express bus. These differ phenomenally in speed. The amazingly slow-in-comparison USB version has a maximum throughput of 480 Mbps. The PCIe version, in contrast, roars in at 2.5 Gbps in unidirectional communication. Woot!

Table 19-4 shows the throughput and variations for the parallel and serial PC cards currently or soon to be on the market.

Standard	Maximum Theoretical Throughput
PC Card using 16-bit bus	160 Mbps
CardBus PC Card using PCI bus	1056 Mbps
ExpressCard using USB 2.0 bus	480 Mbps
ExpressCard using PCIe bus	2.5 Gbps

Table 19-4 PC Card Speeds

Software Support for PC Cards

The PCMCIA standard defines two levels of software drivers to support PC Cards. The first, lower level is known as *socket services*. Socket services are device drivers that support the PC Card socket, enabling the system to detect when a PC Card has been inserted or removed, and providing the necessary I/O to the device. The second, higher level is known as *card services*. The card services level recognizes the function of a particular PC Card and provides the specialized drivers necessary to make the card work.

In today's laptops, the socket services are standardized and are handled by the system BIOS. Windows itself handles all card services and has a large preinstalled base of PC Card device drivers, although most PC Cards come with their own drivers.

NOTE ExpressCards don't require either socket or card services, at least not in the way PC Cards do. The ExpressCard modules automatically configure the software on your computer, which makes them truly plug and play.

Limited-function Ports

All portable PCs and many PDAs come with one or more single-function ports, such as an analog VGA connection for hooking up an external monitor and a PS/2 port for a keyboard or mouse. Note that contrary to the setup on desktop PCs, the single PS/2 port on most laptops supports both keyboards and pointing devices. Most portable computing devices have a speaker port, and this includes modern PDAs. My Compaq iPAQ doubles as an excellent MP3 player, by the way, a feature now included with most PDAs. Some portables have line-in and microphone jacks as well. Finally, most current portable PCs come with built-in NICs or modems for networking support. (See the section "The Modular Laptop" later in this chapter for more on networking capabilities.)

All limited-function ports work the same way on portable PCs as they do on desktop models. You plug in a device to a particular port and, as long as Windows has the proper drivers, you will have a functioning device when you boot. The only port that requires any extra effort is the video port.

Most laptops support a second monitor via an analog VGA port or a digital DVI port in the back of the box. With a second monitor attached, you can display Windows on only the laptop LCD, only the external monitor, or both simultaneously. Not all portables can do all variations, but they're more common than not. Most portables have a special Function (FN) key on the keyboard that, when pressed, adds an additional option to certain keys on the keyboard. Figure 19-15 shows a close-up of a typical keyboard with the Function key; note the other options that can be accessed with the Function key such as indicated on the F5 key. To engage the second monitor or to cycle through the modes, hold the Function key and press F5.

Figure 19-15
Laptop keyboard with (FN) key that enables you to access additional key options, as on the F5 key

NOTE Although many laptops use the Function key method to cycle the monitor selections, that's not always the case. You might have to pop into the Display applet in the Control Panel to click a checkbox. Just be assured that if the laptop has a VGA or DVI port, you can cycle through monitor choices!

General-purpose Ports

Sometimes the laptop doesn't come with all of the hardware you want. Today's laptops usually include several USB ports and a selection of the legacy general-purpose expansion ports (PS/2, RS-232 serial ports, and so on) for installing peripheral hardware. If you're lucky, you might even get a FireWire port so you can plug in your fancy new digital video camera. If you're really lucky, you might even have a docking station or port replicator so you don't have to plug in all of your peripheral devices one at a time.

USB and FireWire

Universal serial bus (USB) and FireWire (or more properly, IEEE 1394) are two technologies that have their roots in desktop computer technology, but have also found widespread use in portable PCs. Both types of connections feature an easy-to-use connector and give the user the ability to insert a device into a system while the PC is running—you won't have to reboot a system in order to install a new peripheral. With USB and FireWire, just plug the device in and go! Because portable PCs don't have multiple internal expansion capabilities like desktops, USB and FireWire are two of the more popular methods for attaching peripherals to laptops (see Figure 19-16).

Figure 19-16
Devices attached to USB or FireWire connector on portable PC

NOTE Almost all PDAs and other handheld devices—such as iPod music players—connect to PCs through USB ports. Most come with a USB cable that has a standard connector on one end and a proprietary connector on the other. Don't lose the cable!

Port Replicators

A *port replicator* plugs into a single port on the portable computer—often a USB port, but sometimes a proprietary port—and offers common PC ports, such as serial, parallel, USB, network, and PS/2. By plugging the port replicator into your notebook computer, you can instantly connect it to nonportable components such as a printer, scanner, monitor, or a full-sized keyboard. Port replicators are typically used at home or in the office with the non-portable equipment already connected. Figure 19-17 shows an Dell Inspiron laptop connected to a port replicator.

Figure 19-17
Port replicator
for a Dell portable
computer

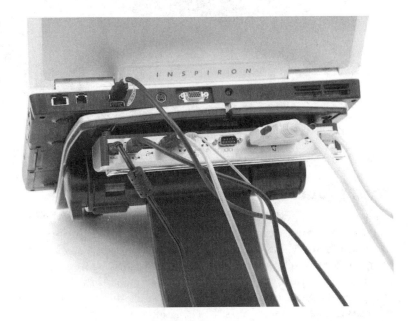

Once connected to the port replicator, the computer can access any devices attached to it; there's no need to connect each individual device to the PC. As a side bonus, port replicators enable you to attach legacy devices, such as parallel printers, to a new laptop that only has modern multifunction ports such as USB and FireWire, and not parallel or serial ports.

 NOTE Although portable PCs most often connect to port replicators via USB ports, some manufacturers have proprietary connections for proprietary port replicators. As long as such a portable PC has a USB port, you can use either the proprietary hardware or the more flexible USB devices.

Docking Stations

Docking stations (see Figure 19-18) resemble port replicators in many ways, offering legacy and modern single- and multi-function ports. The typical docking station uses a proprietary connection, but has extra features built in, such as a DVD drive or PC card slot for extra enhancements. You can find docking stations for most laptop models, but you'll find them used most frequently with the desktop extender and ultralight models. Many ultralights have no internal CD or DVD media drive (because the drives weigh too much), and so must rely on external drives for full PC functionality. Docking stations make an excellent companion to such portables.

Figure 19-18 Docking station

The Modular Laptop

For years, portable PC makers required completely proprietary components for each system model they developed. For the most part, this proprietary attitude still prevails, but manufacturers have added some modularity to today's portable PCs, enabling you to make basic replacements and upgrades without going back to the manufacturer for expensive, proprietary components. You need to surf the Web for companies that sell the components, because very few storefronts stock them. The most common modular components are RAM, hard drives, CPUs, video cards, optical drives, and network cards.

RAM

Stock factory portable PCs almost always come with a minimal amount of RAM, so one of the first laptop upgrades you'll be called on to do is to add more RAM. Economy laptops running Windows XP Home routinely sit on store shelves and go home to consumers with as little 256 MB of RAM, an amount guaranteed to limit the use and performance of the laptop. The OS alone will consume more than half of the RAM! Luckily, every decent laptop has upgradeable RAM slots. Laptops use one of four types of RAM. Most older laptops use either 72-pin or 144-pin SO-DIMMs with SDRAM technology (Figure 19-19). DDR and DDR2 systems primarily use 200-pin SO-DIMMs although some laptops use micro-DIMMs.

Figure 19-19
72-pin SO-DIMM
stick (front and back)

TIP   The amount of RAM needed to run a PC—portable or otherwise—smoothly and stably depends on both the type of applications that it will run and the needs of the OS. When making a recommendation to a client about upgrading a laptop's memory, you should ask the basic questions, such as what he or she plans to do on the laptop. If the laptop will be used for e-mail, word processing, and Web surfing, in contrast, a medium level of RAM, such as 256 MB, might be adequate. If the user travels, uses a high-end digital camera, and wants to use Photoshop to edit huge images, you'll need to augment the RAM accordingly. Then you need to add the needs of the OS to give a good recommendation. Refer back to Chapter 13, "Understanding Windows," for specific OS RAM needs.

How to Add or Replace RAM   Upgrading the RAM in a portable PC requires a couple of steps. First, you need to get the correct RAM. Many older portable PCs use proprietary RAM solutions, which means you need to order directly from Dell, HP, or Sony and pay exorbitant prices for the precious extra megabytes. Most manufacturers have taken pity on consumers in recent years and use standard SO-DIMMs or micro-DIMMs. Refer to the manufacturer's Web site or to the manual (if any) that came with the portable for the specific RAM needed.

Second, every portable PC offers a unique challenge to the tech who wants to upgrade the RAM because there's no standard for RAM placement in portables. More often than not, you need to unscrew or pop open a panel on the underside of the portable (Figure 19-20). Then you press out on the restraining clips and the RAM stick will pop up (Figure 19-21). Gently remove the old stick of RAM and insert the new one by reversing the steps.

Figure 19-20
Removing a
RAM panel

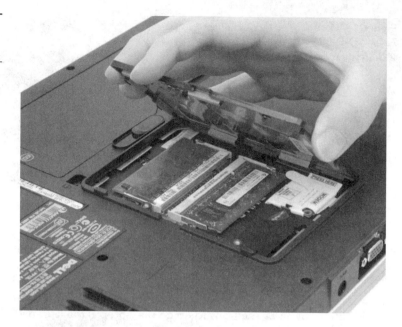

Figure 19-21
Releasing the RAM

Shared Memory Some laptops (and desktops) support *shared memory*. Shared memory is a means of reducing the cost of video cards by reducing the amount of memory on the video card itself. Instead of a video card with 256 MB of RAM, it might have only 64 MB of RAM but can borrow 192 MB of RAM from the system. This equates to a 256-MB video card. The video card uses regular system RAM to make up for the loss.

The obvious benefit of shared memory is a less expensive video card with performance comparable to its mega-memory alternative. The downside is your overall system performance will suffer because a portion of the system RAM is no longer available to programs. (The term *shared* is a bit misleading because the video card takes control of a portion of RAM. The video portion of system RAM is *not* shared back and forth between the video card processor and the CPU.) Shared memory technologies include TurboCache (developed by nVidia) and HyperMemory (developed by ATI).

Some systems give you control over the amount of shared memory while others simply allow you to turn shared memory on or off. The settings are found in CMOS setup and only on systems that support shared memory. Shared memory is not reported to Windows so don't panic if you've got 1 GB of RAM in your laptop, but Windows only sees 924 MB—the missing memory is used for video!

Adding more system RAM to a laptop with shared memory will improve laptop performance. Although it might appear to improve video performance, that doesn't tell the true story. It'll improve overall performance because the OS and CPU get more RAM to work with. On some laptops, you can improve video performance as well, but that depends on the CMOS setup. If the shared memory is not set to maximum by default, increasing the overall memory and upping the portion reserved for video will improve video performance specifically.

Hard Drives

ATA drives in the 2.5-inch drive format now rule in all laptops. Although much smaller than regular ATA drives, they still use all the same features and configurations. These smaller hard drives have suffered, however, from diminished storage capacity compared to their 3.5-inch brothers. Currently, large 2.5-inch hard drives hold up to 120 GB, while the 3.5-inch hard drives can hold more than 750 GB of data! Some manufacturers may require you to set the drive to use a cable select setting as opposed to master or slave, so check with the laptop maker for any special issues. Otherwise, no difference exists between 2.5-inch drives and their larger 3.5-inch brethren (Figure 19-22).

Figure 19-22
The 2.5-inch and 3.5-inch drives are mostly the same.

Modular CPUs

You know from Chapter 3, "Microprocessors," that both AMD and Intel make specialized CPUs for laptops that produce less heat and consume less power, yet only now are folks realizing that they can easily upgrade many systems by removing the old CPU and replacing it with a new one. Be very careful to follow manufacturer's specifications! You should keep in mind, however, that replacing the CPU in a laptop often requires that you disassemble the entire machine. This can be a daunting task, even for professionals. If you want to upgrade the CPU in your laptop, it's often best to let the professionals take care of it.

Video Cards

Some video card makers make modular video cards for laptops. Although no single standard works in all systems, a quick phone call to the tech support department of the laptop maker often reveals upgrade options (if any). Modular video cards are the least standardized of all modular components, but as manufacturers adopt more industry-wide standards, we'll be able to replace video cards in laptops more readily.

Going Inside

To reach most modular components on a laptop, you need to do more than remove an exterior panel. You need to go inside to get access to devices directly connected to the motherboard. Many laptops have an easily removable keyboard that, once removed, gives you access to a metal heat spreader (just a plate that sits over the motherboard) and a half-dozen or more tiny screws. You'll need a special screwdriver to avoid stripping the screws—check a watch or eyeglass shop if your local hardware store doesn't carry anything appropriate.

You need to take major precautions when you remove the keyboard and heat spreader. The keyboard will be attached to a small cable that can easily disconnect if you pull hard. Don't forget to check this connection before you reinsert the keyboard at the end of the procedure! Avoid ESD like you would with any other PC, and definitely unplug the laptop from the wall and *remove the battery* before you do any work inside!

Modular Drives

In order to add functionality to laptops, manufacturers include "modular drives" with their machines. CD-ROM, DVD-ROM, CD-R/RW, and CD-RW/DVD-ROM drives are the most common modular drives that are included with portables. The beauty of modular drives is that you can swap easily back and forth between different types of drives. Need more storage space? Pull out the CD-ROM drive and put in another hard drive. Many laptops enable you to replace a drive with a second battery, which obviously can extend the time you can go before you have to plug the laptop into an AC outlet.

I have a laptop that allows me to swap out my CD-ROM drive for a second battery. If I don't need to access any CDs and don't need super-extended battery life, I just take out the component that's currently installed and put a blank faceplate into the empty slot. Traveling with an empty bay makes my hefty laptop weigh a little bit less, and every little bit helps!

Most modular drives are truly hot-swappable, enabling you to remove and insert devices without any special software. Many still require you to use the Hardware Removal Tool (also known as Safely Remove Hardware) located in the System Tray (Figure 19-23). When in doubt, always remove modular devices using this tool. Figure 19-24 shows the Safely Remove Hardware dialog box. To remove a device, highlight it and click the Stop button. Windows will shut down the device and tell you when it's safe to remove the device.

Figure 19-23
Hardware Removal
Tool in System Tray

Figure 19-24
Safely Remove
Hardware dialog box

Mobile NICs and Mini PCI

Every laptop made in the last few years comes with networking capabilities built in. Laptops have modems for dial-up and Ethernet ports for plugging into a wired network. Because they run Windows, OS X, or some Linux distro, laptops have all the networking software ready to go, just like their desk-bound cousins.

NOTE See Chapter 21 for the scoop on dial-up networking and Ethernet.

Many laptops now come with integrated wireless networking support by way of a built-in Wi-Fi adapter usually installed in a Mini PCI slot on the laptop motherboard. The *Mini PCI* bus is an adaptation of the standard PCI bus and was developed specifically for integrated communications peripherals such as modems and network adapters. Built-in networking support means you don't need an additional PC Card to provide a network adapter. The Mini PCI bus also provides support for other integrated devices such as Bluetooth, modems, audio, or hard drive controllers. One great aspect of Mini PCI is that if some new technology eclipses the current wireless technology or some other technology that uses the bus, you can upgrade by swapping a card.

 EXAM TIP   A typical reason to upgrade a Mini PCI Wi-Fi NIC is to gain access to improved security options such as better encryption.

Officially released in 1999, Mini PCI is a 32-bit, 33-MHz bus and is basically PCI v2.2 with a different form factor. Like PCI, it supports bus mastering and DMA. Mini PCI cards are about a quarter the size of a regular PCI card and can be as small as 2.75 inches by 1.81 inches by .22 inches. They can be found in small products such as laptops, printers, and set-top boxes.

To extend battery life, built-in communication devices such as Wi-Fi and Bluetooth adapters can be toggled on and off without powering down the computer. Many laptops come with a physical switch along the front or side edge allowing you to power on or off the communications adapter. Similarly, you can often use a keyboard shortcut for this, generally by pressing the Function (FN) key along with some other key. The FN key, when pressed, allows other keys to accomplish specific tasks. For example, on my laptop pressing FN-F2 toggles my Wi-Fi adapter on and off; pressing FN-F10 ejects my CD-ROM drive.

 NOTE   Chapter 21, "Local Area Networks," covers wireless networking in great detail.

Managing and Maintaining Portables

Most portable PCs come from the factory solidly built and configured. Manufacturers know that few techs outside their factories know enough to work on them, so they don't cut corners. From a tech's standpoint, your most common work on managing and maintaining portables involves taking care of the batteries and extending the battery life through proper power management, keeping the machine clean, and avoiding excessive heat.

Everything you normally do to maintain a PC applies to portable PCs. You need to keep current on Windows patches and Service Packs, and use stable, recent drivers. Run Check Disk with some frequency, and definitely defragment the hard drive. Disk Cleanup is a must if the laptop runs Windows XP. That said, let's look at issues specifically involving portables.

Batteries

Manufacturers use three different types of batteries for portable PCs and each battery type has its own special needs and quirks. Once you've got a clear understanding of the quirks, you can *usually* spot and fix battery problems. The three types of batteries commonly used in mobile PCs are *Nickel-Cadmium (Ni-Cd)*, *Nickel-Metal Hydride (Ni-MH)*, and *Lithium-Ion (Li-Ion)* batteries. Manufacturers have also started working with fuel cell batteries, although most of that work is experimental at this writing.

Nickel-Cadmium

Ni-Cds were the first batteries commonly used in mobile PCs, which means the technology was full of little problems. Probably most irritating was a little thing called *battery memory,* or the tendency of a Ni-Cd battery to lose a significant amount of its rechargeability if it was charged repeatedly without being totally discharged. A battery that originally kept a laptop running for two hours would eventually only keep that same laptop going for 30 minutes or less. Figure 19-25 shows a typical Ni-Cd battery.

Figure 19-25
Ni-Cd battery

To prevent memory problems, a Ni-Cd battery had to be discharged completely before each recharging. Recharging was tricky as well, because Ni-Cd batteries disliked being overcharged. Unfortunately, there was no way to verify when a battery was fully charged without an expensive charging machine, which none of us had. As a result, most Ni-Cd batteries lasted an extremely short time and had to be replaced. A quick fix was to purchase a *conditioning charger.* These chargers would first totally discharge the Ni-Cd battery, and then generate a special "reverse" current that, in a way, "cleaned" internal parts of the battery so that it could be recharged more often and would run longer on each recharge. Ni-Cd batteries would, at best, last for 1,000 charges, and far fewer with poor treatment. Ni-Cds were extremely susceptible to heat and would self-discharge over time if not used. Leaving a Ni-Cd in the car in the summer was guaranteed to result in a fully discharged battery in next to no time!

But Ni-Cd batteries didn't stop causing trouble after they died. The highly toxic metals inside the battery made it unacceptable simply to throw them in the trash. Ni-Cd batteries should be disposed of via specialized disposal companies. This is very important! Even though Ni-Cd batteries aren't used in PCs very often anymore, many devices, such as cellular and cordless phones, still use Ni-Cd batteries. Don't trash the environment by tossing Ni-Cds in a landfill. Turn them in at the closest special disposal site; most recycling centers are glad to take them. Also, many battery manufacturers/distributors will take them. The environment you help preserve just might be yours—or your kids'!

 EXAM TIP You *must* use disposal companies or battery recycling services to dispose of the highly toxic Ni-Cd batteries.

Nickel-Metal Hydride

Ni-MH batteries were the next generation of mobile PC batteries and are still quite common today. Basically, Ni-MH batteries are Ni-Cd batteries without most of the headaches. Ni-MH batteries are much less susceptible to memory problems, can better tolerate overcharging, can take more recharging, and last longer between rechargings. Like Ni-Cds, Ni-MH batteries are still susceptible to heat, but at least they are considered less toxic to the environment. It's still a good idea to do a special disposal. Unlike a Ni-Cd, it's usually better to recharge a Ni-MH with shallow recharges as opposed to a complete discharge/recharge. Ni-MH is a popular replacement battery for Ni-Cd systems (Figure 19-26).

Figure 19-26
Ni-MH battery

Lithium Ion

The most common type battery used today is Li-Ion. Li-Ion batteries are very powerful, completely immune to memory problems, and last at least twice as long as comparable Ni-MH batteries on one charge. Sadly, they can't handle as many charges as Ni-MHs, but today's users are usually more than glad to give up total battery lifespan in return for longer periods between charges. Li-Ion batteries will explode if they are overcharged, so all Li-Ion batteries sold with PCs have built-in circuitry to prevent accidental over-charging. Lithium batteries can only be used on systems designed to use them. They can't be used as replacement batteries (Figure 19-27).

Figure 19-27
Li-Ion battery

Other Portable Power Sources

In an attempt to provide better maintenance for laptop batteries, manufacturers have developed a new type of battery called the *smart battery*. Smart batteries tell the computer when they need to be charged, conditioned, or replaced.

Portable computer manufacturers are also looking at other potential power sources, especially ones that don't have the shortcomings of current batteries. The most promising of these new technologies are *fuel cells*. The technology behind fuel cells is very complex, but to summarize, fuel cells produce electrical power as a result of a chemical reaction between the hydrogen and oxygen contained in the fuel cell. It is estimated that a small fuel cell could power a laptop for up to 40 hours before it needs to be replaced or refilled. This technology is still a year or two from making it to the consumer market, but it's an exciting trend!

The Care and Feeding of Batteries

In general, keep in mind the following basics. First, always store batteries in a cool place. Although a freezer is in concept an excellent storage place, the moisture, metal racks, and food make it a bad idea. Second, condition your Ni-Cd and Ni-MH batteries by using a charger that also conditions the battery; they'll last longer. Third, keep battery contacts clean with a little alcohol or just a dry cloth. Fourth, *never* handle a battery that has ruptured or broken; battery chemicals are very dangerous. Finally, always recycle old batteries.

NOTE Got an old portable PC battery lying around? Well, you've got to get rid of it, and since there are some pretty nasty chemicals in that battery, you can't just throw it in the trash. Sometimes, you can take old laptop batteries to an auto parts store that disposes of old car batteries—I know it sounds odd, but it's true! See if you can find one in your area that will do this. Many cities offer a hazardous materials disposal or recycling service. Check to see if and how your local government will help you dispose of your old batteries.

Power Management

Many different parts are included in the typical laptop, and each part uses power. The problem with early laptops was that every one of these parts used power continuously, whether or not the system needed that device at that time. For example, the hard drive would continue to spin whether or not it was being accessed, and the LCD panel would continue to display, even when the user walked away from the machine.

The optimal situation would be a system where the user could instruct the PC to shut down unused devices selectively, preferably by defining a maximum period of inactivity that, when reached, would trigger the PC to shut down the inactive device. Longer periods of inactivity would eventually enable the entire system to shut itself down, leaving critical information loaded in RAM, ready to restart if a wake-up event (such as moving the mouse or pressing a key) would tell the system to restart. The system would have to be sensitive to potential hazards, such as shutting down in the middle of writing to a drive, and so on. Also, this feature could not add significantly to the cost of the PC. Clearly, a machine that could perform these functions would need specialized hardware, BIOS, and operating system to operate properly. This process of cooperation among the hardware, the BIOS, and the OS to reduce power use is known generically as *power management*.

System Management Mode (SMM)

Intel began the process of power management with a series of new features built into the 386SX CPU. These new features enabled the CPU to slow down or stop its clock without erasing the register information, as well as enabling power saving in peripherals. These features were collectively called *System Management Mode (SMM)*. All modern CPUs have SMM. Although a power-saving CPU was okay, power management was relegated to special "sleep" or "doze" buttons that would stop the CPU and all of the peripherals on the laptop. To take real advantage of SMM, the system needed a specialized BIOS and OS to go with the SMM CPU. To this end, Intel put forward the *Advanced Power Management (APM)* specification in 1992 and the *Advanced Configuration and Power Interface (ACPI)* standard in 1996.

Requirements for APM/ACPI

APM and ACPI require a number of items in order to function fully. First is an SMM-capable CPU. As virtually all CPUs are SMM-capable, this is easy. Second is an APM-compliant BIOS, which enables the CPU to shut off the peripherals when desired. The third requirement is devices that will accept being shut off. These devices are usually called "Energy Star" devices, which signals their compliance with the EPA's Energy Star standard. To be an Energy Star device, a peripheral must have the ability to shut down without actually turning off and show that they use much less power than the non–Energy Star equivalent. Last, the system's OS must know how to request that a particular device be shut down, and the CPU's clock must be slowed down or stopped.

ACPI goes beyond the APM standard by supplying support for hot-swappable devices—always a huge problem with APM. This feature aside, it is a challenge to tell the difference between an APM system and an ACPI system at first glance.

 NOTE   Don't limit your perception of APM, ACPI, and Energy Star just to laptops! Virtually all desktop systems also use the power management functions.

APM/ACPI Levels

APM defines four different power-usage operating levels for a system. These levels are intentionally fuzzy to give manufacturers considerable leeway in their use; the only real difference among them is the amount of time each takes to return to normal usage. These levels are as follows:

- **Full On**   Everything in the system is running at full power. There is no power management.

- **APM Enabled**   CPU and RAM are running at full power. Power management is enabled. An unused device may or may not be shut down.

- **APM Standby**   CPU is stopped. RAM still stores all programs. All peripherals are shut down, although configuration options are still stored. (In other words, to get back to APM Enabled, you won't have to reinitialize the devices.)

- **APM Suspend**   Everything in the PC is shut down or at its lowest power-consumption setting. Many systems use a special type of Suspend called *hibernation*, where critical configuration information is written to the hard drive. Upon a wake-up event, the system is reinitialized, and the data is read from the drive to return the system to the APM Enabled mode. Clearly, the recovery time between Suspend and Enabled will be much longer than the time between Standby and Enabled.

ACPI handles all these levels plus a few more, such as "soft power on/off," which enables you to define the function of the power button.

Configuration of APM/ACPI

You configure APM/ACPI via CMOS settings or through Windows. Windows settings will override CMOS settings. Although the APM/ACPI standards permit a great deal of flexibility, which can create some confusion among different implementations, certain settings apply generally to CMOS configuration. First is the ability to initialize power management; this enables the system to enter the APM Enabled mode. Often CMOS will then present time frames for entering Standby and Suspend mode, as well as settings to determine which events take place in each of these modes. Also, many CMOS versions will present settings to determine wake-up events, such as directing the system to monitor a modem or a particular IRQ (Figure 19-28). A true ACPI-compliant CMOS provides an ACPI setup option. Figure 19-29 shows a typical modern BIOS that provides this setting.

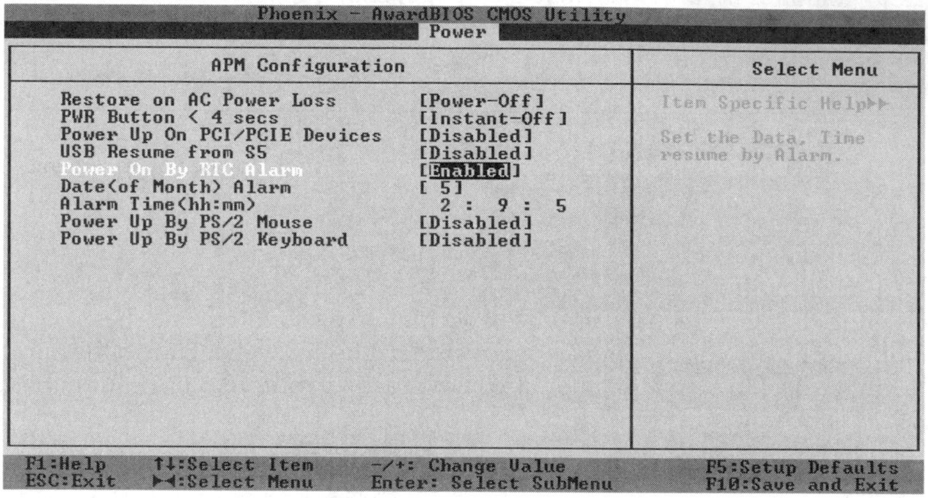

```
          Phoenix - AwardBIOS CMOS Utility
                       Power

      APM Configuration                              Select Menu

   Restore on AC Power Loss      [Power-Off]      Item Specific Help▶▶
   PWR Button < 4 secs           [Instant-Off]
   Power Up On PCI/PCIE Devices  [Disabled]       Set the Data, Time
   USB Resume from S5            [Disabled]       resume by Alarm.
   Power On By RTC Alarm         [Enabled]
   Date(of Month) Alarm          [ 5]
   Alarm Time(hh:mm)              2 : 9 : 5
   Power Up By PS/2 Mouse        [Disabled]
   Power Up By PS/2 Keyboard     [Disabled]


  F1:Help       ↑↓:Select Item    -/+: Change Value       F5:Setup Defaults
  ESC:Exit      ▶◀:Select Menu    Enter: Select SubMenu   F10:Save and Exit
```

Figure 19-28 Setting a wake-up event in CMOS

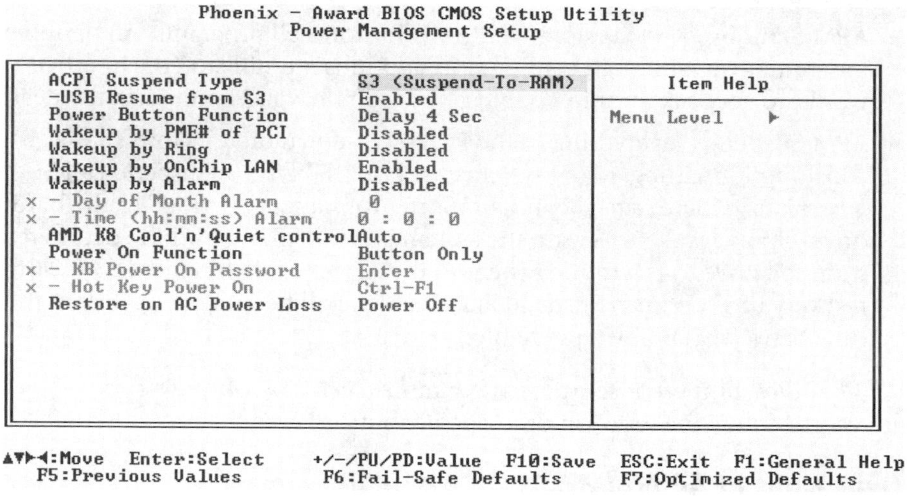

```
         Phoenix - Award BIOS CMOS Setup Utility
                 Power Management Setup

   ACPI Suspend Type           S3 (Suspend-To-RAM)       Item Help
   -USB Resume from S3         Enabled
   Power Button Function       Delay 4 Sec          Menu Level    ▶
   Wakeup by PME# of PCI       Disabled
   Wakeup by Ring              Disabled
   Wakeup by OnChip LAN        Enabled
   Wakeup by Alarm             Disabled
 x - Day of Month Alarm        0
 x - Time (hh:mm:ss) Alarm     0 : 0 : 0
   AMD K8 Cool'n'Quiet control Auto
   Power On Function           Button Only
 x - KB Power On Password      Enter
 x - Hot Key Power On          Ctrl-F1
   Restore on AC Power Loss    Power Off




 ▲▼▶◀:Move   Enter:Select   +/-/PU/PD:Value  F10:Save  ESC:Exit  F1:General Help
    F5:Previous Values        F6:Fail-Safe Defaults   F7:Optimized Defaults
```

Figure 19-29 CMOS with ACPI setup option

APM/ACPI settings can be found in the Windows 2000/XP control panel applet Power Options. The Power Options applet has several built-in *power schemes* such as Home/Office and Max Battery that put the system into standby or suspend after a certain interval (Figure 19-30). You can also require the system to go into standby after a set period of time or turn off the monitor or hard drive after a time, thus creating your own custom power scheme.

NOTE You may also access your Power Options by right-clicking on the Desktop and selecting Properties | Screensavers, and then clicking the Power button in the Monitor Power section of the Screensavers tab.

Figure 19-30
Power Options
Properties

Another feature, Hibernate mode, takes everything in active memory and stores it on the hard drive just before the system powers down. When the PC comes out of hibernation, Windows reloads all the files and applications into RAM. Figure 19-31 shows the Power Options Properties applet in Windows XP.

Figure 19-31
Power Options
Properties

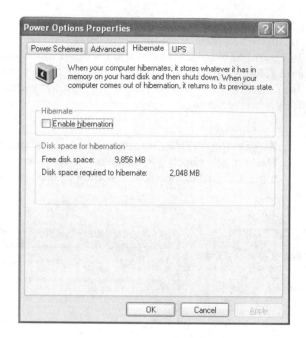

Cleaning

Most portable PCs take substantially more abuse than a corresponding desktop model. Constant handling, travel, airport food on the run, and so on can radically shorten the life of a portable if you don't take action. One of the most important things you should do is clean the laptop regularly. Use an appropriate screen cleaner (not a glass cleaner!) to remove fingerprints and dust from the fragile LCD panel. (Refer to Chapter 17 for specifics.)

If you've had the laptop in a smoky or dusty environment where the air quality alone causes problems, try compressed air for cleaning. Compressed air works great for blowing out the dust and crumbs from the keyboard and for keeping PC Card sockets clear. Don't use water on your keyboard! Even a minor amount of moisture inside the portable can toast a component.

Heat

To manage and maintain a healthy portable PC, you need to deal with issues of heat. Every portable has a stack of electronic components crammed into a very small space. Unlike their desktop brethren, portables don't have lots of freely-moving air space that enables fans to cool everything down. Even with lots of low-power-consumption devices inside, portable PCs still crank out a good deal of heat. Excessive heat can cause system lockups and hardware failures, so you should handle the issue wisely. Try this as a starter guide.

- Use power management, even if you're plugged into the AC outlet. This is especially important if you're working in a warm (more than 80 degrees Fahrenheit) room.

- Keep air space between the bottom of the laptop and the surface on which it rests. Putting a laptop on a soft surface like a pillow on your lap, for example, creates a great heat retention system—not a good thing! Always use a hard, flat surface!

- Don't use a keyboard protector for extended amounts of time.

- Listen to your fan, assuming the laptop has one. If it's often running very fast—you can tell by the high-pitched whirring sound—examine your power management settings and your environment and change whatever is causing heat retention.

- Speaking of fans, be alert to a fan that suddenly goes silent. Fans do fail on laptops, causing overheating and failure. All laptop fans can be replaced easily.

Protect the Machine

While prices continue to drop for basic laptops, a fully loaded system is still pricey. To protect your investment, you'll want to adhere to certain best practices. You've already read tips in this chapter to deal with cleaning and heat, so let's look at the "portable" part of portable computers.

Tripping

Pay attention to where you run the power cord when you plug in a laptop. One of the primary causes of laptop destruction is people tripping over the power cord and knocking the laptop off a desk. This is especially true if you plug in at a public place such as a café or airport. Remember, the life you save could be your portable PC's!

Storage

If your laptop or PDA isn't going to be used for a while, storing it safely will go a long way toward keeping it operable when you do power it up again. It's worth the extra few dollars to invest in a quality case also—preferably one with ample padding. Smaller devices such as PDAs are well protected inside small shock-resistant aluminum cases that clip on to your belt while laptops do fine in well-padded cases or backpacks. Not only will this protect your system on a daily basis when transporting it from home to office, but it will keep dust and pet hair away as well. Lastly, remove the battery if you'll be storing your device for an extended period of time to protect from battery leakage.

Travel

If traveling with a laptop, take care to protect yourself from theft. If possible, use a case that doesn't look like a computer case. A well-padded backpack makes a great travel bag for a laptop and appears less tempting to would-be thieves. Don't forget to pack any accessories you might need, like modular devices, spare batteries, and AC adapters. Make sure to remove any disks, such as CD/DVD or floppies, from their drives. Most importantly—back up any important data before you leave!

Make sure to have at least a little battery power available. Heightened security at airports means you might have to power on your system to prove it's really a computer and not a transport case for questionable materials. And never let your laptop out of your sight. If going through an x-ray machine, request a manual search. The x-ray won't harm your computer like a metal detector will, but if the laptop gets through the line at security before you do, someone else might walk away with it. If flying, keep your laptop out of the overhead bins and under the seat in front of you where you can keep an eye on it.

If you travel to a foreign country, be very careful about the electricity. North America uses ~115-V power outlets, but the rest of the world uses ~230-V outlets. Many portable computers have *auto-switching power supplies,* meaning they detect the voltage at the outlet and adjust accordingly. For these portables, a simple plug converter will do the trick. Other portable computers, however, have *fixed-input power supplies,* which means they run only on ~115-V or ~230-V power. For these portables, you need a full-blown electricity converting device, either a step-down or step-up *transformer.* You can find converters and transformers at electrical-parts stores, such as Radio Shack in the U.S.

Shipping

Much of the storage and travel advice can be applied to shipping. Remove batteries and CD/DVD/floppies from their drives. Pack it well and disguise the container as best you can. Back up any data and verify the warranty coverage. Ship with a reputable carrier and always request a tracking number and, if possible, delivery signature. It's also worth the extra couple of bucks to pay for the shipping insurance. And when the clerk asks what's in the box, it's safer to say "electronics" rather than "a new 20-inch laptop computer."

Security

The fact is, if someone really wants to steal your laptop, they'll find a way. There are, however, some things you can do to make yourself, and your equipment, a less desirable target. As you've already learned, disguise is a good idea. While you don't need to camouflage your laptop or carry it in a brown grocery bag on a daily basis, an inconspicuous carrying case will draw less attention.

Another physical deterrent is a laptop lock. Similar to a steel bicycle cable, there is a loop on one end and a lock on the other. The idea is to loop the cable around a solid object, like a bed frame, and secure the lock to the small security hole on the side of the laptop. Again, if someone really wants to steal your computer, they'll find a way. They'll dismantle the bed frame if they're desperate. The best protection is to be vigilant and not let the computer out of your sight.

An alternative to physically securing a laptop with a lock is to use a software tracking system. Software makers, such as Computer Security Products, Inc. at www.computersecurity.com, offer tracking software that transmits a signal to a central office if stolen and connected to a phone line or the Internet. The location of the stolen PC can be tracked, and sensitive files can even be deleted automatically with the aid of the stealth signal.

Troubleshooting Portable Computers

Many of the troubleshooting techniques you learned about with desktop systems can be applied to laptops. Additionally, there are some laptop-specific procedures to try.

Laptop Won't Power On

- Verify AC power by plugging another electronic device into the wall outlet. If the other device receives power, the outlet is good.

- If the outlet is good, connect the laptop to the wall outlet and try to power on. If no LEDs light up, you may have a bad AC adapter. Swap it out with a known-good power adapter.

- A faulty peripheral device might keep the laptop from powering up. Remove any peripherals such as USB or Firewire devices.

Screen Doesn't Come On Properly

- If the laptop is booting (you hear the beeps and the drives), first make sure the display is on. Press the FN key and the key to activate the screen a number of times until the laptop display comes on.

- If the laptop display is very dim, you may have lost an inverter. The clue here is that inverters never go quietly. They can make a nasty hum as they are about to die and an equally nasty popping noise when they actually fail. Failure often occurs when you plug in the laptop's AC adapter, as the inverters take power directly from the AC adapter.

Wireless Networking Doesn't Work

- Check for a physical switch along the front, rear, or side edges of the laptop that toggles the internal wireless adapter on and off.

- Try the special key combination for your laptop to toggle the wireless adapter. You usually press the FN key in combination with another key.

- You might simply be out of range. Physically walk the laptop over to the wireless router or access point to ensure there are no "out of range" issues.

Handwriting Is Not Recognized

- If your PDA or tablet PC no longer recognizes your handwriting or stylus, you may need to retrain the digitizer. Look for an option in your PDA OS settings to "align the screen." On Windows tablet PCs, you will find a similar option under Start | Settings | Control Panel.

Keypad Doesn't Work

- If none of the keys work on your laptop, there's a good chance you've unseated the keypad connector. These connectors are quite fragile and are prone to unseating from any physical stress on the laptop. Check the manufacturer's disassembly procedures to locate and reseat the keypad.

- If you're getting numbers when you're expecting to get letters, the number lock (NUMLOCK) function key is turned on. Turn it off.

Touchpad Doesn't Work

- A shot of compressed air does wonders for cleaning pet hair out of the touchpad sensors. You'll get a cleaner shot if you remove the keyboard before using the compressed air. Remember to be gentle when lifting off the keyboard and make sure to follow the manufacturer's instructions.

- The touchpad driver might need to be reconfigured. Try the various options in the Control Panel | Mouse applet.

Beyond A+

Centrino Technology

As mentioned previously in this chapter, consumers have always, and will always, demand better performance, more features, and longer battery life from their portable PCs. Intel, for example, promotes a combination of three components—extremely low-power, yet speedy, CPUs; integrated wireless networking technology; and an Intel chipset—that, when combined, produce portable PCs that not only are exceptionally powerful, but also boast an extremely long battery life!

Origami—Ultra-Mobile PCs

Microsoft started pushing the Ultra-Mobile PC (UMPC) standard in 2005 and has started to get some traction in the industry. UMPCs are a small form-factor tablet PC, designed to fill the spot between PDAs and tablet PCs. Most of the versions use a 7-inch widescreen, touch-enabled LCD (although at least one model on the market has a 4.3-inch widescreen LCD) and feature everything you would expect to find in their bigger cousins, with the exception of optical drives. They have internal 30–80 GB hard drives, 512 MB to 1

GB of RAM, built-in Wi-Fi and Bluetooth for connectivity, and more. Some even have USB and FireWire ports! All weigh under 2 pounds and come in at under 1 inch thick.

NOTE Microsoft initially called the UMPC project "Origami." The name has stuck, even though Microsoft has since shifted over to the more generic UMPC name.

The feature that most distinguishes UMPCs from PDAs is that the former runs a fully featured version of Windows XP, just like your desktop and laptop PCs. Most UMPCs run Windows Tablet PC edition, although a few devices run Windows XP Home or Windows Vista. (A few über geeks have even installed versions of Linux on UMPCs!) Figure 19-32 shows a Sony VAIO UX UMPC.

Figure 19-32
Sony VAIO UX
(photo courtesy of
Sony Electronics)

Chapter Review Questions

1. What is the name of the lower level of software drivers that support PC Cards?

   A. PCMCIA services

   B. Socket services

   C. Card services

   D. I/O services

2. How many Type III cards can typically fit into a laptop at one time?

   A. 1

   B. 2

   C. 3

   D. 4

3. Parallel PC Cards come in ____-bit and ____-bit versions. The latter is called CardBus.

   A. 8, 16

   B. 16, 32

   C. 32, 64

   D. 64, 128

4. What is the typical use for Type II PC cards?

   A. Additional RAM

   B. Hard drives

   C. Flash memory

   D. I/O devices such as modems and NICs

5. Which of the following are good ideas when it comes to smart batteries? (Choose all that apply.)

   A. Keep the contacts clean by using alcohol and a soft cloth.

   B. Store them in the freezer if they will not be used for a long period of time.

   C. Toss them in the garbage when they wear out.

   D. Store them in a cool, dry place.

6. What's the typical input device for a PDA?

   A. Keyboard

   B. Mouse

   C. Stylus

   D. Voice

7. Tablet PCs come in which of the following form factors? (Select all that apply.)

   A. Convertible

   B. Desktop

   C. Secure Digital

   D. Slate

8. ExpressCards connect to which buses? (Select all that apply.)

    A. ISA

    B. PCI

    C. PCIe

    D. Hi-Speed USB

9. Clara's laptop has a DVI connector to which she has connected a projector. As she prepares to make her presentation, however, nothing comes on the projector screen. The laptop shows the presentation and the projector appears to be functional, with a bright white bulb making a blank image on the screen. What's most likely the problem?

    A. She needs to plug in the projector.

    B. She's running the laptop on batteries. You need to plug in laptops to use the DVI connector.

    C. She needs to update her PC Card services to support projectors.

    D. She needs to press the Function key combination on her keyboard to cycle through monitor modes.

10. What is the primary benefit to adding more RAM to a laptop that uses shared memory? (Select the best answer.)

    A. Improved battery life

    B. Improved system performance

    C. Improved video performance

    D. None. Adding more RAM is pointless with systems that use shared memory.

Answers

1. **B.** The lower level of software drivers for PC Cards is known as socket services.

2. **A.** Due to their thickness, only one Type III PCMCIA card can fit into a laptop at a time.

3. **B.** Parallel PC Cards come in 16-bit and 32-bit varieties.

4. **D.** The typical use for Type II PC cards is for I/O devices such as modems and NICs.

5. **A, D.** Keeping a battery in the freezer is a good idea in theory, but not in practice. All batteries contain toxic chemicals and should *never* be treated like regular trash.

6. **C.** PDAs (and tablet PCs) use a stylus for input.

7. **A, D.** Tablet PCs come in convertible and slate form factors.

8. **C, D.** ExpressCards connect to either the PCI Express or Hi-Speed USB buses.

9. **D.** Clara needs to press the Function key combination on her keyboard to cycle through monitor modes.

10. **B.** Improved overall system performance is the primary benefit to adding more RAM to a laptop that uses shared memory.

Printers

In this chapter, you will learn how to
- Describe current printer technologies
- Explain the laser printing process
- Install a printer on a Windows PC
- Recognize and fix basic printer problems

Despite all of the talk about the "paperless office," printers continue to be a vital part of the typical office. In many cases, PCs are used exclusively for the purpose of producing paper documents. Many people simply prefer dealing with a hard copy. Programmers cater to this preference by using metaphors such as *page, workbook,* and *binder* in their applications. The CompTIA A+ certification strongly stresses the area of printing and expects a high degree of technical knowledge of the function, components, maintenance, and repair of all types of printers.

Essentials

Printer Technologies

No other piece of your computer system is available in a wider range of styles, configurations, and feature sets than a printer, or at such a wide price variation. What a printer can and can't do is largely determined by the type of printer technology it uses—that is, how it gets the image onto the paper. Modern printers can be categorized into several broad types: impact printers, inkjet printers, dye-sublimation printers, thermal printers, laser printers, and solid ink printers.

Impact Printers

Printers that create an image on paper by physically striking an ink ribbon against the paper's surface are known as *impact printers*. While *daisy-wheel* printers (essentially an electric typewriter attached to the PC instead of directly to a keyboard) have largely disappeared, their cousins, *dot-matrix printers*, still soldier on in many offices. While dot-matrix printers don't deliver what most home users want—high-quality and flexibility at a low cost—they're still widely found in businesses for two reasons: dot-matrix printers have a large installed base in businesses, and they can be used for multipart forms because they actually strike the paper. Impact printers tend to be relatively slow and noisy, but when speed, flexibility, and print quality are not critical, they provide acceptable results. PCs used for printing multipart forms, such as *point of sale (POS)* machines that need to print receipts in duplicate, triplicate, or more, represent the major market for new impact printers, although many older dot-matrix printers remain in use.

Dot-matrix printers (Figure 20-1) use a grid, or matrix, of tiny pins, also known as *printwires,* to strike an inked printer ribbon and produce images on paper. The case that holds the printwires is called a *printhead.* Using either 9 or 24 pins, dot-matrix printers treat each page as a picture broken up into a dot-based raster image. The 9-pin dot-matrix printers are generically called *draft quality,* while the 24-pin printers are known as *letter quality* or *near-letter quality.* The BIOS for the printer (either built into the printer or a printer driver) interprets the raster image in the same way that a monitor does, "painting" the image as individual dots. Naturally, the more pins, the higher the resolution. Figure 20-2 illustrates the components common to dot-matrix printers.

Figure 20-1
An Epson FX-880+ dot-matrix printer (photo courtesy of Epson America, Inc.)

Figure 20-2
Inside a dot-matrix printer

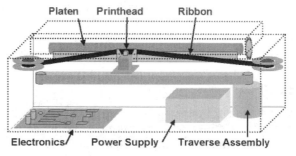

Inkjet Printers

Inkjet printers, also called *ink-dispersion printers,* (like the one in Figure 20-3) are relatively simple devices, consisting of a printhead mechanism, support electronics, a transfer mechanism to move the printhead back and forth, and a paper feed component to drag, move, and eject paper (Figure 20-4). They work by ejecting ink through tiny tubes. Most inkjet printers use heat to move the ink, while a few use a mechanical method. The heat-method printers use tiny resistors or electroconductive plates at the end of each tube (Figure 20-5), which literally boil the ink; this creates a tiny air bubble that ejects a droplet of ink onto the paper, thus creating portions of the image.

Figure 20-3
Typical inkjet printer

Figure 20-4
Inside an inkjet
printer

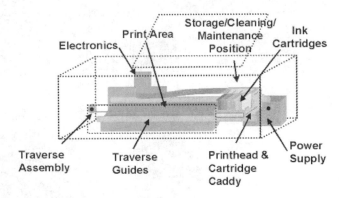

Figure 20-5
Detail of the inkjet printhead

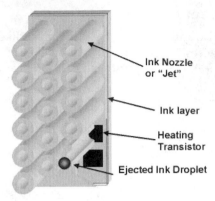

Ink Nozzle or "Jet"

Ink layer

Heating Transistor

Ejected Ink Droplet

The ink is stored in special small containers called *ink cartridges.* Older inkjet printers had two cartridges: one for black ink and another for colored ink. The color cartridge had separate compartments for cyan (blue), magenta (red), and yellow ink, to print colors using a method known as CMYK (you'll read more about CMYK later in this chapter). If your color cartridge ran out of one of the colors, you had to purchase a whole new color cartridge or deal with a messy refill kit.

Printer manufacturers began to separate the ink colors into three separate cartridges, so that printers came with four cartridges: one for each color and a fourth for black (Figure 20-6). This not only was more cost-effective for the user, but it also resulted in higher quality printouts. Today you can find color inkjet printers with six, eight, or more color cartridges. In addition to the basic CMYK inks, the other cartridges provide for green, blue, gray, light cyan, dark cyan, and more. Typically, the more ink cartridges a printer uses, the higher the quality of the printed image—and the higher the cost of the printer.

Figure 20-6
Inkjet ink cartridges

The two key features of an inkjet printer are the *print resolution*—that is, the density of ink, which affects print quality—and the print speed. Resolution is measured in *dots per inch (dpi)*; higher numbers mean that the ink dots on the page are closer together, so your printed documents will look better. Resolution is most important when you're printing complex images such as full-color photos, or when you're printing for duplication and you care that your printouts look good. Print speed is measured in *pages per minute (ppm)*, and this specification is normally indicated right on the printer's box. Most printers have one (faster) speed for monochrome printing—that is, using only black ink—and another for full-color printing.

Another feature of inkjet printers is that they can support a staggering array of print media. Using an inkjet printer, you can print on a variety of matte or glossy photo papers, iron-on transfers, and other specialty media; some printers can print directly onto specially coated CD- or DVD-media discs, or even fabric. Imagine running a t-shirt through your printer with your own custom slogan (how about "I'm CompTIA A+ Certified!"). The inks have improved over the years, too, now delivering better quality and longevity than ever. Where older inks would smudge if the paper got wet or start to fade after a short time, modern inks are smudge proof and of archival quality—for example, some inks by Epson are projected to last up to 200 years.

Dye-Sublimation Printers

The term *sublimation* means to cause something to change from a solid form into a vapor and then back into a solid. This is exactly the process behind *dye-sublimation printing*, sometimes called *thermal dye transfer* printing. Dye-sublimation printers are used mainly for photo printing, high-end desktop publishing, medical and scientific imaging, or other applications for which fine detail and rich color are more important than cost and speed. Smaller, specialized printers called *snapshot* printers use dye-sublimation specifically for printing photos at a reduced cost compared to their full-sized counterparts.

The dye-sublimation printing technique is an example of the so-called CMYK (**c**yan, **m**agenta, **y**ellow, blac**k**) method of color printing. It uses a roll of heat-sensitive plastic film embedded with page-sized sections of cyan (blue), magenta (red), and yellow dye; many also have a section of black dye. A print head containing thousands of heating elements, capable of precise temperature control, moves across the film, vaporizing the dyes and causing them to soak into specially-coated paper underneath before cooling and reverting to a solid form. This process requires one pass per page for each color. Some printers also use a final finishing pass that applies a protective laminate coating to the page. Figure 20-7 shows how a dye-sublimation printer works.

Figure 20-7
The dye-sublimation printing process

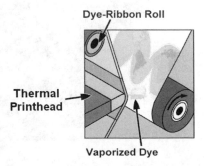

Documents printed through the dye-sublimation process display *continuous tone* images, meaning that the printed image is not constructed of pixel dots, but is a continuous blend of overlaid differing dye colors. This is in contrast to other print technologies' *dithered* images, which use closely packed, single-color dots to simulate blended colors. Dye-sublimation printers produce high-quality color output that rivals professional photo lab processing.

Thermal Printers

You'll see two kinds of thermal printers in use. The first is the *direct thermal* printer, and the other is the *thermal wax transfer* printer. Direct thermal printers use a heated print head to burn dots into the surface of special heat-sensitive paper. If you remember the first generation of fax machines, you're already familiar with this type of printer. It is still used as a receipt printer in many retail businesses. Thermal wax printers work similarly to dye-sublimation printers, except that instead of using rolls of dye-embedded film, the film is coated with colored wax. The thermal print head passes over the film ribbon and melts the wax onto the paper. Thermal wax printers don't require special papers like dye-sublimation printers, so they're more flexible and somewhat cheaper to use, but their output isn't quite as good because they use color dithering.

Laser Printers

Using a process called *electro-photographic imaging, laser printers* produce high-quality and high-speed output of both text and graphics. Figure 20-8 shows a typical laser printer. Laser printers rely on the photoconductive properties of certain organic compounds. *Photoconductive* means that particles of these compounds, when exposed to light (that's the "photo" part), will *conduct* electricity. Laser printers usually use lasers as a light source because of their precision. Some lower-cost printers use LED arrays instead.

Figure 20-8
Typical laser printer

The first laser printers created only monochrome images. Today, you can also buy a color laser printer, although the vast majority of laser printers produced today are still monochrome. Although a color laser printer can produce complex full-color images such as photographs, they really shine for printing what's known as *spot color*—for example, eye-catching headings, lines, charts, or other graphical elements that dress up an otherwise plain printed presentation.

NOTE Some printers use consumables at a much faster rate than others, prompting the industry to rank printers in terms of their cost per page. Using an inexpensive printer (laser or inkjet) costs around 4 cents per page, while an expensive printer can cost more than 20 cents per page—a huge difference if you do any volume of printing. This hidden cost is particularly pernicious in the sub-$100 inkjet printers on the market. Their low prices often entice buyers, who then discover that the cost of consumables is outrageous—these days, a *single* set of color and black inkjet cartridges can cost as much as the printer itself, if not more!

Critical Components of the Laser Printer

The CompTIA A+ certification exams take a keen interest in the particulars of the laser printing process, so it pays to know your way around a laser printer. Let's take a look at the many components of a laser printer and their functions (Figure 20-9).

Figure 20-9
Components inside
a laser printer

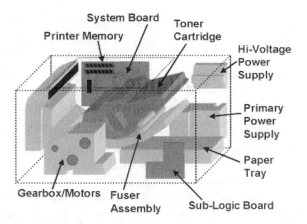

The Toner Cartridge The *toner cartridge* in a laser printer (Figure 20-10) is so named because of its most obvious activity—supplying the toner that creates the image on the page. To reduce maintenance costs, however, many other laser printer parts, especially those that suffer the most wear and tear, have been incorporated into the toner cartridge. Although this makes replacement of individual parts nearly impossible, it greatly reduces the need for replacement; those parts that are most likely to break are replaced every time you replace the toner cartridge.

Figure 20-10
Laser printer's
toner cartridge

The Photosensitive Drum   The *photosensitive drum* is an aluminum cylinder coated with particles of photosensitive compounds. The drum itself is grounded to the power supply, but the coating is not. When light hits these particles, whatever electrical charge they may have had "drains" out through the grounded cylinder.

Erase Lamp   The erase lamp exposes the entire surface of the photosensitive drum to light, making the photosensitive coating conductive. Any electrical charge present in the particles bleeds away into the grounded drum, leaving the surface particles electrically neutral.

Primary Corona   The *primary corona* wire, located close to the photosensitive drum, never touches the drum. When the primary corona is charged with an extremely high voltage, an electric field (or corona) forms, enabling voltage to pass to the drum and charge the photosensitive particles on its surface. The *primary grid* regulates the transfer of voltage, ensuring that the surface of the drum receives a uniform negative voltage of between ~600 and ~1000 volts.

Laser   The *laser* acts as the writing mechanism of the printer. Any particle on the drum struck by the laser becomes conductive, enabling its charge to be drained away into the grounded core of the drum. The entire surface of the drum has a uniform negative charge of between ~600 and ~1000 volts following its charging by the primary corona wire. When particles are struck by the laser, they are discharged and left with a ~100 volt negative charge. Using the laser, we can "write" an image onto the drum. Note that the laser writes a positive image to the drum.

Toner   The *toner* in a laser printer is a fine powder made up of plastic particles bonded to iron particles. The *toner cylinder* charges the toner with a negative charge of between ~200 and ~500 volts. Because that charge falls between the original uniform negative charge of the photosensitive drum (~600 to ~1000 volts) and the charge of the particles on the drum's surface hit by the laser (~100 volts), particles of toner are attracted to the areas of the photosensitive drum that have been hit by the laser (that is, areas that have a *relatively* positive charge with reference to the toner particles).

Transfer Corona To transfer the image from the photosensitive drum to the paper, the paper must be given a charge that will attract the toner particles off of the drum and onto the paper. The *transfer corona* is a thin wire, usually protected by other thin wires, that applies a positive charge to the paper, drawing the negatively charged toner particles to the paper. The paper, with its positive charge, is also attracted to the negatively charged drum. To prevent the paper from wrapping around the drum, a *static charge eliminator* removes the charge from the paper.

In most laser printers, the transfer corona is outside the toner cartridge, especially in large commercial grade machines. The transfer corona is prone to a build-up of dirt, toner, and debris through electrostatic attraction, and it must be cleaned. It is also quite fragile—usually finer than a human hair. Most printers with an exposed transfer corona will provide a special tool to clean it, but you can also—very delicately—use a Q-tip soaked in 90 percent denatured alcohol (don't use rubbing alcohol because it contains emollients). As always, never service any printer without first turning it off and unplugging it from its power source.

Fuser Assembly The *fuser assembly* is almost always separate from the toner cartridge. It is usually quite easy to locate as it will be close to the bottom of the toner cartridge and will usually have two rollers to fuse the toner. Sometimes the fuser is somewhat enclosed and difficult to recognize, because the rollers are hidden from view. To help you determine the location of the fuser, think about the data path of the paper and the fact that fusing is the final step of printing.

The toner is merely resting on top of the paper after the static charge eliminator has removed the paper's static charge. The toner must be permanently attached to the paper to make the image permanent. Two rollers, a pressure roller and a heated roller, are used to fuse the toner to the paper. The pressure roller presses against the bottom of the page while the heated roller presses down on the top of the page, melting the toner into the paper. The heated roller has a nonstick coating such as Teflon to prevent the toner from sticking to the heated roller.

Power Supplies All laser printers have at least two separate power supplies. The first power supply is called the "primary power supply" or sometimes just the "power supply." This power supply, which may actually be more than one power supply, provides power to the motors that move the paper, the system electronics, the laser, and the transfer corona. The high-voltage power supply usually provides power only to the primary corona. The extremely high voltage of the high-voltage power supply makes it one of the most dangerous devices in the world of PCs! Before opening a printer to insert a new toner cartridge, it is imperative that you *always turn off* a laser printer!

Turning Gears A laser printer has many mechanical functions. First, the paper must be picked up, printed upon, and kicked out of the printer. Next, the photosensitive roller must be turned and the laser, or a mirror, must be moved from left to right. Finally, the toner must be evenly distributed, and the fuser assembly must squish the toner into the paper. All these functions are served by complex gear systems. In most laser printers, these gear systems are packed together in discrete units generically called *gear packs* or *gearboxes*. Most laser printers will have two or three gearboxes that a tech can remove relatively easily in the rare case when one of them fails. Most gearboxes also have their own motor or solenoid to move the gears.

System Board Every laser printer contains at least one electronic board. On this board is the main processor, the printer's ROM, and RAM used to store the image before it is printed. Many printers divide these functions among two or three boards dispersed around the printer. An older printer may also have an extra ROM chip and/or a special slot where you can install an extra ROM chip, usually for special functions such as PostScript.

On some printer models you can upgrade the contents of these ROM chips (the *firmware*) by performing a process called *flashing* the ROM. Flashing is a lot like upgrading the system BIOS, which you learned about in Chapter 5, "BIOS and CMOS." Upgrading the firmware can help fix bugs, add new features, or update the fonts in the printer.

Of particular importance is the printer's RAM. When the printer doesn't have enough RAM to store the image before it prints, you get a memory overflow problem. Also, some printers will store other information in the RAM, including fonts or special commands. Adding RAM is usually a simple job—just snapping in a SIMM or DIMM stick or two—but getting the *right* RAM is important. Call or check the printer manufacturer's Web site to see what type of RAM you need. Although most printer companies will happily sell you their expensive RAM, most printers can use generic DRAM like the kind you use in a PC.

Ozone Filter The coronas inside laser printers generate ozone (O_3). Although not harmful to humans in small amounts, even tiny concentrations of ozone will cause damage to printer components. To counter this problem, most laser printers have a special ozone filter that needs to be vacuumed or replaced periodically.

Sensors and Switches Every laser printer has a large number of sensors and switches spread throughout the machine. The sensors are used to detect a broad range of conditions such as paper jams, empty paper trays, or low toner levels. Many of these sensors are really tiny switches that detect open doors and so on. Most of the time these sensors/switches work reliably. Yet occasionally, they can become dirty or broken, sending a false signal to the printer. Simple inspection is usually sufficient to determine if a problem is real or just the result of a faulty sensor/switch.

Solid Ink

Solid ink printers use just what you'd expect—solid inks. The technology was originally developed by Tektronix, a company that was acquired by Xerox. Solid ink printers use solid sticks of non-toxic "ink" that produce more vibrant color than other print methods. The solid ink is melted and absorbed into the paper fibers; it then solidifies, producing a continuous tone output. Unlike dye-sublimation printers, all colors are applied to the media in a single pass, reducing the chances of misalignment. Solid ink sticks do not rely on containers like ink for inkjet printers and can be "topped off" midway through a print job by inserting additional color sticks without taking the printer offline.

These printers are fast, too! A full-color print job outputs the first page in about 6 seconds. Of course, all that speed and quality comes at a price. Xerox's base model starts at about twice the cost of a laser printer, with the expensive model selling for about six times the cost! Solid ink printers become a bit more affordable when you factor in the cost of consumables. A single stick of ink costs about as much as an inkjet cartridge, for example, but with a print capacity of 1000 pages, that completely beats the cost of ink-jet cartridges over time.

Printer Languages

Now that you've learned about the different types of print devices and techniques, it's time to take a look at how they communicate with the PC. How do you tell a printer to make a letter *A* or to print a picture of your pet iguana? Printers are designed to accept predefined printer languages that handle both characters and graphics. Your software must use the proper language when communicating with your printer so that your printer can output your documents onto a piece of paper. Following are the more common printer languages.

American Standard Code for Information Interchange (ASCII)

You might think of ASCII as nothing more than a standard set of characters, the basic alphabet in upper and lowercase with a few strange symbols thrown in. ASCII actually contains a variety of control codes for transferring data, some of which can be used to control printers. For example, ASCII code 10 (or 0A in hex) means "Line Feed," and ASCII code 12 (0C) means "Form Feed." These commands have been standard since before the creation of IBM PCs, and all printers respond to them. If they did not, the PRINT SCREEN key would not work with every printer. Being highly standardized has advantages, but the control codes are extremely limited. Printing high-end graphics and a wide variety of fonts requires more advanced languages.

PostScript

Adobe systems developed the *PostScript* page description language in the early 1980s as a device-independent printer language capable of high-resolution graphics and scalable fonts. PostScript interpreters are embedded in the printing device. Because PostScript is understood by printers at a hardware level, the majority of the image processing is done by the printer and not the PC's CPU, so PostScript printers print faster. PostScript defines the page as a single raster image; this makes PostScript files extremely portable—they can be created on one machine or platform and reliably printed out on another machine or platform (including, for example, high-end typesetters).

Hewlett Packard Printer Control Language (PCL)

Hewlett Packard developed its *printer control language (PCL)* as a more advanced printer language to supersede simple ASCII codes. PCL features a set of printer commands greatly expanded from ASCII. Hewlett Packard designed PCL with text-based output in mind; it does not support advanced graphical functions. The most recent version of

PCL, PCL6 features scalable fonts and additional line drawing commands. Unlike Post-Script, however, PCL is not a true page description language; it uses a series of commands to define the characters on the page. Those commands must be supported by each individual printer model, making PCL files less portable than PostScript files.

Windows GDI

Windows 2000/XP use the *graphical device interface (GDI)* component of the operating system to handle print functions. Although you *can* use an external printer language such as PostScript, most users simply install printer drivers and let Windows do all the work. The GDI uses the CPU rather than the printer to process a print job and then sends the completed job to the printer. When you print a letter with a TrueType font in Windows, for example, the GDI processes the print job and then sends bitmapped images of each page to the printer. The printer sees a page of TrueType text, therefore, as a picture, not as text. As long as the printer has a capable enough raster image processor (explained later in this chapter) and plenty of RAM, you don't need to worry about the printer language in most situations. We'll revisit printing in Windows in more detail later in this chapter.

Printer Connectivity

Most printers connect to one of two ports on the PC: a DB-25 parallel port or a USB port. The parallel connection is the classic way to plug in a printer, but most newer printers use USB. You'll need to know how to support the more obscure parallel ports, cables, and connections as well as the plug-and-play USB connections.

Parallel Communication and Ports

The parallel port was included in the original IBM PC as a faster alternative to serial communication. The IBM engineers considered serial communication, limited to 1 bit at a time, to be too slow for the "high-speed" devices of the day (for example, dot-matrix printers). The standard parallel port has been kept around for backward compatibility despite several obvious weaknesses.

Parallel ports may be far faster than serial ports, but they are slow by modern standards. The maximum data transfer rate of a standard parallel port is still only approximately 150 kilobytes per second (KBps). Standard parallel communication on the PC also relies heavily on software, eating up a considerable amount of CPU time that could be better used.

 NOTE Although the phrase "Centronics standard" was commonly used in the heyday of parallel ports, no such animal actually existed. Prior to the development of IEEE 1284, a very loose set of "standards" were adopted by manufacturers in an attempt to at least reduce incompatibility issues.

Parallel ports are hindered by their lack of true bidirectional capability. While one-way communication was acceptable for simple line printers and dot-matrix printers, parallel communication also became popular for a wide range of external devices that required two-way communication. Although it is possible to get two-way communication out of a standard parallel port, the performance is not impressive.

NOTE Many techs confuse the concept of duplex printing—a process that requires special printers capable of printing on both sides of a sheet of paper—with bidirectional printing. They are two different things!

IEEE 1284 Standard

In 1991, a group of printer manufacturers proposed to the *Institute of Electrical and Electronics Engineers (IEEE)* that a committee be formed to propose a standard for a backward-compatible, high-speed, bidirectional parallel port for the PC. The committee was the IEEE 1284 committee (hence the name of the standard).

The IEEE 1284 standard requires the following:

- Support for five distinct modes of operation: *compatibility mode, nibble mode, byte mode, EPP,* and *ECP*
- A standard method of negotiation for determining which modes are supported both by the host PC and by the peripheral device
- A standard physical interface (that is, the cables and connectors)
- A standard electrical interface (that is, termination, impedance, and so on)

Because only one set of data wires exists, all data transfer modes included in the IEEE 1284 standard are half-duplex: Data is transferred in only one direction at a time.

NOTE The five modes of operation for parallel printing specified in the IEEE 1284 standard (compatibility, nibble, byte, EPP, ECP) are inching closer to obsolescence as USB printers take over the market. You can look up these modes by name using various Web search tools, if you find yourself needing to optimize the performance of a legacy parallel printer.

Parallel Connections, Cabling, and Electricity

Although no true standard exists, "standard parallel cable" usually refers to a printer cable with the previously-mentioned male DB-25 connector on one end and a 36-pin *Centronics* connector on the other (Figure 20-11). The shielding (or lack thereof) of the internal wiring and other electrical characteristics of a standard parallel printer cable are largely undefined except by custom. In practice, these standard cables are acceptable for transferring data at 150 KBps, and for distances of less than 6 feet, but they would be dangerously unreliable for some transfer modes.

Figure 20-11
Standard parallel cable with 36-pin Centronics connector on one end and DB-25 connector on the other

For more reliability at distances up to 32 feet (10 meters), use proper IEEE 1284-compliant cabling. The transfer speed drops with the longer cables, but it does work, and sometimes the trade-off between speed and distance is worth it.

Installing a parallel cable is a snap. Just insert the DB-25 connector into the parallel port on the back of the PC and insert the Centronics connector into the printer's Centronics port, and you're ready to go to press!

 NOTE Some printers come with both USB and parallel connections, but this is becoming increasingly rare. If you need a parallel printer for a system, be sure to confirm that the particular model you want will work with your system!

USB Printers

New printers now use USB connections that can be plugged into any USB port on your computer. USB printers don't usually come with a USB cable, so you need to purchase one at the time you purchase a printer. (It's quite a disappointment to come home with your new printer only to find you can't connect it because it didn't come with a USB cable.) Most printers use the standard USB type A connector on one end and the smaller USB type B connector on the other end, although some use two type A connectors. Whichever configuration your USB printer has, just plug in the USB cable—it's literally that easy!

 NOTE In almost all cases, you must install drivers before you plug a USB printer into your computer. You'll learn about installing printer drivers later in this chapter.

FireWire Printers

Some printers offer FireWire connections in addition to or instead of USB connections. A FireWire printer is just as easy to connect as a USB printer, as FireWire is also hot-swappable and hot-pluggable. Again, make sure you have the proper cable, as most printers don't come with one. If your printer has both connections, which one should you use? The answer is easy if your PC has only USB and not FireWire. If you have a choice, either connection is just as good as the other, and the speeds are comparable. If you already have many USB devices, you may want to use the FireWire printer connection, to leave a USB port free for another device.

Network Printers

Connecting a printer to a network isn't just for offices anymore. More and more homes and home offices are enjoying the benefits of network printing. It used to be that to share a printer on a network—that is, to make it available to all network users—you would physically connect the printer to a single computer and then share the printer on the network. The downside to this was that the computer to which the printer was connected had to be left on for others to use the printer.

Today, the typical printer comes with its own onboard network adapter that uses a standard RJ-45 Ethernet cable to connect the printer directly to the network by way of a router. The printer can typically be assigned a static IP address, or it can acquire one dynamically from a DHCP server. (Don't know what a router, IP address, or DHCP server is? Take a look at Chapter 21, "Local Area Networking.") Once connected to the network, the printer acts independently of any single PC. Some of the more costly network printers come with a built-in Wi-Fi adapter to connect to the network wirelessly. Alternatively, some printers offer Bluetooth interfaces for networking.

Even if a printer does not come with built-in Ethernet, Wi-Fi, or Bluetooth, you can purchase a standalone network device known as a *print server* to connect your printer to the network. These print servers, which can be Ethernet or Wi-Fi, enable one or several printers to attach via parallel port or USB. So take that ancient ImageWriter dot-matrix printer and network it—I dare you!

Other Printers

Plenty of other connection types are available for printers. We've focused mainly on parallel, USB, FireWire, and networked connections. Be aware that you may run into an old serial port printer or a SCSI printer. While this is unlikely, know that it's a possibility.

IT Technician

The Laser Printing Process

The laser printing process can be broken down into six steps, and the CompTIA A+ exams expect you to know them all. As a tech, you should be familiar with these phases, as this can help you troubleshoot printing problems. For example, if an odd line is printed down the middle of every page, you know there's a problem with the photosensitive drum or cleaning mechanism and the toner cartridge needs to be replaced.

You'll look into the physical steps that occur each time a laser printer revs up and prints a page; then you'll see what happens electronically to ensure that the data is processed properly into flawless, smooth text and graphics.

The Physical Side of the Process

Most laser printers perform the printing process in a series of six steps. Keep in mind that some brands of laser printers may depart somewhat from this process, although most work in exactly this order:

1. Clean
2. Charge
3. Write
4. Develop
5. Transfer
6. Fuse

 EXAM TIP Be sure that you know the order of a laser printer's printing process! Here's a mnemonic to help: Clarence Carefully Wrote Down The Facts.

Clean the Drum

The printing process begins with the physical and electrical cleaning of the photosensitive drum (Figure 20-12). Before printing each new page, the drum must be returned to a clean, fresh condition. All residual toner left over from printing the previous page must be removed, usually by scraping the surface of the drum with a rubber cleaning blade. If residual particles remain on the drum, they will appear as random black spots and streaks on the next page. The physical cleaning mechanism either deposits the residual toner in a debris cavity or recycles it by returning it to the toner supply in the toner cartridge. The physical cleaning must be done carefully. Damage to the drum will cause a permanent mark to be printed on every page.

Figure 20-12
Cleaning and erasing the drum

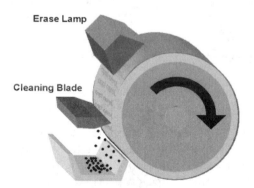

The printer must also be electrically cleaned. One or more erase lamps bombard the surface of the drum with the appropriate wavelengths of light, causing the surface particles to discharge into the grounded drum. After the cleaning process, the drum should be completely free of toner and have a neutral charge.

Charge the Drum

To make the drum receptive to new images, it must be charged (Figure 20-13). Using the primary corona wire, a uniform negative charge is applied to the entire surface of the drum (usually between ~600 and ~1000 volts).

Figure 20-13
Charging the drum
with a uniform
negative charge

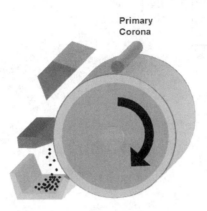

Primary
Corona

Write and Develop the Image

A laser is used to write a positive image on the surface of the drum. Every particle on the drum hit by the laser will release most of its negative charge into the drum. Those particles with a lesser negative charge will be positively charged relative to the toner particles and will attract them, creating a developed image (Figure 20-14).

Figure 20-14
Writing the image
and applying the
toner

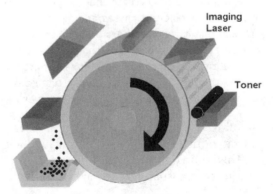

Imaging
Laser

Toner

Transfer the Image

The printer must transfer the image from the drum onto the paper. The transfer corona is used to give the paper a positive charge. Once the paper has a positive charge, the negatively charged toner particles leap from the drum to the paper. At this point, the particles are merely resting on the paper. They must still be permanently fused to the paper.

Fuse the Image

The particles have been attracted to the paper because of the paper's positive charge, but if the process stopped here, the toner particles would fall off the page as soon as the page was lifted. Because the toner particles are mostly composed of plastic, they can be melted to the page. Two rollers—a heated roller coated in a nonstick material and a pressure roller—melt the toner to the paper, permanently affixing it. Finally, a static charge eliminator removes the paper's positive charge (Figure 20-15). Once the page is complete, the printer ejects the printed copy and the process begins again with the physical and electrical cleaning of the printer.

Figure 20-15
Transferring the image to the paper and fusing the final image

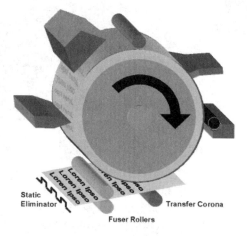

Static Eliminator

Transfer Corona

Fuser Rollers

 NOTE Color laser printers use four different colors of toner (cyan, magenta, yellow, and black) to create their printouts. Most models put each page through four different passes, adding one color at each pass to create the needed results, while others place all the colors onto a special belt and then transfer them to the page in one pass. In some cases, the printer uses four separate toner cartridges and four lasers for the four toner colors, and in others the printer simply lays down one color after the other on the same drum, cleaning after each of four passes per page.

Just be careful to use the right media with a laser printer. The heated roller produces enough heat to melt some types of plastic media, particularly overhead transparency materials. This could damage your laser printer (and void your warranty), so make sure you're printing on transparencies designed for laser printers!

The Electronic Side of the Process

Now that you have looked at the many parts of a laser printer and learned their basic functions, you're ready to delve into some of the electronic functions of laser printing.

Raster Images

Impact printers transfer data to the printer one character or one line at a time, whereas laser printers transfer entire pages at a time to the printer. A laser printer generates a raster image (a pattern of dots) of the page representing what the final product should look like.

It uses a device (the laser) to "paint" a raster image on the photosensitive drum. Because a laser printer has to paint the entire surface of the photosensitive drum before it can begin to transfer the image to paper, it processes the image one page at a time.

A laser printer uses a chip called the *raster image processor (RIP)* to translate the raster image sent to the printer into commands to the laser. The RIP takes the digital information about fonts and graphics and converts it to a rasterized image made up of dots that can then be printed. An inkjet printer also has a RIP, but it's part of the software driver instead of onboard hardware circuitry. The RIP needs memory (RAM) to store the data that it must process. A laser printer must have enough memory to process an entire page. Some images that require high resolutions require more memory. Insufficient memory to process the image will usually be indicated by a memory overflow ("MEM OVERFLOW") error. If you get a memory overflow error, try reducing the resolution, printing smaller graphics, or turning off RET (see the following section for the last option). Of course, the best solution to a memory overflow error is simply to add more RAM to the laser printer.

Do not assume that every error with the word *memory* in it can be fixed simply by adding more RAM to the printer. Just as adding more RAM chips will not solve every conventional PC memory problem, adding more RAM will not solve every laser printer memory problem. The message "21 ERROR" on an HP LaserJet, for example, indicates that "the printer is unable to process very complex data fast enough for the print engine." This means that the data is simply too complex for the RIP to handle. Adding more memory would *not* solve this problem; it would only make your wallet lighter. The only answer in this case is to reduce the complexity of the page image (that is, fewer fonts, less formatting, reduced graphics resolution, and so on).

 NOTE Inkjet printers use RIPs as well, but they're written into the device drivers instead of the onboard programming. You can also buy third-party RIPs that can improve the image quality of your printouts; for an example, see www.colorbytesoftware.com.

Resolution

Laser printers can print at different resolutions, just as monitors can display different resolutions. The maximum resolution that a laser printer can handle is determined by its physical characteristics. Laser printer resolution is expressed in dots per inch (dpi). Common resolutions are 600 × 600 dpi or 1200 × 1200 dpi. The first number, the horizontal resolution, is determined by how fine a focus can be achieved by the laser. The second number is determined by the smallest increment by which the drum can be turned. Higher resolutions produce higher quality output, but keep in mind that higher resolutions also require more memory. In some instances, complex images can be printed only at lower resolutions because of their high-memory demands. Even printing at 300 dpi, laser printers produce far better quality than dot-matrix printers because of *resolution enhancement technology (RET)*.

RET enables the printer to insert smaller dots among the characters, smoothing out the jagged curves that are typical of printers that do not use RET (Figure 20-16). Using

RET enables laser printers to output high-quality print jobs, but it also requires a portion of the printer's RAM. If you get a MEM OVERFLOW error, sometimes disabling RET will free up enough memory to complete the print job.

Figure 20-16
RET fills in gaps with smaller dots to smooth out jagged characters.

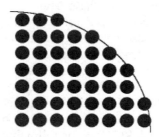 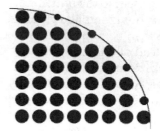

Installing a Printer in Windows

You need to take a moment to understand how Windows 2000 and Windows XP handle printing, and then you'll see how to install, configure, and troubleshoot printers in these operating systems.

 EXAM TIP The CompTIA A+ Essentials exam tests you on installing and troubleshooting printers, so read these sections for all four exams!

To Windows 2000/XP, a "printer" is not a physical device; it is a *program* that controls one or more physical printers. The *physical* printer is called a "print device" to Windows (although I continue to use the term "printer" for most purposes). Printer drivers and a spooler are still present, but in Windows 2000/XP they are integrated into the printer itself (Figure 20-17). This arrangement gives Windows 2000/XP amazing flexibility. For example, one printer can support multiple print devices, enabling a system to act as a print server. If one print device goes down, the printer automatically redirects the output to a working print device.

Figure 20-17
Printer driver and spooler in Windows 2000/XP

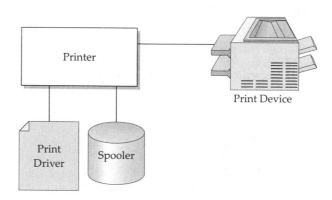

The general installation, configuration, and troubleshooting issues are basically identical in Windows 2000 and Windows XP. Here's a review of a typical Windows printer installation. I'll mention the trivial differences Windows 2000 and XP as I go along.

Setting Up Printers

Setting up a printer is so easy that it's almost scary. Most printers are plug and play, so installing a printer is reduced to simply plugging it in and loading the driver if needed. If the system does not detect the printer or if the printer is not plug and play, click Start | Printers and Faxes in Windows XP to open the Printers applet; in Windows 2000, click Start | Settings | Printers. The icon for this applet can also be found in the Control Panel.

As you might guess, you install a new printer by clicking the Add Printer icon (somehow Microsoft has managed to leave the name of this applet unchanged through all Windows versions since 9*x*). This starts the Add Printer Wizard. After a pleasant intro screen, you must choose to install either a printer plugged directly into your system or a network printer (Figure 20-18). You also have the *Automatically detect and install my Plug and Play printer* option, which you can use in many cases when installing a USB printer.

Figure 20-18
Choosing local or network printer in Windows XP

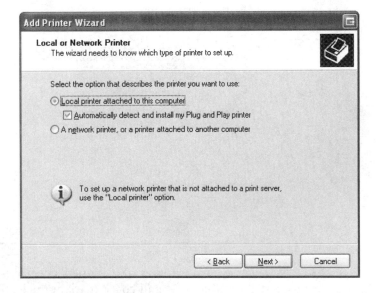

If you choose a local printer (see Chapter 21 for a discussion of networked printers), the applet next asks you to select a port (Figure 20-19); select the one where you installed the new printer. Once you select the port, Windows asks you to specify the type of printer, either by selecting the type from the list or using the Have Disk option, just as you would for any other device (Figure 20-20). Note the handy Windows Update button, which you can use to get the latest printer driver from the Internet. When you click Next on this screen, Windows installs the printer.

Figure 20-19
Selecting a port
in Windows XP

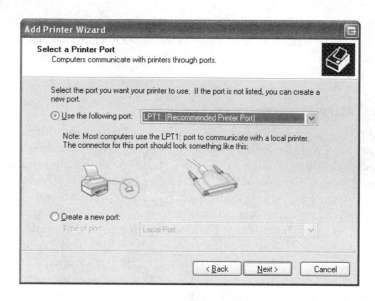

Figure 20-20
Selecting a printer
model/driver in
Windows XP

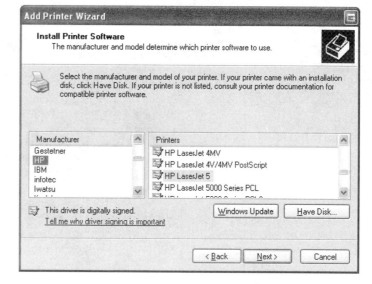

Figure 20-21 shows a typical Windows XP Printers and Faxes screen on a system with one printer installed. Note the small check mark in the icon's corner; this shows that the device is the default printer. If you have multiple printers, you can change the default printer by selecting the printer's properties and checking Make Default Printer.

In addition to the regular driver installation outlined previously, some installations use printer emulation. *Printer emulation* simply means using a substitute printer driver for a printer, as opposed to using one made exclusively for that printer. You'll run into printer emulation in two circumstances. First, some new printers do not come with

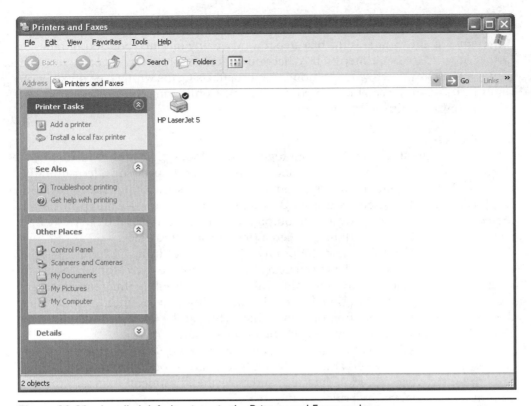

Figure 20-21 Installed default printer in the Printers and Faxes applet

their own drivers. They instead emulate a well-known printer (such as an HP LaserJet 4) and run perfectly well on that printer driver. Second, you may see emulation in the "I don't have the right driver!" scenario. I keep about three different HP LaserJet and Epson ink jet printers installed on my PC as I know that with these printer drivers, I can print to almost any printer. Some printers may require you to set them into an *emulation mode* to handle a driver other than their native one.

NOTE You've seen how to get your system to recognize a printer, but what do you do when you add a brand-new printer? Like most peripherals, the printer will include an installation CD-ROM that contains various useful files. One of the most important, but least used, tools on this CD-ROM is the Readme file. This file, generally in TXT format, contains the absolute latest information on any idiosyncrasies, problems, or incompatibilities related to your printer or printer driver. Usually, you can find it in the root folder of the installation CD-ROM, although many printer drivers install the Readme file on your hard drive, so you can access it from the Start menu. The rule here is *read first to avoid a headache later!*

Optimizing Print Performance

Although a quality printer is the first step toward quality output, your output relies on factors other than the printer itself. What you see on the screen may not match what comes out of the printer, so calibration is important. Using the wrong type of paper can result in less than acceptable printed documents. Configuring the printer driver and spool settings can also affect your print jobs.

Calibration

If you've ever tweaked that digital photograph so it looks perfect on screen, only to discover that the final printout was darker than you had hoped, consider calibrating your monitor. Computer monitors output in RGB—that is, they compose colors using red, green, and blue pixels, as discussed in Chapter 17, "Video"—while printers mix their colors differently to arrive at their output. As mentioned above, the CMYK method composes colors from cyan (blue), magenta (red), yellow, and black.

The upshot of all this is that the printer tries to output using CMYK (or another technique) what you see on the screen using RGB. Because the two color modes do not create color the same way, you see color shifts and not-so-subtle differences between the onscreen image and the printed image. By calibrating your monitor, you can adjust the setting to match the output of your printer. This can be done manually through "eyeballing" it or automatically using calibration hardware.

To calibrate your monitor manually, obtain a test image from the Web (try sites such as www.DigitalDog.net) and print it out. If you have a good eye, you can compare this printout to what you see on the screen and make the adjustments manually through your monitor's controls or display settings.

Another option is to calibrate your printer through the use of an International Color Consortium (ICC) color profile, a preference file that instructs your printer to print colors a certain way—for example, to match what is on your screen. Loading a different color profile results in a different color output. Color profiles are sometimes included on the installation CD-ROM with a printer, but you can create or purchase custom profiles as well. The use of ICC profiles is not limited to printers; you can also use them to control the output of monitors, scanners, or even digital cameras.

Troubleshooting Printers

As easy as printers are to set up, they are equally robust at running, assuming that you install the proper drivers and keep the printer well maintained. But printer errors do occasionally develop. Take a look at the most common print problems with Windows 2000/XP as well as problems that crop up with specific printer types.

General Troubleshooting Issues

Printers of all stripes share some common problems, such as print jobs that don't go, strangely sized prints, and misalignment. Other issues include consumables, sharing multiple printers, and crashing on power-up. Let's take a look at these general troubleshooting issues, but start with a recap of the tools of the trade.

Tools of the Trade

Before you jump in and start to work on a printer that's giving you fits, you'll need some tools. You can use the standard computer tech tools in your toolkit, plus a couple of printer-specific devices. Here are some that will come in handy:

- A multimeter for troubleshooting electrical problems such as faulty wall outlets

- Various cleaning solutions, such as denatured alcohol

- An extension magnet for grabbing loose screws in tight spaces and cleaning up iron-based toner

- A CD-media disc or USB thumb drive with test patterns for checking print quality

- Your trusty screwdriver—both a Phillips-head and flat-head because if you bring just one kind, it's a sure bet that you'll need the other

Print Job Never Prints

If you click Print but nothing comes out of the printer, first check all the obvious things. Is the printer on? Is it connected? Is it online? Does it have paper? Assuming the printer is in good order, it's time to look at the spooler. You can see the spooler status either by double-clicking the printer's icon in the Printers applet or by double-clicking the tiny printer icon in the System Tray if it's present. If you're having a problem, the printer icon will almost always be there. Figure 20-22 shows the print spooler open.

Figure 20-22
Print spooler

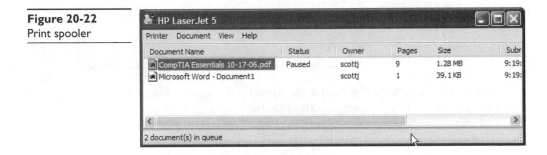

Print spoolers can easily overflow or become corrupt due to a lack of disk space, too many print jobs, or one of a thousand other factors. The status window shows all of the pending print jobs and enables you to delete, start, or pause jobs. I usually just delete the affected print job(s) and try again.

Print spoolers are handy. If the printer goes down, you can just leave the print jobs in the spooler until the printer comes back online. Some versions of Windows require you to select Resume Printing manually, but others will automatically continue the print job(s). If you have a printer that isn't coming on anytime soon, you can simply delete the print job in the spooler window and try another printer.

If you have problems with the print spooler, you can get around it by changing your print spool settings. Go into the Printers and Faxes applet, right-click the icon of the printer in question, and choose Properties. In the resulting Properties window (see Figure 20-23), choose the *Print directly to the printer* radio button and click OK; then try sending your print job again. Note that this window also offers you the choice of printing immediately—that is, starting to print pages as soon as the spooler has enough information to feed to the printer—or holding off on printing until the entire job is spooled.

Figure 20-23
Print spool settings

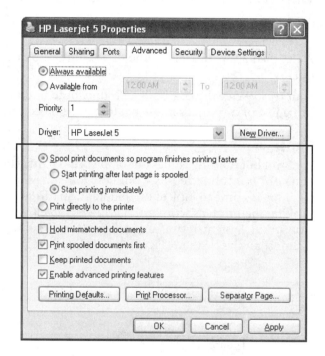

Another possible cause for a stalled print job is that the printer is simply waiting for the correct paper! Laser printers in particular have settings that tell them what size paper is in their standard paper tray or trays. If the application sending a print job specifies a different paper size—for example, it wants to print a standard No. 10 envelope, or perhaps a legal sheet, but the standard paper tray holds only 8.5 × 11 letter paper—the printer will usually pause and hold up the queue until someone switches out the tray or manually feeds the type of paper that's required for this print job. You can usually override this by pressing the OK or GO button on the printer or by manually feeding any size paper you want just to clear out the print queue, but the printer is doing its best to print the job properly.

The printer's default paper tray and paper size options will differ greatly depending on the printer type and model. To find these settings, go into the printer's Properties window from the Printers and Faxes applet, and then select the Device Settings tab. This list of settings includes Form To Tray Assignment, where you can specify which tray (in the case of a printer with multiple paper trays) holds which size paper.

Strange Sizes

A print job that comes out a strange size usually points to a user mistake in setting up the print job. All applications have a Print command and a Page Setup interface. The Page Setup interface enables you to define a number of print options, which vary from application to application. Figure 20-24 shows the Page Setup options for Microsoft Word. Make sure the page is set up properly before you blame the printer for a problem.

Figure 20-24
Page Setup options
for Microsoft Word

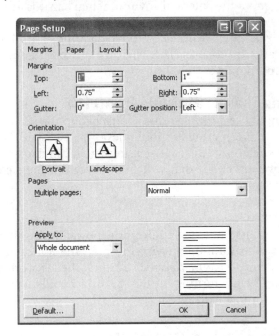

If you know the page is set up correctly, recheck the printer drivers. If necessary, uninstall and reinstall the printer drivers. If the problem persists, you may have a serious problem with the printer's print engine, but that comes up as a likely answer only when you continually get the same strangely sized printouts using a number of different applications.

Misaligned or Garbage Prints

Misaligned or garbage printouts invariably point to a corrupted or incorrect driver. Make sure you're using the right driver (it's hard to mess this up, but not impossible) and then uninstall and reinstall the printer driver. If the problem persists, you may be asking the printer to do something it cannot do. For example, you may be printing to a PostScript printer with a PCL driver. Check the printer type to verify that you haven't installed the wrong type of driver for that printer!

Dealing with Consumables

All printers tend to generate a lot of trash in the form of *consumables*. Impact printers use paper and ribbons, inkjet printers use paper and ink cartridges, and laser printers use paper and toner cartridges. In today's environmentally sensitive world, many laws regulate the proper disposal of most printer components. Be sure to check with the local sanitation department or disposal services company before throwing away any component. Of course, you should never throw away toner cartridges—certain companies will *pay* for used cartridges!

When in doubt about what to do with a component, check with the manufacturer for a *Material Safety Data Sheet (MSDS)*. These standardized forms provide detailed information about the potential environmental hazards associated with different components and proper disposal methods. For example, surf to www.hp.com/hpinfo/globalcitizenship/environment/productdata/index.html to find the latest MSDS for all Hewlett Packard products. This isn't just a printer issue—you can find an MSDS for most PC components.

Problems Sharing Multiple Printers

If you want to use multiple printers attached to the same parallel port, you have to use a switch box. Laser printers should never be used with mechanical switch boxes. Mechanical switch boxes create power surges that can damage your printer. If you must use a switch box, use a box that switches between printers electronically and has built-in surge protection.

Crashes on Power-up

Both laser printers and PCs require more power during their initial power-up (the POST on a PC and the warm-up on a laser printer) than once they are running. Hewlett Packard recommends a *reverse power-up*. Turn on the laser printer first and allow it to finish its warm-up before turning on the PC. This avoids having two devices drawing their peak loads simultaneously.

Troubleshooting Dot-Matrix Printers

Impact printers require regular maintenance but will run forever as long as you're diligent. Keep the platen (the roller or plate on which the pins impact) clean and the printhead clean with denatured alcohol. Be sure to lubricate gears and pulleys according to the manufacturer's specifications. Never lubricate the printhead, however, because the lubricant will smear and stain the paper.

Bad-looking Text

White bars going through the text point to a dirty or damaged printhead. Try cleaning the printhead with a little denatured alcohol. If the problem persists, replace the printhead. Printheads for most printers are readily available from the manufacturer or from companies that rebuild them. If the characters look chopped off at the top or bottom, the printhead probably needs to be adjusted. Refer to the manufacturer's instructions for proper adjustment.

Bad-looking Page

If the page is covered with dots and small smudges—the "pepper look"—the platen is dirty. Clean the platen with denatured alcohol. If the image is faded, and you know the ribbon is good, try adjusting the printhead closer to the platen. If the image is okay on one side of the paper but fades as you move to the other, the platen is out of adjustment. Platens are generally difficult to adjust, so your best plan is to take it to the manufacturer's local warranty/repair center.

Troubleshooting Inkjet Printers

Inkjet printers are reliable devices that require little maintenance as long as they are used within their design parameters (high-use machines will require more intensive maintenance). Because of the low price of these printers, manufacturers know that people don't want to spend a lot of money keeping them running. If you perform even the most basic maintenance tasks, they will soldier on for years without a whimper. Inkjets generally have built-in maintenance programs that you should run from time to time to keep your inkjet in good operating order.

Inkjet Printer Maintenance

Inkjet printers don't get nearly as dirty as laser printers, and most manufacturers do not recommend periodic cleaning. Unless your manufacturer explicitly tells you to do so, don't vacuum an inkjet. Inkjets generally do not have maintenance kits, but most inkjet printers come with extensive maintenance software (Figure 20-25). Usually, the hardest part of using this software is finding it in the first place. Look for an option in Printing Preferences, a selection on the Start menu, or an icon on your desktop. Don't worry—it's there!

Figure 20-25
Inkjet printer
maintenance screen

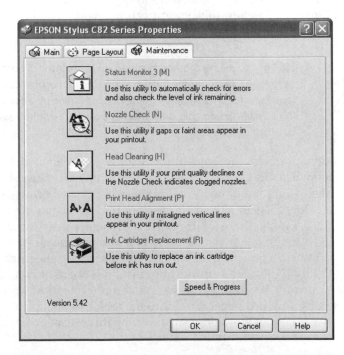

When you first set up an inkjet printer, it normally instructs you to perform a routine to align the printheads properly, wherein you print out a page and select from sets of numbered lines. If this isn't done, the print quality will show it, but the good news is that you can perform this procedure at any time. If a printer is moved or dropped or it's just been working away untended for a while, it's often worth running the alignment routine.

Inkjet Problems

Did I say that you never should clean an inkjet? Well, that may be true for the printer itself, but there is one part of your printer that will benefit from an occasional cleaning: the inkjet's printer head nozzles. The nozzles are the tiny pipes that squirt the ink onto the paper. A common problem with inkjet printers is the tendency for the ink inside the nozzles to dry out when not used even for a relatively short time, blocking any ink from exiting. If your printer is telling Windows that it's printing and it's feeding paper through, but either nothing is coming out (usually the case if you're just printing black text), or only certain colors are printing, the culprit is almost certainly dried ink clogging the nozzles.

 NOTE All inkjet inks are water-based, so water works better than alcohol to clean them up.

Every inkjet has a different procedure for cleaning the printhead nozzles. On older inkjets, you usually have to press buttons on the printer to start a maintenance program. On more modern inkjets, you can access the head cleaning maintenance program from Windows.

 NOTE Cleaning the heads on an inkjet printer is sometimes necessary, but I don't recommend that you do it on a regular basis as preventative maintenance. The head-cleaning process uses up a lot of that very expensive inkjet ink—so do this only when a printing problem seems to indicate clogged or dirty print heads!

Another problem that sometimes arises is the dreaded multi-sheet paper grab. This is often not actually your printer's fault—humidity can cause sheets of paper to cling to each other—but sometimes the culprit is an overheated printer, so if you've been cranking out a lot of documents without stopping, try giving the printer a bit of a coffee break. Also, fan the sheets of the paper stack before inserting it into the paper tray.

Finally, in the maintenance area where the printheads park is usually a small tank or tray to catch excess ink from the cleaning process. If the printer has one, check to see how full it is. If this tray overflows onto the main board or even the power supply, it will kill your printer. If you discover that it's about to overflow, you can remove excess ink by inserting a twisted paper towel into the tank to soak up some of the ink. It is advisable to wear latex or vinyl gloves while doing this. Clean up any spilled ink with a paper towel dampened with distilled water.

Troubleshooting Laser Printers

Quite a few problems can arise with laser printers, but before getting into those details, you need to review some recommended procedures for *avoiding* those problems.

 CAUTION Before you service a laser printer, always, ALWAYS turn it off and unplug it! Don't expose yourself to the very dangerous high voltages found inside these machines.

Laser Printer Maintenance

Unlike PC maintenance, laser printer maintenance follows a fairly well-established procedure. Follow these steps to ensure a long, healthy life for your system.

Keep It Clean   Laser printers are quite robust as a rule. A good cleaning every time you replace the toner cartridge will help that printer last for many years. I know of many examples of original HP LaserJet I printers continuing to run perfectly after a dozen or more years of operation. The secret is that they were kept immaculately clean.

Your laser printer gets dirty in two ways: Excess toner, over time, will slowly coat the entire printer. Paper dust, sometimes called *paper dander*, tends to build up where the paper is bent around rollers or where pickup rollers grab paper. Unlike (black) toner, paper dust is easy to see and is usually a good indicator that a printer needs to be cleaned. Usually, a thorough cleaning using a can of pressurized air to blow out the printer is the best cleaning you can do. It's best to do this outdoors, or you may end up looking like one of those chimney sweeps from *Mary Poppins*! If you must clean a printer indoors, use a special low-static vacuum designed especially for electronic components (Figure 20-26).

Figure 20-26
Low-static vacuum

Every laser printer has its own unique cleaning method, but one little area tends to be skipped in the included cleaning instructions. Every laser printer has a number of rubber guide rollers through which the paper is run during the print process. These little rollers tend to pick up dirt and paper dust over time, making them slip and jam paper. They are easily cleaned with a small amount of 90 percent or better alcohol on a fibrous cleaning towel. The alcohol will remove the debris and any dead rubber. You can also give the rollers and separator pads a textured surface that will restore their feeding properties by rubbing them with a little alcohol on a non-metallic scouring pad.

 CAUTION The photosensitive drum, usually contained in the toner cartridge, can be wiped clean if it becomes dirty, but be very careful if you do so! If the drum becomes scratched, the scratch will appear on every page printed from that point on. The only repair in the event of a scratch is to replace the toner cartridge.

If you're ready to get specific, get the printer's service manual. Almost every printer manufacturer sells these; they are a key source for information on how to keep a printer clean and running. Sadly, not all printer manufacturers provide these, but most do. While you're at it, see if the manufacturer has a Quick Reference Guide; these can be very handy for most printer problems!

Finally, be aware that Hewlett Packard sells maintenance kits for most of its laser printers. These are sets of replacement parts for the parts most likely to wear out on each particular type of HP LaserJet. Although their use is not required to maintain warranty coverage, using these kits when prescribed by HP helps to assure the continuing reliability of your LaserJet.

Periodic Maintenance Although keeping the printer clean is critical to its health and well being, every laser printer has certain components that will need to be replaced periodically. Your ultimate source for determining the parts that need to be replaced (and when to replace them) is the printer manufacturer. Following the manufacturer's maintenance guidelines will help to ensure years of trouble-free, dependable printing from your laser printer.

Some ozone filters may be cleaned with a vacuum and some can only be replaced— follow the manufacturer's recommendation. The fuser assembly may be cleaned with 90 percent or better denatured alcohol. Check the heat roller (the Teflon coated one with the light bulb inside) for pits and scratches. If you see surface damage on the rollers, replace the fuser unit.

Most printers will give you an error code when the fuser is damaged or overheating and needs to be replaced; others will produce the error code at a preset copy count as a preventative maintenance measure. Again, follow the manufacturer's recommendations.

 NOTE Failure of the thermal fuse (used to keep the fuser from overheating) can necessitate replacing the fuser assembly. Some machines contain more than one thermal fuse. As always, follow the manufacturer's recommendations. Many manufacturers have kits that alert you to replace the fuser unit and key rollers and guides at predetermined page counts with an alarm code.

The transfer corona can be cleaned with 90 percent denatured alcohol solution on a cotton swab. If the wire is broken, you can replace it; many just snap in or are held in by a couple of screws. Paper guides can also be cleaned with alcohol on a fibrous towel.

 CAUTION Always let the fuser assembly cool down before cleaning it, because they operate at 200 to 300 degrees Fahrenheit!

Laser Printer Problems

Laser printers usually manifest problems by creating poor output. One of the most important tests you can do on any printer, not just a laser printer, is called a *diagnostic print page* or an *engine test page*. This is done by either holding down the On Line button as the printer is started or using the printer's maintenance software.

Blank Paper   Blank sheets of paper usually mean the printer is out of toner. If the printer does have toner and nothing prints, print a diagnostic print page. If that is also blank, remove the toner cartridge and look at the imaging drum inside. If the image is still there, you know the transfer corona or the high-voltage power supply has failed. Check the printer's maintenance guide to see how to focus on the bad part and replace it.

Dirty Printouts   If the fusing mechanism gets dirty in a laser printer, it will leave a light dusting of toner all over the paper, particularly on the back of the page. When you see toner speckles on your printouts, you should get the printer cleaned.

Ghosting   Ghost images sometimes appear at regular intervals on the printed page. This can be caused either because the imaging drum has not fully discharged (and is picking up toner from a previous image) or because a previous image has used up so much toner that either the supply of charged toner is insufficient or the toner has not been adequately charged. Sometimes it can also be caused by a worn-out cleaning blade that isn't removing the toner from the drum.

Light Ghosting versus Dark Ghosting   A variety of problems can cause both light and dark ghosting, but the most common source of light ghosting is "developer starvation." If you ask a laser printer to print an extremely dark or complex image, it can use up so much toner that the toner cartridge will not be able to charge enough toner to print the next image. The proper solution is to use less toner. You can fix ghosting problems in the following ways:

- Lower the resolution of the page (print at 300 dpi instead of 600 dpi).
- Use a different pattern.
- Avoid 50 percent grayscale and "dot-on/dot-off patterns."
- Change the layout so that grayscale patterns do not follow black areas.
- Make dark patterns lighter and light patterns darker.
- Print in landscape orientation.
- Adjust print density and RET settings.
- Print a completely blank page immediately prior to the page with the ghosting image, as part of the same print job.

In addition to these possibilities, low temperature and low humidity can aggravate ghosting problems. Check your users' manual for environmental recommendations. Dark ghosting can sometimes be caused by a damaged drum. It may be fixed by replacing the toner cartridge. Light ghosting would *not* be solved in this way. Switching other components will not usually affect ghosting problems because they are a side effect of the entire printing process.

Vertical White Lines   Vertical white lines are usually due to a clogged toner preventing the proper dispersion of toner on the drum. Try shaking the toner cartridge to dislodge the clog. If that doesn't work, replace the toner cartridge.

Blotchy Print   This is most commonly due to uneven dispersion of toner, especially if the toner is low. Try shaking the toner from side to side and then try to print. Also be sure that the printer is sitting level. Finally, make sure the paper is not wet in spots. If the blotches are in a regular order, check the fusing rollers and the photosensitive drum for any foreign objects.

Spotty Print   If the spots appear at regular intervals, the drum may be damaged or some toner may be stuck to the fuser rollers. Try wiping off the fuser rollers. Check the drum for damage. If the drum is damaged, get a new toner cartridge.

Embossed Effect   If your prints are getting an embossed effect (like putting a penny under a piece of paper and rubbing it with a lead pencil), there is almost certainly a foreign object on a roller. Use 90 percent denatured alcohol or regular water with a soft cloth to try to remove it. If the foreign object is on the photosensitive drum, you're going to have to use a new toner cartridge. An embossed effect can also be caused by the contrast control being set too high. The contrast control is actually a knob on the inside of the unit (sometimes accessible from the outside, on older models). Check your manual for the specific location.

Incomplete Characters   Incompletely printed characters on laser-printed transparencies can sometimes be corrected by adjusting the print density. Be extremely careful to use only materials approved for use in laser printers.

Creased Pages   Laser printers have up to four rollers. In addition to the heat and pressure rollers of the fusing assembly, other rollers move the paper from the source tray to the output tray. These rollers crease the paper to avoid curling that would cause paper jams in the printer. If the creases are noticeable, try using a different paper type. Cotton bond paper is usually more susceptible to noticeable creasing than other bonds. You might also try sending the output to the face-up tray, which avoids one roller. There is no hardware solution to this problem; it is simply a side effect of the process.

Paper Jams   Every printer jams now and then. If you get a jam, always refer first to the manufacturer's jam removal procedure. It is simply too easy to damage a printer by pulling on the jammed paper! If the printer reports a jam but there's no paper inside, you've almost certainly got a problem with one of the many jam sensors or paper feed sensors inside the printer, and you'll need to take it to a repair center.

Pulling Multiple Sheets   If the printer grabs multiple sheets at a time, first try opening a new ream of paper and loading that in the printer. If that works, you've got a humidity problem. If the new paper angle doesn't work, check the separation pad on the printer. The separation pad is a small piece of cork or rubber that separates the sheets as they are pulled from the paper feed tray. A worn separation pad will look shiny and, well, *worn!* Most separation pads are easy to replace. Check out www.print-erworks.com to see if you can replace yours.

Warped, Overprinted, or Poorly Formed Characters   Poorly formed characters can indicate either a problem with the paper (or other media) or a problem with the hardware.

Incorrect media causes a number of these types of problems. Avoid paper that is too rough or too smooth. Paper that is too rough interferes with the fusing of characters and their initial definition. If the paper is too smooth (like some coated papers, for example), it may feed improperly, causing distorted or overwritten characters. Even though you can purchase laser printer–specific paper, all laser printers will print acceptably on standard photocopy paper. Try to keep the paper from becoming too wet. Don't open a ream of paper until it is loaded into the printer. Always fan the paper before loading it into the printer, especially if the paper has been left out of the package for more than just a few days.

The durability of a well-maintained laser printer makes hardware a much rarer source of character printing problems, but you should be aware of the possibility. Fortunately, it is fairly easy to check the hardware. Most laser printers have a self-test function—often combined with a diagnostic printout but sometimes as a separate process. This self-test shows whether the laser printer can properly develop an image without actually having to send print commands from the PC. The self-test is quite handy to verify the question, "Is it the printer or is it the computer?" Run the self-test to check for connectivity and configuration problems.

Possible solutions include replacing the toner cartridge, especially if you hear popping noises; checking the cabling; and replacing the data cable, especially if it has bends or crimps, or if objects are resting on the cable. If you have a front menu panel, turn off advanced functions and high-speed settings to determine whether the advanced functions are either not working properly or not supported by your current software configuration (check your manuals for configuration information). If these solutions do not work, the problem may not be user serviceable. Contact an authorized service center.

Beyond A+

DOT4

The IEEE 1284.4 standard, commonly known as DOT4, was created for multifunction peripherals (MFPs)—those nifty gadgets that combine the functions of printer, fax, and scanner in one big piece of equipment. The DOT4 protocol enables the individual devices within the MFP to send and receive multiple data packets simultaneously across a single physical channel. All data exchanges are independent of one another, so you can cancel one—for example, a print job—without affecting the others. DOT4 is an enhancement of the IEEE 1284 protocol for parallel printing; look for products that use it the next time you find yourself in a computer superstore.

Chapter Review Questions

1. What mechanism is used by most inkjet printers to push ink onto the paper?

   A. Electrostatic discharge

   B. Gravity

   C. Air pressure

   D. Electroconductive plates

2. With a laser printer, what creates the image on the photosensitive drum?

   A. Primary corona

   B. Laser imaging unit

   C. Transfer corona

   D. Toner

3. What is the proper order of the laser printing process?

   A. Clean, charge, write, develop, transfer, and fuse

   B. Charge, write, transfer, fuse, develop, and clean

   C. Clean, write, develop, transfer, fuse, and charge

   D. Clean, charge, write, develop, fuse, and transfer

4. On a dot-matrix printer, what physically strikes the ribbon to form an image?

   A. Electromagnets

   B. Printwires

   C. Character wheel

   D. Print hammers

5. Which of these items are considered to be dot-matrix printer consumables? (Select all that apply.)

   A. Drive motor

   B. Paper

   C. Flywheel

   D. Ribbon

6. What part must be vacuumed or replaced periodically to prevent damage as a result of the action of the corona?

   A. The rubber rollers

   B. The ozone filter

C. The transfer filter

D. The cleaning blade

7. Which of the following port types commonly support printers? (Select two.)

A. Parallel

B. USB

C. Infrared

D. RS-232

8. A standalone printer will print a test page just fine, but it makes gobbledygook out of your term paper. What's probably wrong?

A. Out of toner

B. Fuser error

C. Printer interface

D. Faulty software configuration

9. What printing process uses heat sensitive plastic files embedded with various color dyes?

A. Dye-sublimation

B. Inkjet

C. Ink-dispersion

D. Dye-dispersion

10. Which tool would help you determine why a print job didn't print?

A. Printer driver

B. Printer setup

C. Print spooler

D. System setup

Answers

1. **D.** Most inkjet printers use electroconductive plates to push the ink onto the paper.

2. **B.** The laser imaging unit creates an image on the photosensitive drum.

3. **A.** Clean, charge, write, develop, transfer, and fuse is the proper process.

4. **B.** Printwires physically strike the ribbon in dot-matrix printers.

5. **B, D.** Both paper and ribbons are considered dot-matrix printer consumables.

6. **B.** The ozone filter should be periodically vacuumed or changed.

7. **A, B.** You'll find almost all printers hooked up to parallel or USB ports.

8. **D.** The application (software) that is trying to print is probably configured incorrectly.

9. **A.** Dye-sublimation printers use heat sensitive plastic files embedded with various color dyes.

10. **C.** The print spooler can help you determine why a print job didn't print.

Local Area Networking

In this chapter, you will learn how to
- Explain network technologies
- Explain network operating systems
- Install and configure wired networks
- Install and configure wireless networks
- Troubleshoot networks

Networks dominate the modern computing environment. A vast percentage of businesses have PCs connected in a small local area network (LAN), and big businesses simply can't survive with connecting their many offices into a single wide area network (WAN). Even the operating systems of today demand networks. Windows XP and Windows Vista, for example, come out of the box *assuming* you'll attach them to a network of some sort just to make them work past 30 days (Product Activation), and they get all indignant if you don't.

Because networks are so common today, every good tech needs to know the basics of networking technology, operating systems, implementation, and troubleshooting. Accordingly, this chapter teaches you how to build and troubleshoot a basic network.

Historical/Conceptual

Networking Technologies

When the first network designers sat down at a café to figure out a way to enable two or more PCs to share data and peripherals, they had to write a lot of details on little white napkins to answer even the most basic questions. The first big question was: *How?* It's easy to say, "Well, just run a wire between them!" Although most networks do manifest themselves via some type of cable, this barely touches the thousands of questions that come into play here. Here are a few of the *big* questions:

- How will each computer be identified? If two or more computers want to talk at the same time, how do you ensure all conversations are understood?

- What kind of wire? What gauge? How many wires in the cable? Which wires do which things? How long can the cable be? What type of connectors?

- If more than one PC accesses the same file, how can they be prevented from destroying each other's changes to that file?

- How can access to data and peripherals be controlled?

Clearly, making a modern PC network entails a lot more than just stringing up some cable! Most commonly, you have a *client* machine, a PC that requests information or services. It needs a *network interface card (NIC)* that defines or labels the client on the network. A NIC also helps break files into smaller data units, called *packets*, to send across the network, and it helps reassemble the packets it receives into whole files. Second, you need some medium for delivering the packets between two or more PCs—most often this is a wire that can carry electrical pulses; sometimes it's radio waves or other wireless methods. Third, your PC's operating system has to be able to communicate with its own networking hardware and with other machines on the network. Finally, modern PC networks often employ a *server* machine that provides information or services. Figure 21-1 shows a typical network layout.

Windows XP Professional workstations

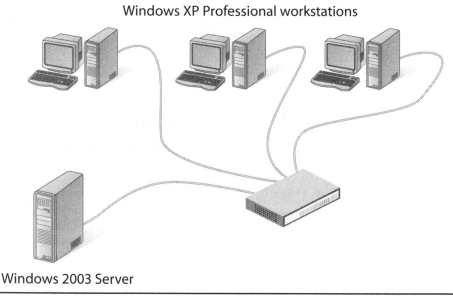

Windows 2003 Server

Figure 21-1   A typical network

This section of the chapter looks at the inventive ways network engineers found to handle the first two of the four issues. After a brief look at core technology, the chapter dives into four specific types of networks. You'll dig into the software side of things later in the chapter.

Topology

If a bunch of computers connect together to make a network, some logic or order must influence the way that they connect. Perhaps each computer connects to a single main line that snakes around the office. Each computer might have its own cable, with all the cables coming together to a central point. Or maybe all the cables from all the computers connect to a main loop that moves data along a track, picking up and dropping off data like a circular subway line.

A network's *topology* describes the way that computers connect to each other in that network. The most common network topologies are called *bus, ring, star,* and *mesh.* Figure 21-2 shows the four types: a *bus topology,* where all computers connect to the network via a main line called a *bus cable;* a *ring topology,* where all computers on the network attach to a central ring of cable; a *star topology,* where the computers on the network connect to a central wiring point (usually called a *hub*); and a *mesh topology,* where each computer has a dedicated line to every other computer. Make sure you know these four topologies!

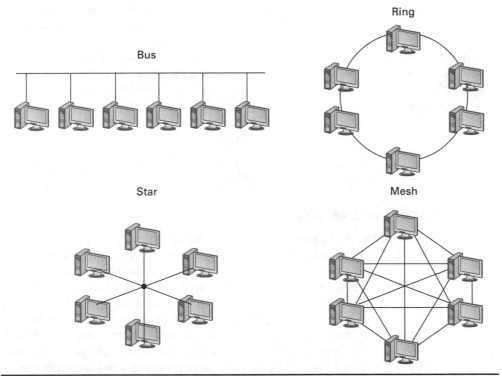

Figure 21-2 Clockwise from top left: bus, ring, mesh, and star topologies

If you're looking at Figure 21-2 and thinking that a mesh topology looks amazingly resilient and robust, it is—at least on paper. Because every computer physically connects to every other computer on the network, even if half the PCs crash, the network still functions as well as ever (for the survivors). In a practical sense, however, implementing a true mesh topology network would be an expensive mess. For example, even for a tiny network with only 10 PCs, you would need 45 separate and distinct pieces of cable to connect every PC to every other PC. What a mesh mess! Because of this, mesh topologies have never been practical in a cabled network.

While a topology describes the method by which systems in a network connect, the topology alone doesn't describe all of the features necessary to make a cabling system work. The term *bus topology*, for example, describes a network that consists of some number of machines connected to the network via the same piece of cable. Notice that this definition leaves a lot of questions unanswered. What is the cable made of? How long can it be? How do the machines decide which machine should send data at a specific moment? A network based on a bus topology can answer these questions in a number of different ways.

Most techs make a clear distinction between the *logical topology* of a network—how the network is laid out on paper, with nice straight lines and boxes—and the physical topology. The *physical topology* describes the typically messy computer network, with cables running diagonally through the ceiling space or snaking their way through walls. If someone describes the topology of a particular network, make sure you understand whether they're talking about the logical or physical topology.

Over the years, manufacturers and standards bodies created several specific network technologies based on different topologies. A *network technology* is a practical application of a topology and other critical technologies to provide a method to get data from one computer to another on a network. These network technologies have names like Ethernet and Token Ring, which will be discussed later in this chapter.

Essentials

Packets/Frames and NICs

Data is moved from one PC to another in discrete chunks called *packets* or *frames*. The terms *packet* and *frame* are interchangeable. Every NIC in the world has a built-in identifier, a binary address unique to that single network card, called a *media access control (MAC) address.* You read that right—every network card in the world has its own unique MAC address! The MAC address is 48 bits long, providing more than 281 *trillion* MAC addresses, so there are plenty of MAC addresses to go around. MAC addresses may be binary, but we represent them using 12 hexadecimal characters. These MAC addresses are burned into every NIC, and some NIC makers print the MAC address on the card. Figure 21-3 shows the System Information utility description of a NIC, with the MAC address highlighted.

 NOTE Even though MAC addresses are embedded into the NIC, some NICs will allow you to change the MAC address on the NIC. This is rarely done.

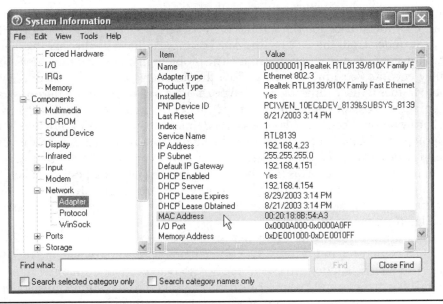

Figure 21-3 MAC address

Hey! I thought we were talking about packets? Well, we are, but you need to understand MAC addresses to understand packets. All the many varieties of packets share certain common features (Figure 21-4). First, packets contain the MAC address of the network card to which the data is being sent. Second, they have the MAC address of the network card that sent the data. Third is the data itself (at this point, we have no idea what the data is—certain software handles that question), which can vary in size depending on the type of frame. Finally, some type of data check (we call it a *cyclic redundancy check* or *CRC*) is performed and information is stored in the packet to enable the receiving network card to verify if the data was received in good order.

Figure 21-4
Generic packet/
frame

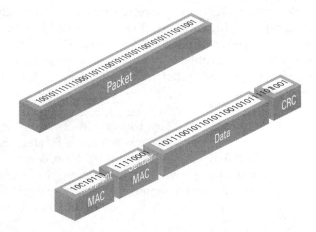

This discussion of packets raises the question, how big is the packet? Or more specifically, how much data do you put into each packet? How do you ensure that the receiving PC understands the *way* that the data was broken down by the sending machine and can thus put the pieces back together? The problem in answering these questions is that they encompass so many items. When the first networks were created, *everything* from the frames to the connectors to the type of cable had to be invented from scratch.

To make a successful network, you need the sending and receiving PCs to use the same hardware protocol. A *hardware protocol* defines many aspects of a network, from the topology, to the packet type, to the cabling and connectors used. A hardware protocol defines everything necessary to get data from one computer to another. Over the years, many hardware protocols have been implemented, with names like Token Ring, FDDI, and ARCnet, but one hardware protocol dominates the modern PC computing landscape: Ethernet. Token Ring contended with Ethernet for many years but has somewhat faded from the mainstream.

A consortium of companies centered on Digital Equipment, Intel, and Xerox invented the first network in the mid-1970s. More than just creating a network, they wrote a series of standards that defined everything necessary to get data from one computer to another. This series of standards was called *Ethernet,* and it is the dominant standard for today's networks. Ethernet comes in three main flavors defined by cabling type: coaxial, unshielded twisted pair, and fiber optic. Because all flavors of Ethernet use the same packet type, you can have any combination of hardware devices and cabling systems on an Ethernet network and all the PCs will be able to communicate just fine.

In the early 1980s, IBM developed the *Token Ring* network standard, again defining all aspects of the network but using radically different ideas than Ethernet. Token Ring networks continue to exist in some government departments and large corporations, but Ethernet has a far larger market share. Because Token Ring networks use a different structure for their data packets, special equipment must be used when connecting Token Ring and Ethernet networks. You'll read about Token Ring later in this chapter; focus on Ethernet for the moment.

Coaxial Ethernet

The earliest Ethernet networks connected using *coaxial cable.* By definition, coaxial cable (*coax* for short) is a cable within a cable—two cables that share the same center or axis. Coax consists of a center cable (core) surrounded by insulation. This in turn is covered with a *shield* of braided cable. The inner core actually carries the signal. The shield effectively eliminates outside interference. The entire cable is then surrounded by a protective insulating cover.

 EXAM TIP   You've seen coaxial cable before, most likely, although perhaps not in a networking situation. Your cable TV and antenna cables are coaxial, usually RG-59 or the highly shielded RG-6. Watch out for questions on the exams dealing specifically with networking hardware protocols, trying to trip you up with television-grade coaxial answers!

Thick Ethernet—10Base5

The original Xerox Ethernet specification that eventually became known as *10Base5* defined a very specific type of coaxial cabling for the first Ethernet networks, called *Thick Ethernet*. (In fact, the name for the cable became synonymous with the 10Base5 specification.) Thick Ethernet, also known as *Thicknet*, was a very thick (about half an inch in diameter) type of coaxial called *RG-8*. *RG* stands for Radio Grade, an industry standard for measuring coaxial cables. The *10* in 10Base5 refers to the fact that data could move through an RG-8 cable at up to 10 Mbps with this Ethernet standard.

Every PC in a 10Base5 network connected to a single cable, called a *segment* or *bus*. Thicknet supported attaching up to 100 devices to one segment. The maximum length of a Thicknet segment was 500 meters—that's what the *5* in *10Base5* meant (Figure 21-5). Networks like 10Base5 are laid out in a bus topology.

Figure 21-5
10Base5

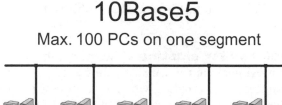

10Base5
Max. 100 PCs on one segment

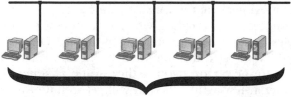

Max. segment length is 500 meters

Bus Topology   The Ethernet bus topology works like a big telephone party line— before any device can send a packet, devices on the bus must first determine that no other device is sending a packet on the cable (Figure 21-6). When a device sends its packet out over the bus, every other network card on the bus sees and reads the packet. Ethernet's scheme of having devices communicate like they were in a chat room is called *carrier sense multiple access/collision detection (CSMA/CD)*. Sometimes two cards talk (send packets) at the same time. This creates a collision, and the cards themselves arbitrate to decide which one will resend its packet first (Figure 21-7).

Figure 21-6
Devices can't send packets while others are talking.

CSMA/CD

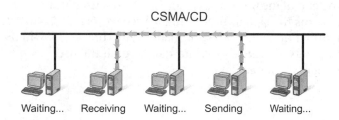

Waiting...   Receiving   Waiting...   Sending   Waiting...

Figure 21-7
Collisions result
when two devices
send simultaneously.

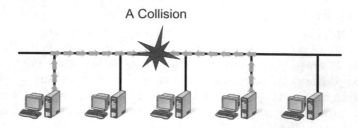

A Collision

All PCs on a bus network share a common wire, which also means they share the data transfer capacity of that wire—or, in tech terms, they share its *bandwidth*. This creates an interesting effect. Ten PCs chatting on a bus each get to use a much higher proportion of its total bandwidth than, for instance, 100 PCs on the same bus (in this case, one-tenth compared to one-hundredth). The more PCs on a bus, the more likely you'll have a communication traffic jam. This problem does not get solved until you get beyond coaxial Ethernet.

Reflection and Termination   The ends of the bus present a bit of a problem for the signal moving along the wire. Any time a device sends voltage along a wire, some voltage bounces back, or *reflects*, when it reaches the end of the wire (Figure 21-8). Network cables are no exception. Because of CSMA/CD, these packets reflecting back and forth on the cable would bring the network down. The NICs that want to send data would wait for no reason because they would misinterpret the reflections as a "busy signal." After a short while, the bus will get so full of reflecting packets that no other card can send data.

Figure 21-8
Reflection

When an electrical signal
reaches the end of a wire...

some of the signal
is reflected back.

To prevent packets from being reflected, a device called a *terminator* must be plugged into the end of the bus cable (Figure 21-9). A terminator is nothing more than a resistor that absorbs the signal, preventing reflection (Figure 21-10). The bus topology's need for termination is a weak spot. If the cable breaks anywhere, the reflections quickly build up and no device can send data, even if the break is not between the devices attempting to exchange data.

Figure 21-9
Terminator on
back of PC

Figure 21-10
No reflection with a
terminator

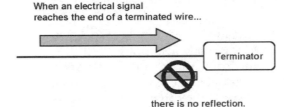

When an electrical signal
reaches the end of a terminated wire...

Terminator

there is no reflection.

Connections Thicknet was clearly marked every 2.5 meters (Figure 21-11). These marks showed where to connect devices to the cable. All devices on a Thicknet connected at these marks to ensure that all devices were some multiple of 2.5 meters apart.

Figure 21-11
Connection mark

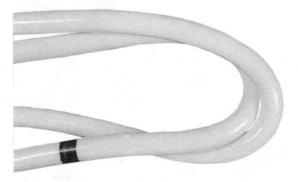

Devices are connected to Thicknet by means of a *vampire connector*. A vampire connector was so named because it actually pierces the cable to create the connection (Figure 21-12). A vampire connector was part of a transceiver—the device that both receives and sends data. Transceivers enable connections between the networked devices and the common cable and detect when collisions take place. Actually, all networks use transceivers, but Thicknet used an external transceiver—often referred to as an *access unit interface (AUI)*. The cable from the vampire connector/transceiver to the device had to be no more than 50 meters in length.

Figure 21-12
10Base5 transceiver
(vampire connector)

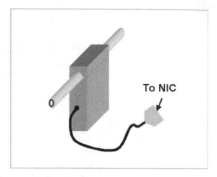

Thick Ethernet used a bus topology so it needed terminators. A very specific 50-ohm terminator was made just for Thicknet. It had to be placed on each end of the segment. Thicknet connected to a PC's network card via a 15-pin DB type connector. This connector was called the AUI or sometimes the *Digital, Intel, Xerox (DIX)* connector. Figure 21-13 shows the corresponding AUI port.

Figure 21-13
DIX or AUI port

Thick Ethernet is on the way out or completely dead. Bus topology is always risky, because one break in the cable will cause the entire network to fail. In addition, Thicknet was expensive and hard to work with. The cable, transceivers, and terminators cost far more than those in any other network.

EXAM TIP The vast majority of 10Base5 networks have gone away, so it's unlikely you'll ever encounter one in the field. The CompTIA A+ certification exams like using older or obscure technology for incorrect answers, though, so watch out for references to 10Base5, AUI, DIX, and Thicknet as wrong answers on exam questions.

Thin Ethernet—10Base2

Thin Ethernet, also known as *Thinnet* or *Cheapernet,* was invented as a cheap alternative to Thicknet. Thinnet used a specific type of coax called RG-58 (Figure 21-14). This type of coax looked like a skinny version of the RG-59 or RG-6 coax used by your cable television, but it was quite different. The RG rating was clearly marked on the cable. If it was not, the cable would say something like "Thinnet" or "802.3" to let you know you had the right cable (Figure 21-15).

Figure 21-14
RG-58 coaxial

Figure 21-15
Cable markings

Although Thin Ethernet also ran at 10 Mbps, it had several big limitations compared to Thick Ethernet. Thin Ethernet supported only 30 devices per segment, and each segment could be no more than 185 meters long (Figure 21-16). The *2* in 10Base2 originally meant 200 meters, but practical experience forced the standard down to 185 meters.

Figure 21-16
10Base2

10Base2
Max. 30 PCs on one segment

Max. segment length is 185 meters

On the plus side, cabling with Thinnet was a snap compared to Thicknet. The cable was much thinner and more flexible than Thicknet. In addition, the transceiver was built into the Thinnet network card, so Thinnet did not require an external transceiver. Each Thinnet network card was simply connected to the bus cable with a T connector (Figure 21-17).

Figure 21-17
T connector

The Thinnet cable had twist-on connectors, called *BNC connectors*, that attached to the T connector to form the network. Termination was handled by twisting small, specialized terminators onto the unused ends of the T connector on the machines at the ends of the chain. When installing Thinnet, it was important that one of the terminators be grounded. Special terminators could be grounded to the case of the PC. The PC also had to be grounded. You *had to* use a T connector! To add another PC to a Thinnet network, you simply removed the terminator from the last PC, added another piece of cable with another T connector, and added the terminator on the new end. It was also very easy to add a PC between two systems by unhooking one side of a T connector and inserting another PC and cable.

Thinnet, like its hefty cousin 10Base5, is on its way out or already dead. Very popular for a time in *small office/home office (SOHO)* networks, the fact that it used a bus topology where any wire break meant the whole network went down made 10Base2 unacceptable in a modern network.

UTP Ethernet (10/100/100BaseT)

Most modern Ethernet networks employ one of three technologies (and sometimes all three), *10BaseT*, *100BaseT*, or *1000BaseT*. As the numbers in the names would suggest, 10BaseT networks run at 10 Mbps, 100BaseT networks run at 100 Mbps, and 1000BaseT networks—called Gigabit Ethernet—run at 1000 Mbps, or 1 Gbps. All three technologies—sometimes referred to collectively as *10/100/1000BaseT*—use a *star bus* topology and connect via a type of cable called *unshielded twisted pair (UTP)*.

Star Bus

Imagine taking a bus network and shrinking the bus down so it will fit inside a box. Then, instead of attaching each PC directly to the wire, you attach them via cables to special ports on the box (Figure 21-18). The box with the bus takes care of termination and all those other tedious details required by a bus network. The bus topology would look a lot like a star topology, wouldn't it?

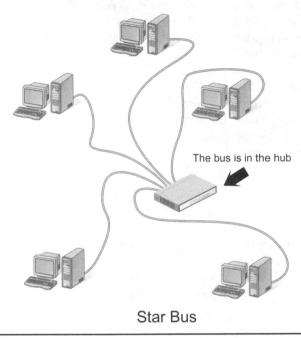

The bus is in the hub

Star Bus

Figure 21-18 Star bus

The central box with the bus is called a hub or switch. The *hub* provides a common point for connection for network devices. Hubs can have a wide variety of ports. Most consumer-level hubs have 4 or 8, but business-level hubs can have 32 or more ports. A hub is the old style device, still in use in many networks. A *switch* is a newer, far superior version of a hub. Figure 21-19 shows a typical consumer-level switch.

Figure 21-19
A switch

A hub provides no cure for the bandwidth-sharing problem of Ethernet networks. If you put 32 PCs on a 32-port 100BaseT hub, you have 32 PCs sharing the 100 Mbps bandwidth. A switch addresses that problem by making each port a separate Ethernet network. Each PC gets to use the full bandwidth available, because a switch stops most collisions. Bottom line? Swap out your old hubs for newer switches and you'll dramatically improve your network performance.

Cheap and centralized, a star bus network does not go down if a cable breaks. True, the network would go down if the hub itself failed, but that is very rare. Even if a hub fails, replacing a hub in a closet is much easier than tracing a bus running through walls and ceilings trying to find a break!

Unshielded Twisted Pair

UTP cabling is the specified cabling for 10/100/1000BaseT and is the predominant cabling system used today. Many different types of twisted pair cabling are available, and the type used depends on the needs of the network. Twisted pair cabling consists of AWG 22—26 gauge wire twisted together into color-coded pairs. Each wire is individually insulated and encased as a group in an common jacket.

CAT Levels   UTP cables come in categories that define the maximum speed at which data can be transferred (also called *bandwidth*). The major categories (CATs) are as follows:

CAT I	Standard phone line	CAT 2	Data speeds up to 4 Mbps (ISDN and T I lines)
CAT 3	Data speeds up to 16 Mbps	CAT 4	Data speeds up to 20 Mbps
CAT 5	Data speeds up to 100 Mbps	CAT 5e	Data speeds up to 1 Gbps
CAT 6	Data speeds up to 10 Gbps		

The CAT level should be clearly marked on the cable, as Figure 21-20 shows.

Figure 21-20
Cable markings
for CAT level

The *Telecommunication Industry Association/Electronics Industries Alliance (TIA/EIA)* establishes the UTP categories, which fall under the TIA/EIA 568 specification. Currently, most installers use CAT 5e or CAT 6 cable. Although many networks run at 10 Mbps, the industry standard has shifted to networks designed to run at 100 Mbps and faster. Because only CAT 5 or better handles these speeds, just about everyone is installing the higher rated cabling, even if they are running at speeds that CAT 3 or CAT 4 would do. Consequently, it is becoming more difficult to get anything but CAT 5, CAT 5e, or CAT 6 cables.

Implementing 10/100/1000BaseT

The 10BaseT, 100BaseT, and 1000BaseT cabling standards require two pairs of wires: a pair for sending and a pair for receiving. 10BaseT runs on CAT 3, CAT 4, or CAT 5 cable.

100BaseT requires at least CAT 5 to run. 1000BaseT is a special case because it needs all four pairs of wires in a CAT 5e or CAT 6 cable. These cables use a connector called an *RJ-45* connector. The *RJ* designation was invented by Ma Bell (the phone company, for you youngsters) years ago and is still used today. Currently, only two types of RJ connectors are used for networking: RJ-11 and RJ-45 (Figure 21-21). RJ-11 is the connector that hooks your telephone to the telephone jack. It supports up to two pairs of wires, though most phone lines use only one pair. The other pair is used to support a second phone line. RJ-11 connectors are primarily used for dial-up networking (see Chapter 22) and are not used in any common LAN installation, although a few weird (and out of business) "network in a box"–type companies used them. RJ-45 is the standard for UTP connectors. RJ-45 has connections for up to four pairs and is visibly much wider than RJ-11. Figure 21-22 shows the position of the #1 and #8 pins on an RJ-45 jack.

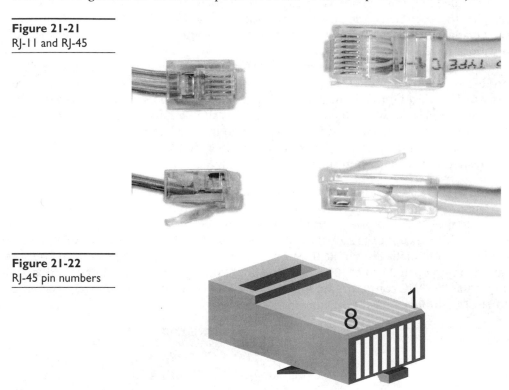

Figure 21-21
RJ-11 and RJ-45

Figure 21-22
RJ-45 pin numbers

The TIA/EIA has two standards for connecting the RJ-45 connector to the UTP cable: the TIA/EIA 568A and the TIA/EIA 568B. Both are acceptable. You do not have to follow any standard as long as you use the same pairings on each end of the cable; however, you will make your life simpler if you choose a standard. Make sure that all of your cabling uses the same standard and you will save a great deal of work in the end. Most importantly, *keep records!*

Like all wires, the wires in UTP are numbered. However, a number does not appear on each wire. Instead, each wire has a standardized color. Table 21-1 shows the official TIA/EIA Standard Color Chart for UTP.

Pin	568A	568B	Pin	568A	568B
1	White/Green	White/Orange	5	White/Blue	White/Blue
2	Green	Orange	6	Orange	Green
3	White/Orange	White/Green	7	White/Brown	White/Brown
4	Blue	Blue	8	Brown	Brown

Table 21-1   UTP Cabling Color Chart

Plenum versus PVC Cabling   Most workplace installations of network cable go up above the ceiling and then drop down through the walls to present a nice port in the wall. The space in the ceiling, under the floors, and in the walls through which cable runs is called the *plenum* space. The potential problem with this cabling running through the plenum space is that the protective sheathing for networking cables, called the *jacket*, is made from plastic, and if you get any plastic hot enough, it will create smoke and noxious fumes.

Standard network cables usually use *PVC (poly-vinyl chloride)* for the jacket, but PVC produces noxious fumes when burned. Fumes from cables burning in the plenum space can quickly spread throughout the building, so you want to use a more fire-retardant cable in the plenum space. Plenum-grade cable is simply network cabling with a fire-retardant jacket and is required for cables that go in the plenum space. Plenum-grade cable costs about three to five times more than PVC, but you should use it whenever you install cable in a plenum space.

Combo Cards   All Ethernet networks share the same language, so you can easily have mixed or combined networks. All it takes is a network card capable of running at multiple speeds or even over multiple cables. Most NICs built into motherboards (Figure 21-23), for example, are 10/100 auto-sensing cards. If you plug into a 10BaseT network, they automatically run at 10 Mbps. If you log into a 100 Mbps network, they'll quickly ramp up and run at 100 Mbps. You might find older cards that have both a RJ-45 port and a BNC connector for 10Base2. These sorts of cards can connect to either a 10BaseT or 10Base2 network (Figure 21-24).

Figure 21-23
NIC built into
motherboard

Figure 21-24
Ethernet 10Base2/
10BaseT combo card

Hubs and Switches In a 10/100/1000BaseT network, each PC is connected to a 10/100/1000BaseT hub or switch, as mentioned earlier. To add a device to the network, simply plug another cable into the hub or switch (Figure 21-25). Remember that 10/100/1000BaseT uses the star bus topology. The hub holds the actual bus and allows access to the bus through the ports. Using a star bus topology creates a robust network; the failure of a single PC will not bring down the entire network.

Figure 21-25
Typical switch
with several cables
connected

In a 10/100/1000BaseT network, the maximum distance from the hub to any device is 100 meters. No more than one PC can be attached to each segment, and the maximum number of PCs that can be attached to any one hub is 1024—although you will be hard pressed to find a hub with that many connectors (Figure 21-26). Most hubs come with 4, 8, 16, or 24 ports. 10/100/1000BaseT hubs act as repeaters, turning received signals into binary data and then re-creating a new signal to send out to devices connected to other ports. They need power, so make sure that the hubs are plugged into a good power source.

Figure 21-26
10BaseT

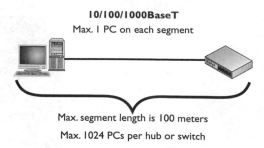

10/100/1000BaseT
Max. 1 PC on each segment

Max. segment length is 100 meters
Max. 1024 PCs per hub or switch

Crossover Cables   You can actually hook two 10/100/1000BaseT network cards together without a hub by using a special UTP cable called a *crossover cable*. A crossover cable is a standard UTP cable but with one RJ-45 connector using the 568A standard and the other using the 568B. This reverses the signal between sending and receiving wires and thus does the job of a hub or switch. Crossover cables work great as a quick way to network two PCs. You can purchase a crossover cable at any computer store.

Duplex and Half-Duplex   All modern NICs can run in full-*duplex* mode, meaning they can send and receive data at the same time. The vast majority of NICs and switches use a feature called *auto-sensing* to accommodate very old devices that might attach to the network and need to run in half-duplex mode. Half-duplex means that the device can send and receive but not at the same time. The walkie-talkies you played with as a kid that required you to press and hold the orange button to transmit—at which time you couldn't hear anything—are an obvious example of a half-duplex device. Half-duplex devices are exceedingly rare in modern computers, but you need to understand this option. Some NICs just can't handle full-duplex communication when you plug them directly to another NIC using a crossover cable—that is, no switch. Dropping both NICs down from full-duplex or auto-sensing can sometimes enable these odd NICs to communicate.

Fiber Optic Ethernet

Fiber optic cable is a very attractive way to transmit Ethernet network packets. First, because it uses light instead of electricity, fiber optic cable is immune to electrical problems such as lightning, short circuits, and static. Second, fiber optic signals travel much farther, up to 2000 meters (compared with 100 meters for 10/100/1000BaseT) with some standards. Most fiber Ethernet networks use *62.5/125 multimode* fiber optic cable. All fiber Ethernet networks that use these cables require two cables. Figure 21-27 shows three of the more common connectors used in fiber optic networks. Square *SC* connectors are shown in the middle and on the right, and the round *ST* connector is on the left.

Figure 21-27
Typical fiber
optic cables with
connectors

Like many other fiber optic connectors, the SC and ST connectors are half-duplex, meaning data flows only one way—hence the need for two cables in a fiber installation. Other half-duplex connectors you might run into are FC/PC, SMA, D4, MU, and LC. They look similar to SC and ST connectors but offer variations in size and connection. Newer and higher end fiber installations use full-duplex connectors, such as the MT-RJ connectors.

NOTE Light can be sent down a fiber optic cable as regular light or as laser light. Each type of light requires totally different fiber optic cables. Most network technologies that use fiber optics use LEDs, or light emitting diodes, to send light signals. These use *multimode* fiber optic cabling. Multimode fiber transmits multiple light signals at the same time, each using a different reflection angle within the core of the cable. The multiple reflection angles tend to disperse over long distances, so multimode fiber optic cables are used for relatively short distances.

Network technologies that use laser light use *single-mode* fiber optic cabling. Using laser light and single-mode fiber optic cables allows for phenomenally high transfer rates over long distances. Except for long distance links, single-mode is currently quite rare; if you see fiber optic cabling, you can be relatively sure that it is multimode.

The two most common fiber optic standards are called 10BaseFL and 100BaseFX. As you can guess by the names, the major difference is the speed of the network (there are some important differences in the way hubs are interconnected, and so on). Fiber optic cabling is delicate, expensive, and difficult to use, so it is usually reserved for use in data centers and is rarely used to connect desktop PCs.

Token Ring

Token Ring remains Ethernet's most significant competitor for connecting desktop PCs to the network, but its market share has continued to shrink in recent years. Developed by IBM, Token Ring uses a combination of ring and star topologies. Because Token Ring has its own packet structure, you need special equipment to connect a Token Ring to an Ethernet network.

Ring Topology

A ring topology connects all the PCs together on a single cable that forms a ring (Figure 21-28). Ring topologies use a transmission method called *token passing*. In token passing, a mini-packet called a *token* constantly passes from one NIC to the next in one direction around the ring (see Figure 21-29). A PC wanting to send a packet must wait until it gets the token. The PC's NIC then attaches data to the token and sends the packet back out to the ring. If another PC wants to send data, it must wait until a free token (one that doesn't have an attached packet) comes around.

Figure 21-28
Ring topology

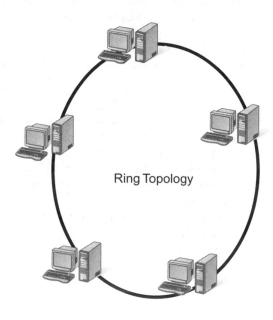

Ring Topology

Figure 21-29
Token passing

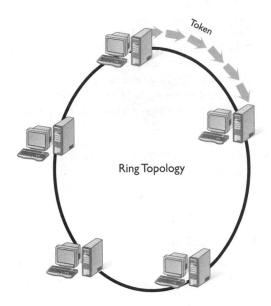

Ring Topology

Implementing Token Ring

The CompTIA A+ certification has a very old-school view of Token Ring networks, focusing on the traditional rather than the current iterations. As such, you'll find the exams test you only on the ancient 4 Mbps or 16 Mbps networks, which depended on the type of Token Ring network cards you bought. Token Ring was originally based around the IBM Type 1 cable. Type 1 cable is a two-pair, *shielded twisted pair (STP)* cable designed to handle speeds up to 20 Mbps (Figure 21-30). Today, Token Ring topologies can use either STP or UTP cables, and UTP cabling is far more common.

Figure 21-30
Type 1 STP Token
Ring cable

NOTE Token Ring manufacturers have not rolled over and given in to the pressure of Ethernet standards, but rather have continued to adapt and innovate. Modern IEEE 802.5t Token Ring networks run at 100 Mbps or faster and, because the ring technology does not suffer from the overhead of CSMA/CD, you get phenomenally faster performance from High Speed Token Ring (HSTR) networks than on comparably speedy Ethernet. Check them out here: www.token-ring.com.

STP Types   STP cables have certain categories. These are called types and are defined by IBM. The most common types are the following:

- **Type 1**   Standard STP with two pairs—the most common STP cable
- **Type 2**   Standard STP plus two pairs of voice wires
- **Type 3**   Standard STP with four pairs
- **Type 6**   Patch cable—used for connecting hubs
- **Type 8**   Flat STP for under carpets
- **Type 9**   STP with two pairs—Plenum grade

Token Ring Connectors   The Type 1 Token Ring connectors are not RJ-45. Instead, IBM designed a unique *hermaphroditic* connector called either an IBM-type Data Connector (IDC) or Universal Data Connector (UDC). These connectors are neither male nor female; they are designed to plug into each other (Figure 21-31). Token Ring network cards use a 9-pin female connector. A standard Token Ring cable has a hermaphroditic connector on one end and a 9-pin connector on the other.

Figure 21-31
IDC/UDC connector

Token Ring can also be used with CAT 3, 4, 5, 5e, and 6 UTP. When combined with UTP, Token Ring uses an RJ-45 connector, so from a cabling standpoint, Token Ring UTP and Ethernet UTP look the same. Many Token Ring network cards are combo cards, which means they come with both a 0-pin connection for STP and an RJ-45 connection for UTP.

As discussed earlier, Token Ring uses a star ring topology. The central connecting device, or concentrator, is sometimes called a hub, but the proper term is *multistation access unit* (*MSAU* or *MAU*). Token Ring MAUs and Ethernet hubs look similar but are *not* interchangeable. Each Token Ring MAU can support up to 260 PCs using STP and up to 72 PCs using UTP. Using UTP, the maximum distance from any MAU to a PC is 45 meters. Using STP, the maximum distance from any MAU to a PC is 100 meters (Figure 21-32). Token Ring can also uses repeaters, but the repeaters can be used only between MAUs. With a repeater, the functional distance between two MAUs increases to 360 meters (with UTP) and 720 meters (with STP).

Figure 21-32
Token Ring
specifications

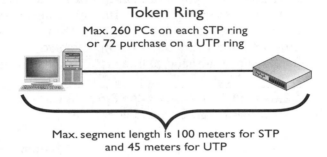

Token Ring

Max. 260 PCs on each STP ring
or 72 purchase on a UTP ring

Max. segment length is 100 meters for STP
and 45 meters for UTP

Parallel/Serial

It would be unfair not to give at least a token nod to the possibility of making direct cable connections using the parallel or serial ports on a pair of PCs. All versions of Windows have complete support for allowing two, and no more than two, systems to network together using either parallel or serial cables. You need crossover versions of IEEE1284 cables for parallel and RS-232 cables for serial. These should be considered only as a last resort option, given the incredibly slow speeds of parallel and especially serial cable transmission compared to that of Ethernet and Token Ring. Direct cable connections should never be used unless no other viable alternative exists.

FireWire

You can connect two computers together using FireWire cables. Apple designed FireWire to be network aware, so the two machines will simply recognize each other and, assuming they're configured to share files and folders, you're up and running. See the section "Sharing and Security" later in this chapter for more details.

USB

You can also connect two computers using USB, but it's not quite as elegant as FireWire. You can use several options. The most common way is to plug a USB NIC into each PC and then run a UTP crossover cable between the Ethernet ports. You can buy a special USB crossover cable to connect the two machines. Finally, at least one company makes a product that enables you to connect with a normal USB cable, called USB Duet.

IT Technician

Network Operating Systems

At this point in the discussion of networking, you've covered two of the four main requirements for making a network work. Through Ethernet or Token Ring hardware protocols, you have a NIC for the PC that handles splitting data into packets and putting the packets back together at the destination PC. You've got a cabling standard to connect the NIC to a hub/switch or MSAU, thus making that data transfer possible. Now it's time to dive into the third and fourth requirements for a network. You need an operating system that can communicate with the hardware and with other networked PCs, and you need some sort of server machine to give out data or services. The third and fourth requirements are handled by a network operating system.

 EXAM TIP The CompTIA A+ Essentials exam assumes you have a working knowledge of network operating systems.

In a classic sense, a *network operating system (NOS)* communicates with the PC hardware—of whichever hardware protocol—and makes the connections among multiple machines on a network. The NOS enables one or more PCs to act as a server machine and share data and services over a network—to share *resources,* in other words. You then need to run software on client computers to enable those computers to access the shared resources on the server machine.

Every Windows OS is an NOS and enables the PC to share resources and access shared resources. But it doesn't come out of the box ready to work on all networks! You need to configure Windows to handle all three tasks to make all this work: install a network protocol to communicate with hardware, enable server software to share resources, and install client software to enable the PC to access shared resources.

All NOSs are not alike, even among Windows. Before you can share resources across a network, you must answer a number of questions. How do you make that happen? Can everyone share his or her hard drives with everyone else? Should you place limits on sharing? If everyone needs access to a particular file, where will it be stored? What about security? Can anyone access the file? What if someone erases it accidentally? How are backups to be handled? Different NOSs answer these questions differently. Let's look at network organization and then turn to protocols, client software, and server software.

Network Organization

All NOSs can be broken into three basic organizational groups: client/server, peer-to-peer, and domain-based. All Windows PCs can function as network clients and servers, so this muddies the waters a bit. Let's take a look at traditional network organization.

Client/Server

The client/server solution to all the sharing resources questions is to take one machine and dedicate it as a resource to be shared over the network. This machine will have a dedicated NOS optimized for sharing files. This special OS includes powerful caching software that enables high-speed file access. It will have extremely high levels of protection and an organization that permits extensive control of the data. This machine is called a *dedicated server.* All of the other machines that use the data are called *clients* (because it's what they usually are) or *workstations.*

The client/server system dedicates one machine to act as a "server." Its only function is to serve up resources to the other machines on the network. These servers do not run Windows 9*x* or Windows XP. They use highly sophisticated and expensive NOSs that are optimized for the sharing and administration of network resources. Dedicated server operating systems include Windows 2003 Server, Novell NetWare, and some versions of Linux.

Novell NetWare servers provide the most pure example of a dedicated server. A NetWare server doesn't provide a user environment for running any applications except for tools and utilities. It just *serves* shared resources; it does not *run* programs such as Excel or CorelDraw. Many network administrators will even remove the keyboard and monitor from a NetWare server to keep people from trying to use it. NetWare has its own commands and requires substantial training to use, but in return, you get an amazingly powerful NOS! While Linux and Windows 2003 server machines can technically run client applications such as word processors, they have been optimized to function as servers and you don't typically use them to run end-user applications.

NOTE The terms *client* and *server* are, to say the least, freely used in the Windows world. Keep in mind that a *client* generally refers to any process (or in this context, computer system) that can request a resource or service, and a *server* is any process (or system) that can fulfill the request.

Novell NetWare provides excellent security for shared resources. Its security permissions are similar to Microsoft NTFS permissions.

Peer-to-Peer

Some networks do not require dedicated servers—every computer can perform both server and client functions. A peer-to-peer network enables any or all of the machines on the network to act as a server. Peer-to-peer networks are much cheaper than client/server networks, because the software costs less and does not require that you purchase a high-end machine to act as the dedicated server. The most popular peer-to-peer NOSs today are Windows 2000/XP and Macintosh OS X.

The biggest limiting factor to peer-to-peer networking is that it's simply not designed for a large number of computers. Windows has a built-in limit (10) to the number of users who can concurrently access a shared file or folder. Microsoft recommends that peer-to-peer workgroups not exceed 15 PCs. Beyond that, creating a domain-based network makes more sense.

Security is the other big weakness of peer-to-peer networks. Each system on a peer-to-peer network maintains its own security.

Windows 2000 Professional and Windows XP Professional enable you to tighten security by setting NTFS permissions locally, but you are still required to place a local account on every system for any user who's going to access resources. So, even though you get better security in a Windows 2000 Professional or Windows XP Professional peer-to-peer network, system administration entails a lot of running around to individual systems to create and delete local users every time someone joins or leaves the network. In a word: bleh.

Peer-to-peer workgroups are little more than a pretty way to organize systems to make navigating through My Network Places a little easier (Figure 21-33). In reality, workgroups have no security value. Still, if your networking needs are limited—such as a small home network—peer-to-peer networking is an easy and cheap solution.

Figure 21-33
Multiple workgroups in a network

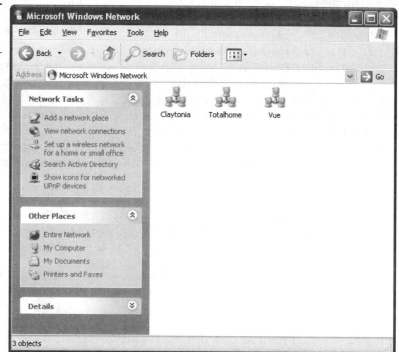

Domain-Based

One of the similarities between the client/server network model and peer-to-peer networks is that each PC in the network maintains its own list of user accounts. If you want to access a server, you must log on. When only one server exists, the logon process takes only a second and works very well. The trouble comes when your network contains multiple servers. In that case, every time you access a different server, you must repeat the logon process (Figure 21-34). In larger networks containing many servers, this becomes a time-consuming nightmare not only for the user, but also for the network administrator.

Figure 21-34
Multiple logins

A domain-based network provides an excellent solution for the problem of multiple logins. In a domain-based environment, one or more dedicated servers called *domain controllers* hold the security database for all systems. This database holds a list of all users and passwords in the domain. When you log on to your computer or to any computer, the logon request goes to an available domain controller, to verify the account and password (Figure 21-35).

Figure 21-35
A domain controller
eliminates the need
for multiple logins.

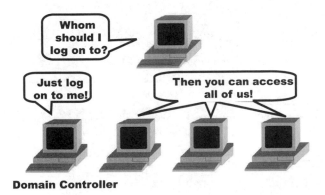

Domain Controller

Modern domain-based networks use what is called a *directory service* to store user and computer account information. Current versions of Novell NetWare move from the strict client/server model described to a directory service-based model implementing the appropriately named *NetWare Directory Service (NDS)*. Large Microsoft-based networks use the *Active Directory (AD)* directory service. Think of a directory service as a big, centralized index, similar to a telephone book, that each PC accesses to locate resources in the domain.

Server versions of Microsoft Windows look and act similar to the workstation versions, but they come with extra networking capabilities, services, and tools to enable them to take on the role of domain controller, file server, *remote access services (RAS)* server, application server, Web server, and so on. A quick glance at the options you have in Administrative Tools shows how much more full-featured the server versions are compared to the workstation versions of Windows. Figure 21-36 shows the Administrative Tools options on a typical Windows XP workstation. These should be familiar to you. Figure 21-37 shows the many extra tools you need to work with Windows 2000 Server.

Figure 21-36
Administrative Tools in Windows XP Professional

Figure 21-37
Administrative Tools in Windows 2000 Server

Every Windows system contains a special account called the *administrator account.* This one account has complete and absolute power over the entire system. When you install Windows 2000 or XP, you must create a password for the administrator account. Anyone who knows the administrator password has the ability to install/delete any program, read/change/delete any file, run any program, and change any system setting. As you might imagine, you should protect the administrator password carefully. Without it, you cannot create additional accounts (including additional accounts with administrative privileges) or change system settings. If you lose the administrator password (and no other account with administrative privileges exists), you have to reinstall Windows completely to create a new administrator account—so don't lose it!

In Windows 2000, open the Properties window for My Computer, and select the Network Identification tab, as shown in Figure 21-38. This shows your current selection. Windows XP calls the tab Computer Name and renames a few of the buttons (Figure 21-39). Clicking the Network ID button opens the Network Identification Wizard, but most techs just use the Change button (Figure 21-40). Clicking the Change button does the same thing as clicking the Network ID button, but the wizard does a lot of explaining that you don't need if you know what you want to do. Make sure you have a valid domain account or you won't be able to log in to a domain.

Figure 21-38
Network
Identification tab
in Windows 2000

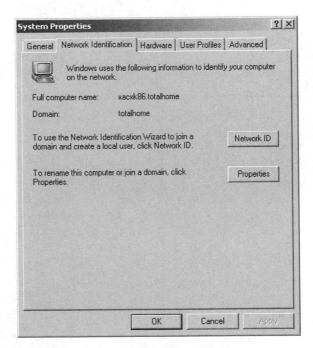

Figure 21-39
Computer Name tab
in Windows XP

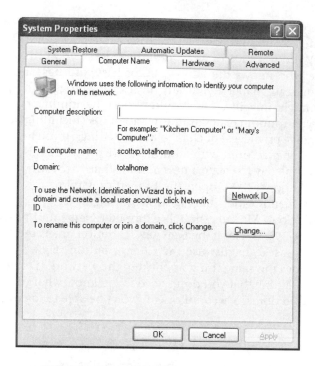

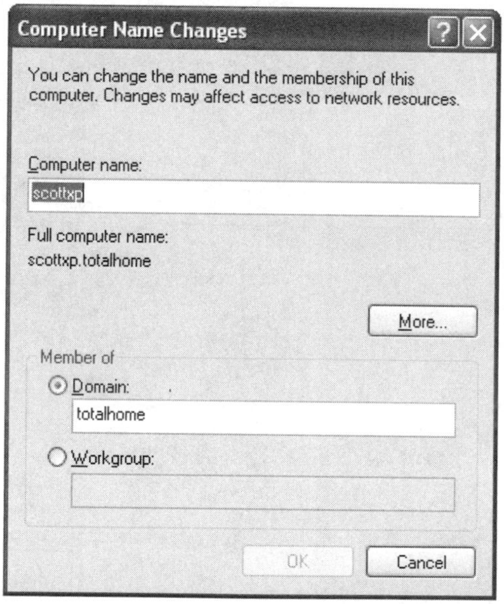

Figure 21-40
Using the
Change button

At this point, you've prepared the OS to network in general, but now you need to talk to the specific hardware. For that, you need to load protocols.

Protocols

Simply moving data from one machine to another is hardly sufficient to make a complete network; many other functions need to be handled. For example, if a file is being copied from one machine to another, something must keep track of all the packets so that the file can be properly reassembled. If many machines are talking to the same machine at once, that machine must somehow keep track of which packets it sends to or receives from each of the other PCs.

Another issue arises if one of the machines in the network has its network card replaced. Up to this point, the only way to distinguish one machine from another was by the MAC address on the network card. To solve this, each machine must have a name, an identifier for the network, which is "above" the MAC address. Each machine, or at least one of them, needs to keep a list of all the MAC addresses on the network and the names of the machines, so that packets and names can be correlated. That way, if a PC's network card is replaced, the network, after some special queries, can update the list to associate the name of the PC with its new network card's MAC address.

Network protocol software takes the incoming data received by the network card, keeps it organized, sends it to the application that needs it, and then takes outgoing data from the application and hands it to the NIC to be sent out over the network. All networks use some protocol. Although many different protocols exist, three dominate the world of PCs—NetBEUI from Microsoft, IPX/SPX from Novell, and TCP/IP from UNIX/Internet.

NetBEUI

During the 1980s, IBM developed *NetBIOS Extended User Interface (NetBEUI)*, the default protocol for Windows for Workgroups, LANtastic, and Windows 95. NetBEUI offers small size and a relatively high speed, but it can't be used for routing. Its inability to handle routing limits NetBEUI to networks smaller than about 200 nodes.

 NOTE A *node* is any device that has a network connection—usually this means a PC, but other devices can be nodes. For example, many printers now connect directly to a network and can therefore be deemed nodes. I use the term *node* extensively in the rest of the chapter in place of *PC* or *networked computer*. This is especially true when I talk about wireless technologies, because that's the term the manufacturers use.

IPX/SPX

Novell developed the *Internetwork Packet Exchange/Sequenced Packet Exchange (IPX/SPX)* protocol exclusively for its NetWare products. The IPX/SPX protocol is speedy, works well with routers, and takes up relatively little RAM when loaded. Microsoft implements a version of IPX/SPX called *NWLink*.

NOTE Although IPX/SPX is strongly associated with Novell NetWare networks, versions of NetWare since version 5 have adopted TCP/IP as their default, native protocol.

TCP/IP

Transmission Control Protocol/Internet Protocol (TCP/IP) was originally developed for the Internet's progenitor, the *Advanced Research Projects Agency Network (ARPANET)* of the U.S. Department of Defense. In 1983, TCP/IP became the built-in protocol for the popular BSD UNIX, and other flavors of UNIX quickly adopted it as well. TCP/IP is the best protocol for larger (more than 200 nodes) networks. The biggest network of all, the Internet, uses TCP/IP as its protocol. Windows NT also uses TCP/IP as its default protocol. TCP/IP lacks speed and takes up a large amount of memory when loaded, but it is robust, well understood, and universally supported.

AppleTalk

AppleTalk is the proprietary Apple protocol. Similar to IPX, it is small and relatively fast. The only reason to use the AppleTalk protocol is to communicate with older Apple computers on a network. Apple Macintosh OS X uses TCP/IP natively, so you won't need AppleTalk to plug a modern Mac into a Windows network.

Client Software

To access data or resources across a network, a Windows PC needs to have client software installed for every kind of server that you want to access. When you install a network card and drivers, Windows installs at least one set of client software, called Client for Microsoft Networks (Figure 21-41). This client enables your machine to do the obvious: connect to a Microsoft network! To connect to a NetWare network, you'd need to add Client Service for NetWare. Internet-based services work the same way. You need a Web client (such as Internet Explorer) to access a Web server. We'll go through the installation and configuration steps for the Microsoft and NetWare clients a little later in this chapter. For now, you need to know that Windows PCs don't just access shared data magically but require that client software be installed.

Figure 21-41
LAN Properties
window showing
Client for Microsoft
Networks installed
(along with other
network software)

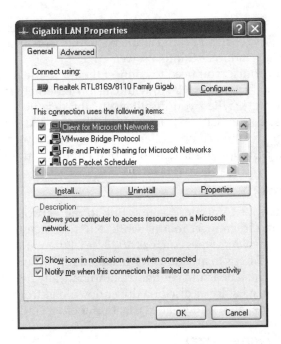

Server Software

You can turn any Windows PC into a server, simply by enabling the sharing of files, folders, and printers. Windows 2000 and XP have File and Printer Sharing installed but not activated by default, but activating it requires nothing more than a click on a check box next to the *File and Printer Sharing for Microsoft Networks* option, as shown in Figure 21-41.

Installing and Configuring a Wired Network

Almost halfway through the chapter and we're finally getting to the good stuff—installing and configuring a network! To have network connectivity, you need to have three things in place:

- **NIC** The physical hardware that connects the computer system to the network media.
- **Protocol** The language that the computer systems use to communicate.
- **Network client** The interface that allows the computer system to speak to the protocol.

If you want to share resources on your PC with other network users, you also need to enable Microsoft's File and Printer Sharing. This installs the services and software that turns a Windows PC into a server.

Plus, of course, you need to connect the PC to the network hub or switch via some sort of cable (preferably CAT 6 with Gigabit Ethernet cranking through the wires, but that's just me!). When you install a NIC, by default, Windows 2000 and XP Professional install the TCP/IP protocol, the Client for Microsoft Networks, and File and Printer Service upon setup. Other versions of Windows require you to jump through a couple more hoops and install some or all of this stuff to get connectivity.

Installing a NIC

The NIC is your computer system's link to the network, and installing one is the first step required to connect to a network. NICs are manufactured to operate on specific media and network types, such as 100BaseT Ethernet or 16 Mbps Token Ring. Follow the manufacturer's instructions for installation. If your NIC is of recent vintage, it will be detected, installed, and configured automatically by Windows 2000 or Windows XP. You might need a driver disc or a driver download from the manufacturer's Web site if you install the latest and greatest Gigabit Ethernet card.

Add Hardware Wizard

The Add Hardware Wizard automates installation of non–plug-and-play devices, or plug-and-play devices that were not detected correctly. Start the wizard by clicking Start | Settings | Control Panel, and double-clicking the icon for the Add Hardware applet. (Note that earlier versions of Windows call this the Add/Remove Hardware applet.) Click the Next button to select the hardware task you wish to perform, and follow the prompts to complete the wizard.

 NOTE If you have the option, you should save yourself potential headaches and troubleshooting woes by acquiring new, name-brand NICs for your Windows installation.

Configuring a Network Client

To establish network connectivity, you need a network client installed and configured properly. You need a client for every type of server NOS to which you plan to connect on the network. Let's look at the two most used for Microsoft and Novell networks.

Client for Microsoft Networks

Installed as part of the OS installation, the Client for Microsoft Networks rarely needs configuration, and, in fact, few configuration options are available. To start it in Windows XP, click Start, and then right-click My Network Places and select Properties. In Windows 2000, click Start | Settings | Network and Dial-up Connections.

In all versions of Windows, your next step is to double-click the Local Area Connection icon, click the Properties button, highlight Client for Microsoft Networks, and click the Properties button. Note that there's not much to do here. Unless told to do something by a network administrator, just leave this alone.

Client Service for NetWare

Microsoft's Client Service for NetWare provides access to file and print resources on NetWare 3.*x* and 4.*x* servers. Client Service for NetWare supports some NetWare utilities and NetWare-aware applications. To connect Microsoft client workstations to NetWare servers running NDS also requires the Microsoft Service for NetWare Directory Services (NDS). Once installed, Client Service for NetWare offers no configuration options.

NOTE Client Service for NetWare does not support the IP protocol used in NetWare 5.*x* and more recent versions of NetWare.

Configuring Simple Protocols

Protocols come in many different flavors and perform different functions on the network. Some, such as NetBEUI, lack elements that allow their signals to travel through routers, making them non-routable (essentially, this protocol is unsuitable for a large network that uses routers to re-transmit data). The network protocols supported by Windows include NetBEUI, NWLink (IPX/SPX), and TCP/IP, although Windows XP drops support for NetBEUI. This section looks at installing and configuring the simple protocols used by Windows 2000: NetBEUI and NWLink.

NetBEUI

NetBEUI is easy to configure, since no network addresses are needed. Generally, all you need to establish a connection between computer systems using NetBEUI is a NetBIOS computer name. NetBIOS names must be unique and contain 15 or fewer characters, but other than that there isn't much to it. To install the NetBEUI protocol in any version of Windows except XP, follow these steps:

1. In Windows 2000, click Start | Settings | Network and Dial-up Connections. Double-click the Local Area Connection icon to bring up the Local Area Connection Status dialog box (Figure 21-42).

Figure 21-42
LAN Status dialog box in Windows 2000

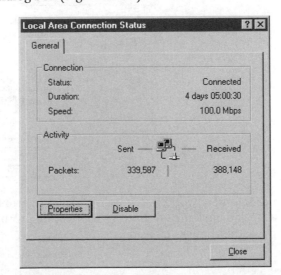

2. Click the Properties button to bring up the Local Area Connection Properties dialog box (Figure 21-43).

Figure 21-43
LAN Properties
dialog box in
Windows 2000

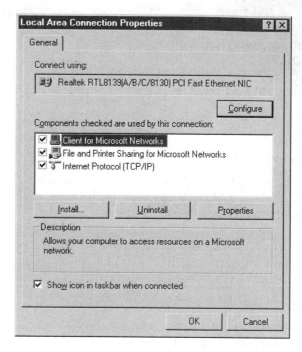

3. Click the Install button. In the Select Network Component Type dialog box, highlight Protocol and click the Add button (Figure 21-44).

Figure 21-44
Adding a protocol

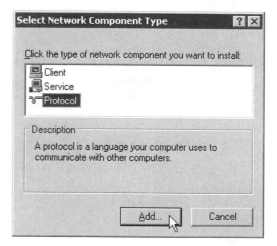

4. In the Select Network Protocol dialog box, select NetBEUI Protocol (Figure 21-45), and click the OK button. You will be prompted to reboot the system to make the changes take effect.

Figure 21-45
Selecting NetBEUI

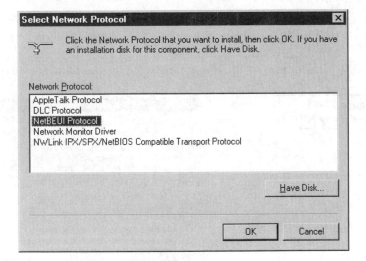

NWLink (IPX/SPX)

As mentioned, NWLink is Microsoft's implementation of the IPX/SPX protocol. The Microsoft version of NWLink provides the same level of functionality as the Novell protocol and also includes an element for resolving NetBIOS names. NWLink packages data to be compatible with client/server services on NetWare networks, but it does not provide access to NetWare File and Print Services. For this, you also need to install the Client Service for NetWare, as noted earlier.

Follow the same steps used to install NetBEUI to install NWLink, except choose NWLink rather than NetBEUI when you make your final selection. You'll be prompted to reboot after adding the protocol.

NWLink is a relatively easy protocol to configure. Normally, the only settings you may need to specify are the internal network number and frame type (usually, however, the default values are sufficient). The internal network number is used by the network for routing purposes. The frame type specifies how the data is packaged for transport over the network. For computers to communicate by NWLink, they must have the same frame types. By default, the frame type is set to Auto Detect.

NOTE When NWLink is set to Auto Detect the frame type, it will detect only one type, searching in the following order: 802.2, 802.3, 802.5.

To configure NWLink properties manually, follow these steps:

1. In Windows XP, click Start | Control Panel and open the Network Connections applet. Double-click the Local Area Connection icon. In Windows 2000, click Start | Settings | Network and Dial-up Connections, and double-click the Local Area Connection icon.

2. Click the Properties button, highlight NWLink IPX/SPX/NetBIOS Compatible Transport Protocol, and click the Properties button.

3. In the NWLink IPX/SPX/NetBIOS Compatible Transport Protocol properties dialog box, set the internal network number and frame type (Figure 21-46).

Figure 21-46
Configuring NWLink

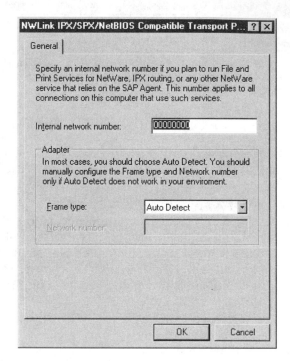

Configuring TCP/IP

This final section on protocols covers TCP/IP, the primary protocol of most modern networks, including the Internet. For a PC to access the Internet, it must have TCP/IP loaded and configured properly. TCP/IP has become so predominant that most network folks use it even on networks that do not connect to the Internet. Although TCP/IP is very powerful, it is also a bit of a challenge to set up. So whether you are installing a modem for a dial-up connection to the Internet or setting up 500 computers on their own private *intranet*, you must understand some TCP/IP basics. You'll go through the following basic sections of the protocol and then you'll look at specific steps to install and configure TCP/IP.

Network Addressing

Any network address must provide two pieces of information: it must uniquely identify the machine and it must locate that machine within the larger network. In a TCP/IP network, the *IP address* identifies the PC and the network on which it resides.

IP Addresses   In a TCP/IP network, the systems don't have names but rather use IP addresses. The IP address is the unique identification number for your system on the network. Part of the address identifies the network, and part identifies the local computer (host) address on the network. IP addresses consist of four sets of eight binary numbers (octets), each set separated by a period. This is called *dotted-decimal notation*. So, instead of a computer being called SERVER1, it gets an address like so:

```
202.34.16.11
```

Written in binary form, the address would look like this:

```
11110010.00000101.00000000.00001010
```

But the TCP/IP folks decided to write the decimal equivalents:

```
00000000 = 0
00000001 = 1
00000010 = 2
...
11111111 = 255
```

IP addresses are divided into class licenses, which correspond with the potential size of the network: Class A, Class B, and Class C. Class A licenses were intended for huge companies and organizations, such as major multinational corporations, universities, and governmental agencies. Class B licenses were assigned to medium-size companies, and Class C licenses were designated for smaller LANs. Class A networks use the first octet to identify the network address and the remaining three octets to identify the host. Class B networks use the first two octets to identify the network address and the remaining two octets to identify the host. Class C networks use the first three octets to identify the network address and the last octet to identify the host. Table 21-2 lists range (class) assignments.

Network Class	Address Range	No. of Network Addresses Available	No. of Host Nodes (Computers) Supported
A	1–126	129	16,777,214
B	128–191	16,384	65,534
C	192–223	2,097,152	254

Table 21-2   Class A, B, and C Addresses

You'll note that the IP address ranges listed above skip from 126.x.x.x to 128.x.x.x. That's because the 127 address range (i.e., 127.0.0.1–127.255.255.255) is reserved for network testing (loopback) operations. (We usually just use the address 127.0.0.1 for loopback purposes, and call it the *localhost* address, but any address that starts off with *127* will work just as well.) That's not the only reserved range, either! Each network class has a specific IP address range reserved for *private* networks—traffic from these networks doesn't get routed to the Internet at large. Class A's private range goes from 10.0.0.1 to 10.255.255.254. Class B's private range is 172.16.0.1 up to 172.16.255.254. Class C has two private addresses ranges: 192.168.0.0 to 192.168.255.254 for manually configured addresses, and 169.254.0.1 to 169.254.255.254 to accommodate the *Automatic Private IP Addressing (APIPA)* function.

NOTE Pinging the loopback is the best way to test if a NIC is working properly. To test a NIC's loopback, the other end of the cable must be in a working switch or you must use a loopback device.

Subnet Mask The subnet mask is a value that distinguishes which part of the IP address is the network address and which part of the address is the host address. The subnet mask blocks out (or "masks") the network portions (octets) of an IP address. Certain subnet masks are applied by default. The default subnet mask for Class A addresses is 255.0.0.0; for Class B, it's 255.255.0.0; and for Class C, 255.255.255.0. For example, in the Class B IP address 131.190.4.121 with a subnet mask of 255.255.0.0, the first two octets (131.190) make up the network address, and the last two (4.121) make up the host address.

EXAM TIP The CompTIA A+ certification exams do not require you to break down IP addresses and subnet masks into their binary equivalents or to deal with non-standard subnet masks like 255.255.240.0, but you should know what IP addresses and subnet masks are and how to configure your PC to connect to a TCP/IP network.

TCP/IP Services

TCP/IP is a very different type of protocol. Although it supports File and Printer Sharing, it adds a number of special sharing functions unique only to it, lumped together under the umbrella term *TCP/IP services.* The most famous TCP/IP service is called *hypertext transfer protocol (HTTP)*, the language of the World Wide Web. If you want to surf the Web, you must have TCP/IP. But TCP/IP supplies many other services beyond just HTTP. Using a service called Telnet, for example, you can access a remote system as though you were actually in front of that machine.

Another example is a handy utility called *Ping.* Ping enables one machine to check whether it can communicate with another machine. Figure 21-47 shows an example of

Ping running on a Windows 2000 system. Isn't it interesting that many TCP/IP services run from a command prompt? Good thing you know how to access one! I'll show you other services in a moment.

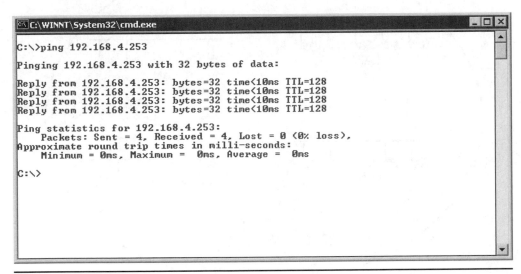

Figure 21-47   Ping in action

The goal of TCP/IP is to link any two hosts (remember, a host is just a computer in TCP/IP lingo), whether the two computers are on the same LAN or on some other network within the WAN. The LANs within the WAN are linked together with a variety of different types of connections, ranging from basic dial-ups to dedicated, high-speed (and expensive) data lines (Figure 21-48). To move traffic between networks, you use specialized computers called *routers* (Figure 21-49). Each host will send traffic to the router only when that data is destined for a remote network, cutting down on traffic across the more expensive WAN links. The host makes these decisions based on the destination IP address of each packets. Routers are most commonly used in TCP/IP networks, but other protocols also use them, especially IPX/SPX.

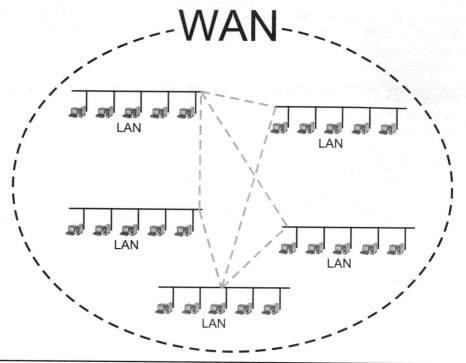

Figure 21-48 WAN concept

Figure 21-49
Typical router

TCP/IP Settings

TCP/IP has a number of unique settings that you must set up correctly to ensure proper network functioning. Unfortunately, these settings can be quite confusing, and there are quite a few of them. Not all settings are used for every type of TCP/IP network, and it's not always obvious where you go to set them.

Windows 2000/XP makes this fairly easy by letting you configure both dial-up and network connections using the My Network Places properties (Figure 21-50). Simply select the connection you wish to configure, and then set its TCP/IP properties.

Figure 21-50
Network
Connections
dialog box showing
Dial-up and LAN
connections

The CompTIA A+ certification exams assume that someone else, such as a tech support person or some network guru, will tell you the correct TCP/IP settings for the network. Your only job is to understand roughly what they do and to know where to enter them so the system works. Following are some of the most common TCP/IP settings.

EXAM TIP The CompTIA A+ certification exams have a rather strange view of what you should know about networking. Take a lot of time practicing how to get to certain network configuration screens. Be ready for questions that ask, "Which of the following steps will enable you to change a particular value?"

Default Gateway   A computer that wants to send data to another machine outside its LAN is not expected to know exactly how to reach every other computer on the Internet. Instead, all IP hosts know the address of at least one router to which they pass all the data packets they need to send outside the LAN. This router is called the *default gateway*, which is just another way of saying "the local router" (Figure 21-51).

Figure 21-51
Setting a default
gateway

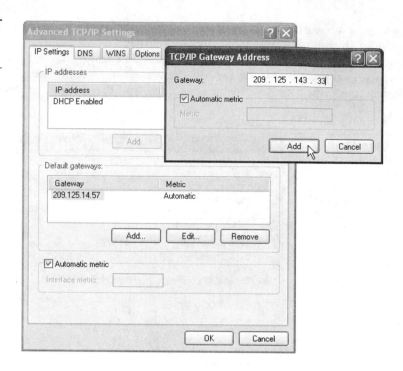

Domain Name Service (DNS)   Knowing that users were not going to be able to remember lots of IP addresses, early Internet pioneers came up with a way to correlate those numbers with more human-friendly computer designations. Special computers, called *domain name service (DNS)* servers, keep databases of IP addresses and their corresponding names. For example, a machine called TOTAL.SEMINAR1 will be listed in a DNS directory with a corresponding IP address, such as 209.34.45.163. So instead of accessing the \\209.34.45.163\FREDC share to copy a file, you can ask to see \\TOTAL.SEMINAR1\FREDC. Your system will then query the DNS server to get TOTALSEMINAR1's IP address and use that to find the right machine. Unless you want to type in IP addresses all the time, a TCP/IP network will need at least one DNS server (Figure 21-52).

Figure 21-52
Adding two
DNS servers in
Windows 2000

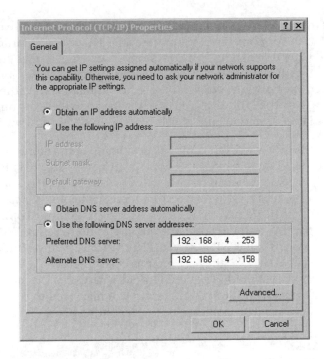

The Internet has very regulated domain names. If you want a domain name that others can access on the Internet, you must register your domain name and pay a small yearly fee. In most cases, your ISP can handle this for you. Originally, DNS names all ended with one of the following seven domain name qualifiers, called *top level domains (TLDs)*:

.com	General business	**.org**	Nonprofit organizations
.edu	Educational organizations	**.gov**	Government organizations
.mil	Military organizations	**.net**	Internet organizations
.int	International		

As more and more countries joined the Internet, an entire new level of domains was added to the original seven to indicate a DNS name in a particular country, such as .uk for the United Kingdom. It's common to see DNS names such as www.bbc.co.uk or www.louvre.fr. The *Internet Corporation for Assigned Names and Numbers (ICANN)* announced the creation of several more new domains, including .name, .biz, .info, and others. Given the explosive growth of the Internet, these are unlikely to be the last ones! For the latest developments, check ICANN's Web site at www.icann.org.

WINS Before Microsoft came fully on board with Internet standards such as TCP/IP, the company implemented its own type of name server: *Windows Internet Name Server (WINS)*. WINS enables Windows network names such as SERVER1 to be correlated to IP addresses, just as DNS does, except these names are *Windows* network names such as SERVER1, not Internet names such as server1.example.com. Assuming that a WINS server exists on your network, all you have to do to set up WINS on your PC is type in the IP address for the WINS server (Figure 21-53). Many Windows 2000/XP–based networks don't use WINS; they use an improved "dynamic" DNS that supports both Internet names and Windows names. On older networks that still need to support the occasional legacy Windows NT 4.0 server, you may need to configure WINS, but on most TCP/IP networks you can leave the WINS setting blank.

Figure 21-53
Setting up WINS to use DHCP

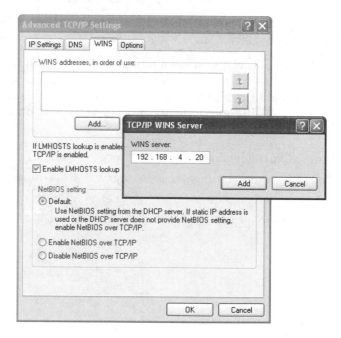

DHCP The last feature that most TCP/IP networks support is *dynamic host configuration protocol (DHCP)*. To understand DHCP, you must first remember that every machine must be assigned an IP address, a subnet mask, a default gateway, and at least one DNS server (and maybe a WINS server). These settings can be added manually using the TCP/IP Properties window. When you set the IP address manually, the IP address will not change and is called a *static IP address* (Figure 21-54).

Figure 21-54
Setting a static
IP address

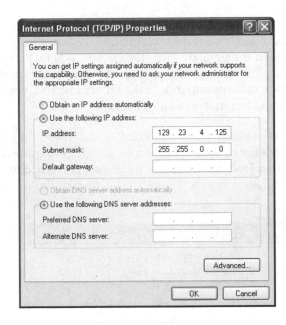

DHCP enables you to create a pool of IP addresses that are given temporarily to machines. DHCP is especially handy for networks that have a lot of laptops that join and leave the network on a regular basis. Why give a machine that is on the network for only a few hours a day a static IP address? For that reason, DHCP is quite popular. If you add a NIC to a Windows system, the default TCP/IP settings are set to use DHCP. When you accept those automatic settings, you're really telling the machine to use DHCP (Figure 21-55).

Figure 21-55
Automatically obtain
IP address

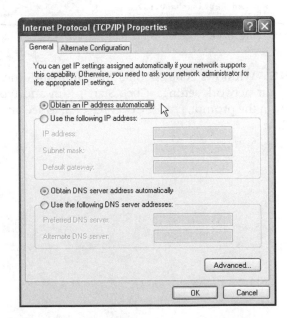

TCP/IP Tools

All versions of Windows come with handy tools to test TCP/IP. Those that you're most likely to use in the field are Ping, IPCONFIG, NSLOOKUP, and TRACERT. All of these programs are command prompt utilities! Open a command prompt to run them—if you just place these commands in the Run command, you'll see the command prompt window open for a moment and then quickly close!

Ping   You've already seen Ping, a really great way to find out if you can talk to another system. Here's how it works. Get to a command prompt and type **ping** followed by an IP address or by a DNS name, such as **ping www.chivalry.com**. Press the ENTER key on your keyboard and away it goes! Figure 21-56 shows the common syntax for Ping.

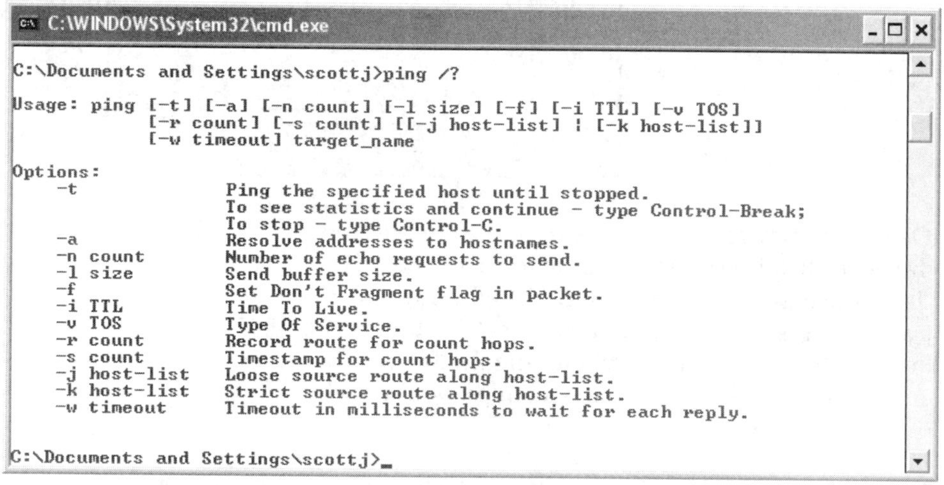

```
C:\WINDOWS\System32\cmd.exe                                    _ □ ×

C:\Documents and Settings\scottj>ping /?

Usage: ping [-t] [-a] [-n count] [-l size] [-f] [-i TTL] [-v TOS]
            [-r count] [-s count] [[-j host-list] ¦ [-k host-list]]
            [-w timeout] target_name

Options:
    -t              Ping the specified host until stopped.
                    To see statistics and continue - type Control-Break;
                    To stop - type Control-C.
    -a              Resolve addresses to hostnames.
    -n count        Number of echo requests to send.
    -l size         Send buffer size.
    -f              Set Don't Fragment flag in packet.
    -i TTL          Time To Live.
    -v TOS          Type Of Service.
    -r count        Record route for count hops.
    -s count        Timestamp for count hops.
    -j host-list    Loose source route along host-list.
    -k host-list    Strict source route along host-list.
    -w timeout      Timeout in milliseconds to wait for each reply.

C:\Documents and Settings\scottj>_
```

Figure 21-56   Ping syntax

IPCONFIG   Windows 2000/XP offer the command-line tool IPCONFIG for a quick glance at your network settings. Click Start | Run and type **CMD** to get a command prompt. From the prompt, type **IPCONFIG /ALL** to see all of your TCP/IP settings (Figure 21-57).

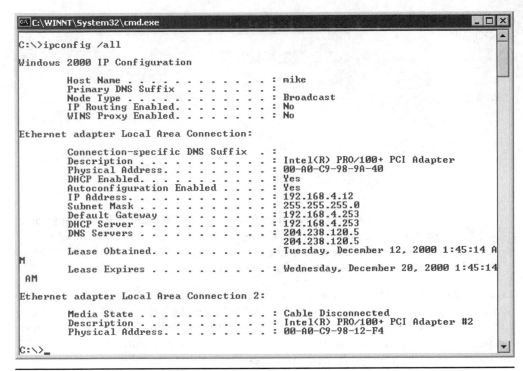

Figure 21-57 IPCONFIG /ALL on Windows 2000

When you have a static IP address, IPCONFIG does little beyond reporting your current IP settings, including your IP address, subnet mask, default gateway, DNS servers, and WINS servers. When using DHCP, however, IPCONFIG is also the primary tool for releasing and renewing your IP address. Just type **ipconfig /renew** to get a new IP address or **ipconfig /release** to give up the IP address you currently have.

NSLOOKUP NSLOOKUP is a powerful command-line program that enables you to determine exactly what information the DNS server is giving you about a specific host name. Every version of Windows makes NSLOOKUP available when you install TCP/IP. To run the program, type **NSLOOKUP** from the command line and press the ENTER key (Figure 21-58). Note that this gives you a little information, but that the prompt has changed. That's because you're running the application. Type **exit** and press the ENTER key to return to the command prompt.

Figure 21-58
NSLOOKUP
in action

```
C:\>nslookup
Default Server:  totalhomedc2.totalhome
Address:  192.168.4.155

>
```

 NOTE You can do some cool stuff with NSLOOKUP, and consequently some techs absolutely love the tool. It's way outside the scope of CompTIA A+ certification, but if you want to play with it, type **HELP** at the NSLOOKUP prompt and press ENTER to see a list of common commands and syntax.

TRACERT The TRACERT utility shows the route that a packet takes to get to its destination. From a command line, type **TRACERT** followed by a space and an IP address. The output describes the route from your machine to the destination machine, including all devices it passes through and how long each hop takes (Figure 21-59). TRACERT can come in handy when you have to troubleshoot bottlenecks. When users complain that it's difficult to reach a particular destination using TCP/IP, you can run this utility to determine whether the problem exists on a machine or connection over which you have control, or if it is a problem on another machine or router. Similarly, if a destination is completely unreachable, TRACERT can again determine whether the problem is on a machine or router over which you have control.

```
C:\>tracert www.chivalry.com

Tracing route to chivalry.com [65.18.214.130]
over a maximum of 30 hops:

  1     2 ms     1 ms     1 ms  192.168.4.151
  2    20 ms    19 ms    21 ms  adsl-208-190-121-38.dsl.hstntx.swbell.net [208.1
90.121.38]
  3    22 ms    19 ms    19 ms  dist1-vlan50.hstntx.swbell.net [151.164.11.126]
  4    20 ms    19 ms    19 ms  bb1-g1-0.hstntx.swbell.net [151.164.11.230]
  5    22 ms    22 ms    23 ms  core1-p6-0.crhstx.sbcglobal.net [151.164.188.1]
  6    25 ms    26 ms    26 ms  core3-p3-0.crdltx.sbcglobal.net [151.164.240.189
]
  7    27 ms    26 ms    26 ms  core2-p8-0.crdltx.sbcglobal.net [151.164.242.113
]
  8    26 ms    26 ms    25 ms  bb1-p14-3.dllstx.sbcglobal.net [151.164.240.97]
  9    28 ms    26 ms    26 ms  bb2-p15-0.dllstx.sbcglobal.net [151.164.243.150]
 10    27 ms    29 ms    29 ms  sl-gw40-fw-3-0.sprintlink.net [144.228.39.225]
 11    29 ms    29 ms    29 ms  sl-bb22-fw-4-3.sprintlink.net [144.232.8.249]
 12    28 ms    29 ms    29 ms  sl-st20-dal-14-1.sprintlink.net [144.232.20.138]
 13    29 ms    29 ms    29 ms  so-1-1-1.edge1.Dallas1.Level3.net [64.158.168.73
]
```

Figure 21-59 TRACERT in action

Chapter 21: Local Area Networking

955

Configuring TCP/IP

By default, TCP/IP is configured to receive an IP address automatically from a Dynamic Host Configuration Protocol (DHCP) server on the network (and automatically assign a corresponding subnet mask). As far as the CompTIA A+ certification exams are concerned, Network+ techs and administrators give you the IP address, subnet mask, and default gateway information and you plug them into the PC. That's about it, so here's how to do it manually:

1. In Windows XP, open the Control Panel and double-click the Network Connections applet. Double-click the Local Area Connection icon. In Windows 2000, click Start | Settings | Network and Dial-up Connections, and double-click the Local Area Connection icon.

2. Click the Properties button, highlight Internet Protocol (TCP/IP), and click the Properties button.

3. In the dialog box, click the Use the Following IP Address radio button.

4. Enter the IP address in the appropriate fields.

5. Press the TAB key to skip down to the Subnet Mask field. Note that the subnet mask is entered automatically (you can type over this if you want to enter a different subnet mask). See Figure 21-60.

Figure 21-60
Setting up IP

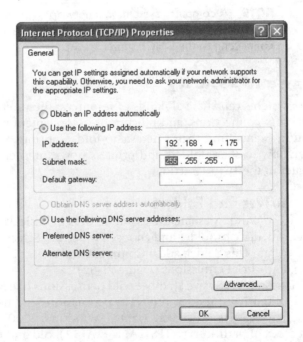

6. Optionally, enter the IP address for a default gateway (router, or another computer system that will forward transmissions beyond your network).

7. Optionally, enter the IP address of a primary and secondary DNS server.

8. Click the OK button to close the dialog box.

9. Click the Close button to exit the Local Area Connection Status dialog box.

10. Windows will alert you that you must restart the system for the changes to take effect.

Automatic Private IP Addressing

Windows 2000 and XP support a feature called Automatic Private IP Addressing (APIPA) that automatically assigns an IP address to the system when the client cannot obtain an IP address automatically. The Internet Assigned Numbers Authority, the nonprofit corporation responsible for assigning IP addresses and managing root servers, has set aside the range of addresses from 169.254.0.0 to 169.254.255.254 for this purpose.

If the computer system cannot contact a DHCP server, the computer randomly chooses an address in the form of 169.254.$x.y$ (where $x.y$ is the computer's identifier) and a 16-bit subnet mask (255.255.0.0) and broadcasts it on the network segment (subnet). If no other computer responds to the address, the system assigns this address to itself. When using APIPA, the system can communicate only with other computers on the same subnet that also use the 169.254.$x.y$ range with a 16-bit mask. APIPA is enabled by default if your system is configured to obtain an IP address automatically.

 NOTE A computer system on a network with an active DHCP server that has an IP address in this range usually indicates that there is a problem connecting to the DHCP server.

Sharing and Security

Windows systems can share all kinds of resources: files, folders, entire drives, printers, faxes, Internet connections, and much more. Conveniently for you, the CompTIA A+ certification exams limit their interests to folders, printers, and Internet connections. You'll see how to share folders and printers now; Internet connection sharing is discussed later in the TCP/IP section.

Sharing Drives and Folders

All versions of Windows share drives and folders in basically the same manner. Simply right-click any drive or folder and choose Properties. Select the Sharing tab (Figure 21-61). Select Share This Folder, add a Comment and a User Limit if you wish (they're not required), and click Permissions (Figure 21-62).

Hey! Doesn't NTFS have all those wild permissions like Read, Execute, Take Ownership, and all that? Yes, it does, but NTFS permissions and network permissions are totally separate beasties. Microsoft wanted Windows 2000 and XP to support many different types of partitions (NTFS, FAT16, FAT32), old and new. Network permissions are Microsoft's way of enabling you to administer file sharing on any type of partition supported by Windows, no matter how ancient. Sure, your options will be pretty limited if you are working with an older partition type, but you *can* do it.

Figure 21-61
Windows Sharing tab
on NTFS volume

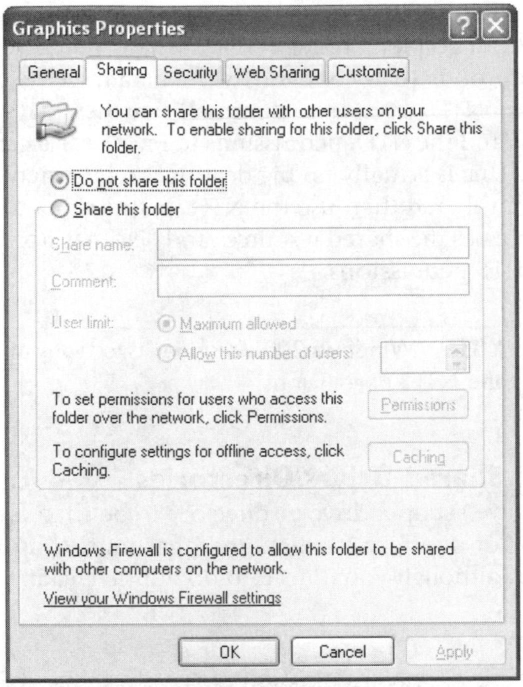

Figure 21-62
Network
permissions

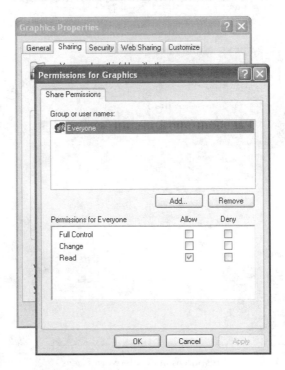

The beauty of Windows 2000/XP is that they provide another tool—NTFS permissions—that can do much more. NTFS is where the power lies, but power always comes with a price: You have to configure two separate sets of permissions. If you are sharing a folder on an NTFS drive, as you normally are these days, you must set *both* the network permissions and the NTFS permissions to let others access your shared resources. Some good news: This is actually no big deal! Just set the network permissions to give everyone full control, and then use the NTFS permissions to exercise more precise control over *who* accesses the shared resources and *how* they access them. Open the Security tab to set the NTFS permissions.

NOTE Windows 2000/XP offer two types of sharing: network permissions and NTFS permissions.

Accessing Shared Drives/Directories

Once you have set up a drive or directory to be shared, the final step is to access that shared drive or directory from another machine. Windows 2000 and XP use My Network Places, although you'll need to do a little clicking to get to the shared resources (Figure 21-63).

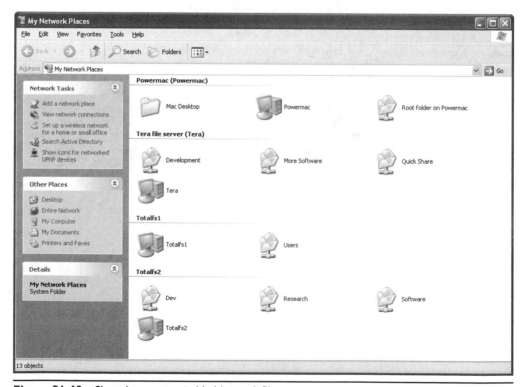

Figure 21-63 Shared resources in My Network Places

Network resources can also be "mapped" to a local resource name. For example, the FREDC share can be mapped to be a local hard drive such as E: or F:. From within any My Computer/Explorer window (such as My Documents or My Network Places), choose Tools | Map Network Drive to open the Map Network Drive dialog box (Figure 21-64). Click the Browse button to check out the neighborhood and find a shared drive (Figure 21-65).

Figure 21-64
Map Network
Drive dialog box

Figure 21-65
Browsing for
shared folders

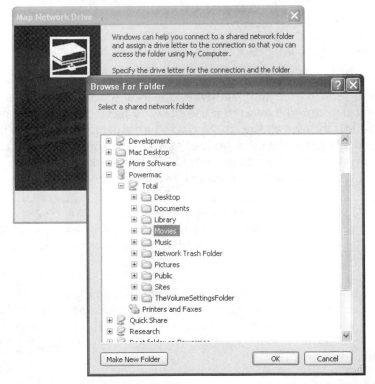

In Windows 2000, you can also use the handy Add Network Place icon in My Network Places to add network locations you frequently access without using up drive letters. Windows XP removed the icon but added the menu option in its context bar on the left. Here's how it looks on a Windows 2000 system (Figure 21-66).

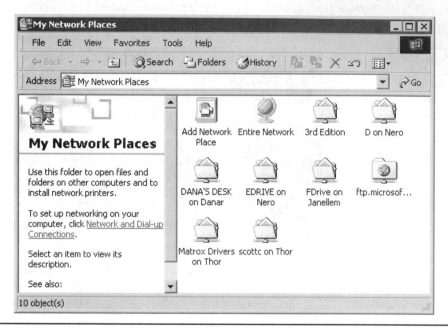

Figure 21-66 My Network Places

Mapping shared network drives is a common practice, as it makes a remote network share look like just another drive on the local system. The only downside to drive mapping stems from the fact that users tend to forget they are on a network. A classic example is the user who always accesses a particular folder or file on the network and then suddenly gets a "file not found" error when the workstation gets disconnected from the network. Instead of recognizing this as a network error, the user often imagines the problem as a missing or corrupted file.

 TIP All shared resources should show up in My Network Places. If a shared resource fails to show up, make sure you check the basics first: Is File and Printer Sharing activated? Is the device shared? Don't let silly errors fool you!

UNC

All computers that share must have a network name, and all of the resources they share must also have network names. Any resource on a network can be described by combining the names of the resource being shared and the system sharing. If a machine called SERVER1 is sharing its C: drive as FREDC, for example, the complete name would look like this:

\\SERVER1\FREDC

This is called the *universal naming convention (UNC)*. The UNC is distinguished by its use of double backslashes in front of the sharing system's name, and a single backslash in front of the shared resource's name. A UNC name can also point directly to a specific file or folder:

```
\\SERVER1\FREDC\INSTALL-FILES\SETUP.EXE
```

In this example, INSTALL-FILES is a subdirectory in the shared folder FREDC (which may or may not be called FREDC on the server), and SETUP.EXE is a specific file.

Sharing Printers

Sharing printers in Windows is just as easy as sharing drives and directories. Assuming that the system has printer sharing services loaded, just go to the Printers folder in the Control Panel and right-click the printer you wish to share. Select Properties, go to the Sharing tab, click Share this printer, and give it a name (see Figure 21-67).

Figure 21-67

Giving a name to a shared printer

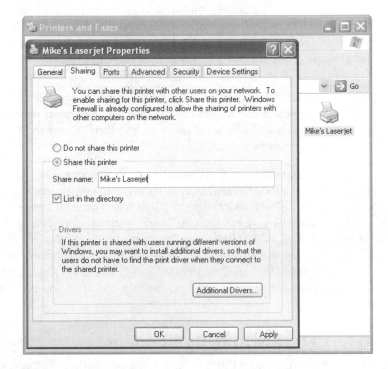

To access a shared printer in any version of Windows, simply click the Add Printer icon in the Printers folder. When asked if the printer is Local or Network, select Network; browse the network for the printer you wish to access, and Windows takes care of the rest! In almost all cases, Windows will copy the printer driver from the sharing machine. In the rare case where it doesn't, it will prompt you for drivers.

One of the most pleasant aspects of configuring a system for networking under all versions of Microsoft Windows is the amazing amount of the process that is automated. For example, if Windows detects a NIC in a system, it will automatically install the NIC driver, a network protocol (TCP/IP), and Client for Microsoft Networks (the NetBIOS part of the Microsoft networking software). So if you want to share a resource, everything you need is automatically installed. Note that while File and Printer Sharing is also automatically installed, you still must activate it by clicking the appropriate check box in the Local Area Connection Properties dialog box, as explained earlier in the chapter.

Essentials

Installing and Configuring a Wireless Network

Wireless networks represent the newest (and to me, one of the coolest) things happening in networking today. The chance to get away from all the cables and mess and just *connect* has a phenomenal appeal. Because I see wireless as one of the most important areas of development in the PC, this section goes a good bit deeper into the technology than the CompTIA A+ exams require. A highly skilled tech today should know this stuff, because that's what your customers will demand. To make it a little easier to study, I've included some exam tips in this section that you can skim before taking the exams.

 EXAM TIP The CompTIA A+ Essentials exam expects you to know the names and connectors (or lack thereof) in wireless networking. This chapter jumps back to Essentials for a bit and then returns to IT Technician and the other advanced exams.

Instead of a physical set of wires running between network nodes, wireless networks use either radio waves or beams of infrared light to communicate with each other. Different kinds of wireless networking solutions have come and gone in the past. The types of wireless radio wave networks you'll find yourself supporting these days are those based on the IEEE 802.11 wireless Ethernet standard *Wireless Fidelity (Wi-Fi)*—and those based on the newer Bluetooth technology. Wireless networks using infrared light are limited to those that use the *Infrared Data Association (IrDA)* protocol. Finally, the cell-phone companies have gotten into the mix and offer access to the Internet through cellular networks.

Wireless Networking Components

Wireless networking capabilities of one form or another are built into many modern computing devices. Infrared *transceiver* ports have been standard issue on portable computers, PDAs, and high-end printers for years, although they're curiously absent from many of the latest PCs. Figure 21-68 shows the infrared transceiver ports on a laptop computer and a PDA. Wireless Ethernet and Bluetooth capabilities are increasingly popular as integrated components, or they can easily be added using USB, PCI, PCI Express, or PC Card adapters. Figure 21-69 shows a PCI card that accepts a wireless PC Card Ethernet card. You can also add wireless network capabilities using external USB wireless network adapters, as shown in Figure 21-70.

Figure 21-68
Infrared transceiver
ports on a PDA
and laptop

Figure 21-69
Wireless PC Card
NIC inserted into
PCI add-on card

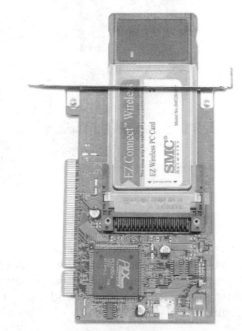

Figure 21-70
External USB
wireless NIC

Wireless network adapters aren't limited to PCs. Many handheld computers and PDAs have wireless capabilities built-in or available as add-on options. Figure 21-71 shows a PDA accessing the Internet through a wireless network adapter card.

Figure 21-71
PDA with wireless
capability

To extend the capabilities of a wireless Ethernet network, such as connecting to a wired network or share a high-speed Internet connection, you need a *wireless access point (WAP)*. A WAP centrally connects wireless network nodes in the same way that a hub connects wired Ethernet PCs. Many WAPs also act as switches and Internet routers, such as the Linksys device shown in Figure 21-72.

Figure 21-72
Linksys device that
acts as wireless
access point, switch,
and DSL router

Wireless communication via Bluetooth comes as a built-in option on newer PCs and peripheral devices, or you can add it to an older PC via an external USB Bluetooth adapter. Figure 21-73 shows a Bluetooth adapter with a Bluetooth-enabled mouse and keyboard.

Figure 21-73
External USB
Bluetooth adapter,
keyboard, and mouse

EXAM TIP The CompTIA A+ Essentials exam loves questions on cables and connectors, so look for questions on USB adapters and WAPs.

IT Technician

Wireless Networking Software

Wireless devices use the same networking protocols and client that their wired counterparts use, and they operate using the CSMA/CA networking scheme. The *CA* stands for *collision avoidance*, a slightly different standard than the *collision detection* standard used in wired Ethernet. Here's the difference. Wireless nodes listen in on the wireless medium to see if another node is currently broadcasting data. If so, it waits a random amount of time before retrying. So far, this method is exactly the same as the method used by wired Ethernet networks. Because wireless nodes have a more difficult time detecting data collisions, however, they offer the option of using the *Request to Send/Clear to Send (RTS/CTS)* protocol. When enabled, a transmitting node that determines that the wireless medium is clear to use sends an RTS frame to the receiving node. The receiving node responds with a CTS frame, telling the sending node that it's okay to transmit. Then, once the data is sent, the transmitting node waits for an acknowledgment (ACK) from the receiving node before sending the next data packet. Very elegant, but keep in mind that using RTS/CTS introduces significant overhead to the process and can impede performance.

EXAM TIP It's tempting if you're studying for the Help Desk or Depot Technician exams (Exams 220-603 and 220-604) to minimize the importance of wireless networking. This could come back to haunt you on the Essentials exam, though, so don't skip this section!

In terms of configuring wireless networking software, you need to do very little. Wireless network adapters are plug and play, so any modern version of Windows will immediately recognize a wireless network adapter when installed into a PCI or PCMCIA slot, or a USB port, prompting you to load any needed hardware drivers. You will, however, need a utility to set parameters such as your *Service Set Identifier (SSID)*, also called a *network name*.

Windows XP has built-in tools for configuring these settings, but for previous versions of Windows, you need to rely on configuration tools provided by the wireless network adapter vendor. Figure 21-74 shows a typical wireless network adapter configuration utility. Using this utility, you can determine your link state and signal strength, configure your wireless networking *mode* (discussed next), and set security encryption, power saving options, and so on.

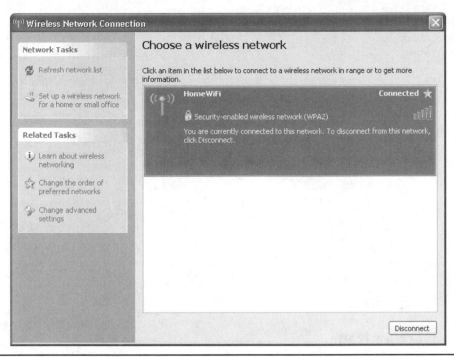

Figure 21-74   Wireless configuration utility

Wireless Network Modes

The simplest wireless network consists of two or more PCs communicating directly with each other *sans* cabling or any other intermediary hardware. More complicated wireless networks use a WAP to centralize wireless communication and bridge wireless network segments to wired network segments. These two different methods are called *ad-hoc* mode and *infrastructure* mode.

Ad-hoc Mode

Ad-hoc mode is sometimes called peer-to-peer mode, with each wireless node in direct contact with each other node in a decentralized free-for-all, as shown in Figure 21-75. Two or more wireless nodes communicating in ad-hoc mode form what's called an *Independent Basic Service Set (IBSS)*. Ad-hoc mode networks are suited for small groups of computers (less than a dozen or so) that need to transfer files or share printers. Ad-hoc networks are also good for temporary networks such as study groups or business meetings.

Figure 21-75
Wireless ad-hoc
mode network

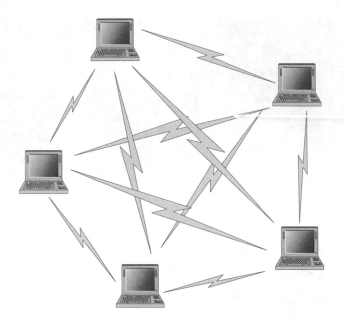

Infrastructure Mode

Wireless networks running in infrastructure mode use one or more WAPs to connect the wireless network nodes to a wired network segment, as shown in Figure 21-76. A single WAP servicing a given area is called a *Basic Service Set (BSS)*. This service area can be extended by adding more WAPs. This is called, appropriately, an *Extended Basic Service Set (EBSS)*.

Figure 21-76
Wireless
infrastructure
mode network

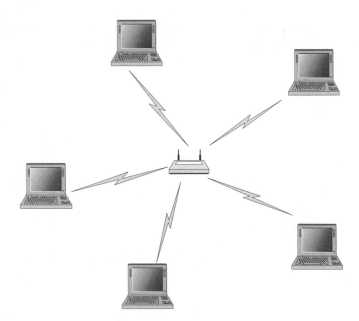

Wireless networks running in infrastructure mode require more planning and are more complicated to configure than ad-hoc mode networks, but they also give you finer control over how the network operates. Infrastructure mode is better suited to business networks or networks that need to share dedicated resources such as Internet connections and centralized databases. If you plan on setting up a wireless network for a large number of PCs or need centralized control over the wireless network, infrastructure mode is what you need.

Wireless Networking Security

One of the major complaints against wireless networking is that it offers weak security. In many cases, the only thing you need to do to access a wireless network is walk into a WAP's coverage area and turn on your wireless device! Further, data packets are floating through the air instead of safely wrapped up inside network cabling. What's to stop an unscrupulous PC tech with the right equipment from grabbing those packets out of the air and reading that data himself?

Wireless networks use three methods to secure access to the network itself and secure the data that's being transferred. The SSID (network name) parameter is used to define the wireless network—very handy when you have a number of wireless networks in the same area!

SSID

One of the main security weaknesses with wireless networks is that, out of the box, there's *no* security configured at all. Wireless devices *want* to be heard, and WAPs are usually configured to broadcast their presence to their maximum range and welcome all other wireless devices that respond.

Always change the default SSID to something unique. Configuring a unique SSID name is the very least that you should do to secure a wireless network. The default SSID names are well known and widely available online. This is intended to make setting up a wireless network as easy as possible, but conversely it creates a security hole you could drive a bullet train through. Each wireless network node and access point needs to be configured with the same unique SSID name. This SSID name is then included in the header of every data packet broadcast in the wireless network's coverage area. Data packets that lack the correct SSID name in the header are rejected.

 EXAM TIP   Changing the default SSID for the WAP is the first step in setting up a new wireless network.

Another trick often seen in wireless networks is to tell the wireless device to not broadcast the SSID. This makes it harder for people not authorized to access the network to know it's there.

MAC Filtering

Most WAPs also support MAC address filtering, a method that enables you to limit access to your wireless network based on the physical, hard-wired address of the units' wireless NIC. MAC filtering is a handy way of creating a type of "accepted users" list to limit access to your wireless network, but it works best when you have a small number of users. A table stored in the WAP lists the MAC addresses that are permitted to participate in the wireless network. Any data packets that don't contain the MAC address of a node listed in the table are rejected.

WEP

Early on, Wi-Fi developers introduced the *Wired Equivalent Privacy (WEP)* protocol to attempt to ensure that data is secured while in transit over the airwaves. WEP encryption uses a standard 40-bit encryption to scramble data packets. Many vendors also support 104-bit encryption. Note that some vendors advertise 128-bit encryption, but they actually use a 104-bit encryption key. Unfortunately, WEP encryption includes a flaw that makes it vulnerable to attack. While better than no encryption at all, keep in mind that WEP will not keep out a determined and knowledgeable intruder.

One important note to consider is that WEP doesn't provide complete end-to-end encryption. WEP provides encryption only between the WAP and the wireless device. Encryption is stripped from the data packet as it travels "up" through the subsequent network layers. For true end-to-end encryption, you need to upgrade to WPA or WPA2.

WPA

The *Wi-Fi Protected Access (WPA)* protocol addresses the weaknesses of WEP and acts as a security protocol upgrade to WEP. WPA offers security enhancements such as an encryption key integrity-checking feature and user authentication through the industry-standard *Extensible Authentication Protocol (EAP)*. EAP provides a huge security improvement over WEP encryption. After all, MAC addresses are fairly easy to "sniff" out, since they're transmitted in unencrypted, clear text format. Usernames and passwords are encrypted and therefore much more secure. Even with these enhancements, WPA was intended only as an interim security solution until the IEEE 802.11i security standard was finalized and implemented.

WPA2

Recent versions of Mac OS X and Microsoft Windows XP Professional support the full IEEE 802.11i standard, more commonly known as *Wi-Fi Protected Access 2 (WPA2)*, to lock down wireless networks. WPA2 uses the Advanced Encryption Standard (AES), among other improvements, to provide a secure wireless environment. If you haven't upgraded to WPA2, you should.

Speed and Range Issues

Wireless networking data throughput speeds depend on several factors. Foremost is the standard that the wireless devices use. Depending on the standard used, wireless throughput speeds range from a measly 2 Mbps to a respectable 54 Mbps. One of the other factors affecting speed is the distance between wireless nodes (or between wireless nodes and centralized access points). Wireless devices dynamically negotiate the top speed at which they can communicate without dropping too many data packets. Speed decreases as distance increases, so the maximum throughput speed is achieved only at extremely close range (less than 25 feet or so). At the outer reaches of a device's effective range, speed may decrease to around 1 Mbps before it drops out altogether.

Speed is also affected by interference from other wireless devices operating in the same frequency range—such as cordless phones or baby monitors—and by solid objects. So-called *dead spots* occur when something capable of blocking the radio signal comes between the wireless network nodes. Large electrical appliances such as refrigerators are *very* effective at blocking a wireless network signal. Other culprits include electrical fuse boxes, metal plumbing, air conditioning units, and similar objects.

NOTE You can see the speed and signal strength on your wireless network by looking at the Wireless NIC's properties.

Wireless networking range is difficult to define, and you'll see most descriptions listed with qualifiers, such as *"around* 150 feet" and *"about* 300 feet." This is simply because, like throughput speed, range is greatly affected by outside factors. Interference from other wireless devices affects range, as does interference from solid objects. The maximum ranges listed in the next section are those presented by wireless manufacturers as the theoretical maximum ranges. In the real world, you'll experience these ranges only under the most ideal circumstances. True effective range is probably about half what you see listed.

NOTE Range can be increased in a couple of ways. You can install multiple WAPs to permit "roaming" between one WAP's coverage area and another's—an EBSS, described earlier in this chapter. Or you can install a signal booster that increases a single WAP's signal strength, thus increasing its range.

EXAM TIP Look for basic troubleshooting questions on the CompTIA A+ certification exams dealing with factors that affect wireless connectivity, range, and speed.

Wireless Networking Standards

To help you gain a better understanding of wireless network technology, here is a brief look at the standards that they use.

IEEE 802.11-Based Wireless Networking

The IEEE 802.11 wireless Ethernet standard defines methods by which devices may communicate using *spread-spectrum* radio waves. Spread-spectrum broadcasts data in small, discrete chunks over the different frequencies available within a certain frequency range. All of the 802.11-based wireless technologies broadcast and receive at 2.4 GHz (with the exception of 802.11a, which uses 5 GHz). The original 802.11 standard has been extended to 802.11*a*, 802.11*b*, and 802.11*g* variations used in Wi-Fi wireless networks, and also *hybridized* (combined with another wireless communication technology) to form the *Shared Wireless Access Protocol (SWAP)* used in the now defunct HomeRF networks.

Wi-Fi is by far the most widely adopted wireless networking type today. Not only do thousands of private businesses and homes have wireless networks, but many public places such as coffee shops and libraries also offer Internet access through wireless networks.

NOTE Technically, only wireless devices that conform to the extended versions of the 802.11 standard, 802.11a, 802.11b, and 802.11g, are Wi-Fi certified. Wi-Fi certification comes from the Wi-Fi Alliance (formerly the Wireless Ethernet Compatibility Alliance, or WECA), a nonprofit industry group made up of more than 175 member companies who design and manufacturer wireless networking products. Wi-Fi certification ensures compatibility among wireless networking devices made by different vendors. First-generation devices that use the older 802.11 standard are not Wi-Fi certified and may or may not work well with devices made by different vendors.

Wireless devices can communicate only with other wireless devices that use the same standard. The exception to this is 802.11g, which is backward compatible with 802.11b devices (although at the lower speed of 802.11b). The following paragraphs describe the important specifications of each of the popular 802.11-based wireless networking standards.

NOTE Devices that use the original 802.11 (with no letter) standard are a rarity these days. You're likeliest to find them in service on some brave early wireless adopter's network. The original 802.11 standard was hampered by both slow speeds (2 Mbps maximum) and limited range (about 150 feet). 802.11 employed some of the same features that are in use in the current wireless standards. 802.11 uses the 2.4-GHz broadcast range, and security is provided by the use of industry-standard WEP, WPA, and WPA2 encryption.

802.11a Despite the "a" designation for this extension to the 802.11 standard, 802.11a was actually developed *after* 802.11b. The 802.11a standard differs from the other 802.11-based standards in significant ways. Foremost is that it operates in a different frequency range, 5 GHz. This means that devices that use this standard are less prone to interference from other devices that use the same frequency range. 802.11a also offers considerably greater throughput than 802.11 and 802.11b at speeds up to 54 Mbps, though its actual throughput is no more than 25 Mbps in normal traffic conditions. While its theoretical range tops out at about 150 feet, in a typical office environment, its maximum range will be lower. Despite the superior speed of 802.11a, it isn't widely adopted in the PC world.

802.11b 802.11b is practically ubiquitous in wireless networking. The 802.11b standard supports data throughput of up to 11 Mbps (with actual throughput averaging 4 to 6 Mbps)—on par with older wired 10BaseT networks—and a maximum range of 300 feet under ideal conditions. In a typical office environment, its maximum range will be lower.

802.11b networks can be secured though the use of WEP and WPA encryption. The main downside to using 802.11b is, in fact, that it's the most widely used standard. The 2.4-GHz frequency is already a crowded place, so you're likely to run into interference from other wireless devices.

802.11g The latest standardized version of 802.11, 802.11g offers data transfer speeds equivalent to 802.11a, up to 54 Mbps, with the wider 300-foot range of 802.11b. More important, 802.11g is backward compatible with 802.11b, meaning that the same 802.11g WAP can service both 802.11b and 802.11g wireless nodes.

Table 21-3 compares the important differences between the versions of 802.11.

Standard	802.11a	802.11b	802.11g
Max. throughput	54 Mbps	11 Mbps	54 Mbps
Max. range	150 feet	300 feet	300 feet
Frequency	5 GHz	2.4 GHz	2.4 GHz
Security	SSID, MAC filtering, industry-standard WEP, WPA	SSID, MAC filtering, industry-standard WEP, WPA	SSID, MAC filtering, industry-standard WEP, WPA
Compatibility	802.11a	802.11b	802.11b, 802.11g
Spread-spectrum method	DSSS	DSSS	DSSS
Communication mode	Ad-hoc or infrastructure	Ad-hoc or infrastructure	Ad-hoc or infrastructure
Description	Products that adhere to this standard are considered "Wi-Fi Certified." Eight available channels. Less prone to interference than 802.11b and 802.11g.	Products that adhere to this standard are considered "Wi-Fi Certified." Fourteen channels available in the 2.4-GHz band (only eleven of which can be used in the U.S. due to FCC regulations). Three non-overlapping channels.	Products that adhere to this standard are considered "Wi-Fi Certified." Improved security enhancements. Fourteen channels available in the 2.4-GHz band (only eleven of which can be used in the U.S. due to FCC regulations). Three non-overlapping channels.

Table 21-3   Comparison of 802.11 Standards

 EXAM TIP   Know the differences between 802.11a, 802.11b, and 802.11g.

Infrared Wireless Networking

Wireless networking using infrared technology is largely overlooked these days, probably due to the explosion of interest in the newer and faster wireless standards. This is a shame, because infrared provides an easy way to transfer data, often without the need to purchase or install any additional hardware or software on your PCs.

Infrared Data Association Standard   Communication through infrared devices is enabled via the *Infrared Data Association (IrDA)* protocol. The IrDA protocol stack is a widely supported industry standard and has been included in all versions of Windows since Windows 95.

> **NOTE**   Apple computers also support IrDA, as do Linux PCs.

Speed- and range-wise, infrared isn't very impressive. Infrared devices are capable of transferring data up to 4 Mbps—not too shabby, but hardly stellar. The maximum distance between infrared devices is 1 meter. Infrared links are direct line-of-sight and are susceptible to interference. An infrared link can be disrupted by anything that breaks the beam of light—a badly placed can of Mountain Dew, a co-worker passing between desks, or even bright sunlight hitting the infrared transceiver can cause interference.

Infrared is designed to make a point-to-point connection between two devices only in ad-hoc mode. No infrastructure mode is available. You can, however, use an infrared access point device to enable Ethernet network communication using IrDA. Infrared devices operate at half-duplex, meaning that while one is talking, the other is listening—they can't talk and listen at the same time. IrDA has a mode that emulates full-duplex communication, but it's really half-duplex. Security-wise, the IrDA protocol offers exactly nothing in the way of encryption or authentication. Infrared's main security feature is the fact that you have to be literally within arm's reach to establish a link. Clearly, infrared is not the best solution for a dedicated network connection, but for a quick file transfer or print job without getting your hands dirty, it'll do in a pinch.

Table 21-4 lists infrared's important specifications.

Table 21-4 Infrared Specs	**Standard**	**Infrared (IrDA)**
	Max. throughput	Up to 4 Mbps
	Max. range	1 meter (39 inches)
	Security	None
	Compatibility	IrDA
	Communication mode	Point-to-point ad-hoc

Bluetooth

Bluetooth wireless technology (named for 9th-century Danish king Harald Bluetooth) is designed to create small wireless *personal area networks (PANs)* that link PCs to peripheral devices such as PDAs and printers, input devices such as keyboards and mice, and even consumer electronics such as cell phones, home stereos, televisions, home security systems, and so on. Bluetooth is *not* designed to be a full-function networking solution, nor is it meant to compete with Wi-Fi. If anything, Bluetooth is poised to replace infrared as a means to connect PCs to peripherals.

The IEEE organization has made Bluetooth the basis for its forthcoming 802.15 standard for wireless PANs. Bluetooth uses the FHSS spread-spectrum broadcasting method, switching between any of the 79 frequencies available in the 2.45-GHz range. Bluetooth hops frequencies some 1600 times per second, making it highly resistant to interference. It transfers data from 723 Kbps to 1—count 'em, *1*—Mbps, with a maximum range of 10 meters (just over 30 feet). Some high-powered Bluetooth devices have throughput speed of a whopping 2 Mbps and a maximum range of up to 300 feet, but these are uncommon.

Bluetooth is *not* designed to be a full-fledged wireless networking solution. Bluetooth is made to replace the snake's nest of cables that currently connects most PCs to their various peripheral devices—keyboard, mouse, printer, speakers, scanner, and the like—but you won't be swapping out your 802.11-based networking devices with Bluetooth-based replacements anytime soon.

Having said that, Bluetooth-enabled wireless networking is comparable to other wireless technologies in a few ways:

- Like infrared, Bluetooth is acceptable for quick file transfers where a wired connection (or a faster wireless connection) is unavailable.
- Bluetooth's speed and range make it a good match for wireless print server solutions.

Bluetooth Wireless Networking Hardware Bluetooth hardware comes either integrated into many newer portable electronic gadgets such as PDAs and cell phones or as an adapter added to an internal or external expansion bus. Bluetooth networking is enabled through ad-hoc styled PC-to-PC (or PDA, handheld computer, or cell phone–to-PC) connections, or in an infrastructure-like mode through Bluetooth access points. Bluetooth access points are very similar to 802.11-based access points, bridging wireless Bluetooth PAN segments to wired LAN segments.

Cellular

Cellular wireless networks enable you to connect to the Internet through a network-aware personal digital assistant (PDA) or cell phone. Figure 21-77 shows a higher end cell phone with an Internet connection. Using an add-on PC Card, you can connect any laptop to a cellular network as well. Figure 21-78 shows a Sprint Mobile Broadband Card.

Figure 21-77
Sony-Erikson phone

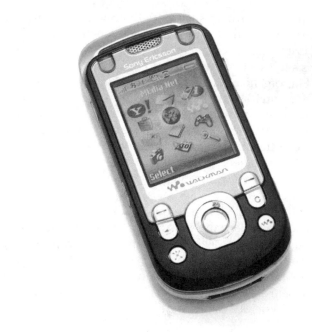

Figure 21-78
Cellular network
card

In areas with broad cell phone coverage, such as big cities, cellular wireless networks offer high-speed access (400 to 700 Kbps download speeds) anywhere you go. Just fire up your device or portable and start surfing the Web! In remote areas, the speed drops down to something closer to modem connection speeds. (See Chapter 22, "The Internet," for the scoop on modems.)

Cellular networks use various protocols to connect, such as Global System for Mobile Communications (GSM), General Packet Radio Service (GPRS), and Code Division Multiple Access (CDMA). These protocols are handled seamlessly by the software and hardware. What the end user sees is TCP/IP, just as if he or she connected through a wired network.

About the only real downside to cellular wireless networks is the price. The cell phone companies (notably Sprint and Cingular) are quite proud of their network service. As the technology matures, competition among the cellular network providers should bring the price down to something affordable for many people. At this point, though, it's usually much more cost-effective to go to a coffee shop or library and connect via Wi-Fi.

Configuring Wireless Networking

The mechanics of setting up a wireless network don't differ much from a wired network. Physically installing a wireless network adapter is the same as installing a wired NIC, whether it's an internal PCI card, a PCMCIA card, or an external USB device. Simply install the device and let plug and play handle detection and resource allocation. Install the device's supplied driver when prompted, and you're practically done. Unless you're using Windows XP, you also need to install the wireless network configuration utility supplied with your wireless network adapter so that you can set your communication mode, SSID, and so on.

As mentioned earlier, wireless devices want to talk to each other, so communicating with an available wireless network is usually a no-brainer. The trick is in configuring the wireless network so that only specific wireless nodes are able to use it and securing the data that's being sent through the air.

Wi-Fi

Wi-Fi networks support ad-hoc and infrastructure operation modes. Which mode you choose depends on the number of wireless nodes you need to support, the type of data sharing they'll perform, and your management requirements.

Ad-hoc Mode   Ad-hoc wireless networks don't need a WAP. The only requirements in an ad-hoc mode wireless network are that each wireless node be configured with the same network name (SSID), and that no two nodes use the same IP address. Figure 21-79 shows a wireless network configuration utility with ad-hoc mode selected. Clicking the Initiate Ad Hoc button on this particular utility opened the Ad Hoc Setting dialog box where you can set the speed and the channel (if necessary.) Other utilities have the options in different dialog box, but a quick glance should find the same options.

Figure 21-79
Selecting ad-hoc
mode in wireless
configuration utility

The only other configuration steps to take are to make sure that no two nodes are using the same IP address (this step is usually unnecessary if all PCs are using DHCP) and to ensure that the File and Printer Sharing service is running on all nodes.

Infrastructure Mode   Typically, infrastructure mode wireless networks employ one or more WAPs connected to a wired network segment, a corporate intranet or the Internet, or both. As with ad-hoc mode wireless networks, infrastructure mode networks require that the same SSID be configured on all nodes and WAPs. Figure 21-80 shows the same NETGEAR Wi-Fi configuration screen, this time set to infrastructure mode and using WPA security.

Figure 21-80
Selecting
infrastructure
mode in wireless
configuration utility

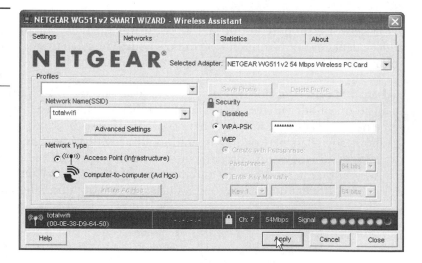

WAPs have an integrated Web server and are configured through a browser-based setup utility. Typically, you fire up your Web browser on one of your network client workstations and enter the WAP's default IP address, such as 192.168.1.1, to bring up the configuration page. You will need to supply an administrative password, included with your WAP's documentation, to log in (see Figure 21-81). Setup screens vary from vendor to vendor and from model to model. Figure 21-82 shows the initial setup screen for a popular Linksys WAP/router.

Figure 21-81
Security login for
Linksys WAP

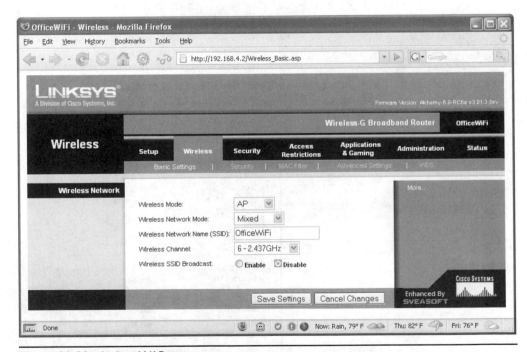

Figure 21-82 Linksys WAP setup screen

Configure the SSID option where indicated. Channel selection is usually automatic, but you can reconfigure this option if you have particular needs in your organization (for example, if you have multiple wireless networks operating in the same area). Remember that it's always more secure to configure a unique SSID than it is to accept the well-known default one. You should also make sure that the option to allow broadcasting of the SSID is disabled. This ensures that only wireless nodes specifically configured with the correct SSID can join the wireless network.

To increase security even more, use MAC filtering. Figure 21-83 shows the MAC filtering configuration screen on a Linksys WAP. Simply enter the MAC address of a wireless node that you wish to allow (or deny) access to your wireless network. Set up encryption by turning encryption on at the WAP and then generating a unique security key. Then configure all connected wireless nodes on the network with the same key information. Figure 21-84 shows the WPA2 key configuration dialog for a Linksys WAP.

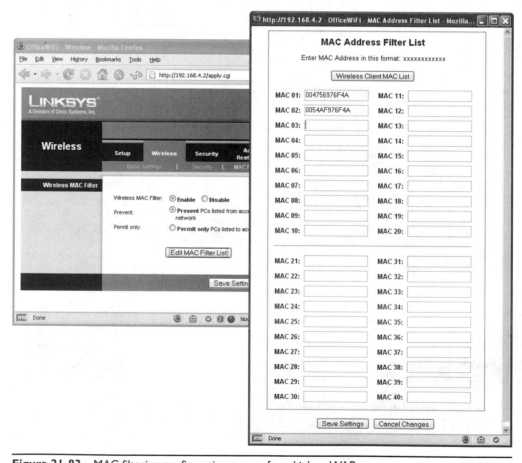

Figure 21-83 MAC filtering configuration screen for a Linksys WAP

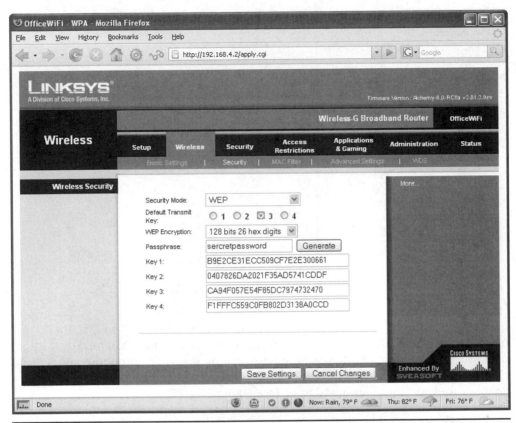

Figure 21-84 Encryption key configuration screen on Linksys WAP

 EXAM TIP As noted earlier in the chapter, the WEP protocol provides security, but it's fairly easily cracked. Use WPA2 or, if you have older equipment, then settle for WPA until you can upgrade.

You have the option of automatically generating a set of encryption keys or doing it manually—save yourself a headache and use the automatic method. Select an encryption level—the usual choices are either 64-bit or 128-bit—and then enter a unique passphrase and click the Generate button (or whatever the equivalent button is called on your WAP). Then select a default key and save the settings. The encryption level, key, and passphrase must match on the wireless client node or communication will fail. Many WAPs have the capability to export the encryption key data onto a media storage device for easy importing onto a client workstation, or you can manually configure encryption using the vendor-supplied configuration utility, as shown in Figure 21-85.

Figure 21-85
Encryption screen
on client wireless
network adapter
configuration utility

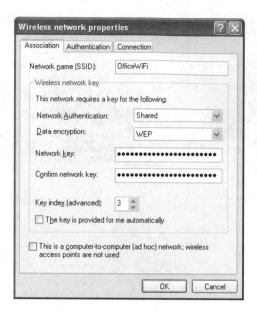

Infrared

IrDA device support is very solid in the latest version of Windows—in fact, there's not much for techs to configure. IrDA links are made between devices dynamically, without user interaction. Typically, there's nothing to configure on an infrared-equipped PC. Check your network settings to ensure that you've got the IrDA protocol installed and enabled, and you should be good to go (see Figure 21-86).

Figure 21-86
Confirming the
presence of IrDA
protocol in Windows
Network settings

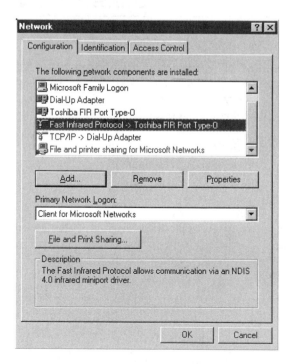

As far as infrared networking goes, your choices are somewhat limited. Infrared is designed to connect only two systems in ad-hoc mode. This can be done simply to transfer files, or with a bit more configuration, you can configure the two PCs to use IrDA in *direct-connection* mode. You can also use a special infrared access point to enable Ethernet LAN access via IrDA.

Transferring Files via Infrared   File transfers via IrDA are simple. When two IrDA-enabled devices "see" each other, the sending (primary) device negotiates a connection to the receiving (secondary) device, and *voilà*. It's just "point and shoot"! Figure 21-87 shows Windows 2000's *Wireless Link* applet. Use this to configure file transfer options and the default location for received files. You can send a file over the infrared connection by specifying a location and one or more files using the Wireless Link dialog box; dragging and dropping files onto the Wireless Link icon; right-clicking the file(s) in My Computer and selecting Send To Infrared Recipient; or printing to a printer configured to use an infrared port.

Figure 21-87
Windows 2000
Wireless Link applet

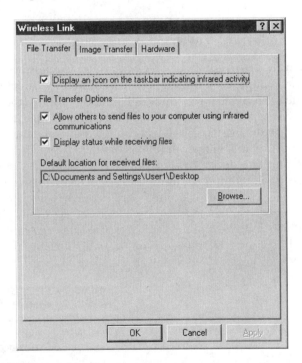

Networking via Infrared   Direct network connections between two PCs using infrared are similar to using a null-modem cable to connect two PCs together via a serial port. Modern versions of Windows make this type of connection extremely easy by employing wizards. Simply select Connect Directly to Another Computer and follow the prompts, choosing your infrared port as the connection device.

An infrared access point combines an infrared transceiver with an Ethernet NIC and translates the IrDA protocol into an Ethernet signal, enabling you to log on to your network and access resources. Figure 21-88 shows a laptop accessing an Ethernet LAN through an infrared access point.

Figure 21-88
Laptop using infrared
access point

Bluetooth Configuration   As with other wireless networking solutions, Bluetooth devices are completely plug and play. Just connect the adapter and follow the prompts to install the appropriate drivers and configuration utilities (these are supplied by your hardware vendor). Once installed, you have little to do: Bluetooth devices seek each other out and establish the master/slave relationship without any intervention on your part.

Connecting to a Bluetooth PAN is handled by specialized utility software provided by your portable device or Bluetooth device vendor. Figure 21-89 shows a Compaq iPAQ handheld computer running the Bluetooth Manager software to connect to a Bluetooth access point. Like their Wi-Fi counterparts, Bluetooth access points use a browser-based configuration utility. Figure 21-90 shows the main setup screen for a Belkin Bluetooth access point. Use this setup screen to check on the status of connected Bluetooth devices; configure encryption, MAC filtering, and other security settings; and use other utilities provided by the access point's vendor.

Figure 21-89
iPAQ Bluetooth
Manager software
connected to
Bluetooth access
point

Figure 21-90
Windows Bluetooth
setup screen

Troubleshooting Networks

Once you go beyond a single PC and enter the realm of networked computers, your troubleshooting skills need to take a giant leap up in quality. Think of the complexity added with networks. Suddenly you have multiple PCs with multiple users who could, at the drop of a hat, do all kinds of inadvertent damage to a fully functional PC. Networked PCs have a layer of networked hardware and resource sharing that adds a completely new dimension to a user's cry for help, "I can't print!"

EXAM TIP The "Troubleshooting Networks" section covers a range of questions you're likely to see on the "Communication and Professionalism" exam domain. See also Chapter 24, "The Complete PC Tech," for more on the topic.

Where can the problem lie in a *non-networked situation* if a person cannot print? Here are the obvious ones:

- Printer is not connected to the PC.
- Printer is out of ink.
- PC doesn't have the proper driver loaded.
- PC points by default to a printer other than the one to which the user thinks should print.

That's about it. Maybe the parallel port configuration is wrong in CMOS or the USB drivers aren't correct, but still…. Now do the same thing with a *networked situation* where a user can't print. Here are the obvious *extra* issues, because all the local machine issues apply as well:

- Print server is down.
- Printer is locked by another user.
- The client PC doesn't have network connectivity.
- The NIC driver is bad or incorrect.
- The client PC doesn't have the proper printer drivers installed for the networked printer.
- The cable between the client PC's NIC and the nearest switch is bad.
- The port to which the cable connects is bad.
- The switch failed.
- Somebody in an office down the hall spilled coffee on the printer inside the mechanism and then didn't fess up to the accident.

That's a lot of variables, and they just scratch the surface of possibilities. You live in a networked world—it's time to elevate your troubleshooting skills and methodologies to the next level. This section offers a series of steps you can use when performing any type of PC or network troubleshooting. You'll look at ways to apply your tech skills and general communication skills to get to the bottom of a problem and get that problem fixed.

Verify the Symptom

The one thing that all PC problems have in common is a symptom. If something odd was happening (or not happening) to users as they tried to do whatever they need to do on their computers, you wouldn't have a problem at all, would you? Unfortunately, the vast majority of users out there aren't CompTIA A+ certified technicians. As a tech, you need to overcome a rather nasty communication gap before you can begin to consider a fix. Let's bridge that gap right now.

 EXAM TIP Look for lots of questions on communication with users on the IT Technician and Help Desk Technician exams.

It usually starts with a phone call:

You: "Tech Support, this is Mike. How can I help you?"

User: "Uh, hi, Mike. This is Tom over in Accounting. I can't get into the network. Can you help me?"

Tom just started over in the Accounting department this week and has been a pain in the rear end so far. Ah, the things you might want to say to this person: "No. I only help non-pain-in-the-rear accountants." Or how about this? "Let me check my appointment schedule.... Ah, yes. I can check on your problem in two weeks. Monday at 4:00 P.M. okay for you?"

But, of course, you had the audacity to choose the beloved profession of IT tech support, so you don't get to ask the questions you want to ask. Rather, you need to take a position of leadership and get to the bottom of the problem, and that means understanding the symptom. Take a deep breath, smile, and get to work. You have two issues to deal with at this point. First, if you're working with a user, you must try to get the user to describe the symptom. Second, whether you're working on a system alone or you're talking to a user on the telephone, you must verify that the symptom is legitimate.

Getting a user to describe a symptom is often a challenge. Users are not techs and as a result their perception of the PC is very different than yours. But by the same token, most users know a bit about PCs—you want to take advantage of a user's skill and experience whenever you can. A personal example of verifying the symptom: Once I got a call from a user telling me that his "screen was blank." I told him to restart his system. To which he responded, "Shouldn't I shut down the PC first?" I said: "I thought you just told me the screen was blank!" He replied: "That's right. There's nothing on the screen but my Desktop."

When Did It Happen?

Once you know the symptom, you need to try to inspect the problem yourself. This doesn't mean you need to go to the system, as many real problems are easily fixed by the user, under your supervision. But you must understand when the problem occurs so that you can zero in on where to look for the solution. Does it happen at boot? It might be a CMOS/BIOS issue. Is it taking place as the OS loads? Then you need to start checking initialization files. Does it take place when the system runs untouched for a certain amount of time? Then maybe the power management could come into play.

What Has Changed?

Systems that run properly tend to continue to run properly. Systems that have undergone a hardware or software change have a much higher chance of not running properly than a system that has not been changed. If something has gone wrong, talk to the user to determine whether anything particular has occurred since the system last worked properly. Has new software been installed? Did the user add some new RAM? Change the Windows Domain? Run a Windows Update? Drop the monitor on the floor? Not only do you need to consider those types of changes, you must make sure that any unrelated changes don't send you down the wrong path. The fact that someone installed a new floppy drive yesterday probably doesn't have anything to do with the printer that isn't working today.

Last, consider side effects of changes that don't seem to have anything to do with the problem. For example, I once had a customer whose system kept freezing up in Windows. I knew he had just added a second hard drive, but the system booted up just fine and ran normally—except it would freeze up after a few minutes. The hard drive wasn't the problem. The problem was that he unplugged the CPU fan in the process. When I discover a change has been made, I like to visualize the process of the change to consider how that change may have directly or indirectly contributed to a problem. In other words, if you run into a situation where a person added a NIC to a functioning

PC that now won't boot, you need to think about what part of the installation process could be fouled up to cause a PC to stop working.

Check the Environment

I use the term *environment* in two totally different fashions in this book. The first way is the most classic definition: the heat, humidity, dirt, and other outside factors that can affect the operation of the system. The other definition is more technical and addresses the computing environment of the user's system and other surrounding systems: What type of system do they run? What OS? What is their network connection? What are the primary applications they use? What antivirus program do they run? Do other people use the system?

Answering these questions gives you an overview of what is affecting this system both internally and externally. A quick rundown of these issues can reveal possible problems that might not be otherwise recognized. For example, I once got a call from a user complaining they had no network connection. I first checked the NIC to ensure it had link lights (always the first thing to check to ensure a good physical connection!) only to discover that they had no link lights—someone decided to turn on a space heater which destroyed the cable!

Reproducing the Problem

My official rule on problems with a PC is this: "If a problem happens only once, it is not a problem." PCs are notorious for occasionally locking up, popping errors, and display-ing all types of little quirks that a quick reboot fixes, and they don't happen again. Why do these things happen? I don't know, although I'm sure if someone wanted me to guess I could come up with a clever explanation. But the majority of PCs simply don't have redundancy built in, and it's okay for them to occasionally "hiccup."

A problem becomes interesting to me if it happens more than once. If it happens twice, there's a much higher chance it will happen a third time. I want to see it happen that third time—under my supervision. I will direct the user to try to reproduce the problem while I am watching to see what triggers the failure. This is a huge clue to help-ing you localize the real problem. Intermittent failures are the single most frustrating events that take place in a technician's life. But do remember that many seemingly in-termittent problems really aren't intermittent—you have simply failed to reproduce the events exactly enough to see the consistency of the problem. Always take the time to match every step that leads to a problem to try to re-create the same error.

Isolating the Symptom

With so many bits and pieces to a PC, you must take the time to try to isolate the symp-tom to ensure your fix is going to the software or hardware that really needs it. In hard-ware, that usually means removing suspect parts until only one possible part remains. In software, that usually means removing background programs, booting into Safe Mode, or trying to create a situation where only the suspected program is running.

Isolation takes on a whole new meaning with networks. One of the greatest tools in networking is isolation—does this problem happen on other systems, on other workgroups, on other PCs running DHCP? Whenever a problem takes place in networking, isolation is the key to determining the problem.

Separating Hardware from Software

Many problems that occur on a PC are difficult to isolate given that it is difficult to determine whether the problem lies in the software or the hardware. If you find yourself in this situation, you can take a few steps to help you zero in on which side of the PC to suspect.

Known Good Hardware

The absolute best way to know whether a problem is hardware or software related is to replace the suspected piece of hardware with a known good part. If you can't tell whether a Windows page fault comes from bad RAM or a software incompatibility, quickly replacing the RAM with known good RAM should help you determine whether the RAM or the software is to blame.

Uninstall/Reinstall

If you can do so easily, try uninstalling the suspected software and reinstalling. Many hardware/software problems magically disappear with a simple uninstall/reinstall.

Patching/Upgrading

Many hardware or software problems take place due to incompatibilities between the two suspect sides. Try upgrading drivers. Download patches or upgrades to software, especially if the hardware and the software are more than two years apart in age.

Virus Check

Last (maybe I should have put this first), always check for viruses. Today's viruses manifest so many different symptoms that failure to check for them is a study in time wasting. I recently got a new hard drive that started to make a nasty clicking noise—a sure sign of a failing hard drive. However, I ran an extensive virus check and guess what—it was a virus! Who would have thought? I checked with the hard drive maker's Web site, and my fears were confirmed. It just goes to show you—even the best of techs can get caught by the simplest problems.

Research

Once you've got your mind wrapped around the problem, it's time to fix it. Unless the problem is either simple (network cable unplugged) or something you've seen before and know exactly how to fix, you'll almost certainly need to research it. The Internet makes this easy. I use one of my favorite tricks when I get some bizarre error text: I type the error message into my search engine—that would be Google, of course—and most times find a quick fix!

Make the Fix and Test

Once you have a good idea as to the problem and how to fix it, it's time to do the fix. Always make backups—or at least warn the user of the risk to the system. If possible, try to remember how the system was configured before the fix so that you can go back to square one if the fix fails to work. After you perform the fix, do whatever you need to do to make sure the system is again working properly. Make sure the user sees that the system is working properly so that he or she can "sign off" on your work.

OSI Seven-Layer Model

A lot of people think about networks and troubleshoot networking issues using the OSI seven-layer model. Using this model (or my four-layer model, described in the next section of this chapter) helps you isolate problems and then implement solutions. Here are the seven layers of the OSI model:

- **Layer 1** Physical
- **Layer 2** Data Link
- **Layer 3** Network
- **Layer 4** Transport
- **Layer 5** Session
- **Layer 6** Presentation
- **Layer 7** Application

The *Physical layer* defines the physical form taken by data when it travels across a cable. Devices that work at the Physical layer include NICs, hubs, and switches. Figure 21-91 shows a sending NIC turning a string of ones and zeros into an electrical signal, and a receiving NIC turning it back into the same ones and zeros.

The *Data Link layer* defines the rules for accessing and using the Physical layer. MAC addresses and Ethernet's CSMA/CD operate at the Data Link layer.

The *Network layer* defines the rules for adding information to the data packet that controls how routers move it from its source on one network to its destination on a different network. The IP protocol that handles IP addressing works on Layer 3.

The *Transport layer*, Layer 4, breaks up data it receives from the upper layers (that is, Layers 5–7) into smaller pieces for transport within the data packets created at the lower layers. In TCP/IP networks, the protocols that typically handle this transition between upper and lower layers are TCP and UDP.

Figure 21-91
The Physical layer
turns binary code
into a physical signal
and back into ones
and zeros.

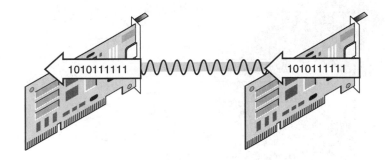

The *Session layer* manages the connections between machines on the network. Protocols such as NetBIOS and sockets enable a computer to connect to a server, for example, and send and receive e-mail or download a file. Each different task you can perform on a server would require a different kind of session.

The *Presentation layer* presents data from the sending system in a form that a receiving system can understand. Most Layer 6 functions are handled by the same software that handles Layer 7 functions.

The *Application layer* is where you (or a user) get to interact with the computers. These are programs that make networking happen, such as Web browsers and e-mail applications. Chapter 22, "The Internet," covers these applications in a lot more detail.

The key to using the OSI seven-layer model is to ask the traditional troubleshooting question: What can the problem be? If Jill can't browse a Web site, for example, could this be a Layer 7 issue? Sure: If her browser software was messed up, this could stop her from browsing. It could also be a lower level problem, though, and you need to run through the questions. Can she do anything over the network? If her NIC doesn't show flashing link lights, that could point all the way down to the Physical layer and a bad NIC, cable, hub, or switch.

If she has good connectivity to the overall network but can't ping the Web server, that could point to a different problem altogether. Figure 21-92 shows the OSI seven-layer model graphically.

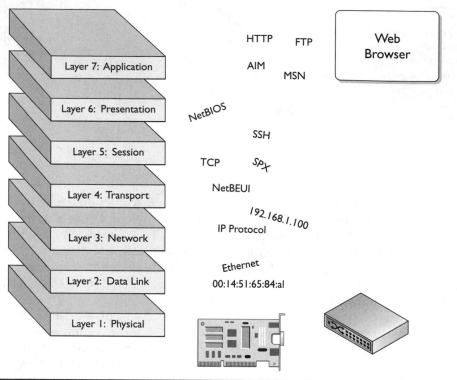

Figure 21-92 OSI

The only drawback to the OSI seven-layer model, in my view, is that it's too complex. I like to conceptualize network issues into fewer layers—four to be precise. Let's take a look.

Mike's Four-Layer Model

Network problems, by the very nature of the complexity of a network, usually make for more complex problems. Given that, I have created a four-step process that I modestly call "Mike's Four-Layer Model." These four things go through my mind every time I have a problem. I think about four distinct "categories" to help me isolate the symptoms and make the right fix.

Hardware

Hardware is probably the most self-explanatory of the four categories. This covers the many different ways data can be moved from one PC to another. Does the system have a good connection—how's the cabling? This also covers network cards—are they installed properly and tested? Plus, the hardware category hits on all of those interesting boxes, such as hubs, switches, and repeaters, among which all of the wires in the network run. If you can see it, it's under this category.

Protocols

This category covers the protocols, such as TCP/IP or NetBEUI. Is the protocol installed? Is it configured properly? Does any particular system's configuration prevent it from working with another system?

Network

The network category has two parts: servers and clients. Network operating systems must differentiate systems that act as servers from those that do not. If a system is a server, some process must take place to tell it to share resources. Additionally, if a system is intended to share, it must be given a name. This category also includes defining and verifying users and groups—does your system need them? Do the right accounts exist, and are they working properly?

Shared Resources

Once all the systems, users, and groups are working properly, you need to identify the resources they will share. If a drive or folder is to be shared, the OS must provide a way to identify that drive or folder as available for sharing. The rules for naming shared resources are called *naming conventions*. A great example would be a system that offers its D:\FRED directory for sharing. This D:\FRED directory needs a network name, such as FRED_FILES. This network name is displayed to all of the devices on the network.

Sharing a resource is only half the battle. Individual systems need to be able to access the shared resources. The network needs a process whereby a PC can look out on the network and see what is available. Having found those available resources, the PC then needs to make them look and act as though they were local resources. A network also needs to control access to resources. A laser printer, for example, might be available for sharing, but only for the accounting department, excluding other departments.

Chapter Review Questions

1. To provide a computer with a physical and electronic connection to a network, what must be installed?

   A. A hub

   B. A router

   C. A NIC

   D. A bridge

2. Which of the following is needed to configure a PnP NIC in a Windows XP system?

   A. CMOS

   B. Configuration software

   C. Device driver

   D. DMA

3. How far apart can two PCs that share the same 100BaseT switch be placed?

   A. 100 meters

   B. 200 meters

   C. 330 meters

   D. 1000 meters

4. Under ideal conditions, the 802.11g standard supports data throughput of up to _____ and has a range of up to _____.

   A. 11 Mbps/150 feet

   B. 11 Mbps/300 feet

   C. 54 Mbps/150 feet

   D. 54 Mbps/300 feet

5. What is the minimum specification of cable types for 100BaseT networks?

   A. CAT 2

   B. CAT 3

   C. CAT 4

   D. CAT 5

6. Joe needs to network two computers in his office together using an Ethernet peer-to-peer connection. What kind of cable does he need?

   A. CAT-5

   B. Crossover

   C. UTP

   D. STP

7. What are the two TIA/EIA standards for connecting an RJ-45 connector to UTP cable?

   A. 10BaseT/100BaseT

   B. CAT5/CAT5e

   C. RG-58/RG-59

   D. 568A/568B

8. Steven's Windows XP system can't connect to the Internet, and he comes to you, his PC tech, for help. You figure out that it's a DHCP problem. What program should you run to get him a new DHCP lease?

   A. IPCONFIG

   B. WINIPCFG

   C. CONFIG

   D. DHCP /RENEW

9. Which encryption protocol offers the best security?

    A. Hi-Encrypt

    B. WEP

    C. WPA

    D. WPA2

10. Bluetooth technology enables computers to link into what sort of network?

    A. Bluetooth area network (BAN)

    B. Personal area network (PAN)

    C. Local area network (LAN)

    D. Wide area network (WAN)

Answers

1. **C.** A system must have a NIC to participate in any type of network.

2. **C.** PnP only requires the proper driver.

3. **B.** Each system can be 100 meters from the switch, so any two systems can be up to 200 meters apart.

4. **D.** Under ideal conditions, the 802.11g standard supports data throughput of up to 54 Mbps and has a range of up to 300 feet.

5. **D.** 100BaseT requires CAT 5 rated cabling.

6. **B.** Joe needs a crossover cable to network two computers in his office together using an Ethernet peer-to-peer connection.

7. **D.** The TIA/EIA has two standards for connecting the RJ-45 connector to the UTP cable: TIA/EIA 568A and TIA/EIA 568B.

8. **A.** You should run IPCONFIG to get a new DHCP lease for Steven's Windows XP system. WINIPCFG was the program used by Windows 9x for this task. /RENEW is a valid switch for both programs, but not for CONFIG.

9. **D.** WPA2 is the best of the encryption technologies listed.

10. **B.** Bluetooth creates personal area networks.

The Internet

In this chapter, you will learn how to
- Explain how the Internet works
- Connect to the Internet
- Use Internet software tools

Imagine coming home from a long day at work building and fixing PCs, sitting down in front of your shiny new computer, double-clicking the single icon that sits dead center on your monitor…and suddenly you're enveloped in an otherworldly scene, where 200-foot trees slope smoothly into snow-white beaches and rich blue ocean. Overhead, pterodactyls soar through the air while you talk to a small chap with pointy ears and a long robe about heading up the mountain in search of a giant monster…a TV show from the SciFi channel? Spielberg's latest film offering? How about an interactive game played by millions of people all over the planet on a daily basis by connecting to the Internet? If you guessed the last one, you're right.

This chapter covers the skills you need as a PC tech to help people connect to the Internet. It starts with a brief section on how the Internet works along with the concepts of connectivity, and then it goes into the specifics on hardware, protocols, and software that you use to make the Internet work for you (or for your client). The "Beyond A+" section is beefier than that of other chapters because, although the CompTIA A+ certification exams don't require it, every tech needs to know how to assist clients with some of the *niceties* of the Internet. Let's get started!

Historical/Conceptual

Understanding the Internet

The Internet enables users to communicate with one another over vast distances, often in the blink of an eye. As a PC tech, you need to know how PCs communicate with the larger world for two reasons. First, knowing the process and pieces involved in the communication enables you to troubleshoot effectively when that communication goes away. Second, you need to be able to communicate knowledgeably with a network technician when he or she comes in to solve a more complex issue.

Internet Tiers

You probably know that the Internet is millions and millions of computers all joined together to form the largest network on earth, but not many folks know much about how these computers are organized. In order to keep everything running smoothly, the Internet is broken down into groups called *tiers*. The main tier, called *Tier 1*, consists of nine companies called *Tier 1 providers*. The Tier 1 providers own long-distance, high-speed fiber-optic networks called *backbones*. These backbones span the major cities of the earth (not all Tier 1 backbones go to all cities) and interconnect at special locations called *network access points (NAPs)*. Anyone wishing to connect to any of the Tier 1 providers must pay large sums of money. However, the Tier 1 providers do not charge each other.

Tier 2 providers own smaller, regional networks and must pay the Tier 1 providers. Most of the famous companies that provide Internet access to the general public are Tier 2 providers. *Tier 3 providers* are even more regional and connect to Tier 2 providers.

The piece of equipment that makes this tiered Internet concept work is called a backbone router. *Backbone routers* connect to more than one other backbone router, creating a big, interwoven framework for communication. Figure 22-1 illustrates the decentralized and interwoven nature of the Internet. The key reason for interweaving the backbones of the Internet was to provide alternative pathways for data if one or more of the routers went down. If Jane in Houston sends a message to her friend Polly in New York City, for example, the shortest path between Jane and Polly in this hypothetical situation is this: Jane's message originates at Rice University in Houston, bounces to Emory University in Atlanta, flits through Virginia Commonwealth University in Richmond, and then zips into SUNY in New York City (Figure 22-2). Polly happily reads the message and life is great. The Internet functions as planned.

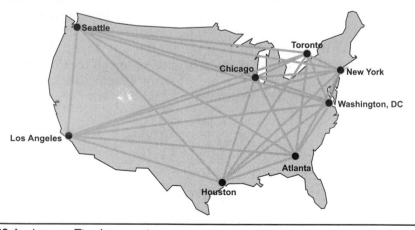

Figure 22-1 Internet Tier 1 connections

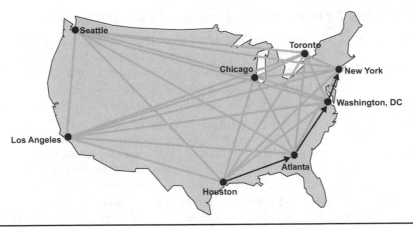

Figure 22-2 Message traveling from Houston to NYC

But what happens if the entire southeastern United States experiences a huge power outage and Internet backbones in every state from Virginia to Florida goes down? Jane's message would bounce back to Rice and the Rice computers. Being smart cookies, the routers would reroute the message to nodes that still functioned—say, Rice to University of Chicago, then University of Toronto, and then SUNY (Figure 22-3). It's all in a day's work for the highly redundant and adaptable Internet. At this point in the game (early 2007), the Internet simply cannot go down fully—barring, of course, a catastrophe of Biblical proportions.

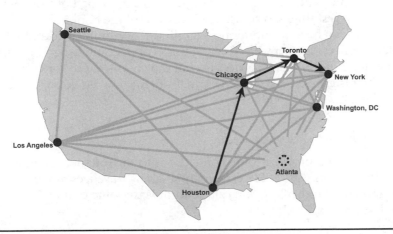

Figure 22-3 Rerouted message from Houston to NYC

TCP/IP—The Common Language of the Internet

As you know from all the earlier chapters in this book, hardware alone doesn't cut it in the world of computing. You need software to make the machines run and create an interface for humans. The Internet is no exception. TCP/IP provides the basic software structure for communication on the Internet.

Because you spent a good deal of Chapter 21 working with TCP/IP, you should have an appreciation for its adaptability and, perhaps more importantly, its extendibility. TCP/IP provides the addressing scheme for computers that communicate on the Internet through IP addresses, such as 192.168.4.1 or 16.45.123.7. As a protocol, though, TCP/IP is much more than just an addressing system. TCP/IP provides the framework and common language for the Internet. And it offers a phenomenally wide-open structure for creative purposes. Programmers can write applications built to take advantage of the TCP/IP structure and features, creating what are called TPC/IP services. The cool thing about TCP/IP services is that they're limited only by the imagination of the programmers.

You'll learn much more about TCP/IP services in the software and "Beyond A+" sections of this chapter, but I must mention one service that you've most likely worked with yourself, whether you knew them by that term or not. The most famous service is the *Hypertext Transport Protocol (HTTP)*, the service that provides the structure for the *World Wide Web* ("the Web" for short), the graphical face of the Internet. Using your *Web browser*—a program specifically designed to retrieve, interpret, and display Web pages—an almost endless variety of information and entertainment is just a click away. I can't tell you how many times I've started to look up something on the Web, and suddenly it's two hours later and I still haven't looked up what I started out wanting to know, but I don't actually care, because I've learned some amazing stuff! But then when I do go look it up, in just minutes I can find out information it used to take *days* to uncover. The Web can arguably claim the distinction of being both the biggest time-waster and the biggest time-saver since the invention of the book!

At this point, you have an enormous, beautifully functioning network. All the backbone routers connect together with fiber and thick copper cabling backbones, and TCP/IP enables communication and services for building applications for humans to interface across the distances. What's left? Oh, that's right: how do you tap into this great network and partake of its goodness?

Internet Service Providers

Every Tier 1 and Tier 2 provider leases connections to the Internet to companies called *Internet service providers (ISPs)*. ISPs essentially sit along the edges of the Tier 1 and Tier 2 Internet and tap into the flow. You can, in turn, lease some of the connections from the ISP and thus get on the Internet.

NOTE Microsoft calls the connections ISPs make to the Internet *access points*, which I think is a very bad name. You'd think we'd be able to come up with new terms for things! Instead, some folks in this industry continue rebranding things with the same phrases or catch words, only serving to confuse already bewildered consumers.

ISPs come in all sizes. America Online (AOL) has a huge pipe into the Internet, enabling its millions of customers (in the U.S. alone) to connect from their local machines and surf the Web. Contrast AOL with Unisono Net, an ISP in San Miguel de Allende, Mexico (Figure 22-4). Billed as the "Best ISP in San Miguel," it services only a small (but delightful) community and the busy tourist crowd. Functionally, though, Unisono Net does the same thing AOL does, just without all the bells, whistles, and mountains of free CD-ROMs!

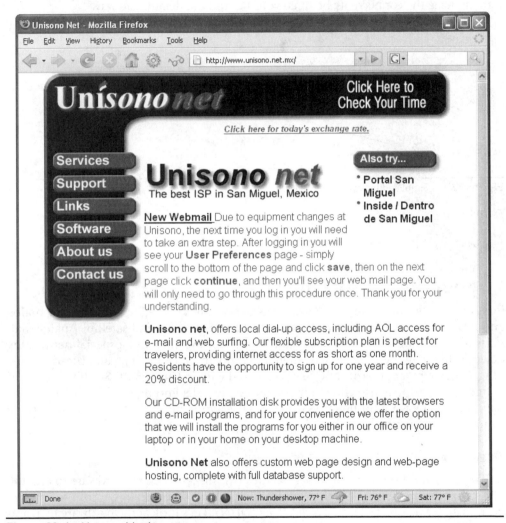

Figure 22-4 Unisono Net homepage

Connection Concepts

Connecting to an ISP requires two things to work perfectly: hardware for connectivity, such as a modem and a working telephone line; and software, such as protocols to govern the connections and the data flow (all configured in Windows), and applications to take advantage of the various TPC/IP services. Once you have a contract with an ISP to grant you access to the Internet, the ISP gives you TCP/IP configuration numbers and data so you can set up your software to connect directly to a router at the ISP that becomes your gateway to the Internet. The router to which you connect at the ISP, by the way, is often referred to as the *default gateway*. Once you configure your software correctly, you can connect to the ISP and get to the greater Internet. Figure 22-5 shows a standard PC-to-ISP-to-Internet connection. Note that various protocols and other software manage the connectivity between your PC and the default gateway.

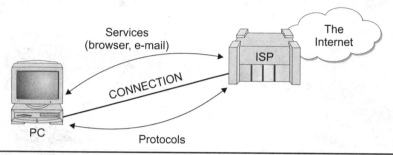

Figure 22-5 Simplified Internet connectivity

Essentials

Connecting to the Internet

PCs commonly connect to an ISP using one of seven technologies: dial-up, both analog and ISDN; dedicated, such as DSL, cable, and LAN; wireless; and satellite. Analog dial-up is the slowest of the bunch and requires a telephone line and a special networking device called a modem. ISDN uses digital dial-up and has much greater speed. All the others use a regular Ethernet NIC like you played with in Chapter 21. Satellite is the odd man out here; it may use either a modem or a NIC, depending on the particular configuration you have, although most folks will use a modem. Let's take a look at all these various connection options.

Dial-up

A dial-up connection to the Internet requires two pieces to work: hardware to dial the ISP, such as a modem or ISDN terminal adapter; and software to govern the connection, such as Microsoft's *Dial-up Networking (DUN)*. Let's look at the hardware first, and then we'll explore software configuration.

Modems

At some point in the early days of computing, some bright guy or gal noticed a colleague talking on a telephone, glanced down at a PC, and then put two and two together: why not use telephone lines for data communication? The basic problem with this idea is that traditional telephone lines use analog signals, while computers use digital signals (Figure 22-6). Creating a dial-up network required equipment that could turn digital data into an analog signal to send it over the telephone line, and then turn it back into digital data when it reached the other end of the connection. A device called a modem solved this dilemma.

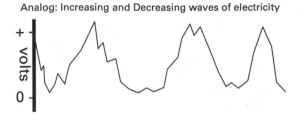

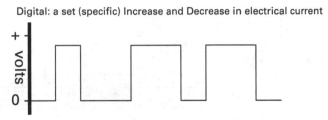

Figure 22-6   Analog signals used by a telephone line versus digital signals used by the computer

Modems enable computers to talk to each other via standard commercial telephone lines by converting analog signals to digital signals, and vice versa. The term *modem* is short for MOdulator/DEModulator, a description of transforming the signals. Telephone wires transfer data via analog signals that continuously change voltages on a wire. Computers hate analog signals. Instead, they need digital signals, voltages that are either on or off, meaning the wire has voltage present or it does not. Computers, being binary by nature, use only two states of voltage: zero volts and positive volts. Modems take analog signals from telephone lines and turn them into digital signals that the PC can understand (Figure 22-7). Modems also take digital signals from the PC and convert them into analog signals for the outgoing telephone line.

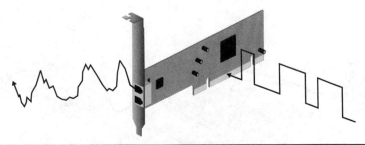

Figure 22-7   Modem converting analog signal to digital signal

A modem does what's called *serial communication:* It transmits data as a series of individual ones and zeroes. The CPU can't process data this way. It needs parallel communication, transmitting and receiving data in discrete 8-bit chunks (Figure 22-8). The individual serial bits of data are converted into 8-bit parallel data that the PC can understand through the *universal asynchronous receiver/transmitter (UART)* chip (Figure 22-9).

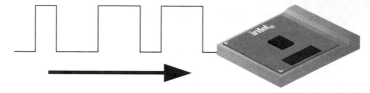

Figure 22-8   CPUs can't read serial data.

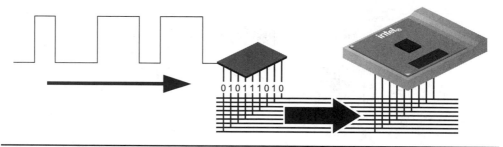

Figure 22-9   The UART chip converts serial data to parallel data.

There are many types of UARTs, each with different functions. All serial communication devices are really little more than UARTs. *External* modems can convert analog signals to digital ones and vice versa, but they must rely on the serial ports to which they're connected for the job of converting between serial and parallel data (Figure 22-10). Internal modems can handle both jobs because they have their own UART built in (Figure 22-11). Table 22-1 shows the UART chips that have been used in PCs.

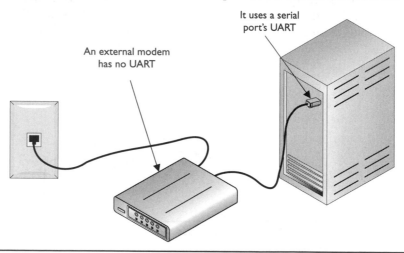

Figure 22-10   An external modem uses a PC's serial port.

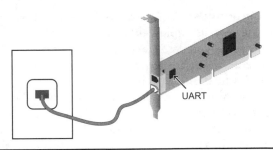

Figure 22-11   An internal modem has UART built in.

Chip	Description
8250	This is the original chip selected by IBM for use in the PC. It had several bugs, but IBM worked around them with built-in routines written in the PC and XT ROM BIOS.
8250A	This chip was developed to fix the bugs in the 8250, but the fix meant it did not work properly with the PC and XT BIOS, although it does work with the AT BIOS. This chip does not work adequately at speeds at or above 9600 bits per second (bps).
8250B	This chip was developed to fix the bugs in the previous chips, but still came with the interrupt enable bug contained in the 8250 chip. This made it compatible with the PC/XT BIOS, and possibly also with the AT BIOS. It retains the problems with rates above 9600 bps.
16450	This chip was initially picked by IBM for its AT systems. It should be seen as the bare minimum for its OS/2 systems; otherwise, the serial ports will not function properly. This chip has a higher throughput than the previous chips and has an added scratch register to aid in speed. The only drawback is that it cannot be used with the PC/XT BIOS due to the interrupt bug being fixed.
16550	This chip was an improvement over the 16450, but it cannot be used for First In First Out (FIFO) buffering modes. It did enable programmers to use multiple DMA channels, however. This chip is not recommended for standard high-speed communication use and should be replaced by the 16550A, even though it has a higher throughput.
16550A	This chip has 16 built-in FIFO registers for receiving and transmitting. It will increase your throughput without loss of characters at higher rates of speed, due to the added registers. This is the only UART installed on today's systems.

Table 22-1   UARTs

Phone lines have a speed based on a unit called a *baud*, which is one cycle per second. The fastest rate that a phone line can achieve is 2,400 baud. Modems can pack multiple bits of data into each baud; a 33.6 kilobits per second (Kbps) modem, for example, packs 14 bits into every baud: 2,400 × 14 = 33.6 Kbps. Thus, it is technically incorrect to say, "I have a 56 K baud modem." The correct statement is, "I have a 56 Kbps modem." But don't bother; people have used the term "baud" instead of bps so often for so long that the terms have become functionally synonymous.

Modern Modem Standards: V.90 vs. V.92   The fastest data transfer speed a modem can handle is based on its implementation of one of the international standards for modem technology: the V standards. Set by the International Telecommunication Union (ITU-T), the current top standards are V.90 and V.92. Both standards offer download speeds of just a hair under 56 Kbps, but they differ in upload speeds: up to 33.6 Kbps for V.90, and up to 48 Kbps for V.92 modems. To get anywhere near the top speeds of a V.90 or V.92 modem requires a comparable modem installed on the other line and connecting telephone lines in excellent condition. In practice, you'll rarely get faster throughput than about 48 Kbps for downloads and 28 Kbps for uploads.

Flow Control (Handshaking)   Flow control, also known as *handshaking*, is the process by which two serial devices verify a conversation. Imagine people talking on a CB radio. When one finishes speaking, he will say "over." That way, the person listening can be sure that the sender is finished speaking before she starts. Each side of the conversation is verified. During a file transfer, two distinct conversations take place that require flow control: local (between modem and COM port) and end-to-end (between modems).

The modems themselves handle end-to-end flow control. PCs can do local flow control between the modem and COM port in two ways: hardware and software. Hardware flow control employs extra wires in the serial connection between the modem and the COM port to let one device tell the other that it is ready to send or receive data. These extra wires are called *ready to send (RTS)* and *clear to send (CTS)*, so hardware handshaking is often called RTS/CTS. Software flow control uses a special character called XON to signal that data flow is beginning, and another special character called XOFF to signal that data transmission is finished; therefore, software handshaking is often called XON/XOFF. Software handshaking is slower and not as dependable as hardware handshaking, so you rarely see it.

NOTE   You can test a modem by plugging in a physical device, called a loopback plug, and then running diagnostics.

Bells and Whistles   Although the core modem technology has changed little in the past few years, modem manufacturers have continued to innovate on many peripheral fronts—pardon the pun and the bad grammar. You can walk into a computer store nowadays, for example, and buy a V.92 modem that comes bundled with an excellent fax machine and a digital answering machine. You can even buy modems that you can call remotely that will wake up your PC (Figure 22-12). What will they think up next?

Modem Connections: PCI, PCI Express, and USB   Modems connect to the PC in two basic ways: internally or externally. Almost all internal modems connect to a PCI or PCI Express expansion bus slot inside the PC, although cost-conscious manufacturers may use smaller modems that fit in special expansion slots designed to support multiple communications features such as modems, NICs, and sound cards (Figure 22-13). On AMD's motherboards this is called an ACR (Advanced Communication Riser) slot, while Intel motherboards use the extremely similar CNR (Communication and Networking Riser) slot. Finally, and least expensive of all, many current motherboards dispense with expansion cards entirely and come with the modem integrated into the motherboard.

Figure 22-12   Some of the many features touted by the manufacturer of the SupraMax modem

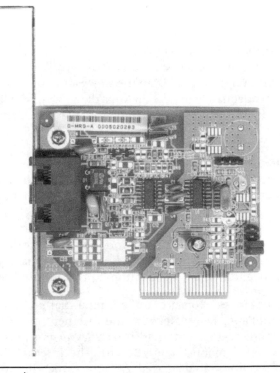

Figure 22-13   A CNR modem

External modems connect to the PC through an available serial port (the old way) or USB port (Figure 22-14). Many PCs come with two 9-pin serial ports, whereas most external modems designed to connect to a serial port come with a 25-pin connector. That means you will probably need a 9-to-25-pin converter, available at any computer store. Virtually all computers today have two or more USB ports in addition to serial ports.

Figure 22-14
A USB modem

If you have the option, choose a USB modem, especially one with a volume control knob. The very low speeds of data communication over a modem make the physical type of the connection unimportant. Even the slowest interface—the aging serial interface—can more than adequately handle 56 Kbps data transfers. USB offers simple Plug and Play and easy portability between machines, plus such modems require no external electrical source, getting all the power they need from the USB connection.

Dial-up Networking

The software side of dial-up networks requires configuration within Windows to include information provided by your ISP. The ISP provides a dial-up telephone number or numbers, as well as your user name and initial password. In addition, the ISP will tell you about any special configuration options you need to specify in the software setup. The full configuration of dial-up networking is beyond the scope of this book, but you should at least know where to go to follow instructions from your ISP. Let's take a look at the Network and Internet Connections applet in Windows XP.

Network Connections To start configuring a dial-up connection in Windows XP, open the Control Panel. Select Network and Internet Connections from the Pick a Category menu (Figure 22-15), and then choose *Set up or change your Internet connection* from the Pick a task menu (Figure 22-16). The Internet Properties dialog box opens with the Connections tab displayed. All your work will proceed from here (Figure 22-17).

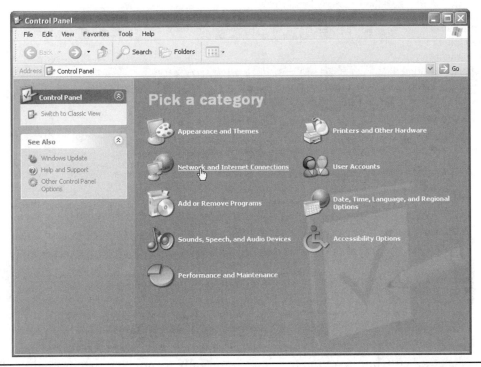

Figure 22-15 Opening the Network and Internet Connections applet

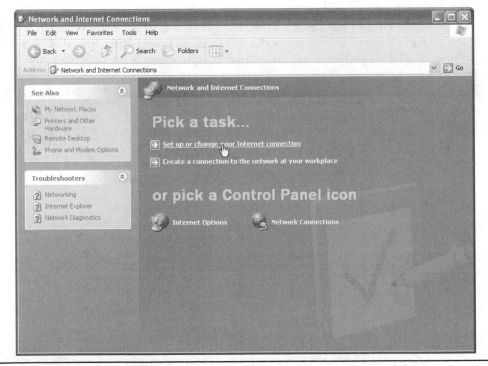

Figure 22-16 Picking a task ... set up or change?

Figure 22-17
The Connections
tab in the Internet
Properties dialog box

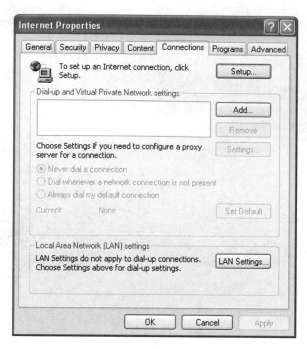

Click the Setup button to run the New Connection Wizard, and then work through the screens (Figure 22-18). At this point, you're going to need information provided by your ISP to configure your connection properly. When you finish the configuration, you'll see a new Connect To option on the Start menu if your system is set up that way. If not, open up Network Connections and your new dial-up connection will be available. Figure 22-19 shows the option to connect to a fictitious ISP, Cool-Rides.com.

Figure 22-18
The New
Connection Wizard

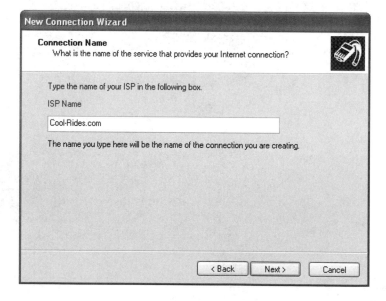

Figure 22-19
Connection
options in Network
Connections

PPP   Dial-up links to the Internet have their own special hardware protocol called *Point-to-Point Protocol (PPP)*. PPP is a streaming protocol developed especially for dial-up Internet access. To Windows, a modem is nothing more than a special type of network adapter. Modems will have their own configuration entry in the Network Connections applet.

Most dial-up "I can't connect to the Internet"–type problems are user errors. Your first area of investigation is the modem itself. Use the modem's properties to make sure the volume is turned up. Have the user listen to the connection. Does she hear a dial tone? If she doesn't, make sure the modem's line is plugged into a good phone jack. Does she hear the modem dial and then hear someone saying, "Hello? Hello?" If so, she probably dialed the wrong number! Wrong password error messages are fairly straightforward—remember that the password may be correct, but the user name may be wrong. If she still fails to connect, it's time to call the network folks to see what is not properly configured in the Dial-up Networking settings.

ISDN
A standard telephone connection comprises many pieces. First, the phone line runs from your phone out to a network interface box (the little box on the side of your house), and into a central switch belonging to the telephone company. (In some cases, intermediary steps are present.) Standard metropolitan areas have a large number of central offices, each with a central switch. Houston, Texas, for example, has nearly 100 offices in the general metro area. These central switches connect to each other through high-capacity *trunk lines*. Before 1970, the entire phone system was analog; over time,

however, phone companies began to upgrade their trunk lines to digital systems. Today, the entire telephone system, with the exception of the line from your phone to the central office, is digital.

During this upgrade period, customers continued to demand higher throughput from their phone lines. The old telephone line was not expected to produce more than 28.8 Kbps. (56 K modems, which were a *big* surprise to the phone companies, didn't appear until 1995.) Needless to say, the phone companies were very motivated to come up with a way to generate higher capacities. Their answer was actually fairly straightforward: make the entire phone system digital. By adding special equipment at the central office and the user's location, phone companies can now achieve a throughput of up to 64 K per line (see the paragraphs following) over the same copper wires already used by telephone lines. This process of sending telephone transmission across fully digital lines end-to-end is called *integrated services digital network (ISDN)* service.

ISDN service consists of two types of channels: Bearer, or B, channels and Delta, or D, channels. B channels carry data and voice information at 64 Kbps. D channels carry setup and configuration information and carry data at 16 Kbps. Most providers of ISDN allow the user to choose either one or two B channels. The more common setup is two B/one D, usually called a *basic rate interface (BRI)* setup. A BRI setup uses only one physical line, but each B channel sends 64 K, doubling the throughput total to 128 K. ISDN also connects much faster than modems, eliminating that long, annoying, mating call you get with phone modems. The monthly cost per B channel is slightly more than a regular phone line, and usually a fairly steep initial fee is levied for the installation and equipment. The big limitation is that you usually need to be within about 18,000 feet of a central office to use ISDN.

The physical connections for ISDN bear some similarity to analog modems. An ISDN wall socket usually looks something like a standard RJ-45 network jack. The most common interface for your computer is a device called a *terminal adapter (TA)*. TAs look much like regular modems, and like modems, they come in external and internal variants. You can even get TAs that are also hubs, enabling your system to support a direct LAN connection.

NOTE Another type of ISDN, called a *primary rate interface (PRI)*, is composed of twenty-three 64-Kbps B channels and one 64-Kbps D channel, giving it a total throughput of 1.5 megabits per second. PRI ISDN lines are rarely used as dial-up connections—they are far more common on dedicated lines.

Digital Subscriber Line (DSL)

Digital subscriber line (DSL) connections to ISPs use a standard telephone line but special equipment on each end to create always-on Internet connections at blindingly fast speeds, especially when compared with analog dial-up connections. Service levels vary around the U.S., but the typical upload speed is ~384 Kbps, while download speed comes in at a very sweet ~2+ Mbps!

NOTE The two most common forms of DSL you'll find are *asynchronous (ADSL)* and *synchronous (SDSL)*. ADSL lines differ between slow upload speed (such as 128, 256, or 384 Kbps) and faster download speed (usually 2 Mbps). SDSL has the same upload and download speeds, but telecom companies charge a lot more for the privilege. DSL encompasses many such variations, so you'll often see it referred to as *xDSL*.

DSL requires little setup from a user standpoint. A tech comes to the house to install a NIC in the Internet-bound PC and drop off a *DSL receiver* (often called a DSL modem) (Figure 22-20). The receiver connects to the telephone line and the PC (Figure 22-21). The tech (or the user, if knowledgeable) then configures the TCP/IP protocol options for the NIC to match the settings demanded by the DSL provider, and that's about it! Within moments, you're surfing at blazing speeds. You don't need a second telephone line. You don't need to wear a special propeller hat or anything. The only kicker is that your house has to be within a fairly short distance from a main phone service switching center, something like 18,000 feet. This pretty much stops everybody but inner-city dwellers from having access to DSL service.

Figure 22-20
A DSL receiver

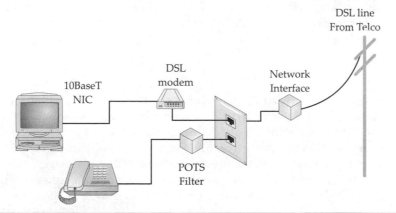

Figure 22-21 DSL connections

Cable

Cable offers a different approach to high-speed Internet access, using regular cable TV cables to serve up lightning-fast speeds. It offers comparable service to DSL with a 384 Kbps upload and 2+ Mbps download. Cable Internet connections are theoretically available anywhere you can get cable TV.

Cable Internet connections start with an RG-6 or RG-59 cable coming into your house. The cable connects to a *cable modem* that then connects to a NIC in your PC via UTP Ethernet cable. Figure 22-22 shows a typical cable setup. One nice advantage of cable over DSL is that if you have a TV tuner card in your PC, you can use the same cable connection (with a splitter) to watch TV on your PC. Both DSL and cable modem Internet connections can be used by two or more computers if they are part of a LAN, including those in a home.

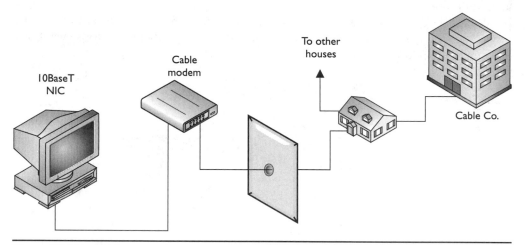

Figure 22-22 Cable connections

NOTE The term *modem* has been warped and changed beyond recognition in modern networking. Both DSL and cable fully-digital Internet connections use the term *modem* to describe the box that takes the incoming signals from the Internet and translates it into something the PC can understand.

LAN

Most businesses connect their internal local area network (LAN) to an ISP via some hardware solution that Network+ techs deal with. Figure 22-23 shows a typical small-business wiring closet with routers that connect the LAN to the ISP. You learned all about wiring up a LAN in Chapter 21, so there's no need to go through any basics here. To complete a LAN connection to the Internet, you need to add a second NIC or a modem to one of the PCs and then configure that PC as the default connection. We'll revisit this idea in a moment with Internet Connection Sharing.

Figure 22-23
A wiring closet

Wireless

Every once in a while a technology comes along that, once the kinks are smoothed out, works flawlessly, creating a magical computing experience. Unfortunately, the various wireless networking technologies out there today don't fulfill that dream yet. When they work, it's like magic. You walk into a coffee shop, sit down, and flip open your laptop computer. After firing up your Internet browser, suddenly you're quaffing lattes and surfing Web sites—with no wires at all.

You spent a good deal of Chapter 21 working through wireless connectivity to a LAN, so I won't rehash any of that here. Suffice it to say that connecting to the Internet via wireless means that you must connect to a LAN that's wired to an ISP or connect to a cellular network. The local Internet café purchases high-speed Internet service from the cable or telecom company, for example, and then connects a wireless access point (WAP) to its network. When you walk in with your portable PC with wireless NIC and open a Web browser, the wireless NIC communicates with the *fully wired* DHCP server via the WAP and you're surfing on the Internet. It appears magically wireless, but the LAN to ISP connection still uses wires.

Cellular networking is even more seamless. Anywhere you can connect with your cell phone, you can connect with your cellular network–aware portable or laptop computer.

NOTE One form of wireless communication does not require local wires. *Wireless Broadband* relies on the ISP putting up a tower, and then any building within the line of sight (perhaps up to 10 miles) can get a high-speed connection.

Satellite

Satellite connections to the Internet get the data beamed to a satellite dish on your house or office; a receiver handles the flow of data, eventually sending it through an Ethernet cable to the NIC in your PC. I can already sense people's eyebrows raising. "Yeah, that's the download connection. But what about the upload connection?" Very astute, me hearties! The early days of satellite required you to connect via a modem. You would upload at the slow 26- to 48-Kbps modem speed, but then get super fast downloads from the dish. It worked, so why complain? Newer technology still requires the initial setup be done via modem, but the download and the upload go through the dish. You really can move to that shack on the side of the Himalayas to write the great Tibetan novel, and still have DSL- or cable-speed Internet connectivity. Sweet!

Satellite might be the most intriguing of all the technologies used to connect to the Internet today. As with satellite television, though, you need to have the satellite dish point at the satellites (toward the south if you live in the U.S.). The only significant issue to satellite is that the distance the signal must travel creates a small delay called the *satellite latency*. This latency is usually unnoticeable unless the signal degrades in foul weather such as rain and snow.

Internet Connection Sharing

Windows 98 SE came out with a number of improvements over Windows 98, and one of the most popular was the inclusion of *Internet Connection Sharing (ICS)*. ICS enables one system to share its Internet connection with other systems on the network, providing a quick and easy method for multiple systems to use one Internet connection. Windows 2000 and Windows XP also provide this handy tool. Figure 22-24 shows a typical setup for ICS. Note the terminology used here. The PC that connects to the Internet and then shares via ICS that connection with machines on a LAN is called the *ICS host* computer. PCs that connect via LAN to the ICS host computer are simply called client computers.

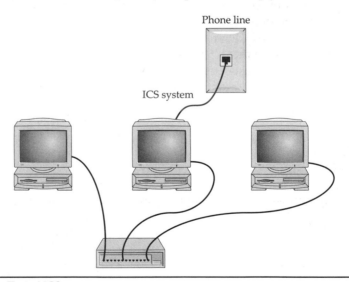

Figure 22-24 Typical ICS setup

To connect multiple computers to a single ICS host computer requires several things in place. First, the ICS host computer has to have a NIC dedicated to the internal connections. If you connect via dial-up, for example, the ICS host computer uses a modem to connect to the Internet. It will also have a NIC that plugs into a hub. Other PCs on the LAN likewise connect to the hub. If you connect via some faster service, such as DSL that uses a NIC cabled to the DSL receiver, you'll need a second NIC in the ICS host machine to connect to the LAN and the client computers.

Setting up ICS in Windows 2000/XP is very simple. Open the properties dialog for My Network Places, and then access the properties of the connection you wish to share. Click the Sharing tab (Windows 2000) or the Advanced tab (Windows XP) and select Enable Internet Connection Sharing for This Connection (Windows 2000) or Allow Other Network Users to Connect Through this Computer's Internet Connection (Windows XP, Figure 22-25). Clients don't need any special configuration but should simply be set to DHCP for their IP address and other configurations.

Figure 22-25
Enabling Internet
Connection Sharing
in Windows XP

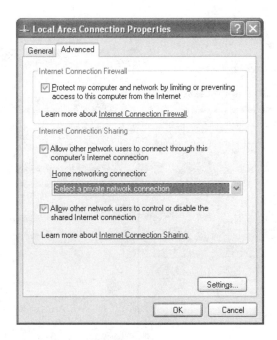

Several manufacturers offer robust, easy-to-configure hardware solutions that enable multiple computers to connect to a single Internet connection. These boxes require very little configuration and provide a level of firewall protection between the primary computer and the Internet. You'll find these boxes more commonly used with DSL and cable connections rather than any sort of dial-up.

Linksys makes a great little DSL/cable router, for example, that offers four 10/100 Ethernet ports for the LAN computers; plus, you can configure it so that to the outside world the router is the PC. It therefore acts as a firewall, protecting your internal network from probing or malicious users from the outside.

The Windows XP Internet Connection Firewall

Once you've established a connection to the Internet, you should start thinking about security. Windows 2000 requires you to use some third-party tool, such as a hardware firewall, but Windows XP offers the *Internet Connection Firewall (ICF)* built into the system. ICF basically stops all uninvited access from the Internet. ICF keeps track of when you initiate communication with a particular machine over your Internet connection and then allows communication back from that same machine. This works whether your connection is a single machine directly dialed into an ISP or a group of networked PCs connecting through an ICS host computer. ICF tracks the communication and blocks anything uninvited. You can implement ICF on the same screen as you would ICS (Figure 22-26).

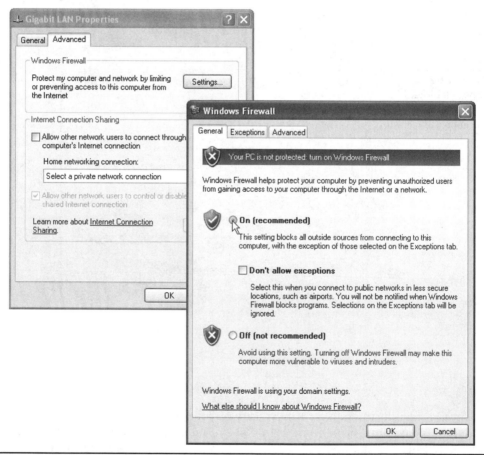

Figure 22-26   Implementing Internet Connection Firewall

NOTE ICF enables you to open up specific computers inside a LAN for specific tasks, such as running an FTP server.

When you're running a LAN, implement ICF only on the machine that directly connects to the Internet. If you enable ICF on other machines on the LAN, you can possibly create problems.

Internet Software Tools

Once you've established a connection between the PC and the ISP, you can do nothing on the Internet without applications designed to use one or more TCP/IP services, such as Web browsing and e-mail. TCP/IP has the following commonly used services:

- World Wide Web
- E-mail
- Newsgroups
- FTP
- Telnet
- VoIP

Each of these services (sometimes referred to by the overused term *TCP/IP protocols*) requires a special application, and each of those applications has special settings. You'll look at all five services and learn how to configure them.

The World Wide Web

The Web provides a graphical face for the Internet. Servers running specialized software called *Web servers* provide Web sites and Web pages that you can access and thus get more or less useful information. Using Web-browser software, such as Internet Explorer or Mozilla Firefox, you can click a link on a Web page and be instantly transported, not just to some Web server in your home town, but anywhere in the world. Figure 22-27 shows Internet Explorer at the home page of my company's Web site, www.totalsem.com. Where is the server located? Does it matter? It could be in a closet in my office or on a huge clustered server in Canada. The great part about the Web is that you can get from here to there and access the information you need with a click or two of the mouse.

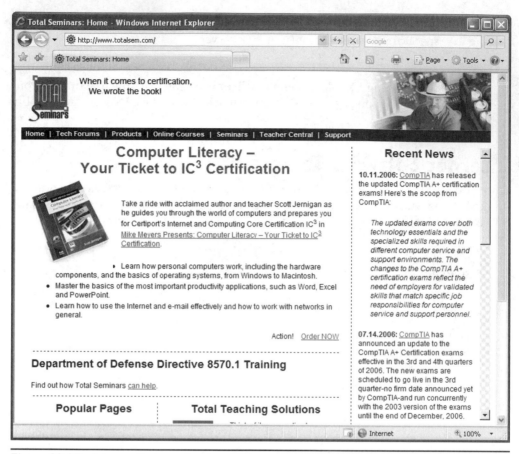

Figure 22-27 Internet Explorer showing a Web page

Although the Web is the most popular part of the Internet, setting up a Web browser takes almost no effort. As long as the Internet connection is working, Web browsers work automatically. This is not to say you can't make plenty of custom settings, but the default browser settings work almost every time. If you type in a Web address, such as the best search engine on the planet—www.google.com—and it doesn't work, check the line and your network settings and you'll figure out where the problem is.

The command-line tool *ping* may be your best friend for diagnosing TCP/IP errors. Ping always works; you don't need to log on to a server or even log on to a system. Simply type in a DNS name or an IP address. To run ping, get to a command prompt (Start | Run | type **CMD** | click OK) and type **ping** followed by a DNS name or IP address, like this:

```
c:\>ping www.whitehouse.gov
```

Then press the ENTER key. If the Web server is up, you'll get a reply to that effect.

You can even ping yourself: just type **ping 127.0.0.1** (127.0.0.1 is known as the loopback address). If you ping an address and get the famous "Request timed out" message, the device you are trying to ping is not available. Be aware, however, that "Request timed out" messages are fairly common when you use ping on the Internet because many servers turn off the ping reply as a security measure.

Configuring the Browser

Web browsers are highly configurable. On most Web browsers, you can set the default font size, whether it will display graphics, and several other settings. Although all Web browsers support these settings, where you go to make these changes varies dramatically. If you are using the popular Internet Explorer that comes with Windows, configuration tools are found in the Internet Options Control Panel applet or under the Tools menu.

Proxy Server   Many corporations use a *proxy server* to filter employee Internet access, and when you're on their corporate network you will have to set your proxy settings within the Web browser (and any other Internet software you want to use). A *proxy server* is software that enables multiple connections to the Internet to go through one protected PC, much like how ICS works on a home network. Unlike ICS, which operates transparently to the client PCs by manipulating IP packets (we say that it operates at Layer 3—the Network layer in the OSI model—see Chapter 21), proxy servers communicate directly with the browser application (operating at Layer 7, the Application layer). Applications that want to access Internet resources send requests to the proxy server instead of trying to access the Internet directly, both protecting the client PCs and enabling the network administrator to monitor and restrict Internet access. Each application must therefore be configured to use the proxy server. To configure proxy settings in Internet Explorer, choose Tools| Internet Options. Select the Connections tab. Then click the LAN Settings button to open the Local Area Network (LAN) Settings dialog box (Figure 22-28).

Figure 22-28
The LAN Settings
dialog box

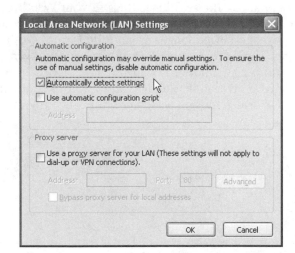

Note that you have three options here, with automatic detection of the proxy server being the default. You can specify an IP address for a proxy server by clicking the third radio button and simply typing it in (Figure 22-29). Your network administrator or a CompTIA Network+ tech will give you information on proxy servers if you need it to configure a machine. Otherwise, you can safely leave the browser configured to search automatically for a proxy server. If proxy servers are not used on your network, the autoconfiguration will fail and your browser will try to connect to the Internet directly, so there is no harm in just leaving Automatically Detect Settings checked.

Figure 22-29
Specifying the proxy
server address

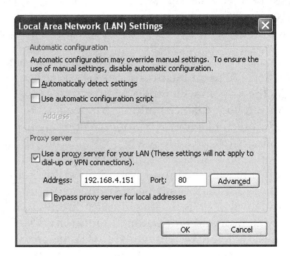

Security and Scripts   While we're on the subject of configuration, make sure you know how to adjust the security settings in your Web browser. Many Web sites come with programs that download to your system and run automatically. These programs are written in specialized languages and file formats with names like Java and Active Server Pages. These programs make modern Web sites very powerful and dynamic, but they can also act as a portal to evil programs. To help with security, all better Web browsers let you determine whether you want these potentially risky programs to run. What you decide depends on personal factors. If your Web browser refuses to run a Java program (you'll know because you'll get a warning message, like in Figure 22-30), check your security settings, because your browser may simply be following orders! To get to the security configuration screen in Internet Explorer, choose Tools | Internet Options and open the Security tab (Figure 22-31).

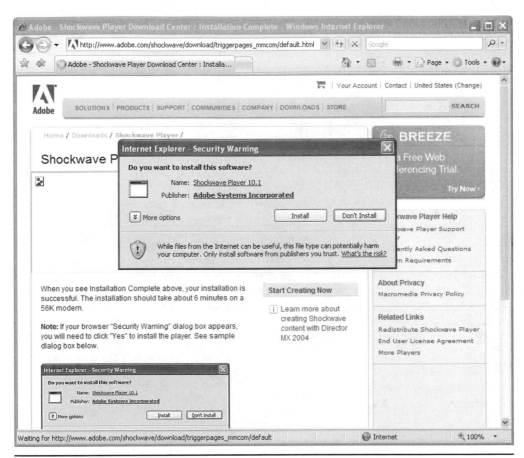

Figure 22-30 Warning message about running ActiveX

Figure 22-31
The Security tab in
the Internet Options
dialog box

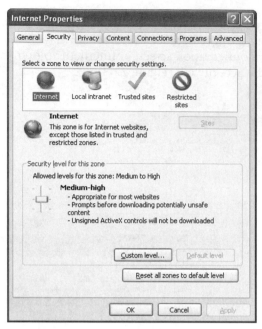

Internet Explorer gives you the option of selecting preset security levels by clicking
the Custom level button on the Security tab and then using the pull-down menu (Figure
22-32). Changing from Medium to High security, for example, makes changes across the
board, disabling everything from ActiveX to Java. You can also manually select which
features to enable or disable in the scrolling menu, also visible in Figure 22-32.

Figure 22-32
Changing security
settings

Security doesn't stop with programs. Another big security concern relates to Internet commerce. People don't like to enter credit card information, home phone numbers, or other personal information for fear this information might be intercepted by hackers. Fortunately, there are methods of encrypting this information, the most common being *HTTP over Secure Sockets Layer (HTTPS)* Web sites. It's easy to tell if a Web site is using HTTPS because the Web address starts with *HTTPS*—instead of just *HTTP*, as shown in Figure 22-33. The Web browser also displays a lock symbol in the lower right-hand corner to remind you that you're using an encrypted connection.

Figure 22-33   A secure Web page (check out the little lock in the lower-right corner)

There's one security risk that no computer can completely defend against: you. In particular, be very careful when downloading programs from the Internet. The Internet makes it easy to download programs that you can then install and run on your system. There's nothing intrinsically wrong with this unless the program you download has a virus, is corrupted, contains a Trojan horse, or is incompatible with your operating system. The watchword here is *common sense.* Only download programs from reliable sources. Take time to read the online documentation so you're sure you're downloading a version of the program that works on your operating system. Finally, always run a good antivirus program, preferably one that checks incoming programs for viruses before you install them! Failure to do this can lead to lockups, file corruption, and boot problems that you simply should not have to deal with.

NOTE See Chapter 23 for the scoop on Trojans and other viruses.

E-mail

You need an e-mail program to access e-mail. The two most popular are Microsoft's Outlook Express and Mozilla's Thunderbird. E-mail clients need a little more setup. First, you must provide your e-mail address and password. All e-mail addresses come in the now-famous accountname@Internet domain format. Figure 22-34 shows e-mail information entered into the Outlook Express Internet Connection Wizard.

Figure 22-34
Adding an e-mail account to Outlook Express

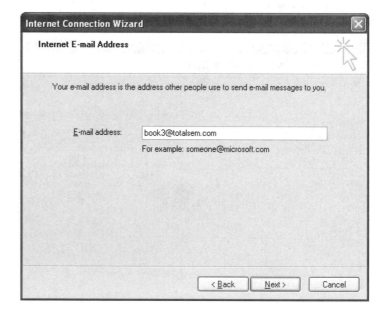

The second thing you must add are the names of the *Post Office Protocol version 3 (POP3)* or *Internet Message Access Protocol (IMAP)* server and the *Simple Mail Transfer Protocol (SMTP)* server. The POP3 or IMAP server is the computer that handles incoming (to you) e-mail. POP3 is by far the most widely used standard, although the latest version of IMAP, *IMAP4*, supports some features POP3 doesn't. For example, IMAP4 enables you to search through messages on the mail server to find specific keywords and select the messages you want to download onto your machine. Even with the advantages of IMAP4 over POP3, the vast majority of incoming mail servers use POP3.

The SMTP server handles your outgoing e-mail. These two systems may often have the same name, or close to the same name, as shown in Figure 22-35. All these settings should be provided to you by your ISP. If they are not, you should be comfortable knowing what to ask for. If one of these names is incorrect, you will either not get your e-mail or not be able to send e-mail. If an e-mail setup that has been working well for a while suddenly gives you errors, it is likely that either the POP3 or SMTP server is down, or that the DNS server has quit working.

Figure 22-35
Adding POP3 and
SMTP information
in Outlook Express

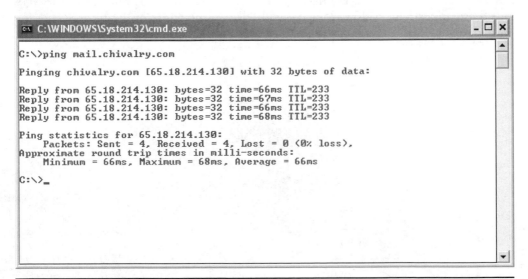

When I'm given the name of a POP3 or SMTP server, I use ping to determine the IP address for the device, as shown in Figure 22-36. I make a point to write this down. If I ever have a problem getting mail, I'll go into my SMTP or POP3 settings and type in the IP address (Figure 22-37). If my mail starts to work, I know the DNS server is not working.

```
C:\WINDOWS\System32\cmd.exe

C:\>ping mail.chivalry.com

Pinging chivalry.com [65.18.214.130] with 32 bytes of data:

Reply from 65.18.214.130: bytes=32 time=66ms TTL=233
Reply from 65.18.214.130: bytes=32 time=67ms TTL=233
Reply from 65.18.214.130: bytes=32 time=66ms TTL=233
Reply from 65.18.214.130: bytes=32 time=68ms TTL=233

Ping statistics for 65.18.214.130:
    Packets: Sent = 4, Received = 4, Lost = 0 (0% loss),
Approximate round trip times in milli-seconds:
    Minimum = 66ms, Maximum = 68ms, Average = 66ms

C:\>_
```

Figure 22-36   Using ping to determine the IP address

Figure 22-37
Entering IP addresses
into POP3 and SMTP
settings

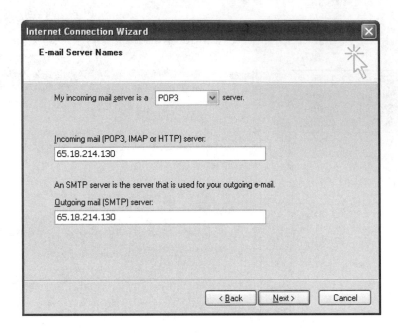

Newsgroups

Newsgroups are one of the oldest services available on the Internet. To access a newsgroup, you must use a newsreader program. A number of third-party newsreaders exist, such as the popular Forté Free Agent, but Microsoft Outlook Express is the most common of all newsreaders (not surprising since it comes free with most versions of Windows). To access a newsgroup, you must know the name of a news server. *News servers* run the *Network News Transfer Protocol (NNTP)*. You can also use public news servers, but these are extremely slow. Your ISP will tell you the name of the news server and provide you with a user name and password if necessary (Figure 22-38).

Figure 22-38
Configuring Outlook
Express for a news
server

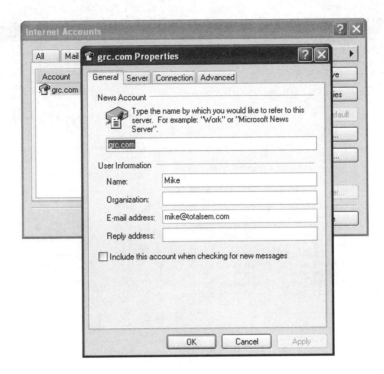

File Transfer Protocol (FTP)

File Transfer Protocol (FTP) is also a great way to share files between systems. FTP server software exists for most operating systems, so FTP provides a great way to transfer data between any two systems regardless of the operating system. To access an FTP site, you must use an FTP client such as WS_FTP, although later versions of Internet Explorer and other Web browsers provide support for FTP. Just type in the name of the FTP site. Figure 22-39 shows Internet Explorer accessing ftp.microsoft.com.

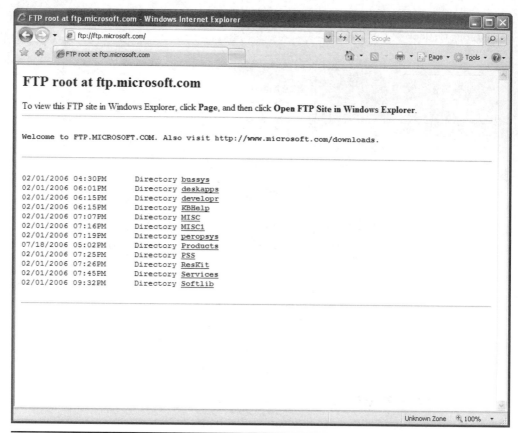

Figure 22-39 Accessing an FTP site in Internet Explorer

Even though you can use a Web browser, all FTP sites require you to log on. Your Web browser will assume that you want to log in as "anonymous." If you want to log on as a specific user, you have to add your user name to the URL. (Instead of typing in **ftp://ftp.example.com**, you would type in **ftp://scottj@ftp.example.com**.) An anonymous logon works fine for most public FTP sites. Many techs prefer to use third-party programs such as WS_FTP (Figure 22-40) for FTP access because these third-party applications can store user name and password settings. This enables you to access the FTP site more easily later. Keep in mind that FTP was developed during a more trusting time, and that whatever user name and password you send over the network is sent in clear text. Don't use the same password for an FTP site that you use for your domain logon at the office!

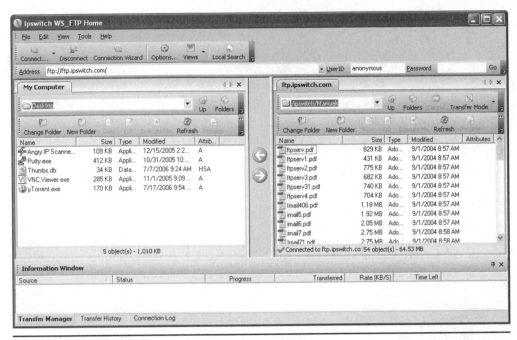

Figure 22-40   WS_FTP

Telnet

Telnet is a terminal emulation program for TCP/IP networks that enables you to connect to a server and run commands on that server as if you were sitting in front of it. This way, you can remotely administer a server and communicate with other servers on your network. As you can imagine, this is rather risky. If *you* can remotely control a computer, what's to stop others from doing the same? Of course, Telnet does not allow just *anyone* to log on and wreak havoc with your network. You must enter a special user name and password to run Telnet. Unfortunately, Telnet shares FTP's bad habit of sending passwords and user names as clear text, so you should generally use it only within your own LAN. If you need a remote terminal that works securely across the Internet, investigate more sophisticated tools such as SSH (Secure Shell).

EXAM TIP   The CompTIA A+ Certification exams test your knowledge of a few networking tools, such as Telnet, but only enough to let you support a Network+ tech or network administrator. If you need to run Telnet (or its more secure cousin, SSH), you will get the details from a network administrator. Implementation of Telnet falls well beyond CompTIA A+.

Voice over IP

Voice over IP (VoIP) enables you to make voice calls over your computer network. Why have two sets of wires, one for voice and one for data, going to every desk? Why not just use the extra capacity on the data network for your phone calls? That's exactly what VoIP does for you.

VoIP doesn't refer to a single protocol, but rather to a collection of protocols that make phone calls over the data network possible. Venders such as Skype and Vonage offer popular VoIP solutions, and many corporations use VoIP for their internal phone networks.

Terminal Emulation

In Microsoft networking, we primarily share folders and printers. At times, it would be convenient to be transported in front of another computer—to feel as if your hands were actually on its keyboard. This is called *terminal emulation*. Terminal emulation is old stuff—Telnet is one of the oldest TCP/IP applications, but the introduction of graphical user interfaces cost it much of its popularity. Today when techs talk about terminal emulation, they are usually referring to graphical terminal emulation programs.

Like so many other types of Windows applications, graphical terminal emulation originally came from third-party companies and was eventually absorbed into the Windows operating system. While many third-party emulators are available, one of the most popular is the University of Cambridge's VNC. VNC is free and totally cross-platform, enabling you to run and control a Windows system remotely from your Macintosh system, for example. Figure 22-41 shows VNC in action.

Figure 22-41   VNC

NOTE All terminal emulation programs require separate server and client programs.

Windows 2000 Server (not Professional) was the first version of Windows to include a built-in terminal emulator called Windows Terminal Services. Terminal Services has a number of limitations: the server software runs only on Windows Server and the client software runs only on Windows—although the client works on *every* version of Windows and is free. Figure 22-42 shows Windows Terminal Services running on a Windows 2000 computer.

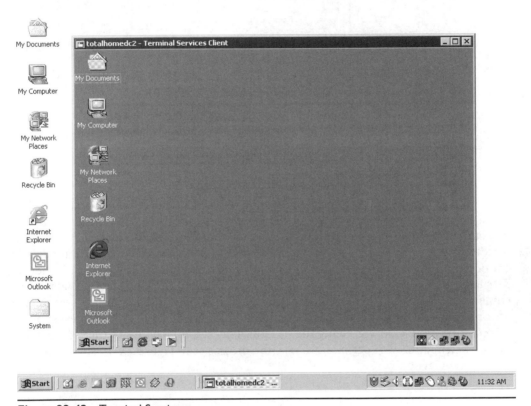

Figure 22-42 Terminal Services

Windows XP offers an alternative to VNC: Remote Desktop. *Remote Desktop* provides control over a remote server with the fully graphical interface. Your desktop *becomes* the server desktop (Figure 22-43). It's quite incredible—although it's only for Windows XP.

Figure 22-43
Windows XP
Remote Desktop
Connection
dialog box

Wouldn't it be cool if, when called about a technical support issue, you could simply see what the client sees? (I'm not talking voyeur cam here.) When the client says that something doesn't work, it would be great if you could transfer yourself from your desk to your client's desk to see precisely what he or she sees. This would dramatically cut down on the miscommunication that can make a tech's life so tedious. Windows XP's Remote Assistance does just that. Based on the Shared Desktop feature that used to come with the popular MSN Messenger program, *Remote Assistance* allows you to give anyone control of your desktop. If a user has a problem, he or she can request support directly from you. Upon receiving the support request e-mail, you can then log into his or her system and, with permission, take the driver's seat. Figure 22-44 shows Remote Assistance in action.

Figure 22-44
Remote Assistance
in action

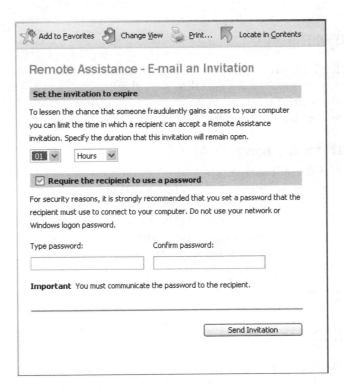

Remote Assistance enables you to do anything you would do from the actual computer. You can troubleshoot some hardware configuration or driver problem. You can install drivers, roll back drivers, download new ones, and so forth. You're in command of the remote machine as long as the client allows you to be. The client sees everything you do, by the way, and can stop you cold if you get out of line or do something that makes him or her nervous! Remote Assistance can help you teach someone how to use a particular application. You can log onto a user's PC and fire up Outlook, for example, and then walk through the steps to configure it while the user watches. The user can then take over the machine and walk through the steps while you watch, chatting with one another the whole time. Sweet!

The new graphical terminal emulators provide everything you need to access one system from another. They are common, especially now that Microsoft provides free terminal emulators. Whatever type of emulator you use, remember that you will always need both a server and a client program. The server goes on the system to access and the client goes on the system you use to access the server. On many solutions, the server and the client software are integrated into a single product.

Beyond A+

While the areas covered by the CompTIA A+ Certification exams do a great job on the more common issues of dealing with the Internet, a few hot topics, although beyond the scope of the CompTIA A+ exams, are so common and important that you need to know them: online gaming, chatting, and file sharing.

Online Gaming

One of the more exciting—and certainly more fun—aspects of the Internet is online gaming. Competing online against a real person or people makes for some amazing games—classics like Hearts and Backgammon. Entire Web sites are devoted to helping you find playing partners and thereby enjoy thousands of different games (Figure 22-45). Another popular genre of online gaming is the "first-person shooters" format. These games place you in a small world with up to 32 other players. A great example is Valve Software's Counter Strike: Source (Figure 22-46).

Figure 22-45
Folks playing games online

• Ghost Recon	33 players
• Ghost Recon Demo	0 players
• Ghost Recon: Desert Siege	0 players
• Giants: Citizen Kabuto	12 players
• Global Operations	96 players
• Global Operations Public Beta	0 players
• Gore	36 players
• Gore Demo	0 players
• Gruntz	0 players
• Gulf War: Operation Desert Hammer	1 players
• Gunman Chronicles	4 players

H

• Half-Life	58219 players
• Halo (Xbox)	102 players
• Harley Davidson: Race Around the World	0 players

Figure 22-46
Counter Strike: Source

No discussion of online gaming is complete without talking about the most amazing game type of all—the massively multiplayer online role-playing game (MMORPG). Imagine being an elfin wizard, joined by a band of friends, all going on adventures together in worlds so large that it would take a real 24-hour day to journey across them! Imagine that in this same world, 2,000 to 3,000 other players, as well as thousands of game-controlled characters, are participating! Plenty of MMORPGs are out there, but the most popular today is World of Warcraft (Figure 22-47).

Figure 22-47
World of Warcraft

Each of these games employs good old TCP/IP to send information using special ports either reserved by the game itself or by DirectX. For instance, the Quake series of games uses port 26000, while DirectX uses ports 47624 and 2300–2400.

Chatting

If there's one thing we human beings love to do, it's chat. The Internet provides you with a multitude of ways to do so, whether it be by typing or actual talking. Keep in mind that chatting occurs in real time. As fast as you can type or talk, the other person or persons hear or see what you have to say. In order to chat, however, you need some form of chat software. The oldest family of chat programs is based on the Internet Relay Chat (IRC) protocol, and the single most common IRC chat program is probably mIRC. IRC protocols allow for a number of other little extras as well, such as the ability to share files.

Today, companies such as AOL, Yahoo!, and Microsoft have made their own chat programs that not only provide text chat but also add features such as voice and video, turning your PC into a virtual replacement for your telephone! Figure 22-48 shows the popular Microsoft Windows Live Messenger software.

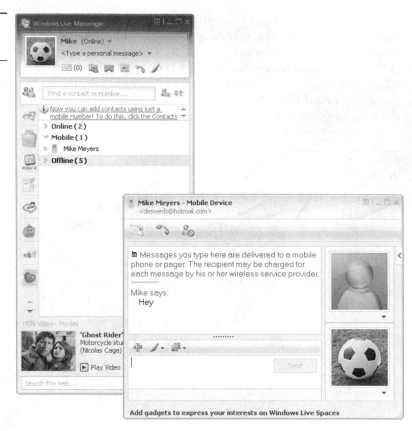

Figure 22-48
Windows Live
Messenger in action

File Sharing

The last extra Internet function to discuss is also probably the most controversial: file sharing. File sharing basically consists of a whole bunch of computers with one program loaded, such as Napster or Kazaa. The file-sharing program enables each of the computers running that program to offer files to share, such as MP3 music files and MPEG movies. Once all the file-sharing computers log onto the Internet, any of them can download any file offered by any other in the group.

File sharing through such *distributed* sharing software becomes almost anonymous and free—and that's the problem. You can share *anything*, even copyright-protected music, movies, and more. The music industry in particular has come out swinging to try to stop file-sharing practices. As a result, the music industry is working on a way to shut down those persons who share lots of files. But software developers have countered, creating Internet protocols such as BitTorrent to handle the distribution and make the file sharers much more difficult to find and punish. Figure 22-49 shows one of the more popular BitTorrent protocol programs called μTorrent (the μ is the symbol for "micro," so you pronounce it "micro torrent"). BitTorrent has many legitimate uses as well—its protocol is extremely efficient for the distribution of large files and has become the method-of-choice for distributing Linux distributions and large open-source applications such as Apache and OpenOffice.

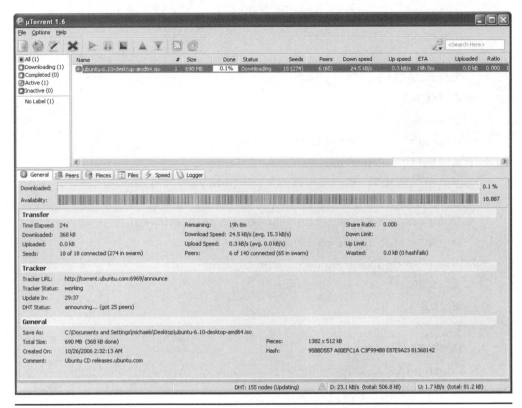

Figure 22-49 μTorrent

These example programs just scratch the surface of the many applications that use the Internet. One of the more amazing aspects of TCP/IP is that its basic design is around 30 years old. We use TCP/IP in ways completely outside the original concept of its designers, yet TCP/IP continues to show its power and flexibility. Pretty amazing!

Chapter Review Questions

1. Of the four Internet connection options listed below, which typically offers the *slowest* connection speed?

   A. Cable

   B. Dial-up

   C. DSL

   D. Satellite

2. Which of the following technologies use dial-up connections? (Select all that apply.)

   A. Cable modem

   B. DSL receiver

   C. ISDN TA

   D. Modem

3. What advantages does dial-up have over DSL?

   A. Dial-up is faster than DSL

   B. You can be farther than 18,000 feet from a main phone service switching center.

   C. You can get a second phone line to use just for dial-up.

   D. None. Dial-up has no advantages over DSL.

4. Which protocol can you use to send e-mail?

   A. IMAP

   B. POP3

   C. PPP

   D. SMTP

5. Which protocols can you use to receive e-mail? (Select all that apply.)

   A. IMAP

   B. POP3

   C. PPP

   D. SMTP

6. What advantage does satellite have over cable for connecting to the Internet?

   A. Satellite is faster than cable.

   B. Cable degrades in stormy weather; satellite does not.

   C. Satellite requires you to be within 18,000 feet of a central switch.

   D. Cable is limited to areas with cable installed; satellite is not.

7. Which Microsoft technology enables you to share a single Internet connection with multiple computers?

   A. Internet Connection Sharing

   B. My Network Places

    C. Remote Access

    D. Remote Desktop

8. What command often enables you to diagnose TCP/IP errors such as connection problems?

    A. FTP

    B. Ping

    C. POP3

    D. VoIP

9. At what layer of the OSI seven-layer model do proxy servers operate?

    A. Layer 1—Physical

    B. Layer 2—Data Link

    C. Layer 6—Presentation

    D. Layer 7—Application

10. Which of the following programs enable you to access and work on a remote computer from your local computer? (Select all that apply.)

    A. FTP

    B. Internet Connection Sharing

    C. Remote Desktop

    D. Telnet

Answers

1. **B.** Dial-up connections are robust and widely-available, but slower than the newer connection types.

2. **C, D.** ISDN terminal adapters and traditional modems use dial-up for connecting to the Internet.

3. **B.** DSL has a fairly short limit of 18,000 feet from a main switch, leaving people in rural areas (in the U.S., at least) out of luck. Dial-up just requires a phone line.

4. **D.** You can use SMTP to send e-mail messages.

5. **A, B.** You can use either IMAP or POP3 to receive e-mail messages.

6. **D.** Clearly, satellite cuts you loose from the wires!

7. **A.** Internet Connection Sharing enables you to share a single Internet connection with multiple computers.

8. **B.** You can often use the ping command to diagnose TCP/IP problems.

9. **D.** Proxy servers operate at Layer 7—the Application layer.

10. **C, D.** Both Telnet and Remote Desktop enable you to access and work on a remote computer. The latter is just prettier!

CHAPTER 23

Computer Security

In this chapter, you will learn how to
- Explain the threats to your computers and data
- Describe how to control the local computing environment
- Explain how to protect computers from network threats

Your PC is under siege. Through your PC, a malicious person can gain valuable information about you and your habits. He can steal your files. He can run programs that log your keystrokes and thus gain account names and passwords, credit card information, and more. He can run software that takes over much of your computer processing time and use it to send spam or steal from others. The threat is real and right now. Worse, he's doing one or more of these things to your clients as I write these words. You need to secure your computer and your users from these attacks.

But what does computer security mean? Is it an antivirus program? Is it big, complex passwords? Sure, it's both of these things, but what about the fact that your laptop can be stolen easily? Before you run out in a panic to buy security applications, let's take a moment to understand the threat to your computers, see what needs to be protected, and how to do so.

Analyzing the Threat

Threats to your data and PC come from two directions: mistakes and malicious people. All sorts of things can go wrong with your computer, from a user getting access to a folder he or she shouldn't see to a virus striking and deleting folders. Files can get deleted, renamed, or simply lost. Hard drives can die, and CD- and DVD-media discs get scratched and rendered unreadable. Even well-meaning people can make mistakes.

Unfortunately, there are a lot of people out there who intend to do you harm. Add that intent together with a talent for computers, and you've got a deadly combination. Let's look at the following issues:

- Unauthorized access
- Data destruction, accidental or deliberate
- Administrative access
- Catastrophic hardware failures
- Viruses/spyware

Historical/Conceptual

Unauthorized Access

Unauthorized access occurs when a user accesses resources in an unauthorized way. Resources in this case mean data, applications, and hardware. A user can alter or delete data; access sensitive information, such as financial data, personnel files, or e-mail messages; or use a computer for purposes the owner did not intend.

Not all unauthorized access is malicious—often this problem arises when users who are randomly poking around in a computer discover that they can access resources in a fashion the primary user did not intend. Unauthorized access can sometimes be very malicious when outsiders knowingly and intentionally take advantage of weaknesses in your security to gain information, use resources, or destroy data!

Data Destruction

Often an extension of unauthorized access, data destruction means more than just intentionally or accidentally erasing or corrupting data. It's easy to imagine some evil hacker accessing your network and deleting all your important files, but consider the case where authorized users access certain data, but what they do to that data goes beyond what they are authorized to do. A good example is the person who legitimately accesses a Microsoft Access product database to modify the product descriptions, only to discover he or she can change the prices of the products, too.

This type of threat is particularly dangerous when users are not clearly informed about the extent to which they are authorized to make changes. A fellow tech once told me about a user who managed to mangle an important database due to someone giving them incorrect access. When confronted, the user said: "If I wasn't allowed to change it, the system wouldn't let me do it!" Many users believe that systems are configured in a paternalistic way that wouldn't allow them to do anything inappropriate. As a result, users will often assume they're authorized to make any changes they believe are necessary when working on a piece of data they know they're authorized to access.

Administrative Access

Every operating system enables you to create user accounts and grant those accounts a certain level of access to files and folders in that computer. As an administrator, supervisor, or root user, you have full control over just about every aspect of the computer. Windows XP, in particular, makes it entirely too easy to give users administrative access to the computer, especially Windows XP Home because it allows only two kinds of users, administrators and limited users. Because you can't do much as a limited user, most home and small office systems simply use multiple administrator accounts. If you need to control access, you really need to use Windows 2000 or XP Professional.

System Crash/Hardware Failure

Like any technology, computers can and will fail—usually when you can least afford for it to happen. Hard drives crash, the power fails—it's all part of the joy of working in the computing business. You need to create redundancy in areas prone to failure (like installing backup power in case of electrical failure) and perform those all-important data backups. Chapter 15, "Maintaining and Troubleshooting Windows," goes into detail about using Microsoft Backup and other issues involved in creating a stable and reliable system.

Virus/Spyware

Networks are without a doubt the fastest and most efficient vehicles for transferring computer viruses among systems. News reports focus attention on the many virus attacks from the Internet, but a huge number of viruses still come from users who bring in programs on floppy disks, writable optical discs, and USB drives. This chapter describes the various methods of virus infection, and what you need to do to prevent virus infection of your networked systems in the "Network Security" section.

Essentials

Local Control

To create a secure computing environment, you need to establish control over local resources. You need to back up data and make sure that retired hard drives and optical discs have no sensitive data on them. You should recognize security issues and be able to respond properly. You need to implement good access control policies, such as having all computers in your care locked down with proper passwords or other devices that recognize who should have access. Finally, and this is particularly important for the IT Technician exam, you need to be able to implement methods for tracking computer usage. If someone is doing something wrong, you and the network or computer administrator should be able to catch him or her!

To mimic the physician's oath, here's the technician's oath: "Technician, first, secure your data." You need to back up data on machines in your care properly. Also, techs need to follow correct practices when retiring or donating old equipment. Let's take a look.

What to Back Up

Systems in your care should have regular backups performed of essential operating system files and, most importantly, data files. Chapter 15, "Maintaining and Troubleshooting Windows," covers the process of backing up data, such as running the Backup or Restore Wizard in Windows 2000 and Windows XP, so the mechanics aren't covered here. Instead, this chapter looks more critically at what files to back up and how to protect those files.

Essential Data

By default, the Backup or Restore Wizard in Windows XP offers to back up your Documents and Settings folder (Figure 23-1). You also have options to back up everyone's documents and settings. That takes care of most, but not all, of your critical data. There are other issues to consider.

Figure 23-1
Backup or Restore
Wizard

NOTE Windows 2000 and 2003 open the Backup Wizard with somewhat different settings. You are prompted to back up the entire drive initially, for example, rather than just Documents and Settings. This is also the case when you run the wizard in Windows XP in Advanced Mode.

First, if you use Microsoft Outlook for your e-mail, the saved e-mail messages—both received and sent—will not be backed up. Neither will your address book. If you don't care about such things, then that's fine, but if you share a computer with multiple users, you need to make certain that you or the users back up both their mail and address book manually and then put the backed-up files in the Documents and Settings folder! That way, the Backup or Restore Wizard will grab those files.

Second, if you or others on the computer use any folders outside the Documents and Settings environment, then you need to select the *Let me choose what to back up* option from the Backup or Restore Wizard when prompted. This opens the Items to Back Up dialog where you can select individual files and folders to back up (Figure 23-2).

Server Environments

If you work in an environment that requires you to back up Windows 2000 Server or Windows Server 2003 computers, you need to back up some extra data. This is espe-

Figure 23-2
Selecting items
to back up

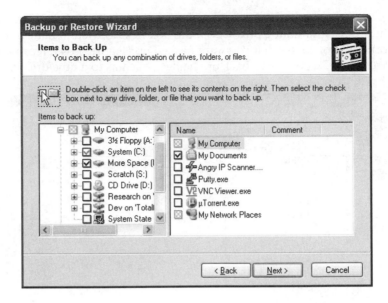

cially true if you have a Windows network running. Windows networking features *Active Directory*, a system that enables you to share files easily within the network, yet still maintain rock-solid security. A user only has to log in once to an Active Directory server and then they have access to resources throughout the Active Directory network (assuming, of course, that the user has permission to access those resources).

To back up the extra data, you need to run the Backup Wizard and select the radio button that says *Only back up the System State data* (Figure 23-3). This takes care of most of the registry, security settings, the Desktop files and folders, and the default user.

Figure 23-3
Backup Wizard

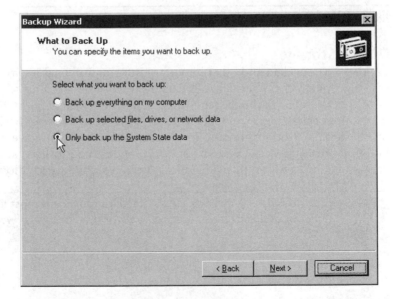

If you want to back up more than that, close the wizard and select the Backup tab in the Backup dialog box. Check the box next to System State and then check off any other file or folder that you want backed up (Figure 23-4). From this same dialog box, you can select where to back up the data, such as to a tape drive or external hard drive.

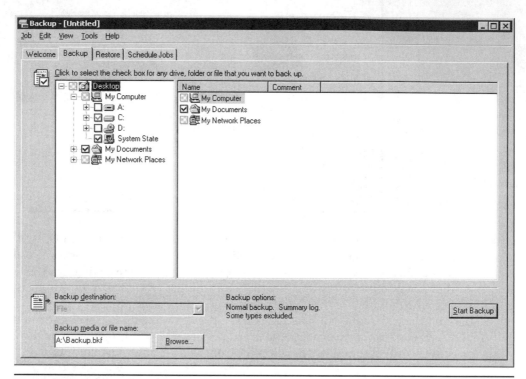

Figure 23-4   Backup tab in the Backup dialog box with System State and My Documents selected

Offsite Storage

Backing up your data and other important information enables you to restore easily in case of a system crash or malicious data destruction, but to ensure proper security, you need to store your backups somewhere other than your office. Offsite storage means that you take the tape or portable hard drive that contains your backup and lock it in a briefcase. Take it home and put it in your home safe, if you have one. This way, if the building burns down or some major flood renders your office inaccessible, your company can be up and running very quickly from a secondary location.

 EXAM TIP   The CompTIA A+ certification exams most likely *won't* ask you about offsite storage, but in today's world, anything less would be illogical.

Migrating and Retiring

Seasons change and so does the state of the art in computing. At a certain point in a computer's life, you'll need to retire an old system. This means you must migrate the data and users to a new system or at least a new hard drive and then safely dispose of the old system. Chapter 15, "Maintaining and Troubleshooting Windows," went through the details of the Documents and Settings Transfer Wizard, so I won't bore you by repeating that here. When talking about migration or retirement in terms of security, you need to answer one question: what do you do with the old system or drive?

All but the most vanilla new installations have sensitive data on them, even if it's simply e-mail messages or notes-to-self that would cause embarrassment if discovered. Most PCs, especially in a work environment, contain a lot of sensitive data. You can't just format C: and hand over the drive.

Follow three principles when migrating or retiring a computer. First, migrate your users and data information in a secure environment. Until you get passwords properly in place and test the security of the new system, you can't consider that system secure. Second, remove data remnants from hard drives that you store or give to charity. Third, recycle the older equipment; don't throw it in the trash. PC recyclers go through a process of deconstructing hardware, breaking system units, keyboards, printers, and even monitors into their basic plastics, metals, and glass for reuse.

Migration Practices

Migrate your users and data information in a secure environment. Until you get passwords properly in place and test the security of the new system, you can't consider that system secure. Don't set a copy to run while you go out to lunch, but rather be there to supervise and remove any remnant data that might still reside on any mass storage devices, especially hard drives.

You might think that, as easy as it seems to be to lose data, that you could readily get rid of data if you tried. That's not the case, however, with magnetic media such as hard drives and flash memory. It's very difficult to clean a drive completely. Repeated formatting won't do the trick. Partitioning and formatting won't work. Data doesn't necessarily get written over in the same place every time, which means that a solid wipe of a hard drive by writing zeroes to all the clusters still potentially leaves a lot of sensitive and recoverable data, typically called *remnants,* on the drive.

Although you can't make data 100 percent unrecoverable short of physically shredding or pulverizing a drive, you can do well enough for donation purposes by using one of the better drive-wiping utilities, such as Webroot's Window Washer (Figure 23-5). Window Washer gives you the ability to erase your Web browsing history, your recent activity in Windows (such as what programs you ran), and even your e-mail messages permanently. As an added bonus, you can create a bootable disk that enables you to wipe a drive completely.

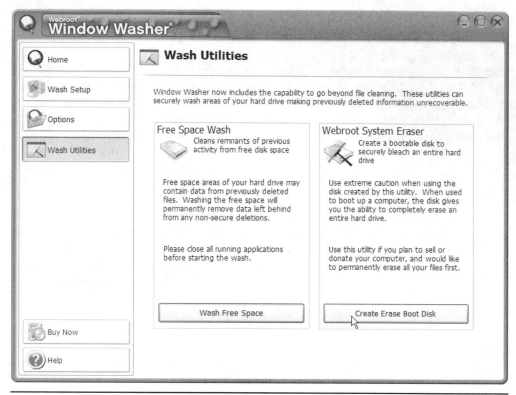

Figure 23-5   Webroot Window Washer security software

Recycle

An important and relatively easy way to be an environmentally conscious computer user is to *recycle*. Recycling products such as paper and printer cartridges not only keeps them out of overcrowded landfills, but also ensures that the more toxic products are disposed of in the right way. Safely disposing of hardware containing hazardous materials, such as computer monitors, protects both people and the environment.

Anyone who's ever tried to sell a computer more than three or four years old learns a hard lesson—they're not worth much if anything at all. It's a real temptation to take that old computer and just toss it in the garbage, but never do that!

First of all, many parts of your computer—such as your computer monitor—contain hazardous materials that pollute the environment. Luckily, thousands of companies now specialize in computer recycling and will gladly accept your old computer. If you have enough computers, they might even pick them up. If you can't find a recycler, call your local municipality's waste authority to see where to drop off your system.

An even better alternative for your old computer is donation. Many organizations actively look for old computers to refurbish and to donate to schools and other organizations. Just keep in mind that the computer can be too old—not even a school wants a computer more than five or six years old.

IT Technician

Social Engineering

Although you're more likely to lose data through accident, the acts of malicious users get the vast majority of headlines. Most of these attacks come under the heading of *social engineering*—the process of using or manipulating people inside the networking environment to gain access to that network from the outside. The term "social engineering" covers the many ways humans can use other humans to gain unauthorized information. This unauthorized information may be a network login, a credit card number, company customer data—almost anything you might imagine that one person or organization may not want a person outside of that organization to access.

 EXAM TIP CompTIA considers security to be an extremely important topic, whether you're at the Essentials level or any of the Technician levels. Unlike other chapters, almost every single topic covered in the IT Technician section of this chapter *applies equally to the Essentials section*. In other words, you need to know everything in this chapter to pass any of the four CompTIA A+ certification exams.

Social engineering attacks aren't hacking—at least in the classic sense of the word—although the goals are the same. Social engineering is where people attack an organization through the people in the organization or physically access the organization to get the information they need. Here are a few of the more classic types of social engineering attacks.

 NOTE It's common for these attacks to be used together, so if you discover one of them being used against your organization, it's a good idea to look for others.

Infiltration

Hackers can physically enter your building under the guise of someone who might have a legitimate reason for being there, such as cleaning personnel, repair technicians, or messengers. They then snoop around desks, looking for whatever they can find. They might talk with people inside the organization, gathering names, office numbers, department names—little things in and of themselves, but powerful tools when combined later with other social engineering attacks.

Telephone Scams

Telephone scams are probably the most common social engineering attack. In this case, the attacker makes a phone call to someone in the organization to gain information. The attacker attempts to come across as someone inside the organization and uses this to get the desired information. Probably the most famous of these scams is the "I forgot my user name and password" scam. In this gambit, the attacker first learns the account name of a legitimate person in the organization, usually using the infiltration method. The attacker then calls someone in the organization, usually the help desk, in an attempt to gather information, in this case a password.

Hacker: "Hi, this is John Anderson in accounting. I forgot my password. Can you reset it please?"

Help Desk : "Sure, what's your user name?"

Hacker: "j_w_Anderson"

Help Desk: "OK, I reset it to e34rd3."

Certainly telephone scams aren't limited to attempts to get network access. There are documented telephone scams against organizations aimed at getting cash, blackmail material, or other valuables.

Dumpster Diving

Dumpster diving is the generic term for anytime a hacker goes through your refuse, looking for information. The amount of sensitive information that makes it into any organization's trash bin boggles the mind! Years ago, I worked with an IT security guru who gave me and a few other IT people a tour of our office's trash. In one 20-minute tour of the personal wastebaskets of one office area, we had enough information to access the network easily, as well as to embarrass seriously more than a few people. When it comes to getting information, the trash is the place to look!

Physical Theft

I once had a fellow network geek challenge me to try to bring down his newly installed network. He had just installed a powerful and expensive firewall router and was convinced that I couldn't get to a test server he added to his network just for me to try to access. After a few attempts to hack in over the Internet, I saw that I wasn't going to get anywhere that way. So I jumped in my car and drove to his office, having first outfitted myself in a techy-looking jumpsuit and an ancient ID badge I just happened to have in my sock drawer. I smiled sweetly at the receptionist and walked right by my friend's office (I noticed he was smugly monitoring incoming IP traffic using some neato packet-sniffing program) to his new server. I quickly pulled the wires out of the back of his precious server, picked it up, and walked out the door. The receptionist was too busy trying to figure out why her e-mail wasn't working to notice me as I whisked by her carrying the 65-pound server box. I stopped in the hall and called him from my cell phone.

Me (cheerily): "Dude, I got all your data!"

Him (not cheerily): "You rebooted my server! How did you do it?"

Me (smiling): "I didn't reboot it—go over and look at it!"

Him (really mad now): "YOU <EXPLETIVE> THIEF! YOU STOLE MY SERVER!"

Me (cordially): "Why, yes. Yes, I did. Give me two days to hack your password in the comfort of my home, and I'll see everything! Bye!"

I immediately walked back in and handed him the test server. It was fun. The moral here is simple—never forget that the best network software security measures can be rendered useless if you fail to protect your systems physically!

Access Control

Access is the key. If you can control access to the data, programs, and other computing resources, you've secured your system. Access control is composed of five interlinked areas that a good, security-minded tech should think about: physical security, authentication, the file system, users and groups, and security policies. Much of this you know from previous chapters, but this section should help tie it all together as a security topic.

Secure Physical Area and Lock Down Your System

The first order of security is to block access to the physical hardware from people who shouldn't have access. This isn't rocket science. Lock the door. Don't leave a PC unattended when logged in. In fact, don't ever leave a system logged in, even as a limited user. God help you if you walk away from a server still logged in as an administrator. You're tempting fate.

For that matter, when you see a user's computer logged in and unattended, do the user and your company a huge favor and lock the computer. Just walk up and press CTRL-L on the keyboard to lock the system. It works in Windows 2000 and all versions of Windows XP and Windows Vista.

 EXAM TIP Expect questions on controlling access to computers and computer rooms on the CompTIA A+ 220-604 Depot Technician exam.

Authentication

Security starts with properly implemented *authentication*, which means in essence, how the computer determines who can or should access it. And, once accessed, what that user can do. A computer can authenticate users through software or hardware, or a combination of both.

Software Authentication: Proper Passwords It's still rather shocking to me to power up a friend's computer and go straight to his or her desktop; or with my married-with-kids friends, to click one of the parent's user account icons and not get prompted for a password. This is just wrong! I'm always tempted to assign passwords right then and there—and not tell them the passwords, of course—so they'll see the error of their ways when they try to log in next. I don't do it, but always try to explain gently the importance of good passwords.

You know about passwords from Chapter 15, "Maintaining and Troubleshooting Windows," so I won't belabor the point here. Suffice it to say that you need to make certain that all your users have proper passwords. Don't let them write passwords down or tape them to the underside of their mouse pads either!

It's not just access to Windows that you need to think about. If you have computers running in a public location, there's always the temptation for people to hack the system and do mean things, like change CMOS settings to render the computer inoperable to the casual user until a tech can undo the damage. All modern CMOS setup utilities come with an access password protection scheme (Figure 23-6).

Figure 23-6
CMOS access
password request

```
IOS Extension v1.0A
ard Software, Inc.

·y Master ... ST10232A
·y Slave  ... None
lary
lary  Enter Password:
```

Hardware Authentication   Smart cards and biometric devices enable modern systems to authenticate users with more authority than mere passwords. Smart cards are credit-card-sized cards with circuitry that can be used to identify the bearer of the card. Smart cards are relatively common for tasks such as authenticating users for mass transit systems, for example, but fairly uncommon in computers. Figure 23-7 shows a smart card and keyboard combination.

Figure 23-7
Smart card and
keyboard reader
(photo courtesy
of Cherry Corp.)

People can guess or discover passwords, but it's a lot harder to forge someone's fingerprints. The keyboard in Figure 23-8 authenticates users on a local machine using fingerprints. Other devices that will do the trick are key fobs, retinal scanners, and PC cards for laptop computers.

Figure 23-8
Microsoft keyboard
with fingerprint
accessibility

NOTE Full disclosure time. Microsoft does not claim that the keyboard in Figure 23-8 offers any security at all. In fact, the documentation specifically claims that the fingerprint reader is an accessibility tool, not a security device. Because it enables a person to log onto a local machine, though, I think it falls into the category of authentication devices.

Clever manufacturers have developed key fobs and smart cards that use radio frequency identification (RFID) to transmit authentication information, so users don't have to insert something into a computer or card reader. The Prevarius plusID combines, for example, a biometric fingerprint fob with an RFID tag that makes security as easy as opening a garage door remotely! Figure 23-9 shows a plusID device.

Figure 23-9
plusID (photo
courtesy of
Privaris, Inc.)

NTFS, not FAT32!

The file system on a hard drive matters a lot when it comes to security. On a Windows machine with multiple users, you simply must use NTFS or you have no security at all. Not just primary drives, but any secondary drives in computers in your care should be formatted as NTFS, with the exception of removable drives, such as the one you use to back up your system.

When you run into a multiple-drive system that has a second or third drive formatted as FAT32, you can use the *CONVERT* command-line utility to go from FAT to NTFS. The syntax is pretty straightforward. To convert a D: drive from FAT or FAT32 to NTFS, for example, you'd type the following:

```
CONVERT D: /FS:NTFS
```

You can substitute a mount name in place of the drive letter in case you have a mounted volume. The command has a few extra switches as well, so at the command prompt, type **a** /? after the CONVERT command to see all your options.

Users and Groups

Windows uses user accounts and groups as the bedrock of access control. A user account gets assigned to a group, such as Users, Power Users, or Administrators, and by association gets certain permissions on the computer. Using NTFS enables the highest level of control over data resources.

Assigning users to groups is a great first step in controlling a local machine, but this feature really shines once you go to a networked environment. Let's go there now.

Network Security

The vast majority of protective strategies related to internal threats are based on policies rather than technology. Even the smallest network will have a number of user accounts and groups scattered about with different levels of rights/permissions. Every time you give a user access to a resource, you create potential loopholes that can leave your network vulnerable to unauthorized access, data destruction, and other administrative nightmares. To protect your network from internal threats, you need to implement the correct controls over user accounts, permissions, and policies.

Networks are under threat from the outside as well, so this section looks at issues involving Internet-borne attacks, firewalls, and wireless networking. The section finishes with discussion of the tools you need to track computer and network activity and, if necessary, lock down your systems.

User Account Control Through Groups

Access to user accounts should be restricted to the assigned individuals, and those accounts should have permission to access only the resources they need, no more. Tight control of user accounts is critical to preventing unauthorized access. Disabling unused accounts is an important part of this strategy, but good user account control goes far deeper than that. One of your best tools for user account control is groups. Instead of giving permissions/rights to individual user accounts, give them to groups; this makes keeping track of the permissions assigned to individual user accounts much easier. Figure 23-10 shows me giving permissions to a group for a folder in Windows 2000. Once a group is created and its permissions set, you can then add user accounts to that group as needed. Any user account that becomes a member of a group automatically gets the permissions assigned to that group. Figure 23-11 shows me adding a user to a newly created group in the same Windows 2000 system.

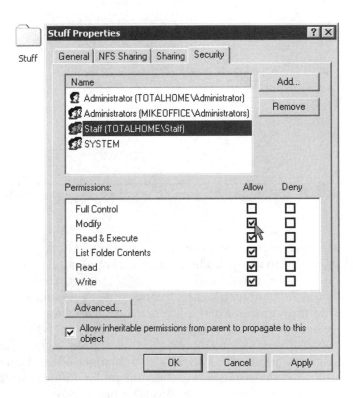

Figure 23-10
Giving a group permissions for a folder in Windows 2000

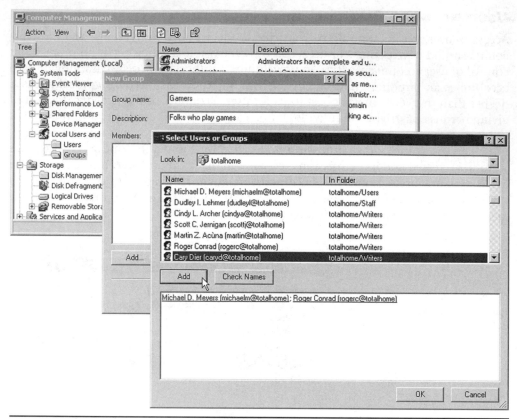

Figure 23-11   Adding a user to a newly created group in Windows 2000

Groups are a great way to get increased complexity without increasing the administrative burden on network administrators, because all network operating systems combine permissions. When a user is a member of more than one group, which permissions does he or she have with respect to any particular resource? In all network operating systems, the permissions of the groups are *combined*, and the result is what you call the *effective permissions* the user has to access the resource. Let's use an example from Windows 2000. If Rita is a member of the Sales group, which has List Folder Contents permission to a folder, and she is also a member of the Managers group, which has Read and Execute permissions to the same folder, Rita will have both List Folder Contents *and* Read and Execute permissions to that folder.

Watch out for *default* user accounts and groups—they can become secret backdoors to your network! All network operating systems have a default Everyone group, and it can be used to sneak into shared resources easily. This Everyone group, as its name implies, literally includes anyone who connects to that resource. Windows 2000 gives full control to the Everyone group by default, for example, so make sure you know to lock this down!

All of the default groups—Everyone, Guest, Users—define broad groups of users. Never use them unless you intend to permit all those folks to access a resource. If you use one of the default groups, remember to configure them with the proper permissions to prevent users from doing things you don't want them to do with a shared resource!

All of these groups and organizational units only do one thing for you: They let you keep track of your user accounts, so you know they are only available for those who need them, and they only access the resources you want them to use.

Security Policies

While permissions control how users access shared resources, there are other functions you should control that are outside the scope of resources. For example, do you want users to be able to access a command prompt on their Windows system? Do you want users to be able to install software? Would you like to control what systems or what time of day a user can log in? All network operating systems provide you with some capability to control these and literally hundreds of other security parameters, under what Windows calls *policies*. I like to think of policies as permissions for activities as opposed to true permissions, which control access to resources.

A policy is usually applied to a user account, a computer, or a group. Let's use the example of a network composed of Windows XP Professional systems with a Windows 2000 Server system. Every Windows XP system has its own local policies program, which enables policies to be placed on that system only. Figure 23-12 shows the tool you use to set local policies on an individual system, called *Local Security Settings*, being used to deny the user account Danar the capability to log on locally.

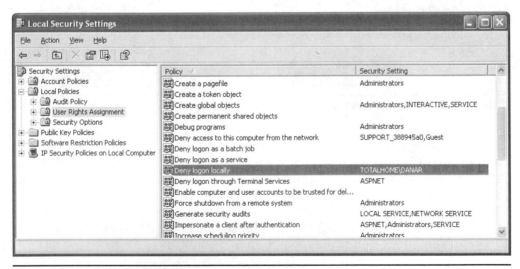

Figure 23-12   Local Security Settings

Local policies work great for individual systems, but they can be a pain to configure if you want to apply the same settings to more than one PC on your network. If you want to apply policy settings *en masse*, then you need to step up to Windows Active Directory domain-based *Group Policy*. Using Group Policy, you can exercise deity-like— Microsoft prefers to use the term *granular*—control over your network clients.

Want to set default wallpaper for every PC in your domain? Group Policy can do that. Want to make certain tools inaccessible to everyone except authorized users? Group Policy can do that, too. Want to control access to the Internet, redirect home folders, run scripts, deploy software, or just remind folks that unauthorized access to the network will get them nowhere fast? Group Policy is the answer. Figure 23-13 shows Group Policy; I'm about to change the default title on every instance of Internet Explorer on every computer in my domain!

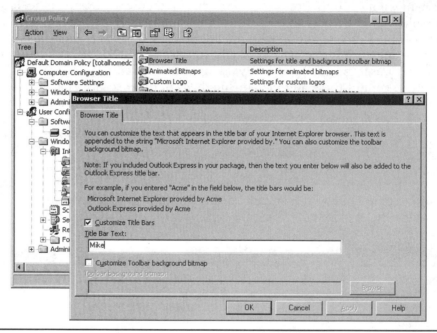

Figure 23-13   Using Group Policy to make IE title say "provided by Mike!"

That's just one simple example of the types of settings you can configure using Group Policy. There are literally hundreds of "tweaks" you can apply through Group Policy, from the great to the small, but don't worry too much about familiarizing yourself with each and every one. Group Policy settings are a big topic in the Microsoft Certified Systems Administrator (MCSA) and Microsoft Certified Systems Engineer (MCSE) certification tracks, but for the purposes of the CompTIA A+ exams, you simply have to be comfortable with the concept behind Group Policy.

NOTE   Linux doesn't provide a single application that you open to set up policies, like Windows does. In fact, Linux doesn't even use the name "policies." Instead, Linux relies on individual applications to set up policies for whatever they're doing. This is in keeping with the Linux paradigm of having lots of little programs that do one thing well, as opposed to the Windows paradigm of having one program try to be all things for all applications.

Although I could never list every possible policy you can enable on a Windows system, here's a list of some of those more commonly used:

- **Prevent Registry Edits**   If you try to edit the Registry, you get a failure message.
- **Prevent Access to the Command Prompt**   This policy keeps users from getting to the command prompt by turning off the Run command and the MS-DOS Prompt shortcut.
- **Log on Locally**   This policy defines who may log on to the system locally.
- **Shut Down System**   This policy defines who may shut down the system.
- **Minimum Password Length**   This policy forces a minimum password length.
- **Account Lockout Threshold**   This policy sets the maximum number of logon attempts a person can make before they are locked out of the account.
- **Disable Windows Installer**   This policy prevents users from installing software.
- **Printer Browsing**   This policy enables users to browse for printers on the network, as opposed to using only assigned printers.

While the CompTIA A+ exams don't expect you to know how to implement policies on any type of network, you are expected to understand that policies exist, especially on Windows networks, and that they can do amazing things in terms of controlling what users can do on their systems. If you ever try to get to a command prompt on a Windows system, only to discover the Run command is grayed out, blame it on a policy, not the computer!

Malicious Software

The beauty of the Internet is the ease of accessing resources just about anywhere on the globe, all from the comfort of your favorite chair. This connection, however, runs both ways, and people from all over the world can potentially access your computer from the comfort of their evil lairs. The Internet is awash with malicious software (*malware*) that is—even at this moment—trying to infect your systems. Malware consists of computer programs designed to break into computers or cause havoc on computers. The most common types of malware are viruses, worms, spyware, Trojan horses, adware, and grayware. You need to understand the different types of malware so you can combat them for you and your users successfully.

Viruses

Just as a biological virus gets passed from person to person, a computer *virus* is a piece of malicious software that gets passed from computer to computer (Figure 23-14). A computer virus is designed to attach itself to a program on your computer. It could be your e-mail program, your word processor, or even a game. Whenever you use the infected program, the virus goes into action and does whatever it was designed to do. It can wipe out your e-mail or even erase your entire hard drive! Viruses are also sometimes used to steal information or send spam e-mails to everyone in your address book.

Figure 23-14
You've got mail!

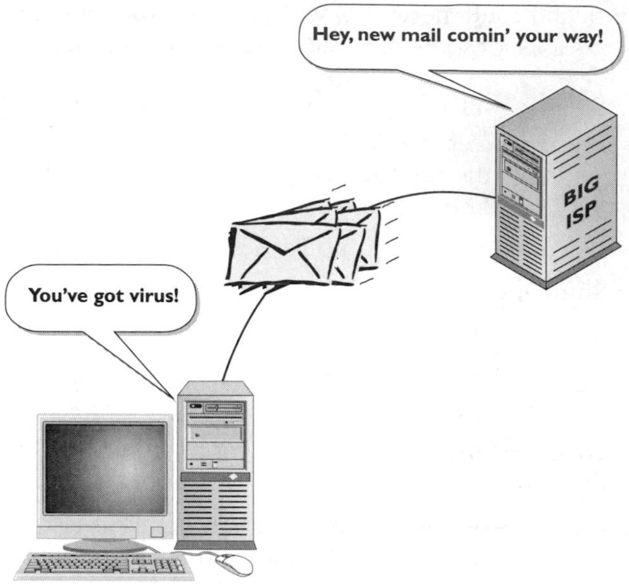

Trojans

Trojans are true, freestanding programs that do something other than what the person who runs the program thinks they will do. An example of a *Trojan virus* is a program that a person thinks is a game but is actually a CMOS eraser. Some Trojans are quite sophisticated. It might be a game that works perfectly well, but when the user quits the game, it causes some type of damage.

Worms

Similar to a Trojan, a *worm* is a complete program that travels from machine to machine, usually through computer networks. Most worms are designed to take advantage of security problems in operating systems and install themselves on vulnerable machines. They can copy themselves over and over again on infected networks, and can create so much activity that they overload the network, in worst cases even bringing chunks of the entire Internet to a halt.

There are several things you can do to protect yourself and your data against these threats. First, make sure you are running up-to-date virus software—especially if you connect to the Internet via an always-on broadband connection. You should also be protected by a firewall, either as part of your network hardware or by means of a software program. (See the sections on antivirus programs and firewalls later in this chapter.)

Since worms most commonly infect systems because of security flaws in operating systems, the next defense against them is to make sure you have the most current version possible of your operating system and to check regularly for security patches. A *security patch* is an addition to the operating system to patch a hole in the operating system code. You can download security patches from the software vendor's Web site (Figure 23-15).

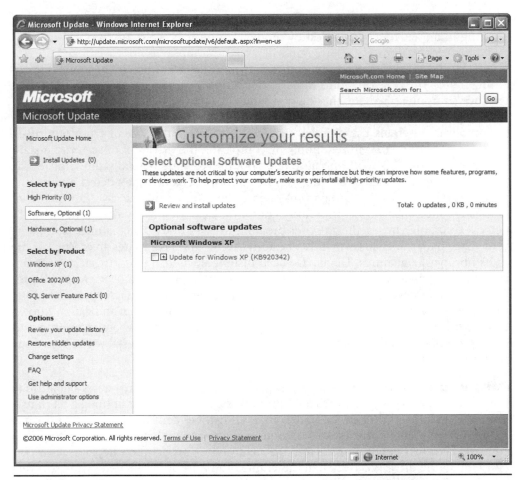

Figure 23-15 Microsoft Update

Microsoft's Windows Update tool is handy for Windows users as it provides a simple method to ensure that your version's security is up to date. The one downside is that not everyone remembers to run Windows Update. Don't wait until something goes wrong on your computer, or you hear on the news that another nasty program is running rampant across the Internet—Run Windows Update weekly (or even better automatically) as a part of your normal system maintenance. Keeping your patches up-to-date is called *patch management,* and it goes a long way toward keeping your system safe!

Antivirus Programs

The only way to protect your PC permanently from getting a virus is to disconnect from the Internet and never permit any potentially infected software to touch your precious computer. Because neither scenario is likely these days, you need to use a specialized antivirus program to help stave off the inevitable virus assaults.

An antivirus program protects your PC in two ways. It can be both sword and shield, working in an active seek-and-destroy mode and in a passive sentry mode. When ordered to seek and destroy, the program will scan the computer's boot sector and files for viruses, and if it finds any, present you with the available options for removing or disabling them. Antivirus programs can also operate as virus shields that passively monitor your computer's activity, checking for viruses only when certain events occur, such as a program executing or a file being downloaded.

Antivirus programs use different techniques to combat different types of viruses. They detect boot sector viruses simply by comparing the drive's boot sector to a standard boot sector. This works because most boot sectors are basically the same. Some antivirus programs make a backup copy of the boot sector. If they detect a virus, the programs will use that backup copy to replace the infected boot sector. Executable viruses are a little more difficult to find because they can be on any file in the drive. To detect executable viruses, the antivirus program uses a library of signatures. A *signature* is the code pattern of a known virus. The antivirus program compares an executable file to its library of signatures. There have been instances where a perfectly clean program coincidentally held a virus signature. Usually the antivirus program's creator will provide a patch to prevent further alarms. Antivirus programs detect macro viruses through the presence of virus signatures or certain macro commands that indicate a known macro virus. Now that we understand the types of viruses and how antivirus programs try to protect against them, let's review a few terms that are often used when describing certain traits of viruses.

Polymorphics/Polymorphs   A *polymorph virus* attempts to change its signature to prevent detection by antivirus programs, usually by continually scrambling a bit of useless code. Fortunately, the scrambling code itself can be identified and used as the signature—once the antivirus makers become aware of the virus. One technique used to combat unknown polymorphs is to have the antivirus program create a checksum on every file in the drive. A *checksum* in this context is a number generated by the software based on the contents of the file rather than the name, date, or size of that file. The algorithms for creating these checksums vary among different antivirus programs (they are also usually kept secret to help prevent virus makers from coming up with ways to beat them). Every time a program is run, the antivirus program calculates a new checksum and compares it with the earlier calculation. If the checksums are different, it is a sure sign of a virus.

Stealth   The term "stealth" is more of a concept than an actual virus function. Most *stealth virus* programs are boot sector viruses that use various methods to hide from antivirus software. The AntiEXE stealth virus will hook on to a little-known but often-used software interrupt, for example, running only when that interrupt runs. Others make copies of innocent-looking files.

Virus Prevention Tips   The secret to preventing damage from a malicious software attack is to keep from getting a virus in the first place. As discussed earlier, all good antivirus programs include a virus shield that will scan e-mail, downloads, running programs, and so on automatically (see Figure 23-16).

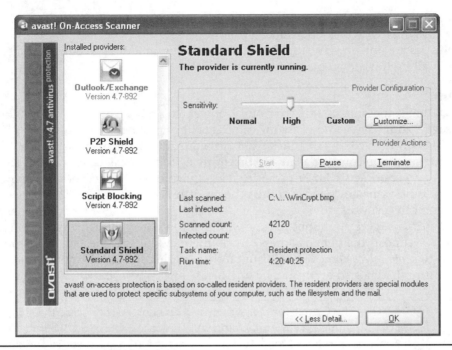

Figure 23-16 A virus shield in action

Use your antivirus shield. It is also a good idea to scan PCs daily for possible virus attacks. All antivirus programs include terminate-and-stay resident programs (TSRs) that will run every time the PC is booted. Last but not least, know where the source of any software before you load it. While the chance of commercial, shrink-wrapped software having a virus is virtually nil (there have been a couple of well-publicized exceptions), that illegal copy of Unreal Tournament you borrowed from a local hacker should definitely be inspected with care.

Keep your antivirus program updated. New viruses appear daily, and your program needs to know about them. The list of viruses your antivirus program can recognize is called the *definition file,* and you must keep that definition file up-to-date. Fortunately, most antivirus programs will update themselves automatically.

Get into the habit of keeping around an antivirus CD-R—a bootable, CD-R disc with a copy of an antivirus program. If you suspect a virus, use the disc, even if your antivirus program claims to have eliminated the virus. Turn off the PC and reboot it from the antivirus disc. (You might have to change CMOS settings to boot to optical media.) Run your antivirus program's most comprehensive virus scan. Then check all removable media that were exposed to the system, and any other machine that might have received data from it or that is networked to the cleaned machine. A virus or other malicious program can often lie dormant for months before anyone knows of its presence.

E-mail is still a common source of viruses, and opening infected e-mails is a common way to get infected. If you view an e-mail in a preview window, that opens the e-mail message and exposes your computer to some viruses. Download files only from sites you know to be safe, and of course the less reputable corners of the Internet are the most likely places to pick up computer infections.

Viruses are not, however, the only malicious software lurking in e-mail. Sometimes the e-mail itself is the problem.

Spam

E-mail that comes into your Inbox from a source that's not a friend, family member, or colleague, and that you didn't ask for, can create huge problems for your computer and you. This unsolicited e-mail, called *spam*, accounts for a huge percentage of traffic on the Internet. Spam comes in many flavors, from legitimate businesses trying to sell you products to scammers who just want to take your money. Hoaxes, pornography, and get-rich-quick schemes pour into the Inboxes of most e-mail users. They waste your time and can easily offend.

You can use several options to cope with the flood of spam. The first option is defense. Never post your e-mail address on the Internet. One study tested this theory and found that *over 97 percent* of the spam received during the study went to e-mail addresses they had posted on the public Internet.

 NOTE The Center for Democracy and Technology conducted the study in 2003, entitled "Why Am I Getting All This Spam? Unsolicited Commercial E-mail Research Six Month Report." Here's the Web link if you're curious: www.cdt.org/speech/spam/030319spamreport.shtml.

Filters and filtering software can block spam at your mail server and at your computer. AOL implemented blocking schemes in 2004, for example, that dropped the average spam received by its subscribers by a large percentage, perhaps as much as 50 percent. You can set most e-mail programs to block e-mail from specific people—good to use if someone is harassing you—or to specific people. You can block by subject line or keywords. Most people use a third-party anti-spam program instead of using the filters in their e-mail program.

Pop-ups, Spyware, and Adware

On most systems, the Internet Web browser client is the most often used piece of software. Over the years, Web sites have come up with more and more ways to try to get you to see what they want you to see: their advertising. When the Web first got underway, we were forced to look at an occasional banner ad. In the last few years, Web site designers have become much more sophisticated, creating a number of intrusive and irritating ways to get you to part with your money in one form or another.

There are basically three irritating Web browser problems: pop-ups, spyware, and adware. *Pop-ups* are those surprise browser windows that appear automatically when you visit a Web site, proving themselves irritating and unwanted and nothing else. *Spyware*, meanwhile, defines a family of programs that run in the background on your PC, sending information about your browsing habits to the company that installed it on your system. *Adware* is not generally as malicious as spyware, but it works similarly to display ads on your system. As such, these programs download new ads and generate undesirable network traffic. Of the three, spyware is much less noticeable but far more nefarious. At its worst, spyware can fire up pop-up windows of competing products on the Web site you're currently viewing. For example, you might be perusing a bookseller's Web site only to have a pop-up from a competitor's site appear.

Pop-Ups   Getting rid of pop-ups is actually rather tricky. You've probably noticed that most of these pop-up browser windows don't look like browser windows at all. There's no menu bar, button bar, or address window, yet they are each separate browser windows. HTML coding permits Web site and advertising designers to remove the usual navigation aids from a browser window so all you're left with is the content. In fact, as I'll describe in a minute, some pop-up browser windows are deliberately designed to mimic similar pop-up alerts from the Windows OS. They might even have buttons similar to Windows' own exit buttons, but you might find that when you click them, you wind up with more pop-up windows instead! What to do?

The first thing you need to know when dealing with pop-ups is how to close them without actually having to risk clicking them. As I said, most pop-ups have removed all navigation aids, and many are also configured to appear on your monitor screen in a position that places the browser window's exit button—the little *X* button in the upper right-hand corner—outside of your visible screen area. Some even pop up behind the active browser window and wait there in the background. Most annoying! To remedy this, use alternate means to close the pop-up browser window. For instance, you can right-click the browser window's taskbar icon to generate a pop-up menu of your own. Select Close, and the window should go away. You can also bring the browser window in question to the forefront by pressing ALT-TAB until it becomes visible, and then press ALT-F4 to close it.

Most Web browsers have features to prevent pop-up ads in the first place, but I've found that these types of applications are sometimes *too* thorough. That is, they tend to prevent *all* new browser windows from opening, even those you want to view. Still, they're free to try, so have a look to see if they suit your needs. Applications such as Ad-Subtract control a variety of Internet annoyances, including pop-up windows, cookies, and Java applets, and are more configurable—you can specify what you want to allow on any particular domain address—but the fully functional versions usually cost at least something, and that much control is too confusing for most novice-level users.

Dealing with Spyware   Some types of spyware go considerably beyond this level of intrusion. They can use your computer's resources to run *distributed computing* applications, capture your keystrokes to steal passwords, reconfigure your dial-up settings to use a different phone number at a much higher connection charge, or even use your Internet connection and e-mail address list to propagate itself to other computers in a virus-like fashion! Are you concerned yet?

Setting aside the legal and ethical issues, and there are many, you should at least appreciate that spyware can seriously impact your PC's performance and cause problems with your Internet connection. The threat is real, so what practical steps can you take to protect yourself? Let's look at how to prevent spyware installation, and how to detect and remove any installed spyware.

Preventing Spyware Installation   How does this spyware get into your system in the first place? Obviously, a sensible person doesn't download and install something that they know is going to compromise their computer. Makers of spyware know this, so they bundle their software with some other program or utility that purports to give you some benefit.

What kind of benefit? How about free access to MP3 music files? A popular program called Kazaa does that. How about a handy *e-wallet* utility that remembers your many screen names, passwords, and even your credit-card numbers to make online purchases easier and faster? A program called Gator does that, and many other functions as well. How about browser enhancements, performance boosters, custom cursor effects, search utilities, buddy lists, file savers, or media players? The list goes on and on, yet they all share one thing—they're simply window-dressing for the *real* purpose of the software. So you see, for the most part spyware doesn't need to force its way into your PC. Instead they saunter calmly through the front door. If the graphic in Figure 23-17 looks familiar, you might have installed some of this software yourself.

Figure 23-17
Gator Corporation's acknowledgment warning

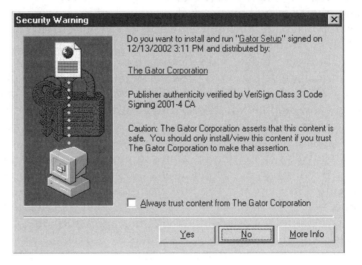

Some spyware makers use more aggressive means to get you to install their software. Instead of offering you some sort of attractive utility, they instead use fear tactics and deception to try to trick you into installing their software. One popular method is to use pop-up browser windows crudely disguised as Windows' own system warnings (Figure 23-18). When clicked, these may trigger a flood of other browser windows, or may even start a file download.

The lesson here is simple—*don't install these programs!* Careful reading of the software's license agreement before you install a program is a good idea, but realistically, it does little to protect your PC. With that in mind, here are a couple of preventative measures you can take to keep parasitic software off of your system.

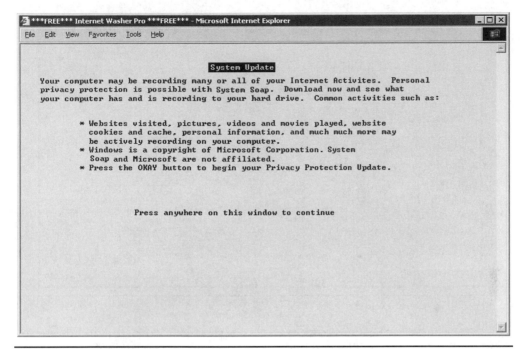

Figure 23-18   A spyware pop-up browser window, disguised as a Windows alert

If you visit a Web site and are prompted to install a third-party application or plug-in that you've never heard of, *don't install it.* Well-known and reputable plug-ins, such as Adobe's *Shockwave* or *Flash,* are safe, but be suspicious of any others. Don't click *anywhere* inside of a pop-up browser window, even if it looks just like a Windows alert window or DOS command-line prompt—as I just mentioned, it's probably fake and the Close button is likely a hyperlink. Instead, use other means to close the window, such as pressing ATL-F4 or right-clicking the browser window's icon on the taskbar and selecting Close.

You can also install spyware detection and removal software on your system and run it regularly. Let's look at how to do that.

Removing Spyware   Some spyware makers are reputable enough to include a routine for uninstalling their software. Gator, for instance, makes it fairly easy to get rid of their programs—just use the Windows Add/Remove Programs applet in the Control Panel. Others, however, aren't quite so cooperative. In fact, because spyware is so—well, *sneaky*—it's entirely possible that your system already has some installed that you don't even know about. How do you find out?

Windows comes with Windows Defender, a fine tool for catching most spyware but it's not perfect. The better solution is to back up Windows Defender with a second spyware removal program. There are several on the market, but two that I highly recommend are Lavasoft's Ad-Aware (Figure 23-19) and PepiMK's Spybot Search & Destroy.

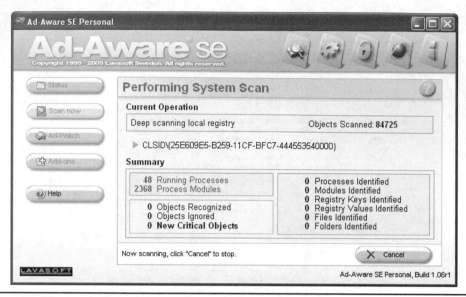

Figure 23-19 Lavasoft's Ad-Aware

Both of these applications work exactly as advertised. They detect and delete spyware of all sorts—hidden files and folders, cookies, registry keys and values, you name it. Ad-Aware is free for personal use, while Spybot Search & Destroy is shareware (Figure 23-20). Many times I've used both programs at the same time because one tends to catch what the other misses.

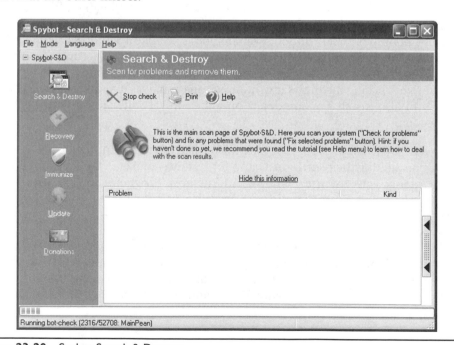

Figure 23-20 Spybot Search & Destroy

Grayware

Some programs, called *grayware*, are not destructive in and of themselves, but they leach bandwidth in networks and can turn a speedy machine into a doddering shell of a modern computer. These programs are called grayware because some people consider them beneficial. They might even be beneficial in the right setting. The primary example of grayware is the highly popular peer-to-peer file sharing programs, such as Bittorrent. Peer-to-peer file sharing programs enable a lot of users to upload portions of files on demand so that other users can download them. By splitting the load to many computers, the overall demand on a single computer is light.

The problem is that if you have a tight network with lots of traffic and suddenly you have a bunch of that bandwidth hogged by uploading and downloading files, then your network performance can degrade badly overall. So, is the grayware bad? Only in some environments. You need to judge each network or computer according to the situation.

Knowledge is Power

The best way to keep from having to deal with malware and grayware is education. It's your job as the IT person to talk to users, especially the ones whose systems you've just spent the last hour cleaning of nasties, about how to avoid these programs. Show them samples of dangerous e-mails they should not open, Web sites to avoid, and the types of programs they should not install and use on the network. Any user who understands the risks of questionable actions on their computers will usually do the right thing and stay away from malware.

Firewalls

Firewalls are an essential tool in the fight against malicious programs on the Internet. Firewalls are devices or software that protect an internal network from unauthorized access to and from the Internet at large. Hardware firewalls protect networks using a number of methods, such as hiding IP addresses and blocking TCP/IP ports. Most SOHO networks use a hardware firewall, such as the Linksys router in Figure 23-21. These devices do a great job.

Figure 23-21
Linksys router
as a firewall

Windows XP comes with an excellent software firewall, called the Windows Firewall (Figure 23-22). It can also handle the heavy lifting of port blocking, security logging, and more.

Figure 23-22
Windows Firewall

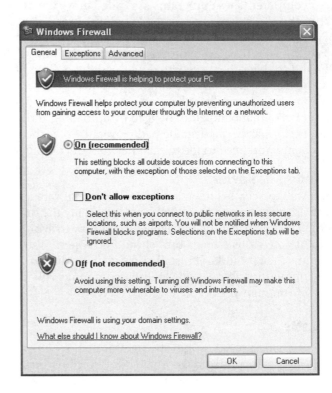

You can access the Windows Firewall by opening the Windows Firewall applet in the Control Panel. If you're running the Control Panel in Category view, click the Security Center icon (Figure 23-23),and then click the Windows Firewall option in the Windows Security Center dialog box. Figure 23-24 illustrates the Exceptions tab on the Windows Firewall, showing the applications allowed to use the TCP/IP ports on my computer.

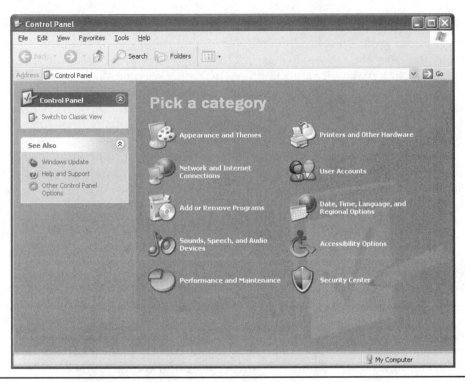

Figure 23-23   Control Panel, Category view

Figure 23-24
Essential programs
(doesn't everyone
need to run
Half-Life 2?)

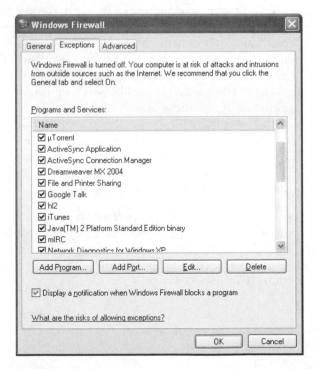

Encryption

Firewalls do a great job controlling traffic coming into or out of a network from the Internet, but they do nothing to stop interceptor hackers who monitor traffic on the public Internet looking for vulnerabilities. Once a packet is on the Internet itself, anyone with the right equipment can intercept and inspect it. Inspected packets are a cornucopia of passwords, account names, and other tidbits that hackers can use to intrude into your network. Because we can't stop hackers from inspecting these packets, we must turn to *encryption* to make them unreadable.

Network encryption occurs at many different levels and is in no way limited to Internet-based activities. Not only are there many levels of network encryption, but each encryption level provides multiple standards and options, making encryption one of the most complicated of all networking issues. You need to understand where encryption comes into play, what options are available, and what you can use to protect your network.

Network Authentication

Have you ever considered the process that takes place each time a person types in a user name and password to access a network, rather than just a local machine? What happens when this *network* authentication is requested? If you're thinking that when a user types in a user name and password, that information is sent to a server of some sort to be authenticated, you're right—but do you know how the user name and password get to the serving system? That's where encryption becomes important in authentication.

In a local network, encryption is usually handled by the NOS. Because NOS makers usually control software development of both the client and the server, they can create their own proprietary encryptions. However, in today's increasingly interconnected and diverse networking environment, there is a motivation to enable different network operating systems to authenticate any client system from any other NOS. Modern network operating systems such as Windows NT/2000/XP/2003 and NetWare 4.*x*/5.*x*/6.*x* use standard authentication encryptions like MIT's *Kerberos,* enabling multiple brands of servers to authenticate multiple brands of clients. These LAN encryptions are usually transparent and work quite nicely even in mixed networks.

Unfortunately, this uniformity falls away as you begin to add remote access authentications. There are so many different remote access tools, based on UNIX/Linux, Novell NetWare, and Windows serving programs, that most remote access systems have to support a variety of different authentication methods.

PAP *Password Authentication Protocol (PAP)* is the oldest and most basic form of authentication. It's also the least safe, because it sends all passwords in clear text. No NOS uses PAP for a client system's login, but almost all network operating systems that provide remote access service will support PAP for backward compatibility with a host of older programs (like Telnet) that only use PAP.

CHAP *Challenge Handshake Authentication Protocol (CHAP)* is the most common remote access protocol. CHAP has the serving system challenge the remote client. A *challenge* is where the host system asks the remote client some secret—usually a password—that the remote client must then respond with for the host to allow the connection.

MS-CHAP *MS-CHAP* is Microsoft's variation of the CHAP protocol. It uses a slightly more advanced encryption protocol.

Configuring Dial-up Encryption

It's the server not the client that controls the choice of dial-up encryption. Microsoft clients can handle a broad selection of authentication encryption methods, including no authentication at all. On the rare occasion when you have to change your client's default encryption settings for a dial-up connection, you'll need to journey deep into the bowels of its properties. Figure 23-25 shows the Windows 2000 dialog box, called Advanced Security Settings, where you configure encryption. The person who controls the server's configuration will tell you which encryption method to select here.

Figure 23-25
Setting dial-up encryption in the Windows 2000 Advanced Security Settings dialog box

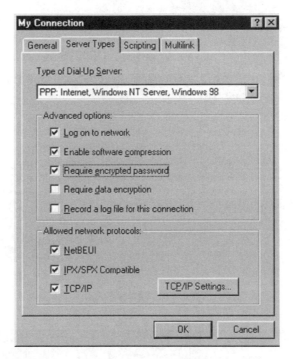

Data Encryption

Encryption methods don't stop at the authentication level. There are a number of ways to encrypt network *data* as well. The choice of encryption method is dictated to a large degree by the method used by the communicating systems to connect. Many networks consist of multiple networks linked together by some sort of private connection, usually some kind of telephone line like ISDN or T1. Microsoft's encryption method of choice for this type of network is called *IPSec* (derived from *IP security*). IPSec provides transparent encryption between the server and the client. IPSec will also work in VPNs, but other encryption methods are more commonly used in those situations.

Application Encryption

When it comes to encryption, even TCP/IP applications can get into the swing of things. The most famous of all application encryptions is Netscape's *Secure Sockets Layer (SSL)* security protocol, which is used to create secure Web sites. Microsoft incorporates SSL into its more far-reaching HTTPS (HTTP over SSL) protocol. These protocols make it possible to create the secure Web sites used to make purchases over the Internet. HTTPS Web sites can be identified by the *HTTPS://* included in their URL (see Figure 23-26).

Figure 23-26   A secure Web site

To make a secure connection, your Web browser and the Web server must encrypt their data. That means there must be a way for both the Web server and your browser to encrypt and decrypt each other's data. This is done by the server sending a public key to your Web browser so the browser knows how to decrypt the incoming data. These public keys are sent in the form of a digital certificate. This certificate not only provides the public key but also is signed by a trusted authority that guarantees the public key you are about to get is actually from the Web server and not from some evil person trying to pretend to be the Web server. There are a number of companies that issue digital certificates to Web sites, probably the most famous is Verisign, Inc.

Your Web browser has a built-in list of trusted authorities. If a certificate comes in from a Web site that uses one of these highly respected companies, you won't see anything happen in your browser; you'll just go to the secure Web page and a small lock will appear in the lower right-hand corner of your browser. Figure 23-27 shows the list of trusted authorities built into the Firefox Web browser.

Figure 23-27
Trusted authorities

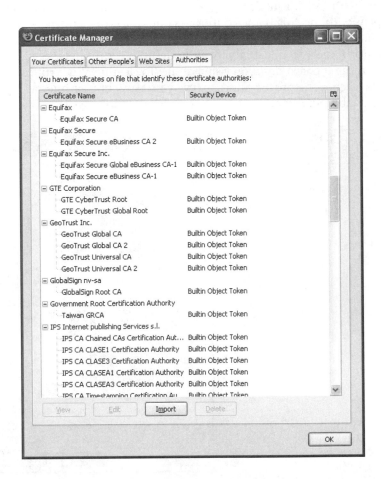

However, if you receive a certificate from someone *not* listed in your browser, the browser will warn you and ask if you wish to accept the certificate, as shown in Figure 23-28.

Figure 23-28
Incoming certificate

What you do here is up to you. Do you wish to trust this certificate? In most cases, you simply say yes, and this certificate is added to your SSL cache of certificates. However, there are occasions where an accepted certificate becomes invalid, usually due to something boring, for instance, it goes out of date or the public key changes. This never happens with the "big name" certificates built into your browser—you'll see this more often when a certificate is used, for example, in-house on a company intranet and the administrator forgets to update their certificates. If a certificate goes bad, your browser issues a warning the next time you visit that site. To clear invalid certificates, you need to clear the SSL cache. The process varies on every browser, but on Internet Explorer, go to the Content tab under Internet Options and click the Clear SSL state button (Figure 23-29).

Figure 23-29
Content tab

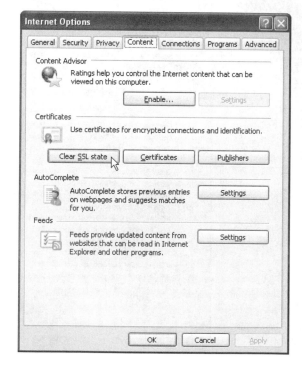

Wireless Issues

Wireless networks add a whole level of additional security headaches for techs to face, as you know from Chapter 21, "Local Area Networking." Some of the points to remember or to go back and look up are as follows:

- Set up wireless encryption, at least WEP but preferably WPA or the more secure WPA2, and configure clients to use them.
- Disable DHCP and require your wireless clients to use a static IP address.
- If you need to use DHCP, only allot enough DHCP addresses to meet the needs of your network to avoid unused wireless connections.
- Change the WAP's SSID from default and disable SSID broadcast.
- Filter by MAC address to allow only known clients on the network.
- Change the default user name and password. Every hacker has memorized the default user names and passwords.
- Update the firmware as needed.
- If available, make sure the WAP's firewall settings are turned on.

Reporting

As a final weapon in your security arsenal, you need to report any security issues so a network administrator or technician can take steps to make them go away. You can set up two tools within Windows so that the OS reports problems to you: Event Viewer and Auditing. You can then do your work and report those problems, which is called *incidence reporting.* Let's take a look.

Event Viewer

Event Viewer is Window's default tattletale program, spilling the beans about many things that happen on the system. You can find Event Viewer in Administrative Tools in the Control Panel. By default, Event Viewer has three sections, Application, Security, and System, and if you've downloaded Internet Explorer 7, you'll see a fourth option for the browser, Internet Explorer (Figure 23-30). As you'll recall from Chapter 15, the most common use for Event Viewer is to view application or system errors for troubleshooting (Figure 23-31).

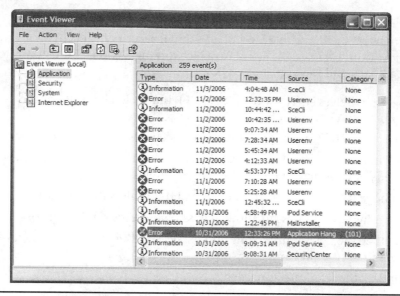

Figure 23-30   Event Viewer

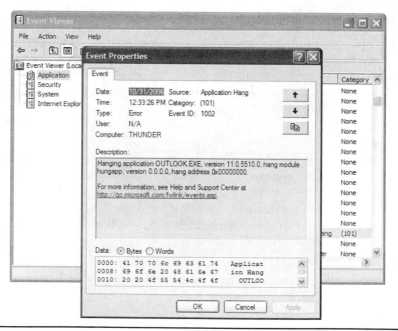

Figure 23-31   Typical application error message

One very cool feature of Event Viewer is that you can click the link to take you to the online Help and Support Center at Microsoft.com, and the software reports your error (Figure 23-32), checks the online database, and comes back with a more or less useful explanation (Figure 23-33).

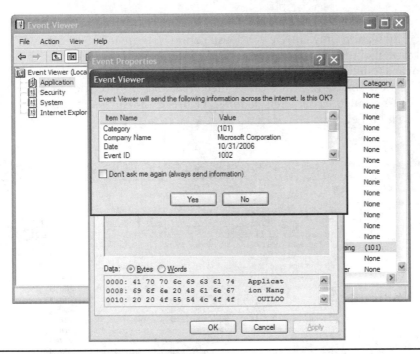

Figure 23-32 Details about to be sent

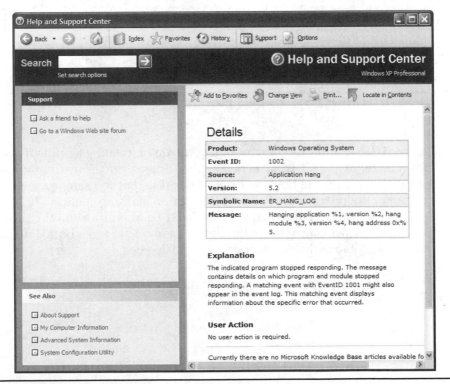

Figure 23-33 Help and Support Center being helpful

Auditing

The Security section of Event Viewer doesn't show you anything by default. To unlock the full potential of Event Viewer, you need to set up auditing. *Auditing* in the security sense means to tell Windows to create an entry in the Security Log when certain events happen, for example, a user logs on—called *event auditing*—or tries to access a certain file or folder—called *object access auditing*. Figure 23-34 shows Event Viewer tracking logon and logoff events.

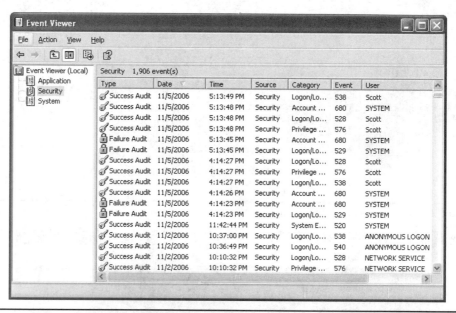

Figure 23-34   Event Viewer displaying security alerts

The CompTIA A+ certification exams don't test you on creating a brilliant auditing policy for your office—that's what network administrators do. You simply need to know what auditing does and how to turn it on or off so that you can provide support for the network administrators in the field. To turn on auditing at a local level, go to Local Security Settings in Administrative Tools. Select Local Policies and then click Audit Policies. Double-click one of the policy options and select one or both of the check boxes. Figure 23-35 shows the Audit object access dialog box.

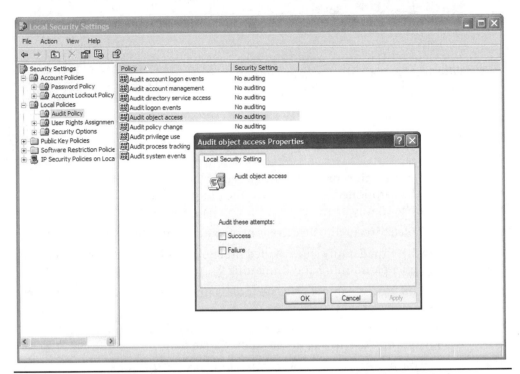

Figure 23-35 Audit object access with the Local Security Settings dialog box open in the foreground

Incidence Reporting

Once you've gathered data about a particular system or you've dealt with a computer or network problem, you need to complete the mission by telling your supervisor. This is called *incidence reporting*. Many companies have pre-made forms that you simply fill out and submit. Other places are less formal. Regardless, you need to do this!

Incidence reporting does a couple of things for you. First, it provides a record of work you've done and accomplished. Second, it provides a piece of information that, when combined with other information that you might or might not know, reveals a pattern or bigger problem to someone higher up the chain. A seemingly innocuous security audit report, for example, might match other such events in numerous places in the building at the same time and thus show conscious, coordinated action rather than a glitch was at work.

Chapter Review Questions

1. Which of the following would you select if you need to back up an Active Directory server?

   A. Registry

   B. System state data

   C. My Computer

   D. My Server

2. Johan migrated his server data to a bigger, faster hard drive. At the end of the process, he partitioned and formatted the older hard drive before removing it to donate to charity. How secure is his company's data?

   A. Completely secured. The drive is blank after partitioning and formatting.

   B. Mostly secured. Only super skilled professionals have the tools to recover data after partitioning and formatting.

   C. Very unsecured. Simple software tools can recover a lot of data, even after partitioning and formatting.

   D. Completely unsecured. The data on the drive will show up in the Recycle Bin as soon as someone installs it on a system.

3. What is the process of using or manipulating people to gain access to network resources?

   A. Cracking

   B. Hacking

   C. Network engineering

   D. Social engineering

4. Which of the following might offer good hardware authentication?

   A. Strong passwords

   B. Encrypted passwords

   C. NTFS

   D. Smart cards

5. Randall needs to change the file system on his second hard drive (currently the D: drive) from FAT32 to NTFS. Which of the following commands would do the trick?

   A. CONVERT D: /FS:NTFS

   B. CONVERT D: NTFS

   C. CONVERT /FS:NTFS D:

   D. CONVERT NTFS D:

6. Which of the following tools would enable you to stop a user from logging on to a local machine, but still enable him to log on to the domain?

   A. AD Policy

   B. Group Policy

   C. Local Security Settings

   D. User Settings

7. Which type of encryption offers the most security?

   A. MS-CHAP

   B. PAP

   C. POP3

   D. SMTP

8. Zander downloaded a game off the Internet and installed it, but as soon as he started to play he got a blue screen of death. Upon rebooting, he discovered that his My Documents folder had been erased. What happened?

   A. He installed spyware.

   B. He installed a Trojan.

   C. He broke the Group Policy.

   D. He broke the Local Security Settings.

9. Which of the following should Mary set up on her Wi-Fi router to make it the most secure?

   A. NTFS

   B. WEP

   C. WPA

   D. WPA2

10. What tool would you use to enable auditing on a local level?

   A. AD Policy

   B. Group Policy

   C. Local Security Settings

   D. User Settings

Answers

1. **B.** Backing up the system state data gets the Registry, Active Directory files, and more.

2. **C.** Although it would take a little work, simple software tools can recover a lot of data, even after partitioning and formatting.

3. **D.** Social engineering is the process of using or manipulating people to gain access to network resources.

4. **D.** Smart cards are an example of hardware authentication devices.

5. **A.** Use the following command to convert from FAT32 to NTFS:
   CONVERT D: /FS:NTFS

6. **C.** Local Security Settings enable you stop someone from logging on to a local machine.

7. **A.** Of the choices here, MS-CHAP offers the most security.

8. **B.** Zander clearly installed a Trojan, a virus masquerading as a game.

9. **D.** Mary should set up WPA2 on her Wi-Fi router.

10. **C.** You can enable local auditing through Local Security Settings.

CHAPTER 24

The Complete PC Tech

In this chapter, you will learn how to
- Describe how computers work
- Explain the nuances of dealing with customers
- Implement a troubleshooting methodology

When a mission-critical computer goes down, regardless of the industry, people get upset. Workers can't work, so they feel guilty. Employers can't get product out on time, so they feel anxious. Supervisors blame employees for fouling things up, or at least the employees fear such blame, even if they did not break the machine.

Into this charged atmosphere comes the tech, ready to fix the computer and move on to the next challenge. Accomplishing this task, though, requires three things: First, a good tech must know the broken machine inside and out—how it's *supposed* to work when working properly. Second, the tech has to calm the workers and supervisors, and get answers to questions to gain relevant information about the problem. Third, the tech must troubleshoot the problem and fix the machine.

This chapter starts with an overview of how computers work and then dives into a section on dealing with customers and how to get them to tell you what you need to know and smile about it. The chapter wraps up with a proven troubleshooting methodology to help you figure out the source of problems and point you to the fix quickly.

Essentials

How Computers Work

You've spent a lot of time going through this book, reading about technologies and components in great detail. Each chapter contained troubleshooting information and methodologies for the components explained in that chapter. In Chapter 3, for example, you learned all about CPUs, from how they work to how to install them. You also learned about issues specific to CPUs, including the potentially difficult task of adding or removing the fan and heat sink assembly that all CPUs require. In Chapters 9 and 10, you dove into hard drives in gory detail. With each chapter, you added more and more information about the pieces that make up the personal computer today.

In this chapter, I want you to distill that knowledge, to think about the computer as a coherent machine. Each of the computer's components works together to enable people to produce some amazing things.

To master the art of troubleshooting as a PC tech, you need to approach a technical problem and answer one question: "What can it be? What can be causing this problem?" (Okay, that was two questions, but you get the idea.) Because every process involves multiple components, you must understand the interconnectedness of those components. If Jane can't print, for example, what could it be? Connectivity? Drivers? Paper jam? Slow network connection? Frozen application? Solar flares? Let's look at the process.

Computing Process

When you run a program, your computer goes through three of the four stages of the computer process: input, processing, and output (Figure 24-1). Input requires specific devices, such as the keyboard and mouse, that enable you to tell the computer to do something, such as open a program or type a word. The operating system (OS) provides an interface and tools so that the microprocessor and other chips can process your request. The image on the monitor or sound from the speakers effectively tell you that the computer has interpreted your command and spit out the result. The fourth stage, storage, comes into play when you want to save a document and when you first open programs and other files.

Figure 24-1
Input, processing, and output

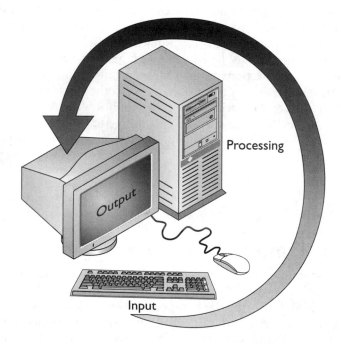

Processing

Output

Input

Making this process work, though, requires the complex interaction of many components, including multiple pieces of hardware and layers of software. As a tech, you need to understand all the components and how they work together so when something doesn't work right, you can track down the source and fix it. A look at a modern program reveals that even a relatively simple-seeming action or change on the screen requires many things to happen within the computer.

Games such as Second Life (Figure 24-2) are huge, taking up multiple gigabytes of space on an Internet server. They simply won't fit into the RAM in most computers, so developers have figured out ways to minimize RAM usage.

Figure 24-2   Second Life

In Second Life, for example, you move through the online world in a series of more or less seamlessly connected areas. Crossing a bridge from one island to another triggers the game to update the information you're about to see on the new island quickly, so you won't be out of the action and the illusion of being in the game world remains intact. Here's what happens when you press the W key on your keyboard and your character steps across the invisible zone line.

NOTE   Second Life is a massively multiplayer online role-playing game (MMORPG) that offers a unique twist on the genre. You can create just about anything you can imagine, as far as your time and talent can take you. Second Life has a functioning economy that spills out into the real world, meaning you can buy and sell things within the game and turn that into real US dollars, although the more common scenario is to spend real money to get virtual possessions.

The keyboard controller reads the grid of your keyboard and, on discovering your input, sends the information to the CPU through the wires of the motherboard (Figure 24-3). The CPU understands the keyboard controller because of a small program it loaded into RAM from the system BIOS stored on the system ROM chip on the motherboard when you first booted the computer.

Figure 24-3 Keyboard to CPU

The CPU and the application determine what should happen in the game, and on discovering that your character is about to cross the zone line, they trigger a whole series of actions. The application sends the signal to the operating system (OS) that it needs a specific area loaded into RAM. The OS sends a signal to the CPU that it needs data stored on the hard drive plus information stored on the Second Life servers. The CPU then sends the commands to the hard drive controller for it to grab the proper stored data and send it to RAM, while at the same time sending a command to the NIC to download the updated information (Figure 24-4).

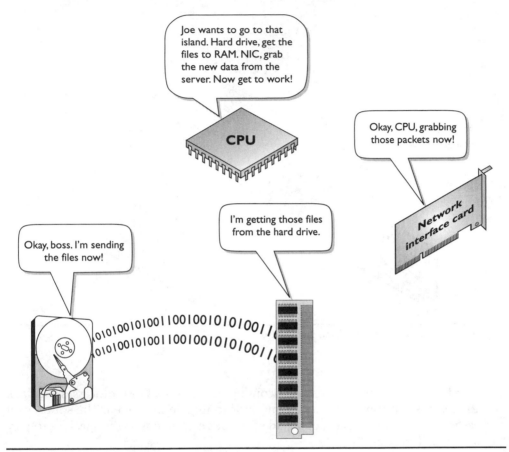

Figure 24-4 CPU to hard drive and NIC

The hard drive controller tells the hard drive to cough up the data—megabytes worth—and then sends that data through the motherboard to the memory controller, which puts it into RAM and communicates with the CPU when it's finished. The network card and network operating system communicate with the Second Life servers and download the necessary updated information. The CPU then uses the application and OS to process the new data, sending video data to the video card and sound data to the sound card, again through the wires on the motherboard (Figure 24-5).

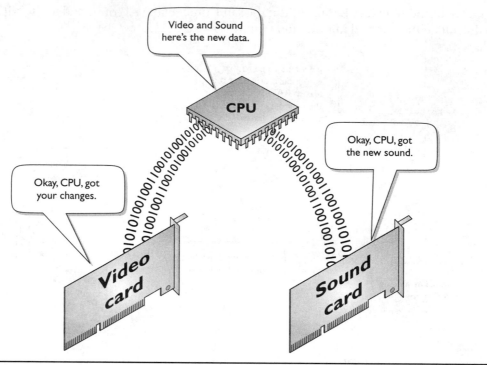

Figure 24-5 CPU to video card and sound card

The video card processor puts the incoming data into its RAM, processes the data, and then sends out commands to the monitor to update the screen. The sound card processor likewise processes the data and sends out commands to the speakers to play a new sound (Figure 24-6).

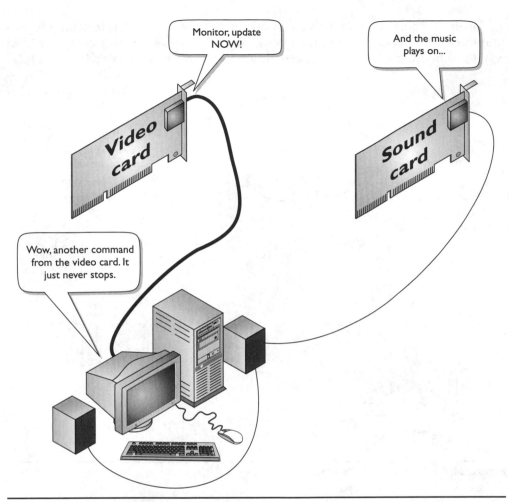

Figure 24-6 Updating the screen and speakers

For all of this to work, the PC has to have electricity, so the direct current (DC) provided by the power supply and the alternating current (AC) provided to the power supply must both be the proper voltage and amperage.

Finally, because Second Life is a network application, the OS has to send information through the NIC and onto the Internet to update everyone else's computer. That way, the other characters in the game world see you move forward a step (Figure 24-7).

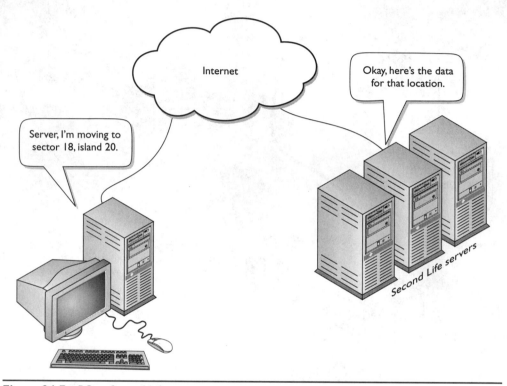

Figure 24-7   PC to Second Life servers

What do you see or hear with all these electrons zipping all over the place? Out of a seemingly blank vista (Figure 24-8), a castle begins to appear, building itself piece by piece as your computer processes the new information and updates the video screen.

You hear music begin to play from your speakers. Within a few seconds, with the data describing the new island fully downloaded and processed, the world on your monitor looks very different (Figure 24-9). That's when all goes well. Many megabytes of data have flowed from your hard drive and across the Internet, been processed by multiple processors, and sent to the monitor and the speakers.

Figure 24-8 New area loading

Figure 24-9 Castle completed

To keep the action continuous and unbroken, Second Life, like many current online games, uses a process of continuous or *stream loading*: your computer constantly downloads updated information and data from the Second Life servers, so the world you see changes with every step you take. When done right, stream loading can do some amazing things. In the GameCube game Zelda, for example, the game anticipates where you will go next and loads that new area into RAM before you take the step. You can be in one area and use a telescope to zoom in on another fully developed area (Figure 24-10), making the experience amazingly seamless, just like real life.

Figure 24-10
Zelda zoomed

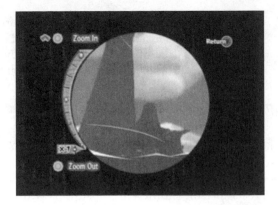

Troubleshooting

Good techs understand the components involved in inputting, processing, and outputting data, including the devices that store data, such as hard drives. That's because if something doesn't work properly, you can start answering the ultimate troubleshooting question—what can it be?—accurately. If your screen freezes or the sound goes wonky, where in the process is the problem located?

As you go into any troubleshooting scenario, always keep the computing process in mind. This helps you sort through possibilities quickly and accurately. If you know all the stages, you won't miss a simple step, such as figuring out that a user can't print because the cleaning service accidentally turned off the print server the night before, or waste time reinstalling printer drivers when the real issue is a stalled print job in the print queue.

Dealing with Customers

When you deal with users, managers, and owners who are frustrated and upset because a computer or network is down and they can't work, your job requires you to take on the roles of detective and psychologist. It takes skill to talk with frazzled and confused people and get answers to questions about how the PC got into the state it's in. It's important to be able to communicate clearly and effectively. Plus, you need to follow the rules of tech-person decorum, acting with personal integrity and respect for the customer. Finally, use assertive communication to empathize with and educate the user. Great techs spend the time needed to develop these essential skills.

EXAM TIP This section has no IT Technician section because the entire chapter applies to Essentials, IT Technician, and Help Desk Technician exams. Expect 1 out of every 5 questions on the 220-603 exam to be on Communication and Professionalism, so you have to know this stuff!

Eliciting Answers

Your job as a tech is to get the computer fixed, and the best way to start that process is to determine what the computer is doing or not doing. You must start by talking to the customer. Allow the customer to explain the problem fully while you record the information. Once the person has described the situation, you must then ask questions.

Although each person is different, most users with a malfunctioning computer or peripheral will be afraid and often defensive about the problem. To overcome this initial attitude, you need to ask the right questions *and* listen to the customer's answers. Then ask the proper follow-up questions.

Always avoid accusatory questions because they won't help you in the least. "What did you do?" generally gets a confused or defensive "Nothing" in reply, which doesn't get you closer to solving the problem. First, ask questions that help clarify the situation. Repeat what you think is the problem after you've listened all the way through the user's story.

Follow up with fact-seeking questions, such as "When did it last work?"; "Has it ever worked in this way?"; "Has any software changed recently?"; or "Any new hardware?"

By keeping your questions friendly and factual, you show the user that you won't accuse them or judge their actions. You also show them that you're there to help them. After the initial tension drops away, you'll often get more information, for instance, a recitation of something the user might have tried or changed. These clues can help lead to a quick resolution of the problem.

It's important to remember that you may know all about computer technology, but the user probably does not. This means they will often use vague and/or incorrect terms to describe a particular computer component or function. That's just the way it works, so don't bother to correct the user. Wherever possible, avoid using jargon, acronyms, or abbreviations specific to computers. They simply confuse the already upset user and can make it sound like you're talking down to them. Just ask direct, factual questions in a friendly tone using simple, non-jargon language to zero in on what the user was trying to accomplish and what happened when things went wrong. Point at the machine or go to a working PC to have the user show what went wrong or what he or she did or tried to do.

Although you don't want to overwhelm them, people do usually want to get a handle on what you are doing—although in a simplified way. Don't be afraid to use simple analogies or concepts to give them an idea what is happening. If you have the time (and the skills), use drawings, equipment, and other visual aids to make technical concepts more clear. If a customer is a "closet tech" and is really digging for answers—to the point it's affecting your ability to do your job—compliment their initiative and then direct them to outside training opportunities. Better yet, tell them where they can get a copy of this book!

Integrity

A computer tech must bring integrity to his or her job, just like any other service professional. Treat anything said to you as a personal confidence, not to be repeated to coworkers or bosses. Respect the privacy and property of the user.

You have a lot of power when you sit in front of someone's computer. You can readily read private e-mail, discover Web sites surfed, and more. With a click of the Start button, you can know the last five programs the user ran, including Word and Solitaire, and the last few documents he or she worked on. Don't do this. You really don't want to know! Plus, if you get caught violating a customer's privacy, you'll not only lose credibility and respect, you could lose your job.

Passwords are a big issue for techs. We have to reboot computers and access shares and other jobs that require passwords. The rule here is to avoid learning other folks' passwords at all costs. If you only need a password once, let the user type it in for you. If you anticipate accessing something multiple times (the more usual situation), ask the user to change his or her password temporarily.

It's funny, but people assume ownership of things they use at work. John in accounting doesn't call the computer he uses anything but "my PC." The phone on Susie's desk isn't the company phone, it's "Susie's phone." Regardless of the logic or illogic involved with this sense of ownership, a tech needs to respect that feeling. You'll never go wrong if you follow the Golden Rule: Treat people's things as you would have other people treat yours. Don't use or touch anything—keyboard, printer, laptop, monitor, mouse, phone, pen, paper, or cube toy—without first asking permission. Follow this rule at all times, even when the customer isn't looking!

Beyond basic manners, never assume that just because you are comfortable with friendly or casual behavior, the customer will be, too. Even an apparently casual user will still expect you to behave with professional decorum. On the flip side, don't allow a user to put you in an awkward or even potentially dangerous or illegal situation. Never socialize with customers while on the clock. Never do work outside the scope of your assigned duties without the prior approval of your supervisor (when possible in such cases, try to direct users to someone who *can* help them). You are not a babysitter—never volunteer to "watch the kids" while the customer leaves the job site, or tolerate a potentially unsafe situation if a customer isn't properly supervising a child. Concentrate on doing your job safely and efficiently, and maintain professional integrity.

Respect

The final key in communicating with the user revolves around respect. You don't do his or her job, but should respect that job and person as an essential cog in your organization. Communicate with users the way you would like them to communicate with you were the roles reversed.

Generally, IT folks are there to support the people doing a company's main business. You are there to serve their needs, and all things being equal, to do so at their convenience, not yours.

Don't assume the world stops the moment you walk in the door and that you may immediately interrupt their work to do yours. Although most customers are thrilled and motivated to help you the moment you arrive, this may not always be the case. Ask the magic question, "May I start working on the problem now?" Give your customer a chance to wrap up, shut down, or do anything else necessary to finish his or her business and make it safe for you to do yours.

Engage the user with the standard rules of civil conversation. Take the time to listen. Don't interrupt a story, but rather let it play out. You might hear something that leads to resolving the problem. Use an even, non-accusatory tone, and although it's okay to try to explain a problem if the user asks, never condescend, and never argue. Remain positive in the face of adversity. Don't get defensive if you can't figure something out quickly and the user starts ragging on you. Remember that an angry customer isn't really angry with you—he's just frustrated—so don't take his anger personally. Take it in stride; smile and assure him that computer troubleshooting sometimes takes awhile!

Avoid letting outside interruptions take your focus away from the user and his or her computer problem. Things that break your concentration slow down the troubleshooting process immensely. Plus, customers will feel insulted if you start chatting on your cell phone with your significant other about a movie date later that night when you're supposed to be fixing their computer! You're not being paid to socialize, so turn those cell phones and pagers to vibrate. That's why the technogods created voicemail. Never take any call except one that is potentially urgent. If a call is potentially urgent, explain the urgency to the customer, step away, and deal with the call as quickly as possible.

If you discover that the user caused the problem, either through ignorance or by accident, don't minimize the importance of the problem, but don't be judgmental or insulting about the cause. We all screw up sometimes, and these kinds of mistakes are your job security! *You get paid because people make mistakes and machines break.* Chances are you'll be back at that workstation six months or a year later, fixing something else. By becoming the user's advocate and go-to person, you create a better work environment. If it's a mistaken action that caused the problem, explain in a positive and supportive way how to do the task correctly and then have the user go through the process while you are there to reinforce what you said.

Assertiveness

In many cases, a PC problem is due to user error or neglect. As a technician, you must show users the error of their ways without creating anger or conflict. You do this by using assertive communication. *Assertive communication* is a technique that isn't pushy or bossy, but it's also not the language of a pushover. Assertive communication first requires you show the other person that you understand and appreciate the importance of his or her feelings. Use statements such as "I know how frustrating it feels to lose data" or "I understand how infuriating it is when the network goes out and you can't get your job done." Statements like these cool off the situation and let the customer know you are on his or her side.

The second part of assertive communication is making sure the problem is clearly stated—without accusing the user directly: "Not keeping up with defragmenting your hard drive slows it down," or "Help me understand how the network cable keeps getting unplugged during your lunch hour." Lastly, tell the user what you need from them to prevent this error in the future. "Please call me whenever you hear that buzzing sound," or "Please check the company's approved software list before installing anything." Always use "I" and "me," and never make judgments. "I can't promise the keyboard will work well if it's always getting dirty" is much better than "Stop eating cookies over the keyboard, you slob!"

Troubleshooting Methodology

Following a sound troubleshooting methodology helps you figure out and fix problems quickly. But because troubleshooting is as much art as science, I can't give you a step-by-step list of things to try in a particular order. You've got to be flexible.

First, make sure you have the proper tools for the job. Second, back up everything important before doing repair work. And third, analyze the problem, test your solution, and complete your troubleshooting.

Tech Toolkit

Way back in Chapter 2, "The Visible PC," you learned the basic tools in every well-prepared tech's toolkit (see Figure 24-11): a Phillips-head and straight-slot screwdriver along with a few other useful tools, such as a Torx wrench and a pair of tweezers. You also should carry some computer components.

Figure 24-11
Typical technician toolkit

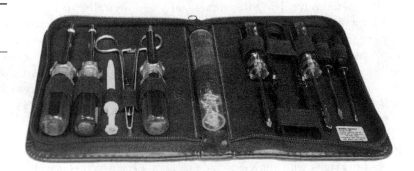

Always carry several *field replaceable units (FRUs)*—a fancy way to say *spare parts*—when going to a job site or workstation. Having several known good components on hand enables you to swap out a potentially bad piece of hardware to see if that's the problem. Different technicians will have different FRUs. A printer specialist might carry a number of different fusers, for example. Your employer will also have a big effect on what is an FRU and what is not. I generally carry a couple of RAM sticks (DDR and DDR2), a PCI video card, a NIC, and a 300-watt power supply.

Backup

In many troubleshooting situations, it's important to back up critical files before making changes to a system. Partly this is a matter of proper ongoing maintenance. If you're in charge of a set of machines for your company, for example, make sure they're set to back up critical files automatically on a regular basis.

 EXAM TIP The CompTIA A+ certification exams assume that all techs should back up systems *every time* before working on them, even though that's not how it works in the real world.

If you run into a partially functional system, where you might have to reinstall the OS but can access the hard drive, then you should definitely back up essential data, such as e-mail, browser favorites, important documents, and any data not stored on a regularly backed-up server. Because you can always boot to a copy of Windows and go to the recovery console, you should never lose essential data, barring full-blown hard drive death.

 NOTE Dead hard drives retain their data, so you can recover it—if you're willing to pay a lot of money. Having a good backup in place makes a lot more economic sense!

Steps

Troubleshooting a computer problem can create a great day for a computer tech—if he or she goes about solving it systematically and logically. Too many techs get into a rut, thinking that when symptom A occurs, the problem must be caused by problem A and require solution A. They might even be right nine times out of ten, but if you think this way, you're in trouble when the problem is really Z and requires a completely different solution. What do you do when the fix doesn't work and you're sure it's got to be problem A? Your customer won't be happy, you'll end up frustrated or embarrassed, and you still won't have the problem fixed. Follow the right methodology: analyze, test, and complete your task.

Analyze

Everything starts with analyzing the problem. Because you know how the process should work, when you run into a computer problem, the first question you should ask is, "What can it be?" Don't limit yourself in the initial analysis, but examine all possibilities.

Make sure you understand the nature of the problem first. A big portion of the initial fact-finding involves talking to the user with your newly-honed customer communication skills. Practice asking friendly, factual questions to get the results you want.

When you run into big problems, such as a completely dead PC, or some weird issue that involves networking as well as a local machine, break the problem down into smaller parts. For a dead PC, for example, organize your inquiry into categories, like this:

- **Power**   Check the AC connections and power switches on the power supply and UPS or surge suppressor.

- **Connectivity**   Check inside the box to make sure nothing is unplugged.

- **CMOS**   If you've got power (you see an LED lit up, for example), then check CMOS to see if the hard drive shows up.

- **Operating system**   If you have some life in the PC, but get no boot option, then try booting to the CD and running the recovery console. Check to see if you can access the hard drive. If you have a boot option, then try booting to Safe Mode or Last Known Good Configuration.

By breaking the problem into discrete chunks, you make a big problem more manageable. You can determine whether the problem is caused by a hardware failure, connection problem, or perhaps an issue with the operating system or other software.

Test

Once you determine what might have caused the problem, test your theories. The testing procedure follows a simple set of rules:

First, check the easy stuff. Is the failed device plugged in? Is it turned on? Does the printer have paper?

Second, use a process of elimination to home in on the problem. Use a notepad to write down what you've tried and what effect that effort had. Do one thing at a time. If you go into CMOS and make a whole series of changes to various settings, for example, and then computer works, how do you know what was wrong? You can't know when you make multiple changes. Worse yet, you risk breaking something else while fixing the first problem!

Third, if hardware seems to be the problem, swap out the suspect parts with known good parts from your stash of FRUs. With a dead or dying piece of hardware, you can generally get almost immediate results. A fried stick of RAM, for example, can create a dead PC. Pop in a good stick, and you'll have a functional machine.

 NOTE   The power supply provides the only exception to the instant gratification rule of part swapping. If you have a wonky computer that has intermittent problems, swap out the power supply and leave your FRU in the computer for a half day or longer. You need the user to road test the PC and report if he or she has the same problems.

Complete

Once you finish the testing phase, you can complete the troubleshooting process with four more steps. First, evaluate the results of your actions. Run the system through its paces; don't just get it working and walk away. Make certain the user can accomplish his or her primary tasks before you consider a job complete.

If you can't get the computer or peripheral working in a fairly short period of time, take the second step and call for help. Because you've taken notes on the symptoms and each troubleshooting step you've tried, you can very quickly get a more senior tech up to speed on the problem and get suggestions for where you might go next.

Third, clean up the work environment. If you installed a drive, for example, do the right thing and tie off the ribbon cables. If you see a mess of cables coming out of the back of the PC or running across the floor, take a moment to tie them off. Good cable management does more than leave your clients with a nice looking computer and workstation area, it also helps prevent accidents.

Finally, document your results. Many companies have specific forms for you to use to describe the problem and its resolution. If not, then make some for yourself and other techs in your workplace. Documenting problems helps you track the trouble-shooting history of a machine over time, enabling you to make longer-term determinations about retiring it or changing out more parts. If you and fellow techs fix a specific problem with Mary's machine several times, for example, you might decide to swap out her whole system rather than fix it a fourth time.

Documenting helps fellow techs if they have to follow up on a task you didn't finish or troubleshoot a machine that you've worked on previously. The reverse is also true. If you get a call about Frank's computer, for example, and check the records to find other service calls on his computer, you might find that the fix for a particular problem is already documented. This is especially true for user-generated problems. Having documentation of what you did also means you don't have to rely on your memory when your co-worker asks what you did to fix the weird problem with Jane's computer a year ago!

Documenting also comes into play when you or a user has an accident on site. If your colleague Joe dropped a monitor on his foot and broke both the monitor and his foot, for example, you need to fill out an incident report, just like you would with any kind of accident—electrical, chemical, or physical. An incident report should detail what happened and where it happened. This helps your supervisors take the appropriate actions quickly and efficiently.

Chapter Review Questions

1. While troubleshooting a fairly routine printing problem, the customer explains in great detail precisely what he was trying to do, what happened when he tried to print, and what he attempted as a fix for the problem. At what point should you interrupt him?

A. After he describes the first problem

B. As soon as you understand the problem

C. As soon as you have a solution

D. Never

2. While manning the help desk, you get a call from a distraught user who says she has a blank screen. What would be a useful follow-up question? (Select two.)

A. Is the computer turned on?

B. Is the monitor turned on?

C. Did you reboot?

D. What did you do?

3. While manning the help desk, you get a call from Sharon in accounting. She's lost a file that she knows she saved to her hard drive. Which of the following statements would direct Sharon to open her My Documents folder in the most efficient and professional manner?

A. Sharon, check My Documents.

B. Sharon, a lot of programs save files to a default folder, often to a folder called My Documents. Let's look there first. Click the Start button and move the mouse until the cursor hovers over My Documents. Then click the left mouse button and tell me what you see when My Documents opens.

C. Probably just defaulted to My Docs. Why don't you open Excel or whatever program you used to make the file, and then open a document and point it to My Documents.

D. Look Sharon, I know you're clueless when it comes to computers, but how could somebody lose a file? Just open up My Documents, and look there for the file.

4. What tool should be in every technician's toolkit?

A. Pliers

B. Hammer

C. Straight-slot screwdriver

D. Phillips-head screwdriver

5. When is it appropriate to yell at a user?

A. When he screws up the second time

B. When he interrupts your troubleshooting

C. When he screws up the fifth time

D. Never

6. Al in marketing calls for tech support, complaining that he has a dead PC. What is a good first question or questions to begin troubleshooting the problem?

A. Did the computer ever work?

B. When did the computer last work?

C. When you say "dead," what do you mean? What happens when you press the power button?

D. What did you do?

7. While manning the help desk, you get a call from Bryce in Sales complaining that he can't print and every time he clicks on the network shared drive, his computer freezes. He says he thinks it's his hard driver. What would be a good follow-up question or statement?

A. Bryce, you're an idiot. Don't touch anything. I'll be there in five minutes.

B. Okay, let's take this one step at a time. You seem to have two problems, one with printing and the second with the network shared drive, right?

C. First, it's not a hard driver, but a hard drive. It doesn't have anything to do with the network share or printing, so that's just not right.

D. When could you last print?

8. When troubleshooting a software problem on Phoebe's computer and listening to her describe the problem, your beeper goes off. It's your boss. Which of the following is the most appropriate action for you to take?

A. Excuse yourself, walk out of the cube, and use a cell phone to call your boss.

B. Pick up Phoebe's phone and dial your boss' number.

C. Wait until Phoebe finishes her description and then ask to use her phone to call your boss.

D. Wait until Phoebe finishes her description and run through any simple fixes; then explain that you need to call your boss on your cell phone.

9. You've just installed new printer drivers into Roland's computer for the big networked laser printer. What should you do to complete the assignment?

A. Document that you installed new printer drivers.

B. Tell Roland to print a test page.

C. Print a test page and go to the printer to verify the results.

D. Print a test page and go to the printer to verify the results. Document that you installed new printer drivers successfully.

10. What's an FRU?

    A. Foreign replacement unit—a cheaper part to replace an expensive American-made part

    B. Field replacement unit—a known good computer part to swap with a suspect part as part of the troubleshooting process

    C. Free repair unit—a gimmick used by some companies to provide free tech support for the first time customer

    D. Short for FRU Linux, a Linux distribution

Answers

1. **D.** Don't interrupt customers. Let them tell you what's happening and then ask questions.

2. **A, B.** Go for the simple answer first. When faced with a blank screen, check to see if the computer and the monitor are on.

3. **B.** Walking customers through the path to a fix, using simple, nontechnical words, is the best way to accomplish tasks over the phone.

4. **D.** Every tech's toolkit should have a Phillips-head screwdriver, at the very least.

5. **D.** Don't get angry or yell at clients!

6. **C.** Asking for clarification is a good first step. This is a tough call because A and B are obviously useful questions that will probably be the second and third questions you ask!

7. **B.** Similar to question 6, asking for clarification and stating the problem as you heard it are good follow-up options.

8. **D.** Focus on the customer and don't use her things!

9. **D.** Always verify the results once you finish troubleshooting. Then document what you accomplished.

10. **B.** A field replacement unit is a known good computer part.

Mapping to the CompTIA A+ Objectives

This appendix contains four charts that show where this book covers the CompTIA A+ objectives for each of the four exams. After you've read through the book the first time, these charts will help focus your studies on the exam you plan to take next. This is especially important for folks taking the Help Desk (220-603) or Depot Technician (220-604) exams because the objectives differ from those of the IT Technician (220-602). Good luck!

CompTIA A+ Essentials Objectives Map

Topic	Chapter(s)
Domain 1.0—Personal Computer Components	
1.1 Identify the fundamental principles of using personal computers	
Identify the names, purposes, and characteristics of storage devices	2, 9, 10, 11
Identify the names, purposes, and characteristics of motherboards	2, 3, 4, 5, 6, 7, 9
Identify the names, purposes, and characteristics of power supplies	8
Identify the names purposes, and characteristics of processors/CPUs	3
Identify the names, purposes, and characteristics of memory	4
Identify the names, purposes, and characteristics of display devices	2, 17
Identify the names, purposes, and characteristics of input devices	16, 18
Identify the names, purposes, and characteristics of adapter cards	9, 16, 17, 18
Identify the names, purposes, and characteristics of ports and cables	2, 18, 20
Identify the names, purposes, and characteristics of cooling systems	3, 8
1.2 Install, configure, optimize, and upgrade personal computer components	
Add, remove, and configure internal and external storage devices	9, 10
Install display devices	17
Add, remove, and configure basic input and multimedia devices	16

Topic	Chapter(s)
1.3 Identify tools, diagnostic procedures, and troubleshooting techniques for personal computer components	
Recognize the basic aspects of troubleshooting theory	24
Identify and apply basic diagnostic procedures and troubleshooting techniques	24
Recognize and isolate issues with display, power, basic input devices, storage, memory, thermal, and POST errors (e.g., BIOS, hardware)	3, 4, 5, 8, 9, 10, 16, 17
Apply basic troubleshooting techniques to check for problems (e.g., thermal issues, error codes, power, connections including cables and/or pins, compatibility, functionality, software/drivers) with components	3, 4, 6, 7, 8, 16, 17
Recognize the names, purposes, characteristics, and appropriate application of tools	5, 9
1.4 Perform preventive maintenance on personal computer components	
Identify and apply basic aspects of preventive maintenance theory	5, 6, 24
Identify and apply common preventive maintenance techniques for devices such as input devices and batteries	16, 19
Domain 2.0—Laptop and Portable Devices	
2.1 Identify the fundamental principles of using laptops and portable devices	
Identify names, purposes, and characteristics of laptop-specific form factors, peripherals, expansion slots, ports, communication connections, power and electrical input devices, LCD technologies, and input devices	19, 21
Identify and distinguish between mobile and desktop motherboards and processors including throttling, power management, and Wi-Fi	3, 19, 21
2.2 Install, configure, optimize, and upgrade laptops and portable devices	
Configure power management	19
Demonstrate safe removal of laptop-specific hardware such as peripherals, hot-swappable devices, and non-hot-swappable devices	19
2.3 Identify tools, basic diagnostic procedures, and troubleshooting techniques for laptops and portable devices	
Use procedures and techniques to diagnose power conditions, video, keyboard, pointer, and wireless card issues	19
2.4 Perform preventive maintenance on laptops and portable devices	
Identify and apply common preventive maintenance techniques for laptops and portable devices	19
Domain 3.0—Operating Systems	
3.1 Identify the fundamentals of using operating systems	
Identify differences between operating systems (e.g., Mac, Windows, Linux) and describe operating system revision levels including GUI, system requirements, and application and hardware compatibility	12
Identify names, purposes, and characteristics of the primary operating system components including registry, virtual memory, and file system	13

Topic	Chapter(s)
Describe features of operating system interfaces	13
Identify the names, locations, purposes, and characteristics of operating system files	13
Identify concepts and procedures for creating, viewing, and managing disks, directories, and files in operating systems	10, 13, 14
3.2 Install, configure, optimize, and upgrade operating systems	
Identify procedures for installing operating systems	12
Identify procedures for upgrading operating systems	12
Install/add a device including loading [and] adding device drivers and required software	6, 13
Identify procedures and utilities used to optimize operating systems	15
3.3 Identify tools, diagnostic procedures, and troubleshooting techniques for operating systems	
Identify basic boot sequences, methods, and utilities for recovering operating systems	15
Identify and apply diagnostic procedures and troubleshooting techniques	24
Recognize and resolve common operational issues such as bluescreen; system lock-up; input/output device; application install, start, or load; and Windows-specific printing problems (e.g., print spool stalled, incorrect/ incompatible driver for print)	15, 20
Explain common error messages and codes	15, 23
Identify the names, locations, purposes, and characteristics of operating system utilities	5, 6, 10, 13, 14, 15
3.4 Perform preventive maintenance on operating systems	
Describe common utilities for performing preventive maintenance on operating systems	15
Domain 4.0—Printers and Scanners	
4.1 Identify the fundamental principles of using printers and scanners	
Identify differences between types of printer and scanner technologies	16, 20
Identify names, purposes, and characteristics of printer and scanner components	16, 20
Identify the names, purposes, and characteristics of interfaces used by printers and scanners including port and cable types	16, 20
4.2 Identify basic concepts of installing, configuring, optimizing, and upgrading printers and scanners	
Install and configure printers/scanners	16, 20
Optimize printer performance	20
4.3 Identify tools, basic diagnostic procedures, and troubleshooting techniques for printers and scanners	
Gather information about printer/scanner problems	16, 20
Review and analyze collected data	16, 20
Identify solutions to identified printer/scanner problems	16, 20

Topic	Chapter(s)
7.2 Identify potential hazards and implement proper safety procedures including ESD precautions and procedures, safe work environment, and equipment handling	2, 8
7.3 Identify proper disposal procedures for batteries, display devices, and chemical solvents and cans	17, 19, 23
Domain 8.0—Communication and Professionalism	
8.1 Use good communication skills, including listening and tact/discretion, when communicating with customers and colleagues	24
8.2 Use job-related professional behavior including notation of privacy, confidentiality, and respect for the customer and customer's property	24

CompTIA A+ 220-602 (IT Technician) Objectives Map

Topic	Chapter(s)
Domain 1.0—Personal Computer Components	
1.1 Install, configure, optimize, and upgrade personal computer components	
Add, remove, and configure personal computer components, including selection and installation of appropriate components	3, 4, 6, 7, 8, 9, 10, 16, 17
1.2 Identify tools, diagnostic procedures, and troubleshooting techniques for personal computer components	
Identify and apply basic diagnostic procedures and troubleshooting techniques	3, 4, 6, 7, 8, 9, 10, 17
Recognize and isolate issues with peripherals, multimedia, specialty input devices, internal and external storage, and CPUs	3, 9, 10, 16, 17, 18, 20
Identify the steps used to troubleshoot components (e.g., check proper seating, installation, appropriate components, settings, and current driver)	3, 4, 6, 7, 8, 16, 17
Recognize the names, purposes, characteristics, and appropriate application of tools	2, 8, 20, 22, 24
1.3 Perform preventive maintenance on personal computer components	
Identify and apply common preventive maintenance techniques for personal computer components	3, 4, 6, 7, 8, 10, 11, 15, 16, 17
Domain 2.0—Laptop and Portable Devices	
2.1 Identify the fundamental principles of using laptops and portable devices	
Identify appropriate applications for laptop-specific communication connections such as Bluetooth, infrared, cellular WAN, and Ethernet	19, 21
Identify appropriate laptop-specific power and electrical input devices and determine how amperage and voltage can affect performance	19
Identify the major components of the LCD including inverter, screen, and video card	19

Topic	Chapter(s)
2.2 Install, configure, optimize, and upgrade laptops and portable devices	
Demonstrate safe removal of laptop-specific hardware such as peripherals, hot-swappable devices, and non-hot-swappable devices	19
Describe how video sharing affects memory upgrades	19
2.3 Use tools, diagnostic procedures, and troubleshooting techniques for laptops and portable devices	
Use procedures and techniques to diagnose power conditions, video issues, keyboard and pointer issues, and wireless card issues	19
Domain 3.0—Operating Systems	
3.1 Identify the fundamental principles of operating systems	
Use command-line functions and utilities to manage operating systems, including proper syntax and switches	14
Identify concepts and procedures for creating, viewing, and managing disks, directories, and files in operating systems	10
Locate and use operating system utilities and available switches	5, 6, 10, 13, 14, 15, 22
3.2 Install, configure, optimize, and upgrade operating systems	
Identify procedures and utilities used to optimize operating systems	15
3.3 Identify tools, diagnostic procedures, and troubleshooting techniques for operating systems	
Demonstrate the ability to recover operating systems	15
Recognize and resolve common operational problems	15, 20
Recognize and resolve common error messages and codes	15
Use diagnostic utilities and tools to resolve operational problems	5, 6, 7, 12, 15, 22
3.4 Perform preventive maintenance on operating systems	
Demonstrate the ability to perform preventive maintenance on operating systems including software and Windows updates (e.g., Service Packs), scheduled backups/restore, restore points	15
Domain 4.0—Printers and Scanners	
4.1 Identify the fundamental principles of using printers and scanners	
Describe processes used by printers and scanners including laser, ink dispersion, thermal, solid ink, and impact printers and scanners	16, 20
4.2 Install, configure, optimize, and upgrade printers and scanners	
Install and configure printers/scanners	16, 20
Install and configure printer upgrades including memory and firmware	20
Optimize scanner performance including resolution, file format, and default settings	16
4.3 Identify tools and diagnostic procedures for troubleshooting printers and scanners	
Gather information about printer/scanner problems	16, 20
Review and analyze collected data	16, 20

Topic	Chapter(s)
Isolate and resolve identified printer/scanner problems including defining the cause, applying the fix, and verifying functionality	16, 20
Identify appropriate tools used for troubleshooting and repairing printer/scanner problems	16, 20
4.4 Perform preventive maintenance of printers and scanners	
Perform scheduled maintenance according to vendor guidelines	16, 20
Ensure a suitable environment	16, 20
Use recommended supplies	20
Domain 5.0—Networks	
5.1 Identify the fundamental principles of networks	
Identify names, purposes, and characteristics of basic network protocols and technologies	21, 22
Identify names, purposes, and characteristics of technologies for establishing connectivity	21, 22
5.2 Install, configure, optimize, and upgrade networks	
Install and configure browsers	22
Establish network connectivity	21, 22
Demonstrate the ability to share network resources	21, 22
5.3 Use tools and diagnostic procedures to troubleshoot network problems	
Identify names, purposes, and characteristics of tools	21
Diagnose and troubleshoot basic network issues	21
5.4 Perform preventive maintenance of networks, including securing and protecting network cabling	24
Domain 6.0—Security	
6.1 Identify the fundamental principles of security	
Identify the purposes and characteristics of access control	15, 23
Identify the purposes and characteristics of auditing and event logging	23
6.2 Install, configure, upgrade, and optimize security	
Install and configure software, wireless, and data security	5, 23
6.3 Identify tools, diagnostic procedures, and troubleshooting techniques for security	
Diagnose and troubleshoot software and data security issues	15, 23
6.4 Perform preventive maintenance for computer security	
Recognize social engineering and address social engineering situations	23
Domain 7.0—Safety and Environmental Issues	
7.1 Identify potential hazards and proper safety procedures including power supply, display devices, and environment	8, 17, 21

Topic	Chapter(s)
Domain 8.0—Communication and Professionalism	
8.1 Use good communication skills, including listening and tact/ discretion, when communicating with customers and colleagues	24
8.2 Use job-related professional behavior including notation of privacy, confidentiality, and respect for the customer and customer's property	24

CompTIA A+ 220-603 (Help Desk Technician) Objectives Map

Topic	Chapter(s)
Domain 1.0—Personal Computer Components	
1.1 Install, configure, optimize, and upgrade personal computer components	
Add, remove, and configure display devices, input devices, and adapter cards including basic input and multimedia devices	6, 11, 16, 17
1.2 Identify tools, diagnostic procedures, and troubleshooting techniques for personal computer components	
Identify and apply basic diagnostic procedures and troubleshooting techniques	3, 4, 6, 7, 8, 9, 10, 11, 17, 18
Recognize and isolate issues with display, peripheral, multimedia, specialty input devices, and storage	9, 10, 11, 16, 17
Apply steps in troubleshooting techniques to identify problems (e.g., physical environment, functionality, and software/driver settings) with components including display, input devices, and adapter cards	6, 16, 17
1.3 Perform preventive maintenance on personal computer components	
Identify and apply common preventive maintenance techniques for storage devices	9, 10, 11
Domain 2.0—Operating Systems	
2.1 Identify the fundamental principles of using operating systems	
Use command-line functions and utilities to manage Windows 2000, XP Professional, and XP Home, including proper syntax and switches	14
Identify concepts and procedures for creating, viewing, and managing disks, directories, and files in Windows 2000, XP Professional, and XP Home	13, 15
Locate and use Windows 2000, XP Professional, and XP Home utilities and available switches	13, 15

Topic	Chapter(s)
2.2 Install, configure, optimize, and upgrade operating systems	
Identify procedures and utilities used to optimize the performance of Windows 2000, XP Professional, and XP Home	13, 15
2.3 Identify tools, diagnostic procedures, and troubleshooting techniques for operating systems	
Recognize and resolve common operational problems	13, 15
Recognize and resolve common error messages and codes	13, 15
Use diagnostic utilities and tools to resolve operational problems	13, 15
2.4 Perform preventive maintenance on operating systems	
Perform preventive maintenance on Windows 2000, XP Professional, and XP Home including software and Windows updates (e.g., Service Packs)	13, 15
Domain 3.0—Printers and Scanners	
3.1 Identify the fundamental principles of using printers and scanners	
Describe processes used by printers and scanners including laser, ink dispersion, thermal, solid ink, and impact printers	16, 20
3.2 Install, configure, optimize, and upgrade printers and scanners	
Install and configure printers/scanners	16, 20
Optimize scanner performance including resolution, file format, and default settings	16
3.3 Identify tools, diagnostic procedures, and troubleshooting techniques for printers and scanners	
Gather information required to troubleshoot printer/scanner problems	16, 20
Troubleshoot a print failure	20
Domain 4.0—Networks	
4.1 Identify the fundamental principles of networks	
Identify names, purposes, and characteristics of basic network protocols and terminologies	21, 22
Identify names, purposes, and characteristics of technologies for establishing connectivity	21, 22
4.2 Install, configure, optimize, and upgrade networks	
Establish network connectivity and share network resources	21, 22
4.3 Use tools, diagnostic procedures, and troubleshooting techniques for networks	
Identify the names, purposes, and characteristics of command-line tools	21
Diagnose and troubleshoot basic network issues	21

Topic	Chapter(s)
Domain 5.0—Security	
5.1 Identify the fundamental principles of security	
Identify the names, purposes, and characteristics of access control and permissions	15, 23
5.2 Install, configure, upgrade, and optimize security	
Install and configure hardware, software, wireless, and data security	5, 15, 23
5.3 Identify tools, diagnostic procedures, and troubleshooting techniques for security issues	
Diagnose and troubleshoot software and data security issues	15, 23
5.4 Perform preventive maintenance for computer security	
Recognize social engineering and address social engineering situations	23
Domain 6.0—Communication and Professionalism	
6.1 Use good communication skills, including listening and tact/discretion, when communicating with customers and colleagues	24
6.2 Use job-related professional behavior including notation of privacy, confidentiality, and respect for the customer and customer's property	24

CompTIA A+ 220-604 (Depot Technician) Objectives Map

Topic	Chapter(s)
Domain 1.0—Personal Computer Components	
1.1 Install, configure, optimize, and upgrade personal computer components	
Add, remove, and configure internal storage devices, motherboards, power supplies, processors/CPUs, memory, and adapter cards	3, 4, 6, 7, 8, 9, 10, 11, 16, 17
Add, remove, and configure systems	3, 4, 6, 7, 8, 9, 10, 11, 16, 17
1.2 Identify tools, diagnostic procedures, and troubleshooting techniques for personal computer components	
Identify and apply basic diagnostic procedures and troubleshooting techniques	3, 4, 6, 7, 8, 9, 10, 17
Identify the steps used to troubleshoot components (e.g., check proper seating, installation, appropriate components, settings, and current driver)	3, 4, 6, 7, 8, 16, 17
Recognize the names, purposes, characteristics, and appropriate application of tools	2, 8, 20, 22, 24

Topic	Chapter(s)
1.3 Perform preventive maintenance on personal computer components	
Identify and apply common preventive maintenance techniques	3, 4, 6, 7, 8, 10, 11, 15, 16, 17
Domain 2.0—Laptop and Portable Devices	
2.1 Identify the fundamental principles of using laptops and portable devices	
Identify appropriate applications for laptop-specific communication connections such as Bluetooth, infrared, cellular WAN, and Ethernet	19, 21
Identify appropriate laptop-specific power and electrical input devices	19
2.2 Install, configure, optimize, and upgrade laptops and portable devices	
Demonstrate safe removal of laptop-specific hardware such as peripherals, hot-swappable devices, and non-hot-swappable devices	19
Describe how video sharing affects memory upgrades	19
2.3 Use tools, diagnostic procedures, and troubleshooting techniques for laptops and portable devices	
Use procedures and techniques to diagnose power conditions, video issues, keyboard and pointer issues, and wireless card issues	19
Domain 3.0—Printers and Scanners	
3.1 Identify the fundamental principles of using printers and scanners	
Describe processes used by printers and scanners including laser, inkjet, thermal, solid ink, and impact printers	16, 20
3.2 Install, configure, optimize, and upgrade printers and scanners	
Identify the steps used in the installation and configuration processes for printers and scanners	16, 20
Install and configure printer/scanner upgrades including memory and firmware	16, 20
3.3 Identify tools, diagnostic methods, and troubleshooting procedures for printers and scanners	
Gather data about printer/scanner problem	16, 20
Review and analyze data collected about printer/scanner problems	16, 20
Implement solutions to solve identified printer/scanner problems	16, 20
Identify appropriate tools used for troubleshooting and repairing printer/scanner problems	16, 20
3.4 Perform preventive maintenance of printers and scanners	
Perform scheduled maintenance according to vendor guidelines	16, 20
Ensure a suitable environment	16, 20
Use recommended supplies	20

Topic	Chapter(s)
Domain 4.0—Security	
4.1 Identify the names, purposes, and characteristics of physical security devices and processes	
Control access to PCs, servers, laptops, and restricted spaces	23
4.2 Install hardware security	
[Install] smart card readers	23
[Install] key fobs	23
[Install] biometric devices	23
Domain 5.0—Safety and Environmental Issues	
5.1 Identify potential hazards and proper safety procedures including power supply, display devices, and environment	8, 17, 21

About the CD-ROM

Mike Meyers has put together a bunch of resources that will help you prepare for the CompTIA A+ exams and that you will find invaluable in your career as a PC Tech. The CD-ROM included with this book comes complete with a sample version of the Total Tester practice exam software with eight full practice exams, an extensive glossary, an electronic copy of the book, a document from CompTIA with a list of acronyms that you should know for the CompTIA A+ exams, a complete list of the objectives for all four of the CompTIA A+ exams, a copy of several freeware and shareware programs that Mike talks about in the book, and a sample of LearnKey's online training featuring Mike Meyers. The practice tests and video software are easy to install on any Windows 98/NT/2000/XP/Vista computer, and must be installed to access the Total Tester practice exams and LearnKey video sample. The glossary, eBook, and CompTIA A+ acronyms list are Adobe Acrobat files. If you don't have Adobe Acrobat Reader, it is available for installation on the CD-ROM.

System Requirements

The software on the CD-ROM requires Windows 98 or higher, Internet Explorer 5.0 or above, and 50 MB of hard disk space for full installation. To access the online training from LearnKey, you must have Windows Media Player 9, which will be automatically installed when you launch the online training.

Installing and Running Total Tester

If your computer's CD-ROM drive is configured to Autorun, the CD-ROM will automatically start upon inserting the disk. If the Autorun feature does not launch the CD's splash screen, browse to the CD-ROM and double-click the Launch.exe icon.

From the splash screen, you may install Total Tester by clicking the *Install A+ Practice Exams* button. This will begin the installation process, create a program group named Total Seminars, and put an icon on your desktop. To run Total Tester, go to Start | Programs |Total Seminars or just double-click the icon on your desktop.

To uninstall the Total Tester software, go to Start | Settings | Control Panel | Add/Remove Programs and select the A+ Total Tester program. Select Remove, and Windows will completely uninstall the software.

About Total Tester

The best way to prepare for the CompTIA A+ exams is to read the book and then test your knowledge and review. We have included a sample of Total Seminars' practice exam software to help you test your knowledge as you study. Total Tester provides you with a simulation of the actual exam. There are four suites of exams: Essentials, 220-602, 220-603, and 220-604. Each suite contains two exams that can be taken in either practice or final mode. Practice mode provides an assistance window with hints, references to the book, an explanation of the answer, and the ability to check your answer as you take the test. Both practice and final modes provide an overall grade and a grade broken down by certification objective. To launch a test, select Suites from the menu at the top, select an exam, and choose from the list of available practice exams. Additional practice exams are available for all four of the CompTIA A+ exams. Visit our Web site at www.totalsem.com or call 800-446-6004 for more information.

Accessing the Glossary, eBook, CompTIA A+ Acronyms List, and CompTIA A+ Exam Objectives

You will find these documents useful in your preparation for the exams. To access these PDF documents, first be sure you have a copy of Adobe Acrobat Reader installed. If you don't have Acrobat Reader installed on your system, you can install it from the CD-ROM by clicking the *Install Adobe Acrobat Reader* button. Once you have installed Acrobat Reader, simply select the document you want to view from the CD-ROM's splash screen to open and view the document.

Shareware and Freeware

Mike has put together copies of some of his favorite freeware and shareware programs that are mentioned in this book. The CD-ROM includes a list with short descriptions of the programs. To use these programs, select the Shareware and Freeware option on the CD-ROM splash screen. The next menu lists each program. Select a program and follow the installation instructions to load the utility on your system.

LearnKey Online Training

If you like Mike's writing style, you will love listening to him in his LearnKey video training. The CD-ROM includes sample videos of Mike covering several different topics. Check out Mike's video training. If you like it, you can purchase the full 21 hours of interactive video training by contacting Mike's company, Total Seminars, at www.totalsem.com or 800-446-6004. The *Install LearnKey demo* button will launch a wizard to install the software on your computer. Follow the instructions on the wizard to complete the installation. To run the LearnKey demo, use Start | Programs | LearnKey or just double-click the icon on your desktop. Enter a user name and password to begin your video training.

Technical Support

For questions regarding the Total Tester software, visit www.totalsem.com or e-mail support@totalsem.com, or e-mail customer.service@mcgraw-hill.com. For customers outside the United States, e-mail international_cs@mcgraw-hill.com.

LearnKey Technical Support

For technical problems with the software (installation, operation, or uninstallation) and for questions regarding LearnKey Video Training, e-mail techsupport@learnkey.com.

INDEX